Topical
Reference Books

Other books in the *Bowker Buying Guide Series*

General Reference Books for Adults
Reference Books for Young Readers

The Bowker Buying Guide Series

Topical Reference Books

Marion Sader
Editor

Charles A. Bunge
Sharon Hogan
Consultants

R. R. Bowker
New Providence, New Jersey

Acknowledgments

R. R. Bowker thanks the following publishers for permission to reprint from their publications:
Page 20: Reprinted by permission of Oxford University Press from N. G. L. Hammond and H. H. Scullard, *Oxford Classical Dictionary,* 2d edition (Oxford: Oxford University Press, 1970).
Page 21: Used with permission of Garland Publishing, Inc., from *Encyclopedia of Human Evolution and Prehistory,* edited by Ian Tattersall, Eric Delson, and John Van Couvering, copyright © 1988. All rights reserved.
Page 23: Reprinted with permission from Stanley J. Kunitz and Howard Haycraft, eds., *American Authors, 1600–1900* (New York: H. W. Wilson, 1966).
Page 24: Excerpt from *The Essential Guide to Nonprescription Drugs* by David R. Zimmerman. Copyright © 1983 by David R. Zimmerman, Inc. Reprinted by permission of HarperCollins Publishers.
Page 26: Reprinted with permission of Andromeda Oxford Ltd. from Donald Matthew, *Atlas of Medieval Europe* (New York: Facts On File, 1983). Copyright © Equinox (Oxford) Ltd.
Page 27: From *America: History and Life,* copyright ABC-Clio, Inc. Reproduced by permission.

Published by R. R. Bowker, a division of Reed Publishing (USA) Inc.

Printed and bound in the United States of America

Library of Congress Cataloging-in-Publication Data

Topical reference books / Marion Sader, editor; Charles A. Bunge, Sharon Hogan, consultants.
p. cm. — (The Bowker buying guide series)
Includes bibliographical references and indexes.
ISBN 0-8352-3087-2 (hard cover)
1. Reference books—Bibliography. 2. Reference services (Libraries). I. Sader, Marion. II. Series.
Z1035.1.T66 1991 91-9706
011'.—dc20 CIP

Editorial Development and Production by Visual Education Corporation, Princeton, NJ

ISBN 0-8352-3087-2

9 780835 230872

Contents

List of Categories

Board of Advisors

Reviewers

M. L. Phoebe Adams
Head Librarian
Sierra Club
William E. Colby Memorial Library
San Francisco, California

Susan M. Allen
Assistant to the Director
Acting Head, Special Collections
The Libraries of Claremont Colleges
Claremont, California

Susan C. Awe
Head, Information Services
Natrona County Public Library
Casper, Wyoming

Sarojini Balachandran
Head, Science and Technology
Auburn University Libraries
Auburn, Alabama

Charlene M. Baldwin
Acting Head Map Librarian
University of Arizona Library
Tucson, Arizona

Daniel Barkley
Assistant Government Documents and Map Librarian
University of Kansas Libraries
Lawrence, Kansas

Jane A. Bealer
Librarian
WNET/Channel 13
New York, New York

Craig W. Beard
Head of Reference
Mervyn H. Sterne Library
University of Alabama at Birmingham
Birmingham, Alabama

Barbara C. Beattie
Librarian
Fort Myers-Lee County Public Library
Fort Myers, Florida

Mel Bohn
Librarian
University of Nebraska at Omaha
Omaha, Nebraska

Lori Bronars
Science Reference Librarian
Kline Science Library
Yale University
New Haven, Connecticut

Mary Jane Brustman
Reference Bibliographer
Dewey Graduate Library for Public Affairs and Policy
State University of New York at Albany
Albany, New York

Barbara A. Burg
Reference Librarian
Widener Library
Harvard University
Cambridge, Massachusetts

Jeris F. Cassel
Reference Librarian, Online Services Coordinator
Rutgers University Libraries
New Brunswick, New Jersey

Erna Beiser Chamberlain
Coordinator of Science Collection and Science Reference
Science Library
State University of New York at Binghamton
Binghamton, New York

Lois Cherepon
Professor
St. John's University
Jamaica, New York

Janet K. Chisman
Librarian
Owen Science and Engineering Library
Washington State University
Pullman, Washington

Dorothy J. Coakley
Librarian
San Francisco Public Library
San Francisco, California

Charla A. Coatoam
Subject Specialist, Literature
Cuyahoga County Public Library System
Cleveland, Ohio

Wendell Cochran
Science Editor
Seattle, Washington

Donald E. Collins
Associate Professor
Department of Library and Information Studies
East Carolina University
Greenville, North Carolina

Mary Ellen Collins
Librarian
Purdue University Libraries
West Lafayette, Indiana

Luren E. Dickinson
Director
Findlay-Hancock County Public Library
Findlay, Ohio

Priscilla L. Drach
Librarian
Cuyahoga County Public Library System
Cleveland, Ohio

John F. Drexel
Writer and Critic
Montclair, New Jersey

Carol L. Ebener
Librarian
Montana State University Libraries
Bozeman, Montana

Dr. Lesley S. J. Farmer
Library Director
San Domenico School
San Anselmo, California

Leslie L. Gale
Research Associate
New Brunswick, New Jersey

Priscilla Cheng Geahigan
Head of Reference
Krannert Management and Economics Library
Purdue University Libraries
West Lafayette, Indiana

Martin E. Gingerich
Professor
Department of English
Western Michigan University
Kalamazoo, Michigan

Dr. M. Patrick Graham
Librarian
Pitts Theology Library
Emory University
Atlanta, Georgia

Helen Guice Groves
Librarian
University of Texas of the Permian Basin
Odessa, Texas

Karla Hahn
Librarian
School of Information Studies
Syracuse University
Syracuse, New York

Celia Hales-Mabry
Librarian
University of Minnesota Libraries
Minneapolis, Minnesota

Diana Hanaor
Adult Services Librarian
Monroe Township Library
Jamesburg, New Jersey

M. Dorcas Hand
Librarian
Episcopal High School, Bellaire
Houston, Texas

Robert D. Harlan
Professor
School of Library and Information Studies
University of California at Berkeley
Berkeley, California

Stephen M. Hayes
Reference and Public Documents Librarian
University Libraries
University of Notre Dame
Notre Dame, Indiana

Lucy Heckman
Reference Librarian, Business and Economics
St. John's University
Jamaica, New York

Atha Louise Henley
Life Sciences Librarian
Auburn University Libraries
Auburn, Alabama

Judith Herschman
Librarian
University Library
University of California at San Diego
La Jolla, California

Gary Holloway
Assistant Professor
Institute for Christian Studies
Austin, Texas

Joseph Holub
Librarian
Van Pelt Library
University of Pennsylvania
Philadelphia, Pennsylvania

Sharon A. Huge
Librarian
Alden Library
Ohio University
Athens, Ohio

Richard David Irving
Librarian
University Libraries
State University of New York at Albany
Albany, New York

Lawrence L. Irwin
Librarian
Cleary College
Livingston County, Michigan

Lorraine A. Jean
Head Reference Librarian
Nyselius Library
Fairfield University
Fairfield, Connecticut

Claudine Arnold Jenda
Science and Technology Librarian
Auburn University Libraries
Auburn, Alabama

Cynthia Stewart Kaag
Librarian
Science and Engineering Library
Washington State University
Pullman, Washington

James R. Kelly
Librarian
Gelman Library
George Washington University
Washington, D.C.

Charlene Kennedy
Head of Reference Services
Carlsbad City Library
Carlsbad, California

Mimi King
Bibliographic Instruction Coordinator
Mabel Smith Douglass Library
Rutgers University
New Brunswick, New Jersey

Bobbie Jean Klepper
Special Services Librarian
University of Texas of the Permian Basin
Odessa, Texas

Shirley D. Knight
Librarian
The Berkeley College of Business
Little Falls, New Jersey

Grove Koger
Librarian
Boise Public Library
Boise, Idaho

Christine Kollen
Map Librarian
University of Arizona Library
Tucson, Arizona

Les Kong
Librarian
University Library
California State University
San Bernardino, California

Sue Kopp
Reference Librarian
Holland Library
Washington State University
Pullman, Washington

Gordon Law
Krannert Management Library
Purdue University
West Lafayette, Indiana

Arla M. Lindgren
Associate Professor
St. John's University
Jamaica, New York

Lill Maman
Reference Librarian, Life Sciences
Mabel Smith Douglass Library
Rutgers University
New Brunswick, New Jersey

Laura Hibbets McCaffrey
Readers Services Librarian
Allen County Public Library
Fort Wayne, Indiana

Doreen J. McCullough
Librarian
College of St. Joseph Library
Rutland, Vermont

Mary Ann McFarland
Science Librarian
Lovejoy Library
Southern Illinois University
Edwardsville, Illinois

Heidi Mercado
Librarian, Science and Technology
University Library
Eastern Michigan University
Ypsilanti, Michigan

Michael A. Miranda
Associate Librarian
Feinberg Library
State University of New York at Plattsburgh
Plattsburgh, New York

Rachelle Moore
Librarian
Bartle Library
State University of New York at Binghamton
Binghamton, New York

Janice G. Newkirk
Reference Librarian
University Library
State University of New York at Albany
Albany, New York

Lawrence Olszewski
Librarian
School of Library Science
Kent State University
Columbus, Ohio

Jennifer F. Paustenbaugh
Assistant to the Dean of Libraries
Indiana University Libraries
Bloomington, Indiana

Pamela J. Peters
Librarian
James M. Milne Library
State University of New York at Oneonta
Oneonta, New York

David M. Pilachowski
Associate University Librarian
Case Library
Colgate University
Hamilton, New York

Jill H. Powell
Librarian
Cornell University Libraries
Ithaca, New York

Susan W. Price
Reference Librarian
Syracuse University Library
Syracuse, New York

Marilyn J. Rehnberg
Reference Librarian, Social Science and Literature
St. Paul Public Library
St. Paul, Minnesota

Philip G. Riley
Librarian
Guilford County Law Library
High Point, North Carolina

Terri J. Robar
Adjunct Associate Professor
Otto G. Righter Library
University of Miami
Coral Gables, Florida

Robert F. Rose
Librarian
The Behrend College
Pennsylvania State University
Erie, Pennsylvania

Steven J. Schmidt
Librarian
Indiana University-Purdue University Libraries
Indianapolis, Indiana

Richard Shotwell
Librarian
The Berkshire Museum
Pittsfield, Massachusetts

Donna L. Singer
Former High School English Teacher
Sarasota, Florida

Phillip A. Smith
Librarian
University Library
University of California at San Diego
La Jolla, California

Dr. Paul Sprachman
Professor
Rutgers University
New Brunswick, New Jersey

Joan Stahl
Department Head, Fine Arts and Recreation
Enoch Pratt Free Library
Baltimore, Maryland

Valsa Varma
Research Librarian
William F. Maag Library
Youngstown State University
Youngstown, Ohio

Tim J. Watts
Public Services Librarian
School of Law Library
Valparaiso University
Valparaiso, Indiana

Janet K. Wright
Arts and Humanities Librarian
Portland State University Library
Portland, Oregon

Andrea M. Yang
Coordinator of Online Services
Montana State University Libraries
Bozeman, Montana

Abby Yasgur
Librarian
Schlesinger Library
Harvard University
Cambridge, Massachusetts

Diane Zabel
Social Science Reference Librarian
Pattee Library
The Pennsylvania State University
University Park, Pennsylvania

Brenda M. Zimmerman
Librarian
Seminole County Public Library System
Seminole County, Florida

Preface

The third volume in the Bowker Buying Guide Series, *Topical Reference Books* represents a continuation of Bowker's commitment to providing librarians with useful tools for developing and maintaining their collections. Like its counterparts in this series, *General Reference Books for Adults* and *Reference Books for Young Readers,* this book offers the librarian a valuable source that collects, in one spot, reviews of a variety of reference books that are recommended for purchase.

Though embracing that shared goal of providing assistance in collection development, *Topical Reference Books* departs from the other two volumes in its focus. Those two works contain authoritative evaluations of general reference books—encyclopedias, dictionaries, atlases, and word books. This volume reviews instead those reference works that address more specific areas of knowledge. Whereas its sister publications in the series evaluate such works as the *World Book Encyclopedia,* the *Oxford English Dictionary,* or the many Hammond world atlases, this work includes reviews of such tools as the *Encyclopedia of Baseball,* the *Dictionary of American History,* and the *Cultural Atlas of Africa.* In addition to taking this topical orientation, the current work also goes farther afield in terms of the types of reference works included. This buying guide contains reviews of such diverse types as Chilton's automobile and truck publications (manuals), the *College Blue Book* (a directory), Congressional Quarterly's *Guide to U.S. Elections* (a handbook), *Contemporary Authors* (a biographical dictionary), *Historical Abstracts* (a bibliography), the *Oxford History of the Classical World* (a history), and the *Statesman's Year-Book* (a yearbook). The works reviewed in this volume range in topical coverage from advertising to zoology and in breadth of appeal from astrology to current events. Included are such different titles as the sober, weighty *Dictionary of American Biography* and the lighter but no less authoritative *Guinness Book of World Records.*

What is shared by all the works reviewed in this guide is their importance in their topical area. Many excellent reference works have been published over the years, and certainly the job of our Board of Advisors in determining which titles to recommend was a difficult one. Their task was not to judge merit alone, but to identify those titles that were most significant to a librarian wishing to build a core collection in each subject. A title that is not recommended, then, is not necessarily without merit. Such a work may be simply too specialized or too narrowly focused to warrant inclusion on the central list of the core collection. The titles that are included, though, clearly deserve serious consideration by any librarian developing a collection. The goal of *Topical Reference Books* is to provide librarians with a list of titles that, taken together, form a strong collection that will meet the needs of their patrons—a core collection of the essential works in a given subject area.

Once selected by the Board of Advisors, the core titles were analyzed by reviewers. These librarians and content experts report on the works' authority, accessibility, clarity, objectivity, scope, and features. Reviews aim to give the librarian a sense of the flavor of the work as well as its structure, content, and features.

Some librarians may desire a broader or deeper collection in a particular subject. For these librarians, *Topical Reference Books* augments each core listing with a list of supplementary and "new and noteworthy" titles. These works, like the core titles, are of outstanding merit. Any librarian building his or her collection would do well to include these titles. Some of these supplementary titles may appear to be old if judged merely by their copyright dates. Many of these works, however, are standards in their fields. It is also the case that in some fields—ancient history, for instance—such classic works remain the essential embodiment of a reference source.

Each category, then, contains a listing of core titles, which a collection should include; supplementary titles, which a collection of greater breadth or depth might include; and new and noteworthy titles, which enhance the collection with the most recent publications. Beyond these rankings, *Topical Reference Books* provides librarians with additional information. Listings of each core and supplementary title identify the type of library—public, academic, or school—for which the work is most suitable. Some titles, of course, are appropriate for all three classes of library. Others are clearly more desirable in one setting than the others. This evaluation is based on the technical nature of the work's content and the level at which the material is written. We feel that this ranking of audience offers a valuable service to librarians.

Chapter 1, "Using This Book," contains more information on how the book is organized, how the titles were chosen, and what issues the reviews address. Here it is more appropriate to consider why *Topical Reference Books* came into being.

The economics of publishing constrain publishers from investing the money required to undertake new, massive general reference works: the amount of material required would make the works of monumental size; the time required to compile, edit, and produce the information would be too long to afford. Yet we live in an age of burgeoning information. Publishers see the need to make that information accessible to librarians and patrons—scholars, students, specialists, laypersons. A solution to the problem is the creation of more focused reference works, works that address one field of study rather than human knowledge in general. The result is a growing trend to more specialized publications that nevertheless serve the main reference function: providing authoritative information in an accessible format.

We concluded that the librarian, faced with publication lists that were increasing exponentially, needed assistance in sifting through the mass of material to separate the indispensable from the desirable and the desirable from the unnecessary. We further reasoned that because these more narrowly focused works are highly specialized, they are often highly technical. It is impossible for even the most conscientious librarian to be expert—or even conversant—in all of the subjects for which they are asked to provide information.

Thus was born *Topical Reference Books.* Our goal is to help the librarian who is mining the rich vein of reference publishing by identifying the purest ore. Our hope is that the librarian faced with collection decisions will, by consulting this work, be better able to determine what publications are most needed by his or her patrons.

Topical Reference Books, then, is Bowker's newest offering in a long tradition of providing valuable professional reference materials for librarians. This tradition, now almost 120 years old, includes such well-known works as *Books in Print* and *The Reader's Adviser.* This title, joining the others in the Bowker Buying Guide Series, makes a vital contribution to Bowker's catalog of tools to aid librarians.

Many people contributed to the creation of *Topical Reference Books.* First I would like to thank our consultants for their insight in reviewing the scope and structure of the book, making suggestions as to fields of study to include, commenting on the title lists, reading through the chapters and headnotes, and recommending potential members of the Board of Advisors and reviewers. The librarians who served on that board were dedicated, hard-working, and responsible professionals whose spirit of service underlies their entire participation in this project. To the reviewers, we can only offer profound thanks. This group of librarians found resourceful ways of obtaining review copies of the titles assigned to them. When resourcefulness failed, they simply relied on perseverance. The results of their efforts were thoughtful, probing reviews.

The editorial staff was certainly instrumental in the creation of this book, and its members should not go unacknowledged. Dick Lidz provided advice to all involved, helping shape the project into its final form. Dale Anderson planned, organized, and managed the editorial and production teams. Maureen Bischoff-Drexel's guidance and even temper helped shepherd this book from idea to manuscript. Kim Nir's organization, editorial sense, and plain stubborn tenacity solved—and prevented—many a problem. Leslie Gale and Gabriela Mouskonas made phone call after phone call and library search after library search in the quest for the definitive price, ISBN, or publication date. Susan Tatiner guided our copy editors and proofreaders in the difficult task of creating consistency out of diversity. Finally, Mary Lyn Sodano skillfully and efficiently managed reams of proof through all stages of production to create a handsome product.

Marion Sader

Marion Sader
Publisher, Professional
and Reference Books
R. R. Bowker
January 1991

Abbreviations of Titles

A Arch	*American Archivist*
A Art	*American Art*
A Lib	*American Libraries*
AB	*AB Bookman's Weekly*
ABC	*American Book Collector*
Acad	*Academy*
Afterimage	*Afterimage*
AH	*American Heritage*
AHR	*American Historical Review*
AL	*American Literature*
Am	*America*
Am Craft	*American Craft*
Ams	*Americas: A Quarterly Review of Inter-American Cultural History*
Analog	*Analog: Science Fiction/Science Fact*
ANQ	*American Notes and Queries*
Ant R	*Antioch Review*
Apo	*Apollo*
Appl Mech Rev	*Applied Mechanics Review*
APSR	*American Political Science Review*
AR	*Accounting Review*
ARBA	*American Reference Books Annual*
Arch	*Archaeology*
Art Bul	*Art Bulletin*
ASBYP	*Appraisal: Science Books for Young People*
Atl	*Atlantic Monthly*
Aud	*Audubon*
B Rpt	*Book Report*
B&B	*Books & Bookmen*
BF	*Book Forum*
BHR	*Business History Review*
BL	*Booklist*
Bloom Rev	*Bloomsbury Review*
BM	*Burlington Magazine*
BOT	*Books of the Times*
BRD	*Book Review Digest*
Brit Bk N	*British Book News*
BS	*Best Sellers*
BSA-P	*Bibliographical Society of America—Papers*
Bus W	*Business Week*
BW	*Book World*
Bwatch	*Bookwatch*
CAY	*Come-All-Ye*
CBR	*Computer Book Review*
CC	*Christian Century*
CE	*Childhood Education*
CG	*Canadian Geographic*
CH	*Church History*
Cha Ti	*Changing Times*
CHE	*Chronicle of Higher Education*
Choice	*Choice*
CJ	*Classical Journal*
CLW	*Catholic Library World*
Cng	*Change*
Col Lit	*College Literature*
Comp Dr	*Comparative Drama*
Conn	*Connoisseur*
CP	*Contemporary Psychology*
CR	*Contemporary Review*
Cr H	*Craft Horizons*
CRL	*College and Research Libraries*
CS	*Contemporary Sociology*
CSM	*Christian Science Monitor*
CT	*Children Today*
Cu H	*Current History*
Cur R	*Curriculum Review*
CW	*Classical World*
Dial	*Dial*
Dr	*Drama: the Quarterly Theatre Review*
Earth S	*Earth Science*
Econ	*Economist*
Econ Bks	*Economic Books Current Selections*
EHR	*English Historical Review*
EJ	*English Journal*
Emerg Lib	*Emergency Librarian*
Enc	*Encounter*
Ethics	*Ethics*

Fant R	*Fantasy Review*
FQ	*Film Quarterly*
FR	*French Review*
Ga R	*Georgia Review*
GJ	*Geographical Journal*
Gov Pub R	*Government Publications Review*
GW	*Guardian Weekly*
HAHR	*Hispanic American Historical Review*
Hisp	*Hispania*
Hist of Photo	*History of Photography*
Hob	*Hobbies*
HRNB	*History: Reviews of New Books*
HT	*History Today*
Hum	*Humanist*
IJ Aging	*International Journal of Aging and Human Development*
ILN	*Illustrated London News*
Indexer	*The Indexer*
Inst	*Instructor*
Intl Dendrology Society YB	*International Dendrology Society Yearly Bulletin*
IRLA	*Information Retrieval & Library Automation*
Isis	*Isis*
J Bark Rev	*John Barkham Reviews*
J Geront	*Journal of Gerontology*
J Hi E	*Journal of Higher Education*
J Hist G	*Journal of Historical Geography*
J Interdis H	*Journal of Interdisciplinary History*
J Pol	*Journal of Politics*
J Read	*Journal of Reading*
JAL	*Journal of Academic Librarianship*
JAS	*Journal of Asian Studies*
JB	*Junior Bookshelf*
JEGP	*Journal of English and Germanic Philology*
JEH	*Journal of Economic History*
JEL	*Journal of Economic Literature*
JHI	*Journal of the History of Ideas*
JLH	*Journal of Library History, Philosophy, and Comparative Librarianship*
JQ	*Journalism Quarterly*
JR	*Journal of Religion*
Kliatt	*Kliatt Young Adult Paperback Book Guide*
KR	*Kirkus Reviews*
LATBR	*Los Angeles Times Book Review*
LIB	*The Library*
Lib Sci Ann	*Library Science Annual*
Lis	*Listener*
Lit D	*Literary Digest*
LJ	*Library Journal*
Lon R Bks	*London Review of Books*
LQ	*Library Quarterly*
LR	*Library Review*
LRTS	*Library Resources and Technical Services*
M Ed J	*Music Educators Journal*
Mag Lib	*Magazines for Libraries*
Mag YA	*Magazines for Young Adults*
MEJ	*Middle East Journal*
Meridian	*Meridian*
MFS	*Modern Fiction Studies*
MFSF	*Magazine of Fantasy and Science Fiction*
MLJ	*Modern Language Journal*
Money	*Money*
MQR	*Michigan Quarterly Review*
Ms	*Ms.*
N Dir Wom	*New Directions for Women*
Nat	*Nation*
Nation and Ath	*Nation and Athenaeum*
Nature	*Nature*
NCR	*National Civic Review*
New R	*New Republic*
New Tech Bks	*New Technical Books*
NGSQ	*National Genealogical Society Quarterly*
NH	*Natural History*
NL	*New Leader*
Notes	*Notes*
NS	*New Statesman*
NW	*Newsweek*
NY	*New Yorker*
NYRB	*New York Review of Books*
NYT	*New York Times*
NYTBR	*New York Times Book Review*
Obs	*Observer*
ON	*Opera News*
Pac A	*Pacific Affairs*
PAR	*Public Administration Review*
Parabola	*Parabola: Myth and the Quest for Meaning*

Prog	*Progressive*
PSQ	*Political Science Quarterly*
PT	*Psychology Today*
Pub Gar	*Public Gardens*
Punch	*Punch*
PW	*Publishers Weekly*
R&R Bk N	*Reference and Research Book News*
RBB	*Reference Books Bulletin*
Ref Bk R	*Reference Book Review*
Rel St Rev	*Religious Studies Review*
Rp B Bk R	*Reprint Bulletin Book Reviews*
RQ	*RQ*
RSR	*Reference Services Review*
RT	*Reading Teacher*
S Fict R	*Science Fiction Review*
S&T	*Sky and Telescope*
SA	*Scientific American*
SAQ	*South Atlantic Quarterly*
SB	*Science Books and Films*
Sch L	*School Libraries*
Sch Lib	*School Librarian*
Sci	*Science*
SciTech	*SciTech Book News*
SE	*Social Education*
Ser Lib	*Serials for Librarians*
Ser Lib 2nd	*Serials for Librarians, 2d edition*
Ser R	*Serials Review*
SF	*Social Forces*
SF&FBR	*Science Fiction & Fantasy Book Review*
SL	*Special Libraries*
SLJ	*School Library Journal*
SLMQ	*School Library Media Quarterly*
Sm Pr R	*Small Press Review*
SMQ	*School Media Quarterly*
Soc	*Society*
Spec	*Spectator*
Sports Ill	*Sports Illustrated*
SR	*Saturday Review*
SS	*Social Studies*
Studio	*Studio International*
Teacher	*Teacher*
TES	*Times Educational Supplement*
Theat A	*Theater Arts*
TLS	*Times Literary Supplement*
TN	*Top of the News*
Trav	*Travel-Holiday*
TT	*Theology Today*
USA T	*USA Today*
VOYA	*Voice of Youth Advocates*
VQR	*Virginia Quarterly Review*
WCRB	*West Coast Review of Books*
WHQ	*Western Historical Quarterly*
WHR	*Western Humanities Review*
Wil Q	*Wilson Quarterly*
WLB	*Wilson Library Bulletin*
WLT	*World Literature Today*
Wom R Bks	*Women's Review of Books*
WSJ	*Wall Street Journal*
YR	*Yale Review*

PART ONE

Introduction

Chapter 1

Using This Book

Topical Reference Books is a collection-development tool that provides librarians with evaluative reviews of reference works that should be acquired to build a core collection of the most essential titles in each of over 90 subject areas. These highly recommended titles—the core titles—are identified by the type of library for which they are appropriate. In addition to the core titles, the volume provides a list of supplementary works that are recommended for acquisition by librarians who wish to develop a more in-depth collection in a given subject area. The titles recommended were selected by a vote of 23 librarians who served on the Board of Advisors. The process was aided as well by the services of two consultants who are prominent in library science.

When appropriate, the book also mentions "new and noteworthy" works—newly published or recently revised titles that, while released subsequent to the selection of core and supplementary lists, are worthy of librarians' attention.

Scope

Topical Reference Books recommends English-language works published or distributed in the United States. Works are classified as being suitable for use in one or more of the following types of libraries: public, academic, or secondary school. The reading level of the works included is high school and up.

Although this buying guide reviews topical reference books, the works considered are broadly rather than narrowly focused. For example, a biographical dictionary such as *Contemporary Dramatists* is included, but a study of Eugene O'Neill would not be included.

Reference works reviewed in *Reference Books for Young Adults* and *General Reference Books for Adults*—the first two volumes in the Bowker Buying Guide series—are also excluded from this volume. These two volumes include reviews of general encyclopedias, dictionaries, atlases, and word books.

Topical Reference Books reviews subject encyclopedias, dictionaries, bibliographies, biographical works, fact books, atlases, and government sources. Anthologies and denominational works are not reviewed. Indexes and directories, for the most part, are not included in this buying guide. A few important indexes and directories were voted for inclusion by the Board and are therefore mentioned in the category headnote. Some indexes or directories are reviewed within this book when the scope of the work includes information that is more extensive than the classification might indicate and when the work is particularly important to the subject category. For example, *The Standard Directory of Advertisers* is reviewed in the Advertising category because directories are the primary reference tools in this field. Other exceptions will be found, for example, in the Business and Folklore and Mythology categories.

Where on-line and CD-ROM versions of print works exist, this fact is noted in the bibliographic profile provided for the print work. These versions are not evaluated as part of this buying guide, although some reviewers may make brief comments about them.

The cutoff date for works considered for review is publication in January 1990. Because valuable works are being published at all times, the editorial staff did not wish to ignore more recent publications. Thus, major reference works published after that date are briefly described in the section titled "New and Noteworthy" at the end of a category.

Topical Reference Books reviews in-print works only. Out-of-print books suggested by the Board of Advisors as worthy of inclusion or works that were suggested by the Board but became out of print during the development of this work are not reviewed. Such titles are, however, mentioned in the headnote. A significant number of books that were in print when the development of this guide began (in May 1988) were no longer in print two years later for a variety of reasons. Publishers no longer maintain a large inventory of backlist titles because of the taxable nature of these items and the cost of warehousing them. Additionally, mergers, acquisitions, and consolidations of publishing companies contribute to more recent books being declared out of print. Because many of these works are integral to collections, librarians should make use of the suggestions in the headnote. To aid the librarian in tapping this important resource, the "List of Publishers and Distributors" at the back of this volume suggests sources through which out-of-print books may be obtained.

Audience

Topical Reference Books was developed to assist public, academic, and school librarians in the selection of core and supplementary works in all subject areas. Patrons of these libraries can also use this guide to identify the most essential works in a given field or to acquire core works for their home libraries.

To create a single reference work recommending specialized titles in all fields—or even in the major areas of academic pursuit: humanities, social sciences, and sciences—would be a monumental task. Further, such a work would appeal only to a few narrowly focused audiences and not to the great body of reference librarians and library patrons. For these reasons, we determined to focus our efforts on topical reference books of more broad-based interest.

Consultants

The consultants for *Topical Reference Books* supplied general expertise through their review of the format and the reviews of selected content areas. Among their duties were: (1) to suggest appropriate librarians to serve as Board of Advisor members and identify qualified reviewers for subject categories; (2) to review the list of selected and new titles to be included; (3) to evaluate and comment on headnotes and reviews in a number of subject areas; (4) to make decisions on how works are to be reviewed and cross-referenced in categories that have titles in common; and (5) to evaluate and comment on the introductory chapters.

Board of Advisors

The Board of Advisors performed the task of selecting titles for inclusion. The Board identified topical reference works suitable for core and supplementary collections in public, academic, and school libraries, working from a compilation of topical reference works currently in print. (See the "Voting" section of this chapter for a description of the voting process.)

Board members were librarians familiar with the reference review process through their previous experience as reviewers or as authors or editors of books in this area. Many Board members also serve on committees for collection development in their own libraries and for various professional associations.

The Board included 23 members: ten currently serve as public librarians, eleven as academic librarians, and two as school librarians. Because of their backgrounds, Board members provided a wider range of expertise than their current position may indicate. Several of the public and academic librarians had previous experience in school libraries, and several academic librarians held prior positions in public libraries. The geographical distribution of the Board is representative. Seven Board members are located in the Northeast; five in the South; seven in the Midwest; and four in the West.

Category Selection

To make *Topical Reference Books* accessible to all types of libraries, the reviews are arranged alphabetically by subject category. (Additional accessibility is provided by separate indexes of core and supplementary works arranged by Dewey Decimal classification numbers and the Library of Congress classification system.) Category titles were selected after an examination of the subject headings used in the *American Reference Books Annual, Guide to Reference Books, Reference Books Bulletin,* and those used in the Dewey and Library of Congress classification systems. Ninety-one subject categories were finally selected.

The organization of titles into categories is a key feature of *Topical Reference Books* and its central organizing logic. The editorial staff believes that evaluative volumes organized by type of book (for instance, all biographical dictionaries) overlook two important points. First, books are creative endeavors not easily pigeonholed into given types; what matters in evaluating reference works is not what a book is called, but what information it contains. Second, although a given type of book may be useful for a certain field of study, other types of books may be equally or more valuable. The study of history is an example. Biographical dictionaries are certainly useful to the librarian building a collection, but atlases, which help fix the area being studied in time and place, are equally essential. If you view each type of book as a way of approaching a field, the importance of including many types of books in the core collection is clear. Biographical dictionaries give the people-oriented view, but many reference questions address other issues such as dates, terms, or places. To answer these questions, the librarian needs chronologies, topical dictionaries, or atlases, each of which takes a different perspective on history and, by doing so, sheds more light on the subject. By focusing on an isolated class or type of book, these nomenclature-oriented volumes rob the librarian—and eventually the patron—of these other perspectives.

The editorial staff determined early on, then, that the focus of this book would be the *category,* the field of study, rather than the type of book. In this way, the titles selected can help the librarian build a core collection that provides a range of views of each subject area in the attempt to offer patrons the best mix of resources.

Compiling Works for Approval by the Board

To develop the list of recommended titles, the editorial staff began by compiling large lists of reference works in the 91 subject categories. Compilations were generated by librarians and researchers who consulted library reference collections in those areas, subject experts and special collections, subject bibliographies, and journals and periodicals that are either aimed at the library market or focus on special subject areas. All titles on the original lists were in print when those lists were compiled.

Voting

The Board members were sent the compiled lists to select the final titles. They were also asked to rate each title as being suitable for one or more of the three types of libraries. Board members were instructed to designate each title as either a core book or a supplementary book and to delete titles that they deemed inappropriate. A *core title* is defined as one that is a must for a collection in a particular subject area. A *supplementary title* is defined as one that would add depth to a collection or would reflect specialized interests among the library's patrons. The Board was further instructed to mention any out-of-print works that might need to be included in a core collection. An important part of the Board's job was to add titles that might have been overlooked in the compilation of the lists. The final total number of books in a category was not to exceed 30, including core and supplements. (In practice, a few categories did exceed this number.)

The results of the voting in each category were then tallied and ranked numerically. The suggested additions to these lists were also tallied and included in the ranking. The total number of votes determined whether a book is a core or supplementary work, as well as the libraries for which it is appropriate. Larger categories (for example, Music) were divided into smaller subcategories to organize titles more clearly and facilitate comparisons. Final listings of core titles were then prepared for the reviewers.

Reviewers and the Review Process

Reviewers were selected by recommendation of the consultants; by contacting major libraries, library schools, and special libraries (for subject expertise); and by recommendation of librarians associated with the first two volumes in the Bowker Buying Guide series.

The intention of the editorial staff was to have only one reviewer per category to ensure comparability among the works reviewed. In most cases, this aim has been achieved. However, in the case of very large categories or instances in which the reviewer was unable to locate all of the books for review, one or more additional reviewers had to be assigned. If a category has more than one reviewer, the initials of the reviewer appear at the end of each review. The names of all reviewers are printed above the category title. The book's front matter lists all reviewers and their affiliations.

It was the task of the reviewer to prepare the reviews and the category headnote according to the structure designed for this buying guide (see "Category Structure" below). It is important to reiterate, however, that the designation of core and supplementary books and the identification of the kind of library for which they are suitable was determined by the vote of the Board of Advisors, not by the reviewers.

Category Structure

Each category contains a headnote, a chart of core works, bibliographic profiles for all titles, core reviews, supplementary reviews, and "new and noteworthy" reviews. (Some few categories have no supplementary titles. A small number of categories have no "new and noteworthy" reviews.) The category structure provides the user with highly selective source material that can be used in a systematic approach to collection development. Each part of the category offers clearly defined and consistent information to the user.

The *headnote* defines and summarizes the scope of the category and the main features of the kinds of works that are standard in the field. This gives the librarian an overview of the subject area and addresses any important issues in that area that affect the composition of the category. The headnote also mentions significant directories, indexes, and out-of-print works, which are not reviewed but which could be acquired to add depth to a collection. Cross-references to related categories appear before the headnote. For ease of identification, titles reviewed in the Buying Guide are set in large and small caps. (This is the case in the body of the reviews as well.)

The *core chart* precedes the reviews. This chart lists all of the core titles with brief bibliographical information and shows for which of the three libraries each title is suitable. Related titles that are applicable to more than one category and are reviewed elsewhere will have a line reading "(See [name of the category])." The core chart is a quick selection aid that a librarian can use to focus only on those core books that are suitable for his or her library.

A *bibliographic profile* precedes each review of core, supplementary, and "new and noteworthy" works. This profile provides the title, edition, author, publisher (and distributor, if appropriate), date of publication (and date of reprint edition, if appropriate), hard or soft binding, number of volumes, number of pages, illustrations, appendix, index, ISBN (for multivolume works which are not sold as sets, the ISBN of the most recent volume is listed), price, type of work, Library of Congress classification number, and Dewey Decimal classification number. If the work being reviewed has an on-line or CD-ROM version, that information also appears. The bibliographic profile also lists the next scheduled revision of the work, if known. Related titles that are reviewed elsewhere will contain the bibliographic profile and a "see" reference to the category in which the full review appears.

The editors sent forms requesting ISBN, price, and revision schedules to all publishers whose works appear in this buying guide. Attempts were made to obtain verification of this information at least twice, with a final check taking place in August 1990. If no response was received from the publisher, the information was obtained from the 1990–1991 edition of *Books in Print.*

Core reviews focus on those books that are *musts* in the subject category. The text of each review defines the scope, authority, accuracy, comprehensiveness, currency, and accessibility of the work. These reviews include comments comparing the work to other works in the category where applicable. The review ends with the Board's recommendation of the type of library for which the work is appropriate.

Depending on the key issues for the field identified in the headnote, the librarian may want to concentrate on certain criteria mentioned in the review. For example, in the category Computers and Artificial Intelligence, currency would be an important factor in evaluating titles. In a category such as American History, where several similar dictionaries are available, the librarian would want to look carefully at the comparative comments made in the reviews.

Supplementary reviews highlight those works that could be purchased to add additional depth to a category, depending on the individual needs of the library. These reviews feature excerpts from previously published reviews that best define the work. Citations for other reviews of the work are listed following these excerpts. The Board's recommendation is the final item provided in this review.

"New and noteworthy" works—those that were published after the voting process was completed—conclude the category. These reviews provide a sentence or two taken from a review in a major periodical that best defines the work.

Structure of the Buying Guide

Topical Reference Books has two main parts: part 1, "Introduction," which includes background information on topical reference books, and part 2, "Evaluations of Topical Reference Books," which contains the reviews of the subject categories. The volume concludes with a bibliography, a list of publishers and distributors, and indexes. A brief overview of the contents is given below.

Chapter 1, "Using This Book," is preceded by a "List of Categories" reviewed in this buying guide. This list also includes all cross-references to related categories. A person consulting the list can use it to locate categories of interest and all related categories without having to search further in the text.

Chapter 2, "About Topical Reference Books," presents a concise look at the history of the reference book in the United States from colonial times to the development of the first reference services in libraries (circa 1898) to information services today. This is followed by a brief overview of reference book publishing, its history in the United States, and current trends in the reference publishing industry.

Chapter 3, "Choosing Topical Reference Books," describes public, academic, school, and special libraries and relates the four philosophies of reference service to the role of the reference librarian. The types of reference books reviewed in this work are then defined. Included are examples of each type of work that is reviewed in this buying guide. Additionally, the chapter includes facsimile pages from several reference works reprinted with annotations highlighting their distinguishing characteristics. The chapter provides an in-depth look at how to use the elements of each category (headnote, chart, reviews) to evaluate reference works. Review criteria for the evaluation of each of the reference works are explained using examples of works reviewed in this book. Finally, the chapter includes a brief discussion of other selection tools.

Following part 2 are two appendixes. There is a bibliography of books and periodicals related to all aspects of reference books, reference book publishing, reference libraries, and reference service. These works address issues of both current and historical interest.

A "List of Publishers and Distributors" follows the bibliography. This list contains addresses and phone numbers for the publisher or distributor of all core and supplementary works reviewed in *Topical Reference Books.* Each entry also contains a list of all titles published by that publisher or distributor that are reviewed in this book. This section concludes with names of sources through which out-of-print titles can be obtained.

Five indexes complete this volume. The title and subject index lists (alphabetically) all works that appear in the volume. This includes all directories, indexes, out-of-print works, new works, or historically significant titles mentioned in the headnotes as well as the core, supplementary, and "new and noteworthy" titles that are reviewed. The second is an author and editor index. The names of all those whose works are mentioned in the volume (not only the core and supplementary titles) are arranged alphabetically. The third index accesses titles by recommendation, as a core work, a supplementary work, or a "new and noteworthy" work. In the fourth index, core and supplementary titles are arranged numerically, according to The Library of Congress classification system. Titles in the fifth index are arranged according to Dewey Decimal classification number. These final two indexes allow librarians using either of these classification systems to have access to the titles reviewed in this guide.

Chapter 2

About Topical Reference Books

The history of reference tools can be traced back as far as the primitive efforts of prehistoric humans to use pictures or symbols to recall events or, more directly, to the development of the Greek lexicon in Alexandria in the first century A.D. This early history is treated at length in "The History of General Reference Books," which is chapter 1 in *General Reference Books for Adults.*

Reference Works in the Colonial Period

Despite their long history, reference books were not a common feature in American libraries until the close of the nineteenth century. The earliest reference works in this country were, in fact, likely to be found in the homes of settlers rather than on library shelves. Because many of our ancestors had come to the New World in order to practice their religious beliefs freely, the Bible and related religious literature were the kinds of books that could usually be found in the home. A Bible could provide guidance for the settlers' daily lives and serve as a primer to teach children to read.

In addition to religious needs, settlers living in an age before the widespread availability of professional services discovered that books teaching self-reliance and guidance in everyday living were very necessary. For example, planters in the South might include among their books works on farming, animal husbandry, and other aspects of country life. Almanacs were also popular works because the information they contained supplied readers with weather predictions; times of sunrise, sunset, and high and low tides; as well as other such data. In colonial times, how-to-do-it manuals taught the pioneers to be their own doctors, architects, and lawyers. William Vaughn's *Directions for Health, Both Natural and Artificial* provided assistance when doctors were unavailable. Michael Dalton's *The Country Justice* served in the absence of practicing attorneys. Domestic affairs were guided by such books as Robert Cleaver's *A Godly Form of Household Government,* and conduct in manners was governed by *The Whole Duty of Man* and *The Academy of Complements.* In these and other ways, reference books aided the growth of a colonial society that stressed practical literature over leisure reading.

From the colonial period and well into the nineteenth century, the reference works that were in the possession of individuals tended to be utilitarian or instructional in nature. College libraries during this time were custodial and generally restrictive institutions catering to faculty, not student, needs. School libraries were nonexistent, and public libraries were few in number.

Some familiar reference titles did make their appearance during this period. The *Encyclopaedia Britannica* was first published in Great Britain between 1768 and 1771, with pirated editions printed in the United States as early as 1798. Samuel Johnson's *Dictionary of the English Language* appeared in England in 1750 and acquired a longstanding reputation as the finest dictionary in the English language in Great Britain and the United States. By the time of the American Revolution, the use of dictionaries was well established in American schools. In his *Ideas of the English School* (1751), Benjamin Franklin had recommended that "Each boy should have an English dictionary to help him over difficulties." Franklin's criticism of the lack of standardization in English spelling served as an inspiration for Noah Webster's *A Compendious Dictionary of the English Language* (1806) and *An American Dictionary of the English Language* (1828), two works that made Webster's name synonymous with the word "dictionary" in the United States.

Reference Works of the Nineteenth Century

Beginning in 1876, several factors combined to create a more favorable atmosphere for the development of a readership for reference works. Heavy immigration brought millions of new inhabitants to our shores. More and more cities and towns began to establish public libraries to meet the needs of the growing population. Meanwhile, changes in teaching methods in academic institutions had a dramatic effect on the demand for reference publications. The beginning of graduate education at Johns Hopkins University in 1876, with emphasis on research and scientific investigation, made libraries and reference works essential for the first time in academic libraries.

The periodical index, later to become an indispensable tool for all levels of twentieth-century library users, made its first appearance in 1848 when William Poole, Assistant Librarian of the Society of Brothers in Unity at Yale University, compiled a manuscript index to the magazines in the society's library. Realizing the value of his "Index to Periodical Literature," Poole submitted it for publication to G. P. Putnam. His index, with its later supplements, is still the standard guide to nineteenth-century periodical literature.

Despite the existence of these and other reference works, a large enough market did not exist to support mass publication of reference books. Even after the Civil War, the sum total of reference works consisted of little more than several general-purpose dictionaries and encyclopedias, including *Bartlett's Familiar Quotations,* the *Annual Register of World Events,* and a handful of other works.

Without corresponding developments in the library field, however, growth in the publication of reference works could not have taken place. When librarians met in Philadelphia in 1876 to found the American Library Association (ALA), librarianship became a profession dedicated to changing its institutions to better serve their patrons. Within 20 years, reference collections and departments were common library features. The development of reference collections and services is discussed later in this chapter.

Publishers responded to the call to supply the necessary reference works. One of the earliest needs in this area was for bibliographies that would enable users to locate books and periodicals in the library and provide information on the availability of new materials on the market. Consequently, numerous bibliographic works began to make their appearance. The need for a national bibliography was met by Frederick Leypoldt's *American Catalog of Books in Print and for Sale,* published between 1880 and 1910, and the *United States Catalog of Books in Print,* which was started in 1898 and is published today as the *Cumulative Book Index.* Other reference works that first appeared during the late 1800s included: the *Statistical Abstracts of the United States* (1879); *Grove's Dictionary of Music and Musicians* (1879–1889); and *Ayer's Directory of Newspapers and Periodicals in the United States and Canada* (now the *Gale Directory of Publications*). All these works continue to be published today. The proliferation of reference works from the late 1880s on makes it difficult to realize that the ideas of a separate reference collection and reference service were at one time revolutionary. The following pages trace the development of these concepts and philosophies in various library settings.

Reference Departments Past and Present

Libraries have not always been receptive to the idea of reference service. Prior to 1876, separate reference collections did not even exist. Although informal help to individuals in the use of collections had long been provided in some institutions as a matter of courtesy, the library was viewed well into the nineteenth century as a place where books were to be stored and preserved. At best, users were allowed to find their own information and materials, and at worst, they were not to disturb the books that had been carefully arranged on the shelves by the librarian. According to A. R. Spofford, the Librarian of Congress from 1864 to 1897, it was not unusual to find the leading encyclopedias, dictionaries, biographies, and other works locked up in cases or placed on remote or inaccessible shelves. However, by 1876, changes were in the wind as a movement for free popular education swept the country. The newly awakening library movement saw a role for itself in uplifting the masses through books and literature. In that year, Spofford wrote of the need for a "central bureau of reference" in every library. "Here would be assembled, whether on a circular case made to revolve on a pivot, or on a rectangular case, with volumes covering both sides, or in a central alcove forming a portion of the shelves of the main library, all those books of reference and volumes incessantly needed by students in pursuit of their various inquiries." This revolutionary call for a separate reference collection was at least partially self-serving, because Spofford's idea would allow patrons to help themselves, thus leaving the librarians free for other labor.

The year 1876 also saw the first public statement calling for actual reference service to readers. Samuel S. Green, in his address to that year's American Library Association Conference, noted that the availability of reference books was not enough. Instead, librarians needed to "mingle with the readers" and provide greater assistance. The formulation of this philosophy marked the beginning of reference librarianship. The next two decades saw the elements needed for modern reference service fall into place. Rapid growth in both academic and public libraries brought concern for the organization of reference collections and access to them. Two solutions included the development of the dictionary catalog and the widespread adoption of Melvil Dewey's scheme for subject classification of books, without which user access in libraries would be severely limited. As was noted above, academic reference collections and service developed largely as a result of the new research-oriented educational methods introduced with the founding of Johns Hopkins University in 1876.

The nation's first full-time reference librarians, George and William G. Baker, were appointed in 1884 by Melvil Dewey, librarian at Columbia University. By 1886, the work of personal assistance at Columbia evolved into a distinct reference department. The next year, a committee at Boston Public Library advised that because the catalog was the only means of linking inquirers with what they sought, library personnel should be on hand who were specialists in such guidance. At this time, reference service was being developed in the large public libraries in Boston, Brooklyn, Chicago, Providence, and St. Louis. In 1891 the term *reference work* appeared for the first time in the *Library Journal*, and by 1893 the theory of reference service was generally accepted by American librarians. By the 1890s, the three distinctive features of modern reference service had also been developed: (1) a staff exclusively devoted to reference work; (2) reference collections in separate rooms specifically designed for that purpose; and (3) efficient guides to the library's resources.

This period was also one of rapid change in the physical facilities that were provided for the new reference collections. Until the early 1880s, the architectural layout prevalent in libraries was one in which all books were placed in a single large room surrounded by alcoves and galleries. In 1881, William Poole, the same librarian who had earlier introduced the periodical index to the library world, called for library buildings that would consist of a number of special subject rooms, plus a reference room in which the general reference collection would be placed. Such was Poole's influence that most of the medium- and large-sized libraries soon came to adopt his plan.

Another major step in the evolution of information services in libraries was the development of subject specialization among reference librarians and in reference collections. Again, it was Melvil Dewey who took the lead. In 1901, he predicted that "as demand . . . warrant[s] we shall have reference librarians each limited to history, science, art, . . . till we shall have . . . a company of men each an authority in his own field." Special libraries soon began to emerge in business and industry as well as in government departments. The larger public libraries were also answering the call. The first known technical division opened in 1889 in the Carnegie Library in Pittsburgh, while the Newark Public Library added a business section in 1904. By 1909, there were enough "special librarians" in various kinds of institutions to form a Special Libraries Association separate from the American Library Association. Further narrowing in subject expertise among reference librarians is reflected in the establishment of library organizations for librarians specializing in law and other areas, and in the growing subject departmentalization in public and academic libraries. By 1910 the idea of a full-time reference librarian appointed to serve businesspersons and other groups of special-interest patrons was firmly established.

Reference librarians of the 1990s continue to use and be influenced by the innovations introduced by the late nineteenth- and early twentieth-century library pioneers. The most obvious of these, the physical form and organization of the reference department itself, unchanged since the early 1900s, is the appropriate place to begin a discussion of the present-day situation.

Upon entering a particular library for the first time, users may observe that all reference books are located in a single department, whereas in another library, they may discover that these titles are separated in different locations according to subject matter. In some instances (for example, in large public, college, or university libraries) the breakdown may be along broad divisional lines, with the social sciences, humanities, and science reference materials located in different areas of the same building or even in separate buildings. In other cases the division will be along narrow subject lines, with separate sections for business, law, art, music, and so on, within the same or different buildings. And while the general reference collection is the standard for most libraries, divided collections in medium- and large-sized libraries are dictated as much by the views of the staff and administration as by the size and type of library.

The general reference plan is the most common, and for small- and medium-sized libraries with limited resources, this may be the only choice. Regardless of the size of the library, this approach has benefits—particularly in view of today's tight budgets—because it requires fewer staff members and the least duplication of materials. This plan, however, sacrifices in-depth knowledge in reference service and collection development to the ability to provide some service to all. Many libraries compensate for this by making each librarian responsible for one or more subject areas in the collection. Although this works well in keeping pace with new reference literature, it can fall short in providing works that provide further depth for answering subject-specific questions.

The divisional plan is more appropriate for libraries with large collections. Normally, it consists of one or more rooms devoted to such broad subject areas as the humanities, social sciences, and science and technology. Each division may possess multiple types of material and include periodicals, nonreference books, and reference books in the same general location. Subject departmentalization is similar to this, except that each unit is responsible for fewer subject areas. Typical breakdowns might include business and finance, history and travel, or sociology and education.

Organization of collections according to subject departmental and divisional plans is an excellent approach from the reference and collection-development point of view. Librarians who work continually in selected areas quickly become more expert in those subjects. Consequently, they can serve both the general public and subject experts alike at a higher level of efficiency, and their familiarity with the literature in their fields enables better selection of reference materials. Of course, there are limitations to this approach. Specialized collections require more personnel, and duplication of materials is inevitable. Additionally, the fact that knowledge does not always fit neatly into specific categories can lead to confusion among users who look for information in one division, only to find it is in another. Some of these problems may be solved by setting up an information desk near the library's catalog or maintaining a general reference collection as part of the divisional or subject plan.

Reference Works Today

The basic character of reference service and reference tools that was established during the late nineteenth and early twentieth centuries has carried through to the present. Reference works continue to become more specialized in subject content to meet the post–World War II information explosion. It is the introduction of the computer, however, that has affected reference publishing more than any invention since Gutenberg's printing press in the fifteenth century. With reference data in machine-readable form available via CD-ROM and online search services, reference works have entered a new age in which books exist side by side with the newer electronic forms.

Reference Book Publishing Today

The reference book publishing industry encompasses the production, distribution, and sale of informational books in which the data have been organized for convenient and easy access by users. Common products include dictionaries, encyclopedias, biographical sources, indexes, directories, and similar works that, by definition, are to be consulted for specific information rather than read straight through.

The reference collection is a major part of any library and, along with the library's catalog, the starting point for research. The publishing industry provides the material that makes the collection possible. Librarians, publishers, and the book trade are tied together in an interdependent chain, each link serving the needs of the other. To develop the reference collection to its utmost potential, librarians working in collection development should familiarize themselves with reference publishers and the publishing industry. The name of the publisher may be the decisive factor in the selection process. A publisher's name can be an indication of that publisher's experience and reputation for authority and quality. When, for example, the name H. W. Wilson appears on the title page of a new periodical index, a librarian's first thoughts are of the experience, authority, and quality of that publisher's reputation. The same may be said of Marquis and the *Who's Who* series, R. R. Bowker and bibliographical works, and so on. Some familiarity with reference publishers, then, is important to those who choose the information sources of the library.

One of the most prominent publishers of books for and about libraries and the book trade is the R. R. Bowker Company, which has served American librarianship since its professional beginnings in the late nineteenth century. The company's publications keep track of industry statistics through the *Bowker Annual of Library and Book Trade Information,* of libraries and book stores with the *American Library Directory* and the *American Book Trade Directory,* and of titles that are currently in print through *Books in Print.*

For over 90 years the products of the H. W. Wilson Company have also been staples in libraries of all levels and types. Librarians, students, and others know Wilson's *Readers' Guide to Periodical Literature* as a "household word," and the company's indexes in education, law, business, and other areas are standards in their fields.

Another well-known name in the field, Gale Research, Inc., was founded as a reprint business in 1954 and has grown to become one of the largest reference publishers of the 1980s and now 1990s. Gale's highly regarded *Contemporary Authors* series is the most comprehensive source of information on writers presently on the market. The *Encyclopedia of Associations* is an indispensable source of information on professional and nonprofit organizations. Gale also publishes bibliographic works such as the *Book Review Index* and other similar titles.

The backbone of any reference collection is its encyclopedias. The average public library may have anywhere from 4 to 12 different sets on its shelves. This field is dominated by four companies: Encyclopaedia Britannica; World Book, Inc.; Grolier, Inc.; and Macmillan Publishing Company. Together, they account for more than four-fifths of all encyclopedias sold. These companies and their products are treated in detail in the Bowker buying guide entitled *General Reference Books for Adults.*

A leader in science, social science, and business publishing, John Wiley & Sons has the distinction of operating under the ownership of the same family for nearly two centuries. In the reference area, Wiley has produced works such as the well-regarded *Kirk-Othmer Concise Encyclopedia of Chemical Technology* and the *Worldmark Encyclopedia of the Nations.* Wiley's *International Encyclopedia of Robotics* was recently honored with an award by the Association of American Publishers. Like many other large publishers, Wiley's products include computer software and electronic data bases.

Simon & Schuster is currently the largest publishing house in the United States. Their presence in the reference book market became notable through the acquisition of Prentice-Hall, Inc., in 1984. Established in New York in 1913, Prentice-Hall was known mainly for publishing textbooks, business-related looseleaf services and books, and general-interest and fiction works. Restructured and revitalized by Simon & Schuster, the reference (or information) division covers legal and financial services, tax and professional services, law, and business. Electronic products are strongly emphasized and account for a major portion of sales. The company's reference books cover topics beyond the specializations stated above and include familiar standards such as *Documents of American History.*

Houghton Mifflin Company is another textbook publisher that makes significant contributions in the reference area. The company's reference division produces a wide variety of reference titles, including the *Encyclopedia of World History* and the *Information Please Almanac.*

Frederick Ungar Publishing Company was established in New York in 1940 after its founder was forced to flee his publishing business in Nazi-occupied Austria. Since its beginning, Ungar has produced over 2,000 books in literature, criticism, history, philosophy, science, and the arts, including the *Encyclopedia of World Literature in the Twentieth Century.* Other works of interest from Ungar are the *Literature and Life* series of literary biographies in approximately 200 volumes and the *Library of Literary Criticism* in 30 volumes.

McGraw-Hill, Inc., produces many fine works in the area of science and technology, many of which are well known in libraries. These include the excellent 20-volume *McGraw-Hill Encyclopedia of Science and Technology* and *McGraw-Hill Dictionary of Scientific and Technical Terms.* McGraw-Hill also owns Standard & Poor's Corporation, a major provider of reference sources in business.

In addition to commercial publishers, a significant portion of the reference materials found in libraries, homes, and elsewhere are produced by university presses. These publishers are particularly important because they produce works on highly specialized or scholarly topics which commercial companies cannot economically produce. On the whole, university presses are doing well financially. A 1988 survey of 11 leading American university presses found them all growing steadily. The American Association of University Presses reported that its members published 3,500 new titles in 1986, with approximately 90,000 other titles in print. Two of the best known academic presses, in England as well as in the United States, are those at Oxford and Cambridge universities.

Oxford University Press was founded in 1478 and has published continuously since 1584. Today Oxford has branches or representatives in more than 50 countries and more than 10,000 titles in print. Oxford University Press, Inc., its American subsidiary, is the largest university press in the United States. Many of their company's publications are regarded as essential to any reference collection. Notable works include the Oxford Companion series, the *Oxford English Dictionary,* the *Dictionary of National Biography,* and the *Oxford Classical Dictionary.*

Cambridge University Press, like Oxford, is regarded as a book trade giant. Up to 70 percent of its books are exported to the United States and other English-speaking countries. Of the long list of familiar Cambridge titles found in American libraries, perhaps the best known are the multivolume *Cambridge Ancient History, Cambridge Medieval History,* and *Cambridge Modern History.*

Foreign competition for reference works in the science, technical, and medical areas is led by Springer-Verlag GmbH & Co. KG, a German company founded in 1842 as a bookstore with a publishing sideline. Bookselling quickly became the dominant business, and Springer rose to a leading position in that field. After World War II, the company made the strategic decision to publish for the English-language market, and Springer-Verlag New York, Inc., was opened in 1964. *Duncan's Dictionary for Nurses* and the *Encyclopedia of Aging* represent two popular reference works published by this company.

Any discussion of reference publishing can only provide a sampling of the literally thousands of publishers in the United States and abroad that produce reference sources for American libraries. For a more extensive listing of publishers of reference works, readers should consult the "List of Publishers and Distributors" that can be found at the end of this book.

Trends and Prospects in Reference Publishing

The economic picture for reference publishers is generally good. The industry is healthy and growing and should enjoy a stable long-term outlook. Because standard book trade statistics are calculated by topic rather than by intended use (such as "reference"), precise figures are difficult to obtain. Nevertheless, data from most review media attest to an increase in reference publishing. Moreover, the average price of reference works is predicted to continue to rise at a significantly lower rate than nonreference books. Comparatively speaking, reference materials remain a bargain within the book trade.

Perhaps the most significant changes in reference publishing come from the introduction of computer technology. Some publishers have already formed electronic publishing divisions to exist alongside or in conjunction with their print sections, which enables them to take advantage of the growing market for CD-ROM products and on-line data bases. Encyclopedias, dictionaries, almanacs, indexes, and other reference works already available on CD-ROM provide library users with approaches to research that were unavailable in the past. For example, Encyclopaedia Britannica's *Compton's MultiMedia Encyclopedia* includes sound; motion; 15,000 still pictures, maps, and charts; the full text of the 26-volume standard *Compton's Encyclopedia;* and the 65,000-entry *Merriam-Webster Intermediate Dictionary.* It should also be noted that Grolier—with its *Academic American Encyclopedia*—and World Book have also entered the CD-ROM encyclopedia market. In at least one instance, CD-ROM technology *(General Periodicals Ondisc)* allows users to identify topical articles via an index on one disk and to retrieve these articles from another.

Other effects of the computerization of publishing include increased efficiency in production due to the reduction of many manual publication tasks and the ability to generate several titles from a single data base. Gale Research, Inc., led the way in this trend by putting all of its publications in machine-readable form and generating products for specific audiences. A good illustration of this now widely adopted practice is provided by H. W. Wilson's *Readers' Guide Abstracts,* which is now available in abridged print form to high school and small public libraries; in complete microfiche versions, on CD-ROM, and on-line through Wilsonline, to larger libraries; and on tape for libraries to mount on their own computers. Bowker's *Books in Print* and *Ulrich's International Periodicals Directory* are also available in CD-ROM versions. Automation has also resulted in a smaller high school edition of *Who's Who in America* and Facts On File's *News Digest.* Computer technology has made it easier to produce a greater number of reference books at more affordable prices and has given librarians a greater variety of works from which to choose.

Changes wrought by computer technology are occurring in libraries at all levels. While the first CD-ROM products were aimed at academic and special libraries, they now abound in public and school libraries and are also being targeted toward the consumer market. A recent article in *Reference Books Bulletin* predicts that lists of "outstanding reference books" published in library trade journals will include a mixture of print and electronic titles in the not-too-distant future.

Second only to technology in its effects on reference publishing is the mania for mergers and acquisitions that continues to rage after two decades. This has changed the corporate face of the industry, as old familiar names disappear and new ones appear or merge as a result of joint ventures under combined corporate names. Few publishers have escaped the effects of the movement. Among reference publishers R. R. Bowker Co. is owned by Reed Publishing (USA) Inc.; Maxwell Communications Corporation acquired Macmillan, which owned Scribner, G. K. Hall, and Marquis *Who's*

Who, among others; Harper & Row was acquired by Rupert Murdoch's News America Corporation and has since become HarperCollins to stress its connection to its British counterpart, Collins Publishers. Gale Research, Inc. was purchased by International Thomson Publishing.

The irony is that what appears to be instability in the industry can be seen as a sign of the vitality of the field, as individuals from inside and outside the publishing field are attracted by the healthy growth in sales. The potential for success can be seen in the example of Facts On File, Inc. Long known for its *World News Digest,* a popular looseleaf reference work found frequently in libraries, Facts On File grew from a publisher of only two print titles in the 1970s to one that produced 120 print and electronic reference works yearly in the 1980s.

In theory, such well-financed large corporations should be in better positions to fund new and expensive reference publishing projects. While this is true, there may also be factors inhibiting the growth of such projects. Debts incurred in corporate acquisitions may cause pressures for immediate profits in a field in which some publishing projects tie up large amounts of money for lengthy periods before any profits are seen. This may cause publishers to think twice before embarking on some potentially worthwhile reference publications. At the present time, however, fears that the ongoing merger and acquisition movement will lead to inferior products have not been borne out, as a supply of quality works continues to be issued from smaller and larger presses alike.

Another significant factor in reference publishing is the increased growth in the production of specialized and topical reference works such as those described in this book. This is a natural response by publishers to the information explosion, which continues to divide and subdivide as research and discoveries open new specializations in academic, professional, and everyday life. Macmillan, for instance, actively seeks to publish topical encyclopedias that could be considered final, authoritative reference works on some very narrow topics, including the *Encyclopedia of the Holocaust* and the popular *Baseball Encyclopedia.* The success of these and other topical reference works are examples that are not lost on other publishers.

The future of reference publishing can be said to be reflected in its present. Mergers and acquisitions will continue to reshape the corporate picture, and electronic publishing technology will bring further changes to both the production and format of information sources. But regardless of changes, the field should remain an attractive one for publishers, who can expect further growth. Libraries will also benefit from the availability of continued and expanded access to new electronic sources, along with the increasing variety of traditional topical print materials.

—Donald E. Collins

Bibliography

Chapter 2 is concerned with the past and present of reference sources, collections, service, and publishing in the United States. Because reference work is primarily a post-1876 phenomenon, treatment of the topic in prior times centers on the relatively small number of reference books available and on the reading and information needs of the population. Social historian Louis B. Wright covers this in a chapter on "Books, Libraries, and Learning" in his book *The Cultural Life of the American Colonies, 1607–1763* (New York: Harper & Row, 1957). Reference books and publishers after the American Revolution are treated in several works, including Elmer D. Johnson, *Communication: An Introduction to the History of Writing, Printing, Books, and Libraries,* 4th edition (Metuchen, N.J.: Scarecrow, 1973). A contemporary view of reference works at the beginning of the modern period is provided by Ainsworth R. Spofford in his chapter, "Works of Reference for Libraries," in the U.S. Bureau of Education's special report, *Public Libraries in the United States of America: Their History, Condition, and Management,* (Washington, D.C.: U.S. Government Printing Office, 1876). The formative years of reference service are detailed in Louis Kaplan's *The Growth of Reference Service in the United States from 1876 to 1893* (A.C.R.L. Monographs, Association of College and Reference Libraries, 1952). A good supplement to this work is James Rettig's brief but informative article "Reference and Information Services" in the *ALA World Encyclopedia of Library and Information Services,* 2d edition (Chicago: ALA, 1986). A useful listing of developments in reference service through the 1950s is provided in Josephine Metcalfe Smith's *A Chronology of Librarianship* (Metuchen, N.J.: Scarecrow, 1968). Information on the historical background of dictionaries, encyclopedias, and other types of reference works may also be found in *General Reference Books for Adults,* part of the Bowker Buying Guide series, Marion Sader, ed. (New York: Bowker, 1988).

Locating literature on publishers of reference works presents a challenge to researchers because it is not an officially recognized subfield of publishing, with the exception of subscription reference books (primarily encyclopedias). In most instances, data must be culled from works that cover publishing in general. John Tebbel's four-volume work, *A History of Book Publishing in the United States* (New York: Bowker, 1978), is useful for background information on the major reference publishers, while a good current treatment of the industry is given by Audrey Eaglen in her *Buying Books: A How-To-Do-It Manual for Librarians* (New York: Neal-Schuman, 1989).

A valuable new column by Sandy Whitely, titled "Trends in Reference Publishing," featured annually in *Reference Books Bulletin* provides a badly needed service for this neglected field. A recent column (May 1, 1990, page 1744) provides insight into the current direction of the reference publishing field. Additional articles of use in providing material for this chapter include: Keith Dawson and Laura Nixon, "Looking It Up," *Publishers Weekly,* July 14, 1989, pages 18–34; Deborah Selsky, "Reference Books: Smallest Gains in Overall Soaring Book Prices," *Library Journal,* April 15, 1990, page 28; John Sutherland, "The Making of Codices and Careers," *Times Literary Supplement,* May 26–June 1, 1989, page 580.

Readers will also find the following publications of particular value in keeping up to date with the reference industry and publishers: *Wall Street Journal, New York Times,* and *Publishers Weekly.*

Chapter 3

Choosing Topical Reference Books

Before librarians can consider which topical reference books are appropriate for acquisition, they must evaluate the kinds of reference service offered in their individual libraries. Reference service can be defined as the aid given by librarians in response to the information needs of patrons. Various writers on librarianship have characterized reference service as falling into three distinct categories. Rather than being categories, however, they are in reality philosophies concerning how a particular library or librarian should treat questions asked by patrons. Although these philosophies can be applied to specific types of libraries and groups of users, the way a librarian approaches answering queries is actually determined by the needs and background of each individual user.

Three Philosophies of Reference Service

The first, and oldest of the three, is the minimum, or conservative, philosophy, advocated by librarians who view libraries as educational institutions and themselves as teachers of library use. The emphasis is on helping the users help themselves by instructing them on the use of books and libraries, rather than on the delivery of information. According to this view, students and new or infrequent patrons, regardless of type of library, are best served when librarians either guide them through the paces or teach library usage.

The second philosophy espouses the other extreme. The maximum or liberal philosophy sees reference as a service in which information or material is provided to the user upon request. The librarian, as the expert in information retrieval, should find, deliver, and, if asked, even guarantee the authenticity and relevance of the information supplied. This approach is most appropriate in situations in which users are either already familiar with reference materials and research or a user's position is such that time spent in searching for information would be inappropriate.

In practice, librarians use neither approach exclusively. In order to take this discrepancy into account, the third philosophy, called the middling or moderate philosophy, was developed. This philosophy combines elements of the minimum and maximum approaches. These three philosophies are perhaps better understood by looking at how they are used in a variety of library settings.

Library Settings for Reference Service

Public Libraries

From the standpoint of use, the public library is the most broad based of all. Set up by the local government to serve the recreational, educational, and informational needs of the entire community, its audience includes everyone who lives within its jurisdiction, as well as visitors from outside.

In reality, no clientele is so diverse. Ideally, the reference collection is as varied as the people in the community because there are no restrictions on what may be asked. Although surveys show that students and businesspersons are among the most frequent users of reference services, persons seeking information come from all age groups and educational backgrounds. This variety, plus the public library's historic view of its role as an educational institution for the community at large, calls for different approaches to handling information requests. Students using the library for homework or research assignments may be best served with an educational approach that teaches library use. Patrons who are businesspersons might not have time for research. These individuals would probably receive the information without instruction. The differences in patrons, therefore, will determine the philosophy or approach used.

Special Libraries

Special libraries, on the other hand, operate under the maximum or liberal philosophy almost exclusively. Created to serve the information needs of their parent institutions, they exist as departments within businesses (for example, insurance companies or banks), industrial concerns (such as those that produce chemicals, computers, or engineering materials), nonprofit organizations (such as hospitals, museums, and professional associations), and government agencies. These collections are usually small in size, narrow in subject matter, and developed to reflect the specific interests of the parent organization, making the clientele the narrowest and most homogeneous of all types of libraries. Because both librarians and users in these circumstances are subject experts, it is, then, not the librarians' job to educate the user, but to provide the information that is needed.

School Libraries and Academic Libraries

Libraries in schools, two- and four-year colleges, and universities exist to serve their students, faculty, and curriculum. In order to do this, their collections must include materials to support faculty research and teaching and contain a wide selection of works in all areas of knowledge. These libraries are positioned somewhere between their public and special library counterparts in the diversity of their clientele. The main variations are found in the ages and education levels of students, the expertise and research levels of faculty, and the level and complexity of courses. The academic librarians will function for the most part as subject specialists, whereas school librarians, with smaller collections, can only be reference generalists.

Reference service in institutions requires the maximum theory approach when dealing with the members of administrative staff and, in most instances, faculty. On the other hand, students from elementary through graduate school are rarely expert in reference book use; consequently, the minimum approach (which calls for educating users in library procedures and reference books) is often called for. This is done either through formal classes held in classrooms or in the library, or through informal guidance or instruction while answering reference questions. The latter is perhaps the most common.

Reference Questions

Four Types of Questions

Reference service in *any* library means answering questions. Although there are differences in the amount and depth of information provided, the basic methodology used by librarians is the same for all library patrons. An examination of the way in which librarians look at reference questions is a useful exercise because the success of the reference department and the quality of its collection are dependent on the sources selected and used to meet these needs.

When a user comes to the reference desk for help, librarians, either consciously or subconsciously, look at the question on at least two levels: difficulty and content. In his *Introduction to Reference Work,* Bill Katz, a leading writer in librarianship and a reference authority, presents one popular school of thought in the following four-part breakdown of reference questions.

1. *Direction.* "Where is the *Business Periodicals Index?*" "Where is the government documents collection?" These examples serve to illustrate the most common kind of questions asked in a library. They require little more from the librarian than a knowledge of the layout of the library and its materials. These requests make up as much as half of the queries received in any given day.

2. *Ready reference.* "On which congressional committees does Representative Jones sit?" "In which of William Faulkner's books did the Snopes family appear as characters?" Inquiries such as these are simple fact questions that a single source can answer. The *Almanac of American Politics* and Benet's *Reader's Encyclopedia* will provide quick, easy answers to these two questions. These are the second-most-common type of inquiry librarians receive. In most libraries, it is a common practice to place anywhere from one to several hundred ready-reference books behind or close to the reference desk for quick answers to these questions. While fact books (such as almanacs, yearbooks, handbooks, directories) are the most commonly found books in these collections, almost any reference book will serve the

purpose other than bulky multivolume encyclopedias and serial publications.

3. *Specific search.* "Where can I find information for a report on Lee Iacocca and the Chrysler Corporation?" "Do you have anything on the Battle of Wounded Knee for a research paper I have to write?" These are different from ready-reference questions in that specific search questions require more time and almost always take the form of giving the user a document (for example, a list of citations, a book, or a report). These queries are often bibliographic in nature. The two sample questions above, for example, would be answered at least in part by the *Business Periodical Index* and *America: History and Life,* two popular topical indexes that provide bibliographic information.

4. *Research.* These questions often require hours or days to answer and more in-depth searching. They form a negligible part of the total questions asked in school and some college libraries, but may be relatively common in special and university libraries. Like specific search queries, research questions tend to be bibliographic in nature. Although the questioner is usually an adult specialist—a professor, businessperson, scientist—it could be anyone who needs data for a decision or for additional information on a problem.

The second approach used by librarians involves examining patrons' queries in terms of content. Another reference specialist, the late Louis Shores, wrote that most questions fall into one of ten categories, each of which can be answered by a specific type of reference book—for example, word questions are best answered by dictionaries. Shores's analysis can be carried a step further, in that each question is either general or subject oriented. Thus, the answer to a question on a business term is found in a business dictionary. This approach, which identifies the type of reference book by subject orientation, leads us to a major consideration of this chapter—identifying types of reference books.

Types of Reference Books

Dictionaries, encyclopedias, yearbooks, handbooks, . . . the words are used by students, librarians, and the public at large. But what do they mean? What is it about a handbook that makes it a handbook? The same question may be asked about bibliographies, manuals, and other categories of reference books. Their characteristics and functions are rarely known to any but those who use them with regularity—reference librarians. The knowledge of reference books by type, content, and commonly held features ensures a better choice in answering queries and a more expertly developed reference collection. The following pages look at the various types of reference books and their distinctive characteristics, focusing on topical works.

One all-too-frequent and misleading occurrence to keep in mind is the practice of some authors and compilers to mislabel the types of works in the titles they choose. Dictionaries are sometimes called "handbooks" or "encyclopedias," directories may be titled "Encyclopedia of . . . ," bibliographies are incorrectly called "indexes," and encyclopedias are all too often termed "dictionaries." Because content is the main factor in determining the type of reference work, librarians and other users should look beyond titles when choosing books for use or purchase.

The following pages treat the various categories of reference works and, through text and sample pages from pertinent reference works, illustrate features one may expect to find when using them. Although directories and indexes are not reviewed in this buying guide, a brief discussion of these works is included.

Dictionaries

A dictionary is defined by the *Encyclopedia of Library and Information Science* as a book containing the words of a language, or terms of a subject, arranged in some definite order, usually alphabetical, with an explanation of their meanings and use. A full history of dictionaries, from earliest times to the present, can be found in *General Reference Books for Adults* (in the Bowker Buying Guide series.)

When the word *dictionary* is mentioned, the public tends to think only in terms of the general dictionaries that one uses every day, but in fact there are many diverse categories of dictionaries. These may be reduced to five main types: (1) general English-language dictionaries; (2) etymological dictionaries that trace the history of words; (3) foreign-language dictionaries that translate the words of one language into another; (4) subject or topical dictionaries that define words in a given area; and (5) "other" dictionaries, including those of slang, usage, abbreviations, and other specialized areas.

This volume is, of course, concerned with subject or topical dictionaries. The characteristics exhibited by subject or topical dictionaries vary, with two formats most commonly found. The first format follows the traditional content line: entries arranged alphabetically, with each containing various elements, including spelling, word division, pronunciation, etymology, synonyms, antonyms, and usage. Slang, abbreviations, and acronyms may also be included as entries, and some works possess word- and language-related articles, and separate sections for geographical terms, biography, and numerous other special features. The

McGraw-Hill Dictionary of Scientific and Technical Terms, reviewed in this work, is a traditional topical dictionary.

An increasing number of topical dictionaries are following an encyclopedic format by including both brief entries that define terms and topical survey articles similar in content to those found in encyclopedias. This characteristic is illustrated in the *Oxford Classical Dictionary* facsimile found on page 20. Other features commonly found in such works are cross-references to related entries, bibliographies at the end of entries, names or initials of authors appearing within entries, illustrations, maps, and indexes to contents.

Other works in the dictionary category that are reviewed in this book include *The New Grove Dictionary of Music and Musicians* (see Music), *The Facts On File Dictionary of Religions* (see Religion), *Dictionary of the Middle Ages* (see European History), and the *Encyclopedia of Electronics* (see Engineering).

Encyclopedias

An encyclopedia may be defined as a reference work that attempts to encompass systematically the whole of human knowledge, or a specialized work that similarly treats a particular field or subject. (A complete history of this type of work is also found in *General Reference Books for Adults.*)

The popular image of encyclopedias being multivolume works is misleading because the majority of specialized or topical works tend to be single volumes. Most are organized alphabetically, although a small number follow classified or other arrangements. An example of the classified arrangement can be seen in *Grzimek's Encyclopedia of Mammals* (see Zoology). This work is arranged by order (or subcategory) of mammals and further broken down into families.

Encyclopedias are best known for providing general information; each entry includes the definition, history, persons involved, and other pertinent information, and a bibliography of related works that leads users to additional data. Entries are typically written by experts whose names or initials are appended. "See" references are almost universally used to lead from terms not used to the preferred entry word, while cross-referencing to related articles is becoming more widespread. Maps and illustrations are also standard encyclopedia features. Indexes are essential for bringing together related facts that are spread throughout the set and for locating facts contained within articles. Several of these features are illustrated in the facsimile page from the *Encyclopedia of Human Evolution and Prehistory* on page 21.

The current trend leans toward increased growth in the topical encyclopedia area. This is true not only with single-volume works, which will probably always dominate the field, but with multivolume sets also. A large number of subject encyclopedias are reviewed in this buying guide. These include the *Encyclopedia of American Economic History* (see Economics); the *Encyclopedia of American Foreign Policy* (see American History); the *Encyclopedia of Artificial Intelligence* (see Computers and Artificial Intelligence); the *Encyclopedia of Physical Education, Fitness, and Sports* (see Sports); and the *Encyclopedia of the American Constitution* (see Law).

Yearbooks

Yearbooks and annuals are sources issued each year to review developments of the previous year and to record current information of a descriptive or statistical nature. These works are frequently limited to a special subject. In the layperson's mind, a yearbook is the annual update that accompanies most well-known encyclopedias. In the library field, however, the definition is much broader, including almanacs and other works on politics, sports, and statistics that appear annually and provide information for that year. Yearbooks and almanacs have existed since the colonial period; the *Annual Register: A Record of World Events,* begun in London in 1758, is perhaps the oldest still in publication. The longevity of yearbooks is confirmed by several current works that date from the mid-nineteenth century, including *The World Almanac* (1868–) and the *Statesman's Year-Book* (1864–).

Yearbooks differ greatly in content and arrangement. Those in the encyclopedia category reflect the characteristics of the parent work. These are alphabetically arranged, with general-survey-type articles covering events of the year preceding the date of publication. Originally related to the calendar, almanacs have evolved into annual compendiums of statistics and facts. A major difference between these and encyclopedia yearbooks is that almanacs include retrospective data, whereas the latter normally cover only the year in question. Subject yearbooks vary greatly in format, with content and arrangement based on the topic and function of the work.

For a discussion of specific yearbooks, see reviews for the following titles in this buying guide: *Facts On File* (see Current Events), *The Europa World Year-Book* (see Current Events), and *Statistical Abstracts of the United States* (see American History).

Biographical Sources

Biographical sources consist of: (1) biographical dictionaries, which may be defined as a collection of descriptions of the lives of people, usually arranged in alpha-

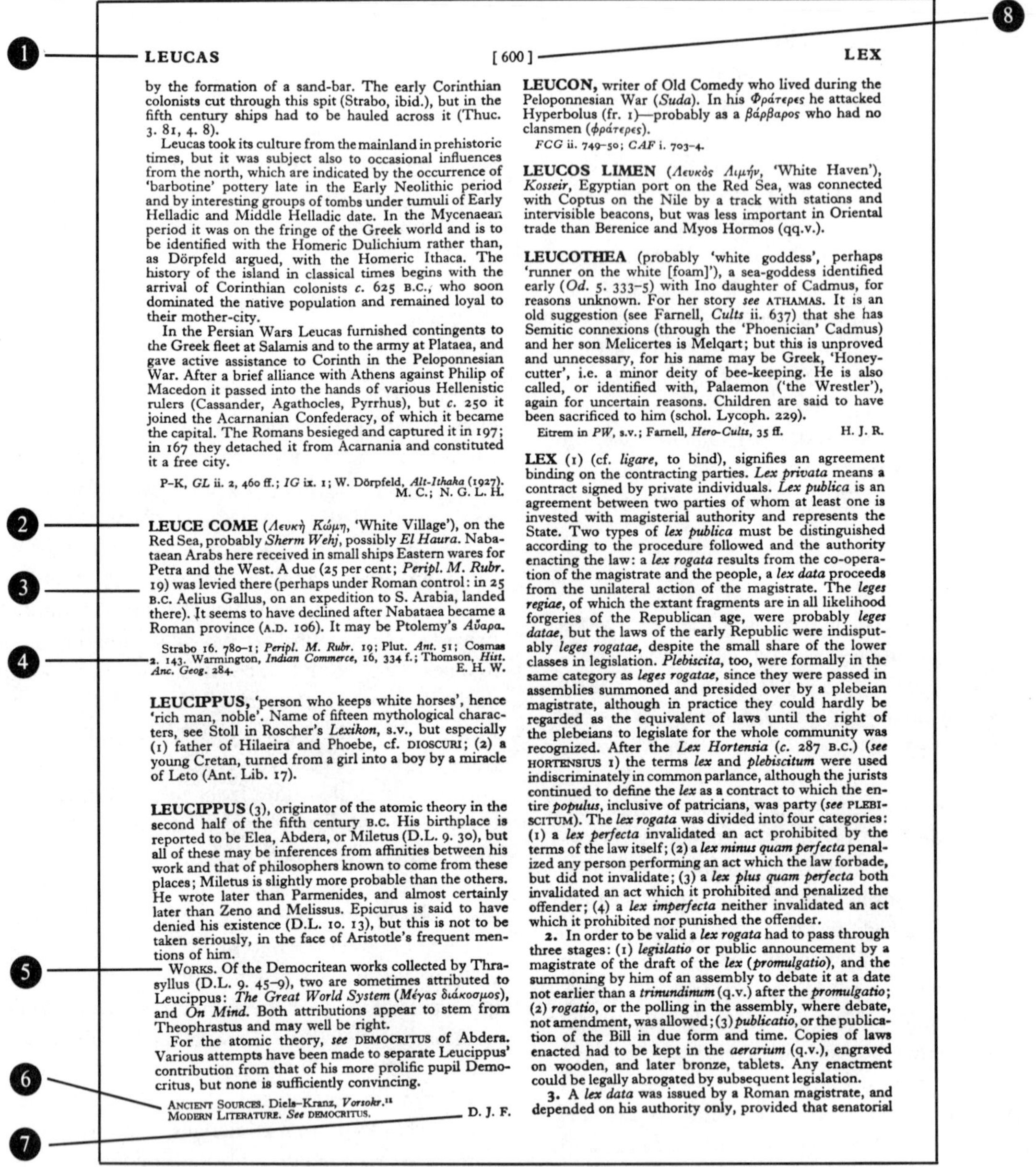

LEUCAS [600] **LEX**

by the formation of a sand-bar. The early Corinthian colonists cut through this spit (Strabo, ibid.), but in the fifth century ships had to be hauled across it (Thuc. 3. 81, 4. 8).

Leucas took its culture from the mainland in prehistoric times, but it was subject also to occasional influences from the north, which are indicated by the occurrence of 'barbotine' pottery late in the Early Neolithic period and by interesting groups of tombs under tumuli of Early Helladic and Middle Helladic date. In the Mycenaean period it was on the fringe of the Greek world and is to be identified with the Homeric Dulichium rather than, as Dörpfeld argued, with the Homeric Ithaca. The history of the island in classical times begins with the arrival of Corinthian colonists *c.* 625 B.C., who soon dominated the native population and remained loyal to their mother-city.

In the Persian Wars Leucas furnished contingents to the Greek fleet at Salamis and to the army at Plataea, and gave active assistance to Corinth in the Peloponnesian War. After a brief alliance with Athens against Philip of Macedon it passed into the hands of various Hellenistic rulers (Cassander, Agathocles, Pyrrhus), but *c.* 250 it joined the Acarnanian Confederacy, of which it became the capital. The Romans besieged and captured it in 197; in 167 they detached it from Acarnania and constituted it a free city.

P–K, *GL* ii. 2, 460 ff.; *IG* ix. 1; W. Dörpfeld, *Alt-Ithaka* (1927).
M. C.; N. G. L. H.

LEUCE COME (*Λευκὴ Κώμη*, 'White Village'), on the Red Sea, probably *Sherm Wehj*, possibly *El Haura*. Nabataean Arabs here received in small ships Eastern wares for Petra and the West. A due (25 per cent; *Peripl. M. Rubr.* 19) was levied there (perhaps under Roman control: in 25 B.C. Aelius Gallus, on an expedition to S. Arabia, landed there). It seems to have declined after Nabataea became a Roman province (A.D. 106). It may be Ptolemy's *Αὔαρα*.

Strabo 16. 780–1; *Peripl. M. Rubr.* 19; Plut. *Ant.* 51; Cosmas 2. 143. Warmington, *Indian Commerce*, 16, 334 f.; Thomson, *Hist. Anc. Geog.* 284.
E. H. W.

LEUCIPPUS, 'person who keeps white horses', hence 'rich man, noble'. Name of fifteen mythological characters, see Stoll in Roscher's *Lexikon*, s.v., but especially (1) father of Hilaeira and Phoebe, cf. DIOSCURI; (2) a young Cretan, turned from a girl into a boy by a miracle of Leto (Ant. Lib. 17).

LEUCIPPUS (3), originator of the atomic theory in the second half of the fifth century B.C. His birthplace is reported to be Elea, Abdera, or Miletus (D.L. 9. 30), but all of these may be inferences from affinities between his work and that of philosophers known to come from these places; Miletus is slightly more probable than the others. He wrote later than Parmenides, and almost certainly later than Zeno and Melissus. Epicurus is said to have denied his existence (D.L. 10. 13), but this is not to be taken seriously, in the face of Aristotle's frequent mentions of him.

WORKS. Of the Democritean works collected by Thrasyllus (D.L. 9. 45–9), two are sometimes attributed to Leucippus: *The Great World System* (*Μέγας διάκοσμος*), and *On Mind*. Both attributions appear to stem from Theophrastus and may well be right.

For the atomic theory, *see* DEMOCRITUS of Abdera. Various attempts have been made to separate Leucippus' contribution from that of his more prolific pupil Democritus, but none is sufficiently convincing.

ANCIENT SOURCES. Diels–Kranz, *Vorsokr.*[11]
MODERN LITERATURE. *See* DEMOCRITUS.
D. J. F.

LEUCON, writer of Old Comedy who lived during the Peloponnesian War (*Suda*). In his *Φράτερες* he attacked Hyperbolus (fr. 1)—probably as a *βάρβαρος* who had no clansmen (*φράτερες*).

FCG ii. 749–50; *CAF* i. 703–4.

LEUCOS LIMEN (*Λευκὸς Λιμήν*, 'White Haven'), *Kosseir*, Egyptian port on the Red Sea, was connected with Coptus on the Nile by a track with stations and intervisible beacons, but was less important in Oriental trade than Berenice and Myos Hormos (qq.v.).

LEUCOTHEA (probably 'white goddess', perhaps 'runner on the white [foam]'), a sea-goddess identified early (*Od.* 5. 333–5) with Ino daughter of Cadmus, for reasons unknown. For her story *see* ATHAMAS. It is an old suggestion (see Farnell, *Cults* ii. 637) that she has Semitic connexions (through the 'Phoenician' Cadmus) and her son Melicertes is Melqart; but this is unproved and unnecessary, for his name may be Greek, 'Honey-cutter', i.e. a minor deity of bee-keeping. He is also called, or identified with, Palaemon ('the Wrestler'), again for uncertain reasons. Children are said to have been sacrificed to him (schol. Lycoph. 229).

Eitrem in *PW*, s.v.; Farnell, *Hero-Cults*, 35 ff.
H. J. R.

LEX (1) (cf. *ligare*, to bind), signifies an agreement binding on the contracting parties. *Lex privata* means a contract signed by private individuals. *Lex publica* is an agreement between two parties of whom at least one is invested with magisterial authority and represents the State. Two types of *lex publica* must be distinguished according to the procedure followed and the authority enacting the law: a *lex rogata* results from the co-operation of the magistrate and the people, a *lex data* proceeds from the unilateral action of the magistrate. The *leges regiae*, of which the extant fragments are in all likelihood forgeries of the Republican age, were probably *leges datae*, but the laws of the early Republic were indisputably *leges rogatae*, despite the small share of the lower classes in legislation. *Plebiscita*, too, were formally in the same category as *leges rogatae*, since they were passed in assemblies summoned and presided over by a plebeian magistrate, although in practice they could hardly be regarded as the equivalent of laws until the right of the plebeians to legislate for the whole community was recognized. After the *Lex Hortensia* (*c.* 287 B.C.) (*see* HORTENSIUS 1) the terms *lex* and *plebiscitum* were used indiscriminately in common parlance, although the jurists continued to define the *lex* as a contract to which the entire *populus*, inclusive of patricians, was party (*see* PLEBISCITUM). The *lex rogata* was divided into four categories: (1) a *lex perfecta* invalidated an act prohibited by the terms of the law itself; (2) a *lex minus quam perfecta* penalized any person performing an act which the law forbade, but did not invalidate; (3) a *lex plus quam perfecta* both invalidated an act which it prohibited and penalized the offender; (4) a *lex imperfecta* neither invalidated an act which it prohibited nor punished the offender.

2. In order to be valid a *lex rogata* had to pass through three stages: (1) *legislatio* or public announcement by a magistrate of the draft of the *lex* (*promulgatio*), and the summoning by him of an assembly to debate it at a date not earlier than a *trinundinum* (q.v.) after the *promulgatio*; (2) *rogatio*, or the polling in the assembly, where debate, not amendment, was allowed; (3) *publicatio*, or the publication of the Bill in due form and time. Copies of laws enacted had to be kept in the *aerarium* (q.v.), engraved on wooden, and later bronze, tablets. Any enactment could be legally abrogated by subsequent legislation.

3. A *lex data* was issued by a Roman magistrate, and depended on his authority only, provided that senatorial

Page shown at 72% of actual size.

1. Guide words indicate the first and last entries on the page.
2. Main entry words appear in boldface capital letters with ample space above to make locating entries easy.
3. Topics for entries range from persons, places, events, and terms to major literary themes. Some long entries, such as *lex* on this page, are usual in topical dictionaries.
4. Bibliographies are provided for most entries. These are often featured in topical dictionaries.
5. In entries for persons, a list of their major works is often included.
6. Cross-references to entries providing additional information are frequently included.
7. Most entries are signed with the initials of the contributor. Full names of contributors are listed at the end of this dictionary.
8. Page number.

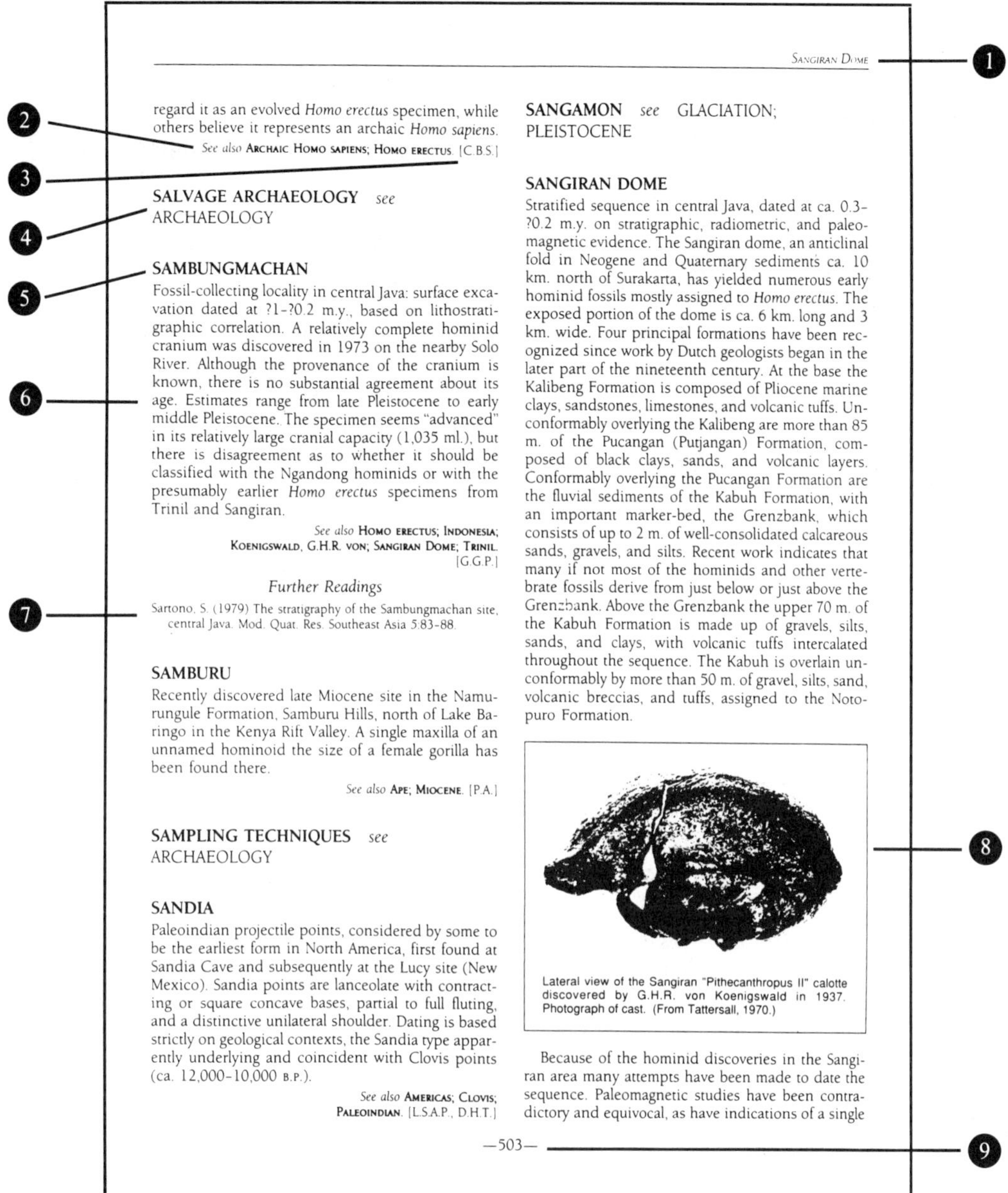

SANGIRAN DOME

regard it as an evolved *Homo erectus* specimen, while others believe it represents an archaic *Homo sapiens*.

See also ARCHAIC HOMO SAPIENS; HOMO ERECTUS. [C.B.S.]

SALVAGE ARCHAEOLOGY *see* ARCHAEOLOGY

SAMBUNGMACHAN

Fossil-collecting locality in central Java: surface excavation dated at ?1–?0.2 m.y., based on lithostratigraphic correlation. A relatively complete hominid cranium was discovered in 1973 on the nearby Solo River. Although the provenance of the cranium is known, there is no substantial agreement about its age. Estimates range from late Pleistocene to early middle Pleistocene. The specimen seems "advanced" in its relatively large cranial capacity (1,035 ml.), but there is disagreement as to whether it should be classified with the Ngandong hominids or with the presumably earlier *Homo erectus* specimens from Trinil and Sangiran.

See also HOMO ERECTUS; INDONESIA; KOENIGSWALD, G.H.R. VON; SANGIRAN DOME; TRINIL. [G.G.P.]

Further Readings

Sartono, S. (1979) The stratigraphy of the Sambungmachan site, central Java. Mod. Quat. Res. Southeast Asia 5:83–88.

SAMBURU

Recently discovered late Miocene site in the Namurungule Formation, Samburu Hills, north of Lake Baringo in the Kenya Rift Valley. A single maxilla of an unnamed hominoid the size of a female gorilla has been found there.

See also APE; MIOCENE. [P.A.]

SAMPLING TECHNIQUES *see* ARCHAEOLOGY

SANDIA

Paleoindian projectile points, considered by some to be the earliest form in North America, first found at Sandia Cave and subsequently at the Lucy site (New Mexico). Sandia points are lanceolate with contracting or square concave bases, partial to full fluting, and a distinctive unilateral shoulder. Dating is based strictly on geological contexts, the Sandia type apparently underlying and coincident with Clovis points (ca. 12,000–10,000 B.P.).

See also AMERICAS; CLOVIS; PALEOINDIAN. [L.S.A.P., D.H.T.]

SANGAMON *see* GLACIATION; PLEISTOCENE

SANGIRAN DOME

Stratified sequence in central Java, dated at ca. 0.3–?0.2 m.y. on stratigraphic, radiometric, and paleomagnetic evidence. The Sangiran dome, an anticlinal fold in Neogene and Quaternary sediments ca. 10 km. north of Surakarta, has yielded numerous early hominid fossils mostly assigned to *Homo erectus*. The exposed portion of the dome is ca. 6 km. long and 3 km. wide. Four principal formations have been recognized since work by Dutch geologists began in the later part of the nineteenth century. At the base the Kalibeng Formation is composed of Pliocene marine clays, sandstones, limestones, and volcanic tuffs. Unconformably overlying the Kalibeng are more than 85 m. of the Pucangan (Putjangan) Formation, composed of black clays, sands, and volcanic layers. Conformably overlying the Pucangan Formation are the fluvial sediments of the Kabuh Formation, with an important marker-bed, the Grenzbank, which consists of up to 2 m. of well-consolidated calcareous sands, gravels, and silts. Recent work indicates that many if not most of the hominids and other vertebrate fossils derive from just below or just above the Grenzbank. Above the Grenzbank the upper 70 m. of the Kabuh Formation is made up of gravels, silts, sands, and clays, with volcanic tuffs intercalated throughout the sequence. The Kabuh is overlain unconformably by more than 50 m. of gravel, silts, sand, volcanic breccias, and tuffs, assigned to the Notopuro Formation.

Lateral view of the Sangiran "Pithecanthropus II" calotte discovered by G.H.R. von Koenigswald in 1937. Photograph of cast. (From Tattersall, 1970.)

Because of the hominid discoveries in the Sangiran area many attempts have been made to date the sequence. Paleomagnetic studies have been contradictory and equivocal, as have indications of a single

—503—

Page shown at 58% of actual size.

1. Guide word indicates first (left-hand page) or last (right-hand page) entry on page.
2. "See also" cross-references to related topics.
3. Initials of contributor; all contributors are listed in front of book.
4. Cross-reference to locations of actual discussion clearly marked.
5. Main entry words appear in boldface capital letters with ample space above to make locating them easy.
6. Entries range from short definitions to longer essays.
7. List of additional readings accompanies some entries.
8. Artwork supplements text.
9. Page number.

betical order; (2) biographical indexes, which lead to information about persons in other sources. Such works have been known throughout history, the best-known early example of which was the bio-bibliographical *Pinakes,* or *Tables of Persons Eminent in Every Branch of Learning,* compiled by Callimachus in the Alexandrian Library between 280 and 250 B.C.

Like other reference works, biographical reference works are organized according to some plan. Most are alphabetical. The second-most-popular plan is chronologically arranged entries, in which persons who lived during the same time period are grouped together. Occasionally titles follow other patterns, including entries arranged by geographical region or occupation.

Biographical data are generally presented in one of two formats: directory or essay. The former is best illustrated by the familiar entries in Marquis *Who's Who* series, in which information is presented in abbreviated form that includes such basic personal information as birth, parents, children, education, occupation, organizations, address, business, and career records. Most data for biographical sketches of this type are supplied by the biographees themselves. In the latter format, the essay entries can vary greatly in length. Some biographical works include brief paragraphs in which only the major events of a person's life are given, such as *Webster's New Biographical Dictionary.* Others contain lengthy biographies of several pages, as in *Current Biography,* and some entries run over 100 pages, as in the monumental *Dictionary of National Biography.* In this type of work, articles are frequently written and signed by specialists.

Biographical dictionaries often include a number of other elements that should be mentioned. Many contain indexes that offer subject access when names cannot be remembered or when persons associated with certain events are wanted. Appendixes frequently provide lists of persons according to offices held, occupation, or other related characteristics. And many works include bibliographies that lead users to additional sources of information. Several of these features are illustrated in the facsimile from *American Authors, 1600–1900,* on page 23.

Examples of other biographical dictionaries included in this work are *Who's Who in American Politics* (see Political Science), *Contemporary Authors* (see American Literature), and *Musicians Since 1900* (see Music).

Handbooks and Manuals

Handbooks and manuals are frequently treated as one category in library texts and dictionaries of librarianship. They will be discussed together here also. Nevertheless, it is important to note that there is a basic distinction between the two. A handbook is defined as a reference book of miscellaneous facts and figures on one or many subjects assembled for ready use. Its primary use is for brief, factual data. *The ALA Glossary of Library and Information Science* defines a manual as: "1. A compact book; a handbook. 2. A book of rules for guidance or instructions in how to perform a task, process, etc., or make some physical object." The primary difference is that the former is a fact source and the latter is a book of instructions. With this distinction in mind, their similarities perhaps outweigh their differences. Both are created in response to a need for specific information, usually on a very narrow topic. In addition, both may be used to answer fact questions. Except in rare cases, manuals are not usually found in reference collections.

Facts may be grouped into so many categories that it is difficult to discuss handbooks in terms of individual characteristics. It is possible, however, to identify at least eight types: (1) curiosity, (2) literary, (3) statistics, (4) calendar, (5) documentary, (6) parliamentary and debate, (7) historical, and (8) specific subject handbooks. Consequently, purpose determines format, and individual works may appear in statistical, directory, dictionary, encyclopedic, or other forms. The facsimile page from *The Essential Guide to Nonprescription Drugs* on page 24 demonstrates the handy factual nature of this type of work.

Handbooks have been in demand for many years. *Robert's Rules of Order* has provided information on the conduct of meetings since 1876. Handbooks form one of the largest of reference fields currently, with titles devoted to even the most specific topics. Some representative titles that are reviewed in this book include *The Rule Book: The Authoritative, Up-to-Date, Illustrated Guide to the Regulations, History, and Object of All Major Sports* (see Sports), and *The Chicago Manual of Style* (see Publishing).

Geographic Sources

Geographic sources may be subdivided into three categories: atlases, gazetteers, and guidebooks. An atlas is defined as a volume of maps, plates, engravings, tables, and so on, with or without text. (A complete history of the atlas can be found in *General Reference Books for Adults.*) A gazetteer is a geographic dictionary, giving spelling, pronunciation, and a varying amount of descriptive, historical, or statistical data about places named on maps. A guidebook is a handbook for travelers that gives information about a city, region, or country, or a similar work about a building, museum, travel

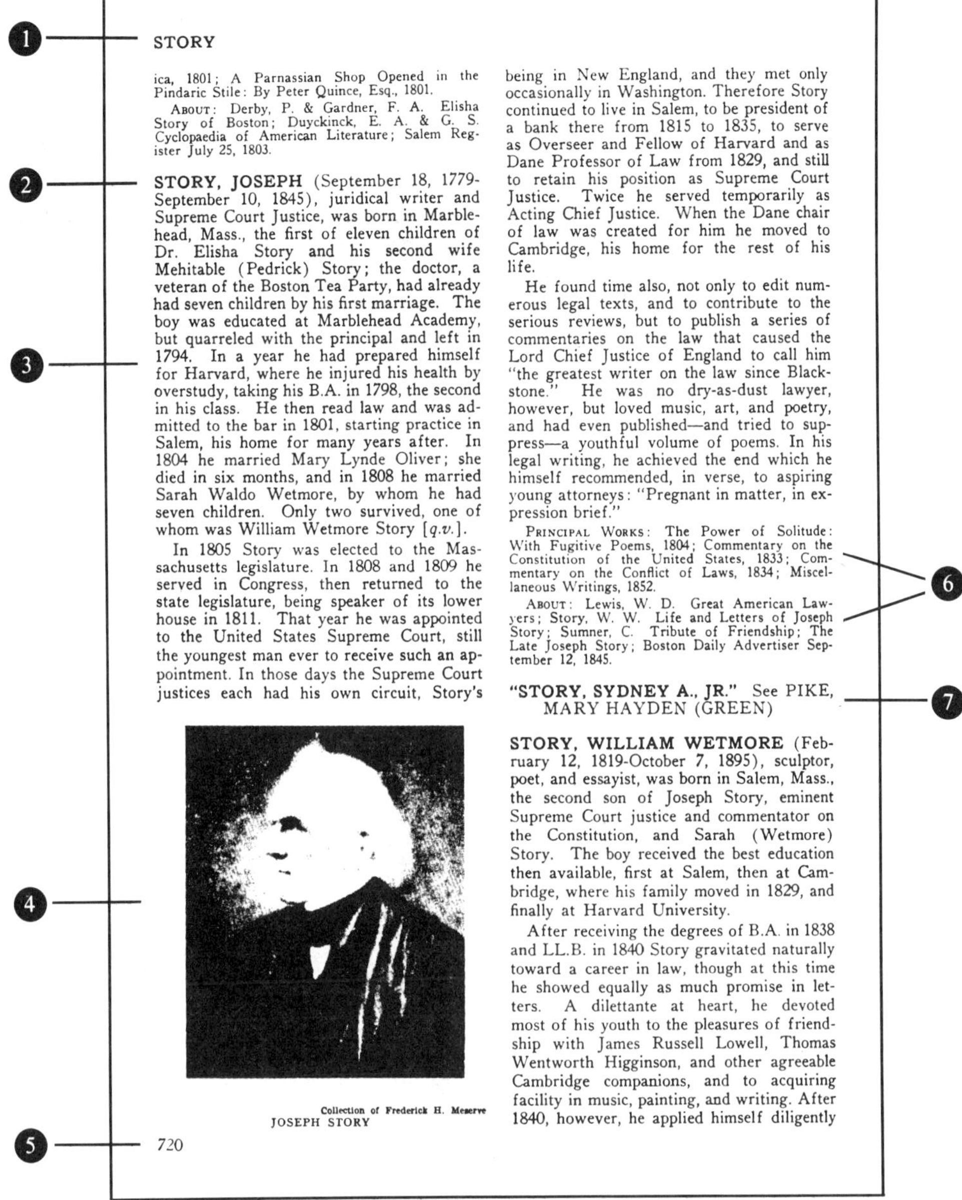

STORY

ica, 1801; A Parnassian Shop Opened in the Pindaric Stile: By Peter Quince, Esq., 1801.

About: Derby, P. & Gardner, F. A. Elisha Story of Boston; Duyckinck, E. A. & G. S. Cyclopaedia of American Literature; Salem Register July 25, 1803.

STORY, JOSEPH (September 18, 1779-September 10, 1845), juridical writer and Supreme Court Justice, was born in Marblehead, Mass., the first of eleven children of Dr. Elisha Story and his second wife Mehitable (Pedrick) Story; the doctor, a veteran of the Boston Tea Party, had already had seven children by his first marriage. The boy was educated at Marblehead Academy, but quarreled with the principal and left in 1794. In a year he had prepared himself for Harvard, where he injured his health by overstudy, taking his B.A. in 1798, the second in his class. He then read law and was admitted to the bar in 1801, starting practice in Salem, his home for many years after. In 1804 he married Mary Lynde Oliver; she died in six months, and in 1808 he married Sarah Waldo Wetmore, by whom he had seven children. Only two survived, one of whom was William Wetmore Story [*q.v.*].

In 1805 Story was elected to the Massachusetts legislature. In 1808 and 1809 he served in Congress, then returned to the state legislature, being speaker of its lower house in 1811. That year he was appointed to the United States Supreme Court, still the youngest man ever to receive such an appointment. In those days the Supreme Court justices each had his own circuit, Story's being in New England, and they met only occasionally in Washington. Therefore Story continued to live in Salem, to be president of a bank there from 1815 to 1835, to serve as Overseer and Fellow of Harvard and as Dane Professor of Law from 1829, and still to retain his position as Supreme Court Justice. Twice he served temporarily as Acting Chief Justice. When the Dane chair of law was created for him he moved to Cambridge, his home for the rest of his life.

He found time also, not only to edit numerous legal texts, and to contribute to the serious reviews, but to publish a series of commentaries on the law that caused the Lord Chief Justice of England to call him "the greatest writer on the law since Blackstone." He was no dry-as-dust lawyer, however, but loved music, art, and poetry, and had even published—and tried to suppress—a youthful volume of poems. In his legal writing, he achieved the end which he himself recommended, in verse, to aspiring young attorneys: "Pregnant in matter, in expression brief."

Principal Works: The Power of Solitude: With Fugitive Poems, 1804; Commentary on the Constitution of the United States, 1833; Commentary on the Conflict of Laws, 1834; Miscellaneous Writings, 1852.

About: Lewis, W. D. Great American Lawyers; Story, W. W. Life and Letters of Joseph Story; Sumner, C. Tribute of Friendship; The Late Joseph Story; Boston Daily Advertiser September 12, 1845.

"STORY, SYDNEY A., JR." See PIKE, MARY HAYDEN (GREEN)

STORY, WILLIAM WETMORE (February 12, 1819-October 7, 1895), sculptor, poet, and essayist, was born in Salem, Mass., the second son of Joseph Story, eminent Supreme Court justice and commentator on the Constitution, and Sarah (Wetmore) Story. The boy received the best education then available, first at Salem, then at Cambridge, where his family moved in 1829, and finally at Harvard University.

After receiving the degrees of B.A. in 1838 and LL.B. in 1840 Story gravitated naturally toward a career in law, though at this time he showed equally as much promise in letters. A dilettante at heart, he devoted most of his youth to the pleasures of friendship with James Russell Lowell, Thomas Wentworth Higginson, and other agreeable Cambridge companions, and to acquiring facility in music, painting, and writing. After 1840, however, he applied himself diligently

Collection of Frederick H. Meserve
JOSEPH STORY

720

Page shown at 68% of actual size.

1. Guide word indicates the first (left-hand page) or last (right-hand page) name on the page.
2. Main entry words appear in boldface capital letters.
3. Main body of entry, which includes nickname, birth and death dates, basic biographical information, and an evaluation of the subject's career.
4. Photograph of subject.
5. Page number.
6. Bibliography at the end of each entry. For this work, a literary biographical dictionary, listings are clearly divided into works by and works about.
7. Cross-reference to location of the actual entry clearly marked.

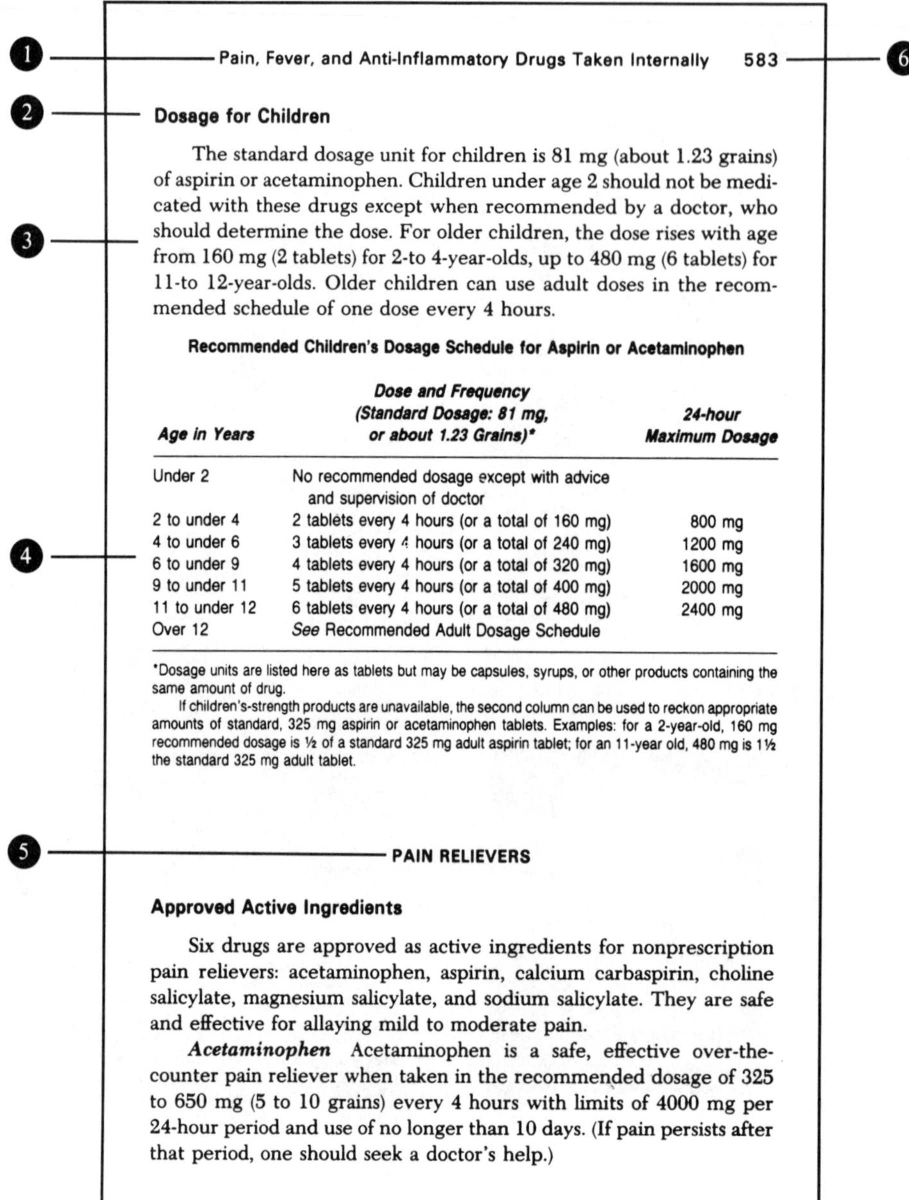

Pain, Fever, and Anti-Inflammatory Drugs Taken Internally 583

Dosage for Children

The standard dosage unit for children is 81 mg (about 1.23 grains) of aspirin or acetaminophen. Children under age 2 should not be medicated with these drugs except when recommended by a doctor, who should determine the dose. For older children, the dose rises with age from 160 mg (2 tablets) for 2-to 4-year-olds, up to 480 mg (6 tablets) for 11-to 12-year-olds. Older children can use adult doses in the recommended schedule of one dose every 4 hours.

Recommended Children's Dosage Schedule for Aspirin or Acetaminophen

Age in Years	*Dose and Frequency (Standard Dosage: 81 mg, or about 1.23 Grains)**	*24-hour Maximum Dosage*
Under 2	No recommended dosage except with advice and supervision of doctor	
2 to under 4	2 tablets every 4 hours (or a total of 160 mg)	800 mg
4 to under 6	3 tablets every 4 hours (or a total of 240 mg)	1200 mg
6 to under 9	4 tablets every 4 hours (or a total of 320 mg)	1600 mg
9 to under 11	5 tablets every 4 hours (or a total of 400 mg)	2000 mg
11 to under 12	6 tablets every 4 hours (or a total of 480 mg)	2400 mg
Over 12	*See* Recommended Adult Dosage Schedule	

*Dosage units are listed here as tablets but may be capsules, syrups, or other products containing the same amount of drug.

If children's-strength products are unavailable, the second column can be used to reckon appropriate amounts of standard, 325 mg aspirin or acetaminophen tablets. Examples: for a 2-year-old, 160 mg recommended dosage is ½ of a standard 325 mg adult aspirin tablet; for an 11-year old, 480 mg is 1½ the standard 325 mg adult tablet.

PAIN RELIEVERS

Approved Active Ingredients

Six drugs are approved as active ingredients for nonprescription pain relievers: acetaminophen, aspirin, calcium carbaspirin, choline salicylate, magnesium salicylate, and sodium salicylate. They are safe and effective for allaying mild to moderate pain.

Acetaminophen Acetaminophen is a safe, effective over-the-counter pain reliever when taken in the recommended dosage of 325 to 650 mg (5 to 10 grains) every 4 hours with limits of 4000 mg per 24-hour period and use of no longer than 10 days. (If pain persists after that period, one should seek a doctor's help.)

Page shown at 75% of actual size.

1. Page heading indicates section of book for easy access to material.
2. Subheadings within entries break text into significant subtopics.
3. Text presents information succinctly; in the case of this book, the need to consult a physician is emphasized.
4. Charts and tables organize information into clear guidance for use. Footnotes to tables provide valuable supplementary information. Note that last table entry is a cross-reference.
5. Headings appear in all capitals with ample space above and below to indicate beginning of new topic.
6. Page number.

route, or other points of interest. The two names most frequently associated with this type of book are the Baedeker and Fodor guides.

In order to qualify as an atlas, a work need only contain maps and index. Some of the best possess only these features. Atlases today, however, range from the bare essentials, to those containing text, illustrations, charts, statistics, timelines, chronologies, vivid use of color, and a variety of other means to bring out more fully the theme or topic illustrated by the maps. Several of these elements are shown in the facsimile page from the *Atlas of Medieval Europe* on page 26. Users of atlases need to be concerned with scale, which may distort relative sizes when it differs between maps; color, which may be poorly printed or cause difficulty in reading names; projections, which indicate map distortion; the clear explanation of map symbols; and the quality of the indexes, which in some atlases give entries only for the maps as a whole and not the locations named on them.

Representative geographic works reviewed in this book include *The World Atlas of Architecture* (see Architecture), *We the People: An Atlas of America's Ethnic Diversity* (see Ethnic Studies), and the *Atlas of the Bible* (see Religion).

Directories

The ALA Glossary of Library and Information Science defines a directory as "a list of persons or organizations, systematically arranged, usually in alphabetic or classed order, giving address, affiliations, etc., for individuals, and address, officers, functions, and similar data for organizations." This is said to be the largest of all reference book categories. Most groups, whether in profit, nonprofit, professional, technical, business, educational, hobby, or other areas, make lists of their members containing varying amounts of data. These are used in numerous instances when information of any kind concerning an organization is needed.

The arrangement and content of directories are usually quite consistent. As previously noted, most are organized in alphabetical or classified order. Some contain as little as name and address for each organization, while others may contain several pages of extensive data, as exemplified in *Standard & Poor's Corporation Records.* The contents of each entry are tied to the purpose of the directory—that is, whether for library, business, or educational use. Whatever the basic organization of the book, it is standard practice to include geographic and other approaches to the organization or indexing of entries. Most directories must be updated regularly because organizations are constantly being formed, merging, dying, dividing, moving, and otherwise changing. The best known book in this category is the *Encyclopedia of Associations,* a work that is considered essential in most libraries.

Bibliographies

Although definitions vary greatly in content and length, a bibliography is basically a list of written, printed, or otherwise produced records of civilization. Although such works were compiled in antiquity, it was the invention of printing in the fifteenth century, and the consequent increase in books, that made bibliographies a necessity.

A more complete description of this reference tool is provided by *Harrod's Librarians' Glossary,* which defines a bibliography as a compilation of books, manuscripts, audiovisual formats, or other publications arranged in a logical order giving author, title, date and place of publication, publisher, details of edition, pagination, series, and literary or information content. Such bibliographies might contain the works of one author or be devoted to one subject or works printed during one period, and so forth. The term *bibliography* also applies to the literature on a subject. Bibliographies may be universal, containing all formats, periods, and subjects; national, including the material from one country or in one language; selective, containing works rated by quality or relevance; trade, compiled for commercial purposes in the book trade; or subject, listing works by topic. Some annotated bibliographies include abstracts or reviews.

The content and organization of bibliographies differ—to the frustration of librarians and library users alike—depending on the type of material, purpose of the work, and background of the compiler. Every bibliography should contain introductory matter that explains the bibliographic makeup of entries to users. This should always be consulted. *America: History and Life,* a facsimile of which appears on page 27, provides an excellent illustration of several bibliographic entries that include books, dissertations, periodical articles, and abstracts.

Other representative bibliographic works reviewed in this book include *Women in the World* (see Women's Studies), the *Bibliography of Bioethics* (see Philosophy), and *Guide to Reference Books* (see Library Science).

Periodical indexes constitute a major bibliographic subfield. Although treated separately by most writers on library science, these everyday tools match the definition given in *Harrod's Librarians' Glossary* in content, organization, and function. Since the introduction of index publications to the library world by William Poole in the mid-nineteenth century, these reference works have increased to the point now where virtually every

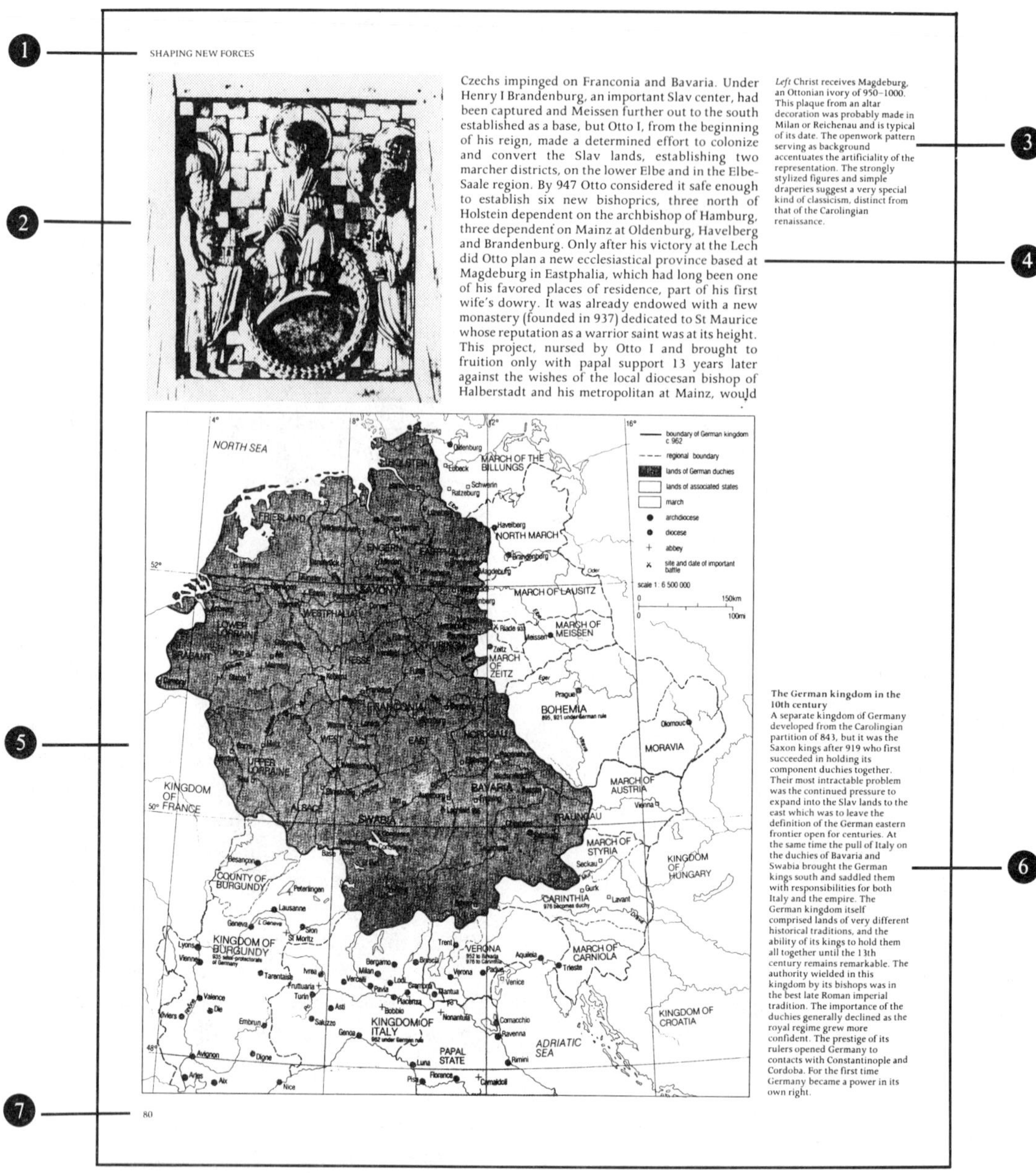

SHAPING NEW FORCES

Czechs impinged on Franconia and Bavaria. Under Henry I Brandenburg, an important Slav center, had been captured and Meissen further out to the south established as a base, but Otto I, from the beginning of his reign, made a determined effort to colonize and convert the Slav lands, establishing two marcher districts, on the lower Elbe and in the Elbe-Saale region. By 947 Otto considered it safe enough to establish six new bishoprics, three north of Holstein dependent on the archbishop of Hamburg, three dependent on Mainz at Oldenburg, Havelberg and Brandenburg. Only after his victory at the Lech did Otto plan a new ecclesiastical province based at Magdeburg in Eastphalia, which had long been one of his favored places of residence, part of his first wife's dowry. It was already endowed with a new monastery (founded in 937) dedicated to St Maurice whose reputation as a warrior saint was at its height. This project, nursed by Otto I and brought to fruition only with papal support 13 years later against the wishes of the local diocesan bishop of Halberstadt and his metropolitan at Mainz, would

Left Christ receives Magdeburg, an Ottonian ivory of 950–1000. This plaque from an altar decoration was probably made in Milan or Reichenau and is typical of its date. The openwork pattern serving as background accentuates the artificiality of the representation. The strongly stylized figures and simple draperies suggest a very special kind of classicism, distinct from that of the Carolingian renaissance.

The German kingdom in the 10th century
A separate kingdom of Germany developed from the Carolingian partition of 843, but it was the Saxon kings after 919 who first succeeded in holding its component duchies together. Their most intractable problem was the continued pressure to expand into the Slav lands to the east which was to leave the definition of the German eastern frontier open for centuries. At the same time the pull of Italy on the duchies of Bavaria and Swabia brought the German kings south and saddled them with responsibilities for both Italy and the empire. The German kingdom itself comprised lands of very different historical traditions, and the ability of its kings to hold them all together until the 13th century remains remarkable. The authority wielded in this kingdom by its bishops was in the best late Roman imperial tradition. The importance of the duchies generally declined as the royal regime grew more confident. The prestige of its rulers opened Germany to contacts with Constantinople and Cordoba. For the first time Germany became a power in its own right.

80

Page shown at 53% of actual size.

1. Page heading provides guidance as to topic under consideration.
2. Illustrations supplement maps with fine art or artifacts that impart a sense of the people, the time, and the place.
3. Captions describe subject, origin, and significance of illustrations.
4. Text provides a narrative highlighting key events, movements, and individuals and setting context for maps.
5. Maps, mostly in color, are the focus of the page. Each treats a given topic. The key (upper right corner of map) clarifies what each symbol or color signifies.
6. Map title and caption explain the background behind the map.
7. Page number.

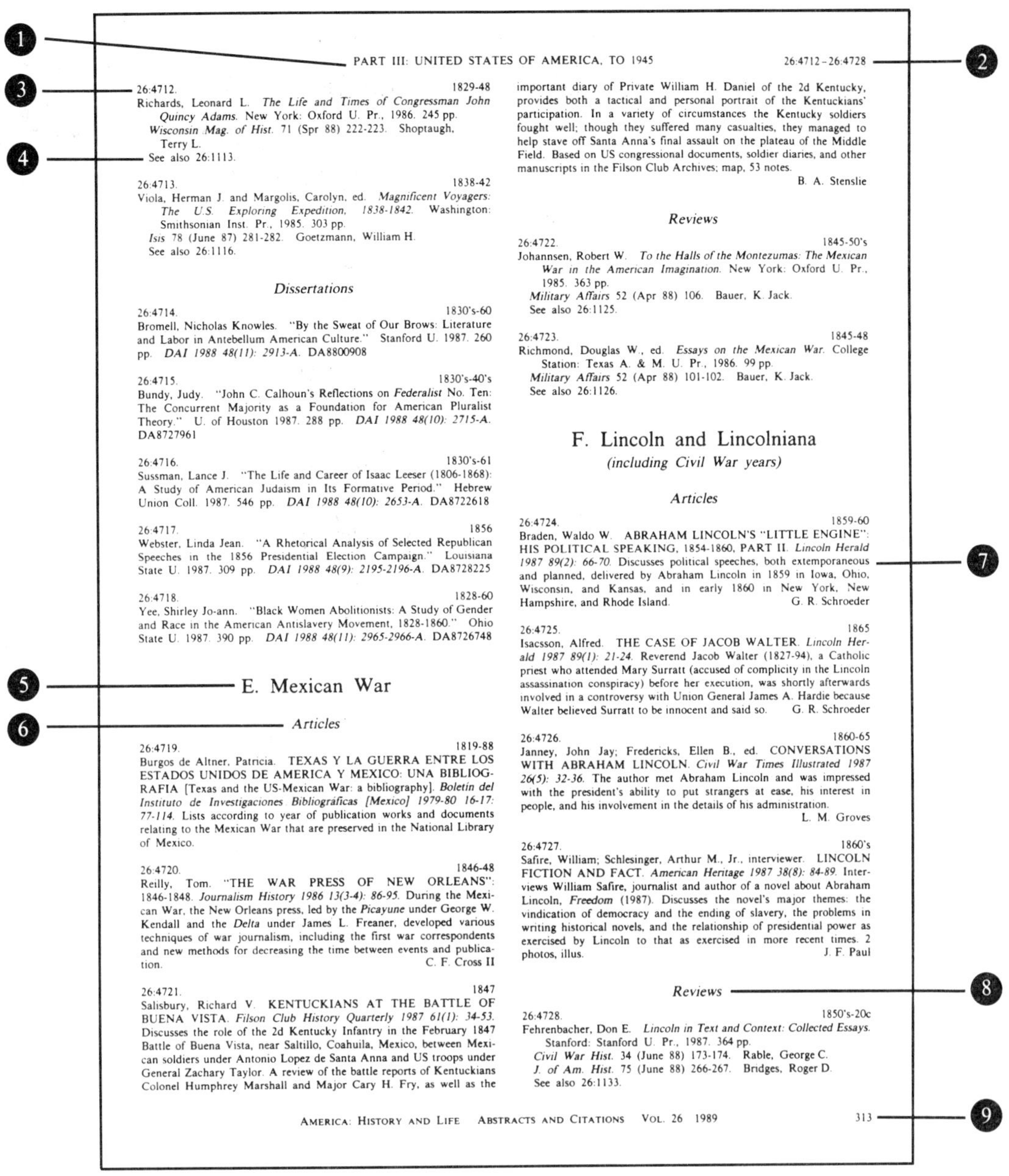

PART III: UNITED STATES OF AMERICA, TO 1945 26:4712–26:4728

26:4712. 1829-48
Richards, Leonard L. *The Life and Times of Congressman John Quincy Adams.* New York: Oxford U. Pr., 1986. 245 pp.
Wisconsin Mag. of Hist. 71 (Spr 88) 222-223. Shoptaugh, Terry L.
See also 26:1113.

26:4713. 1838-42
Viola, Herman J. and Margolis, Carolyn, ed. *Magnificent Voyagers: The U.S. Exploring Expedition, 1838-1842.* Washington: Smithsonian Inst. Pr., 1985. 303 pp.
Isis 78 (June 87) 281-282. Goetzmann, William H.
See also 26:1116.

Dissertations

26:4714. 1830's-60
Bromell, Nicholas Knowles. "By the Sweat of Our Brows: Literature and Labor in Antebellum American Culture." Stanford U. 1987. 260 pp. *DAI 1988 48(11): 2913-A.* DA8800908

26:4715. 1830's-40's
Bundy, Judy. "John C. Calhoun's Reflections on *Federalist* No. Ten: The Concurrent Majority as a Foundation for American Pluralist Theory." U. of Houston 1987. 288 pp. *DAI 1988 48(10): 2715-A.* DA8727961

26:4716. 1830's-61
Sussman, Lance J. "The Life and Career of Isaac Leeser (1806-1868): A Study of American Judaism in Its Formative Period." Hebrew Union Coll. 1987. 546 pp. *DAI 1988 48(10): 2653-A.* DA8722618

26:4717. 1856
Webster, Linda Jean. "A Rhetorical Analysis of Selected Republican Speeches in the 1856 Presidential Election Campaign." Louisiana State U. 1987. 309 pp. *DAI 1988 48(9): 2195-2196-A.* DA8728225

26:4718. 1828-60
Yee, Shirley Jo-ann. "Black Women Abolitionists: A Study of Gender and Race in the American Antislavery Movement, 1828-1860." Ohio State U. 1987. 390 pp. *DAI 1988 48(11): 2965-2966-A.* DA8726748

E. Mexican War

Articles

26:4719. 1819-88
Burgos de Altner, Patricia. TEXAS Y LA GUERRA ENTRE LOS ESTADOS UNIDOS DE AMERICA Y MEXICO: UNA BIBLIOGRAFIA [Texas and the US-Mexican War: a bibliography]. *Boletin del Instituto de Investigaciones Bibliograficas [Mexico] 1979-80 16-17: 77-114.* Lists according to year of publication works and documents relating to the Mexican War that are preserved in the National Library of Mexico.

26:4720. 1846-48
Reilly, Tom. "THE WAR PRESS OF NEW ORLEANS": 1846-1848. *Journalism History 1986 13(3-4): 86-95.* During the Mexican War, the New Orleans press, led by the *Picayune* under George W. Kendall and the *Delta* under James L. Freaner, developed various techniques of war journalism, including the first war correspondents and new methods for decreasing the time between events and publication. C. F. Cross II

26:4721. 1847
Salisbury, Richard V. KENTUCKIANS AT THE BATTLE OF BUENA VISTA. *Filson Club History Quarterly 1987 61(1): 34-53.* Discusses the role of the 2d Kentucky Infantry in the February 1847 Battle of Buena Vista, near Saltillo, Coahuila, Mexico, between Mexican soldiers under Antonio Lopez de Santa Anna and US troops under General Zachary Taylor. A review of the battle reports of Kentuckians Colonel Humphrey Marshall and Major Cary H. Fry, as well as the important diary of Private William H. Daniel of the 2d Kentucky, provides both a tactical and personal portrait of the Kentuckians' participation. In a variety of circumstances the Kentucky soldiers fought well; though they suffered many casualties, they managed to help stave off Santa Anna's final assault on the plateau of the Middle Field. Based on US congressional documents, soldier diaries, and other manuscripts in the Filson Club Archives; map, 53 notes. B. A. Stenslie

Reviews

26:4722. 1845-50's
Johannsen, Robert W. *To the Halls of the Montezumas: The Mexican War in the American Imagination.* New York: Oxford U. Pr., 1985. 363 pp.
Military Affairs 52 (Apr 88) 106. Bauer, K. Jack.
See also 26:1125.

26:4723. 1845-48
Richmond, Douglas W., ed. *Essays on the Mexican War.* College Station: Texas A. & M. U. Pr., 1986. 99 pp.
Military Affairs 52 (Apr 88) 101-102. Bauer, K. Jack.
See also 26:1126.

F. Lincoln and Lincolniana
(including Civil War years)

Articles

26:4724. 1859-60
Braden, Waldo W. ABRAHAM LINCOLN'S "LITTLE ENGINE": HIS POLITICAL SPEAKING, 1854-1860, PART II. *Lincoln Herald 1987 89(2): 66-70.* Discusses political speeches, both extemporaneous and planned, delivered by Abraham Lincoln in 1859 in Iowa, Ohio, Wisconsin, and Kansas, and in early 1860 in New York, New Hampshire, and Rhode Island. G. R. Schroeder

26:4725. 1865
Isacsson, Alfred. THE CASE OF JACOB WALTER. *Lincoln Herald 1987 89(1): 21-24.* Reverend Jacob Walter (1827-94), a Catholic priest who attended Mary Surratt (accused of complicity in the Lincoln assassination conspiracy) before her execution, was shortly afterwards involved in a controversy with Union General James A. Hardie because Walter believed Surratt to be innocent and said so. G. R. Schroeder

26:4726. 1860-65
Janney, John Jay; Fredericks, Ellen B., ed. CONVERSATIONS WITH ABRAHAM LINCOLN. *Civil War Times Illustrated 1987 26(5): 32-36.* The author met Abraham Lincoln and was impressed with the president's ability to put strangers at ease, his interest in people, and his involvement in the details of his administration. L. M. Groves

26:4727. 1860's
Safire, William; Schlesinger, Arthur M., Jr., interviewer. LINCOLN FICTION AND FACT. *American Heritage 1987 38(8): 84-89.* Interviews William Safire, journalist and author of a novel about Abraham Lincoln, *Freedom* (1987). Discusses the novel's major themes: the vindication of democracy and the ending of slavery, the problems in writing historical novels, and the relationship of presidential power as exercised by Lincoln to that as exercised in more recent times. 2 photos, illus. J. F. Paul

Reviews

26:4728. 1850's-20c
Fehrenbacher, Don E. *Lincoln in Text and Context: Collected Essays.* Stanford: Stanford U. Pr., 1987. 364 pp.
Civil War Hist. 34 (June 88) 173-174. Rable, George C.
J. of Am. Hist. 75 (June 88) 266-267. Bridges, Roger D.
See also 26:1133.

AMERICA: HISTORY AND LIFE ABSTRACTS AND CITATIONS VOL. 26 1989 313

Page shown at 59% of actual size.

1. Page heading indicates historical period.
2. Guide numbers indicate the first and last entries on the page.
3. Citation numbers are provided for each item.
4. Cross-reference indicates related titles.
5. Topical divisions organize citations into manageable size.
6. Format of the title is used for grouping like items, that is, articles, dissertations, reviews, and so on.
7. Entries for books and articles include full bibliographic information plus brief descriptions of the work. This bibliography even indicates the time span of the work in question.
8. This bibliography also includes reviews of works that pertain to the time span covered.
9. Page number.

field and many subfields are represented by at least one or more indexes. Many of these, because of the addition of brief descriptions to the basic bibliographic elements, bear the word *abstract* in the title. While the *Reader's Guide to Periodical Literature* is synonymous with this category, the following titles illustrate the variety of the field: *Index Medicus* (see Medicine and Dentistry), *Index to Legal Periodicals* (see Law), and *Psychological Abstracts* (see Psychology and Psychiatry).

Histories

Historical reference works are those that, although not meeting the definition of reference books, treat a topic in such detail that they are included in the reference collection. They are normally topical or subject oriented, and deal with specific areas such as music, art, and literature. The *Cambridge Ancient History* has long been a standard work in college and university libraries.

Histories included in reference collections are usually presented in a standard narrative format. They may be single- or multivolume. In some instances these works are made up of individual volumes that may be used independently or as part of the series. Good, detailed indexes for easy access to specific data are essential. Frequently, such works include other reference-type elements that add to the decision to place them in a reference collection, including maps, chronologies, illustrations, bibliographies, and lists of various kinds.

Reference works in this category that are reviewed in this work include *The Cambridge History of English Literature* (see British Literature), *A History of Italian Literature* (see Italian Literature), and the *Oxford History of the Classical World* (see Ancient History).

Evaluating Reference Sources

The best of all possible situations when purchasing a reference book is a physical examination of a copy of the book under consideration. Although this is not always possible, librarians have a variety of opportunities to see both standard and new reference materials that are on the market. Many libraries use approval plans in which publishers send copies of new materials at regular intervals for examination and possible selection by librarians. These titles are selected by the publisher based on a profile of the interests of the particular library. One of the best and most convenient opportunities for viewing new reference products is at the annual librarians' and teachers' professional association conferences. Exhibit booths set up by individual publishers include copies for examination by those in attendance and sometimes offer titles at discount rates. Even browsing in local bookstores can lead to some finds of value to the local library.

Selection based on a physical examination of a reference book, however, is not always possible, particularly with titles that are more than a year or two old. One alternative method in this decision-making process is for the librarian to evaluate reviews of these works published in reputable periodicals and buying guides. The librarian should become familiar with the criteria used by reviewers to judge these works. While guidelines may vary from publication to publication, there is common agreement on certain aspects that must be looked at before a book can be recommended for purchase or inclusion in the library. The following guidelines were used by librarians and subject specialists in this buying guide for reviewing the almost 2,000 titles that are included in this work. (A detailed description of the specific review process for *Topical Reference Books* can be found in chapter 1, "Using This Book.")

Review Guidelines

Each review states what the book does and why it is a good choice for a collection. The work's authority, format, scope, accessibility, currency, and accuracy are evaluated as part of the review process. The following checklist for each of these elements helped the reviewer evaluate the work.

1. *Authority:* Are the editors, reviewers, or compilers identified? Are these notable figures in the field? What is their reputation? If no author is listed, evaluate the reputation of the publisher. Does the publisher consistently produce well-researched reference works?
2. *Format:* Is there anything positive or negative about the book's size, reproduction of illustrations, typeface, paper quality, or binding?
3. *Scope:* Briefly describe the organization of the book, length of entries, selection criteria, inclusion or exclusion of pertinent material. Depending on the subject of the work being examined, the librarian may need to consider cultural and racial balance in the text, as well as the kind of coverage that is given to women and other minorities.
4. *Accessibility:* Is the reading level of the book intended for specialists or a general audience? Do the arrangement of entries, the use of cross-references, and the methods of indexing contribute to the accessibility of information? Are bibliographies provided to lead users to further information?

5. *Currency:* Does the publication date affect the scope of the book? Is the material now dated due to current scholarship? Is it still valuable for some uses?
6. *Accuracy:* Are there errors or inconsistencies that detract from the book's value?

In addition to these guidelines, one must also take into consideration the kind of library for which the book is intended, budget constraints, and, most important, the needs, both known and anticipated, of the users.

Let's look at how the preceding criteria were used in reviewing several types of reference books selected for this buying guide.

The *Dictionary of the Middle Ages* (Joseph R. Strayer, ed. 13 vols. New York: Scribner, 1982–1989) is, by its title, a dictionary. *Authority* in works of this type is determined by the authors, whose names follow each article, with additional information about them in a list of contributors, which may appear in the front of the first volume or in each volume of the set. Additional authority is guaranteed by the work's sponsoring organization, the American Council of Learned Societies.

Scope is partially indicated in the title of almost any work—thus, the time period is the Middle Ages. A reviewer may further define the scope through an examination of the book's preface or introduction, which, in this instance, limits the scope in time to A.D. 500 to 1500, and geographically to the Latin West, the Slavic world, Asia Minor, the Arab caliphate in the East, and the Muslim-Christian areas of North Africa. The scope is thus broader than most works on the medieval world, and will provide a larger spectrum of information. The breadth of the time period covered and the extent of the coverage (13 volumes) define this work as an encyclopedia, rather than as the "dictionary" of its title.

The *format* for this work is good, as an examination of the readable typeface and sturdy paper quality and binding will show. High production quality indicates that these volumes will withstand the wear and tear of use in a library setting.

Accessibility is determined through an examination of the work's contents. The reading level of the entries in the *Dictionary of the Middle Ages* reveals that it is suitable for use by high school and college students and adults. The alphabetical arrangement of entries, the frequent use of cross-references, and an excellent index indicate that users will find easy access to information anywhere in the set. Bibliographies following most articles give readers leads to additional information on the topic.

The *currency* of information in this dictionary is demonstrated by the recent dates shown in the bibliographic citations that follow the dictionary entries. These show that the most up-to-date research findings were used to compile entries.

Accuracy is not always easy to determine, because the reviewer must have enough expertise in an area to call an author's judgment into question. In encyclopedic works, most persons will know at least one area sufficiently well enough to do this. For example, an examination of the entry on libraries by this writer shows no obvious errors and, therefore, provides no reason to question the accuracy of the work as a whole. The entry for libraries is just over 13 pages in length. Subheadings cover numerous topics from "library historiography" to "collection development." An illustration of the floor plan of a medieval library is provided. An extensive bibliography appears at the end of the article; some of the works cited date from the early 1980s and reflect current research finds. Updated bibliographies are an important factor, even in works of a historical nature.

The Almanac of American Politics 1990 by Michael Barone and Grant Ujifusa (Washington, D.C.: National Journal, 1989) is a political handbook. *Authority* for this type of work can be determined in two ways: the reputation of the publisher, the National Journal, which is one of the two major sources of political information on the federal level in the United States; and the authors, both of whom have backgrounds in political affairs.

An examination of the *format* shows sturdy binding, good-quality paper, and easy-to-read type.

The title actually provides a good, quick summary of each major part of the book's *scope.* Additional content information is found in an introductory "Guide to Usage." A brief scan of the table of contents shows a good, logical geographic breakdown of political data that cover every state and congressional district in the United States, plus charts and text on a variety of congressional and state affairs. This outline of material makes the book significant to any library concerned with giving users current data on the political scene.

In considering *accessibility,* a review of the text shows logical and consistent arrangement of material, aided by a good table of contents and an excellent index. The reading level is aimed at a general audience, making this book easily usable by the patrons of public, academic, school, and even some special libraries.

The *accuracy* of this work can easily be determined by reviewers through a simple examination of the entry for their own senator, congressional representative, or governor to see if the facts are correct. In addition, librarians looking at this title will note that any annual or biennial volume cannot reflect unexpected and interim changes in political offices between editions.

Collection Development Tools

Librarians are fortunate to have an array of collection-development tools at their disposal. Reference books are reviewed regularly in periodicals and books, many of which evaluate good and bad features, recommend user level or type of library for which the title is best suited, and even note the location of additional critical information. Librarians searching for reviews or listings of books, whether suitable for a particular type of audience, library, or subject, will find that selection aids have been created for each circumstance or situation. The list of works initially compiled for voting for *Topical Reference Books* was, of course, compiled through information found in most of the following publications.

General Selection Aids

General selection aids provide information on reference materials in all subject categories, and in some cases, on materials in a variety of formats: print, microform, or computer data bases. Normally, the only real limitation is the date of publication of the works that appear in the following list. Although some include useful titles of any date, old or new, others concentrate on reference books issued during the preceding year or within a stated number of recent years. The following provide a representative sampling of this category of selection aid:

Guide to Reference Books. 10th edition. Eugene P. Sheehy. Chicago: ALA, 1986, and supplements.

Guide to Reference Materials. 5th edition. Albert J. Walford. London: Library Association, 1989.

American Reference Books Annual. 21st edition. Bohdan S. Wynar et al., eds. Englewood, Colo.: Libraries Unlimited, 1990.

Sheehy's *Guide to Reference Books* is so familiar that it has earned a reputation as "the Bible of the reference librarian." This guide has served as a text in library schools and as a standard selection aid in libraries of all kinds. International in scope, but with an emphasis on American, Canadian, and English titles, the *Guide to Reference Books* provides an annotated listing of reference works in all subject areas. Included are many titles that have stood the test of time. Consequently, still-useful reference works from the turn of the century are listed side by side with more recent volumes. A classified arrangement that places like materials together, with related subjects nearby, makes it easy for librarians to survey a topic for pertinent reference titles. Although supplements are issued between editions, the titles listed are generally several years behind the copyright date of either *A Guide to Reference Works* or its supplements. Nevertheless, this is a basic and reliable selection aid that is a standard in the field. Walford's *Guide to Reference Materials* serves as a useful complement to Sheehy, the major difference being that this work, published in England, has an emphasis on English and European reference works.

For more current reference books, librarians will find annual guides such as *American Reference Books Annual (ARBA)* to be valuable supplements to those of Sheehy and Walford. This is one of the best sources available for surveying the best and worst of the annual crop of reference titles. The stated purpose of *ARBA* is to provide reviews of the complete spectrum of English-language reference books published in the United States and Canada during a single year. Since *ARBA* began in 1970, over 34,000 titles have been reviewed in its pages. Reviews are critical, describing good and bad points about a volume, and generally tell the audience or type of library for which a title is best suited.

Aids for Libraries of Varying Sizes

While general selection aids may be used by all librarians, those who work in small- and medium-sized libraries, as well as those in school, public, two-year, and other institutions will find a number of collection-development tools designed specifically for their needs. These vary greatly in content and format. Each of the works in the following list are generally unlimited in subject content, but they were compiled with specific audiences in mind. In addition, some of the best works in this area include both reference and nonreference titles, thus being oriented to the entire collection—not just one part. The following eight titles represent only a sampling of what librarians in specific types of libraries will find available for their needs:

Reference Sources for Small and Medium-Sized Libraries. 4th edition. Jovian Lang and Deborah Master, eds. Chicago: ALA, 1984.

Guide to Reference Books for School Media Centers. 3d edition. Christine Wynar. Englewood, Colo.: Libraries Unlimited, 1986.

Best Books for Children. 4th edition. John T. Gillespie and Corrine J. Naden, eds. New York: Bowker, 1990.

The Elementary School Library Collection; A Guide to Books and Other Media. 16th edition. Lois Winkel. Williamsport, Pa.: Brodart, 1988.

Children's Catalog. 15th edition. New York: Wilson, 1986.

Junior High School Library Catalog. 5th edition. New York: Wilson, 1985.

Senior High School Library Catalog. 13th edition. New York: Wilson, 1987.

Public Library Catalog. 9th edition. New York: Wilson, 1989.

Medium-sized and smaller libraries, whether school, public, or college, have certain reference needs in common. These institutions will find value in *Reference Sources for Small and Medium-Sized Libraries,* which is produced approximately every five years by a committee of the ALA's Reference and Adult Services Division. The recent title change from "books" to "sources" reflects the growing number of reference materials available in microform and on-line formats, as well as traditional print sources. Titles are grouped by topic, annotated, and labeled for suitability for children and young adults.

Librarians serving teachers and students from kindergarten through the twelfth grade are well served by Christine Wynar's *Guide to Reference Books for School Media Centers.*

Elementary school libraries are also well served by a number of other good selection aids, including the *Children's Catalog* (part of H. W. Wilson's Standard Catalog series to be discussed below) and *The Elementary School Library Collection.* Bowker's *Best Books for Children,* which is reviewed in the Children's Literature category, lists and evaluates titles up to the sixth-grade level.

The Standard Catalog series, consisting of the *Children's Catalog,* the *Fiction Catalog* (not discussed here), the *Junior High School Catalog,* the *Senior High School Catalog,* and the *Public Library Catalog,* is familiar to librarians in the types of libraries indicated in the titles. All are similar and can be discussed as a group. Users will find the contents of each arranged according to the Dewey Decimal System (most frequently used by small or medium-sized libraries). Also, users should note some overlapping of use. Materials for advanced sixth graders will be found in the *Junior High* volume, while the *Public Library Catalog,* which only includes books for adults, may be useful in college libraries. All list both old and new titles, with annotations. Reference and nonreference books are interfiled without distinction. The series, with its library-shelf-related organization, specialization by library type, and annual supplements to the bound volumes, offers librarians a wide-ranging collection-development tool.

Recent Reference Publications as Selection Aids

Because all of the selection tools discussed thus far are at least several months out of date by the time they reach a library's shelves, librarians must turn to other sources to identify the most recently published materials. The best sources for identifying new books of quality are reviewing periodicals and review sections in professional library journals. Because of the small number of titles listed in each issue, reference titles are generally listed without subject breakdowns. Because of this, they are best suited for random browsing to identify occasional works that may be of interest rather than a systematic subject or title approach to selection. The following selective list illustrates some of the choices librarians have for surveying current reference sources:

Choice reviews 600 to 700 reference and nonreference works suitable for the undergraduate arts and sciences college curriculum in each monthly issue.

Library Journal is well known to librarians in libraries of every size and type. Its articles feature news, statistics, and, in general, inform the profession in areas of interest. Each bimonthly issue features a small number of brief (100- to 150-word) evaluative reviews of recent reference books. The total per year is approximately 450.

School Library Journal is published in ten issues per year. This periodical is the leading publication for librarians concerned with selecting works for children and young adults. Its contents include reviews, feature articles, and related news, among other information.

The *Wilson Library Bulletin* is a popular monthly containing news, feature articles, and a number of topical reviewing columns aimed at such library interests as science fiction, crime stories, young adult materials, and current reference books.

RQ is the official journal of the Reference and Adult Services Division of the American Library Association (ALA), and as such contains articles, columns, and reviews of interest to reference librarians of all kinds. Approximately 20 to 50 critical and sometimes lengthy reviews appear in each issue.

Reference Books Bulletin is a separate publication issued regularly within *Booklist*, which is, in turn, a more general reviewing journal. *Reference Books Bulletin* provides authoritative, carefully developed, and substantial reviews prepared by members of the editorial board of ALA's Publishing Committee. Approximately 20 to 35 reviews appear twice monthly, September through June, and monthly in July and August.

Publishers' Catalogs as Selection Aids

Publishers' catalogs are excellent sources of information on very recent material as well as forthcoming and older books. These often include illustrations, sample entries and pages, and provide details unavailable in the review sources discussed above. Publishers are more than willing to place any library with an interest in their publications on the mailing lists for catalogs and other publicity packages.

Conclusion

Reference librarianship and reference collections have come a long way in the short time since they were first recognized as legitimate library concerns just a century ago. This book is a recognition of this fact. The century has seen a steady stream of improvements. Gone are the days when the only service a library user could expect was self-service, and the entire reference collection was a small number of dictionaries and encyclopedias locked in cases or located on inaccessible shelves. Today, even the smallest libraries offer information assistance as a normal and expected service. School, public, academic, and special libraries include information sources in forms undreamed of by our grandparents and great-grandparents, who were the patrons of the libraries of Dewey, Poole, and Spofford. On-line data bases, CD-ROMs, microforms, and specialized reference books to meet any need and audience are, or can be, found in libraries of any size and type. A survey of *Topical Reference Books* will illustrate the continually increasing ability of reference librarians to serve their clientele in their varied needs by focusing on formulation of core collections in major subject areas.

—Donald E. Collins

Bibliography

Writings on contemporary reference work and materials are plentiful. While there are several leading authors in the field, perhaps the most widely read is William Katz. His two-volume *Introduction to Reference Work,* 4th edition (New York: McGraw-Hill, 1982), added to this writer's personal experience in reference, supplied much of the material for this chapter. Readers will also find useful three excellent articles in the *Encyclopedia of Library and Information Services* (New York: Marcel Dekker, 1968–). The first, "Reference Books," by Louis Shores, one of this century's leading reference authorities, and Richard Krzy (volume 25, pages 136–202), provides a good general treatment of the topic; Thomas J. Galvin, another widely published author, contributed the article "Reference Services and Libraries" (volume 25, pages 210–226); while the near-book-length article "Reference Books and Alternate Sources," by Martin H. Sable, (supplement 9, pages 284–388) treats a wide range of issues, from reference books to reference publishing and the book trade. The *ALA World Encyclopedia of Library and Information Services,* 2d edition (Chicago: ALA, 1986) provides good survey articles on the various kinds of libraries, including "Academic Libraries—Purposes, Goals, and Objectives," by Beverly P. Lynch (pages 4–8); "Academic Libraries—Services for Users," by Billy R. Wilkinson (pages 8–12); "Public Libraries—Purposes and Objectives" by H. C. Campbell (pages 660–663); "Public Libraries—Services to Users," by Mary Jo Lynch (pages 663–666); "Special Libraries," by Elin B. Christianson (pages 772–782); "School Libraries and Media Centers—Purposes and Objectives," by Jean E. Lowrie (pages 733–736); and "School Libraries—Services to Users," by Elrieda McCauley and Jean E. Lowrie (pages 736–739).

PART TWO

Evaluations of Topical Reference Books

Lucy Heckman

Advertising

See also Graphic Arts

A critical factor in the success of a product or service is often the strength of its advertising campaign. Advertising is very much in evidence in various media, including newspapers and magazines, television and radio broadcasting, and direct-mail campaigns. It is a field that draws upon cultural and psychological concepts, among other factors, to attract a buyer to a product.

The advertising reference works described here are designed for both professionals and nonprofessionals involved or interested in the field. The works fall within the categories of directories, handbooks, and dictionaries. Directories are included in this category because the data they present are germane to the study and analysis of the field. The advertising core collection should include source materials from all three categories.

The STANDARD DIRECTORY OF ADVERTISING AGENCIES and the STANDARD DIRECTORY OF ADVERTISERS are two sources necessary for the advertising collection. Updated several times during the year, the STANDARD DIRECTORY OF ADVERTISING AGEN-

Core Titles

	PUBLIC	ACADEMIC	SCHOOL
The Advertising Handbook Hall, S. Roland. Garland, 1986	✦	✦	
The Dictionary of Advertising Urdang, Laurence, ed. NTC Business Books, 1979		✦	
Dictionary of Advertising and Direct Mail Terms Imber, Jane, and Betsy-Ann Toffler. Barron's, 1987	✦	✦	
Standard Directory of Advertisers National Register, annual	✦	✦	
Standard Directory of Advertising Agencies National Register, published three times per year	✦	✦	

CIES provides information on names, addresses, number of employees, and much more for advertising agencies in the United States and in foreign countries as well as current statistics on advertising expenditures. Another core work, the STANDARD DIRECTORY OF ADVERTISERS, identifies the advertising agencies for corporations and the amount these corporations spend on advertising campaigns. The directories provide valuable current and comprehensive advertising data.

Handbooks representing the advertising field offer practical guidelines and advice on such assignments as preparing layout, proofreading, and writing television commercials. These handbooks may be read cover to cover or referred to as a guide to answering reference questions on a particular aspect of advertising. Also, handbooks often give examples of effective advertising methods.

Dictionaries in advertising provide definitions of terms along with information about various organizations and agencies. The dictionaries also provide a list of frequently used acronyms. Most of the dictionaries that are described in this section are illustrated and give readers a visual picture of an advertising concept.

Several supplementary works should also be considered. These sources are ADVERTISING SLOGANS OF AMERICA, by Harold S. Sharp; INFORMATION SOURCES IN ADVERTISING HISTORY, by Richard W. Pollay; and STANDARD RATE AND DATA SERVICE. Some respected works in this field are now out of print. Librarians may want to obtain three additional titles through out-of-print sources: *The Macmillan Dictionary of Marketing and Advertising*, by Michael J. Baker (Nicholas Publishing, 1984); *Slogans*, by Laurence Urdang (Gale, 1984); and *The Copywriter's Handbook,* by Robert W. Bly (Dodd, Mead, 1985).

Core Titles

The Advertising Handbook. S. Roland Hall. Garland, 1986; reprint of Macmillan, 1921. hard. 1 vol. 743 pp. illus. index. ISBN 0-8240-6732-0. $15. handbook.
HF5823.H29 651.1'13

The title page of the original edition (1921) of *The Advertising Handbook* describes the book as "a reference work covering the principles and practice of advertising." The author, S. Roland Hall, was an advertising counselor and former advertising manager for Alpha Portland Cement Company and the Victor Talking Machine Company. In writing this handbook, Hall drew upon his experiences as practitioner, teacher, researcher, and writer.

The Advertising Handbook is part of a 40-volume facsimile series of books on the history of advertising. Among books in this series are *Psychology for Advertisers* (1930), by D. B. Lucas and C. E. Benson; *Retail Advertising and Selling* (1924), by S. Roland Hall; and *Advertising: The Social and Economic Problem* (1915), by George French. These books offer historical perspectives on advertising principles in use today.

Hall's work, although it predates key developments such as television advertising, films with sound, and computer technology, contributes practical and theoretical guidelines. Among the topics covered are marketing campaigns, copywriting, the role of advertising agencies, magazine advertising, and layout preparation.

Of special value are the black-and-white illustrations of advertisements used in various campaigns. For example, ads for Steinway pianos, Ivory soap, and Colgate toothpaste demonstrate the use of psychological appeal in promoting products. Other illustrations depict effective advertising techniques in newspapers, catalogs, posters, circulars, and magazines.

Of benefit to advertising historians is the section on laws affecting advertising circa 1921, with descriptions of legislation on unfair competition, copyright, and resale price control.

The Advertising Handbook is of major importance to advertising historians. Many of the basic concepts and theories presented are not outmoded and are still very much in evidence in today's ad campaigns. The Board recommends this work for the core collections of public and academic libraries.

The Dictionary of Advertising. Laurence Urdang, ed. NTC Business Bks., 1979. soft. 1 vol. 209 pp. ISBN 0-8442-3040-5. $15.95. dictionary.
HF5803.D5 659.1

The Dictionary of Advertising, an expanded version of the 1977 *Dictionary of Advertising Terms,* provides definitions of words and terms used by marketing professionals, especially those involved in advertising. The work is edited by Laurence Urdang, a noted lexicographer whose past contributions include his work as managing editor of the *Random House Dictionary of the English Language* and editorial director of the reference guide *Slogans. The Dictionary of Advertising* provides definitions for over 4,000 terms used in such fields as marketing planning, copywriting, art direction, media research, consumer research, and media analysis. The work does not include "reference to or the proprietary terminology of such suppliers as project-oriented research houses, advertising agencies, or individual media vehicles" (preface). For these terms, readers are referred to such sources as the Agency Red Books (more formally called the STANDARD DIRECTORY OF ADVERTISING AGENCIES), the Green Book, and STANDARD RATE AND DATA SERVICE.

Entries consist of definitions of terms as well as brief descriptions of the functions and purposes of various major broadcast networks, industry organizations, and syndicated research firms. Each entry contains the term, part of speech, and a brief definition. Some definitions are accompanied by black-and-white illustrations, giving a visual example of how terms are used. For example, an illustration of an airbrush and its components is included with its definition. Cross-references are provided for abbreviations, acronyms, and synonyms. Those looking for the *A.A.A.A.,* or the *Four A's,* will be referred to the *American Association of Advertising Agencies.*

Entries for networks, associations, companies, unions, and firms include brief statements of purpose, often with year of founding and logo.

The Dictionary of Advertising furnishes clear and concise definitions of terms as well as information about organizations. The dictionary is enhanced by the inclusion of the definitions of advertising acronyms. The Board recommends this work for the core collection of academic libraries. Students of the advertising business and experts in the field will find this source highly beneficial.

Dictionary of Advertising and Direct Mail Terms. Jane Imber and Betsy-Ann Toffler. Barron's, 1987. soft. 1 vol. 514 pp. illus. appendixes. ISBN 0-8120-3765-0. $9.95. dictionary.
HF5803.I46 659.1'03'21

The *Dictionary of Advertising and Direct Mail Terms* provides definitions of terms used in advertising and encompasses broadcast, print, direct-mail, direct-response, trade, corporate, and classified advertising. The authors are Jane Imber, marketing manager of Neodata Services, and Betsy-Ann Toffler, a free-lance writer. The work is a part of the Barron's Business Guides series.

Entries are alphabetized letter by letter instead of word by word (thus *pull tab* follows *pulling power.*) Cross-references are included for related and contrasting terms. Definitions are provided for such contemporary terms as *VCR, yuppie, baby boomer,* and *laser printer.* All definitions of terms are succinct, and examples are given of how these terms are used in contemporary advertising. A small number of the definitions are accompanied by black-and-white illustrations. For example, illustrations are furnished for the terms *comprehensive layout, envelope, checkerboard,* and *video display terminal.*

Companies, organizations, and associations—such as the American Marketing Association—are listed in the dictionary with a description of their purpose, history, publications, and founding date. Also defined and described are key publications in advertising, such as the *Creative Black Book, Standard Advertising Register,* and Green Book. The entry for the *Standard Advertising Register,* for example, discusses the purpose, coverage, publisher, and frequency of publication of the STANDARD DIRECTORY OF ADVERTISING AGENCIES and the STANDARD DIRECTORY OF ADVERTISERS.

The appendixes are entitled "Abbreviations and Acronyms," "Proofreading Marks," and "Print Fonts." The appendix entitled "Abbreviations and Acronyms" is designed to answer ready-reference questions on what terms such as *BG* (background) and *IOA* (Institute of Outdoor Advertising) stand for. "Proofreading Marks" is a compilation of commonly used marks. "Print Fonts" gives examples of 18 fonts, including Baskerville, Kabel Ultra, and Times Roman.

The Dictionary of Advertising and Direct Mail Terms is a helpful reference guide for professionals, students, teachers, and librarians. The Board recommends this work for the core collections of public and academic libraries.

Standard Directory of Advertisers. National Register, annual (1915–). Classified Edition published in April. Geographical Edition published in May. Pocket-sized Geographical Directory published in May. soft. index. ISSN 0081-4229. ISBN 08721-7090-X. $357. directory.
HF5805.S7 659

The *Standard Directory of Advertisers* provides listings for over 17,000 companies that employ advertising agencies. Readers can find out names of current advertising agencies for companies representing over 50 product classifications. The Classified Edition arranges entries by product categories, and the Geographic Edition arranges entries by state and city. Information is updated by cumulative supplements issued throughout the year. This directory and the STANDARD DIRECTORY OF ADVERTISING AGENCIES are published by National Register Publishing Company.

The sections of the *Standard Directory of Advertisers* are: "The Largest Advertising Agencies"; "The Largest Advertisers"; "Index of Classification by Government S.I.C. Codes"; "Index of Classification in Numerical Order"; "Key to Abbreviations"; "Key to Advertising Media"; "Number of Parent Companies by Product Classification"; "Breakdown of Parent Companies by State"; "Company Listings with Logos"; "Index of Associations," with names, addresses, telephone numbers, and brief description of organization; "Alphabetical Index (of companies)"; "Trade Name List"; "Index of Classification"; and "Index of Groups."

Comprehensive data about each advertiser company appears in the product classification section. Each entry provides: name, address, business description and trade names, officers, subsidiaries, advertising agencies, advertising appropriation, distribution of company's products, and the month in which the company determines its advertising budget.

As an example of how this directory may be used, those looking for advertising agencies and expenditures of the Ford Motor Company may check the alphabetical index under the company name, then refer to the appropriate page. To compare expenditures of Ford with a competitor, for example, users may consult the "Index of Groups" to find pages for the automobile industry. Researchers may also scan the "Trade Name List" to find out which companies produce various products, including Big Mac hamburgers and Black Flag insecticides.

The Board recommends the *Standard Directory of Advertisers,* along with the STANDARD DIRECTORY OF ADVERTISING AGENCIES, for the core collections of public and academic libraries.

Standard Directory of Advertising Agencies. National Register, published three times per year—February, June, and October (1917–). soft. indexes. ISSN 0085-6614. $247 (1 issue); $487 (3 issues). directory.
HF5805.S72 659

The *Standard Directory of Advertising Agencies,* or Agency Red Book, is a guide to over 4,800 advertising agencies in the United States and overseas. The directory is published three times a year, with nine "Agency News" supplements issued as updates. National Register Publishing Company also issues other business guides, including the STANDARD DIRECTORY OF ADVERTISERS, *The Directory of Corporate Affiliations,* and the *Standard Directory of International Advertisers and Advertising Agencies.*

Important sections of the *Standard Directory of Advertising Agencies* are: "The Largest Advertising Agencies," ranked by annual billings; "Number of Agencies by Billing Classifications"; "Number of Agencies by State"; the "Special Market Index," a list of agencies that specialize in particular markets such as financial services and resort and travel; "Mergers, Acquisitions and Name Changes Since Publication of Last Directory"; "Key to Abbreviations" of advertising agency associations and media membership affiliations; "New Agencies," listed for the first time; the "Geographic Index of Agencies," arranged by states in the United States and foreign countries; the "Alphabetical Listings of Agencies"; "Media Service Organizations"; and "Sales Promotion Agencies."

Each agency entry in the alphabetical listings includes a listing of: name, address, number of employees, association membership, agency's specialization, founding date, annual billing with breakdown, top management, creative marketing personnel, account executives, branch offices, and accounts. A check mark before each account name indicates that it was acquired by the agency since the last issue of the directory. An asterisk before the name of the agency shows that the updating information has been received directly from that organization. Several of the agencies have furnished logos. In addition to the information on advertising agencies, directory information is included for media service organizations and sales promotion agencies. The geographic and special market indexes organize the entries to enable users to target agencies by location and specialization.

The *Standard Directory of Advertising Agencies* is a key source book for students, faculty, and practitioners in the field. Libraries should purchase this title along with the STANDARD DIRECTORY OF ADVERTISERS. The Board recommends this work for the core collections of public and academic libraries.

Supplementary Titles

Advertising Slogans of America. Harold S. Sharp, comp. Scarecrow, 1984. hard. 1 vol. 543 pp. ISBN 0-8108-1681-4. $39.50. dictionary.
HF6135. S53 659.1

Advertising Slogans of America is a "collection of approximately 15,000 slogans used by some 6,000 businesses from (among other sources) television, radio, films, newspapers, letterheads [and] handbills. . . . The slogans, parent organizations, 'and/or the products/services to which [the slogans] pertain' are interfiled in one alphabetical list with slogans appearing both under the company/product name, and individually with the company/product listed underneath." (*BL,* February 1, 1985, p. 770)

"The quality of arrangement and references is good with a triple listing of product, organization, and slogan in a single alphabet. . . . The publisher suggests that this book will assist advertisers, slogan writers, copywriters, students, and teachers, and that it will provide research material for studies in sociology and American popular culture." (*Choice,* November 1984, p. 408)

Also reviewed in: *Ref Bk R,* 1984, p. 6; *WLB,* October 1984, p. 144.

Board's recommendation: Public libraries.

Information Sources in Advertising History. Richard W. Pollay. Greenwood, 1979. hard. 1 vol. 330 pp. ISBN 0-313-214-220. $46.95. bibliography.
Z7164.C81P66 016.6591

Information Sources in Advertising History is "a long overdue bibliographic tool for the researcher in advertising history. . . . Annotations are brief in most cases, but generally direct and useful. The hefty bibliography is followed by an impressive listing of archives and special collections with their addresses and contact persons, along with a description of their holdings. A thorough index is also included. [This work is] essential for any business collection, research library, or large public library." (*LJ,* July 1979, p. 1442)

Also reviewed in: *ARBA,* 1980, p. 364; *BHR,* Summer 1980, p. 247; *Choice,* March 1980, p. 50.

Board's recommendation: Academic libraries.

Standard Rate and Data Service. Standard Rate and Data Service, frequency varies. 32 vols. to date. ISBN varies. directory.
659.1.016

The *Standard Rate and Data Service* is an "excellent source of information on rates and advertising media. [It is] published in various sections with varying titles. [It] includes newspapers, magazines, radio and television, films, transportation and gives Canadian and Mexican rates as well as those for United States. [The volumes are composed of a] . . . series of separate publications of [the] Standard Rate and Data Service, Inc., most of them beginning 1951 and assuming the volume numbering of the *Standard rate and data service*; most are monthly, some quarterly, some semiannual. Titles have varied; sections current in 1985 include: *Business publication rates and data,* 1951–; *Canadian advertising rates and data,* 1953–; *Community publication rates and data,* 1978–; *Consumer magazine and farm publication rates and data,* 1951–; *Co-op service directory,* 1981; *Direct mail list rates and data,* 1967–; *Network rates and data,* 1951–; [and so on]. . . . Several international editions are also available (e.g., England, France, Italy, Mexico, West Germany)." (*RSR*, Winter 1986, p. 110)

Board's recommendation: Public libraries.

Charlene M. Baldwin

African History

See also Middle Eastern History; World History

Reference sources in African history actually cover African studies. This is because the history of Africa is very closely related to the continent's physical geography, human geography, and prehistory of complex indigenous civilizations as well as to the modern record of a large continent's changing political climate, cultural diversity, and economic and technological development from earliest times to the present.

Africa spans many ecological and climatic zones and represents millennia of recorded human presence. The small core collection that has been selected must represent generalized information about a diverse region and yet also provide specific, accurate, and timely information concerning the discrete political and administrative units that govern each nation.

The most successful reference works are the annuals, which not only provide necessary historical perspective but also are able to report, often in succinct tabular or statistical format, the most recent data available. Annuals can present new biographical information and the most recent statistics on economic development, land-use statistics, population, and so on. These works can best reflect the rapidly changing political and economic climate of Africa.

Annuals, however, by their nature do not offer the in-depth coverage of encyclopedias. The encyclopedias complement the annuals by offering in-depth and illustrated texts with bibliographies.

Atlases provide a varied approach to the study of African history. These works may combine maps and text to chronicle the history of the continent or add other illustrative material to show cultural, political, and economic aspects of Africa and its people.

The core collection under review here consists of six works: a historical atlas, two annuals, and three encyclopedias. No one of these works provides all the information needed to stay current and provide in-depth information about all of Africa. A library with a larger reference collection might wish to supplement this list with more specific works on individual countries, additional resources from the list of supplementary titles, and other general works. One useful supplement to this category, which is now out of print, is *African Political Facts Since 1945* (Chris Cook and David Killingray, Facts On File, 1983). Librarians may want to obtain a copy through out-of-print sources.

Core Titles

	PUBLIC	ACADEMIC	SCHOOL
Africa South of the Sahara. Europa, annual; distrib. by Gale	✦	✦	
The Cambridge Encyclopedia of Africa Oliver, Roland, and Michael Crowder, gen. eds. Cambridge, 1981	✦	✦	
The Cambridge Encyclopedia of the Middle East and North Africa Mostyn, Trevor, exec. ed. and Albert Hourani, adv. ed., Cambridge, 1988 (See Middle Eastern History)	✦	✦	
Encyclopedia of the Third World, 3d edition, 3 vols. Kurian, George Thomas. Facts On File, 1987	✦	✦	✦
Historical Atlas of Africa Ade Ajayi, J. F., and Michael Crowder, gen. eds. Cambridge, 1985	✦	✦	✦
The Middle East and North Africa Europa, annual; distrib. by Gale (See Middle Eastern History)	✦	✦	

Core Titles

Africa South of the Sahara. Europa, annual; distrib. by Gale. hard. 1 vol. 1,163 pp. illus. index. ISBN 0-946653-51-8. $225. yearbook.
DT351 916.7

Africa South of the Sahara is a major resource for current information about Africa. Data have been obtained from various United Nations publications and authoritative sources in the United States, England, and France. This annual is well organized and contains many signed articles. Sections that are newly revised for this edition are noted in the table of contents. *Africa South of the Sahara* is a large work, using a small typeface. There is almost no illustrative material—only ten maps and no photographs. However, the many tables that accompany the articles are clear and easy to read. This work does not include all of Africa, and the companion volume, THE MIDDLE EAST AND NORTH AFRICA (see Middle Eastern History), also an annual, is required for complete continental coverage.

The work is divided into three parts. Part 1 is "Background to the Continent." This part includes lengthy articles on past African history, economics, physical geography, politics, religion, and so forth. The yearbook is introduced by an essay entitled "Africa in Historical Perspective," by Basil Davidson, the author of, among other works, *A History of West Africa: 1000–1800.* Many articles in this section conclude with bibliographies for further reading.

Part 2 is a directory of regional organizations. Here are details of many organizations that have operations in Africa, including the United Nations and its subsidiary units, the Organization of African Unity and the African Development Bank. The one-page citations include addresses, names of those in positions of leadership, and their activities in Africa. A name index completes this section.

Part 3, "Country Surveys," is probably the most useful part of this work and will be the most consulted. The information collected here is what makes *Africa South of the Sahara* the best work in the core collection for looking up current facts about a specific country. The profiles vary from 10 to 30 pages in length. Each profile is divided into six sections: "Physical and Social Geography," "Recent History," "Economy," "Statistical Survey," "Directory," and "Bibliography." The directories contain copious information about each country's constitution, current government officials, legislative bodies, and judicial system. Financial institutions, religious organizations, and trade and industry listings are just a few of the other listings that appear.

Africa South of the Sahara is a valuable reference work filled with useful, current, accurate, and reliable information. The Board recommends this work for the core collections of public and academic libraries.

The Cambridge Encyclopedia of Africa. Roland Oliver and Michael Crowder, gen. eds. Cambridge, 1981. hard. 1 vol. 492 pp. illus. index. ISBN 0-521-23096-9. $49.50. encyclopedia.
DT3.C35 960.03

The Cambridge Encyclopedia of Africa serves more as a concise history of Africa than as an encyclopedia. The volume is easy to read, with well-prepared maps, many of them in color; tables in certain sections; and color and black-and-white photographs.

The work is divided into four major sections: "The African Continent," "The African Past," "Contemporary Africa," and "Africa and the World." The first section deals with Africa's physical environment and traditional ethnic groups. The second section discusses precolonial Africa, European occupation, European rule, and the struggle for independence. For the most part this section offers a regional treatment; all regions seem to have been treated equally.

The third section deals with the history of contemporary Africa on a country-by-country basis. This is followed by general discussions of governmental systems, natural resources, economy, society, religion, and arts and recreation. The final section deals with Africa and the world: inter-African relations, international relations, and the "Black Diaspora."

The placement of some topics may seem arbitrary and confusing if the user is seeking quick information. For example, the origins of the traditional arts in Africa, dating back 5,000 years, are found in the section entitled "Contemporary Africa," not in "The African Past." Similarly, the section on natural resources is found in "Contemporary Africa," in part because it is meant to be a discussion of the *utilization* of natural resources in the twentieth century, but the user might possibly expect to find such information in "The African Continent," the section on the physical environment.

The biggest drawback of this reference work is the 1981 copyright date. Many changes have taken place in Africa since then, making much of the work dated. For example, the section "Africa Since Independence" provides facts and narrative about each country in an alphabetical arrangement; however, some of these countries have changed names, renamed their cities, and developed and grown in many ways in the years since publication. Additionally, the work contains tables that present data from the mid-1970s. A user seeking current information on, for example, commercial energy consumption or electricity generation in Africa would need facts more recent than 1976. For the most recent data, the user should consult the two annuals in this category: AFRICA SOUTH OF THE SAHARA and THE MIDDLE EAST AND NORTH AFRICA.

Despite these drawbacks, *The Cambridge Encyclopedia of Africa* is a readable and sensitive presentation of the whole continent. The combination of a thorough table of contents and a detailed index makes the volume accessible to the user. The Board recommends this work for the core collections of public and academic libraries.

The Cambridge Encyclopedia of the Middle East and North Africa. Trevor Mostyn, exec. ed., and Albert Hourani, adv. ed. Cambridge, 1988. hard. 1 vol. 504 pp. illus. index. ISBN 0-521-32190-5. $49.50. encyclopedia.
DS44.C37 956

See Middle Eastern History.

Encyclopedia of the Third World, 3d edition. George Thomas Kurian. Facts On File, 1987. hard. 3 vols. 2,384 pp. appendixes. ISBN 0-8160-1118-4 (set). $195 (set). encyclopedia.
HC59.7 909.09724

In his preface to the *Encyclopedia of the Third World,* author George Thomas Kurian defines the Third World as "the politically nonaligned and economically developing and less industrialized nations of the world." Kurian selected 126 countries for inclusion in the 3d edition of this three-volume work (up from 114 in the 1st edition in 1978). The author acknowledges the U.S. State Department, the World Bank, and the United Nations as leading sources of information.

While African countries are represented in this work, this is not a reference tool only about Africa. Nor does the *Encyclopedia of the Third World* include all of Africa: Namibia, Reunion, South Africa, and the Western Sahara are not represented.

The work will be heavily used in any library reference collection because of the concise, readable entries and current information contained in the text.

Volume 1 begins with a detailed description of the outline of information used to compile each country's entry. This "Notes and Information Classification System" explains the source of data for each heading, the kinds of information represented, and the sources and formulas used to obtain these statistics. The author also notes three difficulties in collecting data for Third World countries: official manipulation of data; discontinuities in the publication of data due to political instability and civil war; and differing definitions of statistical terms that render data useless. This information on how data were compiled is invaluable in validating and interpreting the material in the encyclopedia. A helpful section on acronyms and abbreviations (mostly of political parties and regionally based organizations) follows. Information on 42 organizations operating within the Third World is presented next. Many of these entries are unique to the Third World and do not duplicate similar lists of organizations contained in other works in this core collection.

Individual entries on each country comprise the bulk of the three volumes. Countries are presented in alphabetical order, regardless of their regional or continental context. The entry for each country includes an introductory outline map and a boxed "Basic Fact Sheet." Each entry runs approximately 10 to 20 pages. The information in each entry follows a similar outline as described in the "Notes and Information Classification System" mentioned previously. Some of the topics covered include location and area, weather, population, ethnic composition, languages, religions, government, freedom and human rights, foreign policy, budget, finance, agriculture, industry, energy, education, food, media and culture, and social welfare. Each entry concludes with a short glossary, a chronology of the country's history, and a bibliography for further reading.

The third volume includes the balance of the country entries and 17 appendixes, a number of which show comparative statistical tables on a variety of economic topics for Third World countries in relation to other parts of the world. The final appendix is a general bibliography of the Third World. An index to the entire work completes volume 3. This encyclopedia has an attractive design, with a large typeface for the text and a liberal use of section headings in boldface type.

The *Encyclopedia of the Third World* will be a popular addition to any reference collection. The Board recommends this work for the core collections of public, academic, and school libraries.

Historical Atlas of Africa. J. F. Ade Ajayi and Michael Crowder, gen. eds. Cambridge, 1985. hard. 1 vol. unpaged. illus. index. ISBN 0-521-25353-5. $90. atlas.
G2446.S1 911.6

The result of ten years of research and preparation, the *Historical Atlas of Africa* is an excellent addition to a core collection in African history. J. F. Ade Ajayi and Michael Crowder, the general editors, are eminently qualified Africanists who undertook this distinguished effort to portray the prehistory and history of the entire African continent in a single volume.

The atlas contains unpaginated, full-page color plates, accompanied by text on facing pages. The lack of page numbers is a bit disconcerting, but because each map plate and full page of explanatory text make up one numbered unit, it is still possible to consult the atlas easily. The atlas begins with several maps dealing with physical geography: relief and rainfall; vegetation and soils; geology and natural resources; language classification; insect, parasite, and livestock distribution; and past climates and vegetation changes. These early sections are valuable for general background information.

The balance of the atlas deals with human activity in Africa. The arrangement is chronological: Continental maps concerned with prehistory are followed by maps treating regional history. The final map shows decolonization and independence up to 1980. There are no maps on individual countries; this is a continental and regional profile. For treatment of the peoples of Africa, country by country, a better volume to consult would be the CULTURAL ATLAS OF AFRICA.

An extremely valuable index, which lists all place names and persons mentioned on the maps or in the text, follows the maps. An introduction to the index explains certain cross-reference and orthographic conventions used by the indexer.

The maps in the *Historical Atlas of Africa* are sharp and clear. Photographs included in the text portions add visual reinforcement to the explanations. This was the first full-color atlas on Africa and is still extremely useful even though the work makes no reference to events more recent than 1980.

The Board recommends this work for the core collections of public, academic, and school libraries.

The Middle East and North Africa. Europa, annual; distrib. by Gale. hard. 1 vol. 949 pp. illus. appendix. ISBN 0-946653-44-5. $210. yearbook.
DT160 961.04805

See Middle Eastern History.

Supplementary Titles

Africa Contemporary Record: Annual Survey and Documents. Colin Legum and John Drysdale. Holmes & Meier, annual (1969–). hard. 1 vol. 1,182 pp. illus. ISBN 0-8419-0658-4. $395. yearbook.
DT1.L43 915.005

The *Africa Contemporary Record* answers such questions as "Where does Botswana stand in its foreign policy? How many banks are there in Gambia? What were the terms of the memorandum of understanding on the Ethiopia-Sudan border dispute in August, 1968?" (*TLS,* August 21, 1989, p. 928)

"The three parts of this book [are comprised of] (1) current issues . . . (2) country by country review . . . [and] (3) documents 1967–68 (divided into sections on international relations, political issues, social developments and public administration, economic developments and trade, agriculture, health, education, and literature). There are [also] . . . treatments of the Rhodesian crisis and the Nigerian civil war." (*Choice,* September 1970, p. 817)

"The object of this venture is to provide an annual abstract of essential data for the whole continent. . . . The records will be a valuable part of the African journalist's equipment." (*NS,* October 17, 1960, p. 541)

Also reviewed in: *Econ,* August 16, 1969, p. 44; *Obs,* August 17, 1969, p. 21.

Board's recommendation: Public and academic libraries.

Atlas of African History. Colin McEvedy. Facts On File, 1980. hard. 1 vol. 148 pp. index. ISBN 0-87196-480-5. $17.50. atlas.
G2446.SIM3 911.6

The *Atlas of African History* "highlight[s] the evolution of Africa from the breakup of Gondwanaland 160 million years ago to the end of white rule in Rhodesia in 1978. . . . Some dozen maps are devoted to the BC period; another 17 maps show the movements of people from AD 1 [to AD] 1460. The remaining 30 maps cover the more familiar ground of the early European voyages, the age of imperialism, and the growth of nationalism." (*Choice,* December 1980, p. 508)

"A very thorough Index helps pinpoint such information as the naming of the Libyan Pentapolis, or the origin of the official language of Ethiopia, [which is] Geez. . . . The narrative portion provides interesting factual reading. The greatest appeal may be its succinctness and clarity. . . . The account only covers the period through mid-1978, but a prediction of what to expect by the year 2000 is provided." (*BL,* February 15, 1981, p. 836)

Also reviewed in: *ARBA,* 1981, p. 207.

Board's recommendation: Public, academic, and school libraries.

The Cambridge History of Africa. Cambridge, 1975–1987. hard. 8 vols. illus. indexes. ISBN 0521-334-608 (set). $665 (set). history.
DT20.28 960

The Cambridge History of Africa is "an eight-volume series on Africa from 'earliest times' to the 1970's.

"This series will be read mainly by specialists . . . but it will be an invaluable reference tool for a larger constituency. Every chapter in each volume has a long bibliography and a bibliographical essay that discusses archival as well as secondary sources. The [indexes are] extraordinarily thorough. . . . The numerous maps are precise and detailed." (*Choice,* June 1977, p. 585)

"The authors ably use the rich array of primary and secondary sources available to them. Impressive syntheses are offered by M. Hiskett on west Africa, D. Birmingham on central Africa, and J. D. Omer-Cooper on southern Africa." (*LJ,* May 1, 1977, p. 1014)

"Chapters like Shinnie's on Christian Nubia are the first brief, authoritative surveys in English. . . . [Some] individual chapters are of such scholarly importance that this work belongs in all public and university libraries." (*Choice,* November 1979, p. 1220)

Also reviewed in: *AHR,* June 1977, p. 709; December 1977, p. 1303; February 1978, p. 244; June 1983, p. 276; *Brit Bk N,* September 1982, p. 585; February 1984, p. 77; *Choice,* February 1976, p. 1615; *Econ,* October 25, 1975, p. 120; *EHR,* January 1977, p. 146; January 1979, p. 137, April 1979, p. 371; *GJ,* November 1976, p. 534; November 1977, p. 480; March 1980, p. 129; July 1983, p. 236; *HRNB,* May 1977, p. 510; July 1977, p. 177; *LJ,* March 1, 1976, p. 712; June 1, 1979, p. 1253; *LR,* Autumn 1979, p. 194; *MEJ,* Winter 1976, p. 108; *TLS,* June 3, 1977, p. 670; June 18, 1982, p. 673; *VQR,* Winter 1977, p. 22.

Board's recommendation: Academic libraries.

Cultural Atlas of Africa. Jocelyn Murray, ed. Facts On File, 1981. hard. 1 vol. 240 pp. illus. index. ISBN 0-87196-558-5. $40. atlas.
DT14.C83 920

The *Cultural Atlas of Africa* "aims to provide an introduction to the continent of Africa as a whole through text, illustrations, and maps. Part One, 'The Physical Background,' gives [an] outline of both the physical and social geography of the continent with maps illustrating each aspect. [Part Two] 'Cultural Background' presents languages and peoples, religions, prehistory, kingdoms and empires, recent history, art, architecture, music and dance, education, and health. [Part Three provides] a section on each region and each nation within these regions.

"[The photographs] make the real Africa, in all its complexity, come to life on the pages. . . . The credentials of the contributors are given, and a good index, list of illustrations, gazetteer, and bibliography enhance the volume's usefulness. Murray has succeeded in presenting a great deal of information in an extraordinarily attractive book." (*Choice,* September 1981, p. 52)

Also reviewed in: *ARBA,* 1982, p. 183; *BL,* July 15, 1981, p. 1432; May 1, 1982, p. 1182; *Brit Bk N,* December 1981, p. 760; *BW,* December 6, 1981, p. 10; *CRL,* July 1982, p. 336; *HT,* November 1981, p. 58; *LJ,* August 1981, p. 1526; May 15, 1982, p. 962; *PW,* July 3, 1981, p. 139; *SLJ,* May 1983, p. 22; *TES,* August 7, 1981, p. 18; *TLS,* February 26, 1982, p. 230; *WLB,* December 1981, p. 301.

Board's recommendation: Public, academic, and school libraries.

New and Noteworthy

African Studies Companion: A Resource Guide and Directory. Hans Zell. Saur, 1989. hard. 1 vol. 200 pp. ISBN 0-905-45080-9. $47.50. handbook.
DT19.8.Z45

The *African Studies Companion* "provides librarians with a convenient quick reference guide to resources, . . . [and] also serves as a desk-top compendium for the African studies scholar or teacher developing an African studies program. The book contains a wealth of information on sources related to African studies, including major directories and reference sources; journals and periodicals; descriptive listings of the top libraries and documentation centers in the field; publishers . . .; professional societies and associations . . .; [and] awards and prizes in African studies." (Excerpted from publisher's announcement)

An Annotated Bibliography of Exploration in Africa. James A. Casada. Saur, 1990. hard. 1 vol. 400 pp. indexes. ISBN 0-905-45027-2. $85. bibliography.

An Annotated Bibliography of Exploration in Africa "provides the first detailed, annotated bibliography on African exploration from the earliest recorded expeditions to the twentieth century. Featuring an analytical introduction as well as an overview of the history of the continent's exploration, this comprehensive work covers books and articles published in English and in other languages as well. Author and subject indexes provide ready access to this wealth of information." (Excerpted from publisher's announcement)

Apartheid: A Selective Annotated Bibliography, 1979–1987. Sherman E. Pyatt. Garland, 1990. hard. 1 vol. 169 pp. ISBN 0-8240-7637-0. $25. bibliography.
DT763.P93 016.3058'00968

The purpose of *Apartheid* is "to present a concise listing of writings dealing with the 'effects of apartheid on the people of South Africa and [apartheid's] indirect effect on the world.' Most of the English-language literature selected for inclusion was published between 1979 and 1987, serving to measure the effects of the Reagan and Botha presidencies. . . . Most entries have a brief descriptive annotation." (*BL,* June 15, 1990, p. 2023)

Handbooks to the Modern World: Africa. Sean Moroney, ed. Facts On File, 1989. hard. 2 vols. 1,248 pp. index. ISBN 0-8160-1623-2. $95. handbook.
DT3.H36 960

"Volume 1 [of *Handbooks to the Modern World: Africa*] provides country-by-country entries, each covering geography, population, constitutional system, recent history, economy, social services, education, mass media, and biographies of prominent people. . . . Volume 2 contains 32 clearly written articles by contributors representing academia, journalism, government, civil engineering, and broadcasting. Together, these articles are designed to serve as a 'thorough examination of the crucial political, economic, and social issues affecting Africa as a whole.' " (*BL,* January 15, 1990, p. 1042)

The United States in Africa: A Historical Dictionary. David Shavit. Greenwood, 1989. hard. 1 vol. 298 pp. index. ISBN 0-313-25887-2. $59.95. dictionary.
DT38.1.S53 303.482730

The United States in Africa is "a biographical dictionary of missionaries, academics, artists, leaders, diplomats, educators, soldiers, engineers, etc. (dead and alive), who established relationships between the US and Africa. The entries include information on institutions, organizations, business firms, even ships that were involved in these contacts." (*Choice,* December 1989, p. 616)

Women of Northern, Western, and Central Africa: A Bibliography, 1976–1985. David A. Bullwinkle. Greenwood, 1989. hard. 1 vol. 601 pp. index. ISBN 0-313-26609-3. $55. bibliography.
Z7964.A337B4 016.305409

Women of Northern, Western, and Central Africa "is the second in a projected three-volume series. . . . This series will constitute a major, comprehensive bibliography of English-language works (over 4,100 will be cited in all) on women in Africa for the period 1976–1985." (*Choice,* November 1989, p. 456)

Charla A. Coatoam

African Literature

See also World Literature

African literature has come into prominence only in the last 20 years. The novel *The Palm-wine Drinkard* (published in translation in 1952) by Nigerian author Amos Tutuola was the first work by an African to receive international acclaim, and the flourishing of interest in contemporary African literature is generally agreed to date from that publication.

As the copyright dates on the following core and supplementary titles will attest, interest in academic research on African literature started with a flurry of publishing activity in the early 1970s. The editorial tone of many of these new publications was introductory in nature, presenting authors, titles, and evidence of a vast literary output that had heretofore been unmined as far as study and research was concerned. The steady efforts of Hans M. Zell (editor of A NEW READER'S GUIDE TO AFRICAN LITERATURE) and Bernth Lindfors (compiler of the BLACK AFRICAN LITERATURE IN ENGLISH series) have assured that this field will not go untended. There is need for updating of many of these publications, however. In 1986, Wole Soyinka became the first African writer to be awarded a Nobel Prize in Literature. This recognition may encourage publishers to return to activity in the field of African literature.

There is particular need for a current, comprehensive reference source dealing with authors and works of the entire continent. The absence of such a work is understandable. The multiplicity of cultures and languages would make this a prodigious task (40 or 50 written languages are represented in the work of this continent), and the difficulty of finding some method to organize material on the subject is apparent in all of the books reviewed. Most of the titles reviewed in this category concentrate on black authors only, but this system of selection neglects many fine South African authors, Nadine Gordimer and J. M. Coetzee among others, as well as North African authors, such as the recent winner of the Nobel Prize for Literature, Naguib Mahfuz of Egypt.

It should be noted that there are variants in the spellings of names, depending upon the book you consult. Ezekiel Mphahlele, for example, is Es'Kia Mphablete in more recent sources.

Of the books reviewed here only AFRICAN LITERATURES IN THE 20TH CENTURY deals with authors of all countries and ethnic backgrounds, but it is taken from a source with a 1981 copyright and is already dated. The excellent and consistently current bibliography, BLACK AFRICAN LITERATURE IN ENGLISH, is an outstanding title for academic libraries. A NEW READER'S GUIDE TO AFRICAN LITERATURE is the only choice

Core Titles

	PUBLIC	ACADEMIC	SCHOOL
African Authors: A Companion to Black African Writing, vol. 1: 1300–1973 Herdeck, Donald E., ed. Gale; reprint of Black Orpheus, 1973	✦	✦	
Black African Literature in English: A Guide to Information Sources Linfors, Bernth, comp. Gale, 1979 o.p.		✦	
Black African Literature in English: 1977–1981 Supplement Linfors, Bernth, comp. Holmes & Meier, 1986		✦	
Black African Literature in English: 1982–1986 Supplement Linfors, Bernth, comp. Saur, 1989		✦	
A New Reader's Guide to African Literature, 2d edition Zell, Hans M., Carol Bundy, and Virginia Coulon, eds. Africana/Holmes & Meier, 1983	✦	✦	

for up-to-date information on African authors, and it is recommended for all libraries.

African literature is a rich and rewarding field of study, and it is to be hoped that future publications will continue with the enthusiasm which is evident in the efforts reviewed here.

A number of notable works in this field are no longer in print. Librarians wishing to add depth to their collection might try to obtain some of the following titles through out-of-print distributors: *Nigerian Literature: A Bibliography of Criticism, 1952–1976* (Claudia Baldwin, G. K. Hall, 1980); *Selected Black American, African, and Caribbean Authors: A Bio-Bibliography* (James A. Page and Jae Min Row, Libraries Unlimited, 1985); *The South African Novel in English Since 1950: An Information and Resource Guide* (G. E. Gorman, G. K. Hall, 1978); and *Twelve African Writers* (Gerald Moore, Indiana Univ. Pr., 1980).

Core Titles

African Authors: A Companion to Black African Writing, Volume 1: 1300–1973. Donald E. Herdeck, ed. Gale; reprint of Black Orpheus, 1973. 1 vol. hard. 605 pp. illus. appendixes. ISBN 0-8103-0076-1. $70. biographical dictionary.
PL8010.H38 809.896

Almost 600 black authors of sub-Saharan Africa are included in *African Authors: A Companion to Black African Writing.* Entries for the main body of the work are alphabetical by author's name with biographical information ranging from a paragraph to 12 pages for well-known author Wole Soyinka.

In the biographical section, authors included range in dates from approximately 1300 to 1973. Only five of the authors predate 1500; the majority of the entries deal with twentieth-century authors. Most entries represent the genres of fiction, drama, and poetry, although a few deal with writers of "market literature"—pamphlets containing short novels and plays—which are popular in some urban centers of Africa.

The introductory heading for each entry contains birth date, place of birth, type of writing, and other professions. If the place of birth is not clear, the geographical location is cited. For example, Chinua Achebe was born in "Agidi, Ibo country (a few miles east of the Niger River, in eastern Nigeria)." The biographical information that follows includes education, themes in works, some quotations from the author, and a listing of the author's publications with titles, dates, and publishers. A list of biographical and critical sources often concludes the entry. A pronunciation guide to authors' names would have been useful.

The format is very easy to use. The text is set up in two columns per page, with an easily readable typeface, excellent illustrations (photographs of authors and/or book covers), and well-spaced entries. Entries are arranged alphabetically, with the authors' last names first (in boldface type, all capitals), followed by the first names in bold print. The introductory heading is set apart by double spacing from the main body of the entry, as are the lists of writings and the biographical and critical sources. The guide word at the top of each page is the author's name for the entry on that page.

The guide words are in boldface type for the easy location of an entry without an index.

There are several appendixes. The first part, "Critical Essays," contains four essays by various authors: "The Development of Contemporary African Literature," "Black Writers and the African Revolution," "Vernacular Writing in Southern Africa," and "Three Key Afro-Caribbean Writers: Aimé Césaire, René Maran, Léon Damas." These critical essays are five to ten pages long, set in a much smaller type from that used in the main "Biographical Entries."

Other appendixes include listings of authors by chronological period; authors by genre (including storytellers); authors by language; major publishers of African literature; and listings of journals, bookshops, and book distributors. The appendix on African journals, including the classic *Présence Africaine* and *Black Orpheus,* is of particular interest.

The only drawback of this useful, attractive, well-organized reference book is the copyright date. The work was planned as volume 1 of a series of biennial reference works, with hopes that there would be a complete revision every six years. To this reviewer's knowledge, *African Authors: A Companion to Black African Writing* is the only volume published in the projected series.

The Board recommends this work for the core collections of public and academic libraries.

Black African Literature in English: A Guide to Information Sources. Bernth Lindfors, comp. Gale, 1979. hard. 1 vol. 482 pp. index. ISBN 0-8103-1206-9. $68. bibliography. O.P.
Z3508.L5 016.82

Black African Literature in English: 1977–1981 Supplement. Bernth Lindfors, comp. Holmes & Meier, 1986. 1 vol. 382 pp. indexes. ISBN 0-8419-0962-8. $45. bibliography.
Z3508.L5 016.82

Black African Literature in English: 1982–1986 Supplement. Bernth Lindfors, comp. Saur, 1989. 1 vol. hard. 500 pp. indexes. ISBN 0-905-450-75-2. $85. bibliography.
Z3508.L5 016.82

Black African Literature in English: A Guide to Information Sources contains 3,305 consecutively numbered entries. This first volume in the series has been followed by two supplements. The parent volume is currently out of print; however, the format is discussed below because it is followed in the two supplements. Also, librarians compiling a core collection in this area will want to try to obtain the first volume if it is not already on the shelf.

Part 1 contains studies by genre (including biographies, interviews, children's literature) and broad topics such as censorship, teaching, conferences, and festivals. Part 2 contains citations of secondary sources on individual authors. This section is arranged alphabetically by the author's last name, with sources listed by type (criticism, bibliography, interview). Entries are easily located using the table of contents and the four indexes (author, title, subject, and geographical).

There is usually only one numbered listing per entry, and there are extensive cross-references. Entries are not annotated. Occasionally a few words are supplied to help the reader identify a work where the title of the cited publication is unclear or ambiguous, for example, "Introduction to Poet Banned in South Africa," or "Study Guide."

The individual author section is indispensable for the study of major authors. As an example, the numbered entries on *Chinua Achebe* range from 2263 to 2447, or almost 15 pages.

Subject headings appear at the top of each page; the margins and the space between entries are adequate. The typeface is clear, making the text easy to read. The system of chronological numbering per entry makes this an easy format to use, regardless of subject heading.

A continuation of the bibliography *Black African Literature in English, Black African Literature in English: 1977–1981 Supplement* uses exactly the same format and continues with entries numbered 3306 to 6136. Another supplement, *Black African Literature in English: 1982–1986,* has been published, but it was not available for examination at the time this review was written.

Black African Literature in English is the standard source for bibliographical information on black African literature in English and, with its frequent supplements, is unlikely to be superseded by anything else in the near future. The Board recommends this work for the core collection of academic libraries.

A New Reader's Guide to African Literature, 2d edition. Hans M. Zell, Carol Bundy, and Virginia Coulon, eds. Africana/Holmes & Meier, 1983. 1 vol. soft. 553 pp. illus. appendixes. index. ISBN 0-8419-0640-8. $29.50. biographical source/bibliography.
PN849.A35 809.8896

For the most part, *A New Reader's Guide to African*

Literature is an extensive annotated booklist of titles published up to June 1981 by and about African authors. The focus is on contemporary authors. This is the second edition of a book first published ten years previously. The preface states that the new edition has changed slightly in theme because colonial experiences are no longer the major topic of writing—contemporary urban life in Africa is now the major subject. Social problems and politics have also come into the foreground as themes for writing, as has regional language. More women authors are included in this edition than in the previous one, and some authors who were in the first edition now appear in different genre sections because they have changed their literary form of expression. The publishing industry in Africa has also expanded, and the book now includes a directory of African publishers, booksellers, and international libraries with African collections.

The book is divided into two parts: "Bibliography" and "Biography." "Bibliography" includes general works: bibliography, reference, criticism (general and monographs), anthologies, folklore, and oral literature. This is followed by three separate sections on works in English, French, and Portuguese organized by author's country of origin. The value of the "Bibliography" is that it includes so much: "3,091 works by black African authors south of the Sahara writing in English, French, and Portuguese." Annotations are generous, sometimes extending the length of one full column of the two-column page, with original publishing data, extensive quotations from reviews, and plot summaries included. No attempt at critical evaluation is made.

The three language sections are subdivided by region, then by country, alphabetically. For example, under English-speaking Africa we have "West Africa," with the nations of Cameroon, the Gambia, Ghana, and so forth, listed. Some sections include the same countries—Nigeria and Cameroon are listed under both French- and English-speaking Africa; the titles listed in these sections are those published in the specified language. Translations are also noted, and sometimes it is only translations themselves that are reviewed.

"Biographies" contains entries of two to four pages per author, with some quotations from the authors themselves pertaining to influences, interests, and other factors. A small photograph of an author sometimes accompanies an entry. This section is arranged in alphabetical order by author's name, and thus is much easier to use than the "Bibliography" section.

This paperbound edition is set in a small typeface, with two columns of text per page. Countries, names, and subjects serve as guide words to aid easy locating. Entry headings are in boldface type, double-spaced. A general index of all names in the text appears in three columns, in small print. Inner margins are tight.

A New Reader's Guide is initially difficult to use because of the multiplicity of headings and subheadings in the "Bibliography." If used carefully, the table of contents and index, however, will enable the reader to find entries. A listing of authors by country would have been useful. There is a wealth of information packed into these pages—a boon for the researcher and a joy for the enthusiast of African literature. The section on magazines, now out of date, is still useful for research. The Board recommends this work for the core collections of public and academic libraries.

Supplementary Titles

African Literatures in the 20th Century: A Guide. Leonard S. Klein, ed. Ungar, 1986. soft. 1 vol. 245 pp. index. ISBN 0-8044-6362-X. $12.95. handbook.
PL8010A.43 809.889′6

African Literatures in the 20th Century: A Guide "has pulled together articles verbatim from the *Encyclopedia of World Literature in the 20th Century,* and includes a sampling of writers from the early part of this century, up through the 1960s, but who may continue to be published today. Missing are . . . writers such as Mongane Wally Serote (South Africa), Bessie Head (Botswana), Meja Mwangi and Grace Ogot (Kenya), Femi Osofison, Buchi Emecheta and Flora Nwapa (Nigeria), and others. . . . To its credit though, this volume has exceptionally fine introductory essays, and includes the North African countries as well." (*ARBA,* 1989, p. 493)

Board's recommendation: Public, academic, and school libraries.

Bibliography of Creative African Writing. Jahnheinz Jahn and Claus Peter Dressler. Kraus International, 1973. hard. 1 vol. 446 pp. index. ISBN 0-527-451050-9. $45. bibliography.
Z3508.L5 016.8088

"In 1971, when *Bibliography of Creative African Writing* was first issued, it received praise for its thoroughness and accuracy in assimilating and recording in logical fashion the creative work of Black African writers. . . . A language map is provided, translations are listed, forgeries are identified, and indexes cover books in African languages, and by countries of origin. The very necessary 'Instructions for Use,' appearing in English, German, and French, are a model of bibliographic intelligence." (*ARBA,* 1977, pp. 608–609)

Also reviewed in: BL, July 15, 1976, p. 1626; *LRTS,* April 1982, p. 119.

Board's recommendation: Academic libraries.

Black African Literature in English Since 1952. Barbara Abrash, comp. Johnson Reprint, 1967. soft. 1 vol. 91 pp. index. ISBN 0384-00201-3. $9. bibliography.
Z3508.L5A25 016.82

"*Black African Literature in English Since 1952* is an impressive list of 463 bibliographies, general critical books and articles, and anthologies. A list of authors is alphabetically arranged. Information provided includes listings of their full length works with citations to reviews, their short stories in periodicals, inclusion in anthologies and general critical articles on their work. The date and country of each author are given. A list of thirty pertinent periodicals is appended." (*WLB,* March 1968, p. 736)

Also reviewed in: *CRL,* January 1969, p. 78.

Board's recommendation: Academic libraries.

A Reader's Guide to African Literature. Hans M. Zell and Helene Silver, comps. Africana/Holmes & Meier, 1971. soft. 1 vol. 218 pp. illus. index. ISBN 8419-0019-1. $9.50. handbook.
PR9798.Z4 809.8967

A Reader's Guide to African Literature is the earlier edition of A NEW READER'S GUIDE TO AFRICAN LITERATURE. *A Reader's Guide* "includes 820 works, mostly by contemporary black Africans writing in English or French, and quote excerpts from favorable reviews." Also included is "a separate bibliography of children's books by African authors, a listing of a group of 'politically committed' works, an annotated selected list of magazine articles on creative African literature, and 51 short biographies (44 of which have photos) of 'major' authors, including quotations from their views on their own and others' works." (*LJ,* August 1972, p. 2604)

Also reviewed in: *AB,* May 15, 1972, p. 1790; *A Lib,* May 1972, p. 559; *B&B,* June 1972, p. 67; *BSA-P,* October 1972, p. 454; *CRL,* July 1972, p. 325; *LJ,* April 15, 1973, p. 1244; *Lis,* March 30, 1972, p. 246.

Board's recommendation: Public, academic, and school libraries.

Stephen M. Hayes

Aging

The study of aging, or gerontology, is a rapidly expanding field that may pose a problem for librarians wishing to build a comprehensive core collection. The field of aging covers many disciplines including sociology, psychology, nutrition, recreation, medicine, psychiatry, biology, nursing, and more. Reference works range from directories or sourcebooks such as the SOCIOLOGY OF AGING: AN ANNOTATED BIBLIOGRAPHY AND SOURCEBOOK to highly specific bibliographies such as RETIREMENT: AN ANNOTATED BIBLIOGRAPHY, or self-help works such as THE SENIOR CITIZEN HANDBOOK: A SELF-HELP AND RESOURCE GUIDE.

Perhaps the most important factor for librarians in developing a core reference collection is to define their user population and limit the collection to meet their patrons' needs. For some academic libraries, the collection will most likely consist of annotated bibliographies that survey the literature and apprise users of the wealth of research-oriented, scholarly material available. For other academic or public libraries, the core collection may consist entirely of directories or sourcebooks. These will be critical for library patrons who need up-to-date information on available services or products aimed at the elderly. However, keeping these

Core Titles

	PUBLIC	ACADEMIC	SCHOOL
Current Literature on Aging National Council on the Aging, quarterly		✦	
Encyclopedia of Aging Maddox, George L., ed. Springer, 1987	✦	✦	
Sociology of Aging: An Annotated Bibliography and Sourcebook Harris, Diana K. Garland, 1985		✦	
Statistical Handbook on Aging Americans Schick, Frank L., ed. Oryx, 1986	✦	✦	

sourcebooks and directories current will require a significant budgetary commitment. These works tend to become obsolete quickly because the elderly population is growing quite rapidly, as are the number of services aimed toward them. In order to stretch their budgets, libraries may wish to limit acquisition of directory or sourcebook materials to those their patrons find most helpful. For example, some collections will consist mainly of retirement information while others may have a concentration in health care or recreational information. Some titles that merit consideration are: the *Directory of Nursing Homes* (3d edition, Oryx, 1988), the *Encyclopedia of Senior Citizens Information Sources* (Gale, 1987) the *National Continuing Care Directory: Retirement Communities with Nursing Care* (American Assn. Homes, 1988), and the *National Directory of Retirement Facilities* (Oryx, 1988).

Core Titles

Current Literature on Aging. National Council on the Aging, quarterly. soft. annual index. ISSN 1047-4862. $48 (per year). bibliography.
Z7164.0437 301.435

Current Literature on Aging is a quarterly guide to a selection of "recent books and journals, [and] articles in gerontology" (copyright page). The bibliography is produced by the National Council on the Aging, Inc. The National Council, "founded in 1950 to improve the quality of life for older Americans, protect their rights and expand the opportunities available to them . . . serves as the national resource for information, training, technical assistance, advocacy, publication and research . . .," abstracts journals designated as core, and selectively reviews others. English-language materials predominate. Various journals are indexed and journals not thought of as gerontological in content are often included. For example, *Art Education, Monthly Labor Review,* and *Library Quarterly* are all included. The journals themselves range from the scholarly (such as the *Journal of Applied Gerontology*) to legal (such as *Issues in Law and Medicine*) to popular magazines (such as *Psychology Today*).

Entries are arranged by subject heading. Unfortunately, there is no overall listing of subject headings, and the reader must try every possible heading, which is a drawback, as the search can become time consuming. A cumulative author and subject index is included in the fourth issue of each year. The cumulative subject index lists the same entry under as many different subjects as possible. It is unfortunate that these useful cumulative indexes are not in all issues throughout the year. A list of "Additional Publications of Interest to the Field of Aging" is also included.

Nearly all of the entries include an abstract; a few, however, simply list the author and title of the article. Abstracts are very brief, but rather than just describing the book or article, most include a summary of results or findings and give key statistics.

Although *Current Literature on Aging* provides a library with a basic bibliography of articles dealing with aging, the bibliography is not a comprehensive guide to all such articles. This reference work indexes a limited number of different journals each quarter. There is no list of the "core" journals, which are abstracted in their entirety.

Current Literature on Aging is, however, still an excellent initial source for any library developing a basic collection on the subject of aging. Libraries wishing to expand their core collection will want to subscribe to multidisciplinary indexes that include abstracts of articles related to aging such as PSYCHOLOGICAL ABSTRACTS (see Psychiatry and Psychology), and SOCIOLOGICAL ABSTRACTS (see Sociology). Because of the breadth of subjects related to aging many other indexes also can be consulted for appropriate material.

An additional benefit from the title is that cited books are available through interlibrary loan from the Center's Randall Library in Washington, D.C. The Board recommends this work for the core collection of academic libraries.

Encyclopedia of Aging. George L. Maddox, ed. Springer, 1987. hard. 1 vol. 915 pp. index. ISBN 0-8261-4840-9. $96. encyclopedia.
HQ1061.E53 305.2′6′0321

Springer Publishing Company is one of the important publishers in the field of aging and gerontology. Springer's *Encyclopedia of Aging* is a work aimed at the "educated inquirer who needs a brief, authoritative introduction to the key topics and issues in aging." The editors are associated with various gerontological centers around the United States, and the book contains contributions from over "200 leading gerontologists from universities, hospitals, and governmental agencies." The reference comprises bylined entries, arranged alphabetically by subject. Each entry is clearly written and citations are provided. The entries provide basic information and, where necessary, graphs, charts, and illustrations. The entries are scholarly yet readable. Because the information contained is often historical in nature, it will not become obsolete. Many entries include "Research Trends" or "Prospects for the Future" or similar subheadings. For example, under the entry for *poverty,* "Future Prospects" are suggested by the contributor. For example, it is stated that "the key to reducing poverty in old age is to eliminate income disabilities at earlier life stages." There are some unusual entries such as *future trends* and *federal expenditures, year 2,000,* which the reader should find thought provoking. The entry entitled *life satisfaction* covers information such as "Discontentment with Past Research," "Current Research," and "Future Research Needs." It is critical and visionary passages like these that make the encyclopedia unusual and exciting.

An index is provided at the end of this reference tool and will prove useful in locating needed information given under a less obvious heading. For example, *living wills* is a separate index entry but is also cross-referenced under *death* and *euthanasia.* There are "see also" references in both the index and in various entries in the main text. Patrons will find these cross-references adequate and very useful. Because only the author's name and publication year appear in reference notes found in individual entries, a full list of cited sources is given in the "References" section.

The physical layout of the encyclopedia is attractive, and the print is easy to read. The traditional encyclopedia format will enable users to locate the needed entries quickly and easily. The major drawback to the work is its lack of further references after the entries. It seems clear that each entry has been written by an expert in the field, so the information is very reliable. However, for those patrons who desire more in-depth knowledge, suggestions for further readings or references should have been included at the end of each entry.

The *Encyclopedia of Aging* is an impressive collection of information, arranged in a readable format. The Board recommends this work for the core collections of public and academic libraries.

Sociology of Aging: An Annotated Bibliography and Sourcebook. Diana K. Harris. Garland, 1985. hard. 1 vol. 312 pp. index. ISBN 0-8240-9046-2. $44. bibliography.
Z7164.04.H374 016.3052′6

The *Sociology of Aging* is an annotated bibliography that covers the years 1960 through 1980. Because of the multidisciplinary nature of aging, the author has decided to focus primarily on one aspect of the topic: sociology. The information has been derived from journal, monographic, and book materials. The work comprises eight parts covering the following areas: "Introduction" (including theory and research methods); "Culture and Society"; "Social Inequality"; "Social Institutions"; "Environment and Aging"; "Periodicals"; "Resource Materials on Aging"; and "Offices, Associations and Centers on Aging." Within these broad parts a variety of subjects are covered, including religion, crime and deviance, retirement, and death and dying. All are linked by a common "sociological emphasis . . . or [contain] substantial parts relating to the sociological aspects of aging."

There is no subject index; the table of contents is, unfortunately, the only guide to subject matter. Although this lack of detailed subject indexing makes access to the work more difficult, it is not unusual. Most bibliographies with a narrow scope do not contain subject indexes. This work does include an author index.

Parts 1 through 5 cover the literature of the field, and while monographic and book materials are liberally included in these sections, periodical and journal materials predominate. The journals selected range from the scholarly *Gerontologist* and *Research on Aging* to the more popular *Psychology Today.* The reviews of the literature such as *Annual Review of Gerontology and Geriatrics* are also represented. Government publications are included, but they are cited infrequently. Annotations are brief and to the point; they supply a frame of reference rather than simply summarizing the content. The annotations allow the reader to judge the appropriateness of the source prior to locating it in the library.

Parts 6 and 7, "Periodicals" and "Resource Materials on Aging," respectively, are the librarian-oriented sections. Their usefulness is limited due to the limited scope of time period (1960–1980), but these sections will prove useful as starting points in collection development.

Part 8, which concerns "Offices, Associations and Centers on Aging," may be useful as a survey of organizations to consult for aging information. As a directory, it is somewhat out of date. This part is of lesser importance than others within the work because of the lack of currency.

The author, an educator at the University of Tennessee, appears to be familiar with works in the field, as is evidenced by the content of the annotations and the use of appropriate sociological vocabulary. She has also authored a DICTIONARY OF GERONTOLOGY (Greenwood, 1988) and several other works.

The *Sociology of Aging* will be very useful as a survey of the literature. Librarians responsible for collection development will appreciate its comprehensiveness and the many sources listed. The typeface is readable, and the book is printed on acid-free paper, which is desirable given the importance of collection preservation today.

The Board recommends this work for the core collection of academic libraries.

Statistical Handbook on Aging Americans. Frank L. Schick, ed. Oryx, 1986. hard. 1 vol. 294 pp. index. ISBN 0-89774-259-1. $42.50. handbook.
HQ1064.U5S343 305.2'6'0973021

The *Statistical Handbook on Aging Americans* is a collection of tables and charts reproduced from various sources and arranged in six broad topical sections: "Demographics," "Social Characteristics," "Health Aspects," "Employment Conditions," "Economic Status," and "Expenditures for the Elderly." Each section is preceded by a brief narrative that shows how the statistics relate to the elderly. Some brief conclusions are also drawn. The handbook also includes a "List of Sources" from which the tables and charts were derived, a "Guide to Relevant Information Sources" which lists journal articles, books, pamphlets, reports, and on-line data bases, and an index.

The usefulness of the handbook is somewhat limited, because the information is easily dated. Although the source of each table is clearly given, the user may have difficulty locating updated material because data sources for the specific figures within the table are not consistently identified. The currency problem is further complicated because many of the sources used were monographs or one-time reports, and more recent figures have since become available. The book does have redeeming qualities. Some interesting and unusual demographics have been included, such as religion (which covers the percentage of adults who are church or synagogue members), spiritual commitment, time activities (which gives the percentage of persons receiving assistance with meal preparation), and life satisfaction.

Although many valuable and interesting statistics are given, some sections give broad information that is not related to the elderly. For example, seven charts are given for the general consumer price index, but no special comparison to the concerns of the elderly is made. There is no information given on how the elderly spend their money. Furthermore, the statistics presented do not always cover the full range of situations in which the elderly live. One example is that household expenditures are reported for older women and married couples but not older men.

The handbook is printed on acid-free paper and the reproduction quality of the tables and charts is excellent.

The *Statistical Handbook on Aging Americans* can be a quick source of data and, using its references, a helpful one-volume guide to statistics (current as of the early 1980s). However, users may sometimes become frustrated at the lack of more up-to-date statistics. Librarians will have to supplement this work with periodicals and reports that provide more recent information. The Board recommends the *Statistical Handbook on Aging Americans* for the core collections of public and academic libraries.

Supplementary Titles

Dictionary of Gerontology. Diana K. Harris. Greenwood, 1988. hard. 1 vol. 201 pp. illus. ISBN 0-313-25287-4. $39.95. dictionary.
HQ1061.H338 612.1

"This dictionary is intended to 'further the development of a specialized gerontological terminology; and, because of the multidisciplinary nature of gerontology, to assist students, scholars, researchers, and practitioners in the field in understanding the terminology that is used in the various disciplines that gerontology encompasses.' . . . The definitions range from one to five sentences. . . . Internal cross-references are noted by asterisks, and see also references are given for related terms. . . . The author states that the Dictionary also serves as a bibliography because, following each definition, from one to four citations to works on the subject are given. Also, when possible, the name of the person who originated the term and the date of its first use are mentioned.

"[The definitions in this dictionary] are clear, concise, and as jargon-free as possible. . . . The cross-references are well done. The Dictionary includes well-known terms (pet therapy, living well, elderhostel, empty nest, hot flash, pigeon drop); common terms applied to the field or aging (adaptation, cholesterol, community, introversion, social strata); vocabulary related to medicine and research methods; and specialized theories, studies, terms, and organizations in the field. . . . Users will find most bibliographic citations helpful; some appear to be contrived and seem to be given only to fulfill the intention to include a citation for each entry. . . . Several diagrams and graphs give additional information. . . . The Dictionary of Gerontology is a good and useful effort that will be helpful in academic and public libraries." (*BL,* November 1, 1988, p. 462)

Also reviewed in: *ARBA,* 1989, p. 301; *Choice,* December 1988, p. 628; *R&R Bk N,* February 1989, p. 15; *SciTech,* January 1989, p. 4.

Board's recommendation: Public and academic libraries.

A Guide to Research in Gerontology: Strategies and Resources. Dorothea R. Zito and George V. Zito. Greenwood, 1988. hard. 1 vol. 130 pp. indexes. ISBN 0-313-25904-6. $35.95. bibliography.
Z7164.04257 016.3052

"The authors explain how to design a research strategy, how to evaluate different information sources (primary, secondary, tertiary, and nondocumentary), and the role of various kinds of reference sources (e.g., handbooks, directories, encyclopedias, abstracts) in research. They also explain how to get information from agencies (with a list of appropriate agencies and their addresses), computerized data services, and community resources. The book contains four appendixes that list and annotate references books, indexes and abstracts, databases, and journals.

"The intended audience for this work includes information specialists and professionals concerned with gerontology in all of its aspects—psychological, social, and medical. Persons trained in any of these disciplines will find the work readable. The use of examples from gerontological experience and literature is especially helpful. *A Guide to Research in Gerontology* will be a desirable addition to libraries serving students and professionals in disciplines concerned with any aspect of gerontology. Large public libraries may also consider purchasing it as a good introduction to information strategy in any discipline." (*BL,* July 1989, p. 1883)

Also reviewed in: *Choice,* April 1989, p. 1315; ***R&R*** *Bk N,* February 1989, p. 15.

Board's recommendation: Public and academic libraries.

Handbook of Aging and the Social Sciences, 2d edition. Robert H. Binstock and Ethel Shanas, eds. Van Nostrand Reinhold, 1985. hard. 1 vol. 809 pp. index. ISBN 442-26480-1 $84.95. handbook.
HQ1061.H336 305.2′6

"The editors of this [second edition of the *Handbook of Aging and the Social Sciences*] have assembled once again a distinguished set of scholars in social gerontology to create a . . . definitive reference work for the field. There are enough familiar chapter titles and authors to indicate that the first edition was developed soundly. Six new chapters and 23 new authors or coauthors suggest, however, the volume is fresh and organizes information on topics in social gerontology that have exploded during the past decade.

"The editors have organized the variety of topics covered into five sections: (a) the study of aging, (b) social aspects of aging, (c) aging and social structure, (d) aging and social systems, and (e) aging and social intervention. Although the sociological perspective is prevalent, a number of other disciplines are represented including anthropology, law, political science, and social work.

"Generally speaking, over 60% of the references are recent.

"Binstock and Shanas have orchestrated a major contribution to our understanding of the social context of aging." (*J Geront,* January 1986, p. 120)

Also reviewed in: *IJ Aging,* 1986, p. 61 and p. 64.

Board's recommendation: Public and academic libraries.

Handbook on the Aged in the United States. Erdman B. Palmore, ed. Greenwood, 1984. hard. 1 vol. 458 pp. index. ISBN 0-313-23721-2. $59.95. handbook.
HQ1064.45H23 305.2

Handbook on the Aged in the United States "is intended as a state-of-the-art report on what is known about aging and aged persons in the U.S. The contents are divided into four parts, one each for demographic, religious, and ethnic groups and one for groups representing special concerns. Within each part are chapters on subgroups: e.g., demographic groups include centenarians, veterans, and the widowed, while the section on special groups has material on criminals, the disabled, homosexuals, and the institutionalized.

"Chapters generally include discussions of current demographic and socioeconomic data about subgroups of the elderly. Also covered are the subgroup's history, special problems and advantages, psychological characteristics, research issues, organizations and services, and lists of sources for additional information. . . . Other features of the book are a list of academic research centers on aging, a bibliography of texts and handbooks, a list of contributors, and an Index." (*BL,* April 1985, p. 1167)

"[This] collection was compiled by a leading scholar, and the chapters were written by experts. . . . This information-packed book will be widely used by scholars and helping professionals." (*LJ,* December 1984, p. 2292)

Also reviewed in: *J Geront,* July 1985, p. 526; *RQ,* Summer 1985, p. 498.

Board's recommendation: Public and academic libraries.

International Handbook on Aging: Contemporary Developments and Research. Erdman B. Palmore, ed. Greenwood, 1980. hard. 1 vol. 529 pp. illus. appendixes. index. ISBN 0-313-20890-5. $50.95. handbook.
HQ1061.I535 301.43′5

International Handbook on Aging: Contemporary Developments and Research contains "information on programs and research throughout the world [which] is summarized and arranged alphabetically by country, providing a concise, comparative study of aging. . . . The articles are written at the scholar's level; they will be of interest primarily to researchers, educators, and students." (*BL,* July/August 1981, p. 1467)

"This book is a real boon to the field of gerontology; it has no peer. . . . The editor has carefully arranged the work of 28 prominent scientists who have, in turn, elaborated upon developments in their countries [30 in all]—this includes Palmore's own version of the status of the field in the U.S. The countries included represent a wide range in terms of economic and governing systems. . . . A number of charts and graphs have been included in the text, and the references and bibliographies at the chapter ends will be useful to those who wish to pursue particular points. The appendixes include names and addresses of gerontological organizations." (*Choice,* February 1981, p. 822)

Also reviewed in: *CS,* November 1981, p. 782; *SF,* September 1982, p. 343.

Board's recommendation: Academic libraries.

Retirement: An Annotated Bibliography. John J. Miletich, comp. Greenwood, 1986. hard. 1 vol. 147 pp. indexes. ISBN 0-313-24815-X. $35. bibliography.
Z7164.R5M3 016.306

"This comprehensive bibliography [*Retirement: An Annotated Bibliography*] covers a 10-year period, 1975–1985. Topics of current interest such as mandatory retirement, pensions, Social Security and employment benefit plans are well covered. . . . In addition to providing a wealth of material for researchers, the bibliographic citations within this volume provide a useful resource to assist retirees and those who are associated with them.

"There are 633 citations that include 200 separate periodical references. Each complete bibliographic citation is numbered and has a 10- to 50-word descriptive annotation. The citations represent books, articles, theses, and government publications published in the U.S., Canada, Europe, and Australia. . . . There is an author index and a general subject index." (*BL,* April 15, 1987, p. 1266)

Also reviewed in: *ARBA,* 1987, p. 307; *Choice,* January 1987, p. 746; *J Geront,* March 1987, p. 237; *R&R Bk N,* Winter 1987, p. 37.

Board's recommendation: Public and academic libraries.

The Senior Citizen Handbook: A Self-Help and Resource Guide. Marjorie Stokell and Bonnie Kennedy. Prentice-Hall, 1985. hard and soft. 1 vol. 260 pp. illus. index. ISBN 0-13-806522-5 (hard); 0-13-806514-4 (soft). $21.95 (hard); $9.95 (soft). handbook.
HQ1062 646.7′9

The Senior Citizen Handbook is a "combination advice/resource guide for the elderly [which] is designed to make senior citizens' lives more pleasurable and comfortable. The range of alphabetically arranged entries is impressively wide, with information included on the removal of age spots, on Alzheimer's disease, on the role of foster grandparenting, . . . and on much, much more. Bibliographies and addresses of sources for further information appear throughout this most useful handbook. [In addition, the reference is illustrated,] indexed and cross-referenced." (*BL,* September 1, 1985, p. 14)

Board's recommendation: Public libraries.

Lill Maman

Agriculture

See also Botany; Horticulture and Gardening

The word *agriculture* stems from the Latin words *ager,* meaning "field," and *cultura,* meaning "cultivation of the land." The science of agriculture provides us not only with food, but also with our other basic necessities: shelter and clothing. Agricultural products and materials create some of the largest industries in the world. Agriculture encompasses all aspects of life and includes horticulture (treated in this buying guide as a separate category), fruit and vegetable farming, dairy farming, and livestock breeding; the use of land for grazing; meadowland; market gardens; nurseries and woodlands.

It is not easy to choose a reference collection that will cover all aspects of agriculture. An index, such as the *Biological and Agricultural Index* (Wilson, annual), will give the user access to the biological and agricultural literature published in some of the major journals in the field, which will, in turn, provide information on most of the important research going on in the many subfields of agriculture. A core collection must also include statistical data in agricultural production, supplies, consumption, facilities, cost, and returns. A work such as the YEARBOOK OF AGRICULTURE provides a useful overview of specific topics, while BLACK'S AGRICULTURAL DICTIONARY clarifies terms for farmers as well as students of agriculture.

Other important agriculture-related works included in this volume are THE NEW YORK BOTANICAL GAR-

Core Titles

	PUBLIC	ACADEMIC	SCHOOL
Agricultural Statistics U.S. Dept. of Agriculture. U.S.G.P.O., annual	✦	✦	
Black's Agricultural Dictionary, 2d edition Dalal-Clayton, D. B., ed. Rowman & Littlefield/Barnes & Noble, 1985	✦	✦	
Yearbook of Agriculture U.S. Dept. of Agriculture. U.S.G.P.O., annual	✦	✦	

DEN ILLUSTRATED ENCYCLOPEDIA OF HORTICULTURE, a ten-volume set that explains the scientific cultivation of fruits, vegetables, flowers, and shrubs, and HORTUS THIRD: A CONCISE DICTIONARY OF PLANTS CULTIVATED IN THE UNITED STATES AND CANADA. These titles are reviewed in the Horticulture and Gardening category.

AGRICULTURAL & VETERINARY SCIENCES INTERNATIONAL WHO'S WHO, a supplementary work, will aid the user in locating information about agricultural workers, teachers, and researchers.

Encyclopedia of American Agricultural History (Edward L. Shapsmeier and Frederick H. Schapsmeier, Greenwood, 1975), now out of print, presents a historical overview of all topics relating to agriculture in the United States and is worth tracking down through out-of-print sources. Depending upon their patrons, public libraries may want to enlarge their core collection with works such as these.

Core Titles

Agricultural Statistics. U.S. Dept. of Agriculture. U.S.G.P.O., annual. index. ISBN 0-318-22873-4. $20. yearbook.
HD1751.A43 338.109

Agricultural Statistics is an annual reference book providing statistical data in agricultural production, supplies, consumption, facilities, costs, and returns. Many different government agencies participate in the preparation of this manual, which may explain why the publication of this "annual" is often delayed. The latest edition was published in 1988; this volume covers data from 1973 through 1987, although some tables cite data only through 1986.

The estimates for crops, livestock, and poultry are based on data obtained by sample surveys of farmers and distributors doing business with the farmers. Information from the agricultural census (taken every five years) is also included. Foreign agricultural trade statistics include government and civilian shipments of products from the United States to foreign countries. They exclude shipments to U.S. Armed Forces abroad for their own use.

The introduction covers weights, measures, and conversion factors used in the book. The book itself is divided into 14 main chapters that furnish statistics on the following subjects: grain; cotton, tobacco, sugar crops, and honey; oilseeds, fats, and oils; vegetables and melons; fruits, tree nuts, and horticultural specialties; hay, seeds, and minor field crops; cattle, hogs, and sheep; dairy and poultry products; farm resources, income, and expenses; taxes, insurance, cooperatives, and credit; stabilization and price-support programs; agricultural conservation and forestry; consumption and family living; and miscellaneous statistics.

The miscellaneous statistics include information on fishery, refrigeration, and agricultural imports and exports.

All of the statistics are cross-referenced to an index at the end of the volume. The index entries are arranged with main headings and subheadings that aid the reader in locating a particular topic. The statistics are often quite detailed. For example, chapter 5, "Vegetables and Melons," contains a table on tomatoes that gives specific information on area, production, and value per ton of the tomatoes produced in 20 states between 1985 and 1987. This table is further divided into columns for fresh tomatoes and those that will be processed.

Agricultural Statistics is a valuable source of information. The Board recommends this work for the core collections of all public and academic libraries.

Black's Agricultural Dictionary, 2d edition. D. B. Dalal-Clayton, ed. Rowman & Littlefield/Barnes & Noble, 1985. hard. 1 vol. 432 pp. illus. appendix. ISBN 0-389-20556-7. $42.50. dictionary.
S411.D245 630

The first edition of *Black's Agricultural Dictionary* appeared in 1981 and, as the preface states, "was intended as a reference source for farmers, students of agriculture, and all those involved in or associated with the agricultural industry in whatever capacity." This dictionary, which was published originally in England, is slanted toward agriculture in Great Britain. Entries are included for terms from the fields of agriculture, horticulture, biology, chemistry, geography, and so forth. The second edition adds 78 new entries covering legislation, organization, techniques, and developments in the industry between 1981 and 1985. The new edition also includes an extended list (18 pages) of abbreviations, acronyms, and initials, which is a very useful part of the dictionary.

Entries are arranged alphabetically. The main entry word appears in boldface type. Cross-references to related entries are set in small capital letters. Terms that are defined in another entry are set in small capital letters and preceded by an arrow. The entries in this dictionary vary in length, from a few words (such as for *kip,* meaning "the hide of a young animal") to three and a half pages (for *land use*), depending upon the relevance of the material and the complexity of the definition. However, the average entry is about a quarter of a page. Some statistics are presented in tabular form to help clarify the entries, and photographs or line drawings are used where words alone cannot convey the meaning. Because agriculture in Great Britain is affected by the policy of the European Economic Community (EEC), terms used by the EEC are also included. "See" and "see also" references are indicated by an arrow pointing to the name of the main entry where the information can be found.

Because of the inclusion of terminology for Great Britain and the EEC in *Black's Agricultural Dictionary,* this work will be useful to students and researchers with an interest in agriculture on an international level. The only comparable work with a U.S. orientation, *A Dictionary of Agricultural and Allied Terminology,* was published nearly 30 years ago and is, of course, lacking in current terminology. The Board recommends this work for the core collections of public and academic libraries.

Yearbook of Agriculture. U.S. Dept. of Agriculture. U.S.G.P.O., annual. hard. illus. ISSN 0082-97214. $20. yearbook.
S21.A351988

The *Yearbook of Agriculture* was first published by the United States Patent Office in 1849. In 1862, the United States Department of Agriculture assumed the rights to the publication. There were several changes of title until the current one emerged in 1938. The format used for the yearbooks since 1938 is to focus each volume on a single issue. Each chapter in the volume contains a succinct overview of one aspect of the central topic. All volumes are illustrated and include statistical information in the text and in charts. Each volume is approximately 300 pages long and contains an index.

The 1986 yearbook was subtitled *Research for Tomorrow* and, as stated in the preface, gave a "glimpse into just a few aspects of research generated by or involving dedicated people in the U.S. Department of Agriculture and the 56 State Agricultural Experiment Stations." Four chapters were devoted to the biotechnology aspects of research. Other topics included insects, weeds, human nutrition and food, forest resources, and the careers in agriculture.

The yearbook for 1987 was subtitled *Our American Land* and presented a historical view of land use in the United States. The text covered the history of agricultural institutions as well as territorial expansion, farming, and conservation. As noted earlier, each chapter presented a concise overview of issues related to the main topic, such as: "The Land and the Constitution," "Changing Patterns of Settlement," "Understanding Land," "Managing Land Use," and "Coping with Nature."

The 1988 *Yearbook of Agriculture: Marketing U.S. Agriculture* is the latest edition. This reference tool introduces the reader to marketing strategies and the promotion of agricultural products. The text explains why marketing is an important factor in the agricultural industry. For example, the change to a more healthful, diet-conscious life style in the 1980s has increased consumer demand for fresher and healthier food products. This demand has had great impact on the food industry. The 1988 yearbook covers such topics as marketing in a changing world, marketing strategies, discovering what buyers want, and new and better products to meet buyer demands.

Agriculture spans many different fields and topics, and a subscription to this annual will give the library patron a yearly overview of specific areas of agriculture. The Board recommends this work for the core collections of public and academic libraries.

Supplementary Titles

Agricultural & Veterinary Sciences International Who's Who, 3d edition. Longman, 1987; distrib. by Gale. hard. 2 vols. 1,195 pp. ISBN 0-582-90159-6 (set). $450(set). biographical dictionary.
S415.W48 630.92′2

These useful books present "biographical profiles on some seventy-five hundred senior agricultural and veterinary scientists from over one hundred countries . . . in such disciplines as agricultural economics, agricultural engineering, botany, aquaculture, food science and technology, horticulture, microbiology, soil science, oceanography, forestry, plant production, veterinary medicine, and zoology. Each entry includes name, birth date, higher education, present job, experience, appointments, memberships, publications, interests, and telephone number and address, or as much information as was made available. Part 2 lists the experts by subject area/country. Individuals and subject entries are easily located, as they are set in boldface type. This set is nicely bound, and the information is presented in an easy to read/use manner. Agricultural firms, consultants, agricultural libraries, and others who need this type of information will want to purchase this set." (*ARBA,* 1988, p. 596)

Also reviewed in: *R&R Bk N,* June 1988, p. 26; *SciTech,* January 1988, p. 23.

Board's recommendation: Academic libraries.

Guide to Sources for Agricultural and Biological Research. J. Richard Blanchard and Lois Farrell, eds. Univ. of California Pr., 1982. hard. 1 vol. 746 pp. indexes. ISBN 0-520-03-226-8. $55. bibliography.
Z5071.G83 016.63

Guide to Sources for Agricultural and Biological Research is a "valuable, comprehensive, and unique reference tool.

"[The reference] recognizes the position of agricultural research in the mainstream of biology and has encompassed new technologies with a chapter on computer databases.

"The agriculture/biology universe is grouped into seven broad sections with such headings as plant sciences, animal sciences, and environmental sciences. Within each section, the materials are arranged by type, such as bibliographies, abstracts and indexes, dictionaries, encyclopedias, and handbooks. Citations are complete and the annotations are informative and concise. . . . An in-depth outline precedes each section, and there are separate author, subject, and title indexes, as well as a glossary of acronyms and abbreviations.

"This guide, with its 5,779 citations, fills a need that has existed for some years." (*RQ,* Summer 1982, p. 417)

Also reviewed in: *ARBA,* 1983, p. 703; *Choice,* July 1982, p. 1538; November 1983, p. 392; *Ser R,* July 1981, p. 10.

Board's recommendation: Academic libraries.

New and Noteworthy

The State of Food and Agriculture. Food and Agriculture Organization of the United Nations, 1989; distrib. by UNIPUB. soft. 1 vol. 161 pp. ISBN 92-5-102660-2. $36. yearbook.
S401.U6A317 338.106

"Like all FAO publications, [*The State of Food and Agriculture*] contains the most current information (and in many cases the only data available) on world food and agriculture. [The work contains] a glossary of acronyms and definitions, . . . regional review[s], . . . changing priorities for agricultural science and technology in developing countries, . . . [and] 54 pages of annex tables covering such areas as exports, imports, importance of agriculture to the economy, [and] consumer prices." (*Choice,* November 1989, p. 471)

Bobbie Jean Klepper

American History

See also World History

The richness of materials available in the field of American history should yield many classic works for a core collection. With a vast number of records and publications in print, there should be some sort of short cut to allow the scholar and the browser quick and easy access to this information. Fortunately, there are reference tools that fulfill these needs—standard works that supply the answer to most questions about historical figures or events.

In selecting which of these compilations should form a core collection, several criteria should be considered, including the quality of the publication, depth of coverage of material, expertise of the writer or compiler, factual accuracy, and date of publication, as well as the type of information desired. Unless the information is fairly current, it is likely to be of little value for most research projects in American history.

When biographical facts are needed, one of the compilations devoted to profiles of historical figures, such as GREAT LIVES FROM HISTORY, American series, would be a useful source. A core collection should also have a bibliography to point the user in the direction of other works in the field. One useful bibliography is WRITINGS ON AMERICAN HISTORY, 1962–1973: A SUBJECT BIBLIOGRAPHY OF BOOKS AND MONOGRAPHS.

Extremely valuable or even indispensable sources of information for keeping abreast of significant advances in knowledge are topical encyclopedias. These offer greater coverage of subject areas and tend to be works of strict, objective scholarship tailored to satisfy basic informational needs. On the subject of American history, several excellent choices have been listed as part of the core collection. These include THE ENCYCLOPEDIA OF AMERICAN FACTS AND DATES and the ENCYCLOPEDIA OF AMERICAN FOREIGN POLICY: STUDIES OF THE PRINCIPAL MOVEMENTS AND IDEAS. The *Encyclopedia of American History* (Richard Morris, ed., Harper & Row, 1982) is another highly regarded source, but it is now out of print.

Other basic tools in historical research are statistical abstracts, atlases, almanacs, and guides. The STATISTICAL ABSTRACT OF THE UNITED STATES, published yearly by the Government Printing Office, is an essential part of the core collection in American history.

Librarians will want to note that the *Atlas of American History* (Scribner, 1985), which is now out of print and which was originally chosen as part of the core collection, will be replaced by a new edition in the near future.

The works reviewed in this category deserve to be called "core" and may well contain all the required

Core Titles

	PUBLIC	ACADEMIC	SCHOOL
The Almanac of American History Schlesinger, Arthur M., Jr., ed. Putnam, 1984	✦	✦	
Concise Dictionary of American History Scribner, 1983	✦	✦	✦
Dictionary of American Biography, 18 vols. American Council of Learned Societies. Scribner, 1958–1981 (See Biography)	✦		
Dictionary of American History, rev. and enl. edition Martin, Michael, and Leonard Gelber. Rowman & Littlefield, Adams, 1981	✦	✦	
Dictionary of American History, rev. edition, 8 vols. Ketz, Louise Bilebof, ed. Scribner, 1976–1978	✦	✦	✦
Documents of American History, 10th edition, 2 vols. Commager, Henry Steele, ed. Prentice-Hall, 1988	✦	✦	✦
Encyclopedia of American Economic History: Studies of the Principal Movements and Ideas, 3 vols. Porter, Glenn, ed. Scribner, 1980 (See Economics)		✦	
The Encyclopedia of American Facts and Dates, 8th edition Carruth, Gordon. Harper & Row, 1987	✦	✦	✦
Encyclopedia of American Foreign Policy: Studies of the Principal Movements and Ideas, 3 vols. DeConde, Alexander, ed. Scribner, 1978	✦	✦	✦
Encyclopedia of American Political History: Studies of the Principal Movements and Ideas, 3 vols. Greene, Jack P., ed. Scribner, 1984 (See Political Science)		✦	✦
Great Lives from History, American series, 5 vols. Magill, Frank N., ed. Salem, 1987			✦
Harvard Guide to American History, rev. edition Freidel, Frank, ed., with the assistance of Richard K. Showman. Belknap/Harvard, 1974	✦	✦	
The Oxford Companion to American History Johnson, Thomas H., in consultation with Harvey Wish. Oxford, 1966	✦	✦	✦
Statistical Abstract of the United States U.S.G.P.O., annual	✦	✦	✦
Who's Who in American Politics: 1989–1990, 12th edition Bowker, 1989 (See Political Science)	✦	✦	
Worldmark Encyclopedia of the States, 2d edition Sachs, Moshe Y., ed. Worldmark, 1986; distrib. by John Wiley	✦	✦	✦
Writings on American History, 1962–1973: A Subject Bibliography of Books and Monographs, 10 vols. Masterson, James R., comp. Kraus International, 1985		✦	

facts for the average library patron; however, the needs of the clientele of some libraries may require supplementing these key works with additional titles. The supplementary list contains a number of bibliographic and statistical sources that can satisfy further research requirements.

Core Titles

The Almanac of American History. Arthur M. Schlesinger, Jr., ed. Putnam, 1984. soft. 1 vol. 623 pp. illus. index. ISBN 0-399-51082-6. $13.95. almanac.
E174.A4 973.02′02

The Almanac of American History is a chronological survey that spans the years 986 through 1982. This volume is divided into five time periods, each prefaced by a scholar's essay. The author's name, title, and institutional affiliation appear with each essay. Each section documents the events of a certain time period, for example, a segment called "Expanding Resources" covers the years 1901 through 1945. The four chronological periods that cover from 986 to 1945 receive 100 to 130 pages each. The most recent time period—from 1946 to 1982—receives 106 pages of coverage.

Entries are arranged chronologically in a two-column format, with running heads in boldface type displaying the dates. The entries run from 2 or 3 lines to 30 lines or more. The text is enhanced by well-chosen and effectively placed photos. There are approximately 200 illustrations in this volume. Two hundred eighty-six boxed articles also accompany the text. About 60 percent of these are biographical profiles; the remainder are topical—for example, Civil Service reform. Each article is half to two-thirds of a column long. Uniform subheadings (such as "National," "Industry," "Westward Movement," and so forth) are used to define the nature of several different entries under one date. Each year's list of events concludes with a brief summary of trends and developments in areas such as education and the arts.

The Almanac of American History emphasizes social and political history in its chronological entries. The entries are factually correct, and the editor (noted historian Arthur Schlesinger, Jr.) and consultants (the name of a distinguished academic is listed for each major section) are well qualified. One weakness of this work is the shortness of the index, which occupies only eight pages in the text. Some names in the chronology are in the index; others are not and can only be located if the user consults broader subject categories. Boxed entries receive the same inadequate treatment. The boxed article *The Salvation Army* has no index entry nor is there an entry for its founder, William Booth. Only the page number on which *The Salvation Army* appears can be found under the index entry *social services, voluntary.*

Although a stronger index would be desirable to adequately access information in the text, *The Almanac of American History* is a useful volume, combining features of chronologies such as Gordon Carruth's THE ENCYCLOPEDIA OF AMERICAN FACTS AND DATES with the expanded text format of a work such as Richard Morris's *Encyclopedia of American History* (now out of print). The Board recommends this work for the core collections of public and academic libraries.

Concise Dictionary of American History. Scribner, 1983. hard. 1 vol. 1,140 pp. ISBN 0-684-17321-2. $95. dictionary.
E174.D522 973.0321

The *Concise Dictionary of American History* is a one-volume abridgment of the eight-volume DICTIONARY OF AMERICAN HISTORY, published by Scribner in 1976–1978, which was, in turn, a revision of the *Dictionary of American History* begun by James Truslow Adams in 1936. The purpose of the abridgment is to provide one readily available source containing scholarly accounts of all the major movements and ideas in American history. This abridgment retains all the entries of the parent work, albeit much shortened. The entries in the concise version are not signed; the ones in the parent work are. New entries, covering events up to 1982, have been added. Mentions of events of 1980 and 1981 can be found, for example, in entries for *Job Corps* and *Texas.* The entry for *Afro-Americans* contains information on the effect of school desegregation and the progress of Afro-Americans in housing and income as of 1980. The entry for *Latin America, U.S. relations with* notes that new centers of power emerged in the 1980s which were expected to alter U.S. relations in this hemisphere.

Arranged in alphabetical order, the entries cover all the events that have played an important part in the development of the United States, such as major battles, concepts, acts of Congress, Supreme Court decisions, and scientific and technological advancements. Complete texts of the Declaration of Independence and the Constitution of the United States are included, as well as a comprehensive list of presidents and vice-presidents. Topical essays give brief overviews of various aspects of American life, such as painting, literature, medicine, philosophy, religion, banking, immigration, and labor. As in the multivolume work, major entries have been devoted to Native American cultures and Afro-Americans.

The *Concise Dictionary of American History* contains many excellent entries. For example, the entries on *Cuba,* the *Philippine Islands,* and *Puerto Rico* are informative and well written, depicting their role in U.S. history up to the 1970s. Omissions of significant subjects are few but include the right-to-life and pro-choice movements, although women's issues are discussed under the entry *women's rights movement.* Much future updating will be needed to provide information as events in Central and South America, Europe, and the Middle East continue to affect the United States and its foreign policy.

Bibliographies have been omitted in the concise version. Many entries are cross-referenced to others to provide more comprehensive information.

Librarians concerned with the deterioration of their collections will appreciate that the dictionary is printed on paper that meets the guidelines of the Committee on Production Guidelines for Book Longevity of the Council on Library Resources.

Although not a substitute for the complete eight-volume set, the *Concise Dictionary of American History* is an excellent reference source for anyone who needs quick access to information on all aspects of American history up to 1983. The Board recommends this work for the core collections of public, academic, and school libraries.

Dictionary of American Biography. American Council of Learned Societies. Scribner, 1928–1988. hard. 18 vols. ISBN 0-19075 (set). $1,499 (set). biographical dictionary.
E176.B562 920.073

See Biography.

Dictionary of American History, rev. and enl. edition. Michael Martin and Leonard Gelber. Rowman & Littlefield, Adams, 1981. soft. 1 vol. 742 pp. ISBN 0-8226-0124-9. $11.95. dictionary.
E174.M3 973.03

This ready-reference volume is a revised and enlarged edition of the work first published in 1952 by the Philosophical Library under the title *The New Dictionary of American History.* It is a paperback and contains over 4,000 entries, of which about two-thirds are biographical. There are approximately six entries per page. The text is clearly written and concise, furnishing the essential data in capsule form, as would be expected in a one-volume dictionary of this type. There are no illustrations, maps, or graphics of any kind. The complete text of the Constitution of the United States is reprinted at the back of the book.

The publisher calls this book a "revised and enlarged edition," but the enlargement is not easily ascertained. This edition has changed very little from the 1952 version and includes fewer than 20 additional pages. There is some evidence of updating, which can be identified as readily from the differences in inking of the new type from the old, as from the actual content; however, in many cases information presented has not been revised. Thus the various state entries list 1950 Census Bureau population data. Surely the figures from a more recent census were readily available and could have been inserted in the text. Readers needing more current figures would not find this volume an accurate source, which limits its value as a ready-reference tool.

The *Dictionary of American History* is liberally cross-referenced with words or phrases shown in small capital letters to indicate that they appear as separate entries elsewhere in the volume. This cross-referencing and its alphabetical arrangement make the dictionary easy to use.

There are several similar references within this category that are clearly superior in terms of currency. Most users will prefer Scribner's multivolume DICTIONARY OF AMERICAN HISTORY. If a smaller publication is desired, Richard B. Morris's *Encyclopedia of American History* (now out of print) and THE OXFORD COMPANION TO AMERICAN HISTORY are better choices.

While it has limitations, *The Dictionary of American History* can be of assistance to students and the general reader, especially in those areas in which the facts have long been established and the patron needs concise information quickly. For this reason, the Board recommends it for the core collections of public and academic libraries.

Dictionary of American History, rev. edition. Louise Bilebof Ketz, ed. Scribner, 1976–1978. hard. 8 vols. index. ISBN 0-684-13856-5 (set). $625 (set). dictionary.
E174.D521976 973.03

The revised edition of the *Dictionary of American History* consists of eight volumes containing 7,200 entries describing the political, economic, social, and cultural history of the United States. First published in 1940, this edition is completely revised and contains 500 new entries, 1,200 entries that have been rewritten, and 4,200 entries that have been edited and updated.

The revised and rewritten entries are often characterized by fuller coverage, better organization, and, in some cases, greater objectivity. For example, the entry *pure food and drug acts* has been retitled *pure food and drug movement* and now has four times the number of pages. In addition, major improvements have been made in coverage of Afro-Americans, Native Americans, science and technology, and the history of the arts, with thorough articles on both general and specific topics.

The entries are arranged alphabetically and range in length from a few lines (for example, *flag, presidential)* to several pages (for example, *newspapers*). Many entries are followed by short bibliographies ranging from one line (or one work) to half a page. The bibliographical entries contain author and title only and do not have publisher and date of publication. Lack of this helpful information for tracing sources is a weakness, as is the heavy reliance on monograph materials in bibliographies. Another minor drawback is that the entries almost never include an indication of articles on related topics. For example, there are no cross-references included in the entry for *race relations* to refer the reader to related entries such as *Afro-Americans* or *Chinese immigration and labor,* both of which are topics discussed in the entry.

The major drawback to this publication is the 1976 copyright date. A set that is more than 15 years old cannot help but be outdated, even though the information within it is complete to that time.

The entries are well written, and all are signed. Volume 7 contains the list of 800 contributors, chosen for expertise in the field, along with the articles they wrote. No other information is given about the authors; however, some research on the part of the user will reveal that their credentials, for the most part, are impeccable. The entry for *New England* was prepared by James Truslow Adams, author of *History of New England,* while Perry Miller, co-author of *The Puritans,* had written the entry on *Puritans.* Sidney Ratner, author of a classic work on taxation *(Taxation and Democracy in America)* had contributed the entry for *taxation.* Even entries on less well known topics such as *cattle drives* and *cattle brands* were prepared by experts; J. Evetts Haley (author of *Charles Goodnight*) wrote the former, and folklorist J. Frank Dobie prepared the latter.

Although there are no biographies included in the dictionary, the index in volume 8 can be consulted for names of individuals who can then be located through the references to the topical entries in which they are mentioned. The index is heavily cross-referenced. Each page has guide words identifying the first entry on the left-hand page and the last entry on the right-hand page. There are some helpful "see" references within entries.

The handsome binding as well as the quality of the paper and the typeface used make this edition easier to read and more attractive than the previous edition.

The *Dictionary of American History* is the basic work in the field because of its scope and accuracy. The Board recommends this work for the core collections of public, academic, and school libraries.

Documents of American History, 10th edition. Henry Steele Commager, ed. Prentice-Hall, 1988. hard. 2 vols. appendix. index. ISBN 0-21724-7 (vol. 1); 0-13-217282-8 (vol. 2). $39 (vol. 1); $39 (vol. 2). sourcebook.
E173.C66 973.08

The two-volume *Documents of American History* is "designed to illustrate the course of American history from the Age of Discovery to the present" (preface). Published first in 1934, this is the tenth edition covering the texts of significant American historical documents from 1492 through 1987. The set contains 727 documents, including treaties, letters, speeches, Supreme Court decisions, historic acts, proclamations, and other documents within this time frame, including "*Roe* v. *Wade,*" "Nixon's Resignation," and "The Iran-Contra Affair." Selections are introduced by brief notes on the historical significance of the documents along with additional references on the topic.

The documents are arranged chronologically. Volume 1 of this edition is the same as the previous edition, covering documents from Columbus's voyage in 1492 to the documents of 1898. In volume 2, as in previous editions, some documents, focusing mainly on civil rights and civil disobedience (Truman's Civil Rights Message of 1948, for example) have been dropped to make room for documents from 1966 through 1987. Volume 2 also contains an appendix with the text of the Constitution of the United States as well as an easy-to-use index. The entries in the index are arranged by topic and personal name and keyed to document numbers, not page numbers. However, the index is still relatively easy to consult.

Having the complete text of original documents in two easy-to-use volumes saves valuable time searching through other and perhaps multiple sources.

The *Documents of American History* is an excellent reference tool for students of American history. The Board recommends this work for the core collections of public, academic, and school libraries.

Encyclopedia of American Economic History: Studies of the Principal Movements and Ideas. Glenn Porter, ed. Scribner, 1980. hard. 3 vols. index. ISBN 0-684-16271-7 (set). $250 (set). encyclopedia.
HC103.E52 330.9′73

See Economics.

The Encyclopedia of American Facts and Dates, 8th edition. Gordon Carruth. Harper & Row, 1987. hard. 1 vol. 1,008 pp. index. ISBN 0-06-181143-2. $35. encyclopedia.
E174.5.C3 1987 973.0202

First published in 1956, *The Encyclopedia of American Facts and Dates* presents in one volume a vast amount of information about America's past up to June 1986. Gordon Carruth, an editor of reference books for many years, has been responsible for all eight editions. Other titles edited by Carruth include the *Oxford American Dictionary* and *The Encyclopedia of Historic Places.* According to the preface, the new information in this eighth edition was developed from both original research and standard sources, such as the *New York Times.* Some features introduced in previous editions (such as the introductions that summarize important events in each year) have been expanded to the rest of the text.

The facts and dates covered for each year are formatted chronologically and concurrently in four columns appearing on two facing pages. Each column contains entries on specific topics. The first column contains entries covering 21 subjects, such as exploration, government, wars, disasters, and temperature. The second column covers 18 subjects, such as drama, publishing, arts, entertainment, and architecture. The third column also covers 18 subjects, including business, industry, science, education, agriculture, philosophy, and religion. Finally, the fourth column covers 13 subjects, including social issues, sports, and crime. Reading across the two pages provides a panoramic view of the important events of a year. Some readers may have some difficulty in adjusting to the two-page-spread format that continues the left-hand columns on subsequent left-hand pages and the right-hand columns on subsequent right-hand pages. Once the user becomes accustomed to the format, however, it is possible to get an informative and enjoyable picture of a specific point in time. In July of the bicentennial year of 1976, death penalty laws in several states were struck down; the tranquilizer Valium and alcohol were reported to be the leading cause of drug-related ailments; former President Nixon was declared ineligible to practice law; Lyme arthritis was discovered; the first ballet was broadcast live; and Operation Sail took place in New York harbor.

Specific topics are found through an extensive index that can be used to find events as well as to trace themes through American history. The index directs the reader not only to the date but also to the column where the item will be found. Only those names that appear in boldface type in the main entries are indexed. However, many other persons can be located as subentries under main entries for topics with which they are most closely associated. The index is preceded by a helpful explanatory note on how to use it.

The Encyclopedia of American Facts and Dates is the most up-to-date and all-inclusive chronology covering historic events in the United States. The Board recommends this work for the core collections of public, academic, and school libraries.

Encyclopedia of American Foreign Policy: Studies of the Principal Movements and Ideas. Alexander DeConde, ed. Scribner, 1978. hard. 3 vols. 1,201 pp. index. ISBN 0-684-155036-6 (set). $250 (set). encyclopedia.
JX1407.E53 327.73

The *Encyclopedia of American Foreign Policy* is a three-volume set containing 95 essays that analyze and interpret the development, application, and meaning of basic concepts in American foreign policy. The essays cover broad concepts, such as isolationism and national self-determination, and specific topics, such as the Monroe Doctrine and the Marshall Plan. Historiography is included as well, with essays on such topics as revisionism.

This outstanding set is the work of leading scholars—such as George C. Herring, Robert Freeman Smith, and Theodore A. Wilson—representing a variety of political positions and ideologies. Most of the contributors are American historians who are authorities in their fields, and many are included in the *Directory of American Scholars.* The editor of the encyclopedia, Alexander DeConde, is also a well-known historian.

The three-volume set has an attractive layout, and the typography is clear and readable. The essays are not footnoted; however, there are cross-references and, at the end of each essay, there is a bibliographic essay that contains the references used to write the entries as well as references to other literature. There is also a useful index.

Volume 3 contains a separate 150-page biographical section, most of which is reprinted from the CONCISE DICTIONARY OF AMERICAN BIOGRAPHY or condensed from the DICTIONARY OF AMERICAN BIOGRAPHY supplements (both reviewed in the Biography category). The biographical sketches include both past and present contributors to the development of foreign policy. These sketches are not listed in the table of contents.

The *Encyclopedia of American Foreign Policy* is not a substitute for a single-volume reference work containing short entries on a large number of specific topics, nor does it replace conventional texts that cover the history of foreign relations chronologically; however, it is a comprehensive supplement of thoughtful analyses of foreign policy and the concepts associated with it. It is obvious that given the 1978 copyright date, the user must look elsewhere for information on more recent policy developments.

The Board recommends this work for the core collections of public, academic, and school libraries.

Encyclopedia of American Political History: Studies of the Principal Movements and Ideas. Jack P. Greene, ed. Scribner, 1984. hard. 3 vols. index. ISBN 0-684-17003-5 (set). $250 (set). encyclopedia.
E183.E5 320.973′03′21

See Political Science.

Great Lives from History, American series. Frank N. Magill, ed. Salem, 1987. hard. 5 vols. 2,592 pp. index. ISBN 9-89356-529-6 (set). $325 (set). biography.
CT214.G76 920.073

The first of a projected biographical series, *Great Lives from History,* American series, is a five-volume set containing biographical sketches. According to the preface, the most important criterion for selection was the individual's contribution to the culture and development of society and that he or she "be judged historically to have gone beyond his or her immediate field of endeavor to affect the everyday lives of most, if not all, Americans" (preface). Entries range from early explorers to contemporary figures, both living and dead, and encompass politics, science, literature, sports, and entertainment. Among those included are Neil Armstrong, Sandra Day O'Connor, John Muir, William Faulkner, George Washington, and Daniel Boone.

Generally 2,000 to 3,000 words long, the entries follow a standard format. Each entry begins with a section listing the name, birthplace, birth and death dates, and areas of achievement of the subject, along with a sentence or two summarizing the person's contribution. This is followed by material on the subject's early life and influences, a discussion of his or her life's work, and a summary section. After the summary, there is an annotated six- to eight-item bibliography of major works on the subject.

The fifth volume includes a biographical index, which lists the subjects covered alphabetically, and an "Areas of Achievement" index. All index entries include volume and page numbers. While these are helpful, a general subject index would make this work easier to use.

All the entries are clearly written, and all are signed. The list of contributors is quite lengthy and represents a generous sampling of scholars from colleges and universities across the country. Although their institutions are listed, biographical details are scanty; therefore, it is difficult to judge the quality of the scholars. The series editor, Frank N. Magill, is a well-known editor of reference works.

Great Lives from History is written more for the layperson and not for the serious researcher. Most of the entries are well covered in other standard works, such as the DICTIONARY OF AMERICAN BIOGRAPHY (see Biography).

The Board recommends this work for the core collection of school libraries.

Harvard Guide to American History, rev. edition. Frank Freidel, ed., with the assistance of Richard K. Showman. Belknap/Harvard, 1974. soft. 1 vol. 1,312 pp. indexes. ISBN 0-674-37555-6. $20. bibliography. Currently out of stock.
Z1236.F77 973

The *Harvard Guide to American History* actually began in 1896 when Albert Bushnell Hart and Edward Channing prepared a small book containing an outline and key bibliography for a course in American history to 1865. The book was so successful that in 1912, Hart and Channing, joined by Frederick Jackson Turner, revised it as the *Guide to the Study and Reading of American History* and included material up to 1910. In 1953, Oscar Handlin; Arthur Meir Schlesinger; Arthur Meir Schlesinger, Jr.; Samuel Eliot Morison; Frederick Merk; and Paul Herman Buck, under sponsorship of the Harvard University Department of History, brought out an essentially new volume covering the intervening 40 years. The current edition, edited by Frank Freidel and published in 1974, was expanded and contains an outstanding collection of books, articles, documents, and reference sources on the political, social, economic, and constitutional history of America published through mid-1970. About a third of the material in this edition is new.

Both volumes are now contained in a one-volume paperback. The first volume contains four major parts: "Research Methods and Materials," "Biographies and Personal Records," "Comprehensive and Area Histories," and "Histories of Special Subjects." The special subjects include topics such as politics, demography and social structure, immigration and ethnicity, social ills, and reform, education, and religion. Part 1, "Research Methods and Materials," has been revised to reflect newer research approaches; however, the sections on history as a literary art, book reviewing, and note taking are retained virtually unchanged.

The second volume is arranged in five historical periods, beginning with "America to 1789" and ending with the "Twentieth Century." It includes many of the same sociological subjects contained in volume 1 (for example, religion, social ills, and reform.)

This second volume also contains three indexes: a detailed name index to cited materials, an author index, and a subject index. A title index and a more detailed subject index would be helpful. In addition to the indexes, readers will find the detailed tables of contents and the alphabetical list of biographies extremely useful tools.

Any library attempting to support the reading and study of American history should have the *Harvard Guide to American History.* Although hampered by a 1974 copyright date, it is the basic reference bibliography and major source to consult for detailed study of American history. Also, libraries can use this work for collection development. If this guide is revised in the future, there is a need for a more comprehensive subject index and more bibliographic detail in the entries than just the author, title, and date—all that is currently provided.

A good companion to this volume, although similarly dated, is THE OXFORD COMPANION TO AMERICAN HISTORY.

The Board recommends this work for the core collections of public and academic libraries.

The Oxford Companion to American History. Thomas H. Johnson, in consultation with Harvey Wish. Oxford, 1966. hard. 1 vol. 912 pp. ISBN 0-19-500597-X. $49.95. encyclopedia.
E174.J6 973.03

The Oxford Companion to American History is a complementary volume to THE OXFORD COMPANION TO AMERICAN LITERATURE (see American Literature), emphasizing the historical importance of people and events rather than the literary importance of writers. It is a very serviceable biographical and historical guide to American civilization containing summaries of lives, events, and places significant in the founding and growth of the nation. There are articles on social, political, and labor movements, as well as art, science, commerce, literature, education, and law. Articles on sports and entertainment are also included, and the text of the Constitution and its amendments is reprinted in an appendix.

There are 4,710 entries, including 1,835 biographies. There are 699 "see" references, along with about 5,500 cross-references within the entries. The major "see" references are indicated by italics, while those within entries are indicated by small capitals, a typical format for works of this sort. Longer entries have references for additional information (for example, the article "Frontier" has five cross-references to related entries.) There are entries for presidents, vice-presidents, cabinet members, and members of the Supreme Court. Tables give names and dates of persons who held high offices, a useful device for quick reference. However, the volume does not contain an index.

The entries are arranged alphabetically. Most of the entries are short, not exceeding 2,000 words. The longer entries are reserved for the more important subjects, for example, Benjamin Franklin and George Washington. The entries are well written by reputable authors. The authors' credentials are given on the book's cover. Since many libraries do not retain book covers, it would be better if this information appeared within the volume. The book is designed for everyday use by anyone who needs a reliable, ready source of information on any point of importance in the history of America. This work is not designed to be a scholarly reference tool.

The Oxford Companion to American History is a convenient reference volume, with accurate information presented concisely and clearly. Although this volume is still a solid resource, the book is badly dated. This work should be revised and updated to include the important people and events that have emerged since publication in 1966 (such as Presidents Jimmy Carter, Ronald Reagan, and George Bush and the first woman Supreme Court Justice, Sandra Day O'Connor).

The Board recommends this work for the core collections of public, academic, and school libraries.

Statistical Abstract of the United States, 109th edition. U.S.G.P.O., annual. hard and soft. 1 vol. 984 pp. illus. index. S/N 003-024-06906-7 (hard); S/N 003-024-06788-1 (soft). $33 (hard); $26 (soft). yearbook.
HA202.U54 317.3

The *Statistical Abstract of the United States* is a one-volume standard summary of statistics on the social, political, and economic organization of the United States. It also provides references to other statistical publications and sources in the introductory matter to each of the 31 sections, the source notes for each table, and appendix 1, which is a guide to sources of statistics.

First published in 1878, the 1989 edition is the 109th edition, and it reflects changes in coverage of marriage and divorce, AIDS, and housing. New areas covered include age differences of bride and groom, home improvements and repairs, and 1988 presidential election results. One hundred six new tables were added. Statistics given in the tables usually cover a period of about 15 to 20 years, with some tables giving figures for as long ago as 1789. Statistical methodology and reliability are explained in appendix 3 (one of five appendixes).

Most of the information is presented in tabular form; however, there are a few graphs and charts. For example, on page 786 of the 1989 edition, there is a graph showing the annual percentage change of U.S. exports and imports during the years 1970 through 1986. On the front endpaper, there is a useful map of the United States showing census divisions and regions. At the end of the volume is a detailed index that keys the subject entries to the appropriate table numbers. The index also contains numerous helpful "see" and "see also" references.

The *Statistical Abstract of the United States* is an indispensable collection of statistical data selected from public and private statistical publications. The Board recommends this work for the core collections of public, academic, and school libraries.

Who's Who in American Politics: 1989–1990, 12th edition. Bowker, 1989. hard. 1 vol. 1,936 pp. index. ISBN 0-8352-2577-1. $174.95. handbook.
E176.W6424 920

See Political Science.

Worldmark Encyclopedia of the States, 2d edition. Moshe Y. Sachs, ed. Worldmark, 1986; distrib. by John Wiley. hard. 1 vol. 690 pp. ISBN 0-471-83213-8. $99.95. encyclopedia.
E156.W67 973.03'21

The one-volume 1986 *Worldmark Encyclopedia of the States* is a second edition, completely revised and updated, of the one issued in 1981 as a companion volume to an earlier work, the WORLDMARK ENCYCLOPEDIA OF THE NATIONS. According to the preface, it is intended to be "a practical guide to the geographic, demographic, historical, political, economic and social development of the United States." The format of this encyclopedia reinforces the idea that the United States is a federal union of separate states, each with its own history, traditions, resources, laws, and economic interests.

The statistics given are based on the latest federal and state data available at the time of publication, including January 1985 state population estimates. The text is the work of over 50 eminent academicians and journalists. The entries in this encyclopedia are not signed. An alphabetical list of contributors and their credentials does appear in the volume with no indication of attribution. Each state is treated in an individual chapter, which has a framework of 50 standard subject headings. The District of Columbia and the Commonwealth of Puerto Rico are discussed in separate chapters, and two additional articles summarize the other Caribbean and Pacific dependencies.

Arrangement is alphabetical by state. Factual and statistical information on the individual states is exhibited in uniform format under such topics as topography, climate, flora and fauna, and history. The format is explained in the "Notes" section, and a "Key to Subject Headings" is given. Each entry begins with introductory material for the state that includes the origin of such things as its name, song, motto, and flag. Each entry contains a map showing standard features for that state such as county names, state capitals, and elevations. Tables of counties, county seats, county areas, and county populations accompany the entries on the 14 most populous states. In addition, each entry is followed by a short bibliography containing the references used to write the entry. Article length varies; the more populous states usually receive the longest entries (for example, the entry for Alaska is 6 pages and the entry for California is 30 pages).

The concluding chapter is a 50-page overview of the state of the nation. Tables of conversions, a list of abbreviations and acronyms, a glossary, black-and-white maps, and data on the U. S. presidents supplement the main text.

The end matter contains colored maps of the United States, including insets of Hawaii and Alaska, showing state capitals and city populations, which are based on U.S. Census Bureau mid-1984 estimates.

The *Worldmark Encyclopedia of the States* constitutes a well-written and aptly arranged gathering of timely information pertaining to the states of the Union with treatment of the states on a par with those of the major encyclopedias—*Collier's, World Book,* and *Americana.* Although it does not contain photographs, maps and statistical data are plentiful and fairly current. Other strengths are the clear description of the state and local governmental structure, the state historical background, and the bibliographies.

The one-volume *Worldmark Encyclopedia of the States* is a convenient source for comparative data on the states. However, researchers in need of current data may find the 1986 copyright a drawback, and academic libraries might be better served by a more comprehensive multivolume work. The Board recommends this work for the core collections of school, public, and academic libraries.

Writings on American History, 1962–1973: A Subject Bibliography of Books and Monographs. James R. Masterson, comp. Kraus International, 1985. hard. 10 vols. 6,530 pp. index. ISBN 0-527-98268-7 (set). $1,300 (set).
Z1236.W773 016.973

Writings on American History, 1962–1973: A Subject Bibliography of Books and Monographs is a ten-volume set listing over 50,000 book-length works relevant to the study of American history published during the years specified in the title. Based on a compilation by James R. Masterson, it is a companion set to *Writings on American History, 1973–74: A Subject Bibliography of Articles.* Both are components of the Writings on American History series, begun in 1902 by the American Historical Association, and as such are considered standard reference works in the field.

The entries are organized into five broad categories: "History and Historians," "Chronological Classification," "Subject Classification," "Geographical Classification," and "Biography." These categories are further subdivided to provide more specific topics. For example, the "Geographical Classification" has nine subdivisions, one for each section of the country, such as the "Great Plains" and the "Southwest." Also, the "Southwest" entry is divided into "General," "Arizona," "New Mexico," and "Texas."

Each entry is a reproduction of a Library of Congress catalog card and provides full bibliographic information, including author, title, publication data, classification numbers, and so forth. In addition, a number has been added to each entry. The inclusive entry numbers are displayed on the spines of the volumes. Each of the ten volumes contains about 650 pages. The entire work is printed on acid-free paper and is sturdily bound. This handsome set will withstand heavy use.

Volume 10 contains two indexes: the "Index to Authors, Editors, and Compilers" and the "Index to Personal Names as Subjects." The latter index lists all people who are subjects of the books cited in the work. The work relies on this extensive index to locate all citations rather than providing cross-references.

The index lists all the entry numbers of all the locations for the entry. This results in very long citations, for example, 326 for *John F. Kennedy.* Checking entry numbers in such cases can prove tedious and frustrating for researchers.

On the other hand, a helpful feature is that the table of contents for the entire set is repeated at the front of each volume, with the inclusive page numbers for every volume listed at the bottom of all contents pages.

Using the Library of Congress holdings for listings provides access to the world's most extensive resource for publication information. However, the Library of Congress does not always acquire a work as quickly as it is published, and cataloging is slow as well. Thus many newer volumes are not included in this bibliography. Compilations such as *Books in Print* could serve as alternative resources for the most current works.

Academic libraries, especially those supporting graduate study, will need this bibliography. Its cost may preclude its purchase by most other libraries, and the material covered is not likely to be needed in public libraries.

The Board recommends this work for the core collection of academic libraries.

Supplementary Titles

Album of American History. J. T. Adams. Scribner, 1981. hard. 3 vols. 2,260 pp. index. ISBN 0-684-16848-0 (set). $290 (set). sourcebook.
E178.5.A48 973.022′2

In the *Album of American History,* "the pictures themselves *are* the history, and the text assumes the subordinate role which pictures have had in the past. . . . In this book we have a thread of text which explains the pictures, instead of scattered pictures which only scantily illustrate the text.

"To gain entrance to these volumes, 'a picture must answer to certain questions; was it made during the period it represents and does it illustrate some significant aspect of the life of the times?'.

"Naturally, the Civil War is lavishly covered. . . . But the great event was the driving of the last gold spike that united the eastern and western lines at Promontory Point.

"There is an agreeable absence of pomposity in the choice of pictures.

"It remains to say that the index volume is a most entertaining, as well as most useful, coda to a very successful piece of pictorial recording." (*TLS,* March 14, 1968, p. 247)

Board's recommendation: Public, academic, and school libraries.

America: History and Life. Eric H. Boehm, ed. ABC-Clio, annual (1974–). 5 issues (per year). soft. ISSN 0002-7065. $175 (per year). bibliography.
Z1361.W39S56 016.9173′06′96073

"*America: History and Life* scans nearly 2,000 journals in 38 languages. (The abstracts, however, are always in English.) It is currently arranged in four parts: Part A contains the abstracts, Part B is an index to book reviews from 130 journals in history and related fields, Part C, 'American History Bibliography,' arranges the citations from the first two parts (articles, books, and dissertations) alphabetically by author, under the same table of contents as Part A, and Part D is the annual index. . . . It has subject, biographic, geographic, and chronological terms and there is also an author index. Much white space in the format makes this an easy-to-read and attractive reference work." (*RSR,* July/September 1979, p. 18)

Also reviewed in: *A Arch,* January 1977, p. 44; *ARBA,* 1976, p. 190; 1979, p. 208; *BL,* January 15, 1977, p. 745; October 1, 1978, p. 319; *JQ,* Autumn 1977, p. 634; *Mag Lib,* 1982, p. 2; *RSR,* October 1977, p. 49; April 1981, p. 15.

Board's recommendation: Public and academic libraries.

Bibliographies in American History, 1942–1978: Guide to Materials for Research. Henry Putney Beers. Research Pubs., 1982. hard. 2 vols. 946 pp. ISBN 0-89235-038-5. $275. bibliography.
Z1236.B39 016.016973

"*Bibliographies in American History,* published in 1942, is a staple of library reference collections. Long considered essential for historical research, it has been reprinted twice. Now Beers has produced a two-volume continuation that covers bibliographies issued 1942–78 plus and he has added pre-1942 bibliographies not included in the original work." (*BL,* October 1, 1983, p. 242)

"This work lists 11,784 bibliographies relating to American history in various formats, including 'articles, compilations in progress and manuscript bibliographies' that were published or compiled during the 1942–78 period. . . . Chapters I–III are arranged by broad categories such as general aids, periodical indexes, dissertations, published works, archives and manuscripts, with some division into subsections as applicable: government documents, secondary works by period and by types, cartography, exploration and travel, women, etc." (*CRL,* January 1983, p. 52)

Also reviewed in: *A Arch,* Winter 1983, p. 83; *ARBA,* 1984, p. 179; *Choice,* February 1983, p. 51; *RSR,* Fall 1983, p. 72.

Board's recommendation: Academic libraries.

The Civil War Dictionary. Mark M. Boatner III. McKay, 1988. hard. 1 vol. 974 pp. ISBN 0-812-916-89-1. $29.95. dictionary.
E468.B7 973.7'03'21

"First published in 1959, *The Civil War Dictionary* covers every aspect of the struggle with more than four thousand entries that range from biographical sketches—there are about two thousand of them—to accounts of twenty major campaigns that are both comprehensive and well written. Along with the expected entries on a host of skirmishes, weapons, and army organization are others that suggest the author's lively interest in his subject." (*AH,* March 1989, p. 110)

Board's recommendation: Public, academic, and school libraries.

Facts About the Presidents: From George Washington to George Bush, 5th edition. Joseph Nathan Kane. Wilson, 1989. hard. 1 vol. 419 pp. ISBN 0-8242-0774-2. $45. biographical dictionary.
E176.1.K3 973.09'92

"In Part I [of *Facts About the Presidents*] a chapter is devoted to each president [from Washington to Bush] in the chronological order in which he took office. . . . A genealogical compilation presents . . . material about the President's parents, brothers and sisters, wives, and children. Family history is followed by data on elections, congressional sessions, cabinet and Supreme Court appointments, and the Vice President, as well as highlights of the President's life and administration. In Part II material is presented in comparative form, with collective data and statistics on the Presidents as individuals and on the office of the presidency." (preface)

A review of the fourth edition said: "Topics covered . . . vary from obvious ones such as presidents by state of birth, by age at inauguration, and so forth to rather esoteric comparisons such as presidents who have married widows. . . . Organization in the biographical section of the work is clear enough to make its use easy. . . . The [work] will be a welcome addition to most general reference collections." (*BL,* June 15, 1982, p. 1385)

Also reviewed in: *ARBA,* 1977, p. 254; 1983, p. 273; *BL,* January 1, 1975, p. 469; July 1, 1976, p. 1527; December 1, 1981, p. 481; *Choice,* April 1978, p. 197; December 1981, p. 488; *RSR,* January 1975, p. 19; July 1982, p. 68; *WLB,* October 1968, p. 177; September 1972, p. 21; November 1974, p. 249.

Board's recommendation: Public, academic, and school libraries.

Great Events from History, American series. Salem,

1975. hard. 3 vols. 2,047 pp. index. ISBN 0-89356-112-6 (set). $115 (set). handbook.

Board's recommendation: Public and school libraries.

Historical Statistics of the United States. U.S. Bureau of the Census. U.S.G.P.O., 1975. hard. 2 vols. approx. 1,200 pp. S/N 003-024-0012-9 (set). $56 (set). sourcebook.
HA202.B87 317.3

The *Historical Statistics of the United States* series "is prepared with the cooperation of the Social Science Research Council. This is a compilation of more than 8,000 statistical time series, largely annual, on American social and economic development. . . . Each chapter includes definitions of terms and descriptive text. Specific source notes provide a basic guide to original published sources for further reference and additional data. [There is a] detailed alphabetical subject index." (*WLB,* April 1972, p. 753)

"The first volume in the series, *Historical Statistics of the United States: 1789–1945,* was published in 1949, and a *Continuation to 1952* appeared in 1954. *Historical Statistics of the United States: Colonial Times to 1957* came out in 1960, and a *Continuation to 1962 and Revisions* was issued in 1965. 'The present edition presents more than 12,500 time series, a 50-percent increase over the last edition.' " (*LJ,* June 1, 1976, p. 1276)

Also reviewed in: *ARBA,* 1977, p. 364; *Choice,* October 1976, p. 964; *RSR,* October 1976, pp. 11 and 18; July 1977, p. 36; October 1981, p. 71; *SF,* December 1976, p. 575; *SMQ,* Fall 1976, p. 52.

Board's recommendation: Public, academic, and school libraries.

The Presidents: A Reference History. Henry F. Graff. Scribner, 1984. hard. 1 vol. 700 pp. ISBN 0-684-17607-6. $75. biobibliography.
E176.1.P918 973.09'92

In *The Presidents: A Reference History,* "academic scholars of the presidency have contributed . . . 35 original essays that describe the administrations of the 38 presidents from Washington through Carter. The articles, ranging from 10 to 30 pages, include some brief biographical information as well." (*Choice,* September 1984, p. 70)

"Each essay is a careful appraisal of the accomplishments and impact of the administrations, followed by a bibliography of the most important primary and secondary sources. . . . Written in a readable style without the burden of scholarly documentation, they are suitable both for reference and general reading." (*BL,* January 1, 1985, p. 632)

Also reviewed in: *ARBA,* 1985, p. 158; *CRL,* January 1986, p. 77; *LJ,* April 15, 1985, p. 42; *WLB,* September 1984, p. 65.

Board's recommendation: Public, academic, and school libraries.

New and Noteworthy

The American Presidents: The Office and the Men. Norman S. Cohen. Frank N. Magill, ed. Grolier, 1989. hard. 3 vols. 284 pp. (vol. 1); 290 pp. (vol. 2); 303 pp. (vol. 3). illus. index. ISBN 0-7172-7166-8 (set). $150 (set). biographical source.
E176.1 016.973

"Individual articles in [*The American Presidents*] . . . detail basic biographical information, tracing the subject's early years, political career, and ascent to the presidency. . . . An assessment of his personal and psychological qualities and the strengths and weaknesses of his unique contributions to the evolution of the institution of the presidency is provided." (*SLJ,* May 1990, p. 27)

Chronicle of America. Chronicle Publications, 1989; distrib. by Prentice Hall. hard. 1 vol. 1,400 pp. illus. index. ISBN 0-13-133645-9. $49.95. chronology.

Chronicle of America "is a chronology of America from prehistory through 1988, lavishly illustrated with more than 3,000 illustrations, many of them in color. Appendixes include an immigration map, a list of presidents, and brief descriptions of the 50 states. A detailed index concludes the book." (*BL,* January 15, 1990, p. 1031)

The Complete Book of U.S. Presidents, 2d edition. William A. DiGregorio. Dembner, 1989; distrib. by Norton. hard. 1 vol. 740 pp. illus. index. ISBN 0-942637-17-8. $29.95. biographical dictionary.
E176.1.D43 973.09

The Complete Book of U.S. Presidents "gives readable, thorough information on each president, arranged in chronological order through George Bush (with Grover Cleveland listed twice). Included in each chapter is a full-page black-and-white portrait; . . . physical description; information on personality, family, marriage, career, nomination, campaign, cabinet, administration, Supreme Court appointments, retirement, and death; quotes from and about each president; and books by and about each." (*BL,* March 1, 1990, p. 1382)

Dictionary of American Diplomatic History, 2d edition. John E. Findling, ed. Greenwood, 1989. hard. 1 vol. 674 pp. index. ISBN 0-313-26024-9. $59.95. dictionary.
E183.7.F5 327.73

"Of the more than 1,200 entries [in the *Dictionary of American Diplomatic History*], approximately half are biographical sketches of the major 'movers and shakers' in American diplomatic history; the remainder focus on the principal treaties, incidents, interventions, and conferences since 1776. . . . Most useful is the list of key diplomatic personnel arranged by presidential administration. A very detailed index concludes the book." (*BL,* December 15, 1989, p. 854)

The Encyclopedia of Colonial and Revolutionary America. John M. Faragher, ed. Facts On File, 1989. hard. 1 vol. 448 pp. illus. index. ISBN 0-8160-1744-1. $50. dictionary.
E188.E63 973.3'03

The Encyclopedia of Colonial and Revolutionary America contains "1,500 entries [that] are alphabetically arranged from *Abortion* to *Peter Zenger.* . . . While including standard topics like discoveries and battles, [this work] . . . also provide[s] coverage of social, economic, and cultural topics such as crafts, disease, food, insurance, lotteries, and witchcraft. Longer articles are generally signed and describe topics such as Afro-Americans, agriculture, French colonies, geography and culture, religion, war, women, and each of the 13 colonies." (*BL,* February 1, 1990, p. 1112)

The Historical Atlas of Political Parties in the United States Congress, 1789–1989. Kenneth C. Martis, ed. Macmillan, 1989. hard. 1 vol. 518 pp. illus. index. ISBN 0-02-920170-5. $190. atlas.
G1201.F9M25 912

"Specialists viewing the detailed multicolored maps [in *The Historical Atlas of Political Parties in the United States Congress*] will see new possibilities for historical inquiry as the dynamics of local, regional, and national elections are made graphically evident. The party affiliation of each member of Congress is clarified, with sources cited. . . . The introductory section helps place the vast amount of information . . . into proper historical and political context." (*LJ,* June 15, 1989, p. 52)

Martin E. Gingerich

American Literature

See also British Literature; World Literature

American literature is a broad category, with a wide range of reference books available for public, academic, and school libraries. The category covers all aspects and types of literature (drama, fiction, nonfiction, poetry) by writers who were either born in the United States or who, if born elsewhere, nonetheless contributed to the body of literature identified as American. Thus, a definition of American literature is not based solely on geography; this is what makes American literature sometimes difficult to define and what makes assembling a basic reference collection in this subject a complex task.

Another kind of complexity arises when we consider the relationship of American literature to literature as a general category. In compiling and maintaining a core collection of reference materials on American literature, librarians must not only choose biographical reference works; they must also consider a large mass of publications on criticism, history, and bibliography, as well as encyclopedic "guides" to literature. When the words "American" or "United States" form part of the title, at least the national aspect of the coverage will be obvious. However, when a title simply indicates that the work focuses on novels or novelists, poems or poets,

Core Titles

CRITICISM	PUBLIC	ACADEMIC	SCHOOL
Contemporary Literary Criticism: Excerpts from Criticism of the Works of Today's Novelists, Poets, Playwrights, and Other Creative Writers, 58 vols. Gale, annual (1973–) (See World Literature)	✦	✦	
The Critical Temper: A Survey of Modern Criticism on English and American Literature from the Beginnings of the Twentieth Century, 3 vols., 2 suppls. Tucker, Martin, ed. Ungar, 1969– (See British Literature)	✦		

DRAMA	PUBLIC	ACADEMIC	SCHOOL
Contemporary Dramatists, Contemporary Writers series, 4th edition Kirkpatrick, D. L., ed. St. James, 1988 (See British Literature)	✦	✦	
Critical Survey of Drama, English Language series, 6 vols., 1 suppl. Magill, Frank N., ed. Salem, 1985 (See British Literature)	✦	✦	
FICTION			
Contemporary Novelists, 4th edition D. L. Kirkpatrick, eds. St. Martin's, 1986 (See World Literature)	✦	✦	✦
Critical Survey of Long Fiction, English Language series, 8 vols., 1 suppl. Magill, Frank N., ed. Salem, 1983	✦	✦	✦
Critical Survey of Short Fiction, 7 vols., 1 suppl. Magill, Frank N., ed. Salem, 1981, 1987 (See World Literature)	✦	✦	✦
Masterplots II, American Fiction series Magill, Frank N., ed. Salem, 1986	✦	✦	✦
GUIDES			
American Authors, 1600–1900: A Biographical Dictionary of American Literature, The Authors series Kunitz, Stanley J., and Howard Haycraft, eds. Wilson, 1986	✦	✦	✦
American Women Writers: A Critical Reference Guide from Colonial Times to the Present, 4 vols. Mainiero, Lina, ed. Ungar, 1979–1982	✦	✦	
American Writers: A Collection of Literary Biographies, 4 vols., 2 suppls. Unger, Leonard, and A. Walton Litz, eds. Scribner, 1974–1981	✦	✦	
Contemporary Authors: A Bio-Bibliographical Guide to Current Writers in Fiction, General Nonfiction, Poetry, Journalism, Drama, Motion Pictures, Television, and Other Fields, 129 vols. May, Hal, and Susan Trosky, eds. Gale, 1962– (See Biography)	✦	✦	✦
Contemporary Authors, New Revision series, 30 vols. May, Hal, and James J. Lesniak, eds. Gale, 1990	✦	✦	✦

essays or essayists, and the like, without a specific national designation, the work will usually address aspects of foreign literature in addition to American literature.

Several core reference works whose contents are not strictly limited to American literature are reviewed in the American Literature category. See, for example, CONTEMPORARY AUTHORS, New Revision series, and CRITICAL SURVEY OF LONG FICTION. These critical-biographical titles all include entries on British and non-English-language authors, as well as Americans. However, because American authors and their works make up the plurality of entries, these titles are considered in this category. On the other hand, works that include some American writers but focus primarily on foreign authors have cross-reference entries under

American Literature, while they are reviewed in the British Literature or World Literature categories. CRITICAL SURVEY OF DRAMA and CRITICAL SURVEY OF SHORT FICTION are two such titles. The reader may also want to turn to the Theater category, where reviews of several books dealing with American plays will be found, although the emphasis in these works is on performances.

Certain titles deal with technical matters of form or prosody rather than with specific authors or literary works. These titles are reviewed under the World Literature category and are not cross-referenced here. Titles that deal with genres such as mystery, fantasy, and science fiction are reviewed in that category as well.

There are two indexes that the Board noted as being essential to a core collection in American literature. These are *The Columbia Grainger's Index to Poetry* (9th edition, Edith P. Hazen and Deborah J. Fryer, eds., Columbia, 1990) and the *Short Story Index* (Juliet Yaakov, Wilson, 1984). Four out-of-print titles were recommended as being worthy of inclusion. They are: Max J. Herzberg's *The Reader's Encyclopedia of American Literature* (Crowell, 1962); Peter J. Brier and Anthony Arthur's *American Prose and Criticism: A Guide to Information Sources* (Gale, 1981); the *Literary History of the United States,* 4th edition, revised (Robert E. Speller et al., Macmillan, 1974); and *The Cambridge History of American Literature* (W. P. Trent et al., Putnam, 1917–1921; reprinted Macmillan, 1945 and 1972).

Core Titles

Criticism

Contemporary Literary Criticism: Excerpts from Criticism of the Works of Today's Novelists, Poets, Playwrights, and Other Creative Writers. Gale, annual (1973–). hard. 58 vols. illus. appendix. indexes. ISBN 0-8103-4432-7 (vol. 58). $99 (vol. 58). criticism.
PN771.C59 809

See World Literature.

The Critical Temper: A Survey of Modern Criticism on English and American Literature from the Beginnings to the Twentieth Century. Martin Tucker, ed. Ungar, 1969–. hard. 3 vols. plus 2 suppls. 1,704 pp. (set). index. ISBN 0-804-4330-38 (set). $225 (set). criticism.
PR85.C77 820.C934

See British Literature.

Drama

Contemporary Dramatists, 4th edition, Contemporary Writers series. D. L. Kirkpatrick, ed. St. James, 1988. hard. 1 vol. 785 pp. appendix. index. ISBN 0-912289-62-7. $105. biobibliography.
PR737.C57 822.9

See British Literature.

Critical Survey of Drama, English Language series. Frank N. Magill, ed. Salem, 1985. suppl. 1987. hard. 6 vols. plus suppl. 2,575 pp. (set); 408 pp. (suppl.). index. $350 (set); $80 (suppl.). ISBN 0-89356-375-7 (set); 0-89366-389-7 (suppl.). criticism.
PR623.C5 822.009
PN1625.C74 (suppl.)

See British Literature.

Fiction

Contemporary Novelists, 4th edition. D. L. Kirkpatrick, ed. St. Martin's, 1986. hard. 1 vol. 1,003 pp. appendix. index. ISBN 0-312-16731-8. $79.95. biographical dictionary.
PR.883.C64 823.9

See World Literature.

Critical Survey of Long Fiction, English Language series. Frank N. Magill, ed. Salem, 1983. hard. 8 vols. plus 1 suppl. 3,352 pp. index. ISBN 0-89356-359-5 (set); 0-89536-368-4 (suppl.): $375 (set); $80 (suppl.). criticism.
PR821.C7 (set) 813

Magill's *Critical Survey of Long Fiction* follows the format of many of his series, with several volumes of authors arranged alphabetically supplying biographical, bibliographical, and critical information and a volume of essays on the subject of the series. In this work the first seven volumes survey long fiction as represented by 272 authors from the eighteenth century to the present (Daniel Defoe to Gore Vidal, for example). Entries also follow a format Magill has pretty much standardized in his various collections. A headnote gives brief, necessary information about the author followed by lists of the author's principal long fiction and other literary forms. A paragraph of the author's achievements relates the literary and critical reputation and in the case of recent writers also honors and awards; a biography relates and to a limited extent interprets the life of the author; an analysis surveys and critiques an author's major works and places them in thematic and critical perspective; these are all followed by a list of major publications other than long fiction (quite often a repeat in standard bibliographical form of other literary forms previously mentioned), and a bibliography of secondary studies points the reader toward an in-depth investigation of the author. These entries are informative and accurate, the critical sections very thoughtfully written. There do seem to be more misprints in this set of volumes than in most of the Magill-edited texts, but these are primarily just a nuisance to the reader.

Volume 8 contains 20 essays on such subjects as the history of the novel, the American novel, types of novels (picaresque, epistolary, gothic, western), and the like. These are generally good, workmanlike essays, informative and substantial. The essay on the novella, the longest in the volume (127 pages), traces the sources and follows the development of this form through place and time. It is very informative but is marred by such locutions as "center around," "thrust of the story," and numerous split infinitives, disfigurements that will, of course, not irritate everyone. The author of this essay includes a selective but substantial bibliography of studies of the novella, quite useful to students who wish to pursue the subject.

Volume 8 concludes with a kind of handbook that lists and defines 86 terms such as *defamiliarization, motif,* and *structuralism.*

Critical Survey of Long Fiction is a very useful set of volumes for a library to have, particularly one used by beginning students of literature. Libraries whose clientele comprises high school or college students will find it a good addition to their reference collection. The Board recommends this work for the core collections of public, academic, and school libraries.

Critical Survey of Short Fiction. Frank N. Magill, ed. Salem, 1981, 1987. hard. 7 vols. plus 1 suppl. index. ISBN 0-89356-210-7 (set); 0-89356-218-1 (suppl.) $375 (set); $80 (suppl.). criticism.
PN3321.C7 809.31

See World Literature.

Masterplots II, American Fiction series. Frank N. Magill, ed. Salem, 1986. hard. 4 vols. index. ISBN 0-89356-456-7 (set). $300 (set). handbook.
PN846.M37 809.3

Masterplots II, the successor to *Masterplots,* includes South American and Canadian writers as well as U.S. writers. Magill has made an effort to achieve some racial and minority balance as well, and has entries on works by 53 women and 32 black writers. Another improvement over the original is that the essays are less plot summaries and more critical assessments than in the past. Although there are plot summaries, teachers at every level will much prefer these to the essays in the original *Masterplots.* A note of essential information about the author leads off each entry, followed by the type of plot, time of plot, locale of plot, and when the work was first published. These notes lead into a plot summary of the novel, an analysis of major characters, and a description of themes and meanings that is really an interpretive essay. The editor then puts the novel into its critical context, including critical views of it and its place among the author's other works. Finally, a brief bibliography supplies a few sources for further study. The judgments of the various contributors seem fair and studious. Entries are arranged alphabetically by title of work. An index allows readers to find works whose titles are forgotten or remembered inaccurately by looking up the author's name.

Many of the works selected from the canon of a major author are of the second rank, such as Ernest Hemingway's *Across the River and into the Trees.* Works range from 1900 to 1985 and are chosen from various genres of fiction. Here are, for example, Joyce Carol Oates's *Bellefleur,* Isaac Asimov's *Foundation Trilogy,* and Raymond Chandler's *Farewell, My Lovely.*

Masterplots II is very well done and serves a function in a core collection of American literature reference works. The Board recommends this work for the core collections of public, academic, and school libraries.

Guides

American Authors 1600–1900: A Biographical Dictionary of American Literature, The Authors series, 8th edition. Stanley J. Kunitz and Howard Haycraft, eds. Wilson, 1977. hard. 1 vol. 846 pp. illus. ISBN 0-8242-0001-2. $60. biographical dictionary.
PS21.K8 928

American Authors is a one-volume biographical dictionary first published in 1938 and reissued many times since. It contains entries for "almost 1,300 authors, of both major and minor significance, who participated in the making of our literary history from the time of the first English settlement at Jamestown in 1607 to the close of the nineteenth century" (preface). Entries are arranged alphabetically by author, and range from 150 to 2,500 words in length.

The figures represented in this volume are not limited to authors who may be studied in American literature courses, but also include politicians, clergy members, historians, and others whose published works have had some bearing on American culture, however superficial or temporary. This truly is an A to Z dictionary, beginning with the minor nineteenth-century poet Henry Abbey and concluding with the eighteenth-century journalist and printer John Peter Zenger. For example, there are entries for the naturalists Alexander and Louis Agassiz and John James Audubon. Diplomat John Hay is represented, as are the naval historian Alfred Thayer Mahan and the educator Horace Mann. Members of the illustrious and prolific Adams family who have entries include Abigail, Brooks, Charles Follen, Charles Francis Jr., Hannah, Henry, and Samuel. Of course, the reader will also find substantial entries on the great figures of American literature of this period, including Hawthorne, Melville, Dickinson, James, Twain, and Whitman.

Because *American Authors* has not been revised in the more than 50 years since it first appeared, the book obviously does not reflect recent scholarship or the critical reevaluations of many authors that have taken place over these 50-plus years. The bibliographies of authors' works remain definitive, but the lists of articles and books "about" that follow each entry are rather out of date. The "dated" quality of this reference work also shows through in the editors' often highly personal judgments of their subjects' lives and works. We are told, for example, that Horatio Alger "never grew up. . . . The fat, pale little man with the clouded eyes was the unhappiest creature on earth." Herman Melville is described as "the most neglected of all American geniuses," and "the man who has written the only novel worthy to stand on the pinnacle with *Wuthering Heights,* the man who might be called the American Blake." And "it is unlikely that Whitman ever had a deep emotional interest in any human being except a few younger men . . . and, above all, himself." Yet while such appraisals are out of fashion in reference books in the 1980s, it is precisely such characterizations, at once direct and stylish, that give *American Authors* its color, strength, and authority. The biographical profiles in this work never beat around the bush, are never pedestrian or colorless.

The other great strength of *American Authors* is its comprehensiveness. No other single-volume biographical dictionary on this subject contains as much information on so many figures. Here are obscure and forgotten writers who may only be of interest to the graduate student, but, thanks to the Depression-era scholarship of Kunitz and Haycraft, that student is bound to find useful gems of information on these figures that is not readily available elsewhere. Although the volume does not include an index or table of contents, *American Authors* remains a reference work of first resort. The Board recommends this work for the core collections of public, academic, and school libraries.

American Women Writers: A Critical Reference Guide from Colonial Times to the Present. Lina Mainiero, ed. Ungar, 1979–1982. hard. 4 vols. index. ISBN 0-8044-3150-7 (set). $300 (set). biographical dictionary.
PS147.A4 016.8

American Women Writers: A Critical Reference Guide from Colonial Times to the Present includes more than 1,000 writers of all degrees of skill and from all fields. The four-volume series includes women of all classes, colors, and economic levels. Here are literary artists of critical acclaim such as Louisa May Alcott, Emily Dickinson, Lorraine Hansberry, Sylvia Plath, and Katherine Anne Porter; popular writers such as Grace Livingstone Hill and Gene Stratton-Porter; nontraditional writers of letters, diaries, and biographies such as Louisa Adams and Elizabeth Hawthorne; children's writers of critical acclaim and authors of well-known stories such as Frances Hodgson Burnett, Eleanor Porter, and Kate Douglas Wiggin; and essayists such as Rachel Carson, Suzanne K. Langer, and Margaret Mead.

The entries are generally from one to two pages in length. Biographical details are included, but the main focus is on the writer's work, not her life. Each entry concludes with a list of the author's works, plus a bibliography of selected works about her. The entries are signed, and all the contributors, apparently, are women; most are university teachers or writers themselves. The entries are concise and to the point. In fact, at times there seems to be an effort to be blunt and bluff, as in this statement about Sylvia Plath: "P. [all authors are referred to by the initial of their last name] gassed herself at the age of thirty-one."

The problem of what name to list the women under (in the case of women who write under their married names or use pseudonyms) is solved by following the practice of the Library of Congress in cataloging the subject. Each volume contains in its front matter a list of "Writers Included" that covers all the writers contained in the four volumes with cross-references to the name used for the entry. The index in the final volume also supplies cross-references. Grace Livingstone, for example, married Frank Hill. After Hill died, she married Flavius Lutz. She wrote most of her novels as Grace Livingstone Hill, but she also wrote as Grace Livingstone Hill Lutz and as Marcia MacDonald, her mother's maiden name. Readers familiar with her work under the name of Hill would not find her entry except by chance without looking in the index or the list of

"Writers Included." The index includes no titles of literary works so that a reader who remembers titles but not authors must first find the name of the author in another reference work and then return to *American Women Writers.* Who wrote *Pollyanna,* for example, or *Girl of the Limberlost?* Quite often when people read these they are at an age when the least interesting thing about the book is who wrote it.

Despite these quibbles *American Women Writers* is an important work. The Board recommends this work for the core collections of public and academic libraries.

American Writers: A Collection of Literary Biographies. Leonard Unger and A. Walton Litz, eds. Scribner, 1974–1981. 4 vols. plus 2 suppls. (each in 2 vols). index. ISBN 0-684-17322-0 (set). $625 (set). biographical dictionary.
PS129.A55 810.9

According to the opening comments in the introduction, the essays in *American Writers: A Collection of Literary Biographies* are intended for a wide audience from scholars to general readers, including young readers in high schools and colleges. They derive from essays written and published as the "University of Minnesota Pamphlets on American Writers" (1959–1972). In some cases, the pamphlets have been revised for publication in these volumes and are reprinted in their entirety.

Each essay of 20 to 25 pages is evaluative and interpretive as well as factual and is followed by a "Selected Bibliography" of both primary and secondary works. The essays are arranged alphabetically by subject. For example, volume 1 begins with an essay on historian Henry Adams by Louis Auchincloss, and volume 4 ends with an essay on novelist Richard Wright by Robert Bone. The index to volume 4 lists names and titles appearing throughout the four volumes. Leonard Unger's introduction itself is a brief essay that surveys some of the generalizations about American writers.

Supplement 1, which appeared in 1979, extends the range of the earlier volumes and includes a larger proportion of black and women writers than the previous volumes. Again, essays in these two volumes range over the whole history of American literature from colonial poet Anne Bradstreet to contemporary novelist Toni Morrison. The authors of the essays in this supplement are all "new," with only one essay by each.

Supplement 2 was published in 1981 with much the same intent as were the original four volumes and supplement 1. Although supplement 2 emphasizes contemporary writers (and also attempts to improve the representation of black and women writers), it too ranges over American history with essays on clergyman Cotton Mather and poet Philip Freneau of the colonial era and on novelists Joyce Carol Oates and Thomas Pynchon of the twentieth century. One innovation of supplement 2 is to include essays on writers like R. P. Blackmur and Lewis Mumford, literary critic and social historian, respectively. Essays in both supplements, like those in the original volumes, are also evaluative and interpretive. All the essays in *American Writers,* it might be added, are well written and interesting but are not more "authoritative" than other thoughtful, well-written essays.

These four volumes and two supplements of *American Writers* are probably a good set for all libraries to own. Academic libraries should have them just to have the additional critical assessments of writers in one series to supplement the various collections of critical articles shelved throughout their holdings. The style of the essays, plain and straightforward prose that avoids the esoteric, makes *American Writers* attractive also to public libraries. The Board recommends this work for the core collections of public and academic libraries.

Contemporary Authors: A Bio-Bibliographical Guide to Current Writers in Fiction, General Nonfiction, Poetry, Journalism, Drama, Motion Pictures, Television, and Other Fields. Hal May and Susan Trosky, eds. Gale, 1962–. hard. 129 vols. 503 pp. index in even-numbered volumes. ISBN 0-8103-1954-3 (vol. 129). $99 (vol. 129). biobibliography.
PN771.C66X 928.1

See Biography.

Contemporary Authors, New Revision series. Hal May and James J. Lesniak, eds. Gale, 1990. hard. 30 vols. index in even-numbered volumes. ISBN 0-8103-1984-5 (vol. 30). $99 per vol. biobibliography.
Z1224.C62X 803

The New Revision series of *Contemporary Authors* was devised to avoid the expensive and often unnecessary method of unit revision by which Gale Research Company had previously revised and published all biographical sketches in a given volume. For example, according to Ann Evory, who edited the first volumes of this new series, *Contemporary Authors* volumes 41 to 44, First Revision, contained revised versions of all the 2,252 sketches that appeared in the original volumes.

The New Revision series only includes *revised* sketches of authors whose careers have developed significantly since their original appearance in an earlier edition of the First Revision series was last published. The New Revision series, therefore, replaces *no* earlier volumes of *Contemporary Authors;* and consequently, libraries should maintain most of the Permanent series (volumes of which are still being published). To aid reference librarians in that task, a chart at the end of the preface in each New Revision series volume shows which of the previous volumes may be safely discarded.

Information in each biographical sketch follows the order employed in previous volumes, an obvious and logical choice since these sketches are merely updatings of earlier ones. The arrangement of the data, which seems logical and sensible, follows:

- Personal—family, education, current address.
- Career—employment history, memberships, awards.
- Writings—a full bibliography, including edited works.
- Work in Progress—data revealing changes in interests or lack of change.
- Sidelights—comments by the author, critics, and reviewers along with editorial comments by the compilers or contributing editors.
- Biographical/Critical Sources—bibliography of secondary source materials.

Entries are alphabetical in each volume, making a volume index unnecessary. But each author entry is indexed in the latest *even-numbered* volume of the Permanent series. Thus to find a specific author in a volume, one must look in the index of the latest even-numbered volume. Even if the author one seeks is *not* in the New Revision series, the index in the Permanent series will list all the volumes of the complete *Contemporary Authors* in which a sketch for that author appears, a very useful, even essential, feature.

Because most of the authors represented in *Contemporary Authors,* New Revision series, are Americans, it is not too much to say it belongs in a core collection of reference works on American literature. The Board recommends this work for the core collections of public, academic, and school libraries.

Supplementary Titles

Criticism

American and British Poetry: A Guide to the Criticism, 1925–1978. Harriet Semmes Alexander. Swallow, 1984. hard. 1 vol. 486 pp. appendixes. ISBN 0-0840-0848-5. bibliography.
Z1231.P7A44 [P5303] 821.008

American and British Poetry: A Guide to the Criticism, 1925–1978 "covers critical references to poets from Spenser to Dickey. Criticism has been included only of poems up to 1,000 lines long. Generally, only criticism or explanations have been included if little information was found on a given poem or the criticism was especially significant. Books on specific poets were not included in the sources. . . . Arrangement is alphabetical by the poet's name and then by title of poem. Books and journals cited are listed at the back of the volume." (*Choice,* December 1984, p. 531)

Also reviewed in: *LJ,* December 1984, p. 2263.

Board's recommendation: Public and academic libraries.

American Drama Criticism: Interpretations 1890–1977, 2d edition. Floyd Eugene Eddleman, ed. Shoe String, 1979. hard. 1 vol. plus 2 suppl. 488 pp. (2d). appendixes. index. ISBN 0-208-01713-5 (2d); 0-208-01978-2 (suppl. 1); 0-208-02139 (suppl. 2). $42.50 (2d); $34.50 (suppl. 1); $42.50 (suppl. 2). bibliography.
Z1231.D7P3[PS332] 016.792

American Drama Criticism: Interpretations 1890–1977 includes "critiques and reviews of American plays appearing in some 200 books and monographs and in more than 400 periodicals. Published primarily between 1890 and 1977, these items are arranged by playwright and then by play title. . . . Excluded from this edition are interviews, biographies, author bibliographies, listings on non-American dramatists, nondramatic works of playwrights, and newspaper references. Added, usefully, for musicals are the names of all authors: of the book, lyrics, and music." (*ARBA,* 1980, p. 451)

Also reviewed in: *WLB,* February 1980, p. 398.

Board's recommendation: Public and academic libraries.

Drama

Twentieth-Century American Dramatists. John MacNicholas. Gale, 1981. hard. 2 vols. 345 pp. (vol. 1); 475 pp. (vol. 2). illus. appendix. index. ISBN 0-8103-0928-9 (set). $206 (set). biographical source.
PS129.D5XV.7 812.509

"The lives and works of 78 twentieth-century American dramatists are examined in *Twentieth-Century American Dramatists* . . . [which] is part of Gale's

Dictionary of Literary Biography series. *Twentieth-Century American Dramatists* focuses on 19 major and 57 lesser-known American playwrights whose works have been published since 1900. . . . Entries are arranged alphabetically and vary in length from a few pages . . . to between 20 and 30 pages. . . . Critical essays are preceded by a list of the playwright's works (both plays and books). . . . Primary bibliographies. . . . provide a list of the dramatists' works other than their original book-length writings. Secondary bibliographies include titles [of]. . . . the most relevant books and articles. . . . illustrated." (*ARBA,* 1982, p. 651)

Board's recommendation: Public, academic, and school libraries.

Fiction

Dickinson's American Historical Fiction. Virginia Brokaw Gerhardstein. Scarecrow, 1986. hard. 1 vol. 352 pp. index. ISBN 0-8108-1867-1. $32.50. bibliography.
Z1231.F4D47 [PS374.M5] 016.813

Dickinson's American Historical Fiction "lists 3,048 novels published between 1917 and 1984, and it also includes 'authors and titles from the past that have come to be standard names in historical fiction regardless of publication date.' Brief descriptive . . . annotations follow the standard bibliographical information of each entry. . . . Ending the bibliography are two indexes—one for authors and titles and one for subjects that are keyed to entry numbers of each citation." (*BL,* October 15, 1986, p. 334)

Board's recommendation: Public, academic, and school libraries.

Guides

The Concise Oxford Companion to American Literature. James D. Hart. Oxford, 1986. hard and soft. 1 vol. 497 pp. appendix. index. ISBN 0-19-503982-3 (hard); 0-19-504771-0 (soft). $24.95 (hard); $13.95 (soft). handbook.
PS21.H32 810.9

The Concise Oxford Companion to American Literature is an abridgment of the fifth edition of the *Oxford Companion to American Literature.* "All the plot summaries seem to be here and remain some of the most carefully written to be found anywhere. . . . Much has been deleted however. . . . The listing of Pulitzer Prize winners found in the fifth edition has been omitted, but the excellent 'Chronological Index' included in the parent work is complete and updated through 1985. In addition, some entries have been updated. . . . This concise guide to American Literature is carefully edited and is a most attractive book. As in the parent work, typography aids use." (*BL,* January 15, 1987, p. 766)

Board's recommendation: Public, academic, and school libraries.

Modern American Literature, 4th edition. Dorothy Nyren Curley, Maurice Kramer, and Elaine Fialka Kramer, comps. and eds. Ungar, 1969. hard. 3 vols. plus 2 suppls. index. ISBN 0-8044-3046-2 (set); 0-8044-3050-0 (suppl. 1); 0-8044-3265-1 (suppl. 2). $225 (set); $75 (suppl. 1); $75 (suppl. 2). handbook.
PS221.C8 810.9

Modern American Literature, fourth edition, a "very valuable source book and index[,] excerpts hundreds of critical books, essays, articles, and reviews dealing with the works of nearly 300 important 20th-Century American novelists, poets, dramatists, and essayists with citations to original sources. . . . A judiciously chosen representative survey of and key to modern criticism of American authors of our century." (*LJ,* September 15, 1969, p. 3039)

Board's recommendation: Public, academic, and school libraries.

The Oxford Companion to American Literature, 5th edition. James D. Hart, ed. Oxford, 1983. hard. 1 vol. 896 pp. ISBN 0-19-503074-5. $49.95 handbook.
PS21.H3 810.9

A reviewer of the fourth edition of *The Oxford Companion to American Literature* wrote: "this edition of a standard 'companion' has added 223 authors, 62 summaries, . . . and rewritten the entries of 343 authors carried over from the third edition (1956). Though this is a definite edition, it supplements rather than supersedes earlier editions; for the substance of this reference work has withstood time and tastes since its first edition (1941)." (*Choice,* June 1966, p. 291)

Also reviewed in: *AB,* October 11, 1965, p. 1325; *ABC,* March 1966, p. 6; *AL,* March 1966, p. 6; *BL,* February 1, 1966, p. 493; *CC,* November 3, 1965, p. 1355; *Econ,* July 9, 1966, p. 154; *Ga R,* Fall 1966, p. 371; *KR,* August 1, 1965, p. 804; September 1, 1965, p. 923; *Lib,* September 1967, p. 273; *LJ,* November 15, 1965, p. 4952; *NYT,* November 2, 1965, p. 35M; *SA,* February 1966, p. 34; *SAQ,* Summer 1966, p. 418; *SR,* March 19, 1966, p. 36; *TLS,* June 23, 1966, p. 556; *WLB,* December 1965, p. 367.

Board's recommendation: Public, academic, and school libraries.

Poetry

Critical Survey of Poetry, English Language series. Frank N. Magill, ed. Salem, 1983, hard. 8 vols. plus 1 suppl. 3,753 pp. (8 vols); 411 pp. (suppl.). index. ISBN 0-89356-340-4 (set); 089356-349-8 (suppl.). $375 (set); $80 (suppl.). criticism.
PR502.C85 (set) 809.1
PN1021.C7 (suppl.)

See British Literature.

New and Noteworthy

African American Writers. Valerie Smith, A. Walton Litz, and Lea Baechler. Scribner, 1990. hard. 1 vol. 540 pp. ISBN 0-684-19058-3. $75. biography.

In *African American Writers,* "the essence of the African American spirit is revealed through 34 essays on the lives and literary achievements of authors from the colonial times to the present, including such well-known figures as James Baldwin, Ralph Ellison, Langston Hughes, and Toni Morrison. Authors less likely to be found as widely . . . are also included." (Excerpted from publisher's announcement)

Biographical Dictionary of Hispanic Literature in the United States: The Literature of Puerto Ricans, Cuban Americans, and Other Hispanic Writers. Nicholas Kanellos. Greenwood, 1989. hard. 1 vol. 357 pp. index. ISBN 0-313-24465-0. $49.95. biographical dictionary.
PQ7420.2.K3 016.86'09

In its introduction, the *Biographical Dictionary of Hispanic Literature in the United States* "gives an overview of Puerto Rican literature and then of Cuban American and Cuban exile literature, presenting the historical development of each and placing writers in context. The entry for each writer includes a biography, major themes, survey of criticism, and bibliography of works by and about the author." (*BL,* November 1, 1989, p. 600)

Black American Women in Literature: A Bibliography. Ronda Glikin. McFarland, 1989. hard. 1 vol. 251 pp. appendixes. index. ISBN 0-89950-241-5. $35. bibliography.
Z1229.N39657 016.810809

Black American Women in Literature "names works by and about some 300 writers of essays, poetry, novels, short stories, and plays. . . . Appendix A: 'Works about Black Women Writers' and Appendix B: 'Authors by Genre' identify the collective body of material that has already been published in this area and combine to make this a guide to the literature as well." (*Choice,* October 1989, p. 286)

Black Writers: A Selection of Sketches from Contemporary Authors. Linda Metzger, s.ed. Gale, 1989. hard. 1 vol. 619 pp. ISBN 0-8103-2772-4. $80. biographical dictionary.
PN490.B53 810.9'896

"Biographical and bibliographical information on more than 400 black authors active during the 20th century are found in [*Black Writers*]. . . . Individuals . . . who have written books but are better known for their activities in political or social areas, are also included. The table of contents contains a brief but helpful description of each writer." (*SLJ,* May 1990, p. 28)

Dictionary of American Literary Characters. Benjamin V. Franklin. Facts On File, 1989. hard. 1 vol. 512 pp. index. ISBN 0-8160-1917-7. $60. dictionary.
PS374.C4305 813.009230

The *Dictionary of American Literary Characters* "lists alphabetically more than 11,000 American literary characters taken from significant popular novels as well as from the works of major authors. Entries are brief . . . and meticulously objective. A three-level index lists the authors represented, their novels, and the characters themselves." (*LJ,* August 1989, p. 122)

Guide to American Poetry Explication, Colonial and Nineteenth-Century. James Ruppert. G. K. Hall, 1989. hard. 1 vol. 239 pp. ISBN 0-8161-8919-6. $40. bibliography.
Z1231.P7R66 016.811'009

Guide to American Poetry Explication, Modern and Contemporary. John R. Leo. G. K. Hall, 1989. hard. 1 vol. 546 pp. ISBN 0-8161-8918-9. $50. bibliography.
Z1231.P7L46 016.811'509

Volumes 1 and 2 of the *Guide to American Poetry Explication* are part of "a projected five-volume set that revises *Poetry Explication: A Checklist of Interpretation Since 1925.* . . . The other three volumes will cover British poetry. . . . Entries are arranged by the poet's name, then by the poem, and finally by the last name of the critic." (*BL,* October 1, 1989, p. 392)

Literature in America: An Illustrated History. Peter Conn. Cambridge, 1989. hard. 1 vol. 587 pp. illus. index. ISBN 0-521-30373-7. $29.95. history.
PS88.C65 810.9

Literature in America "weaves together biography and critical analysis into a rich and entertaining essay. . . . Most useful is the information about the authors' styles, motivations, and the contributions to the 'schools,' movements, and periods in the development of American literature. A rather lengthy bibliography provides additional sources for general literary history, biographical information on authors, and material relating to the specific chapters." (*SLJ,* May 1990, p. 30)

Modern American Women Writers. E. Showalter, A. W. Litz, and L. Baechler. Scribner, 1990. hard. 1 vol. 500 pp. ISBN 0-684-19057-5. $75. biography.

"Recorded here [in *Modern American Women Writers*] are the lives and literary contributions of 41 representative American women writers from Emily Dickinson to present-day authors. Many are . . . popular and as well known . . .—but some are as controversial as Mary McCarthy [and] Dorothy Parker." (Excerpted from publisher's announcement)

Roth's American Poetry Annual: A Reference Guide to Poetry Published in the United States. Roth, 1989. hard. 1 vol. 727 pp. index. ISBN 0-89609-285-2. guide.
PS507.S8272 811.008

Roth's American Poetry Annual "incorporates three former titles [*The Annual Survey of American Poetry, The Annual Index to Poetry in Periodicals,* and *American Poetry Index*] . . . [and] functions as one sourcebook of poetry for the year. [This work contains] an anthology of . . . poems, . . . [and sections entitled] 'American Books and Articles about Poetry and Poets,' 'Grants, Fellowships, Writing Colonies, and Schools,' 'Supporting Organizations and Newsletters,' and 'Periodicals and Publishers.' " (*Choice,* October 1989, p. 292)

Susan M. Allen

Ancient and Classical Literature

See also Folklore and Mythology

Studied under the rubric of "the Classics" is everything that is now known of the people of the Mediterranean until about A.D. 500, or the reign of Justinian. Traditionally this meant only the study of their languages and literature—Greek and Latin—and their philosophy, religion, and history as expressed in the writings of classical authors. The object of an education in the classics was to achieve command of the languages and a knowledge of a fixed set of texts. But in the last 100 years, the emphasis has shifted from language proficiency in Greek and Latin to the study of literature in translation and the civilization, augmented by information from the fields of archaeology, anthropology, and art history. Material evidence has come to stand side by side with the written word. As a consequence, there has been a necessary shift in emphasis in reference sources toward secondary source material and classical literature in translation. Contemporary reference collections must reflect this change in emphasis in order to serve their patrons, whether they be the general public, high school students, or advanced scholars.

Harper's Dictionary of Classical Literature and Antiquities, edited by H. T. Peck, was perhaps one of the first reference books written to help students study the classics from this new perspective. Peck wrote in the preface to the first edition (1896): "Even the undergraduate Classical courses in our universities and colleges . . . are no longer restricted to the mere reading of ancient authors and the formal study of their language. An early familiarity with the conditions of ancient life is expected . . .; some knowledge of art and archaeology is a further requisite; and at least a moderate acquaintance with the best and most obvious sources of information is asked of all. It is, therefore, evident that to aid the student . . . some manual is needed." His dictionary was just such a "manual." A second edition appeared in 1897, and it was reprinted throughout much of the twentieth century.

Ironically, as time passed, the important bibliographic entries Peck included as a key to the secondary literature became sadly dated. In the early 1980s the dictionary went out of print, and the other reference tools reviewed here have filled the void it left. Those librarians who still have *Harper's Dictionary* in their collections would do well to retain it for its coverage of biography, mythology, history, and literature. THE OXFORD CLASSICAL DICTIONARY or the two-volume THE CAMBRIDGE HISTORY OF CLASSICAL LITERATURE—or both—could be added for more current bibliographical coverage. (The latter will require a larger investment of precious acquisition funds.) GREEK AND LATIN AUTHORS 800 B.C.–A.D. 1000 stands alone in

Core Titles

	PUBLIC	ACADEMIC	SCHOOL
Ancient Writers: Greece and Rome, 2 vols. Luce, T. James, ed. in chief. Scribner, 1982	✦	✦	✦
The Cambridge History of Classical Literature, 2 vols. Easterling, P. E., et al., eds. Cambridge, 1982–1985	✦	✦	
Greek and Latin Authors 800 B.C.–A.D. 1000 Grant, Michael. Wilson, 1980	✦	✦	✦
The Oxford Classical Dictionary, 2d edition Hammond, N. G. L., and H. H. Scullard, eds. Clarendon/Oxford, 1970	✦	✦	
The Oxford Companion to Classical Literature, 2d edition Howatson, M. C., ed. Oxford, 1989	✦	✦	✦

providing coverage to the year A.D. 1000, and with ANCIENT WRITERS: GREECE AND ROME would provide for ready reference as well as meet more in-depth biographical information needs. *Crowell's Handbook of Classical Drama,* by Richmond Y. Hawthorn (Crowell, 1967), *Crowell's Handbook of Classical Literature,* by Lillian Feder (Crowell, 1974), and the *Dictionary of Greek and Roman Biography and Mythology,* edited by William Smith (Little, Brown, 1890; reprinted by AMS, 1967), have gone out of print. However, they remain authoritative, and if they can be obtained they should be included for the accessibility to the subject matter they provide to a general audience.

Core Titles

Ancient Writers: Greece and Rome. T. James Luce, ed. in chief. Scribner, 1982. hard. 2 vols. 1,148 pp. illus. index. ISBN 0-684-16595-3 (set). $160 (set). criticism.
PA3002.A5 880.09

Ancient Writers: Greece and Rome is a compilation of 47 signed biographical essays on the chief literary figures of the ancient world born before the middle of the fourth century A.D. These essays have been written entirely by classics scholars, mostly at American institutions of higher education, with outstanding records of publication, including translations.

The work contains a list of subjects (table of contents), an introduction by the editor, chronological table, list of contributors with reference to their publications, critical essays on individual writers, and an index. The chronological table is laid out in three columns—time period, historical periods and events, and writers' names and dates, respectively. These columns are aligned in such a way as to make clear the historical period in which each writer flourished.

The somewhat lengthy essays were not intended to follow a rigid formula. "The aim here has been rather for the authors to write personal, even idiosyncratic, essays in order to show what in their eyes constitute the significant achievements of the writers of the ancient world" (introduction). The length of the essays ranges from a low of 10 pages ("Josephus") to a high of more than 50 pages ("Aeschylus"). Most are critical accounts of individual writers, although a few encompass two or more individuals. Quality varies, to be sure, but a certain uniformity is imposed by the selected bibliography that completes each essay. These bibliographies usually list English translations, Greek or Latin editions, and modern works through the 1970s. The essays are arranged according to the chronological table; pagination is continuous. For the most effective use, both volumes must be available.

To overcome the awkwardness of two volumes, created by a text too lengthy to fit in one book, the names of ancient writers included in each volume are listed on the spine and the front cover of each volume. This handy external "table of contents" facilitates movement between the volumes. Internally, the text of the essays is laid out in two readable columns, and ample white space surrounding the type block adds to the legibility.

Ancient Writers: Greece and Rome is quite useful for those who require in-depth information about early Greek and Roman writers. The Board recommends this work for the core collections of public, academic, and school libraries.

The Cambridge History of Classical Literature. P. E. Easterling and B. M. W. Knox, eds., vol. 1. E. J. Kenney, ed., and W. V. Clausen, adv. ed., vol. 2. Cambridge, 1982–1985. hard and soft. 2 vols (hard); 6 vols. (soft). 1,910 pp. illus. appendixes. index. ISBN 0-521-21042-9 (vol. 1, hard); 0-521-21043-7 (vol. 2, hard). $97.50 (vol. 1, hard); $122.50 (vol. 2, hard). criticism.
PA3001 (vol. 1) 880.09 (vol. 1)
PA6003.L3 (vol. 2) 870.9 (vol. 2)

The scholarly stamp of the Cambridge University Press is evident throughout the two-volume *Cambridge History of Classical Literature.* The general editors of the series are fellows of Cambridge University, the Center for Hellenic Studies in Washington, D.C., and Harvard University, respectively. Volume 1, *Greek Literature,* has a few more contributions from American scholars than British, while volume 2, *Latin Literature,* is dominated by contributions from faculty of British institutions. Whether British or American, most contributors come from prestigious universities known for the high quality of their classics departments.

The hefty volumes are sturdily bound; paper and typography are pleasing to the eye, especially in volume 1, where a clear, legible typeface is used for Greek characters. However, in both volumes the illustrations are lost in the many pages of text and might have been omitted. As they stand in obscurity, they seem an afterthought.

The content of both volumes follows the same format. Preliminary pages consist of a table of contents, a listing of plates, a preface, and a list of abbreviations. The text, which forms the bulk of each volume, consists of critical essays on classical writers and literary genres written by the large group of contributors mentioned previously. Individual works are not treated in separate essays, but are discussed under the genre subheadings devoted to specific writers. For example, in volume 1, chapter 6, entitled "Monody," the user will find a definition and historical background of the form, brief biographies of the writers Sappho, Alcaeus, Ibycus, and Anacreon, who were its leading proponents, and an analysis of their poetic works as they relate to the form of monody. Introductory essays to various genres are usually five to ten pages long. Other essays average from 20 to 30 pages in length.

These essays represent "the results of recent and current scholarship" (preface). Volume 1, *Greek Literature,* pays particular attention "to texts discovered in recent years" (preface). In both volumes, a loose chronological arrangement unites the essays. The history, background of events, and general culture of the classical world "have had to be treated only incidentally" (preface). Following the text are two appendixes. Biographical details and complete bibliographical listings for each author, including texts, commentaries, and criticism are given in the "Appendix of Authors and Works." The "Metrical Appendix" in each volume spells out this crucial aspect of Greek or Latin versification; however, at least some familiarity with the language is required to use each appendix. "Works Cited in the Text," a listing of the secondary literature cited in the essays, seems to be as current as 1983 for volume 1, published in 1985, while volume 2, published in 1982, is no more current than 1979. The index for each volume gives access to all material on a given writer that may be spread throughout the essays and appendixes.

Cambridge University Press has also issued a six-volume paperback edition of this two-volume work. The prefaces from both hardcover volumes are omitted, as are the first chapters in each volume (which provide historical background). The remaining chapters, as divided, emphasize the genre approach to the material. According to an editorial note, the paperback edition updates, where available, bibliographic information and sources of original text. The multivolume approach allows the individual user to focus on specific genres and time periods, but the two-volume hardcover edition will probably be the version preferred by most libraries.

As a comparative literary history, *The Cambridge History of Classical Literature* will serve the serious researcher well, providing current critical views and bibliographic access to the primary and secondary sources. It will however, prove less helpful as a ready-reference tool to the librarian or general reader, who may refer to it infrequently. The Board recommends this work for the core collections of public and academic libraries.

Greek and Latin Authors 800 B.C.–A.D. 1000. Michael Grant. Wilson, 1980. hard. 1 vol. 490 pp. illus. appendixes. ISBN 0-8242-0640-1. $49. biographical dictionary.
PA31.G7 880.9[920]

Greek and Latin Authors 800 B.C.–A.D. 1000 was written by Michael Grant, an extensively published, British classics historian. The work fits into the Wilson Authors series as a biographical dictionary covering the classical period to A.D. 1000, linking the ancient world to the next volume in the series, *European Authors 1000–1900.* Most reference tools in the classics cover very little beyond A.D. 300 or 400 (or the advent of the Christian world); Grant's work, covering seven more centuries (the so-called Dark Ages), is much more comprehensive.

The volume includes a "List of Authors Included"; "List of Illustrations with Credits"; preface; "Key to Pronounciation"; "Biographical Sketches"; some 480 pages of the body of the work; and two appendixes: "Works of Doubtful Attribution" and "Chronological List of Authors Arranged by Century." Each of the more than 370 biographical sketches generally consists of five or six elements. The life of the figure—poet, philosopher, dramatist, historian, or scientist—is recounted concisely. When an artistic representation of the person exists, a photograph of this is reproduced. The writer's works are then listed and described, followed by commentary and a discussion of their influence. The entry concludes with a bibliographical listing of works, including translations, editions, and some critical studies. References are made to modern editions and related works published in the 1960s and 1970s (the publication date of this volume is 1980). Each entry is roughly 1,000 to 4,000 words in length.

Because the period A.D. 300 to A.D. 1000 is included, many more Roman figures appear than one might expect in a work entitled *Greek and Latin Authors.* For example, entries appear for well-known figures such as *Saint Ambrose, Saint Augustine, Eusebius, Saint Hilary, Saint Jerome, Saint Benedict, and Boethius.*

The relatively large typeface makes this volume particularly easy to read. Entry headings and running heads are set off in boldface type; generous white space punctuates the end of each entry. The brief bibliographical listings are set off from the body of the entry by appearing in smaller typeface—the standard style for the Wilson Authors series.

Greek and Latin Authors 800 B.C.–A.D. 1000 provides coverage for a variety of well-known and lesser-known literary figures of this period. The Board recommends this work for the core collections of public, academic, and school libraries.

The Oxford Classical Dictionary, 2d edition. N. G. L. Hammond and H. H. Scullard, eds. Clarendon/ Oxford, 1970. hard. 1 vol. 1,198 pp. appendix. indexes. ISBN 0-19-869117-3. $49.95. dictionary.
DE5.09 913.38003

The Oxford Classical Dictionary, now in its second edition, continues to live up to the fine reputation of other Oxford University Press publications. In order to bring the dictionary up to date in terms of current scholarship (circa 1970), the editors decided that every article in the original edition should be either revised or replaced. Therefore, many new articles, signed by scholars, appear in the second edition. Those that were revised carry both the initials of the original contributor and those of the contributor responsible for the revision. According to the editors, the briefest entries, "which were merely cross references for the most part," were dropped to make room for new entries (preface).

The contents include prefaces from the first and second editions; a list of abbreviations used in the present work; the body of the dictionary; a general bibliography; an index of names that are not titles of entries; and an index to initials of contributors.

The dictionary is arranged alphabetically by topic. Entries range in length from the two or three lines that one will find for *Capys,* a companion of Aenaeas, to the nine or ten pages for *Rome.* The entry for Rome covers the history of the Empire from the Bronze Age through its fall (A.D. 330). *Women, positions of* is given about one page. This entry presents a chronological review of the position of women in Greece and Rome as well as philosophers' views of women's roles in society.

More space has been given in this edition to archaeological background; to places, peoples, and persons; and to the later portion of the Roman Empire than in the previous edition. However, the emphasis remains on the biographical information and literary terminology. The bibliographies accompanying longer entries are up to date to the years 1967–1968 when this edition went into production. The more general bibliography that appears as an appendix lists works "currently in use in 1969." The index of names (added for the first time in this edition) improves access to the volume by cross-referencing names that appear within entries but not as headings. Cross-references within entries are given as "see" references. Small capital letters are used for the entry being cross-referenced.

The book is a comfortable size. Although the light weight of the paper and the small size of the typeface are annoying, their use prevents the book, which is already more than 1,100 pages long, from being cumbersome. Other elements of the design live up to the customary high standards of the Oxford University Press.

The Oxford Classical Dictionary is a general but scholarly work that covers every aspect of ancient Greek and Roman life. The Board recommends this work for the core collections of public and academic libraries.

The Oxford Companion to Classical Literature, 2d edition. M. C. Howatson, ed. Oxford, 1989. hard. 1 vol. 627 pp. illus. appendixes. ISBN 0-19-866121-5. $39.95. dictionary.
PA31.H69 880.9′001

The first edition of *The Oxford Companion to Classical Literature* was edited by Sir Paul Harvey and published in 1937. This second edition, selected by M. C. Howatson (Fellow, St. Anne's College, Oxford University), maintains the high standard set by Harvey and the Oxford University Press.

The text is organized into four parts: the preface; main text; a chronological table; and maps. The preface, written by Howatson, indicates that the dictionary is not limited to books and authors but rather "is for any reader who is curious to find out about the classical world." As a consequence, the text retains Harvey's summaries of books and biographical entries and adds entries that illuminate the culture, history, geography, philosophy, and political institutions of the ancient world for readers who may not have studied Greek or Latin. For example, there are lengthy entries (seven to ten paragraphs) for *women, position of* and *education,* as well as *Homeric Age, money and coins,* and entries for important cities, regions, and groups of people. The knowledge gained from recent archaeological discoveries is incorporated into entries, as the entry on *Linear A and B* attests.

The 605 pages of entries are followed by a chronological table, which places a timeline of major historical events beside one on literature that gives the dates for authors and their books. The maps section completes the volume with six maps illustrating Asia Minor and the Middle East, Greece and the Aegean Islands, Italy, the Western Roman Empire, and Roman Britain. Only places mentioned in the companion section are indicated on the maps.

Physically, the volume can be immediately identified as a well-made product of the Oxford University Press. Sound binding, good-quality paper, and printing in a legible typeface all work together to form a book that will last and be easily read. The contents are readily accessible through the double-column format of the body of the text. Simple and attractive section headings, entry headings in boldface type, and "see also" references (indicated by an asterisk placed before the word or name referenced) contribute to the ease with which this work may be used. Entries are arranged alphabetically.

The depth of information presented so concisely, combined with the format's ease of use, makes *The Oxford Companion to Classical Literature* invaluable for reference librarians and students alike. The Board recommends this work for the core collections of public, academic, and school libraries.

New and Noteworthy

Classical Greek and Roman Drama. Robert J. Forman. St. John's Univ. Pr., 1989. hard. 1 vol. 200 pp. ISBN 0-89356-659-4. $40. criticism.
PA3024.F57

"The comprehensive introduction [to *Classical Greek and Roman Drama*] thoughtfully examines the evolution of classical drama, providing a firm grounding for the student. The works selected include the best-known works of the classical Greek and Roman theater. . . . The bibliography is arranged alphabetically by author and title. . . . There are citations pointing the student to the best available translations of these plays." (Excerpted from publisher's announcement)

A Concise Dictionary of Classical Mythology. Pierre Grimal. Basil Blackwell, 1990. hard. 1 vol. 350 pp. illus. index. ISBN 0-631-16696-3. $34.95. dictionary.
BL715.G713 292.13

"*A Concise Dictionary of Classical Mythology* is a distillation into brief form of the leading single source dictionary of ancient Greek and Roman myths and legends. . . . The concise version covers virtually all major characters, and eight genealogical tables present the principal complex relationships between gods and men. . . . The entries concentrate on principal versions of each legend, and only the most significant variations are covered." (Excerpted from publisher's announcement)

Laura Hibbets McCaffery

Ancient History

See also World History

Ancient history covers the period from the time ancient peoples mastered the art of writing, and therefore were able to set down a record of history, into the fourth and fifth centuries of the Roman Empire, although the end date varies among historians. Prehistory is often included in treatments of this subject because the foundations for the ancient civilizations were established then. The geographic emphasis given to the subject in libraries is generally Rome, Greece, and the civilizations of the Near East as they existed at that time. Although libraries are slowly including other areas of the world due to growing awareness of the achievements of other civilizations, this Eurocentric treatment still exists.

As with any field, the needs of users of an ancient history collection vary with age and interests. A considerable amount of information will be found at all levels in such standard general reference tools as encyclopedias, biographical sources, and bibliographies.

The core and supplementary reference works described in this category are devoted specifically to ancient history and its constituent parts. THE CAMBRIDGE ANCIENT HISTORY SERIES is an essential title for academic and large public libraries. The broad scope, detailed bibliographies, numerous maps, chronologies, illustrations, and genealogies will satisfy many needs in this area. While there are no good multivolume encyclopedias on ancient history in the English language, THE OXFORD CLASSICAL DICTIONARY (see Ancient and Classical Literature) includes good survey articles on Greek and Roman life, law, economy, and other aspects of their history. Similar treatment on a wider scope will be found in the superb GREAT EVENTS FROM HISTORY, edited by Frank Magill. The need for historical maps, geographical place names, biographical data, date information, and pictorial materials can be met through the atlases, biographical dictionaries, and chronology reviewed in this category.

Bibliographies and indexes to the literature are of great importance in academic libraries, particularly to history majors and professors and to any students doing research papers. The standard work in this area is *L'Année Philologique: Bibliographie Critique et Analytique de L'Antiquité Gréco-Latine,* which is international in scope but in the French language. While no similar work exists in English, several broader titles serve the user in search of articles and books in ancient history. These include the bibliographies in Magill's GREAT EVENTS FROM HISTORY and THE CAMBRIDGE ANCIENT HISTORY SERIES, which are particularly useful. Also of value to the researcher are: the now out-of-print American Historical Association's *Guide to Historical Literature;* the *Social Sciences Citation Index;* the *Arts & Humanities Citation Index;* and *C.R.I.S.: The Combined Retrospective Index Set to Journals in History 1838–1974.*

Core Titles

	PUBLIC	ACADEMIC	SCHOOL
Atlas of Ancient Egypt Baines, John, and Jaromír Málik. Facts On File, 1980 (See Archaeology)	✦	✦	✦
Atlas of the Ancient World Fagg, Christopher, and Frances Halton. Crescent/Crown, 1979			✦
Atlas of Classical History Talbert, Richard J. A., ed. Macmillan (hard); Routledge, Chapman & Hall (soft), 1985			✦
Atlas of the Greek World Levi, Peter. Facts On File, 1981	✦		✦
Atlas of the Roman World Cornell, Tim and John Matthews. Facts On File, 1982	✦		
The Cambridge Ancient History Series, 1st, 2d, and 3d editions, 12 vols., 7 vols. of plates Cambridge, 1930–1988	✦	✦	
Great Events from History, Ancient and Medieval series, 3 vols. Magill, Frank N., ed., and E. G. Weltin, assoc. ed. Salem, 1972			✦
The Oxford Classical Dictionary, 2d edition Hammond, N. G. L., and H. H. Scullard, eds. Clarendon/Oxford, 1970 (See Ancient and Classical Literature)	✦	✦	✦
Oxford History of the Classical World Boardman, John, Jasper Griffin, and Oswyn Murray, eds. Oxford, 1986		✦	

Two recommended titles are no longer in print: *Who Was Who in the Roman World,* edited by Diana Bower (Washington Square Press, 1984) and *The Roman Emperors: A Biographical Guide to the Rulers of Ancient Rome, 31 B.C.–A.D. 476,* by Michael Grant (Scribner, 1985). Librarians may want to locate these titles to broaden the biographical scope of their collection.

—*D. E. C.*

With contributions by Donald E. Collins.

Core Titles

Atlas of Ancient Egypt. John Baines and Jaromír Málek. Facts On File, 1980. hard. 1 vol. 240 pp. illus. index. ISBN 0-87196-334-5. $45. atlas.
DT56.9.B34 932

See Archaeology.

Atlas of Classical History. Richard J. A. Talbert, ed. Macmillan, 1985 (hard); Routledge, Chapman & Hall (soft). 1 vol. 217 pp. illus. index. ISBN 0-02-933110-2 (hard); 0-415-03463-9 (soft). $50 (hard); $18.50 (soft). atlas.
G1033.A833 911

The *Atlas of Classical History* is a comprehensive work that contains well over 100 maps, each accompanied by supporting text, covering ancient history up to the time of Constantine. The atlas also includes a list of the reigns of the Roman emperors, a list of abbreviations, a list of equivalents to Roman measurements, an extensive list of suggestions for further readings, and a gazetteer. The "Further Readings" section, arranged by subject heading to coincide with the text, contains both American and British publications.

This atlas is one of the many works about ancient history originally published in Great Britain. Richard

J. A. Talbert, the editor, is a teacher at Queen's University and the author of several other books and articles about Rome and Greece. The other contributors are also scholars from the United Kingdom.

The book has many attractive features: the size (about 7½ by 9¾ inches) makes the atlas comfortable to use; the binding allows the book to be opened easily; and the two-column layout is easy to read. In addition, the reading level is suitable for almost any audience. The atlas is produced in black and white. Some color would have been nice, particularly with the physical maps, but it would probably have increased the cost of the book significantly.

The atlas, which is chronologically arranged, begins with the Aegean Age and ends with the time of Constantine and the Dioceses and Provinces of the Roman Empire in A.D. 314. There are many full-page maps, several maps on two-page spreads, and many small maps and diagrams that locate settlements, boundaries, wars, cities, and religious cults. Text that accompanies the maps ranges from half a page to two pages in length. Users will find entries on *Troy, Dark Age Greece, archaic Greece, archaeological sites of Greece, republican Rome, trade in the Roman World,* and *Roman Egypt,* among many others. Troy is depicted in its various stages. The map of Dark Age Greece includes settlements, cemeteries, and sanctuaries. The map of archaic Greece includes major city-states, religious centers such as Dodona, and important battle locations such as Thyrea. Other maps show the Greek and Phoenician trade routes as well as the type of trade conducted in the various regions. The city maps are superbly done and easy to read. The drawing of Ostia is finely detailed, and the maps of Pompeii, Sparta, Herculaneum, Masada, and others are clean and crisp and highly legible. Here, the use of black and white enhances the maps. The map of the Homeric world would be helpful to any reader of *The Iliad* or *The Odyssey.*

The comprehensive indexing gazetteer and the chronological arrangement make the atlas easy to use. The table of contents leads the reader to the general geographic location, and the gazetteer provides specific references. However, most monuments and features of battles or site plans are not listed in the 27-page gazetteer.

Concise entries and sharply drawn maps make the *Atlas of Classical History* an excellent introduction to classical history. The material represents the latest in thinking from some leading teachers and scholars. The Board recommends this work for the core collection of school libraries. If the price of the hardcover is prohibitive, a less expensive paperback edition is available.

—*L. H. M.*

Atlas of the Ancient World. Christopher Fagg and Frances Halton. Crescent/Crown, 1979; distrib. by Random House. hard. 1 vol. 59 pp. illus. index. ISBN 0-517-295253. atlas. out of stock.
G1033.F3 913.3

The *Atlas of the Ancient World* is another fine reference work that originated in Great Britain. Co-author Christopher Fagg has written two other atlases of Greek and Roman history.

This atlas is suitable for young readers. It is oversize, and its large print makes it easy to read. There are a limited number of entries and a large number of colorful illustrations. Many of the fine photographs are attributed to the British Museum. The entries are brief, as is the text that accompanies the illustrations. As a result, young readers can scan the atlas easily. One outstanding feature of the atlas is the use of sidebars to give readers a short chronology of the entry and to highlight important features and facts.

There are 24 entries plus an introductory essay, an index, and a glossary. The small number of entries makes this a very general atlas. The entries range from an overview of the past, the first people, and the first religions, to China, Barbarians, and the Americas. The entry for *China* is two pages long and contains seven illustrations, one of which is a map. The three sidebars in the *China* entry deal with chronology, travel, and agriculture. In addition, the text of the entry contains information on geography, climate, traditions, and government. The entries for the world in 1500 B.C., 500 B.C., A.D. 117, and A.D. 500 provide good, simple maps showing where civilizations existed at those times.

The atlas has a few minor problems. For example, in addition to the photographs, the book includes artists' renderings, or interpretations, of ancient times and places. The authors note in their introductory essay, "Looking at the Past," that this technique is appropriate because historians and artists view the past through the perspective of the future. Unfortunately, this approach does not always work, and some of the renderings appear to depict modern people dressed in costumes from the past. Another minor problem: The entry entitled "Mastering Skills" discusses alphabets, but it would have been more helpful if the entry had been expanded to include a complete example of several alphabets.

These minor problems are outweighed by the colorful and open arrangement that makes the atlas so easy to use. Many entries in the extensive index have several subentries. Young students will appreciate the ease with which they can find materials on one subject (for example, there are 24 subentries under the entry *building.*)

Some new interpretations of the facts and theories of ancient history may have been promulgated since the *Atlas of the Ancient World* was published in 1979. It is, however, still valid enough to be used today. This atlas will fill the needs of young students and will supplement, with illustrations and maps, the needs of intermediate-grade students. The Board recommends this work for the core collection of school libraries.

—*L. H. M.*

Atlas of the Greek World. Peter Levi. Facts On File, 1981. hard. 1 vol. 239 pp. illus. index. ISBN 0-87196-448-1. $45. atlas.
DF77.L43 913.38

The *Atlas of the Greek World* creatively combines maps, photographs, drawings, and text to acquaint the reader with the ancient Greeks. Their mental, spiritual, physical, and artistic worlds are described as well as their achievements in medicine, science, economics, law, and theater.

The atlas is authored by the distinguished British teacher and classics scholar Peter Levi, of Oxford University. Two other Oxford scholars, John Boardman and Thomas Braun, served as art and archaeological advisor and historical and cartographic advisor, respectively. This atlas and the ATLAS OF THE ROMAN WORLD are part of a series of atlases published by Facts On File, whose reputation for quality reference materials is well established.

The *Atlas of the Greek World* has an attractive, easy-to-use format. The binding is such that the book opens easily and stays flat, an important feature in an atlas with many double-page spreads for maps and other illustrations. The multicolumn text is profusely illustrated with 60 specially drawn maps and 500 illustrations (350 in color), making the atlas easy to read and aesthetically pleasing. The maps portray a wide variety of topics, such as Greece's modern geographical setting, Homeric Greece, origin of Olympic foot-race winners, poets and philosophers, the Athenian empire, the campaigns of Alexander, and the silk and spice routes. Many of the illustrations appear in special feature spreads, which are pictorial essays on various aspects of the civilization, or in "site" feature spreads, which focus on significant places in ancient history. Detailed captions accompany all maps and illustrations.

The atlas is divided into six parts that are further broken down into chapters. The first part sets the stage by briefly describing the geography and the study of ancient Greece through the ages. The second part concentrates on the flourishing of the Bronze Age and covers the palace civilizations of Crete and Mycenae, the survival of Mycenaean influences, and Homer's world. Part 3 discusses the Age of Tyranny and includes the renaissance of the eighth century B.C., archaic religious practices, the birth of the city-states, and the growth of literature. Site features depict Dodona, Eleusis, Delphi, and other notable locations of this age.

The Age of Pericles is the subject of the fourth part. The topics covered include fifth-century Athenian society, the Persian and Peloponnesian wars, and the classical revolution. Part 5 deals with the Age of Alexander. This section describes the trends in literature and religion, the rise of Macedon, and the Alexandrian expansion followed by the Roman conquest in the second century B.C. The final part, part 6, deals with the fate of Hellenism. The text covers the classical impact of Hellenism, postclassical revivals, and the principal inheritance of the modern Greeks—language.

The atlas also contains an excellent two-page illustrated chronological table arranged by subject and date. The dates range from 3000 B.C. to A.D. 200, and the subjects include the Aegean and Greek mainland; pottery style; art and architecture; literature, philosophy, and science; Egypt, Asia Minor, and the East; Western Mediterranean; and elsewhere in Europe. For example, readers can see from this table that Stonehenge was built at about the same time as palaces in Crete, circa 2000 B.C. A detailed list of illustrations with sources, a glossary, an extensive bibliography, a gazetteer, and an index provide access to this comprehensive introduction to the ancient Greek world.

The *Atlas of the Greek World* is an excellent choice for the general reader as well as the student. It presents scholarly information in an informal manner. This atlas is enjoyable to read and may well meet the author's purpose to "stir the imagination of readers I have never met" (introduction). The Board recommends this work for the core collections of public and school libraries.

—*L. H. M.*

Atlas of the Roman World. Tim Cornell and John Matthews. Facts On File, 1982. hard. 1 vol. 240 pp. illus. index. ISBN 0-87196-652-2. $45. atlas.
DG77.C897 937.0211

The *Atlas of the Roman World* provides a complete, albeit general, view of the Roman Empire in its physical as well as cultural settings. It covers a period of over 1,330 years, from the founding of Rome to the collapse of the empire in Italy and the establishment of a Greek empire in the east.

The book's authors and advisory editor have impressive academic credits. The authors, Tim Cornell and John Matthews, are experts on early republican Rome and fourth century A.D., respectively. Cornell is a lecturer in ancient history at University College, London, and Matthews is Fellow and Tutor in ancient history at Queens College, Oxford. Advisory editor Peter Brown, formerly at Oxford, is Professor of Ancient History and Mediterranean Archaeology at the University of California, Berkeley. The publisher, Facts On File, is well known for producing quality reference publications. This atlas and the ATLAS OF THE GREEK WORLD are part of a series of atlases published by Facts On File.

The purpose of this atlas is to give a complete although general view of the physical and cultural aspects of the Roman world to a general user. It covers the period from the early development of the city of Rome through the period of conquest and expansion until the collapse of the Roman West. The atlas is basically a survey course of Roman history that covers over 1,300 years.

The book has an attractive, oversized format. The pages open easily, and the book lies flat, making it possible to examine the many maps without hindrance. The multicolumn text, 62 specially drawn full-color maps, and 470 illustrations (257 in color) are combined into a layout that is accessible and aesthetically pleasing. The maps portray a wide range of topics such as rainfall, geology, the first and second Punic Wars, the rise of Julius Caesar, shipwrecks, and the provinces of the empire. Many of the illustrations appear in special feature spreads that are pictorial essays on various aspects of the civilization. All maps and illustrations are accompanied by detailed captions.

Graphic features, such as tables, display information on important elements of Roman life and culture. For example, the table depicting the distribution of the legions in the provinces at three different time periods is a unique feature, as is the use of aerial photography to show, for example, how the Roman roads in England contrast with the modern roadway. Aerial photography is used several times to show the existence of villas and settlements under present-day fields.

The atlas is divided into four parts that are further broken down into chapters. Part 1 focuses on early Italy and the Roman Republic. It covers the foundation and development of Rome, the conquest of Italy and the Mediterranean, and the crisis and reform that followed. There are special features highlighting early Latium, the Etruscans, and archaic Rome.

Part 2 details the transition from republic to empire and includes the Roman revolution and the character of the emerging empire. Some special features depict town life in Pompeii, early imperial Rome, festivals of the state religion, and the emperors from Augustus to Justinian.

Part 3 concentrates on the possessions of imperial Rome at the height of its power. The provinces examined include Africa, Spain, Gaul, Germany, Britain, the Danube, Greece, Asia Minor, the East, Egypt, and Cyrenaica.

Part 4 details the empire in decline starting with an economic crisis in the third century, continuing with the rise of Constantine in the fourth century and the subsequent fall of the Western Roman Empire, and ending with the rise of the Greek Empire. Here, special features include, among others, Roman portraiture, mills and technology, public shows, late imperial Rome, and the legacy of Rome. The special feature on public shows is a two-page spread that includes scenes of gladiatorial combat, circus halls, hunting scenes, and chariot races. These illustrations are taken from mosaics, re-creations, and artworks, and complement a brief text.

The atlas also contains an excellent two-page, illustrated chronological table arranged by subject and date. The dates range from 800 B.C. to A.D. 500, and the subjects include Rome and Italy; art and architecture; Latin literature; Africa, Spain, and the Western Mediterranean; Gaul, Britain, and Central Europe; and Greece and the East. A list of maps, a detailed list of illustrations with sources, a list of special features, bibliography, gazetteer, and index provide access to this comprehensive introduction to the Roman world.

The *Atlas of the Roman World* is intended for the general reader. It does assume that the reader has some knowledge of Latin and Roman history. However, it is an excellent reference tool. The Board recommends this work for the core collection of public libraries.

—L. H. M.

The Cambridge Ancient History Series. 1st, 2d, and 3d editions. Cambridge, 1930–1988. hard. 12 vols. plus 7 vols. of plates. illus. appendixes. history.
D57.C25 913.32

The Cambridge Ancient History Series presents the history of Europe from its "remote and dim beginnings . . . down to the victory of Constantine the Great in 324 A.D." (preface, volume 1, 1923 edition). This work and THE CAMBRIDGE MEDIEVAL HISTORY (see World History) form the most comprehensive and authoritative history of Europe and the Middle East available. For decades, these series have been regarded as the standard works in their respective areas. The content of *The Cambridge Ancient History Series* reflects Europe's indebtedness to prehistory and the older civilizations of the Middle East, and devotes considerable attention to such areas as primitive humanity, the beginnings of language, and the earliest populations of Europe, western Asia, and northern Africa. Similarly, the histories of the ancient Egyptian, Sumerian, Hittite, Semitic, Greek, and Roman civilizations and the peoples of northeastern Africa and southwestern Asia are treated extensively.

Each volume is composed of scholarly, readable essays by leading historians writing in their areas of expertise. Readers are aided by an outstanding variety of supplementary maps, historical chronologies, genealogies, black-and-white illustrations, and bibliographies that, taken together, provide a much greater understanding of the period than text alone. There is excellent access to each volume through detailed tables of contents and indexes, although a general series index is lacking. The text volumes are accompanied by volumes of black-and-white photographic plates.

Volume 7, part 1, *The Hellenistic World,* serves as a good example of the overall series. In 641 pages the work covers the 106-year period from the death of Alexander the Great to 217 B.C. in a wide array of topics from politics, economics, and religion, to "War and Siegecraft," "Building and Townplanning," and "Monarchies and Monarchic Ideas." Genealogical charts and king lists place the lineages of the Ptolemies and other leading families in historical perspective, while chronologies in tabular format provide readers with quick surveys of major events. An 87-page bibliography leads readers to additional material in categories as broad as ancient authors and as specific as ceramics and jewelry. The companion plate volume, *The Hellenistic World to the Coming of the Romans,* illustrates the life of the period through well-chosen black-and-white photographs, including, for example, medical practice, technology, burial practices, ornaments, coinage, education, sports, theater, commerce, homes, and weapons. These illustrations add to the value of the text and will satisfy some pictorial reference needs.

The Cambridge Ancient History Series is not without problems. The 12-volume set is being revised and updated in a sporadic and piecemeal manner, with the result that the set now contains volumes from the first through third editions. The publication dates of volumes currently in print range from 1930 through 1988. While all volumes are still of value, the later editions are greatly expanded and include recent research findings. The revised text volumes remain true to the original purpose and structure of the series; however, the new plate volumes vary in arrangement and function. While first-edition plate volumes are tied closely to their respective text volumes and are illustrated without significant comment, more recent works, particularly plate volumes 3 (1984), 4 (1988), and 7, part 1 (1984), are divided into chapters, include maps and narrative comment, and can be used without reference to the text volume.

Despite the variation in age between volumes, *The Cambridge Ancient History Series* is still the standard work on the period and continues to be of value. The Board recommends this work for the core collections of public and academic libraries. —*D. E. C.*

Great Events from History, Ancient and Medieval series. Frank N. Magill, ed., E. G. Weltin, assoc. ed. Salem, 1972. hard. 3 vols. 1,854 pp. index. ISBN 0-89356-108-8 (set). $115 (set). history.
D59.M26 909.09'812

Great Events from History, Ancient and Medieval series, is very much the product of its notable editor, Frank N. Magill, assisted by associate editor E. G. Weltin. Magill presents over 300 political, military, intellectual, scientific, literary, sociological, and cultural events that he determined changed the course of Western history, and he summarizes each event in his characteristic brief style. Each account is followed by two review essays of scholarly literature about the event and citations for further readings. The list of scholars who have contributed to the essays for *Great Events from History* represents a good cross-section of American university thought.

Although the volumes have tight bindings that make them unwieldy and difficult to keep flat, the print is easy to read and the design is the one used by Salem Press for Magill's other reference titles.

The events summarized in volume 1 cover from 4000 B.C. and the domestication of the horse to 1 B.C. and the birth of Jesus. Other topics include the introduction of the wheel, the origin of writing, the transmission of the alphabet, the founding of the Olympic games, the invention of coinage, the formalization of geometry, the use of the arch, the start of the Julian calendar, and the establishment of history as a literary genre.

Volume 2 covers from A.D. 1—Ovid and the *Metamorphoses*—to A.D. 950—the court of Cordoba. The second volume also includes events from the ministry of Jesus, the martyrdom of Peter at Rome, the writings of Marcus Aurelius, and the commissioning of the Vulgate Bible.

Volume 3 covers from A.D. 951 and the creation of the Holy Roman Empire to A.D. 1500 and the revival of classicism in painting. This volume also includes three indexes, a list of literature reviewed, and suggested readings. The indexes include an alphabetical list of events, a keyword index, a category index, and a name index.

Most entries are about five pages long. In addition to a summary of the event, each entry contains information about the type of event, when and where it took place, pertinent literature, and suggested reading. People are included when applicable. For example, in the entry *Rise of Parthia*—described as a political event that took place in northwestern Iran—five principal personages are listed, including Tiridates and Mithridates. The synopsis of this event is two pages long. The review essays from two scholarly books on Parthia follow, and three books are cited for further reading.

Great Events from History is suitable for teachers, students, librarians, and researchers who require brief information quickly. The Board recommends this work for the core collection of school libraries. —*L. H. M.*

The Oxford Classical Dictionary, 2d edition. N. G. L. Hammond and H. H. Scullard, eds. Clarendon/ Oxford, 1970. hard. 1 vol. 1,198 pp. appendix. indexes. ISBN 0-19-869117-3. $49.95. dictionary.
DE5.091970 913.38003

See Ancient and Classical Literature.

The Oxford History of the Classical World. John Boardman, Jasper Griffin, and Oswyn Murray, eds. Oxford, 1986. hard. 1 vol. 882 pp. illus. appendix. index. ISBN 0-19-872112-9. $49.95. history.
DE59.094 938

The Oxford History of the Classical World provides a comprehensive view of the Graeco-Roman world, covering its political and social history as well as its literature, philosophy, and art. The work covers the period from the time of Homer to the fall of the Roman Empire in the West. The book's editors, John Boardman, Jasper Griffin, and Oswyn Murray, are recognized authorities in their fields, as are the 30 contributors who wrote the individual chapters, such as Peter Levi, author of the ATLAS OF THE GREEK WORLD and John Matthews, co-author of the ATLAS OF THE ROMAN WORLD.

The Oxford History of the Classical World is physically attractive, and the typeface is readable. The book is profusely illustrated with 16 pages of color plates and over 250 black-and-white illustrations integrated within the text. The book opens easily and, when open, stays flat. This is an important feature for users who want to take notes.

An excellent introduction, written by Jasper Griffin, defines the scope of the book and gives a brief overview of the important characteristics of the Greek and Roman civilizations. The main text is divided into three sections. The first section covers Greece from the eighth to the fourth centuries B.C. This section has 12 chapters that treat the history of the archaic and classical periods; Homer; Greek myth; lyric and elegiac poetry; early and classical Greek philosophy; Greek historians; and culture and life in classical Greece. The chapter on Greek historians, written by Oswyn Murray, is illustrative of the depth with which topics are discussed. This material includes, in part, the origins of history; Herodotus (dubbed the "father of history"); local history and chronography and those writers who worked within this form; and the historians Thucydides and Xenophon.

The second section, which focuses on Greece and Rome, covers roughly from 336 B.C. to A.D. 14. Nine chapters cover the history of the Hellenic period; Hellenistic culture; early Rome and its growth; the first Roman literature; the poets of the late republic; and Hellenistic and Graeco-Roman art.

The third section focuses entirely on Rome. Eleven chapters cover the founding of the empire; the arts of government; Augustan poetry and society; Roman historians; literature and the arts; and Roman life and culture. The chapter "The Arts of Living," written by Roger Ling, provides an intimate look at Roman houses and villas, interior decoration, gardens, eating and drinking customs, and dress and personal effects. An envoi discusses some aspects of the later empire and its influence on Western civilization.

The Oxford History of the Classical World is easy to use and includes many helpful features, such as an extensive list of further readings after each chapter and a detailed "Table of Events." This table is an extremely valuable tool that spans from approximately 3000 B.C. to A.D. 1453 and provides a basis for comparing the Mediterranean world with the Greek world and the Roman world with the Hellenic world. The work also includes a list of color plates, a list of maps, a list of illustrations with detailed descriptions where possible, bibliographies, and an index.

The Oxford History of the Classical World is one of the most current books considered in this category. The Board recommends this work for the core collection of academic libraries. This work is also a worthwhile purchase for any library where there is a reader population interested in classical history. —*L. H. M.*

Supplementary Titles

Chronology of the Ancient World, 2d edition. E. J. Bickerman. Cornell, 1980. hard. 1 vol. 223 pp. ISBN 0-8014-1282-X. $32.50. chronology.
D54.5.B5 529.32

This is the second edition of the *Chronology of the Ancient World,* which was first published in English in 1968. A review of the 1968 edition noted that the work was "originally written to answer a simple question in the author's mind—how are we able to date an event in ancient history?—the book provides the answers in a chapter, 'Applied Chronology'. . . . The volume also serves as an up-to-date bibliographical guide on the subject."

The text also contains "lists of kings and rulers of the East, including those of even tiny states . . . Roman emperors to Constantine; chronological tables of early Roman history; of Greek and Roman history; . . ." and much more. (*CW,* October 1968, p. 6)

Also reviewed in: *AJP,* October 1969, p. 478; *ARBA,* 1981, p. 184; *CJ,* March 1969, p. 282.

Board's recommendation: Academic libraries.

Civilization of the Ancient Mediterranean: Greece and Rome. Michael Grant and Rachel Kitzinger, eds. Scribner, 1987. hard. 3 vols. 1,980 pp. illus. ISBN 0-684-17594-0 (set). $250 (set). history.
DE59.C55 938

Civilization of the Ancient Mediterranean "contains essays on classical Greece and Rome from prehistory to the fall of Rome. The first volume begins with a chronological table and historical summaries.

"The editors of this three-volume set . . . assembled an impressive group of scholars . . . to write 97 essays on topics ranging from Greek and Roman building techniques, engineering, class structure, and government to cooking, folklore, clubs, games, and attitudes toward sex and gender. . . . Encyclopedic in coverage, the set provides a comprehensive overview of current thinking about the classical world. Following a contemporary trend to emphasize topics germane to ordinary, everyday life, the set includes admirable coverage of domestic and personal concerns and attitudes while not slighting the traditional socioeconomic/political topics." (*BL,* June 15, 1988, p. 1716)

"This unparalleled reference work for the nonspecialist is characterized by accessibility, a broad range of topics covered, currency of information or theory, and authority of contributors. . . . Even though these essays are meant for lay readers, the scholarliness of the contributors is striking." (*LJ,* May 1, 1988, p. 71)

Also reviewed in: *Choice,* January 1989, p. 776; *CRL,* January 1989, p. 91; *Isis,* March 1989, p. 177; *NYTBR,* January 22, 1989, p. 16; *SLJ,* May 1989, p. 26; *WLB,* May 1988, p. 108.

Board's recommendation: Public and academic libraries.

A Guide to the Ancient World: A Dictionary of Classical Place Names. Michael Grant. Wilson, 1986. hard. 1 vol. 728 pp. illus. ISBN 0-8242-0742-4. $65. dictionary.
DE25.G72 913.8′003

A Guide to the Ancient World is "a geographical dictionary of 'locations in the ancient Greek, Etruscan, and Roman world' from 1000 BCE to 500 CE. It covers the Mediterranean, Western and Central Europe, the Black Sea, and Western Asia to the borders of India. There are entries for 900 places, mostly towns and cities, but also nations, provinces, rivers, seas, straits, mountains, plains and battle sites.

"The well-written and informative entries, which run from a few lines to four and one-half pages, reflect current knowledge and contain geographical, historical, archaeological, and, when appropriate, artistic and mythological information." (*Choice,* January 1987, p. 742)

"Grant's sources include ancient Latin and Greek and other writers (briefly identified in the first part of the bibliography), the sites themselves, archaeological reports, inscriptions, and coins. . . . [This title] will be useful to classicists, archaeologists, students of art and literature, travelers, and general readers served by academic and public libraries." (*BL,* March 1, 1987, p. 1001)

Also reviewed in: *ARBA,* 1987, p. 191; *B Rpt,* March 1987, p. 48; *Rel St Rev,* July 1987, p. 258; *VOYA,* June 1987, p. 103; *WLB,* January 1987, p. 80.

Board's recommendation: Public and academic libraries.

Pictorial Dictionary of Ancient Rome. Ernest Nash. Praeger, 1968; repr. by Hacker, 1981. hard. 2 vols. 1,076 pp. illus. ISBN 0-87817-265-3 (set). $150 (set). pictorial dictionary.
NA310.N28 720.94563

The *Pictorial Dictionary of Ancient Rome* is a "two-volume pictorial survey of all Roman monuments and buildings, containing pictures of every extant relic in the Eternal City." (publisher's note)

[The dictionary] "has an extensive index, which includes all modern streets, churches, squares, palaces, all artists, coins, temples, and even the respective parts of the ancient Marble Plan." (*Art Bul,* March 1963, p. 62)

"Nash is to be commended for the manner in which he presents material to capture not only the imagination of the specialist, but of the informed layman as well. . . . Originality of plan and scholarly thoroughness of the work make it a very special publication. . . . [It is] recommended . . . to all academic, special, and larger public libraries." (*LJ,* November 15, 1962, p. 4176)

Also reviewed in: *CW.* February 1963, p. 141; *TLS,* April 26, 1963, p. 285.

Board's recommendation: Public and academic libraries.

Who Was Who in the Greek World, 776 B.C.–30 B.C. Diana Bowder, ed. Cornell, 1982. hard. 1 vol. 227 pp. illus. ISBN 0-8014-1538-1. $35. biographical dictionary.
DF208.W48 920.038

Who Was Who in the Greek World contains "biographies of men and women who played important roles in the history of ancient Greece. Greek politicians, philosophers, military leaders, and poets are included." (publisher's note)

"This is an excellent resource for the interested student or smaller reference collection. Its major virtue is to bring together in short compass the most recent biographical and historical information on a large number of ancient Greek (and a few non-Greek) personages along with maps, chronological tables, and genealogical and dynastic trees." (*Choice,* April 1983, p. 1116)

"The average standard of the articles . . . is high. [The writers] are familiar with the literature of their subjects. . . . The illustrations . . . are an important and attractive feature. . . . [This] will be a valuable acquisition for anyone interested in the ancient world, and for undergraduates [it is] ideal." (*NYRB,* December 16, 1982, p. 48)

Also reviewed in: *A Lib,* May 1984, p. 300; *Ant R,* Winter 1983, p. 121; *ARBA,* 1984, p. 176; *Arch,* July 1983, p. 76; *BL,* February 1, 1983, p. 712; *CC,* December 15, 1982, p. 1292; *HT,* February 1983, p. 54; *LJ,* January 15, 1983, p. 122; *NYTBR,* January 16, 1983, p. 11; August 19, 1984, p. 30; *Rel St Rev,* July 1983, p. 271; *WSJ,* December 7, 1982, p. 32.

Board's recommendation: Public and academic libraries.

Janice G. Newkirk

Anthropology

See also Sociology

Anthropology is in many respects the broadest academic discipline. By definition, anthropology is the study of humankind from all perspectives—throughout time and geography. And within anthropology there are subfields in which the depth of research can be as involved as in any of the most scientific technical fields. If a library supports a specialization in anthropological research, it should have available for users an extraordinary amount of material.

Anthropology is generally divided into four subfields: archaeology, physical anthropology, linguistics, and social and cultural anthropology. While study of any artifact, behavior, or system associated with humankind is fair game for anthropologists, preliterate and non-Western societies and early humans have traditionally been the primary focus. Recently, however, study of behaviors, systems, and artifacts associated with urban Western societies has increased dramati-

Core Titles

	PUBLIC	ACADEMIC	SCHOOL
Abstracts in Anthropology, 2 vols. Moeller, Roger W., and Jay F. Custer, eds. Baywood, 1970–		✦	
Dictionary of Anthropology Seymour-Smith, Charlotte. G. K. Hall, 1986	✦	✦	
The Dictionary of Human Geography, 2d edition Johnston, R. J., Derek Gregory, and David M. Smith, eds. Basil Blackwell, 1986		✦	
Encyclopedia of Human Evolution and Prehistory Tattersall, Ian, Eric Delson, and John Van Couvering, eds. Garland, 1988		✦	

cally. A core reference collection should certainly touch on all four subdisciplines. The basic sources should provide solid support for specialized needs within an academic setting. These choices are based on several of the following considerations. If the library is part of an academic institution, the librarian must ascertain the research interests of the academic community and the courses taught. In the case of a public library, the librarian must determine community interest in this subject and the needs of the students who consult the collection.

The reference collection on anthropology will overlap with other disciplines. For example, social anthropology and sociology are sometimes indistinguishable—especially for urban anthropologists and others who study Western societies. Archaeology and cultural anthropology overlap with the fine and performing arts and literature. Users may wish to consult the corresponding categories in this buying guide for other works supporting the anthropology collection.

By recognizing the interrelationships of certain categories, the librarian can avoid unnecessary duplication. If the library subscribes to *Index Medicus* to support the life sciences category, for example, the need to purchase an anthropological index that emphasizes the scientific literature is diminished.

General social science sources and reference sources in related fields are important to a core collection for anthropology. Sources such as the INTERNATIONAL ENCYCLOPEDIA OF THE SOCIAL SCIENCES (see Sociology) explain many of the theoretical issues in the field and can serve all the social sciences. Directories such as *The Directory of Practicing Anthropologists* (which identifies museum as well as academic personnel) provide a quick reference to current anthropologists.

In addition to the works reviewed here, an academic collection can be supplemented with annual reviews, yearbooks, and book-reviewing sources, especially the quarterly *Reviews in Anthropology,* which provides the most current information available in monographs. Bibliographies, the most important and expensive of which is *The Author and Subject Catalogues of the Library of the Peabody Museum of Archaeology and Ethnology,* offer access to retrospective information. Finally, for culture-specific information as well as cross-cultural study, *Sixty Cultures: A Guide to the HRAF Probability Sample Files*—a huge manual "data base"—contains published books, articles, and unpublished manuscripts and is a primary source library in itself.

Many of the most elaborate and expensive sources are beyond the scope and budgets of smaller libraries, but as long as the collection contains some dictionary or encyclopedic work and some indexing source to serve the research interests of the community, the most elementary requirements of a core reference collection are met.

Core Titles

Abstracts in Anthropology. Roger W. Moeller and Jay F. Custer, eds. Baywood, 1970– . 2 vols. 8 issues per year. soft. ISSN 0001-3455. $239 per year (per 2 vols). abstract/index.
GN1 572.016

Abstracts in Anthropology is an essential core reference source for any library supporting study in anthropology. Although no single source can do justice to the field, *Abstracts in Anthropology* comes as close as possible to covering the wide range of information—from the very scientific to the humanistic.

Each issue contains approximately 750 references with abstracts. Fifty to 150 journals per issue are indexed. Some journals are indexed selectively.

The periodicals indexed include the standards in the field (such as *Man,* the *Journal of Anthropological Research*) and key foreign journals (such as *L'Anthropologie*), abstracts from which appear in English. General scientific journals, such as *Science* and *Nature,* as well as a broad selection of life science periodicals—*Gene* and *Behavioral Neuroscience,* for example—are indexed as well. In fact, the overindexing of science material may be a problem because the inclusion of many esoteric and technical references is peripheral to anthropology, at best. Certain article cites, such as the olfactory EEG and behavior of rabbits, are of questionable use to any anthropological application.

The arrangement of *Abstracts in Anthropology* may be a bit confusing to the new user. The four subfields of anthropology are divided between two issues. The first issue of each volume contains abstracts in archaeology and physical anthropology. The second issue covers linguistics and cultural anthropology. The coverage of subfields alternates throughout a year's issues.

Each issue contains a subject index, an author index, and a list of periodicals indexed in the issue. Currently each volume contains cumulated author and subject indexes; volumes up through 1985 did not contain cumulated indexes.

The subject index is straightforward, including most major themes, such as geographic regions, archaeological sites, ethnic studies, behaviors, artifacts, and physical and social systems.

The abstracts themselves are variable in quality. Those abstracts about scientific topics fully describe the nature of the research, goals, and methodology. Abstracts about the more humanistic topics are more general and sometimes only amount to notes (for example, "The relationship between Jews and Nietszche are [*sic*] reconsidered" [volume 17, p. 74] or "Contemporary discrimination in the Netherlands is examined" [volume 17, p. 75]). Although the treatment of humanistic topics is not as comprehensive, *Abstracts in Anthropology* does serve all the subdisciplines.

For those libraries supporting departments emphasizing physical anthropology, the *Abstracts* are the best option. While not perfect, *Abstracts in Anthropology* comes as close as any source extant to accomplishing the task. The Board recommends this work for the core collection of academic libraries.

Dictionary of Anthropology. Charlotte Seymour-Smith. G. K. Hall, 1986. hard. 1 vol. 305 pp. ISBN 0-8161-8817-3. $45. dictionary.
GN11.D48 306.03′21

The *Dictionary of Anthropology* by Charlotte Seymour-Smith is technically less a dictionary than a mini-encyclopedia. In the foreword the author explains that she intends "to convey the critical spirit of anthropological inquiry to students of social and cultural anthropology" and that "many entries here are not 'definitive': they are designed instead to open up debate." And the entries certainly do more to explain anthropological inquiry than to define its terminology.

Seymour-Smith has a Ph.D. in anthropology from the London School of Economics and is an authority in the field. The writing style in the entries is crisp and lucid, qualities especially valuable in a reference source. Her discussions of legal and social structures are especially valuable and interesting. This dictionary was originally published in Great Britain, so British spellings are used, and there is a certain bias toward British schools of thought. While this emphasis creates little real confusion, it sometimes results in uneven coverage of some American and continental research and diminishes the relative importance of some non-British scholars. This is not an across-the-board indictment, however, because—especially in the longer entries, such as *ritual* and *marriage payments*—the author makes a considerable effort to compare how various schools explain social and cultural phenomena.

The dictionary is arranged alphabetically with approximately 950 text entries and over 160 "see" references. As the author also states in the foreword, the topics included concern issues related almost exclusively to social and cultural anthropology. Some mention is made of basic terms in linguistics, physical anthropology, and archaeology, but the text cannot be considered a source in those areas.

The entries run from a few words to more than two pages in length, with the longer entries often including reference to important personalities, publications, and additional cross-references to other entries. About 90 of the entries are on individual anthropologists, specifically limited by the author to those born before 1920. These entries tend to be short, with just a brief mention of their areas of research and principal works.

A 13-page bibliography of significant works and suggested readings at the end of the *Dictionary of Anthropology* further contributes to the value of the work. Seymour-Smith has created a source that is a starting point for research. Entries explain general areas of anthropology and give overviews of the work done and the principles involved in the field. References within the text and the bibliography point to specific sources for further research.

This source is most valuable for undergraduates and laypersons interested in the field. The biggest criticism of the *Dictionary of Anthropology* may be that its title is misleading; in many respects this work is more than a dictionary, a fact that adds to its value. The Board recommends the *Dictionary of Anthropology* for the core collections of public and academic libraries.

The Dictionary of Human Geography, 2d edition. R. J. Johnston, Derek Gregory, and David M. Smith, eds. Basil Blackwell, 1986. hard and soft. 1 vol. 592 pp. index. ISBN 0-631-14655-5 (hard); 0-631-14656-3 (soft). $75 (hard); $15.95 (soft). dictionary. next revision: 1991.
GF4 304.2′03′21

The Dictionary of Human Geography is an unusual and exciting reference source for anthropologists, who tend to focus on human beings in social and cultural environments, sometimes overlooking the spatial context of human activities, which are important and sometimes crucial to research. This excellent dictionary answers questions about the spatial contexts of populations, settlements, and models of change.

This work is a scholarly and somewhat technical source. The list of contributors to the dictionary is 36 strong, with all but three associated with British universities. The individual articles are signed. British spelling is used, as might be expected, but little scholarly bias is evident. The text tends to explain models rather than to argue for their validity.

At first glance, *The Dictionary of Human Geography*

does not look like an anthropological reference source at all—and in some ways it is not. To many, human (or social) geography may seem like a subdiscipline in geography, having little to do with anthropology. In fact, however, the relationship between humankind and area is part of the essence of anthropology. *The Dictionary of Human Geography* simply reflects the differences in the way American and British (or European) scholars categorize subject disciplines. Much of what American anthropologists do is undertaken in Great Britain and on the continent by scholars calling themselves something other than "anthropologists." While this work is a good source for graduate and undergraduate geography students, there is much to recommend the dictionary to anthropologists, demographers, planners, and sociologists as well.

The Dictionary of Human Geography is an alphabetic presentation of entries, with definitions and explanations of major concepts concerning the human geographic milieu as it reflects and is affected by social characteristics. The dictionary includes about 350 entries, of which approximately 45 are simple "see" entries. Cross-references are common in the textual entries, and the index uses further cross-references. The great majority of the entries are more than simple definitions, and about 30 entries are two or more pages in length. Entries are clear and well written. Diagrams, charts, graphs, and formulas accompany many theoretical discussions and reflect the highly organized presentation of the material.

The briefer entries include specific activities, institutions, phenomena, and analytic terms in geography, mathematics, economics, and social science in general. Examples include *dry farming, isodapane,* and *gross domestic product.* References to corporate bodies, covering primarily international organizations, are also brief. The longer entries involve areas of theory, philosophical and methodological approaches to analysis, and processes of change. Examples of these include *structuration theory, Marxian geography,* and *von Thunen model.* Personalities in the field do not receive entries but can be located through the index, which refers to entries in which they are discussed in the context of their contribution. This work is revised every five years. The next scheduled revision is set for 1991.

As a core reference work in anthropology, *The Dictionary of Human Geography* has no real competition. Standard anthropological dictionaries include only a few of the most basic terms referring to the spatial environment of human beings. *The Dictionary of Human Geography* will be of the most use to anthropologists with a geographic interest. The Board recommends this work for the core collection of academic libraries.

Encyclopedia of Human Evolution and Prehistory. Ian Tattersall, Eric Delson, and John Van Couvering, eds. Garland, 1988. hard. 1 vol. 900 pp. illus. ISBN 0-8240-9375-5. $87.50. encyclopedia.
GN281.E53 573.2'03'21

Human evolution and prehistory are important subject areas to physical anthropologists, archaeologists, primatologists, and, to a lesser degree, social anthropologists. The *Encyclopedia of Human Evolution and Prehistory,* edited by Ian Tattersall, Eric Delson, and John Van Couvering—all on the staff of the American Museum of Natural History—is an extremely solid and complete reference source on the subject.

The editors' aim, stated in "A Brief Introduction to Human Evolution and Prehistory," is to cover the following: systematics, evolutionary theory, genetics, primatology, primate paleontology, and Paleolithic archaeology. The 600 or so text entries contain data, models, descriptions, and explanatory information. Included are descriptions of important archaeological sites, primate and prehuman anatomy and physiology, and comparisons of evolutionary theories.

Several organizational aspects of this source are especially useful for the novice researcher. A brief section on how to use the book explains the organization of the work and the arrangement of the entries. A subject list by topic places entries in their theoretical context and demonstrates at a glance relationships between concepts. A section entitled "A Brief Introduction to Human Evolution and Prehistory" provides a comprehensive overview of the entire area by providing "a context for each of the longer entries."

Additionally, a primate-classification scheme outlines orders (infra- and sub-), families (sub- and supra-), tribes, genera, and species into what the editors call a "consensus" rather than a "definitive" classification system. In this section, as in the encyclopedia entries, the editors strive for a balanced presentation. They realize that the considerable disagreement on explanatory models and the continuous addition of new information to the field render definitive statements unreliable. Finally, the introductory section contains a time chart comparing geologic epochs to the various continental strata of mammalian fauna, accompanied by a full-page explanation.

The editors of this volume have overseen the work of 40 contributors, who are listed along with their institutional affiliations. The contributors represent several British and American museums as well as colleges, universities, and medical schools. The articles in the encyclopedia are all signed, making this a highly authoritative source.

Unfortunately, there is no index, and the approximately 600 cross-references within the text are no adequate substitute. Someone looking for quick information may not have time to peruse cross-references to articles, many of which are long and complex. This is the encyclopedia's most serious limitation.

The editors claim that the text has been written to be "accessible to those with no prior knowledge of the subject" (preface). This objective may not have been fully realized, because the articles use only scientific names for organisms, apparatuses, anatomy, and procedures. Additionally, archaeological discussions refer liberally to sites, findings, and eras that are unfamiliar to most novice readers. The extensive use of technical terms may have made the encyclopedia too sophisticated a source for a lay audience. However, the clarity of the writing; the number of charts, photographs, and diagrams; and the fully descriptive text of the entries give any user quick access to the subject matter, once basic terminology has been mastered.

While the book is very heavy (both physically and informatively), the especially solid binding and clear, large typeface on nonglare, acid-free, heavy paper make it a purchase that will stand up to heavy use and the ravages of time.

The *Encyclopedia of Human Evolution and Prehistory* is an excellent reference source. No other encyclopedic reference source exists that covers this subject area in such breadth, depth, and currency. The Board recommends this work for the core collection of academic libraries.

Supplementary Titles

Bibliographic Guide to Anthropology and Archaeology, 1987. G. K. Hall, 1988. hard. 1 vol. 382 pp. ISBN 0-8161-7069-X. $180. bibliography.
Z5119.B43 016.3012

The *Bibliographic Guide to Anthropology and Archaeology, 1987* "lists materials cataloged between June 1986 and August 1987 by Harvard University's Tozzer Library [formerly the Peabody Museum of Archaeology and Ethnology]. It is the first annual supplement to the *Author and Subject Catalogues of the Tozzer Library,* second enlarged edition, on microfiche (G. K. Hall, 1988). . . . This book contains full cataloging information, compiled from OCLC records, for books and other materials on topics related to cultural anthropology, physical anthropology, archaeology, and liguistics, most published from 1982 through 1986. There are entries for authors, titles, subjects, etc., in a dictionary arrangement. Both LC and Dewey Decimal Classification numbers are given.

"This is an attractive, well-done work . . . [and] will . . . be a useful work, especially for subject access, not available on OCLC." (*ARBA,* 1989, p. 137)

Board's recommendation: Academic libraries.

New and Noteworthy

Atlas of World Cultures: A Geographical Guide to Ethnographic Literature. David H. Price. Sage, 1989. hard. 1 vol. 156 pp. index. ISBN 0-8039-3240-5. $35. atlas.
G1046.E1P7 912.13058

The *Atlas of World Cultures* lists "the geographical locations of 3,500 cultural groups . . . on a series of 40 numbered maps. . . . A bibliography of 1,237 numbered entries of 'classic' ethnographic studies provid[es] detailed information on the 3,500 groups. . . . A culture index provides access to both the maps and the bibliography. . . . The index indicates on which particular map a given ethnic group is found and which bibliographic entries pertain to that group." (*Choice,* December 1989, p. 615)

James R. Kelly

Archaeology

See also Ancient History

Archaeology embodies a remarkable juxtaposition of the ancient and the modern, the erudite and the primitive, the obvious and the mysterious. Coming into its own as a major discipline in the nineteenth century through the efforts, discoveries, and scholarship of such individuals as Heinrich Schliemann and Sir Flinders Petrie, archaeology proved to be a fertile ground for the efforts of self-taught amateur explorers and a burgeoning number of professional researchers. Using traditional methods of excavation and collection, these forebears of today's scientists rapidly brought to light hundreds of sites and countless artifacts, while at the same time building renowned aggregations of their finds at such places as the Egyptian Museum in Cairo and the British Museum in London.

As interest in the field spread (and tools and techniques became more sophisticated due to the heady strides occurring throughout the scientific world), the place of archaeology as a worthwhile field of endeavor became firmly entrenched. The familiar land locales were joined by a plethora of undersea sites, places in which work had been impossible before the advent of submarine vehicles, diving apparatus, and the pioneering efforts of Jacques-Yves Cousteau and others.

Water and earth may be the elements of exploration proper, but the atmosphere plays a role too. Aerial photography is an invaluable aid in terms of mapping and locating sites. Indeed, reconnaissance satellites now add to this capability, joining hands with methods derived from geophysical prospecting to continue the search for our past as read in structures and implements. Nowadays, an archaeologist makes use of knowledge from and methodologies of such disparate fields as computer science, botany, zoology, geology, and soil science, among others. Lastly, it would be a grievous oversight to omit mention of the role of radioactive carbon dating (from the arena of atomic physics) and its derivatives in the tremendous advances made in prehistoric archaeology.

To be sure, the basic reference collection for this field needs a variety of atlases devoted to the ancient and classical worlds, a specialized encyclopedia or two, as well as a dictionary, particularly an up-to-date one dealing with terminology from the intersections of archaeology and modern technology.

Librarians may wish to obtain the following titles, which were recommended by the Board but have since gone out of print. These are *The Atlas of Archaeology*

Core Titles

	PUBLIC	ACADEMIC	SCHOOL
Atlas of Ancient America Coe, Michael, Dean Snow, and Elizabeth Benson. Facts On File, 1986	✦	✦	✦
Atlas of Ancient Egypt Baines, John, and Jaromír Málek. Facts On File, 1982	✦	✦	✦
Dictionary of Terms and Techniques in Archaeology Champion, Sara. Everest House, 1980; repr. by Books on Demand		✦	
The Encyclopedia of Ancient Civilizations Cotterell, Arthur, ed. Mayflower, 1980; distrib. by Smith Bks.	✦	✦	
The Facts On File Dictionary of Archaeology Whitehouse, Ruth D., ed. Facts On File, 1983	✦	✦	✦
The Princeton Encyclopedia of Classical Sites Stillwell, Richard, ed. Princeton Univ. Pr., 1976		✦	

(K. Branigan, ed., St. Martin's, 1982); the *Cambridge Encyclopedia of Archaeology* (Andrew Sharratt, ed., Cambridge, 1980); *Archaeology: A Bibliographic Guide to the Basic Literature* (Robert R. Heizer et al., eds., Garland, 1980); and *The Amateur Archaeologist's Handbook* (Maurice Robbins and Mary B. Irving, Harper & Row, 1981).

Core Titles

Atlas of Ancient America. Michael Coe, Dean Snow, and Elizabeth Benson. Facts On File, 1986. hard. 1 vol. 240 pp. illus. index. ISBN 0-8716-334-5. $45. atlas.
E61.C66 970.11

Authored by a trio of academic anthropologists, each a prolific scholar, the *Atlas of Ancient America,* published by Facts On File, is a solid and useful addition to the literature of pre-Columbian studies. This atlas follows its related predecessor, the ATLAS OF ANCIENT EGYPT, in form, shape, and purpose. The book is full of first-rate maps, plans, and illustrations that do all that one could want in the way of making the atlas appealing to the eye and satisfying to the intellect.

The text is divided into large sections (New World, first Americans, North America, Mesoamerica, South America, and pre-Columbian survivals) that allow the user to find specific information or survey larger portions. Each section contains one or more explanatory essays as well as a variety of specialized essays on features such as "Hopi Ritual Drama" and "Mimbres Pottery," or site features, such as those of Mesa Verde in Colorado and the ruins of Cuzco in Peru. The prose, which is interesting and readable, bolsters the primary function of a traditional atlas, namely the accurate presentation of maps.

Intended for the general reader, the *Atlas of Ancient America* is designed to provide "an introduction to the hemisphere as a whole" (preface). Again, as with the ATLAS OF ANCIENT EGYPT, there is a detailed subject index, a bibliography, and a gazetteer with coordinates of sites and places together with the relevant page numbers for the maps. Accessibility is also enhanced by the detailed chronological table at the beginning of the reference work. The typeface is distinct and clear. Unfortunately, pages are lacking in adequate white space (a drawback both in the matter of book art and in the case of future rebinding, should that be necessary).

All in all, in the limited space available, the authors succeed in their attempt to render a pictorial and textual overview of the broad spectrum of indigenous Americans and their cultures. The Board recommends this work for the core collections of public, academic, and school libraries.

Atlas of Ancient Egypt. John Baines and Jaromír Málek. Facts On File, 1982. hard. 1 vol. 240 pp. illus. index. ISBN 0-87196-334-5. $45. atlas.
DT56.9.B34 932

The *Atlas of Ancient Egypt* originates from the familiar and competent publishers Facts On File and is further recommended by the authorial abilities of Oxford University's John Baines, a professor of Egyptology, and Egyptologist Jaromír Málek. These two have produced a volume that is uniform in visual appearance, form, topic, and style with Facts On File's ATLAS OF ANCIENT AMERICA.

The atlas is divided into three major sections: cultural setting, geographically sequential view of the Nile, and aspects of the society. Each section contains several essays on such topics as "Art and Architecture" and "Women in Society." Some essays have specialized charts or pictorial features within them; for example, within the essay on historical background is a listing of the kings of Egypt and hieroglyphic writings of selected kings' names.

The intent is "to provide a systematic survey of the most important sites with ancient Egyptian monuments, an assessment of their historical and cultural importance, and a brief description of their salient features" (introduction). To accomplish this, Baines and Málek have sensibly and pragmatically limited the work's scope to that area described by the Egyptian frontiers along the Nile River, from its source to the junction with the sea, including lower Nubia. Their chronological boundaries for material are set at 2920 B.C. and 332 B.C.

This is clearly a work for the general population. The heavily illustrated text, numerous special features, and uncomplicated prose invite dipping into parts of the whole as well as reading from cover to cover. The reference takes the reader on a verbal and visual tour of the Nile from south to north, following the river's flow. This introduction to the terrain is made more convenient through the appending of a lengthy index, bibliography, glossary of specialized terms, and a gazetteer with longitude and latitude coordinates keyed to the appropriate maps by page number. In addition, a list of selected museums that have strong Egyptian collections and a very helpful chronological table are included.

Visually attractive and easily manipulated, the book has double columns of text accompanied by marginal illustrations. The book is sturdily bound and will hold up to library use. Moreover, the volume opens flat when turned to any page, an important quality in an atlas.

The *Atlas of Ancient Egypt* remains quite current and is unlikely to need significant alteration or emendation in the near future. The book rewards its readers with high-quality illustrations and a lucid, error-free text. The Board recommends this work for the core collections of public, academic, and school libraries.

Dictionary of Terms and Techniques in Archaeology. Sara Champion. Everest House, 1980; repr. by Books on Demand. soft. 1 vol. 147 pp. illus. ISBN 0-89696-162-1. $36. dictionary.
CC70.C48 930.10321

The *Dictionary of Terms and Techniques in Archaeology* is authored by Sara Champion. At the time this work was published, Champion was a Fellow at Southampton University specializing in the application of current, advanced scientific theory and practice to archaeology. This dictionary is a dependable, utilitarian guide to terminology in the field, especially that portion of the lexicon that has become increasingly burdened with scientific vocabulary. The author notes in her introduction that she has not attempted a general dictionary of the field but rather a collection of words and phrases that "describe a technique applied to archaeological material either in the past or as part of modern analysis." Occasionally, there is evidence of a British bias in spelling and usage. This dictionary has a substantial number of entries (in nearly all cases, one paragraph in length) on such new or abstruse topics as *locational analysis, ceramic petrology,* or *X-ray fluorescence spectrometry.* The entries are not only concise, clear, and thoroughly cross-referenced, but are also supplemented with 60 black-and-white and two-color photographs and 60 maps and diagrams. A list of books for further reading concludes the reference.

The book itself is basically solid and free from distracting slips or oversights. However, the *Dictionary of Terms and Techniques in Archaeology* is now ten years old and is, of course, in need of updating to reflect the continuing, rapid change in things scientific and technological. The Board recommends this work for the core collection of academic libraries.

The Encyclopedia of Ancient Civilizations. Arthur Cotterell, ed. Mayflower, 1980; distrib. by Smith Bks. hard. 1 vol. 367 pp. illus. index. ISBN 0-8317-2790-X. $29.95. dictionary. out of stock.
CB311.E53 930.03

The Encyclopedia of Ancient Civilizations boasts approximately 38 distinguished scholars as contributors. These contributors are broad based and have been recruited from the British Commonwealth, the United States, Sweden, Mexico, and Kenya. Among this well-qualified and respected group are such well-known individuals as Richard E. Leakey, J. M. Plumley, and R. A. Markus, whose efforts have helped to produce a solid and authoritative work on ancient civilizations. Each essay is signed by its author. The reference work begins with two excellent essays on "Prehistory" by Leakey and "The Emergence of Civilization" by Colin Renfrew.

Aiming "to provide a comprehensive view of ancient history through the study of its civilizations," the encyclopedia is designed as an introduction to humanity's early history as it has been archaeologically revealed in Sumer and Egypt, the Indus Valley, the Yellow River Valley, Crete, Mexico, and Peru. To this end, the work is divided into six major sections that contain from 6 to 16 essays each. Each essay averages six pages in length, and details various regions and peoples. For example, the "America" section contains essays on the Olmecs, Maya, and Teotihuacán, among others.

The encyclopedia is for the general reader and beginning student in this field. The text is made accessible not only through the organization of the book as a whole, but also through an in-depth index. Keyed to the table of contents is a bibliography of six pages.

The text is set in a clear, if small, typeface and arranged in two columns. The numerous black-and-white illustrations, plus the occasional full-color pages, are clear and complement the text admirably.

Although *The Encyclopedia of Ancient Civilizations* is of a certain age, it is still of good service and should remain reliable, timely, and accurate enough for its purpose for at least another decade. The Board recommends this work for the core collections of public and academic libraries.

The Facts On File Dictionary of Archaeology. Ruth D. Whitehouse, ed. Facts On File, 1983. hard and soft. 1 vol. 597 pp. illus. index. ISBN 0-87196-048-6 (hard); 0-8160-1893-6 (soft). $35 (hard); $16.95 (soft). dictionary.
CC70.F32 930.1

Entries for *The Facts On File Dictionary of Archaeology* were contributed by nearly 100 academic and professional archaeologists from the English-speaking world (chiefly Great Britain). The only small reservation here is that the contributors' specialties were not identified and their individual entries were not signed. The editor, Ruth Whitehouse, is a lecturer in prehistoric archaeology at the University of Lancaster.

Entries are arranged alphabetically in a two-column format. Most of the "more than 3500 definitions and identifications" are one brief paragraph in length; an occasional entry reaches one column in length. Entries range from aging of skeletal material and mosaic to the Moroccan site of Douar Doum and the TRB culture. Famous archaeologists, such as Sir Flinders Petrie and Heinrich Schliemann, as well as those who influenced the field, such as Captain James Cook, are included. The text is augmented by a few dozen illustrations as well as by nine tables. The introduction to the dictionary states that the coverage is somewhat uneven due to the availability and disproportionate quantities of research accessible in the various topical and geographic areas it aims to cover. Also, the biases of the editors may have prevailed in determining the amount of space given to different subjects. For example, there is no entry for cylinder seals, which were of great importance in Mesopotamia, or for keftiu, the types of ambassadors depicted in tomb paintings in Egypt.

The reference is intended for students, scholars in the field, and nonspecialists alike. The language is such that the least sophisticated user should not be deterred; moreover, explanations and cross-references to technical terms help to guide the reader through any of the thornier parts. As the dictionary includes a number of Chinese words, it is unfortunate that the choice was not made to insert cross-reference entries from the Wade-Giles spelling system to the Pinyin system chosen for this text (except in the cases where the most severe orthographic discrepancies occur). In the instance of other languages, the authors have arbitrarily favored what they perceive to be the predominant form of words. Similarly, in the matter of site names they have vacillated between the ancient and modern appellations, but have at least made reference to the form(s) not selected. On the other hand, there are useful appendixes, one of which is a select subject bibliography and the other a subject index that lists significant terms under a number of subject headings such as dating, geology, period, and geographic locale.

The hardcover edition was originally published in 1983. The 1988 paperback edition of *The Facts On File Dictionary of Archaeology* claims to be a revised and expanded edition, but this reviewer was unable to find any evidence to substantiate that boast. For example, the site of Khirbet-Iskander was under excavation in 1982, but has not been added to this dictionary. The text is nonetheless quite current, and will be of good service to the user. Its currency is further enhanced by the collaborative editorial efforts that have resulted in a generally error-free presentation of an extensive number of clear, concise, and effective entries. The Board recommends this work for the core collections of public, academic, and school libraries.

The Princeton Encyclopedia of Classical Sites. Richard Stillwell, ed. Princeton Univ. Pr., 1976. soft. 1 vol. 1,019 pp. illus. index. ISBN 0-691-013179. $29.95. encyclopedia.
DE59.P7 938.003

The Princeton Encyclopedia of Classical Sites is a monumental and magisterial production of Princeton University Press in collaboration with the Samuel H. Kress Foundation, Andrew W. Mellon Foundation, and the National Endowment for the Humanities, among others. The underlying project was directed by an advisory board that also recommended the authors (some 375 in all from throughout the Western world and including such scholars as Barry Cunliffe of Oxford's Institute of Architecture and Richard P. Harper of the Dumbarton Oaks Center for Byzantine Studies). Entries were written in nine languages, but all have been translated into English for this work.

The encyclopedia provides coverage of approximately 3,000 sites. The advisory board defined the locations acceptable for inclusion as primarily those with actual remains and excluded most early sites of the fourth and fifth centuries. Entries are arranged alphabetically, employing the names used in classical times followed by the modern name, if different. Copius and meticulous cross-referencing aids greatly in quickly finding the chosen form of entry. Cross-references are also made between subsites of and the larger locales under which they have been incorporated. All entries are signed and vary in length from one paragraph to three pages, with most occupying some middle ground.

The most regrettable omission (though necessary for size purposes) is the exclusion of site plans, maps, and illustrations. This is remedied in some measure through the practice of noting the sources for such pictorial matter in the works cited in each entry's bibliography and by appending 16 area maps that denote all 3,000 sites. Map indexes, which group the sites by country, provide easy accessibility for using the maps. Throughout the work, Greek spelling of sites and terms has been favored. A glossary helps the user deal with the terminology of the field.

Intended for scholars and serious students, the entries are clear and thoroughly readable while remaining terse and nondiscursive in keeping with the volume's encyclopedia aim. Nonetheless, the casual user would find the work congenial both for clarity of prose and comprehensive internal cross-references.

Although the nearly 15 years that have passed since publication do inevitably cause *The Princeton Encyclopedia of Classical Sites* to be somewhat dated, the nature of the subject and the vigor of the fundamental effort expended make this work a necessary and timely source today. This, coupled with the skillful and painstaking editing, leaves the work in a secure niche on the reference shelves.

The Board recommends this work for the core collection of academic libraries.

Supplementary Titles

Larousse Encyclopedia of Archaeology, 2d edition. Gilbert Charles-Picard, ed.; Anne Ward, trans. Larousse, 1983. hard. 1 vol. 432 pp. illus. ISBN 0-88332-316-8. $15.95. encyclopedia.
CC165.A64213 930.1

The *Larousse Encyclopedia of Archaeology* seeks "to trace the development of archaeological research and to describe progress in reconstructing the past in selected places and times. Part one provides information on: selective preservation of monuments; methods of locating, excavating, and dating remains; and procedures for restoring, exhibiting, and publishing. Part two summarizes the history of investigations in chapters on prehistoric Europe, western Asia before Alexander, the Aegean world, Classical Greece, the Romans, the Etruscans, Bronze and Iron Age Europe, the Far East, and the Americas.

"The authors are trained in the classical historical rather than the anthropological tradition; consequently, their summaries draw mainly on temples, tombs, sculptures, ornaments, and similar traditional sources." (*SB* May/June 1984, p. 294)

Also reviewed in: *ARBA,* 1984, p. 170; *Atl,* January 1973, p. 100; *BL,* January 1, 1973, p. 425; *BL,* January 15, 1973, p. 489; *BL,* October 15, 1984, p. 431; *Choice,* March 1973, p. 62; *CSM,* November 22, 1972, p. 85; *LJ,* May 1, 1973, p. 1471; *LJ,* November 1, 1983, p. 2074; *RSR,* October 1973, p. 49; *SR,* November 25, 1972, p. 76; *WLB,* May 1973, p. 793.

Board's recommendation: Public and academic libraries.

The New International Dictionary of Biblical Archaeology. Edward M. Blaiklock and R. K. Harrison, eds. Zondervan, 1983. hard. 1 vol. 560 pp. illus. index. ISBN 0-310-21250-2. $30.95. dictionary.
BS622.N48 220.9'3'0321

The New International Dictionary of Biblical Archaeology "offers entries for personal and place names, deities, terms, texts, [and other items] important in biblical archaeology. Except for some brief definitions, all articles are signed with the initials of the contributors; bibliographic references follow most articles; [and there are] numerous cross references. A section of 33 colored maps (on unnumbered pages) has its own index. [The dictionary is] intended for a broad readership [as reflected in the editors' statement in the preface]: 'Our object has not been primarily polemical or evidential. We have sought, within prescribed limits, to present basic facts. Those who use the book must, for the most part, draw their own theological conclusions.' " (*Guide to Reference Books,* 1976, p. 357)

Also reviewed in: *ARBA,* 1985, p. 1292.

Board's recommendation: Public and academic libraries.

The World Atlas of Archaeology. Michael Wood, ed. G. K. Hall, 1985. hard. 1 vol. 423 pp. illus. index. ISBN 0-8161-8747-9. $95. atlas.
G1046.E15W6 912

The World Atlas of Archaeology "is arranged geographically and chronologically, with sections on prehistoric Europe, the classical world, the Middle Ages, Byzantium, Islam, the modern period, and 12 major geographic areas, including the New World. . . . [There are some] 1,000 color illustrations. . . . [Thematic maps] illustrate topics such as trade routes . . . and plant defense areas in Nigeria.

"Detailed contents pages and an index help users locate subjects and cultures. . . . The glossary is useful and a bibliography contains current materials primarily from the 1970s and 1980s. Many of the sources cited are in French, but English works are included in all subject categories. The translation into English reads smoothly." (*BL,* May 15, 1986, p. 1383)

"This atlas aims at presenting material from the perspective of 'new archaeology,' reconstructing diverse peoples' lives based on their material culture. The articles, written largely by French contributors are . . . unsigned. . . . [Overall,] the atlas draws attention both to recent archaeological techniques and to international concern for preserving the past, while encompassing a rich diversity of source material. It will be of interest to both laypersons and scholars." (*LJ,* December 1985, p. 92)

Also reviewed in: *ARBA,* 1986, p. 175; *Choice,* March 1986, p. 1046; *LATBR,* December 1, 1985, p. 8; *SB,* September 1986, p. 43; *TLS,* October 10, 1986, p. 1145; *WLB,* February 1986, p. 66.

Board's recommendation: Public and academic libraries.

New and Noteworthy

Historical Dictionary of North American Archaeology. Edward B. Jelks and Juliet C. Jelks, eds. Greenwood, 1988. hard. 1 vol. 760 pp. index. ISBN 0-313-24307-7. $95. dictionary.
E77.9.H57 970.01

"Invaluable both for reference and collection development (with a 150-page bibliography), . . . [the *Historical Dictionary of North American Archaeology* is a] guide to mainly prehistoric sites, cultures, and artifacts in the United States and Canada [which] features some 1800 signed entries by 151 expert contributors that highlight the information upon which present North American prehistory is based." (*LJ,* April 15, 1989, p. 40)

Judith Herschman

Architecture

In determining the choices for a basic reference collection in the field of architecture, it is first necessary to recognize the variety of aspects that constitute the discipline. Gaining an overall knowledge of the field requires consideration of historical trends, aesthetic elements, stylistic criteria, and structural and technical data. Second, it is necessary to realize that this is a subject that touches people's lives directly and can be a source of great interest to them. Because of these factors, the core collection must be able to provide the answers to a broad spectrum of questions ranging from who designed a particular building to what is a joist. In addition, the field relies heavily on illustrations to convey information to the reader.

The titles reviewed in this buying guide, although few in number, constitute a core collection that should satisfy most of the information needs of the patrons of public and school libraries. Many students and professionals in the field will find the works reviewed useful as well; however, professionals and students will need to consult more technical and specialized sources, such as bibliographies for particular periods of time or architectural styles; handbooks for various aspects of design and construction; and historical reference books for the field.

As Donald Ehresmann says in the preface to his *Architecture: A Bibliographic Guide to Basic Reference Works, Histories, and Handbooks* (Libraries Unlimited, 1984), "of all the media in the fine arts, architecture has the most extensive and complex literature." Although his comprehensive bibliography is no longer in print, it is worth tracking down because it provides access to much of this literature. Ehresmann's bibliography can be supplemented by more specialized works such as *American Architecture and Art: A Guide to Information Sources* (David M. Sokol, Gale, 1976), which unfortunately has recently gone out of print, and by lists of publications on individual architects found in the MACMILLAN ENCYCLOPEDIA OF ARCHITECTS and CONTEMPORARY ARCHITECTS. The last two titles are the best biographical dictionaries in the field and, used together, provide comprehensive historical and international coverage. *Encyclopedia of American Architecture* (McGraw-Hill, 1982) is a good biographical source for historical coverage of American architects. However, this important source has also recently gone out of print.

Although information on style, structure, decoration, social context, and individual architects is included in general art reference works, the depth of a

Core Titles

	PUBLIC	ACADEMIC	SCHOOL
Contemporary Architects, 2d edition Morgan, Ann Lee, and Colin Naylor. St. James, 1987	✦	✦	
Dictionary of Architectural and Building Technology Cowan, Henry J., and Peter R. Smith. Elsevier, 1986	✦	✦	
Macmillan Encyclopedia of Architects, 4 vols. Placzek, Adolf K., ed. Free Pr./Macmillan, 1982	✦	✦	
The World Atlas of Architecture G. K. Hall, 1984	✦	✦	✦

collection can be increased by including a more focused and heavily illustrated source that is exclusively architectural in content. THE WORLD ATLAS OF ARCHITECTURE is one excellent resource of this type.

When more technical information is required, the collection should include the DICTIONARY OF ARCHITECTURAL AND BUILDING TECHNOLOGY and the rich and versatile ARCHITECTURAL GRAPHIC STANDARDS. Where patron interest is high in the area of restoration and preservation, librarians may want to seek out *Historic Preservation: A Guide to Information Sources* (Arnold L. Markowitz, ed., Gale, 1980), now out of print, to add to the collection.

The basic and current periodical literature in architecture is largely included in the *Art Index* (Wilson, annual). Only more specialized or research library collections would need to purchase the more extensive *Avery Index to Architechural Periodicals* (G. K. Hall, 1989).

Core Titles

Contemporary Architects, 2d edition. Ann Lee Morgan and Colin Naylor. St. James, 1987. hard. 1 vol. 1,038 pp. illus. ISBN 0-912289-26-0. $135. biographical dictionary.
NA40 720.92′2

Originally published in 1980, this second edition of *Contemporary Architects* adds entries for 40 architects, while deleting a number whose activity ceased before World War II, for a total of nearly 600 entries. This biographical dictionary is a parallel work to others issued by St. James Press as part of the Contemporary Arts series. Companion volumes are CONTEMPORARY ARTISTS (see Art) and CONTEMPORARY PHOTOGRAPHERS (see Photography).

An international advisory board selected the architects to be included in the volume. Although the criteria for inclusion are not specified in this book, the resulting coverage is international in scope. The term *architect* is broadly defined, and the entries, therefore, include planners, theorists, structural engineers, and landscape architects. Most of the entrants were alive when the biographical dictionary was compiled (1987). An exception to this policy was made to include some deceased twentieth-century figures of importance, such as Le Corbusier, Louis Kahn, and Frank Lloyd Wright. A list of names and architectural firms included appears at the beginning of the volume. Occasionally an architect receives two entries, one in his or her own name and one as part of a collaboration. This occurs when he or she has done major work independent of a firm or, conversely, when a firm has continued to do work without the founder. Such is the case, for example, with the entries for *Louis Skidmore* and *Skidmore, Owings and Merrill,* and *George Hellmuth* and *Hellmuth, Obata and Kassabaum.*

Alphabetically arranged entries contain detailed biographical information; a comprehensive list of works chronologically arranged (dating through 1985); and a list of publications, including monographs and periodical and newspaper articles, by and about the architect. Following this factual section is a statement by the architect about his or her work and a signed commentary by one of the contributing architectural historians or critics. A list of the credentials of the advisors and contributors appear at the end of the volume. Many entries are accompanied by a black-and-white illustration of a typical example of the biographee's work. Unfortunately, there is no separate list of illustrations to guide the reader to a particular building shown.

While this is a wonderful reference source, which complements the comprehensive, more historically oriented MACMILLAN ENCYCLOPEDIA OF ARCHITECTS, it is not the place to go for information on younger, less well known figures in the field. Those listed here have already established reputations (although there are occasional gaps, such as the omission of Emilio Ambasz). For the newer and more obscure names in the field or for regional figures, a potential source of identification—apart from the periodical literature accessed through indexes—would be *Profile: The Official Directory of the American Institute of Architects.*

Contemporary Architects maintains the same high quality as the other titles in the Contemporary Arts series, with the same attractive format and ease of use. The Board recommends this work for the core collections of public and academic libraries.

Dictionary of Architectural and Building Technology. Henry J. Cowan and Peter R. Smith. Elsevier, 1986. hard. 1 vol. 287 pp. illus. ISBN 0-85334-402-7. $36. dictionary.
NA31.C63 720.3'21

First published in 1973, this edition of the *Dictionary of Architectural and Building Technology* has been completely revised. Terms no longer in use have been dropped, and 1,500 new ones have been added. The authors consulted a variety of standard references in their preparation of the dictionary, including the *Encyclopaedia Britannica* and Harris's *Dictionary of Architecture and Construction.*

The authors intend the dictionary to be comprehensive within the areas of architectural technology, building science, and building technology. The field of building technology includes structures, materials, acoustics, lighting, thermal environment, sun control, building services, scientific management studies, architectural computing, and so forth. The dictionary does not include definitions of styles or decorative elements; for definitions of these terms readers might refer to the glossary in the MACMILLAN ENCYCLOPEDIA OF ARCHITECTS.

Because authors Cowan and Smith are Australian, the dictionary is directed at British and Australian audiences. American users will be able to access the entries easily due to the use of cross-references to alternate spellings. In this dictionary the official entry word used is determined by the preferred form of the term found in the *Shorter Oxford English Dictionary.* Cross-references abound to alternative terms, with the definition appearing under the preferred term or expression. Thus the entry for *chipboard* indicates that it is the same as *particle board,* and the term *centring* is said to be the same as *centering.* Sometimes terms that are not related exclusively to architecture are included, such as *interactive* and *mouse.*

Definitions tend to be brief, straightforward, and nontechnical. Sometimes they can be amusing in their simplicity. *Freshness,* for example, is defined as the "opposite of STUFFINESS. It is produced by air movement and cooler temperatures." Words in definitions that are in capital letters are cross-references to separate entries that contain the relevant information. Only SI (Système International, or International System) metric units are used in scientific entries, but both SI metric and Imperial units are used in applied entries. Schematic illustrations occasionally accompany entries, but the logic behind what is illustrated and what is not is unclear.

The *Dictionary of Architectural and Building Technology* is a handy reference source that is as useful for the layman as it is for the practitioners to whom it is directed. The Board recommends this work for the core collections of public and academic libraries.

Macmillan Encyclopedia of Architects. Adolf K. Placzek, ed. Free Pr./Macmillan, 1982. hard. 4 vols. 2,701 pp. illus. appendix. index. ISBN 0-02-925000-5 (set). $400 (set). biographical encyclopedia.
NA40.M25 720.92'2[B]

In the foreword to the four-volume *Macmillan Encyclopedia of Architects,* its editor, Adolf Placzek (the distinguished former librarian of the Avery Art and Architecture Library at Columbia University), characterizes the work as the most comprehensive assemblage of architectural biography ever published. And, indeed, 2,400 architects spanning nearly 5,000 years are described in this monumental work.

However, no one born after December 31, 1930, is included. Architectural visionaries (such as Ledoux and Sant'Elia) and writers on architecture (such as Vitruvius and Ruskin) can be found in these volumes, even though they were not practicing architects. Noted engineers, bridge builders, landscape architects, and town planners are also included. Many names often omitted from similar biographical sources, such as the Egyptian Imhotep (probable architect of a third-dynasty pyramid), or the Turkish architect Sinan (sixteenth-century designer of the most significant buildings in the Ottoman Empire), receive entries here.

A distinguished editorial board, whose members' names are listed opposite the title page, selected the architects to be included and determined the length of the entries (which ranges from 50 to 10,000 words). The chief considerations for inclusion and the determination of the length of the entry were the historic importance of the architect, the availability of information, the nature and quality of the surviving buildings, and the influence exerted by the architect. Over 600 experts from 26 different countries contributed the various essays.

The longer biographical entries contain discussions of the "artistic, technical, and historical perspectives which contributed to the development of the architect's ideas and approach to design, and the extent to which each architect furthered existing styles or developed new techniques" (introduction). Although there are variations in writing style, the entries on the whole provide lively and interesting reading. Following the textual portion of each entry is a selected list of works actually built by the subject, with the name, place, and date of the work provided. Plans and unexecuted structures are discussed in the text. Bibliographies of selected monographs and articles about the architect complete the entry. The *Macmillian Encyclopedia of Architects* contains 1,500 black-and-white illustrations, which include photographs of structures, drawings, engravings and woodcuts, plans, models, and elevations.

Several extremely useful features appear in volume 4. These include a chronological table of contents (that is, a list of architects in somewhat chronological order); a general bibliography of basic biographical sources and standard architectural histories; a 21-page glossary of architectural terms; an index of names that lists those mentioned in the text of the entries as well as the subjects of separate entries; and a 121-page index of works listed by common name and by type of structure. A list of biographies and a directory of contributors and the entries appear in the front of the first volume.

The *Macmillan Encyclopedia of Architects* is one of the most important reference resources in the field of architecture. The Board recommends this work for the core collections of public and academic libraries.

The World Atlas of Architecture. G. K. Hall, 1984. hard. 1 vol. 408 pp. illus. index. ISBN 0-8161-8716-9. $95. atlas.
NA200.W671984 720.9

The World Atlas of Architecture is an English translation of *Le Grand Atlas de l'Architecture Mondiale,* which itself is a revision and expansion of Mitchell Beasley's *Great Architecture of the World,* published in 1975. This edition is a profusely and luxuriously illustrated work that encompasses the whole history of architecture. The atlas is replete with photographs of structures, maps indicating locations of monuments, charts, comparative timelines, plans, and diagrams. The intent of the atlas is to increase sophistication in looking at architecture and to encourage awareness of cultural context, structure and form, space, and ornament. The volume offers guidelines on how to approach, or "read," a building and how to appreciate "not only the social and cultural forces that led to the creation of various styles, but also the technical and practical considerations that shaped their development" (introduction). *The World Atlas of Architecture* successfully achieves these lofty goals.

The atlas is divided into six major parts: "Non-European Civilizations," "The Ancient World," "Late Antiquity and the Early Middle Ages," "The Middle Ages," "The Age of Classicism," and "The Modern Era." The table of contents gives a detailed listing of the chapters and their subdivisions. Each part typically contains a sometimes lengthy introductory article with accompanying maps, timelines, charts, and other visual materials needed to convey an overview of the era, the predominant styles, and its relationship to the architectural history of the rest of the world. The chapter subdivisions (for example, "Stone Walls of Zimbabwe," "Early Gothic in France," or "Critical Rationalism") are supported by many illustrative examples, axonometric plans, and other materials explanatory of the theme. The captions to the illustrations are a descriptive and informative supplement to the text.

A two-page bibliography at the back of the atlas lists general works published in English and more specialized titles relating to the topics of specific chapters. Publishers are not given in this bibliography. Although the "Index/Glossary" is 14 pages long, it does not even attempt to be comprehensive. The list combines definitions of terms and page references to the text and illustrations. Birth and death dates are given for artists or architects, so that the index itself can be a quick reference source. Selected photographs are included in the index as well. A separate list of illustrations would have been a useful addition to this atlas.

In addition to its many virtues, *The World Atlas of Architecture* is a handsomely designed book with an attractive typeface, format, and reproductions. This atlas is oversize, not only in its dimensions, but also in its scope. The Board recommends this work for the core collections of public, academic, and school libraries.

Supplementary Titles

American Architecture and Art: A Guide to Information Sources. David M. Sokol. Gale, 1976. hard. 1 vol. 341 pp. index. ISBN 0-8103-1255-7. $68. bibliography.
Z5961.U5S64 [N6505] 016.709'73

American Architecture and Art is the "second volume in Gale's American Studies Information Guide series [and it] does a good job of providing access to the basic and specialized literature on American architecture and art. The term 'art' is broadly defined, and 'American' includes Europeans who produced significant works with American subjects for American consumption. The 1,590 items cited and briefly annotated are grouped in 11 chapters. The publications range from the standard general monographs to specialized periodical articles and exhibit catalogs. Works by and about a good selection of individual architects, painters, and sculptors are included. The volume is well indexed and will serve as a good guide in all types of libraries." (*WLB,* December 1976, p. 363)

Also reviewed in: *A Art,* March 1977, p. 13; *ARBA,* 1977, p. 421.

Board's recommendation: Public and academic libraries.

Architectural Graphic Standards, 8th edition. John Ray Hoke, Jr., ed. John Wiley, 1988. hard. 1 vol. 854 pp. illus. appendix. index. ISBN 0-471-81148-3. $150. handbook. revised every 6 to 8 years.
TH2031.A84 721.022'2

Architectural Graphic Standards "contains seventeen chapters, covering such topics as masonry, wood, doors and windows, furnishings, and conveying systems. The pages are made up almost entirely of illustrations—drawings, tables, etc.—showing standard dimensions for such things as a Mickey Mouse phone, a dartboard, a knife, fork, and spoon, a wok, various types of file cabinets, desks, chairs, as well as larger items such as escalators and cooling towers. An index is included. According to its publisher, the book's audience includes architects, builders, draftsmen, engineers, students, interior designers, real estate agents and brokers, homeowners, insurance underwriters, and lovers of fine books." (*Ser Lib 2nd,* 1985, p. 175)

Approximately 50 percent of *Architectural Graphic Standards* is revised every six to eight years.

Also reviewed in: *Choice,* September 1971, p. 813.

Board's recommendation: Public and academic libraries.

Encyclopaedia of Architecture. Doreen Yarwood. Facts On File, 1986. hard. 1 vol. 446 pp. illus. index. ISBN 0-8160-1423-X. $35. encyclopedia.
NA31.Y37 720.3'21

The *Encyclopaedia of Architecture* is " 'a copiously illustrated and easy-to-use reference work . . . [describing] architects, materials, building methods and architectural terms.' There are more than 1,200 articles and more than 1,000 illustrations.

"The drawings are notable for their clarity. Doreen Yarwood has written all the articles, done all of the drawings, and taken most of the photographs. Entries are arranged alphabetically and can be categorized into three types: 1) Short glossary definitions. . . . 2) Longer articles [that] discuss broader topics in an encyclopedic manner. . . . [and] 3) . . . biographical entries." (*BL,* September 15, 1986, p. 114)

"This is really two works in one: a general dictionary of architectural terms such as roof, window, lintel, etc., and an encyclopedia of British architects. Many of the write-ups are excellent and are well illustrated." (*Choice,* September 1986, p. 96)

Also reviewed in: *ARBA,* 1987, p. 391; *Brit Bk N,* November 1985, p. 679; *R&R Bk N,* Summer 1986, p. 13; *WLB,* June 1986, p. 80.

Board's recommendation: Public and academic libraries.

New and Noteworthy

American Architects: A Survey of Award-Winning Contemporaries and Their Notable Works. Les Krantz. Facts On File, 1989. hard. 1 vol. 301 pp. ISBN 0-8160-1420-5. $40. biographical dictionary. out of stock.
NA736.K7 720.92

American Architects is "a one-volume guide, in dictionary format, to 400 living American architects. Each entry includes the architect's name and date of birth, . . . plus information on where [he or she] studied, awards won, and most notable works. A brief description of [the architect's] style of architecture and some of the buildings follows." (*Choice,* February 1990, p. 933)

Encyclopedia of Architecture Design, Engineering, & Construction. Joseph A. Wilkes and Robert T. Packard, eds. John Wiley, 1988–1990. hard. 5 vols. illus. index. ISBN 0-471-63351-8 (set). $850 (set). encyclopedia.
NA31.E59 720.3

The *Encyclopedia of Architecture, Design, Engineering, & Construction* "will become the standard in the field. Its broad coverage focusing on architectural processes and technology, but encompassing history, aesthetics, and biography . . . offers lucid accounts by architects, architectural historians, and academics. . . . [The work contains] 3000 illustrations and 500 tables." (*LJ,* April 15, 1989, p. 39)

Judith Herschman

Art

See also Architecture; Decorative and Applied Arts; Graphic Arts; Painting and Sculpture; Photography

Art is an enormous field that touches all of our lives in fairly direct ways. The core reference collection in art must serve a variety of users, ranging from the casual museum visitor who buys a print of a Monet painting and wants to find out more about the artist to the historian who is studying gesture in Renaissance art. This core collection should be able to accommodate the interests of such a diverse readership. In order to do so, it must include a number of different kinds of titles.

A comprehensive reference source such as the *Encyclopedia of World Art* (now out of print) will fulfill many purposes, providing background information on art styles, periods, and cultures as well as answering a multitude of questions about artists, techniques, and specific works. For quicker reference, the more compact THE OXFORD COMPANION TO ART might be the work of first choice for similar information. Both titles provide extensive bibliographies that guide readers to additional material, as do many of the other core and supplementary works.

There is, of course, keen interest in artists themselves, their work, and their lives. It is relatively easy to find information on well-known artists, but the average reader may find information about lesser-known and contemporary artists more difficult to obtain. A large number of biographical dictionaries in the field of art are particularly useful and therefore form a major component of a core reference collection. This accounts for the fact that six of the core titles reviewed are specialized biographical sources that sometimes duplicate, but largely complement, each other as resources for material on individual artists. Many of these dictionaries (for example, CONTEMPORARY ARTISTS and WORLD ARTISTS, 1950–1980) also contain valuable bibliographic information.

In assessing reference works in this field, the librarian may wonder how important the quantity and quality of illustrations in a work are. Illustrations, in general, enhance a reference work, and good illustrations make it even better. The purpose of the work, however, dictates whether or not the quality of the reproductions makes a difference. In the case of CONTEMPORARY ARTISTS, for example, the reproductions are nothing out of the ordinary, but the library needs this source for the biographical information it imparts. Of the titles reviewed here, THE OXFORD COMPANION TO TWENTIETH-CENTURY ART contains the best reproductions. The work is improved by the high quality of the illustrations, but their inclusion is not a deciding factor in the selection of this book. Certain reference works con-

Core Titles

	PUBLIC	ACADEMIC	SCHOOL
Contemporary Artists, 3d edition Naylor, Colin, ed. St. James, 1989	✦	✦	✦
Dictionary of Contemporary American Artists, 5th edition Cummings, Paul. St. Martin's, 1988	✦	✦	
Dictionary of Women Artists: An International Dictionary of Women Artists Born Before 1900 Petteys, Chris. G. K. Hall, 1985	✦	✦	
Mantle Fielding's Dictionary of American Painters, Sculptors, and Engravers, 2d edition Opitz, Glenn B., ed. Apollo, 1987	✦	✦	✦
The Oxford Companion to Art Osborne, Harold, ed. Clarendon/Oxford, 1970	✦	✦	✦
The Oxford Companion to Twentieth-Century Art Osborne, Harold, ed. Oxford, 1981	✦	✦	✦
Who's Who in American Art, 1989–1990, 18th edition Bowker, 1989	✦	✦	
World Artists, 1950–1980 Marks, Claude. Wilson, 1984	✦	✦	✦

sist solely of reproductions (none are included in this collection), and the quality of these reproductions would indeed be a significant criterion for purchase.

For reference to current and retrospective information on all aspects of art, as well as information on contemporary artists, *Art Index* (Wilson, annual) is an essential source. Although not reviewed in this buying guide, this index provides important coverage of the domestic and foreign periodical literature and cannot be excluded from a core reference collection. Other periodical indexes may be more comprehensive in scope, but *Art Index* remains the easiest and most familiar to use. It is available in print format, on-line, or on CD-ROM. The *American Art Directory, 1989–90* (Bowker, 1989) is another work not reviewed but important to include in a basic collection for the variety of information on institutions and organizations it contains.

Sources of great value but that tend to be more specialized either because of subject focus (such as AMERICAN POPULAR ILLUSTRATION: A REFERENCE GUIDE) or because of audience (for example, GUIDE TO THE LITERATURE OF ART HISTORY) have been listed as supplementary titles. For those libraries that can afford them, they provide additional depth to an art reference collection.

A number of art reference works are no longer in print. Librarians may wish to locate the following titles through out-of-print sources to extend the breadth of their collection: *Encyclopedia of World Art* (McGraw-Hill, 1959; supplements 1983 and 1987), already mentioned; *American Folk Art: A Guide to the Sources* (Simon J. Bronner, Garland, 1984); and *The Artist's Handbook of Materials and Techniques,* 4th edition (Ralph Mayer, Viking-Penguin, 1981). *The Artist's Handbook,* however, will be issued in a fifth edition in 1991.

Core Titles

Contemporary Artists, 3d edition. Colin Naylor, ed. St. James, 1989. hard. 1 vol. 1,059 pp. illus. appendix. ISBN 0-912289-96-1. $120. biographical dictionary. revised every 5 years.
N6490.C6567 709.2′2

Contemporary Artists is a biographical dictionary, international in scope, containing entries for 850 artists, most of whom are still alive. Some artists who died after 1960 (such as Mark Rothko and Marcel Duchamp) are included if their work continues to influence current art activity.

Although selective in its entries, *Contemporary Artists* is broader in scope and coverage than most other art biographical sources and is the place to go first for information on important living artists. An international panel of art historians, museum directors, curators, and art critics selected the artists for inclusion based on the following criteria: the artist has worked as a professional for at least five years, has exhibited his or her work at important galleries, has been a participant in large-scale museum survey shows, and is represented in permanent collections of major museums throughout the world. Younger, lesser-known artists are included if they have attracted serious critical attention. Painters, sculptors, and graphic, video, and performance artists are included, but photographers are not. Architects, photographers, and designers are covered in parallel sources by the same publisher: CONTEMPORARY ARCHITECTS (see Architecture) and CONTEMPORARY PHOTOGRAPHERS (see Photography).

Contemporary Artists is revised every five years. An examination of the 1989 edition reveals considerable overlap between artists covered in this volume and the 1977 and 1983 editions, except for deletions of entries for those who have died in the interim or whose importance has diminished. While the panel has come up with a sophisticated list of artists, there are some significant omissions. Noticeably underrepresented are West Coast, black, feminist, and video and performance artists. But for this weakness, one might reasonably expect to find such figures as Kim McConnell, Joyce Treiman, Faith Ringgold, Suzanne Lacy, and Bill Viola. Artists who cross media boundaries, such as Duane Michaels, and therefore might be expected to be included here, are listed in CONTEMPORARY PHOTOGRAPHERS (see Photography) instead. But why Cindy Sherman is excluded from both works is inexplicable.

Each entry includes biographical data; a list of individual exhibitions and up to ten group exhibitions; a bibliography of books, articles, and exhibition catalogs by and about the artist; comments by the artist (when provided); and a signed critical essay on the artist's work. Each article has been updated with current information. Many of the entries (but not all) are accompanied by a representative black-and-white illustration of the artist's work. Although one illustration obviously cannot adequately represent an artist's range, even a single picture can be useful. The format of the entries makes them very easy to read. A list of artists included is provided in the front of the book for quick reference, as is an appendix that supplies the credentials of the 13 advisors and 125 contributors to the work.

An occasional annoying misspelled name in the index list (such as Jose *de Riva* instead of *de Rivera* or Joel *Shiparo* instead of *Shapiro*) slightly mars *Contemporary Artists.* This biographical dictionary is otherwise an outstanding and essential title notable for the scope of its coverage, the comprehensiveness of its information, the currency of the data, and the quality of the commentary. This work is recommended by the Board for the core collections of public, academic, and school libraries.

Dictionary of Contemporary American Artists, 5th edition. Paul Cummings. St. Martin's, 1988. hard. 1 vol. 738 pp. appendixes. indexes. ISBN 0-312-00232-7. $15. biographical dictionary.
N6536.C8 709.2′2

First published in 1966, *Dictionary of Contemporary American Artists* is in its fifth edition and, according to the author, has been extensively revised. The 900 artists included were chosen on the basis of their representation in museums and collections, their participation in major American and international exhibitions, their influence as teachers, and recognition by other professionals. Author Paul Cummings, director of the oral history program of the Archives of American Art at the Smithsonian Institution from 1967 to 1978, has written and edited several art books and reference works. The information that comprises the entries was gathered from questionnaires, personal interviews, and research.

Entries are arranged alphabetically by artist's last name. Each entry contains biographical data, including the artist's education, teaching experience, extensive exhibition history, commissions executed, awards received, address, and dealer. While many listings are brief, those artists who exhibit frequently (such as Christo) can have more than a page of summary data. The numbers at the end of an entry refer to briefly annotated titles, relating to the artist's life and work, that are listed in the bibliography in the back of the volume.

The 40-page bibliography is quite extensive, with a supplementary 9-page addition of books of general interest. Boldface numbers designate the more important titles among those listed. If the artist's papers or taped interviews are available at the Archives of American Art of the Smithsonian Institution, mention is made of that fact.

In addition to a preface entitled "How to Use This Book," Cummings includes a list of illustrations, which refers to the occasional black-and-white photographs scattered throughout the volume; an index of artists and pronunciation guide, which designates the medium in which the artist is best known (for example, painting, watercolor, assemblage, drafting, and so on); a key to museums and institutions and their schools that own works of art by the artists in the book; and a useful list of galleries representing the artists cited.

By virtue of its bibliography and its references to archival materials, the *Dictionary of Contemporary American Artists* is also extremely helpful in directing the reader to additional information, both published and unpublished, on individual artists. Because 127 artists were dropped and 87 added in the most recent edition, it makes sense to keep previous editions in the library collection. The Board recommends this work for the core collections of public and academic libraries.

Dictionary of Women Artists: An International Dictionary of Women Artists Born Before 1900. Chris Petteys. G. K. Hall, 1985. hard. 1 vol. 851 pp. ISBN 0-8161-8456-9. $60. biographical dictionary.
N43.P47 709.2'2

A field of legitimate academic study as well as of increasing general public attention, women and the arts has generated a number of significant reference sources in recent years. Significant among them is *Dictionary of Women Artists: An International Dictionary of Women Artists Born Before 1900,* which brings together in a single work a comprehensive list of female artists of all nationalities. The result is a compilation of biographical information on more than 21,000 women painters, sculptors, printmakers, and illustrators. Photographers, architects, craftsworkers, and designers have been excluded.

The author, a collector of women's art and an active supporter of the arts in Colorado, has gathered her data from secondary sources, such as books, pamphlets, articles, periodicals, exhibition and auction catalogs, newspapers, and unpublished manuscripts, as well as from living individuals. Standard biographical dictionaries of artists (for example, Bénézit's *Dictionnaire des peintres, sculpteurs, dessinateurs et graveurs de tous les temps* and Thieme and Becker's *Allgemeines Lexikon der bildenden Künstler von der Antike bis zur Gegenwart*) were systematically consulted for names.

Individual entries, arranged alphabetically, contain the artist's name (maiden, married, and pseudonym); birth and death dates; media; place of residence or activity; education and training; summary of exhibition record; awards; and bibliographic references. Sources of the entry data are given, but unfortunately in some cases what is cited in the *Dictionary of Women Artists* is all that is available in the original source. For example, the entry for *Florat, Anne Elizabeth,* reads, "French painter active Paris 1764. *Bénézit.*" When one turns to Bénézit, the same information is repeated. The length of an entry is not based on the subject's relative importance; lesser-known artists are sometimes given more extensive treatment because the information is not readily available elsewhere.

In addition to a list of contributors and a list of abbreviations, an extremely useful 70-page bibliography of books, articles, and surveys on women artists is provided.

The only criticism one might level is that the typewriter typeface gives the book an amateurish appearance. This tends to diminish the sense of the solidity and permanence of this resource. The content, however, is thoroughly professional and authoritative, and the importance of the *Dictionary of Women Artists* for art collectors and dealers, museum staff, art historians, and women's studies researchers remains undiminished. The Board recommends this work for the core collections of public and academic libraries.

Mantle Fielding's Dictionary of American Painters, Sculptors and Engravers, 2d edition. Glenn B. Opitz, ed. Apollo, 1987. hard. 1 vol. 1,081 pp. ISBN 0-938290-04-5. $95. biographical dictionary.
N6536.F5 709.2'2

Originally published in 1926 and updated in 1965, 1974, and 1983, this second, newly revised and enlarged edition of *Mantle Fielding's Dictionary of American Painters, Sculptors and Engravers* includes 2,500 additional artists, bringing the total number of entries to over 12,000. Moreover, 60 percent of the entries from the previous edition have been updated. Editor Glenn B. Opitz had already incorporated the *Dictionary of American Artists* (reprint of the *American Art Annual,* 1929) into the 1983 edition, resulting in the addition of 6,000 new entries primarily of nineteenth- and early twentieth-century artists.

In addition to expanding the 1983 edition, the editor and publisher have markedly improved the format and typeface in this new edition, making it easy to read and giving it a more professional look.

A good source for regional artists and lesser-known historical figures, the dictionary broadly defines "American" to include immigrant artists. Thus, for example, there is an entry for portrait painter *John Butler Yeats,* William Butler Yeats's father, who died in New York City in 1922, although he is usually regarded as an Irish national. In a touch of quaintness, he is identified as the father of artist Jack B. Yeats and not of the poet. While coverage is generally stronger for earlier artists, the latest two editions provide entries for about 1,000 contemporary artists. Inclusion is somewhat unpredictable, however; for example, Peter Voulkos and Joyce Treiman have entries, but such major figures as Alan Kaprow, Richard Estes, Gene Davis, and Jennifer Bartlett are omitted.

When the information is available, entries include biographical data, awards, exhibitions, commissions, and latest known address. Some of the entries are extremely brief; one of the shortest, for example, is: "Peratee, Sebastian. Image maker. Worked in NYC in 1918." Another entry that is even less informative but charming reads: "Felch. This name is signed to some poorly executed landscape work published in 1855, with no indication of place." Incomplete as they may be, such entries sometimes provide the only existing information available on minor artists—or, as the dedication calls them, the "second and third 'stringers' of artists who never really made it with the big galleries and critics." The length of an entry has little to do with the subject's importance in the art world, but rather is often based simply on availability of data.

Unlike the DICTIONARY OF WOMEN ARTISTS, *Fielding's Dictionary* does not cite the source of information for each entry. However, an eight-page bibliography at the end of the work guides the reader to further material for study. The titles are a good representation of nineteenth- and early twentieth-century historical sources for American art, although by now many of these may be out of print. Some later titles (circa 1974) are included.

A list of abbreviations at the front of the volume includes the institutions, societies, and terms most commonly used in the entries. A somewhat unnecessary list of city and state abbreviations is also provided.

Art dealers, collectors, curators, students, and librarians will all find *Mantle Fielding's Dictionary of American Painters, Sculptors and Engravers* a critical and necessary resource for identifying painters, sculptors, and graphic artists, even though the work is relatively expensive. The Board recommends this work for the core collections of public, academic, and school libraries.

The Oxford Companion to Art. Harold Osborne, ed. Clarendon/Oxford, 1970. hard. 1 vol. 1,277 pp. ISBN 0-19-866107-X. $49.95. encyclopedia.
N33.09 703

The Oxford Companion to Art is a handy one-volume art reference source that includes alphabetically arranged information on artists, stylistic periods and schools, materials, museums, and terms. The work includes entries for *prehistoric art, folk arts, photography,* and *architecture* but specifically excludes practical arts, handicrafts, textiles, furniture, and book design. The reference is not intended to be encyclopedic in scope, but rather to provide ready reference—that is, quick information and general background—for readers who are not already experts or specialists. Another stated purpose is to guide readers to further study.

There are over 100 contributors to this companion, all listed in the front of the book. Although credentials are not given, the list includes such notable scholars as E. H. Gombrich, L. H. Ettlinger, Quentin Bell, and Edmund Leach, as well as many other art historians. Most entries are clearly written with extensive cross-references to other entries in the book. These cross-references are given either as terms in capital letters in the text or as "see also" references at the end of the entry. Black-and-white illustrations accompany many entries where visual clarification is necessary (for example, architectural devices and ornaments). More illustrations would have been helpful; for example, there is a picture of a woodcut, but not an etching.

At the end of many of the entries are numbers that refer to the items in a 46-page bibliography of over 3,000 titles at the end of the work. The bibliography is also designed for the general reader and contains works in five categories: (1) dictionaries, encyclopedias, general histories of art, and bibliographies; (2) general works on art theory and criticism; (3) general works on nineteenth- and twentieth-century art; (4) works on materials and techniques; and (5) books that have special bearing on individual entries or groups of entries in *The Oxford Companion to Art.* Because this work was published in 1970, the bibliography obviously does not include current material.

International in scope, *The Oxford Companion to Art* has a slight European (particularly British) emphasis. For example, the entry on *Scottish art* has three accompanying illustrations, while there are none for American art. Similarly, the *English Arts and Crafts Movement* has an entry, but its American counterpart does not. This bias may account for a curiously short and uninformative entry under *Berenson, Bernhard [sic].* The positive aspect of this orientation is that coverage of European artists is quite good. This is not to say that other areas of the world are neglected; there are good entries for *Melanesian art* and *African art.* For more modern movements such as happenings, kinetic art, or even art deco, the reader should turn first to the related THE OXFORD COMPANION TO TWENTIETH-CENTURY ART.

The Oxford Companion to Art offers quick access to concise information that is well written and easy to use. The Board recommends this work for the core collections of public, academic, and school libraries.

The Oxford Companion to Twentieth-Century Art. Harold Osborne, ed. Oxford, 1981. hard. 1 vol. 656 pp. illus. ISBN 0-19-866119-3 $49.95. encyclopedia.
N6490.094 709.04

The Oxford Companion to Twentieth-Century Art supplements THE OXFORD COMPANION TO ART by providing more comprehensive coverage of this century than is possible in the broader chronological scope of the latter work. Although it overlaps somewhat with other contemporary biographical sources, *The Oxford Companion to Twentieth-Century Art* also contains accounts of movements and associations, elucidations of special terms, and historical essays describing the development of arts in particular countries or regions. Latin America, Africa, South Africa, Australia, and Canada are among the regions covered. According to the editor, an authority on aesthetics and art appreciation, *The Oxford Companion to Twentieth-Century Art* is intended to be less of an encyclopedia and more of a handbook and guide for students to find their way through the complexities, confusions, and riches of contemporary art. Emphasis is on the "fluctuations of artistic ideas" and "changing aesthetic presuppositions" (preface).

For the most part, separate entries are not provided for influential precursors of twentieth-century art when the major portion of their work was done in the previous century. However, there are ample cross-references to other entries where information on these artists is found. The achievements of living artists are only addressed up to the mid-1970s unless a significant development, radical change of style, or important retrospective exhibition occurred after that time.

Like THE OXFORD COMPANION TO ART, this work is international in scope, and there is particularly strong European and British coverage. According to the editor, no attempt is made to match the length of a given entry with the importance of its subject. Other factors such as availability of information, eventful lives, and need for more information not easily accessible elsewhere have often resulted in longer entries than a figure's reputation might warrant. There appear to be very few gaps in coverage. Performance art and Fluxus are not listed, and Frida Kahlo does not get a separate entry, but these are relatively minor omissions.

Although entries in *The Oxford Companion to Twentieth-Century Art* contain extensive cross-references to concepts and artists discussed elsewhere, there are no references from the essays to the bibliography at the end of the work. However, this valuable 48-page bibliography includes books and exhibition catalogs on artists or subjects within the scope of the title. Periodical articles are not included, and publishers of specific titles are not given.

An additional feature of *The Oxford Companion to Twentieth-Century Art* that distinguishes it from THE OXFORD COMPANION TO ART is the large collection of illustrations in both color and black-and-white of representative works of art. The plates are organized into sections: "Fauvism and Expressionism," "Cubism," "Surrealism and Independent Works," "Constructivism and *Art Informel,*" "American Art to 1960," "Abstract Art after 1960," "Pop Art," and "Artists and Countries Outside Major Movements." A list by artist in the back of the book provides an index to these illustrations.

The scholarly quality of the entries and the richness of the information included distinguish *The Oxford Companion to Twentieth-Century Art.* The Board recommends this work for the core collections of public, academic, and school libraries.

Who's Who in American Art, 1989–1990, 18th edition. Bowker, 1989. hard. 1 vol. 1,341 pp. appendix. indexes. ISBN 0-8352-2477-5. $129.95. biographical source. revised every 2 years.
N6536.W5 709.22

Who's Who in American Art, 1989–1990 profiles 11,373 "contributors to visual arts fields in the United States, Canada, and Mexico." Originally part of the American Art Annual series, the biographical material has been issued separately under this title since 1953. This work is revised every two years. The next revision is scheduled for publication in 1991.

Who's Who in American Art includes all segments of the art world: artists, administrators, historians, educators, collectors, librarians, critics, curators, and dealers. Because *Who's Who in American Art* attempts such broad coverage, however, the work cannot be judged to be either comprehensive or intentionally selective in any area, either geographically or occupationally. Like similar sources, inclusion is based on responses to questionnaires. In some other Who's Who–type publications, those who do not return the form are included, but their entries are identified in some way as being the product of research rather than personal information. In *Who's Who in American Art,* those who do not return their form are omitted no matter how important they are. However, even though one cannot count on finding a particular name, *Who's Who in American Art* is a particularly useful source for regional artists, nonartists associated with the arts (such as gallery owner Leo Castelli, architecture critic Ada Louise Huxtable, and Columbia professor James Beck), and artists who work in media not covered in other directories (such as potter Paul Soldner or cartoonist Patrick Oliphant).

Although the publisher claims no connection to Marquis's *Who's Who* publications, the format of this work is remarkably similar. Arranged alphabetically, each entry includes brief biographical data, exhibition and employment history, awards, a two- to three-item bibliography of works by or about the entrant, media worked in, and mailing addresses for dealer and entrant. There are two useful indexes—geographic and professional classifications—and a necrology, which lists people from previous editions who have died between 1953 and 1988. The geographic index is broken down by state and city with the professional classification of the person also given, enabling the user to identify, for example, all silk screen artists in Wyoming. The "Professional Classifications Index" is arranged by type of art, with headings such as "assemblage artist," "conceptual artist," "muralist," "illuminator," "goldsmith," and "filmmaker," among others. Some categories, such as "painting," are further subdivided by technique or medium. Headings for nonartists include "museologist," "patron," and "librarian," among others.

Even though *Who's Who in American Art* is revised and reissued every two years, entries do not necessarily contain up-to-date information, because some entrants do not return a completed questionnaire to the publisher.

Despite its flaws, *Who's Who in American Art* is an important reference work because the variety of biographical information it contains simply cannot be found elsewhere. While some entrants will also be found in more general sources, many others will be listed only in more highly specialized titles or not at all. The Board recommends this work for the core collections of public and academic libraries.

World Artists, 1950–1980. Claude Marks. Wilson, 1984. hard. 1 vol. 912 pp. illus. ISBN 0-8242-070-6. $78. biographical source. on-line.
N6489.M37 709.2′2[B]

In *World Artists, 1950–1980* Claude Marks attempts to document the modernist period through biographical essays on 312 selected outstanding and influential international art figures who represent a variety of styles and movements. Marks, a British-born poet and writer, prefaces the entries with a 4½-page summary of the major artistic developments of the period and the seminal artists who influenced them. The author chose 1950 as a starting point because it represents the approximate beginning of the international ascendancy of American art. The next volume, covering the years 1980 to 1985, was scheduled for release in late 1990 and was not available for review.

The graphic artists, painters, and sculptors selected for inclusion must have been alive during 1950 to 1980; thus, Henri Matisse squeaks by, but Piet Mondrian does not. While Marks's choices may not agree entirely with those of other sources, such as CONTEMPORARY ARTISTS (Maurice de Vlaminck and Peter Voulkos are missing, and *Bernard Buffet* and *Al Hirschfeld* are in this dictionary but not in the other), most of the notable names of the period covered are included.

Alphabetically arranged, the extensive biographical entries are generally to 2½ to 4 pages long. Such major figures as Picasso and Duchamp do get more attention, but on the whole the length of an entry does not necessarily correspond to the relative importance of the artist. The entries are narrative in form, not just listings of factual data as in most other biographical dictionaries. Often more anecdotal and descriptive than analytical in his writing, Marks does attempt to evaluate the contemporary and historical impact of each artist's work and personality. The entries are filled with interesting information. We find out, for example, that Matisse's "L'Atelier Quai Saint Michel" influenced Richard Diebenkorn; that Joseph Cornell was a "highly sensitive youth prone to nightmares and stomach problems"; that Jasper Johns's visual experience while driving a car led to his use of crosshatching; and that Philip Pearlstein supported himself by drafting industrial trade catalogs with Bauhaus graphics designer Ladislav Sutner. Sources from the popular literature are heavily quoted, although not all of the quotes are well documented. While each entry is followed by a list of exhibitions and a bibliography that includes articles in popular newspapers and journals, these lists are not as current as might be expected, given the publication date. The latest exhibition recorded for Richard Diebenkorn, for example, is 1975 and the last cited work, 1977, while CONTEMPORARY ARTISTS lists a major exhibition in 1979 and catalogs with publication dates of 1980 and 1981. Black-and-white photographs of the artists are included with roughly a third of the entries. A convenient reference list of artists appears at the beginning of the volume, and keys to pronunciation and abbreviations precede the main section.

Although it is less current and less comprehensive than other reference books, *World Artists, 1950–1980* is nevertheless an interesting, lively, and useful visual arts resource that makes for enlightening and enjoyable reading. The Board recommends this work for the core collections of public, academic, and school libraries.

Supplementary Titles

American Popular Illustration: A Reference Guide. James J. Best. Greenwood, 1984. hard. 1 vol. 171 pp. appendixes. index. ISBN 0-313-23389-6. $36.95.
NC975.B45 741.64′0973

American Popular Illustration "is a significant contribution to the literature of this important art form. . . . "This work analyze [s] critically the major works in each of the following categories: histories; illustrated works; bibliographies; biographies of American illustrators; and works dealing with technique, with illustration media, and with the social and artistic context of illustration. . . . Each section [ends] with a comprehensive bibliography of the important articles and books cited. . . .

"Students of art history, of American popular culture, and of American Studies will find this an excellent and informative guide to the literature." (*ARBA,* 1985, p. 328)

Also reviewed in: *BL,* April 15, 1985, p. 1166; *Choice,* April 1985, p. 1135; *JAL,* November 1984, p. 303; May 1985, p. 102.

Board's recommendation: Public and academic libraries.

A Dictionary of Art Terms and Techniques. Ralph Mayer. Harper & Row, 1981. soft. 1 vol. 447 pp. illus. ISBN 0-06-463531-7. $8.95. dictionary.
N33.M36 703

A Dictionary of Art Terms and Techniques "contains more than 3,200 . . . definitions of terms encountered in the study and practice of the visual arts and in their literature. It includes within its coverage every major art form of the Western world except architecture. . . . There are entries on schools, styles, and periods, with photographs of representative works, but the chief emphasis of the book is on the materials and methods of the artist. . . .

"Materials, such as paints and resins, are defined according to composition, characteristic properties, and use. . . . The dictionary will serve artists, especially commercial artists, and students, particularly in the fields of painting and graphic art." (*LJ,* January 7, 1970, p. 57)

Also reviewed in: *A Art,* December 1969, p. 16; *AB,* December 15, 1969, p. 2101; *BL,* December 15, 1969, p. 484; *Conn,* November 1970, p. 215; *LJ,* April 15, 1970, p. 1439; *PW,* June 15, 1970, p. 57; *SR,* December 6, 1969, p. 50; *Studio,* July 1970, p. 64; *TLS,* October 16, 1970, p. 1201; *WLB,* February 1970, p. 661.

Board's recommendation: Public and academic libraries.

Guide to the Literature of Art History. Etta Arntzen and Robert Rainwater. ALA, 1980. hard. 1 vol. 616 pp. index. ISBN 0-8389-0263-4. $75. bibliography.
Z5931.A67[N380] 016.709

Guide to the Literature of Art History aims to supplement "Mary W. Chamberlin's *Guide to Art Reference Books.* . . . The bibliography is divided into four . . . categories: general reference sources, general primary and secondary sources, particular arts (i.e., sculpture, prints, etc.), and serials. Each category is further broken down by subject or genre and is alphabetically arranged.

"There is a very useful subject index that complements the overall subject arrangement and brings together material by country, region, culture, period, and major art movement." (*Choice,* July/August 1981, p. 1525)

"This annotated bibliography is without doubt the most complete with 4147 citations. . . . A must for all libraries supporting art research." (*LJ,* June 1, 1981, p. 1209)

Also reviewed in: *AB,* June 22, 1981, p. 4940; *ANQ,* March 1983, p. 123; *ARBA,* 1982, p. 456; *BL,* October 15, 1982, p. 330; *BM,* March 1982, p. 200; *Choice,* November 1983, p. 391; *Conn,* January 1982, p. 13; *LQ,* October 1981, p. 474; *RQ,* Summer 1981, p. 422; *RSR,* October 1981, p. 13; *Ser R,* October 1981, p. 61.

Board's recommendation: Public and academic libraries.

Who Was Who in American Art. Peter Hastings Falk, ed. Sound View Pr., 1985. hard. 1 vol. 750 pp. illus. ISBN 0-932087-00-0. $115. biographical dictionary.
N6512.F26 709.22

Who Was Who in American Art lists the artist's "full name, profession codes, last known address, birth and death dates, art education, memberships, exhibitions, permanent locations of works, and the last volume of the [American Art] Annual in which the artist was listed. . . .

"The dictionary arrangement permits quick access, but the uninitiated will find it necessary to consult the section 'How to Read an Entry' in order to interpret the data. Death dates have been added to the entries, and some new biographies were included . . . [however] the *Who Was Who* title is somewhat misleading since some artists . . . are still living." (*BL,* March 1, 1986, p 967)

"The arrangement of entries is alphabetical by artist's name with cross-indexes by maiden name and 'brush' name. . . . This is an invaluable source for all libraries academic, public, or other with or without copies of the *American Art Annual* on their shelves." (*Choice,* February 1986, p. 855)

Also reviewed in: *LJ,* November 15, 1985, p. 88.

Board's recommendation: Public and academic libraries.

New and Noteworthy

American Women Artists, Past and Present: A Selected Bibliographical Guide. vol. 2 Eleanor Tufts. Garland, 1989. hard. 1 vol. 491 pp. illus. ISBN 0-8240-1511-8. $61. bibliography.
N6505 016.704′042

"Five years after the publication of *American Women Artists,* Tufts has brought out a second volume of the bibliography 'to supplement (not replace) the first volume.' Alphabetically arranged by artist, [the work lists] selected English-language reference books and journals with bibliographical information on U.S. women painters, sculptors, and photographers. Architects are omitted, but a few fiber artists, printmakers, and weavers are included. . . . The first volume lists 519 artists; the second lists approximately 1,250." (*BL,* December 15, 1989, p. 852)

Black Arts Annual. Donald Bogle. Garland, 1989. hard. 1 vol. 228 pp. illus. index. ISBN 0-8240-0834-0. $40. yearbook.
700

Black Arts Annual "is composed of . . . thoughtful, analytical essays on the year's events in art, dance, literature, movies, popular music, jazz and classical music, photography, television, and theater. Each writer uses an individual voice so that the opinions are fresh, lively, angry, and insightful, in turn. . . . [There are] dramatic photographs on almost every page. . . ." (*Choice,* October 1989, p. 280)

David M. Pilachowski

Asian History

See also European History; World History

Asian history is a complex field. The first consideration adding to its complexity is geography. Asia is the largest continent, covering nearly one-third of the earth's land area and including some 30 countries. Asia extends from the eastern shore of the Mediterranean south and east to encompass India and Sri Lanka, Southeast Asia, China, Korea, Japan, the Indonesian archipelago, and the Philippine Islands. To the north, the area of the Soviet Union east of the Ural Mountains is also considered part of Asia; however, the U.S.S.R. is not included in this category of the Buying Guide.

The second consideration is the diverse nature of the history of Asia due to the sheer number of countries that must be included. Although history can narrowly be considered as a chronological record of past events, the core reference books reviewed here expand that definition to include political, religious, and cultural history and development. This increases the scope of the topic, better places events in context, and helps explain why certain events and developments occurred. The tremendous amount of cross-pollination of ideas among the Asian nations, particularly China, Japan, and Korea, adds to the complexity of the field. Additionally, some of the countries in Asia share the experience of having been European colonial possessions. The European and World History categories, therefore, contain reference works that comment upon this experience from a different perspective.

Library users interested in Asian history will need reference sources that provide information on individual countries and subregions of Asia, including background on people influential in the development of these countries. These sources should contain relevant Eastern religions, which have been important historically and have drawn increasing attention from the West with the political and economic rise of Asian nations. Likewise, the historical relations of the countries of Asia with each other and with the West will be pertinent as users seek to understand the place of Asian nations on the contemporary international scene.

Not surprisingly, no one reference book covers Asian history completely, although the ENCYCLOPEDIA OF ASIAN HISTORY is quite comprehensive. Until recently, Japanese and Chinese history and culture have been the subject of more English-language reference works than other Asian countries. Two recent additions to the field, the aforementioned encyclopedia and THE CAMBRIDGE ENCYCLOPEDIA OF INDIA, PAKISTAN, BANGLADESH, SRI LANKA, NEPAL, BHUTAN AND THE MALDIVES, have substantially expanded and improved treatment of Asian history. Readers desiring additional information about Asia can use the

Core Titles

	PUBLIC	ACADEMIC	SCHOOL
The Cambridge Encyclopedia of China Hook, Brian, gen. ed. Cambridge, 1982		✦	✦
The Cambridge Encyclopedia of India, Pakistan, Bangladesh, Sri Lanka, Nepal, Bhutan and the Maldives Robinson, Francis, ed. Cambridge, 1989		✦	✦
Cultural Atlas of China Blunden, Caroline, and Mark Elvin. Facts On File, 1983	✦	✦	✦
Cultural Atlas of Japan Collcutt, Martin, Marius Jansen, and Isao Kumakura. Facts On File, 1988	✦	✦	✦
Encyclopedia of Asian History, 4 vols. Embree, Ainslie T., ed. in chief. Scribner, 1988	✦	✦	✦
Kodansha Encyclopedia of Japan, 9 vols. Itosaka, Gen, ed. in chief. Kodansha, 1983		✦	

bibliographies in the core reference books and can consult the comprehensive annual BIBLIOGRAPHY OF ASIAN STUDIES, recommended as a supplement.

Core Titles

The Cambridge Encyclopedia of China. Brian Hook, gen. ed. Cambridge, 1982. hard. 1 vol. 492 pp. illus. index. ISBN 0-521-23099-3. $49.50. encyclopedia. DS705.C35 950.03

The Cambridge Encyclopedia of China is an outstanding source of information published by the prestigious Cambridge University Press. The encyclopedia lives up to the standards established by other distinguished books from this publisher. The individuals involved with the work have been well chosen. General editor Brian Hook is senior lecturer and head of the Department of Chinese Studies at the University of Leeds. The long and distinguished list of contributors includes prominent figures in Chinese studies, such as Joseph Needham, Herbert Franke, Stuart Schram, and Roderick MacFarquhar. The result of this collaboration is an authoritative work with well-written essays on all important aspects of Chinese history by experts in the field.

The encyclopedia covers China's geography, people, society, history, culture, and scientific accomplishments in sections ranging from 20 to 150 pages. The coverage of Chinese history is detailed and thorough, spanning some 150 pages, or nearly one-third of the entire work. This section begins with China's prehistory, contains entries on each dynasty, and concludes with entries on the Republican Period and the People's Republic. The more recent periods are given more detailed entries. The dynastic coverage ranges from two pages (the *Shang,* ca. 1480 B.C. to 1050 B.C.) to 26 pages (the *Ch'ing,* 1644 to 1912). Typically, key emperors and officials are described, as are accomplishments or important trends of the period. For instance, the Great Wall and the Grand Canal are discussed under the Sui dynasty; the fiscal reforms of the emperor Wang Anshih and the development of printing are described as part of the advancements made during the Sung dynasty. Of course, the 1982 publication date precludes any mention of recent political events in China.

While the greatest strength of the encyclopedia is the coverage of China's history, the work is also an important source of information about the country's society and institutions, major philosophical schools and religions, and unique cultural and scientific contributions. A useful discussion of traditional educational and examination systems contributes to an understanding of significant institutions that shaped China's history. As these informative essays illustrate, divination and ancestor worship—together with Confucianism, Taoism, and Buddhism—collectively influenced Chinese society. Gunpowder, paper, and movable type were invented in China; the final section of the encyclopedia describes the history and evolution of Chinese science and technology.

The generous use of maps, charts, diagrams, and color illustrations enhances the effectiveness of the work. Two of the more interesting graphic treatments of information depict the evolution of Chinese writing and the cycle of years in the Chinese calendar. Unfortunately, the index to the encyclopedia is not as useful as one might wish in a reference book. Charts, maps, and illustrations are not indexed. The text is not thoroughly indexed; for example, a discussion of gold and silver metalwork during the Tang dynasty is indexed under *gold* and under *silver—art* but not under *metalwork* or *jewelry.*

Despite the shortcomings of the index and the fact that the 1982 copyright excludes a record of more recent events, *The Cambridge Encyclopedia of China* is an important reference source for Chinese history and, due to the country's impact on the region, for the Asian History category. The Board recommends this work for the core collections of academic and school libraries.

The Cambridge Encyclopedia of India, Pakistan, Bangladesh, Sri Lanka, Nepal, Bhutan and the Maldives. Francis Robinson, ed. Cambridge, 1989. hard. 1 vol. 520 pp. illus. appendixes. index. ISBN 0-521-33451-9. $49.50. encyclopedia.
DS334.9.C36 954.033

The Cambridge Encyclopedia of India, Pakistan, Bangladesh, Sri Lanka, Nepal, Bhutan and the Maldives is a useful addition to reference coverage of South Asia. The strength of the work is the attention given to many facets of the history—economic, political, religious, and cultural—of countries that, except for India, have received comparatively little attention in reference works published in the West.

A well-qualified team of scholars has collaborated on this encyclopedia, headed by editor Francis Robinson, a lecturer in history at the University of London's Royal Holloway and Bedford New College. Among Robinson's works is the ATLAS OF THE ISLAMIC WORLD SINCE 1500 (see Middle Eastern History). The advisory editors include scholars in the fields of political science, geography, sociology, Islamic thought, language, and anthropology who hold important positions at universities in the United States, Great Britain, India, and Australia. The essays in the encyclopedia have been written by a distinguished group of scholars who are experts on various aspects of South Asia. Each subsection within this work is signed.

The encyclopedia is divided into sections: "Land," "Peoples," "History to Independence," "Politics," "Foreign Relations," "Economies," "Religions," "Societies," and "Culture." Each section contains between 4 ("Foreign Relations") and 16 ("History to Independence") subsections. Not surprisingly, India and Pakistan receive the most detailed coverage within most sections. However, the other countries are not ignored, with the result that a picture of South Asia emerges.

"History" and "Culture" are the sections treated in the most depth; each is 100 pages long. "History" encompasses prehistory to the era of Indian nationalism (1858–1947), with subsections on Sri Lanka, Nepal, Bhutan, and the Maldives.

The "Culture" section includes discussion of literature, dance, music, the fine and decorative arts, food, dress, cinema, the press, publishing, radio and television, and science and technology. Each topic averages 5 pages, with the exception of language, which is 35 pages long. Each subsection in *The Cambridge Encyclopedia* includes references to additional books on the topic.

Illustrations play an important role in the work. Seventy-five maps are included throughout the volume on aspects of South Asia, such as India in 1600, countries with communities of over 40,000 in South Asia, and physical features and climate. Tables are also used abundantly and are especially effective in illustrating a wide variety of data on economic conditions for the various countries in the 1980s.

The Cambridge Encyclopedia of India, Pakistan, Bangladesh, Sri Lanka, Nepal, Bhutan and the Maldives is an affordable reference work that is useful for Asian history topics and, more particularly, for topics on all aspects of South Asia. The index enhances the reference value of the work. The Board recommends this work for the core collections of academic and school libraries.

Cultural Atlas of China. Caroline Blunden and Mark Elvin. Facts On File, 1983. hard. 1 vol. 237 pp. illus. appendixes. index. ISBN 087196-132-6. $40. atlas.
G2305.B56 912.51

The *Cultural Atlas of China* is an interesting hybrid reference work useful for an understanding of Chinese history. The work includes maps, as one would expect of an atlas, but relies more on text and excellent photographs and illustrations to tell of China's early and recent past. The combined modes of presentation result in a picture of Chinese civilization not possible in a dictionary or encyclopedia. The focus of the work extends beyond history to include a broader picture of Chinese civilization and culture.

Mark Elvin has written and translated extensively in the field of Chinese history and is at Oxford University's Oriental Institute, while the *Cultural Atlas* is Caroline Blunden's first book. The work is an example of a graphically pleasing reference source produced by Facts On File, a respected publisher of such materials.

This work is divided into three sections. The first,

"Space: The Land and Its People," describes the social, economic, and political geography of China. The second section, "Time," is the major focus of the atlas, filling over one-half of the book, while the third section, "Symbols and Society," is relatively short. The emphasis here on history is intentional. As the authors explain in the preface, "It is one of the primary purposes of this cultural atlas to bring them [changes in China over time] as vividly before the reader's consciousness as possible." This goal is achieved through the well-written text and the carefully selected and effective illustrations and maps.

The effective use of specialized maps and illustrations is the distinguishing characteristic of this reference work. The *Cultural Atlas* includes 47 maps and 14 tables to convey information. Among the more intriguing examples of the former are maps of the overextension of the empire during the Tang dynasty, of relations with cultures and countries beyond China, of the various rebellions that took place in the mid-nineteenth century, and of numerous depictions of the wax and wane of dynasties. Perhaps the most informative chart is the chronological table found in the beginning of the book. This illustrative timeline includes dynastic periods and notations on thought and religion, politics, arts, agriculture, money, population growth, and writing throughout these periods.

Of the aspects of culture covered, art is by far the most thoroughly discussed. Compared to the two pages each in the "Symbols and Society" section on theater, architecture, and ceramics and the four pages on music, five chapters of the "Time" section are devoted to art. In addition, the historical text is interspersed with illustrations taken from Chinese art.

The *Cultural Atlas of China* provides a good introduction to the history and culture of China. The value of the work is enhanced by the use of numerous effective illustrations. The index is brief but detailed and includes reference to illustrations. A bibliographic essay—divided according to the chapters of the book—suggests sources of additional reading. The Board recommends this work for the core collections of public, academic, and school libraries.

Cultural Atlas of Japan. Martin Collcutt, Marius Jansen, and Isao Kumakura. Facts On File, 1988. hard. 1 vol. 240 pp. illus. appendixes. index. ISBN 0-8160-1927-4. $40. atlas.
DS821.C62 952

The *Cultural Atlas of Japan* is another in the series of fine cultural atlases published by Facts On File. The authors state that this work "is written for general readers and travelers who would like to relate the rich cultural history of Japan to the physical environment in which it has developed" (preface).

The authors are well qualified for their task. All three are noted scholars with several favorably received books on Japanese history or culture to their credit. Martin Collcutt contributed the chapters on geography, ancient history, and the medieval age, while the lengthy section on Edo culture was provided by Isao Kumakura (translated by Akiko Collcutt). The Meiji and modern periods were written by Marius Jansen.

The *Cultural Atlas* features coverage of history—specifically cultural history and geography—and is divided into three major sections. The first, "Origins," discusses the archaeological origins of Japanese civilization and culture and the geography of the island archipelago. Text and maps place Japan within its geographic context in Asia by focusing on features such as topography, climate, geology and soil, energy resources and minerals, and population and settlement patterns.

The second section, "The Historical Period," covers ancient times to the end of the Edo period in 1867. Like the rest of the *Cultural Atlas,* the second section makes good use of maps, color photographs, and examples of works of art to convey the rich cultural development of the area. This is the longest section of the atlas, encompassing 119 pages.

The third section, "Modern Japan," begins with the Meiji restoration and extends to the present time. Discussion of the Meiji era is the strongest aspect of this section; economic conditions and contact with the West receive the most thorough treatment. World War II and subsequent events are covered only briefly. More detail on Japan's postwar culture would have been welcome if the atlas were to completely fulfill the authors' stated objective of serving the needs of travelers.

The 19 "Special Features" comprise a noteworthy element of this work. Through text and rich illustrations, each feature depicts and explains such cultural institutions and traditions as Kabuki theater, Japanese gardens, Noh drama, and the tea ceremony. The "Special Features" present topics in sufficient detail to be interesting and informative.

The 53 maps contained in the atlas use color effectively to depict such topics as sixteenth- and seventeenth-century trade, peasant uprising and Western intrusions, and early day and modern prefecture boundaries. Informative notes accompany the maps. Useful tables, such as the "Rulers of Japan" and the "Chronological Table," also contribute to the usefulness of the *Cultural Atlas.*

The clear discussion of Japanese culture and history, complemented by the "Special Features" and numerous maps and illustrations, makes the *Cultural Atlas of*

Japan a useful source on Asian history. The Board recommends this work for the core collections of public, academic, and school libraries.

Encyclopedia of Asian History. Ainslie T. Embree, ed. in chief. Scribner, 1988. hard. 4 vols. 2,050 pp. illus. appendixes. index. ISBN 0-684-18619-5 (set). $360 (set); $85 (each vol.). encyclopedia.
DS31.E53 950

The *Encyclopedia of Asian History,* prepared under the auspices of the Asia Society, is a major reference work in the field of Asian history. Editor in chief Ainslie T. Embree, a noted historian of modern India at Columbia University, has assembled a group of distinguished academicians to serve as editors. Likewise, the contributors to the four-volume set bring strong backgrounds to their work. All entries are signed.

In his preface, Embree describes the aim of the encyclopedia as "an attempt to bring some . . . modern scholarly knowledge produced in North America, Europe, and Asia to a wider audience in an accessible form." He also points out that history is clearly the focal point of the work, with less attention given to art, religion, literature, and geography. "Asia" is defined as Iran and Central Asia eastward, including the islands of the Indonesian archipelago and the Philippines.

The entries, which are clearly written and use a minimum of jargon, range in length from one paragraph to a dozen pages. In the former range, individuals, places, and events are briefly described. Examples include *Cao Ba Quat,* the Vietnamese poet; *Cao Kun,* a prominent Chinese militarist; and *Peradeniya,* a suburb of Kandy, Sri Lanka. All short entries usually include reference to another entry in the encyclopedia where the term is put into context, and most conclude with reference to a book in English in which further information is available.

The longer entries cover the history of a country or of an important event in Asian history. These entries are usually further subdivided into chronological periods. All entries on countries—even the one-page entry on *Burma* and the three pages devoted to *Bangladesh*—include a full-page black-and-white map of the country showing political and physical features. These entries include multiple cross-references to other entries in the encyclopedia as well as bibliographic references to standard works on the country.

A noteworthy feature of the *Encyclopedia of Asian History* is the inclusion of entries that treat topics from the perspective of several countries. Examples of such pan-Asian topics include cities, refugees, warfare, and women.

The encyclopedia has been designed to expedite accessibility. In addition to a detailed index that refers users to the volume and page of pertinent information, the work includes a two-part synoptic outline. The first part lists basic concepts and historical eras of the countries of Asia; the second and more useful feature, an "Outline of Contents," lists the countries included, by region, as well as all pertinent entries in the encyclopedia. This outline makes previous knowledge of terminology or historical events unnecessary.

The *Encyclopedia of Asian History* is a scholarly treatment of the topic that is accessible to the nonspecialist. Entries are informative and well written, with abundant cross-references and useful suggestions for further reading. The Board recommends this work for the core collections of public, academic, and school libraries.

Kodansha Encyclopedia of Japan. Gen Itosaka, ed. in chief. Kodansha, 1983. hard. 9 vols. 3,334 pp. illus. index. ISBN 0-87011-620-7 (set). $720 (set). encyclopedia.
DS805.K633 952.003'21

The *Kodansha Encyclopedia of Japan* is a reference work that opens Japan to the English-speaking world in an unprecedented way. The encyclopedia is a comprehensive work in nine volumes (volume 9 is an index) that covers all aspects of Japan. This work is the result of a strong international collaborative effort that involved nearly 700 Japanese scholars and over 500 of their counterparts from around the world. To coordinate the project, editorial services were established in Tokyo (under the leadership of Shigeto Tsuru, past president of Hitotsubashi University) and in Cambridge, Massachusetts (under the late Edwin O. Reischauer, the renowned American scholar of Japan).

The overriding goal of the *Kodansha Encyclopedia of Japan* is to promote international understanding of Japan. The work includes coverage of Japan's past as well as the contemporary scene. This broad scope makes the encyclopedia valuable to students and scholars of Japan as well as to business people and the educated public.

The encyclopedia includes several types of entries. Long introductory entries on major topics and issues of Japanese culture are one feature of the work. Lengthy entries are included for a detailed examination of the history of Japan, nearly 50 pages in length; a discussion of the history of women in Japan; and coverage of traditional theater, economic history, art, the martial arts, and religion. The encyclopedia also includes many long entries on specific topics and short identification entries on people and places. Most entries are signed and usually include references to additional readings, although many of these are in Japanese.

The long entries are customarily further divided into subsections. The entry on *Buddhism* includes the following subsections: "Early Buddhism," "The Spread of Buddhism," "Diffusion of Buddhism in Asia," "Introduction of Buddhism into Japan," "Characteristics of Japanese Buddhism," and "Japanese Buddhism Today." Other entries feature the historical and present-day relations between Japan and other countries. (These entries are found under the name of the other country—for example, *Australia and Japan*).

The *Kodansha Encyclopedia of Japan* uses cross-references and an excellent index to make the work more accessible. "See" references are given under the names of entries not used, and capitalized words and phrases within the text direct users to the treatment of those concepts in other entries. For instance, the entry *armed forces, imperial Japanese* includes 58 cross-references to other entries. The volume 9 index is impressive. It includes only one page reference under each term *(World Bank)* or subentry topic *(World War I—economic impact)* indexed so that users do not have to dig through long lists of page references to locate appropriate information.

The *Kodansha Encyclopedia of Japan* is an excellent source of information on historical and present-day Japan. Unfortunately, the high price and detailed scope of the work make this encyclopedia out of the reach of most public libraries. The publishers plan to issue a one-volume condensed encyclopedia in 1991. The Board recommends this work for the core collection of academic libraries.

Supplementary Titles

The Asian Political Dictionary. Lawrence Ziring and C. I. Eugene Kim. ABC-Clio, 1985. hard and soft. 1 vol. 438 pp. illus. ISBN 0-87436-368-3 (hard): 0-87436-369-1 (soft). $40 (hard); $17 (soft). dictionary.
DS31.Z57 950

The Asian Political Dictionary is the "tenth to be published in a series of subject dictionaries that will eventually consist of 15 separate volumes. . . . The unique arrangement of [this dictionary] enables users to review major political events (twentieth-century political events are emphasized). The interesting discussions have an infectious quality; users finding one term might well continue to the next.

The Asian Political Dictionary "is arranged by topic (e.g., political parties and movements, militarism, diplomacy). It includes Middle Eastern nations as well as China, India, etc. [This dictionary] has more than 300 entries and begins with a guide to countries that indexes all references to countries in the entries. The definitions range from 100 words to more than 1,000 words and reflect current scholarship. Definitions are given in two sections: the first gives an explanation of the topic and the second, labeled 'Significance,' analyzes historical and current relevance." (*BL,* July 1986, p. 1594)

The Asian Political Dictionary's "treatment of East and South Asia and the absence of a comparable work justify its consideration for reference collections." (*Choice,* April 1986, p. 1199)

Also reviewed in: *ARBA,* 1986, p. 255; *Ref Bk R,* 1986, p. 28; *WLB,* March 1986, p. 63.

Board's recommendation: Academic and school libraries.

Atlas of the Islamic World since 1500. Francis Robinson. Facts On File, 1982. hard. 1 vol. 238 pp. illus. appendix. index. ISBN 0-87196-629-8. $45. atlas.
G1786.S1R5 911.17671

See Middle Eastern History.

Bibliography of Asian Studies. Wayne Surdam, man. ed. Assoc. for Asian Studies. University of Michigan, 1963–1985. soft. approx. 340 pp. per vol. index. ISSN 0067-7159. $70 (1985 vol.). bibliography.
Z3001 950.016

The *Bibliography of Asian Studies* "presents comprehensive coverage of western language scholarly monographs and articles dealing with East, South, and Southeast Asia. The basic arrangement is geographic—by region then by country. Entries are provided for the following categories: anthropology and sociology, arts, biography, economics, education, geography, history, language, library and information sciences, literature, philosophy and religion, politics and government, psychology and psychiatry, and science and technology." (*Ser Lib 2nd,* 1985, p. 225)

This book "remains the finest bibliography on Asia . . . [and is] invaluable for libraries and researchers with any interest at all in Asia." (*ARBA,* 1986, p. 52)

Also reviewed in: *ARBA,* 1983, p. 150; *Choice,* November 1972, p. 1091; *Mag Lib,* 1982, p. 116.

Board's recommendation: Academic libraries.

The Cambridge History of China. John K. Fairbanks and Denis Twitchett, gen. eds. Cambridge, 1978–1987. hard. 14 vols. illus. ISBN 0-521-24336-X (vol. 14). $100 (vol. 14). history.
DS736.C3145 951

The essays in *The Cambridge History of China* are "lucid, definitive, and, within the standard of the genre, remarkably readable." (*LJ,* December 15, 1983, p. 2330)

"Each entry is written by an authority in his or her field. . . . Also useful is a short but definitive bibliographical essay. . . . By design, this book does not include methodological debates nor does it seek to pass historical judgment. It is invaluable as a historical reference." (*Choice,* April 1984, p. 1184)

"A bibliographical essay for each chapter, an extensive bibliography in Western and Asiatic languages, and a glossary-index enhance the usefulness of the work. This is a major publication, necessary to all college and university libraries. Even in institutions where Chinese studies have little or no part it should be on the shelves as the reference work on the development of one of the greatest human cultures." (*Choice,* January 1981, p. 710)

"It is the great merit of [this] series that, while it presents the latest scholarship, it can be read or dipped into by anybody interested in China." (*LJ,* 1983, p. 2330)

"The . . . collaborators who have prepared . . . [this work] are all Asian specialists. . . . In a collection of this nature the essays are often of uneven quality. Fortunately, this is not true here. [The work is] extremely useful to a wide readership ranging from undergraduates to college and university faculty. The essays may even inspire undergraduates to delve further into the complexities of modern Chinese history." (*Choice,* February 1987, p. 24)

Also reviewed in: *AHR,* February 1988, p. 209; *Brit Bk N,* May 1987, p. 245; *Choice,* February 1987, p. 924; October 1987, p. 364; March 1988, p. 1149; July 1989, p. 1884; *Econ,* October 31, 1987, p. 81; *HT,* April 1988, p. 55; January 1989, p. 58; *JAS,* February 1988, p. 131; May 1988, p. 342, 356; February 1989, p. 145; *J Interdis H,* Autumn 1988, p. 285; *NS,* October 3, 1986, p. 37; *NYTBR,* June 5, 1988, p. 40; *Pac A,* Winter 1987, p. 660; Spring 1988, p. 138; Fall 1988, p. 503; *TLS,* March 18, 1988, p. 299; *VQR,* Winter 1988, p. 15.

Board's recommendation: Academic libraries.

Chronology of the People's Republic of China 1970–1979. Peter P. Cheng. Scarecrow, 1986. hard. 1 vol. 629 pp. appendixes. index. ISBN 0-8108-1751-9. $57.50. chronology.
DS777.55C445669 951.05

The *Chronology of the People's Republic of China 1970–1979,* "a continuation of Peter Cheng's earlier book, *A Chronology of the People's Republic of China from October 1, 1949,* provides a daily account of cultural, social and political events which occurred in China during the 1970s.

"Compiled from newspapers, periodicals and other publications in China, England, France, India, Japan and the United States, the chronology traces the decade's growth in China's economy and the country's aggressive diplomatic campaign.

"Both events and personalities appear in the chronology; recorded are China's efforts to return to stability following the Great Proletarian Cultural Revolution.

"An introductory section for each chapter provides an overview of that year's major events and trends, and is followed by brief daily entries highlighting significant events.

"The volume includes appendixes of bibliographical sources and selected further reading, and indexes to names and subjects." (*AB,* February 23, 1987, p. 783)

This chronology "should prove the more popular of the two volumes, covering as it does the period in which American interest in China began to increase as a result of Richard Nixon's visit there in February, 1972. In addition to the reversal of a quarter of a century of bitter antagonism between the United States and China, the eventful decade saw China's effort to recover from the Cultural Revolution of the late 1960s, the deaths of Mao and Zhou Enlai in 1976, the disgrace and trial of the Gang of Four and the brief flowering of the 'democracy Wall' in Beijing. These culminating events, along with the events leading up to and following them, Cheng records as well as domestic and international political, economic, cultural, social, diplomatic, and military happenings. . . . Libraries that have Cheng's chronology of China's first twenty years ought to add the next ten." (*WLB,* February 1987, p. 64)

Also reviewed in: *ARBA,* 1988, p. 210; *Choice,* June 1987, p. 1599; *Cu H,* September 1987, p. 270.

Board's recommendation: Academic and school libraries.

Companion to Chinese History. Hugh B. O'Neill. Facts On File, 1987. hard and soft. 1 vol. 397 pp. illus. ISBN 0-87196-841-X (hard); 0-8160-1825-1 (soft). $24.95 (hard); $14.95 (soft). handbook.
DS705.063 951

The *Companion to Chinese History* "covers Chinese history from earliest times to 1985. Geographical and personal names . . . include foreigners important in Chinese history (Marco Polo and Matteo Ricci) as well as Chinese emperors, military leaders, and dynasties. Other entries range from . . . articles on the calendar and romanization to . . . literary classics, the family, railroads, and secret sects. . . . [A] chronology covering 1506–1985 is appended.

The *Companion to Chinese History* is a "readable handbook. . . . Most of the copiously cross-referenced articles have brief bibliographies of one or more English-language titles, usually recent. . . . [This] up-to-date book will augment earlier works . . . in a field of great current interest." (*BL,* December 15, 1987, p. 684)

Also reviewed in: *ARBA,* 1988, p. 210; *Choice,* March 1988, p. 1068; *Kliatt,* September 1988, p. 48; *LJ,* September 1, 1987, p. 173; *Ref Bk R,* 1989, p. 15; *RQ,* Winter 1987, p. 274; Winter 1988, p. 265; *TES,* February 19, 1988, p. 27; January 6, 1989, p. 24.

Board's recommendation: Academic and school libraries.

A Social and Economic Atlas of India. Oxford, 1988. hard. 1 vol. 254 pp. illus. ISBN 0-19-562041-0. $65. atlas.
G2281.G1 912.1330954

A Social and Economic Atlas of India includes "250 multicolor maps, 370 charts, and over 100 statistical tables. . . . The right-hand page is reserved for cartography, the left facing page contains explanatory text and any accompanying tables. . . . [There are nine topical sections]: the land (basic physical and political features, administrative subdivisions, parliamentary constituencies); population (distribution, growth, language and religion, literacy, employment); . . . [climate]; natural resources (water resources, land use, minerals); . . . infrastructure (welfare, education, transportation, communications irrigation and power, banking); . . . production (animal husbandry and fisheries, agriculture, industry); . . . [tourism]; the national economy (key industrial and fiscal indicators); . . . [and] world maps illustrating exports, imports, and aid from and to India.

"A wealth of socioeconomic information is presented in fairly limited space through the well-designed, legible, and clearly annotated thematic maps and charts. The accompanying text and tables enable this atlas to serve to a considerable extent as a handbook and statistical abstract as well. It will be a basic reference source on the world's largest democracy and second most populous nation." (*BL,* 1989, p. 988)

A Social and Economic Atlas of India "is a no-nonsense, technically proficient volume, permitting at a glance a view of where India is now, and where its future lies. . . . For an overview of India this is an important reference volume." (*Choice,* 1989, p. 788)

Also reviewed in: *Meridian,* 1989, p. 48; *WLB,* 1988, p. 127.

Board's recommendation: Academic and school libraries.

New and Noteworthy

Atlas of Southeast Asia. Richard Ulack and Gyula Pauer. Macmillan, 1989. hard. 1 vol. 171 pp. index. ISBN 0-02-933200-1. $95. atlas.
G2360.U4 912.59

"The first chapters of [the *Atlas of Southeast Asia*] . . . provide an overview of Southeast Asian environment, history and politics, culture and population; there follow chapters focusing on the individual countries of Southeast Asia. The atlas includes more than 50 color photographs in addition to 70 maps and 66 diagrams. . . . The clearly written chapters are like general encyclopedia articles. . . ." (*Choice,* October 1989, p. 294)

Japan's Economy: A Bibliography of Its Past and Present. William D. Wray. Markus Wiener, 1989. hard. 1 vol. 303 pp. ISBN 0-910129-79-7. $39.95. bibliography.
HC462 016.330952

"The arrangement [of *Japan's Economy*] is by historical divisions ('Tokugawa Period,' 'Restoration Era,' 'World War II,' . . . [etc.]) with topical subdivisions (history, business, management, labor, government and international relations, finance, taxation, social aspects, specific industries, etc.). The entries . . . encompass materials from the late 19th century to 1989." (*Choice,* January 1990, p. 781)

Political and Economic Encyclopedia of the Pacific. Gerald Segal, ed. St. James, 1989. hard. 1 vol. 450 pp. ISBN 1-55862-033-8. $85. encyclopedia.
DU10.P77

The *Political and Economic Encyclopedia of the Pacific* "is organized as a background reference work to current affairs news stories. . . . The main focus is on providing information to explain what is going on [in the Pacific region] today. . . . The material is laid out with entries in alphabetic order in true encyclopedic format. Basic background statistical information for each country is provided. . . . [Also included are] details of political parties, important people, treaties, scandals, important industrial companies, [and] major bilateral relations (e.g., Japan-China)." (Excerpted from publisher's announcement)

David M. Pilachowski

Asian Literature

See also Asian History; World Literature

Asian literature offers an interesting, informative, and enjoyable perspective on the cultures of the world's largest continent. Literature both demonstrates the values and mores that shape society and presents a picture of life in that culture. Asian literature includes the Western forms of poetry, fiction, essays, and drama. Yet, just as Asia is different from the West, so too is its literature a reflection of the values of the East. The philosophical texts of China, the great epics of India, and the influence of poetry in Japan are particular features of the literature of the region. Additionally, Buddhism has had a marked impact on the literature of the three dominant cultures of the region.

Reference works about Asian literature are numerous, but specialized rather than comprehensive. Most of the works focus on the literature of a single country such as the SELECTIVE GUIDE TO CHINESE LITERATURE, 1900–1949 or a period such as the PRINCETON COMPANION TO CLASSICAL JAPANESE LITERATURE. One exception to the specialized reference works is the recently updated GUIDE TO ORIENTAL CLASSICS. Another excellent comprehensive treatment of Asian literature is unfortunately out of print: Jaroslav Prusek's three-volume *Dictionary of Oriental Literature* (Basic Bks., 1974). A number of other useful resources are also out of print including: *Asian Literature in English: A Guide to Information Sources* (George L. Anderson, Gale, 1981); the *Literature of India: An Introduction* (Edward C. Dimock, Jr., et al., Univ. of Chicago, 1978); *Indian Literature in English, 1827–1979: A Guide to Information Sources* (Gale, 1981); *Guide to Chinese Prose* (Jordan D. Paper, G. K. Hall, 1984); *Modern Chinese Fiction* (Winston L. Y. Yang and Nathan K. Mao, eds., G. K. Hall, 1981); *Indian Fiction in English* (Dorothy M. Spencer, comp., Univ. of Pennsylvania, 1960; reprinted by Greenwood, 1985); *Biographical Dictionary of Japanese Literature* (Sen 'ichi Hisamatsu, ed., Kodansha, 1976); *Guide to Japanese Drama* (Leonard Cabell Pronko, G. K. Hall, 1984); *Guide to Japanese Poetry* (J. Thomas Rimer and Robert E. Morrell, G. K. Hall, 1984); *Japanese Folk Literature: A Core Collection and Reference Guide* (Joanne P. Algarin, comp., Bowker, 1982); and *Modern Japanese Literature in Translation* (Harper & Row, 1979). Additionally, the *Encyclopedia of Indian Literature* (distributed by South Asia Bks., 1983); the *Guide to Chi-*

Core Titles

	PUBLIC	ACADEMIC	SCHOOL
GENERAL			
Guide to Oriental Classics, 3d rev. edition de Bary, William Theodore, Ainslie Thomas Embree, and Amy Vladeck Heinrich, eds. Columbia, 1989		✦	
CHINA			
Bibliography of Studies and Translations of Modern Chinese Literature, 1918–1942 Gibbs, Donald A., and Yun-chen Li. Harvard, 1975		✦	
Indiana Companion to Traditional Chinese Literature Nienhauser, William H., Jr., ed. and comp. Indiana Univ. Pr., 1985		✦	
Selective Guide to Chinese Literature, 1900–1949, 3 vols. Dolezelova-Velingerova, Milena, Zbigniew Slupski, and Lloyd Haft, eds. Brill, 1988–1989	✦	✦	
JAPAN			
Princeton Companion to Classical Japanese Literature Miner, Earl, Hiroko Odagiri, and Robert Morrell. Princeton, 1985		✦	
A Reader's Guide to Japanese Literature Rimer, J. Thomas. Kodansha, 1988	✦	✦	

nese Poetry and Drama (Richard J. Lynn, G. K. Hall, 1984); and the *Kabuki Encyclopedia: An English Language Adaption of Kabuki Jiten* (Samuel L. Leiter, Greenwood, 1979) were recommended by the Board, but were not accessible to the reviewers or obtainable from the publishers.

The core reference books reviewed are almost evenly divided between bibliographies of and guides to the primary literature, and bibliographies of critical studies about that literature. To both categories should be added two standard annual reference sources, the Modern Language Association *Bibliography* and the *Bibliography of Asian Studies.* The former is the more up-to-date of the two and has the advantage of including West Asian Literature. East Asian, Southeast Asian, and South Asian literatures are covered in both works. Both bibliographies should be consulted not only for their coverage of Indian, Japanese, and Chinese literatures, but especially because they include citations to the literature of all Asian countries.

In addition to the core references, there are many supplemental references that are recommended. Academic libraries, especially, may wish to augment their core collections with such highly specialized works as the BIBLIOGRAPHY OF PANJABI DRAMA and THE KABUKI HANDBOOK: A GUIDE TO UNDERSTANDING AND APPRECIATION.

Core Titles

General

Guide to Oriental Classics. William Theodore de Bary, Ainslie Thomas Embree, and Amy Vladeck Heinrich, eds. 3d rev. edition. Columbia, 1989. hard and soft. 1 vol. 324 pp. ISBN 0-231-06674-0 (hard); 0-231-066-75-9 (soft). $53 (hard); $17 (soft). handbook.
PJ307 016.89

Now in its third edition, the *Guide to Oriental Classics* provides a useful, approachable introduction to English translations of the classical literature of Japan, China, India, and the Islamic world. The guide was developed by the faculty and staff of Columbia University's course in the Oriental humanities. The purpose of the work remains the same for the third edition as for the first: "to provide an aid to both teachers and students in reading and discussing the major texts of the four traditions represented" (preface). This aim, combined with the belief that the work should be useful for nonspecialists, results in a publication that serves as a basic, clearly written guide to classical Oriental literature.

The *Guide to Oriental Classics* includes four main sections, one for each of the four traditions treated by the work: China, Japan, India, and Islam. Each section begins with a briefly annotated bibliography of basic reference works and studies of the literature, history, religion, and philosophy of that tradition. This portion of each section serves to place the literature of the tradition into a broader context.

The remainder of each section consists of chapters that focus on individual works or types of literature within that tradition. The Islamic tradition is detailed in 16 chapters that cover the literature through 1500; India receives 26 chapters of coverage, ending with Gandhi's *Autobiography;* China's literature is treated in 29 chapters through approximately A.D. 1000; and Japan receives 19 chapters, taking its literary tradition to the end of the nineteenth century.

The approach and scope of each chapter varies. For example, one chapter might discuss an individual text, such as the *Qur'an* or the *Ruba'iyyat of 'Umar Khayyan* from the Islamic tradition, while other chapters might treat several works or authors. For example, the discussion of Chinese poetry includes chapters on *Book of Songs, Songs of the South,* and individual poets.

The *Guide to Oriental Classics* is most valuable for identifying basic complete and selected translations as well as major secondary readings. Virtually all entries include brief, evaluative annotations that help unfamiliar readers sort out the works most appropriate for their particular needs. For instance, an annotation reveals that Edward Seidentsticker's translation of *Tale of Genji* includes "an excellent complete translation, with lists of the principal characters, and a brief introduction." Similarly, James Legge's translation of Chuang-tzu "loses much of the wit and fancy of the original" (p. 180), while his rendition of Mencius is "still the standard scholarly translation" (p. 184).

The editors of the *Guide to Oriental Classics* were well prepared for their task. William de Bary has taught Chinese and Japanese literature and history at Columbia and has published extensively on Asian history, culture, and literatures. Ainslie Embree is a specialist in modern Indian history at Columbia and editor of the ENCYCLOPEDIA OF ASIAN HISTORY (see Asian History). Amy Heinrich, editor of this third edition of the guide, is a librarian at Columbia's Starr East Asian Library.

The *Guide to Oriental Classics* provides a useful introduction to the field of Asian literature. While the work would benefit from an index, the arrangement and annotations help users identify basic literary texts and secondary works on Chinese, Japanese, Indian, and Islamic literature. The Board recommends this work for the core collection of academic libraries.

China

Bibliography of Studies and Translations of Modern Chinese Literature, 1918–1942. Harvard East Asian monographs, no. 61. Donald A. Gibbs and Yun-chen Li. Harvard, 1975. hard. 1 vol. 239 pp. appendixes. index. ISBN 0-674-07111-5. $24.50. bibliography.

PL2302 016.8951

Donald Gibbs and Yun-chen Li have produced an extensive bibliography on a narrow but important period of Chinese literature in their *Bibliography of Studies and Translations of Modern Chinese Literature, 1918–1942.* Gibbs and Li prepared their work while at Harvard University; both are now in the Department of Chinese Studies at the University of California at Davis. This reference grew out of a desire to "introduce modern Chinese literature into the undergraduate and secondary school curricula" (introduction).

The Bibliography of Studies and Translations of Modern Chinese Literature, 1918–1942 differs from the out-of-print *Modern Chinese Fiction* in that this other bibliography aims to identify all English-language translations and studies rather than to be selective. Furthermore, the focus is on a more narrow time period than is *Modern Chinese Fiction.* The chronological boundaries of the bibliography are the publication of the first of Lu Hsun's short stories in 1918 and the publication of Mao Tse-tung's *Talks at the Yenan Forum* in 1942.

The *Bibliography of Studies and Translations* consists of several sections and appendixes. The appendixes include lists of major sources consulted, Chinese sources, conference papers, and unpublished works. There is also an index of the authors of studies and translations, which adds to the accessibility of the volume.

The two main components of the work are a list of general critical literary studies and a longer section devoted to English-language translations and studies of individual authors. The greatest strength of this reference is the section on individual authors. A useful feature of this section is the inclusion of references to entries in Howard Boorman and Richard Howard's *Biographical Dictionary of Republican China* and in Donald Klein and Anne Clark's *Biographic Dictionary of Chinese Communism, 1921–1965.* One hundred thirty-three authors are included in the *Bibliography.* Coverage is limited to literary figures and the literary accomplishments of people who have made other contributions to society.

The entries on individual authors typically include the formal name and pen name of the person, with the entry under the name by which the author is more commonly known. Dates, all known studies, and translations arranged by genre (short stories, essays, poems, novels) complete each entry. Studies include not only books, articles, master's theses, and doctoral dissertations but also "biographical summaries, prefaces, some newspaper accounts, and even politically motivated propaganda if it is germane to an understanding of a writer's status" (introduction). Any critical study that discusses more than one author is repeated under each author. Only basic bibliographic information is given for studies and translations.

The *Bibliography of Studies and Translations of Modern Chinese Literature, 1918–1942,* is an important contribution to the study of modern Chinese literature. While there is some overlap with *Modern Chinese Fiction,* this reference work includes more authors, studies, and translations for the period covered. However, because that time period is limited and because of their own unique contributions, the two works complement each other. The Board recommends this work for the core collection of academic libraries.

Indiana Companion to Traditional Chinese Literature. William H. Nienhauser, Jr., ed. and comp. Indiana Univ. Pr., 1985. hard. 1 vol. 1,050 pp. appendix. indexes. ISBN 0-253-32983-3. $75. handbook.
PL2264 895.109

The *Indiana Companion to Traditional Chinese Literature* is an impressive scholarly work that describes and evaluates Chinese literature from the earliest times until the end of Imperial China in 1912. Literature is broadly defined to include philosophical or religious texts and histories (such as Ssu-ma Ch'ien's classic *Shih-chi*), as well as the more traditional poetry, drama, and fiction.

Editor and compiler William H. Nienhauser, Jr., professor of Chinese language and literature at the University of Wisconsin, assembled a team of nearly 200 international experts on Chinese literature. He was assisted in his efforts by three associate editors, all scholars in their areas of responsibility. Charles Hartman of SUNY at Albany was responsible for poetry, Y. W. Ma of the University of Hawaii for fiction, and Stephen H. West of the University of Arizona for drama. Their well-conceived and -executed work has become the standard, single-volume discussion of Chinese literature, and will prove especially useful and appropriate for scholars and graduate students.

The work is divided into two sections. The first 194 pages consists of ten essays on important topics of Chinese literature. The chapter titles best indicate their scope and range: "Buddhist Literature," "Drama," "Fiction," "Literary Criticism," "Poetry," "Popular Literature," "Prose," "Rhetoric," "Taoist Literature," "Women's Literature." Averaging ten pages each, the essays give good overviews of their topics, and include bibliographies of editions of pertinent literature, translations into English, Japanese, German, and French, and selected critical studies. Each essay defines its topic within a literary and historical context. For instance, the essay on Buddhist literature by Jan Yun-hua begins: "Of all religious literature written in Chinese, the body of Buddhist literature is the largest and the most varied in theme and style."

The second, longer section of the *Indiana Companion to Traditional Chinese Literature* devotes 774 pages to dictionary entries on authors, works, and genres. The signed entries are longer than those found in most of the well-known Oxford "companions," which were the original inspiration for this volume. Entries on classic works such as the *Dream of the Red Chamber* are often five pages long. Author entries provide brief biographical information, discuss the person's major works, and conclude with an attempt to evaluate the importance and place of the author in Chinese literature. The evaluation of individual authors is particularly helpful to people who are unfamiliar with an individual. For instance, poet, musician, and critic Chiang-K'uei is described as having "unusual competence as both a creative artist and a scholar." Each entry concludes with a bibliography.

The *Indiana Companion to Traditional Chinese Literature* is a formidable work that is not always approachable by a novice in Chinese literature. Attempts have been made to increase the accessibility and usefulness of the book. Several appendixes list all cited sources, frequently cited sources, and a chronology of Chinese literature. Comprehensive name, title, and subject indexes increase access to this handbook. An asterisk appears in the text of individual entries when a term, person, or work is mentioned that has its own individual article.

There are a few minor drawbacks in trying to use this reference, however. Users unfamiliar with the Chinese language may be distracted by the practice of including both the romanized and Chinese character versions of all names. A more serious difficulty of the work is the arrangement of all entries on works by their romanized Chinese names without providing a cross-reference to the English translated title in either the entry section or the title index. As a result, many of the entries are written with the assumption that users are familiar with the subject at hand.

Nonetheless, the *Indiana Companion to Traditional*

Chinese Literature is an ambitious work that will serve advanced users well. It is valuable as a source on Chinese literature, history, and culture due to its broad coverage. The Board recommends this work for the core collection of academic libraries.

Selective Guide to Chinese Literature, 1900–1949. Milena Dolezelova-Velingerova, Zbigniew Slupski, and Lloyd Haft, eds. Brill, 1988–1989. hard. 3 vols. indexes. ISBN 90-04-08960-8 (vol. 3). $67.50 (vol. 3). guide.
PL2302 895.109

Selective Guide to Chinese Literature, 1900–1949, a three-volume work, makes an important contribution to the study of modern Chinese literature. Each volume is devoted to a different genre; volume 1 to the novel, volume 2 to the short story, and volume 3 to the poem. The preface to volume 1 states that "the aim of these volumes is to facilitate the first stage of research for anyone interested in twentieth century Chinese literature." The three volumes are now available. A fourth volume on drama is projected. Each volume includes approximately 100 entries ranging in length from two to four pages.

The *Selective Guide* was a long-term project initiated by the European Association of Chinese Studies and funded by the European Science Foundation. This multinational project was directed by Nils Malmquist, who has written on Chinese language and literature. The editors of each volume are recognized scholars in the genre covered by that volume. Each entry is written and signed by one of the more than 100 specialists in Chinese and Asian literature.

The volumes in the *Selective Guide to Chinese Literature* have several common features. The format of each includes a bibliographical note on important critical sources and anthologies and a scholarly introduction to the genre covered in the volume. The entries are arranged alphabetically by author's last name. Brief indexes of publishers and of author's names, pseudonyms, and alternative names are provided.

The introduction in each volume is especially useful for the reader new to the genre covered therein. Milena Dolezelova-Velingerova's introduction in volume 1 sets the stage for the series by discussing modern Chinese literature in general before detailing the evolution of the novel. In volume 2, Zbigniew Slupski discusses the alternating rise and fall of interest in and the publication of the short story in China, especially after the May Fourth Movement of 1919. Lloyd Haft's introduction in volume 3 describes at length the challenges facing modern Chinese poetry, particularly the difficulty in overcoming the strong tradition of classical poetry that remained in vogue even with the rise of Mao Zedong and the Cultural Revolution.

The entries make up the heart of each volume. Each entry includes: the name and dates of the author; basic bibliographic information about the literary work; a summary of its contents, including an informative appraisal of the work; and reference to contemporary reviews, important secondary sources, and translations into English. The bibliographic information for short story collections includes the names of each story in the anthology, while those for the collections of poetry include the number of poems in the volume.

The description of each work gives a flavor of the piece. Each entry in volume 1 outlines the plot, discusses major themes, presents analysis, and places the novel in the context of modern Chinese literature. For instance, Lao She's *Camel Xiangzi,* also known as the *Rickshaw Boy,* is described "as a parable of the fate of the Chinese people, but the book's worldwide popularity is due more to its other literary qualities." In volume 2, the main short stories of each collection are discussed, together with the place of the anthology within the genre as a whole. The entries in volume 3 also include analysis, but differ from those in other volumes because liberal use is made of excerpts from individual poems.

Access to the literature discussed in the *Selective Guide to Chinese Literature* could have been improved by increased indexing. There is no index to works by title or to the critical studies listed at the end of most entries. An index by theme and subject also would have increased the usefulness of the reference.

Despite this drawback, the *Selective Guide to Chinese Literature* is an important addition to the reference material available on modern Chinese literature. The entries provide a clear introduction to and appraisal of each work included. The *Selective Guide to Chinese Literature, 1900–1949* should be considered for acquisition by libraries with an interest in modern Chinese literature, although its price may be a deterrent to purchase for some. The Board recommends this work for the core collections of public and academic libraries.

Japan

Princeton Companion to Classical Japanese Literature. Earl Miner, Hiroko Odagiri, and Robert Morrell. Princeton, 1985. hard. 1 vol. 570 pages. illus. index. ISBN 0-691-06599-3 (hard); 0-691-00825-6 (soft). $59 (hard); $16.95 (soft). guide.
PL726.1 895.6

The *Princeton Companion to Classical Japanese Literature* is an ambitious, multifaceted work devoted to Japanese literature from the earliest times to the Meiji Restoration (1868). The work is divided into ten parts and includes an index. The listing of parts in the table of contents gives a sense of the scope of the volume: part 1, "A Brief Literary History"; part 2, "Chronologies"; part 3, "Major Authors and Works"; part 4, "Literary Terms"; part 5, "Theaters"; part 6, "Collections, Kinds, Criticism"; "Buddhism and Confucianism"; "Dictionaries"; part 7, "Time, Directions, Related Symbolism, and Annual Celebrations"; part 8, "Geography, Maps, Poetic Place Names"; part 9, "Ranks, Offices, and Certain Incumbents"; part 10, "Architecture"; "Clothing, Armor, and Arms"; "Illustrated Popular Books and Other Genre Representations."

This reference work contains short definitions of literary terms (part 4), longer entries that average 500 words but can extend to 4 pages on important authors and works (part 3), and 10- to 20-page essays on topics such as the development of poetry, historical periods, (part 1), or the five kinds of Japanese theater (part 5).

Beyond the range of subjects covered in the *Princeton Companion,* the work benefits from the combination of text and illustrations. The variety of types of illustrations makes this work different from other literary companions. For instance, charts are used for chronologies (part 2); for depicting time, season, and symbols (part 7); and for describing court ranks and offices (part 9). Maps are featured in part 8 to illustrate Japanese provinces throughout history, while part 10 makes use of frequent illustrations to show architecture, clothing, armor, and arms.

The authors of the *Princeton Companion to Classical Japanese Literature* use several editorial conventions to facilitate access to the work. The user is repeatedly advised to heed the "Notice to Readers" and to read the explanatory comments at the beginning of each part. An asterisk before an author name or title signifies an individual entry in part 3 ("Major Authors and Works"). Any italicized term, other than a title, is included in part 4. In addition, some entries in parts 3 and 4 also contain references to other sections of the volume.

The scholarly approach and depth of coverage of the *Princeton Companion to Classical Japanese Literature* are due to the background of the three authors. Earl Miner is a professor of English and comparative literature at Princeton and has written widely on the literature of Japan, England, and the United States. Robert Morrell, a professor of Japanese language and literature at Washington University in St. Louis, has written on the connection between Buddhism and early Japanese literature. Hiroko Odagiri is at the Institute of Japanese Culture and Classics of Kokugakuin University and was instrumental both in writing and in locating illustrations for the this work.

While the differences are mainly positive, the *Princeton Companion to Classical Japanese Literature* does, as its authors claim, differ significantly from any other literary companion. This reference work does present some obstacles to the user. For example, it is not always apparent where one should begin a search for a topic because the volume has ten parts. Unlike other literary companions, this work does not list all entries alphabetically. Although there is an index, it covers only parts 1, 3, and 6, with some material from part 4 also included. Important information such as the ten-page essay on Nō (or Noh) drama from part 5 is not included in the index. In addition, references are not given to any English-language titles of Japanese works included.

Despite these difficulties, the *Princeton Companion to Classical Japanese Literature* is an important source. The Board recommends this work for the core collection of academic libraries.

A Reader's Guide to Japanese Literature. J. Thomas Rimer. Kodansha, 1988. soft. 1 vol. 208 pp. appendix. index. ISBN 0-87011-896-X. $14.95. handbook. PL717 895.609

A Reader's Guide to Japanese Literature attempts to identify important works available in sound translations for the general reader. The increase in interest in Japan's literature has resulted in numerous translations of a variety of works. As a result, people unfamiliar with Japanese literature who desire to read representative works can easily be overwhelmed by the possibilities. To assist patrons in choosing a work, the author, J. Thomas Rimer, identifies and discusses 50 important works of literature; 20 are classical works (dating from 712–1819), and 30 date from the late nineteenth century to the present (1887–1967). Readers interested in a more complete list of translations of modern Japanese literature may turn to *Modern Japanese Literature in Translation: A Bibliography* (Kodansha, 1979), now out of print.

The reference is a welcome introduction to important translated works of Japanese literature, and reflects the authority of the author. Rimer is presently the head of East Asian Studies at the University of Maryland. His previous positions included Chief of the Asian Division of the Library of Congress and professor of Japanese language and literature at Washington University in St. Louis. In addition, Professor Rimer has written extensively on Japanese fiction, drama, and poetry.

A Reader's Guide to Japanese Literature provides three- to four-page essays on each work included. The types of literature covered range from fiction to drama, essays, and poetry. Each entry includes biographical information about the author, an outline of the work, comments about its place within the author's literary contributions and within world literature, translations available, and, in some instances, comments on the availability of translations of the author's other works.

The essays assume no familiarity with Japanese literature and make useful literary connections. For example, Yasunari Kawabata's debt (in his *Snow Country*) to Murasaki's *Tale of Genji* is noted, as are the stylistic and thematic similarities between Abe Kōbō (author of *The Woman in the Dunes*) and Gabriel García Márquez, Samuel Beckett, and Eugene Ionesco. The essays are clearly written and give a strong sense of the flavor of the work being described.

Rimer's introductory "Some Observations on Reading Japanese Literature" sets the stage for the essays with a straightforward, illuminating discussion of the evolution of the country's literature. Other helpful features in the reference work are a section on "Further Readings" that includes anthologies of literature and critical studies and indexes by author, title, and subject.

A Reader's Guide to Japanese Literature is a very useful addition to the reference material on Japanese literature. The book is written in an informative, approachable style, and highlights important works available in English translation. The Board recommends this work for the core collections of public and academic libraries.

Supplementary Titles

General

Asian/Pacific Literatures in English: Bibliographies. Robert E. McDowell and Judith H. McDowell, eds. Three Continents, 1978. hard and soft. 1 vol. 132 pp. illus. index. ISBN 0-89410-072-6 (hard); 0-89410-073-4 (soft). $26 (hard); $15 (soft). bibliography.
Z3008.L58A8 016.820'8'095

Asian/Pacific Literatures in English: Bibliographies is a "collection of six bibliographies [containing a total of 2,612 items] of literature in the English language from Sri Lanka, the Philippines, Malaysia/Singapore, Papua New Guinea, Hong Kong, and the aboriginal culture of Australia. Each of the bibliographies was compiled by an authority on the country or area. . . . All bibliographies contain sections listing works of fiction, poetry, drama, and criticism; most have sections for bibliography, autobiography, folklore and mythology, and translations from the native languages. Some have special features. [For example,] the bibliography on the Australian aboriginals includes works of a political, sociological, and educational nature and articles depicting aboriginals in white Australian literature. The Philippine bibliography lists 52 novels and picture books for children.

"While the bibliographies vary in length and in the number of categories included, all appear to have been carefully prepared and thoroughly researched. A regional map precedes each bibliography. A common index for all six bibliographies lists names of authors, editors, translators, and compilers appearing in the entries." (*ARBA,* 1979, p. 182)

Board's recommendation: Academic libraries.

Far Eastern Literature in the 20th Century: A Guide, rev. edition. Leonard S. Klein, ed. Ungar, 1986. soft. 1 vol. 205 pp. ISBN 0-8044-6352-2. $12.95. handbook.
PL493.F37 895.03

Far Eastern Literature in the 20th Century: A Guide offers "succinct introductions to the literatures of Burma, Cambodia, China, Indonesia, Japan, Korea, Laos, Malaysia, Mongolia, the Philippines, Singapore, Thailand, Tibet, Vietnam, and the Pacific Islands. [The entries] are written by recognized authorities in the field (such as Donald Keene, Wu-chi Liu, Irving Lo, Leon Zolbrod, Peter H. Lee), and . . . are, for the most part, fair and accurate. The brief profiles of the national literatures are . . . useful because they are not to be found in the three-volume *Dictionary of Oriental Literature* (Basic Books, 1974)." (*MLJ,* Winter 1987, p. 451)

Board's recommendation: Public and academic libraries.

Introduction to Thai Literature. Robert C. Jones and Ruchira C. Mendiones. Southeast Asia Programs/Cornell, 1970. soft. 1 vol. 563 pp. ISBN 0-87727-505-X $7. handbook.
PL4200.J6 895.9'1

Board's recommendation: Academic libraries.

China

Chinese Fiction: A Bibliography of Books and Articles in Chinese and English. Tien-Yi Li. Yale Far Eastern Publications/Yale University, 1968. hard. 1 vol. 356 pp. appendixes. index. ISBN 0-88710-017-1. $11.95. bibliography.
Z3018.L5L4 016.8951'3

Chinese Fiction: A Bibliography of Books and Articles in Chinese and English, "as stated in the Preface, is not intended to be an exhaustive bibliography, but rather as an extensive and yet selective bibliographical listing of 'books and articles in Chinese and English that have been published in the field of Chinese fiction over the past few decades.' (p. v). Also included are reference works and general studies relevant to Chinese fiction. Specialized studies are listed under the individual titles of fiction for classical fiction but are listed under the names of individual writers for modern fiction. Original works of fiction are excluded, but English translations of novels and short stories are listed. Four highly useful appendices are found at the end of the volume: (1) A List of Periodicals and Newspapers, (2) A List of Publishers, (3) A List of Pen Names, Sobriquets, etc., and (4) An Index to Authors and Translators.

"It is obvious that the compiler made every effort to insure easy identification of publications. Not only all necessary bibliographical details, but also all Chinese characters necessary for identification are supplied. . . . For the convenience of its users cross references to pen names and joint authors and translators are made." (*JAS,* August 1972, p. 924)

Board's recommendation: Academic libraries.

The Chinese Theatre in Modern Times: From 1840 to the Present Day. Colin Mackerras. Univ. of Massachusetts Pr., 1975. hard. 1 vol. 256 pp. illus. index. ISBN 0-87023-196-0. $25. guide.
PN2871.M3 792.0951

The Chinese Theatre in Modern Times: From 1840 to the Present Day is "an attempt to provide a general account of the development of Chinese drama over the past 150 years. . . . The first part [deals] with Peking Opera until 1949. . . . The second part deals with the theatre outside Peking until 1949, and . . . [the] third section [concerns] the theatre in China since 1949." (*TLS,* June 4, 1976, p. 680)

"Although intended for the general reader, this book is essential for anyone wishing to initiate or continue serious study of the Chinese theatre. . . . Mackerras writes clearly, objectively, and with authority—presenting Chinese theatre as both an aural and visual art, constantly uniting it with its political/historical/cultural environment. He sketches the lives and styles of leading performers and playwrights; he is also careful to include discussions of rural popular theatre as well as the theatre of the city and of the upper classes. The book concludes with two particularly valuable 'extras': an annotated bibliography and a chronological table (matching reign-title or period with political events in China and events in Chinese theatre)." (*Choice,* July/August 1976, p. 677)

Also reviewed in: *Brit Bk N,* September 1983, p. 540; *Pac A,* Winter 1978, p. 698; *WHR,* Winter 1978, p. 87.

Board's recommendation: Academic libraries.

Contemporary Chinese Novels and Short Stories, 1949–1974: An Annotated Bibliography. Meishi Tsai. Harvard, 1979. hard. 1 vol. 408 pp. ISBN 0-674-16681-7. $30. bibliography.
Z3018.LST78 016.8951'3'09

Contemporary Chinese Novels and Short Stories, 1949–1974: An Annotated Bibliography "covers fiction from mainland China . . . [and] is divided into four major sections—index of authors, list of authors and their works, index of titles, and subject index of selected topics. Entries are arranged alphabetically according to the Wade-Giles romanization. When available, a short biography of the author is included and entries are selectively annotated. Chinese characters and English equivalents precede the romanization of all titles.

"[In addition,] all titles listed can be found in major U.S. libraries. . . . This [volume] is an invaluable tool for the study of contemporary China." (*LJ,* July 1979, p. 1442)

Also reviewed in: *ARBA,* 1980, p. 589; *JAS,* May 1980, p. 587; *Pac A,* Summer 1980, p. 328; *WLT,* Summer 1980, p. 487.

Board's recommendation: Academic libraries.

The History of Chinese Literature: A Selected Bibliography, 2d edition. Tien-Yi Li. Yale Far Eastern Publications/Yale University, 1970. hard. 1 vol. 98 pp. ISBN 0-88710-030-9. $7.95. bibliography.
P623 895.1'09

The History of Chinese Literature: A Selected Bibliography provides "a list of [about] 300 books in Chinese, English, French, German, and Japanese [which are divided into] 11 sections: [for example,] 1. Bibliographies—2. Glossaries—3. Anthologies and sources . . . 10. Biographical dictionaries and monographs—11. Others. [There are] no annotations or index." (*Guide to*

Reference Material, 3d edition, 1977, p. 623)
Board's recommendation: Academic libraries.

Twenty-five T'ang Poets: An Index to English Translations. Sydney S. K. Fung and S. T. Lai, comps. Chinese Univ. of Hong Kong Pr., 1984; distrib. by Univ. of Washington Pr. hard. 1 vol. 696 pp. ISBN 0-295-96155-4. $75. index.
Z3108.L5F86 895.1

With *Twenty-five T'ang Poets: An Index to English Translations,* "students of Chinese poetry have the first comprehensive collection of translations of poems from the T'ang dynasty (AD 618–907). The availability of 4,000 poems attributed to the 25 most popular and representative of the T'ang poets, with 12,000 entries for English translations, is a major contribution to the study of Chinese literature. The index is first listed alphabetically by the poets. Under each poet, the poems are arranged alphabetically by the transliteration of the titles, followed by the titles and the first lines in Chinese, page reference to the *Ch'üan T'ang Shih* or other sources, translator, bibliographic location of the translation, and first line of the translation. Coverage extends from 1902 to 1981. [An] index of first lines of translations is an added merit." (*Choice,* April 1985, p. 1142)

Also reviewed in: *ARBA,* 1985, p. 413.
Board's recommendation: Academic libraries.

India

Bibliography of Panjabi Drama. Joginer S. Bajwa. Modern Library Prakasham, 1985, distrib. by South Asia Bks. hard. 1 vol. ISBN 0-8364-1307-5. $11. bibliography.
016.954

Board's recommendation: Academic libraries.

Translations of Bengali Works into English: A Bibliography. Dipali Ghosh. Mansell, 1986; distrib. by Wilson. hard. 1 vol. 264 pp. indexes. ISBN 0-7201-1809-3. $64. bibliography.
Z3201.G48 016.954'14

In *Translations of Bengali Works into English: A Bibliography* the compiler "has assembled citations to 711 Bengali works that have been translated into English. Both books and journal articles are included, but only works found in the British Library, the India Office Library, and the School of Oriental and African studies at the University of London are listed. . . . Entries are listed by subject [for example,] 'Art and Aesthetics,' 'Conferences,' 'Drama,' 'Fiction' . . . . Eight authors have more than half the entries; [Rabindranath] Tagore alone has 216. [Though] names are given in Indian rather than Anglicized form . . . a name index refers from Anglicized to Indian forms of names." (*Choice,* January 1987, p. 742)

Also reviewed in: *TLS,* August 29, 1986, p. 951.
Board's recommendation: Academic libraries.

Japan

Dawn to the West: Japanese Literature of the Modern Era. Donald Keene. Holt, 1984. hard and soft. 2 vols. 2,012 pp. index. ISBN 0-03-062814-8 (vol. 1, hard); 0-03-062816-4 (vol. 2, hard); 0-8050-0607-9 (vol. 1, soft); 0-8050-0608-7 (vol. 2, soft). $60 (vol. 1, hard); $40 (vol. 2, hard); $29.95 (vol. 1, soft); $19.95 (vol. 2, soft). history.
PL726.55.K39 895.6'09

These two volumes (of *Dawn to the West: Japanese Literature of the Modern Era*] "provide a treatment of modern Japanese literature which surveys . . . figures and literary movements since 1868 when Japan was opened to the West. Starting with the 'new' literature begun with the denial of traditional writing (under the impetus of a flow of translations of Western writers in the 1880s), Keene gives examples of imitations and influences while [attempting to] account for the emergence of new [literary] forms.

"The approach used by Keene is straightforward: he surveys major and minor works by individual authors, providing fairly detailed plot summaries.

"[Volume 1 on fiction and Volume 2 on poetry, drama, and criticism] constitute . . . [the] definitive history of modern Japanese literature, destined to become the standard work on the subject." (*Choice,* July/August 1984, p. 1615)

Also reviewed in: *BW,* May 6, 1984, p. 10; *LATBR,* April 22, 1984, p. 1; *LJ,* May 15, 1984, p. 983; *New R,* June 25, 1984, p. 28; *NYT,* May 5, 1984, p. 13; *NYTBR,* May 13, 1984, p. 11; *PW,* February 3, 1984, p. 393.

Board's recommendation: Public and academic libraries.

Guide to Japanese Prose, 2d edition. Alfred H. Marks and Barry D. Bort. G. K. Hall, 1984. hard. 1 vol. index. ISBN 0-8161-8630-8. $32.95. bibliography.
PL782.E8 016.8956'8'08

The *Guide to Japanese Prose* is an "annotated bibliography of Japanese prose in English translation.

Works annotated are listed chronologically within two sections which cover the pre-Meiji [27 works] and the modern [94 works] periods. Complete bibliographical data, including the romanized form of the Japanese title, is provided with each entry.

"Annotations are informative and gracefully written, and often include brief plot summaries and critical comments. The introduction attempts to place the works listed in their historical context. . . . [This work is] a significant reference tool for librarians, nonspecialist readers, and students interested in Japanese literature." (*LJ,* October 1, 1975, p. 1812)

Also reviewed in: *Choice,* April 1976, p. 206; *WLB,* April 1976, p. 647.

Board's recommendation: Academic libraries.

A History of Japanese Literature. Shuichi Kato; David Chibbett and Don Sanderson, trans. Kodansha, 1979–1983. hard (vols. 2 and 3) and soft (vol. 1). 3 vols. index. ISBN 0-87011-491-3 (vol. 1); 0-87011-568-5 (vol. 2); 0-87011-569-3 (vol. 3). $6.25 (vol. 1); $35 (vol. 2); $35 (vol. 3). history.
PL716.K2413 895.6109

A History of Japanese Literature was "originally written for a Japanese audience, . . . [and contains] many sensible, insightful critical observations about literary works and their immediate social context, and [much] space [is] devoted to important lesser-known works, particularly those having to do with religion." (*Choice,* March 1980, p. 80)

"[The first volume] focuses on Japanese literature before the 16th Century and covers its development and relation to the Japanese language and world view.

"[In all volumes] discussion of texts is complemented by frequent quotations and expert re-creations of the social and cultural milieu from which the literature emerged. A great deal of information is conveyed in the most painless way—a laudable achievement!" (*LJ,* January 1, 1980, p. 104)

Also reviewed in: *BL,* February 1, 1980, p. 750; *JAS,* August 1980, p. 771; *JAS,* August 1984, p. 761; *Lon R Bks,* March 1, 1984, p. 20; *TLS,* December 7, 1979, p. 100.

Board's recommendation: Academic libraries.

A History of Japanese Literature: Vol. 1, The Archaic and Ancient Ages. Jin'ichi Konishi; Earl Miner, ed.; Aileen Gatten and Nicholas Teele, trans. Princeton, 1984. hard. 1 vol. 475 pp. illus. index. ISBN 0-691-06592-6. $62.50. history.
PL717.K6213 895.6'09

A History of Japanese Literature: Vol. 1, The Archaic and Ancient Ages "is the first of a projected five volumes, published in translation prior to publication in the original. It ends with the early ninth century.

"[The author] combines encyclopedic mastery of his own tradition with a catholic interest in other literatures and forms of criticism." (*Choice,* January 1985, p. 690)

"[The author] proceeds by genre, rather than chronologically, since different geographic areas reached different levels of literary sophistication at different times. . . . Konishi offers extensive comparisons with other world literatures; the bibliography leans heavily towards comparative literature in the Western works cited and to technical commentaries in the Japanese. [This is] a well-translated and -edited, highly significant work for specialized collections." (*LJ,* November 1, 1984, p. 2067)

Also reviewed in: *JAS,* August 1985, p. 842; *Rel St Rev,* July 1986, p. 318.

Board's recommendation: Academic libraries.

A History of Japanese Literature: Vol. 2, The Early Middle Ages. Jin'ichi Konishi; Earl Miner, ed.; Aileen Gatten, trans. Princeton, 1986. hard and soft. 1 vol. 461 pp. illus. index. ISBN 0-691-06655-8 (hard); 0-691-10177-9 (soft). $62.50 (hard); $22.95 (soft). history.
PL717.K6213 895.6

A History of Japanese Literature: Vol.2, The Early Middle Ages, the "second of five projected volumes, discusses Japanese literature from the ninth to the mid-twelfth centuries, coinciding with the Heian period of political history. Konishi argues that the cult of beauty and courtly love for which this period is . . . known was not indigenous but inspired by the Chinese Six Dynasties' pursuit of . . . 'an idealized sphere of worldly pleasures'. . . ." (*TLS,* December 11–17, 1987, p. 1382)

"[Thus,] Konishi's aim is interpretation rather than the listing of facts, and he states personal views on a number of controversial topics. He is concerned both with the works and with their readers; what emerges from his discussion is the unique shape of the literary tradition itself. The translation preserves Konishi's idiom; yet large portions of his dense original are rendered so fluently that the reader is scarcely conscious that they were not composed in English—a remarkable achievement." (*Choice,* March 1987, p. 1076)

"Konishi's special concern is with the technical aspects of Japanese literature: questions of genre, prosody, narrative technique, patronage, author and audience, anthologizing techniques, and so on. . . . The excellence of [this] work lies . . . in its international perspective and transcendence of parochial barriers. Konishi is unusually well read in comparative literature, and his work is rich in elegant cross-cultural comparisons." (*TLS,* December 11–17, 1987, p. 1382)

Also reviewed in: *JAS,* May 1988, p. 377; *Rel St Rev,* October 1987, p. 364.

Board's recommendation: Academic libraries.

The Kabuki Handbook: A Guide to Understanding and Appreciation. Aubrey S. Halford and Giovanna M. Halford. Tuttle, 1956. soft. 1 vol. 487 pp. ISBN 0-8048-0332-3. $14.95. handbook.
PN2921.H3 792.0952

Board's recommendation: Public and academic libraries.

Helen Guice Groves

Astrology, Parapsychology, and the Occult

See also Astronomy; Folklore and Mythology

While the term *occult* indicates the hidden, the mysterious, or what is known only to initiates, its meanings often diverge into such areas as black or white magic, alchemy, demonology, ghosts, or poltergeists. The occult also has astronomical as well as astrological significance. For example, when one heavenly body, such as the moon, obscures a planet or star, this is meaningful. *Parapsychology* refers to the paranormal or paraphysical concerning unusual phenomena such as telepathy, clairvoyance, precognition, psychokinesis or telekinesis, extrasensory perception (ESP), or any matters that are not yet understood fully.

From the late 1920s through 1940, Drs. J. B. and Louisa Rhine and Professor William McDougall used scientific methodology to study the extranormal and establish a scientific validation for these events. Their work at Duke University's Parapsychology Laboratory is frequently cited in reference works on parapsychology and the occult, although meaningful validation of paranormal events in the laboratory is difficult. In addition to those who have an interest in the scientific aspects of parapsychology and the occult, readers (and writers) of fiction in which these elements appear will often request information on these subjects.

Astrology is a discipline that requires the use of mathematical formulas to produce charts from the movements of the sun, moon, and planets, and the interpretation of these movements to explain our basic natures and our probable responses to celestial influences. Those who are knowledgeable about astrology find the use of signs and symbols to be no more occult than the use of signs and symbols in mathematics, chemistry, or music. The alphabet of astrology is "occult" only to those who are unfamiliar with it and cannot translate its symbols into a form of information. Even the U.S. space program makes use of the same calculations of celestial and planetary movements used in astrology, in a coherent way, to find a "window" to launch another mission into space, while a former president was said to have been guided by astrological advice to time important political events.

The librarian's goal in acquiring materials in astrology, parapsychology, and the occult should be to stress the use of information to dispel misinformation in this area and, particularly, to obtain a selection of books that may be understood and used by the novice as well as the expert. The reviews that follow can also help librarians build a strong core collection in astrology, parapsychology, and the occult. Several books that are out of print would be welcome additions to the core collection. They are the *Dictionary of Occult, Hermetic, and Alchemical Sigils* (Fred Gettings, Methuen, 1981),

Core Titles

	PUBLIC	ACADEMIC	SCHOOL
The Astronomical Almanac Nautical Almanac Office, U.S.G.P.O., annual (See Astronomy)	✦	✦	
Encyclopedia of Occultism and Parapsychology: A Compendium of Information on the Occult Sciences, Magic, Demonology, Superstitions, Spiritism, Mysticism, Metaphysics, Psychical Science & Parapsychology, 2d edition, 3 vols. Shepard, Leslie, ed. Gale, 1984	✦	✦	✦
Heaven Knows What, 8th edition, rev. Lewi, Grant. Llewellyn Publications, 1989	✦		
Man, Myth and Magic: The Illustrated Encyclopedia of Mythology, Religion and the Unknown, 3d edition, 12 vols. Cavendish, Richard, and Yvonne Deutch, eds. Marshall Cavendish, 1985	✦	✦	✦
The New A to Z Horoscope Maker and Delineator, 13th edition Llewellyn, George. Llewellyn Publications, 1987	✦		
The New Compleat Astrologer, rev. edition Parker, Derek, and Julia Parker. Harmony/Crown, 1984	✦		

the *Larousse Encyclopedia of Astrology* (Helen Weaver, ed., NAL/Penguin, 1982), the *Dictionary of Astrology* (Fred Gettings, Routledge, Chapman & Hall, 1985), and the *Dictionary of Mysticism and the Occult* (Nevill Drury, Harper & Row, 1985). —*H. G. G.*
With contributions by Shirley Knight.

Core Titles

The Astronomical Almanac. Nautical Almanac Office. U.S.G.P.O., annual. hard. 1 vol. unpaged. illus. index. S/N 008-054-001297. $23. almanac.
D213.8 528

See Astronomy.

Encyclopedia of Occultism and Parapsychology: A Compendium of Information on the Occult Sciences, Magic, Demonology, Superstitions, Spiritism, Mysticism, Metaphysics, Psychical Science & Parapsychology, 2d edition. Leslie Shepard, ed. Gale, 1984. hard. 3 vols. 1,617 pp. indexes. ISBN 0-8103-0196-2. $285. encyclopedia.
BF1407.E52 133.03′21

The *Encyclopedia of Occultism and Parapsychology* is based on two out-of-print volumes, the *Encyclopedia of Occultism* by Lewis Spence (1920) and the *Encyclopedia of Psychic Sciences* by Nandor Fodor (1934). This encyclopedia represents a substantial merging of information from those two sources, which was revised and supplemented with new material written by Leslie Shepard. Over 1,000 new entries have been added to the more than 3,000 entries of the first edition. The original entries have been updated where necessary.

Entries vary in length, from only a few lines for the entries for periodicals to the nine-page entry for *astrology* or the 11½-page entry for *apparitions.* The entries are broad in topical and conceptual scope and range from biographical entries, organizations, cults, phenomena, and occult terms, to entries on *acupuncture, earthquake, prediction, witchcraft,* and a periodical called *Elvis Still Lives!*

The table of contents is repeated in all three volumes, and volume 3 contains a comprehensive general index and a helpful topical index that includes such headings as "Animals, Birds, Insects," "Gems," "Geographical Places of Phenomena," "Paranormal Phenomena" (with 51 subheadings), "Gods," "Demons," "Plants and Flowers," "Periodicals," and "Societies and Organizations." Historical background in the longer articles and bibliographical references appended at the end of entries provide rich sources of information easily accessible through indexes.

Current subjects are included, because the range of

topics reflects the universal curiosity about the unknown. Perspectives on the past and the present are linked in Shepard's entry on witchcraft: "The witchcraft of the Middle Ages arose from the theological problem of the place of evil in human affairs. . . . But the witchcraft and black magic of today is primarily a malady of an affluent and permissive society. . . . It has flourished on dreams of power over others and over the forces of nature."

The large, attractive typeface, the excellent quality of the paper and binding, and the ease of handling add to the merits of this encyclopedia. This reference work is arranged alphabetically in two columns, with large, boldface headings for each entry. The cross-references, "Recommended Reading" at the end of the lengthier articles, and clarity of the text make this an excellent reference source. The editor avoids sensationalism in the controversial subjects by presenting several points of view and bibliographical references for further study.

Altogether, the *Encyclopedia of Occultism and Parapsychology* is exemplary in conception and execution, and the Board recommends this work for the core collections of public, academic, and school libraries.

—H. G. G.

Heaven Knows What, 8th edition, rev. Grant Lewi. Llewellyn Publications, 1989. soft. 1 vol. 223 pp. illus. appendix. ISBN 0-89542-444-9. $12.95. handbook.
BF1728 133.5

Heaven Knows What is one of the more durable handbooks for those interested in astrology. This edition is the 35th printing, dating from the original publication in 1936. This handbook was the first astrology book to achieve substantial sales in hardcover. Author Grant Lewi worked for *American Astrology* and was the editor of *Horoscope,* a best-selling popular astrology magazine. Lewi has made astrology accessible to the general public by simplifying the erection of the natal chart without the need for other reference books, complex calculations, or knowledge other than basic literacy. Because Lewi focuses on the relationships in the horoscope, *Heaven Knows What* can be used as a reference work by professional astrologers and by individuals who merely want to explore astrology in greater depth.

Very simple directions for erecting the natal chart are given on the first two pages of the book and summarized in the back of the book in "How to Cast Your Own Horoscope." Horoscope blanks are included after the "Table of Years" (in the appendix), along with wheels to be superimposed on the horoscope blanks in order to determine the aspects, or relationships, among the sun, moon, and the eight planets.

Any book in its eighth edition and 35th printing evidences validity far beyond the original publication. There is no simpler way to cast a horoscope or interpret the aspects in the natal chart than the one described in this book. The interrelatedness of these aspects is the factor that makes this book superior to most astrology manuals. The complex relationships in a horoscope are delineated in a comparable manner in only one other source—Ivy Goldstein-Jacobson's basic textbook, *Here and There in Astrology* (now out of print).

To bring *Heaven Knows What* as up to date as possible, the numbered paragraphs for the aspects to Pluto have been added, with the positions of Pluto given from 1890 through 1990. The current softcover edition is easy to use, the print large and attractive. The paper quality of this softcover edition is superior to that of many hardcover books and should survive even heavy use. The boldface headings above the sun-moon aspects and the planetary aspects are numbered and correspond to those in the "Table of Years" in the back of the book. The "Table of Years" is Lewi's simplified ephemeris, and it covers 1890 to 1999. The Board recommends this work for the core collection of public libraries. *—H. G. G.*

Man, Myth and Magic: The Illustrated Encyclopedia of Mythology, Religion and the Unknown, 3d edition. Richard Cavendish and Yvonne Deutch, eds. Marshall Cavendish, 1985. hard. 12 vols. illus. index. ISBN 0-86307-041-8. $409.95. encyclopedia. 4th edition scheduled for 1991.
BF1411.M25 291.1'3'0321

The first edition of *Man, Myth and Magic* was published in 1970. The third edition is edited by Richard Cavendish and Yvonne Deutch. Both are renowned authorities in a wide variety of areas such as magic, folk medicine, mythology, and black arts. This 12-volume set is a "comprehensive guide to the world's religions, mythologies and magical belief systems from the distant past to the present day. Also major faiths, philosophies, legends, folklore, literature, symbolism, superstition and the supernatural" ("A Reader's Guide" to *Man, Myth and Magic*).

The encyclopedia is arranged alphabetically by subject. Entries range in length from 30 pages to a few concise paragraphs. Typical entries, such as those on the *Antichrist, Amida,* and *Amazons,* are one-page long. Cross-references are given within the entry as well as at the end of the entry. Major areas covered in the encyclopedia are treated in longer entries, such as those for *alphabet, alchemy,* and *Athene.* Bibliographies are included for further reading at the end of major entries. Major entries are usually signed by their authors. The "Editorial Board" section notes that unsigned entries have been researched and edited by special consultants or contributors.

Cross-references are set in full capitals and appear in parentheses at the end of entries. Readers who desire additional reading on major areas of interest can refer to individual bibliographies at the end of each volume.

Accompanying the bibliography is a "series of special classified thematic subject guides [that have] been created along with recommended sources of further reading." Under the major heading "Magic," the reader will find an alphabetical listing of subject guides, entries within the encyclopedia (*Abracadabra, alchemy, ashes, astral body,* and more) that can be consulted for an in-depth study of the subject.

Access to the set is supplied by volume 12, a one-volume subject index that is arranged alphabetically. The index provides the volume number and page number for each index entry. The illustrations are very appealing, an asset to the work. The average reader, as well as students and teachers, will find this an invaluable reference tool. The price of this multivolume work may be a hindrance in adding this work to a collection. If it can be afforded, *Man, Myth and Magic* is certainly a valuable addition. The Board recommends this work for the core collections of public, academic, and school libraries. —*S. K.*

The New A to Z Horoscope Maker and Delineator, 13th edition. George Llewellyn; rev. and ed. by Marylee Bytheriver. Llewellyn Publications, 1987. soft. 1 vol. 592 pp. illus. index. ISBN 0-87542-264-0. $12.95. handbook.
BF1728.A2G36 133.5

Since the first edition of *The New A to Z Horoscope Maker and Delineator* was published in 1910, the book has become a classic in the field of astrology and is now in its 56th printing. Major revisions have been made over the years. Some were prompted by the discovery of Pluto in 1930, which caused the section of the work dealing with interpretation to be revised.

The New A to Z Horoscope Maker and Delineator is truly comprehensive in scope, living up to its title. The book is composed of 6 parts, including principles of astrology; constructing and interpreting the horoscope; a 29-page astrological dictionary; and a 7-page index. The brief index is balanced by a detailed table of contents that makes the topics accessible easily when consulted by the user.

A special feature of this book is the inclusion of the Arabian parts. Thirty-two parts are used, historically, and formulas are given for determining all of the parts. It must be noted, however, that these Arabian parts are significant only when the chart is correct or has been rectified. Just as a watch or clock is useless if not set to the proper time, a horoscope, or map of the hour, is affected by the same limitations.

Comprehensive coverage of subjects for both the beginner and the advanced student make this book one of the best introductory handbooks on astrology available. However, in order for readers to use the text to best advantage, they will need to consult a number of other sources for specific tables and charts. *The New A to Z Horoscope Maker and Delineator* instructs readers in the use of these astrological tools and also provides an excellent reference source.

The handbook is printed on paper of excellent quality, using an easy-to-read typeface. The book contains 42 figures and 22 tables, almost all of which are well reproduced. Larger, boldface type is used for headings within the text, marking effectively divisions of subject matter.

While HEAVEN KNOWS WHAT bestows an almost instant understanding, *The New A to Z Horoscope Maker and Delineator* is more complex and requires lengthy study before proficiency in astrology is acquired. No matter what level of learning the user wishes to achieve, for 80 years this reference work has been an excellent guide. The Board recommends this work for the core collection of public libraries.

—*H. G. G.*

The New Compleat Astrologer, rev. edition. Derek Parker and Julia Parker. Harmony/Crown, 1984. 1 vol. hard. 288 pp. illus. indexes. ISBN 0-517-55503-4. $20. history.
BF1708.1.P36 133.5

The New Compleat Astrologer attempts to present a comprehensive history of astrology, from its origins in Mesopotamia as early as 8000 B.C., to the present time. The authors, well-known British astrologers, rush through the historical background, with little textual substance but plenty of lavish illustrations. Users will appreciate the color plates showing the Ziggurat of Ur, Babylonian and Egyptian astrological motifs, Stonehenge, a Mayan observatory, and the Middle East Arab astrologers, among other illustrations, which also include pertinent pictorial information up to the present day.

Part 1 is an overview of the history of astrology. A historical chart covers the period from circa 2872 B.C. to A.D. 1977. Readers will find interesting facts relating to historic figures in these pages. For example, the text notes that Hippocrates (c. 460 B.C.) studied the timing of elective surgery, warning that hemorrhages are more common at the time of the full moon. However, the authors do not quote Hippocrates' actual dictum, "Cut not with iron that part of the body ruled by the sign the Moon is in." Part 1 also discusses Oriental psychology, the Age of Aquarius, and the uses of astrology.

Part 2 deals with the zodiac, the signs, and the planets; part 3 presents interpretations based on the birth chart with aspects, progressions, chart patterns, midpoints and house divisions, harmonics, and harmonic charts. In part 4, a who's who provides biographical information about astrologers from Ramses II, the Pharaoh of the Exodus, to John Addey (1920–1982). Astrology and its usefulness in psychotherapy is also discussed.

Part 5 contains the basic tools for casting a chart for a horoscope. Part 5 also includes astrological tables, planetary positions, sun-sign changes, and sidereal times from 1910–2001. The print used for the tabular material is small and is particularly crowded in the table for sidereal times. Houses for northern latitudes are small and confusing to the eye, but the print is clearer in the ephemeris for the moon nodes, 1910–2001, and shortened ephemeris for 2000–2020. A noon date card is given, as well as zone standard times, but these times should be checked for variations in dates and daylight saving times.

This large, handsome book has excellent color plates and striking graphic details. The paper quality is slick and likely to deteriorate in time, but the binding is excellent and should wear well.

A reading list of mainly British astrologers, a brief general index, and a technical index conclude the book. Although *The New Compleat Astrologer* contains material of less interest to the experienced astrologer, the illustrative material makes this an attractive introductory work for readers looking for a general overview of the field. The Board recommends this work for the core collection of public libraries. —*H. G. G.*

Supplementary Titles

The Astrologer's Handbook. Frances Sakoian and Louis S. Acker. Harper & Row, 1973 (hard), 1989 (soft). hard and soft. 1 vol. 480 pp. illus. index. ISBN 0-06-013734-7 (hard); 0-06-091495-5 (soft). $19.95 (hard); $9.95 (soft). handbook.
BF1708.1.S24 133.5

The Astrologer's Handbook is an "ambitious volume [which] deals with the major factors of horoscope analysis in an exhaustive . . . listing of every planet, in every sign, in every house, in every major aspect to every other planet." (*LJ,* April 1973, p. 1178)

"[It moves] beyond the common 'sun signs' to the important planetary aspects—trines, squares [etc.] . . .—discussing their impact on the human personality and exploring their . . . influence on our lives. . . . [The authors explain] the central concepts and provide . . . instructions for doing [an] interpretation—both general and specific—of any natal chart." (*CC,* May 9, 1973, p. 548)

"[The volume also contains a] glossary, [a] general index, [and a] cross index of aspects." (publisher's note, *Book Review Digest,* 1973, p. 1143)

Board's recommendation: Public and academic libraries.

A Dictionary of Superstitions. Sophie Lasne and Andre Pascal Gaultier; Amy Reynolds, trans. Prentice-Hall, 1984. soft. 1 vol. 355 pp. illus. index. ISBN 0-13-210873-9. $10.95. dictionary.
BF1775.L3713 001.96

"Translated into English from French, . . . [the *Dictionary of Superstitions* has] nine chapters [which] have been grouped thematically according to beliefs and practices. . . . [E]ach is preceded by a brief synoptic introduction. Chapters cover the keys of superstitions, minerals, plants, animals, the weather, the calendar, the human body, the great stages of life and objects, the house, and clothing.

"This dictionary was authored by Sophie Lasne, a history and geography instructor, and Andre Pascal Gaultier, a film editor who has written for television and theater. The translator, Amy Reynolds, generally appears to have presented a fine interpretation. . . . [The reference also contains] a four-page introduction [which] covers the origin of superstitions, the motives behind superstitions, and the classifications of superstitions. An index completes the book, which will be a useful addition to public and school libraries." (*ARBA,* 1986, p. 290)

Board's recommendation: Public, academic, and school libraries.

Knock on Wood: An Encyclopedia of Talismans, Charms, Superstitions, and Symbols. Carole Potter. Beaufort Bks., 1983. soft. 1 vol. 263 pp. illus. ISBN 0-8253-0144-0. $10.95. encyclopedia.
BF1775.P67 001.9

"Abracadabra opens . . . [*Knock on Wood*'s] alphabetically arranged collection. . . . Entries—e.g. evil eye, divining rod, and mistletoe—are combined with such notions as singing before breakfast, passing a priest, crossed knives and forks, and phrases like up to snuff or tying the knot. Also included are holiday customs, zodiac data, and charts of names, colors, plants, months, trees, flowers, and their meanings." (*LJ,* July 1983, p. 1354)

"[The reference has an] informal tone and lightness of touch. . . . It even features a good (if brief) bibliography packed with data." (*BL,* November 1, 1984, p. 353)

Also reviewed in: *ARBA,* 1985, p. 448; *CAY,* Spring 1984, p. 9.

Board's recommendation: Public and school libraries.

New and Noteworthy

Encyclopedia of Witches and Witchcraft. Rosemary Ellen Guiley. Facts On File, 1989. hard and soft. 1 vol. 488 pp. illus. index. ISBN 0-8160-1793-X (hard); 0-8160-2268 (soft). $45.00 (hard); $19.95 (soft). encyclopedia.
BF1566.G85 133.4303

"Consisting of over 500 essay entries and 100 photographs, [the *Encyclopedia of Witches and Witchcraft*] . . . is an excellent source of information on witchcraft for all ages. It presents well researched entries on modern Wiccan philosophy, practices, and beliefs plus a wealth of historical information on the various witch trials in Europe and American during the period of persecution. . . ." (*LJ,* June 1, 1989, p. 98)

Philip G. Riley

Astronomy

See also Science and Technology

Astronomy is currently undergoing one of the most dynamic periods in decades. In recent years, new discoveries have been made with such frequency that even the most basic assumptions are not above reexamination. Thus, while currency is always an important consideration in any branch of science, it is especially so with astronomy. A library reference collection in astronomy must include materials covering all aspects of the topic and should contain both specialized and general works. Librarians must also consider that unlike other branches of science, astronomy is available to everyone on some level. For example, not everyone has access to the sophisticated equipment that allows the human eye to view the smallest particles of matter, but most of us can view the cycles evident in our evening sky with little or no mechanical aid. Because astronomy is of interest to both the hobbyist and the scientist, the library must provide usable materials for the casual observer as well as the specialist.

The collection should contain many different types of books, including histories, which are important in helping readers grasp interrelated developments in the field; encyclopedias of astronomy, which give the reader an overview of the subject; and yearbooks and almanacs, which provide up-to-date information on recent statistics and discoveries. Astronomical almanacs

Core Titles

	PUBLIC	ACADEMIC	SCHOOL
The Astronomical Almanac Nautical Almanac Office. U.S.G.P.O., annual	✦	✦	
The Cambridge Atlas of Astronomy, 2d edition Audouze, Jean, and Guy Israël, eds. Cambridge, 1988	✦	✦	✦
The Facts On File Dictionary of Astronomy, rev. edition Illingworth, Valerie, ed. Facts On File, 1985	✦	✦	✦
McGraw-Hill Encyclopedia of Astronomy Parker, Sybil P., ed. McGraw-Hill, 1983	✦	✦	

contain pertinent data arranged by weeks and months. In this type of work, tables and statistics are used to illustrate projected astronomical events. A topical atlas is also an important reference tool. Such works can provide diagrams and maps of the evening sky in a form that can be invaluable to people with an interest in the field. Subject dictionaries are also very appropriate for inclusion in astronomy collections. These works contain alphabetical listings of astronomical terms and are important for ready-reference information.

Outstanding among the supplementary works are THE INTERNATIONAL ENCYCLOPEDIA OF ASTRONOMY and the annual YEARBOOK OF ASTRONOMY, both edited by Patrick Moore. These are extremely useful works that will expand the scope of a reference collection. —*P. G. R.*

With contributions by Wendell C. Cochran.

Core Titles

The Astronomical Almanac. Nautical Almanac Office. U.S.G.P.O., annual. hard. 1 vol. unpaged. illus. index. S/N 008-054-00129. $23. almanac.
D213.8 528

This 1990 edition of *The Astronomical Almanac* is the ninth in the series. This almanac is the result of a merger in 1980 of *The American Ephemeris and Nautical Almanac* and *The Astronomical Ephemeris* (its British counterpart). *The Astronomical Almanac,* first published in 1981, was designed to provide accurate astronomical data for observations for the knowledgeable observer or professional.

An ephemeris such as *The Astronomical Almanac* can be defined as a publication giving the computed location of celestial bodies for each day of the year. Presenting an enormous amount of information, the volume contains observational data from the times of moonrise to orbital schedules for planetary satellites. Most information is given in the form of tables that are arranged with adequate white space and printed in a legibly sized typeface. The data are provided by the U.S. Naval Observatory and the Royal Greenwich Observatory, which accounts for the work's authoritativeness. However, some features of the work may hamper access to the information. Topics are divided into sections (labeled by letter) that are listed in the table of contents. The work has no continuous pagination; however, each section is paginated separately, using a letter-number arrangement. Each section also has its own separate list of contents. There is no pagination provided in the main table of contents. If readers want to locate information on galaxies, they must first locate the topic in the general table of contents. They must then check the contents page of the appropriate section to discover that "Bright Galaxies" are located on page H44. This can make the search for information somewhat frustrating and time consuming. Readers can use the index at the end of the work for much easier access to information. There the reader can determine that the section on galaxies does indeed begin on page H44, and even though it takes some time to locate Section H, a step is still saved.

As in other works of this type, there are few visual aids. Most diagrams are located in the section on "Orbits of Planetary Satellites." These black-and-white configurations are particularly effective in illustrating daily position of the Jovian moons.

The Astronomical Almanac is an excellent work; in fact, it is considered by authorities in the field as one of the best works available. It is not intended, however, for the casual user. Even though a short glossary is included, considerable subject knowledge is often necessary for the information to be useful. For example, moonrise and moonset are defined as, "The times at which the apparent upper limb of the moon is on the astronomical horizon, i.e., when the true zenith distance, referred to the center of the Earth of the central point of the disk is $90°34'+s-\pi$, where s is the moon's semidiameter, π is the horizontal parallax, and 34′ is the adopted value of horizontal refraction." Although certainly precise, the additional explanation is hardly useful to the inexperienced reader.

Complexities aside, *The Astronomical Almanac* is a very useful reference tool. The format is usable once the reader adjusts to the lack of pagination. The volume should be included in libraries that need an in-depth almanac for users who are knowledgeable astronomy students, teachers, scientists, or hobbyists. The Board recommends this work for the core collections of public and academic libraries. —*P. G. R.*

The Cambridge Atlas of Astronomy, 2d edition. Jean Audouze and Guy Israël, eds. Cambridge, 1988. hard. 1 vol. 432 pp. illus. appendix. index. ISBN 0-521-36360-8. $90. atlas.
QB43.2 520

The Cambridge Atlas of Astronomy is the English-language edition of *Le Grand Atlas de l'Astronomie* (1986). The authority of this translation can be judged by considering the fine reviews received by the first edition, the reputation of the Cambridge University Press, and the impressive number of English astronomers who made the translation of the original work from the French. The two dozen contributors to the original work are leading French astronomers, mostly from the National Research Council of France; the translators are, for the most part, from the Institute of Astronomy at Cambridge.

The oversize pages accommodate more than 1,000 illustrations—perhaps half of which are in color, some filling whole pages and occasional double-page spreads—and an extensive text.

The organization is systematic and logical: the work opens with an introduction and an essay on "Astronomy Today." The main body of the atlas opens with a section on "The Sun." The second and longest section in the work (180 pages) is devoted to "The Solar System," including articles on the planets, our moon, and the asteroids. Articles within this section deal with meteorites and the *Voyager* and related space missions. The amount of space devoted to a topic seems to be in proportion to current knowledge: 28 pages on Mars, 22 on Jupiter and its moons, 6 on Uranus, 1 on Pluto. As an example, the article on Mars includes a discussion of the red planet's topography, volcanism and tectonics, the surface relief, the soil, Martian activity (mainly atmospheric), and the Martian moons. As is the case elsewhere in the book, photos abound.

The third section in the atlas concerns the stars and our home galaxy; the fourth, the extragalactic domain or galaxies other than our own; and the fifth, current scientific perspectives including that on cosmology, the debate over the possible existence of extraterrestrial life, observational equipment and resources such as the Hubble Space Telescope, and the history of astronomy. The book concludes with a sky map, a short bibliography of titles for further reading (grouped by subject), a five-page glossary, and a six-page index.

The level of writing will not disappoint professional scientists, even though this work is intended for nonprofessionals. Numerous tables illustrate data and make questions easy to answer. The logical arrangement, table of contents, index, and glossary enable rapid searching for general background information or for specific data. Text and illustrations are interrelated, but the photos alone (with their captions) yield a reliable view of our overall knowledge of the universe.

Information throughout the text is quite up to date; the text includes material about the volcanic eruptions on Jupiter's moon Io; the rings of Uranus; and plans for the Hubble Space Telescope.

The Cambridge Encyclopedia of Astronomy efficiently depicts the current state of planetary science, astronomy, astrophysics, and cosmology. This work would be a worthwhile addition to any reference collection. The Board recommends this work for the core collections of public, academic, and school libraries.

—*W. C. C.*

The Facts On File Dictionary of Astronomy, rev. edition. Valerie Illingworth, ed. Facts On File, 1986. hard and soft. 1 vol. 438 pp. ISBN 0-8160-1357-8 (hard); 0-8160-1892-8 (soft). $29.95 (hard); $12.95 (soft). dictionary.
QB14.F3 520.32

This second edition of *The Facts On File Dictionary of Astronomy* is updated from the original published in 1979. According to the editor, over 250 new terms have been added, bringing the total number of entries to over 2,300.

One of the major disadvantages of any scientific reference tool is that parts of the text are often dated by the time of publication. This is especially true in the rapidly changing field of astronomy. However, Facts On File has made an effort not only to update the 1979 edition but also to maintain currency through the use of "projections." A projection is the estimated outcome of a situation or event that was still in the planning stage when this work was being published. For example, in 1985 the Hubble Space Telescope was still two years away from its "projected" space shuttle launch. Its launch was further delayed for several years by the *Challenger* disaster and other misfortunes. Yet the *Facts On File Dictionary of Astronomy* supplies an entry on the *Hubble Space Telescope,* its capabilities, and its possible revolutionary effects on observational astronomy. Another example of a projection is an entry on the *Galileo* probe. Mention of this probe's mission to Jupiter and the plans for gathering data in the Jovian system effectively use a scheduled future event to keep a work current past the 1985 publication date. Of course, this approach is not foolproof, as it cannot anticipate the unexpected, such as the *Challenger* tragedy and the various delays it caused.

In typical dictionary fashion, entries in this volume are arranged alphabetically in a two-column page format. Main entry words are set in boldface type, making terms easy to locate. Entries are separated by sufficient white space, which adds to the work's readability. "See" references are used for very specific or technical entries to refer one to a broader category. For example, under the entry for *fission* the user is advised to "see nuclear fission." Under *E-layer* one is directed to "see ionosphere." This feature is useful because it allows readers to narrow their search quickly to appropriate listings. In addition to "see" references, an asterisk placed before any word within the body of an entry indicates that the reader will find an entry for that word, which provides additional information.

There are drawings, diagrams, and tables throughout the dictionary, providing a useful visual representation to sometimes complex topics. One can use any number of words to describe the various equatorial telescope mountings, but the well-constructed comparison drawing can immediately illustrate the differences. There are many such figures in the text designed to help the user.

Several tables, placed at the end of the volume, give the reader easy access to planetary satellites, meteor shower dates, and Messier objects, among other useful information. There is no index, but terms can be accessed readily through the alphabetical arrangement of the dictionary.

The accessible format and readable text make *The Facts On File Dictionary of Astronomy* an excellent choice for patrons at all levels. The Board recommends this work for the core collections of public, academic, and school libraries. —*P. G. R.*

McGraw-Hill Encyclopedia of Astronomy. Sybil P. Parker, ed. McGraw-Hill, 1983. hard. 1 vol. 450 pp. illus. index. ISBN 0-07-045251-2. $79.50. encyclopedia.
QB14.M3725 523.003'21

Published in 1983, the *McGraw-Hill Encyclopedia of Astronomy* is a compilation of relevant articles arranged alphabetically and covering a broad spectrum of subjects in the field. Topics chosen for inclusion were selected by the editorial staff. All 230 entries have been taken from the 5th edition (1982) of the McGRAW-HILL ENCYCLOPEDIA OF SCIENCE AND TECHNOLOGY (see Science and Technology). The contributing authors are considered very knowledgeable in their fields. Professor George O. Abell, at that time in the UCLA Department of Astronomy, served as consulting editor and shaped this one-volume encyclopedia.

Arranged alphabetically, the entries usually average from one to four pages, and most include a bibliography, which is a very useful feature. In many instances, the bibliography includes journal citations as well as other sources of information. Longer entries are divided into smaller segments and ample use is made of "see" references. For example, the entry for *galaxy* is broken into five related subheadings with "see" references after each. Under the subheading "structure," the reader is referred to, among other entries, *interstellar matter.* And conversely, when reviewing that entry one is referred back to *galaxy.* Thus by using the internal cross-reference system, much more information can be located on a given topic.

Another positive feature is the ample use of graphs, tables, drawings, and photographs (both black and white and color). Nearly every lengthy article is accompanied by some type of visual aid. For example, under the entry for *Messier catalog,* a complete listing of Charles Messier's nebulae and star clusters is given. Also provided are the NGC numbers, right ascension, declination, apparent magnitude, and a description of each of these objects.

The boldface subheadings in entries make the text easy to follow and provide topical divisions at appropriate intervals. There is also an excellent index that provides access to each major subject by using the entry subheadings as index entries. The volume is sturdy and well bound and should hold up well to repeated use.

This work is not meant to be a reference tool for the casual reader, because the entries are taken from the McGRAW-HILL ENCYCLOPEDIA OF SCIENCE AND TECHNOLOGY, with its detailed approach and liberal use of mathematics. The *Encyclopedia of Astronomy* gives the student or casual user little or no preliminary explanation and assumes some degree of knowledge on the part of the user. For example, the entry for *space probe* discusses the energy levels necessary to launch a spacecraft toward the sun. Within this definition, it is mentioned that 1 AU $= 1.496 \times 10^8$ km. No effort is made to explain what an AU (astronomical unit) is. The assumption is made that readers will know that 1 AU is the distance between the earth and the sun.

Because astronomy is such a dynamic field, this volume is in need of updating in view of its 1983 publication date. Nevertheless, the *McGraw-Hill Encyclopedia of Astronomy* remains a very authoritative reference source. The Board recommends this work for the core collections of public and academic libraries.

—*P. G. R.*

Supplementary Titles

The International Encyclopedia of Astronomy. Patrick Moore, ed. Crown/Orion, 1987. hard. 1 vol. 464 pp. illus. ISBN 0-517-56179-4. $40. encyclopedia.
QB14.I58 520'3'21

The International Encyclopedia of Astronomy contains "2,500 alphabetically arranged entries [which] vary in length. Included are seven 'essays on topics such as exploring space and superclusters; . . . articles on subjects such as black holes, the Apollo program, and neutrinos; and brief entries on individual meteors, satellites, astronomers, astronauts, observational techniques, and space research. Most entries are signed. . . . Some entries are followed by see also references, plus terms within entries are set in capital letters to indicate they are also entries in the book.

"More than 100 astronomers from universities and

observatories throughout the world have collaborated to produce this substantial and up-to-date book. . . . The encyclopedia makes excellent use of color illustrations, tables, and diagrams, most of which are adequately labeled." (*BL,* March 1, 1988, p. 1121)

Also reviewed in: *A Lib,* May 1988, p. 356; *ARBA,* 1988, p. 687; *ASBYP,* Spring 1988, p. 25; *Bloom Rev,* November 1988, p. 29; *BW,* December 6, 1987, p. 10; *Choice,* December 1987, p. 601; *CSM,* December 8, 1987, p. 20; *LATBR,* November 29, 1987, p. 10; *LJ,* April 15, 1988, p. 33; *S & T,* July 1988, p. 44; *WLB* December 1987, p. 94.

Board's recommendation: Public libraries.

Yearbook of Astronomy. Patrick Moore, ed. Norton, annual. hard. 1 vol. ISBN 0-393-0-2926-3 (1991 edition). $22.95 (1991 edition). yearbook.
QB1.Y4 520

The *Yearbook of Astronomy* "is a well-organized, handy-sized reference guide to [yearly] celestial events . . . that contains a good variety of information, including star charts, monthly notes, eclipses, occultations, comets, and so on." (*SB,* September 1987, p. 13)

"This well-established yearbook is intended for a general, popular audience. . . . Contents are in three parts. The first, compiled through the Royal Greenwich Observatory, provides the reader with dates, times, and positions of astronomical phenomena that will occur in the calendar year. The information is in diagrammatic or descriptive form and the positions of familiar objects may be found on the numerous star charts of both the northern and southern hemispheres. The second part consists of about ten short articles, each by a different author, pertaining to current trends or noteworthy events in the field. A third section covers miscellaneous objects such as telescopic variable stars, double stars, clusters, and nebulae." (*Ser Lib 2nd,* 1985, p. 165)

Also reviewed in: *ARBA,* 1987, p. 660; *SB,* September 1985, p. 36; *SB,* September 1987, p. 13; *SciTech,* September 1986, p. 6; July 1988, p. 8; *S & T,* February 1988, p. 161; *TES,* December 27, 1985, p. 23; *TES,* April 15, 1988, p. 25.

Board's recommendation: Public, academic, and school libraries.

New and Noteworthy

Magill's Survey of Science, Space Exploration series. Frank N. Magill, ed. Salem, 1989. hard. 5 vols. 2,328 pp. ISBN 0-89356-600-4 (set). $400 (set). encyclopedia.
TL790.M24 629.4

Magill's Survey of Science is an "easy to read series [that covers] . . . discoveries, exploration and technology development from the 1950's through the Challenger disaster and discusses projects currently in the planning stage. 350 articles of 6 to 8 pages in length are organized chronologically in a clear, easy reference format with annotated bibliography and thorough indexing. Space travel, the astronauts, Apollo and Mariner Missions, Black Holes, and other solar systems are just some of the subjects covered in this special series." (Excerpted from publisher's announcement)

Space Almanac. Anthony R. Curtis. Arcsoft Pubs., 1989. soft. 1 vol. 955 pp. illus. index. ISBN 0-86668-065-9. $19.95. almanac.
QB500.C87 520

"*Space Almanac* contains an assortment of information on space exploration and astronomy. . . . It is divided into seven chapters (e.g., 'Space Shuttles,' 'Rockets,' 'Satellites'), each of which is further subdivided. . . . The information provided is current . . . and international in scope. Many lists in this book provide quick reference to astronauts, cosmonauts, spacewalks, NASA acronyms, spaceports, planetariums, etc. Entries range in length from a few paragraphs to several pages and are written for the layperson." (*BL,* December 15, 1989, p. 858)

M. L. Phoebe Adams

Biography

See also Ethnic Studies; Genealogy

A core collection of biographical reference sources should enable the reference librarian and library user to find information on individuals, living and dead, of various nationalities and professions, from the most famous to the relatively obscure, and from the beginning of recorded history to the present. The nine works included in this core collection were selected as finding guides or reference sources for such a broad range of names and should serve as an adequate basic collection for most libraries.

When little is known about an individual, the best place to start a biographical search would be one of two indexes. The epic *Biography and Genealogy Master Index* (Gale, 1980) contains literally millions of names from all nationalities and eras and cites locations from hundreds of biographical reference sources: collective biographies, name directories, dictionaries for persons of specific nationalities or professions, sex, and race. It leads to short-entry data sources, such as the many *Who's Who* publications, as well as to essay-type sources, such as CONTEMPORARY AUTHORS or the DICTIONARY OF NATIONAL BIOGRAPHY. For more detailed research questions, *Biography Index* (Wilson, 1947–), a more affordable source that is unlimited in scope by time or country, will lead to periodical articles and to books (collections, as well as biographies, autobiographies, and biographical novels). Often *Biography Index* alone can serve as a ready-reference source giving not only citations to sources but vital dates, nationality, and profession of names listed. *The New York Times Obituary Index* (New York Times, 1968; supplement 1980) is an excellent supplementary index choice. This index includes death notes for people from all walks of life, not just the rich and famous.

The core collection recommended here should be sufficient in scope to answer most questions concerning British and American persons, living or dead, and to a lesser degree international figures of renown. Researchers of all ages should be able to find at least some reference to individuals as removed in time and place as Virginia Dare and Salman Rushdie.

One out-of-print source that was recommended by the Board was the *National Cyclopedia of American Biography* (T. C. White, 1984). Libraries may be able to acquire this series through out-of-print book sources. Libraries may also want to include in their core collections biographical sources that reflect the demography of the communities they serve.

Core Titles

	PUBLIC	ACADEMIC	SCHOOL
Chambers Biographical Dictionary, rev. edition Thorne, J. O., and T. C. Collocott, eds. Chambers, 1984; reprinted 1986	✦	✦	✦
Contemporary Authors: A Bio-Bibliographical Guide to Current Writers in Fiction, General Nonfiction, Poetry, Journalism, Drama, Motion Pictures, Television, and Other Fields, 129 vols. May, Hal, and Susan M. Trosky, eds. Gale, 1962–	✦	✦	✦
Current Biography Yearbook Moritz, Charles, ed. Wilson, 1940–	✦	✦	✦
Dictionary of American Biography, 18 vols. (including suppls. 1–8) American Council of Learned Societies. Scribner, 1928–	✦	✦	✦
Dictionary of National Biography, 22 vols. Lord Blake, and C. S. Nicholls, eds. Oxford, 1982–		✦	
Notable American Women, 1607–1950, 3 vols. James, Edward T., ed. Belknap/Harvard, 1974	✦	✦	✦
Notable American Women, the Modern Period Sicherman, Barbara, and Carol Hurd Green, eds. Belknap/Harvard, 1980	✦	✦	✦
Who Was Who in America with World Notables, 10 vols. Marquis, 1942–1985	✦	✦	
Who's Who in America, 2 vols. Marquis, annual (1899–)	✦	✦	✦

Core Titles

Chambers Biographical Dictionary, rev. edition. J. O. Thorne and T. C. Collocott, eds. Chambers, 1984; reprinted 1986. hard. 1 vol. 1,493 pp. index. ISBN 0-550-16010-8. $29.95. biographical dictionary. revised edition published in October 1990 as *Cambridge Biographical Dictionary.* ISBN 0-521-395-6. $34.50.
CT103.C4 920.02

The revised edition of *Chambers Biographical Dictionary* incorporates the 1961 edition (which contained over 15,000 entries), its supplement, plus an additional several hundred entries. (In October 1990, this edition was revised and renamed the *Cambridge Biographical Dictionary.* This revision was not available at the time this category was completed.)

Most of the entries in the *Chambers Biographical Dictionary* are of the brief identification type, ranging from one line to several hundred lines. Previously existing entries have been revised, if deemed appropriate, and expanded (for example, *T. S. Eliot*'s from 6 to 144 lines), reduced, or in some cases deleted as dictated by the "vagaries of fashion" and "critical assessments of modern research" (preface).

In order to determine whether to include a specific entry, the editors asked themselves the question, "Is he (or she) likely to be looked up?" In addition to the expected entries for royalty, politicians, composers, and authors, this work also includes murderers, traitors, forgers, and war criminals. Chambers is intended to be international in scope and to cover world history, yet its emphasis is decidedly on British and European figures. In testing the "likely to be looked up" question for six movie directors, there are entries for *Akira Kurosawa* and *Rainer Werner Fassbinder,* but not for Bernardo Bertolucci, Robert Altman, Werner Herzog, or Wim Wenders. For female authors, there were entries for *Germaine Greer, Doris Lessing, Iris Murdoch,* and *Barbara Cartland.* Neither Margaret Atwood nor Toni Morrison had an entry, and under the name *Sylvia Plath* was a "see" reference to poet *Ted Hughes,* in whose entry was the note: "In 1956 he married Sylvia Plath (1932–63), also an outstanding poet," followed by references to her collections of poetry and her novel, *The Bell Jar.* American architect *Frank Lloyd Wright* has an entry, but there is none for Robert Venturi or I. M. Pei. In general, *Chambers* is an excellent source for the ancients and for those firmly established in the fabric of history (Elvis Presley is included), but the reference cannot be expected to include all modern people of interest.

The structure of the entries in the revised edition has been standardized so that essential information such as surnames, given names and titles, pronunciation (if given), designation (or occupation), and birthplace begin the biographical text. Bibliographical notes end most of the entries, which are arranged alphabetically in two columns for each compact page. The typeface is small, and there is a minimum of white space. The last name of the individual is in boldface capitals and overhangs the text. There is no blank space between the last line of one entry and the first line of the next. Collective entries are used for individuals with common last names; thus, for example, *Samuel Johnson* is number 12 under *Johnson,* while *Lyndon Baines Johnson* is number 9. There is no name index but there is ample cross-referencing within the text.

The 35-page supplementary subject index is exemplary. It lists the names of literary and artistic works of art, musical compositions, and under the heading "Exploration and Geography," the name of the country leads to the names of its primary explorers. Another useful category within this index is "Nicknames and Personalities," with *Brown Bomber* leading to *Joe Louis* and *The Greatest* to *Muhammud Ali.*

Chambers Biographical Dictionary enjoys a well-deserved reputation for accuracy and authority among biographical reference sources. The Board recommends this work for the core collection of public, academic, and school libraries.

Contemporary Authors: A Bio-Bibliographical Guide to Current Writers in Fiction, General Nonfiction, Poetry, Journalism, Drama, Motion Pictures, Television, and Other Fields. Hal May and Susan M. Trosky, eds. Gale, 1962–. hard. 129 vols. 503 pp. ISBN 0-8103-1954-3 (vol. 129). index in even-numbered vols. $99 (per vol.). biographical source.
PN771.C66X 928.1

Published since 1962, the *Contemporary Authors* series is the most comprehensive of the biographical sources for twentieth-century writers. One hundred twenty-nine volumes have been published to date. Volume 129 brings the total number of authors represented up to 94,000. *Contemporary Authors* has a universal scope and includes "nontechnical writers in all genres—fiction, poetry, drama, etc.—whose books are issued by commercial, risk publishers or by university presses." Non-American and non-English-language writers are included providing that "their works have been published in the United States or translated into English."

The primary focus of *Contemporary Authors* is on authors of published books, but the series also encompasses those who have achieved prominence in communications, including television reporters, photojournalists, syndicated cartoonists, and others. Since the publication of volume 104, "authors deceased since 1900 whose works are still of interest to today's readers" have fallen within the scope of this series. In volume 125, Nathaniel West, H. L. Mencken, and Margaret Mitchell are representative of this category.

The information for *Contemporary Authors* usually comes directly from the author being profiled. In the case of dead authors or living authors who fail to respond to *Contemporary Authors'* queries and questionnaires, the entries are compiled from material gathered from reliable reference sources, published interviews, feature stories, and book reviews. If the author is deceased, the completed entry is sent for verification, whenever possible, to a family member, agent, or publisher. Living authors usually review their own entries; an asterisk marks those listings that were compiled from secondary sources but not personally verified for the current edition by the subject of the entry.

Contemporary Authors presents biographical and bibliographical information in three kinds of listings: sketches, brief entries, and obituary notices. In volume 125, thirty-four authors and media people are specially featured in lengthy sketches. Among those included are entrepreneur Lee Iacocca, filmmaker Spike Lee, and deceased philosopher Martin Buber. Included in the lengthy sketches are separate paragraphs with rubrics such as *personal, addresses, career, awards, honors, writings* (each title begins a new line), *work in progress* (for living authors), *avocational interests,* and *biographical/critical sources.* Books and periodicals are listed separately. No page numbers are given for periodicals.

Many sketches are accompanied by an interesting feature called "Sidelights," a narrative that includes absorbing details of the author's work and career. Spike Lee's sidelight gives a production history of the film *She's Gotta Have It,* and places the film in the context of current cinematography by using quotes from film reviews and interviews with Lee.

The brief entries give short, factual information in a *Who's Who* style, and, like the sketches, are followed by a biographical/critical sources list. Obituary notices are about the same length as the brief entries and provide a list of citations for other obituaries and additional sources on the subject. In addition to these three types of entries, there are also occasional exclusive interviews with authors chosen because of their particular interest for readers.

Recent volumes of *Contemporary Authors* are attractive, well-bound books. Each page has two columns set off by ample margins. The typeface is not overly small, and an unobtrusive variety of fonts is used. Guide words (surnames) are printed at the outer edge of each two-page spread. Listings are separated by space. Volume 125 was thoroughly cross-referenced, with nicknames referring back to given names (cross-references for each of H. L. Mencken's over 20 pseudonyms are included). Given names are used for entries even if the nickname is preferred.

Even-numbered volumes include an index to all previous volumes in the *Contemporary Authors* series plus all other Gale literary series, including CONTEMPORARY LITERARY CRITICISM, DICTIONARY OF LITERARY BIOGRAPHY, and CONTEMPORARY AUTHORS, New Revision series (for the first two, see World Literature; for the last, see American Literature). The index to volume 124 has also been published (intact, with the same pagination) as a separate volume.

Contemporary Authors is an authoritative, well-documented source. The Board recommends this work for the core collections of public, academic, and school libraries.

Current Biography Yearbook. Charles Moritz, ed. Wilson, annual (1940 –). hard. 1 vol. 700 pp. illus. index. ISSN 0084-9499. $52. biographical source.
CT100 920

Current Biography Yearbook, a "dictionary of contemporary biography," has been published annually since 1940. Each volume, a cumulation of the monthly *Current Biography,* contains objective essays on approximately 200 individuals prominent in a wide variety of fields. Its subjects are chosen from the world of sports, art, politics, medicine, entertainment, and literature, among other areas. Although the coverage is international in scope, most essays are about Americans or persons who have in some way made their mark on the American consciousness. Content is derived from newspaper and magazine articles, books, encyclopedias, reference sources (a complete list of which is appended to the text under the heading "Biographical References"), and sometimes from interviews with the subjects. The personalities covered are given the opportunity to revise or update information contained in their biographical essays before the yearbook is sent to press. The main source of direct information is questionnaires supplied to the subjects by the editors.

A photograph of the subject precedes each essay, which opens with a headnote that includes the subject's name in boldface type, followed by date of birth (if obtainable), profession, and address. The essays, which are unsigned, are lively and contain personal information, anecdotes, education, and details of the subject's professional development. The essays are about 2,500 words long and are followed by a list of references used in compiling them. Any source not noted in the references will appear in parenthesis within the essay following the information it documents.

Professional names are not cross-referenced, but "when a biographee's preferred forename is a nickname, the full original name is usually given in a cross reference as well as in the article thus Jimmy Carter and James Earl Carter are cross-referenced. When a nickname is tantamount to a professional name, the cross reference is sometimes dispensed with." Thus Pee-Wee Herman's given name, Paul Rubenfeld, appears in the article but not in the index.

Each yearbook contains a rather specific subject index that classifies by profession. A person is not limited to one category, however, so that Germaine Greer's name is found under the categories of social activism, nonfiction, and education. There is also an obituary section for those recently deceased whose biographies have appeared in the yearbooks. The one-paragraph obituaries cite the issue of *Current Biography* in which the biography appeared as well as the source for the obituary, more often than not *The New York Times.* Keys to abbreviations and pronunciation appear in the beginning of the volume.

Accessibility is provided by the newest cumulated index, which covers the years 1940 to 1985. The latest edition of each yearbook provides a supplementary index for all the volumes issued to date during that decade. The 1988 volume, for example, indexes 1981 to 1988.

Current Biography fills the need for easily accessible information about mainstream individuals who figure prominently in the news and in popular culture from 1940 until the present day. All the yearbooks are in print. Since 1985 it has had a rival in the Gale series entitled NEWSMAKERS (formerly *Contemporary Newsmakers*), a publication that excludes writers and is somewhat more expensive but devotes more space to less established personalities.

The Board recommends this work for the core collections of public, academic, and school libraries as a well-established and reliable contemporary biographical source.

Dictionary of American Biography. American Council of Learned Societies. Scribner, 1928–1988. hard. 18 vols. (including suppls. 1–8). index. ISBN 0-684-19075-3 (set). $1,499 (set). biographical source.
E176.B562 920.073

The *Dictionary of American Biography* is this country's counterpart to the classic British publication DICTIONARY OF NATIONAL BIOGRAPHY. Volume 1 of the original set of 11 volumes (volume 11 comprises supplements 1 and 2 to the main work) was published in 1928. With its eighth supplement, published in 1988, the entire set includes alphabetical biographical essays on 18,110 notable deceased Americans. Foreigners who lived in the United States for a significant portion of time and in some way contributed to its history are also included.

Beginning with the fifth supplement to the *Dictionary of American Biography,* authors of the essays were asked to fill out extensive two-part data sheets on their subjects. These sheets are kept on file in the Library of Congress along with other *Dictionary of American Biography* papers so that researchers may have access to them. All the essays in the dictionary are signed.

The most recent volume, supplement 8, covers 454 notable Americans who died between the years 1966 and 1970. The biographies range in length from a few paragraphs to several pages. Each page is laid out in two columns with guide words (surnames) at the top of each column. Entrants' names, in the form they are best known, are printed in boldface capitals that begin the first sentence of the essay. Each essay closes with a bracketed appendix (in smaller type) that lists publications not noted in the essays; locations of manuscripts, letters, and so on; works of art; nonprint sources such as films; and additional sources of biographical material.

The diversity of individuals who are elected for inclusion in this most exclusive collective American biography reflects the richness of our culture and history. The eighth supplement, for example, includes entries for *Helen Keller, Lenny Bruce, Dwight D. Eisenhower, Janis Joplin, Martin Luther King, Jr., Walter Gropius, Elizabeth Arden,* and *Vito Genovese.*

The perceived necessity for a separate retrospective biography for women, which precipitated the publication of NOTABLE AMERICAN WOMEN, is emphasized by this latest supplement, in which women comprise only about 25 percent of the total number of biographees. Although this may be due to the continued paucity of women in positions of political power, American women who *are* included receive, in general, briefer coverage in the *Dictionary of American Biography* than in NOTABLE AMERICAN WOMEN. *Dorothy Parker,* for example, is allotted six columns in NOTABLE AMERICAN WOMEN and little more than half that in the *Dictionary of American Biography.*

Black Americans represented include *Martin Luther King, Jr., John Coltrane, Jimi Hendrix,* and others, but representation is perhaps not as full as it might be.

In 1937 an index to the main set was published, and indexes to the supplements have appeared with each new addition. The 1981 guide is a combined alphabetical listing. Roman numerals indicate main-set volumes, and Arabic numerals indicate the supplements. This latest supplement includes, as did the earlier ones, an index guide to all previous supplements.

Small libraries might consider purchasing the CONCISE DICTIONARY OF AMERICAN BIOGRAPHY, but it is really a poor substitute for the original *Dictionary of American Biography.* The Board recommends this work for the core collections of public, academic, and school libraries.

Dictionary of National Biography. Lord Blake and C. S. Nicholls, eds. Oxford, 1882–. hard. 22 vols. indexes. ISBN 0-19-865101-5 (set). $1,100 (set); $98 (per vol.). biographical source.
CT774 920.041

A British publication, the *Dictionary of National Biography* is preeminent among the retrospective essay forms of national collective biographies. It is the model for the DICTIONARY OF AMERICAN BIOGRAPHY and, indirectly, NOTABLE AMERICAN WOMEN. The core set of 22 volumes was edited by Sir Leslie Stephen, father of Virginia Woolf, and is extended by ten-year supplements. The *Dictionary of National Biography* is devoted to preserving the memory of the most reputable of deceased British and Irish subjects.

Whenever possible, the editors chose as contributors persons who actually knew the subjects whose essays they would compose; thus, "private information" or "personal knowledge" often serves in lieu of, or along with, a list of references to secondary sources. The signed essays are informative on a personal as well as on a professional level, and their authors are often as famous as those about whom they write. For example, the ninth supplement lists among its contributors three prime ministers.

The essays vary in length. The essay on *Winston Churchill* is over 22 pages long. Pages are arranged in a two-column format. Surnames of the entrants are used as guide words on the outer corners of each two-page spread.

With the eighth supplement, which covers figures who died between 1961 and 1970, the editors gradually began to include fewer Canadians and Australians than previously; by this time, Canadian and Australian national biography series had been established in those countries. This supplement also marks the first time in this dictionary that homosexuality is openly discussed where it would "make more intelligible" the careers of persons such as *E. M. Forster, Joe Orton, W. Somerset Maugham,* and, to a lesser extent, *Vita Sackville-West.* The careers of notable secret service agents are also revealed in this volume, whereas previously these careers had been judiciously circumvented. Among the 745 entries in this volume is the previously mentioned biography of *Winston Churchill,* clearly the most prominent person included, and long essays on *Nehru, T. S. Eliot, Augustus John,* and *Bertrand Russell.*

The ninth supplement, including 748 entries, covers those who died between 1971 and 1980 and continues the practice of "keeping down the Commonwealth numbers." Among the entrants included are *Lord Mountbatten, Alfred Hitchcock* (a Briton who adopted American nationality), *Edward VIII* (the Duke of Windsor), *W. H. Auden,* and *John Lennon.*

The *Dictionary of National Biography* is noted for its high standards of accuracy and its fine writing. In many cases the comprehensive essays contained within these volumes are the sole source of authoritative biography in print for the individual represented. The ninth supplement includes a "Cumulative Index to the Biographies Contained in the Supplements of the Dictionary of National Biography 1901–1980." The index includes birth and death dates and is completely cross-referenced. Vita Sackville-West, for example, is cross-referenced from her married name, "Nicholson," and from "West, Victoria Mary Sackville-."

The *Dictionary of National Biography* represents the highest standard of achievement in retrospective national biographies. The Board recommends this work for the core collection of academic libraries.

Notable American Women, 1607–1950. Edward T. James, ed. Belknap/Harvard, 1974. soft. 3 vols. 2,141 pp. appendix. ISBN 0-674-62734-2 (set). $40 (set). biographical dictionary.
CT3260N57 920.7N843

Notable American Women, 1607–1950 is a retrospective biographical dictionary based on the model provided by the DICTIONARY OF AMERICAN BIOGRAPHY, to which it is an invaluable supplement. Only 706 of the 15,000 subjects covered in the DICTIONARY OF AMERICAN BIOGRAPHY (excluding the supplementary volumes) are women. Of those, 179 names have been omitted from *Notable American Women,* mainly because the subjects lacked lasting significance.

In total there are 1,337 essays (22 are joint biographies combining two or more related figures). The subjects, all of whom died no later than the end of 1950, are women who distinguished themselves by their own accomplishments and whose work took them in some way beyond local significance and into the public eye. The only exceptions to this criterion are presidents' wives, all of whom are included. Included under the blanket "American" are noncitizens who "had lived for a number of years in the United States and engaged in important activity during that period." Women from all walks of life, establishment or nonestablishment, are included within the scope of *Notable American Women.* The 1,359 women were chosen from general biographical works, from works pertaining to fields in which women were known to be active, and from obituaries found in professional journals, state historical societies, and other sources.

The entries are arranged alphabetically. The two-column pages are well laid out, with ample white space between entries. There is no name index, so cross-referencing appears within the body of the dictionary. The subject's last name in boldface capitals forms the first word of a sentence that generally includes birth and death dates, area of prominence, place of birth, and parentage. Virtually all entries are signed by one of the more than 700 contributors; the entries range in length from 400 to 7,000 words. Many of the entries, such as the ten-page essay on *Mary Baker Eddy* (1921–1910), read like short monographs.

The editors have obviously put a great research effort into the entries, verifying the basic facts of birth, death, marriage, and heritage. However, the preface advises that for "women's lives generally, documentation tends to be scanty. . . . Problems of falsified birth dates, hidden divorces, and even disappearances from the historical record" have been known to occur. The articles themselves are authoritatively composed, well documented, and often evoke the flavor of the times in which the subject lived. We learn that painter *Cecilia Beaux,* for example, could not attend the Pennsylvania Academy of the Fine Arts and study under Thomas Eakins because of "her uncle's conservatism, especially in the matter of life drawing classes." Many of the bibliographies at the end of entries are annotated. They include both primary and secondary sources and, where appropriate, give locations for manuscript collections.

A special feature of these volumes is found in the single appendix, "Classified List of Selected Biographies," which categorizes over 700 of the biographies included in the volumes. The categories are quite diverse and include "Indian captives" as well as "librarians."

Notable American Women is not intended to be comprehensive but rather to present influential women whose activities figured in the making of American history. This volume is an intelligent and skillfully executed reference source, equally geared to browsing. The Board recommends this work for the core collections of public, academic, and school libraries.

Notable American Women, the Modern Period. Barbara Sicherman and Carol Hurd Green, eds. Belknap/Harvard, 1980. hard and soft. 1 vol. 795 pp. appendix. ISBN 0-674-62732-6 (hard); 0-674-62733-4 (soft). $48 (hard); $12.95 (soft). biographical dictionary.
CT3260.N573 920.720973

Notable American Women, the Modern Period is a one-volume supplement to NOTABLE AMERICAN WOMEN, 1607–1950. The volume includes 442 biographies of women who died between January 1, 1951, and December 31, 1975. The birth years of subjects range from 1857 for *Marian Nevins MacDowell* to 1943 for *Janis Joplin.* Criteria for inclusion in this volume "favored individuals who had founded new fields or institutions, those who had made important discoveries, and those who had worked to advance opportunities for their sex" (preface, volume 1).

The format of this volume differs only slightly from that of NOTABLE AMERICAN WOMEN, 1607–1950. A headnote giving the subject's name in boldface type is followed by vital dates and the subject's profession. The headnote is set off from the entry by a two-line space. Within the entries, names of subjects who appear either in this volume or in the 1607–1950 volumes are printed in small capital letters. A classified list of biographies by profession is appended to the text, and persons are not limited to one field. For example, *Zora Neale Hurston* can be found under "Anthropology & Folklore" as well as "Literature" (subhead: "Writers").

The entries in *Notable American Women, the Modern Period* retain the same high standard set by the earlier volumes. They are both scholarly and entertaining to read, interspersing details of the subject's personal life with the narrative of her career. Bibliographies refer to both primary and secondary sources.The Board recommends this work for the core collections of public, academic, and school libraries.

Who Was Who in America with World Notables. Marquis 1942–1985. hard. 10 vols. ISBN 0-8379-0216-9 (set). $560 (set). biographical source. revised every 4 years.
CT101.W627A 927.0973

Who Was Who in America with World Notables is a series of ten volumes (including an unnumbered historical volume, which covers from 1607 to 1896, and a one-volume index to the series) that provides entries on deceased biographees from *Who's Who in America with World Notables.* The ten-volume set covers the years from 1897 through 1985. It also includes entries for "Marquis biographees known to be 95 years of age or older"; these are indicated by a dagger mark at the end of the entry. The preface of volume 7 mentions that deceased subjects or those over age 95 are included from the four regional *Who's Who* publications, but the preface to volume 8 does not repeat this information, leaving a question as to whether the regionals are included.

The entire series includes some 112,000 biographical entries that comprise, according to the preface to volume 8, the "autobiography of America." It is stressed that in most cases *Who's Who* biographies, unless otherwise indicated, are compiled from information provided by the subjects. An asterisk is used to indicate entries compiled by the editors without the assistance of the subject. The place of interment is given only for subjects from *Who's Who in America,* and the date of death is often missing. In some cases, the entry simply ends with "deceased" or "died."

The entries are arranged in alphabetical order, with entrants' names in boldface capitals, on pages of three columns each. The volume is relatively small for a reference book and easy to handle. There is ample white space between the end of one entry and the beginning of the next.

As with other Marquis publications, entries vary in length; entry length does not always reflect the subject's significance. It should also be noted that this publication is by no means exhaustive or comprehensive in its content. For example, the prominent art collector and philanthropist Joseph H. Hirshhorn is not included in this edition, nor is the late Egyptian president Anwar el-Sadat, who was surely a "world notable." Moreover, although volume 8 has as part of its title *1982–1985,* it includes entries for many people who died in the second part of 1981. The preface to volume 7 (1977–1981) notes that its contents include up to mid-1981, but volume 8 makes no mention of that year. This sort of ambiguity can cause confusion for the user. Fortunately a single-volume index is now available. It covers all eight volumes of *Who Was Who in America,* including the historical volume.

Most libraries have WHO'S WHO IN AMERICA—at least the most current edition. A companion work, *Who Was Who in America with World Notables,* is also a useful biographical resource. The Board recommends this work for the core collections of public and academic libraries.

Who's Who in America. Marquis, annual (1899–). hard. 2 vols. 3,627 pp. indexes. ISBN 0-8379-0145-6 (set). $335 (set). biographical dictionary. on-line.
CT101.W628A 920.073

This latest edition of *Who's Who in America* (45th edition) contains 77,000 concise biographies of notable Americans as well as leading officials of the Mexican and Canadian governments. (Altogether, this is about 2,000 more entries than the 44th edition.) The guiding principle behind *Who's Who* is to "chronicle the lives of individuals whose achievements and contributions to society made them subjects of widespread reference interest and inquiry." A board of 37 advisors—including photographer Jill Krementz, economic commentator Louis Rukeyser, producer Joseph Papp, and writer-physician Lewis Thomas—nominate individuals with demonstrated public achievements for inclusion.

Standards of admission are based on the individual's "reference interest." A position of high responsibility alone can mark a person as worthy of inclusion. High-ranking officials in all branches of the U. S. government, officials of state and territorial governments, officials of principal city governments, and judges of highest appellate courts in states and territories are arbitrarily included by virtue of their position. Active members of the military (major general and above), highly visible individuals such as top officers of major national and international corporations, head administrators of leading colleges and universities, heads of prominent institutions and associations (cultural, philanthropic, educational, and scientific), and winners of major awards, such as the Nobel Prizes and the Academy Awards, are also ensured inclusion. Individuals may also be admitted on the basis of significant achievements, "noteworthy accomplishments beyond those of the vast majority of contemporaries."

Biographical information is usually supplied by the subjects themselves. After the potential subjects are identified, they are sent forms requesting complete biographical and career information. This information is reviewed and confirmed by Marquis staff members. Not all candidates respond, however, so some entries are compiled by the Marquis staff and marked with an asterisk. Of the living former U.S. presidents, only one, Jimmy Carter, supplied his own information to the publisher.

Information in the biographies includes birth date; names of parents, spouses, children; education; professional certification; career; writings and creative works; civic and political activities; military service; awards and fellowships; professional and association memberships; political affiliations; religion; clubs; lodges; avocation; and home and office addresses. In rare instances a quote from the subject ("Thoughts of My Life") is included as the last entry item. "Avocation" is a new category in the 45th edition.

Length of entries can range from fewer than five lines to close to 100 and does not depend on the relative significance of the individual but on how much of the categorical information mentioned above is available to the publisher.

Each large page of *Who's Who* contains three columns. Entry names are printed in boldface capitals in the form that the person is best known. *Madonna* (actress/singer) appears under that name with her given name following in parentheses. There is adequate white space in the margins and between the entries; the typeface is small but readable. Thin white paper with minimal see-through is used. The large volumes are heavy but firmly bound.

Special features include a retiree index for persons whose names were deleted from the 43rd through 45th editions; a necrology of individuals whose entries appeared in the previous edition; and "Biographees in Marquis Who's Who Regional and Topical Directories," a feature that lists all the names in other Marquis publications and thereby broadens the usefulness of this reference source.

Who's Who in America remains an excellent ready-reference source in spite of the fact that its inclusions are admittedly arbitrary. The work has a long history of reliability (since 1899). The Board recommends this work for the core collections of public, academic, and school libraries.

Supplementary Titles

The Annual Obituary. Patricia Burgess, ed. St. James, annual (1980–). hard. 1 vol. 723 pp. index. ISBN 0-912289-82-1. $85. biographical dictionary.
CT100 920.0205

In *The Annual Obituary,* "obituaries are arranged chronologically by death date with noteworthy points highlighted at the end of each. An alphabetical list of names, an index of professions, an index of the obituary writers, and a list of abbreviations are included. . . . The editors have included people of major historical importance or national or international prominence, a large number of whom are from the United States, Canada, the United Kingdom, and other English-speaking countries. Although many of the individuals covered were given obituaries in the *New York Times,* many others were not; and good, current biographical information about those people is sometimes hard to find." (*LJ,* June 15, 1981, p. 1298)

Also reviewed in: *ARBA,* 1982, p. 77; *BL,* January 1, 1982, p. 613; *Choice,* November 1981, p. 354; *LJ,* May 15, 1982, p. 958; *RQ,* Fall 1981, p. 89; *RSR,* Summer 1983, p. 45; *WLB,* September 1981, p. 58.

Board's recommendation: Public and academic libraries.

Biographical Books: 1876–1949. Gertrude Jennings, ed. Bowker, 1983. hard. 1 vol. 1,768 pp. index. ISBN 0-8352-1603-9. $135. bibliography.
CT.104.B56 016.92002

"As the foregoing volume to *Biographical Books 1950–1980, Biographical Books 1876–1949* completes a bibliography spanning over a century and listing—according to Bowker—'virtually every biography published or distributed in the U.S.' Autobiographies, published letters, diaries, journals, biographical dictionaries, directories, and collective works are included. Access to the biographees in collective works is not given unless the names appeared in the original cataloging notes. . . . [T]he Library of Congress . . . cataloging [is] used as the basis for Bowker's *American Book Publishing Record* and its cumulations. The *ABPR* database in turn provided the entries for the various indexes in the bibliographies of biographical books. The items in this book are alphabetically arranged in a name/subject index. . . . Headings from original cataloging, occasionally changed for uniformity, sort the more than 40,000 entries under 16,500 personal names and 3,500 LC subjects. The information includes main entry, full title, imprint, collation, series, notes, LC and Dewey Decimal class numbers, and tracings.

"Additional indexes are the author, title, and vocation indexes. The vocation index . . . is a finding aid identifying relationships between individuals and topics.

"[T]his work (extended by *Biographical Books 1950–1980*) is a major contribution. . . . Because of its coverage and retrospective nature, its reference value will not diminish." (*ARBA,* 1984, p. 40)

Also reviewed in: *ANQ,* May 1983, p. 197; *BL,* January 15, 1984, p. 730.

Board's recommendation: Academic libraries.

Biographical Books: 1950–1980. Gertrude Jennings, ed. Bowker, 1980. hard. 1 vol. 1,557 pp. index. ISBN 0-8352-1315-3. $135. bibliography.
CT104.868 016.92002

"*Biographical Books* provides access to full-length biographies and autobiographies. Letters, diaries, journals, and other similar materials are listed. Collective biographies, dictionaries, and directories are included, but individual entries are not analyzed.

"*Biographical Books* is comprised of five separate indexes. The body of the work is contained in the 'Name/Subject Index,' which lists a biographee's name . . . or a topic . . . and provides full entries on all the books available on the subject. Full cataloging and inprint information appears. . . . Separate author and title indexes are included.

"In total, [over 43,000] titles are included in *Biographical Books.* . . . [It] will find a place in both the library and bookstore." (*ARBA,* 1981, pp. 48–49)

Also reviewed in: *BL,* September 15, 1981, p. 127; *Choice,* March 1981, p. 928; *CRL,* July 1981, p. 349; *LJ,* January 15, 1981, p. 135; *LQ,* July 1981, p. 351; *WLB,* February 1981, p. 461.

Board's recommendation: Academic libraries.

Biographical Dictionaries and Related Works, 2d edition. Robert B. Slocum, ed. Gale, 1986. hard. 2 vols. 1,319 pp. indexes. ISBN 0-8103-0243-8 (set). $150 (set). bibliography.
Z5301.S55 016.92

The "*Biographical Dictionaries and Related Works,* 2d edition includes 16,000 sources, thus updating previous editions and supplements with a net increase of approximately 4,000 titles. The arrangement and execution of this work remain the same: coverage is international in scope, each entry provides basic bibliographic information (author, title, imprint, and pagination) plus brief annotations—usually one or two sentences. All entries are arranged under numerous headings within three main categories: 'Universal Biography,' 'National and Area Biography,' and 'Biography by Vocation.' Related material is also included, primarily biobibliographies, collections of epitaphs, some genealogical works, dictionaries of anonyms and pseudonyms, historical and subject dictionaries, government and legislative manuals (with biographical material), biographies of individuals and collective biographies, biographical indexes, and selected portrait catalogs.

"Slocum's *Biographical Dictionaries* is the most comprehensive source of this kind available now." (ARBA, 1987, p. 12)

Also reviewed in: *AB,* March 30, 1987, p. 1384; *BL,* January 1, 1987, p. 694; *R&R Bk N,* Summer 1986, p. 27.

Board's recommendation: Academic libraries.

Concise Dictionary of American Biography, 3d edition. American Council of Learned Societies. Scribner, 1980. hard. 1 vol. 1,333 pp. ISBN 0-684-16631-3. $125. biographical dictionary.
E176.D564 920.073

"Each entry [in the *Concise Dictionary of American Biography*] contains, when known, year and place of birth and of death and a brief identification of the person, e. g., manufacturer, author, etc. Typically, this information is then supplemented by a few sentences describing the person's major accomplishments. In addition to statements of fact, many entries include succinct assessments of personality or reputation." (*BL,* January 15, 1981, p. 1362)

"The chief virtue of the *Concise Dictionary of American Biography* is its easy access to biographies taken from the *Dictionary of American Biography.* [However,] the third edition . . . [has] a separate list of 1,000 biographies . . . [which forces] the researcher to peruse two alphabetic listings." (*Choice,* January 1981, p. 634)

Also reviewed in: *AHR,* April 1965, p. 797; *ARBA,* 1978, p. 67, 1981, p. 55; *Choice,* September 1977, p. 827; *Econ,* May 8, 1965, p. 649; *EHR,* January 1967, p. 210; *HT,* May 1965, p. 367; *NS,* March 19, 1965, p. 452; *RSR,* April 1981, p. 15; *SLJ,* May 1982, p. 23; *WLB,* May 1977, p. 782, October 1980, p. 140.

Board's recommendation: Public, academic, and school libraries.

Dictionary of Scientific Biography. American Council of Learned Societies. Scribner, 1970–1980. hard. 16 vols. plus suppl. index. ISBN 0-684-16962-2 (set); 0-684-18294-7 (suppl.). $1,080 (set); $160 (suppl. 2, 2 vols.). biographical dictionary.
Q141.D5 920.03

"Organized alphabetically by name of subject, the articles in volume[s] I-XIV [of the *Dictionary of Scientific Biography*] . . . focus on the professional lives of their subjects and the history of their thoughts and contributions. . . . A number of articles include passing bibliographic references, and each article concludes with a bibliography . . . normally divided into 'Original Works' and 'Secondary Literature.' . . .

"The supplementary volume (v. XV) is comprised of two sections: additional biographies of subjects who were for various reasons not included in the main set; and topical essays . . . designed to provide thematic overviews of science in certain regions/countries where it was judged not feasible to attempt biographical coverage.

"A thorough Subject Index . . . occupies most of volume XVI. It is preceded by a detailed Note on the Index, which clearly states its scope. . . . Entries for persons include birth and death dates and the volume, page, and column designations for primary references (all in boldface) and secondary references.

"The *Dictionary of Scientific Biography* is an authoritative work. . . . [It is] highly recommended." (*BL,* January 1, 1982, pp. 612–613)

Also reviewed in: *AB,* May 11, 1981, p. 3960; *BOT,* May 1980, p. 185; *CHE,* November 3, 1980, p. 21; *NYTBR,* August 31, 1980, p. 6; *RSR,* April 1981, p. 11; *SA,* August 1980, p. 35; *SB,* January 1981, p. 129, *SR,* November 25, 1972, p. 74; *TLS,* November 28, 1980, p. 1367.

Board's recommendation: Public, academic, and school libraries.

International Who's Who. Europa, (1935–); distrib. by Gale. hard. 1 vol. 1,700 pp. ISBN 0-946653-42-9. $200. biographical source.
CT120 920.01

"The *International Who's Who* is an invaluable tool for finding 'biographies of people from almost every country in the world and in almost every sphere of human activity.' . . . Persons represented are far more than the expected section of politicians and diplomats; archaeologists, business executives, librarians, mathematicians, pharmacists, and theologians are only a few of the professions represented. Entries concisely state date of birth, nationality, area of prominence, education, career data, accomplishments, honors and awards, publications, leisure interests, address, and telephone number. The biography section is preceded by brief data about reigning royal families. . . . An obituary section lists names and dates of death of prominent persons. . . . *International Who's Who* . . . remains the best single source for worldwide biographical data." (*ARBA,* 1981, pp. 51–52)

Also reviewed in: *ARBA,* 1976, p. 79, 1980, p. 51, 1983, p. 44; *BL,* June 15, 1977, p. 1593; *Choice,* March 1974, p. 62; *Econ,* August 31, 1968, p. 47, September 5, 1970, p. 63, October 21, 1972, p. 67; *Punch,* October 12, 1965, p. 565; *RSR,* April 1974, p. 17, January 1975, p. 103, October 1979, p. 56; *TLS,* December 29, 1966, p. 1208, September 12, 1968, p. 985, September 18, 1969, p. 1016, October 16, 1970, p. 1183, September 28, 1973, p. 1104, October 18, 1974, p. 1168; *WLT,* Spring 1965, p. 225, Autumn 1982, p. 763.

Board's recommendation: Public and academic libraries.

McGraw-Hill Encyclopedia of World Biography. McGraw-Hill, 1975. hard. 12 vols. ISBN 0-07-079633-5. $550. encyclopedia.
CT103.M3 920.02

The *McGraw-Hill Encyclopedia of World Biography* is "an excellent biographical encyclopedia [which] contains entries for both the living and the dead. The 5,000 well written, critical biographies are worldwide in scope and were prepared by several hundred contributors. . . . For quick reference, a brief sketch of the biographee is included for each entry at the beginning of the essay. . . . A bibliography for each entry is an added plus and directs the reader to the study guide in Vol. 12, to other appropriate biographies, or to other topical books. Vol. 12 consists of a topical index, a study guide, and a list of consultants." (*LJ,* April 15, 1975, p. 732)

Also reviewed in: *BL,* July 1, 1974, p. 1161; *Choice,* April 1974, p. 236; *CLW,* May 1974, p. 499; *RSR,* April 1974, p. 17.

Board's recommendation: Public and school libraries.

Newsmakers: The People Behind Today's Headlines. Peter M. Gareffa and Michael L. LaBlanc, eds. Gale, quarterly. hard. approx. 563 pp. ISBN 0-8103-2209-9. $85 per year. periodical.
CT120.C663 920.02

Newsmakers is "a periodical covering news personalities prominent in the previous year. It goes beyond any such works published in the past in that it combines lengthy biographical texts with photographs. Want the story on A. Bartlett Giamatti ([late] czar of baseball) or Rupert Murdock (newspaper executive and publisher)? You will find them covered in words and photographs in this 563-page volume. It is an extremely useful addition to the reference shelf." (*J Bark Rev,* June 1989)

Board's recommendation: Public and school libraries.

Webster's New Biographical Dictionary. Merriam-Webster, 1983. hard. 1 vol. 1,152 pp. ISBN 0-87779-543-6. $21.95. dictionary.
CT103 920.02

Board's recommendation: School libraries.

New and Noteworthy

Biographies of American Women: An Annotated Bibliography. Patricia E. Sweeney. ABC-Clio, 1990. hard. 1 vol. 290 pp. index. ISBN 0-87436-070-6. $59. bibliography.
Z7963.B6588 016.92072′0973

Biographies of American Women is an "annotated bibliography [that] 'examines 1,391 biographies of American Women that comprise at least 50 pages and are written in English.' Seven hundred American women are covered; early immigrants who were born outside of America are included, as are Americans who became nationals of another country. Entries are alphabetical. . . . There are cross-references from maiden name to married name when a woman was known under both forms." (*BL,* August 1990, p. 2195)

Black Biography, 1790–1950: A Cumulative Index. Henry Louis Gates, Jr., ed. Chadwyck-Healey, 1990. hard. 3 vols. ISBN 0-89887-085-2. $900. biographical index.

Black Biography "is a centralized, alphabetical listing of 30,000 individuals listing vital data with each name including: gender, birth date, death date, place of birth, occupation (over 40 categories), [and] religious affiliation (over 50 denominations). Cumulative listings by occupation, religion, and gender complete a unique sociological portrait of Black America." (Excerpted from publisher's announcement)

Chambers Concise Dictionary of Scientists. David, Ian, John, and Margaret Millar. Chambers/Cambridge, 1989. hard. 1 vol. 461 pp. illus. index. ISBN 1-85296-354-9. $29.95. biographical dictionary.
CT103 925

"The 1000 biographical sketches in [the *Chambers Concise Dictionary of Scientists*] profile men and women . . . who have contributed significantly to knowledge in the fields of physical, life, earth, and space science. A few major mathematicians are also included. The entries are generally two to three paragraphs in length and concentrate on the subject's scientific work and contributions. . . . A list of Nobel Prize winners up to 1988 is also included." (*SLJ,* May 1990, p. 29)

The Continuum Dictionary of Women's Biography, rev. edition. Jennifer S. Uglow, comp. Crossroad/

Continuum, 1989. hard. 1 vol. 621 pp. illus. index. ISBN 0-8264-0417-0. $37.50. biographical dictionary.
CT3202.C66 920.72

The Continuum Dictionary of Women's Biography "is a revised edition of *The International Dictionary of Women's Biography*. . . . The number of women covered has been increased by 250 over the 1,500 of the previous volume. . . . Women of all nations and times are included. . . . Biographies [are] arranged alphabetically by last name. . . . The *Dictionary* ends with a classified subject index and an outline of the subject-index categories." (*BL,* September 1, 1989, p. 102)

The Nobel Peace Prize and the Laureates: An Illustrated Biographical History, 1901–1987. Irwin Abrams. G. K. Hall, 1988. hard. 1 vol. 288 pp. illus. ISBN 0-8161-8609-X. $40. biographical history.
JX1962.A2A25 327.172092

The Nobel Peace Prize and the Laureates "is the only current, comprehensive, single-volume reference on the Nobel Peace Prize. It comprises both an incisive historical survey of the award and a biographical encyclopedia of all 87 Laureates. . . . [This reference is] designed for accessibility and packed with quick reference features, including . . . an annotated bibliography of sources on the general history of the prize[,] selected bibliographies of sources on all the Laureates[,] the portion of Nobel's will establishing the prize[,] the invitation to nominate candidates[, and] a chronology of the Laureates." (Excerpted from publisher's announcement)

Notable Black American Women. Jessie Carney Smith. Gale, 1990. hard. 1 vol. approx. 800 pp. illus. index. ISBN 0-8103-4749-0. $49.95. biographical dictionary.

"Of the 500 notable women [covered in *Notable Black American Women*], approximately 425 are contemporary figures. These profiles are balanced by coverage of about 75 forerunners, women of historical impact who are no longer living. Throughout the book, the emphasis is on women whose achievements make them noteworthy, and women active in all fields of endeavor are represented. Profiles range from one-half to three pages and are arranged in a single alphabet. . . . Entries include basic biographical data and a list of sources for additional study." (Excerpted from publisher's announcement)

Political Leaders of the Contemporary Middle East and North Africa: A Biographical Dictionary. Bernard Reich. Greenwood, 1990. hard. 1 vol. 570 pp. ISBN 0-313-26213-6. $79.95. biographical dictionary.
DS61.5.P65 920.056

Political Leaders of the Contemporary Middle East and North Africa "is one of the few systematic examinations of the political personalities and leaders in this area of the world. The book focuses on the period since World War II . . . and examines the roles of these Middle Eastern/North African statesmen in the evolution of political life in their own countries. . . . The geographical area covered is more extensive than that usually considered in works on the Middle East. . . . The profiles include basic 'who's who' information . . . [and cover the leaders'] methods, programs, and goals, and their contributions to the political past, present, and probable future of . . . the Middle East and North Africa." (Excerpted from publisher's announcement)

Who's Who Among Hispanic Americans. Amy L. Unterburger, ed. Gale, 1990. hard. 1 vol. 550 pp. indexes. ISBN 0-8103-7451-X. $89.95. biographical dictionary.
920

"Brief yet detailed entries on 6,000 notable contemporary Hispanic Americans make [*Who's Who Among Hispanic Americans*] . . . your first choice when searching for biographical information on those who trace their lineage to Mexico, Puerto Rico, Cuba, Spain, or . . . Central and South America. . . . The work includes individuals from a broad range of professions. . . . Entries are arranged alphabetically by surname and include date and place of birth; parents' names; marital status and children's names; educational background; career history; awards and honors; [and] other noteworthy achievements." (Excerpted from publisher's announcement)

Who's Who in the Socialist Countries in Europe. Juliusz Stroynowski. Saur, 1989. hard. 3 vols. 2,000 pp. ISBN 3-598-10636-X. $350. biographical dictionary.
CT120.L44 920.047

"*Who's Who in the Socialist Countries in Europe* lists approximately 13,000 'eminent individuals from the sphere of party, government, military, diplomacy, economics, sciences, literature, religion, art, and press,' plus 350 dissidents from European socialist states other than the Soviet Union. The alphabetically arranged entries provide full name, nationality, profession, date and place of birth, family background, biographical sketch, publications, honors, decorations, and prizes." (*Choice,* October 1989, p. 296)

Who's Who in the Soviet Union Today: Political and Military Leaders. Ulrich-Joachim Schultz-Torge. Saur, 1990. hard. 2 vols. 800 pp. ISBN 3-598-10810-9 (set). $375 (set). biographical dictionary.
CT759 920.047

Who's Who in the Soviet Union Today is a "two-volume reference [that] provides full and up-to-date biographical information on over 2,000 leading personalities in the political and military life of the Soviet Union today. Volume One lists the leading figures in the Communist Party of the Soviet Union (CPSU) at both central and regional levels. Volume Two provides each entrant's full name, dates, nationality, distinctions, training, and career." (Excerpted from publisher's announcement)

Mary Ann McFarland

Biology

See also Zoology

Biology is a rapidly changing and expanding field; it is a complex discipline, and this is reflected in the complexity of its information sources. H. V. Wyatt's INFORMATION SOURCES IN THE LIFE SCIENCES provides an excellent overview of the variety and abundance of sources in this area. The core collection in biology should be broad enough to answer the most basic questions in such areas as natural history, microbiology, anatomy, genetics, entomology, and evolution, as well as provide the specialized information in one discipline that a researcher from another discipline may need for background reading.

Dictionaries and encyclopedias play an important role in defining and clarifying a host of terms relating to biological concepts, methods, nomenclature, substances, and techniques. With a diverse field such as biology, it is difficult even for the professional to keep abreast of current developments in areas outside one's immediate interest. In complex and rapidly developing areas such as genetics, dictionaries and encyclopedias require regular revision. For example, King and Stansfield's A DICTIONARY OF GENETICS has undergone three revisions since its first edition. Each library will have to assess its patrons' needs when contemplating the purchase of new editions.

Access to journal literature is of primary importance to the biological sciences. Major coverage of periodical sources is provided through the *Biological and Agricultural Index* (Wilson, monthly) and *Biological Abstracts* (BIOSIS, semimonthly). Excellent bibliographies such as those found in the CAMBRIDGE ENCYCLOPEDIA OF LIFE SCIENCES can also provide additional access to scholarly sources.

Illustrative materials are also necessary for the core biology collection because clear and precise illustrations can enhance understanding of difficult concepts. LIFE SCIENCES ON FILE provides explicit, uncluttered diagrams suitable for a wide variety of needs. The CAMBRIDGE ILLUSTRATED DICTIONARY OF NATURAL HISTORY and THE CAMBRIDGE ENCYCLOPEDIA OF LIFE SCIENCES are richly illustrated volumes.

In addition to keeping up with the tremendous proliferation of biological literature, the librarian assembling a collection faces a need to acquire additional materials in related fields. This reflects the trend toward interdisciplinary research in the biological sciences. A comprehensive collection for biology is quickly becoming more difficult and expensive to maintain. However, the titles included herein should provide a useful starting point.

Core Titles

	PUBLIC	ACADEMIC	SCHOOL
The Cambridge Encyclopedia of Life Sciences Friday, Adrian, and David S. Ingram, eds. Cambridge, 1985	✦	✦	
Concise Dictionary of Biology Martin, Elizabeth, ed. Oxford, 1985			✦
A Dictionary of Genetics, 3d edition King, Robert C., and William D. Stansfield. Oxford, 1985		✦	
The Facts On File Dictionary of Biology, rev. and exp. edition Tootill, Elizabeth. Facts On File, 1988	✦	✦	✦
Life Sciences on File The Diagram Group. Facts On File, 1986			✦
The Oxford Dictionary of Natural History Allaby, Michael, ed. Oxford, 1985	✦	✦	✦

Core Titles

The Cambridge Encyclopedia of Life Sciences. Adrian Friday and David S. Ingram, eds. Cambridge, 1985. hard. 1 vol. 432 pp. illus. index. ISBN 0-521-25696-8. $57.50. encyclopedia.
QH307.2.C36 574

The *Cambridge Encyclopedia of Life Sciences* is a richly illustrated volume that attempts to summarize the available information on the living organisms that inhabit or have inhabited the earth.

This work from Cambridge is similar in format to other well-received Cambridge encyclopedias, such as THE CAMBRIDGE ENCYCLOPEDIA OF EARTH SCIENCES (see Earth Science). According to its editors, *The Cambridge Encyclopedia of Life Sciences* provides a "synthesis which draws both on the observations of the naturalist tradition and on the findings of the experimental approach" (introduction). The encyclopedia attempts to explain the whys and wherefores of the life sciences, rather than merely to define terminology. There are 31 contributors listed for this work. Nearly two-thirds of the writers are from Cambridge University; they include biologists, biochemists, botanists, zoologists, plant scientists, parasitologists, earth scientists, and geneticists. The essays, however, are unsigned.

The encyclopedia is divided into three parts. Part 1, "Processes and Organization," contains essays on the cell, the organism, genetics, behavior, and sociobiology and ecology. The essays in part 2, "Environments," survey marine, coastal, terrestrial, freshwater, wetlands, and living organisms as environments. Part 3, "Evolution and the Fossil Record," has essays that examine the evolutionary process, paleontology, early events in evolution, the origin and development of the land, and the recent history of fauna and flora.

The *Encyclopedia of Life Sciences* is arranged by broad concepts rather than alphabetical entries, and this approach supports the editors' argument that all biological phenomena are indissolubly linked, as each chapter builds upon the last. The organization of the text is logical and effective.

The encyclopedia includes a 20-page review of the classification of living organisms, ample suggestions for additional reading, a species index, and a subject index. Chapters are divided into major concepts by use of subheadings set in boldface type. The maps, charts, and diagrams dispersed throughout, both black and white and color, are particularly attractive and easy to read. The photographs are also exceptional. Nearly every page in the volume is enhanced by artwork.

The Cambridge Encyclopedia of Life Sciences is well organized, attractive, and interesting. The Board recommends it for the core collections of public and academic libraries.

Concise Dictionary of Biology. Elizabeth Martin, ed. Oxford, 1985. hard and soft. 1 vol. 261 pp. illus. ISBN 0-19-866144-4 (hard); 0-19-286109-3 (soft). $17.95 (hard); $7.95 (soft). dictionary.
QH302.5C7441985 574.0321

The *Concise Dictionary of Biology* contains entries

taken from the *Concise Science Dictionary* (also published by Oxford University Press), which relate specifically to biology and biochemistry and those geological, physical, chemical, and medical terms necessary for an understanding of biology. The more chemical aspects of biochemistry and chemistry itself are not included in the scope of this work.

The arrangement of entries is alphabetical, and most entries are brief. There are a few black-and-white illustrations. Pronunciation, etymology, and division of syllables are not provided. A comparable work in this category, THE FACTS ON FILE DICTIONARY OF BIOLOGY, which also focuses on brief definitions, includes many illustrations that enhance its accessibility.

The editor, Elizabeth Martin, has edited several other works including medical dictionaries. The quality of paper is somewhat poor, and the binding may not withstand repeated uses. Also, in a field where currency is of the utmost importance, a dictionary over five years old has some limitations. The Board recommends this work for the core collection of school libraries.

A Dictionary of Genetics, 3d edition. Robert C. King and William D. Stansfield. Oxford, 1985. hard and soft. 1 vol. 480 pp. illus. appendixes. index. ISBN 0-1950-34945 (hard); 0-1950-34953 (soft). $32.50 (hard); $21.95 (soft).
QH427.K551985 575.1

A Dictionary of Genetics is more than its name implies. This title is a compendium of genetic information. The third edition is one third larger than the second edition, which was published in 1972. (A fourth edition has recently been published; however, the publisher was unable to supply a review copy for this publication.) The main body consists of 5,920 entries, compared with the 3,800 in the second edition. The text is enhanced with 225 illustrations. Most definitions are simple and concise; however, more complex concepts such as meiosis and deoxyribonucleic acid run considerably longer.

There are four useful appendixes to the dictionary. Appendix A is the "Classification of Living Organisms" down to the level of orders. Appendix B lists "Domesticated Species"; it provides the common and scientific names of a variety of economically important domesticated organisms. Appendix C is a 22-page "Chronology of Genetics"—from the introduction of the compound microscope in 1590 to the Nobel Prize laureates of 1984. Although the selection of significant events for inclusion is subjective, it does provide a historical perspective of genetics. This chronology also includes an index of scientists and a bibliography of major sources used for the compilation. Appendix D is a lengthy list of "Periodicals Cited in the Literature of Genetics, Cytology and Molecular Biology" followed by a list of "Foreign Words Commonly Found in Scientific Titles." These four appendixes add another dimension to the usefulness of the volume.

The compilers, Robert C. King and William D. Stansfield, are notable scientists—both are listed in *American Men and Women of Science.* King has also edited the five-volume *Handbook of Genetics.*

Genetics is a field of rapid and complex changes. Even the most experienced geneticist may have need for this dictionary. Oxford University Press has produced many excellent reference works, and *A Dictionary of Genetics* is no exception. The Board recommends this work for the core collection of academic libraries.

The Facts On File Dictionary of Biology, rev. and expan. edition. Elizabeth Tootill, ed. Facts On File, 1988. hard. 1 vol. 326 pp. illus. ISBN 0-8160-1865-0 (hard); 0-8160-23689-9 (soft) $24.95 (hard); $12.95 (soft). dictionary.
QH13.F351988 574'.0321'219

The Facts On File Dictionary of Biology is a good basic dictionary for laypersons or students. This revision of the 1981 edition includes approximately 3,000 entries in an alphabetical arrangement. The entries vary from one sentence to almost half a page, however, most are short. The definitions are quite easy to read; in some cases numbering is used within longer definitions to delineate major points. Key terms within definitions are italicized for easy referral.

The coverage is broad and includes traditional fields such as anatomy and botany and newer fields such as immunology and molecular biology. There are plentiful "see" and "see also" references in the dictionary.

The quality of the illustrations definitely enhances this work. The black-and-white diagrams are clear, simple, and attractively presented. The illustration of the alimentary canal, for example, is ideally suited for an elementary school lesson, and the illustration of meiosis is exceptionally clear.

The Facts On File Dictionary of Biology is comparable to the CONCISE DICTIONARY OF BIOLOGY, which is also reviewed in this section. The dictionaries are very similar in scope, content, and appearance. Definitions tend to be slightly longer in this work than in the CONCISE DICTIONARY OF BIOLOGY, and there may be a few more cross-references. The Facts On File volume is a bit sturdier, and the larger typeface makes it much easier to read. The paper is also better quality than the CONCISE DICTIONARY OF BIOLOGY.

The Facts On File Dictionary of Biology is a good basic dictionary for all types of libraries. It is reasonably priced, up to date, accurate, and attractive. The editor, Elizabeth Tootill, also compiled THE FACTS ON FILE DICTIONARY OF BOTANY (see Botany) and the *Penguin Dictionary of Botany* as well as several other reference works. The Board recommends this work for the core collections of public, academic, and school libraries.

Life Sciences on File. The Diagram Group. Facts On File, 1986. looseleaf. 1 vol. 304 pp. illus. index. ISBN 0-8160-1284-9. $145. atlas.
QH318.L45 574.022'2

Life Sciences on File is an ideal visual aid for students or teachers. The sturdily bound volume contains over 300 well-constructed charts and diagrams on heavy looseleaf stock. These plates pertain to the study of biology, botany, and zoology. Also included are a simple decimal classification system and a comprehensive subject index.

All illustrations are printed in black and white and can easily be removed for photocopying; they are also very clearly labeled. The publisher authorizes the reproduction of any of the diagrams for nonprofit educational or private use without any further permission or fees. Anyone who has struggled to make a photocopy from a tightly bound volume will appreciate the easy access that this looseleaf binder affords.

The volume is divided into six sections: "Unity," "Continuity," "Diversity," "Maintenance," "Human Biology," and "Ecology." The scope of each section is indicated by the contents at the beginning of each chapter. The first section, "Unity," includes such topics as photosynthesis, enzymes, DNA, and RNA. "Continuity," the second section, covers cell division, meiosis, fetal development, and mutation. The "Diversity" section includes the classification of living organisms. Section 4, "Maintenance," includes life functions such as nutrition, respiration, and secretion. Human physiology (digestion, coordination, locomotion, and so on) is covered in the next chapter. "Ecology" constitutes the last section. This section contains only eight diagrams and is considerably shorter than the others.

The primary strength of this collection is the clarity of the drawings; however, because there is no accompanying written information, the illustrations should be used in conjunction with a reliable biology text.

The Diagram Group is a team of artists, designers, and editors that specializes in the creation of heavily illustrated reference books. Other volumes produced by this group include *Surgery on File, Physical Sciences on File, Earth Sciences on File,* and *Timelines on File.*

Life Sciences on File will be a welcome addition to any school library; both the teacher in need of overhead projection material and the student who needs a clear diagram can take advantage of this well-conceived reference tool. The Board recommends this work for the core collection of school libraries.

The Oxford Dictionary of Natural History. Michael Allaby, ed. Oxford, 1985. hard. 1 vol. 688 pp. ISBN 0-19-217720-6. $45. dictionary.
QH13.03 508.03'21

The Oxford Dictionary of Natural History is intended for students, amateur naturalists, and "all those who would pursue their interest in natural history beyond the more popular books, articles and television programs." In the preface, the editor points out the great need for both professionals and amateurs to master vocabularies and the concepts underlying them; this is the need the dictionary addresses.

The dictionary contains over 12,000 entries pertaining to the earth sciences (geology, geomorphology, pedology, and mineralogy), the atmospheric sciences, genetics, cell structure, biochemistry, parasitology, and other disciplines. The entries in the dictionary are generally short (two to three sentences). Approximately half the entries pertain to living organisms, listed to the family level with cross-references from the common names. Abbreviations have been kept to a minimum, and there are helpful "see also" references within the entries. Technical terms are defined within the entry. One of the longer entries (eight sentences) in the work is devoted to Charles Darwin; however, Darwin's is the only biographical entry found in the dictionary.

There are no illustrations in the work. A comparable title to this volume, the well-illustrated THE CAMBRIDGE ILLUSTRATED DICTIONARY OF NATURAL HISTORY, examined in the supplementary portion of this section, may be preferred by some patrons.

Coverage was intended to be global; however, the 25 contributors are predominantly British. The list of contributors and consultants includes their affiliations but not their credentials, although perhaps it would have been useful to list the contributors' areas of expertise. The dictionary includes a three-page bibliography of publications consulted by the contributors or used as authorities for taxonomic systems.

This dictionary is an attractive and easy-to-use volume. Its attempt at comprehensiveness is admirable although only partially successful. In any scientific discipline there is a need for currency; the 1985 publication date does reflect the need for some additional material. However, *The Oxford Dictionary of Natural History* remains generally reliable and reasonably priced. The Board recommends this work for core collections in public, academic, and school libraries.

Supplementary Titles

The Cambridge Illustrated Dictionary of Natural History. R. J. Lincoln and G. S. Boxshall. Cambridge, 1987. hard. 1 vol. 413 pp. illus. ISBN 0-521-30551-9 (hard); 0-521-59941-6 (soft). $27.95 (hard); $14.95 (soft). dictionary.
QH13.L56 508.03'21

The Cambridge Illustrated Dictionary of Natural History "contains more than 10,000 entries covering 'the entire spectrum of life—plants, animals, and micro-organisms.' . . . Definitions include the types of organisms within a classification, the approximate number of the species, habitat, geographical distribution, and other characteristic features of the group. . . . In addition, the dictionary defines ecological terms related to feeding, reproduction, population biology, behavior, soils, habitats, and life histories. . . . [There are] about 700 black-and-white line drawings.

"[The] dictionary briefly explains Latinized terms like canidae (dogs and foxes) and violaceae (violets and pansies). . . . In most cases taxonomic groups are included to the level of order. [While] present-day species are emphasized, . . . some fossil groups are included. . . . [In addition,] cross-references from common names are extensive." (*BL,* March 1, 1988, p. 1115)

Also reviewed in: *ARBA,* 1988, p. 609; *Choice,* February 1988, p. 887; *Earth S,* Fall 1988, p. 29; *SciTech,* December 1987, p. 14; *WLB,* November 1987, p. 87.

Board's recommendation: Academic libraries.

Five Kingdoms: An Illustrated Guide to the Phyla of Life on Earth, 2d edition. Lynn Margulis and Karlene V. Schwartz. Freeman, 1987. hard. 1 vol. 338 pp. illus. index. ISBN 0-7167-1885-5 (hard); 0-7167-1912-6 (soft). $37.95 (hard); $24.95 (soft). handbook.
QH83.M36 574.012

Five Kingdoms: An Illustrated Guide to the Phyla of Life on Earth explains "the five-kingdom plan of organization [which was first proposed by R. H. Whittaker in the 1960s and is now universally accepted by biologists]. [All organisms are classified within the following five kingdoms]: the Monera include all the prokaryotes (mainly bacteria); the Protoctista, including all the eukaryotic microorganisms and their derivatives; the Fungi; the Animalia; and the Plantae. A system of classification is presented for each kingdom, and the phyla are described (87 in all) for each kingdom. . . . For each phylum a short description is given of dominant anatomical and ecological characteristics; several principal genera are listed; and a picture and generalized sketch are included of one example of the particular phylum.

"Serious students will welcome the bibliography listed at the end of each kingdom." (*Choice,* June 1982, p. 1427)

"For each kingdom there is offered an illustrated family tree of the descent of the phyla described. . . . A thousand genera of organisms are listed at the end in a helpful directory with such common names as exist, each assigned to the right phylum. An indispensable glossary is not forgotten." (*SA,* April 1982, p. 32)

Also reviewed in: *ARBA,* 1989, p. 564; *B Watch,* March 1988, p. 1; *Sm Pr R,* January 1988, p. 2.

Board's recommendation: Public and academic libraries.

The Human Body on File. The Diagram Group. Facts On File, 1983. looseleaf. 1 vol. 300 pp. illus. index. ISBN 0-87196-706-5. $145. atlas.
QM25.H85 611.0022'2

The Human Body on File "consists of black-and-white line drawings of the various systems/parts of the human body. All are . . . labeled with numbers keyed to terms which appear below each drawing. . . . Sections 1 and 2 cover anatomical positions and cellular structure respectively. Sections 3 through 12 are devoted to systems, [for example] nervous, muscular, skeletal, digestive, . . . with section 13 covering human development from infancy to adulthood. Each section is preceded by a one-page introduction.

"The diagrams are clear and concise and progress from general to specific in each of the 13 sections. . . . The heavy paper should endure frequent heavy use. . . . Purchasers may make copies of any part by any means for nonprofit educational or private use without obtaining any further permission or payment of fees." (*BL,* April 15, 1984, p. 1174)

Also reviewed in: *Choice,* November 1983, p. 402; *RQ,* Spring 1984, p. 363; *TES,* September 7, 1984, p. 30; *WLB,* November 1983, p. 226.

Board's recommendation: Public, academic, and school libraries.

Information Sources in the Life Sciences, 3d edition. H. V. Wyatt, ed. Saur, 1987. hard. 1 vol. 191 pp. index. ISBN 0-408-11472-X. $90. bibliography.
QH303.6.I54 01'6.574

Information Sources in the Life Sciences is one of a series of guides (Butterworths Guides to Information Sources series) whose aim "is to bring a great variety of sources and channels together in a single convenient form and to present a picture of the international scene in each of the disciplines already covered . . . and those to be covered. This particular [volume] is actually a revision of the 2nd edition (1971) of *Use of Biological Literature*. . . . As far as possible, the chapter authors—all British, incidentally—only cite recent books. . . .

"There are 13 chapters, but only 8 deal with specific subjects: biochemical sciences, microbiology, . . . biotechnology, genetics, zoology, ecology, botany, and history of biology. Five essays precede all this by covering areas that prepare the reader or user for the more specific literature to follow.

"[The] preliminary areas covered are [an introduction dealing with search techniques and finding expert help], current awareness, literature searching by computer, secondary sources (abstracts, indexes, and bibliographies), databanks, . . . and guides to the literature.

"Each subject chapter (6-13) also contains an essay on different aspects of searching (in that subject), as well as a thorough guide to the related literature." (*SL,* Winter 1988, p. 79)

Also reviewed in: *ARBA,* 1988, p. 607; *Choice,* May 1988, p. 1382; *New Tech Bks,* October 1987, p. 266; *Ref Bk R,* 1989, p. 27; *Ref Bk R,* 1988, p. 24; *SciTech,* September 1987, p. 13.

Board's recommendation: Academic libraries.

International Dictionary of Medicine and Biology. Sidney I. Landau, ed. John Wiley, 1986. hard. 3 vols. 3,200 pp. index. ISBN 0-471-01849-X (set). $395 (set). dictionary.
R121.I58 610.3'21

"The *International Dictionary of Medicine and Biology (IDMB)* is probably the most significant and comprehensive medical dictionary to date. . . . *IDMB* has a distinguished editorial board and highly qualified contributors who are scientists and physicians from all over the world. According to Landau, it was conceived to be an unabridged dictionary of medicine in the broadest sense and to include much of the related biological sciences as well. Subjects covered include the branches of biology and medicine as well as anthropology, biomedical engineering, environmental health, and veterinary medicine.

"*IDMB* is in three volumes and contains more than 150,000 terms and definitions. There are also entries for commonly used abbreviations, although abbreviations are in no way treated comprehensively.

"Entries . . . are arranged alphabetically letter by letter. Subentries are included under main entries, which are printed in bold letters and are set off from subentries by a double line. . . . Entries are concise but are geared to those with some familiarity with medical terminology. Word derivations or etymologies are given in square brackets immediately after the term. Usage information is also provided, for example, to note if a term is outmoded, seldom used, or popular.

"Although quite expensive, this comprehensive and authoritative set will be an invaluable resource for academic and large public libraries." (*BL,* October 1, 1986, p. 209)

Also reviewed in: *ARBA,* 1987, p. 618; *Choice,* July 1986, p. 1658; *LJ* June 15, 1986, p. 61; *LJ,* April 15, 1987, p. 35; *Nature,* April 17, 1986, p. 428; *R & R Bk N,* Summer 1986, p. 20; *SciTech,* June 1986, p. 16; *WLB,* April 1986, p. 66.

Board's recommendation: Academic libraries.

Synopsis and Classification of Living Organisms. Sybil P. Parker, ed. McGraw-Hill, 1982. hard. 2 vols. 2,398 pp. illus. appendix. index. ISBN 0-07-079031-0 (set). $295 (set). handbook.
QH83.S89 574.012

The *Synopsis and Classification of Living Organisms* "contains more than 8,000 synoptic articles devoted to the classification and description of all living organisms. The scheme used in these volumes recognizes four kingdoms: Virus, Monera, Plantae, and Animalia, arranged in two superkingdoms—the Prokaryotae and the Eukaryotae.

"Each article is a well-written synthesis of the literature from a wide variety of sources. . . . The 174 international contributors are among the leading authorities in their fields. There are more than 300 pages of illustrations—160 pages of drawings and 150 pages of excellent photographs. The appendix contains a classification outline, an essay on the history of naming organisms, and an article on biological classification. An extensive index of more than 35,000 entries includes both scientific and common names." (*Choice,* September 1982, p. 60)

"This incredibly ambitious reference covers all living things, viruses to vertebrates, down to the family level. Full technical characterizations are given together with typical habits and life histories. . . . Major references are given for each family. Some of the information is not otherwise available in English. . . . [This is] an enormously valuable first source of information for scientists, students, and instructors." (*LJ,* May 1, 1982, p. 878)

Also reviewed in: *ARBA,* 1983, p. 618; *BL,* May 15, 1983, p. 1211; *LJ,* March 1, 1983, p. 445; *LJ,* May 15, 1983, p. 964; *Nature,* January 6, 1983, p. 96; *RQ,* Summer 1982, p. 421; *WLB,* April 1982, p. 76.

Board's recommendation: Public and academic libraries.

New and Noteworthy

Atlas of Human Anatomy. Frank H. Netter. CIBA-Geigy, 1989. hard and soft. 1 vol. 592 pp. illus. index. ISBN 0-914168-18-5 (hard); 0-914168-19-3 (soft). $86.50 (hard); $39.95 (soft). atlas.
611.0022

The *Atlas of Human Anatomy* "is divided into seven broad sections: Head and Neck, Back and Spinal Cord, Thorax, Abdomen, Pelvis and Perineum, Upper Limb, and Lower Limb. Each of these is in turn broken down into intricate subsections that detail all parts of the human anatomy. Illustrations are clearly labeled and follow nomenclature adopted by the Eleventh International Congress of Anatomists in 1980." (*SLJ,* May 1990, pp. 27–28)

The Biological Sciences in the Twentieth Century. Merriley Borell. Scribner, 1989. hard. 1 vol. 306 pp. illus. index. ISBN 0-684-16483-3. $75. encyclopedia.
QH305.B67 574.09

The Biological Sciences in the Twentieth Century covers "the life sciences from large- and small-scale biology, evolution, and agriculture to biology in a social context. Separate chapters are devoted to each discipline. . . . Each chapter opens with a brief outline of major discoveries, principles, and participants in the field, followed by a collection of pictures. Each volume's approximately 400 photographs and drawings show scientists, scientific discoveries, manuscripts, and popular public images. Each picture is accompanied by a descriptive caption." (*BL,* January 1, 1990, p. 942)

The Encyclopedia of Evolution. Richard Milner. Facts On File, 1990. hard. 1 vol. 500 pp. illus. index. ISBN 0-8160-1472-8. $45. encyclopedia.
GN281.M53 573.2′03

"The more than 500 insightful and wide-ranging entries in Milner's [*The Encyclopedia of Evolution*] cover every aspect of evolutionary thought from the most scholarly to the most popular. You'll find entries on 'Fantasia,' 'Tarzan,' 'Planet of the Apes,' and P. T. Barnum rubbing shoulders with entries on Fossils, Teilhard de Chardin, Panda's Thumb, and Binomial Nomenclature." (Excerpted from publisher's announcement)

Robert D. Harlan

Book Arts

See also Graphic Arts; Publishing

The book arts encompass several fields which in one way or another focus upon the book as a physical object. The crafts of binding, papermaking, and fine printing have experienced a revitalization during the past three decades, creating an enthusiastic and growing group of practitioners and connoisseurs for relevant reference and bibliographical sources. By and large existing works can meet those patrons' requirements. Book collecting, particularly of the rare or antiquarian book, has generated its own compilations to assist the specialist as well as the amateur in answering questions on the physical state as well as the monetary value of books.

Practitioners, students, and patrons of the book arts may request specific information on aspects of the crafts of binding, papermaking, and printing. Manuals, guides, dictionaries, and histories will be obvious sources of assistance. Examples of this material are Laura S. Young's *Bookbinding and Conservation by Hand: A Working Guide* (Bowker, 1981) and Lewis Allen's excellent *Printing with the Handpress: Herewith a Definitive Manual* (1969) which, unfortunately, are now out of print. Another source for instruction or description, this time in a historical context, is Philip Gaskell's standard *A New Introduction to Bibliography,* which provides excellent descriptions of the processes

Core Titles

	PUBLIC	ACADEMIC	SCHOOL
Bookman's Glossary, 6th edition Peters, Jean, ed. Bowker, 1983	✦	✦	
Bookman's Price Index: A Guide to the Values of Rare and Other Out-of-Print Books McGrath, Daniel F., ed. Gale, annual	✦	✦	

of typefounding and composition, papermaking, and binding up to the middle of this century. BOOKMAN'S GLOSSARY assembles a basic vocabulary shared by the book arts as well as more specialized terms, as does Glaister's *Glossary of the Book: Terms Used in Papermaking, Printing, Bookbinding & Publishing* (Berkeley: Univ. of California Pr., 2d edition, 1979), which contains double the number of entries in BOOKMAN'S GLOSSARY as well as diagrams and illustrations. However, obtaining this book will be problematic for those libraries that do not already own a copy because the book is out of stock. It was impossible to obtain a copy from the publisher for review purposes. A good directory for practicing fine printers is *The International Directory of Private Presses: Letterpress* (Bowker, annual), which includes a listing of hand bookbinders, paper manufacturers, and suppliers.

Two important questions about the rare or antiquarian book are its monetary value and its physical state. These questions are best answered, if at all, in dealers' and auction catalogs, which are conveniently indexed in such sources as BOOKMAN'S PRICE INDEX. Although the scope of this buying guide generally excludes indexes, this work is reviewed because of its great relevance to the category. The vocabulary employed by antiquarian book dealers is only partially treated in such works as BOOKMAN'S GLOSSARY. More comprehensive listings may be found in John Carter's *ABC's of Book Collecting* (1963); unfortunately, this publication is now out of print. Directories, such as *Sheppards' Book Dealers in North America* (Scarecrow, 1986) and *Buy Books Where—Sell Books Where* (Robinson Bks., 1988) provide the names, locations, and specializations of both antiquarian and second-hand book dealers. Two out-of-print works are also useful additions to the book arts collection, including *American Book Prices Current* (Katharine Keyes Leab and Daniel J. Leab, Bancroft-Parkman, 1989), and *Bookbinding and the Care of Books* (Douglas Cockerell, Taplinger, 1978). One final reference that should be considered for a core collection is the *American Book Trade Directory* (Bowker, annual).

Core Titles

Bookman's Glossary, 6th edition. Jean Peters, ed. Bowker, 1983. hard. 1 vol. 23 pp. appendix. ISBN 0-8352-1686-1. $34.95. glossary.
Z118.B77 070.5'03

First published in 1925, the *Bookman's Glossary* has been considerably expanded in this edition to cover new concepts and terms. According to the preface, this edition attempts "to provide a practical guide to the terminology used in the production and distribution of books old and new . . . and the words in common use in the publisher's office, in a bookstore, or among book collectors." The clause "in common use" allows for the exclusion of the more technical terms and definitions employed specifically in each field. In addition to definitions of terms, biographies of "men and women of historic importance in bibliography, the graphic arts, and book publishing" are included (preface). Although not stated, only deceased persons are listed.

The glossary is arranged in alphabetical order. The 1,800 entries are primarily of the ready-reference type, averaging four to five lines each, with several entries one line in length. Why some topics have been chosen for the longer entries (for example, *calendars, Benjamin Franklin, Thomas J. Wise*) is not obvious. The treatment of related topics can also seem imbalanced. For example, the *Doves Press* receives 36 lines, but the equally distinguished *Kelmscott Press* (founded by William Morris and noted for the beauty of its bookmaking), only 9. Cross-references throughout the book are helpful but too few in number. Separate topics are sometimes buried under related terms: for example, Shaw and Shoemaker's *American Bibliography* is only discussed in the entry for *Charles Evans.* The *American Bibliography* receives only a cross-reference to the Evans entry. However, the clarity of the definitions for bibliographical terms is notable. Seminal bibliographies are also represented, sometimes under personal names and sometimes under title. The more common words of the antiquarian book trade and book collectors receive entries as well.

The attempt to provide terms in electronic publishing and computer application is less successful, in large measure because of the rapid and profound changes in these fields. Now eight years old, this edition of *Bookman's Glossary* is seriously out of date in this area. One might also argue about certain omissions, such as Joachim Ibarra, John Peter Zenger, and fakes and forgeries. The latter is particularly glaring in light of the long entry accorded *Thomas J. Wise.* In addition, some of the entries are impossibly truncated, such as the three-line definition of *Library of Congress classification.* The most successful aspect of the work is the treatment of the current vocabulary of book publishing and distribution in North America. The comprehensiveness of the treatment of these topics is commendable. Terms range from different publishing activities (there are entries for *alternative publisher, private press, trade list, mass market paperback*) to working vocabulary (for example, *coffee table book, breakeven point, line editor, slushpile*). Entries for terms from library science are restricted to those most likely to be encountered in other fields, such as *divided catalogue* or *corporate entry.*

Bookman's Glossary serves the useful function of providing, in one source, a convenient and reasonably comprehensive compilation of several terms likely to be employed in more than one of the several fields concerned with "the book." Although some of the information in selected entries was outmoded at the time of this editor's publication (for example, the bibliographic citations under the entries for *Benjamin Franklin* and the *Gesamtkatalog der Wiegendrucke*), *Bookman's Glossary* is an effective starting point for definitions and identifications. The Board recommends this work for the core collections of public and academic libraries.

Bookman's Price Index: A Guide to the Values of Rare and Other Out-of-Print Books. Daniel F. McGrath, ed. Gale, annual (1964–). 2 vols. per year. hard. ISBN 0-8103-1814-8. $190 (per year). index.
Z1000.B66 018

First published in 1964, the *Bookman's Price Index (BPI)* serves as an index to current prices and to the availability of antiquarian books in America, Canada, and Great Britain. An antiquarian book is defined as "important (or in demand) and scarce." In addition to its usefulness to the antiquarian book trade and to rare book librarians, *BPI* can be of assistance to library patrons in determining the availability and current value of a particular book.

The 60,000 to 70,000 entries in each year's two volumes provide prices asked in the catalogs of about 150 to 180 antiquarian book dealers. Prices asked are not always prices paid, but overall this work is a reasonably accurate gauge of the market. The total number of dealers listed in any given year represents only a fraction of all the dealers, and the names listed are not always the most important. The policy for the selection of names is not provided.

Each volume of *BPI* is arranged alphabetically by the name of the personal or corporate author. In the case of anonymous books, listings are by title. A helpful feature is the standardization of names. The works of an author are listed alphabetically by title, with collected works placed at the end of the list. A further subdivision by date of publication under a given title is provided. These features make for easy accessibility to *BPI*'s long listings.

The descriptions provided for the entries are detailed and give information not always available in the more standard bibliographies and catalogs. To meet the needs of the dealer and the collector, the compilers have taken care to incorporate information on such topics as issue, state, and "points." Size by format, pagination, and, when appropriate, information on paper, bindings, and illustrations are given as well.

The condition of the copies listed here is crucial in their pricing and accounts for great variations in the value placed upon different copies of the same work. In consulting this work, it is important for the novice to be apprised of this fact. Three levels of condition are used: good, very good, and fine. The rankings have been determined by dealers, not the compilers of the work.

A final section provides separate listings for association copies (copies having once belonged to particular persons) of works also included in the main section of *BPI,* for fine bindings, and for fore-edge paintings.

BPI is not exhaustive, of course. The fact that a book does not happen to be listed in *BPI* does not mean that it may not be rare. The *Bookman's Price Index* is useful in both its cumulative and current editions. In the work's cumulative form it provides bibliographical details for thousands of antiquarian books. In the current volume *BPI* serves as an indicator of the range of prices one may expect to pay for a book. The Board recommends this work for the core collections of public and academic libraries.

Supplementary Titles

Bookman's Guide to Americana, 9th edition. J. Norman Heard and Charles F. Hamsa. Scarecrow, 1986. hard. 1 vol. 476 pp. ISBN 0-8108-1894-9. $42.50. handbook.
Z1207.H43 016.97

"This new edition of . . . [*Bookman's Guide to Americana*] is a compilation of price quotations gathered from out-of-print booksellers' catalogs. It is arranged alphabetically by author of fiction and nonfiction works of Americana. There is a directory of book dealers in front.

"This edition concentrates on history, business and industry, and agriculture of all the Americas. There are a considerable number of national and state publications. Although many of the books are rare and expensive, most of them are listed to sell at a price between $10 and $25. There is no repetition of price quotations from any of the other editions. Consequently, libraries should not discard old editions of this title. . . . This edition consists of . . . almost 10,000 titles." (*ARBA,* 1987, p. 250)

"This work is a time-saving compilation for a subject field of interest to most libraries, is unique in its presentation of actual market prices, and is a fuller listing of Americana titles than any previous list compiled locally or regionally to serve the same purpose." (*Sub Bks,* April 1954, p. 17)

Also reviewed in: *ANQ,* September 1983, p. 24; *ARBA,* 1978, p. 30; *ARBA,* 1982, p. 18; *BL,* November 1, 1978, p. 495; *BL,* September 15, 1982, p. 135; *CLW,* December 1971, p. 214; *LJ,* April 1, 1977, p. 789; *LR,* Spring 1965, p. 37; *RQ,* Summer 1969, p. 285; *RQ,* Winter 1971, p. 176; *R&R Bk N,* Spring 1987, p. 36; *WLB,* January 1968, p. 532; *WLB,* December 1971, p. 363.

Board's recommendation: Public and academic libraries.

Dictionary and Encyclopedia of Paper and Paper-Making, 2d edition. E. J. Labarre, 1952; distrib. by Swets NA. hard. 1 vol. 500 pp. ISBN 90-265-0037-8. $80. dictionary.
TS1085.L3 676.03

The *Dictionary and Encyclopedia of Paper and Paper-Making* "is the most comprehensive dictionary-encyclopedia of paper terms [with equivalents of the technical terms given in French, German, Dutch, Italian, Spanish, and Swedish]. It is also a good source for the etymology of the terms. Labarre is thorough and comprehensive, going to great lengths to describe all kinds of papers." (*AB,* September 8, 1980, p. 1332)

Board's recommendation: Academic libraries.

New and Noteworthy

Book Collecting: A Comprehensive Guide. Allen Ahearn. Putnam, 1989. hard. 1 vol. 320 pp. ISBN 0-399-13456-5. $24.95. handbook.
Z897.A39 002.075

"The major part of [*Book Collecting*] . . . is a price list of about 3,500 titles. Special coverage is given to the first published books of major authors, mostly English and American. . . . The prices represent the authors' estimates." (*BL,* January 15, 1990, p. 1038)

First Editions: A Guide to Identification, rev. edition. Edward N. Zempel and Linda A. Verkler. Spoon River Pr., 1989. hard. 1 vol. 312 pp. ISBN 0-930358-08-2. $20. handbook.
Z1033.F53F57 010

In *First Editions,* "Zemple and Verkler have collected statements from some 1700 20th-century publishers of English-language books—about 700 more than in their 1984 edition—indicating current practices and earlier methods [of designating first printings] as far back as 1928. The guide also helps track down acquisitions and publishers' name changes." (*LJ,* August 1989, p. 128)

Richard Shotwell

Botany

See also Horticulture and Gardening

Botany, the science of plant life, has been of serious interest to human beings since the first hunters-and-gatherers began passing on their hard-won knowledge of plants to the next generation. Such knowledge was as essential to their survival and progress as our greatly augmented fund of knowledge is to modern society. Thus botany, while not generally considered a basic science such as chemistry or physics (upon which botany builds), is an important scientific discipline in itself. Botany also serves as a foundation science for such vital and diverse fields as ecology, agriculture, pharmacology, and biotechnology. Although the books selected for this category provide much useful information for those interested in gardening, the horticulture category should be consulted for works in that area.

The scope of botany and its corresponding literature is extraordinarily wide, covering detailed description, classification, and naming of plants, to their evolution, ecology, physiology, and pathology from the aspect of the descriptive to the functional. The descriptive aspect encompasses the primitive herbals of the medieval period to the specialized taxonomic journals of the late twentieth century. This in itself is an immense literature, covering all continents and oceans, in all languages. Here the oldest literature is often as important as the newest.

Conversely, an important component of the functional literature is a collection of current serials, especially journals, the number and cost of which have been rising exponentially. Both the descriptive and the functional aspects of the study of botany utilize the journal article as a record of research, which makes many journals almost indispensable. One recent useful guide to the literature, the *Guide to Information Sources in the Botanical Sciences* (Elizabeth B. Davis, Libraries Unlimited, 1987), is already out of print, and librarians will want to try to obtain this bibliography through out-of-print sources.

On the other hand, botany in general makes use of more books and monographs than do some other scientific fields. Although the basic literature is relatively stable, multidisciplinary and multilingual serial literature can include literally thousands of titles, making botany one of the most difficult literatures for librarians to survey, acquire, store, and access.

Librarians need to acquire a knowledge of the literature, their clientele, and their institutional needs. Interest in and knowledge of botany varies widely, from the beginning student to the serious amateur to the professional.

In some cases, the needs of the amateur botanist are as extensive and specialized as those of the professional

Core Titles

	PUBLIC	ACADEMIC	SCHOOL
Exotica, Series 4 International: Pictorial Cyclopedia of Exotic Plants from Tropical and Near-tropic Regions, 2 vols. Graf, Alfred Byrd. Roehrs, 1982	✦	✦	
The Facts On File Dictionary of Botany Blackmore, Stephen, consult. ed., and Elizabeth Tootill, gen. ed. Facts On File, 1984	✦		✦
The Trees of North America Mitchell, Alan. Facts On File, 1987	✦		

scientist. Most libraries cannot be all things to all people, and botanical libraries in particular must shape their collections and services for their particular clientele and institution; certain institutions have a tradition of being more interested in some aspect of the botanical sciences than in some others (for example, in taxonomy). The reference librarian needs to be aware of a broad range of materials, from basic data bases, such as *BIOSIS,* to regional publications and serial publications in a related area of interest, such as biochemistry or climatology. To do this requires interest, organization, attention to detail, networking with other librarians and institutions, and a thorough knowledge of the particular library's mission, goals, and physical and financial resources.

The popular *Encyclopedia of Plants* (Vernon H. Heywood, ed., Cambridge, 1982) was recommended by the Board, but is now out of print. The scope of this work was exceptionally broad, covering 800 genera of economic worth and several hundred important ornamental ones. The text was authoritative enough for the patrons of academic libraries, as well as being accessible enough for the patrons of public libraries. This would be a worthwhile work to add to a botany collection if a copy can be located through an out-of-print book dealer.

Core Titles

Exotica, Series 4 International: Pictorial Cyclopedia of Exotic Plants from Tropical and Near-tropic Regions. Alfred Byrd Graf. Roehrs, 1982. hard. 2 vols. 2,580 pp. illus. appendix. indexes. ISBN 0-911-266-17-8 (set). $187 (set). encyclopedia.
SB407.G7 635.965

The *Exotica, Series 4 International* (subtitled *Pictorial Cyclopedia of Exotic Plants from Tropical and Near-tropic Regions*) is a "comprehensive and contemporary pictorial record of ornamental or fruited plants and trees, introduced from far-flung tropical and warm-climate regions of the world, as known to horticulture, and . . . for their decorative qualities. . . . They may be grown indoors in home or office . . . or the home greenhouse; or on occasion outdoors, on the sheltered patio, or the summer garden" (introduction).

Persons coming upon the *Exotica* series for the first time often describe the work as "awesome," "unbelievable," or "monumental." These volumes are all of these and more, especially the later editions (series 3 and 4). Habitual users—and there are many—consider the work exhaustive, authoritative, practical, and encouraging, a source of information and inspiration. The title derives from the source of the plants—the tropics (hence foreign, curious, unusual, or "exotic"). The work is indeed monumental: series 4 includes 16,300 photographs, 405 plants in color, and 300 drawings. Although *Exotica* is primarily an authoritative source for photographs of plants that might be grown indoors in most of North America, the volumes also are a guide to plant care, decorating, tropical botany and gardens, plant geography, ecology, and propagation.

Near the beginning of volume 1 is a "Botanic Index to Genera" illustrated, which is an index of Latin names for the plants in the illustrations. The nomenclature is based on the HORTUS THIRD (see Horticulture), a standard reference in the field. Volume 1 also contains a section on caring for indoor plants and a section on propagation. Orchids, palms, woody plants, cacti and succulents, and ferns are all illustrated. There is also a brief review of botanical families. The bulk of the volume is devoted to photographs of the plants. The photographs are exceptionally large and clear, showing detail that is more than adequate, in most cases, for identification.

Illustrations continue in the second volume, followed by a major section entitled "Plant Descriptions Combined with Code to Care and Photo Index." The code refers to a section on directions for culture ("International Key to Care"), written in English, Spanish, French, German, and Russian. This descriptive section, beginning with *Albelia* (Caprifoliaceae family) and ending with *Zygostates* (Orchidaceae family), includes information on the plant's origins, synonyms, common name, and characteristics (mainly habit of growth), and the shape, texture, and color of its foliage, flowers, and fruit. A two-page bibliography, an index of common names, and a repeat of the index given in volume 1 concludes this volume. The inside back cover is a horticultural color guide for identifying plant hues.

Because *Exotica* is accessible both to specialists and to a general audience, and serves both botanical and horticultural interests, the work is especially versatile. Although the work is aimed at people interested in indoor plants, a large and enthusiastic group, *Exotica* also serves anyone interested in plants in general.

The printing and binding are exceptional. Although both volumes are heavy and awkward to handle, they lie flat when open.

Exotica, Series 4 International should remain relevant for years to come. The Board recommends this work for the core collections of public and academic libraries.

The Facts On File Dictionary of Botany. Stephen Blackmore, consult. ed., and Elizabeth Tootill, gen. ed. Facts On File, 1984. hard. 1 vol. 400 pp. illus. appendixes. ISBN 0-87196-861-4. $21.95. dictionary.
QK9.F33 580.3'21

The Facts On File Dictionary of Botany is a dictionary of modern general botany, British in origin, and current as of the 1984 publication date. The dictionary was compiled by ten British scientists, all of whom have at least a bachelor's level degree, with three having higher degrees. This degree of expertise, while not particularly impressive, is adequate for a work of this nature. Although a more recent work would be desirable, there is no real substitute for this dictionary at this time. The text should remain reasonably current for some time, although users must recognize that changes in certain areas, such as biotechnology and taxonomy, may require more recent sources for up-to-date information.

The scope of *The Facts On File Dictionary of Botany* embraces the major fields of the botanical sciences, including some entries for related areas such as horticulture, agricultural botany, microbiology, and laboratory techniques and equipment. The dictionary omits entries for named genera or species, but includes some higher ranks of groups and families (for example, *Leguminosae*). Thus this work is not a substitute for a dictionary of plant names.

As in any good dictionary devoted to a specific discipline, the entries provide fuller descriptions and more terms than do more general dictionaries that cover the biological sciences as a whole. The 3,000-plus entries are arranged alphabetically. There are relatively few illustrations, although some definitions are made clearer by the use of line drawings or charts. The definitions are clear and concise, well suited to the primary audience—undergraduate students and amateur botanists. The work should also be suitable for advanced high school students. Although some entries may seem simplistic to professional botanists, this feature makes the work more accessible to students. A typical short entry runs for three to four lines. Other entries stretch on for one or two long paragraphs, giving a thorough explanation. Because of this depth of treatment, the total number of entries is just over 3,000, compared to over 5,000 in a comparable but older work, *A Dictionary of Botany,* by R. J. Little and C. E. Jones (Van Nostrand Reinhold, 1980, now out of print). Depth for quantity is, however, a reasonable compromise. Further clarification is achieved by the use of cross-references to direct the user to entries for technical terms or concepts. Although this practice is not carried out throughout the work, the diligent searcher can find more information.

The printing and binding of *The Facts On File Dictionary of Botany* are excellent, and the two appendixes, covering scientific epithets and recommended chemical names for some common organic compounds, are useful. The Board recommends this work for the core collections of public and school libraries.

The Trees of North America. Alan Mitchell. Facts On File, 1987. hard. 1 vol. 208 pp. illus. index. ISBN 0-8160-1806-5. $29.95. handbook.
QK115.M5 582.16

The Trees of North America is a handsome work that is a credit to the author, illustrator, and publisher. Written by the foremost tree specialist in Great Britain (or in Europe, for that matter) and illustrated by one of the best British artists of trees, this book is attractive enough for coffee table display.

The team of editor Alan Mitchell and illustrator David More had previously produced the well-received *Complete Guide to Trees of Britain and Northern Europe.* As with that work, the combination of clearly written, authoritative text and artistic, detailed botanical illustrations in the North American volume is a winning one. The arrangement of the book is simple and logical: broadleaved trees are followed by conifers. Over 500 species and 250 varieties are described under these broad categories, listed by common names. For example, *alders* and *yews* are separate entries, while *torreyas, cowtail pines and monkey-puzzles* are grouped together, as are *mulberries and Osage orange.* (A British orientation is evident here in the common names used.)

Each text entry consists of a common name, a botanical name, the place of origin, and a taxonomic description: leaf, flower, fruit, and bark, as well as the size of the tree and the range, which is indicated by symbols for the individual states. Each entry takes up two pages. The text occupies about two-thirds of a two-page spread, with the illustrations filling the bottom one-third of each page. This design is both efficient and pleasing to the eye, successfully integrating the text and drawings. The full-color drawings are beautifully detailed, showing major taxonomic details as well as landscape effects (such as a view of mature trunks and representative trees in summer, and often in autumn and winter). Small-scale geographic range maps shaded to show the range in North America for native and exotic species are also included in this section. The species are listed by common name—*flowering dogwood* or *Russian olive.* One can always quibble over choices of trees, but the selection included in this work is an appropriate, slightly unusual, and stimulating one.

The Trees of North America is a superior work of its kind that should be a standard for years to come. The Board recommends this work for the core collection of public libraries.

Supplementary Titles

Conifers. D. M. van Gelderen. Royal Boskoop Horticultural Society by Timber Pr.; distrib. by Internatl. Specialized Bk. Svcs., 1986. hard. 1 vol. 375 pp. illus. ISBN 0-88192-153-X. $65. dictionary.
SB428.G45 635.97752

Conifers is a "visual dictionary, which represents a monumental amount of travel, thought, and aesthetic appreciation. The work contains 1,180 color photographs of common and rare needled evergreens.

"*Conifers* has a variety of uses. The images of overall forms will help landscape designers select plants and show clients how the plants look. Horticulturalists will use the close-ups of cones and twigs as visual keys in the identification and learning of conifers." (*Pub Gar,* January 1987, p. 21)

"Only 48 of the total 375 pages are devoted entirely to text but into them, van Gelderen has packed a lot of interesting and useful information. . . . [There is] a popular account of all the genera illustrated, with their countries of origin, and their uses, both ornamental and economic, followed by a list of species. For the more serious minded dendrologist and gardener there is also a *Summary of Characteristics of the Gymnosperms* plus an illustrated *Outline of Botanical Terms and Their Meanings,* and a *Botanical Key to the Coniferous Genera.*" (*Intl Dendrology Soc YB,* 1986, p. 127)

"Aesthetically, *Conifers* will appeal to anyone who has any eye for color or form. . . . The price is remarkably modest for the product." (*For Chron,* February 1987, p. 69)

"*Conifers* is an absolute must for anyone with a horticultural library." (*Pub Gar,* January 1987, p. 21)

Also reviewed in: *ARBA,* 1987, p. 584.

Board's recommendation: Public libraries.

Familiar Flowers of North America: Eastern Region. Richard Spellenberg. Knopf/Random House, 1986. soft. 1 vol. 192 pp. illus. index. ISBN 0-394-74843-3. $5.95. handbook.
QK110 582.13

Familiar Flowers of North America: Western Region. Richard Spellenberg. Knopf/Random House, 1986. soft. 1 vol. 192 pp. illus. index. ISBN 0-394-74844-1. $4.95. handbook.
QK133.F34 582.130978

"The nature guides sponsored by the Audubon Society have been of uniformly high quality. These [two volumes of *Flowers of North America*] are no exception.

"Each of these . . . pocket guides describes eighty of the most common wildflowers found in their respective regions. Entries are arranged by flower color and shape, with an excellent full-page color photograph of each species. On the opposite page are a description, the habitat and range, and a discussion of look-alike species and relatives.

"The author has been careful to include representative plants from all the important plant families, and the introductory material discusses how knowing the family characteristics is the key to more complete wildflower knowledge. The books also include a glossary and graphic material, which go a long way toward supplying the reader with that knowledge." (*ARBA,* 1988, p. 613)

Board's recommendation: Public libraries.

Familiar Trees of North America: Eastern Region. Ann H. Whitman, ed. Knopf/Random House, 1986. soft. 1 vol. 192 pp. illus. index. ISBN 0-394-74851-4. $5.95. handbook.
QK477 582.1609

Familiar Trees of North America: Western Region. Ann H. Whitman, ed. Knopf/Random House, 1986. soft. 1 vol. 192 pp. illus. index. ISBN 0-394-74852-2. $4.95. handbook.
QK477 582.1609

The two volumes of *Familiar Trees of North America* "are two guides in a new series of nature guides sponsored by the Audubon Society . . . and limited in coverage to sections of the United States and Canada. These . . . pocket-sized guides . . . contain beautiful color photographs showing a leaf cluster for each tree included. . . . Other identification aids are a small but good quality photograph of a tree's bark and a silhouette showing the adult tree. The brief printed descriptions are good . . . [and] include information on characteristics of the genus, specific information concerning height, diameter, foliage, and seeds. Habitat and range are given for every tree included. Common and scientific names are used and the index includes both in one alphabetical arrangement." (*ARBA,* 1988, p. 620)

Also reviewed in: *NH,* May 1987, p. 68.

Board's recommendation: Public libraries.

New and Noteworthy

American Horticultural Society Encyclopedia of Garden Plants. Christopher Brickell, ed. Macmillan, 1989. hard. 1 vol. 608 pp. illus. index. ISBN 0-02-557920-7. $49.95. encyclopedia.
SB403.2.A46 635.9'03

"The [*American Horticultural Society Encyclopedia of Garden Plants*] is arranged in two major sections: the 'Plant Catalog' and the 'Plant Dictionary.' The catalog . . . is arranged by plant type, size, season, and color. . . . The 'Plant Dictionary' is a guide to the characteristics and cultivation of more than 8,000 plants—the 4,000 listed in the 'Plant Catalog' and an additional 4,000." (*BL,* March 15, 1990, p. 1496)

The Encyclopedia of Wood: A Tree-by-Tree Guide to the World's Most Versatile Resource. Aidan Walker, ed. Facts On File, 1989. hard. 1 vol. 192 pp. illus. index. ISBN 0-8160-2159-7. $29.95. dictionary/encyclopedia.
TA419.E53 674.03

The Encyclopedia of Wood "has four major sections. The first is an excellent description of the living tree. . . . This is followed by a chapter on logging that points out some of its pitfalls and what is being done to correct these sometimes damaging operations. . . . The largest section of the book is the 'Directory of Wood' [where] seventy-five different woods are described. . . . [Finally, there is] 'The World of Wood,' where 19 of the woods are further described in terms of their uses, properties, and products manufactured." (*BL,* January 15, 1990, p. 1040)

Lawrence L. Irwin

British History

See also World History

Few countries have as rich a past as Great Britain. From the Battle of Hastings to the battle for the Falkland Islands, British history is full of significant and colorful places, people, events, and objects. The reference works in this category offer patrons in public, academic, and school libraries useful guides that cover these events as well as many other aspects that constitute a nation's history.

A good collection on British history would include volumes that cover the nation's entire history, touching on all the likely areas of interest to library users. The kinds of books the core collection should include are a historical encyclopedia that would include a definition of Magna Carta and the War of the Roses; a standard history of Anglo-Saxon or Victorian England; a biographical dictionary with entries for Beatrice Webb and Anthony Eden; and a bibliography suggesting additional sources for the study of Florence Nightingale and the Crimean War. A historical fact book should provide such details as an accurate chronology of the American Revolution or the members of William Gladstone's last administration. An atlas or historical encyclopedia with maps is needed to show the growth and decline of the British Empire and the campaigns of

Core Titles

	PUBLIC	ACADEMIC	SCHOOL
Bibliography of British History, 1789–1851 Brown, Lucy M., and Ian R. Christie, eds. Clarendon/Oxford, 1977		✦	
The Cambridge Historical Encyclopedia of Great Britain and Ireland Haigh, Christopher, ed. Cambridge, 1985		✦	✦
Dictionary of National Biography, 22 vols. Lord Blake, and C. S. Nicholls, eds. Oxford, 1986 (See Biography)	✦	✦	

World War II. A core collection in British history that includes these tools will be able to provide an answer to any likely question in British economic, cultural, or political history.

The core collection included here offers reference works that fulfill most of the aforementioned requirements. The DICTIONARY OF NATIONAL BIOGRAPHY has long set the international standard for biographical dictionaries that cover politicians, princesses, painters, and other leading national figures. For further biographical information, the patron may be directed to bibliographies, such as the BIBLIOGRAPHY OF BRITISH HISTORY, 1789–1851, which includes a variety of sources (such as original manuscripts, periodical articles, and books). The *British Historical Facts* series offers two or three monographs for each person and also includes information on other topics germane to British history. Unfortunately, this useful series has recently gone out of print, but libraries possessing copies should not discard them as the information remains topical.

In addition to information on particular persons, patrons will want information on trends, such as the Industrial Revolution or the effect of the Reformation and Counter-Reformation in England. Historical encyclopedias will provide information for both the micro and macro types of information needs. *The Oxford History of England,* another important work that is no longer in print, provides detailed discussions of the background causes and the course of such long-term events.

The *Historical Atlas of Britain* (Continuum, 1981; distrib. by Crossroad), originally chosen by the Board as a core work in this category, is no longer in print. Librarians will have to obtain a copy from out-of-print sources if they wish to add this work to their collections. The *Dictionary of British History* (Stein & Day, 1983), another fine reference work, is also no longer in print and presents similar acquisition problems.

Most of the core volumes take a general approach to British history. For additional insight, librarians might seek out the supplementary work THE LONGMAN HANDBOOK OF MODERN BRITISH HISTORY. However, the core works reviewed should be sufficient to meet the needs of most library patrons.

Core Titles

Bibliography of British History, 1789–1851. Lucy M. Brown and Ian R. Christie, eds. Clarendon/Oxford, 1977. hard. 759 pp. ISBN 0-19-822-390-0. $110. bibliography.
Z2019.B76 016.942073

The *Bibliography of British History: 1789–1851,* one of a distinguished series of volumes published by Oxford University Press, is one of the seminal books of British history and surely the premier bibliography for this time period. No other volume compares to this work in scope and coverage.

Editors Brown and Christie, leading British scholars, utilize their skills well in making a wide variety of materials (manuscripts, pamphlets, memoirs, hymnals, and others) available to the public. The user will find entries for famous men, such as *Wellington, Pitt, Darwin,* and the *Prince Consort.* There are numerous individual entries for noted women, such as *Mary W. Shelley, Queen Charlotte, Princess Charlotte,* and *Emma Hamilton* as well as citations for materials on Victorian women and women's rights and duties. There are also entries for *deer stalking,* the *Irish potato famine,* and the *Aborigines of New Zealand.* There are also references to works on British history from the perspective of the French, Spanish, Italians, Canadians, and Americans, cited in the original language. The bibliography is wonderful for putting all these subjects together under one cover. To be sure, there are uneven points in the volume, owing partly to greater publishing activity in certain areas such as law, economics, and religion. In general, works from Great Britain receive the primary emphasis. The volume is well organized and interesting just to browse through.

The bibliography is divided into 15 main sections, starting with a useful section entitled "General Reference Works," which includes the leading historical journals (British, American, and Canadian), guides to research libraries in several countries, and previous bibliographies relating to this subject. Following that section are broad subject headings, such as "Political History," "Military History," "Economic History," and "Cultural History," with other sections devoted to the British Empire (including India) as well as Ireland, Scotland, and Wales. The main sections are then subdivided into four further levels. This system allows one to find works on noted actor Edward Kean, John Cardinal Newman, General John Burgoyne, a French study of Waterloo, and so on. The editors' comments vary from a one-line review to several lines in smaller italic type noting further works on the subject. The entries are arranged in a single column, with an average of nine entries per page. Cross-references refer the reader to related entries. The section on literature (under "Cultural History") is restricted to main entries on works about noted authors, such as Dickens, with brief notes about the standard editions of the collected works and letters. The introduction, table of contents, cross-references, and index make accessing the 10,000 or so entries a pleasant task. The type is easy to read, and the binding is very sturdy.

One can understand why the Victorian Age and the British Empire are so often the object of study after looking through the multiplicity of resources listed in this fine bibliography. Although a researcher with access to manuscript collections in British libraries will be able to make maximum use of the *Bibliography of British History, 1789–1851,* many of the sources listed are available in most large academic libraries. The Board recommends this work for the core collection of academic libraries.

The Cambridge Historical Encyclopedia of Great Britain and Ireland. Christopher Haigh, ed. Cambridge, 1985. hard. 1 vol. 393 pp. illus. appendix. index. ISBN 0-521-25559-7 (hard); 0-521-39552-6 (soft). $44 (hard); $15.95 (soft). encyclopedia.
DA34.C28 941.00321

The Cambridge Historical Encyclopedia of Great Britain and Ireland is a recent addition to the esteemed ranks of Cambridge University Press encyclopedias. Christopher Haigh, editor of the encyclopedia, is a lecturer in modern history at Oxford and the author of several works on British history in the Tudor period. Additional editorial consultants and advisors, all professors at leading British and Irish universities, are listed opposite the title page.

The Cambridge Historical Encyclopedia is divided into seven main sections, along with an extremely useful "Who's Who" appendix. Signed "Overviews," written by distinguished contributors, provide a good survey of each period. Each period is discussed under several headings that remain constant through the work, such as "War and International Relations," "Economy," and "Culture." In addition, "Overview" sections trace the development of Wales, Ireland, and Scotland through the centuries. The text is augmented by 930 short summaries of events and institutions mentioned by name in the text. These summaries, three to five sentences in length, are set in smaller type than the main text and are placed in the margins. While the summaries tend to make the pages appear crowded, they add a great deal to the work's accessibility. The summaries cover a wide variety of topics, such as the Magna Carta, the Black Death, the Popish Plot, and the 1678 and 1944 Education Acts. The one full-color map and several black-and-white maps per "Overview" section cover a variety of subjects. In the "Britons and Romans" section, for example, there are at least six maps showing, among other subjects, Hadrian's Wall, the tribes of Britain, and Roman forts. In the same section are photos and illustrations of Roman roads and textiles, a "reconstruction" drawing of Roman soldiers and the Roman governor's palace in London, and a reconstruction of a Celtic fighting chariot.

The "Who's Who" appendix contains brief biographies of people discussed in this section, such as the Roman Emperor Hadrian and the British King Cunobelinus.

The overall accuracy of the volume is outstanding. The only drawbacks are the lack of pictures of all members of the British monarchy throughout the ages and the exclusion of cultural features, such as paintings by John Constable and William Turner (although both men are listed in the "Who's Who" appendix), and contemporary cultural icons, such as the Beatles. One assumes these exclusions are due to space limitations because the work of significant cultural figures such as George Stubbs, Josiah Wedgewood, and the Lake poets are mentioned, among others. However, modern culture receives only the briefest of discussions in general, with Al Jolson(!) being the only entertainer mentioned by name.

The index and several pages of further reading (divided by topic) add to the value of the encyclopedia. Students from high school on can use the book as a good introduction to the subject or to quickly check the identity of a person or place. Works such as the out-of-print *British Historical Facts* series and *The Oxford History of England* and the comprehensive DICTIONARY OF NATIONAL BIOGRAPHY should be used to supplement the volume.

Given the many courses on British history and culture, the Board recommends *The Cambridge Historical Encyclopedia of Great Britain and Ireland* for the core collections of academic and school libraries.

Dictionary of National Biography. Lord Blake and C. S. Nicholls, eds. Oxford, 1882–. hard. 22 vols. indexes. ISBN 0-19-865101-5 (set). $1,100 (set); $98 (per vol.). biographical source.
CT774 920.041

See Biography.

Supplementary Titles

The Longman Handbook of Modern British History, 1714–1986, 2d edition. Chris Cook and John Stevenson. Longman, 1988. soft. 1 vol. ISBN 0-582-48582-7. $20.50. handbook.
DA470C65 941.07

The Longman Handbook of Modern British History, 1714–1986 "attempts to bring together in a condensed form a wide range of information on politics, social and economic history, foreign affairs and religion. . . . [T]his handbook contains some valuable features . . . : a valuable chronology of political events, brief but informative studies of minor political parties, a useful glossary of terms, and a good bibliographical guide." (*Brit Bk N,* November 1983, p. 715)

Also reviewed in: *CRL,* January 1984, p. 54; *HRNB,* February 1984, p. 74; *HT,* April 1984, p. 51; *Sch Lib,* December 1983, p. 398; *TES,* January 6, 1984, p. 21.

Board's recommendation: Public and academic libraries.

New and Noteworthy

Atlas of Prehistoric Britain. John Manley. Oxford, 1989. hard. 1 vol. 160 pp. illus. index. ISBN 0-19-520807-2. $39.95. atlas.
GN805.M36 936.1

The *Atlas of Prehistoric Britain* "summarizes nearly one-half million years of prehistory in the four chapters covering circa 500,000 B.C. to A.D. 43 (the date of the final Roman invasion of Britain). Then follow two date charts, a highly selective list of sites to visit (museums, heritage centers, theme parks), and a brief list of significant texts and guidebooks on British prehistory. The detailed index pinpoints sites . . . , places . . . , and a diverse range of topics from *climate, diet,* and *fauna* to *pottery, tools,* and *weapons.*" (*BL,* February 15, 1990, p. 1184)

Atlas of the British Empire. C. A. Bayly, ed. Facts On File, 1989. hard. 1 vol. 256 pp. illus. index. ISBN 0-8160-1995-9. $40. atlas.
DA16.A8 912

The *Atlas of the British Empire* "contains 39 specially commissioned maps and more than 200 photographs. Illustrations include drawings, documents, and paintings, many of them in color, all of which enrich the text. . . . The book is arranged in five sections that describe the expansion and decline of the British Empire. . . . The table of contents lists 41 chapters, each of which is 3–4 pages in length; there is also a list of the maps." (*BL,* February 1, 1990, p. 1110)

The Cambridge Guide to the Historic Places of Britain and Ireland. Kenneth Hudson and Ann Nicholls. Cambridge, 1989. hard. 1 vol. 326 pp. illus. index. ISBN 0-521-36077-3. $29.95. handbook.
DA660.H89 914.104'858

The Cambridge Guide to the Historic Places of Britain and Ireland "describes more than 1,500 historic places in Great Britain and Ireland. . . . [The editors] have included the expected cathedrals, great houses, and archaeological remains, but have added canals, factories, state quarries, hotels, shops, prisons, cemetaries, clubs, battlefields, and homes of notable persons. There is a single alphabetical arrangement of towns and cities with the sites listed under the name of the nearest town. . . . Dates and hours of opening are listed. . . . Descriptions of each site follow; they are most readable, combining background information, description, and anecdotes." (*BL,* February 1, 1990, p. 1110)

Celia Hales-Mabry

British Literature

See also African Literature; Canadian History and Literature; World Literature

Librarians assembling a core reference collection in British literature are well served with a variety of first-class works. The core reference titles reviewed in this section fall into several categories.

Biographical dictionaries (such as BRITISH AUTHORS BEFORE 1800, BRITISH AUTHORS OF THE NINETEENTH CENTURY, and CONTEMPORARY NOVELISTS) give readers access to information about famous and little-known authors alike. Guides to criticism (such as CONTEMPORARY AUTHORS, MODERN BRITISH LITERATURE, and THE CRITICAL TEMPER: A SURVEY OF MODERN CRITICISM ON ENGLISH AND

Core Titles

GENERAL	PUBLIC	ACADEMIC	SCHOOL
British Authors Before 1800: A Biographical Dictionary Kunitz, Stanley J., and Howard Haycraft, eds. Wilson, 1952	✦	✦	✦
British Authors of the Nineteenth Century Kunitz, Stanley J., and Howard Haycraft, eds. Wilson, 1936	✦	✦	✦
British Writers, 8 vols, 1 suppl. Scott-Kilvert, Ian, gen. ed. Scribner, 1979–1984	✦	✦	
The Cambridge Guide to Literature in English Ousby, Ian, ed. Cambridge, 1988	✦	✦	
The Cambridge History of English Literature, 15 vols. Ward, A. W., and A. R. Waller, eds. Cambridge, 1908–1927; distrib. by UMI Demand		✦	
The Concise Oxford Dictionary of English Literature, 2d edition Eagle, Dorothy, ed. Oxford, 1970			✦

	PUBLIC	ACADEMIC	SCHOOL
Contemporary Authors: A Bio-Bibliographical Guide to Current Writers in Fiction, General Nonfiction, Poetry, Journalism, Drama, Motion Pictures, Television, and Other Fields, 129 vols. May, Hal, and Susan Trosky, eds. Gale, 1962– (See Biography)	✦	✦	✦
Contemporary Authors, New Revision series, 30 vols. May, Hal, and James J. Lesniak, eds. Gale, 1990– (See American Literature)	✦	✦	✦
Contemporary Literary Criticism: Excerpts from Criticism of the Works of Today's Novelists, Playwrights, and Other Creative Writers Gale, annual (1973–) (See World Literature)	✦	✦	
The Critical Temper: A Survey of Modern Criticism on English and American Literature from the Beginnings to the Twentieth Century, 3 vols., 2 suppls. Tucker, Martin, ed. Ungar, 1969–1989		✦	
Modern British Literature, 3 vols., 2 suppls. Temple, Ruth Z., and Martin Tucker, eds. Ungar, 1966–	✦	✦	
New Cambridge Bibliography of English Literature, 5 vols. Watson, George, ed. Cambridge, 1969–1977; rev. 1-vol. edition, 1987		✦	
The Oxford Companion to Australian Literature Wilde, William H., Joy Hooton, and Barry Andrews. Oxford, 1985		✦	
The Oxford Companion to Canadian Literature Toye, William, gen. ed. Oxford, 1983 (See Canadian History and Literature)	✦	✦	
The Oxford Companion to English Literature, 5th edition Drabble, Margaret, ed. Oxford, 1985	✦	✦	✦
The Oxford History of English Literature, 13 vols. Wilson, Frank Percy, and Bonamy Dobrée, eds. Oxford, 1945–		✦	

GENRE

	PUBLIC	ACADEMIC	SCHOOL
British Novelists 1600–1800, 1 vol. in 2 parts Battestin, Martin C., ed. Gale, 1985		✦	
Contemporary Dramatists, 4th edition Kirkpatrick, D. L., ed. St. James, 1988	✦	✦	
Critical Survey of Drama, English Language series, 6 vols., 1 suppl. Magill, Frank N., ed. Salem, 1985	✦	✦	
Critical Survey of Long Fiction, English Language series, 8 vols., 1 suppl. Magill, Frank N., ed. Salem, 1983 (See American Literature)	✦	✦	✦
Critical Survey of Short Fiction, 7 vols., 1 suppl. Magill, Frank N., ed. Salem, 1981 (See World Literature)	✦	✦	✦
Masterplots II, British and Commonwealth Fiction series, 4 vols. Magill, Frank N., ed. Salem, 1987	✦	✦	✦

AMERICAN LITERATURE FROM THE BEGINNINGS TO THE TWENTIETH CENTURY) excerpt reviews and critical essays on authors and their works, presenting the insights and opinions of important scholars and critics. "Companions," or guides to literature, generally use a short-entry format to give basic information on authors, books, literary characters, movements, and terms. Prominent among works of this type are THE CAMBRIDGE GUIDE TO LITERATURE IN ENGLISH and the various OXFORD COMPANIONS to Australian, Canadian, and English literature.

Histories or historical surveys are usually in narrative form and often occupy several volumes; they discuss the various periods and movements within British literature, with special attention to major authors and works in the context of their times. Ideally, a complete historical survey of British literature will follow the subject from Celtic or at least Saxon Britain through the post–World War II period. The multivolume CAMBRIDGE HISTORY OF ENGLISH LITERATURE and OXFORD HISTORY OF ENGLISH LITERATURE are the two premiere works of this kind.

General surveys (sometimes called "critical surveys," but not to be confused with guides to criticism or historical surveys) provide general synopses and descriptions of a wide range of literary works. Among titles of this kind are the CRITICAL SURVEY OF POETRY and the CRITICAL SURVEY OF DRAMA, both edited by Frank Magill.

Most important works in the British Literature category are still in print and available through their original publisher as reprints. However, *Contemporary Novelists* (D. L. Kirkpatrick, St. Martin's, 1986), which was chosen by the Board as a core work, and the *Reader's Encyclopedia of Shakespeare* (Oscar Campbell, Crown), which was chosen as a supplementary title, are no longer in print. Librarians may wish to obtain these works through out-of-print dealers.

There is inevitably some overlap among works in these various categories. However, this is not necessarily a drawback, nor does it render one work less useful than another.

The story of English—both as a language and as a body of literature written in that language—is a long, glorious, and complex one, as the works in this section testify. More than any other language, English has spread beyond the country of its origin to become the single most dominant language in the world today. In this context, the term *British literature* is often applied to literature in English written outside the geographical confines of the British Isles, most notably (but not only) in Ireland, Canada, and Australia as well as New Zealand, India, South Africa, and the West Indies, among other places. The distinction between British and world literature is no longer absolute; the blurring of this distinction is reflected in some reference titles. Readers of *Topical Reference Books* are reminded that several of the titles reviewed in the American Literature, Canadian Literature, and World Literature sections are germane to British literature. (Cross-reference entries are found in this section.) Some biographical dictionaries, for example, include American, British, and non-English-language authors under a single title. Moreover, reference books that address the technical aspects of literature—form, poetics, structure, and critical terms, for example—are as pertinent to British literature as they are to American or world literature. Additional literature of British Commonwealth writers can be found in African Literature and Latin American Literature.

School and academic librarians have much to choose from when it comes to compiling a collection of core reference titles for their particular institutions. Certain titles are appropriate either for researchers with a specialized interest (such as, for example, THE NEW CAMBRIDGE BIBLIOGRAPHY OF ENGLISH LITERATURE) or for junior high and high school readers with only a rudimentary knowledge, at best, of the subject (for example, MASTERPLOTS II: BRITISH AND COMMONWEALTH FICTION). Public librarians, on the other hand, usually serve a wide variety of patrons, from those with a casual or intermittent interest (such as general readers who may wish to satisfy a personal curiosity about their favorite authors from time to time) to those who may require more scholarly or in-depth resources (for example, professional writers doing research for a book or article). Needless to say, some sources that belong in a core public library collection will not be appropriate for all the patrons who consult that collection. The board members feel that the core titles reviewed here are of exceptional value and will suit the needs of the various types of patrons who consult reference works in British literature.

—*C. H.-M.*

With contributions by Martin E. Gingerich and Donna L. Singer.

Core Titles

General

British Authors Before 1800: A Biographical Dictionary. Stanley J. Kunitz and Howard Haycraft, eds. Wilson, 1952. hard. 1 vol. 584 pp. ISBN 0-8242-0006-3. $48. biographical dictionary.
PR105.K9 820.9

The biographical dictionaries edited by Kunitz and Haycraft have received critical acclaim, and *British Authors Before 1800* was added in 1952 to four biographical dictionaries published previously by H. W. Wilson. *British Authors Before 1800* covers a strikingly wide period of time. Some 650 authors, major and minor, were selected for inclusion. Bacon, Boswell, and Shakespeare are among the authors found in these pages. The sketches range from 300 to 1,500 words, roughly proportional to the importance of the author.

The entries are arranged alphabetically, and cross-references for pseudonyms are used when needed. Each essay gives pertinent biographical and critical information and is followed by a list of principal works by the author and a list of selected secondary resources.

The writing style is similar to other volumes in the Wilson Author series by Kunitz and Haycraft: anecdotal, chatty, detailed, but sparkling with originality and wit. *Library Journal* gives some credit to the authors themselves as a "diversified and cantankerous lot," adding that their "life-histories often make very stimulating reading." But, of course, it is the editors' ideas about style in biographical dictionaries that make all of this "stimulating reading" possible.

Black-and-white portraits accompany 220 of the longer biographies. Concerning these portraits, the preface states: "a special effort was made to discover authentic and representative portrayals of the subjects." The portraits were "taken from life," and "fanciful or imaginary depictions were shunned." This becomes quite a feat with authors prior to 1800. Again the editors have chosen wisely, an attention to detail making their contribution all the more worthwhile.

British Authors Before 1800 is a fine one-volume reference that is interesting and informative. It contains some authors not always included in more recent single-volume references (for example, Mary Wollstonecraft Godwin, who is not in the 5th edition of THE OXFORD COMPANION TO ENGLISH LITERATURE). The material is not out of date, but the user will want to consult more recently published reference books for current secondary resources, especially for the major authors.

Library Quarterly suggested that *British Authors Before 1800: A Biographical Dictionary* belongs particularly in small libraries that lack the DICTIONARY OF NATIONAL BIOGRAPHY (see Biography), the *Cambridge Bibliography of English Literature,* or *Britannica.* The Board recommends this work for the core collections of public, academic, and school libraries.

—C. H.-M.

British Authors of the Nineteenth Century. Stanley J. Kunitz and Howard Haycraft, eds. Wilson, 1936. hard. 1 vol. 677 pp. ISBN 0-8242-0007-1. $50. biographical dictionary.
PR451.K8 820.9

British Authors of the Nineteenth Century contains biographical essays on approximately 1,000 literary figures, both major and minor, of this period. The rubric "British authors" covers not only writers from the British Isles but also English-language authors from the then British colonies of Canada, Australia, South Africa, and New Zealand.

Authors were included on the basis of their contribution to belles lettres, but there is also a representative sample of writers of nonliterary works that had a major impact on the life of the time. Among the authors included are Byron, the Brontës, and Tennyson. The focus is on the nineteenth century, as the title indicates, although some writers who lived well into the twentieth century are included because their most important works were produced before 1900. A case in point is the inclusion of Thomas Hardy, who is variously regarded as a late Victorian, an early modern, or a transitional literary figure. Although most of his poetry and two of his dramas appeared after the turn of the century, he is included with the nineteenth-century authors because his major novels were published prior to 1900.

The typical entry details the author's life, giving insight into the person's thoughts and ideas, as with Charlotte Brontë, who "disliked children" and "hated the monotony and drudgery" of being a teacher and governess. Major literary works are noted but not discussed in any great depth. Principal works and selected secondary sources are listed at the end of each entry.

Scholars will note that, as a review in *Commonweal* pointed out, "Not all the desirable information is provided, and there are numerous errors of detail." An example of this difficult-to-prove factual detail is the assertion in the sketch on John Keats of a conflict in celebrating his birthday: "The official register shows October 31 [1795], but Keats himself always observed the 29th." In this case, Kunitz and Haycraft are right, but the unsuspecting reader would have no way of knowing how accurate his or her favorite anecdote from this volume might be.

Some early reviewers noted the editors' lively and subjective opinions. These are even more apparent today. An example of this subjectivity can be found in the entry on Thomas Hardy, which details Hardy's realization that *Tess of the D'Urbervilles* was "strong meat for the conventional tastes of that stodgy era." Therefore, "he had to mutilate the story badly for magazine publication," later restoring its "shattered limbs" for reissue in book form. Similarly, the boy Keats is called "generous but extremely pugnacious," and the man Keats is called "the incarnation of the romantic spirit." Bits of his poetry are quoted, giving the reader a sense of this spirit of the romantic in Keats.

Most students would find criticism dating from 1936 to be of limited usefulness today. Thus, the passing of time has diminished the value of the list of secondary resources given at the end of each entry, but the list of primary or principal works of each author remains accurate and worthwhile.

It is a monument to the originality and scholarship of Kunitz and Haycraft that *British Authors of the Nineteenth Century* remains a major biographical dictionary. As evidenced by the copyright date of 1936, it has stood the test of time, and it set the format for later works in the publisher's Authors series. For concise and interesting background on the British literary giants (and some of the smaller folk) of the nineteenth century, it is unsurpassed. The Board recommends this work for the core collections of public, academic, and school libraries. —*C. H.-M.*

British Writers. Ian S. Scott-Kilvert, gen. ed. Scribner, 1979–1984. hard. 8 vols. plus 1 suppl. index. ISBN 0-684-18253-X (set); 0-684-18612-8 (suppl.). $625 (set); $85 (suppl.). biographical source.
PR85.B688 820.9

British Writers was designed to complement AMERICAN WRITERS (see American Literature), a six-volume set first published in 1974 and based upon a series of pamphlets published by the University of Minnesota. *British Writers* is based upon a series of separate articles initiated by the British Council in 1950 titled *Writers and Their Work.* In 1980, *Choice* counseled that this set was not needed if the separate articles were held by the library; in the years since, however, the original works have become less widely available. Thus, the place of this set in any reference collection has grown in importance with the publication of each succeeding volume in the set.

Authors were selected for inclusion in *British Writers* not on the basis of completeness or uniformity in presentation, but rather "to provide an introduction to the work of writers who have made a significant contribution to English literature. . . ." Thus, each contributor "sets out to explain what are the qualities that make an author worth reading" (introduction, all volumes). An important criterion for selecting current authors represented in supplement 1 was the "quality of critical attention that a given writer has attracted" (introduction, supplement 1).

There are a maximum of 25 essays per volume, with each volume bounded by significant dates (volume 7 ends with World War II and supplement 1 begins with the postwar writers). Some overlapping occurs chronologically, as with Graham Greene, who wrote both before and after World War II but is included only in supplement 1. Special features in each volume include an introduction detailing the scope of the volume, a chronological table, a list of contributors with their credentials, and a selected bibliography after each entry. Some of the introductions in the later volumes are quite lengthy, placing the representative authors within the larger context of literary, historical, and social movements.

The arrangement of the writers in the set is chronological by date of birth. The volumes can be a bit clumsy to use; the authors discussed within each volume are listed on the spine of the book in chronological, not alphabetical, order.

Not an encyclopedia or a literary history, *British Writers* is much more of an appreciation written by enthusiasts for their individual writer favorites. Writers from the fourteenth to the twentieth centuries are included in the series. According to the preface, the set is not meant to establish a canon of the "greats," although how this can be avoided is not entirely clear. The essays are informative in tone, not critical, and are written by many of the most outstanding critics and literary figures of this century. These contributors (such as Donald Coggan, the former Archbishop of Canterbury, writing on the English Bible, and Stanley Wells, head of the Shakespeare Department of Oxford University Press, writing on Shakespeare) ensure the high standard of scholarship. There is a diversity of critical approaches, from Nevill Coghill's selection on Chaucer, which focuses on medieval civilization as related to Chaucer's works, to Frank Kermode's essay on John Donne, which stresses the analysis of Donne's poetry. Most selections have numerous quotations from the author's works to illustrate points.

The brilliance of the critics, each a recognized scholar (an "expert," if you will) on his or her writer, ensures that errors will be of tone—too much enthusiasm for the writer and his or her place in history—not ignorance of the subject.

The thoroughness and scholarship that is the hallmark of this series is exemplified by Stanley Wells's essay on Shakespeare. In his discussion of the publication of Shakespeare's works, Wells focuses on the "often unreliable and conflicting evidence" of what Shakespeare actually wrote as revealed in the early printed editions of his works. The essay also includes sections on "Shakespeare in Performance" and "Shakespeare's Critics" (vol. 1).

Some biographical discussion is included in each essay, but the primary feature is an analysis of the works—analytical, but not critical, as mentioned above. Each essay averages about 15 pages in length and concludes with a bibliography of editions of the works as well as secondary sources. There is a separate index volume that lists exhaustively each mention of a name as well as each mention of a work.

British Writers is meant to serve the student of literature foremost—and, in particular, the undergraduate who needs background information on his or her assigned British author. Because of its tendency to discuss without drawing critical conclusions, the set has become a favorite of librarians who deal with undergraduates lacking a grounding in the fundamentals and needing help before proceeding to other sources. The Board recommends this work for the core collections of public and academic libraries. —*C. H.-M.*

The Cambridge Guide to Literature in English. Ian Ousby, ed. Cambridge, 1988. hard. 1 vol. 1,109 pp. illus. index. ISBN 0-521-26751-X. $39.50. handbook.
PR85.C29 820.9

According to the editor's note, *The Cambridge Guide to Literature in English* is designed "to provide a handy reference guide to the literature in English produced by all the various English-speaking cultures." This reference fulfills its purpose quite effectively with three main types of entries: entries for authors, many of whom are still publishing; entries for major individual works; and entries for critical concepts, genres, literary movements, and so on. Neither works in translation nor those by non-English writers are covered, although the latter may be mentioned in entries on literary movements or concepts. As a major exception, significant works of medieval literature originally written in Latin, Anglo-Norman, or Gaelic are included because they "influenced" or "flourished beside" literature in English, according to the editor's note.

The entries are listed in alphabetical order, with headings for authors, terms, and movements appearing in boldface type, and headings for titles in boldface italic type. Writers who are best known under their pseudonyms (such as George Eliot) are listed under those names rather than their real names. For each author entry, basic biographical data and major works are given, whereas for entries on literary works, synopses are given without critical comment. Other types of entries (for example, *schools of criticism*) contain a basic identification and description. Entries vary in length from 5 lines to 5½ pages (for the entry on *libraries*).

This comprehensive, up-to-date reference contains entries that cover such diverse writers as American children's author Frank Baum, South African novelist Alan Paton, and contemporary poets Dorothy Livesay (Canada) and Okot p'Bitek (Uganda). Readers can also find information on such diverse items as the Royal Shakespeare Company or Lincoln Center for the Performing Arts, and such literary terms as *anagnorsis* and *ottava rima.* There is even an entry for Herman Melville's book of poems on the Civil War *(Battle-Pieces and Aspects of the War).*

Though the size of this reference is a bit cumbersome, the typeface is easy to read, and the organization of material and numerous cross-references make it easily accessible to the general reader as well as to the student of literature. Some 300 illustrations, and the foreword by Canadian novelist and poet Margaret Atwood on the variety of the English language add to the usefulness of the reference. *The Cambridge Guide* appears to be very accurate and authoritative; a list of contributors is given, but their specific qualifications are not presented.

The Cambridge Guide to Literature in English is an excellent reference source with a somewhat broader scope than THE OXFORD COMPANION TO ENGLISH LITERATURE. It includes some authors that THE OXFORD COMPANION doesn't (such as black American poet Claude McKay), yet other authors found in THE OXFORD COMPANION (biographer Michael Holroyd for one) are missing. However, THE OXFORD COMPANION and *The Cambridge Guide* do complement each other.

The Board recommends this work for the core collections of public and academic libraries. —*D. L. S.*

The Cambridge History of English Literature. A. W. Ward and A. R. Waller, eds. Cambridge, 1908–1927; distrib. by UMI Demand. hard and soft. 15 vols. $113 (vol. 15, hard); $107 (vol. 15, soft). history.
PR83.C2 820.9

A classic, *The Cambridge History of English Literature,* available through UMI Demand in a number of reprints at varying prices, deserves a place in all comprehensive collections that support English literature. Written over a period of about 20 years up to 1927, the 14 volumes of the history proper are a treasure trove for the serious student of literature. Entries cover the breadth of English literature from *Beowulf* to the end of the Victorian age, the lesser-known figures as well as the greats, and are supported by bibliographies that drew the unanimous praise of critics when the series was first published.

The Cambridge History of English Literature is organized according to successive movements of literature within a general framework of chronological history. As the editors stated in the preface (vol. 1), the series would present writers of primary and secondary importance, and include discussion of the interaction between foreign literatures and the developing English literature, "unfettered by any preconceived notions of artificial eras or controlling dates." Thus, the volumes have headings such as "Renaissance and Reformation" (vol. 3), "The Drama to 1642" (vol. 5), and "Cavalier and Puritan" (vol. 7).

The writers used quite a bit of restraint in their analyses, careful to a fault to avoid error (which drew the praise of series editors Ward and Waller in the last volume). It is clear that the editors similarly chose caution over controversy, and in a work that supports the serious student in research at the graduate school level, the choice is fortuitous.

The extent to which the contributors went to achieve a balanced discussion can be seen in George Saintsbury's essay on Shakespeare (vol. 5). He prefaced his presentation of Shakespeare's life with a careful discussion of fact versus supposition, ending with the statement that "the following summary will give the certain facts with those which are generally accepted as the most probable, distinguishing the two classes, so far as is possible, . . . but avoiding altogether mere guesswork, unless it has assumed such proportions in ordinary accounts that it cannot be passed by."

It is difficult to evaluate the degree of expertise of the various authors at this distance in time. Some early critics faulted the editors for failing to attract more essays by the truly outstanding scholars of the era. The result of their labors was said to be more of a reference tool than a genuine history; certainly time has proved this to be correct, as every reference librarian in a research collection well knows.

The flavor of the various periods is given in some depth, thanks to the emphasis upon lesser figures. Editors Ward and Waller indicated that their rationale for this was "to consider subsidiary movements and writers . . . and to trace, in apparently arid periods, processes which were often carried on, as it were, underground" (volume 1, preface). Biography is not overlooked, nor is critical commentary on sample passages, which are quoted briefly by some of the scholars. As a point of departure, the serious student may read the essays and then give attention to the excellent bibliographies, which are still a truly outstanding feature. The essays remain accurate—a fact that will delight any budding scholar who faces orals.

The work also has the virtue of easy accessibility. Volume 15 consists of a comprehensive index of the whole set as well as an abbreviated table of contents, a useful feature that is easy for the casual reader to overlook.

Although twentieth-century British literature is not included in the set, *The Cambridge History of English Literature* remains the definitive "history" of English literature. The Board recommends this work for the core collection of academic libraries. —*C. H.-M.*

The Concise Oxford Dictionary of English Literature, 2d edition. Dorothy Eagle, ed. Oxford, 1970. hard and soft. 1 vol. 638 pp. ISBN 0-19-886108-8 (hard); 0-19-881233-7 (soft). $35. (hard); $10.95 (soft). dictionary.
PR19.C65 820.3

The Concise Oxford Dictionary of English Literature, 2d edition, takes as its point of departure THE OXFORD COMPANION TO ENGLISH LITERATURE. In this instance, the work is based upon the fourth edition of the larger work, copyright 1967. A fifth edition of THE OXFORD COMPANION has now been published (1985), and so a revision of *The Concise Oxford Dictionary of English Literature*, published in 1970, may follow eventually.

The work is arranged alphabetically by subject; there are no indexes or appendixes. Authors' names are in boldface upper- and lowercase type, while titles of literary works are in boldface italics. Real people and fictional characters are entered under their surnames, in most cases. (Further explanation of the format is given in a note at the beginning of the volume.) Cross-references are adequate. A handy little volume in paperback as well as hardcover and measuring only 5 by 7½ inches, this is good as a student's reference, easy to use, and convenient to carry about.

The Concise Oxford Dictionary follows a format similar to that of THE OXFORD COMPANION. All of the principal entries on authors, works, and so on that appeared in the fourth edition of that work have been included here, and there are new entries for authors who have become "established" since the original publication of the COMPANION and the *Concise* (for example, Samuel Beckett). As the editor, Dorothy Eagle, states in the preface, articles on general literary topics have been revised to reflect the research and developments in the 30 years since the original volume (such literary movements as Imagism and stream of consciousness have been added). What is missing in this volume is the tone of Harvey's original COMPANION, his astute asides and personal creative touch. This dictionary contains the bare bones; it is complete (as far as its "concise" format permits) and efficient to use, but it is also dry and impersonal. Yet, in addition to the main works and figures of English literature, the reader will still find such unlikely entries at *Gettysburg, Hocus-pocus, Scheherazade,* and *Trojan.*

Abridgement does have its drawbacks. The entry for *King Lear,* for example, is barely a column and a half, and the outline of the play is so brief as to be misleading to some readers. Lear is said to "die from grief," which is true, but what is left unsaid speaks volumes; the reader must go to the play itself and other secondary sources in order to understand character motivation and layers of meaning. In the abridgement, unlike the entry for *King Lear* in the COMPANION, little is done except summation, and the loss of meaningful, though brief, analysis is a major one in a book that purports to accompany the reading and study of literature.

The entry for John Keats is similarly truncated. Little more than a chronology, this entry gives only the briefest summary of his life experiences ("In the same year he nursed his brother Tom until his death.") in addition to his major works and their dates. The entry on Shakespeare is concise, with brief mention given to Shakespeare's early life but with no mention of the controversy over authorship of the plays and poems. However, there is an entry, *Shakespeare-Bacon controversy* (which is cross-referenced to *Baconian theory*), that does briefly state one of the controversial theories of authorship.

For libraries that do not hold THE OXFORD COMPANION, *The Concise Oxford Dictionary of English Literature* is a good choice. The prices of hardcover editions of the two books, however, would suggest that one might well forego this briefer version and opt for the complete work. This concise dictionary fulfills a need for an authoritative, basic reference tool which is easy to use. The Board recommends this work for school libraries. —*C. H.-M.*

Contemporary Authors: A Bio-Bibliographical Guide to Current Writers in Fiction, General Nonfiction, Poetry, Journalism, Drama, Motion Pictures, Television, and Other Fields. Hal May and Susan Trosky, eds. Gale, 1962–. hard. 129 vols. 503 pp. index in even-numbered volumes. ISBN 0-8103-1954-3 (vol. 129). approx. $99 per vol. biobibliography.
PN771.C66X 810.9

See Biography.

Contemporary Authors, New Revision series. Hal May and James J. Lesniak, eds. Gale, 1990. hard. 30 vols. index in even-numbered volumes. ISBN 0-8103-1984-5 (vol. 30). approx. $99 per vol. biobibliography.
Z1224.C62X 803

See American Literature.

Contemporary Literary Criticism: Excerpts from Criticism of the Works of Today's Novelists, Poets, Playwrights, and Other Creative Writers. Gale, annual (1973–). hard. 58 vols. illus. indexes. ISBN 0-8103-4432-7 (vol. 58). approx. $99 per vol. criticism.
PN771.C59 809

See World Literature.

The Critical Temper: A Survey of Modern Criticism on English and American Literature from the Beginnings to the Twentieth Century. Martin Tucker, ed. Ungar, 1969–1989. hard. 3 vols plus 2 suppls. 1,704 pp. index. ISBN 0-804-4330-8 (set). $225 (set); approx. $75 per suppl. criticism.
PR85.C77 820.C934

If a collection of selected critical excerpts is desired, *The Critical Temper: A Survey of Modern Criticism on English and American Literature from the Beginnings to the Twentieth Century* is a mandatory title. Martin Tucker is the editor of the A Library of Literary Criticism series, published by Ungar, of which this work is a part. *The Critical Temper* covers English and American literature for the entire period from beginnings to 1900.

Selections were made by a panel of scholars who are acknowledged in the volumes. This is an excellent feature that is missing in others in the series, notably the MODERN BRITISH LITERATURE. As the foreword says, *The Critical Temper* is thus a "record of the taste of modern critics as well as a source for study of the writers included." The four volumes are arranged by literary periods, and within these divisions, alphabetically by author. The authors and works are indeed the principal ones that one would expect to find in a comprehensive sweep of the centuries. *Beowulf* is here, and John Greenleaf Whittier concludes the fourth volume, a supplement published in 1979 that updates various authors covered in the previous volumes and covers a few authors left out of the original volumes (Mary Shelley, Kate Chopin, among others). A second supplement was issued in 1989.

At the head of each entry, the editors have briefly characterized the life of the author and have given bibliographic references. Within the body of the entry, the author's works are taken up in alphabetical order, with the excerpted criticism in chronological order, excepting the concluding "general" criticism. In volumes 3 and 4 there are cross-reference indexes to authors and critics. The cross-reference index to authors is arranged alphabetically according to the author's last name, with the name of the author section referred to in parentheses, followed by volume number and page number.

The foreword to volume 1 states that the reference work attempts to reflect "quality and controversy" in its selection of critical excerpts, rather than quantity of an author's appearance in critical works. Therefore, the great variation in the extent of coverage from one author to another is due in part to the fact that some authors, such as John Donne, have provoked less controversy than others, such as Lord Byron; thus, fewer critical points of view need to be represented for Donne. The vast diversity of opinion, however, is amply represented by the criticism, culled from a wide choice of reviews, periodicals, and books.

The Critical Temper succeeds in its intention to present a "panoramic view of the best of twentieth-century criticism on English and American literature. . . ." and simultaneously "show the wide range of thought and perceptiveness within that criticism" (foreword, volume 1). It is also successful in its choice of writers to represent the vast sweep of literature in the English language—British and American. This work will be of particular value to libraries where backfiles of periodicals are limited.

The Board recommends this work for the core collection of academic libraries. —*C. H.-M.*

Modern British Literature. Ruth Z. Temple and Martin Tucker, eds. Ungar, 1966– . 3 vols. plus 2 suppls. 1,442 pp. (set); 664 pp. (suppl. 1, vol. 4); 681 pp. (suppl. 2, vol. 5). ISBN 0-8044-3275-9 (set); 0-8044-3279-1 (vol. 4); 0-8044-3140-X (vol. 5). $225 (set); $75 (vol. 4); $75 (vol. 5). criticism.
PR473.T4 820.9

It is particularly fortunate to have excerpts from the best criticism of recent times in a modern reference collection. *Modern British Literature,* part of the Library of Literary Criticism series, is intended as a sequel to Charles Wells Moulton's classic *Library of Literary Criticism of English and American Authors.* The introduction states its purpose succinctly: "For each of the authors included, excerpts from criticism have been chosen to describe his qualities, define his status, indicate, if he is well known, something of his life and personality, and specify, if he is notable otherwise than as author, his other pursuits."

On the whole this work has stood the test of time. Any choice of criticism is likely to be controversial, but editors Temple and Tucker were judicious in their choice. They selected from a wide range of sources, both British and American: reviews, periodical articles, general books, books on particular authors. Moreover, with two supplements, the work has been kept up to date. The first volume was published in 1966; the fifth volume in 1985. This work is revised extensively every two years.

The special features of the five-volume set are noteworthy. The introduction is a helpful overview of intent and practice. For the first three volumes, published as a set, the authors to be included are listed at the beginning.

The authors are arranged alphabetically within each volume, and the critical selections on each author are arranged chronologically. Full reference is made to the original sources of criticisms, and a complete index to critics, as well as a cross-reference index to authors, can be found at the end of volume 2.

In general, "British," in this set, means English, Irish, Welsh, or Scottish writers or those of Commonwealth—or former Commonwealth—origin who have lived mainly in the British Isles. Many of the writers chosen are not household names. The variation in the amount of coverage from one author to another partially results from the "difference in the authors' output, ... and reputation" (introduction, volume 1). The length of selections may reveal the fluctuation of literary reputations; hence, E. M. Forster merits about 12 pages in volume 1, but only receives half that amount in the volume 4 supplement. Another reason for this variation in length is that some authors have provoked less controversy than others; thus, fewer critical viewpoints need to be presented (for example, W. Somerset Maugham receives 8 pages of criticism while the more controversial D. H. Lawrence receives over 20 pages). On the whole, however, the criticism is well balanced and fair, although more laudatory than analytical.

The volume 4 supplement aims (1) to bring criticism up to date on approximately one-third of the authors included in the original three-volume set; and (2) to add other writers (49 in number) who have come to critical attention since 1965, such as Tom Stoppard and John Fowles. The emphasis in this volume is more on American critical sources than in the original set in order to reflect the increased role of American critics and scholars in interpreting contemporary British writing.

The volume 5 supplement contains 11 new writers, some writers dropped from the previous supplement but now included due to renewed interest in their works, and new and updated bibliographies for all entries selected. Of particular interest is the inclusion of criticisms by such highly regarded authors as Margaret Drabble and Kingsley Amis.

Modern British Literature has a place in comprehensive collections that are likely to own Moulton's *Library of Literary Criticism.* For smaller collections, the more concise THE CRITICAL TEMPER would be a more likely purchase choice. As a compendium of criticism gleaned from a variety of sources to represent differing viewpoints, however, *Modern British Literature* works well. The Board recommends this work for the core collections of public and academic libraries.

—*C. H.-M.*

New Cambridge Bibliography of English Literature. George Watson, ed. Cambridge, 1969–1977; rev. edition, 1987. hard. 5 vols. index. ISBN 0-521-34378-X. $420 (set). bibliography.
Z2011.N45 016.82

The *New Cambridge Bibliography of English Literature* is based upon the acclaimed *Cambridge Bibliography of English Literature* (Cambridge, 1940, followed by a supplement in 1957). In the editor's preface to the 1969–1977 set, the parent work is declared, along with the *Oxford English Dictionary,* the "greatest of all reference books in English studies." Deference is paid the original, and it is clear that format and content closely parallel the older set. As bibliography, the *Cambridge Bibliography* and the *New Cambridge Bibliography* are without equal.

The *New Cambridge Bibliography* comes in five volumes (the fifth an index), and revises, updates, and integrates the listings for the parent work. The political and social background of the era were deleted from the new work as being more appropriate to bibliographies of literary histories. Otherwise, the selection is very similar. Such categories of material as dissertations, reviews of secondary works, encyclopedia articles, and so on, are excluded. Both primary and secondary material are listed, of course—the works of the author, in all editions, and the criticism (with the exceptions noted above). Organization is by genre, which is one of the most distinguishing features of both the original and this new edition.

The index (volume 5) lists primary authors and major anonymous works, certain headings in the parent work, plus several other categories of lesser importance. The index is particularly helpful because the *New Cambridge Bibliography* remains difficult to use as a quick reference source. It is necessary to use the table of contents in conjunction with the index. The editors found this a "distinguishing" fact (because genre divisions are retained), but this requires the reader to examine the table of contents in order to use the index successfully.

Although the *New Cambridge Bibliography* is still important, the fact remains that between 10 and 20 years have now intervened between the publication of the various volumes and the current day. This makes these volumes less useful than a few years ago, in much the same way that the volumes under discussion were needed to update the original. Cambridge University Press has published a one-volume 1987 edition of this work, but it is currently unavailable from the publisher. Therefore, Cambridge was unable to provide a review copy for this buying guide.

The *New Cambridge Bibliography of English Literature* belongs as a historical source on the shelves of academic libraries. This is a title that faculty members who teach English literature will pass along to their students, and it is a title that is worthy of all serious reference collections. The Board recommends this work for the core collection of academic libraries.

—*C. H.-M.*

The Oxford Companion to Australian Literature. William H. Wilde, Joy Hooton, and Barry Andrews. Oxford, 1985. hard. 1 vol. 760 pp. ISBN 0-19-554233-9. $49.95. dictionary.
PR96043 820.9

The Oxford Companion to Australian Literature is a well-researched work on a literary tradition that is still developing. Like other "companions" published by Oxford University Press, this work is arranged alphabetically by topic, with topics ranging from literary works to authors to national trends, as well as some characters in the fiction, historical, and cultural entries that give basic information on Australian life. Also, some overseas writers who visited Australia (Robert Louis Stevenson, for one) or who exerted significant influence (for example, Dickens, Shakespeare) are included.

Australia has a young tradition, and therefore this book includes living writers. Because the writers are still producing, it will be necessary not only to update *what* they have produced but also to reevaluate their contributions to Australia's canon in the near future.

There are over 3,000 entries, most of which are brief, but some are quite lengthy, especially those on important themes (the role of the bushranger and the role of the aborigine in Australian literature are examples). Written in a lively tone, this *Oxford Companion* gives an overview of the life and culture of the country, with such diverse entries as *billabong* (a water hole), the song, "*Waltzing Matilda,*" the *great Australian adjective* ("bloody"), and such aboriginal words as *waratah* (a bright flowering shrub). There is even an entry on the famous race horse, Phar Lap. At the beginning of the volume is a list of abbreviations used, and a note on the format of the *Companion.* The names of authors and other persons are in boldface capitals, while literary works appear in upper- and lowercase boldface italics, making for easy reading and scanning. There are no bibliographies, indexes, or other accompanying material, but the whole is remarkably comprehensive for a work of this type. Acknowledgment for the authority of this work is given primarily to the *Australian Dictionary of Biography,* E. Morris Miller's bibliography of Australian literature, and specialist studies by individual authors. In addition, an extensive list of additional credits is given in the preface. Some entries are signed by the contributor (the entry on poet Peter Porter was written by Jeff Doyle).

The Oxford Companion to Australian Literature contains entries on writers who have received international recognition, such as Colleen McCullough *(The Thorn Birds),* Morris West *(The Devil's Advocate),* Nancy Cato *(All the Rivers Run),* and the 1973 Nobel Prize winner, Patrick White *(The Eye of the Storm),* as well as selections on authors known primarily within Australia, such as Jack Hibberd (whose play *Dimboola* "has become part of the national folklore.").

The treatment of one popular writer, "Nevil Shute" (Nevil Shute Norway) is representative of the approach of the book. Shute is given not only a listing for himself but also an entry for *A Town Like Alice,* one of his better-known works. Analysis is kept limited, with a recitation of the main facts of his life and a chronology of his works receiving attention. The entry for *Alice* is limited to summation. Consequently, readers will be disappointed if looking for unusual insight. The whole work is conservative in approach, as would befit a volume in which living writers (Shute is an exception) are represented. Although not exclusively a biographical dictionary, most of the entries are for authors, which will be helpful because information on Australian individuals in other sources is quite limited.

Since so many Australian authors are gaining international acclaim, and Australian colloquialisms (such as "sheila" and "walkabout") are finding their way into the common pool of spoken English, it is important that a comprehensive work such as this volume be readily available. *The Oxford Companion to Australian Literature* is a scholarly reference tool. The Board recommends this work for the core collection of academic libraries. —*C. H.-M.*

The Oxford Companion to Canadian Literature. William Toye, gen. ed. Oxford, 1983. hard. 1 vol. 864 pp. ISBN 0-19-540283-9. $49.95. dictionary.
PS8015.C93 810.32

See Canadian History and Literature.

The Oxford Companion to English Literature, 5th edition. Margaret Drabble, ed. Oxford, 1985. hard. 1 vol. 1,168 pp. ISBN 0-19-866130-4. appendix. $45. dictionary.
PR19.D73 820.321

Margaret Drabble, English novelist, critic, and the editor of this fifth edition of *The Oxford Companion to English Literature,* has striven to remain true to the vision that inspired the original editor, Sir Paul Harvey. Drabble is conscious of the central place that *The Oxford Companion* has occupied for countless students and scholars, and this awareness surely has helped to dictate the judicious changes that she has made.

In its current edition, *The Oxford Companion* has been updated to include newly accepted genres, such as science fiction and detective stories, and new literary movements, such as structuralism. Many new entries on composers who have adapted English texts to music (like Prokofiev), and visual artists inspired by literary works (Henry Fuseli, inspired by Shakespeare and Milton) have also been added. Some more recent foreign-language authors who are well known in translation (such as Albert Camus and Hermann Hesse) have also been included, although these authors are not part of the English literary tradition.

The entries are organized alphabetically. Main entry words that are the names of actual people are in boldface capital letters, while others (including fictional characters) are in boldface upper- and lowercase type. Titles of novels, plays, and other full-length works are in italics. The entries vary in length from two lines for *Aaron the Moor* to three pages for *The Canterbury Tales,* but the length by no means indicates importance, as Drabble notes in her preface. Following is an example of a typical entry: "Morddure, in Spenser's

Faerie Queene (II. viii. 20-1), the name of the sword made by Merlin for Prince Arthur. Its more general name is *Excalibur." A cross-reference to another entry is shown by an asterisk.

The Oxford Companion provides easy accessibility to information with its alphabetizing system, a list of abbreviations used, and extensive cross-referencing (as previously mentioned, indicated by an asterisk), making an index unnecessary.

This much-loved volume has been gracefully updated to include authors born in 1939 and before. The absence of younger writers is a disappointment, although it is justified because these writers' significance cannot yet be determined. Many of the more common literary allusions from earlier editions, such as *piece of eight* and *the devil,* have been eliminated. (The reader is now referred to other, more specialized works such as Brewer's *Dictionary of Phrase and Fable.*) The majority of the entries have been rewritten to consider the most recent literary scholarship and contemporary trends, a fact that makes the 1939 cutoff not only disappointing but also perplexing. The volume focuses primarily on British authors and their works but also includes some American, Commonwealth, and foreign-language author entries, particularly when the authors cited are British favorites. Among the latter are Margaret Atwood, Alan Paton, and Teilhard de Chardin. Henry James and T. S. Eliot are considered British authors in this work.

Other changes that have been made improve the clarity of presentation as, for example, Drabble's characterization of *realism* as "a literary term so widely used as to be more or less meaningless. . . ." She is not merely controversial, as in the inclusion of *the Beatles* and *comics* as entries, however; because she has chosen to be more courageous than the restrained Harvey, the companion has benefited from her editorship and is a more comprehensive work than its predecessors.

The New York Times Book Review lightly asks "where else, in one volume, can we learn a little about Copernicus, circulating libraries, the Clapham sect and find a chart enabling us to figure out the day of the week for any date after 1066?"

Library Journal declares this work "indispensable for literary reference collections." At a price of $45, it is a bargain as well. As in its predecessors, the emphasis has been upon primary information rather than critical appreciation. Works and authors are described and characterized rather than judged. Neither "literary merit nor celebrity" has been Drabble's only criterion, and indeed she includes, by her own admission, some authors who are noted for their lack of skill, such as William McGonagall and Amanda Ros. In the preface to *The Oxford Companion to English Literature,* Drabble says her intention was to follow the original plan (of *The Oxford Companion*) to present authors, works, and literary movements that are of historical and contemporary importance, and to "quickly, easily, and clearly satisfy the immediate curiosity of the common reader."

The Board recommends this work for the core collections of public, academic, and school libraries.

—C. H.-M.

The Oxford History of English Literature. Frank Percy Wilson and Bonamy Dobrée, eds. Clarendon/Oxford, 1945– . hard (some vols. soft). 13 vols. index (for each volume). history.

820.9'001

The Oxford History of English Literature is a multivolume work that provides a continuous history of English literature from before the Norman Conquest in 1066 to the writers of the first half of the twentieth century (including James Joyce and G. B. Shaw). Some volumes are divided into two parts, and each volume or half-volume is designed to be an independent work. The volumes have not been published in chronological order; thus, volume 11, part 2, *English Literature, 1832–1890,* was published in 1989, while volume 4, part 2, *The English Drama 1586–1642,* had yet to be released at the time this review was written. The former is the most recent book of the series to be published.

Recently some volumes have gone out of print; however, Oxford University Press planned to reissue the entire series beginning in 1990. The numbering of the volumes is being changed with this reissue so that each part will now receive a separate volume number. Additionally, some volumes are being retitled for uniformity in the series and to give more information to the reader. The volume numbers used in this review refer to the earlier set, which was the only one available at the time this buying guide was being prepared.

Each author of a volume or half-volume is an expert on that particular area of English literature. For example, John Innes Mackintosh Stewart, author of volume 12, *Eight Modern Writers,* is a noted scholar and critic of twentieth-century literature, especially Rudyard Kipling (included in the volume), and Henry Stanley Bennett, author of volume 2, part 1, *Chaucer and the Fifteenth Century,* is an authority on the medieval period. In addition, the general editors of the series are distinguished scholars: Frank Percy Wilson is known for his work on Shakespeare's use of language and authored volume 4, part 1, *The English Drama, 1485–1585,* and Bonamy Dobrée is a distinguished poet and prolific writer on many aspects of English literature.

All volumes or half-volumes of the *Oxford History* follow the same organizational format. After the main body of the text, they include detailed chronological tables, a bibliography, and an alphabetical index of authors, works, and topics for the volume. The books vary in size from 244 pages for volume 4, part 1, *The English Drama, 1485–1585,* to 704 pages for volume 12, *Eight Modern Writers.* Most books in the series have a preface that explains the scope of the material covered and the selection policy. For example, in the preface to volume 12, *Eight Modern Writers,* the author states that he chose the writers on the basis of his own personal literary enjoyment, though he acknowledges that they will "remain important landmarks" of their age. Thus, analysis of a period may be somewhat uneven. The depth of coverage is left to the judgment of the writer, so that the end result may not represent a considered evaluation of the era.

The *Oxford History of English Literature* is very accurate and authoritative, although the bibliographies need to be updated (especially those in the earlier published volumes). As of this writing, Oxford has not announced any plans to extend this history to include contemporary English literature after D. H. Lawrence (volume 12, *Eight Modern Writers*). Some users may find access to the series as a whole confusing, since each book is cataloged individually by the Library of Congress system according to specific subject; therefore, the history series is not found together as a set in libraries that employ this system of classification.

The *Oxford History of English Literature* has an academic orientation and would be most useful to the serious student of literature. The accessibility and usefulness of individual volumes are enhanced by comprehensive indexing, chronological tables, and bibliographies. The Board recommends this work for the core collection of academic libraries. —*C. H.-M.*

Genre

British Novelists 1600–1800. Martin C. Battestin, ed. Gale, 1985. hard. 1 vol. in 2 parts. 665 pp. appendix. index. ISBN 0-8103-1717-6 (set). $196 (set). biographical dictionary.
PR851.B7 823′009

British Novelists 1600–1800 is a two-part reference work presenting in-depth biographies of 50 authors recognized as pioneers of the English novel. It is one volume (volume 39) of the Dictionary of Literary Biography series, which was designed as a comprehensive biographical dictionary of major contributors to literature. According the the "Plan of the Series," given in the prefatory material, each volume is organized around a topic, literary or historical period, or genre; this specific volume can stand alone as a reference on literary history.

British Novelists is arranged alphabetically by author's last name, with part 1 covering A through L and part 2 covering M through Z. Each part contains a table of contents that lists the author, the author's dates, and the name of the contributor who wrote the article. In addition, part 1 contains a foreword on the rise of the English novel, and part 2 has an appendix incorporating essays on the novel by 21 novelists and a list of books for further reading. A list of contributors with their university affiliations is given, although there is no statement of their specific qualifications.

Each entry has the name of the author centered and in boldface type, with the dates underneath in parentheses, followed by the name of the contributor. Each entry begins with an alphabetical list of works, often divided into sections, such as books, plays, editions, translations, and so on. This list is followed by the biographical essay, which discusses the author's life and works, and critically evaluates his or her accomplishments. The entry concludes with a list of biographies or bibliographies (if any) and references for further study, followed by an endnote on the location of any extant original manuscripts. The entries vary in length from 6 pages for a lesser-known figure like Arthur Blackamore to 28 pages for a major writer like Henry Fielding.

An outstanding feature of this reference is the use of illustration. Numerous drawings, paintings of the authors or their families and places of residence, and facsimile pages from novels add to the reader's understanding of the author's life and works. The accurate and detailed analysis of each author is enhanced by the easily accessible format of this excellent reference work. The reader can find comprehensive coverage on such writers as forerunner of the novel Jonathan Swift *(Gulliver's Travels),* early master of the novel Samuel Richardson *(Pamela),* or a lesser-known novelist like Ann Radcliffe *(The Mysteries of Udolpho).* A cumulative index to the entire series concludes the volume. There is also a useful bibliography.

British Novelists can fulfill the general reader's interest in the early British novel as well as provide the serious student of literature with information on novelists who gained critical acclaim in their own age but may be forgotten now. (Entries for Aphra Behn or Mary Wollstonecraft are examples of this.) The material on the authors is quite current as seen in the entry on Aphra Behn, which reflects the resurgence of interest in her work since the late 1970s.

The Board recommends this work for the core collection of academic libraries. —*D. L. S.*

Contemporary Dramatists, 4th edition. D. L. Kirkpatrick, ed. St. James, 1988. hard. 1 vol. 785 pp. index. $85. ISBN 0-912289-62-7. biographical source. revised every 5 years.
PR737.C57 822.9

Contemporary Dramatists holds more than 300 critical entries on living English-language (but not necessarily British) writers for the stage as well as supplementary sections (which are purely bibliographical) treating the output of screenwriters, radio writers, television writers, musical librettists, and theater groups. Among the main entries are such diverse, well-known figures as Samuel Beckett, Harvey Fierstein, Brian Friel, Dennis Potter, Neil Simon, and Wendy Wasserstein. A number of writers (such as Robertson Davies, Iris Murdoch, and John Mortimer) who are primarily novelists or poets but who have written plays are also included.

Each entry in the main section has a brief biography of the author, a complete list of produced and/or published plays, a list of other separately published works, a bibliography of secondary sources, and a signed essay. Author comments in some entries appear just before the signed essay. Seven dramatists who have died since 1963—and who were not included in previous editions—receive full entries in an appendix.

Supplementary sections do not contain full entries and only list publications for each writer. In fact they do not even list dates of birth, only dates for publications, which are listed chronologically. For each supplement, a signed essay introduces (and sometimes defends) the profession treated in that supplement and surveys the field. All of these introductory essays are well done and illuminating as history and survey, especially that on theater groups in Britain and the United States. The extensive index lists play titles; the author's name appears in parentheses after the title, and the date of the first performance or publication is given.

Contemporary Dramatists is an excellent volume in this series on contemporary writers. Casual playgoers, as well as avid ones, will find most of the information necessary to satisfy their curiosity. Beginning students will find it especially useful as a starting place for their research on many dramatists and stage-related subjects. Advanced students and scholars will use it from time to time to keep abreast of subjects related to their specialties and even to brush up on what they have forgotten. The Board recommends this work for the core collections of public and academic libraries.

—M. E. G.

Critical Survey of Drama, English Language series. Frank N. Magill, ed. Salem, 1985. suppl. 1987. hard. 6 vols. plus suppl. 2,575 pp. (set); 408 pp. (suppl.). index. ISBN 0-89356-375-7 (set); 0-89356-389-7 (suppl.). $350 (set); $80 (suppl.). criticism.
PR623.C5 (set) 822.009
PN1625.C74 (suppl.)

The *Critical Survey of Drama* is part of the 45-volume genre series published by Salem Press. Series editor Frank N. Magill has developed a fairly standard format for all his critical survey books and employs it in this work. A headnote gives essential biographical information about the dramatist, which is followed by a list of principal dramatic works, a list of works in other literary forms, and a paragraph or so on the dramatist's achievements. A brief biography leads the reader into an analysis of the dramatist's work. A bibliography of secondary sources completes each entry.

A list of the 158 contributors of author articles and essays on aspects of the drama, which appear in volume 6, is given. No credentials for these contributors are included. However, qualifications of some contributors are reflected in the bibliography of secondary sources, where specific books or articles on the dramatist under discussion have been authored by the contributor of the article (for example Richard N. Coe, author of a book on Samuel Beckett, wrote the essay on Beckett.)

Critical Survey of Drama includes 198 English-language writers from all literary periods since the Elizabethans, a range necessary to honor the "critical survey" aspect of the title. But because entries are arranged alphabetically by dramatist, little impression of the chronology or the progression of drama, as implied by "survey," is made. Contemporary playwright Peter Shaffer, for example, appears between restoration dramatist Thomas Shadwell and Elizabethan playwright William Shakespeare.

The achievement and biography sections of each entry are well done and accurate. The analysis essays vary in quality since they depend on the interpretive skills of the essayists. However, most essays are carefully researched and critically adept, covering such specific subjects as the "theatre of immobility" of Samuel Beckett, the theme of redemption in the plays of T. S. Eliot, and the stage history of Shelley's *The Cenci* with expertise. Bibliographies of secondary sources list readily available works rather than the most recent or most comprehensive; thus readers with deeper interest in the dramatist should seek out the latest individual bibliographies, often ignored by these editors and compilers.

Volume 6 contains a collection of essays that cover many aspects of drama, including history along with genres, national drama, opera and musical drama, cinema, and the like. These essays are arranged in chronological order and establish a historical orientation that is missing in the first five volumes. They vary in length and skill, as might be expected, but in general are of very high quality. This volume also includes a fairly complete list of definitions of terms and movements in drama, as well as a comprehensive index which provides easy access to information about authors, titles, terms, and movements.

The single-volume supplement to *Critical Survey of Drama* functions as a supplement to both the English Language series and the Foreign Language series. The supplement's primary function is to add about 50 dramatists who were not included in the earlier volumes and to update entries for a few dramatists who were. All of the writers listed in this volume are modern or contemporary dramatists currently on the international scene. Included are American performer/choreographer Martha Clark and Polish painter/director Tadeusz Kantor. Both of these figures reflect a trend in contemporary theater to emphasize music, dance, and spectacle.

The *Critical Survey of Drama* is as useful in finding analyses of such classic dramatic works as William Congreve's *Way of the World* as it is for gaining some insight into the plays of such contemporaries as Edward Bond (whose plays, such as *Lear* and *Bingo,* have elicited much controversy.) The Board recommends this work for the core collections of public and academic libraries. —*M. E. G.*

Critical Survey of Long Fiction, English Language series. Frank N. Magill, ed. Salem, 1983. hard. 8 vols., 1 suppl. 3,352 pp. index. ISBN 0-89356-359-5 (set). $375 (set). criticism.
PR821.C7 (set) 813

See American Literature.

Critical Survey of Short Fiction. Frank N. Magill, ed. Salem, 1981. hard. 7 vols. plus 1 suppl. 2,901 pp. index. ISBN 0-89356-210-7 (set); 0-89356-218-1 (suppl.). $375 (set). criticism.
PN3321.C7 809.31

See World Literature.

Masterplots II, British and Commonwealth Fiction series. Frank N. Magill, ed. Salem, 1987. hard. 4 vols. 1,959 pp. index. ISBN 0-89356-468-0 (set). $300 (set). handbook.
PR881.M39 823.00924

Masterplots II is one of the better titles in the Magill series, particularly because of its scope. This work encompasses three areas of literature: (1) British and Irish writing, largely from the 1950s to the present (and therefore missing from the original *Masterplots,* published in 1954). *Masterplots II* includes recent novels by established writers, such as Irish Murdoch and William Golding, works by the younger writers, such as Pat Barker, and works by contemporary, well-known writers, such as John le Carré and Salman Rushdie. (2) Commonwealth literature, which is thoroughly represented, including works from the early twentieth century, with emphasis on the postwar period (for example, Canadian novelist Margaret Atwood's *The Handmaid's Tale* and Nigerian author Wole Soyinka's *The Interpreters*); (3) Major writers of the English language whose principal works were summarized in the original *Masterplots,* but whose other works, though excluded from that title, are represented here as worthy of note (Virginia Woolf's *Jacob's Room,* an early [1922] novel that previews themes and techniques developed in such later masterworks as *To the Lighthouse,* is an example). Although Magill is widely acknowledged as the master of plot summaries, *Masterplots II* is also a guide with basic analysis (emphasis upon "basic") that covers characterization, theme, techniques, critical context, and includes a brief bibliography.

Entries are arranged alphabetically by title. Within each entry, individual essays are divided into six sections. A section on publication information and classification of the work is given first. A list of secondary reference materials, which offers a starting point for further research, concludes each entry (for example, the source list at the conclusion of Soyinka's *The Interpreters* includes three books on African novelists and three books on Soyinka himself). A list of all the writers who contributed articles to this four-volume set, which covers more than 400 novels, is printed at the beginning of volume 1.

Magill is quite popular with students, especially less serious students, and the days of keeping him under lock and key are gone forever. Some caution should be exercised, however, in recommending the series. For one thing, the "analyses" cannot really be called that, in any real sense of the term; they are heavy on summation, as always, and light on in-depth critical comment.

The list of what is included in the Magill works, versus what is not, is difficult to ascertain. The lack of good indexing of the entire series is the reason. *Masterplots II* does have title and author indexes in the fourth column. These allow a reader to locate material under variant titles and to know which works by a given author are available in the series. The complete list of titles with cross-references from all titles under which a work may have been published is useful and does not present any real confusion due to variant titles. (As an example, R. K. Narayan's novel *The Vendor of Sweets* [its publication title in the United States, and its entry title in *Masterplots II*] was first published in Great Britain under the title *The Sweet-Vendor*).

Should plot summaries and rather mundane analyses have a place on library reference shelves? Magill's *Masterplots II* does have a place, although with the qualifications mentioned above. Not all library patrons are scholars, and it is a good idea to provide the "helps" that can make their reading more pleasurable. Moreover, *Masterplots II* has the added bonus of covering Commonwealth literature from Canada, Australia, the West Indies, Africa, and India. The Board recommends this work for the core collections of public, academic, and school libraries. —*C. H.-M.*

Supplementary Titles

American and British Poetry: A Guide to the Criticism 1925–1978. Harriet Semmes Alexander. Swallow/Ohio Univ. Pr., 1984. hard. 1 vol. 486 pp. ISBN 0-8040-0848-5. $46. criticism.
Z1231.P7A44[P5303] 821.008

See American Literature.

Critical Survey of Poetry, English Language Series. Frank N. Magill, ed. Salem, 1983. hard. 8 vols. plus 1 suppl. 3,753 pp. (8 vols.); 411 pp. (suppl.). index. ISBN 0-89356-340-4 (set); 0-89356-349-8 (suppl.). $375 (set); $80 (suppl.). criticism.
PR502.C85 (set). 809.1
PN1021.C7 (suppl.)

In the *Critical Survey of Poetry* which is "arranged by poet or anonymous title, [the text offers] critical essays [of] about ten pages in length, with brief bibliographies of poets and poetry in English from *Beowulf* to the present; v. 8 presents longer essays on particular periods and various aspects of peotry criticism. All essays are signed; index in v. 8." (*Guide to Reference Books, 1986,* Sheehy, p. 433)

The *Critical Survey of Poetry* is "designed to supplement the *Critical Survey of Poetry, English Language Series* (1982) and *Foreign Language Series* (1984). This supplement was developed to give more detailed coverage to contemporary poets who were treated selectively in the earlier volumes.

"The poets included in *Current Survey of Poetry* represent wide geographical areas: the United States, Scotland, Ireland, South Africa, Australia, Eastern and Western Europe, the Soviet Union, the Middle East, Brazil, Turkey, and Japan. . . . [T]here are ten women poets and a good representation of younger poets.

"The critical essays are arranged in alphabetical order by author. The format is uniform, with the headings in boldface print. . . .

"The concluding section, entiteld 'Updates,' includes recent information about poets in earlier volumes of *Critical Survey of Poetry.* The index is comprehensive for all volumes." (*ARBA,* 1988, p. 460)

Board's recommendation: Academic and school libraries.

Elizabethan Dramatists (Dictionary of Literary Biography, vol. 62). Fredson Bowers, ed. Gale, 1987. hard. 492 pp. illus. index. bibliography. ISBN 0-8103-1740-0. $103. biographical dictionary.
PR651.E48 822.309

"Fredson Bowers' *Elizabethan Dramatists* . . . provides a biographical-bibliographical guide and overview for a particular area of literature. Individual entries . . . start with a list of the author's play productions and his books in their first and last authoritative editions (compiled as accurately as evidence permits); and . . . ends . . . with a catalog of bibliographies, secondary references, and manuscripts. Covering nineteen dramatists (Shakespeare among them) and five anonymous plays, *The Elizabethan Dramatists* contains an introduction by Bowers and three appendixes on theater, publication, and source for study . . . . [This work] provide[s] a useful resource for any student of English Renaissance drama." (*Studies in English Literature,* 1988)

Also reviewed in: *ARBA,* 1988.

Board's recommendation: Public, academic, and school libraries.

English Novel Explication: Criticisms to 1972. Helen Palmer and Anne J. Dyson. Shoe String, 1973. hard. 1 vol. 329 pp. index. ISBN 0-208-01322-9. $24.50. bibliography.
Z2014.F5P26 016.823009

English Novel Explication Supplement III, Through 1984. Christian J. Kloesel and Lynn F. Kloesel. Shoe String, 1986. hard. 1 vol. 533 pp. index. ISBN 0-208-02092-6. $57.50. bibliography.
Z2014.F5P26 016.823009

In the *English Novel Explication* series "authors appear in alphabetical order with an alphabetical listing of their novels. Critical references are recorded under the title of each novel. Emphasis has been placed on including as many references for the novels as possible so that the reader may have a choice between types of articles." (*Choice,* December 1973, p. 1531)

"[The compilers] have attempted to limit their citations to articles concerned with each particular novel as a whole. The impressive list of books and periodicals indexed are of the type to be found in any basic literature collection. Since the researcher would have to consult several indexes to get comparable results, it is difficult to see how any library beyond the high school level could justify not buying this bibliography." (*LJ,* September 1, 1973, p. 2424) Supplement II, criticisms to 1975, is currently out of print.

Board's recommendation: Public and academic libraries.

William Shakespeare: His World, His Work, and His Influence. John F. Andrews. Scribner, 1985. hard. 3 vols. 954 pp. illus. appendix. index. ISBN 0-684-17851-6 (set). $210 (set). criticism.
PR2976.W5354 822.33

In the *William Shakespeare* set, "Volume I, His World, discusses various aspects of life in Elizabethan England: the state, the church, economic life, science, travel, manners, dress, and decorum, among others. Volume II, His Work, has articles on Shakespeare's comedies, tragedies, sonnets and other poems, along with discussion of his treatment of history, use of language, music, and prose. Volume III, His Influence, describes Shakespeare's influence on modern directors, actors, playwrights, and critics, and covers such topics as teaching Shakespeare and major Shakespeare-related institutions (libraries, museums, organizations). . . . Each article concludes with a bibliography, and Volume III contains an index to the set.

The reference value of this beautifully produced set derives not only from the authority of its contributors, . . . but also from the presence of bibliography and analytic indexing. . . ." (*BL,* March 1, 1986, p. 968)

Also reviewed in: *Choice,* March 1986, p. 1068; *LJ,* January 1986, p. 87.

Board's recommendation: Public, academic, and school libraries.

New and Noteworthy

British Women Writers: A Critical Reference Guide. Janet Todd, ed. Crossroad/Ungar/Continuum, 1989. hard. 1 vol. 762 pp. index. ISBN 0-8044-3334-8. $165. biographical dictionary.
PR111.B75 820.9

"Intended as a companion to Ungar's four-volume *American Women Writers . . . , British Women Writers* has 447 essays on women writing from the Middle Ages to the present. . . . Entries are arranged alphabetically by last name and begin with dates and places of birth and death (when appropriate) and a few words characterizing the writer's form or genre (e.g., dramatist, essayist, historian, writer for children, diarist, journalist, pamphleteer). The signed essays range from one to four pages and are both biographical and critical." (*BL,* November 15, 1989, p. 688)

Great Writers of the English Language. Marshall Cavendish, 1989. hard. 14 vols. illus. indexes. ISBN 1-85435-000-5 (set). $429.95 (set). biographical dictionary.
PR85 820.9

"*Great Writers of the English Language* is a beautifully and lavishly illustrated survey of English and American literature. The works of 56 authors are discussed here, and vivid portraits of their lives are drawn against the backdrop of their times. The set is comprised of 13 volumes of text and an index volume. . . . Within the volume, each chapter is divided into four sections: 'The Writer's Life,' 'Reader's Guide,' 'The Writer at Work,' and 'Sources and Inspiration.' " (*BL,* February 15, 1990, p. 1186)

Reference Works in British and American Literature. James K. Bracken. Libraries Unlimited, 1990. hard. 2 vols. 252 pp. (vol. 1); approx. 400 pp. (vol. 2). ISBN 0-87287-699-3 (vol. 1); 0-87287-700-0 (vol. 2). $38 (vol. 1); $40 (vol. 2). bibliography.
Z2011.B74 016.82

Reference Works in British and American Literature "will provide essential critical bibliographic guidance to the myriad reference works now available for individual English and American writers that have been largely ignored by existing guides. Volume 1, *English and American Literature,* includes more than 500 annotated entries, with extensive subentries, for general and specialized research guides; dictionaries; encyclopedias; handbooks and histories; indexes and abstracts; [etc.] . . . Volume II, *English and American Writers,* . . . will focus on over 500 . . . writers, covering bibliographies; dictionaries; encyclopedias and handbooks; indexes and concordances; journals; and associations and research centers." (Excerpted from publisher's announcement)

Restoration Drama. Thomas J. Taylor. Salem/Magill Bks., 1990. hard. 1 vol. 225 pp. ISBN 0-89356-657-8. $40. bibliography.
PR691 822.4'09

"The criteria for insertion in . . . [*Restoration Drama*] are simple: Playwrights are included whose dramatic output begins between 1660 and 1700 and responds to the changed social and political atmosphere of London. . . . References to the works of Aphra Behn, Colley Cibber, William Congreve, John Dryden, George Villiers, and William Wycherley appear alphabetically under each playwright's name. The bibliography is selective rather than exaustive. . . ." (Excerpted from publisher's announcement)

Shakespeare A to Z: The Essential Reference to His Plays, His Poems, His Life and Times, and More. Charles Boyce and Professor David White. Facts On File, 1990. hard. 1 vol. 768 pp. illus. appendix. ISBN 0-8160-1805-7. $39.95. handbook.
PR2892.B69 822.33

"*Shakespeare A To Z* is the first and only one-volume reference work to include virtually everything one needs to know about the Bard. It incorporates nearly 3,000 entries that provide authoritative information on: *every play, . . . every character, . . . contemporaries, . . . theatrical terms, authors, scholars and publishers, . . . literary works, . . . places, . . .* [and] *Shakespeare's non-dramatic poetry.*" (Excerpted from publisher's announcement)

The Stanford Companion to Victorian Fiction. John Sutherland. Stanford, 1989. hard. 1 vol. 696 pp. ISBN 0-8047-1528-9. $60. handbook.
PR871.S87 823.8

"The amount of material published between 1837 and 1901 is reflected in the number of entries [found in *The Stanford Companion to Victorian Fiction*]. The 878 entries on Victorian novelists (9566 men and 312 women) are economically worded biographies that assess the authors' lives and summarize their literary contributions. . . . Brief descriptions of novels form part of biographical entries, but the *Companion* also features 554 evaluative synopses of novels. . . . The arrangement is alphabetical with authors' names in boldface. . . . Two appendixes provide lists of alternative names: proper names, . . . pseudonyms, . . . [and] maiden and married names." (*BL,* September 1, 1989, p. 108)

The Victorian Novel: An Annotated Bibliography. Laurence W. Mazzeno. Salem, 1989. hard. 1 vol. 222 pp. index. ISBN 0-89356-653-5. $40. bibliography.
PR871 823.03

The Victorian Novel focuses "on 13 Victorian novelists. . . . Entries are arranged by author; a 'general' section is followed by citations to specific novels. Chapters from works named in the general sections are also cited repeatedly under individual novels. Annotations are straightforward and descriptive." (*Choice,* May 1990, p. 1480)

Jane A. Bealer

Broadcasting

See also Film

Broadcasting is a subject that is wide in scope and in recent years has become increasingly more complex. Not long ago, the field of broadcasting referred almost exclusively to the media of radio and television. Throughout the 1980s, however, new technologies and the proliferation of already established systems greatly enhanced and expanded the options available to the public. Where three television networks once were prominent, there now exist numerous cable stations and independent networks. Satellite broadcast is becoming more readily available, and the home VCR is nearly ubiquitous. For the librarian building a core collection of broadcasting materials, these changes make the job more complex. The broadcasting collection should be representative of all these media. Unfortunately, in some instances, such as guides to cable programming, the reference sources have not kept pace with the industry changes.

An adequate core collection should reflect the many facets of the category. Industry guides providing information on television, radio, or cable stations and the markets that they serve are a necessary acquisition. Biographical sources, which include information about actors, actresses, and the on-air personalities familiar to the public, as well as behind-the-scenes producers and network executives, will be consulted often. Guides providing information on programming will be as essential to the public patron seeking the answer to a trivia question as to the broadcasting scholar. Although video is not truly a broadcasting medium, it is included in this category, and a librarian will want to acquire a reference guide that lists the increasing catalog of video titles available to the public. Also, as video cassettes become more readily available as a part of library collections, a directory of available titles becomes essential as a tool for collection development.

The core titles reviewed in this section are very broad in scope and provide a comprehensive overview of an entire medium (such as television or radio). The librarian who wants to build a more substantial broadcasting collection would probably choose to augment this list with more specialized works. For example, reference books dealing with a specific time period, such as the "golden age" of radio or television programs of the 1960s, might be considered useful. Works that focus on a particular genre (such as children's programming, television news, or comedy) would also be valuable additions to a larger collection.

Several other titles not reviewed in this buying guide should also be considered as part of a core collection. Directories which are out of the scope of the Buying Guide but which would be extremely useful are the annual *Audio Video Marketplace* (Bowker, 1991), *Complete Directory to Prime Time T.V. Stars* (Ballan-

Core Titles

	PUBLIC	ACADEMIC	SCHOOL
The Broadcasting Yearbook West, Donald V., ed. Broadcasting Publications, annual	✦	✦	
International Television and Video Almanac Klain, Jane, ed. Quigley Pub., annual	✦	✦	✦
Radio: A Reference Guide Greenfield, Thomas Allen. Greenwood, 1989		✦	
Television and Cable Factbook, 2 vols. Taliaferro, Michael C., man. ed. Warren, annual	✦	✦	
Total Television: A Comprehensive Guide to Programming from 1948 to the Present, 2d edition McNeil, Alex. Penguin, 1984	✦	✦	✦
Video Source Book, 11th edition, 2 vols. Weiner, David J. Gale, 1990	✦	✦	✦
World Radio and TV Handbook Sennitt, Andrew G., ed. Billboard Bks./Watson-Guptill, annual	✦	✦	

tine, 1987), and *Complete Directory to Prime Time Network T.V. Shows, 1946–Present* (Ballantine, 1988). In addition, two works by Vincent Terrace were out of print at the time of this compilation, but any librarian able to obtain them would want to consider them as part of a broadcast collection: *Encyclopedia of Television* (Zoetrope, 1986) and *Encyclopedia of Television Series, Pilots and Specials, 1974–1984* (Ballantine, 1985).

Core Titles

The Broadcasting Yearbook. Donald V. West, ed. Broadcasting Publications, annual. soft. 1 vol. 1,386 pp. illus. index. $95. yearbook.
HF6146.R3.B731 384.554

The Broadcasting Yearbook is a one-volume reference source that provides coverage of television, radio, cable, satellite, and related professional industries. For over 50 years, it has been published annually by Broadcasting Publications, one of the foremost publishers of industry-related journals. With the 1990 edition, the yearbook reverts to its earlier name of *The Broadcasting Yearbook* after an interim title change to *Broadcasting/Cable Yearbook.*

The scope of *The Broadcasting Yearbook* is broad, and the book is divided into nine sections, each focusing on a different segment of the industry. These are: "The Fifth Estate," "Radio," "Television," "Cable," "Satellites," "Programming," "Advertising," "Technology," and "Professional Services." Coverage is limited to the United States and Canada, and brief historical or background information for each section (called "A Short Course in . . .") is provided in addition to current comprehensive data. *The Broadcasting Yearbook* is a valuable source for locating information on U.S. and Canadian television and radio stations by geographic location, call number, channel, or frequency. Other sections of the book focus on listings of cable stations, programming producers and distributors, satellite owners, equipment manufacturers, public broadcasting stations, major awards, labor unions, associations, books on broadcasting, and schools or universities with programs in broadcasting. For the advertising or marketing professional, the yearbook provides breakdowns and rankings of television and radio markets according to Arbitron data, and a chapter is devoted to advertising-related information. A comprehensive index at the front of the yearbook facilitates access to this reference work, and an additional index refers to advertisers in the volume.

Overall, *The Broadcasting Yearbook* is an outstanding reference book that is highly regarded within the industry. This is the book that broadcasting and marketing professionals will request by name, but the binding on this softcover edition often will not hold up through a year of heavy usage. The librarian considering this purchase may notice, however, that there is a good deal of overlap between *The Broadcasting Yearbook* and the TELEVISION AND CABLE FACTBOOK. While both works are appropriate for academic or public libraries, the librarian with a limited budget may want to buy only one of these. Although the TELEVISION AND CABLE FACTBOOK provides much more extensive coverage of the television and cable industries, *The Broadcasting Yearbook* includes information on radio, which the other work does not, and the yearbook's clear index and single-volume size make it easier to use. Because the yearbook is also significantly less expensive, the librarian forced to choose between the two would probably prefer to include *The Broadcasting Yearbook* as part of the collection. The Board recommends this work for the core collections of public and academic libraries.

International Television and Video Almanac. Jane Klain, ed. Quigley Pub., annual. hard. 1 vol. 685 pp. index. ISBN 0-900610-39-5. $58. yearbook.
HE8698.I55 791.4505

For over 35 years, the *International Television and Video Almanac* has been the self-proclaimed "who, what, where, and when" of the television and video industries. In a single, compact volume, the almanac provides information on television and cable companies, producers, distributors and services, biographies of television and film personalities, program information, listings of festivals and award winners, trade publications, organizations, advertising agencies, and an overview of the industry for the previous year. In 1987, the almanac changed its name from the *International Television Almanac* to the *International Television and Video Almanac* in recognition of the rapidly growing video industry, and an extensive section on video market data was added. The volume is published annually, with extensive updating and revision of the text for each new edition. Although the almanac's emphasis is on U.S. broadcasting activities, brief sections devoted to world television and video markets provide information on international markets that is often difficult to find.

Like its counterpart, the INTERNATIONAL MOTION PICTURE ALMANAC (see Film), this work is noteworthy for its inclusion of a broad range of industry categories rather than for its depth of coverage in any one category. Librarians considering the purchase of both almanacs should be aware that approximately 50 percent of the material, including the extensive "Who's Who" section, is duplicated in both reference works.

Any library serving members of the broadcasting industry will want to supplement the almanac with a few more specialized reference works. For example, the *Audio Video Marketplace* (see headnote) provides a far more exhaustive listing of industry suppliers and services, and the TELEVISION AND CABLE FACTBOOK gives a more complete description of television and cable stations. In addition, the program information in the *International Television and Video Almanac* covers only the most recent television season. The librarian who seeks historical information would have to retain all of the past volumes of the work.

Despite these drawbacks, the *International Television and Video Almanac* is a first-stop source of industry information. Because of its broad range of subjects; compact, single-volume size; ease of use; and low cost (relative to some of the other television reference works), the librarian who can afford only one purchase in the category would want to consider the almanac. The *International Television and Video Almanac* is appropriate for all types of libraries. The Board recommends this work for the core collections of public, academic, and school libraries.

Radio: A Reference Guide. Thomas Allen Greenfield. Greenwood, 1989. hard. 1 vol. 172 pp. index. ISBN 0-313-22276-2. $39.95. bibliography.
Z7224.U6G74 016.38454

Radio: A Reference Guide is an evaluative bibliography of materials on radio history and programming. Published by Greenwood Press as part of its series on American popular culture, the book focuses in particular on radio as a medium of popular culture. Thomas Allen Greenfield, the author and a professor of English at Bellarmine College, is highly selective in his choices for inclusion, and, as he points out in the preface, he omits well-known works on radio such as Eric Sevareid's autobiography, *Not So Wild a Dream,* if he finds them of little historical or scholarly value. The over 500 works listed include books, Ph.D. dissertations, and articles from both scholarly journals and the popular press.

Greenfield embellishes his bibliography with well-written overviews of radio's history and its various genres. He begins with a historical introduction in which he divides radio broadcasting into four periods: (1) the pioneer era to 1926, (2) the network era or "golden age" of radio from 1926 to 1948, (3) the period from 1949 to 1960 when television surpassed radio as the primary communications medium, and (4) the time period from 1969 to the present when "narrowcasting," or the practice of gearing radio programming to a specific locale and format, has prevailed. Subsequent chapters in the book focus on individual subjects: radio networks and station histories, drama, news, music, comedy and variety, sports, shortwaves, and a final segment on miscellaneous subjects, including, among other topics, women in radio, advertising, religious broadcasting, and armed forces radio. Reference sources are discussed in the context of a knowledgeable essay on each subject. Complete publication information is included for all reference works mentioned in bibliographies appended to each chapter.

The final chapter includes listings of major radio collections in the United States, organizations, industry journals, and indexes. The book concludes with an index which lists subjects and individuals mentioned but excludes the titles of references covered in the bibliographies.

Radio: A Reference Guide will be of most interest to serious students and researchers of radio broadcasting and popular culture. Librarians who are building an extensive collection on this topic will also find the guide useful even though many of the sources cited are Ph.D. dissertations, magazine articles, or out-of-print books. The essays are entertaining and informative, and any library patron with a serious interest in radio would appreciate this book. The Board recommends this work for the core collection of academic libraries.

Television and Cable Factbook. Michael C. Taliaferro, man. ed. Warren, annual. soft. 2 vols. 4,054 pp. index. ISBN 0-911486-42-9 (set). $345 (set). handbook.
TK6540.T45 621.388

The *Television and Cable Factbook* is the most comprehensive and exhaustive source of information on the television and cable industries. The *Factbook* is issued annually in two volumes by Warren Publishing, a major publisher of journals and newsletters focusing on the broadcast industry. The first volume focuses on television stations; the second is devoted to cable broadcasting and services. Information that does not specifically fall into one of these categories may appear in either volume, and the user will need to consult the annotated table of contents at the front of each volume in order to locate the desired information. All entries are industry related, and the *Factbook* has no information on actual television programming.

The scope of information contained in the *Television and Cable Factbook* is vast, and it would be impossible within the context of this review to list all the tables and chapters contained therein. Among the highlights, however, are detailed descriptions of each television station in the United States with maps and the Arbitron Area of Dominant Influence market names. (This section alone runs over 1,200 pages.) Other sections include listings of public and educational television stations; U.S. and Canadian television market rankings; ownership of television stations by groups, newspapers, or book publishers; Canadian television stations; listing by call number of foreign-language programming; a directory of cable systems and cable group ownership; pay TV and satellite services; and information on direct broadcast satellites and satellite communication services. Additional sections focus on listings of congressional committees handling broadcast matters, associations, labor unions, attorneys practicing before the FCC, publications on television, and the names of companies involved in television manufacturing, sales, financing, or public relations. The *Television and Cable Factbook* also contains charts of industry statistics and a buying guide.

If there is one criticism of the *Television and Cable Factbook,* it is not that information is omitted, but rather that the breadth and comprehensiveness of the book make it cumbersome to use. The two volumes are immense; each contains nearly 2,000 pages and is heavy and unwieldy to handle. In addition, while there is an index at the front of each volume, the inclusion of all companies and organizations listed in the volume, along with subject headings, makes the index a bit confusing for a novice user.

Overall, the *Television and Cable Factbook* is an outstanding reference source and the most comprehensive book of its type. Any library establishing a core collection on broadcasting will want to include the *Factbook.* The *Factbook* is, however, an expensive acquisition. Because some of the material is duplicated in THE BROADCASTING YEARBOOK, the librarian on a limited budget may want to weigh carefully the advantages of each reference book. The Board recommends this work for the core collections of public and academic libraries.

Total Television: A Comprehensive Guide to Programming from 1948 to the Present, 2d edition. Alex McNeil. Penguin, 1984. soft. 1 vol. 1,027 pp. appendix. index. ISBN 0-14-007377-9. $14.95. handbook.
PN1992.3U5M3 791.4575

Total Television is a guide to all television series that aired from 1948 through the 1984 season. For the purposes of this book, the author, Alex McNeil, defines a series as "open-ended, regularly scheduled programs, regardless of their duration." He includes all programs meeting that description, even if the duration was a single episode. He also includes in the listings any miniseries that contained four or more episodes (such as *Rich Man, Poor Man*). McNeil limits his compendium to those series airing on the three major networks (ABC, CBS, NBC), DuMont (a small network that ceased operating in 1955), public television, and syndication. He does not attempt to include any cable programming, even though this had become a major force in broadcasting at the time of the book's second edition in 1984. He does, however, list those first-run series that have since moved to cable channels.

The main portion of the book is devoted to entries for the program listings, which include, at the minimum, the popular title of the series, the dates of airing, and the network; a brief description of the program with the names of the cast and the roles they played; and, usually, the producer. Many of the entries are lengthy, and McNeil often embellishes his commentary with the history of the series, mention of any noteworthy guest appearances, discussion of controversies surrounding a series, or pertinent trivia. Included in *Total Television* are such facts as the dates of Elvis Presley's and the Beatles' guest appearances on *The Ed Sullivan Show,* discussion of the censorship battles over antiwar material which plagued *The Smothers Brothers Comedy Hour,* and even the names of the actors who competed with Raymond Burr for the role of *Perry Mason.* The book's anecdotal information is well written and often fascinating, making *Total Television* of interest to both the broadcast scholar and the average television fan.

Additional chapters of the book are devoted to a listing of noteworthy television specials, the network's prime-time fall schedules from 1948 to 1984, and names of Emmy and Peabody Award winners. Two indexes provide access to the names of series and the names of the individuals involved in the programs (for example, actors, game show hosts, producers).

The second edition is a durable trade paperback and is an extremely inexpensive acquisition. The main drawback is, of course, that the text only covers programming schedules up to 1984 and totally omits cable programming. Hopefully, the author will continue to update this valuable reference work and expand coverage to include cable networks, which are taking an increasingly active role as producers of original programming.

Total Television is a highly informative and entertaining reference work. The Board recommends this volume for the core collections of public, academic, and school libraries.

Video Source Book, 11th edition. David J. Weiner, ed. Gale, 1990. hard. 2 vols. 2,371 pp. ISBN 0-8103-4299-5. $210. guide.
PN1992.95.V53 011.37

The *Video Source Book (VSB)* is a comprehensive guide to programs currently available on video. Published annually, with two supplements automatically provided to buyers, the *VSB* serves as a *Books in Print* for the video industry and much more, as the description of the typical entry below will show. The scope of the guide is broad, and the *VSB* includes business, educational, children's, instructional, health, sports, fine arts, and general interest videos in addition to the popular entertainment videos most often requested by the home VCR owner. With the eleventh edition in 1990, the *VSB* expands from one volume to two volumes and includes over 55,000 programs from more than 1,300 sources.

Entries in the *VSB* are compiled from video catalogs, press releases, and information provided by the program source. Each program is listed alphabetically by title, and the brief entries are succinct and informative. (One of the few drawbacks to the *VSB* is the small size of type used in entries, making any extensive use of the guide difficult on the eyes. Unfortunately, the expansion to two volumes has not rectified this problem.) In addition to the title and year of release, each listing includes such information as an assigned broad subject category and a more precise subject designation, length, format, availability in color or black and white, close captioning, MPAA rating, credits, television standards, a short description (such as the major subject, theme, or plot), the number and title of programs in a series, availability of ancillary materials, awards, languages, and an identification of the appropriate audience for each video. Ordering and locating desired videos is aided by an indication of the producer, the distributor of the program, and information on the manner in which the video may be obtained (for example, loan or purchase).

The librarian who uses the *VSB* as a buying guide, however, will notice one major omission: no pricing information is given. The absence of pricing indications is deliberate because the prices of videos can change significantly over even a short period of time. The clearly written "Use Guide" at the front of the *VSB* helps users interpret the entries.

Several indexes provide enhanced access to the *VSB.* A subject index categorizes every program using over 400 subject headings. The subject headings are unique to the *VSB,* and while extremely useful, they do contain some idiosyncracies. For example, "Korean War" is a heading but "Korea" is not. To find videos on the land of Korea, a viewer would have to look under the broader heading of "Asia." A credits index lists the works available in video of major film stars and directors, and additional indexes list those programs available on laser optical disk, on 8-millimeter videocassette format, or captioned for the hearing impaired.

The last section of the *VSB* is devoted to an alphabetical listing of program distributors and wholesalers with addresses and telephone numbers. Where applicable, information on format availability and any additional ordering instructions are included.

By virtue of its comprehensiveness, currency, and ease of use, the *Video Source Book* is a valuable reference guide. For the librarian, the *VSB* is a useful buying guide for videos, which are becoming more and more a part of the library collection. For the patron—a teacher in need of educational films for the classroom, a businessperson wanting videos on a particular industry, or a film fan in search of a favorite movie—the *VSB* is an essential reference source. This work is recommended by the Board for the core collections of public, academic, and school libraries.

World Radio and TV Handbook. Andrew G. Sennitt, ed. Billboard Bks./Watson-Guptill, annual. hard. 1 vol. 576 pp. ISBN 0-8230-5920-0. $19.95. handbook.
HE8689.W67 384.5

The World Radio and TV Handbook (WRTH) is a guide to the radio and television stations of the world. Published annually, this handbook provides the most current available information on radio broadcasting stations, including addresses, frequencies, languages, hours of operation, and transmitter powers. Entries are arranged geographically, and virtually every nation having a broadcast station is included, from the United States and Soviet Union to Vatican State and the island nation of Tristan de Cunha. Although a large section is devoted to the listing of world television stations, the primary focus of the *WRTH* is on international radio broadcasting. Through the use of this handbook, the operator of a shortwave or world band radio receiver can locate and tune in stations from foreign countries and identify received signals. (Because of the incompatibility of world television systems, the *WRTH* is of more limited use in tuning in international television signals; however, the listings of major networks on a country-by-country basis with addresses, names of personnel, and technical details of the transmission system provide information that is valuable and often difficult to obtain.) Although the handbook is truly international in scope and is likely to be useful to radio receiver operators anywhere in the world, special attention is paid to worldwide broadcasts in English.

Additional chapters are devoted to tables, in frequency order, of shortwave, mediumwave, and longwave stations. Through the use of these tables, which are divided into broad geographic regions, a radio operator can identify a received signal. Other features of the handbook are listings of broadcast organizations and clubs, maps of worldwide principal transmitter sites, signed articles on such topics as solar activity, equipment reviews, and highlights from the previous year's activities. With the 1990 edition, the *WRTH* has added a section on world satellite broadcasts with information on frequency allocations and addresses of satellite broadcasters. The handbook contains advertising, and an index of advertisers is at the back of the handbook.

The *World Radio and TV Handbook* is written for the radio operator specialist, and the entries are therefore likely to be confusing or even incomprehensible to the novice user. To best understand the handbook, the reader should first consult the "User's Guide to the WRTH" in the front of the book, written in English, French, German, and Spanish. Yet despite the highly specialized nature of the material, most libraries serving the public would want to consider this purchase. The information is comprehensive and current, and the handbook is a very inexpensive acquisition. In fact, the library patrons who are operators of shortwave or world band radio receivers would probably choose to buy a copy of their own. The Board recommends this work for the core collections of public and academic libraries.

Supplementary Titles

Radio Amateur's Handbook, 15th rev. edition. A. Frederick Collins; revised by Robert Hertzberg. Harper & Row, 1983. hard. 1 vol. 416 pp. illus. index. ISBN 0-06-181366-4. $16.95. handbook.
TK9956.C73 621.3841

The *Radio Amateur's Handbook* "is a beginner's handbook that presents the fundamental theories of ham radio operations." (*BL,* September 1, 1984, p. 44)

Also reviewed in: *ARBA,* 1977, p. 539; *BL,* July 1, 1979, p. 1568; *BL,* May 15, 1965, p. 907; *BL,* June 15, 1969, p. 1168; *BL,* March 15, 1970, p. 885; *BL,* April 1, 1970, p. 968; *BL,* June 15, 1971, p. 856; *BL,* June 15, 1972, p. 890; *BL,* July 1, 1972, p. 941; *SB,* September 1970, p. 160; *SB,* May 1977, p. 32; *SB,* September 1971, p. 165; *SB,* September 1972, p. 169; *SLJ,* September 1979, p. 172.

Board's recommendation: Public libraries.

Radio Soundtracks: A Reference Guide, 2d edition. Michael R. Pitts. Scarecrow, 1986. hard. 1 vol. 349 pp. appendix. index. ISBN 0-8108-1875-2. $32.50. discography.
PN1991.9P58 016.79144'75'0973

"Most of [*Radio Soundtracks: A Reference Guide*] is a list, alphabetically arranged by program title, of 'Radio Programs Available on Tape Recordings.' . . . [There are] 1,040 numbered entries, including see references. Then come briefer sections: 'Radio Specials on Tape,' 'Performers' Radio Appearances on Long Playing Records,' and 'Compilation Record Albums.' The volume concludes with an appendix, 'Tape and Record Resources,' and an index to titles and performers.

"Many public and academic libraries will want to consider this second edition of Radio Soundtracks, whether in response to demand from radio buffs or in support of studies of an important development in the history of the performing arts." (*BL,* October 1, 1986, p. 212)

Also reviewed in: *ARBA,* 1977, p. 540; *ARBA,* 1987, p. 349; *Choice,* June 1977, p. 515; *JQ,* Winter 1987, p. 898; *R & R Bk N,* Fall 1986, p. 17; *RSR,* January 1977, p. 17; *WLB,* March 1977, p. 603.

Board's recommendation: Public libraries.

Special Edition: A Guide to Network Television Documentary Series and Special News Reports, 1955–1979. Daniel Einstein. Scarecrow, 1987. hard. 1 vol. 1,069 pp. indexes. ISBN 0-8108-1898-1. $87.50. handbook.
PN1992.8.D6E56 791.45'1

Special Edition: A Guide to Network Television Documentary Series and Special News Reports, 1955–1979 "contains entries for more than 7,000 individual TV programs and more than 120 series of programs (four or more related programs constituting a series in this context). The work is divided into three parts: part 1, 'Network Television Documentary Series Programming, 1955-1979' . . . (757 pages); part 2, 'Documentary Programming Produced by David L. Wolper,' . . . (10 pages); and part 3, 'Network Television News Specials and Special Reports, 1955–1979,' covering an additional 220 pages. Arrangement within part 1 is alphabetical by series title. . . . [In parts 2 and 3], arrangement is chronological. . . . Each entry gives the date the program aired, its full title, a . . . summary of its content, and the names of the writer, director, narrator, producer, etc., connected with it.

"There are two indexes, but they are of names only—personalities and production/technical personnel." (*BL,* December 15, 1987, p. 689)

Also reviewed in: *ARBA,* 1988, p. 379; *Choice,* February 1988, p. 884; *JQ,* Spring 1988, p. 219; *R & R Bk N,* April 1988, p. 20; *WLB,* January 1988, p. 103.

Board's recommendation: Public and academic libraries.

Video Classics: A Guide to Video Art and Documentary Tapes. Deirdre Boyle. Oryx, 1986. soft. 1 vol. 160 pp. illus. indexes. ISBN 0-89774-102-1. $23.50. handbook.
PN1992.95B6 621.3841

Video Classics: A Guide to Video Art and Documentary Tapes consists of "reviews of 101 independently produced art and documentary videos from the last 15 years. . . . The entries are arranged alphabetically by title and each includes creator, copyright date, length, color or black-and-white note, distributor(s), formats, credits, and awards won. . . . The book also contains an index of artists/producers and a subject index listing the videos under 26 broad categories from Adolescence to Women's issues. It concludes with a list of distributors' names and addresses.

"The perceptive reviews range from 250 to 750 words and are accompanied by black-and-white stills from the videos. . . . These tapes document current American culture and concerns. Though some of them were made by amateurs, they all demonstrate innovative techniques." (*BL,* November 1, 1986, p. 399)

"This small book is a model of what all mediagraphies should be: selective, purposive, detailed, and authoritative. . . . Included are major works by [Nam June] Paik, John Alpert, Bill Viola, . . . and productions of the Top Value Television, Downtown Community Television, and Paper Tiger television collectives." (*Choice,* July/August 1986, p. 1651)

Also reviewed in: *Afterimage,* November 1986, p. 17; *A Lib,* June 1986, p. 496; *ARBA,* 1987, p. 353; *B Rpt,* November 1986, p. 48; *Emerg Lib,* May 1986, p. 35; *JQ,* Winter 1987, p. 896; *VOYA,* February 1987, p. 306; *WLB,* December 1986, p. 75.

Board's recommendation: Public and academic libraries.

Priscilla Cheng Geahigan

Business

See also Careers and Occupations; Economics

The number of business reference sources published within the last decade has increased tremendously. With the advent of computer technology, librarians have more options for accessing these sources, such as microfiche, computer tapes, floppy disks, on-line data bases, and compact disks. The compact disk read-only-memory (CD-ROM) technology is a dream come true for many information professionals. CD-ROM provides the flexibility of keyword and field capability similar to on-line data bases, but (with few exceptions) the cost of unlimited searching is contained in a single subscription fee. CD-ROM is an ideal format for users who wish to do their own searching.

Business reference CD-ROMs are favorite reference sources for many library users. A few of these, which are government sponsored (such as data from the various censuses), are priced reasonably. Other commercially produced CD-ROMs are, unfortunately, priced much higher than printed reference sources and are difficult for many libraries to acquire. Because many of the items reviewed in this section are available on CD-ROM, librarians need to decide which format to purchase to best fulfill their users' needs.

Business information requires both accuracy and currency. It is crucial to provide library users with the most up-to-date information possible. For that reason, reference works that include periodical sources are more desirable than those without. Personal investors may use information obtained at the library to invest their retirement money. Businesspeople may use the library to do corporate research, such as finding the recent market shares of their competitors, and then revising their business strategy accordingly.

The familiar names in business and investment publishing are Dun & Bradstreet, Moody's, Standard & Poor's, and Value Line. They publish many reference sources that are similar, and in many ways their products compete with one another. Within this section, you will find reviews of some of the basic reference sources that would constitute a balanced core collection for most small- to medium-sized libraries. Large libraries should look beyond the titles in these reviews and examine other reference sources.

In order for a core collection in business to be complete, it should include an index, such as the *Business Periodical Index* (Wilson, annual). A directory, such as the *Directory of Corporate Affiliations* (National Register, 1985), would help round out the collection. Some out-of-print sources may also be helpful, such as Carl Hayel's *Encyclopedia of Management* (Van Nostrand Reinhold, 1982) and the *Labor Almanac* by Grace and Adrian Paradis (Libraries Unlimited, 1983).

Core Titles

	PUBLIC	ACADEMIC	SCHOOL
Biographical Dictionary of American Labor, rev. edition Fink, Gary M., ed. Greenwood, 1984		✦	
Brands and Their Companies: Consumer Products and Their Manufacturers with Addresses and Phone Numbers, 8th edition, 2 vols. Wood, Donna, ed. Gale, 1990	✦	✦	
Business Information Sources, rev. edition Daniells, Lorna M. Univ. of California Pr., 1985	✦	✦	
Business Serials of the U.S. Government, 2d edition Geahigan, Priscilla C., and Robert F. Rose, eds. ALA, 1988	✦	✦	
Dictionary of Business and Economics, rev. and exp. edition Ammer, Christine, and Dean S. Ammer. Macmillan/Free Pr., 1984 (See Economics)	✦	✦	
The Dow Jones-Irwin Business and Investment Almanac Levine, Sumner N., ed. Business One Irwin, annual	✦	✦	
The McGraw-Hill Handbook of Business Letters, 2d edition Poe, Roy W. McGraw-Hill, 1988	✦	✦	✦
Million Dollar Directory: America's Leading Public and Private Companies, 5 vols. Dun's Marketing Svcs., annual	✦	✦	
Moody's Manuals Moody's Investors Svc., annual	✦	✦	
Rand McNally Commercial Atlas and Marketing Guide Rand McNally, annual	✦	✦	
Small Business Sourcebook, 3d edition Dorgan, Charity Anne, ed. Gale, 1989	✦		
Standard & Poor's Register of Corporations, Directors and Executives, 3 vols., 3 suppls. Standard & Poor's, annual	✦	✦	
Standard & Poor's Stock Market Encyclopedia, Including the S&P 500 Standard & Poor's, quarterly	✦		
Standard & Poor's Stock Reports, 12 vols. Standard & Poor's, quarterly	✦		
Thomas Register of American Manufacturers, 23 vols. Thomas Publishing, annual	✦	✦	
Webster's Secretarial Handbook, 2d edition Eckersley-Johnson, Anna L., ed. Merriam-Webster, 1983	✦	✦	

With the increasing interest in mutual funds by personal investors, libraries should have a mutual fund source guide in core business collections. To complete a basic investment collection, a general-purpose investment newsletter would also be desirable.

Bibliographies such as Lorna M. Daniells's *Business Information Sources* would be able to provide guidance for building a business reference collection beyond what this business section can do. —*P. C. G.*
With contributions by Les Kong and Gordon Law.

Core Titles

Biographical Dictionary of American Labor, rev. edition. Gary M. Fink, ed. Greenwood, 1984. hard. 1 vol. 767 pp. illus. appendixes. index. ISBN 0-313-22865-5. $56.95. biographical dictionary.
HD8073.A1B56 331.88'09'2'2

Gary Fink's *Biographical Dictionary of American Labor* is a significantly expanded version of his earlier *Biographical Dictionary of American Labor Leaders* (1974). In this century, there have been few major efforts to publish substantive compilations of labor biographies. The 1925 Hanford Press *American Labor Who's Who,* and *Who's Who in Labor* published by Dryden Press in 1946, are still useful, and served as a guide for selecting figures to be included within the 1974 edition of this work.

The preface to the *Biographical Dictionary of American Labor* states that the dictionary is intended to be representative of the broad diversity of individuals active in the American labor movement, rather than a definitive roster of those most important. The panel of consultant editors assembled by Fink includes many distinguished chroniclers of the American labor movement.

In addition to the over 500 biographical entries from the first edition, the 1984 revised edition includes more than 200 additional entries. Entries average 325 words in length. Representation of women has been enhanced with entries for Emma Goldman, Jane Addams, and Florence Kelly, as well as more contemporary figures such as Delores Huerta of the United Farm Workers. However, Frances Perkins, the first woman Secretary of Labor and the advocate of some of the most important legislation affecting labor conditions and income security programs in this century, is not included. A stated objective in revising the first edition was more complete representation of Afro-Americans who were active in the labor movement, but the editors state that this was not fully achieved.

This revised edition provides expanded coverage of academicians, labor intellectuals, politicians, and observers of the American scene; there are entries for figures such as John R. Commons, the dean of labor historians, and Selig Perlman, contemporary and colleague of Commons at the University of Wisconsin in the 1920s.

The index is detailed and appears to include practically every event, person, place, and institution referenced in the dictionary. Publications by and about the subjects themselves, however, are not included in the index. Such additional accessibility would have been welcomed by researchers new to the field. Additionally, there are no cross-references in the index; the user must be thorough and creative to extract the most information from the listing. The U.S. Commission on Industrial Relations, for example, is indexed under "Commission."

The bibliographies of primary and secondary sources that appear at the end of each entry reflect recent scholarship (as of 1984). These citations constitute a conveniently available baseline from which to begin tracing relevant manuscript collections. This feature significantly enhances the usefulness of this work for scholars of the American labor movement.

The *Biographical Dictionary of American Labor* is essential for any academic research collection because of its depth of coverage afforded the over 700 individuals included. Students and scholars with varying levels of interest in the American labor movement will find it indispensable. The Board recommends this work for the core collection of academic libraries. —*G. L.*

Brands and Their Companies: Consumer Products and Their Manufacturers with Addresses and Phone Numbers (formerly: ***Trade Names Dictionary***), 8th edition. Donna Wood, ed. Gale, 1990. hard. 2 vols. 2,047 pp. ISBN 0-8103-6964-8 (set). $330 (set). directory.
T223.V4A22 929.9'7'093

Brands and Their Companies: Consumer Products and Their Manufacturers with Addresses and Phone Numbers is a two-volume set that provides the names, addresses, and phone numbers of manufacturers of consumer products. The major categories of products listed in this work include such items as apparel, appliances, automobiles, beverages, candy, computer software, cosmetics, decorative accessories, drugs, fabrics, food, furniture, games, glass products, hardware, jewelry, paper products, pet supplies, tobacco products, and toys. The information in this eighth edition was updated by questionnaires sent to manufacturers and other companies between editions.

The two-volume set covers 2,047 pages. The largest section of the set contains a listing of 210,000 consumer brand names and trademarks. The "Company Yellow Pages" follows that section, and consists of about 40,000 listings of manufacturers and importers of goods.

The trademarks and brand names in the listing include both those that are registered and unregistered, and those that are active as well as inactive. Inactive trademarks are noted in the listing, as are entries with incomplete information such as "product description unknown" or "company address unknown."

Each entry in the listing gives brief information about the product and the manufacturer. For example, the entry for *Kleenex* reads: "Kleenex—Table napkins, tissue, towels, disposable diapers—Kimberly-Clark Corp.—DRB." *DRB* is the source of the information in the *Kleenex* entry. *DRB* stands for *Drug Topics Red Book,* one of 110 titles included in the "List of Sources Used" printed at the beginning of each volume.

In the "Company Yellow Pages," the company entries provide corporate addresses. If you looked at the *Kimberly-Clark* entry, you would find the following: "Kimberly-Clark Corp., 401 N. Lake St., Neenah, WI 54956—TGR (414) 721-2000." The abbreviation *TGR* means that the information for this entry was provided by *Thomas Grocery Register.* If you needed more complete information on companies, you could consult other sources, such as the *Directory of Corporate Affiliations* (see headnote).

Many reference users will consult *Brand Names and Their Companies* to find information on product brand names. Users may range from graduate students conducting market research to consumers who wish to register a complaint against a product. The Board recommends this work for the core collections of public and academic libraries. *—P. C. G.*

Business Information Sources, rev. edition. Lorna M. Daniells. Univ. of California Pr., 1985. hard. 1 vol. 673 pp. index. ISBN 0-520-05335-4. $40. bibliography.
Z7164.C81D16 016.33

Business Information Sources is a completely revised version of an edition that was published under the same title in 1976. The first edition was regarded as a classic reference work in the field. Daniells's long tenure as head of reference at the library serving Harvard's Graduate School of Business has established her as one of the senior people in the profession.

This guide to sources of information in business is aimed at three audiences. These are business decision makers, who need to obtain data for problem solving; business students; and librarians, who can benefit from having a standard guide for answering business questions at the reference desk. Clear, concise annotations averaging about 125 words are provided on each source, detailing its usefulness. As Daniells points out in her preface, these annotations are more descriptive than critical in nature, though inclusion within the guide reflects judgment regarding quality as an authoritative source.

The first eight chapters constitute a descriptive tour through fundamental business sources of information. The chapter titles indicate the aspect of business that is considered as exemplified by the following: "U.S. Business and Economic Trends," "Basic U.S. Statistical Sources," and "Foreign Statistics and Economic Trends." Chapters 6 ("Industry Statistics") and 7 ("Locating Information on Companies, Organizations, and Individuals") will provide guidance on answering some of the questions most frequently asked of public and academic research library staff. Chapter 8 on "Investment Sources" is the most detailed, reflecting the abundance of services in this area and the accurate, timely information needed when, for example, brokers put funds at risk in the market.

The remaining chapters are devoted to other aspects of the management function—such as accounting, management information systems, corporate finance, banking, quantitative methods, operations management, human resources and personnel management, and international business. A separate chapter is provided on insurance and real estate (which this book categorizes as industries rather than functions of the management process).

Summary overviews at the beginning of each chapter highlight the subheadings to be covered within each topic, and these labels are retained throughout the specific chapter. Therefore, users can see at the outset, for instance, that the chapter on "Marketing" is subdivided into "Marketing Models," "Consumer Behavior," "Marketing Channels," "Industrial Marketing," and "Pricing."

It is important to invest time becoming familiar with the work because its organization is not readily apparent. Performance data for franchises, department stores, and discount chains, for example, are found in the chapter on "Marketing" rather than "Industry Statistics." Similarly, the data relating to insurance and real estate are contained within one topical chapter rather than within "Industry Statistics." The index is exceptionally detailed and can be used to access the appropriate section. The overall approach and arrangement of the work emerges through continued use.

The latest edition of *Business Information Sources* remains a classic. The Board recommends this work for the core collections of public and academic libraries. *—G. L.*

Business Serials of the U.S. Government, 2d edition. Priscilla C. Geahigan and Robert F. Rose, eds. ALA, 1988. 1 vol. soft. 86 pp. indexes. ISBN 0-8389-3349-1. $12.50. bibliography.
Z7165.U5B88 016.330973

Business Serials of the U.S. Government is a selected

annotated bibliography of U.S. government documents that users will find useful in business applications. The preface states that it is "aimed primarily toward the business information needs of librarians in small- and medium-sized academic and public libraries, essentially those who cannot afford to subscribe to the *American Statistics Index.*" The editors of *Business Serials of the U.S. Government,* Geahigan and Rose, are well known in business librarianship.

This bibliography is divided into 14 chapters, the most important of which include economic conditions, demographics, international business, agriculture, environment, labor, small business, taxation, and consumers. About one-fourth of the book is devoted to a chapter on industry.

The editors state that a consistent annotation length for entries was not possible, given the varied nature of the sources included. Indeed, some annotations consist of one sentence, while others typically are one-fourth of a page. In some instances, there are annotations that run well over a page. There are a total of 183 entries included in this edition. Annotations were written by members of the Business Reference Services Committee of the Reference and Adult Services Division of the American Library Association.

The editors have broadly defined a serial to be any title published on a continuing basis. Those titles determined to be primarily business or business related in nature have been included. Ephemera, court decisions (except for IRS publications), annual reports of agencies (unless primarily statistical), and inactive titles were excluded. Citations include title, initial date of publication, frequency, previous title(s) and dates of publication, special features, and Superintendent of Documents (SuDocs) number. A useful feature is the list of known indexing sources at the end of each citation.

The annotations were authored by academic librarians and were intended for public librarians. However, the reading level is quite suitable for a general audience. The annotations are well written, and each one succinctly describes, evaluates, and compares the sources with other documents. Separate title and subject indexes are also provided. Both indexes refer to specific entry numbers and are straightforward to use.

The second edition is a large-size paperback. The typeface, on the whole, is quite readable. Chapter headings and titles are set in a clear boldface type. The paper is of excellent quality stock.

The 1988 publication date means that some titles will have ceased or changed titles. *Business Serials* will not reflect new versions of census publications available on CD-ROM. A spot check of the entries shows that less than 5 percent of the titles are no longer published. Therefore, this source is still quite valuable and relatively current.

Business Serials of the U.S. Government is an outstanding reference work. The Board recommends this work for the core collections of public and academic libraries. —*L. K.*

Dictionary of Business and Economics, rev. and exp. edition. Christine Ammer and Dean S. Ammer. Macmillan/Free Pr., 1984. 1 vol. hard and soft. 507 pp. illus. ISBN 0-02-901480-8. $40 (hard); $22.95 (soft). dictionary.
HB61.A53 330.03'21

See Economics.

The Dow Jones-Irwin Business and Investment Almanac. Sumner N. Levine, ed. Business One Irwin, annual. soft. 1 vol. 720 pp. index. ISBN 1-55623-254-3. $40. almanac.
HF5003.D68a 330.9'005

Since 1982 *The Dow Jones-Irwin Business and Investment Almanac* has been published to reflect an increased emphasis on information for investment decisions. This compendium has been edited for many years by Sumner N. Levine, who also edits the *Financial Analyst's Handbook.* With the 1991 edition, the title of this work will change to *The Business One Irwin Business and Investment Almanac.* This edition will be available in hardcover only.

This useful almanac makes available in one convenient place an amalgam of business statistics, directory listings, and investment data. Each edition begins with "Business in Review," a chronology of major business and economic developments, running from September to September. Approximately two-thirds of the volume is investment oriented, with major sections devoted to "Stock Market: U.S. & Foreign"; "Industry Surveys"; "Options & Futures"; and "Investing in Real Estate." The information found in these sections is quite detailed and useful. Included in "Options & Futures," for example, is a glossary of terms, commodity charts, and introductory guides to speculating in these areas.

Other useful sections include "General Business & Economic Indicators," "Bank Failures," and "America's Top 100 Growth Companies." Many of these sections contain reprints of tables and articles from other publications, such as *Fortune* and the STATISTICAL ABSTRACT OF THE UNITED STATES (see American History). Sources are consistently documented in footnotes. Another valuable feature is the "Business Information Directory," consisting of about 100 pages of general reference, state information guide, international, and selected bibliography information. For smaller libraries that cannot afford these sources, the almanac is a necessity.

Designed for the lay investor, the almanac includes numerous guides to interpreting investment listings. An excellent example is "How to Read the New York . . . and American Stock Exchange Quotations." Explanatory features such as these are reprinted by permission of the *Wall Street Journal,* another Dow Jones publication.

Indexing in the almanac is somewhat inconsistent. For example, there are listings under both *assets, tangible* and *current assets.* Entries are frequently listed by the first words of phrases, such as *commercial banking* or *world debt problems.* Cross-references are also a rarity in the index. Acronyms are both inconsistently used and alphabetized, sometimes as words, other times at the beginning of the alphabetical listing. If users are unable to locate an item through the index, it may be helpful to scan the table of contents for the major sections in boldface capital letters.

The typeface is generally readable, with the exception of the microscopic print in "Financial Statement Ratios by Industry," "Sources of Venture Capital," and "Taxes."

The almanac, in short, is packed with reference material that a library may typically need to refer to on a daily basis. Questions regarding the performance of mutual funds, gross national product, consumer price indexes, and interest rates may all be answered through this one source. Though updated annually, information contained in the volume generally runs two years behind the publication date.

The Dow Jones-Irwin Business and Investment Almanac is an outstanding reference work. The Board recommends this work for the core collections of public and academic libraries. —*L. K.*

The McGraw-Hill Handbook of Business Letters, 2d edition. Roy W. Poe. McGraw-Hill, 1988. hard. 1 vol. 306 pp. index. ISBN 0-07-050369-9. $44.95 handbook.
HF5726.P55 808.066651

Books about business writing, such as *The McGraw-Hill Handbook of Business Letters,* are popular in libraries because many people are not confident about their writing abilities. People who own small businesses use these sources for sample business forms and contracts. Students use business sources for sample letters to follow when they have business writing courses, or when they have to write a letter of inquiry for a job.

Like many other business letter writing handbooks, this book provides many sample letters. The author, Roy W. Poe, is an experienced business writer and a business education consultant who has also written *The McGraw-Hill Guide to Effective Business Reports* (McGraw-Hill, 1986) and *The Business Communication: A Problem-Solving Approach* (McGraw-Hill, 1989). In *The McGraw-Hill Handbook of Business Letters,* Poe presents guidelines for writing a good business letter. Then he provides nearly 200 model letters that cover various types of business correspondence related to both professional and social obligations. The letters include topics such as submitting a job application, accepting or rejecting a job offer, offering congratulations to an employee, recommending or terminating an employee, accepting or rejecting an invitation, writing a sales letter, and writing a goodwill letter to a customer.

One distinguishing feature of this book is that, with each sample letter, it includes a one-paragraph description of the "Situation" and an "Analysis of the Letter." The "Situation" explains the background of the sample letter. The "Analysis of the Letter" analyzes the organization, style, tone, and underlying psychology of the letter's construction. The analysis also discusses the pros and cons for each paragraph of the letter. This allows unsophisticated business letter writers to adapt the format and tone of the sample to their own circumstances. At the end of the handbook, a detailed subject index is provided to assist the user in finding letters that are of interest.

The McGraw-Hill Handbook of Business Letters is a no-nonsense handbook that is revised and expanded from the first edition. The Board recommends this work for the core collections of public, academic, and school libraries. —*P. C. G.*

Million Dollar Directory: America's Leading Public and Private Companies. Dun's Marketing Svcs., annual. hard. 5 vols. 9,270 pp. index. ISSN 0734-2661. $350. directory. on-line.
HC102.D8 338.7'4'0973

The basic series of each annual *Million Dollar Directory: America's Leading Public and Private Companies* contains five volumes. The first three volumes provide an alphabetical listing of companies. The fourth volume, titled *Cross-Reference by Industry,* provides cross-references from businesses to Standard Industrial Classification (SIC) codes. These codes are assigned to companies according to the industry and the line of business they are in. A fifth volume, titled *Cross-Reference by Geography,* provides cross-references from businesses to geographical locations. An additional volume called the *Million Dollar Directory Top 50,000* is available. This volume lists the 50,000 companies with tangible net worth exceeding $2,500,000. There is a separate 50-page "Master Index" for users who want to check on the inclusion of a specific company.

The 1990 five-volume basic set has expanded coverage to include 160,000 U.S. businesses. Although the directory focuses on headquarters and single-location businesses, company subsidiaries are also included if they file a separate operating statement and meet the listing criteria. No branch locations or divisions are listed because they do not report a separate net worth from their parent company. The majority of the listings (about 140,000) are for privately owned businesses.

The first three volumes of the 1990 set provide an alphabetical listing of companies. Entries on individual companies vary from five or six lines to half a column. Each entry includes the company's address and telephone number, the primary SIC code, major line of business, and the DUNS number. The majority of entries include additional information such as annual sales volume, number of employees, secondary SIC codes, and the name of at least one company executive and his or her title or position. Many also provide the names of the company's bank, accounting firm, and legal counsel.

The volume titled *Cross-Reference by Industry* provides valuable information about specific industries. For example, there are 122 businesses listed under the manufacturing of natural and processed cheeses (SIC 2022). By examining this list, any cheese manufacturer can immediately tell who its major competitors are. Furthermore, the individual company record would reveal the sales volume and number of persons employed by each competitor. Job seekers interested in working in the cheese industry would have immediate access to the addresses and executive names of 122 potential employers. Each business can potentially be listed by up to six SIC codes in this set. Therefore, a business could be located under its major business code as well as up to five of its minor lines of business codes.

The volume titled *Cross-Reference by Geography* lists businesses in alphabetical order within states and cities, and includes SIC codes. This information can be useful to job seekers trying to relocate, marketing analysts attempting to avoid concentrated markets, and companies looking for new plant sites.

As stated in the *Million Dollar Directory*'s introduction, Dun & Bradstreet Corporation maintains its data through in-person and telephone interviews. Because the directory covers a larger company base than the STANDARD & POOR'S REGISTER OF CORPORATIONS, DIRECTORS AND EXECUTIVES, libraries of all sizes should find the *Million Dollar Directory* valuable for their collection in addition to the STANDARD & POOR'S REGISTER. Libraries serving a large business community might wish to investigate the CD-ROM version, *Dun's Million Dollar Disc.* It provides quarterly updates and includes executive biographical information from Dun's four-volume set *Reference Book of Corporate Managements: America's Corporate Leaders.* For libraries that only occasionally need to find company information, however, the same information is available on the D&B *Million Dollar Directory* on-line data base.

The Board recommends this work for the core collections of public and academic libraries. —*P. C. G.*

Moody's Manuals. Moody's Investors Svc., annual. hard. 8 series in 16 vols. illus. ISSN 0545-0233. manual. on-line. CD-ROM.
HG4961.M67 332.6

The *Moody's Manuals* include the following series: *Moody's Bank and Financial Manual* (4 volumes); *Moody's Industrial Manual* (2 volumes); *Moody's International Manual* (2 volumes); *Moody's Municipal and Government Manual* (3 volumes); *Moody's OTC Industrial Manual; Moody's OTC Unlisted Manual; Moody's Public Utility Manual* (2 volumes); and *Moody's Transportation Manual.* The *Moody's Manuals* are the best-known sets of financial manuals for investment purposes. They provide factual and financial information about publicly held companies traded on U.S. stock exchanges. The *Moody's International Manual* series covers major foreign companies.

A package subscription to the *Moody's Manuals* includes service to all of the above series, but each one can also be purchased individually. Besides the annual hardcover manuals, a complete subscription will also provide weekly or biweekly "News Reports" of each manual and the *Moody's Complete Corporate Index.* The "News Reports" contain current information on personnel changes, financial updates, mergers and acquisitions, plant openings, new products, and descriptions of new bond and stock issues. *Moody's Complete Corporate Index* is a separate pamphlet that serves as a guide for finding specific company profiles among the various manuals. The profiles cover a total of over 25,000 corporations and institutions.

Companies are covered by each manual according to their major industry groups as indicated in the titles of the manuals. The company profiles vary in length from one-sixth of a page to several pages. Each profile provides basic information on the company, including its history, capital structure, recent development, property, subsidiaries and affiliates, officers, directors, auditors, general counsel, and number of stockholders. Additional information includes, among other items, mergers and acquisitions, joint ventures, consolidated income account and balance sheet, long-term debt, credit loan agreements, and a letter to stockholders from the chief executive officer.

Each series of the *Moody's Manuals* has a "Special Features Section" that includes tables and charts containing data of special interest. Topics in the *Industrial Manual* include "Exchange Rates," "Chronological List of Maturing Bonds and Notes," "Stock Splits," "Gold Reserves," and "Business Financing Costs." The *Transportation Manual* features tables ranging from "Air Transport Data" and the "Trucking Industry" to "Railroad Labor: Employees, Hours and Compensation." The *Bank and Financial Manual* provides listings such as "100 Largest Banks in World, Ranked by Size of Deposits," "Top 100 Thrift Institutions," and "300 Largest Life Insurance Companies." Some of this information would otherwise be difficult to find in libraries with limited business and economic sources.

Moody's Manuals are relatively easy to understand and use. They are well-prepared products. Libraries with a business and investment section should definitely include this set of manuals. The CD-ROM version provides similar information for the *Industrial Manual,* the *OTC Industrial Manual,* and selected companies for the other manuals. Libraries that answer a minimal number of business questions might want to subscribe to at least the *Industrial Manual* and the *OTC Industrial Manual* series. On-line access is available on Dialog's Moody's Corporate News and Moody's Corporate Profiles.

The Board recommends these works for the core collections of public and academic libraries.

—*P. C. G.*

Rand McNally Commercial Atlas and Marketing Guide. Rand McNally, annual. hard. 1 vol. 568 pp. illus. indexes. $295. atlas.
G1201 912

Now in its 120th edition, the *Rand McNally Commercial Atlas and Marketing Guide* "brings current economic and geographic information together in a reference work designed to provide both maximum statistical coverage and authoritative interpretation of business data" (introduction). Rand McNally has a much-deserved reputation for high-quality mapmaking and research. The *Commercial Atlas and Marketing Guide* is the oldest annually published reference atlas in existence.

The 1989 edition is organized in six sections. These are: U.S. and Canadian metropolitan area maps; U.S. transportation and communications data; U.S. economic data; U.S. population data; U.S. maps; and indexes by state.

The metropolitan area maps section presents U.S. state, county, and city maps with detailed coverage of 14 major U.S. and Canadian metropolitan areas. Other sections provide data on U.S. highway, railroad, and airline networks, and telephone, postal service, and zip code areas as marketing areas. The zip code data are detailed, providing data on population, households, passenger car registrations, and retail sales. The economic data are also quite extensive, describing business activity for states, counties, cities, metropolitan statistical areas, basic trading areas, and the largest corporations engaged in such activities as banking, manufacturing, retailing, and transportation. Data are reprinted from market statistics in *Sales and Marketing Magazine*'s "Survey of Buying Power" issue. Corporation rankings are reprinted with permission from such sources as *Fortune* and *Advertising Age.*

Population data from the 1980 U.S. Census are provided for states, counties, cities, metropolitan statistical areas, and "Ranally metro areas" (Rand McNally–defined areas). Marketing statistics such as income, food store and drugstore sales, and effective buying income are indicated for major trading areas.

The U.S. maps, tables of statistics, and index of places make up the last sections. These features provide data on states, give basic business data for counties, and list principal cities, towns, and inhabited places.

While designed primarily for business and marketing personnel, the atlas is also useful to business students, urban and regional planners, and other government personnel. The table of contents is easy to follow, indicating detailed sections. Geographic areas are also easily located through an excellent index to the state maps. Throughout the publication, there are a judicious use of color in the maps, sufficient detail, clear typefaces, and easy-to-follow legends.

The atlas is much more than a volume of maps, because the work also provides a variety of marketing statistics and reference information concerning major markets in the United States. Although the atlas is updated annually, information contained in the volume will generally run two years behind the publication date.

This large-sized atlas uses a very legible typeface and a paper stock of an excellent quality. The binding is exceptional for a volume of these dimensions. Given its size and weight, libraries will need to provide special shelving arrangements for this title.

The *Rand McNally Commercial Atlas and Marketing Guide* is an outstanding reference work. The Board recommends this work for the core collections of public and academic libraries. —*L. K.*

Small Business Sourcebook, 3d edition. Charity Anne Dorgan, ed. Gale, 1989. hard. 2 vols. 1,913 pp. appendix. index. ISBN 0-8103-2648-5. $199. handbook.
HD2346.U5.S.65 658.022'07032'19

The *Small Business Sourcebook* states that it is "an annotated guide to live and print sources of information and assistance for 163 specific small businesses, with a detailed listing of similar sources for the small business community in general." This is not a book that provides actual information, such as how to start up a small business, but a handbook that provides a listing of sources of information about 163 kinds of small businesses. A supplement, which lists additional profiles, is also available from Gale.

There are two major parts to the book. Part 1 contains a listing of the 163 kinds of business and information sources. The businesses range from air charter services, bicycle shops, children's daycare centers, fish farms, and videocassette rental stores, to word-processing services. Information sources about these businesses include names of trade organizations and titles of books, pamphlets, and serials. Each business entry is broken down into categories, such as start-up information, primary associations, educational programs, reference works, statistical sources, trade shows and conventions, among other information sources.

Part 2 provides general information on small businesses and a listing of general assistance sources. Some sections in this volume would be of special interest to novice entrepreneurs, such as "Small Business Development Consultants" and "Venture Capital Firms." A section entitled "State Governments" contains a list of government agencies that would be helpful to all entrepreneurs. Another listing of "State Small Business Development Centers" could also be very useful to users, but since these centers are mostly federally funded, the listing is hidden under the "Federal Government" section.

Another useful source of information in part 2 is a rather selective listing of small business incubator centers that offer assistance such as office space at below-market rates, shared services, counseling, and more to start-up companies, as well as a listing of educational institutions that have a special interest in small business.

The present edition is much expanded over the previous two. It is a unique reference tool for libraries that deal with small business questions on a frequent basis. This volume lists titles ranging from simple pamphlets issued by individual trade associations to research sources such as the *Almanac of Business and Industrial Financial Ratios* (Troy, 1986). Although a useful resource, many of the trade publications cited would only be found in a limited number of libraries. In addition, most users of the *Small Business Sourcebook* will require further assistance for document retrieval and ordering because the government document citations do not include Superintendent of Document classification numbers or Government Printing Office stock numbers.

The Board recommends this work for the core collection of public libraries. —*P. C. G.*

Standard & Poor's Register of Corporations, Directors and Executives. Standard & Poor's, annual. hard. 3 vols. plus 3 suppls. $498. ISSN 0361-3623. on-line.
HG4057.A4 338.8'025'73

For over 60 years, the Standard & Poor's Corporation has been publishing *Standard & Poor's Register of Corporations, Directors and Executives,* a major reference work profiling companies and their major personnel.

Volume 1 consists of 50,000 company listings in alphabetical order. The criteria for inclusion are not stated anywhere in the publication; however, it is evident that it uses guidelines based on company size. Typical entries include names, titles, and functions of officers and directors; names of company's accounting, bank, and law firms; stock exchange(s) on which company's stock is traded; description of company's products/services; standard industrial classification (SIC) codes; annual sales and number of employees; division names and functions; zip codes; and telephone numbers. Subsidiary listings are separate, with references to parent companies.

Volume 2, the "Directors and Executives Section," consists of 70,000 individual listings in alphabetical order. The individuals listed serve as officers, directors, trustees, and partners. The listings provide principal business affiliations with official titles, business addresses, residence addresses, and, where obtainable, year and place of birth, and college and year of graduation. Individuals who serve on numerous corporate boards (that is, interlocking directorships) are indicated.

Volume 3 consists of seven color-coded indexes. They are the "SIC Index," "SIC Codes," "Geographic Index," "Corporate Family Indexes," "Obituary Section," "New Individual Additions," and "New Company Additions."

One of the primary reasons for using the register is to develop direct-mail lists of prospective customers. General audiences may also use this work to obtain the names and addresses of appropriate persons in specific companies. Job seekers may use the register to identify key personnel.

The annual volumes are updated by three supplements published in April, July, and October. Each supplement is cumulative, so only the latest needs to be retained. Users concerned with the most up-to-date information may want to monitor developments in business periodicals and newspapers.

Perhaps due to listing criteria and compilation methods, users may note inconsistencies on company information when comparing entries with such sources as the MILLION DOLLAR DIRECTORY and *Directory of Corporate Affiliations* (see headnote for information on the latter). It is suggested that users consult as many of these directories as are available and verify company data through primary sources, such as Securities and Exchange Commission Form 10-Ks. The accuracy and reliability of subsidiary and parent company data can be problematic in these sources.

The paper used for the register is rather thin, so that the print from the left pages bleeds through. Pages tear easily and become ragged through heavy use. The largest of the set, volume 1, may experience binding problems over time.

The Board recommends the *Standard & Poor's Register of Corporations, Directors and Executives* for the core collections of public and academic libraries.

—*L. K.*

Standard & Poor's Stock Market Encyclopedia, Including the S&P 500. Standard & Poor's, quarterly. soft. 1 vol. unpaged. illus. ISSN 0882-5467. $43 (one copy); $65 (semiannual). encyclopedia.
HG4057.A46 338.7'4'073

Standard & Poor's Stock Market Encyclopedia, Including the S&P 500 is a single-volume quarterly that includes the investment profiles of 750 major companies, including the companies listed in the "Standard & Poor's 500." The S&P 500 refers to the S&P 500 stock index that many investors use to gauge the fluctuations of stock market performance. Among all of the U.S. stock indexes, the Dow Jones Average and the Standard & Poor's 500 index are the two most well known to the general public. As its name implies, the S&P 500 index tracks the stock performance of 500 companies. The index comprises industrial companies, utilities, financial institutions, and transportation firms. These companies trade on the New York Stock Exchange and the American Stock Exchange, as well as the over-the-counter market. Therefore, the companies covered by this volume represent a broad array of large, actively traded stocks in the United States. These stocks are spread across about 100 industry subgroups.

In order to help users with different investment objectives, the editors provide specialized stock selection tables that are based upon information about the 750 stocks covered in the volume, such as "Companies with Five Straight Years of Rising Profit Margins," "Rapid Growth Stocks," "Stocks with High Rankings," "Higher Dividends for Ten Years," and more. For new investors, a glossary is included in which terms such as *earnings* and *P/E ratio* are clearly explained.

The company profiles of the 750 stocks included in this volume are identical to those of their counterparts in the three sets of *Standard & Poor's Stock Reports.* STANDARD & POOR'S STOCK MARKET ENCYCLOPEDIA will be useful for investors who wish to stay informed about the most actively traded stocks or those who do not wish to be bothered with the multivolume *Standard & Poor's Stock Reports.*

The Board recommends this work for the core collection of public libraries. —*P. C. G.*

Standard & Poor's Stock Reports. Standard & Poor's, quarterly. soft or looseleaf. 12 vols. index. ISSN 0191-1112. $795 (yearly). handbook.
HG4905.S44 332.322

Standard & Poor's Stock Reports covers about 4,500 companies. These continually updated, two-page company reports are published in three separate sets of four books each. The books are available in looseleaf or bound form. One set of books, the *New York Stock Exchange Reports,* provides a profile of every company listed on the New York Stock Exchange (NYSE). Another set, the *American Stock Exchange Reports,* covers every company on the American Stock Exchange (ASE). The *Over-the-Counter Reports* set describes the most widely held and actively traded companies on the over-the-counter (OTC) and regional stock exchanges. An accompanying paperback that is published three times a year, the *OTC Profiles,* covers 700 smaller and less actively traded OTC companies. These companies are profiled in concise ⅓-page reports instead of the full two-page treatment accorded other companies.

In all three series and the *OTC Profiles,* companies are listed alphabetically by name. For users who do not know which set to use, a quarterly *Stock Reports Index* presents companies on the NYSE, ASE, and OTC series in one alphabetical sequence. The index indicates each company's stock exchange affiliation and stock report number. A seven-page glossary is included at the end of the index in order to clarify some of the terms used.

The two-page profile of each company in the *Standard & Poor's Stock Reports* gives investors a good summary of the company's recent development and financial situation. Each profile includes a business summary, current outlook, and important developments in the company. Financial data include the company stock's recent price range, P/E ratio, dividend, yield, Standard & Poor's ranking, beta, earnings, and the company's income and balance sheet data. A small but precise chart showing a five-year trading trend of the stock is also included.

The looseleaf service has a useful feature not found in the bound version. It provides additional pages containing information on pertinent changes in company status such as name changes, mergers and acquisitions, changes from public to private ownership, and changes in stock exchange affiliation. These pages will direct users to the new company name, or will explain why a company's report is no longer available.

Public libraries that serve a community interested in personal investing will find *Standard & Poor's Stock Reports* quarterly service desirable. The Board recommends this work for the core collection of public libraries. —*P. C. G.*

Thomas Register of American Manufacturers. Thomas Publishing, annual. hard. 23 vols. illus. index. ISSN 0362-7721. $210. on-line. CD-ROM.
T12.T6 338.7′6′02573

The *Thomas Register of American Manufacturers* provides information on which products are made in the United States, where they are made, and which manufacturers make them. The number of volumes in this set has been growing over the years. The 1990 set is divided into three sections totaling 23 volumes. Each volume contains over 2,000 pages. Over 148,000 U.S. manufacturers are included in the set. Of the 23 volumes, the *Products & Services Section* comprises volumes 1 through 14; the *Company Profiles Section,* volumes 15 and 16; and the *Catalog File Section,* volumes 17 through 23.

The *Products and Services Section* covers more than 52,000 product and service headings. The headings are listed alphabetically, under controlled subject terms established by the editors. A detailed index is included at the end of volume 14. The index is helpful in locating individual products in specific volumes and pages. For instance, the heading "Lawn Mowers" will refer users to vol. 8, page 16,476. Here, the user will also see other related headings such as "Lawn Mower Bags," "Lawn Mower Blades," "Lawn Mower Handles," "Lawn Mower Housings," "Lawn Mower Sharpeners," "Lawn Mower Tractors," and "Lawn Mower Trailers." First-time users will be able to find products more easily by consulting the index. Once the register page has been found, the user will see a list of manufacturers of that product arranged alphabetically by state and then by city. Advertisements from the listed manufacturers, many of which contain pictures of the products, are also found on the same page.

Within volume 16 of the *Company Profiles Section* there is a 633-page, alphabetically arranged American trademark index. This index includes both registered and unregistered trademarks and brand names along with the name and address of the manufacturer of that product. For example, "Kimberly Clark Corp." and its address are given as the manufacturer under the index entry for Kleenex brand facial tissues.

Individual entries in the *Company Profiles Section* are arranged alphabetically by company name. Most include such basic information as major line of business, address, telephone number, and a tangible asset rating assigned by the publisher. Many entries also include fax and telex numbers, and names of company executives.

The seven-volume *Catalog File Section* contains over 10,000 pages of company product catalogs from more than 1,500 companies. The catalogs are arranged alphabetically by company name. These catalogs provide much useful information because many include pictures, schematic drawings, and specifications of individual products.

For more current information, librarians can access the biannually updated *Thomas Register Online Database.* The directory's CD-ROM version is also updated biannually.

There is an enormous amount of information contained in this set. Companies are charged for the advertisements and catalogs reproduced in the *Thomas Register,* and this helps to reduce the price per set and make it more affordable for libraries. It is a bargain for those libraries that need this sort of information. The Board recommends this work for the core collections of public and academic libraries. —*P. C. G.*

Webster's Secretarial Handbook, 2d edition. Anna L. Eckersley-Johnson, ed. Merriam-Webster, 1983. hard. 1 vol. 578 pp. illus. appendix. index. ISBN 0-87779-136-8. $10.95. handbook.
HF5547.5.W4 651

A complete guide to developing and maintaining professional secretarial skills is contained in the second edition of *Webster's Secretarial Handbook.* The table of contents quickly establishes the layout of this handbook, and a few moments spent reviewing the 15 chapter headings easily leads users to the appropriate entry. Each chapter addresses one broad skill area, such as oral communication, corporate etiquette, and interpersonal relations; organizing conferences and meetings; techniques for dictation and transcription; word processing, style, and usage in business correspondence; handling office mail and records management; photocopying equipment; basic accounting; telecommunications; and international business. The handbook is prefaced with information about "career-path development" in the secretarial profession. Subsections are clearly delineated at the outset of each chapter, and headings in boldface type throughout the text simplify access to the information.

The panel of contributors to the handbook represents a balance of perspectives between college educators and private sector executives. Such broad-based input is reflected in the comprehensiveness of this handbook. The chapter on travel and functioning in an international business environment is excellent and is typical of the wealth of detail evident throughout the handbook.

Despite an effort to focus on new equipment and procedures in this current edition, the handbook is dated with respect to many changes in technology that have transformed the corporate office this past decade. Terms such as *personal computer, spreadsheet, relational data bases,* and *information systems* came into vogue after this second edition was published. The next edition will require substantial revision to help secretaries understand how information is created and shared within the organization, as well as how it is obtained outside the corporation via electronic means of access.

Nevertheless, the *Webster's Secretarial Handbook* contains more than enough data and cues to make it an essential reference source for secretaries and executives at all levels of experience. The Board recommends this work for the core collections of public and school libraries. —*L. K.*

Supplementary Titles

Business and Economics Books, 1876–1983. Bowker, 1983. hard. 4 vols. 5,171 pp. index. ISBN 0-8352-1614-4 (set). $199 (set). bibliography.
Z7164.C81B927 016.33

These volumes include "books both in and out of print. More than 143,000 titles are listed under 40,547 LC subject headings, with Author and Title Indexes (in v.4) offering page references to the main entries in the Subject Index (v.1–3). The entries, selected from the 1.8 million titles in the American Book Publishing Record (ABPR) database, initially were chosen by Dewey decimal and Library of Congress classification numbers for business and economics, with some titles included from identifiable related areas. Then each entry was reviewed for appropriateness.

"This set was produced in response to the desire expressed by users of business information for a retrospective tool that could be used for reference, research, collection development, and interlibrary loan efforts." (*BL,* July 1984, p. 1530)

Also reviewed in: *ARBA,* 1984, p. 346; *LJ,* March 1, 1984, p. 439; *WLB,* December 1983, p. 305.

Board's recommendation: Public and academic libraries.

Dictionary of Business and Management, 2d edition. Jerry M. Rosenberg. John Wiley, 1983. hard. 1 vol. 631 pp. ISBN 0-471-86730-6. $36.95. dictionary.
HF1001.R79 330.0321

The expanded *Dictionary of Business and Management* includes "more than 10,000 entries providing . . . definitions of terms covering business topics. Examples of new terms include Subchapter S corporation, beachhead demands, floppy disk, leniency bias, and level payment mortgage.

"Some definitions have been updated and sexist language changed. . . . The . . . Appendixes are included as before with corrections to the foreign currency listing, new quotations, and additional chronology items. While, as before, these can be helpful (especially in an office setting), the word list with its clear, concise definitions is the most valuable portion. With its extensive expansion, providing more terms than other such dictionaries, the second edition of [this book] should prove useful to libraries serving business clienteles and to individuals as a desk reference." (*BL,* April 15, 1984, p. 1170)

Also reviewed in: *LJ,* March 1, 1984, p. 440.

Board's recommendation: Public and academic libraries.

Direct Marketing Market Place. Edward L. Stern, ed. Hilary House, 1987. soft. 1 vol. 664 pp. index. ISBN 0-934464-09X. $85. directory.
HF5415.1.D57 016.33

The *Direct Marketing Market Place,* "introduces a reference work intended to serve as a marketing tool 'for all those engaged in the business of direct marketing.' It is arranged in three major sections ('Direct

Marketers of Products and Services to Consumers & Industry,' 'Service Firms & Suppliers to Direct Marketing Companies,' 'Creative & Consulting Services'), which are subdivided by categories *(Catalog & Retail Sales, Nurseries & Seed Companies . . .)*. Entries in each category are listed alphabetically and give company name, address, phone number, key personnel, and brief descriptions of firms' services. Some entries also give number of employees, sales volume, and direct marketing advertising budget. The three major sections end with Geographical Indexes to the firms listed therein.

"The list of readings includes publications of the Direct Mail/Marketing Association and trade publishers.

"A directory of names, addresses, and phone numbers of companies and individuals serves also as an Index to the entries in DMMP. A code guides the user to the section and category in which the listing appears." (*BL,* December 15, 1980, p. 589)

Also reviewed in: *ARBA,* 1980, p. 360; *Choice,* May 1980, p. 362; *Ser Lib,* 1985, p. 57.

Board's recommendation: Public and academic libraries.

Encyclopedia of Business Information Sources, 6th edition. James Way, ed. Gale, 1988. hard. 1 vol. plus suppl. 878 pp.; 125 pp. (suppl.). index. ISBN 0-8103-0364-7; 0-8103-2764-3 (suppl.). $220. bibliography.
HF5353.89 016.33

The *Encyclopedia of Business Information Sources* "aims to be a bibliographic guide for the business person on just about any subject in which he or she might have an interest: for example, the banana industry, libraries, explosives, home economics, and tax shelters. Under each subject are listed handbooks, bibliographies, periodicals, directories, statistics sources, general works, etc." (*LJ,* September 1, 1980, p. 1723)

"No business collection can do without [this book]. . . . The 1,300-plus topics it covers have been expanded. . . . The internal changes are more subtle and far-reaching. The lists of sources on each of the 1,300 topics have been updated extensively. Some topics are more volatile than others, thus there are more changes in the lists for personnel topics than for many of the industry-specific topics (e.g., lead industry). Many of the new entries are for databases, making this useful not only as a 'Sheehy' for business sources, but also as a database selection guide. The *Encyclopedia* remains an essential source." (*WLB,* March 1984, p. 515)

"If your requirement is for bibliographic assistance, . . . [this book remains] your best bet." (*LJ,* March 1, 1981, p. 537)

Also reviewed in: *ARBA,* 1987, p. 70; *Ref Bk R,* 1987, p. 11.

Board's recommendation: Public and academic libraries.

Kohler's Dictionary for Accountants, 6th edition. W. W. Cooper and Yuji Ijiri, eds. Prentice-Hall, 1983. hard. 1 vol. 574 pp. ISBN 0-13-516658-6. $68.80. dictionary.
HF5621.K6 657.0321

The editors of *Kohler's Dictionary for Accountants* "indicate that there are 4,538 terms defined in this edition, compared with some 3,000 entries in the fifth edition, 2,660 of which were carried over. Due to extensive revisions within existing entries, the editors estimate that well over half the material is new or substantially revised. . . . The length of entries ranges from around 15 words for simple identifications to well over 2,500 words for key accounting concepts such as 'depreciation.' Entries average between 75 and 100 words.

"The new editors . . . have maintained the structure and a good deal of the substance of Kohler's earlier work. . . . Although the title of the volume indicates coverage of accounting terminology, its appeal is broader. In addition to brief explanations of such terms as discounted cash-flow method, one will find scores of definitions of general terms from such areas as statistics, management, and economics. . . . The style of presentation is unusually clear." (*BL,* December 1, 1983, p. 555)

Also reviewed in: *AR,* October 1983, p. 843.

Board's recommendation: Public and academic libraries.

Standard Handbook for Secretaries. Lois Irene Hutchinson. McGraw-Hill, 1969. soft. 1 vol. 616 pp. index. ISBN 0-07-031537-X. $16.95. manual.
HF5547.H77 651

The *Standard Handbook for Secretaries* is a well-established reference. "Besides chapters on English, grammar, letter writing, postal information, filing, etc., this handbook gives help on specialized subjects such as legal and court papers, banking papers, securities, financial statements, etc. There are also lists of abbreviations, holidays, weights and measures, and reference books." (*BL,* January 1937, p. 146)

Also reviewed in: *LJ,* March 1, 1970, p. 866.

Board's recommendation: Public and school libraries.

New and Noteworthy

Banking Terminology, 3d edition. American Bankers Assn. 1989. soft. 1 vol. 409 pp. ISBN 0-89982-360-2. $30. dictionary.
HG151.B268 332.1′03

"This third edition [of *Banking Terminology*] defines approximately 6,100 terms and concepts used in banking. . . . Some of the subject areas covered are auditing, bank cards, commercial lending, electronic funds transfer, real estate finance, securities, and trusts. A typical definition is from one to five sentences in length. . . . There are acronyms and abbreviations for approximately 325 terms. . . ." (*BL,* April 1, 1990, p. 1573)

Doing Business in New York City. Thomas E. Crain and Jeffrey P. Levine. Dow Jones-Irwin, 1989. soft. 1 vol. 1,006 pp. illus. index. ISBN 1-55623-137-7. $21.95. directory.
HF5068.N52C73 338.7′4

Doing Business in New York City "is an inexpensive directory of 400 large and 100 small public companies and 1,000 private firms doing business in the New York City metropolitan area. . . . The first 32 pages are a short travel guide to New York City. . . . This is followed by the alphabetical list of the 400 large public companies with addresses and telephone number, type of business, and a short, six- or seven-sentence description. Also presented are a list of the main officers and two years of revenue, assets, and income data. The 100 smaller companies follow with similar information in somewhat abbreviated form." (*BL,* November 1, 1989, p. 604)

Encyclopedia of Telemarketing. Richard L. Bencin and Donald J. Jonovic, eds. Prentice-Hall, 1989. hard. 1 vol. 798 pp. illus. index. ISBN 0-13-275-918-7. $69.95. encyclopedia.

The *Encyclopedia of Telemarketing* is a "weighty volume [that] brings together 30 experts to comment on virtually every aspect of telemarketing, including training; developing and selling scripts; generating lists; organizing telemarketing stations; as well as dealing with international problems and using telemarketing systems for fund-raising. . . . [There is] an excellent index along with a glossary." (*LJ,* September 1, 1989, p. 178)

Encyclopedic Dictionary of Accounting and Finance. Jae K. Shim and Joel G. Siegel. Prentice-Hall, 1989. hard. 1 vol. 572 pp. illus. index. ISBN 0-13-275801-6. $49.95. dictionary.
HF1001.S525 657.03

The "*Encyclopedic Dictionary of Accounting and Finance* is intended for practitioners in the fields of accounting, finance, investments, and banking. It is arranged alphabetically and contains approximately 600 entries. Entries vary from a paragraph to several pages long and are abundantly illustrated with charts, tables, and diagrams. A typical entry includes a number of examples demonstrating the concept." (*BL,* November 15, 1989, pp. 690–692)

Executives on the Move. A. Dale Timpe, ed. Gale, quarterly (1989–). soft. 262 pp. indexes. ISBN 0-8103-6885-4. $150. directory.
338.7

"*Executives on the Move* lists nearly 5,400 executives, middle and high-level managers, and directors in U.S. business and industry who have recently changed or assumed new positions. . . . Data are taken from 21 newspapers and business-oriented newspapers such as the *Chicago Tribune, USA Today, Barron's, Forbes, Fortune,* and the *Wall Street Journal.* . . . Entries are arranged alphabetically under the name of the executive. . . . All entries include new title; . . . an indication of the nature of the change in position; . . . name of company; and the newspaper or periodical that was the source of information." (*BL,* November 1, 1989, pp. 604–606)

Facts On File—National Quotation Bureau Directory of Publicly Traded Bonds. Facts On File, semiannual (1989–). hard (including 10 monthly paper supplements). ISBN 0-8160-2162-7. $80. directory.
HG4651 332.6323025

Facts On File—National Quotation Bureau Directory of Publicly Traded Stocks. Facts On File, semiannual (1989–). hard (including 10 monthly paper supplements). ISBN 0-8160-2160-0. $90. directory.
HG4921 332.6322025

"Presented here are 'comprehensive summarizations of essential market data' from the daily NQB 'Pink Sheets' for stocks and NQB 'Yellow Sheets' for bonds. . . . The *Directory of Publicly Traded Stocks* includes more than 23,000 companies whose securities are publicly traded in the U.S., plus an additional 10,000 companies that have merged, changed their names, gone out of business, or gone private. . . . The *Directory of Publicly Traded Bonds* provides information on 16,500 bonds traded publicly in the U.S. . . . Listings include issuer, coupon rate, maturity, and interest date; where listed; if there are conversion privileges; trustee; default date and nature if this has occurred; terms on which offered; if called, . . . if recognized; notes on mergers, etc." (*BL,* November 1, 1989, pp. 606–607)

Home Business Resource Guide. Cheryl Gorder. Blue Bird Publishing, 1989. soft. 1 vol. 144 pp. illus. indexes. ISBN 0-933025-15-7. $11.95. handbook.
658.041

The *Home Business Resource Guide* "includes an introduction to home business today, four thumbnail sketches of people working out of the home, and selected, annotated lists of information on starting or developing home businesses. These include books; courses and speakers; magazines; organizations; mailing lists; distributorships; dealerships and sales opportunities; wholesale products; and equipment and supplies." (*BL,* April 1, 1990, p. 1576)

The Manager's Desk Reference. Cynthia Berryman-Fink. American Management Assn., 1989. hard. 1 vol. 288 pp. index. ISBN 0-8144-5904-8. $24.95. manual.
HD30.33.B47 658.3

The Manager's Desk Reference "is a helpful and practical reference tool for the busy manager who doesn't have time to stop and research a topic. Forty-three areas, ranging from assertiveness to women and minorities in the workplace, are presented in alphabetical arrangement. Each subject is discussed in an essay averaging about eight pages and is followed by an annotated bibliography. Emphasis is on the human relations aspect of management and how to deal with 'peers, supervisors, subordinates, customers, the public, the press, etc.' " (*LJ,* June 1, 1989, p. 96)

Setting Up a Company in the European Community: A Country by Country Guide. Brebner & Co., comp. Oryx, 1989. hard. 1 vol. 251 pp. ISBN 0-89774-601-5. $49.50. handbook.
KJE2448.S47 346.4'006

"There are 12 chapters to [*Setting up a Company in the European Community*]. . . . Each chapter is divided into two parts. The first part details the requirements for setting up a private company, the second for a public company. The information in both sections includes documents, registration requirements, capital requirements, ownership, management, formation expenses and taxation, and fundamental legislative texts. Each of these areas is further subdivided into subsections with more detail." (*BL,* January 15, 1990, p. 1046)

The States & Small Business: A Directory of Programs and Activities. Office of Advocacy, U.S. Small Business Administration. U.S.G.P.O., 1989. soft. 1 vol. 411 pp. ISBN 0742-843X. $12. directory.
HD2346.U5D57 350.82'048

The States & Small Business is a "biennial publication . . . designed to help potential and existing business owners seeking management, financial, or procurement information and assistance at the state level. . . . The book is arranged alphabetically by state . . . ; the information for each state is in five broad categories. The first three categories provide descriptions, addresses, telephone numbers, and key contact persons for executive departments and agencies, independent boards, semipublic corporations, governor's advisory councils, and legislative committees and subcommittees concerned with small business. . . . The fourth category provides an . . . overview of small business legislation. . . . The final category provides information on any small business conferences sponsored by the state or cosponsored with the private sector." (*BL,* December 1, 1989, p. 766)

Mel Bohn

Canadian History and Literature

See also British History; British Literature; World Literature

For most Americans, Canada is a little-known landmass to the north of the United States. Yet Canada is the United States' second biggest trading partner, just behind Japan and well ahead of the Federal Republic of Germany, which places a distant third. Additionally, nearly three-fourths of Canada's foreign trade is with the United States.

Canada, the second largest nation on earth in area, shares a 5,525-mile border with the United States. Its ten provinces and two territories are home to just over 25 million Canadians. Yet with this population and an area of nearly 4 million square miles, there are only 6 Canadians per square mile, compared to 68 persons per square mile in the United States.

Even though over 35 million Americans travel to Canada every year, the average American's knowledge of Canada is still rather scanty. The five reference books that form the core collection help to meet the need for information about Canada. Included are an encyclopedia, an almanac, a biographical dictionary, an atlas, and a literary guide. These five titles provide a good basic introduction to Canada. It should be noted

Core Titles

	PUBLIC	ACADEMIC	SCHOOL
Canadian Almanac and Directory Copp Clark Pittman, annual; distrib. by Gale	✦	✦	
The Canadian Encyclopedia, 2d edition, 4 vols. Marsh, James A., ed. Hurtig, 1988; distrib. by Gale	✦	✦	
Dictionary of Canadian Biography, 11 vols. Univ. of Toronto, 1966–		✦	
Historical Atlas of Canada Harris, R. Cole, ed. Univ. of Toronto, 1987		✦	
The Oxford Companion to Canadian Literature Toye, William, gen. ed. Oxford, 1983	✦	✦	

that except for the multivolume biographical dictionary, these works, though intended primarily for public and academic libraries, may also be suitable supplements to school library collections.

Reference works cited in the categories of British Literature, British History, and World Literature will also include sources in the Canadian literature and history category. Additionally, specialized sources for Canadian art, music, politics, history, and other disciplines can be chosen to supplement this basic core collection. The librarian building a more extensive collection of materials on Canada should have access to *Canadian Books in Print,* published by the University of Toronto Press, to locate those sources not published in the United States (and, therefore, not listed in *Books in Print*).

Core Titles

Canadian Almanac and Directory. Copp Clark Pittman, annual (1848–); distrib. by Gale. hard. 1 vol. approx. 1,150 pp. index. ISBN 0-7730-4912-6. $90. almanac.
AY414.C2 917.1.C161

The *Canadian Almanac and Directory* is without question a well-established publication; 1989 marked the 142d year of publication. There are 50,000 items, all fully indexed, in the 1989 edition.

The almanac is organized into seven sections. Section 1 provides addresses and phone numbers for financial institutions, libraries, publishers, radio and television stations, transportation companies, hospitals, chambers of commerce, and other related institutions. Section 2 provides similar information for various organizations, such as religious denominations, foundations, and trade unions. Section 3 is a directory of educational institutions, including universities, public school districts, and private schools. Government agencies at various levels are found in section 4, and detailed information on municipalities continues in section 5. Section 6 treats topics more traditionally associated with an almanac, such as holidays, honors and awards, statistics, weights and measures, and astronomical data, such as times for sunrise and sunset. The final section is a legal directory.

The major part of the publication is devoted to directory information, with only a small portion serving the usual role of an almanac. For the reader who needs the kind of information more traditionally associated with that type of reference work, the *Canadian World Almanac and Book of Facts,* which is the Canadian edition of the *World Almanac and Book of Facts,* or the *Corpus Almanac and Canadian Sourcebook* would be a better choice. However, these books are not distributed in the United States and must be ordered from Canadian publishers.

Several features are unique to this work. In addition to the table of contents, there is a guide to frequently used sections (such as population figures). There is also an "Alphabetical Fastfinder" and a "Topical Table of Contents" that is really an abbreviated index rather than a traditional table of contents. The "Topical Table of Contents" includes listings under such categories as "Geographic Information" and "Commerce and Finance." Finally, there is an extensive index at the end of the volume.

Because the *Canadian Almanac and Directory* is an annual publication, currency is a prime consideration, and the editors work right up to deadline in order to get the most current data they can. To this end, an addenda section is provided, which informs the reader about changes that have occurred too late for inclusion in the main text.

The *Canadian Almanac and Directory* will be of great value to anyone who has dealings with or needs information about a myriad of aspects of Canadian life. The almanac is a good starting point for further research as the entries will allow the user to identify sources that can provide information on Canadian government, educational and social organizations, and business groups. The Board recommends this work for the core collections of public and academic libraries.

The Canadian Encyclopedia, 2d edition. James A. Marsh, ed. Hurtig, 1988; distrib. by Gale. hard. 4 vols. illus. index. ISBN 0-76442-9958-4 (set). $225 (set). encyclopedia.
F1006.C36 971.00321

The Canadian Encyclopedia is the only reference of its kind currently available. The success of the first edition of this encyclopedia (published in 1985) enabled the publishers to bring out this second edition in 1988. The publisher does not expect to bring out a third edition until 1992 or later; the possibility of interim updating by supplementary volumes is being investigated. The publisher also projects that the encyclopedia will be made available by electronic means during the 1990s.

The National Advisory Board, which was instrumental in bringing a focus to this work, consisted of faculty members in a variety of disciplines from universities all across Canada. More than 275 consultants were drawn from universities, museums, government, and private agencies. In addition, the editorial team assembled 2,500 authorities in many disciplines to provide the entries for this work. All entries are signed by the contributors.

The more than 9,700 entries in *The Canadian Encyclopedia* are arranged alphabetically and include the expected references to places, public figures, and physical features. They also include distinctly Canadian topics, such as the New Democratic Party (one of Canada's secondary political parties), myths and legends of Inuit people (one of the two native populations in Canada), and the *voyageur* (a special name for persons in the early Canadian fur trading industry who transported workers to distant places). Over 3,500 of the entries are of a biographical nature, focusing on those persons who have made a significant contribution to Canadian culture.

The entries range in length from a single paragraph to several pages. For example, there are brief entries for the *Toronto Symphony* and *Great Bear Lake* (the largest lake entirely in Canada), but much more extensive coverage is given to the various provinces and to topics such as literature in English and the *Métis* (persons of French-Canadian and American Indian descent). Canada's major political subdivisions are covered in much greater detail than in any U.S. encyclopedia. It is noteworthy that the editorial focus of the work is such that there are no entries for Washington, D.C., or George Bush.

The index, which accounts for nearly half of the fourth volume, provides additional subject access with over 140,000 entries. Cross-references are indicated in small capitals within entries and refer the reader to other relevant entries. Additional suggested readings are provided at the end of many entries.

Each volume is approximately 675 pages long. The page numbering is consecutive throughout the four volumes. However, no volume numbers are provided in the index entries. Therefore, the reader is forced either to guess which volume contains the page being referenced or to memorize the page breaks.

Attractive, well-reproduced photographs and maps, in black and white and full color, illustrate the articles. Use of illustrations is conservative when compared to the *World Book Encyclopedia,* but the outstanding quality of the illustrations more than makes up for their frugal use. The type is quite readable, and the white paper used is easy on the eyes.

The edition is as current as can be expected given the date of publication. It is the only ready-reference source of information for relatively obscure Canadian subjects and offers much better coverage of most things Canadian than is available in comparable American encyclopedias.

The Canadian Encyclopedia would be an excellent addition to a high school collection. The Board recommends this work for the core collections of public and academic libraries.

Dictionary of Canadian Biography. Univ. of Toronto, 1966–. hard. 11 vols. indexes. ISBN 0-8020-3367-9 (vol. 11). $150 (vol. 11). biographical dictionary. vol. 12 of the series is forthcoming.
F1005.1049 920.071

The *Dictionary of Canadian Biography* is an ongoing project, with 12 planned volumes that will provide biographical information on Canadians from the year 1000 to the year 1900. Beyond these 12 volumes, the editors intend to expand the dictionary to include the twentieth century. The scope of these volumes is similar to the DICTIONARY OF NATIONAL BIOGRAPHY and the DICTIONARY OF AMERICAN BIOGRAPHY (see Biography for both). The intention, according to the work's general introduction, was to create "a biographical reference work for Canada of truly national importance." The dictionary was modeled after the DICTIONARY OF NATIONAL BIOGRAPHY. This work was the result of a bequest by Canadian businessman James Nicholson, whose will defined the inclusion criteria for the work: that the volumes include concise biographies of all "noteworthy inhabitants" of Canada not still living at the time of publication.

The work includes persons of foreign birth who achieved success in Canada and those of Canadian birth who gained distinction elsewhere.

In keeping with the bilingual nature of Canada, the dictionary is published in two editions, one in English and one in French.

Volume 1 (published in 1966) is devoted to persons who died between the years 1000 and 1700. Volume 2 (1969) treats those persons who died between 1701 and 1740, volume 3 (1974) covers the years to 1770, and volume 4 (1979) ends with 1800. An index to these four volumes was published in 1981. Volume 5 (1983) covers 1801 to 1820; volume 6 (1987), 1821 to 1835; volume 7 (1988), 1836 to 1850. The years 1851 to 1860 are covered by volume 8 (1985), and volume 9 (1976) treats subjects from 1861 to 1870. Volumes 10 (1972) and 11 (1982) continue to 1890 in ten-year increments. Volume 12 (in preparation at press time) will bring the dictionary to 1900.

Many experts have contributed biographical articles to the volumes. Using the most recently published volume as an example, 326 contributors were selected to write entries on subjects of which they have a special knowledge. All entries are signed. Entries in each volume are arranged alphabetically, with indexing by categories (for example, business, educators, explorers, and politicians). There is also a geographical index, allowing access by province.

Each volume attempts to be as inclusive as possible, spotlighting native Canadians who have been tribal or religious leaders as well as Anglo-Canadians and others of Eskimo, French, German, and Ukranian stock. Most of the subjects are not household names. Among those whose lives are summarized are priests, actors, doctors, sculptors, lawyers, educators, and explorers. The entries range from a few hundred words to several thousand. The introductory pages of the later volumes provide a quick reference guide to the subjects of the biographies. This is a handy feature. Cross-references to other volumes are also noted.

Because each volume is limited to 10 or 15 years, a master index to all 12 volumes would be useful, but the editors have not indicated any plans to produce one. However, the dual access, by category or by geographical area, of each volume makes this reference easy to use. Also, each of the 7-by-9-inch volumes is bound in a relatively sturdy red binding, and the paper is a durable stock.

The Board recommends this work for the core collection of academic libraries.

Historical Atlas of Canada. R. Cole Harris, ed. Univ. of Toronto, 1987. hard. 1 vol. 198 pp. illus. ISBN 0-8020-2495-5. $100. atlas.
G1116.51H56 911.71

The *Historical Atlas of Canada,* nearly 20 years in the making, was conceived as a multidisciplinary resource that would reflect the knowledge and interests of scholars in history, geography, and other related fields. The atlas is based on social and economic themes, which makes this a unique work among other atlases that treat Canada. Two hundred fifty scholars and research assistants from such diverse disciplines as archaeology, geology, botany, history, anthropology, linguistics, geography, and demography participated in its creation. In addition, an eight-person editorial board, made up of distinguished scholars from six universities and the Canadian Museum of Civilization, was established to comment on the work's development and to contribute essays.

The general editor is a professor of geography at the University of British Columbia and the author of two books and numerous articles relating to Canadian history. The cartographer and designer has designed 16 other atlases, one of which won the Leipzig award in 1970 for the most beautiful book produced in the world that year.

This atlas provides a record of Canada's early development from 18,000 B.C. to about A.D. 1800. It is primarily concerned with the relationship of the land and its people. The many maps, graphs, and tables illuminate the social and economic impact of European exploitation, trade, and settlement. This volume emphasizes the details of ordinary life (for example, house construction) rather than geopolitical events. Six major sections, comprised of 69 lavishly illustrated subsections designated as plates, treat: Canada's prehistory; four broad geographic realms—"The Atlantic Realm," "Inland Expansion," "The St. Lawrence Settlements," and "The Northwest"; and "Canada in 1800." Within these six sections the plates, which are two-page spreads, cover topics such as "The Coast Tsimshian, ca. 1750," "The Fishery in Atlantic Commerce," "Indian War and American Invasion [1763–1783]," "Ecological Regions, ca. A.D. 1500," and "The House, 1660–1800."

The thick, sturdy pages are enlivened by bright, rich, and varied colors. The cartography is done with great care and precision. However, the maps are often so full of information and the colors used on the plates are often so many and so varied that it is difficult to sort out all the details. Another drawback of the work is the lack of an index, making access to the maps difficult.

In spite of the complexity of many of the plates, the *Historical Atlas of Canada* would be a good supplementary choice for public and high school library collections because other atlases do not match its scope. The Board recommends this work for the core collection of academic libraries.

The Oxford Companion to Canadian Literature. William Toye, gen. ed. Oxford, 1983. hard. 1 vol. 864 pp. ISBN 0-19-540283-9. $49.95. dictionary.
PS8015.C93 810.32

The Oxford Companion to Canadian Literature is a handy, one-volume reference work. The Oxford University Press series of "companions" has such a well-established reputation that one naturally approaches any volume in the series with confidence in the reliability of the work. This is the first volume in the series "to be devoted solely to Canadian literature" (introduction). It replaces *The Oxford Companion to Canadian History and Literature* published in 1967.

All entries in the work are signed, and a list of the 192 contributors, along with their affiliations, is provided in the front of the volume. Among the contributors are such well-known writers as Leon Edel and George Woodcock.

The straightforward alphabetical arrangement of

the entries, with no index or table of contents, makes this a pure dictionary of Canadian literature. The 750 entries are generally quite short; most are less than a page in length. But some entries are several pages long, such as the one on *Indian legends and tales.* Both English-Canadian and French-Canadian literature are discussed in this volume, with an emphasis on the English works. There are entries on the native literatures, such as the Inuit, and references to writers who are not Canadians but who have strong Canadian ties, such as Jack London and Wallace Stegner. Entries cover such diverse topics as children's literature, foreign writers on Canada, pioneer memoirs, and science fiction and fantasy. There are also the usual author entries for standard genres. Some of the entries added in the new companion, which were not found in the original, are those on regional literatures, literary journals, and separate entries on popular titles, such as *Anne of Green Gables.* While the emphasis is on modern literature, obscure writers from the early periods of Canadian literature are mentioned briefly as well.

The lack of an index could cause some problems in locating entries, but there are many cross-references within the volume. For example, the entry for *Jacob, Fred* says "See NOVELS IN ENGLISH 1920 TO 1940: 3," which takes the reader to section 3 of that entry, where a discussion of Jacob's work can be found. Also, cross-references are provided in the text of articles, with those items having separate entries being noted by the use of small capital letters. Overall, this compact, easy-to-hold book is sturdy and well bound.

In spite of the 1983 publication date, *The Oxford Companion to Canadian Literature* is still reasonably current. However, a new edition in the near future would be welcome.

This volume will be useful in those high school libraries in which better insight into the literature of North America is needed. The Board recommends this work for the core collections of public and academic libraries.

Robert F. Rose

Careers and Occupations

Library users of career and occupational-related material bring with them a wide spectrum of information interests and needs. A sampling of users might include junior or senior high school students seeking information or vocational guidance on available career options or training facilities, recent college graduates seeking information on potential employers, unemployed or otherwise displaced workers looking for information on alternative careers, persons reentering the work force trying to learn more about effective job search strategies, or dissatisfied workers seeking new jobs.

The resources available to such users are as diverse as the users themselves; a core collection in the subject area must reflect that diversity. Such a collection must include encyclopedias that provide background information on careers, job search manuals that outline possible strategies for finding employment, directories that list potential employers, and sources that provide up-to-date supplemental information on salaries and other topics.

Although directories are not discussed in detail here, they have an essential role in rounding out both core and supplemental collections.

The Career Guide: Dun's Employment Opportunities Directory (Dun's Marketing Svcs.) is the most comprehensive source providing basic information on the largest employers in the United States and should be acquired by public and academic libraries. Those libraries should also include *The National Job Bank,* which lists employment information (hiring policies, training or experience required of applicants, and benefits) for hundreds of firms. Academic, public, and school libraries should own the *Summer Employment Directory,* which lists specific opportunities for jobs available during the summer months. These three titles can be considered part of a core collection.

Librarians should consider such directories as *Lovejoy's Career and Vocational School Guide* and *The Directory of Special Opportunities for Women* as possible supplements to their collection. The former lists institutions offering vocational education on a state-by-state basis. The latter, though now somewhat out of date, lists sources of information on educational opportunities, career knowledge, networks, and peer counseling assistance for women.

Such topics as job search strategies and résumé writing are not black and white. Users need to examine all the important sources that provide information on such topics and then select the approach that is best for them. Moreover, rapid changes in the workplace, corporate mergers, bankruptcies, turnover in the work force, the introduction of new technologies, and wide-

Core Titles

	PUBLIC	ACADEMIC	SCHOOL
The American Almanac of Jobs and Salaries, 3d edition Wright, John W., ed. Avon Bks., 1987	✦	✦	✦
Career Information Center, 4th edition, 13 vols. Visual Education Corp. for Glencoe/Macmillan, 1989	✦		✦
Dictionary of Occupational Titles, 4th edition, 1 vol., 2 suppls. U. S. Department of Labor, U.S.G.P.O., 1977	✦	✦	✦
The Encyclopedia of Careers and Vocational Guidance, 7th edition, 3 vols. Hopke, William E., ed. J. G. Ferguson, 1987	✦	✦	✦
Occupational Outlook Handbook U.S. Bureau of Labor Statistics, U.S.G.P.O., biannual	✦	✦	✦
What Color Is Your Parachute? A Practical Manual for Job-Hunters and Career Changers Bolles, Richard Nelson. Ten Speed Pr., annual	✦	✦	✦

scale salary cuts or raises mean that the information presented in even the best career reference works can quickly become out-dated. Librarians of course should make sure that only the most current edition of these works are kept on the reference shelves, and patrons should be advised that even the most up-to-date reference works will contain some names, addresses, and statistics that may have changed by the time the patron consults the work.

Users and librarians should also be aware of additional sources not covered here that may be useful. For example, although a number of the sources included here provide some information on writing résumés, libraries should also seriously consider adding books to their collection devoted solely to that topic. Additionally, many books exist on career opportunities in specific fields, and libraries may wish to add some of these books, depending on the information needs of their primary users.

The American Almanac of Jobs and Salaries, 3d edition. John W. Wright, ed. Avon Bks., 1987. soft. 1 vol. 743 pp. index. ISBN 0-380-75307-3. $12.95. almanac.
HD8038.U5W74 331.11'9042

The American Almanac of Jobs and Salaries, edited by John W. Wright, is an essential reference tool for any library whose patrons ask for salary information. Although virtually all the data it contains are available elsewhere, no other source brings it all together in quite the same way or in the same depth.

The almanac is arranged in 11 broad chapters, ranging from science and technology to government jobs to the professions to blue-collar employment. Its purpose is to "provide a comprehensive survey of hundreds of occupations and their pay rates in a wide variety of industries and business organizations." That it does, although its orientation is toward white-collar and service sector occupations. In fact, there is a very strong orientation toward jobs on the upper end of the scale, with tables and anecdotes about celebrities' incomes. While this makes the book more entertaining, this aspect is of little practical value for the majority of users.

In addition to salary data, the various sections also provide—in greater or lesser detail—background information and basic analyses of the occupations or industries being examined. For example, the chapter on working for the government provides detailed information on the general structure of the federal pay system. It indicates specific salary levels for individual positions in the federal government, such as the Assistant Commissioner for Patents in the Department of Commerce. State and local government positions are also covered. In some chapters, the almanac provides information on such topical issues as women's wages and minority incomes. A number of sections or subsections, including those on engineering, computer science, and the movie business, were written by people familiar with the field.

On the negative side, the salary data are somewhat out of date. Almost all the data in this third edition are from 1982–1983. Also, the book's format may be inconvenient for the general user. The chapters deal with broad job categories, but within those categories, specific professions and jobs are not arranged alphabetically. On the positive side, the salary figures were compiled from statistics gathered by the Bureau of Labor Statistics and from professional organization salary surveys. Sources of data are provided in table footnotes. A useful feature of the index is that it lists entries by state and city, with subentries for jobs described therein.

Well written, *The American Almanac of Jobs and Salaries* can easily be read for entertainment value and as a reference work. The Board recommends this work for the core collections of public, academic, and school libraries.

Career Information Center, 4th edition. Visual Education Corp. for Glencoe/Macmillan, 1989. soft. 13 vols. 2,560 pp. illus. index. ISBN 0-02-642601-3 (set). $179 (set). encyclopedia.
HF5382.5.U5C3 331.7

This fourth edition of the *Career Information Center* provides information on more than 3,000 jobs in approximately 650 occupational profiles. The book is arranged in 13 volumes. The first 12 volumes cover occupations in various fields, such as "Engineering, Science, and Technology," "Health," "Marketing and Distribution," "Public and Community Service," and "Construction." Volume 13 is concerned with employment trends that will affect the workplace and work force through the year 2000. It also contains a master index to the entire set, plus career information for Canada.

The first 12 volumes all follow a similar format. They include "Looking Into" sections, which provide background information on the occupational field in question, and "Getting Into" sections, which assist readers in deciding which jobs would be best for them and how to enter the field. Also included in the latter section is information on résumés, application forms, and interviewing.

The principal section of each volume contains career profiles of specific occupations, divided into three levels: those requiring no specialized training or experience, some specialized training or experience, and advanced training or experience. Immediately preceding each occupational description is a "Job Summary" box, a graphic aid that allows the reader to scan such facts as education and training required, average salaries, and the employment outlook for that occupation before reading the profile. The career information and job statistics are derived from the Bureau of Labor Statistics and other government sources. Also included in each volume are bibliographies of additional resources and a directory of accredited institutions offering career training. Each volume is individually indexed; a cumulative index appears as part of volume 13.

One interesting and valuable feature of the *Career Information Center* is that the articles are written at a level appropriate for those entering the occupation discussed. The well-designed layout and graphics make the work easily accessible and easy to read. This is an exceptionally attractive work, enhanced by its frequent use of black-and-white photographs, charts, and tables.

The *Career Information Center* provides information on more occupations than virtually any other source, including some occupations that either are not covered, or not covered well, elsewhere—such as media buyers. Revised every three years, the *Career Information Center* is up to date.

This career encyclopedia is a strong candidate for inclusion in academic library collections. The Board recommends this work for the core collections of public and school libraries.

Dictionary of Occupational Titles, 4th edition. U.S. Department of Labor. U.S.G.P.O., 1977. soft. 1 vol. plus 2 suppls. 1,371 pp. indexes. ISBN 0-318-04550-8. $32. dictionary.
HB2595.A5 331.7

The *Dictionary of Occupational Titles* was created by the U.S. Department of Labor to provide a uniform occupational language for use by employment services and related organizations. It categorizes and defines approximately 20,000 occupations in its main volume. Occupation "refers to [a] collective description of a number of individual jobs performed, with minor variations, in many establishments." The descriptions or definitions have been based on the results of actual on-site job analyses conducted by the U.S. Department of Labor.

Each occupation has been assigned a nine-digit code, called a DOT number. The first three digits refer to the broad category of which the occupation is a part. There are nine such categories: professional, technical, and managerial; clerical and sales; service; agriculture, fishery, forestry, and related occupations; processing; machine trades; bench work; structural work; and miscellaneous. The middle three digits denote worker function ratings, assigned according to how the worker's responsibilities relate to data, people, and things. The final three digits refer to the alphabetical order of titles within the previous six-digit groups.

The pages are set up in a two-column format. Broad category divisions are printed in full capitals in boldface type. DOT number and the title of the occupation are printed in initial capitals and boldface type.

The formal occupational definitions—usually a paragraph in length—provide an official title, industry designation, and alternate title (if applicable). The body of the definition describes the worker's actions, the purpose of those actions, the machines or other equipment used by the worker, and the instructions followed or judgments made by the worker. Task element statements—the specific tasks performed and additional tasks which may be performed—are also included.

The principal section of the dictionary is arranged by the occupational group codes, so that similar occupations are grouped together. There is an introduction which explains the origin of the work, followed by separate sections which describe how the fourth edition is organized, how to find an occupational title and code, and how to use the DOT for job placement. Additional access is provided through an alphabetical index of occupational titles, an industry index, and a list of occupational titles arranged by industry designation.

There have obviously been many changes in the world of work since this edition of the dictionary was published in 1977, particularly in the technology used in many occupations. Two supplements, published in 1982 and 1986, update these changes and provide additional information.

Because the *Dictionary of Occupational Titles* provides standard, accepted definitions for occupations, and because many other occupation information reference works have based their definitions on this source, it deserves a place in libraries with collections in the areas of careers and occupations.

The Board recommends this work for the core collections of public, academic, and school libraries.

The Encyclopedia of Careers and Vocational Guidance, 7th edition. William E. Hopke, ed. J. G. Ferguson, 1987. hard. 3 vols. 1,933 pp. illus. index. ISBN 0-89434-083-2 (set). $89.95 (set). encyclopedia.

HF5381.E52 331.7'02

The Encyclopedia of Careers and Vocational Guidance is a standard source for occupational information. First published in 1967, it is currently in its seventh edition. The encyclopedia is divided into three volumes: "Reviewing Career Fields," "Selecting a Career," and "Selecting a Technician's Career." Altogether, more than 900 occupations are covered.

Volume 1 provides general information about career planning, as well as specific information about various fields of work or industries, such as teaching, law, chemistry, and real estate; altogether, some 70 fields are covered. The volume also includes some basic salary information and indicates the best and worst job prospects for the coming decade. The encyclopedia describes ways "to learn about and land a job," and how to use test results in helping to plan for a career. The section on fields of work covers major manufacturing and service industries and public sector employment.

The second volume provides overviews of specific careers in nine occupational categories: professional, administrative, and managerial; clerical; sales; service; agriculture, forestry, and conservation; processing; machine trades; bench work; structural work; and miscellaneous. The information provided for each field follows a standard format: the occupation is defined and set in its historical context; the nature of the work and the requirements for employment in the field are described, along with methods of entering the occupation and advancement opportunities in the field. The employment outlook, average earnings, working conditions, and social and psychological factors related to the occupation are reported. Finally, additional sources of information are provided.

Volume 3, "Selecting a Technician's Career," is devoted strictly to technician occupations. Its first section is concerned with emerging technical careers in high-technology industries, while the remainder of the volume provides specific information on individual careers for technicians. The information provided follows the same format as in volume 2.

According to its editor, the articles "are written by acknowledged leaders and authorities in each field." However, with the exception of some of the general articles in volume 1, the articles are not signed.

Volumes 2 and 3 contain the same index, with entries to all three volumes included. Volume 1 is not indexed; instead, users must rely on the table of contents.

The language used in this set is clear and understandable, and should be read easily by junior high school students and up. The consistent, well-structured format adds to the work's readability and to the accessibility of the information it contains. The encyclopedia's information is fairly up to date, given the fact that such items as salary data are constantly changing. However, because the information is not updated on an annual basis, readers should be aware that some significant changes may have taken place for some careers since the publication date. (The work is revised every three years.) Contacting the additional sources of information listed should help to overcome this problem.

The set as a whole is extremely well done and is an excellent source of career and occupational information. The third volume of *The Encyclopedia of Career and Vocational Guidance* would probably receive more use by patrons of public and school libraries. The Board recommends this work for the core collections of public, academic, and school libraries.

Occupational Outlook Handbook. U.S. Bureau of Labor Statistics. U.S.G.P.O., biannual. hard and soft. 1 vol. 466 pp. illus. appendixes. index. S/N 029-001-02941-1 (hard); 029-001-02942-0 (soft). $24 (hard); $22 (soft). handbook.
HD8051.A623 331.7′09

The *Occupational Outlook Handbook* is *the* standard source of occupational information. It is highly reliable, authoritative, and well written. This volume is revised every two years.

The handbook provides descriptive information on approximately 225 occupations. Those occupations requiring advanced education or training receive the most attention. After an introductory chapter on tomorrow's job needs, the handbook is arranged in sections according to broad occupational groupings: managerial and management-related occupations; engineers, surveyors, architects; natural, computer, and mathematical scientists; teachers, librarians, and counselors; health technologists and technicians; marketing and sales; service occupations; mechanics, installers, and repairers; and a final section on job opportunities in the armed forces.

The information provided for each of the 225 occupations is arranged in a standard format. The nature of the work (what people in that occupation do) is defined; working conditions (including typical working hours, environments, and any particular hazards faced by workers in the field) are described; training, other qualifications, and advancement paths are given; the short-term and long-term (through the year 2000) outlook for employment in the field is projected; earnings data from a variety of sources, primarily governmental, are presented, usually in the form of median earnings for full-time salaried employees; related occupations (which may or may not be described elsewhere in the handbook) are listed; and sources of additional information are listed. All occupations are cross-referenced by their DICTIONARY OF OCCUPATIONAL TITLES (or DOT) codes. An additional 125 occupations in various fields and at different levels (from unskilled to advanced) are described briefly in an appendix. All occupations in the book are indexed by their titles and also by their DOT codes.

Revised every two years, the *Occupational Outlook Handbook* is an essential work. If a library budget allows for only one book in the category of occupations and careers, this should be the one. Nothing quite matches it for its combination of comprehensiveness, ease of use, easily understood writing style, authority, and price.

The Board recommends this work for the core collections of public, academic, and school libraries.

What Color Is Your Parachute? A Practical Manual for Job-Hunters and Career Changers. Richard Nelson Bolles. Ten Speed Pr., annual. hard and soft. 1 vol. 361 pp. illus. appendixes. index. ISBN 0-89815-386-7 (hard); 0-89815-385-9 (soft). $16.95 (hard); $9.95 (soft). handbook.
HF5383.B56 650.1′4

Arguably the most popular of the "how to find a job" manuals, *What Color Is Your Parachute?* has become a classic of the genre, and its author, the late Richard Bolles, has been described as a "career development guru." *Parachute's* first edition appeared in 1970; since 1975 it has been revised annually, a testament to its continued popularity.

Although the book is entertaining, Bolles's emphasis is on the practical, and his goal is to show job seekers what they need to do in order to find the type of position that best suits their needs. He does so, in part, by guiding readers through a personal skills analysis to help them better understand the specific skills they possess.

The book is arranged in six chapters, under three broad headings: "The Way the Job Hunt Really Is"; "Improving Your Chances: Some Quick Hints"; and "The Most Effective Method: A Systematic Approach to Job-Hunting and Career Change."

Some of the most valuable information provided by Bolles is his listing of additional information sources in the appendixes. These resources address such subjects as interviewing, salary negotiation, résumés, and how to overcome special problems that may be faced by job seekers generally or by special classes of job seekers, such as the handicapped. Each edition also includes other appendixes on special topics of interest, which vary from year to year. Bolles makes extensive use of illustrations in his work. These range from charts and tables to cartoon reproductions to clip art to sample résumés and cover letters. In some cases, the illustrations and layout enhance the content of the book; in others, they detract from it.

Bolles takes a highly personalized approach in presenting his information, and he is not afraid to reveal his opinions or biases. His hortatory method of presentation will no doubt inspire some readers, but it may turn others off. Nevertheless, *What Color Is Your Parachute?* has to be considered an essential reference source for all types of libraries. In fact, this is one work which many libraries will want to buy in multiple copies, particularly in uncertain economic times, when it will undoubtedly be in high demand. The Board recommends this work for the core collections of public, academic, and school libraries.

Supplementary Titles

College to Career: The Guide to Job Opportunities. Joyce Slayton Mitchell. College Board, 1986; distrib. by Macmillan. soft. 1 vol. 259 pp. ISBN 0-87447-249-0. $9.95. handbook.
HF5382.5.U5M564 331.7'02

College to Career: The Guide to Job Opportunities "discusses about 100 jobs including, for most, a description of the work; education and skills required; the number of employees and where they work; salary information; employment prospects; related careers; and addresses of professional associations. . . . Mitchell includes brief comments from people employed in particular fields, lists the level of computer skills needed to perform a job, and gives some statistics on women and minorities. As the title implies, Mitchell concentrates on jobs that require a college education. . . ." (*LJ,* November 15, 1986, p. 92)

This book is completely revised every four years to include the latest U.S. Department of Labor data. The next revision was scheduled for May 1990.

Also reviewed in: *Kliatt,* Winter, 1987, p. 32; *WLB,* November 1986, p. 63.

Board's recommendation: Public, academic, and school libraries.

The CPC Annual. College Placement Council, annual. soft. 4 vols. illus. index. ISSN 0069-5734. $39.95. handbook.
HF5382.5.U5C601 331.7'02

Board's recommendation: Public and academic libraries.

The Encyclopedia of Second Careers. Gene Hawes. Facts On File, 1984. hard. 1 vol. 450 pp. index. ISBN 0-87196-692-1. $49.95. encyclopedia.
HF5384.H382 650.14

The Encyclopedia of Second Careers "is designed to help persons planning a career change, and as such it presents data on a . . . range of jobs/professions. . . . [It] leads users to several lists of careers, first accessed according to interests and then by abilities; skeletal information is given for each career. Other tables list highest income careers, those with easiest entry, education needed (from on-the-job to doctorate), and helpful prior experience. Almost two-thirds of *The Encyclopedia of Second Careers* consists of more detailed descriptions of the jobs listed, organized topically.

"[This work covers] some 200 occupations. . . . The Table of Contents is thorough, but the index refers to career titles only. . . . [I]ts contents are not restricted to seekers of second careers." (BL, March 1985, p. 932)

Board's recommendation: Public and academic libraries.

Jobs of the Future: The 500 Best Jobs—Where They'll Be and How to Get Them. Marvin Cetron with Marcia Appel. McGraw-Hill, 1984. hard. 1 vol. 258 pp. appendix. index. $15.95. ISBN 0-07-010342-9. handbook.
HF5381.C422 331.12'8

Jobs of the Future "discusses jobs in offices, personal services, health, engineering, manufacturing, communication, and entertainment. A general discussion of trends is followed by . . . brief descriptions of particular jobs, number of employees needed, starting and midcareer salaries, and educational requirements. . . .

"After a general forecast for each field, there are long lists of very specific, short job descriptions (just two or three sentences) for new or expanding positions. Also included are four appendices, the most useful of which are two college ranking studies. . . . Because the job descriptions are so short and the quantity so large (500 altogether), a [reader] needs to know what field and level of job he/she will consider." (*LJ,* June 1984, p. 1126)

Also reviewed in: *VOYA,* December 1984, p. 270.

Board's recommendation: Public and academic libraries.

Jobs Rated Almanac. Les Krantz. World Almanac, 1988; distrib. by Ballantine. soft. 1 vol. 349 pp. ISBN 0-88687-307-X. $14.95. handbook.
HF5382.5.U5K7 331.7'02'0973

Board's recommendation: Public, academic, and school libraries.

New York Times Career Planner: A Guide to Choosing the Perfect Job from the 101 Best Opportunities of Tomorrow. Elizabeth M. Fowler. Times Bks., 1987. soft. 1 vol. 351 pp. index. ISBN 0-8129-1212-8. $9.95. handbook.
HF5382.5.U6F68 650.1′4

The *New York Times Career Planner* "describes 'the 101 best jobs of tomorrow' (i. e., interesting fields, not necessarily those in which workers will be in demand). . . ." (*LJ,* November 15, 1987, p. 78)

"The first half of [the *New York Times Career Planner*] offers advice to students who are planning for college and a career. The second half is an alphabetical listing of 101 careers which represent . . . the best job possibilities for the future . . . [from] accountants and retailers . . . to palynologists and hortitherapists. Each career is given two to three pages and includes a description of the work, . . . consideration of the pros and cons of the field, entry level salary ranges, and trends.

[The author] "helps students to choose careers, offering many practical and creative hints. . . . Fowler . . . not only cover[s] the planning of a career, she also extends the process to include resumés, the first day on the job, and 'what to do if you are fired.' . . . A practical and useful book." (*SLJ,* May 1988, p. 121)

Board's recommendation: Public, academic, and school libraries.

The Relocating Spouse's Guide to Employment: Options and Strategies in the U. S. and Abroad. Frances Bastress. Woodley, 1989. soft. 1 vol. 258 pp. illus. appendix. index. ISBN 0-937623-01-6. $12.95. handbook.
HF5382.7.B375 650.1′4

The Relocating Spouse's Guide to Employment "attempts to counsel the job-seeking person who is living in a new location and who may be looking for a complete career change. Chapters on portable careers, self-employment, government jobs, and alternative work arrangements (job sharing, flextime, and temporary work) outline alternatives to the traditional 9–5 work structure. Also discussed are the job market and employment trends, interviewing, résumés and cover letters, and courses and workshops available for strengthening business skills. In addition, personal histories of relocated spouses are supplied, and tips on jobs most likely to 'travel' well are offered. Appended [is] an excellent bibliography and a list of professional associations and federal job centers." (*BL,* February 1, 1987, p. 813)

Board's recommendation: Public and academic libraries.

VGM's Careers Encyclopedia, 2d edition. Craig T. Norback. VGM Career Horizons, 1988. hard. 1 vol. 484 pp. index. ISBN 0-8442-6132-7. $29.95. encyclopedia.
HF5382.5.U5C337 331.7′02

In *VGM's Careers Encyclopedia,* "career descriptions are arranged alphabetically for quick reference. Each entry begins with a general description of the job, followed by more detailed information on places of employment, qualifications, working conditions, education, training, advancement, income, and additional sources of information. This revised, second edition includes more information on places of employment, working conditions, advancement potential, and salary for each career . . . VGM does list a few jobs not found [in some other reference books on careers], e.g., auctioneer, elected public official, and golf/tennis professional. Smaller libraries on a limited budget will find *VGM's Careers Encyclopedia* a good starting point." (*BRD,* 1988, p. 1780)

The next revision of this work is scheduled for 1991.

Board's recommendation: Public and school libraries.

New and Noteworthy

Career Discovery Encyclopedia. E. Russell Primm. J. G. Ferguson, 1990. hard. 6 vols. illus. indexes. ISBN 0-89434-106-5 (set). $109.95 (set). encyclopedia.
HF5381 331.7′02

"The *Career Discovery Encyclopedia* describes 504 careers in alphabetical . . . order. Two-page spreads include information about 'what the work is like, what kind of education and training is required, what the salary and future prospects for the job are like, and how to get more information.' . . . Photographs with each entry are nonsexist and multicultural, and are descriptive of the work performed. Each entry also lists three to six other related occupations to look up. . . ." (*BL,* March 1, 1990, p. 1836)

Occu-Facts: Information on 565 Careers in Outline Form. Elizabeth Handville, ed. Careers, 1989. soft. 1 vol. 624 pp. index. ISBN 0-9623657-0-X. $38. handbook.
HF5382 331.7

Occu-Facts "summarizes more than 565 white- and blue-collar occupations in an easy-to-follow, one-page outline format. While the majority of jobs require at least a two-year college degree, there are many that require no formal education beyond high school. . . . Each career profile opens with a summary of general duties, followed by types of working conditions, . . . physical surroundings, . . . physical demands, . . . and relationships with data, people, and things." (*BL*, April 1, 1990, p. 1580)

Professional Careers Sourcebook: An Information Guide for Career Planning. Kathleen M. Savage et al., eds. Gale, 1990. hard. 1 vol. 1,049 pp. index. ISBN 0-8103-4901-9. $69.95. handbook.
HF5382.5.U5P76 331.7

"*Professional Careers Sourcebook* focuses on career planning for college graduates interested in . . . [professional, technical, and other high-level] occupations. Information on 111 jobs has been excerpted from the *Occupational Outlook Handbook* (duties, responsibilities, salaries, career growth potential) and is presented here with other types of occupational information. . . . For each job are listed related career guides, professional associations, accreditation and licensing agencies, study guides for professional certification, scholarships and grants, professional and trade publications, basic reference sources used by people already in the field, . . . as well as dates and locations of professional meetings and conferences." (*BL*, April 1, 1990, p. 1581)

The Resume Reference Book. Howard Lauther. McFarland, 1990. soft. 1 vol. 160 pp. illus. index. ISBN 0-89950-498-1. $19.95. handbook.
HF5383.L35 650.14

The Resume Reference Book "encourages the development of 'promotional' information and discourages the use of . . . traditional—but useless—data often found on resumes. Users are led from the blank-paper stage into . . . [the] information gathering process and then through . . . editing and design stages, resulting in a document that highlights one's best credentials with the aim of generating an interview. The special needs of . . . executives, new graduates, and those discharged from the military are recognized and addressed at every stage of resume development." (Excerpted from publisher's announcement)

Where the Jobs Are: A Comprehensive Directory of 1200 Journals Listing Career Opportunities. S. Norman Feingold and Glenda Ann Hansard-Winkler. Garrett Park Pr., 1989. soft. 1 vol. 126 pp. ISBN 0-912048-67-0. $15. directory.
HF5382.5.U5F46 016.33112′4

Where the Jobs Are "is a guide to periodicals that contain help-wanted ads. The authors begin with three short chapters discussing types of classified ads, how ads are organized, how an applicant should read an ad, salary considerations, follow-ups, and other topics. . . . Access to the directory is through the index chapter, which is alphabetical by occupation and cites numbers in the journal list. . . . Among the . . . occupations listed are accounting and finance, plumbing and heating industries, pharmacy, quality control, and writing and editing." (*BL*, March 15, 1990, p. 1501)

The Work-at-Home Sourcebook, 3d edition. Lynie Arden. Live Oak Publications, 1990. soft. 1 vol. 219 pp. illus. indexes. ISBN 0-911781-08-0. $14.95. handbook.
HD2336.U5H73 338.7′4

"*The Work-at-Home Sourcebook* lists more than 1,000 companies that pay people to work at home. The jobs include making crafts at home, computer-based jobs, telemarketing and market research, translating and medical transcribing, hand assembly of circuit boards, and cosmetics and encyclopedia sales. Each entry gives the address of the company, the kind and sometimes number of positions available, any special equipment or training necessary, and sometimes the rate of pay." (*BL*, April 1, 1990, p. 1576)

Wendell Cochran

Chemistry

See also Science and Technology

Chemistry is ubiquitous: it deals with the entire physical universe at the atomic and molecular levels. Beginning with the hundred or so elements and their compounds, chemists study the composition, structure, and properties of substances, and their transformation together with changes in energy. However, here the definition falters, because chemistry applications appear in other sciences, in industry, and in everyday life. Boundaries are hard to draw.

Any adequate core reference collection in chemistry involves problems in selection. The subject, and its literature, is so vast, and growth and change are rapid and accelerating. For example, one abstracting and indexing service processes more than 8,500 technical papers a week.

In the field of chemistry, library users range from practicing chemists to newspaper readers who are curious about the latest report of a hazardous substance found in a common soap or paint. Among them are industrial chemists moving into new specialties as well as teachers and students. Government employees and manufacturers are concerned with regulations for hazardous substances. Consumers, singly and in groups, try to reconcile the earth's environment with the manifest benefits of chemistry.

In a core collection, dictionaries and encyclopedias are essential guides to names and terms, descriptions, definitions, and principles and properties. However, no one reference source can cover to the same depth all the main branches of chemistry—analytical, inorganic, organic, and physical.

Fundamental to sources in core collections are the chemical elements and their compounds, adding up to millions of known chemical substances. Many common reference questions that involve chemicals take the form "how much?" and many thick reference works consist largely of tables listing data for properties of chemical substances. Another common reference question is "how do I make it?", with answers in works of technology, including formulas, recipes, and techniques. Libraries will, of course, want to have Chemical Abstracts Service from the American Chemical Society to help answer some of these questions.

Finally, a basic reference collection must have a source that explains the multitudinous sources of chemical information—the tools and how to use them.

Core Titles

	PUBLIC	ACADEMIC	SCHOOL
The Chemical Formulary: Collection of Commercial Formulas for Making Thousands of Products in Many Fields, 29 vols. Bennett, Harry, ed. Chemical Publishing, 1989		✦	
CRC Handbook of Chemistry and Physics Weast, Robert C., ed. CRC Pr., annual (See Physics)	✦	✦	✦
The Facts On File Dictionary of Chemistry, rev. edition Daintith, John, ed. Facts On File, 1988	✦		✦
Hawley's Condensed Chemical Dictionary, 11th edition Sax, Irving N., and Richard J. Lewis, eds. Van Nostrand Reinhold, 1987			✦
How to Find Chemical Information: A Guide for Practicing Chemists, Educators, and Students, 2d edition Maizell, Robert E. John Wiley, 1987	✦	✦	
Kirk-Othmer Concise Encyclopedia of Chemical Technology Kirk, Raymond E., Donald F. Othmer, Martin Grayson, and David Eckroth, eds. John Wiley, 1985		✦	
Lange's Handbook of Chemistry, 13th edition Dean, John A., ed. McGraw-Hill, 1985	✦	✦	✦
The Merck Index: An Encyclopedia of Chemicals, Drugs, and Biologicals, 11th edition Susan Budavari, ed. Merck, 1989	✦	✦	
Van Nostrand Reinhold Encyclopedia of Chemistry, 4th edition Considine, Douglas M., ed. Van Nostrand Reinhold, 1984	✦	✦	✦

Core Titles

The Chemical Formulary: Collection of Commercial Formulas for Making Thousands of Products in Many Fields. Harry Bennett, ed. Chemical Publishing, 1989. hard. 29 vols. appendix. index. ISBN 0-8206-0338-4 (vol. 29). approx. $60 each vol. handbook.

TP151.C53 660.C424

Through the many volumes published since 1933, *The Chemical Formulary* has established itself as a universal recipe book for both chemists and nonchemists. Practicing chemists use it when moving into new professional areas; nonchemists use it when compounding products for themselves. Consumers, too, may use this book to compare the essential ingredients as given in this reference work with those listed for a commercial product.

Each volume seems deceptively small (and handy), but any one of them contains hundreds of straightforward formulas for products, such as adhesives; foods and beverages; cosmetics; coatings; detergents; drugs; metal treatments; polishes; and elastomers, polymers, and resins. The cumulative index for the first 25 volumes reveals a more extensive list of categories than can be detailed here.

Whether an entry is called a recipe, receipt, or formula, each is typically one-third to one-half page long. For an example of recipe format, look at any traditional cookbook that first lists the ingredients and then gives the procedure. The main difference is that instead of an amount for each ingredient, *The Chemical Formulary* gives a proportion. Names and terms throughout the book are technical and precise (the editor warns readers against substitutions), and the procedure rigidly maintains clinical exactness.

The reading level, and the readership, of *The Chemical Formulary* may be judged from the preface: "The only repetitious material is the introduction (Chapter 1) which is used in every volume for the benefit of those who may have bought only one volume and who have no educational background or experience in chemical compounding." In reading, most nonchemists will only find difficulty with names of unfamiliar substances, and the problem is more apparent than real.

The introduction itself is simple, clear, and blunt—it might have been the model for any primer in cookery to be presented to any inexperienced cook. The introduction gives many examples of recipes for hand creams, foot powders, baking powders, saddle soap, laundry bluing, and photographic solutions.

The appendix in each volume commonly discusses federal laws regulating foods, drugs, and cosmetics; lists chemicals that should not be stored together; gives conversion tables for weights and measures; describes first aid for chemical injuries; lists trademark chemicals and tells where to buy them. All back volumes of *The Chemical Formulary* are available, as well as a cumulative index for volumes 1 through 25 (which covers more than 115,000 formulas). The Board recommends this work for the core collection of academic libraries.

CRC Handbook of Chemistry and Physics. Robert C. Weast, ed. CRC Pr., annual. hard. 1 vol. 2,528 pp. illus. index. ISBN 0-8493-0470-9. $97.50. handbook.
QD65.C911 540.212'12'19

See Physics.

The Facts On File Dictionary of Chemistry, rev. edition. John Daintith, ed. Facts On File, 1988. hard and soft. 1 vol. 256 pp. illus. ISBN 0-8160-1866-9 (hard); 0-8160-2367-0 (soft). $24.95 (hard); $12.95 (soft). dictionary.
QD5.D26 540.321

The authority of *The Facts On File Dictionary of Chemistry* rests on the generally positive reception accorded its first edition (1981) as well as on the excellent reputation of the many other dictionaries published by Facts On File. This dictionary is quite up to their standard.

The book itself is handy, being far less intimidating than the other sources in this section. This work contains about 2,500 definitions (compared with tens of thousands in grander works). Yet for many chemistry questions, library users need only consult this comparatively little book.

The scope of this work covers materials, techniques, and applications. According to the foreword, the entries that are new in this edition stress terms for "new materials, new techniques, and for topics affecting the environment."

The entries are arranged alphabetically. Definitions are as short as one line long, such as "rutherfordium. *See* element 104" and as long as one page. The typical length is ten lines. The longer definitions are those for individual terms. An example is the entry for *polyester.* It is defined as "a synthetic polymer made by reacting alcohols with acids, so that the monomers are linked by the group—O—CO—. Synthetic fibres such as Terylene and Dacron are polyesters."

The reading level of this dictionary is suitable for the readership intended: students and (to quote the foreword) "anyone interested in the life sciences." The text is neither jargon-laden nor oversimplified. British spelling prevails, but no one should be inconvenienced by this.

Cross-references are common, and only the most elementary terms used are not defined in their alphabetical place. Pages are in a two-column format, and each page has one catchword on it. All text is flush left, with no indent for successive paragraphs, and definitions are separated by one-line spaces. This work is extremely legible, readable, and easy to use.

In judging accuracy and currency, it may be worth noting some inconsistency (which appears harmless) in reference to names of the transactinide elements. As the book went to press, apparently, the competition to name element 104 had not yet been settled.

The tedium induced by solid text in *The Facts On File Dictionary of Chemistry* is relieved by 45 line drawings, most of which are structural formulas such as that for the benzene ring. An appendix lists the chemical elements, physical constants, elementary particles, the Greek alphabet, and the periodic table.

The Board recommends *The Facts On File Dictionary of Chemistry* for the core collections of public and school libraries.

Hawley's Condensed Chemical Dictionary, 11th edition. N. Irving Sax and Richard J. Lewis, eds. Van Nostrand Reinhold, 1987. hard. 1 vol. 1,288 pp. illus. appendixes. ISBN 0-442-28097-1. $57.95. dictionary.
QD5.C5 540.3'21

Hawley's Condensed Chemical Dictionary has been a classic source for the chemical industry and elsewhere since 1919. (The dictionary was long known as *Hawley's* before the name was added to the title.) The word *condensed* may seem misleading for a work with nearly 1,300 double-column pages and more than 20,000 entries. As the editors point out, this work is not a dictionary but "a compendium of technical data and descriptive information covering many thousand chemicals and chemical phenomena" (introduction).

The editors classify the information as "(1) descriptions of chemicals, raw materials, processes, and equipment; (2) expanded definitions of chemical entities, phenomena, and terminology; and (3) description or identification of . . . trademarked products." Also included are abbreviations, biographical sketches of important chemists, and notes on technical associations and trade groups.

Over the years, the principles of selection have changed, and the editors of this latest edition note "the growing importance, to chemists, and to the general public as well, of environmental and health hazards." Therefore, there is increased editorial stress on the many facets of hazardous materials and practices in modern technology. Appendixes concern the origin of some chemical terms, the history of chemistry (new in this edition), and two lists (alphabetical and numerical) of trademarked products.

The content ranges so widely as to make sampling difficult, but here is one entry: "emeralds, synthetic. Artificial crystals produced by a high pressure–high temperature process from beryllium aluminum silicate containing a small amount of chromium. Use: Lasers, masers, semiconductors."

Typically, an entry is about six lines long. It may be as short as one line for abbreviations and synonyms, such as "dibenzofuran. See diphenylene oxide," or as long as a page, such as for polyethylene.

In the eleventh edition, perhaps 3,000 entries bear Chemical Abstracts Service registry numbers, which enables identification of a compound of any of its synonyms throughout the vast literature of chemistry. In that and other ways, this reference work is easy to use, even by readers who are not chemists.

Publication date aside, the currency of *Hawley's Condensed Chemical Dictionary* may be adjudged from the periodic table, which shows the latest transactinide elements 104 (Unq), 105 (Unp), 106 (Unh), and 107 (Uns).

The Board recommends this work for the core collection of school libraries.

How to Find Chemical Information: A Guide for Practicing Chemists, Educators, and Students, 2d edition. Robert E. Maizell. John Wiley, 1987. hard. 1 vol. 402 pp. illus. indexes. ISBN 0-471-86767-5. $40. handbook.
QD8.5.M34 540.7

Now in its second edition, *How to Find Chemical Information* upholds the reputation of both the author and the Wiley-Interscience imprint. At 402 pages, this work is handier than almost any other book reviewed in this section, and it is dense with useful information and guidance.

This work encompasses the traditional printed sources as well as electronic means of searching for—and obtaining and manipulating—information available from on-line services.

The reading level is helpfully low, and there are separate indexes to names and subjects that speed searching for information. The table of contents is nine pages long, and is itself an efficient entry point for research. In the table of contents, chapter sections are numbered, such as "7–16, Coverage of Documents from the Soviet Union," the same as they are in heads (on an isolated line, in bold caps) in the text.

The appearance and organization of the text may be characterized by the numbered section headings, which greatly aid scanning for specific facts or advice. The chapter on "Search Strategy" lacks numbered sections, but it lists 22 questions—some of them multiple choice—to ask when systematically searching for information.

In general, the author first describes an information source or service, then tells how to use it. The size of the field, and its inherent complexity and diversity, precludes such a simple and unified treatment throughout the book. However, the result is an advantage to the reader, since most discussion of a subject can be found in one place. Cross-references help to compensate for the inevitable scattering.

Major topics include the Chemical Abstracts Service (which has two chapters covering nearly 60 pages, as befits the largest and most comprehensive organization of its kind), other abstracting and indexing services, technical information sources of the U.S. government, encyclopedias and similar references, patents, and the finding and use of physical properties of substances. One chapter that is not easily predictable concerns marketing and business information; another one concerns safety and related subjects. The text closes with a summary of trends and developments in chemical information.

Most of the 19 chapters of *How to Find Chemical Information* end with lists of references to pertinent literature and also with addresses of information sources mentioned in the text. A remarkable feature is a five-page list of topics, volume by volume, covered in the 24-volume *Kirk-Othmer Encyclopedia of Chemical Technology* (the concise edition titled the KIRK-OTHMER CONCISE ENCYCLOPEDIA OF CHEMICAL TECHNOLOGY is reviewed elsewhere in this section). The chapter covering on-line data bases—a topic vulnerable to aging—seems quite up to date.

The Board recommends *How to Find Chemical In-*

formation for the core collections of public and academic libraries.

Kirk-Othmer Concise Encyclopedia of Chemical Technology. Raymond E. Kirk, Donald F. Othmer, Martin Grayson, and David Eckroth, eds. John Wiley, 1985. hard. 1 vol. 1,318 pp. illus. appendixes. index. ISBN 0-471-86977-5. $59.95. encyclopedia.
TP9.K54 660.03′21

In condensing a widely known 24-volume reference work (then in its third edition), the editors of the *Kirk-Othmer Concise Encyclopedia of Chemical Technology* have produced a new reference that is more up to date and easier to use. The new volume is big and heavy—the pages are business-letter size—but it packs 2 million words by perhaps 1,200 contributors onto its 1,300 pages.

The scope is vast, covering dozens of industrial fields including agricultural chemicals, chemical engineering, inks, energy conversion, textiles, fossil fuels, ceramics, water supply, and wood and paper.

The book was intended primarily for chemists, other scientists, and engineers; however, teachers and students will also find the encyclopedia useful. Chemists in particular will appreciate the use of Chemical Abstracts Service registry numbers, which can solve the problem of synonyms for chemical names.

The book is arranged alphabetically, aided by frequent citations of related articles as well as secondary entries and cross-references leading to main articles. The index is large—24 pages—and helpful when searching for information in this huge volume. In the front matter is a list of conversion factors, abbreviations, and symbols.

Double columns and generous white space aid reading, and at least two levels of subheads (in boldface type) make it easier to find specific information. There are many figures, graphs, and tables. At the end of articles, there are usually references to literature. (For more extensive citations, the editors refer readers to the original 24-volume work.)

The length of entries ranges from one line to many pages. One example, which is not atypical, is the discussion of lithium and its compounds, covering three columns, with subheadings for sources, production, manufacture, inorganic compounds (specifically discussing 16 compounds, such as lithium perchlorate), organolithium compounds (discussing 7), and ending with two citations to literature.

Data seem as current as can be expected from a 1985 source. The latest bibliographic citation noted is for 1983; the latest chemical element listed is element 105 (unnilpentium). The price of the *Kirk-Othmer Concise Encyclopedia of Chemical Technology* is high, and some buyers may wish to weigh the cost against the work's considerable utility.

The Board recommends this work for the core collection of academic libraries.

Lange's Handbook of Chemistry, 13th edition. John A. Dean, ed. McGraw-Hill, 1985. hard. 1 vol. 1,856 pp. illus. index. ISBN 0-07-016192-5. $73. handbook.
QD65.L36 540

Lange's Handbook of Chemistry is edited specifically for chemists. As suggested by "Thirteenth Edition" on the title page, *Lange's* has long been accepted by chemists (since 1934).

The handbook's coverage may be summed up by the section titles: "Mathematics," "General Information and Conversion Tables," "Atomic and Molecular Structure," "Inorganic Chemistry," "Analytical Chemistry," "Electrochemistry," "Organic Chemistry," "Spectroscopy," "Thermodynamic Properties," "Physical Properties," and "Miscellaneous."

In the current edition, new data are included for 3,600 inorganic compounds as well as for about 7,600 organic compounds. Chemists will notice that the compounds are listed alphabetically and not by Chemical Abstracts Service registry numbers. The editor, who has held his post since 1968, contends that for most readers, and most chemicals, his scheme is simpler. He includes a formula index intended to help find organic compounds. In recognition of the calculator (not to mention the microcomputer), he has dropped tables of logarithms and trigonometric functions, which results in a net gain of many pages. However, the back endpapers bear tables of common logarithms, and many integrals and differential equations have been restored.

This handbook consists largely of tables and illustrations of structural formulas. Therefore, the nonchemist will find that searching for specific information tends to be slow if sure. In fact, Table 7–15, "Physical Constants of Organic Compounds," is more than 600 pages long. As one indication of currency, the periodic table stops with element 103, lawrencium.

The text is rare, but useful. The glossary occupies about 50 pages and includes a brief introduction to the indexing system used by Chemical Abstracts. Shorter discussions cover the physical chemistry of gases, separation processes, spectroscopic methods, techniques for measuring pH, and ways to use statistics. The index fills 38 two-column pages, and for many people will be the most efficient place to begin searching for information.

The Board recommends *Lange's Handbook of Chemistry* for the core collections of public, academic, and school libraries.

The Merck Index: An Encyclopedia of Chemicals, Drugs, and Biologicals, 11th edition. Susan Budavari, ed. Merck, 1989. hard. 1 vol. 1,962 pp. illus. appendixes. indexes. ISBN 0-911910-28-X. $35. encyclopedia. on-line.
RS356.M524 615.103

A hundred years after its first publication (in 1889), *The Merck Index: An Encyclopedia of Chemicals, Drugs, and Biologicals* seems to be on reference shelves to stay. This encyclopedia has established a tradition (as the editor remarks) of service to chemists, pharmicists, physicians, and their colleagues as a "one-volume compendium of information on the most important chemicals, drugs and biological substances"—information they can quickly find and use in their everyday work.

The bulk of *Merck* (1,606 pages) consists of more than 10,000 "drug monographs," the term being used here in the sense of an extremely condensed and technical description of a chemical. Typically, the monograph includes the chemical's name; identifying number; generic name; the name used by Chemical Abstracts Service; alternate names; molecular formula, molecular weight, and percentage composition; literature references; structure; physical data; derivatives; therapeutic use; and indexes.

This reference work cannot be exploited fully without considerable knowledge and practice, but the encyclopedia is an invaluable mine of information. Also, not all of the monographs are as esoteric as that of No. 5460, lovastatin. For example, see the monographs under *W* for *water, water gas, watermelon, wheat germ oil,* and *whisky.*

Under the entry *water* (monograph 9951), for example, there is the molecular weight, percentage composition of hydrogen and oxygen, temperature at maximum density, melting point, boiling point, critical temperature, and pressure. Then the editor remarks that water expands on freezing, and that it is the most nearly universal solvent known. A separate note on pyrogen-free water (for injection) gives a source for a method of its preparation, and refers the reader to the monograph for *pyrogens.* Few reference works yield so much condensed information about a substance as common as water.

In this edition, hundreds of monographs are new, half have been revised or updated, and about 500 from the tenth edition (1983) have been deleted or combined with other monographs. (Monographs appearing in the ninth and tenth editions but not in the eleventh are listed in a cross-index of names.) New subjects in the eleventh edition include drugs used against AIDS and cancer, drugs with novel mechanisms of action, products of recombinant technology, and chemicals of environmental concern. A "Therapeutic Category and Biological Activity Index" is intended to provide "an additional entry point to drug monographs." The category for substance—CAS registry numbers—has been expanded; indexes to CAS numbers remain in both alphabetical and numerical order. The "Organic Name Reactions" section has been dropped.

Librarians whose collections stress chemistry and medicine should consider the *Merck Index Online* as a supplement to the print edition of *The Merck Index,* as the electronic version of the monograph section is brought up to date semiannually.

The Board recommends *The Merck Index* for the core collections of public and academic libraries.

Van Nostrand Reinhold Encyclopedia of Chemistry, 4th edition. Douglas M. Considine, ed. Van Nostrand Reinhold, 1984. hard. 1 vol. 1,082 pp. illus. index. ISBN 0-442-22572-5. $124.95. encyclopedia.
QD5.E58 540.3'21

Now in its fourth edition, the *Van Nostrand Reinhold Encyclopedia of Chemistry* confirms its publisher's reputation for outstanding reference works. The encyclopedia is large, heavy, and expensive as well as authoritative and useful.

The content covers perhaps 1,300 topics—about double that of the third edition—discussed by 113 principal contributors. This edition reflects the tendency for chemistry to become increasingly interdisciplinary as workers in other fields draw on chemistry and apply it in their own areas. In addition to topics usual in a chemical encyclopedia (as the editor says), the fourth edition concerns these areas: advanced processes, strategic raw materials, chemistry of metals, energy sources and conversion, wastes and pollution, analytical instrumentation, food chemistry, structure of matter, new and improved materials, plant chemistry, and biochemistry and biotechnology.

The encyclopedia is arranged alphabetically. To use this book effectively, readers must systematically exploit both cross-references in the text and the index. The index runs 44 three-column pages with 8,000 entries. The names of main entries are set in boldface type to make searching for information easier.

The reading level is commendably low despite the demands of chemical terminology and editorial condensation. Blank lines between entries help to keep the reading level easy, as do boldface subheads, italic sideheads, and boldface cross-references to other main articles. Pages are set in double columns. Illustrations, such as line drawings, charts, flow sheets, and structural formulas are frequently used. Articles commonly end with related bibliographic references.

Discussions range from one line (usually cross-references to synonyms) to several pages. One of the longer discussions, on petroleum, runs 12 pages of text including three tables, two flowcharts, two figures (geological cross-sections and block diagrams showing the relationships of rock strata and oil), and seven references to literature. First-level subheads are "Petroleum Fuels," "Basic Physical Characteristics of Petroleum Fuels," and "Refining and Processing of Petroleum." Boldface type refers the reader to other articles, such as those on natural gas, oil shale, tar sands, catalytic converters, alkylation, cracking processes, distillation, and hydrotreating.

The currency of the material in the *Van Nostrand Reinhold Encyclopedia of Chemistry* may be judged from the literature cited, the latest apparently dated 1981, and by the table of electron structure of atoms, which ends with element 103, lawrencium.

The *Van Nostrand Reinhold Encyclopedia of Chemistry* is among the most expensive on the core list for chemistry. The Board recommends this work for the core collections of public, academic, and school libraries.

Supplementary Titles

Dictionary of Organic Compounds, 5th edition. John Buckingham, ed. Routledge, Chapman & Hall, 1982. hard. 7 vols. 1,300 pp. illus. indexes. ISBN 0-412-17050-7 (set). $675 (set). dictionary.
QD246.D5 003.21

The *Dictionary of Organic Compounds,* a "well-known and highly accepted reference work, first compiled by [I. M.] Heilbron in 1934, is the retrospective authority on 150,000 of the most important and frequently referred to organic compounds. Alphabetically arranged, this edition claims revision and updating of 65 percent of the material in the 1965 edition and its 15 annual supplements with the remaining 35 percent being entirely new. References to primary and secondary literature have been updated and more 'spectroscopic references [have been added], hazard and toxicity information and Chemical Abstracts Service Registry Numbers' structure diagrams have been redrawn to a new standard with stereochemical features given special attention. Entries are under names accepted by the editorial board of the *Dictionary of Organic Chemistry* (DOC).

"There are four indexes. The Name Index includes every name that appears in the dictionary. . . . The molecular formulas of all main compounds and important derivatives are included in the Molecular Formula Index. The Heteroatom Index includes the 'molecular formulae of compounds containing atoms other than carbon, hydrogen, nitrogen, oxygen, or halogens,' sorted in heteroatom order. . . . The Chemical Abstracts Service Registry Numbers are arranged in numerical order in the CAS Registry Number Index.

"Annual supplements [have appeared since 1983] and . . . include some 2,000 new and revised entries and cumulative indexes. . . . The entire work is also on a magnetic database, and . . . will be marketed as an online database." (*BL,* September 15, 1983, p. 149)

Also reviewed in: *ARBA,* 1978, p. 639; *ARBA,* 1981, p. 634; *Choice,* January 1972, p. 1438; *LJ,* February 15, 1966, p. 934; *RSR,* January 1975, p. 106; *RSR,* January 1976, p. 53; *Sci,* December 3, 1965, p. 1280.

Board's recommendation: Academic libraries.

Handbook of Organic Chemistry. John A. Dean. McGraw-Hill, 1987. hard. 1 vol. 976 pp. illus. index. ISBN 0-07-01693-3. $78. handbook.
QD251.2.D43 547

The *Handbook of Organic Chemistry* "provides a one-volume source of information specifically for the organic chemist. Of the 11 sections, the first and longest is a compilation of the physical properties of 4,000 organic compounds; the second section is a compilation of the physical properties of inorganic compounds useful to the organic chemist. Remaining sections consist of tables grouped under various headings: properties of atoms, radicals and bonds, physical properties, thermodynamic properties, spectroscopy, physiochemical relationships, electrolytes, electromotive forces, chemical equilibrium, laboratory manipulations, and polymers, rubbers, fats, oils, and waxes. . . . The outstanding feature of this book is the remaining nine sections that contain an encyclopedic presentation of pertinent data." (*SB,* May 1988, p. 282)

Also reviewed in: *New Tech Bks,* February 1987, p. 67; *SciTech,* April 1987, p. 13.

Board's recommendation: Academic libraries.

Hazardous Chemicals Desk Reference. N. Irving Sax and Richard J. Lewis. Van Nostrand Reinhold, 1987. hard. 1 vol. 1,084 pp. ISBN 0-442-28208-7. $79.95. handbook.
T55.3.H3H39 604.7

In *Hazardous Chemicals Desk Reference* "information is given for more than '4700 of the most hazardous chemicals . . . used in industry, manufacturing, laboratories, and the workplace.' Hazards such as chemicals, pesticides, dyes, detergents, lubricants, plastics, drugs, food additives, preservatives, ores, and soaps are some of the corrosives, flammables, poisons, irritants, carcinogens, and explosives that are included. Specific data in this very thorough book give name, hazard rating, Chemical Abstract Service Registry number, DOT code and rating, Registry of Toxic Effects of Chemical Substances number, molecular weight, properties, exposure limits, and toxicity. The properties section lists the melting point, density, vapor pressure, refractive index, flashpoint, auto-ignition temperature, solvents, solubility, and explosive limits. Other chapters treat chemical handling and storage, respirators, protective clothing, fire protection, and first aid in the workplace. Cross-references abound." (*Choice,* December 1987, p. 600)

Also reviewed in: *ARBA,* 1988, p. 693; *New Tech Bks,* November 1987, p. 334.

Board's recommendation: Public and academic libraries.

How to Use Chemical Abstracts, Current Abstracts of Chemistry and Index Chemicus, Brian Livesey. Gower, 1987. 65 pp. ISBN 0-566-03567-7. $38.95. handbook.
QD9.L58 025.0654

Board's recommendation: Academic libraries.

New and Noteworthy

The Nobel Prize Winners, Chemistry. Frank N. Magill, ed. Salem, 1990. hard. 3 vols. approx. 1,350 pp. ISBN 0-89356-561-X (set). $210 (set). biographical dictionary.
920

In *The Nobel Prize Winners, Chemistry* "the lives, accomplishments, and major contributions of these scientists are discussed. . . . Each 7 to 10 page article is structured with the same categories and headings as articles in the previous Nobel Prize Winners Series. There is a major introductory essay that discusses the foundation, the selection process, and the history of the Chemistry award itself. A time line presents all laureates, their countries and their specializations in chronological order." (Excerpted from publisher's announcement)

Sue Kopp

Children's Literature

The number of reference works in the field of children's literature has proliferated since the 1960s. Some of the newer titles have already become classics; others, however, are superficial and of dubious value. This review section identifies those reference sources in children's literature that will be of most assistance to librarians, teachers, students, and parents in the identification and use of worthwhile titles in children's literature.

Selection tools comprise the largest share of this section. An example of a selection tool from the general category is THE BEST IN CHILDREN'S BOOKS: THE UNIVERSITY OF CHICAGO GUIDE TO CHILDREN'S LITERATURE, a three-volume set covering the years 1966 to 1984.

Many of the titles are author biographical sources. Multivolume sets, such as the 60-volume SOMETHING ABOUT THE AUTHOR series, are included, as is the one-volume TWENTIETH CENTURY CHILDREN'S WRITERS. These sources contain biographical sketches.

Other kinds of works include dictionaries of children's literature; books on awards and honors, drama, poetry, and multimedia; and general reference sources.

Genre and specialty core and supplementary titles include FANTASY LITERATURE FOR CHILDREN AND YOUNG ADULTS and SUPERNATURAL FICTION FOR TEENS. Two significant titles are A GUIDE TO NONSEXIST CHILDREN'S BOOKS and MORE NOTES FROM A DIFFERENT DRUMMER: A GUIDE TO JUVENILE FICTION PORTRAYING THE DISABLED. Two valuable works selected by the Board as genre and specialty core works are now out of print: *Poetry Anthologies for Children and Young People* (Marycile E. Olexer, ALA, 1985) and *Sequences: An Annotated Guide to Children's Fiction in Series* (Susan Roman, ALA, 1985).

One consideration peculiar to children's literature is that of reading levels. Most of the reference works reviewed here give age or grade level information along with other standard bibliographical data for individual children's books. However, as children's reference editors are well aware, reading abilities vary not only from one age to another, but also among children of the same age or grade. Therefore, it is understood that age or grade notations are intended as a general guide rather than as a hard-and-fast rule.

FICTION FOR YOUTH: A GUIDE TO RECOMMENDED BOOKS is the only one of the reviewed titles that contains citations to works for youngsters 14 and over; there are not enough reference works designed for

Core Titles

	PUBLIC	ACADEMIC	SCHOOL
Best Books for Children: Preschool Through the Middle Grades, 4th edition Gillespie, John T., and Christine B. Gilbert, eds. Bowker, 1990	✦		
The Best in Children's Books: The University of Chicago Guide to Children's Literature, 1966–1972 Sutherland, Zena, ed. Univ. of Chicago, 1973	✦		
The Best in Children's Books: The University of Chicago Guide to Children's Literature, 1973–1978 Sutherland, Zena, ed. Univ. of Chicago, 1980	✦		
The Best in Children's Books: The University of Chicago Guide to Children's Literature, 1979–1984 Sutherland, Zena, ed. Univ. of Chicago, 1986	✦		
Children's Catalog, 15th edition Isaacson, Richard H., Ferne E. Hillegas, and Juliette Yaakov, eds. Wilson, 1986	✦		✦
Fiction for Youth: A Guide to Recommended Books, 2d edition Shapiro, Lillian L., ed. Neal-Schuman, 1986			✦
Newbery and Caldecott Medal and Honor Books: An Annotated Bibliography Peterson, Linda Kauffman, and Marilyn Leathers Solt. G. K. Hall, 1982	✦		✦
The Oxford Companion to Children's Literature Carpenter, Humphrey, and Mari Prichard. Oxford, 1984.	✦	✦	✦
Sixth Book of Junior Authors and Illustrators Holtze, Sally Holmes, ed. Wilson, 1990	✦		✦
Something About the Author: Facts and Pictures About Authors and Illustrators of Books for Young People, 60 vols. Commire, Anne, ed. Gale, 1971–	✦		✦
Twentieth-Century Children's Writers, 2d edition Kirkpatrick, D. L., ed. St. Martin's, 1983			✦

teenagers to warrant a separate review section. While so much effort is made to interest young children in reading, it is amazing that reference works pay little attention to literature for "young adults." It is true that teens are not as captive an audience as younger children, but teachers, librarians, and parents need to meet the challenge of encouraging them to continue reading.

There are several standard indexes in the children's literature field. *The Index to Children's Poetry: A Title, Subject, Author, and First Line Index to Poetry in Collections for Children and Youth* (Wilson, 1942) remains comprehensive and valuable, if not up to date. It is now supplemented by *The Index to Poetry for Children and Young People,* a two-volume set covering the years 1970–1975 and 1976–1981. THE STORYTELLER'S SOURCEBOOK: A SUBJECT, TITLE, AND MOTIF INDEX TO FOLKLORE COLLECTIONS FOR CHILDREN is the definitive index for the serious storyteller. Finally, the *Index to Collective Biographies for Young Readers* is also of interest, as is the *Index to Collective Biographies.*

Like books for adults, books (both fiction and nonfiction) for young readers tend to go into and out of print without warning. Some of the reference books reviewed in this section—whether designed as selection tools or for general floor reference—list out-of-print as well as current titles.

Core Titles

Best Books for Children: Preschool Through the Middle Grades, 4th edition. John T. Gillespie and Christine B. Gilbert, eds. Bowker, 1990. hard. 1 vol. 595 pp. indexes. ISBN 0-8352-2668-9. $44.95. bibliography.
Z1037.G48[PN1009.A1] 011.62

Best Books for Children: Preschool Through the Middle Grades includes over 9,000 individual entries for books aimed at readers from preschool through advanced sixth grade, with lesser depth for readers in junior high school. This one-volume reference tool thus provides comprehensive coverage of children's literature. Some titles included here were selected from the revised second edition of *Best Books.* Titles that have gone out of print since that edition were dropped. (Titles were originally chosen for the second edition on the basis of availability, currency, accuracy, and usefulness; each title was also recommended by at least three of the sources from which the final title list was compiled.) New titles, making up approximately half the entries, were selected on the basis of multiple recommendations from such standard critical sources as *Booklist, Horn Book, Children's Catalog,* and *Notable Children's Books.* The volume can be used for book selection, evaluating current collections, reading guidance, and in the preparation of bibliographies and reading lists.

The contents are divided into broad subjects and may be subdivided. For example, the heading "Christmas" appears under the broad topic "Holidays and Holy Days" and is further broken down into Christmas-related books under the subheadings "Fiction," "Crafts," "Music," "Plays," and "Poetry." Books under the heading "Fiction" are arranged in individual sections for "Animal Stories," "Family Stories," "Friendship Stories," and "Adventure and Mystery," to name but a few. Some fiction categories—notably, "Historical Fiction"—are divided into subsections on various continents and nations. Fiction about the United States is further categorized by historical period or theme ("Indians of North America," "Colonial Period," "The Revolution," "Westward Expansion and Pioneer Life," and so forth). Such distinct categories, which are detailed clearly in the table of contents, make it easy for the user to find titles on virtually any subject of interest to children. Moreover, effective indexing provides access to the entries by author-illustrator, title, biographic subject, and subject with cross-references. All indexing refers to entry numbers. Needless to say, accessibility is excellent.

Within each topic section, entries are in alphabetical order by author. Each entry includes author, title, age range, illustrations or illustrator, publisher, data, and price. Also included is a one- or two-sentence annotation, the type of binding available, sequels (if appropriate) with date and price, and occasional references to a similar title.

Best Books for Children is an excellent one-volume reference tool for current children's publications. The Board recommends this work for the core collection of public libraries.

The Best in Children's Books: The University of Chicago Guide to Children's Literature, 1966–1972. Zena Sutherland, ed. Univ. of Chicago, 1973. hard. 1 vol. 484 pp. appendixes. indexes. ISBN 0-226-78057-0. approx. $25. bibliography.
Z1037.A1S9[PN1009.A1] 810.9′9282

The Best in Children's Books: The University of Chicago Guide to Children's Literature, 1973–1978. Zena Sutherland, ed. Univ. of Chicago, 1980. hard. 1 vol. 547 pp. appendixes. indexes. ISBN 0-226-78059-7. approx. $25. bibliography.
Z1037.A1S92 [PN1009.A1] 810.9′9282

The Best in Children's Books: The University of Chicago Guide to Children's Literature, 1979–1984. Zena Sutherland, ed. Univ. of Chicago, 1986. hard. 1 vol. 547 pp. appendixes. indexes. ISBN 0-226-78060-0. approx. $25. bibliography.
Z1037.A1S93 [PN1009.A1] 016.81′09′9282

The Best in Children's Books series emanates from the *Bulletin of the Center for Children's Books* sponsored by the University of Chicago Graduate Library School; the center, established at the university in 1945, evaluates books "in terms of uses, appeals, and literary quality" (introduction). Zena Sutherland, the series editor, is a member of the *Bulletin*'s editorial board. The volumes are excellent reference tools and selection aids. Covering both fiction and nonfiction, the series includes the most distinctive books published in each given year. Literary quality is the primary selection consideration.

Each volume follows the same format: a general introduction, suggestions for use, annotated entries, appendix of publishers' addresses, and multiple indexes. Each entry is numbered and listed in alphabetical order by author. A full bibliographic citation is given, including price, ISBN, and Library of Congress card numbers. The annotations are well written, with an emphasis on plots and interwoven themes.

Previous reviews have mentioned the unwieldy indexes of this series. The "Developmental Values Index" has far too many listings on each topic; for example, 53 page numbers are listed under "Family Relations." Similarly, the "Reading Level Index" is too confusing, with such listings as grades 3–4, 3–6, 3–7, 4–5, 4–6, 4–7, 4–8, 4–9, and grades 4 up. Because suggested grades of readers are listed in the margins, it seems easier to flip through the text than to follow the 162 references suggested for the grades 4–6 category. The title index refers to the author's name, which one can then look for in alphabetical order in the text. This index is helpful, as it refers the reader to the entry number; however, the final index, "Type of Literature Index," gives far too many page numbers without any subdivision, making it difficult to use. Future editions would benefit from more detailed indexing.

Despite these problems with the indexes, *The Best in Children's Books* series remains a respected reference tool by a trusted editor. The Board recommends this series for the core collection of public libraries.

Children's Catalog, 15th edition. Richard H. Isaacson, Ferne E. Hillegas, and Juliette Yaakov, eds. Wilson, 1986. hard. 1 vol. 1,298 pp. indexes. ISBN 0-8242-0743-2. $72. bibliography.
Z1037.C5443 [PN1009.A1] 011.62

For book selection, the *Children's Catalog* is a standard in the field. The fifteenth edition offers the best books for children as determined by a distinguished advisory committee and voted on by a consulting group of experienced children's librarians. The advisory committee and consultants are listed in the volume.

The work begins with a section instructing users on how to use this reference tool. The volume contains 5,715 entries for fiction and nonfiction books for ages preschool through sixth grade. Nonfiction entries are arranged according to Dewey Decimal numbers and then listed in alphabetical order by author. Fiction is divided into three sections: "Fiction," "Story Collections," and "Easy Books." These entries are also arranged alphabetically by author.

All entries include the author's name in boldface type, a full bibliographic citation, an age notation, and ISBN and Library of Congress card numbers. An annotation in the form of an excerpt from a book review is provided and the reviewing source is identified—*Horn Book, Booklist,* and *School Library Journal* are examples of sources included. If the title is part of a series, only the first title in the series has a full annotation.

An excellent "Author, Title, Subject, and Analytical Index" comprises almost half of the volume, referring the reader back to the Dewey Decimal number (or to the "Fiction" section) where the entry can be found. Index entries, like the main entry itself, identify the appropriate age level for each title. A "Directory of Publishers and Distributors" is included. Even this list is cross-referenced (from publishers to distributors) for convenience.

The *Children's Catalog,* first published in 1909, has been a trusted reference source and buying guide for children's librarians since that time. For the most part, this volume does not include those children's books that have gone out of print since the last edition. Should some of these titles return to print, they will be included in the supplements, which, according to the preface, "purchasers of the fifteenth edition will receive . . . without further charge."

The Board recommends this work for the core collections of public and school libraries.

Fiction for Youth: A Guide to Recommended Books, 2d edition. Lillian L. Shapiro, ed. Neal-Schuman, 1986. soft. 1 vol. 264 pp. indexes. ISBN 0-918212-94-4. $29.95. bibliography.
Z1037.S485 [PN1009.A1] 016.80883

Addressing fiction intended for mature young adults, ages 14 to 18, *Fiction for Youth: A Guide to Recommended Books* is an annotated bibliography of 619 titles that fills a gap in "children's" literature for that age group. The second edition continues the same arrangement as the first with regard to purpose, audience, criteria, and methodology, as defined in the introduction, as well as adding 125 additional titles and deleting 94 that have gone out of print.

The bulk (over 200 pages) of *Fiction for Youth* consists of single-paragraph descriptions of the recommended titles arranged alphabetically by author. Some of the descriptions are basic plot summaries; some also provide a critical comment on the work. When a book deals with sensitive subject matter (sex or violence), this is noted as well. Complete bibliographic information is given for every title. All the books listed were written in the twentieth century.

Supplementary sections at the back of *Fiction for Youth* include a list of recommended out-of-print titles, a directory of publishers, a title index, and a subject index. Among the "A" titles are such classics as Faulkner's *Absalom, Absalom,* Wharton's *The Age of Innocence,* Remarque's *All Quiet on the Western Front,* Warren's *All the King's Men,* Orwell's *Animal Farm,* and Rand's *Atlas Shrugged*—which give a good idea of the type of "mature" books covered in this work. The subject index breaks down titles by genre (short stories, suspense, sea stories), geographical location (Latin America, Israel), ethnic group, and topic (anti-Semitism, apartheid). These indexes greatly enhance both the usefulness and the accessibility of *Fiction for Youth.*

In "A Nation at Risk," the preface to *Fiction for Youth,* editor Lillian L. Shapiro details her concern with the mediocrity of American education as well as with the popularity of television, home computers, and formula novels. Shapiro encourages adults to work with young adults in such activities as book talks and reading aloud of the recommended literature to further their education: "It is time for all the adults who are responsible for this generation to provide more guidance" (preface).

The Board recommends this work for the core collection of school libraries.

Newbery and Caldecott Medal and Honor Books: An Annotated Bibliography. Linda Kauffman Peterson and Marilyn Leathers Solt. G. K. Hall, 1982. hard. 1 vol. 427 pp. appendixes. indexes. ISBN 0-8161-8448-8. $57.50. bibliography.
Z1037.P45 [PN1009.A1] 011.62'079

Newbery and Caldecott Medal and Honor Books: An Annotated Bibliography is a complex reference tool that is far more than a listing of Newbery and Caldecott winners. As the brief historical essay in this work notes, the Newbery Award was first given in 1922 and the Caldecott in 1938. Because there may be more than one outstanding children's book published in a year, this volume also cites the Honor Books for each award, giving them the same treatment as the award winners.

The preface explains the purpose of this reference work and gives details of the work's scope and arrangement, the literature genres covered, and suggestions for use. The introduction continues with information about the origin and terms of the awards, how they were named, who comprises the selection committee, voting procedures, how the awards are announced, the celebration for winners, and the significance of the awards.

The main text lists the award and honor books—first the Newbery books, in chronological order, and then the Caldecott winners in the same fashion. Each title is assigned an entry number. An annotation, which contains a story summary as well as a critical analysis, is given for each title. Preceding each annotation are bibliographic information, a reference to the type of literature represented (such as fantasy, biography, and so forth), and a statement of intended grade level of the book's audience. Of particular value are the "Characteristics and Trends" essays that preface the listing of award winners.

The four appendixes and two indexes provide highly detailed information. Appendix A is a title list of entries in chronological order, with reference to the title number in the main text. Appendix B provides the terms, definitions, and criteria for each award. Appendixes C and D detail the winning books by literary genre. The "Author/Illustrator/Title Index" refers the reader back to the title number. The final "Subject Index" is less useful; under the subject "Animals in Picture Books" are 65 entry numbers. As many subjects list 30 or more numbers, this index is somewhat impractical to use.

Although there are other reference tools available that list Newbery and Caldecott winners, *Newbery and Caldecott Medal and Honor Books* stands out for its detailed information about the organization and distribution of the awards, along with annotations and critical essays. The Board recommends this work for the core collections of public and school libraries.

The Oxford Companion to Children's Literature. Humphrey Carpenter and Mari Prichard. Oxford, 1984. hard. 1 vol. 586 pp. illus. ISBN 0-19-211582-0. $45. handbook.
PN1008.5.C37 809.89282

The exquisite *Oxford Companion to Children's Literature* is a fascinating collection of informational tidbits relating to children's literature. Concentrating on the historical aspect of this topic, *The Oxford Companion* contains some 2,000 entries as well as many beautiful illustrations reproduced in black and white. Biographical sketches on authors run from a few sentences to several columns. Because this is a British publication, it is perhaps understandable that British authors receive greater attention and longer entries than do American authors. For example, *Robert McCloskey, Beverly Cleary, Judy Blume, Lois Lenski,* and *James Marshall* are among successful and popular American authors whose entries are somewhat abbreviated. Caldecott winner Chris Van Allsburg and Newbery medalist Ellen Ruskin are not included, while *William Pène Du Bois* and *Tomie de Paola* receive brief entries.

In the preface, the compilers credit such sources as TWENTIETH-CENTURY CHILDREN'S WRITERS, *Children's Books in England,* third edition (F. J. Harvey Darton), and the head of the Children's Book Section of the Library of Congress as those consulted for selection of material to be included.

The entries are in alphabetical order with spaces and

hyphens ignored. Foreign titles are entered under their English title in translation (for example, *Le Petit Prince* is under the title *The Little Prince*). Entry words are in boldface type, while words in small capitals are used as cross-references to other entries. Many titles of children's literature are included, some with quite lengthy annotations (such as *Peter Pan, Alice's Adventures in Wonderland,* and *The Adventures of Huckleberry Finn*).

The volume identifies storybook characters: "Miss Pickerell, spinster space traveller in stories by Ellen MCGREGOR" and "Miss Piggy, one of the MUPPETS," are examples. Additionally, there are entries for such classic characters of children's literature as *Mickey Mouse* and *Babar the Elephant,* and such innovative works as Walt Disney's animated film *Fantasia* and the TV series *Sesame Street* are included. Entries range from *McGuffey Eclectic Readers* to *penny dreadfuls* to foreign-language children's books in English translation, such as Astrid Lindgren's *Pippi Longstocking.* Of particular interest is the inclusion of brief summaries of the "state of children's literature in all languages, countries, or continents" for which there was "reliable information available" (preface).

Not only is *The Oxford Companion to Children's Literature* an excellent source of information, especially for historical British children's literature, but it is also great fun to sit down and browse through. The strength of *The Oxford Companion* rests on the quality of its brief critical judgments on many of the authors and books included. The entries are incisive, and the lengthy discussions of such legendary writers as J. M. Barrie and Beatrix Potter are quite authoritative. The Board recommends this work for the core collections of public, academic, and school libraries.

Sixth Book of Junior Authors and Illustrators. Sally Holmes Holtze, ed. Wilson, 1990. hard. 1 vol. 345 pp. illus. index. ISBN 0-8242-0777-7. $40. biographical dictionary.
PN1009.A1F47 809.89282

The *Sixth Book of Junior Authors and Illustrators* is the latest addition to a series of autobiographical sketches of authors that was first published in 1935. Illustrated with photographs of most of the authors, the book is well laid out and easy to read. It is appropriate for both librarians and interested older school-age children.

The *Sixth Book* contains sketches of 236 authors and illustrators who have come to popular or literary prominence since 1983, when the *Fourth Book* was published. The types of books written by the authors included in the volume span the age levels of children's literature. Marc Brown is an example of an author for the younger set, Paula Danziger *(The Cat Ate My Gymsuit)* represents the middle years, and Anne McCaffrey's "Dragon" series (including *Dragonsong, Dragonsinger,* and others) is popular with young adults.

The criteria for selection and the names of members of the selection committee are listed in the preface. The committee is composed primarily of librarians, such as Margaret N. Coughlan, reference specialist in children's literature at the Library of Congress.

The entries are arranged alphabetically by the author's or illustrator's name. Each begins with an autobiographical or biographical sketch, followed by a list of selected works with publication dates, and a list of books and articles about the subject that are readily available. In those cases where authors or illustrators did not provide an autobiographical sketch, biographical sketches were written by free-lance contributors, who are listed in the front of the volume. Some of these biographical sketches were written by someone who knew the subject personally or who is an authority on his or her work; these sketches are signed by the contributors. When the editor felt that the autobiographical sketch was incomplete, she added such important details as information on degrees, honors, and awards.

A cumulative index to the entire series began with the *Third Book* and continues with each subsequent volume. The index provides cross-references for all names and pen names.

This series does present an awkward classification problem. National cataloging rules require cuttering by main entry, which is the title. As a result, unless a library is willing to bend national standards, the six editions of the *Book of Junior Authors and Illustrators* series will not be located together on the shelf.

If one had to make a choice, the SOMETHING ABOUT THE AUTHOR series would be preferred, but the *Sixth Book of Junior Authors and Illustrators* and its other editions are quite useful as well. The Board recommends this series for the core collections of public and school libraries.

Something About the Author: Facts and Pictures About Authors and Illustrators of Books for Young People. Anne Commire, ed. Gale, 1971–. hard. 60 vols. illus. index. ISBN 0-8103-2270-6 (vol. 60). approx. $74 per vol. biographical dictionary.
PN497.S66 028.5′092′2

Delightful to browse through, the *Something About the Author* series is the premiere biographical tool in children's literature. The first volume of this 60-volume series was published in 1971. Aimed at students from about the fifth grade on as well as librarians, teachers, education students, parents, and the general public interested in children's literature, each volume has approximately 300 to 400 pages. Beautifully illustrated in black and white, each volume includes an introduction that explains the types of genres covered (virtually all), revisions of author entries as their careers progress, obituaries, and the "highlights" of the volume. The introduction also details the individual entries, which include name, dates, education, and addresses; career notations; awards and honors received; writings; adaptations of writings; and the "Sidelights" area, which may include an autobiographical statement as well as commentary on the person's life and achievements. Entries, which run from one to several pages, include a photograph of the author. There are usually reproductions of examples from an illustrator's works. Illustrations are considered an integral part of an entry.

Cumulative indexing for the complete series in each volume is another strong facet of this reference tool. Illustrators and authors are indexed separately. Authors with entries in the *Something About the Author* autobiography series (SAAS), *Children's Literature Review,* and *Yesterday's Authors of Books for Children* are also included. A "Character Index" appeared for the first time in volume 50 and is repeated in volume 54. According to the introduction, this feature will eventually appear in each volume.

The *Something About the Author* series covers many more authors and illustrators than does the SIXTH BOOK OF JUNIOR AUTHORS AND ILLUSTRATORS, a reference work of similar orientation. Also, the *Something About the Author* series is much easier for children to use, and scrupulous attention has been paid to giving as complete coverage as possible, including obituaries (since volume 20) that give concise overviews of individual writers' or illustrators' careers.

The *Something About the Author* series is an outstanding reference tool. The Board recommends this series for the core collections of public and school libraries.

Twentieth-Century Children's Writers, 2d edition. D. L. Kirkpatrick, ed. St. Martin's, 1983. hard. 1 vol. 1,024 pp. appendix. index. ISBN 0-312-82414-9. $75. biographical dictionary.
PN1009.A1T9 809.89282'19

Listing over 700 English-language writers, *Twentieth-Century Children's Writers* is a comprehensive reference work in one volume. Among the authors included are *Joan Aiken, Vivian Alcock, Enid Bagnold,* and *Roald Dahl.* Each entry provides biographical information, a complete list of published books, a signed critical essay about each author, and in many cases, an essay on writing for children written by the featured author. A valuable feature of this work is the essay on the historical perspective of children's literature. Although the volume is well laid out and well organized, it would not be as accessible for children to consult for information about their favorite authors as the SOMETHING ABOUT THE AUTHOR series.

Besides merely listing the advisors and contributors, a section at the end of this authoritative volume annotates their professional involvement with children's literature. The section also identifies which of the critical essays they wrote within the volume. Some children's authors also served as contributors (for example, Jane Yoland and Mary Rayner).

An appendix provides a representative sampling of 38 important nineteenth-century writers, such as *Lewis Carroll* and *Edward Lear.* Each entry in the appendix consists of a biographical sketch that includes a list of published books and a signed critical essay. An essay on important foreign-language authors followed by a list of over 60 foreign-language writers (for example, *Mitsumasa Anno* and *Jean de Brunhoff*) is included, with titles and dates of their publications. A 110-page title index, which provides publication date and author's name, completes the volume.

Twentieth-Century Children's Writers is a standard work for research on children's literature. The Board recommends this work for the core collection of school libraries.

Supplementary Titles

American Writers for Children Before 1900. Glenn E. Estes, ed. (*Dictionary of Literary Biography,* vol. 42.) Gale, 1985. hard. 1 vol. 441 pp. illus. index. ISBN 0-8103-1720-6. $103. biographical dictionary.
PS490.A44 810.9'9282

American Writers for Children, 1900–1960. John Cech, ed. (*Dictionary of Literary Biography,* vol. 22.) Gale, 1983. hard. 1 vol. 412 pp. illus. index. ISBN 0-8103-1146-1. $103. biographical dictionary.
PS490.A43 810.9'9282[B]

American Writers for Children Since 1960: Poets, Illustrators, and Nonfiction Authors. Glenn E. Estes, ed.(*Dictionary of Literary Biography,* vol. 61.) Gale, 1987. hard. 1 vol. 430 pp. illus. index. ISBN 0-8103-1739-7. $103. biographical dictionary.
PS490.A45 810.9'9282

The *American Writers for Children* series "is arranged alphabetically by biographee. Within each entry is listed the corpus of the writer's works, with full bibliographic information. Following is a description of the person's career, along with germane personal information. Entries [seek to] outline the influences on the writing of the biographees and place them within the context of the period in which they wrote. Pictures of the subjects as well as illustrations from their works are included. Concluding each entry is a list of references.

"At the end of the book is a bibliography of historical and critical material on children's literature found in books and journals. . . . Finally, there is a cumulative index to all volumes in the DLB [Dictionary of Literary Biography] series, including the Yearbooks and the Documentary Series. . . . [These volumes are] a valuable addition to reference material on children's literature criticism and would be useful in many academic and public libraries." (*BL,* May 15, 1986, p. 1372)

Also reviewed in: *AB,* November 17, 1986, p. 2032; *ARBA,* 1986, p. 434; *BL,* March 15, 1988, p. 1230; *JB,* August 1988, p. 177; *Lib Sci Ann,* 1986, p. 123; *WLB,* February 1988, p. 96.

Board's recommendation: Public, academic, and school libraries.

Black Authors and Illustrators of Children's Books: A Biographical Dictionary. Barbara Rollock. Garland, 1988. hard. 1 vol. 130 pp. illus. ISBN 0-8240-8580-9. $27. biographical dictionary.
Z1037.R63 [PN1009.A1] 011.62'08996073

Black Authors and Illustrators "contains very brief sketches of 115 well-known and less familiar authors and illustrators; authors of books for adults are excluded. Entries, arranged alphabetically, include facts on each subject's birthplace, accomplishments, positions held, and awards. A list of the subject's publications follows each one- to two-paragraph entry. Included is an eight-page insert of photographs of some authors/illustrators and a few book covers showing artwork. . . . Rollock presents only factual information.

"Students in the middle grades and up, librarians, and others who are searching for information about black writers or illustrators, will find this . . . book useful for beginning that search." (*SLJ,* November 1988, p. 54)

Board's recommendation: Public and school libraries.

The Bookfinder: A Guide to Children's Literature About the Needs and Problems of Youth Aged 2–15. Sharon Spreadmann Dreyer. American Guidance Service, 1977–. hard and soft. 4 vols. (vol. 1 out of print.) illus. indexes. ISBN 0-913476-50-1 (vol. 4, hard); 0-913476-51-X (vol. 4, soft). $69.95 (vol. 4, hard); $34.95 (vol. 4, soft). bibliography.
Z1037.A1D78 011.62

The Bookfinder: A Guide to Children's Literature About the Needs and Problems of Youth Aged 2–15 is a four-volume set "describing and categorizing [over] 725 books according to 450 psychological, behavioral, and developmental topics of concern to children and adolescents.

"The unique split-image format of the former volumes is not used in [volume 3.] Instead, the volume is arranged . . . with the main section containing the annotations followed by the indexes: subject, author, and title. The hardcover edition also includes a cumulated subject index to all three volumes.

"Each entry in the annotation section includes full bibliographical information for each book, a listing of primary and secondary themes, an annotation, commentary, reading level, and other forms available, such as braille, large print, cassette, or paperbound. . . .

"This work will be useful to . . . anyone who is attempting to match children with books in an effort to help them cope with specific behavioral and developmental needs and problems." (*ARBA,* 1986, p. 432)

Also reviewed in: *A Lib,* March 1978, p. 171; *BL,* September 1, 1979, p. 60; *B Rpt,* January 1983, p. 48; *Cur R,* May 1982, p. 190; *EJ,* May 1979, p. 73; *Inst,* April 1978, p. 162; January 1981, p. 86; October 1981, p. 29; *RT,* May 1978, p. 962; January 1979, p. 443; December 1981, p. 377; *SLJ,* January 1978, p. 66; *SLMQ,* Summer 1982; *TN,* Spring 1978, p. 302; Summer 1980, p. 347; Winter 1980, p. 93; *Teacher,* April 1978, p. 114; *VOYA,* December 1981, p. 52; *WLB,* February 1978, p. 507.

Board's recommendation: Public and school libraries.

Child Drama: A Selected and Annotated Bibliography, 1974–1979. Carol Jean Kennedy. Children's Theatre Assn. of America, 1981. soft. 1 vol. 51 pp. index. ISBN 0-8191-3524-0. $7.75. bibliography.
Z5784.C5K46 [PN3157] 016.792'0226'0973

Board's recommendation: Academic libraries.

Dictionary of American Children's Fiction, 1859–1959: Books of Recognized Merit. Alethea K. Helbig and Agnes Regan Perkins. Greenwood, 1985. hard.

1 vol. 666 pp. index. ISBN 0-313-22590-7. approx. $70. dictionary.
PS374.C454H45 813.009′9282

Dictionary of American Children's Fiction, 1960–1984: Recent Books of Recognized Merit. Alethea K. Helbig and Agnes Regan Perkins. Greenwood, 1986. hard. 1 vol. 914 pp. index. ISBN 0-313-25233-5. approx. $70. dictionary.
PS374.C454H45 813.54′099282

Within the *Dictionary of American Children's Fiction,* "an extensive index includes all items entered, plus major characters for whom there are no separate entries, special settings by place and period, and themes and subjects. It is possible, therefore, to look up novels about small-town life, subdivided by place (e.g., Italy, Maine, etc.); books that discuss siblings or dogs; or stories that are set in the seventeenth century. According to the Preface, [the] companion volume will cover children's fiction published after 1959. These two volumes will be useful to anyone concerned with children's literature—librarians, teachers and students." (*BL,* March 15, 1986, p. 1067)

"Browsers will be ensnared by this book, which gives extremely detailed (if rather rigorously critical) plot summaries, character sketches, and brief author biographies for 420 children's books . . . A few errors were detected; one, in the index, was slight, but citing Laura Ingalls Wilder's *By the Shores of Silver Lake* [BRD 1939] as On the Shores of Silver Lake is confusing at best. . . . There are no actual lists of award books, but one can track them down . . . through the index, which is also extremely useful for locating books by subject or theme, a welcome feature for librarians and students of children's literature. Although there are other recent reference works that are broader in coverage (Jon Stott's *Children's Literature from A to Z* . . .; *Twentieth-Century Children's Writers,* 2nd ed., 1983), they do not attempt the depth of detail that is the chief attribute of this sturdy though expensive book." (*Choice,* June 1986, p. 1520)

Also reviewed in: *AB,* November 17, 1986, p. 2032; *A Lib,* May 1986, p. 316; January 1987, p. 526; *ARBA,* 1987, p. 428; April 1987, p. 1198; *JAL,* September 1987, p. 240; *LJ,* November 15, 1985, p. 86; *R & R Bk N,* Winter 1987, p. 20; *Ref Bk R,* 1986, p. 19; *RQ,* Summer 1986, p. 535.

Board's recommendation: Public and school libraries.

Exciting, Funny, Scary, Short, Different, and Sad Books Kids Like About Animals, Science, Sports, Families, Songs, and Other Things. Frances Laverne Carroll and Mary Meacham, eds. ALA, 1984. soft. 1 vol. 210 pp. index. ISBN 0-8389-0423-8. $10. bibliography.
Z1037.C29 [PN1009.A1] 016.80806′8

"The editors [of this book] surveyed a number of children's librarians to determine two things. First they wanted to learn what subjects children request books about these days. Second, they wanted to learn what books the librarians recommend on these subjects. The result is *Books Kids Like,* an annotated guide to books on thirty-five broad topics such as those listed in the lengthy title as well as holidays, computers, war, dinosaurs, cars, and history. Genre books (historical fiction, mystery) are treated as well as popular series such as the 'Little House' books and the Will Stanton series. Many of the broad subject sections are subdivided; for example, the section entitled 'I Like to Read About Kids Like Me' breaks down into kids at school, being blind, black children, doing fun things, friends, in the city, super kids, kids who can't hear, and kids with handicaps. There is no particular order to the sections since 'there is not any reason from a child's point of view to put Halloween books with Christmas books, for example, together in a division of holiday books.' This may or may not be true; since the index lists authors and titles of the recommended books but not the subject sections, one must scan the table of contents carefully lest a desired topic be overlooked. The arrangement implies that children themselves should use the book as a selection guide and indeed the annotations of a sentence or two are written so that children can comprehend them. Perhaps this explains the absence of grade or age level indicators which children might find patronizing or off-putting. When used carefully, in the hands of either a young reader or a children's librarian, *Books Kids Like* will be a helpful reader's advisory tool. Librarians may also want to comb it systematically as a collection development/evaluation guide." (*WLB,* May 1985, p. 624)

Also reviewed in: *AB,* August 19, 1985, p. 1221; *ARBA,* 1986, p. 43; *SLJ,* September 1985, p. 44; *TN,* Spring 1985, p. 305.

Board's recommendation: Public and school libraries.

Fantasy Literature for Children and Young Adults: An Annotated Bibliography, 3d edition. Ruth Nadelman Lynn. Bowker, 1988. hard. 1 vol. 771 pp. indexes. ISBN 0-8352-2347-7. $39.95 bibliography.
Z1037.L97 [PN1009.A1] 016.80883′876

Fantasy Literature for Children and Young Adults "is an annotated bibliography of 3,300 fantasy novels and story collections. (The second edition was published as *Fantasy for Children.*) . . . Now in its third revision, the work has seen many improvements: 1,600 books have been added to the 1,700 books from the last edition. . . . The scope now includes books for young adults—those students in grades 8 through 12.

"Part 1 lists novels and story collections published in English in the U.S. between 1900 and 1988. Out-of-print books continue to appear in the bibliography, which is an asset since many of these works still are found in libraries. The titles are arranged in 10 sections by type of fantasy—animal, ghost, time travel, etc.—and then alphabetically by author. Each book has a one-sentence annotation that gives the gist of the story. This is followed by citations to reviews of the book. Symbols to designate the quality of the works have been placed in the left margin . . . [and] indicate the appropriate audience for each book. . . . Part 2 is the research guide, the bibliography of secondary sources for adults.

"This work is a valuable resource that should be on the shelf of every librarian who works with children." (*Ref Bks Bul,* May 1, 1989, p. 1516)

Board's recommendation: Public and academic libraries.

A Guide to Non-sexist Children's Books, Volume II: 1976–1985. Denise Wilms and Ilene Cooper, eds. Academy Chicago, 1987. hard and soft. 1 vol. 240 pp. illus. indexes. ISBN 0-89733-161-3 (hard); 0-89733-162-1 (soft). $17.95 (hard): $8.95 (soft). bibliography.
Z1037.A1W64 [PN1009.A1] 011.62

A Guide to Non-sexist Children's Books, Volume II: 1976–1985 "contains 685 role-free titles representing preschool-grade 12 picture books, novels, poetry, folktales, and nonfiction. Entries are arranged by grade categories . . . [and] are annotated, [there is a] note if the title is an award winner, and full bibliographic information, including grade level, is provided. Other helpful sections are a directory of small press publishers, an age-grade comparison chart, and the inclusion of black-and-white illustrations to break up the monotony of the text.

"The intent of providing an annotated guide to contemporary, role-free children's literature is noteworthy. One hopes that volume 3 [which is to be published in the fall of 1990] will contain a detailed introduction of the title selection process, and a cumulative author, title, and subject index to the earlier volumes." (*ARBA,* 1988, p. 451)

Also reviewed in: *B Rpt,* January 1988, p. 49; *Wom R. Bks,* December 1987, p. 15.

Board's recommendation: Public libraries.

More Notes from a Different Drummer: A Guide to Juvenile Fiction Portraying the Disabled. Barbara H. Baskin and Karen H. Harris. Bowker, 1984. hard. 1 vol. 495 pp. illus. index. ISBN 0-8352-1871-6. $39.95. bibliography.
Z1037.9.B36 [PN1009.Z6] 808.06'8

More Notes from a Different Drummer examines "more than 400 books of juvenile fiction published between 1976 and 1981 that portray the disabled. . . . [There are] two introductory chapters. . . . Chapter 3, representing more than three quarters of the book, is devoted to the annotated guide to the selected juvenile fiction, which appears alphabetically by author's name. Each annotation consists of a description of the plot and an analysis of the literary treatment. . . . Books are coded in four rough reading levels from YC (young child 5–8 years old) to MA (mature adolescent 16–18 years old). . . . The bibliographic information is accompanied by the approximate reading range and, also, the major disability that is presented in the story—auditory, cosmetic, intellectual, neurological, orthopedic, speech or visual impairment, emotional dysfunction, learning disability, or special health problems." (*Choice,* April 1985, p. 1154)

"[*More Notes*] is useful for pinpointing books on disability, many of which would not otherwise be easily identified. The authors' determination that books must stand up both as literature and as having accurate portrayals of disability results in tough, knowledgeable critiques. . . . [This] is a high-quality reference." (*BL,* June 1, 1985, p. 1384)

Also reviewed in: *ARBA,* 1985, p. 371; *J Read,* April 1985, p. 664; *LQ,* October 1985, p. 482.

Board's recommendation: Public and school libraries.

A Reference Guide to Modern Fantasy for Children. Pat Pflieger. Greenwood, 1984. hard. 1 vol. 690 pp. index. ISBN 0-313-22886-8. $69.95. reference guide.
PR830.F3G84 823.0876'099282

A Reference Guide to Modern Fantasy for Children "employs brief-entry dictionary format to describe authors, book titles, major and minor characters, places, and magical objects. . . . The author has selected fantasies concerning place, time, conflict between good and evil, incredible beings, and animals.

"Plot synopses and descriptions of characters are good, and the author entries are also a strong feature, providing biographical information, themes, a well-prepared bibliography of primary works, and a selection of the best available literature covering these works." (*BL,* February 15, 1985, p. 833)

"A very thorough guide to the fantasies and fantasists . . . this is unlike any other guide to the genre. . . . The index and the multitude of cross-references appear to be thorough and accurate." (*Choice,* January 1985, p. 664)

Also reviewed in: *A Lib,* May 1986, p. 318; *CE,* September 1985, p. 65; *SLJ,* May 1986, p. 31; *TN,* Summer 1986, p. 430.

Board's recommendation: Public and school libraries.

The Storyteller's Sourcebook: A Subject, Title, and Motif Index to Folklore Collections for Children. Margaret Read MacDonald. Neal-Schuman, 1982. hard. 1 vol. 818 pp. ISBN 0-8103-0471-6. $95. handbook.
GR74.6.M3 016.3982′088054

The Storyteller's Sourcebook "is a source for locating variants of folktales and brief descriptions of them. Access is through the use of motif, title, subject, ethnic, and geographic indexes. Over 550 folktale collections and 389 picture books have been represented, plus titles extracted from other reviewing sources.

"The motif index is based on Stith Thompson's classification for his six-volume Motif-Index of Folk Literature (1955–58), but MacDonald has tailored it for the particular use of those working with children. . . . Accuracy and quality of the indexing and coverage [are] impressive. . . . Careful reading of the preface and 'How to Use This Book' section is essential. . . . Storytellers, children's librarians, and students of children's literature will readily welcome this valuable source." (*Choice,* October 1982, p. 244)

Also reviewed in: *LJ,* August 1982, p. 1451.

Board's recommendation: Public, academic, and school libraries.

Supernatural Fiction for Teens: 500 Good Paperbacks to Read for Wonderment, Fear, and Fun. Cosette Kies. Libraries Unlimited, 1987. soft. 1 vol. 127 pp. index. ISBN 0-87287-602-0. $17.50. bibliography.
Z1037.K485 [PN1009.A1] 016.80883′937

Board's recommendation: Public and school libraries.

New and Noteworthy

Beacham's Guide to Literature for Young Adults. Kirk H. Beetz and Suzanne Niemeyer. Beacham Publishing, 1989. hard. 3 vols. 1,545 pp. illus. index. ISBN 0-933833-11-3 (set). $189 (set). bibliography.
PN1009.A1 028.1′62

The "214 books chosen [for *Beacham's Guide to Literature for Young Adults*] . . . are popular with young adults, possess literary merit, and are classics over time, critically acclaimed, and appropriate for junior high or high school. . . . Entries are signed, thorough, well written, and range from 5 to 10 pages. Each includes information about the author, an overview of the work, and sections on setting, themes and characters, literary qualities, social sensitivity, . . . ideas for papers, and a brief bibliography. . . ." (*BL,* July 1990, p. 2113)

Beyond Picture Books: A Guide to First Readers. Barbara Barstow and Judith Riggle. Bowker, 1989. hard. 1 vol. 336 pp. indexes. ISBN 0-8352-2515-1. $39.95. bibliography.
Z5818.E5B37 011.6250543

"The criteria for inclusion [in *Beyond Picture Books*] are books that are well written and contain accurate information, material of interest to primary grade children, and illustrations that complement the text and are appealing to children. . . . The book begins with a list of 200 outstanding first readers, old and new, all currently in print. This list offers a mix of informational and entertaining titles." (*BL,* October 1, 1989, p. 388)

Dictionary of British Children's Fiction: Books of Recognized Merit. Alethea K. Helbig and Agnes Regan Perkins. Greenwood, 1989. hard. 2 vols. 1,632 pp. index. ISBN 0-313-22591-5. $125. dictionary.
PR830.C513H4 823.009

The *Dictionary of Children's Fiction* "contains 1,626 entries based on 387 books published from 1687 to 1985. Books chosen for inclusion were drawn from 21 award and citation lists. . . . A comprehensive index and a system of asterisks that provide cross-referencing between various entries for each book make the *Dictionary* easy to use." (*BL,* November 15, 1989, p. 688)

The Horn Book Guide to Children's and Young Adult Books. Ann A. Flowers. Horn Book, semiannual (1990–). soft. 1 vol. 176 pp. indexes. ISBN 0-87675-036-6. $50. bibliography.
PN1009 028

The Horn Book Guide to Children's and Young Adult Books "reviews nearly 1,600 titles. . . . Each book has been assigned a rating by the reviewers, and within each class, books are arranged by rating with the best books first, then alphabetically by author within each rating. . . . Reviews are brief (usually two or three sentences) but critical." (*BL,* July 1990, p. 2116)

Literature for Young People on War and Peace: An Annotated Bibliography. Harry Eiss, comp. Greenwood, 1989. hard. 1 vol. 131 pp. index. ISBN 0-313-26068-0. $35. bibliography.
Z1037.E38 016.8088′0358

"The preface [of *Literature for Young People on War and Peace*] describes the different types of literature described here—picture books, poetry, Holocaust diaries, pacifist biographies, and materials for adults who work with children. More than 380 books are listed alphabetically by author; an author-title-subject index concludes the work. Each entry notes the appropriate audience, from preschool through young adult." (*BL,* April 1, 1990, p. 1578)

They Wrote for Children Too: An Annotated Bibliography of Children's Literature by Famous Writers for Adults. Marilyn Fain Apseloff. Greenwood, 1989. hard. 1 vol. 202 pp. indexes. ISBN 0-313-25981-X. $37.95. bibliography.
PN1009.A1 011.62

They Wrote for Children Too "is an annotated bibliography of books for children by such well-known writers as William Faulkner, Gertrude Stein, Alice Walker, Gian-Carlo Menotti, Emily Dickinson, Rabelais, Chaucer, Tennyson, Tolstoy, and about 150 others. . . . The book is divided into three chapters covering pre-nineteenth-, nineteenth-, and twentieth-century literature. . . . Titles are arranged by such categories as picture books, poetry and verse, tales and legends, history and culture, biography and informational books, and drama." (*BL,* November 1, 1989, p. 612)

Wendell Cochran

Computers and Artificial Intelligence

See also Science and Technology

Ever since the first microcomputers appeared in 1975, the world of computer science has been evolving rapidly and expanding into new and unexpected areas. The field's most advanced (and controversial) developments are probably in artificial intelligence (AI), which involves manipulation not only of numbers but also of symbols and patterns—the Holy Grail being the creation of a model of the human brain. The technical complexity of computers, the advancing technology, and the growth of applications may overwhelm both librarians and library users.

A core collection in this field should cover the science of computers, the machines themselves, the operating systems that control them, and the application programs that demonstrate the power of what computers can do. In other words, the core collection should cover the underlying science plus hardware and software. Readers' interests can range from how computers work to how to write programs in a variety of languages, and from how to design a computer to how to use a specific application program. (Books in this latter category are more likely to be in circulation than in the reference collection.)

To satisfy readers' interests and concerns, core references should include general as well as specialized dictionaries, such as telecommunications and data-processing dictionaries; encyclopedias, including engineering and electronics encyclopedias; bibliographies; books describing computer functions; books about peripheral equipment, such as mice, printers, and modems; guides to periodical literature; industry directories listing manufacturers, publishers, service companies, consultants, and computer-user groups; computer-language textbooks; and software manuals and guides to the thousands of programs that make computers entertaining, challenging, and useful.

Frequent technical advances force publishers of computer books to make frequent revisions. This often leads to short press runs and high prices. Obsolescence, expense, variety, clarity, and technical accuracy are important factors that must be considered carefully when selecting a small shelf of reference works in computer science and artificial intelligence.

Core Titles

Computer Dictionary, 4th edition. Charles J. Sippl. Sams, 1985. soft. 1 vol. 576 pp. illus. ISBN 0-672-22205-1. $24.95. dictionary.
QA75.133S51 004.0321

The *Computer Dictionary* is an excellent general-purpose reference that has been refined through four

Core Titles

	PUBLIC	ACADEMIC	SCHOOL
Computer Dictionary, 4th edition Sippl, Charles J. Sams, 1985	✦	✦	✦
Dictionary of Computers, Information Processing, and Telecommunications, 2d edition Rosenberg, Jerry M. John Wiley, 1987	✦	✦	✦
Dictionary of Information Technology, 2d edition Longley, Dennis, and Michael Shain. Oxford, 1986		✦	
Encyclopedia of Artificial Intelligence, 2 vols. Shapiro, Stuart C., ed. in chief. John Wiley, 1990	✦	✦	
McGraw-Hill Encyclopedia of Electronics and Computers, 2d edition Parker, Sybil P., ed. in chief. McGraw-Hill, 1988	✦	✦	
The Software Encyclopedia, 1989, 4th edition, 2 vols. McElroy, Brenda A., exec. ed., and Michael Olenik, man. ed. Bowker, 1989	✦	✦	

editions by Charles J. Sippl, author of a dozen other computer dictionaries and many other works on computers and related fields. Sippl is also the author of the article on computers in the *Encyclopaedia Britannica.*

This dictionary contains about 12,000 terms stressing basic knowledge. Most of the 1,000 new terms added in this edition are from the fields of robotics, artificial intelligence, and factory automation.

Coverage is light on hardware and history (there are few biographical details) and very good on other topics, such as applications, computer architecture, communications, and programming and programming languages. According to the author, the range of expected readers is from novice to expert; this expectation accounts for the readability of the definitions. Nonspecialists should appreciate the preface, which contains an overview of computer science and applications.

Terms are alphabetized word by word. Many multiword terms are inverted to be listed under the keyword rather than the modifying term. For example, there are entries for *conversion, binary to decimal* and *conversion, code.* This approach gathers together related topics and makes the main entries more useful. Other helpful features include a how-to-use page, many cross-references, and explanations of the abbreviations and acronyms that characterize virtually all writing about computers and computer uses. Occasional illustrations aid the definitions.

Each page contains two columns of entries. Guide words at the top of the page show the first and last terms on the page. The terms are set in boldface type, and run-on lines of the definitions are indented under the terms. If a term has several definitions, they are numbered and run in as part of the entry. Entries are separated by extra space.

The preface includes predictions concerning the technical developments in microchips, breakthroughs in robotics and artificial intelligence, and future dominance of operating systems by UNIX. This by-product of lexicography provides a context for serious dictionary users.

The *Computer Dictionary* stresses basic terms and concepts and covers a wide spectrum of topics for a large variety of readers. The Board recommends this work for the core collections of public, academic, and school libraries.

Dictionary of Computers, Information Processing, and Telecommunications, 2d edition. Jerry M. Rosenberg. John Wiley, 1987. hard and soft. 1 vol. 734 pp. appendix. ISBN 0-471-85558-8 (hard); 0-471-85559-6 (soft). $49.95 (hard); $19.95 (soft). dictionary.
QA76.15.R67 001.64′03′21

The *Dictionary of Computers, Information Processing, and Telecommunications* focuses on terms related to the major functions of computers, which are storing, manipulating, and transmitting information. In the title of this second edition, "Information" has replaced the "Data" of the first edition, underlining the important point that computers are capable of a great deal more than number crunching. The author, Jerry M. Rosenberg, is chairman of the Department of Business Administration at Rutgers University. He has authored other dictionaries, including one in his own field of artificial intelligence and robotics.

The dictionary contains about 12,000 entries. As the author explains in the preface, definitions are of two kinds: the umbrella kind, covering the general idea, and the specialized kind, dealing with more technical usage. In each case, the umbrella comes first, preparing readers for details and differences. The dictionary contains few historical terms; for example, ENIAC, the first digital computer, is not covered. This work also does not emphasize hardware. Specialists may think that some definitions are insufficiently detailed. However, nonspecialists and general readers will appreciate the work's readability and will welcome concepts cut to bite size.

Each term is set in boldface type. The term is followed immediately by the definition. Run-on lines of the definition are indented under the term. If more than one definition applies to a term, each definition is numbered and begins on a new line. The definitions contain many synonyms, acronyms, abbreviations, and cross-references. Some definitions are followed by a capital letter in parentheses that identifies the source of the definition. All sources are given in a bibliography that follows the collection of entries. All type is sans serif.

An unusual glossary lists about 600 terms in English with their equivalents in Spanish and French.

The *Dictionary of Computers, Information Processing, and Telecommunications,* with its emphasis on information management and its accurate and readable definitions, is a desirable supplement to computer dictionaries of more general scope. The coverage is as up to date as can be expected from the publication date. The Board recommends this work for the core collections of public, academic, and school libraries.

Dictionary of Information Technology, 2d edition. Dennis Longley and Michael Shain. Oxford, 1986. hard. 1 vol. 381 pp. illus. ISBN 0-19-520519-7. $29.95. dictionary.
QA76.15.L63 020.3′21

The *Dictionary of Information Technology* contains entries that stress the roles of computing, communications, and microelectronics in the handling of information. This work is an important resource because, as the authors point out, their special subject of information technology has become a discipline of its own. One author, Dennis Longley, is head of the Department of Computing and Cybernetics at Brighton Polytechnic; the other, Michal Shain, is a consultant who has worked at British Telecom. The two authors have also written three books on microcomputers. In the first edition, this dictionary was commended by the American Library Association as an "Outstanding Reference Source." For this second edition, Terry Curtis of California State University, Chico, has helped adapt the work for the American market.

The technical level of this dictionary is somewhat high for general use, but a how-to page is helpful, as are the word-by-word arrangement of terms and the multitude of cross-references ("compare," "see," and "synonymous with"). Most definitions are brief, but important topics are covered in detail. For example, the entry on *word processing* is four pages long.

Considering the complexity inherent in the subject, readability is very good. Definitions are forthright and clear, and some are accompanied by line drawings. Only the most specialized readers might criticize currency or accuracy.

Reading is made easier by the simple and functional typography and format: a serif typeface, boldface terms, two columns per page, and extra space between entries.

In comparison with the DICTIONARY OF COMPUTERS, INFORMATION PROCESSING, AND TELECOMMUNICATIONS by Jerry M. Rosenberg, which stresses computer architecture, this dictionary deals with computer applications and programming. This work defines 6,000 terms. This is a smaller number of terms than Rosenberg's book defines, but the definitions here are given in greater detail. The DICTIONARY OF COMPUTERS, INFORMATION PROCESSING, AND TELECOMMUNICATIONS may serve somewhat better as a general dictionary of computers and computing; however, the *Dictionary of Information Technology* does include extended discussions of key topics, such as data communications, expert systems, local area networks, programming, and typesetting. The Board recommends this work for the core collection of academic libraries.

Encyclopedia of Artificial Intelligence. Stuart C. Shapiro, ed. in chief. John Wiley, 1990. hard. 2 vols. 1,219 pp. illus. index. ISBN 0-471-52079-9 (set). $195 (set). encyclopedia.
Q335.E53 006.3′03′21

The *Encyclopedia of Artificial Intelligence* attempts to define artificial intelligence (AI) by providing a comprehensive knowledge base of research efforts and achievements in making computers perform tasks that would be called intelligent if they were performed by humans.

The topics and the authors were chosen by an editorial advisory board of distinguished authorities, and each article is written by a recognized research expert on the topic. Articles are signed. Moreover, each article has been reviewed by the author's peers. Therefore, the authority of this encyclopedia and its importance for reference shelves are firmly established.

As stated in the editor's foreword, "The articles are written primarily for the professional from another discipline who is seeking an understanding of AI, and secondarily for the lay reader who wants an overview of the entire field or information on one specific aspect."

Some articles are only a paragraph, but most range from two to ten pages. There are long landmark articles on subjects such as cognitive psychology, computer chess, limits of AI, robotics, social issues of AI, and the LISP programming language. Most articles (except for brief definitions) are followed by a numbered bibliography. The numbers correspond to parenthetical figures embedded in the text and provide leads to much more information elsewhere. (The bibliography for *control structures* runs to 89 citations.) Some entries are also supplemented by an unnumbered list of general references.

There is no contents page to help the nonspecialist, but the index fills 52 three-column pages. In addition, there are seven pages devoted to explaining approximately 500 abbreviations and acronyms. As another aid to accessibility, extensive cross-referencing can lead a reader from almost any article to almost every other article in the encyclopedia.

The nonspecialist should read the guest foreword by Nobel laureate Herbert A. Simon of Carnegie-Mellon University for an authoritative, concise, and readable survey of this almost unmanageable field. The nonspecialist should also read the entry on *artificial intelligence* for history and other background.

In books dealing with difficult subjects, page design is especially important. In this encyclopedia, reading is aided by a large two-column page format, a guide word at the top of each page, and several levels of subheads in the text. More than 450 tables and figures break up the text.

General computer dictionaries discuss AI and define some of its terms, but none can approach the detail given in the *Encyclopedia of Artificial Intelligence* or the recognized expertise of its many authors. The Board recommends this work for the core collections of public and academic libraries.

McGraw-Hill Encyclopedia of Electronics and Computers, 2d edition. Sybil P. Parker, ed. in chief. McGraw-Hill, 1988. hard. 1 vol. 1,047 pp. illus. index. ISBN 0-07-045499-X. $75. encyclopedia.
TK7804.M43 621.381

The *McGraw-Hill Encyclopedia of Electronics and Computers* is an effective resource for information about electronic devices, especially those employing semiconductors. This encyclopedia joins a long line of similar works, including many (like this one) derived from the McGRAW-HILL ENCYCLOPEDIA OF SCIENCE AND TECHNOLOGY (see Science and Technology).

This second edition contains 520 articles; 45 articles are new, and 120 have been completely rewritten. They are arranged alphabetically by subject name and range from a few paragraphs *(open circuits)* to many pages *(integrated circuits).* The articles, which are signed, are written by about 325 specialists in the fields of government, academia, and industry. The selection of articles and authors was aided by Robert D. Briskman of Geostar Corporation, John K. Galt of Aerospace Corporation, and David Turnbull of Harvard University.

The articles stress the science of semiconductors and electronics as well as the design and use of computers. As an example of scope, the article on programming languages describes, in some detail, the general principles of programming and discusses 11 languages. Other entries in the encyclopedia include: *artificial intelligence, computer-aided engineering, computer storage technology, fault-tolerant systems, high-temperature electronics, holes in solids, junction diodes, molecular electronics, negative-resistance circuits,* and *radar.*

Many articles are quite technical and contain mathematical equations and terms from specialized fields. Some are supplemented by illustrations. Most articles end with a bibliography.

The typographic treatment makes it easy for readers to skim articles to find a specific topic or to answer a question. Each article title is set in boldface type and set off by two rules. In longer or more complex articles, important divisions are marked with more than one level of subheads. The entry *operating systems* demonstrates how the articles are structured. The article lists five types of systems (with three cross-references), and then discusses four of their major aspects, which are marked by boldface subheads: control programs (with one cross-reference), processing programs (with two cross-references), time-sharing applications (with ten cross-references), and microcomputer systems (with two cross-references). The bibliography at the end of the article gives one citation.

Accessibility is aided by a liberal use of cross-references (as the *operating systems* example above showed). The cross-references, which appear at the point of relevance, are set in italic type and small capitals, making them stand out readily from the text. The index (14 four-column pages) tags the titles of main articles with asterisks and is so detailed that many readers will benefit from using it first when searching for information.

The *McGraw-Hill Encyclopedia of Electronics and Computers* is as up to date as publishing schedules allow. The Board recommends this work for the core collections of public and academic libraries.

The Software Encyclopedia 1989, 4th edition. Brenda A. McElroy, exec. ed.; Michael Olenik, man. ed. Bowker, 1989. soft. 2 vols. 2,105 pp. ISBN 0-8352-2649-2 (set). $189.95 (set). encyclopedia. revised 1990.
QA76.755.S64 005.36029

The Software Encyclopedia 1989 is to computer programs what *Books in Print* (Bowker, annual) is to books. The encyclopedia contains over 40,000 listings of software programs from nearly 4,000 publishers. The accuracy of the listings and their arrangement in print have been refined in three previous editions.

In this fourth edition, software for schools has been omitted (it appears in a companion volume), and 44,000 new programs have been added. The newest entries are remarkably recent.

The encyclopedia consists of two volumes. In the first volume, programs are listed alphabetically by title. Under each title is a short description that includes version, author, release date, compatible hardware, microprocessor type, operating system, required memory, price, ISBN, and publisher's name. This information is followed by a description of the program, ranging in length from a few words to a long paragraph. After the list of programs the volume contains a list of publishers and their addresses.

In the second volume (called "System Compatibility/Applications"), the programs are grouped under 38 major headings (such as "Accounting," "Library Services," "Music and Sound," and "Spreadsheets") subdivided into hundreds of subsidiary applications (such as "Acquisitions," "Interlibrary Loan," and "Serials"). These headings are grouped under 14 sections for different operating systems such as MS-DOS, UNIX, Apple II series, Macintosh, and Commodore 8-bit micros. For example, under MS-DOS, the user will find the headings "Accounting," "Spreadsheet," "Word Processing," and so on.

The structure of the two volumes allows readers to research software either by program name or operating system. Thus, if you know the name of the program you want, such as *WordPerfect,* you can go on to volume 1 to look up either the entry or the publisher's name and address. However, if you know only what you want the program to do, such as word processing, you would begin with volume 2. Then you would look for the name of your computer's operating system—such as MS-DOS—and under that you would look for "Word Processing" (one of the 38 major headings mentioned earlier). Under that heading you would find *WordPerfect* and the program names of other word-processing programs, each accompanied by a condensed version of the main entry. Then you would go back to the list of titles (volume 1) to compare specifications of the various programs you find interesting.

Both volumes contain a how-to-use section describing the encyclopedia's structure. One page lists the 14 operating systems represented. Another short section lists the 38 major headings and the subsidiary applications under them. This listing contains entries for those applications cross-indexed to their major headings.

Along with commercial programs, *The Software Encyclopedia* lists shareware, programs for which the user is honor-bound to pay a fee (usually much less than $100) only if satisfied after trial use. However, the encyclopedia does not include programs in the public domain.

Legibility is high even though the concentration of information is extreme. An irritant is the excessive use of capital letters in the program descriptions.

The Software Encyclopedia is a one-of-a-kind encyclopedia that provides the most complete list of software programs available. Though the price is high, the book is essential. The Board recommends this work for the core collections of public and academic libraries.

Supplementary Titles

ACM Guide to Computing Literature. Assn. for Computing Machinery, annual (1977–). hard. 1 vol. ISSN 0149-1199. $175. index.
QA75.5 001.64'016

"Although [the *ACM Guide to Computing Literature*] serves as an annual index to the monthly current awareness and review publication *Computer Reviews,* . . . [it] provides full bibliographic citations and thus can also serve as a stand-alone index to the computer science literature. Books, journal articles, conference proceedings, technical reports, and theses are indexed, in all fields of computer science and its applications." (*Guide to Reference Books,* p. 1258)

"[The *Guide* contains] a listing of 14,000 current scientific books, papers, and reports. Approximately 17,000 authors are included. . . . It is composed of six indexes: titles, authors, keywords, topics, sources, and reviewers." (*SL,* 1977, p. 170)

Board's recommendation: Public and academic libraries.

The Computer Dictionary: A User-Friendly Guide to Language Terms and Jargon. John Prenis, ed. Running Pr., 1983. hard and soft. 1 vol. 109 pp. illus. ISBN 0-89471-232-2 (hard); 0-89471-231-4 (soft). $12.90 (hard); $4.95 (soft). dictionary.
QA76.15.C64 001.64′03′21

The Computer Dictionary "defines the terms and jargon associated with computers in language that is clearly understandable to the novice. Within definitions, terms that are defined elsewhere in the book are italicized. The book is attractively laid out and illustrated with excellent line drawings." (*ARBA,* 1985, p. 583)

Also reviewed in: *Emerg Lib,* September 1984, p. 45; *LJ,* February 1, 1985, p. 60.

Board's recommendation: Public, academic, and school libraries.

Computer Industry Almanac. Karen Juliussen and Egil Juliussen, eds. Simon & Schuster/Brady Bks., annual. soft. 1 vol. approx. 750 pp. index. ISBN 0-13-154122-6. $29.95. almanac.
HD9696.C62J85 338.7′61004

In the *Computer Industry Almanac,* "the editors have gathered . . . statistical, financial, directory, and general information from countless industry sources (company reports and newsletters, journals, magazines, and newspapers) reporting on the people, products, and trends in this fascinating industry.

"Sections include rankings of computer companies by size, by growth rate, by type—nationally and internationally, industry forecastings, directories of computer trendsetters, and salaries of professionals in the field. A 'Bits and Mips' (million instructions per second) section contains information on computer chess winners, which computers are fastest, and a tantalizing section on computer industry trivia. Also included are sections on award winners in the field; advertising industry data; educational, organizational, and publisher information and directory listings." (*ARBA,* 1988, p. 674)

Board's recommendation: Public and academic libraries.

Dictionary of Computing and New Information Technology, 3d edition. A. J. Meadows, M. Gordon, and A. Singleton. Nicholas, 1987. hard. 1 vol. illus. ISBN 0-8939-7273-8. $39.50. dictionary.
QA7615.D52636 001.64

The *Dictionary of Computing and New Information Technology* "is oriented toward nonspecialists who, nevertheless, have either interest or expertise in some aspect of information technologies. Entries are arranged letter by letter, and the definitions for the terms are concise, well written, and generally informative. Many entries go beyond providing brief definitions by including relatively extensive information on the topic. Cross-references both explicit and implicit are ample." (*BL,* June 1, 1985, p. 1382)

Also reviewed in: *CBR,* January 1985, p. 13; *Sci-Tech,* September 1987, p. 5.

Board's recommendation: Public, academic, and school libraries.

The Illustrated Dictionary of Microcomputers, 2d edition. Michael F. Hordeski. TAB Bks., 1986. hard and soft. 1 vol. 352 pp. illus. ISBN 0-8306-0488-X (hard); 0-8306-2688-3 (soft). $26.95 (hard); $16.60 (soft). dictionary.
TK7885.A2H67 004.16′03′21

The Illustrated Dictionary of Microcomputers "is an engineer's dictionary of more than 8,000 microcomputer terms, numerous engineering-type illustrations, some cross-references, and two and one-half pages of symbols and programming information. Certain entries of the work have an encyclopedic bent; e.g., the 'Boolean algebra' entry is 21 lines plus 5 illustrations and some equations. Although the preface guarantees acronyms, new words, and old words with new meanings, there is no explanation of how specific entries have been selected. There is a fine sampling of the normal jargon: ROM and RAM, time-sharing, and network; and FORTRAN, BASIC, and PL/1 programming language. The definitions and illustrations seem to have integrity. This is a relatively inexpensive, dependable dictionary." (*Choice,* November 1986, p. 454)

Also reviewed in: *ARBA,* 1987, p. 651; *New Tech Bks,* December 1986, p. 662.

Board's recommendation: Academic libraries.

McGraw-Hill Personal Computer Programming Encyclopedia. William J. Birnes, ed. McGraw-Hill, 1985. hard. 1 vol. 696 pp. illus. index. ISBN 0-07-005389-8. $95. encyclopedia.
QA76.6.M414 001.6412

The *McGraw-Hill Personal Computer Programming Encyclopedia* seeks to "explain the various functions, commands, and course codes for 19 major programming languages, including BASIC, C, COBOL, and

PASCAL. It . . . [also] compares and contrasts the complexities of various software packages and thereby [attempts to help] select a suitable programming language for a personal computer. Explanations are intended for beginning programmers and introductory chapters explain the principles of programming." (*BL,* January 1, 1986, p. 670)

"For libraries seeking to provide a quick technical reference for many of the software aspects of personal computing, this encyclopedia would be a fine choice. . . . Numerous charts and diagrams complement the well-written text. Users will find the extensive bibliography and language keyword index especially helpful. The book is physically attractive and solidly built with a strong binding." (*Choice,* January 1986, p. 728)

Also reviewed in: *ARBA,* 1986, p. 664; *BL,* April 15, 1986, p. 1210; *CBR,* October 1985, p. 56; *LJ,* September 1, 1985, p. 191; *LJ,* March 1, 1986, p. 46.

Board's recommendation: Public and academic libraries.

New and Noteworthy

Facts On File Dictionary of Artificial Intelligence. Raoul Smith. Facts On File, 1989. hard. 1 vol. 211 pp. illus. ISBN 0-8160-1595-3. $24.95. dictionary.
Q334.2.F33 006.303

The *Facts On File Dictionary of Artificial Intelligence* "covers all of the major subfields of artificial intelligence, including search, logic, vision, and natural-language processing. . . . Approximately one-third of the more than 2,000 entries are for specific programs or languages used in artificial intelligence, with the rest covering basic concepts in the field. Most entries contain at least one cross-reference, and a few of the entries are accompanied by drawings or diagrams." (*BL,* September 1, 1989, p. 104)

Microcomputer Software Sources: A Guide for Buyers, Librarians, Programmers, Business People, Educators. Carol Truett. Libraries Unlimited, 1990. hard. 1 vol. approx. 300 pp. ISBN 0-87287-560-1. $23.50. handbook.
QA76.754.T78 016.005302

Microcomputer Software Sources "lists and evaluates guides to software selection—directories, catalogs, review services, bibliographies, and journals with regular software review sections. [This guide] includes sources for 'freeware' or 'shareware.' [The] final chapters cover software marketing guides and online sources of microcomputer software, including electronic bulletin boards and hardware selection tools." (Excerpted from publisher's announcement)

Jill H. Powell

Consumer Health

See also Medicine and Dentistry

Reference works in the field of consumer health contain information on medical topics directed to the general public. These volumes encompass the topics of wellness, nutrition, physical fitness, patient education, management of illnesses, substance abuse, and more. Due to the high costs of medical care and the development of new technologies, consumers are increasingly pressured to make informed choices about their health care. The focus of health care today is on prevention and informed consent rather than seeking the most costly cure or accepting a doctor's advice without question. If they are to assume primary responsibility for their own health, consumers must keep informed of the benefits, risks, and costs of a variety of health care alternatives. Today's health-conscious consumers are concerned with understanding the ingredients listed on food labels, maintaining a healthy diet, exercising more, and preventing serious illnesses. They are demanding more information from a wide variety of sources, and libraries need to meet these demands.

A library serving this clientele should have sources on almost every conceivable illness, drug, medical treatment, and health service. While much of this information is readily available to doctors and other health care professionals, it is written in very technical language that is not understood easily by the layperson. Books such as the PHYSICIANS' DESK REFERENCE (see Medicine and Dentistry) fit this description. On the other side, popular books of questionable value abound on a variety of subjects, such as fad diets and controlling arthritis, cancer, or cholesterol. These publications and the media reporting them provide a constant stream of unscientific information to the public. The key for libraries is to ascertain the availability of authoritative information sources in a readable format. Books published by federal organizations (such as the National Institutes of Health), medical professional societies (such as the American Medical Association), nonprofit associations (such as the American Heart Association), consumer groups, and well-known medical experts with good credentials are excellent sources of authoritative information intended for the consumer. On-line data bases, including *Health Periodicals Database* from Dialog, *Consumer Drug Information* (CDIF) from Dialog and BRS, and *Combined Health Information Database* (CHID from BRS), are valuable sources of journal articles and patient education materials.

The books reviewed in this category will enable librarians to direct their patrons to sources that competently answer many questions in the area of consumer health in lay language. The handbooks, dictionaries, and directories included here define medical terms and diseases, contain information on emergency first aid, analyze symptoms, and list medical organizations. In

Core Titles

	PUBLIC	ACADEMIC	SCHOOL
Advice for the Patient: Drug Information in Lay Language, vol. 2, 9th edition U.S. Pharmacopeial Convention. Bantam, 1989	✦		
AMA Handbook of Poisonous and Injurious Plants Lampe, Kenneth F., and Mary Ann McCann. Chicago Review Pr., 1985; distrib. by American Medical Assn.	✦	✦	
American Cancer Society Book of Cancer: Prevention, Detection, Diagnosis, Treatment, Rehabilitation, Cure Holleb, Arthur I., ed. Doubleday, 1986	✦		
American Medical Association Family Medical Guide, rev. edition Kunz, Jeffrey R. M., and Asher J. Finkel, eds. Random House, 1987	✦	✦	✦
The Essential Guide to Nonprescription Drugs Zimmerman, David R. Harper & Row, 1988	✦	✦	
The Essential Guide to Prescription Drugs Long, James W. Harper & Row, annual	✦	✦	
The Patient's Guide to Medical Tests, 3d edition Pinckney, Cathey, and Edward R. Pinckney. Facts On File, 1986	✦		
The Prentice-Hall Dictionary of Nutrition and Health Anderson, Kenneth, and Lois Harmon. Prentice-Hall, 1985 (See Food and Nutrition)	✦		

addition, librarians should consider purchasing books from the supplementary titles list, especially HEALTH CARE U.S.A., which is a unique directory that describes many diseases, identifies those hospitals and clinics specializing in the disorder, and lists the physicians doing research. The book also provides phone numbers and addresses of support groups across the country, along with a very useful bibliography of books and free materials available on each illness.

The *Consumer Health Information Source Book,* which is an extremely useful out-of-print source, describes principal sources of health information for laypersons. The work was written by Alan M. Rees and Judith Jones, and was published by Bowker in 1984; it consists of bibliographies on special topics such as cancer, children's health, diet, drug abuse, and heart disease. The books listed include those written by patients as well as by doctors. Addresses and phone numbers of health information clearinghouses and hotlines are also listed. Other useful supplementary titles that have recently gone out of print include *The Marshall Cavendish Illustrated Encyclopedia of Family Health* (Edward Horton, ed., Marshall Cavendish, 1986) and *Standard First Aid & Personal* Safety (American National Red Cross, Doubleday, 1987). Librarians may wish to locate these works through out-of-print book dealers.

In a rapidly changing field such as health, currency is an important issue. The books in the core collection are up to date, but advances in medicine occur at all times and, because these advances are widely discussed in the media, consumers must have reliable information in order to sort out the truth. This kind of constant updating goes beyond the capacity of books. To supplement these titles with timely information, the on-line indexes previously mentioned and print indexes are very important for meeting consumers' needs. *Consumers Index to Product Evaluations and Information Sources* includes a section on health, nutrition, and personal care. This index, *Consumer Health & Nutrition Index,* and *The Cumulated Index to Nursing and Allied Health Literature* index health articles in popular journals, such as *Ladies Home Journal, American Health, Consumer Reports,* and *FDA Consumer* as well as more scholarly journals, such as the *New England Journal of Medicine.* These indexes cover the latest medical developments on contact lenses, contraceptives, drugs, and all diseases, including their complications, treatment, and rehabilitation. Directories, such as the *Medical and Health Information Directory,* 3d edition (Anthony T. Kruzas, Kay Gill, and Karen Backus, eds., Gale, 1985–1986) should be made available in most public and academic libraries.

Librarians may wish to purchase additional books (such as those in the field of holistic medicine), depending on their patrons' main interests. However, the core collection listed here will provide an excellent base from which consumers can seek information to make knowledgeable decisions about issues affecting their health.

Core Titles

Advice for the Patient: Drug Information in Lay Language, vol. 2, 9th edition. U.S. Pharmacopeial Convention. Bantam, 1989. soft. 1 vol. 1,503 pp. illus. appendix. index. ISBN 0-913595-35-7. $35. handbook.
RS51.U65 615.1′219

At over 1,500 pages, *Advice for the Patient: Drug Information in Lay Language,* volume 2, is a very thorough guide to the proper use of thousands of drugs. It gives detailed directions on the what, when, where, and how of medications. *Advice for the Patient* also includes bimonthly supplements that update information on new and existing drugs and bibliographies. The other volumes in the series are oriented more toward health professionals and are not reviewed here. These volumes address approved drug products and legal requirements.

The drugs listed in *Advice for the Patient* are arranged alphabetically by generic name. Entries are given for drugs such as minoxidil, used for treating high blood pressure; atropine, used to dilate eye pupils for eye exams and treat eye diseases; and ergotamine, used to treat migraine headaches. Each entry contains common names, steps to take before using the medicine, proper use of the drug, precautions to take while using it, and side effects that might occur. Entries indicate whether these side effects are merely bothersome or require prompt medical attention, a useful addition. Drugs are categorized according to how they should be administered—for example, as systemic (general), topical (skin), or ophthalmic (eyes).

The entries also describe how the drugs work and act in the body and whether alcohol, foods, or smoking might affect their performance. Side effects are given in detail (for example, nausea from the use of ergotamine or sensitivity to light from the use of atropine). Exacting instructions on how to take the drug are also included because the same drug can be administered several ways (for example, by capsule or topically). Because side effects can be different, each form of the drug is presented separately.

The appendix includes a discussion of combination chemotherapy, tips against tampering, pictograms as directions for taking medications, and a listing of drugs to avoid during pregnancy. Drugs are indexed by category of use. Color photographs of the most frequently prescribed medicines in the United States are included.

Under each entry in *Advice for the Patient* there are lengthy warnings to consumers (keep the drug out of children's reach, do not use the drug for any condition other than the condition for which it was prescribed, follow the directions exactly, and so on). These warnings considerably lengthen the book, but such repetition is probably warranted. The Board recommends this work for the core collection of public libraries.

AMA Handbook of Poisonous and Injurious Plants. Kenneth F. Lampe and Mary Ann McCann. Chicago Review Pr., 1985; distrib. by American Medical Assn. soft. 1 vol. 432 pp. illus. index. ISBN 0-89970-183-3. $28. handbook.
RA1250.L27 615.9′52

The *AMA Handbook of Poisonous and Injurious Plants* was originally intended as a guide to the management of plant poisonings for physicians and health care professionals. The format of this book, however, makes it suitable for use by the lay reader as a field guide for the recognition of dangerous and injurious plants, such as poison ivy and chokeberry. The writing style is very readable throughout and is accessible to a nonprofessional audience.

The book begins with an informative introduction on treating plant poisonings, including recommended antidotes and the role of poison centers. Statistics on common plant ingestions are presented.

Section 1, "Systemic Plant Poisoning," lists entries in alphabetical order by botanical name. (There is a common name index in the back of the book.) For example, under the plant *wisteria,* text is included on its family, trivial names, description, geographic location, toxic parts, toxin, symptoms of injection, and treatment. Some three to five references are given for each of the approximately 150 plant entries.

Section 2, "Plant Dermatitis," has a general discussion and brief descriptions of individual plants, which refer to the pictures in the figures section. Section 3,

"Mushroom Poisoning," is very brief, but includes commonly asked questions with answers. Section 3 also discusses symptoms of mushroom poisoning and possible treatments.

The conciseness and size of the *AMA Handbook of Poisonous and Injurious Plants,* and the inclusion of 437 color photographs, make it very easy for the user to locate a particular plant or mushroom. The inclusion of a bibliography for each section adds value to the work. The Board recommends this volume for the core collections of public and academic libraries.

American Cancer Society Book of Cancer: Prevention, Detection, Diagnosis, Treatment, Rehabilitation, Cure. Arthur I. Holleb, ed. Doubleday, 1986. hard. 1 vol. 650 pp. illus. index. ISBN 0-385-17847-6. $24.95. handbook.
RC263.C64 616.99'4

The *American Cancer Society Book of Cancer: Prevention, Detection, Diagnosis, Treatment, Rehabilitation, Cure* is an authoritative handbook, written by over 34 physicians and scientists who specialize in various types of cancer. This book presents reliable and understandable information on cancer and treatment and the various support organizations that can supply information on medical specialists, rehabilitation, transportation services, and home health care.

The first part of the book is devoted to describing useful and practical information on cancer prevention, early detection, and treatment—dealing with pain associated with cancer, rehabilitation, and questionable cancer remedies—genetics and cancer, and many other topics related to all aspects of the disease. Tables are used to facilitate the understanding of risk factors, preventive action, warning signs, and guidelines for checkups by age group for different types of cancer. The second and largest portion of the book contains a separate chapter for each of 20 major types of cancer, including bone, breast, colon, liver, lung, lymphoma, leukemia, skin, and cancer of the male and female reproductive systems. Diagrams of the human anatomy with the relevant parts labeled are provided in every chapter. For example, in the section "Tumors of the Brain," clearly labeled cross-sectional drawings are presented. Each type of cancer is presented with a brief history of research and treatment, current statistics, symptoms, diagnosis, progression of the disease, recommended treatment, odds for recovery, and causes, if known. Cancer patients and their families will benefit from the directory of resources that follows the main text. The directory includes the addresses and phone numbers of American Cancer Society offices throughout the nation as well as those of other organizations providing medical information, and emotional and financial support. There is also a detailed glossary and index.

The one weakness of this book is the lack of a good bibliography. A short bibliography (five books) appears following the first chapter, with a list of suggested reading. This is very useful and should have been expanded because many patrons will want to read further on the subject. Although it is beyond the scope of the book to include patient narratives and detailed medical discussions, these areas could also have been addressed through a longer bibliography.

While cancer affects 30 percent of all Americans, many of this number could be cured. This book can dispel myths and provides the public with authoritative information that could bring about an improvement in the cancer survival rate. The *American Cancer Society Book of Cancer* is an outstanding reference work. The Board recommends this work for the core collection of public libraries.

American Medical Association Family Medical Guide, rev. edition. Jeffrey R. M. Kunz and Asher J. Finkel, eds. Random House, 1987. hard. 1 vol. 832 pp. illus. appendix. index. ISBN 0-394-55582-1. $29.95. handbook.
RC81.A543 616

The *American Medical Association Family Medical Guide* is the single most important book to have in a consumer health collection. Filled with photographs, drawings, diagrams (1,350 in all, 130 of these in full color), and self-diagnostic flowcharts, this handbook enables consumers to determine their medical condition based on particular symptoms and make a decision on whether to seek medical attention or to apply home treatment. This book is indispensable to the public, who can use it to avoid unnecessary doctor visits or seek help earlier for a potentially serious illness.

The *American Medical Association Family Medical Guide* is clear and easy to understand. The text is divided into four parts. Part 1, "The Healthy Body," enables the reader to learn how to maintain the best health; this is done through discussions of fitness, nutrition, environmental health, and cancer facts. The reader is given additional guidance through instructive self-tests and questionnaires. Part 1 concludes with a long section called the "Atlas of the Body," which discusses virtually every organ, nerve, bone, and muscle. Part 2, "Symptoms and Self-Diagnosis," uses 162 pages of excellent self-diagnostic flowcharts with conversational questions about symptoms that direct the reader to possible options for treatment, both self- or professionally administered. The symptoms described are wide ranging—from chest pain, hearing loss, or fever to "feeling under the weather" or difficulty in sleeping. Many children's health problems are described—from common childhood diseases to sleep disorders. Detailed color photographs—called "Visual Aids to Diagnosis"—follow this section for conditions such as skin and eye diseases. Cross-references are made from the flowcharts and visual aids to part 3, "Diseases and Other Disorders and Problems," which includes articles on almost every major and minor disease and special problems of different age groups. Each disorder entry includes descriptions of symptoms, risks, self-treatment, and professional treatment. Part 4, "Caring for the Sick," provides information on choosing a physician, hospital tests, and home care.

There is neither a bibliography nor suggestions for further reading in this volume. Three indexes and a glossary are included at the end of the book. The indexes include a drug index, illustrated first aid index, and general index. The topics discussed throughout the text are fully accessible through this extensive indexing.

Few other books on the market can compete with the *American Medical Association Family Medical Guide* in quality and breadth of coverage. This comprehensive and well-organized reference work stands alone in providing the most information in one volume. The Board recommends this work for the core collections of public, academic, and school libraries.

The Essential Guide to Nonprescription Drugs. David R. Zimmerman. Harper & Row, 1988. hard. 1 vol. 886 pp. index. ISBN 0-06-014915-9. $27.50. handbook.
RM671.A1Z55 615.1

The Essential Guide to Nonprescription Drugs is a unique, well-organized guide that will help the consumer determine which over-the-counter drugs to use based on certain symptoms or problems. By consulting the text, a consumer interested in a particular product can also see how it is rated by medical experts for safety and effectiveness. This book discusses the suitability of nonprescription drugs for a condition or symptom, their effectiveness, and the safe dosage. The text also discusses which symptoms or conditions require medical attention. Evaluations of the drugs listed were performed by a panel of over 200 independent medical and scientific experts who served on 17 advisory review panels convened by the Food and Drug Administration (FDA). As a result of their work, some prescription drugs can now be purchased over the counter (such as weak hydrocortisone anti-itch medications, formerly available only by prescription). Also resulting from the work of these panels, products deemed unsafe when used in self-treatment have been removed from nonprescription status by the FDA. Mercury, used to treat skin conditions, and phenol, a toxic disinfectant, are examples from this latter group.

The main section of the book presents the panel's evaluations of these nonprescription drugs in alphabetical order by category (such as acne medications; antacids; antibiotics for skin infections; anti-inflammatory drugs; antiperspirants; antiseptics; cold, cough, allergy drugs; and many more). Under each entry, a short history and description of the symptom or condition is given, followed by claims of product advertising (and warnings of side effects), how the medical problem originates, how treatment works, and charts that rate safety and effectiveness of active ingredients. Following these sections are valuable drug "product rating" charts that list the products and their active ingredients and enable the consumer to distinguish between false or misleading advertising by grading the products as A, B, or C (best to worst). The panel's comments in these charts provide additional information.

Consumers looking for nonprescription drugs to treat a symptom have access to the text in several ways. They can consult the general index, the table of contents, or the "unit finder" of general problems located in the "How to Use This Book" section. Those already using a product can look up the active ingredients of the drug in the main index. A second index contains brand names and generic products.

For thorough and readable product reviews as well as descriptions of the conditions the products treat, *The Essential Guide to Nonprescription Drugs* is an excellent source. The Board recommends this work for the core collections of public and academic libraries.

The Essential Guide to Prescription Drugs. James W. Long. Harper & Row, annual. hard and soft. 1 vol. 1,094 pp. index. ISBN 0-06-055171-2 (hard); 0-06-096394-8 (soft). $27.50 (hard); $14.95 (soft). handbook.
RM300.L84 615.1

Providing detailed information in an easy-to-read format, *The Essential Guide to Prescription Drugs* describes 220 of the most commonly prescribed drugs in comprehensible terms. There are many more drugs listed if brand names are counted. While far fewer drugs are covered than in ADVICE FOR THE PATIENT, this book presents the information more clearly on the drugs it does cover, and it has added features that are extremely valuable for the consumer. The text includes information on the role of drugs in treating 25 common chronic disorders, tables grouping drugs by the disorders they treat and by side effects, a glossary, and a bibliography.

The book begins with a section on guidelines for safe and effective drug use and the use of drugs in treating chronic diseases. The largest section of the text is devoted to the use of drugs in treating chronic disorders (such as acne, Alzheimer's disease, angina pectoris, and depression). The profiles, arranged alphabetically, include a description of the disorder, statistics on prevalence of the illness, drugs that can cause the disorder, and drugs used to treat the illness. National organizations and support groups are listed following each profile.

The main section of the book (over 800 pages) consists of drug profiles, which range from two to five pages long and have a uniform sequence of 42 or more separate subheadings of information. (These subheadings are thoroughly explained in the introductory chapter.) Some of the subheadings include drug name, class, benefits versus risks, principal uses, the way a drug works, usual dosage range, dosing instructions, precautions to take, counterindications, side effects, and interaction with other drugs. Specific information is very easy to locate because of the appropriate use of boldface type for subheadings, the uniform repetition of these subheadings throughout the book, and the use of boxed tables to highlight important information.

Among the many drugs listed are insulin for diabetes, nitroglycerin for angina, nizatidine for peptic ulcers, prednisolone for inflammatory conditions, and some nonprescription drugs such as aspirin, ibuprofen, and calcium carbonate. The drug profiles will answer the majority of questions a consumer may have about a drug and even recommend certain foods to eat or to avoid during medication. Following the final section, devoted to a glossary, there are tables of drugs according to known side effects (such as excitability, depression, confusion, loss of vision, and so forth).

When selecting a reference book, authorship, currency, quality, scope, and readability are important, and *The Essential Guide to Prescription Drugs* scores high on all five points while maintaining a good balance. The Board recommends this work for the core collections of public and academic libraries.

The Patient's Guide to Medical Tests, 3d edition (formerly *The Encyclopedia of Medical Tests*). Cathey Pinckney and Edward R. Pinckney. Facts On File, 1986. hard and soft. 1 vol. 385 pp. ISBN 0-8160-1292-X (hard); 0-8160-1593-7 (soft). $27.95 (hard); $12.95 (soft). handbook.
RC71.P56 616.07'5

The Patient's Guide to Medical Tests, an expansion and revision of *The Encyclopedia of Medical Tests,* contains descriptions of over 1,000 medical tests. This book outshines most other guides in size, coverage, and readability. The text includes a frank introduction that covers patient rights, interpretation of tests, how patient behavior influences test results, why doctors order so many tests, and the risks versus the benefits of testing. The introduction emphasizes the prevalence of inaccurate test results due to profit-seeking by hospitals (50 percent of their income is produced by testing), the lack of accuracy of most test equipment, and the attempt by doctors to avoid malpractice suits. The text keeps the reader's interest by using relevant examples from studies of patients who have benefited from medical tests as well as patients who have been harmed, as a caution to readers not to rely exclusively on test results for a diagnosis. This handbook also provides a list of outmoded tests, which may not be covered by insurance companies, and answers to ten commonly asked questions about medical testing.

The bulk of the book is devoted to the tests themselves, which are listed alphabetically by the name commonly used by physicians. There are cross-references and "see" references from many diseases to the appropriate tests. Specific tests range from serious to common, such as amniocentesis for birth defects, hematocrit for anemia, computerized tomography for cancer, and blood pressure for hypertension. Each entry includes a complete description of the test and its purpose, what factors (for example, age or symptoms) precipitate its use, specific normal and abnormal levels and results, any health risks, pain or discomfort associated with the test, expense, accuracy, and diagnostic value.

The main drawback to *The Patient's Guide to Medical Tests* is the lack of an index, and it is most unfortunate that this new edition does not include one. Entries for tests to diagnose certain conditions, such as Parkinson's, Hodgkin's, and Lou Gehrig's disease, were not found under the name of the disease. One must know the name of the test in order to locate the information. A section on medical tests patients can do at home would be a useful addition to future revisions.

The Patient's Guide to Medical Tests will help many patrons make an informed decision regarding whether or not to undergo medical tests. This clear and accurate book presents valuable information in an easy-to-understand format. The Board recommends this work for the core collection of public libraries.

The Prentice-Hall Dictionary of Nutrition and Health. Kenneth Anderson and Lois Harmon. Pren-

tice-Hall, 1985. hard and soft. 1 vol. 257 pp. appendix. ISBN 0-13-695610-6 (hard); ISBN 0-13-695602-5 (soft). $21.95. dictionary.
TX349.A54 613.2'03

See Food and Nutrition.

Supplementary Titles

Complete Guide to Prescription & Nonprescription Drugs. H. Winter Griffith. Price/Stern/Sloan, 1989. hard and soft. 1 vol. 1,232 pp. index. ISBN 0-317-66061-6 (hard); 0-89586-860-1 (soft). $25 (hard); $14.95 (soft). encyclopedia.
RM302.5.G75 615.1

"This paperback compendium of information on 400 generic drugs is an ideal ready reference tool. Organized alphabetically, by generic name, with cross-references to brand names, this is one of the most complete and easy-to-use consumer drug books currently on the market. With two pages of detailed information for each generic drug, there is room for information on usage, dosage, overdose, adverse reactions, side effects, precautions, interactions with other drugs, and interactions with substances such as alcohol, tobacco, foods, marijuana, and cocaine. Descriptions of effects on lactating and pregnant women, patients over 60, and children is [*sic*] included for each drug. [It would be useful for public libraries to] consider purchasing additional copies for circulation." (*A Lib,* May 1985, p. 291)

This book contains "information about approximately 400 generic drugs, alphabetically arranged, representing more than 2500 brand names. At two pages per drug, there is room for concise details. . . . The legible tabular format makes the book easy to use for quick reference." (*LJ,* February 1, 1984, p. 173)

This title is revised annually.

Also reviewed in: *ARBA,* 1985, p. 575; *Cha Ti,* November 1986, p. 72; *Kliatt,* Winter 1984, p. 43; *LATBR,* December 18, 1983, p. 7; *SciTech,* March 1985, p. 19.

Board's recommendation: Public libraries.

Drug Information for the Consumer. U.S. Pharmacopeial Convention, 1989. soft. 1 vol. 1,503 pp. illus. appendix. index. ISBN 0-89043-178-7. $25. handbook.
RM300.4557 615.1

Board's recommendation: Public libraries.

Health Care U.S.A. Jean Carper. Prentice-Hall, 1987. hard and soft. 1 vol. 653 pp. ISBN 0-13-609686-7 (hard); 0-13-609694-8 (soft). $19.95. directory.
R118.4U6C37 362.1'02573

Health Care U.S.A. "includes names and telephone numbers of clinics, hospitals, and researchers that specialize in [particular] disorders, as well as publications, associations, and agencies. The book is arranged by health problem [such as] AIDS, burns, drug abuse, . . . or service (genetic counseling, hospices, rehabilitation). Each entry contains a brief description of the disease or service; a roster of experts, including centers, clinics, hospitals, and physicians; a list of books, pamphlets, and audio- and video tapes on the subject; a list of voluntary self-help groups and federal government organizations; and information [about] where experimental therapy is being done.

"This directory of medical information is designed to help consumers find the resources to cope with more than 120 serious medical problems. . . . The primary source for the information in this book was the National Institutes of Health, along with professional medical and health associations and health-related accrediting and government agencies. . . . The listings are not endorsements, but those named have credentials in those areas in which they perform research or provide care." (*BL,* October 15, 1987, p. 379)

Also reviewed in: *ARBA,* 1988, p. 650; *BL,* August 1988, p. 1876; *Choice,* December 1987, p. 648; *LJ,* July 1987, p. 67; *R&R Bk N,* April 1988, p. 24.

Board's recommendation: Public libraries.

New and Noteworthy

Directory of Pain Treatment Centers in the U.S. and Canada. Oryx, 1989. soft. 1 vol. 207 pp. indexes. ISBN 0-89774-529-9. $65. directory.
RB127.D57 362.1'960472

"*Directory of Pain Treatment Centers* [*in the U.S. and Canada*] attempts to aid both 'patients and physicians in their search for treatment of chronic pain' by providing 'enough information so that a physician or chronic pain sufferer can request additional information' from more than 700 centers described here. Treatment centers include general pain-management centers and centers specializing in certain types of pain, such as headache, or specific causes of pain, such as cancer or arthritis." (*BL,* November 1, 1989, p. 604)

Drugs, Vitamins, Minerals in Pregnancy. Ann Karen Henry and Jill Feldhausen. Fisher Bks., 1989. soft. 1 vol. 412 pp. index. ISBN 1-55561-017-X. $14.95. handbook.
RG528.H46 618.2

"The purpose of [*Drugs, Vitamins, Minerals in Pregnancy*] is 'to describe the benefits, risks, and special medical concerns associated with the use of medications, vitamins, minerals, and other substances during pregnancy and lactation.' . . . The book is arranged in three major sections: 'Medications'; 'Vitamins, Minerals, and Supplements'; and 'Other Substances.' Each section is arranged alphabetically, and a chart is used to present information in each entry." (*BL,* September 1, 1989, p. 103)

The Encyclopedia of Alternative Health Care. Kristin Gottschalk Olsen. Pocket Bks., 1990. soft. 1 vol. 325 pp. ISBN 0-671-66256-2. $9.95. encyclopedia.
R733.047 615.8

"Thirty-three healing arts, such as acupuncture, aromatherapy, biofeedback, herbalism, iridology, past life therapy, relaxation techniques, rolfing, and yoga are covered in [*The Encyclopedia of Alternative Health Care*]. The author's purpose is to 'demystify holistic health' and to encourage readers to take 'a participatory role' in their own health care." (*BL,* September 1, 1989, p. 103)

The Family Mental Health Encyclopedia. Frank J. Bruno. John Wiley, 1989. hard. 1 vol. 422 pp. index. ISBN 0-471-63573-1. $24.95. encyclopedia.
RA790.B76 616.8′003

The Family Mental Health Encyclopedia "provides a basic introduction to the language of the mental health field for the layperson. . . . There are approximately 700 subject entries and 130 name entries, arranged alphabetically. . . . Almost every entry ends with several *see also* entries, so the user can see how a term fits into broader concepts." (*BL,* March 15, 1990, p. 1498)

The New A–Z of Women's Health: A Concise Encyclopedia, rev. edition. Christine Ammer. Facts On File, 1989. hard. 1 vol. 544 pp. illus. ISBN 0-8160-2073-6. $29.95. dictionary.
RA778.A494 613.04244

The New A–Z of Women's Health "provides up-to-date information about women's health in clear, simple language but also is careful to encourage users to seek clinical care and to obtain second opinions. . . . The more than 1,000 entries . . . appear in alphabetical order, letter by letter. *See* references direct users from unused terms to those employed in the work." (*BL,* January 15, 1990, p. 1044)

Sickness and Wellness Publications. Janet R. Utts. John Gordon Burke Publisher, biennial (1989–). soft. 1 vol. 288 pp. ISBN 0-934272-21-2. $50. bibliography.
Z6658 016.616′05

Sickness and Wellness Publications "is a directory of publications for laypersons about diseases, chronic conditions, and wellness. It provides access to about 400 newsletters and magazines offering updates on current medical research, support groups, personal narratives, and other information related to a given condition that would be useful to to patients and their families, friends, and caregivers." (*BL,* November 1, 1989, p. 612)

Traveler's Guide to Healing Centers and Retreats in North America. Martine Rudee and Jonathan Blease. John Muir Publications, 1989; distrib. by Norton. soft. 1 vol. 217 pp. illus. ISBN 0-945465-15-7. $11.95. directory.
R733.R83 362.1′78

The *Traveler's Guide to Healing Centers and Retreats in North America* "describes healing centers and retreats in the U.S. and Canada. . . . [These centers] offer New Age programs for relieving the stress associated with modern society. . . . The centers listed are holistic and nondenominational. They were chosen from 750 institutions that received a questionnaire from the compilers." (*BL,* November 15, 1989, p. 700)

The World Book Health and Medical Annual. World Book, annual. hard. 1 vol. approx. 400 pp. illus. index. ISBN 0-7166-1189-9. $22.90. handbook.
RA431.W65 610

"Within the text [of *The World Book Health and Medical Annual*] terms are defined (e.g., 'tendons—thick, strong bands of tissue that attach muscle to bone'). Many articles have short bibliographies citing three or four works, and there are frequent citations to associations. . . . As with other World Book products, [this] annual is designed with a wide-ranging audience in mind." (*BL,* September 15, 1989, p. 200)

Susan C. Awe

Current Events

Current events is a broad category of information, of interest to nearly everyone. Reference sources in this category are generally factual or statistical in nature. Almanacs, yearbooks, and news digests provide indexed records of recent events, current conditions, and up-to-date statistics. Most of these sources are broad enough in scope to cover a wide range of subjects and specialties. Because of the frequency with which these reference sources are referred to, they are usually part of the ready-reference collection; many are needed in both public and academic libraries.

Almanacs and yearbooks are annual retrospective publications using governmental statistical sources, covering broad geographical areas, and emphasizing their country of publication. It is useful to have several different almanacs in a reference core collection. The core list recommended by the Board has seven such titles. News digests are weekly publications that cover world events as they happen by taking their information from large, well-known newspapers. FACTS ON FILE fills this need in the core list. Besides these relatively short information sources, several more detailed references are also needed, such as an encyclopedia containing background articles for various countries of the world. The WORLDMARK ENCYCLOPEDIA OF THE NATIONS provides such a resource, going beyond the information found in more general encyclopedias. The PUBLIC AFFAIRS INFORMATION SERVICE BULLETIN provides access to periodical articles, thereby helping to keep users of this reference collection current.

Current events information is needed by the student, the businessperson, and the traveler. Questions range from what is the address of the Australian embassy in San Francisco to when is Arbor Day to what is the world long-distance water skiing record, and so on. Library patrons will consult the current events section for the answers to both specific and general questions. Depending upon the needs of the patrons, additional sources may be needed. The list of supplementary titles provides some suggestions. The United Kingdom's ANNUAL REGISTER is a useful source, as it provides some insight into the events and developments of another country. Both the pro and con sides of questions are discussed in Wilson's REFERENCE SHELF, and detailed comparative country and city statistics are found in THE NEW BOOK OF AMERICAN RANKINGS and THE NEW BOOK OF WORLD RANKINGS.

Currency is, of course, the preeminent concern for the librarian and user seeking information from books in this category. It is not surprising that of the 19 core and supplementary titles reviewed here, 12 are annuals and 3 are issued even more frequently (weekly, semi-

Core Titles

	PUBLIC	ACADEMIC	SCHOOL
An Almanack J. Whitaker, annual; distrib. by Gale	✦	✦	
Chase's Annual Events Contemporary Bks., annual	✦	✦	✦
Demographic Yearbook United Nations, annual	✦	✦	
The Europa World Year Book, 2 vols. Europa, annual; distrib. by Gale	✦	✦	
Facts On File Hitchings, Thomas E., ed. Facts On File, weekly (1940–)	✦	✦	✦
Guinness Book of World Records McFarlan, Donald, ed. Sterling, annual (1955–)	✦	✦	✦
Information Please Almanac Houghton Mifflin, annual (1947–)	✦	✦	✦
The International Year Book and Statesman's Who's Who Reed Information Svcs., annual (1953–) (See Political Science)		✦	
Political Handbook of the World Banks, Arthur S., ed. CSA Publications, annual (See Political Science)	✦	✦	
Public Affairs Information Service Bulletin Sloan, Gwen, ed. Public Affairs Information Service, annual		✦	
The Statesman's Year-Book: Statistical and Historical Annual of the States of the World Paxton, John, ed. St. Martin's, annual (See Political Science)	✦	✦	✦
The World Almanac and Book of Facts Hoffman, Mark S., ed. Pharos Bks., annual (1868–)	✦	✦	✦
World Facts and Figures, 3d edition Showers, Victor. John Wiley, 1989	✦	✦	
Worldmark Encyclopedia of the Nations, 6th edition, 5 vols. Sachs, Moshe Y., ed. Worldmark, 1984; distrib. by John Wiley	✦	✦	✦

monthly, or bimonthly). Some of these titles are quite inexpensive, making acquisition a feasible proposition. In addition to currency, accuracy is a significant concern—the student or businessperson wants reliable data. Because the sources of information or statistics are often official bodies (for example, the United Nations in the case of the DEMOGRAPHIC YEARBOOK), reliable publishers (Facts On File, Public Affairs Information Service), or books with long pedigrees (THE STATEMAN'S YEAR-BOOK), that need for accuracy is well met by this core collection. —*S. C. A.*
With contributions by Donald E. Collins.

Core Titles

An Almanack. J. Whitaker, annual; distrib. by Gale. hard. 1 vol. 1,241 pp. illus. index. ISBN 0-85021-197-2. $60. almanac.
AY754.A445 031

Usually called *Whitaker's Almanac, An Almanack* has been published annually since 1868 in London, England. This work contains "a vast Amount of Information respecting the Government, Finances, Population, Commerce, and General Statistics of the various

Nations of the World with an Index containing nearly 10,000 References [*sic*]," with an emphasis on statistics of the British Commonwealth.

In comparison to U.S. almanacs, this book has smaller type and is physically smaller, making it a bit more difficult to read. However, the paper quality is superior.

Entries are grouped by topic and vary in length from a few lines to several pages. Sample topics include "Shipping Forecast Areas Map," "Education in the U.K.," "New Towns," and "Patron Saints/Cinque Ports." This edition has been made up to date by including recent events such as the United Kingdom's elections for the European parliament in June 1989, education reforms, and "the structure of the water industry after privitization" (preface).

In addition to the detailed table of contents, an extensive index makes entries very accessible. Information is presented for the general public at a high school reading level. As a bonus that may delight some patrons, *An Almanack* includes a quiz.

An annual publication, *An Almanack* contains current information, generally from the past year, as in "Sport 1988–89," "Literature 1988–89," and "Archaeology 1988–89" in the 1990 edition. Some of the information found in this work will also be found in THE WORLD ALMANAC AND BOOK OF FACTS or INFORMATION PLEASE ALMANAC; however, *An Almanack* contains many more details pertaining to the United Kingdom.

At about $60, *An Almanack* is a bargain source of information about the United Kingdom and the world. The Board recommends this work for the core collections of public and academic libraries. —*S. C. A.*

Chase's Annual Events. Contemporary Bks., annual. hard. 1 vol. 368 pp. illus. index. ISBN 0-8092-4292-3. $27.95. almanac.
D11.5C48 529.3

William and Helen Chase first published this much-used reference source in 1958. The 1990 *Chase's Annual Events* is now in its thirty-second edition and is being published by Contemporary Books, with numerous editors.

Quality paper, the convenient 8½-by-11-inch size, and boldface headings make this book very easy to use. Each entry (organized chronologically by day) gives current happenings, festivals, tournaments, and celebrations of all types, plus historic anniversaries, celebrity birthdays, and foreign holidays and special events. The 1,500 special days, weeks, and events included range from Buzzard's Day (when the buzzards return to Hinckley, Ohio, every March 15) to the Earth Day Anniversary (April 22) and Pearl Harbor Day (December 7).

The reading level is rather basic, and the nearly 40-page detailed index makes the information very accessible. Besides the main entries, lists at the back of the book contain information about astronomical phenomena and national and international calendars, plus a list of recent presidential proclamations. Events are for the current year of the volume. Thus the 1990 edition lists the dates for events such as the Indian Market in Phoenix, Arizona, on December 8–9, 1990, and the Rwanda Feast of Harvest on August 1, 1990. This book is very useful, as many of these foreign special days and festivals are not found in other sources. Accuracy of entries in *Chase's Annual Events* seems impeccable; many anniversaries fall on the same day each year, of course, but many of the entries do change annually.

The Board recommends this work for the core collections of public, academic, and school libraries.

—*S. C. A.*

Demographic Yearbook. United Nations, annual. soft. 1 vol. 1,232 pp. index. ISBN 92-1-051072-0. $85. yearbook.
HA17.D45 312.025

The *Demographic Yearbook* is an annual treatise on international demographic data. Official statistics from competent individuals and organizations in over 250 geographic areas of the world are included. The book is published annually by the United Nations, but there is a time lag between the date of statistics and publication. Thus, the *1986 Demographic Yearbook* was published in 1988. Therefore, other comparable sources, such as THE STATESMAN'S YEAR-BOOK, would have more current worldwide statistics.

The 8½-by-11-inch format of the volume makes it easy to read and use. All of the statistics are presented in tables and grouped under topics. For example, the "World Summary" tables include: population, rate of increase, and birth and death rates; estimates of population and its percentage distribution, by age and sex and sex ratio of total population; population by sex and rate of population increase; and vital statistics rates, natural increase rates, and expectation of life at birth for the latest available year.

Other major subjects covered are "Population," "Infant and Maternal Mortality", "General Mortality," "Nuptiality," and "Divorce." Also included are nine other "Special Topic Tables." Besides the table of contents, there is a 17-page subject-matter index that facilitates access to the information. The information in the tables of the *Demographic Yearbook* is useful and easy to read, although THE STATESMAN'S YEAR-BOOK may contain more detailed, current information and statistics on governments and populations of the world.

The Board recommends this work for the core collections of public and academic libraries. —*S. C. A.*

The Europa World Year Book. Europa, annual; distrib. by Gale. hard. 2 vols. 3,034 pp. indexes. ISBN 0-946653-57-7 (set). $400 (set). yearbook.
JN1.E85 320.9

The Europa World Year Book, formerly titled *The Europa Year Book: A World Survey,* and more popularly referred to simply as *Europa,* is regarded by many as a first stop when ready-reference information is needed on international organizations and countries of the world.

First published in 1926, *Europa* became a two-volume annual in 1959. The contents of the 1990 edition are divided into three sections. The first, "International Comparisons," provides brief comparative statistical data on the area, population (numbers, density, and yearly increase), life expectancy, and gross national product of the world's countries.

The second section, comprising most of volume 1, is devoted to data on international political, economic, and commercial organizations. As in the country section, the amount of information varies according to the importance of the institution. The entry for the Junior Chamber of Commerce (Jaycees) International, for example, consists of a single paragraph containing such standard directory-type data as address, telephone, purpose, top officials, total membership, and publication titles. The United Nations (UN), with its affiliate organizations and agencies, on the other hand, is treated extensively in 86 pages that provide such information as names and addresses of officials, diplomatic representatives, and subagencies; the complete text of the UN Charter; background data; member (and nonmember) nations; publication titles; observer organizations; financial data; and much more. The UN is followed, in alphabetical order, by substantial entries for approximately 55 other major international organizations, including, for example, the North Atlantic Treaty Organization (NATO), the Organization of the Petroleum Exporting Countries (OPEC), the International Olympic Committee, and the World Council of Churches. The international organizations section concludes with brief single-paragraph entries, topically grouped, for over a thousand smaller organizations.

The third section is devoted to surveys of the nations of the world, arranged alphabetically, and takes up the remainder of volume 1 and all of volume 2. Each national entry consists of three main parts. The "Introductory Survey" section is divided into subdivisions that provide data on location, climate, language, religion, flag, and capital city; recent history; government; defense; economic affairs; social welfare; education; public holidays; and weights and measures. This is followed by a "Statistical Survey" that provides tables covering such topics as area, population, vital statistics, immigration, agriculture, industry, currency and other financial data, tourism, education, and more. The final section, the "Directory," begins with information on the national constitution (ranging from a summary of the main provisions to full text) and follows with directory-type data on government officials, political organizations, embassies, the judicial system and judiciary, religious denominations, the press, news agencies, publishers, radio and television, financial and trade institutions, trade unions, transportation information and companies, tourism data and agencies, and atomic energy organizations. While these categories are standard, the content of different country surveys may vary.

Europa is easy to use. Access is reasonably easy through the table of contents, the logical and consistent format of individual entries, and two indexes—one to international organizations and one to countries and territories. Sources of data are provided only in the statistical sections of the book and in a rather general statement in the foreword. Nevertheless, *Europa* is widely regarded for its accuracy and reliability.

For libraries that wish more data provided in a similar format, Europa Publications also publishes six regional books: THE MIDDLE EAST AND NORTH AFRICA (see Middle Eastern History); AFRICA SOUTH OF THE SAHARA (see African History); *The Far East and Australasia;* SOUTH AMERICA, CENTRAL AMERICA, AND THE CARIBBEAN (see Latin American History); *Western Europe;* and *The USA and Canada.*

For those libraries whose budgets preclude the cost of *Europa,* THE STATEMAN'S YEAR-BOOK is an excellent alternative that, while not as detailed, provides good coverage of nations and international organizations at a more modest price. The Board recommends the *Europa World Year Book* for the core collections of public and academic libraries. —*D. E. C.*

Facts On File. Thomas E. Hitchings, ed. Facts On File, weekly (1940–). hard. 1 vol. illus. index. ISSN 0014-6641. $575 (annual subscription). yearbook.
AY40.F119 905.8

Facts On File is an indexed world news digest published by Facts On File, Inc., which puts out mainly reference sources and is a subsidiary of Commerce Clearing House, a very reputable publisher since 1927. Currently, the editor in chief of this work is Thomas E. Hitchings.

The 8½-by-11-inch looseleaf sheet is attractive and easy to read. Good paper and legible print add to the user-friendly format.

Facts On File is a useful, time-saving weekly service that paraphrases the significant news of the day from metropolitan daily newspapers. Some of the headings under which news is classified include: "Soviet Union," "Deaths," "Aviation," "Air Terrorism," "Abortion," and "Savings and Loan Industry." The work can be used to verify miscellaneous data such as key government appointments and resignations, price indexes, and the results of sporting events. A sample entry (a death announcement) reads as follows: "Kelly, Patrick, 40, black American-born fashion designer who won a following in Paris in the 1980s with his snug-fitting jersey dresses covered in brightly-colored buttons; Jan. 1 in Paris of a reported bone marrow disease."

The reading level of this reference tool is comparable to the average newspaper. Indeed, *Facts On File* is sometimes easier to understand than the large newspapers from which the information is derived. The format makes it easy to locate winners of prizes, awards, and so on. Indexing is thorough, detailed, and excellent; it is cumulated continually from the beginning of the year. Access is further enhanced by the detailed instructions on how to use the index and news digest printed on the inside covers of the annual binder.

Information is very current and locating the date of a particular event is relatively easy. No easily discernible errors in information are apparent. A similar publication directed more toward the United Kingdom is THE ANNUAL REGISTER.

Facts On File is an important reference source. The Board recommends this work for the core collections of public, academic, and school libraries. —*S. C. A.*

Guinness Book of World Records. Donald McFarlan, ed. Sterling, annual (1955–). hard. 1 vol. 447 pp. illus. index. ISBN 0-8069-5791-3. $21.95. handbook. 1991 edition to be published by Facts On File.
AG243.G87 032

Since the first edition was published in 1955, the *Guinness Book of World Records* has been a top seller every year that it has been published. In fact, the editors list this book as the top-selling copyright book in publishing history.

The format of the volume is attractive, and information is very easy to read. Records are grouped in related subject areas. Some color and numerous black-and-white pictures are included. Entries include an endless variety of records such as the oldest insect, the smallest bicycle, the push-up champion, the longest fight between a fish and an angler, the largest mosque, the longest wedding dress train, and so on. Entries vary in length from one sentence to several paragraphs. Records set in very hazardous endeavors are no longer published, and categories that have "reached the limits of safety such as sword swallowing and Volkswagen stuffing, have been retired." No new claims will be published in retired categories.

Besides a general table of contents, there is a detailed index at the end of the volume. The records are grouped by topics such as "The World's Structures," "The Sports World," and "The Universe and Space." Records are updated whenever a claimant submits documentation that supports the record and the claim is approved by the editors. Information about documentation and verification is given in the introductory pages. The publication remains the authority in this field. The editors note in the preface that *Guinness* "is not a compendium of every record ever set, but a rather subjective selection of those that the editors *in their sole discretion* find to be the most significant and/or interesting."

All libraries will want to include a copy of the *Guinness Book of World Records* in their collections because this type of information is often requested, and this work is virtually the only source available. Perhaps locating the names of the first test-tube quintuplets (Alan, Brett, Connor, Douglas, and Edward) is not essential to scientific research, but it is an interesting bit of knowledge. The Board recommends this work for the core collections of public, academic, and school libraries. —*S. C. A.*

Information Please Almanac. Houghton Mifflin, annual (1947–). soft. 1 vol. 992 pp. illus. index. ISBN 0-395-55133-1. $12.95. almanac.
AY64.155 317

The *Information Please Almanac* is an accumulation of statistics and facts. Since 1832, Houghton Mifflin has been a renowned publisher of reference books. It has published this volume, now in its 43rd edition, since 1984. Like THE WORLD ALMANAC, this inexpensive volume contains information on current affairs, associations, countries of the world, U.S. federal taxes, and worldwide statistics.

The comprehensive index makes using this source a

pleasure. Lists of "Special Articles," "Special Features," and the table of contents, all in the front of the book, also provide easy access to various types of useful information. Entries vary in length from one line to several pages. Sources are often given for statistical tables and are occasionally provided for articles as well. This almanac can be used by high school students as well as adults. It is suitable for fact-finding as well as pleasure reading. An outstanding feature is the accurate, timely articles on subjects of current interest such as "Eight Forecasts for U.S. Banking," "AIDS Watch," and "1990 Census." Also, the "Year in Pictures" is a popular feature.

The nearly 1,000 pages of the *Information Please Almanac* are packed with sports records; motion picture, theatrical, and literary awards; color maps; useful lists; and important toll-free telephone numbers.

The Board recommends this work for the core collections of public, academic, and school libraries.

—*S. C. A.*

The International Year Book and Statesman's Who's Who. Reed Information Svcs., annual (1953–). hard. 1 vol. 637 pp. appendix. ISBN 0-611-00738-X. $230. yearbook.
JA51.I57 320.05

See Political Science.

Political Handbook of the World. Arthur S. Banks, ed. CSA Publications, annual. hard. 1 vol. 910 pp. illus. appendixes. indexes. ISBN 0-933199-05-8. $89.95. handbook.
JF37.P6XC 320.3

See Political Science.

Public Affairs Information Service Bulletin. Gwen Sloan, ed. Public Affairs Information Service, annual. soft. 1 vol. 1,321 pp. index. ISBN 1-877874-06-X. $495. on-line. CD-ROM. magnetic tape.
AI1.P96 016

The *Public Affairs Information Service Bulletin* is one of the most widely known and used periodical indexes. Usually abbreviated as *PAIS,* it is published by the nonprofit educational corporation, Public Affairs Information Service, Inc., which was chartered in 1954 by the Regents of the University of the State of New York. PAIS is housed in the New York Public Library and "makes extensive use of the Library's collections" (copyright page). In some cases, photocopies of the information are available from the Photographic Services of the New York Public Library. The *Bulletin* has been published since 1915.

The *PAIS Bulletin* is published monthly, cumulated three times per year, and published annually in a permanent volume. This reference tool is a subject index to current periodicals, government documents, reports, pamphlets, books, and other materials relating to economics, politics, social conditions, and international public affairs. The *Bulletin* selectively indexes over 1,000 English-language publications from around the world. The format is easy to use and read, and the book is printed on quality paper.

Entries are organized alphabetically by author under subject headings set in boldface type. Subjects include "Computers and Crime," "Corporations," "Diabetes," "Shoppers and Shopping," and "Stock Brokers." Besides the full bibliographic citation, entries often include notes. Special features including illustrations, bibliographies, tables, diagrams, charts, and maps are noted. Selections are based on the relevance of the material to issues of public policy, with an emphasis on factual and statistical information.

This index is written at a high school level and is easy to use, although the sources themselves vary in difficulty. "See" and "see also" references are used extensively. Currency is excellent, as may be expected from the frequency of publication. Research for the publication is thorough and accurate.

The *Bulletin,* with two sister publications—*PAIS Foreign Language Index* and *PAIS International*—is available electronically as *PAIS on CD-ROM.*

The Public Affairs Information Service Bulletin is an important source for research in the social sciences, including political science, business, international affairs, education, social issues, and law. The Board recommends this work for the core collection of academic libraries. —*S. C. A.*

The Statesman's Year-Book: Statistical and Historical Annual of the States of the World. John Paxton, ed. St. Martin's, annual. hard. 1 vol. 1,691 pp. indexes. ISBN 0-312-03235-8. $65. yearbook.
JA51.S7 310.58

See Political Science.

The World Almanac and Book of Facts. Mark S. Hoffman, ed. Pharos Bks., annual (1868–). hard and soft. 1 vol. 960 pp. illus. index. ISBN 0-88687-580-3 (hard); 0-88687-578-1 (soft). $14.95 (hard); $6.95 (soft). almanac.
AY67.N5W7 317

Since 1868, one of the best-known and bestselling almanacs has been *The World Almanac and Book of Facts,* because of its reliability and excellent reputation with librarians and researchers everywhere. The typeface is small but legible, and the overall organization of entries is logical and consistent. The annual article on "U.S. Changing Population Patterns" is very useful, and a great deal of information relative to relocation can be found in this almanac. There is a detailed general index in the front of the book as well as a quick reference index at the back. As the title implies, statistics from the United Nations and all the countries of the world are included.

The 960 pages contain entries varying in length from one line to several pages. For example, this work includes a 28-page list of "all accredited undergraduate degree-granting institutions in the United States and U.S. territories that have a total enrollment of 600 or more." Additional information about these institutions includes address, year of founding, governing official, control, highest degree offered, enrollment, and faculty. As with this information on colleges, taken from PETERSON'S GUIDE (see Education), many of the articles and tables have clearly identified sources.

Each year's edition includes a useful chronology of the previous year's events (from November of the prior year to October of the year before publication). The 1990 volume adds an interesting article entitled "The Decade in Review." Like the INFORMATION PLEASE ALMANAC, the reading level is about that of the average high school student.

Information is generally current. For example, a graph on "Network TV Program Ratings" is based on the Nielsen Media Research of February 1989, as is the chart on "America's Favorite Television Programs: 1988." Lists of famous people are given, from individuals born in the 1600s to present-day personalities. Another section gives basic information on countries of the world.

The Board recommends this work for the core collections of public, academic, and school libraries.

—*S. C. A.*

World Facts and Figures, 3d edition. Victor Showers. John Wiley, 1989. hard. 1 vol. 665 pp. index. ISBN 0-471-85775-0. $59.95. handbook.
G109.S52 910.212

In 1973, Victor Showers wrote his first book, *The World in Figures.* The third edition of that work, now titled *World Facts and Figures,* is published by the well-known John Wiley & Sons. Showers has proved to be conscientious and accurate in his research in preparing this unique collection of comparative statistics on countries, cities, and geographic features. Data were collected from embassies and many libraries.

The paper quality, size, and typeface of this work combine to produce an attractive format. The "Country Tables," the first major section, are grouped by continent and subject (demography, economy, transportation and communication, and education) and cover 222 countries. The "City Tables," organized by continent and country, cover 2,045 cities. Following these tables are "Country Comparisons" and "City Comparisons." These sections provide lists ranging from largest area and population to largest number of telephones, radios, and televisions. City comparisons focus on size, altitude, and climate.

"Comparisons of Cultural Features," including largest universities, libraries, buildings, bridges, tunnels, and dams, are listed next. The final six sections are "Geographic Tables and Comparisons," which cover the following subdivisions: seas, islands, rivers, mountains, natural lakes, and waterfalls. A bibliography and index complete the volume. The bibliography provides the reader with additional sources, should further research be necessary.

The information in *World Facts and Figures* is arranged logically and consistently, making this an excellent quick-reference tool. The book has no easily detectable inconsistencies. The third edition updates the two previous versions, making this a very current source. Because this collection of information is unparalleled, it is difficult to compare it with a similar reference book.

The Board recommends this work for the core collections of public and academic libraries. —*S. C. A.*

Worldmark Encyclopedia of the Nations, 6th edition. Moshe Y. Sachs, ed. Worldmark, 1984; distrib. by John Wiley. hard. 5 vols. 1,746 pp. ISBN 0-471-88622-X (set). $285 (set). encyclopedia.
G63.W67 910.3'21

The *Worldmark Encyclopedia of the Nations* is "a practical guide to the geographical, historical, political, social, and economic status" of nearly 200 countries of the world (preface). Volume 1 covers the United Nations and its organization, procedures, and subsidiary agencies; volumes 2 through 5 cover the continents of Africa, North and South America, Asia and Australia, and Europe.

John Wiley & Sons, a very reputable name in book publishing, distributes this work internationally. The contributors are listed at the beginning of the work.

The format makes this work easy to read. The 8½-

by-11-inch format packs a great deal of information on every page.

The United Nations volume contains a very thorough description of the UN, with articles such as "Comparison with the League of Nations," "Economic and Social Development," "Narcotic Drugs Control," and "Peaceful Uses of Outer Space." The articles detailing the United Nations' specialized and related agencies cover the following subjects: background, creation, purposes, membership, structure, budget, activities, and bibliography. In volumes 2 through 5, 50 standard subjects are covered for each country. Some of the subjects briefly covered include population, religion, transportation, animal husbandry, political parties, libraries and museums, taxation, press, and organizations. The entries range from 4 pages for Bhutan to over 30 pages for the United States. The alphabetical, consistent entries make access to the information very simple, and the material is written in basic, easy-to-understand language. The subject headings are in boldface type and are numbered to make comparing data even easier.

The material in the *Worldmark Encyclopedia of the Nations* is now somewhat dated. The EUROPA WORLD YEAR BOOK and THE STATESMAN'S YEAR-BOOK may be better ready-reference sources for country information, as both give a larger number of statistics and both are updated annually. However, the *Worldmark Encyclopedia* provides more in-depth data and information and incorporates many more topics about each country. Small maps and flags of the country are also included. For the United States, information for each state includes area, date of admission to the union, capital, population of state at entry, population for two censuses, and rank (in population). The data included are very accurate. The biographical information provided for famous individuals is also very useful, as is the reading list at the end of each entry.

Although somewhat expensive, the *Worldmark Encyclopedia of the Nations* is a worthwhile purchase. The Board recommends this work for the core collections of public, academic, and school libraries. —*S. C. A.*

Supplementary Titles

The Annual Register: A Record of World Events. H. V. Hodson, ed. Longman, annual; distrib. by Gale. hard. 1 vol. illus. index. ISBN 0-8103-5382-2. $123. yearbook.
D2.A7 909.82′8

The Annual Register, now 232 years old, "discusses the important events of the world for the year in essay form. The first and most comprehensive chapter is on Great Britain. Other chapters cover the Americas and the Caribbean; the U.S.S.R. and Eastern Europe; Western, Central, and Southern Europe; the Middle East and North Africa; Equatorial Africa; Central and South Africa; South Asia and the Indian Ocean; Southeast and East Asia; and Australia and the South Pacific. After the regional essays, events are discussed by subject, such as religion, science, law, sports, economics, and social affairs. One chapter is devoted to documents and references which contain diplomatic statements and United Nations resolutions. Also included are an obituary list, a chronology of the year's events, a subject index, maps, and illustrations." (*Ser Lib 2nd,* 1985, p. 1)

"The register is a venerable yearbook; its first editor was Edmund Burke. It is an excellent source for quick background on the most important events of [any given year]. . . . The articles are written by recognized experts. Various subject areas are . . . covered; however, [these areas] focus on British achievements." (*CuH,* November 1985, p. 385)

Also reviewed in: *ARBA,* 1987, p. 271; *ARBA,* 1983, p. 29; *ARBA,* 1980, p. 221; *BL,* May 1, 1986, p. 963; *BL,* May 15, 1975, p. 974; *BL,* May 15, 1981, p. 1267; *CR,* September 1984, p. 168; *CR,* October 1982, p. 224; *Econ,* June 30, 1973, p. 111; *Econ,* September 1, 1979, p. 97; *EHR,* January 1986, p. 316; *ILN,* August 1978, p. 50; *ILN,* September 1979, p. 109; *ILN,* October 1982, p. 93; *MEJ,* Winter 1984, p. 172; *RSR,* October 1974, p. 130; *RSR,* January 1975, p. 18; *TES,* October 14, 1977, p. 18; *TLS,* August 18, 1972, p. 971; *TLS,* September 21, 1973, p. 1091; *WLB,* February 1965, p. 493.

Board's recommendation: Academic libraries.

Editorials On File. Facts On File, semimonthly (1970–). hard. 1 vol. index. ISBN 0-685-54985-2. $345 (annual subscription). handbook.
D839 070.016

"The 'most provocative and articulate editorials' from 125 U.S. and Canadian newspapers are gathered [into *Editorials On File*]. A brief factual summary of background events introduces each of the ten to twelve crucial issues selected for the semimonthly publication. Fifteen to twenty-five editorials probe each issue; the editorials are reprinted in full text as they appeared in the newspaper editions. About 60 prepunched pages make up the semimonthly. Indexes are provided monthly and are cumulated quarterly. The service includes the *Editorial Survey,* which is the twice-monthly publication, the indexes, and the annual buckram-bound post binder. The topics selected are very timely. . . . [T]here is no other source that brings together the commentaries from so many important newspapers." (*Mag YA,* 1984, p. 97)

Board's recommendation: Public and academic libraries.

The New Book of American Rankings. For Your Information Services, Inc. Facts On File, 1984. hard. 1 vol. 312 pp. appendix. index. ISBN 0-87196-254-3. $35. handbook.
HA214.N49 317.3

The New Book of American Rankings "contains 'tables which compare such topics as climate, cost of living, health, crime rate, etc., in the 50 states. There are 33 broad categories with approximately 332 key topic subsections and tables. The broad topics cover geography, population, family unemployment, income, taxes, energy, pollution, sports, and politics. Within each major topic is . . . comparative information on such subjects as divorce/marriage ratio, average farm acreage, pupil/teacher ratio, average residential gas bills, and the number of registered automobiles, etc. . . . Appended to the main body of this volume are short summaries on each state. Profiles are listed alphabetically along with their ranking in several different areas. A Bibliography and an alphabetical Subject Index conclude the work.'

"An introduction to each major topic provides an overview. Then follow specific data presented with an interpretive, well-written narrative. . . . On the whole, [this work] provides an excellent portrait of each state's standing in many various categories." (*BL,* May 15, 1985, p. 1320)

Also reviewed in: *ARBA,* 1986, p. 45; *Ref Bk R,* 1985, p. 2.

Board's recommendation: Public libraries.

The New Book of World Rankings, 3d edition. George Thomas Kurian, comp. Facts On File, 1989. hard. 1 vol. 490 pp. index. ISBN 0-8160-1931-2. $40. handbook.
HA155.K87 310

The New Book of World Rankings contains "chiefly 1980 statistics for more than 190 nations and for 349 discrete subjects [which] were derived for the most part from UN, World Bank, International Monetary Fund, and the U.S. Agency for International Development statistics. These are arranged under 23 [topics] . . . Politics, Military Power, Crime, Education, Economy, Geographical Climate, etc., selected by the same criteria: availability, comparability, usability, reliability, and rankability.

"Kurian has held here to the patterns of his 1979 *Book of World Rankings,* but has added a number of new subjects (liquor consumption, slum population) and dropped 32 old ones. . . . This source on a wide variety of data reflects Kurian's experience as a compiler of reference books, . . . and will be an excellent ready-reference tool in almost any library where a question like 'Who has the most . . . ?' is an everyday occurrence." (*BL,* September 15, 1984, p.118)

Also reviewed in: *ARBA,* 1985, p. 266; *CLW,* September 1985, p. 93; *Econ Bks,* June 1984, p. 80; *LJ,* May 1, 1984, p. 888; *Ref Bk R,* 1984, p. 2; *SLJ,* May 1985, p. 37; *VOYA,* December 1985, p. 342; *WLB,* April 1984, p. 595.

Board's recommendation: Public libraries.

Reference Shelf. Wilson, bimonthly. soft. 1 vol. approx. 200 pp. index. $52 (annual subscription); $13 per single title. bibliography.
PN4181.R332 308

"The *Reference Shelf* consists of six familiar blue and white paperback issues per year. Five cover topics of contemporary interest, and the sixth (not always the same issue number in each volume) comprises the subseries *Representative American Speeches.* Approximately fifteen speeches selected to give representative coverage of events of the year are included in each issue. . . . There is a cumulative speaker index at the end of each current issue, as well as at the end of each decade. Biographical information on each speaker is included, and there is a two- or three-page introduction discussing the selection of the speeches.

"The subject issues of the *Reference Shelf* follow a standard format. A two-page general introduction defines the scope of the subject. The approximately twenty articles reprinted from easily accessible periodicals and books are arranged in three or four sections, and each section has a brief introduction. The articles selected cover a range of viewpoints and provide a balanced approach to the timely topic. The unannotated bibliographies at the end of each issue are in two parts: books and periodical articles. Each bibliography includes at least one hundred recent citations; the mix of books and periodicals vary according to the subject.

". . . The primary audience for the *Reference Shelf* is likely to be college undergraduates rather than high school students. . . . [In addition, *Reference Shelf* could be useful in many specialized libraries.]" (*RSR,* 1988, p. 106)

Board's recommendation: Public and academic libraries.

New and Noteworthy

Atlas of World Issues. Nick Middleton. Facts On File, 1989. hard. 1 vol. 63 pp. illus. index. ISBN 0-8160-2022-1. $16.95. atlas.
G1046.E1M57 912.1304

The *Atlas of World Issues* "includes such themes as pollution, population, energy, education, and government. [This work also] treat[s] the topics of desertification, transportation, and war. . . . A typical article . . . consists of a world map showing a global aspect of the subject with smaller maps and charts showing specific examples of the phenomenon. A few paragraphs discuss the problem in general and explain each map or chart." (*BL,* November 1, 1989, p. 599)

Facts On File News Digest CD-ROM. Facts On File, annual. ISBN 0-8160-2019-1 (IBM/MS-DOS); 0-8160-2020-5 (Macintosh). $695 (FOF print subscribers); $795 (nonsubscribers). handbook. CD-ROM.
909.82

"*Facts On File News Digest CD-ROM* uses CD-ROM technology to search and retrieve the full extent of all Facts On File articles published from 1980 through 1988 using keywords, Boolean logic, or controlled index terms. Users can limit searches by date and examine and print maps. They can also create their own article titles lists and store them on disk for future retrieval." (*BL,* December 15, 1989, p. 849)

Human Rights. Lucille Whalen. ABC-Clio, 1990. hard. 1 vol. 218 pp. index. ISBN 0-87436-093-5. $39. handbook.
K3240.4.W46 016.342′085

Human Rights "offers a concise overview of the topic plus detailed descriptions of the resources listed. . . . A chronology shows the dates of major human rights documents and events. There are biographical sketches of leaders in the human rights arena and a listing of international, national and regional organizations committed to human rights advocacy. Each citation gives the address and phone number of the organization, name of the director, purpose and scope of the organization, and a list of its publications." (*SLJ,* May 1990, p. 29)

NBC News Rand McNally World News Atlas. Rand McNally, 1990. soft. 1 vol. 96 pp. illus. index. ISBN 0-528-83371-5. $7.95. atlas.
909.82

The *NBC News Rand McNally World News Atlas* "provides the user with basic pertinent information on selected global topics and key geographic areas. The *Atlas* consists of five sections: world themes, world hot spots, world maps, world information table, and the map index. . . . The *Atlas* concludes with a map index of approximately 11,000 place names." (*BL,* April 1, 1990, p. 1578)

The Nuclear Weapons World: Who, How and Where. Patrick Burke, ed. Greenwood, 1989. hard. 1 vol. 383 pp. illus. indexes. ISBN 0-313-26590-9. $95. handbook.
U264.B87 355.0217

The Nuclear Weapons World "treats five countries (U.S., U.S.S.R., U.K., France, People's Republic of China) and two organizations (North Atlantic Treaty Organization and Warsaw Treaty Organization). The chapters . . . begin with essays that provide background information, along with organization charts that illustrate complex intergovernmental agencies and help explain the decision-making process. . . . The seven chapters also provide biographical information for 750 people concerned with weapons development, including scientists." (*BL,* September 15, 1989, pp. 207–209)

Donna L. Singer

Dance

Dance is an eclectic field, encompassing not only classical ballet and modern dance but also such categories as jazz, tap, ballroom, folk, ethnic, and disco. All of the reference works reviewed here focus primarily on classical ballet and modern dance, although some of the dictionaries do include other dance categories.

A core reference collection in dance should contain works that present the history, personalities, cultural influences, and technical aspects of dance as well as synopses of major dance pieces. The library patron looking for information on classical ballet dancer Vaslav Nijinsky should be served as well as the patron seeking to learn about popular dancer Fred Astaire. In addition, the serious researcher's quest to understand the technique of the *pas de deux* or to find a concise definition of *rond de jambe* should be accommodated along with the ballet enthusiast's desire to find a concise synopsis and data on the first performance of *The Nutcracker.*

A dictionary of ballet terms is essential in order to access French, the international language of ballet. THE CONCISE OXFORD DICTIONARY OF THE BALLET and THE LANGUAGE OF BALLET are two core works that fulfill this need. The Oxford title also provides brief biographical information on important dancers and dance figures, as well as articles on broader aspects of

Core Titles

	PUBLIC	ACADEMIC	SCHOOL
The Concise Oxford Dictionary of Ballet, 2d edition Koegler, Horst. Oxford, 1982 (updated 1987)	✦	✦	✦
The Language of Ballet: A Dictionary Mara, Thalia. Princeton Bks., 1987		✦	
101 Stories of the Great Ballets Balanchine, George, and Francis Mason. Anchor, 1975	✦		✦

the dance, such as historical movements that influenced dance. Some patrons will want even more biographical information on the personal and professional lives of composers, choreographers, and dancers. Barbara Naomi Cohen-Stratyner's *Biographical Dictionary of the Dance* (Schirmer Bks., 1982), now out of print, provides those patrons with the information they will want. This title had initially been selected by the Board for the core list.

An important directory would be a useful addition to the core collection. Margaret T. DeVaney and Phyllis A. Penney have edited *The Dance Directory: Programs of Professional Preparation in American Colleges and Universities* (American Alliance for Health, Physical Education, Recreation, and Dance, 1986), providing a guide to institutions that teach dance. Public and school libraries in particular may wish to consider acquiring this title.

Another type of book popular in the category of dance is the collection of stories of ballets. Balanchine and Mason's 101 STORIES OF THE GREAT BALLETS, on the core list, is one such title. Another work, with somewhat different coverage, had been selected for the core list but is now out of print: George Balanchine and Francis Mason's *Balanchine's Festival of Ballet,* a two-volume work originally published by Doubleday in 1977 and reissued in 1989 by Princeton Books.

Librarians may wish to supplement the core collection with the supplementary titles that are briefly discussed in the following pages. As the needs and the interests of their patrons warrant, librarians may also wish to include reference works that are specifically concerned with ballroom dancing or folk and ethnic dancing.

In addition to the reference works discussed, *The Dance Encyclopedia* by Anatol Chujoy and P. W. Manchester (1967) was considered by the Board to be a valuable reference work on dance. Although the work is currently out of print, librarians may wish to obtain a copy through an out-of-print book source. The *Encyclopedia of Dance and Ballet* (Mary Clarke and David Vaughn, Putnam, 1977) is also now out of print. The Board had recommended this title as a valuable supplementary work.

Core Titles

The Concise Oxford Dictionary of Ballet, 2d edition. Horst Koegler. Oxford, 1982 (updated 1987). soft. 1 vol. 458 pp. illus. ISBN 0-19-311330-9. $17.95. dictionary.
GV1787 792.8'03'21

This update of the second edition of *The Concise Oxford Dictionary of Ballet* contains more than 5,000 entries that span all aspects of ballet from personalities, companies, and specific works to places of performance and technical terms for nearly 400 years of ballet history. Also included are special entries for cities that played a role in ballet history *(Paris* and *Leningrad),* literary subjects set to dance movement (for example, *The Odyssey*), and dramatists and composers whose works have been adapted for ballets *(Pushkin, Shakespeare,* and *Beethoven).* A number of dancers not involved directly in the ballet are included: *Gwen Verdon, Merce Cunningham, Gene Kelly,* and *Antonio Gades* are accorded entries. Nonballet dance forms, such as *jig, flamenco, jota,* and *squaredancing,* are also described.

The author, a well-known German ballet critic, has drawn his information directly from dance experts, such as Marilyn Hunt (United States) and Nöel Goodwin (Britain), and from such standard reference works as *The Dance Encyclopedia* by Anatol Chujoy and P. W. Manchester (1967) as well as from other books and periodicals, which are listed in a select bibliography at the beginning of the dictionary.

The main word of each entry is printed in boldface type. Entries are arranged in alphabetical order. The length of entries varies from two lines to one and one-half pages. Although essential information on a ballet is given only under the title accepted in Anglo-American usage, all titles by which a ballet is known are cross-referenced as "see" entries. Special notes on alphabetization and spelling are given in a reprint of the foreword of the first edition. A list of bibliographical references is given at the end of some entries. It should be pointed out, however, that these references are by no means exhaustive. Many could be supplemented with more recent material.

The only selection criterion given is the author's acknowledgment that many entries which appeared in the first edition have been deleted in the second edition and its 1987 update (for example, Maurice Béjart's 1968 ballet *Neither Flowers nor Wreaths*) and replaced by "topical new subjects" because "some names, titles, and events need to be registered only once, and not perpetuated from one edition to another" (foreword to second edition). Koegler also states that he has not included an entry on postmodern dance because of a lack of a "workable definition" (foreword to second edition).

However, questions arise about the selection process. For example, dancer/choreographer *Choo San Goh* has been added but dancer/choreographer Karole Armitage has not, although both have international reputations as avant-garde artists. Also, there is a brief entry for French dancer *Jean-Charles Gil,* who has become prominent recently, but no entries for American dancers Susan Jaffe or Robert LaFosse, who have assumed major roles since the second edition was published in 1982. Again one wonders at the inclusion of choreographer *Peter Gennaro* and the exclusion of Hermes Pan, who created many famous dance sequences for Astaire and Rogers. Most of the entries, however, have been made current in this update of the second edition (for example, entries for *Edward Villella* and *Helgi Tomasson* include their current positions as ballet directors).

Despite some inconsistencies in updating and some puzzling exclusions, *The Concise Oxford Dictionary of Ballet* is an excellent, concise repository of pertinent information, with an especially strong representation of the European ballet scene. However, due to the deletions in this updated second edition, librarians may want to keep a copy of the first edition. The work remains a convenient, quite comprehensive, modestly priced reference source on ballet that is easily accessible to the generalist and the specialist alike. The judicious use of cross-references and illustrations of leading dance companies in well-known productions adds to the dictionary's usefulness. The Board recommends this work for the core collections of public, academic, and school libraries.

The Language of Ballet: A Dictionary. Thalia Mara. Princeton Bks., 1987. hard and soft. 1 vol. 120 pp. illus. ISBN 0-87127-144-3 (hard); 0-87127-037-4 (soft). $18.95 (hard); $9.95 (soft). dictionary.
GV1585.M37 792.8203

The Language of Ballet: A Dictionary is a practical guide for dance students, teachers, and interested laypersons who need to find clear and accurate identification and description of the basic steps and exercises in ballet. Written by Thalia Mara, author, teacher, and former ballerina, this reference book is based on a dictionary developed for use in the Graded Syllabus of the National Academy of Ballet. As stated in the foreword, the aim of this reference work is to standardize ballet terminology so that "teaching ideas may be more easily transmitted from teacher to student" and so that these ideas can "flow more freely between teachers of differing schools and countries." Therefore, the terms included are those that are most commonly and widely used. In addition, many variations of names by which a step or exercise may be known, such as *battement dégagé,* which is also called *battement tendu jété* (Russian school) and *battement glissé* (French school), are indicated through cross-references.

The dictionary also contains a few brief descriptions of famous dancers/teachers (such as *Agrippina Vaganova* and *Enrico Cecchetti*) and schools of dance (such as *French school* and *Italian school*) that have figured prominently in the development of techniques and methods of teaching. Over 100 line drawings provide clear illustrations of the way to perform various dance movements.

All entries are arranged in alphabetical order, with main entries in boldface capitals. Any terms that are subsidiary to the main entry are indented in boldface type in upper- and lowercase letters. For example, the main entry *Chassé, pas* is followed by the related terms *Chassé, Chassé en tournant,* and *Chassé passé en avant,* which are indented. A phonetic pronunciation is given in parentheses for almost every entry—English or foreign language—as well as for personal names. A literal translation of foreign-language terms is provided. This is followed by a basic description of how the movement is performed. There are more than 600 entries, which vary in length from one line to a full page.

The Language of Ballet is a concise, clearly written, easy-to-use dictionary that contains such familiar terms as *leotard* and *virtuoso* as well as more technical terms, such as *saut de Basque* and *piqué detourné.* Since the basic terms for ballet movement, its techniques, and rules were codified in French over 300 years ago, the language of ballet has remained fairly constant; thus this reference work should remain current. *The Language of Ballet* is easily accessed by the interested layperson as well as by the more serious student or teacher of ballet. The Board recommends this work for the collection of academic libraries.

---

101 Stories of the Great Ballets. George Balanchine and Francis Mason. Anchor, 1975. soft. 1 vol. 541 pp. index. ISBN 0-385-03398-2. $9.95. handbook.
MT95.B3 792.8′4

George Balanchine, an acknowledged master of dance, and Francis Mason, a well-known dance writer and critic, have compiled a paperback reference, *101 Stories of the Great Ballets,* that presents synopses of and commentaries on 101 classical and contemporary ballets that are performed by the world's leading ballet companies. According to the preface, 50 of the ballets are standard classical works that form the core of dance companies' repertoires *(Giselle* and *The Sleeping Beauty)* or are of "major historical importance" *(Les Noces* and *The Three-Cornered Hat).* The remaining 51 ballets are among the new works (such as *Eugene Onegin* and *Goldberg Variations*) that have appeared since the 1968 publication of the now out-of-print *Balan-*

chine's Complete Stories of the Great Ballets.*

The entries are arranged alphabetically by ballet title, which appears at the top of each entry in capital letters. An italicized block of information detailing the choreographer, composer, set and costume designers, and data on first performance begins each entry. The main section of the entry is a vivid description of the ballet, often supplemented with comments by a well-known dance critic (such as Edwin Denby or Patricia Barnes) or a discussion by someone identified with a particular role in that ballet (such as Erik Bruhn's impressions of the role of Albrecht in *Giselle*).

Entries vary in length from a half a page for *After Eden* to several pages for the many different ballet versions of *Romeo and Juliet.* An alphabetical index, which includes dancers, choreographers, companies, ballet titles, and composers, adds to the usefulness and accessibility of this reference work.

The publication date does affect the scope of the book, for much has happened in the dance world since 1975. (For example, Balanchine himself choreographed such major ballets as *Vienna Waltzes* [1977] and *Davidsbündler tänze* [1980] before his death in 1983.) Also, the limits imposed by the book's paperback format dictate that many standard classical ballets, which can be found in the more comprehensive two-volume paperback edition, *Balanchine's Festival of Ballet*, now out-of-print, be excluded (for example, *The Afternoon of a Faun*). However, the material that is presented provides excellent background on several standard ballets and accurate information on selected ballets composed between 1968 and 1975.

101 Stories of the Great Ballets is a convenient, inexpensive, ready reference on specific ballets for the general reader and the balletomane alike. However, librarians who purchase the two-volume *Balanchine's Festival of the Ballet* may not need to acquire this more selective reference, as the two-volume set contains entries on all the ballets in *101 Stories.* On the other hand, smaller libraries, or those that may not need the more comprehensive set, will find *101 Stories* an excellent reference of its kind. The Board recommends this work for the core collections of public and school libraries.

Supplementary Titles

Ballet Goer's Guide. Mary Clarke and Clement Crisp. Knopf, 1981. hard. 1 vol. 352 pp. illus. index. ISBN 0-394-51307-X. $22.50. handbook.
GV1787.C563 792.8′4

The *Ballet Goer's Guide* "provides authoritative information on the choreography, plot, and historical background of today's 143 most performed ballets. One of the most interesting features in [the main] section is the discussion of the various stagings of the same ballet by different companies, such as *Swan Lake* by Stuttgart Ballet and the National Ballet of Canada. The descriptions of the ballets are greatly enhanced by numerous color and black and white photographs.

"The introductory essay on the history of ballet is a model of precision and comprehensiveness. The brief biographical sketches of leading choreographers and dancers and the photographic essay on ballet steps and positions are also very useful." (*ARBA,* 1983, p. 455–456)

Board's recommendation: Public libraries.

Bibliographic Guide to Dance. G. K. Hall, annual (1975–). hard. 2 vols. ISBN 0-816-17071-1. $345. bibliography.
Z7514.D2 792.016

The *Bibliographic Guide to Dance* is "a comprehensive annual subject bibliography which also serves as a yearly supplement to the *Dictionary Catalog of the Dance Collection* of the New York Public Library. It provides complete bibliographical information on all dance materials collected, including films, photographs, music, scores, videotapes, books, etc. Access is provided through main entries, added entries, titles, series, and subject headings." (*Ser Lib 2nd,* 1985, p. 92)

Also reviewed in: *ARBA,* 1982, p. 535.

Board's recommendation: Academic libraries.

Black Dance: An Annotated Bibliography. Alice J. Adamczyk. Garland, 1989. hard. 1 vol. 213 pp. illus. index. ISBN 0-8240-8808-5. $31. bibliography.
GV1595.H33 016.7932

Black Dance is a bibliography that "is composed of nearly 1,400 citations to books, articles, reviews, and dissertations. Journals indexed range from the *Village Voice* and *Ebony* to the *University of Pennsylvania Museum Journal* and *Journal of American Folklore.* Entries are listed in alphabetical order by author or main entry, and most have brief annotations. There is a subject index that includes names of individuals . . . , dance groups . . . , types of dance . . . , and other topics. . . . The index is generally well done. . . . Nine illustrations of historical interest enliven the text." (*Ref Bks Bul,* June 15, 1989, p. 1794)

"In the index the user will find some 81 references under 'Africa,' . . . 'Jamaica,' . . . 'Big Apple,' . . . and . . . 'Break Dancing.' A large portion of the references deal with black dance as seen in the U.S. over the past

50 years on stage, television, and in the movies. . . . The compiler states her aim as wishing to 'assist researchers in their quest for more information on black dance.' With its large number of entries, the book accomplishes this purpose, and will be useful to upper-division undergraduates." (*Choice,* September 1989, p. 75)

Also reviewed in: *Ref Resources,* September 1989.

Board's recommendation: Academic libraries.

A Dictionary of Ballet Terms. Leo Kersley and Janet Sinclair. Da Capo, 1979. soft. 1 vol. ISBN 0-306-80094-2. $8.95. dictionary.
GV1585.K45 792.8′2′03

Board's recommendation: Public and academic libraries.

New and Noteworthy

The Dance Handbook. Allen Robertson and Donald Hutrea. G. K. Hall, 1990. hard. 1 vol. 278 pp. ISBN 0-8161-9095-X. $25. handbook.
GV160.R63

The Dance Handbook is "organized in rough chronological order by dance tradition, to cover romantic, classical and modern ballet, the Ballets Russes, modern dance, the ballet boom, the dance explosion and alternative dance. [This work] includes a brief introduction to each tradition. [It also covers] 200 dancers, dance companies, and choreographers in alphabetical order by name." (Excerpted from publisher's announcement)

Donna L. Singer

Decorative and Applied Arts

The decorative and applied arts are regarded as those that have a practical purpose yet exhibit fine craftsmanship. These arts encompass a wide area of endeavor from glassmaking and woodworking to jewelry and fashion design. Actually, the distinction between the fine arts and the decorative arts is a product of Western culture, a division that did not become established until the emergence of public museums in the nineteenth century. To some extent, the classifications are arbitrary. For example, ceramics and architecture are areas that might fall into either fine or decorative arts. In general reference works on the decorative arts as a whole, the authors and editors clearly define the parameters of what constitutes decorative or applied art. However, most of the core reference works reviewed deal with a specific decorative or applied art, such as ceramics, fashion, or jewelry; taken together, these books effectively represent this diversified field.

Ideally, the reference collection in the decorative and applied arts should serve the needs of the antique collector who wants to know the value of an eighteenth-century Delftware vase as well as the curiosity of the patron seeking to identify the work of Renaissance miniaturist Nicholas Hilliard. It should accommodate the researcher who wants to find out the distinguishing characteristics of Ming dynasty pottery or the

Core Titles

	PUBLIC	ACADEMIC	SCHOOL
The Encyclopedia of Fashion O'Hara, Georgina. Abrams, 1986	✦		
Fairchild's Dictionary of Fashion, 2d edition Calasibetta, Charlotte Mankey. Fairchild, 1988		✦	
An Illustrated Dictionary of Jewelry Newman, Harold. Thames & Hudson, 1987	✦		
Kovels' Antiques and Collectibles Price List Kovel, Ralph, and Terry Kovel. Crown, annual	✦		
The Oxford Companion to the Decorative Arts Osborne, Harold, ed. Oxford, 1985	✦	✦	

tools needed for woodcarving, or provide the theatrical costumer with details on the Watteau coat.

The dictionaries, encyclopedias, companions, and price guides reviewed here should provide the breadth of information and specifics necessary to answer patron queries on the decorative and applied arts. In addition, most of these references have copious illustrations that enhance their usefulness to patrons. Many librarians will want to supplement these core works with additional titles in certain areas. Especially recommended are AN ILLUSTRATED DICTIONARY OF GLASS, THE ENCYCLOPEDIA OF FURNITURE, and THE DICTIONARY OF INTERIOR DESIGN. Because FAIRCHILD'S DICTIONARY OF FASHION is part of the recommended core collection, librarians may also wish to acquire FAIRCHILD'S DICTIONARY OF TEXTILES as a supplementary volume. In addition, librarians who have many patrons with an interest in the performing arts may wish to add the COSTUME DESIGNER'S HANDBOOK as a supplement to their reference shelf. School librarians will also find that this work is a useful guide for students and teachers who are involved in the study and production of plays.

Several valuable titles selected by the Board for this category are no longer in print. Three of those titles were voted to the core collection: Louise Ade Boger's *Dictionary of World Porcelain and Pottery* (Scribner, 1971); Doreen Yarwood's *Encyclopedia of World Costume* (Scribner, 1978); and Harold Newman and George Savage's *Illustrated Dictionary of Ceramics* (Thames & Hudson, 1985). Among the titles selected as supplementary works but now out of print, we find Simon J. Bronner's *American Folk Art: A Guide to the Sources* (Garland, 1984); John Fleming and Hugh Honour's *Dictionary of Decorative Arts* (Harper & Row, 1977); Laura Torbet's *Encyclopedia of Crafts* (Scribner, 1980); Martin Grayson's *Encyclopedia of Textiles, Fibers, and Non-Woven Fabrics* (John Wiley, 1984); and Dora Ware and Maureen Stafford's *Illustrated Dictionary of Ornament* (St. Martin's, 1985). The librarian who wishes to build an extensive collection in this field may wish to obtain some of these titles from out-of-print book sources.

Core Titles

The Encyclopedia of Fashion. Georgina O'Hara. Abrams, 1986. hard. 1 vol. 272 pp. illus. ISBN 0-8109-0882-4. $27.50. encyclopedia.
GT507.053 391.003'21

More than 1,000 entries are included in *The Encyclopedia of Fashion,* which covers the world of fashion from the 1840s to the mid-1980s. During this time the sewing machine transformed the making of clothing from a small business or home enterprise that produced custom-made clothes into a major industry that manufactured ready-to-wear clothes through mechanized operations. The author, a writer and editor for women's magazines in London and Paris, approaches fashion as "a history lesson, a geography lesson, an economics lesson, and a mathematics lesson" (introduction). She concentrates on the world's five major fashion capitals during the nineteenth and twentieth centuries: Paris, London, New York, Rome, and more recently, Milan.

The entries, arranged alphabetically in a single-column dictionary format, with the main entry word in boldface type, are short in length; very few entries are more than one page long. Each entry contains a brief definition or a biography that highlights the subject's significant contributions to the fashion world. One shortcoming of these entries is the lack of any key to pronunciation, which would be especially helpful because so many proper names are foreign. Small capital letters are used to indicate cross-references. Over 350 illustrations and photographs are cross-referenced in text by use of an asterisk. The 27 color plates are identified in text by the abbreviation "col. pl."

Entries span a wide variety of material. Included are biographies of designers, clothing manufacturers, art directors, hairdressers, illustrators, fashion photographers, couturiers, and costume designers. Art movements, such as *art nouveau* and *cubism,* are defined. Store owners such as *Thomas Burberry* and *Arthur Lazenby Liberty* also receive entries. Various types of clothing are described (such as *leotard, jodphurs, car coat*). Fashion terms (such as *decolleté* and *kick pleat*), kinds of fabric and trims (for example, *crepe* and *lamé*), and famous stores *(Marks and Spencer, Tiffany and Co.)* receive entries. Magazines (from the *La Gazette du Bon Ton* to *Vogue*) are covered, and styles of dress (such as *Edwardian, Ivy League,* and *hippy*) are described. Celebrities who had an impact on fashion also appear, such as *Brigitte Bardot* and the *bikini.*

The variety and quality of the illustrations are excellent, which is important in a work of this nature. "Sources of Illustration" are provided throughout the text. Illustrations are captioned and are usually dated. Many designers and companies have granted permission to reproduce original sketches and photographs from their archives. Photographs include designer gowns, such as designer Emanuel's sketch for the wedding gown of Diana, Princess of Wales; advertisements from Liberty's and Sears Roebuck's catalogs; magazine front covers and posters; jewelry, hairstyles, and accessories; swatches of fabrics and laces. Reproductions of paintings from the 1800s detail the styles of an earlier time. The illustrations for the limited number of entries on children's clothing are often taken from children's books, such as those of Kate Greenaway.

A four-page bibliography is included, arranged by topic, and a fine preface gives a brief overview of the changing fashion world.

The Encyclopedia of Fashion is comprehensive, concise, easy to read, and well illustrated. The Board recommends this work for the core collection of public libraries.

Fairchild's Dictionary of Fashion, 2d edition. Charlotte Mankey Calasibetta. Fairchild, 1988. hard. 1 vol. 749 pp. illus. appendix. index. ISBN 0-87005-635-2. $50. dictionary.
TT503.C34 391.003'21

The second edition of *Fairchild's Dictionary of Fashion* is a complete revision of the 1975 edition and contains over 15,000 entries, 1,700 of which are new. Most of the 1,000 pen-and-ink drawings (400 more than in the 1975 edition) were done by the author and appear near the relevant entries. In addition, there are 16 pages of full-color illustrations cross-referenced to the text; their sources are acknowledged at the beginning of the volume. Drawings depicting the historical development of costume appear on the endpapers. A special feature of this dictionary is an appendix containing biographical entries for famous fashion designers, including photographic portraits and examples of each designer's work. Entries for outstanding contemporary designers such as *Herbert de Givenchy, Donna Karan,* and *Christian Lacroix* are included here. The designers' names are listed alphabetically in the dictionary proper and are cross-referenced to the appendix.

The author, a professor of fashion, has utilized the publisher's connection with fashion trade magazines such as *Women's Wear Daily,* as well as Fairchild's Costume Library, as sources of material for the dictionary. Judith Straeten, former assistant curator of the Costume Institute at the New York Metropolitan Museum of Art, was a consultant.

The broad scope of this dictionary includes clothing terminology from classical to contemporary times—from the Greek mantle, the *limation,* to the *flashdance top,* inspired by the 1983 movie. Also included as entries are fashion trademark names such as *Burberry,* fashion magazines such as *Vogue,* fashion authorities such as *Diana Vreeland,* technical terms such as *cross-dyed,* and ethnic or nationalistic terms such as *yashmak* (a Turkish veil).

Individual entries are arranged alphabetically in a two-column format with the main entry word in boldface type, followed by a succinct definition or identification. Cross-referencing, shown by small capital letters, is used for related terms; a pronunciation guide and foreign word derivations are provided where applicable. The individual entries are interrupted throughout by 98 broad categories that contain groups of related terms representing different styles of a particular article of clothing. For example, after the individual entry for *button,* there is a black bar, and the category main entry word *buttons* is centered and set in boldface capital letters. Under this heading the various types of buttons are arranged alphabetically (for example, *blazer, brass, covered,* and so forth). These terms also appear in the individual alphabetical listing in the main text but are not defined; rather the reader is referred to the category for explanation. An index for the categories appears at the beginning of the volume.

Fairchild's Dictionary of Fashion is comprehensive and visually attractive, with an easy-to-use format. However, a bibliography for further reading would have added to the reference's usefulness, especially because many entries are so brief (about one line). The dictionary is extremely current, with such entries as *Boy George* (as a representative of the *androgynous* look). This volume will aid students; designers; people involved in theater, film, or opera; and those just interested in fashion. The Board recommends this work for the core collection of academic libraries.

An Illustrated Dictionary of Jewelry. Harold Newman. Thames & Hudson, 1987. soft. 1 vol. 334 pp. illus. ISBN 0-500-23309-8. $18.95. dictionary.
NK7304.N43 739.27'03'21

Jewelry has been used for adornment for millennia, and its appeal reaches into all cultures. *An Illustrated Dictionary of Jewelry,* which has 2,530 entries, is a fine one-volume guide that provides an overview of the variety of styles, gemstones, materials, processes, designers, and jewelry makers from antiquity to the present. In the preface, jewelry is defined as "any decorative article that is made of metal, gemstones and/or hard organic material of high quality, contrived with artistry or superior craftsmanship, and intended to be worn on a person." More than 50 important gemstones that are usually set in jewelry are included, but technical terms relating to their chemical composition are omitted. Also included are entries on decorative buttons, hat ornaments, jeweled dress ornaments, and examples of "royal regalia" (such as crowns and scepters). Excluded are objects with a utilitarian purpose, such as eyeglasses, lighters, and decorative accessories such as hand mirrors. The author has been selective in including entries for contemporary designers (there are no entries for persons born after 1950) and jewelry firms due to the large number of each and the lack of consensus among experts in evaluating their influence or contributions. However, such highly regarded designers as *René Lalique* and jewelry firms such as *Garrard & Co.* are represented.

Harold Newman, the author of this accurate and authoritative reference volume, has written on many aspects of the decorative arts, including two companion volumes to this one, *An Illustrated Dictionary of Ceramics* and AN ILLUSTRATED DICTIONARY OF GLASS. Newman acknowledges the contributions of other authorities, such as Dr. Reynold Higgins on pre-Christian jewelry.

Entries are in word-by-word alphabetical order with the main entry word in boldface type. In biographical entries, this is followed by birth and death dates or dates of reigns (where applicable) in parentheses. A definition, a description, or brief biographical data, often including some historical background or references to related topics, forms the heart of each entry. Selected bibliographical references often conclude the entry. Extensive cross-references within the entries—indicated by small capital letters—add to the accessibility of this dictionary. Appropriate black-and-white illustrations (a total of 669) show significant types or examples of jewelry in various museums and collections. These are placed adjacent to the relevant entry. In addition, 16 pages of color photographs are interspersed throughout the dictionary. All black-and-white illustrations have captions containing the name of the object, the date (or approximate date) of the object, and the source of the picture. The captions for the color illustrations also describe the objects in basic terms.

This dictionary serves the needs of the curious reader who wants to know the distinction between *smoky quartz* and *smoky topaz* or the historical significance of the *Phoenix Jewel,* as well as the needs of the collector or more serious student who wants basic information on the decorative art of *dot-repoussé,* the characteristics of *Mycenaean jewelry,* or the jewelry-making process of *colloid hard-soldering.*

The readable typeface and visual effectiveness of the illustrations that enhance the written material add to the attractive format of this dictionary. *An Illustrated Dictionary of Jewelry* is a useful reference for collectors of jewelry and those patrons interested in the wonderful variety of jewelry produced throughout history. The Board recommends this work for the core collection of public libraries.

Kovels' Antiques and Collectibles Price List. Ralph Kovel and Terry Kovel. Crown, annual. soft. 1 vol. approx. 804 pp. illus. index. ISBN 0-517-58095-0. approx. $11.95. guide.
NK1125.A39 708.05

Kovels' Antiques and Collectibles Price List is rewritten annually. It has been published previously under several titles, such as *Kovels' Antiques Price List* and *Kovels' Complete Antiques Price List.* Categories are added and omitted with each new edition. The goal is to keep the book at about 800 pages and up to date with the most current prices. Over 50,000 appraiser-approved prices were included in the 1989 edition. The items included were selected at random from pieces offered for sale during the preceding 12 months. The last entries are dated in June, and the book is available in October of the same year. Each edition has a short introduction to some trends of that particular year. (Older editions of the work should be saved for reference and appraisal information.)

The guide reflects purchases made in U.S. or Canadian markets. Most prices are transactions from a shop or show; very few are from an auction. Not too many items have sold for over $5,000. No price is based on an estimate. This is one of the reasons why the Kovel guide has become a staple in the antiques and collectibles field. It should be noted that this guide does not include price listings for paintings, books, comic books, stamps, coins, and several other categories.

Each antique or collectible is listed alphabetically by category or object (such as *Abingdon pottery, animal trophy,* or *art deco*). The main entry word appears in boldface type followed by a one-line description, which includes material composition of the object, color, date, size, and significant markings. The price quotes are listed in a column on the right of the page. Bold rectangular boxes interspersed throughout the guide provide additional information on preservation of antiques and collectibles ("Don't put crazed pottery or porcelain in the dishwasher. It will often break even more") or sometimes dispel a rumor ("Billy Beer cans are not worth hundreds of dollars even though this myth appears in newspapers every six months").

Cross-references, which appear in boldface type, are found in the index and in the introductory notes to each category. The index includes references to proper names, categories, and individual items. References to *trap* are found under *fishing-trap, minnow,* and under the main entry *trap,* which lists various kinds of animal traps. Using the index, information about a Lalique perfume bottle is found under *Lalique,* not *art deco* or *perfume bottle.* A reference note is provided in the category description for *perfume bottles:* "Glass or porcelain examples will be found under the appropriate name such as Lalique, Czechoslovakia, etc."

It should be noted that all items listed were presumed to be in good condition when sold. Regional differences account for the fact that some prices may seem high and others low.

Each edition of the guide is fully illustrated. Over 500 photographs in color and black and white are updated as necessary in each new edition. The only exceptions are pictures representing patterns for Depression glass and pressed glass. In addition, small line drawings have been inserted between many of the categories. Many of these represent pottery marks, silver marks, and so forth. They are part of the introductory descriptions to each category.

The *Kovels' Antiques and Collectibles Price List* is a necessity for the professional, the dealer, the collector, and the general interested reader. The Board recommends this work for the core collection of public libraries.

The Oxford Companion to the Decorative Arts. Harold Osborne, ed. Oxford, 1985. soft. 1 vol. 865 pp. illus. ISBN 0-19-281863-5. $18.95. dictionary.
NK30.093 745.03

The paperback edition of *The Oxford Companion to the Decorative Arts* is a reprint of the 1975 hardcover edition. The more than 3,000 entries and many illustrations contained in that earlier edition remain unchanged in the current reprint. The only addition is a corrigenda at the end, which is a bibliography for the lengthy article entitled "Decorative Papers." This broad-based reference work is meant to serve as an introduction to those arts made for utilitarian purposes that "are nevertheless prized for the quality of their workmanship and the beauty of their appearance" (preface). Included are time-honored crafts such as woodworking and papermaking; specialized crafts such as enameling; and practical arts such as landscape gardening and costuming. Also selected for coverage are certain "borderline" areas between the fine arts and the decorative arts: ceramics, bookbinding, typography. Excluded are items related to the art of architecture and crafts such as shipbuilding. Ultimately, the basic selection criterion was the "idea of fine craftsmanship" that forms the "unifying concept" of this reference work (preface). Although *The Companion* purports to have international coverage, the emphasis is on the decorative arts of Great Britain, the United States, and Western Europe.

Harold Osborne, the editor of this volume, has edited several arts journals as well as THE OXFORD COMPANION TO ART (see Art). He provides an acknowledgments page and includes a list of the 75 contributors, but no credentials are presented for these experts. Furthermore, the longer entries are not signed. Individual articles in *The Companion,* however, are generally authoritative, strong in content, and accurate.

The Companion has general entries on particular crafts (such as *glass-making*), groups of entries on specific historical periods or cultures (such as, *ancient Egypt* and *pre-Columbian*), and entries on techniques and materials (for example *weaving* and *pewter*). Readers can also find short biographical entries on outstanding craftsmen (such as *Ikkan,* a nineteenth-century Japanese netsuke carver), as well as brief entries on aspects of design such as styles in furniture. The entries are arranged alphabetically in a two-column format with the main entry word in boldface capital letters, followed by the definition, a description of the item, an explanation of use, and the method of production (or by biographical data where appropriate). The decorative arts of European countries and the United States are not given separate entries; rather they are included within the entries on particular arts. For example, the entry on *furniture* is subdivided into sections on "European," "English," "American," and "Modern." Countries and cultures outside the Western world have their own entries, which are subdivided into sections on specific arts and crafts (for example, *China* is subdivided into sections for bronzes, jade, mirrors, and so forth). All subdivisions within an entry are numbered consecutively, Cross-references—which appear in small capital letters—abound, and secondary sources are often cited within the text of an article. Most entries end with numerical references that refer to books listed in a general bibliography at the end of the volume. This bibliography is alphabetized by author.

The Oxford Companion to the Decorative Arts is an excellent reference source for the general reader and the specialist. Its value is enhanced when used in conjunction with THE OXFORD COMPANION TO ART (see Art). The Board recommends this work for the core collections of public and academic libraries.

Supplementary Titles

Color Encyclopedia of Gemstones, 2d edition. Joel E. Arem. Van Nostrand Reinhold, 1987. hard. 1 vol. 288 pp. illus. index. ISBN 0-442-20833-2. $53.95. encyclopedia.
QE392.A69 553.8032

"Approximately 250 gems are described [in the *Color Encyclopedia of Gemstones*] according to the basic properties necessary to identification: chemical formula, crystallography, color, luster, hardness, density, cleavage, spectra, luminescence, where it occurs, and size. Additional comments are added where appropriate. Photographs of gems are in a separate section, printed on glossy paper. They are in alphabetical order and one can turn quickly from description to appropriate illustration. The illustrations are excellent and it is obvious that care has been taken in their presentation. Information describing the gems has been derived from standard reference works and periodicals in mineralogy and gemology and is presented in a highly condensed form. Brief discussions of color measurement, thermal properties, and growing of synthetic gems provide additional information. . . . [This] is a guide for the knowledgeable individual who desires specific descriptive information and color photographs that are an accurate representation of the gem in question.

"A brief bibliography and lists of gemstone species and mineral groups, plus an index, complete this well-conceived and well-presented basic reference tool." (*ARBA,* 1988, p. 697)

Also reviewed in: *R&R Bk N,* February 1988, p. 18.

Board's recommendation: Public and academic libraries.

The Complete Guide to Furniture Styles, enl. edition. Louise Ade Boger. Scribner, 1982. soft. 1 vol. 688 pp. illus. indexes. ISBN 0-684-17641-6. $29.95. handbook.
NK2270.B63 749.2

"Each chapter [of *The Complete Guide to Furniture Styles*] is in two sections, the first providing a short but good general account of the history of the period or style, while the details of various pieces of furniture are dealt with in the second part, headed 'Articles of Furniture.' Subheadings (beds, settees, etc.) set out in the margin make them easy to locate. This plus a fine index (general, and of artists and craftsmen) make this both a readable and 'referable' book. The plates depicting 637 pieces of furniture, each with a short annotation, are of excellent quality.

"For those that own the 1959 edition, the present edition has four new chapters (23–26), English Victorian, American Victorian, Art Nouveau, and Twentieth Century. The other chapters (1–22 and 27) are exactly the same as those in the 1959 edition, except that there is a slight change in the numbering of the chapters." (*RQ,* Summer 1970, p. 368)

"The bib[liography] includes many museum catalogs of special exhibitions and is quite comprehensive. The text is clean double-column, well-written and presented in attractive format." (*AB,* November 10, 1969, p. 1555)

Also reviewed in: *A Art,* November 1970, p. 73; *SR,* December 6, 1969, p. 50.

Board's recommendation: Public libraries.

The Costume Designer's Handbook: A Complete Guide for Amateur and Professional Costume Designers. Rosemary Ingham and Liz Covey. Prentice-Hall, 1983. hard and soft. 1 vol. 264 pp. illus. index. ISBN 0-13-181289-0 (hard); 0-13-181271-8 (soft). $24.95 (hard); $15.95 (soft). handbook.
TT507.I46 792.026

"Not only do the authors [of *The Costume Designer's Handbook*] proceed thoughtfully and clearly through the stages of actual design for a theatrical performance, but they also offer advice for a potential designer including discussions of necessary training, business acumen, equipment, and work space. Advice is given on how to read and effectively analyze a script; on working with the director, cast, and other production staff; on performing theatrical research; and on cumulating the creative effort. These practicalities are supplemented by suggested reference works and other sources, including an extensive list of painters whose work is helpful for costume design and a national shopping list arranged by key cities (New York, Chicago, San Francisco, Boston, and Los Angeles). [This is] a thorough guide, helpful for current designers and neophytes involved in theater at any level—professional, amateur, or school." (*LJ,* September 1, 1983, p. 17)

Also reviewed in: *BL,* September 1, 1983, p. 17; *VOYA,* December 1983, p. 287.

Board's recommendation: Public and school libraries.

The Dictionary of Costume. Ruth Turner Wilcox. Scribner, 1969. hard. 1 vol. 406 pp. illus. ISBN 0-684-15150-2. $50. dictionary.
GT507.W5 391.003

"*The Dictionary of Costume* . . . describes briefly more than 3,000 articles of clothing, many of them with black-and-white drawings by the author. [The dictionary] includes brief biographies of top couturiers of the twentieth century—Chanel, Dior, Cassini. Perhaps illustrations were included for less familiar clothing, for

American-Indian costume is illustrated only with the head of an Indian in war paint, while Eighteenth Century costume is represented by dozens of corsets, chemises, and bustles. Adequate cross-references and convenient alphabetical arrangements of entries recommend it for quick identification of the 'New Look' or an angel sleeve." (*WLB,* April 1970, p. 876)

"Incorporating foreign words recently added to the language of fashion, biographies of leaders in costume design, and many drawings to illustrate the text, Wilcox includes descriptions of wearing apparel, jewelry, cosmetics, hair and beard styles, tailoring and dressmaking tools and terms, and clothing materials such as leather, furs, and both natural and synthetic textiles. An attractive reference volume of interest to general readers and to students of costume history. A bibliography is appended." (*BL,* March 15, 1970, p. 869)

Also reviewed in: *A Art,* February 1970, p. 8; *Choice,* July 1971, p. 662; *Dr,* Winter 1971, p. 76; *KR,* November 15, 1969, p. 1248; *LJ,* April 15, 1971, p. 1326.

Board's recommendation: Public and academic libraries.

The Dictionary of Interior Design. Martin M. Pegler. Fairchild, 1983. hard. 1 vol. 217 pp. illus. ISBN 0-87005-447-3. $25. dictionary.
NK1165 747.03

The Dictionary of Interior Design "is an illustrated glossary of approximately 4,300 terms and names from the field of interior design. Intended for beginning students or laypersons, the alphabetically arranged entries provide concise definitions and, if appropriate, historical origins of the terms.

"The entries treat furniture, design motifs, fabrics, porcelain, architects, and designers. French, German, Italian, Spanish, and Indian terms are interfiled, and many entries are followed by *see* references. The difference between the 1966 and the 1983 versions is the omission of almost all entries dealing with architecture.

"The entries are arranged in the outer columns of each three-column page of this straightforward work; the center column contains small but clear black-and-white line illustrations to support the adjacent definitions. . . . *The Dictionary of Interior Design* presents information efficiently and will have reference value in libraries which do not own the 1966 edition." (*BL,* March 1, 1984, p. 953)

Also reviewed in: *BL,* July 1, 1967, p. 1125; *Choice,* December 1983, p. 557; *Conn,* May 1969, p. 42; *LJ,* November 1, 1966, p. 5379; *SR,* May 20, 1967, p. 50; *TLS,* June 22, 1967, p. 564.

Board's recommendation: Public libraries.

Dictionary of Ornament. Philippa Lewis and Gillian Darley. Pantheon, 1986. hard. 1 vol. 319 pp. illus. ISBN 0-394-50931-5. $29.95. dictionary.
NK1165.L48 745.4

The *Dictionary of Ornament* is a "survey of motifs in the applied arts and architecture [which] cover[s] European and North American buildings and objects from the Renaissance to the present. The more than 1,000 alphabetically arranged entries cover specific styles, patterns and motifs, themes of decoration (e.g., mourning), origins of motifs (e.g., the eagle in America), techniques of ornamentation (e.g., ormolu), publications, and designers and architects. [There are] more than 1,000 black-and-white illustrations (photographs, engravings, and line drawings), . . . cross-references and a two-page bibliography. An 11-page visual key . . . groups together and labels with the entry term motifs from antiquity; plant, animal, human, and part-human forms; linear and surface decoration; and architectural and decorative features.

"This encyclopedia provides commendable coverage of pattern books (collections of ornamental designs by artists and architects) that influenced decoration and fashion from the fifteenth to the nineteenth centuries. The entry 'pattern books' refers the reader/researcher to numerous other entries for decorative elements and specific designers of the patterns. . . . It is a reasonably priced, handy guide that should be useful to art students, collectors, and reference librarians in public and academic libraries. But it also can serve the browser or any reader interested in this aspect of the arts." (*BL,* April 1, 1987, p. 1191)

Also reviewed in: *Apo,* February 1987, p. 148; *BM,* January 1987, p. 42; *Choice,* February 1987, p. 864; *Obs,* December 7, 1986, p. 29.

Board's recommendation: Public and academic libraries.

The Encyclopedia of Furniture, 3d rev. edition. Joseph Aronson. Crown, 1986. soft. 1 vol. 202 pp. illus. ISBN 0-517-03735-1. $19.95. encyclopedia.
NK2205.47 749

The Encyclopedia of Furniture "cover[s] all phases of furniture design from early times to the present. The major part of this book consists of monographs of the important items of furniture knowledge, supplemented by some 2500 separate definitions and descriptions. The larger subjects or classifications—America, Chairs, Construction, France, Gothic, Modern, Woods, etc. are treated at some length and are related to the arrangements of pictures. More than half of the book is devoted to photographs" (foreword).

An "excellent bibliography [is] included. [This is] a delightful volume." (*SL,* January 1939, p. 26)

Also reviewed in: *AB,* December 20, 1965, p. 2493; *BL,* January 1, 1939, p. 154; *LJ,* February 1, 1966, p. 681; *SR,* March 19, 1966, p. 38.

Board's recommendation: Public and academic libraries.

The Facts On File Dictionary of Design and Designers. Simon Jervis. Facts On File, 1984. hard. 1 vol. 533 pp. ISBN 0-87196-891-6. $35. dictionary.
NK1165.J47 745.1075

The Facts On File Dictionary of Design and Designers contains "biographical entries, 50 to 1,000 words in length [that] emphasize the biographee's work in design, e.g., as in Aalto's contribution as a designer rather than as an architect or urban planner. Entries for design journals are evaluated as to their usefulness as sources. Movements (Art Nouveau) and societies (Art-Workers' Guild) include many cross-references in their texts. . . . In a field 'where modern literature is both sketchy and patchy,' [this] is a convenient source of identification of major and minor figures, as well as organizations and journals." (*BL,* February 1, 1985, p. 772)

Also reviewed in: *Choice,* December 1984, p. 538; *LJ,* August 1984, p. 1438; *Ref Bk R,* 1984, p. 8.

Board's recommendation: Public and academic libraries.

Fairchild's Dictionary of Textiles, 6th edition. Isabel B. Wingate. Fairchild, 1979. hard. 1 vol. 691 pp. illus. appendix. ISBN 0-87005-198-9. $40. dictionary.
TS1309.F34 677.003'21

The sixth edition of *Fairchild's Dictionary of Textiles* "adds about 1,000 definitions to the 13,000 included in its predecessor (1967), reflecting developments in synthetic fiber technology, advances in mechanical and electronic equipment, and new methods of dyeing, printing, and finishing fabrics. Many terms brought forward from the previous edition have been revised and expanded. Trademarks are updated, with their owners identified. An appendix annotating trade associations and institutes has been added." (*LJ,* May 15, 1979, p. 1131)

The Dictionary of Textiles is "an indispensable source of reference to people in all branches of that industry and related ones (clothing, designers, retailers, advertising personnel, etc.). Libraries serving teachers and students of textile courses will also find this volume essential. . . . [This is] a most complete and up-to-the-minute guide for serious students and professionals, covering the total range of the subject, from fibers and yarns, through construction and finishing, to inventors and government regulations." (*Choice,* July 1979, p. 646)

Also reviewed in: *ARBA,* 1980, p. 421; *BL,* May 15, 1980, p. 1382; *WLB,* November 1979, p. 196.

Board's recommendation: Public and academic libraries.

An Illustrated Dictionary of Glass. Harold Newman. Thames & Hudson, 1987. soft. 1 vol. 315 pp. illus. ISBN 0-500-27451-7. $18.95. dictionary.
TP788.N48 748.2

An Illustrated Dictionary of Glass is a 1987 paperback revision of the hardcover edition published in 1977 by the same publisher. A reviewer of the first edition found that the work was "a comprehensive and highly organized text. . . . The text coupled with the informative and wide-ranging selections of photographs helps bring clear understanding of the subject to the reader. The illustrations cover over a quarter of the entries and include fine examples of vessels, styles, and details. The scope of the contents is primarily European and English with an emphasis on historical rather than contemporary information. This volume is a necessary reference for all libraries servicing art history or studio art departments. In addition, it may be included in most general libraries because of its fascinating material and straightforward presentation." (*Choice,* September 1978, p. 843)

Also reviewed in: *ARBA,* 1979, p. 451; *Apo,* December 1979, p. 532; *Arch,* November 1978, p. 64; *BL,* April 1, 1979, p. 1240; *BM,* August 1978, p. 562; *CSM,* March 9, 1978, p. 24; *Conn,* July 1978, p. 241; *Cr H,* Fall 1979, p. 18; *Hob,* September 1978, p. 101; *LJ,* April 15, 1978, p. 862.

Board's recommendation: Public and academic libraries.

The Illustrated Encyclopedia of Costume and Fashion: 1550–1920. Jack Cassin-Scott. Sterling, 1986. hard. 1 vol. 160 pp. illus. index. ISBN 0-7137-1811-0. $19.95. encyclopedia.
GT580 391.009

The Illustrated Encyclopedia of Costume and Fashion contains "some 150 colorplates of men, women, and children dressed in period fashions. . . . From the stiff silhouette of the mid-sixteenth-century Spanish court dress to the 1920s flapper outfit, each sample includes a brief description of the costume and an illustration (many of which often resemble two-dimensional paper dolls). [This work is] a handy, easy-to-use guide for novice costume designers and artists." (*BL,* September 15, 1986, p. 85)

Also reviewed in: *Ref Bk R,* 1987, p. 13.

Board's recommendation: Public libraries.

Miller's International Antiques Price Guide. Judith Miller and Martin Miller. Penguin, annual. soft. 1 vol. 696 pp. ISBN 0-670-82478-5. $24.95. guide.
NK1125 745.1075

Board's recommendation: Public libraries.

Warman's Americana and Collectibles, 3d edition. Harry L. Rinker, ed. Warman, 1988. soft. 1 vol. 560 pp. illus. index. ISBN 0-911594-12-4. $13.95. handbook.
AM231 790.132

Warman's Americana and Collectibles is a "companion volume to Warman's Antiques and Their Prices. . . . The work includes 250 categories of collectibles (25,000 items). Included are broad categories such as glassware, pottery, and toys and narrow categories such as aeronautica, cigarette items, cowboy heroes, fishing collectibles, padlocks, scouting, snowdomes, stock and bond certificates, and Tarzan collectibles. Entries for each of these categories include the following headings: Collecting Hints, History, References, Collectors' Clubs, and Periodicals, followed by the listing of individual items and suggested purchase prices.

"The item descriptions are, perforce, brief and intended more for readers already familiar with a collectible category. The casual user may not be able to identify a specific item but will get an impression of market values and the variety of items available for purchase. Illustrations are good; usually one item is pictured for each category. . . . The index serves to bring together types of items listed in more than one category. . . . This work is one of many guides to collectibles. The concentration on inexpensive items and the number of categories included makes it a good purchase for libraries not wishing to purchase the specialized guides that concentrate on one type of collectible." (*BL,* August 1988, p. 1908)

This work is completely revised biennially. The price for the fourth edition is $14.95.

Also reviewed in: *BL,* February 15, 1984, p. 839; *Hob,* July 1984, p. 60; *LATBR,* February 19, 1984, p. 60.

Board's recommendation: Public libraries.

Warman's Antiques and Their Prices. Harry L. Rinker, ed. Warman, annual. soft. 1 vol. 720 pp. illus. index. ISBN 0-911594-15-9. $12.95. handbook.
NK1125 708.05

Warman's Antiques and Their Prices "is a general price guide covering almost 500 collecting categories. More than 50,000 items are listed with prices. Objects are listed alphabetically by category, e.g., advertising, clocks, games, pattern glass, samplers, and toy trains. . . . Each category begins with a brief history of that item followed by a list of references to books and periodicals as well as collector clubs and museums specializing in the item. The description of each object is briefly noted with dimensions, descriptors, and prices.

"[In this work], a comprehensive index provides easy access to the specific objects. . . . An explanation of the prices cited is given thorough treatment in the prefatory material. Illustrations are limited in number (about 1,000), small, and in black and white." (*BL,* October 1, 1987, p. 249)

This work is completely revised each year.

Board's recommendation: Public libraries.

New and Noteworthy

Decorative Arts and Household Furnishings in America, 1650–1920: An Annotated Bibliography. Kenneth L. Ames and Gerald W. R. Ward. Winterthur Museum, 1989; distrib. by Univ. of Virginia Pr. hard. 1 vol. approx. 400 pp. ISBN 0-912724-19-6. $60. bibliography.
Z5956.D3D43 016.745097

Decorative Arts and Household Furnishings in America "is the combined work of twenty-two specialists, each devoted to a specific aspect of decorative arts and household furnishings used in America from the seventeenth century to the First World War. Each chapter contains a brief essay outlining the development of scholarship in the field and pointing toward new directions for research, followed by annotated entries on the most significant works on the subject. The book is divided into three sections: [a guide] to basic reference tools and surveys of American art and architecture . . . a section on materials . . . [and a section] on themes." (Excerpted from publisher's announcement)

Claudine Jenda

Drug Abuse

See also How-To and Self-Help

Drug abuse, a subject with a long history, is being viewed with growing seriousness. The term *drug* is used to refer to any chemical substance taken into the body that alters the physical or mental condition. The term includes medicines, which technically are substances used in the prevention, treatment, cure, or diagnosis of a disease or an abnormal condition in humans or animals. The term also includes nonmedicinal substances such as caffeine and alcohol, as well as the array of controlled substances.

Drug abuse most often involves drugs that affect the brain and nervous system, of which there are five main groups. Depressants decrease the activity of the central nervous system; barbiturates, tranquilizers, and alcohol are examples. Stimulants have the opposite effect; cocaine and amphetamines are stimulants. Drugs in the third category, analgesics, relieve pain. This group includes over-the-counter medicines such as aspirin and acetaminophen, as well as the highly addictive narcotics (morphine, heroin, and codeine). A fourth kind of drug that affects the nervous system is anesthetics, used by medical professionals to eliminate sensation either generally or at a specific part of the body. The fifth group, hallucinogens, causes the user to sense some-

Core Titles

	PUBLIC	ACADEMIC	SCHOOL
The Encyclopedia of Alcoholism, 2d edition Evans, Glen, Robert O'Brien, and Morris Chafetz, eds. Facts On File, 1990	✦	✦	✦
The Encyclopedia of Drug Abuse, 2d edition O'Brien, Robert, and Sidney Cohen, eds. Facts On File, 1990	✦	✦	✦
Rehab: A Comprehensive Guide to Recommended Drug-Alcohol Treatment Centers in the United States Hart, Stan. Harper & Row, 1988	✦		

thing that exists solely in the mind. Marijuana and LSD are hallucinogens.

Drug abuse occurs when drugs are not used as recommended or prescribed. Dependence and tolerance are two serious effects of drug abuse. Dependence is the physical or mental craving for a dose of a specific drug. Tolerance, as it relates to drug abuse, means that the user must take increasingly more of a drug to obtain the same effects he or she previously got from lower doses.

Drug abuse is a highly interdisciplinary subject that draws from medical science, chemistry, biological science, pharmacology, and other areas—including health care. For a core reference collection to be of any meaningful service, it should reflect this subject diversity. Necessary reference works include encyclopedic dictionaries that define terms and explain concepts for both general readers and diverse professionals. Librarians may need to supplement these titles with more specialized subject dictionaries. For example, some chemical dictionaries may be outside the scope of drug abuse core titles; however, they should be considered when building a core collection because they provide chemical data on drugs.

This category also includes directories of drug-alcohol treatment centers to enable librarians to identify and recommend rehabilitation centers when patrons ask for help. One directory—REHAB—appears on the core list because its thorough evaluations of treatment centers are far more useful than a mere list of locations would be.

The bibliographic titles in this category will be useful for librarians who need to answer requests for additional information or to locate earlier literature for collection development or research. One bibliography was voted by the Board as a core title but is now out of print: Theodora Andrews's *Substance Abuse Materials for School Libraries: An Annotated Bibliography* (Libraries Unlimited, 1985). Jean Moore's bibliography *Road to Recovery* (Collier Books, 1986), selected as a supplementary title, is also out of print. Librarians may feel the need, depending on the clientele they serve, to include other titles from related disciplines as core reference titles. —*C. J.*

With contributions by Atha Louise Henley.

Core Titles

The Encyclopedia of Alcoholism, 2d edition. Glen Evans, Robert O'Brien, and Morris Chafetz. Facts On File, 1990. hard. 1 vol. 331 pp. illus. appendixes. index. ISBN 0-8160-1955-X. $45. dictionary.
HV5017.E5 362.29'2'03-dc20

The Encyclopedia of Alcoholism is a dictionary covering alcoholism and alcohol abuse authored by three men reputable in this field. O'Brien has published some similar works on drug abuse. Chafetz, the founding director of the National Institute on Alcohol Abuse and Alcoholism, is a medical practitioner who has worked, researched, and published extensively in this field and in clinical psychiatry. His publications focus on the treatment, prevention, and dynamics of alcoholism and alcohol-related disorders.

The terms and topics in this dictionary are listed alphabetically. Each term or topic is defined or explained as it relates to alcoholism. For example, *metabolism* is defined as it relates to the ingestion of alcohol. The entries average about 100 words. A few topics have been described in greater detail. These longer entries range from one to several pages and give an overview of specific subjects, such as *Alcoholics Anonymous, alcoholism,* and *driving while intoxicated.* Such articles end with a list of references for additional information.

The entries on terms and topics make up about two-thirds of the book. The last third of the book contains two appendixes, a bibliography, and the index. The first appendix includes tables and figures; the second appendix is a list of sources of information, primarily organizations and periodicals, with addresses included. The listing is organized by country; listings for the United States and Canada are further subdivided by state or province. A 30-page bibliography follows the appendixes; the titles are not grouped topically. The book ends with a brief subject index that includes cross-references to help users find related information.

The Encyclopedia of Alcoholism makes it easy for a wide readership to find facts, information, and literature on alcoholism. This reference work has the added benefit of being much more up to date than most other dictionaries in print on the subject. (This review is based on the book's galleys, since the book was not yet in print at the time this review was written.)

Those who deal with alcoholism and alcohol-related disorders as researchers, medical professionals, psychologists, counselors, social workers, or teachers can turn to *The Encyclopedia of Alcoholism* for help in understanding the technical terminology related to alcoholism. This work can also help laypersons by introducing them to the terms and concepts they need to know in order to better understand alcoholism. The Board recommends this work for the core collections of public, academic, and school libraries. —*C. J.*

The Encyclopedia of Drug Abuse, 2d edition. Robert O'Brien and Sidney Cohen, eds. Facts On File, 1990.

hard. 1 vol. 370 pp. illus. appendixes. index. ISBN 0-8160-1956-8. $45. dictionary.
HV5804.024 362.2′9

The Encyclopedia of Drug Abuse is an authorative, comprehensive, well-written, and easy-to-understand one-volume work that is more dictionary than encyclopedia in format. Eight contributors on the editorial board are from the following well-recognized organizations: the National Institute on Drug Abuse, the Federal Bureau of Investigation, the U.S. Department of Health and Human Services, the National Institute on Alcohol Abuse and Alcoholism, and the World Health Organization. A new edition of this work was published by Facts On File in 1990. This review reflects an examination of material from that revision provided by the publisher.

This work presents an overall view of drug abuse and information on the medical and physical effects of drugs, psychological factors of drug use and abuse, and the political and legal aspects of drugs in more than 25 countries. This work includes tables of statistics on the use of specific drugs, such as opium, heroin, morphine, marijuana, and LSD. These tables are invaluable to any researcher.

The first part of *The Encyclopedia of Drug Abuse* is a "History of Drugs and Man," beginning with an ancient Egyptian papyrus from 1500 B.C. A "Drug Classification Chart" classifies specific drugs under 11 different types of headings, such as "Antidepressants" and "Volatile Inhalants."

Subject entries are arranged alphabetically. Their length varies from one line (for "see" and "see also" notes) to three lines (for short descriptions) to more than three pages (for the entry on *amphetamines,* which includes a history from 1887 to the 1980s). Among the more than 500 topics covered are entries on *caffeine, cocaine, heroin, nicotine,* and over-the-counter drugs that could lead to physical or psychological damage.

Four appendixes greatly enhance the value of this encyclopedia: a glossary of street-language terms, a slang list of synonyms for drugs, 55 tables of detailed statistical data about drug use and abuse in the United States through the late 1980s, and sources of information, such as names and address of institutes and agencies in the United States, Canada, and foreign countries.

The bibliography is arranged alphabetically by the author's surname. For example, in the bibliography, four titles were listed under *Cohen, Sidney,* a co-author of this book. The citations include publications with dates ranging from 1926 to 1989. Forty to fifty titles are being added in the new edition to provide up-to-date information. The volume ends with a helpful subject index.

A companion volume is THE ENCYCLOPEDIA OF ALCOHOLISM, published in 1990. However, *The Encyclopedia of Drug Abuse* is the principal reference work on drug abuse and is a valuable resource for libraries, community leaders, laypersons, and health professionals. The Board recommends this work for the core collections of public, academic, and school libraries.

—*A. L. H.*

Rehab: A Comprehensive Guide to Recommended Drug-Alcohol Treatment Centers in the United States. Stan Hart. Harper & Row, 1988. soft. 1 vol. 513 pp. index. ISBN 0-06-096296-8. $10.95. directory.
RC564.73.H365 362.2′9′02573

Rehab: A Comprehensive Guide to Recommended Drug-Alcohol Treatment Centers in the United States is a directory of drug and alcohol treatment centers throughout the United States. This directory lists about 146 chemical-dependency rehabilitation centers offering inpatient care of adults. The author, who has published two similar works on this subject, personally visited and evaluated each center described in this directory.

The work begins with a four-page introduction in which the author explains how he collected the information in the directory. Hart highlights the factors he considers important in a drug-alcohol rehabilitation center—factors that he uses later to rate each center. The listings of drug-alcohol treatment centers follows the introduction. The centers are listed alphabetically by state, and then alphabetically within each state.

The entries make up the main part of the directory. A typical entry for each center includes the following: name, address, and phone number of the rehabilitation center; names and titles of the individuals from each center who were interviewed by the author; a brief description of the center, including who owns it, when it was founded, and the types of cases and patients treated there; physical setting and condition of the facility; location of the center from the nearest interstate and airports; descriptions of residential accommodations; average attendance record; dominant age group; duration of treatment; cost estimates, including the types of insurance accepted by the center; primary therapeutic staff and their areas of specialization; type of treatment and type of therapy (individual or group, and aftercare program); availability of a hospital on the center's premises; family program and visiting hours; and key personnel at the center. Hart comments on each center and gives each one a rating ranging from *good* or *very good* to *excellent.*

A special 11-page section on centers for women follows the main section. A section titled "Honorable Mention," which follows the section on women's centers, lists centers whose standards are not adequately developed (in the author's opinion). The work concludes with a glossary that gives definitions of acronyms and unfamiliar terms used in the directory and a name index of all the centers.

Rehab is better than other standard directories on the subject because this work provides information that a person needing rehabilitation for chemical dependency is likely to inquire about. Librarians should find the detailed information useful for answering queries. Because the author is the only person describing and rating each center, the assessment of the quality of the centers is consistent, reliable, and unique. Moreover, the information and figures in the directory are relatively current.

Rehab's main shortcoming is that it is not as comprehensive as some other directories. However, medical practitioners, teachers, psychologists, counselors, social workers, and laypeople seeking to identify a suitable center for drug-alcohol treatment will still find *Rehab* a valuable information source, especially if they need an independent assessment of specific centers. The Board recommends this work for the core collection of public libraries. —*C. J.*

Supplementary Titles

Alcohol Use and Alcoholism: A Guide to the Literature. Penny Booth Page. Garland, 1986. hard. 1 vol. 164 pp. ISBN 0-8240-9020-9. $30. bibliography.
Z7721.P33 016.3622

Alcohol Use and Alcoholism is "a selective annotated bibliographic guide to the general literature on alcohol use and alcoholism. Most of the English-language material was published between the late 1970s and 1985. The 405 cited items include books, pamphlets, leaflets, and government documents. . . . The first part of the volume is a . . . brief introduction to the topic of alcohol use and problems and a short section on how to use the guide. This is followed by 16 chapters on subjects such as general reference guides and handbooks, [and] audiovisual guides. . . . Two appendixes list some alcohol-related periodicals and resource organizations to write [to] for more information. Access to the bibliography is by the general subject division of the chapters or by the author and title indexes.

"Specifically excluded are technical and research reports, periodical articles, and audiovisual materials. . . . There is no subject index. All items are consecutively numbered and arranged alphabetically within each chapter. Each item is cited completely and has a 50- to 70-word annotation. Where appropriate, the annotations detail the intended audience (e.g., junior high), whether there is a bibliography, and whether there is a glossary of terms. Other unique features, such as pictures, charts, self-tests, etc., are also noted in the annotations. This bibliography does an excellent job of identifying numerous pamphlets and leaflets not published by mainstream publishers. . . . This guide fills a void in identifying some of the recent literature on alcoholism." (*BL,* 1987, p. 764)

Also reviewed in: *ARBA,* 1987, p. 309; *Choice,* December 1986, p. 609; *R&R Bk N,* Fall 1986, p. 29; *WLB,* November 1986, p. 62.

Board's recommendation: Public and academic libraries.

The 100 Best Treatment Centers for Alcoholism and Drug Abuse. Linda Sunshine and John W. Wright. Avon Books, 1988. soft. 1 vol. 452 pp. index. ISBN 0-380-75489-4. $10.95. encyclopedia.
RC564.73.S96 362.2

In this up-to-date reference book, *The 100 Best Treatment Centers for Alcoholism and Drug Abuse,* "Sunshine and Wright include an introduction that covers the signs and symptoms of chemical dependency, how to seek help, what to look for in a treatment program, and how to select the best treatment center. They also have appendixes with lists of therapists, organizations offering help for families, selected books, and support groups. . . . The main body of [this] directory is a list of centers, organized alphabetically by state and city or center name. Each entry consists of an overview of the center's treatment philosophy, statistics, admissions policy, social programs offered, costs and insurance coverage, staff, address, and telephone number.

"[The information given in the book] is based on recommendations from professionals actively working in the chemical-dependency field and on responses to detailed questionnaires sent to almost 200 centers. All centers included in [this] book have been highly recommended by professionals. . . . [It] has an excellent detailed subject index that lists types of addictions (gambling, cocaine), special groups served (gays, professionals, senior citizens), types of treatment (outpatient, antabuse), and types of admission and payment. Both [this book and Stan Hart's REHAB, Harper & Row, 1988] will be useful additions to consumer, health, and social-science collections. They will help those faced with substance-abuse problems in the family or workplace to make some difficult decisions. *The 100 Best Treatment Centers* offers a more complete and impartial overview of the chemical-dependency field." (*BL,* March 15, 1989, p. 1266)

Board's recommendation: Public libraries.

New and Noteworthy

Prevention Education: A Guide to Research. William J. Derivan and Natalie Anne Silverstein. Garland, 1990. hard. 1 vol. 282 pp. appendixes. indexes. ISBN 0-8240-3716-2. $35. bibliography.
Z7164.N17D44 016.36229'17

Prevention Education "lists more than 600 citations to literature on the prevention of abuse of alcohol and drugs. . . . Chapters deal with topics like school-based prevention programs (including teacher training), reports on model prevention programs, curricula for prevention programs, community-based prevention programs, and the family and prevention (including therapeutic interventions). . . . Each citation has a brief descriptive annotation. Appendixes list organizations providing information on substance abuse and periodicals in the field." (*BL,* August 1990, p. 2205)

Wendell Cochran

Earth Science

See also Science and Technology

Earth science embraces many different aspects of other science and adds one vital, pervasive concept—geological time. The mix of science in this category usually involves geology; geophysics; geochemistry; mineralogy and petrology; seismology, climatology, and meteorology; and paleontology. The component sciences often overlap, but the overall object of study remains the planet Earth—its structure, composition, natural processes, history, and life forms. (Readers can consult Marine Science and Astronomy for works that treat the oceans and extraterrestrial worlds in greater detail.)

The comprehensive nature of earth science makes the librarian's job difficult, whether answering specific questions or assembling resources. Inquiries in this area may be at any level, from the lower grades (pupils unaware of formal academic boundaries) to professionals (scientists seeking an interdisciplinary approach).

A core collection that helps to deal with such diversity of material and inquirers will include dictionaries, glossaries, bibliographies, and encyclopedias that also may contain extensive bibliographies leading to primary sources in periodicals, maps, and monographs.

In general, the works in the core collection should set the stage for further study of Earth's place in the solar system and narrate the development of its continents and oceans (with explanations of the processes involved) as well as the evolution of life and humankind's interaction with our planet. THE CAMBRIDGE ENCYCLOPEDIA OF EARTH SCIENCES is one work that takes this approach. Dictionaries may be generalized or specialized, though "geology" tends to cover the solid and liquid Earth and its fossil life. The core and supplementary lists include a selection of dictionaries with both broad and narrow scopes. The three other encyclopedias selected should facilitate the search for descriptions and explanations of places, things, and ideas in the field of earth science.

Finally, in evaluating works to be included a collection in earth science, librarians should bear in mind that earth scientists often search the older literature for observations made in the past, so less recent publications should not necessarily be dismissed, because they may still contain relevant information.

Core Titles

	PUBLIC	ACADEMIC	SCHOOL
The Cambridge Encyclopedia of Earth Sciences Smith, David G., ed. Cambridge, 1981	✦	✦	✦
Dictionary of Geological Terms, 3d edition Bates, Robert L., and Julia A. Jackson, eds. Anchor, 1984		✦	
Encyclopedia of Climatology Oliver, John E., and Rhodes W. Fairbridge, eds. Van Nostrand Reinhold, 1987		✦	
Glossary of Geology, 3d edition Bates, Robert L., and Julia A. Jackson, eds. American Geological Institute, 1987		✦	
McGraw-Hill Dictionary of Earth Science Parker, Sybil P., ed. in chief. McGraw-Hill, 1984	✦	✦	✦
McGraw-Hill Encyclopedia of the Geological Sciences, 2d edition Parker, Sybil P., ed. in chief. McGraw-Hill, 1988	✦	✦	

Core Titles

The Cambridge Encyclopedia of Earth Sciences. David G. Smith, ed. Cambridge, 1981. hard. 1 vol. 496 pp. illus. index. ISBN 0-521-23900-1. $44.50. encyclopedia.
QE26.2.35 550

The Cambridge Encyclopedia of Earth Sciences encompasses the whole story of the Earth in one volume. This reference work was written by 32 earth scientists who are all widely known and active in the fields they discuss. Throughout the text they describe the Earth, recount its history, and explain its dynamic properties.

The contents are divided into six section topics, with chapters that elaborate on each topic. Part 1 is entitled "The Earth Sciences in Perspective"; part 2, "Physics and Chemistry of the Earth"; part 3, "Crustal Processes and Evolution"; part 4, "Surface Processes and Environments"; part 5, "Evaluation of Earth Resources and Hazards"; and part 6, "Extraterrestrial Geology."

This work is not concerned solely with the physical Earth; nearly a sixth of the book pertains to the study of life: its origins and early evolution, the interpretation of fossils, colonization of the Paleozoic seas, development of life on land, and evolution itself. A chapter on historical geology introduces detective procedures that have been developed for deciphering Earth's past.

The final chapter, on the geology of the solar system, shows how principles of geology, as developed on the Earth, are applied to the rocks of the moon, Mars, and the satellites of Jupiter.

According to the editor, the encyclopedia is meant primarily as a reference work and secondarily as a source for general readers and students. The text can be read straight through as a synthesis of the earth's history or may be searched for specific information by consulting the extensive, 3,500-entry index (which includes entries for figures and tables). The list of "Further Reading"—found at the end of the book and divided by chapter—is a guide with over 100 titles for users who wish to locate other sources for more in-depth information. A glossary of more than 500 terms, including many minerals and their chemical compositions, helps to clarify the work's scientific language.

The typeface is large and extremely readable. The double-column format has been well designed to accommodate many maps, cross sections, and detailed drawings. Much of the illustrative material is in color.

Scrutiny of the list of authors and their affiliations reveals a preponderance of British academics, but that in no way reduces accuracy of observation history, although the geographical areas covered favor the British Isles only as necessary in discussing the work of the first geologists.

The Cambridge Encyclopedia of Earth Sciences will be frequently used in all libraries. The Board recommends this work for the core collections of public, academic, and school libraries.

Dictionary of Geological Terms, 3d edition. Robert L. Bates and Julia A. Jackson, eds. Anchor, 1984. soft. 1 vol. 576 pp. ISBN 0-385-18101-9. $10.95. dictionary.
QE5.D55 550.3'21

The authority of the *Dictionary of Geological Terms* lies in its reliance on the much more extensive *Glossary of Geology*, also edited by Bates and Jackson. It compresses approximately 8,000 terms into a work of manageable size.

This reference is intended for the nonspecialist, although the editors declare that the terms they define were drawn from "the working vocabulary of earth scientists." In this context, the term *earth scientists* embraces specialists such as geomorphologists, glacial geologists, marine scientists, mineralogists and petrologists, paleontologists, seismologists, stratigraphers, structural geologists, and geologists in engineering, groundwater, petroleum, planetary studies, environmental studies, and natural hazards.

Definitions are arranged in two columns per page (each column with its own guide word), and each entry term is set in boldface type with subsequent lines indented.

Usage is generally North American; in particular the stratigraphic divisions are restricted to North American systems and series (the rocks) and periods (the geological time represented by the rocks).

Terms and their definitions occupy the entire book, except for a geological time chart that notes characteristic features of geological ages and periods. For example, by consulting the chart the reader can learn that the Devonian period was from 405 to 425 million years ago, that it was a part of the Paleozoic era, and that it is sometimes known as "the age of fishes." The chart also provides the information that the Devonian period was notable for the first appearance of amphibians and ammonite cephalopods.

Alphabetization is strictly letter by letter. Definitions can be as short as one line (usually synonyms) but may run half a column. About six lines constitutes a typical entry. However, some terms may have multiple meanings or may be used differently in different specialties. When this situation arises, the definitions are numbered as 1, 2, 3. Cross-references are common. Etymologies are rare, but the chemical composition is given for minerals. Entry words are commonly divided by syllables and their accents shown.

In terms of accuracy, currency, and ease of use, the *Dictionary of Geological Terms* scores high. The Board recommends this work for the core collection of academic libraries.

Encyclopedia of Climatology (vol. 11 of *Encyclopedia of Earth Sciences*). John E. Oliver and Rhodes W. Fairbridge, eds. Van Nostrand Reinhold, 1987. hard. 1 vol. 986 pp. illus. appendix. index. ISBN 0-879-33009-0. $105.95. encyclopedia.
QC854.E25 551.5'03'21

The *Encyclopedia of Climatology* covers an impressive range of topics in climatology, each in considerable detail. This coverage is the result of efforts by 132 specialists in the field whose articles were subject to peer review before publication. The authors and their affiliations are listed in the front of the book. The book is large (almost 1,000 pages), heavy, and expensive.

There are 213 signed entries, arranged alphabetically. The entries are set up in a two-column page layout. The entries are listed separately in the front of the book and are also accessible through three indexes of personal names (and organizations), geographical names, and subjects. Each index is exhaustive. The reading level of the text tends to be somewhat technical, and a general reader has to refer to a separate dictionary in order to fully understand the material.

The format of the book makes information easily accessible. Each page has a guide word; in addition, subheads and side heads in boldface type are often used. Within the article, reference sources are briefly noted in parentheses and given in full bibliographic form at the end of the article. Illustrations include maps, halftones, charts, diagrams, and tables.

Some topics are discussed more than once in order to present distinctive points of view, and for certain standard items the reader is referred to an earlier volume in the series. The following are random samples of main entries illustrating the range of topics, the length, the number of references to other literature, and other notable features. The entry for *climatic classification* takes up more than 16 pages, with about 2 columns of reference citations and 13 cross-references to other main entries. *Horse latitudes* occupies less than a column, with 2 reference citations given, and 4 cross-references provided. *Ice-age theory* is about 10 pages long with 4 columns of reference citations and 13 cross-references. *Tornadoes* receives a discussion of nearly 10 pages, 45 reference citations, 4 cross-references, and other main entries. It should be mentioned that such unusual topics as *art and climate* and *crime and climate* receive entries, giving an unusually broad scope to the work.

The information contained within the encyclopedia is reasonably current, although few reference citations are as recent as 1985. The price of the *Encyclopedia of*

Climatology, like the volume itself, is hefty, and for some libraries this will be a barrier. The Board recommends this work for the core collection of academic libraries.

Glossary of Geology, 3d edition. Robert L. Bates and Julia A. Jackson, eds. American Geological Institute, 1987. hard. 1 vol. 788 pp. ISBN 0-913312-89-4. $75. dictionary.
QE5.B38 550'3'21

The reliability of the *Glossary of Geology* can be seen in its long history (the parent edition dates to 1957) and its approximately 150 contributors, who are specialists in geology and related sciences. Also, one of the editors, Robert Bates, has been a geologist in industry and academia for many years and is well respected in the field.

The book is somewhat bulky (as it must be in order to contain 37,000 terms). However, despite the small type size used, the text is still legible. Since the second edition in 1980, the editors have added about 1,000 terms and increased the references (cited parenthetically within the entries and given as full bibliographic citations at the end of the book) to over 2,000. The bibliography is one of the most notable features of this work. This list will enable students to further their research in many different geological areas.

The glossary consists of 750 pages with text arranged in two columns. Each page contains about 50 definitions.

Entries are arranged alphabetically, letter by letter. Terms that have meanings in more than one subspecialty are identified by bracketed tags, as in *old age,* with definitions tagged, for example, as "[coast]" for coastal geology "[streams]," and "[topog]" for topography.

Some entries are included for terms that are now seldom used or used inaccurately, an example being *tidal wave,* defined as an "erroneous syn. of both *storm surge* and *tsunami.*" The introduction explains the reason for this practice: geologists are more likely than other physical scientists to search the older publications for evidence and observations, where they will often encounter archaic or obsolete terms.

Usage is primarily North American, though British (and other) terms are sometimes included. Pertinent terms conform to recommendations of the North American Stratigraphic Code of 1983.

Primary users will be students and specialists in the field; general readers may prefer the DICTIONARY OF GEOLOGICAL TERMS (reviewed in this section) by the same editors.

The *Glossary of Geology* is a bargain in terms of authoritative definitions per dollar. The Board recommends this book for the core collection of academic libraries.

McGraw-Hill Dictionary of Earth Science. Sybil P. Parker, ed. in chief. McGraw-Hill, 1984. hard. 1 vol. 850 pp. ISBN 0-07-045252-0. $44.50. dictionary.
QE5.M365 550.321

The *McGraw-Hill Dictionary of Earth Science* stems from a long line of authoritative science and technology encyclopedias and dictionaries published by McGraw-Hill. Some of its more than 15,000 terms were drawn from related McGraw-Hill books; others were written especially for this volume.

The scope of the dictionary is multidisciplinary; *earth science* includes not only the sciences of the solid earth and its oceans and atmosphere, but also its life and resources, with the addition of geodesy, engineering, and mining. No other book reviewed in this section attempts to cover a range so great. However, the work does not always succeed in fulfilling its ambitious scope. There are occasions when the definitions are unclear and the reader must look elsewhere in the dictionary to discern the meaning of terms within the definition.

Over 15,000 entries are alphabetically arranged in two columns in 837 pages. To accommodate such a range of subject matter, definitions must be brief and concise. As a result, most definitions are more suitable for the casual reader rather than the critical specialist. Even so, definitions are generally adequate. The definition for *guyot* reads as follows: "[GEOL] A seamount, usually deeper than 100 fathoms (180 meters), having a smooth platform top. Also known as tablemount."

Not all of the technical terms that appear within a definition are defined elsewhere. For example, the word *crura* is found in the definition for *Spiriferida,* but *crura* itself is never defined. Some widely used terms, such as hot spot and plume, are not included, despite the appearance of other terms with similar meaning.

When attempting to encompass so many fields, some will inevitably be less thorough than others. This dictionary lists *Ammonoidea* but not cephalapod; *Spiriferida* (an order of brachiopods) but not brachiopod; mollusk does not appear, and all in all, the coverage of paleontology is uneven. In seismology, *magnitude* (for earthquakes) is defined, but *intensity* is found only as *earthquake intensity.* Similarly, *tidal wave* is not restricted to a tidal mechanism, and it is not cross-referenced to *tsunami,* the preferred term. Readers may find cross-references less than complete.

For most mineral names, the chemical composition is specified. Some entries, although brief, may aid the reader in determining the geological origin of the word: *Granby car [MIN ENG], Grand Banks [GEOGR]* and *Asia [GEOGR]*. For some readers the most interesting feature may be a page headed "Scope of Fields," which defines the 18 disciplines represented in this work, from climatology through petrology. Scientific disciplines almost always overlap, and it is useful to be able to differentiate these 18 at a glance. However, few geophysicists will agree with the designation of their special field as a branch of geology, and other ambiguities occur in this classification of disciplines.

This work does best in providing general definitions to a wide range of science and technology terms. THE CAMBRIDGE ENCYCLOPEDIA OF EARTH SCIENCES provides more comprehensive coverage of the field.

The Board recommends this work for the core collections of public, academic, and school libraries.

McGraw-Hill Encyclopedia of the Geological Sciences, 2d edition. Sybil P. Parker, ed. in chief. McGraw-Hill, 1988. hard. 1 vol. 722 pp. illus. ISBN 0-07-045500-7. $85. encyclopedia.
QEM29 551.03'21

Articles in the *McGraw-Hill Encyclopedia of the Geological Sciences* were drawn from the MCGRAW-HILL ENCYCLOPEDIA OF SCIENCE AND TECHNOLOGY (see Science and Technology) or were written especially for this work; its 233 contributors represent subfields within geology, geochemistry, mineralogy, petrology, and geophysics. (This edition comprises 520 articles, 40 of which are new, with half of the rest revised or rewritten.) The consulting editors were a mineralogist and a sedimentologist, both eminent in their fields.

Physical products and processes are the dominant subject of entries in this book. Earth history is outlined in entries for plate tectonics, evolution of continents, and geologic eras (such as the Paleozoic and Mesozoic) and periods (such as the Cretaceous), but details of paleontology and the evolution of life are comparatively scant.

Entries are arranged alphabetically in two columns per page and range in length from a few lines to several pages; one page per topic is typical. The frequent use of subheads and side heads in boldface type makes reading and searching for information quick and easy. Maps, sketches, and other artwork abound. The reading level is raised by the technical terms made necessary by the content, but is lowered by judicious sentence length and structure; general readers should have little trouble. Content is uniformly up to date and accurate, as shown in the entry for *plate tectonics.* Nearly all articles include cross-references, and they usually end with a bibliography.

The following is a sample of the scope of an average entry: *Paleomagnetism* covers slightly over two pages, including a map of polar wandering, a sketch showing how a magnetometer works, and a diagram of a magnetic pole and its components. Side heads draw the reader's attention to discussions of magnetic field behavior, magnetization of rocks, collection and measurement of samples, and interpretation of the data. Cross-references in this entry direct the reader to *plate tectonics, rock magnetism, geomagnetism,* and *geophysical exploration.* Finally, there is a bibliography with titles of two journal articles and two books.

The index is large and detailed, with a dozen four-column pages; asterisks identify names of articles among index entries.

In addition to the *McGraw-Hill Encyclopedia of the Geological Sciences,* a balanced reference shelf may call for the addition of comprehensive works on historical geology, including paleontology, and on planetary materials and processes. The Board recommends this work for the core collections of public and academic libraries.

Supplementary Titles

Bibliography and Index of Geology. John Mulvihill, ed. Geological Society of America in cooperation with the American Geological Institute, monthly with annual cumulation (1969–). soft. 1 vol. approx. 160 pp. ISBN 0-913312-66-5. $8.95. bibliography.
Z6081.B57 016.55'05

The latest edition of the *Bibliography and Index of Geology* represents "a change of title for the *Bibliography and index of geology exclusive of North America,* and continues its numbering. Coverage includes North American geology. The bibliography is now produced with the use of data-processing equipment. [It follows] the classed arrangement of the preceding volumes (i.e., v. 31–32 of the earlier title); a series of descriptors or keywords is sometimes provided in place of the abstracts which were a feature of v. 31–32. Each monthly issue includes author and subject indexes. The annual index is in four parts: [parts] 1–2 cumulate the bibliography in author arrangement, giving the full bibliographical citation, but omitting the descriptors supplied in the monthly issues; [parts] 3–4 cumulate the monthly subject indexes, giving authors' names and references to item numbers in the monthly issues.

"[The book is] photocomposed from citations in GeoRef, a database produced at the American Geological Institute." (*Guide to Reference Books,* 10th edition, Sheehy, p. 1199)

Board's recommendation: Academic libraries.

Challinor's Dictionary of Geology, 6th edition. Anthony Hyatt, ed. Oxford, 1986. soft. 1 vol. 392 pp. index. ISBN 0-19-520506-5. $16.95. dictionary.
QE5.C45 550.3

Challinor's Dictionary of Geology "contains approximately 2600 entries, including nearly 400 that refer the reader to other terms for their definitions. Descriptions include mineral and rock names and descriptive terms; structural, stratigraphic, geomorphic and paleontologic terms; fossil groups; and geologic processes. Some terms are defined in a few words, while others receive encyclopedic treatments of more than a page. The amount of space for a term is not necessarily related to the term's importance; for example, fossilology is given more space than fractional crystallization. Quotations from ancient and modern publications are used extensively." (*Sci Bks & Films,* December 1979, p. 145)

Also reviewed in: *ARBA,* 1980, p. 655; *Earth S,* Winter 1979, p. 43; *TES,* April 25, 1980, p. 51.

Board's recommendation: Academic libraries.

Climates of the States, 4th edition. Frank Blair, ed. Gale, 1991. 2 vols. hard. 1,575 pp. ISBN 0-8103-0449-X. $255. encyclopedia.
QC983.C56 551.6

Climates of the States brings together the "fifty-one individual state climatological reports issued during the last decade by the National Oceanic and Atmospheric Administration. . . . Each section contains a general summary of climatic conditions followed by . . . tables of freeze data; normals of temperature and precipitation by climatic divisions and stations; normals, means, and extremes of selected individual stations; and maps showing temperature, precipitation and locations of stations. Also included are miscellaneous data on snowfall, sunshine and occurrence of tropical storms. Altogether the two volumes contain [over] 395 tables and 310 maps.

"The volumes have a sturdy binding which will hold up under frequent use, and the pages lie flat when open. . . . Since this is an accumulation of previously issued reports, there is no index. This, however, is not a serious drawback since the states are listed in alphabetical order in each volume. . . . [This work] can be recommended to researchers, libraries, and individuals wishing climatic information for specific sections of the country." (*BL,* May 1, 1975, p. 919)

Also reviewed in: *ARBA,* 1979, p. 701; 1981, p. 691; *BL,* February 15, 1980, p. 852; *Choice,* June 1979, p. 558; *GJ,* March 1981, p. 113; *RSR,* October 1974, p. 31; Fall 1982, p. 72; *WLB,* March 1979, p. 525.

Board's recommendation: Public, academic, and school libraries.

The Facts On File Dictionary of Geology and Geophysics. Dorothy Farris Lapidus. Facts On File, 1987. hard and soft. 1 vol. 347 pp. ISBN 0-87196-703-0 (hard); 0-8160-2367-0 (soft). $24.95 (hard); $12.95 (soft). dictionary.
QE52.29 550

"Many people have a need for this uncomplicated dictionary of working definitions for terms used in geology and geophysics: middle-school, high-school, and college students as well as professionals. Given that this dictionary only covers some 3,000 technical words, one can't expect to always find the terms sought; however, the coverage is good." (*SB,* September 1988, p. 23)

Also reviewed in: *Choice,* June 1988, p. 1538; *RQ,* Spring 1988, p. 426; *WLB,* December 1987, p. 92.

Board's recommendation: Public and academic libraries.

New and Noteworthy

Magill's Survey of Science, Earth Science series. Frank N. Magill, ed. Salem, 1989. hard. 5 vols. 2,804 pp. index. ISBN 0-89356-600-4. $400. handbook.
QE28.M33 629.4

"The five volumes of *Magill's Survey of Science: Earth Science Series* contain 377 alphabetically arranged articles authored by 171 authorities; each article averages seven pages in length. . . . Each article is in the same format, with a title followed by labels giving the type of earth science and field of study and a brief definition. Then follows a glossary of terms that are encountered in the article. . . . Each volume includes an alphabetical and a categorical list of all articles in the set." (*BL,* September 1, 1990, pp. 394–395)

Jennifer F. Paustenbaugh

Eastern European Literature

See also Russian Literature; World Literature

Eastern European literature is a very broad field not only because it encompasses so many languages (and language groups) but also because it embraces such a wide variety of literary and historical traditions. The majority of reference works included in this category treat the literature of their respective countries at a fairly general level yet often contain information of great value to the specialist as well.

In selecting these works every attempt has been made to provide some treatment of the literatures of all the countries of Eastern Europe—Albania, Bulgaria, Czechoslovakia, Greece, Hungary, Poland, Romania, and Yugoslavia. However, a number of significant works in this area are no longer in print or are not currently available in the United States. This means that countries with an extensive literary tradition that is not well known in the West may not receive proportionately as much coverage in this category as they might deserve within the context of world literature. Current events in many of these countries are quickly bringing some of the more obscure literatures to the attention of Western readers and should encourage future publishing activity in this area.

A core reference collection in Eastern European literature should accomplish three things. First, it should provide biographical information about the writers in the area. In addition, a dictionary type of treatment of genres, literary movements, and trends should also be included. Second, it should provide bibliographic information about translations of works into English. Without this type of information, the literature of Eastern Europe will remain undiscovered by most Western readers. Third, it should provide some basic criticism of the literature. Works containing excerpts of criticism or citations to criticism are also very valuable and have been included.

In the case of most of the Eastern European literatures covered, this goal is realized through the combination of sources recommended herein—not by a single source. In two instances it cannot be realized at all. Works about modern Greek and Romanian literature in English have not been included because none are currently in print. An excellent out-of-print work on modern Greek literature is Linos Politis's *A History of Modern Greek Literature* (Clarendon, 1973). *The Slavic Literatures* (Richard C. Lewanski, Ungar, 1967) and *Czech and Slovak Literature in English: A Bibliography* (George J. Kovtun, Library of Congress, 1988) are also worthwhile out-of-print sources. Librarians may wish to obtain these works through out-of-print book dealers. No recommendation can be made for Romanian literature. We can hope that this particular gap will be recognized by English-speaking scholars and that this lacuna will be filled before too long.

Core Titles

	PUBLIC	ACADEMIC	SCHOOL
A Comprehensive Bibliography of Yugoslav Literature in English, 1593–1980 Mihailovich, Vasa D., and Mateja Matejic. Slavica, 1984		✦	
First Supplement to A Comprehensive Bibliography of Yugoslav Literature in English, 1981–1985 Mihailovich, Vasa D. Slavica, 1988			
Dictionary of Albanian Literature Elsie, Robert. Greenwood, 1986		✦	
A History of Bulgarian Literature, 1865–1944 Moser, Charles A. Mouton, 1972		✦	
The History of Polish Literature, 2d edition Milosz, Czeslaw. Univ. of California Pr., 1983		✦	
Modern Slavic Literatures: Bulgarian, Czechoslovak, Polish, Ukranian, and Yugoslav Literatures, vol. 2 Mihailovich, Vasa D., ed. Ungar, 1976	✦	✦	
The Oxford History of Hungarian Literature: From the Earliest Times to the Present Czigany, Lóránt. Clarendon/Oxford, 1984	✦	✦	

Core Titles

A Comprehensive Bibliography of Yugoslav Literature in English, 1593–1980. Vasa D. Mihailovich and Mateja Matejic. Slavica, 1984. hard. 1 vol. 586 pp. index. ISBN 0-89357-136-9. $29.95. bibliography.
Z2958.L5M53 016.8918′1

First Supplement to A Comprehensive Bibliography of Yugoslav Literature in English, 1981–1985. Vasa D. Mihailovich. Slavica, 1988. soft. 1 vol. 338 pp. index. ISBN 0-89357-188-1. bibliography.
Z2958.L5M3 016.8918′1

A Comprehensive Bibliography of Yugoslav Literature in English, 1593–1980, which incorporates all of the 1976 volume *Yugoslav Literature in English: A Bibliography of Translations and Criticism (1821–1975),* by the same authors, not only updates the earlier volume to 1980 but also extends the coverage back to 1593 and fills in gaps in the existing bibliographic record. Vasa D. Mihailovich, working with Mateja Matejic, has brought together in one volume a very high percentage of the Yugoslav literature translated into English during a 388-year period. Mihailovich is also the editor of MODERN SLAVIC LITERATURES.

Also, as suggested by the title, the book attempts to be comprehensive. The authors note in the preface that "it covers all literature that has been written or is being written within the boundaries of Yugoslavia and abroad. It is an all-inclusive rather than selective bibliography, for the editors believe that what may seem trivial to one person may be of great importance to another."

The book contains references to the earliest known English translation from any of the four major Yugoslav literatures—a Thomas Lodge translation of four sonnets of Ludovik Paskvalic—as well as the first known critical mention of South Slavic literature, the comments in 1603 of Richard Knolles on Serbo-Croatian folk poetry.

The bibliography is divided into three parts: translations, criticism, and indexes. The first two sections contain a combined total of 5,255 entries. The translations section is divided into folk literature and individual writers, with the majority of the coverage being devoted to individual writers. Multiple translations of the same work are listed chronologically. The criticism section comprises entries in reference works, books and articles, reviews, and dissertations.

The indexes complete the volume and complement the excellent organization of the first two parts. The four indexes, each providing unique access to the volume's contents, are to English titles or first lines of translations, original titles or first lines of original, periodicals and newspapers, and subject names.

A very attractive feature of this work is its supplements, scheduled for publication at five-year intervals. The first supplement, *First Supplement to A Comprehensive Bibliography of Yugoslav Literature in English, 1981–1985* appeared in 1988. This work follows the same structural pattern established in the parent volume and contains a combined total of 3,127 entries in the first two sections. Most of the entries refer to works published during 1980 to 1985, although an effort has been made to add to and correct entries from the previous period. Mihailovich notes in the preface that the *First Supplement* includes addenda—"newly unearthed data stretching back to 1495."

A second supplement, scheduled to be published sometime in 1991, will include material for the years 1986 to 1990.

The contents of both the original volume and the supplement are presented in a very straightforward manner; the citation style is well explained in the prefaces to each volume. All alphabetization is done without regard to diacritical marks, making the volumes very accessible to the English-speaking reader.

A Comprehensive Bibliography of Yugoslav Literature in English would be a useful acquisition for any public library that has sufficient patron interest in Eastern European subject areas. The Board recommends this work for the core collection of academic libraries.

Dictionary of Albanian Literature. Robert Elsie. Greenwood, 1986. hard. 1 vol. 170 pp. index. ISBN 0-313-25186-X. $36.95. dictionary.
PG9602.E47 891.991'03

For all but the devoted Albanologist, the world of Albanian literature is an obscure one. Through the *Dictionary of Albanian Literature* Robert Elsie, who is a translator for the Federal Republic of Germany, makes available for the first time an English-language dictionary-style work that will satisfy the curiosity of the generalist and provide a starting point for the specialist.

The approximately 500 entries include Albanian writers—those living both in Albania and abroad—and literature-related topics. The author notes in the preface that inclusion does not signify literary merit nor exclusion the lack of it.

The book is arranged alphabetically according to English-language conventions so that the entry for *dhosi* comes before *dodani* and not vice versa, as would be the case in Albania. Among the 500 entries are extensive cross-references leading the reader from assorted variations of names to the best-known form of the name. This is especially helpful for Arbëresh (Albanians who settled in Italy) and Muslim writers. Thus, there is a full entry for the Arbëresh poet Frano Krispi Glavjano under the Albanian form of his name and references from two variants of the Italian form, "Glaviano, Francesco Crispi" and "Crispi Glaviano, Francesco." In addition, terms referred to in entries that are also defined in this work are noted with the notation "(q.v.)" following the term.

All entries appear in the index, including cross-references from variations of names to the most commonly used form of the name. The index is especially useful for the terms that are not personal names. For example, anyone wanting to see all the Arbëresh writers in the text or all the writers of the Rilindja period could look under the entries for those terms in the index and be led to all entries in the main text with that information.

One problem that the author notes in the preface is that of accuracy. According to Elsie, "Primary sources for Albanian literature are frequently difficult and occasionally impossible to trace; and secondary sources . . . are eminently unreliable." A significant problem, he observes, is that titles and years of publication "contradict one another from source to source with an alarming regularity."

Entries vary in length but do not exceed two paragraphs. In addition to any relevant biographical information, the author's major works are included with their original title and place and date of publication, with the English title parenthetically noted. Many entries also include a short bibliography of works about the writer or subject, including those in Albanian, English, German, French, and other languages.

Most readers will be frustrated by the paucity of good English-language translations of the literary works cited. While Elsie provides basic information about many important Albanian literary figures, he does not include information about the availability or existence of English-language translations—good or bad—of their works. Thus the door to Albanian literature is only partially opened for those not reading Albanian.

In spite of these limitations, in the *Dictionary of Albanian Literature,* Elsie has done a remarkable job in providing an authoritative, comprehensive, and up-to-date work in an area that has traditionally been one of the most difficult literatures for the American reader to learn about.

Because this dictionary is accessible to the general reader, the volume is suitable for public libraries where patron interest in this area would warrant its inclusion. The Board recommends this work for the core collection of academic libraries.

A History of Bulgarian Literature, 1865–1944. Charles A. Moser. Mouton, 1972. hard. 1 vol. 282 pp. index. ISBN 90-2792-008-7. $53.50. history.
PG1001.M67 891.8′1′09

A History of Bulgarian Literature, 1865–1944 does what its title suggests: it traces the history of Bulgarian literature from its earliest times up to the Communist takeover in 1944. Moser, a professor of Slavic languages at George Washington University and the author of several texts on Russian literature, provides an accurate and lively treatment of this subject.

The work is divided into five major sections: "Old Bulgarian Literature," "The Bulgarian Renaissance," "The Post-Liberation Epoch," "The Age of Modernism and Individualism," and "From War to War (1917–1944)." The body of the text is roughly divided in half, with literature before 1896 covered in the first 119 pages and literature of the next 50 years covered in the remaining 131 pages. Moser states that this is "a division which in my opinion accurately reflects the literary—though not historical—value of works published before and after 1896."

With his lucid prose, Moser paints an interesting picture of Bulgarian literature in its historical context; he tells a story rather than compiling a list of names, dates, and works. The coverage of persons and themes varies with the degree of importance played over this time span. In his foreword, Moser notes that he has "tried not even to mention an author if I could not give him at least a paragraph which would convey a notion of his literary personality," and he is very faithful to this principle. Figures such as novelist Ivan Vazov (1850–1921)—considered Bulgaria's most important writer—and poet and dramatist Peyo Iavorov (1878–1914)—the most important exponent of Bulgarian Modernism—receive the extensive treatment they deserve; lesser figures such as Cerkovski receive a few paragraphs.

In addition to biographical and historical information, the author also provides what are assumed to be his own translations of excerpts of important works. Unfortunately, he does not include the original text, which is usually of greater interest to the user who is a specialist.

One other drawback is that the author's transliteration system is not explained in his foreword. While the system is rather simple to figure out for the speaker of Bulgarian, it may not be apparent to someone unfamiliar with the language. This becomes especially disconcerting when using the index, as some terms do not occur in the order one might expect. Outside of the transliteration problem, the index is very thorough, with ample and appropriate cross-references.

The book contains an excellent bibliography that is divided according to the five sections of the book. Each section includes not only works relevant to the general period covered but also works on specific writers. Most entries are for Bulgarian-language works, although there are few entries for works in other languages.

Although the coverage is only through 1944, "for the sake of completeness" the author includes brief descriptions in the foreword of the post-1944 careers of those writing before that time. At the time the book was published the author felt that a general summary of literary events in Bulgaria after 1944 should not be attempted, "since this period is still unfolding and cannot yet be considered objectively." Almost 20 years later, regrettably, there is still no source available in English that adequately covers the period after 1944.

Although *A History of Bulgarian Literature* is intended more for the specialist, the knowledgeable generalist can also profit from this volume. The Board recommends this work for the core collection of academic libraries.

The History of Polish Literature, 2d edition. Czeslaw Milosz. Univ. of California Pr., 1983. hard and soft. 1 vol. 583 pp. index. ISBN 0-520-04465-7 (hard); 0-520-04477-0 (soft). $37.50 (hard); $11.95 (soft). history.
PG7012.M48 891.8′5′09

The History of Polish Literature is the work of the eminently qualified and distinguished Nobel laureate for literature, Czeslaw Milosz. As the work of both a scholar of Polish literature and a poet and writer of remarkable talent, Milosz's compendium is all one would expect it to be: incisive, comprehensive, and authoritative. As one reviewer has previously noted, "No other study thus far, published in the West or in Poland, covers the span of a thousand years as completely and comprehensively as Milosz's work" (*Commonweal,* August 10, 1984, p. 446).

The book is divided chronologically into 11 major sections that reflect both literary and historical periods. Within each section are subsections covering major literary events and trends of the period as well as the major writers. The works of minor writers are also incorporated in the narrative text about the literary trends and events. Entries for minor writers range in length from a few sentences to several paragraphs. Entries for major writers (those who appear in their own subsection) vary in length from a few pages to 25 pages for the great nineteenth-century poet and writer Adam Mickiewicz. This varying coverage seems to reflect both the writer's actual stature in the field as well as Milosz's personal literary tastes.

Although the book is intended for the specialist—or someone very familiar with literary terminology—it can be used without difficulty by general audiences.

The index is one of the weak points of the volume and is mainly useful if you are looking for references to a writer or to a particular piece of literature. Someone looking for an explanation of *Arianism,* or another term specifically associated with Polish literature, will not be led to it through the index but must figure out in which major section the term appears, in this case "Humanism and Reformation."

The second edition differs from the first in that it contains a brief epilogue covering the 1960s and 1970s as well as some updating of the bibliography. Even with the epilogue, the book is still only comprehensive up through the mid-1960s. Notable writers after this period are mentioned in the epilogue, but there are no examples of their works with the accompanying textual translations, analyses, and criticism found in the earlier sections.

Milosz makes no attempt to provide information about the availability of English translations of the works mentioned, although there are perhaps more good English translations of Polish literature than of any other East European literature. *The Slavic Literatures* (now out-of-print), by Richard C. Lewanski, does provide this information through the early 1960s. To have a complete picture of Polish literature it would be necessary to acquire both titles.

The bibliography at the back of the volume, which is arranged chronologically using the same divisions as the main text, is very helpful to the researcher needing more in-depth information. Citations in the bibliography are predominantly to English-language sources.

This work is available in both hard and soft covers. The publisher has provided one particularly nice typographic feature which aids accessibility in the form of italicized headings, printed in the margins, which draw the readers' attention to writers, literary movements, and other topics of importance. These are very helpful for quickly locating information in the somewhat densely set text.

The History of Polish Literature is truly a work without equal in this area. The Board recommends this work for the core collection for academic libraries.

Modern Slavic Literatures: Bulgarian, Czechoslovak, Polish, Ukrainian, and Yugoslav Literatures, vol. 2. Vasa D. Mihailovich, ed. Ungar, 1976. hard. 1 vol. 720 pp. index. ISBN 0-8044-3175-2. $60. criticism.

PG501.M518 891.7′009

The compilers and editor of volume 2 of *Modern Slavic Literatures* have done a commendable job in bringing together criticism on the works of 196 major writers of the twentieth century who wrote or write in Bulgarian, Croatian, Czech, Macedonian, Polish, Serbian, Slovak, Slovenian, or Ukrainian—including natives of these lands and émigrés.

The compilers of each section are noted American, Canadian, and British scholars in their respective fields. In selecting writers for inclusion and the amount of space to be devoted to each literature, there were several criteria that guided the compilers. These included familiarity with and critical reputation of the writer in the West; continuity of critical interest in either the native country or in the West; and the availability of criticism of sufficiently high quality. In addition to these guidelines, each compiler was asked to "present at least three critical excerpts per writer and to stress major figures." With these limitations in mind, the coverage is very good.

As one would expect, truly major figures such as Andric, Capek, and Milosz are allotted more space in their respective literatures than are other writers. In the cases of Czechoslovakia and Yugoslavia, where writers are writing in more than one language, the representation of writers is very fair and indicative of the place of these literatures within the country's total literary context. For example, of the four languages and 47 writers represented in the Yugoslav section there are 20 Serbian, 16 Croatian, 7 Slovenian, and 4 Macedonian writers included.

One earlier review of the work observed that "the volume's worth lies not in breaking new ground or in offering necessarily coherent or complete pictures of the individual writers but rather in bringing together first-rate critical commentary from a wide variety of sources, much of it from Slavic languages themselves and presented here for the first time in English translation" (*World Literature Today,* Spring, 1977, p. 307).

The book is arranged first alphabetically by country; second alphabetically by writer; and finally, chronologically by the date the criticism was published. This arrangement makes the location of writers within the volume very easy, and it provides the reader with a perspective on the development of the particular writer's work.

In addition to the excellent arrangement of the text, the book also includes several very useful indexes. These include a "List of Authors Included, by Literature," in the front of the volume, and an index to critics at the back of the book.

Modern Slavic Literatures is now 15 years old and as such excludes newer writers who have recently gained importance or later and important works of writers who are included, such as those of Milan Kundera or Andrzej Kuśniewicz. In spite of this, the volume is very valuable for presenting a historical perspective for these writers through the words of their critics.

Modern Slavic Literatures is intended for a somewhat specialized audience. This volume will not be very helpful to anyone who does not have some previous knowledge of the writers and their works. However, public libraries that have English translations of at least some of the works of the writers included will want to acquire this work. The Board recommends this work for the core collections of public and academic libraries.

The Oxford History of Hungarian Literature: From the Earliest Times to the Present. Lóránt Czigany. Clarendon/Oxford, 1984. 1 vol. hard. 582 pp. appendix. index. ISBN 0-19-815781-9. $79. history.
PH3012.C94 894.511′09

Although written several years ago, Dr. Lóránt Czigany's *Oxford History of Hungarian Literature* is still the only work on Hungarian literature intended primarily for the English-speaking reader. While a few works in English do exist—such as *Hungarian Authors* (Albert Tezla, Harvard, 1964), *Introductory Bibliography to the Study of Hungarian Literature* (Albert Tezla, Harvard, 1964), and *A History of Hungarian Literature* (Tibor Klaniczay and H. H. Remak, eds., Ungar, 1984)—these are English translations of Hungarian works not originally aimed at a Western audience.

This excellent text is divided into 25 chapters, beginning with the origins of Hungarian literature and going through the postwar era. Approximately one-sixth of the text deals with literature before 1800; the remainder of the text is devoted to the nineteenth and twentieth centuries, a very equitable balance for most students of the subject.

As stated in the introduction, the author's aim in writing this book was twofold: to provide a work "as comprehensive as possible within the limits of space, for students of literature whose mastery of the language is not sufficient to study Hungarian literature in the original and . . . to serve as a guide to one aspect of Hungarian intellectual history for those whose interest in Hungary is broader than, but includes, its literature."

Czigany does a fine job of placing Hungarian literature into the context of religious, historical, social, and political conditions of the time—many of which may be unfamiliar to the average Western reader. All major writers are included and treated in some depth, while minor writers receive an appropriately shorter discussion. For example, the poet Sandór Petófi, whom Czigany compares in stature for Hungarians to Shakespeare for the English-speaking world, receives an entire chapter of coverage. In addition to providing biographical information about Petófi, the author outlines the plots of his major works, provides translations of small portions of a number of his works, and discusses a few of his many imitators.

One very notable feature of this work is the comparisons that the author makes of Hungarian writers with writers of other literatures. Petófi is compared with other Eastern European poets (Vazov, Mickiewicz, and Kollar), with other Hungarians writing during the same time (Vörösmarty), and with other Western poets (Byron and Shelley). It is this total attention to context that sets this work apart from most attempts to treat the history of a particular literature.

The author does not make assumptions about the reader's prior knowledge of the subject and does several things to make this text very accessible to the nonspecialist. There is a very helpful glossary of Hungarian words and less familiar terms and geographical names at the back of the book as well as a thorough index. The author also includes a good bibliography that not only contains supporting readings for each chapter but also provides information about Hungarian and English translations of works mentioned in each chapter.

A weak area of the book is its treatment of writers of the postwar era. The chapter on this period does, however, contain a section on the literature and literary figures of the Hungarian diaspora. Because very little has been written about Hungarian émigré writers, this is very useful.

The Oxford History of Hungarian Literature treats Hungarian literature within the context of European intellectual life. The Board recommends this work for the core collections of public and academic libraries.

Supplementary Titles

Comparative History of Slavic Literatures. Dmitrij Čiževskij. Vanderbilt Univ. Pr., 1971. soft. 1 vol. 225 pp. ISBN 0-8265-1159-7. $12.95. history.
PG501.C513 891.8

In the *Comparative History of Slavic Literature* the author "unfolds the development of Slavic literature against a background of succeeding literary periods, schools, and movements. . . . [Each chapter] establishes first the literary themes and style of a given period, and then examines the literary achievements of the various

Slavic peoples in relation to the general European literary trends and developments.

"A work such as this has long been overdue, for while there existed many histories of Slavic literature, none of them dealt with this subject from a strictly comparative point of view. . . . [Čiževskij] is the first scholar to approach his subject from a topical vantage point. . . . He has rendered an immeasurable service to the field of comparative literature and provided an indispensable tool to the graduate student and those involved in advanced work in Slavistics." (*Choice,* December 1971, p. 1334)

"Despite all of the limitations characteristic of any pioneering work, this book is an ambitious step forward in the comparative presentation of Slavic literatures. Being by nature an observant comparatist, Čiževskij is able throughout his study to demonstrate a profound understanding of his subject and of all its complexities; he shows his keen appreciation of comparative history's timelessness which obliges the reader to reconsider some new questions. . . . Čiževskij's study of the baroque is most enlightening and original. . . . The ambitious treatment of material in a limited space of some 225 pages is impressive. . . . The author's tone of writing is cautious and modest . . . [and his] many astute observations on style and characterizations of various literary periods are of the greatest interest and value." (*MLJ,* January 1973, p. 64)

Board's recommendation: Academic libraries.

Czech Literature. Arne Novák; William E. Harkins, ed. Michigan Slavic Publications, Univ. of Michigan Pr., 1976. hard. 1 vol. 375 pp. ISBN 0-930042-64-6. $15. encyclopedia.
PG5001.N6313 891.8′6′09

"There are precious few studies in English of Czech literature, and . . . practically no monographs devoted to individual authors. Given this state of affairs, one can only greet [*Czech Literature*] with mixed feelings: on the one hand, there is gratitude for the attempted panorama; on the other, frustration at the inevitable ellipsis. . . . *Czech Literature* can only stand as a fair interim measure.

"In his seven chapters Novák traces the growth of Czech literature from the nineteenth century to the twentieth, dealing in movements and literary fashions rather than in straight chronology. Consequently, he obviates pedantry but perhaps spreads his enthusiasm too evenly. As is admitted in a footnote, with a little longer to live Novák may have given more weight to Hašek and Čapek. Harkin's supplement covering the period from 1946–74 is balanced and fairly comprehensive. . . . Taken as a whole, the volume is a reasonable starting point for anyone interested in Czech literature." (*WLT,* Spring 1977, p. 300)

Also reviewed in: *LR,* Summer 1977, p. 165; *TLS,* August 19, 1977, p. 1012.

Board's recommendation: Academic libraries.

Karla Hahn

Ecology

Ecology is a diverse and interdisciplinary field encompassing many other fields such as biology, science and technology, and public policy. The works reviewed in this section can assist the biologist, the nuclear technologist, or the layperson interested in the environmental threats posed by various human activities. The diversity of the subject matter and reading levels poses a challenge to the collection-development librarian. It is important that the core reference collection reflect the needs of expert and novice users alike.

Also, because ecology is a young and developing field, maintaining the currency of the materials in the core collection is particularly important. Materials become dated relatively quickly, and it is necessary to stay aware of the most recent editions and purchase titles that are more likely to enjoy some longevity.

As in most scientific fields, technical jargon is often a problem. Several dictionaries should be included in the collection to aid the user who is not familiar with this language. Such works must be comprehensive in their scope and clear in the definitions they offer.

Handbooks and encyclopedias provide information on theoretical concepts or baseline data. These may be comprehensive in their coverage, like the *McGraw-Hill*

Core Titles

	PUBLIC	ACADEMIC	SCHOOL
Dictionary of Energy, 2d edition Slesser, Malcom, ed. Nichols, 1988		✦	
A Dictionary of the Environment, 3d edition Allaby, Michael. New York Univ. Pr., 1989		✦	
The United States Energy Atlas, 2d edition Cuff, David J., and William J. Young. Macmillan, 1986	✦	✦	✦

Encyclopedia of Environmental Science (now out of print), which examines several environmental issues and explains many broad ecological topics. Also important to the collection are works that are narrower in focus, such as DANGEROUS PROPERTIES OF INDUSTRIAL MATERIALS, HAZARDOUS SUBSTANCES, and TOXIC AND HAZARDOUS MATERIALS, which are among the supplementary titles in this category.

A useful directory to the field is the *Conservation Directory: A List of Organizations, Agencies, and Officials Connected with Natural Resource Use and Management* (National Wildlife Federation, 1987). This work includes both U.S. and Canadian agencies and officials, sources of audiovisual materials, and a list of national parks and wildlife refuges.

Core Titles

Dictionary of Energy, 2d edition. Malcolm Slesser, ed. Nichols, 1988. hard. 1 vol. 300 pp. illus. ISBN 0-89397-320-3. $57.50. dictionary.
TJ163.16.05 621.042′03′21

An updated version of the first edition published in 1983, the *Dictionary of Energy* draws on the works of specialists from the disciplines of nuclear energy, engineering, physics, chemistry, economics, ecology, and bioenergy. It is the expertise of the contributors, combined with Malcolm Slesser's reputation as a leading British chemical engineer, that lends authority to a work broad in scope, yet accessible to readers from a variety of backgrounds.

The emphasis of the work is on the interdisciplinary nature of the field of energy research. As such, it is designed to provide access for specialists to terms from fields outside their expertise. As a result, it is also an excellent work for students or lay users, since no particular familiarity with any of the specific subjects is assumed. However, terms available in standard dictionaries are sometimes excluded.

This concise volume is well organized and convenient to use. Each definition begins with the term in boldface type, which makes for easy reading. The diagrams are well drafted, making them clear and informative, although some diagrams are not titled, and a few do not appear on the same page as the relevant entry.

Over 1,000 terms are defined; each definition identifies the writer. As an additional aid to the reader, words defined elsewhere in the dictionary are indicated with an asterisk. Entries cover the entire range of the discipline and include both general and specific terms. For instance, the explanation for the word *capital* is lucid enough for the engineer as well as the economist. Similarly, the economist will be able to understand the definition for the *Haber process.* The clarity of definitions allows both specialists and laypersons to access vocabulary from fields related to energy.

Entries vary in length from one sentence to a column or more. The definition for *nuclear reactor* is over nine pages long and includes ten diagrams. In contrast, *ethyne* is defined in one line. Much of the terminology is illustrated with detailed but concise diagrams, and equations are provided as needed. Unfortunately, pronunciation is not provided, but this is a common omission in technical dictionaries.

The most recent edition of the *Dictionary of Energy* differs from the previous edition not in its increased length but in its revision of the entries. In fact, this newer edition is only one page longer than its predecessor. However, updating and revision of the entries have made this edition even more comprehensive than the first.

Compared to A DICTIONARY OF THE ENVIRONMENT, the *Dictionary of Energy* includes more technological and economics terminology and fewer terms from the basic sciences. This reference tool also makes effective use of diagrams, a technique particularly helpful to the nonspecialist. The diversity of terminology is impressive, and thanks to the contributors, the quality of the definitions offered is consistently high. The Board recommends this work for the core collection of academic libraries.

A Dictionary of the Environment, 3d edition. Michael Allaby. New York Univ. Pr., 1989. hard. 1 vol. 304 pp. ISBN 0-8147-0591-X. $70. dictionary.
QH540.4A44 508.03′21

This work, by the author of a variety of works on the subject of ecology and natural history, represents a remarkable effort to compile the terminology of a young and still rapidly changing discipline.

Most entries are drawn from the basic sciences—but biology and geology are particularly well represented. More nuclear energy terms have been added since the previous edition. One can locate basic statistical terms such as *logarithmic mean* or *classificatory nomenclature* or more complicated terms such as the *family Hepaticae.* This technical dictionary also includes some rather unusual entries. For example, entries exist for Swiss architect and city planner Charles Edouard Jeanneret and for literary works such as the *Tragedy of Commons,* a drama with an ecological theme.

Most definitions are fairly technical, which makes this work most useful to the reader with some familiarity with scientific terminology. Definitions also tend to be fairly brief, usually only a sentence or two. There are no illustrations.

The dictionary has several features that are designed to enhance its accessibility. One particularly useful feature is the inclusion of abbreviations, particularly common chemical abbreviations, and acronyms such as *JOIDES,* the Joint Oceanographic Institutions for Deep Earth Sampling. This type of information is commonly excluded from technical dictionaries. The numerous cross-references are also helpful. Equations are included where appropriate.

A Dictionary of the Environment is an invaluable addition to the ecology section of any reference collection. Although somewhat technical in nature, this reference tool provides broad coverage of many of the subdisciplines of the field. The Board recommends this work for the core collection of academic libraries.

The United States Energy Atlas, 2d edition. David J. Cuff and William J. Young. Macmillan, 1986. hard. 1 vol. 387 pp. illus. appendix. index. ISBN 0-02-691240-6. $100. atlas.
TJ163.25U6C83 333.79′0973

Compiled from government documents by two energy resource specialists from the faculty of Temple University, this reference work combines graphic and textual information with maps to provide the reader with a variety of data about energy resources. It is composed of three parts: "Nonrenewable Resources," "Renewable Resources," and "Overview of Energy Resources and Issues." Included are estimates of the amounts and geographic locations of crude oil, coal, natural gas, radioactive fuels, geothermal resources, and hydroelectric potential. All material is supported with source citations.

The great strength of this work lies in its ability to combine the text, maps, and figures to make the information accessible and comparable. For example, the chapter on crude oil reserves provides a written explanation on the way crude oil is recovered, photos of drilling operations, a diagram of the products of the refinery process, tables of crude oil production by country, bar charts of reserves versus production, and maps of recovery rates in the United States by state. The maps and charts are colored to highlight various data. The legends and figure headings are clear and self-explanatory, and the text is well positioned to correspond to the figures. The index allows the reader to easily identify the location of the desired information.

The organization of the various sections is logical. The first section on nonrenewable resources covers coal, oil and gas, oil shales and tar sands, nuclear fuels, and geothermal sources. The renewable energy sources section covers solar radiation, wind, hydroelectric power, energy from the ocean, and biomass (the use of biological materials—generally plant life—to generate energy). The final section offers analysis of issues related to energy resource management. All of the information provided is well supported by an introduction explaining the purpose and use of the work along with some background on interpreting charts and tables. A glossary of basic terminology is also included in one of the appendixes.

The straightforward organization and diverse format make this work accessible to the layperson or student, although the attention to detail makes the work equally useful to the specialist.

However, the *Energy Atlas* does not merely present information in a palatable format, it also provides analysis of the amounts and locations of energy resources. Furthermore, this book explains the uncertainties involved in determining the quantities of fuels, emphasizes the geographic parameters that affect utilization of renewable resources, and attempts to provide both national and regional overviews of the energy resources available in the United States. These features greatly increase the value of the atlas by providing a broad context for the information presented.

The United States Energy Atlas is a unique reference source providing information of general usefulness in a variety of formats. As such it provides an uncommon viewpoint on energy information and issues. The Board recommends this work for the core collections of public, academic, and school libraries.

Supplementary Titles

Dangerous Properties of Industrial Materials, 7th edition. N. Irving Sax and Richard J. Lewis, Sr. Van Nostrand Reinhold, 1988. hard. 3 vols. 4,000 pp. illus. index. ISBN 0-442-28020-3 (set). $395 (set). handbook.
T55.3.H353 604.7

See Medicine and Dentistry.

Hazardous Substances: A Reference. Melvin Berger. Enslow, 1986. soft. 1 vol. 128 pp. ISBN 0-89490-116-8. $15.95. dictionary.
RA1193.B475 604.7

Hazardous Substances is a "guide to more than 230 substances that threaten life by contaminating food and the environment. What these are and how they affect the human body and our planet is explained.

"A straightforward, jargon-free introduction explains the scope and arrangement of the book, and there is a glossary of often-used terms in the entries. Although some terms may seem too common to need such explanation (cancer, diarrhea, birth defect, law, risk), the compiler takes no chance that the annotations will be misunderstood. Other terms (parts per billion—ppb, Pollution Standard Index—PSI, structure-activity relationship, nematocide) are less familiar and need defining. . . . The dictionary itself has cross-references from acronyms and alternative names. . . . Drugs are not included." (*BL,* November 15, 1986, p. 494)

Also reviewed in: *ARBA,* 1987, p. 570; *ASBYP,* Spring 1987, p. 12; *B Rpt,* March 1987, p. 49; *SLJ,* May 1987, p. 24; *VOYA,* April 1987, p. 51.

Board's recommendation: Public and academic libraries.

Toxic & Hazardous Materials: A Sourcebook and Guide to Information Sources. James K. Webster, ed. Greenwood, 1987. hard. 1 vol. 430 pp. index. ISBN 0-313-24575-4. $49.95. bibliography.
Z7914.S19T69 016.3631'7

This work lists "monographs, periodicals, newsletters, loose-leaf services, reports and documents, conference proceedings, indexes, audiovisual materials, databases, associations, government agencies, research organizations, libraries, and reviews. . . . Topics covered in the chapters include effects of hazardous materials on the air, land, and water; acid rain; health; disposal of wastes; radioactive materials; laws and regulations; transportation; and accidents, spills, and cleanup.

"A typical chapter begins with a one- to three-page introduction followed by lists of materials under such groupings as books, periodicals, abstracts, reviews, etc. . . . Each list is presented alphabetically by title or author, with complete bibliographic information for each citation, including frequency and length of publication. Citations for associations, government agencies, etc., provide complete addresses and telephone numbers. Most include a brief annotation. . . . Access to citations is through a detailed index that is organized alphabetically by title of the resources cited in the text, with a few subject entries added. . . . [The book] will be a valuable collection-development tool and will prove useful to both the educated novice and specialist." (*BL,* August 1987, p. 1731)

Also reviewed in: *ARBA,* 1988, p. 604; *Choice,* June 1987, p. 1539; *LJ,* April 15, 1988, p. 34; *R&R Bk N,* Summer 1987, p. 35.

Board's recommendation: Academic libraries.

New and Noteworthy

Atlas of Environmental Issues. Dr. Nick Middleton. Facts On File, 1989. hard. 1 vol. 64 pp. ISBN 0-8160-2023-X. $16.95. atlas.
QH75.M486 363.7

The *Atlas of Environmental Issues* "is an in-depth analysis of today's major environmental issues. This *Atlas* provides an understanding of how human activities—urban, industrial, agricultural, and others—affect the world's vegetation, soils, water and animals, as well as the very air we breathe. . . . [This work covers] the environmental issues that will be of increasing importance to future generations." (Excerpted from publisher's announcement)

The Atlas of the Living World. David Attenborough et al. Houghton Mifflin, 1989. hard. 1 vol. 220 pp. illus. index. ISBN 0-395-49481-8. $39.95. atlas.
G1046.C1A7 574.9'022

The Atlas of the Living World "examine[s] the physical, biological, and environmental processes that shape the living world and speculates on what changes will take place in the future. The book is organized in five main sections treating the environment and human impact on it. Within these main sections, narrower topics are surveyed in two-page chapters. Some of the topics include the origins of life, the ice ages, origins of agriculture, tropical rain forests, acid rain, and AIDS." (*BL,* January 1, 1990, p. 242)

The Atmosphere Crisis: The Greenhouse Effect and Ozone Depletion. Eleanor Goldstein et al., eds. Social Issues Resource series, 1989. looseleaf binding. 1 vol. index. ISBN 0-89777-841-3. $80. handbook.
TD883 363.739

"*The Atmosphere Crisis* contains more than 100 reprints [from newspapers and popular periodicals], most from 1988 and 1989, that cover the scientific, sociological, political, and medical aspects of the greenhouse effect and ozone depletion. . . . The newspapers represent a cross-section of the U.S., including New York City, Los Angeles, Fort Lauderdale, Anchorage, and Omaha. SIRS intends to publish annual supplements of 20 articles 'as long as the crisis remains.' The source of each article is identified with the title and date of the periodical and pagination." (*BL,* November 1, 1989, p. 599)

Priscilla Cheng Geahigan

Economics

See also Business

"You cannot understand anything in economics until you have already understood it all" is a statement that describes how most of us feel about economics. The underlying reason for this may have been given in 1938 by Barbara Wootton, a British economist, when she said, "What is lacking [in economics] is any effective means of communication between abstract theory and concrete application." Fortunately, the situation has improved since then. We now see more books on the topic of applied economics and more television programs on the topics of business and economics. Elementary schools are even offering class projects on subjects that relate to economics.

Fortunately, an ample number of economics reference sources—in print and in computerized format—are also available. Printed sources include single or multivolume encyclopedias, dictionaries, indexes, and handbooks. Computerized sources include bibliographical data bases such as the *Economic Literature Index,* which covers the years from 1969 to the present, and numerical data bases such as *Econbase: Time Series and Forecasts,* which is prepared by the WEFA Group and contains historical data back to 1948. Like many data bases in other subject areas, economics data bases can be accessed on-line for a fee and may soon be available on a compact disk format for a fixed-price subscription.

What would constitute a good core collection in economics? The sources recommended in the core review section are exemplary print titles. They range from a good basic dictionary, the DICTIONARY OF BUSINESS AND ECONOMICS, to definitive encyclopedias such as the NEW PALGRAVE: A DICTIONARY OF ECONOMICS. A good alternative dictionary is the second edition of the MCGRAW-HILL DICTIONARY OF MODERN ECONOMICS; it is a well-written dictionary with precise and useful definitions. Unfortunately, the *American Dictionary of Economics* (Douglas A. L. Auld, Facts On File, 1983), a fine introductory dictionary, and *Economics Dictionary* (Donald W. Moffat, Elsevier Science, 1983) are now out of print and would have to be obtained through out-of-print sources.

The annual *Index of Economic Articles* (American Economic Assn.) remains an important acquisition for academic libraries, though most of its volumes are now out of print. This index is a comprehensive source that includes not only articles in journals and periodicals but also chapters in anthologies and collective works in the field of economics. One drawback of this index is that it is updated rather infrequently, at three- to four-year intervals. For more recent information, users can consult the *Economic Literature Index* data base, which is the on-line counterpart of the *Index of Economic Articles.*

Core Titles

	PUBLIC	ACADEMIC	SCHOOL
Dictionary of Business and Economics, rev. and exp. edition Ammer, Christine, and Dean S. Ammer. Macmillan/Free Pr., 1984	✦	✦	
Encyclopedia of American Economic History: Studies of the Principal Movements and Ideas, 3 vols. Porter, Glenn, ed. Scribner, 1980	✦	✦	✦
Encyclopedia of Economics Greenwald, Douglas, ed. in chief. McGraw-Hill, 1982	✦	✦	
Handbook of United States Economic and Financial Indicators O'Hara, Frederick M., Jr., and Robert Sicignano. Greenwood, 1985.	✦	✦	
New Palgrave: A Dictionary of Economics, 4 vols. Eatwell, John, Murray Milgate, and Peter Newman. Stockton, 1987.		✦	

Any library collection should supplement its economic reference sources with an introductory book that explains basic economic concepts for the general public. Any classic college textbook on that level would be an excellent choice.

Core Titles

Dictionary of Business and Economics, rev. and exp. edition. Christine Ammer and Dean S. Ammer. Macmillan/Free Pr., 1984. 1 vol. hard and soft. 507 pp. illus. ISBN 0-02-900790-9. $40 (hard); $22.95 (soft). dictionary.
HB61.A53 330.03′21

This 1984 edition of the *Dictionary of Business and Economics* is a revised and expanded version of the 1977 edition. As implied by the title, the entries in this dictionary cover subject areas in both business and economics. Short biographies of prominent economists, but not business people, are also included.

This work is clearly written and well organized. Topics are fully explored through related entries. For example, when looking under the entry for *stock,* the user will find full-paragraph subentries for the following: *stock certificate* (accompanied by a reproduction of a stock certificate), *stock clearing corporation, stock dividend,* a rather lengthy discussion of *stock exchange* (including a table listing leading North American exchanges by name and location), and *stock market.* The dictionary also supplies many cross-references. The entry for *stockbroker* directs the reader to *broker; stock index* to *average;* and *stock split* to *split.* Additional "see also" references are sometimes provided. For instance, within the discussion of *stock exchange,* readers are directed to other entries, such as *floor traders, pure competition, third market, New York Stock Exchange, American Stock Exchange, commodity exchange, options exchange, over-the-counter market, security,* and *stock clearing corporation.*

Because this reference work was published in the first half of the 1980s, no entries are included for more recent economic activities, such as leveraged buyouts of corporations, a term that came into popular use in the second half of the decade.

A three-page selected bibliography is included at the end of the book listing classic works in business and economics.

With its straightforward approach and clearly illustrated charts, tables, and graphs, the *Dictionary of Business and Economics* may be useful in school libraries. The Board recommends this work for the core collections of public and academic libraries.

Encyclopedia of American Economic History: Studies of the Principal Movements and Ideas. Glenn Porter, ed. Scribner, 1980. hard. 3 vols. illus. appendix. index. ISBN 0-684-16271-7 (set). $250 (set). encyclopedia.
HC103.E52 330.9′73

The preface of the *Encyclopedia of American Economic History* states that this work attempts to make available the views of many specialists, in more or less cohesive form, and assemble the "collective American economic experience as it is understood in the latter part of the 1970s." The encyclopedia contains 72 signed essays on major economic and related topics in American social history. The length of the essays ranges from 6 pages ("Business Cycles, Panics, and Depressions") to 30 pages ("Urbanization"); 16 pages is the average length. These essays are the work of a panel of experts in each subject field, mostly professors in economics or history. The essay "Business Cycles, Panics, and Depressions," written by Geoffrey H. Moore, author of *Business Cycle Indicators,* illustrates the exemplary matches of topics and contributors. Another example can be found in the essay "Socialism," contributed by the late Michael Harrington, a major figure in American socialism. A list of contributors with their credentials is included at the end of volume 3.

This three-volume encyclopedia is divided into five parts. Part 1, "The Historiography of American Economic History," contains an introductory essay on this topic. Part 2, "The Chronology of American Economic History," provides brief overviews of major economic trends within the boundaries of political history. Part 3, "The Framework of American Economic Growth," discusses the economic growth related to business cycles, productivity, population, prices and wages, foreign trade, money supply, and so forth. Part 4, "The Institutional Framework," covers the development of labor organizations, farmers' movements, and the rise and evolution of big business. Part 5, "The Social Framework," concentrates on changing social issues with article topics ranging from bureaucracy, family, women, blacks, to poverty.

The detailed index, contained in volume 3, is 26 pages long. Because the work is a collection of individual essays, the index helps to connect various pieces of information on similar topics spread out over many pages. However, the pages are numbered consecutively throughout all three volumes, and the user will encounter the usual problems in determining in which volume a particular topic appears. Bibliographic references in each essay provide sources for further research.

Contributors to the *Encyclopedia of American Economic History* were instructed to write for the "educated, intelligent layman, not just for the specialist," and the editor and his advisory board have done an admirable job organizing the material to fulfill this goal.

The Board recommends this work for the core collections of public, academic, and school libraries.

Encyclopedia of Economics. Douglas Greenwald, ed. in chief. McGraw-Hill, 1982. hard. 1 vol. 1,070 pp. illus. appendixes. indexes. ISBN 0-07-024367-0. $79.95. encyclopedia.
HB61.E55 330.03'21

Douglas Greenwald, the editor of the *Encyclopedia of Economics,* also edited the popular McGRAW-HILL DICTIONARY OF MODERN ECONOMICS. This one-volume encyclopedia includes 303 entries by 178 contributors from academia, business, and government. All entries are signed. A listing of all contributors with their qualifications is given at the beginning of the book. The encyclopedia covers subjects from the related fields of economics, econometrics, and statistics. The advantage of the encyclopedia approach over the dictionary format is in the greater scope of information provided. For instance, the term *commercial paper* yields a 20-line explanation in the McGRAW-HILL DICTIONARY OF MODERN ECONOMICS. In this encyclopedia, however, a user looking for the same term will find a three-page essay entitled "Financial Instruments," which includes not only a 10-line paragraph on commercial paper but also provides users with information pertaining to how commercial paper relates to other kinds of financial instruments.

Although no biographical articles are included in this encyclopedia, a detailed "Name Index" at the end of the book will lead readers to articles mentioning specific economists or statisticians (for example, the index entry for *John Maynard Keynes* shows that he is mentioned in 35 entries in this work). A comprehensive subject index is also included. Each essay contains bibliographical references that will provide useful sources for further research.

The encyclopedia has two appendixes that contribute to its accessibility. Appendix 1, "Classification of Articles by Economic Fields," groups all articles into subject categories such as economic growth, monetary and fiscal theory, and so on. Appendix 2, "A Time Table of Economic Events, Technological Developments, Financial Developments, and Economic Thought," dates notable events throughout history (for example, the first financial development cited is the use of metal coins in 700 B.C., around the time of Homer).

A collection of well-written, concise essays make up the *Encyclopedia of Economics.* Although contributors were instructed to write for a graduate-level audience, the complexity of the final work varies. Most entries, however, can be easily understood by undergraduate college students.

The Board recommends this work for the core collection of public and academic libraries.

Handbook of United States Economic and Financial Indicators. Frederick M. O'Hara, Jr., and Robert Sicignano. Greenwood, 1985. hard. 224 pp. appendixes. indexes. ISBN 0-313-23954-1. $38.95. handbook.
HC106.8.047 330.973

The *Handbook of United States Economic and Financial Indicators* helps users identify economic trends that will help them evaluate U.S. economic activity. An indicator is defined as "any standard measure of economic activity that reveals to the user where it is heading in the future" (preface). Author Frederick O'Hara, Jr., is a consultant in technical communication; Robert Sicignano is a business and industry librarian. The two authors examined 126 printed sources published by the government and profit and nonprofit agencies. On-line sources are not included. Over 200 indicator entries ranging from *gross national product* to *appliance factory sales* to *Standard & Poor's 500 dividend-price ratio* have been selected for inclusion.

The handbook is arranged alphabetically by indicator, with entries varying from one-half to one and one-half pages in length. Each entry encompasses several sections, including the name and a brief description of the indicator, an explanation of how the data are derived, a short suggestion on how the information could be used, the publisher and source of the indicator, the announcement frequency, and a "Cumulations" section that includes other sources that reprint the information or provide the data in various cumulated frequencies. Most of these cumulation sections have two subsections, "Tables" and "Graphs." A third subsection, "Projections," is included when available. Almost all entries cite articles or book chapters that give further information.

There are three appendixes: "Nonquantitative Indicators," "Abbreviations List and Guide to Sources," and "List of Compilers of Indicators." The "Nonquantitative Indicators" appendix provides information for some tongue-in-cheek indicators (such as the *hemline index*) included in popular industry literature. The other two appendixes provide further information for users who wish to contact the agencies that originated the indicator data. At the end of the book, all the indicators are indexed under broad subject categories such as business, employment, stocks, and transportation.

This handbook is especially useful for novices. The descriptions within each entry will also be valuable to librarians who are unfamiliar with economic and financial concepts. First-time users, however, will have to become accustomed to the book's format. Because all lines and sections within each entry start flush with the margin, with no spaces used to separate sections, the reader may have some difficulty differentiating one type of material from another.

The *Handbook of United States Economic and Financial Indicators* has some minor drawbacks. Although each "Cumulations" section lists sources that enable the reader to access data, specific pages, sections, and issues are not given. Also, some information has changed since its publication in 1985. For instance, *Dun's Business Month* is now simply called *Business Month.* Dun & Bradstreet has since added *Business Starts Record* as a companion series to its *Business Failure Record.* Finally, a major series covering five separate titles, the *Economic Indicators of the Farm Sector,* has regrettably not been included in the listing of sources. However, the book will be especially helpful for libraries in which general reference staff answer business and economics questions.

Despite these few drawbacks, the Board recommends the *Handbook of United States Economic and Financial Indicators* for the core collections of public and academic libraries.

New Palgrave: A Dictionary of Economics. John Eatwell, Murray Milgate, and Peter Newman. Stockton, 1987. hard. 4 volumes. 1,025 pp. appendixes. ISBN 0-935859-10-1. $750. dictionary.
HB61.N49 330.03'21

The *New Palgrave: A Dictionary of Economics* is named for R. H. Inglis Palgrave, who was the joint editor of *The Economist* from 1877 to 1883. He was also the author of the *Dictionary of Political Economy* published between 1894 and 1899, which was later revised by Henry Higgs and published during the years 1923 and 1926 as *Palgrave's Dictionary of Political Economy.* The *New Palgrave* is intended to succeed these two works.

The *New Palgrave* was coedited by John Eatwell of Trinity College, Cambridge; Murray Milgate of Harvard University; and Peter Newman of Johns Hopkins University. The completion of this work was a four-year endeavor for the editors, who assembled a distinguished and knowledgeable group of more than 900 contributors, including 12 Nobel Prize–winning economists. The four-volume set covers a wide array of subjects, including contemporary and historic economic thought, theories, controversies, and methods. According to the editor's preface, they have aimed at "reasonably complete coverage of the important economists who have written primarily in English, especially in

Britain itself, and a substantial treatment of major economists who have written in other languages." Of the 1,261 subject essays, 50 are reprinted from the earlier *Palgrave's Dictionary.* Another 655 entries are biographies of eminent economists (to be included, living economists had to be 70 years of age before January 1, 1986). With few exceptions, all entries include a listing of bibliographic sources, some very lengthy. In addition, 450 cross-references direct readers to related terms discussed within the text of entries but having no direct coverage. There is a subject index, but not all of the cross-references are included therein.

It is misleading to call the *New Palgrave* a dictionary; it is actually an encyclopedia. The text comprises essays that vary widely in both content and length and demonstrate a variety of styles and approaches. Most entries give a thorough discussion of a subject rather than a brief definition. The editors state that they "have tried to capture diversity and vivacity of view by having multiple entries, under similar but different titles." The intention was "to obtain essays that present the results and methods of research with fairness and accuracy, but not necessarily from a 'balanced' point of view." This means that two essays—each written from a different perspective—might be included on related topics. For example, the entry on *arbitrage* is written by the author of the theory, while the entry on *arbitrage pricing theory* is written by a critic. However, both entries cover essentially the same ground. Readers must be sophisticated enough, therefore, to draw their own "balanced" conclusions. Although some of these essays present advanced views in a manner that nonspecialists can understand, many are written with technical and mathematical symbols as well as terminology that requires a fair level of economic expertise. The *New Palgrave* is not a source for students wanting a simple explanation of gross national product but rather is intended primarily for researchers.

The Board recommends this work for the core collection of academic libraries.

Supplementary Titles

McGraw-Hill Dictionary of Modern Economics: A Handbook of Terms and Organizations, 3d edition. Douglas Greenwald et al. McGraw-Hill, 1983. hard. 1 vol. 656 pp. ISBN 0-07-024376-X. $57.50. dictionary.
HB61.M3 330.0321

"With a business orientation, this new edition [of the *McGraw-Hill Dictionary of Modern Economics*] has reworked some of the 1,300 definitions of the first and added about 125 new terms, mostly reflecting the econometric directions of much current economic thinking. . . . [Included also is a] description of approximately 225 public agencies, associations, and private organizations in a separate section.

"[This work] has become a standard reference tool. . . . Very useful are the many graphs and tables. The suggestions for further reading at the end of many definitions are invaluable. . . . No reference collection can afford to be without this new edition." (*Choice,* October 1973, p. 1168)

Also reviewed in: *ARBA,* 1984, p. 350; *BL,* April 15, 1984, p. 1177; *Bus W,* April 18, 1983, p. 114; *Choice,* September 1983, p. 57; *LJ,* December 15, 1973, p. 3623; *PAR,* November 1983, p. 568; *TES,* October 7, 1983, p. 27.

Board's recommendation: Public and academic libraries.

New and Noteworthy

Directory of Economic Institutions. Forrest Capie, ed. Stockton, 1990. hard. 1 vol. 480 pp. ISBN 0-935859-41-1. $90. directory.
HB74.5.C37 330

"*The Directory of Economic Institutions* is a comprehensive guide that enables you to readily locate a wide variety of information about economic institutions throughout the world. . . . [This work] is arranged alphabetically by country to make . . . [it] geographically comprehensive. All information was obtained directly from the institutions themselves." (Excerpted from publisher's announcement)

The Handbook of Financial Market Indexes, Averages, and Indicators. Howard M. Berlin. Business One Irwin, 1990. hard. 1 vol. 262 pp. illus. index. ISBN 1-55623-125-3. $65. handbook.
HG4636.B49 332.63'222

The Handbook of Financial Market Indexes, Averages, and Indicators includes "descriptions for more than 200 financial market averages and indexes from over 24 countries. For each index there is an easy-to-understand description of one to several paragraphs in length. . . . In addition, graphs and tables are used liberally. . . . Sources for every table and graph are given. In addition to these indexes there is a chapter on miscellaneous financial indexes, averages, and indicators." (*BL,* July 1990, p. 2116)

Nobel Laureates in Economic Sciences: A Biographical Dictionary. Bernard S. Katz, ed. Garland, 1989. hard. 1 vol. 339 pp. index. ISBN 0-8240-5742-2. $75. biographical dictionary.
HB101 330.092

Nobel Laureates in Economic Sciences contains alphabetical entries of "10–15 pages in length. They give biographical information on the winner and attempt to explain the theory for which the prize was given. The signed articles include a selected bibliography of works by and about the laureate. A name index concludes the volume." (*BL,* January 1, 1990, p. 948)

World Economic Data. ABC-Clio, 1989. hard. 1 vol. 240 pp. ISBN 0-87436-273-3. $29.95. handbook.
HC59.W643 330.904

"*The World Economic Data* volume lists country data (including budgets, GNP, imports/exports, labor, tourism, trade, balance of payments, industrial and agricultural products, and natural resources) and information on employment, monetary reserves, stocks/bonds, gold, banking, inflation, and trade. It contains a glossary. . . . Countries [are listed] alphabetically and [the work] includes a bibliography." (*B Rpt,* May/June 1990, p. 61)

Jeris Cassel

Education

A core collection on the subject of education must meet the needs of a diverse clientele—individuals working and studying in the field of education as well as individuals seeking further or alternative forms of education for themselves or others.

Sources that identify the concepts, terms, jargon, and trends in education are especially important to students and professionals in education, whereas descriptive guides to colleges or specialized schools—such as AMERICAN UNIVERSITIES AND COLLEGES or THE COLLEGE BLUE BOOK—are demanded by prospective college students on the undergraduate and graduate level. Guides to correspondence courses or occupational training schools are needed by individuals exploring options other than the traditional four-year higher education institutions. Among the titles in this field are THE MACMILLAN GUIDE TO CORRESPONDENCE STUDY and OCCUPATIONAL EDUCATION (part of THE COLLEGE BLUE BOOK). The parents of elementary and secondary school–age children want resources when they seek alternative educational institutions or different educational environmental settings for their children. These users might consult the HANDBOOK OF PRIVATE SCHOOLS or PETERSON'S GUIDE TO INDEPENDENT SECONDARY SCHOOLS. This section describes and evaluates these and other sources appropriate to meet the needs of such a varied group of patrons.

Other sources important to a core collection, are not actually reviewed in these pages but should be considered by the librarian. These include indexes to current literature in the field of education and related fields needed by students, professionals, school board members, and other interested individuals. The standard *Education Index,* indexing yearbooks and over 300 periodicals, is recommended as a core item for academic, public, and school libraries. *Current Index to Journals in Education,* indexing over 700 periodicals in education and related fields, is recommended as a core item for academic libraries. Two directories also belong in core collections. They are the annual *The Directory for Exceptional Children: A Listing of Educational and Training Facilities,* recommended for public libraries, and *The HEP Higher Education Directory,* recommended for public and academic libraries. A useful supplement to these works in the more specialized area of testing is the *Directory of Selected National Testing Programs.*

Core Titles

	PUBLIC	ACADEMIC	SCHOOL
American Educators' Encyclopedia Dejnozka, Edward., and David E. Kapel. Greenwood, 1982		✦	
American Universities and Colleges, 13th edition American Council on Education, comp. and ed. Walter de Gruyter, 1987	✦	✦	✦
Barron's Profiles of American Colleges: Descriptions of the Colleges, 17th edition College Division of Barron's Educational series, comp. and ed. Barron's, 1990	✦	✦	✦
The College Blue Book, 22d edition, 5 vols. Macmillan, 1989	✦	✦	✦
The College Cost Book College Board, annual	✦		✦
The College Handbook, 1990–1991, 27th edition, 1 vol., 2 suppls. College Board, 1990	✦		✦
Comparative Guide to American Colleges for Students, Parents and Counselors, 14th edition Cass, James, and Max Birnbaum. HarperCollins, 1989	✦	✦	✦
Encyclopedia of Educational Research, 5th edition, 4 vols. Mitzel, Harold E., et al., eds. Free Pr., 1982		✦	
Guide to American Graduate Schools, 5th edition Doughty, Harold R. Viking-Penguin, 1986	✦	✦	
Handbook of Private Schools: An Annual Descriptive Survey of Private Education Porter Sargent, annual	✦	✦	
Lovejoy's College Guide, 19th edition Straughn, Charles T. II, and Barbarasue Lovejoy Straughn, eds. Simon & Schuster, 1989	✦	✦	✦
The Macmillan Guide to Correspondence Study, 3d edition Modoc Press, comp. and ed. Macmillan, 1988	✦		
Patterson's American Education Moody, Douglas, ed. Educational Directories, annual	✦	✦	✦
Peterson's Annual Guides to Graduate Study, 6 vols. Moore, Theresa C., series ed. Peterson's Guides, annual	✦	✦	
Peterson's Guide to Four-Year Colleges Lehman, Andrea E., and Eric A. Suber, eds. Peterson's Guides, annual	✦	✦	✦
Peterson's Guide to Independent Secondary Schools Peterson's Guides, annual	✦		✦
Requirements for Certification of Teachers, Counselors, Librarians, Administrators for Elementary and Secondary Schools Univ. of Chicago, annual (1935–)	✦	✦	

Core Titles

American Educators' Encyclopedia. Edward L. Dejnozka and David E. Kapel. Greenwood, 1982. hard. 1 vol. 634 pp. illus. index. ISBN 0-313-20954-5. $85. encyclopedia.
LB15.D37 370.3

The *American Educators' Encyclopedia* is intended as a ready-reference source on American education for professionals, graduate students, and laypersons. It provides brief definitions; basic explanations; and identifications of terms, concepts, and names commonly found in the professional literature of elementary, secondary, and higher education.

Alphabetically arranged, this work covers 22 broad areas of education (e.g., administration and supervision, minority education, art and music education, and counseling and guidance). Each of the approximately 2,000 entries consists of a brief article followed by an average of two to four references for further reading and information on the topic. A limited number of entries are accompanied by illustrations to assist in understanding a concept.

After selecting the entries and writing 100- to 200-word explanations for each, Dejnozka and Kapel chose subject experts to review the entries for accuracy and comprehensiveness, as well as for appropriateness of the references accompanying each entry. The names of these experts (the Board of Consulting Editors), their qualifications, and the broad topical area of entries each reviewed are provided in the front of the volume.

With a few exceptions (e.g., the commonly used acronyms ERIC and I/D/E/A), acronyms or abbreviations are not used as entry headings. A lengthy list of abbreviations and acronyms in the front of the volume enables readers who are more familiar with the shortened forms to access their full-name entries. This list, which includes only those acronyms and abbreviations relevant to the entries in the encyclopedia, is also convenient for quick reference and identification.

Like any ready-reference encyclopedia, the *American Educators' Encyclopedia* does not include entries on all the subjects about which a reader might wish to find basic information. However, other than the editorial constraints of space and time, it is hard to determine why some items were chosen for inclusion and not others. For example, *dissertation* is given an entry, but not thesis; *school library media specialist* is included, but not librarian; some higher education institutions that made significant contributions to education history are included, but others (such as Oberlin College and Hampton University) are not. A number of landmark law cases are listed, but *Regents of University of California* v. *Bakke* (1978) is not among them. Further information on the criteria for inclusion and exclusion by the authors would have been helpful.

Despite some imbalance in the entries, however, the authors of the *American Educators' Encyclopedia* are to be commended for their efforts in producing this useful reference source. It is the most comprehensive and up-to-date work of its kind currently available. Moreover, in addition to providing basic information on a wide range of topics, it includes valuable information in the appendixes, such as the Code of Ethics of the Education Profession and a list of regional accrediting associations. The Board recommends this work for the core collection of academic libraries.

American Universities and Colleges, 13th edition. American Council on Education, comp. and ed. Walter de Gruyter, 1987. hard. 1 vol. 2,024 pp. appendixes. index. ISBN 0-89925-179-X. $119.50. handbook.
LA226.A65 378.73

American Universities and Colleges is a compilation of general historical information on higher education and specific factual and statistical information on four-year American institutions. This work is especially useful to education researchers, institution officials, students, and others wanting background and comparative information on higher education. This one-volume source covers a diversity of information otherwise found in several separate publications and through other resources.

The text of *American Universities and Colleges* is divided into three parts. Part 1 provides surveys on the evolution and structure of higher education; the common characteristics of undergraduate, graduate, and professional education; state and federal support; and foreign student enrollment. Numerous tables are interspersed throughout the text and provide comparative information related to areas such as enrollment, programs, disciplines, revenues, expenditures, and financial support.

Part 2 is devoted to professional education in the United States. It includes a listing of professional fields, a description of the accrediting agency for each field, and a state-by-state listing of fully accredited degree-granting institutions and programs. Nonregionally accredited independent schools that have specialized accreditation receive descriptive entries. For descriptions of the regionally accredited schools, users must turn to part 3.

Part 3, the bulk of the work, is an alphabetical state and territory listing of approximately 1,700 regionally accredited or about-to-be-accredited institutions. The lengthy entries cover such information as characteristics and history of the institution, enrollment of full-time and part-time students by level and gender, institutional structure, undergraduate degree requirements, financial aid, a detailed accounting of departments and number of faculty by rank and gender in each department, finances of the institution, distinctive educational programs, and library collections. The various information subdivisions under each institution are in boldface type, making it easy to find specific information quickly.

The appendixes include information on the history of and etiquette for academic costumes and academic ceremonies; tables of the number of earned doctorates and master's degrees conferred since 1861; a list of institutions with ROTC units, summary data in tabular form for the institutions included in part 3, and an essay on the American Council on Education. The usefulness of this work is enhanced with an institutional index and a general index.

Since this reference work is published irregularly (approximately every four years), it should not be referred to for the most up-to-date information on individual institutions. For that, annual publications such as PETERSON'S GUIDE TO FOUR-YEAR COLLEGES or THE COLLEGE HANDBOOK should be consulted. However, given the wealth of analytical and comparative data in *American Universities and Colleges,* as well as historical information on higher education, the work is valuable. The Board recommends this work for the core collections of public, academic, and school libraries.

Barron's Profiles of American Colleges: Descriptions of the Colleges, 17th edition. College Division of Barron's Educational series, comp. and ed. Barron's, 1990. soft. 1 vol. approx. 1,400 pp. illus. index. ISBN 0-8120-4351-0. $16.95. handbook.
L901.B3 378.73'219

Barron's Profiles of American Colleges is written for prospective college students and their parents. This one-volume, four-part guide to colleges and universities provides information in varying levels and formats to assist prospective students and their parents in thinking about a college education. *Barron's Profiles* is revised on a biennial basis. (This review is based on an examination of the 1988 16th edition; the 1990 edition will be available as this book goes to press.)

Preliminary background information begins in part 1, "An Introduction to College," with a series of informative advisory essays on selecting a college, getting financial aid, taking college entrance examinations, applying to colleges, and choosing a major.

Part 2, "A Close Look at the Colleges," provides profiles of approximately 1,500 colleges and universities in the United States, as well as selected foreign institutions. Entries are arranged by state, territory, and foreign country, respectively. Each state and territory institution profile begins with a capsule of basic information, including number of students within general status categories (that is, part time, full time, and graduate), application deadline, tuition, entrance examinations required, student:faculty ratio, number and average salary rate of faculty, and selectivity rating. This information is followed by narrative descriptions, divided and subdivided into categories of information. Entries for institutions outside of the United States are briefer. In addition to the profiles, part 2 includes colleges categorized in lists according to selectivity, ranging from most competitive to noncompetitive to special.

College locator maps are supplied at the beginning of each state section, but are not as detailed or as large as those found in THE COLLEGE BLUE BOOK: NARRATIVE DESCRIPTIONS. Since many small college towns are not included on the maps, the map locator code assigned to each institution indicates only the general location of the institution within a state.

Barron's profiles are broken down into more detailed categories than those found in LOVEJOY'S COLLEGE GUIDE, although the information presented is much the same. The use of space between categories and larger print make the entries inviting to read, while the detailed categories within profiles make it possible to find specific information easily.

Part 3, "An Overview of Specialized Data," presents comparative tables of the factual and statistical information found in part 2. It also provides advice and information for international students on application procedures, TOEFL (Test of English as a Foreign Language) test centers, and a state-by-state listing of institutions with information on the precentage of international students, the existence of intensive English programs, special organizations, and special counseling. The information presented for international students (in part 3) is more useful than that found in the foreign student section of AMERICAN UNIVERSITIES AND COLLEGES and is comparable to that found in THE COLLEGE HANDBOOK: FOREIGN STUDENT SUPPLEMENT.

Tables in part 4, "Meeting Career Needs," show the percentage of students enrolled in major fields of study, postgraduate activity, and career resources and services offered by each institution.

The abundance of conveniently arranged information on colleges in *Barron's Profiles of American Colleges* makes its acquisition desirable. The Board recommends this work for the core collections of public, academic, and school libraries.

The College Blue Book, 22d edition. Macmillan, 1989. hard. 5 vols. illus. indexes. ISBN 0-02-695969-0 (set). $200 (set). handbook. CD-ROM.
LA226.C685 378.73

The College Blue Book is a standard reference work on colleges and universities in the United States and Canada. This five-volume set is comprehensive in its range of coverage of varied aspects of higher education and occupational education. The introduction provides advice and information to the student on appraisal of self, interests, and characteristics as a basis for proceeding with an evaluation of higher education institutions. The preface also gives general information on entrance examinations and admission policies along with information on two-year colleges, liberal arts colleges, universities, and specialized institutions.

Each volume focuses on a particular aspect of information pertinent to colleges, universities, or schools offering occupational education programs. Three volumes—*Narrative Descriptions; Tabular Data;* and *Degrees Offered by College and Subject*—pertain to two-year schools, four-year schools, universities, and specialized institutions. *Narrative Descriptions* includes approximately 3,000 institutions of higher education. Two parts, corresponding to the United States and Canada, are divided alphabetically by state or province, within which the schools are listed alphabetically. Each state and province section begins with a full-page map showing the location of the institutions included. These maps are more detailed and accurate than those found in BARRON'S PROFILES OF AMERICAN COLLEGES or in THE COLLEGE HANDBOOK.

The subdivisions for each entry are nicely accented with space between them. Much of the information in the *Narrative Descriptions* volume can be found in other college guides, but the emphasis here tends to be on the college and community environment more than in a number of the other guides. Users desiring a more precise outline of factual and statistical information on institutions can find it in the *Tabular Data* volume.

A third volume, *Degrees Offered by College and Subject,* offers a two-part arrangement for finding degrees offered. Part 1 lists schools by state, with fields of study shown after each school. Part 2 lists fields of study, with the schools that offer these programs listed after the appropriate degree. The diversity of fields of study or subjects is greater than that found in other college guides because of *The College Blue Book*'s diverse coverage of institutions.

Occupational Education is the title of the fourth volume, which became part of this set in the early 1970s. Information for this volume has been compiled through questionnaires sent to the schools, state education offices, and various professional and accrediting agencies. The reader is cautioned in the preface "to check institutions thoroughly" through a variety of means because of rapid changes in the schools in this field.

This volume includes over 9,000 business, trade, and technical schools listed alphabetically under city or town headings arranged by state. This listing of occupational schools makes up the first part of this volume. Each state section begins with a list of state education officials, with their addresses, and state regulatory information regarding occupational education or programs for training in technical and semiprofessional jobs. This is followed by a brief description of each institution, including such statistical information as tuition, enrollment, curriculum, degrees or certificates awarded, and accreditation. The second part of the volume lists curricula and programs of instruction.

The final volume, *Scholarships, Fellowships, Grants, and Loans,* covers information on sources of financial aid. This volume is divided into nine broad subject areas that are further divided into more specific categories (for example, "Physical Science" lists the categories of chemistry, geology, geophysics, among others). This volume focuses on private sources of financial aid grouped according to the subject areas supported by the sources. Four indexes assist the user in seeking out the appropriate information by education level, sponsoring organization, title of award, or subject.

The College Blue Book is a reliable, comprehensive source of varied information. The five volumes are well-organized and convenient to use. The Board recommends this work for the core collections of public, academic, and school libraries.

The College Cost Book. College Board, annual. soft. 1 vol. 295 pp. illus. ISBN 0-87447-375-6. $13.95. handbook.
LB2342.C633a 378.3′0973

The College Cost Book is devoted to information on the cost and cost management required for pursuing formal postsecondary education. This annual handbook offers practical information to potential college students and their parents. It does not offer false hopes, but is straightforward and honest in its approach.

The first two chapters in part 1 explore the components of college costs, evaluating family income and assets and identifying possible student monetary contributions. A total expense budget and a table showing the average resources generally available from students are provided.

Chapters 3 through 5 offer strategies, suggestions, and information on how to make the most of time, money, and human resources in order to meet the costs of higher education. Tables assist in clarifying and demonstrating financial possibilities. There is also information on financial aid, including types and eligibility requirements, with specific information on federal and state government assistance programs. Chapters 6 and 7 offer tips on completing financial aid application forms and comparing financial aid awards.

Chapter 8 focuses on long-range planning and is addressed to parents. This chapter outlines the steps for planning the financing of a college education and presents sample family case studies. The final chapter in part 1 is devoted to tables, student case studies, and worksheets. This graphic presentation is designed to help students and parents understand and work out financial planning strategies. A glossary of terms completes part 1.

Part 2 comprises four appendixes that present tables of information on college expenses and financial aid for colleges and universities in the United States and selected foreign countries. Appendix 1 contains tables—arranged by states, territories, and foreign countries—that make it easy to compare the costs of tuition, books and supplies, room and board, and other expenditures for institutions within a particular state. Appendix 2 is an alphabetical listing of institutions in the United States and selected foreign countries.

In addition to this information, appendix 3 presents a state-by-state listing of grant programs as well as a list of agencies (with addresses) for information on guaranteed student loan programs. The final appendix lists institutions that offer special tuition payment plans.

This work has a direct, helpful, and friendly approach to the student and parent. *The College Cost Book* is not only a reference book on various aspects of college costs, but a self-help book to inform and prepare families for the costs. Most chapters end with a set of questions and answers about the topic just discussed; this material is realistic and informative. Tables and case studies, intermingled with the text, clarify information, while worksheets and checklists provide an opportunity for immediate application of the information. Even though a reader may not be interested in using the worksheets and the case studies, the information found in the text on college costs can stand alone. The Board recommends this work for the core collections of public and school libraries.

The College Handbook, 1990–1991, 27th edition. College Board, 1990. soft. 1 vol. plus 2 suppls. 2,017 pp. index. ISBN 0-87447-313-6. $17.95. handbook. LB2351.AI.C6 371.214

Written in the same practical style as THE COLLEGE COST BOOK by the same publishers, *The College Handbook* offers strategies, suggestions, advice, and straightforward information on choosing a college, applying to colleges, and paying for college. Worksheets and checklists are incorporated in the text for practical application. (*The College Handbook* is a biennial publication. The 1988–1989 edition was examined for this review; a new edition was available as this book went to press.)

Under the heading "College Decisions," the text presents a logical strategy for students to follow as they begin seriously thinking about a college education. Students are guided through a checklist of basic preferred characteristics to help them identify the college of their choice.

To facilitate the decision-making process, *The College Handbook* categorizes institutions into "College Indexes." An "index" that is not found in other college guides divides two- and four-year institutions by campus environment (urban, suburban, and rural) and general size (small, medium, large, and very large). Other indexes group colleges according to religious affiliations, ROTC programs, open admissions programs, and specialized programs (such as art, music, or business.) Other indexes list colleges with late or no closing application dates; colleges that accept the Common Application; and colleges with special admission programs (such as Candidates' Reply Agreement and Early Decision Plan Agreement).

The section "College Descriptions" provides information on over 3,100 institutions, arranged alphabetically by state, including two- and four-year colleges, specialized colleges (for example, seminaries, conservatories, and military colleges), and universities. Each description begins with what is referred to as the "College ABC's"—admissions, background, and completion—covering admissions policy, the percentage of applicants admitted to the previous year's freshman class, the percentage of freshmen who complete the year in good standing, the percentage of freshmen who graduate, and the percentage of students who enter graduate study. A number of institution profiles include a category "College Comment" in which school officials contribute remarks on their institutions.

The current academic year's registration and administration dates for the various achievement tests are provided, as well as a bibliography of books on choosing colleges, majors, and careers; admissions and financial aid; college preparation and testing; books for parents; and other pertinent topics.

The College Handbook: Foreign Student Supplement, a supplementary volume, was issued for the first time in 1987. This supplement is directed at students from other countries and provides much the same content as *The College Handbook* but with additional information on services and financial aid available for foreign students at individual institutions. Information on institutions is presented in separate tables for undergraduate and graduate study. This supplement is convenient for foreign students interested in studying in the United States.

An *Index of Majors,* available as a separate publication, covers majors offered in two-year through graduate institutions, but is not a necessary purchase if the library already owns THE COLLEGE BLUE BOOK.

The Board recommends *The College Handbook* for the core collections of public and school libraries.

Comparative Guide to American Colleges for Students, Parents and Counselors, 14th edition. James Cass and Max Birnbaum. HarperCollins, 1989. hard. 1 vol. 777 pp. indexes. ISBN 0-06-055160-7. $35. handbook.
L901.C33 378.73

More than 20 years ago, James Cass and Max Birnbaum designed the *Comparative Guide to American Colleges for Students, Parents and Counselors* as a consumer's guide to college selection for students and parents. This volume continues to serve that purpose today by providing analytical and comparative data for the selection process.

The bulk of the text is devoted to a description of accredited colleges in the United States. The entries are arranged alphabetically by institution name. Each entry features a brief history of the institution, admission information, academic environment, percentage of faculty holding doctorates, faculty compensation, campus life, career data on graduates, and annual costs. The most important institutional data are set off to the top right of each college description for quick reference. This information includes the selectivity index; affiliation; year established; tuition and fees; the percentage of students receiving financial aid, with the average amount received per student; and the telephone numbers for the admissions and financial aid offices. Numerous indexes provide listings of institutions by state, selectivity rating, and religious affiliation.

The authors make a concerted effort in the introduction, preface, and section notes to ensure that users understand the meaning of the data presented. Recognizing the multitude of factors involved in selecting a college suited to the needs of various individuals, the authors do not offer their own judgments on the colleges. Rather, they present the facts and statistics for the individuals to judge and decide for themselves. The emphasis on scholastic achievements, academic opportunities, and campus environment makes this work a valuable decision-making tool for parents and students alike. The Board recommends this work for the core collections of public, academic, and school libraries.

Encyclopedia of Educational Research, 5th edition. Harold E. Mitzel et al., eds. Free Pr., 1982. hard. 4 vols. 2,126 pp. index. ISBN 0-02-900450-0 (set). $400 (set). encyclopedia.
L901.E57.1982 370.718073

The *Encyclopedia of Educational Research* was first published in 1941 in a one-volume format and continued as such until the publication of the fifth edition in 1982, which expanded to fill four volumes. This work approaches topics from a research perspective rather than from a philosophical, historical, or theoretical one. Focusing on current trends and developments, as well as traditional topics, the *Encyclopedia of Educational Research* has no entries for individuals or institutions.

Locating subjects in the encyclopedia is relatively easy. In addition to the general index located in the back of volume 4, volume 1 includes an alphabetical list of article titles for all four volumes of the encyclopedia. An outline of the overall scheme (or structure) of the reference work is also provided in the front of volume 1.

This scheme consists of 18 broad topics into which the encyclopedia entries fall. Related entries are listed under the broader entry heading. For example, under the broad topic of "Teachers and Teaching" are seven articles, ranging from "Faculty Development" to "Teacher Selection and Retention" and "Academic Freedom and Tenure."

The encyclopedia entries are nicely subdivided and conclude with lengthy bibliographies. Cross-references are used frequently to direct the user from one article to other related articles. As with most specialized encyclopedias, the general index should be used before delving into the body of the set.

This work does not cover a comprehensive range of topics, and the general index is not as detailed or specific as would be desirable with an encyclopedic work whose entries are arranged conceptually rather than alphabetically. Nevertheless, the articles, written by subject specialists, are well researched and well documented. The *Encyclopedia of Educational Research* is thus a valuable resource for its synthesis of research related to current trends and developments. The Board recommends this work for the core collection of academic libraries.

Guide to American Graduate Schools, 5th edition. Harold R. Doughty. Viking-Penguin, 1986. soft. 1 vol. 581 pp. indexes. ISBN 0-14-046725-4. $15.95. handbook.
L901.D65 378.1553.02573

The *Guide to American Graduate Schools* focuses on graduate and professional education and is directed to individuals interested in pursuing study beyond the undergraduate level. In a straightforward manner, in his introduction, Doughty addresses the differences between graduate and undergraduate study; the history of graduate and professional education; selecting a graduate or professional school; and the issues of quality, admission, and financial aid. The introduction dispels myths and unrealistic expectations regarding professional and graduate education.

Descriptive entries for American graduate schools make up the main part of the book. This material is preceded by a chapter on understanding the entries and a key to abbreviations used in the entries. The entries for institutions are clear and concise, outlining information on the general characteristics of each school, including founding date, location of nearest major city, type of student body (for example, coed, men only, or women only), type of control or the primary source and sponsor of financial support, term system, major research facilities and library collection, as well as tuition and housing information. Also provided are admission requirements and standards and data on the types of aid awarded, including the percentage of students awarded grants and scholarships. Each entry includes a list of the graduate or professional divisions for that institution. The same type of information is provided for each graduate and professional division if the information differs from the main school entry.

The final part of each entry presents the degree requirements and fields of study offered. The degree requirements category covers minimum required credits, number of credits required in residence, and options offered for completion of a master's. For sixth-year degrees or certificates and doctoral degrees, the minimum total of credits required beyond the master's is given. The fields-of-study list is arranged alphabetically and is occasionally followed by explanations of special majors. Special degree or admission requirements, if they are not covered in the general admissions requirements, and types of degrees awarded are given.

Three indexes provide ample accessibility to this work. There is an index to the location of institutions, by state, and an index of institutional abbreviations. The third index, to fields of study, lists institutions offering these areas.

The detail of this work reflects the expertise and experience of the author as a director of admissions. Unfortunately, this work is published irregularly, so it should be supplemented with information from college catalogs or with PETERSON'S ANNUAL GUIDES TO GRADUATE STUDY.

The *Guide to American Graduate Schools* is packed full of general and specific information needed by students in the process of selecting a graduate or professional school. The Board recommends this work for the core collections of public and academic libraries.

Handbook of Private Schools: An Annual Descriptive Survey of Independent Education. Porter Sargent, annual. hard. 1 vol. 1,488 pp. illus. index. ISBN 0-87558-126-9. $60. handbook.
L901.H3 373.73

The *Handbook of Private Schools: An Annual Descriptive Survey of Independent Education* is the leading compilation of information on American elementary, secondary, and postgraduate private schools. Updated annually, this work provides information from the viewpoints of the publisher and officials of the individual institutions.

The major section of this volume, "Leading Private Schools," provides information on prestigious, historic, and internationally renowned schools. Arranged according to eight geographical sections of the United States, the text lists schools within each state alphabetically by city or town. Each geographical section begins with sectional state maps that include a list of institutions within each state and map locator numbers for each institution.

Each school entry may include up to 12 informational parts, depending upon the availability of information from the individual institutions. The first 11 parts include basic factual and statistical information, such as school name; category (that is, day or boarding); address; key administrative officials; grade levels; curriculum orientation (that is, college preparatory or general); number of graduates in previous academic year; the number entering colleges; the six colleges entered by the largest number of the school's graduates; and financial information that ranges from the monetary value of the school buildings to tuition costs and scholarship figures.

The twelfth part is a descriptive summary of the school, highlighting particular developments, special or unique programs, historical significance, or other unique aspects of the institution. Page references are given keyed to another component of the book, "Private Schools Illustrated," in which institutions pay for the opportunity to portray the school as they wish in descriptions and photographs. Fewer than one-sixth of the 1,765 schools listed opted for this feature in the 1989 edition. The "Leading Private Schools" section is followed by "Features Classified," which lists schools by the type of programs offered.

For schools not listed in "Leading Private Schools," there is a "Concise Listing of Schools." This includes schools that have not provided complete information or that have restricted enrollment. Also included in this handbook is a directory of summer academic programs and summer camps.

Several indexes located throughout the book provide access to institutions by name, adding to the previously mentioned access by category section, which supplies information only for the "Leading Schools." A bothersome, but admittedly potentially helpful feature to users, is the appearance of advertisements for publications by Porter Sargent throughout the work.

Sargent's handbook offers a comprehensive coverage of private schools, an excellent layout for the entries, and a balanced outline of information in the school descriptions, making this work suitable for comparative analyses of different institutions.

The *Handbook of Private Schools* is especially useful for parents looking for a private school for their children. The Board recommends this work for the core collections of public and academic libraries.

Lovejoy's College Guide, 19th edition. Charles T. Straughn II, and Barbarasue Lovejoy Straughn, eds. Simon & Schuster, 1989. hard and soft. 1 vol. 872 pp. ISBN 0-617-68756-5 (hard); 0-671-68757-3 (soft). $32.95 (hard); $18.95 (soft). handbook.
LA226.L6 378.73

Lovejoy's College Guide has its antecedents in Dr. Clarence E. Lovejoy's *So You're Going to College,* first published in 1940. The current incarnation is a one-volume work organized into four sections, containing a core range of information, from financial aid and career guidance to descriptive profiles of colleges and universities.

Section 1, "So You're Going to College," bears the same title as the guide's forerunner. This section clearly and concisely explains terms commonly associated with financial aid and financial aid forms. Federal financial aid packages are also described, and the types of student aid programs frequently available through states and colleges are identified. Guidance is provided to families concerned with managing their financial contributions to postsecondary education by identifying possible loans; recommending literature on financial aid possibilities; and providing the name, address, and telephone number of an agency in each state and U.S. territory that can provide information on guaranteed student loan programs. In addition, this section provides information and guidance concerning the college selection process, the application essay, the college interview, the admissions process, and the tests frequently required for admission to colleges.

Section 2 provides advice on areas of study divided into two parts, "Professional Curricula" and "Special Programs." Approximately 500 majors in professional curricula and 45 special programs are listed alphabetically within the respective sections. Beneath each major or program is an alphabetical listing of institutions offering them.

Section 3, "The Colleges," provides a description of the institutions in the United States and its territories, as well as selected institutions in foreign countries. The schools included are two- and four-year institutions that are regionally, professionally, or nationally accredited, or are candidates for regional accreditation. Each entry begins with admissions selectivity information based on a formula provided by the editors. This formula is explained in the introductory pages to the section. Other information provided with the profiles is typically found in other college guides: enrollment, admissions, tuition, financial aid, academic programs, and student life. Individual institutions provide the descriptions and other information for this section.

Section 4, "Sports Index," is an alphabetical listing of intercollegiate and varsity sports and special-interest activities. Following each sport or activity is a list of institutions at which these activities are offered; indications of the availability of the activity for men and women; and the scholarship opportunities available at each institution.

Lovejoy's College Guide is a concise and well-written guide on undergraduate education. Although it does not have a regular publishing cycle, it is revised approximately every two years. The monthly *Lovejoy's Guid-*

ance Digest is intended to keep the information updated between revisions. Thus libraries may want to subscribe to this service or rely on one of the annual college guides for up-to-date data to supplement the valuable information in this volume.

The Board recommends this work for the core collections of public, academic, and school libraries.

The Macmillan Guide to Correspondence Study, 3d edition. Modoc Press, comp. and ed. Macmillan, 1988. hard. 1 vol. 676 pp. index. ISBN 0-02-921641-9. $85. handbook.
L901.M26 374.4′025′73

The Macmillan Guide to Correspondence Study is a well-organized and clearly printed guide to correspondence courses offered by public, private, and governmental establishments in the United States. This guide compiles the information gathered through questionnaires sent to educational institutions and from catalogs and brochures published by the institutions. An informative and thorough introduction addresses matters such as prerequisites, credit, and opportunities for military personnel.

Four main sections make up this guide. Section 1 lists accredited colleges and universities offering correspondence courses transferable to a formal degree program, noncredit courses of a professional nature, and career enrichment courses. Section 2 lists proprietary schools offering correspondence courses and programs in vocational subjects on the high school, college, and professional levels. Section 3 lists correspondence schools operated by private foundations, nonprofit organizations, and the U.S. government. Section 4 is a guide to computer-based courses.

The first three sections are arranged alphabetically by the name of the institution. Each entry includes the addresses and telephone numbers of the appropriate offices to contact, as well as descriptions of the institutions, their contributions to independent study, and highlights of the programs. This is followed by information on academic levels, degrees or certificates, tuition, enrollment periods, equipment requirements, credit and grading, and accreditations. Courses, listed alphabetically by subjects and arranged by academic levels, are described at the end of the entry.

The length of an entry depends upon the extent of an institution's offerings, varying from one paragraph to 16 pages. The briefest entries are for institutions functioning as a part of a consortium administered at another institution. In this case, the course offerings are listed only under the administrative institution.

Section 4 features computer-based programs offered by institutions. Programs are described that allow online and teleconferencing activities between instructor and student and among students at remote locations.

Institution and subject indexes direct the reader to appropriate sections. The subject index lists names of institutions under the subject area in which courses are offered.

Lack of currency is a drawback to *The Macmillan Guide to Correspondence Study.* It took approximately three years for the current edition (1988) to appear. Competitive guides may be published more frequently, but they lack the course descriptions provided in this volume. The Board recommends this work for the core collection of public libraries.

Patterson's American Education. Douglas Moody, ed. Educational Directories, annual. 752 pp. ISBN 0-910536-43-0. $57.50. directory.
L901.P3 370.25′73

Published annually since 1904, *Patterson's American Education* is known for its comprehensive information on secondary education in the United States. It not only includes public, private, and church-affiliated secondary schools but also school districts; accredited colleges and universities; teaching hospitals; and vocational, technical, and trade schools. Divided into two parts, this reference work packs a wealth of information compactly into its pages.

Part 1 provides alphabetical listings of secondary schools by locality within each state and territory. Each state and territory section begins with the address, telephone number, and names of key officials in the respective department of education. For states, this is followed by other pertinent state education offices, organizations, and associations, which also includes the names and addresses of key officials. A number of state sections also include a list of names and addresses of county or regional superintendents of schools.

Each entry for a locality begins with the city and county name; the city population; the school district name; the total enrollment; and the name and address of the superintendent. Information on the community schools—name, address, and principal—follows. Postsecondary and private and parochial secondary schools in a locality are separated from the public school entries; only addresses are provided for these institutions. Part 1 has separate listings for diocesan superintendents of Roman Catholic schools, district superintendents of Lutheran schools, and conference superintendents of Seventh-Day Adventist conferences.

Part 2, also published separately as *Patterson's Schools Classified,* provides more complete information on accredited postsecondary schools. This part is divided into three sections: the first is arranged alphabetically by type of school; the second is arranged by academic subjects and broad subjects related to education (such as graduate schools, home study and correspondence, women's colleges, art, nursing, photography, study abroad, summer sessions, and oceanography). Each entry includes an address and the name of a key official. Some of the entries include descriptive information supplied by the school.

The third section of part 2 is a useful classified listing of educational associations and societies by type (for example, learned and honor societies, liberal arts and humanities, and accreditation). The last section of part 2 is an index of postsecondary schools classified by type of school (such as colleges and universities and prep schools).

Accessibility is generally good. However, a confusing typographic feature of part 2 is the appearance of a number of schools in boldface type and in larger print than the state subdivisions, making it difficult to find the subdivisions quickly on some pages. This emphasis is apparently at the request of the schools. The introduction explains that this use of boldface type should be interpreted as "an indication of the school's desire to attract qualified students." An error appears in the user's guide to the classifications at the beginning of part 2, which mistakenly says that schools for the handicapped can be found alphabetically under *schools* rather than under *handicapped,* where they are actually listed.

Despite these minor flaws, *Patterson's American Education* is valuable for its general comprehensiveness and unique for its comprehensiveness on secondary education. The Board recommends this work for the core collections of public, academic, and school libraries.

Peterson's Annual Guides to Graduate Study. Theresa C. Moore, series ed. Peterson's Guides, annual. hard and soft. 6 vols. illus. appendixes. indexes. ISBN 0-87866-744-X (book 1, hard); 0-87866-743-1 (book 1, soft). handbook. on-line. L901.P4612 378.73

Peterson's Annual Guides to Graduate Study is a multivolume set of college guides focusing on graduate and professional education. This work, published annually, is the standard source for comprehensive information on postbaccalaureate education. Each of the six volumes focuses on a particular area of interest, but all begin with a section called "The Graduate Advisor," consisting of several essays written by authorities in the areas of professional and graduate education. These essays cover information on the differences between graduate and undergraduate education, the competition for talented candidates between graduate education and private industry, minority students in graduate education, and the international student.

Book 1, *Graduate and Professional Programs: An Overview,* includes a directory of graduate and professional programs by field; 301 fields and the institutions that award degrees in those fields are listed. The volume also contains a second directory with the same information, but listed alphabetically by the school's name, followed by the information on fields. The third directory in this volume includes institutions with combined-degree programs, organized alphabetically by field. Profiles and two-page essays of selected institutions offering graduate and professional programs are given.

Books 2 through 6 are guides to graduate programs in specific subject areas: the humanities and social sciences; biological and agricultural sciences; physical sciences and mathematics; engineering and applied sciences; and business, education, health, and law, respectively. These five volumes have the same format and include the same type of information for the broad areas of study. Each volume includes a directory of institutions with programs in their respective areas, followed by a directory of academic and professional programs with profiles, and full descriptions of the institutions offering these programs. The latter directory in each volume is subdivided into sections according to the major fields of study within each broad discipline. Each section begins with a table of contents for the section and brief background summaries of the subfields into which the section is divided. These summaries are written by educators in the field. There are three indexes in each volume. Two are specific to the schools in the particular volume, and the other is a separate index to the directories and subject areas found in books 2 through 6. Useful appendixes in each volume include: "Institutional Changes Since the 1988 Edition"; a list of abbreviations used; and a list of additional references.

Emphasis in the institutional profiles is on degree requirements, enrollment, entrance requirements, financial aid, and faculty research for the appropriate school, department, or college of an institution. Announcements written by officials of the institutions are appended to some of the profiles. The full descriptions focus on these specific schools, departments, or colleges, and are provided by the individual institutions. These descriptions include general information on programs of study and research facilities and a list of faculty and their research areas.

Peterson's Annual Guide to Graduate Studies is the

most thorough work available on graduate and professional education. The Board recommends this work for the core collections of public and academic libraries.

Peterson's Guide to Four-Year Colleges. Andrea E. Lehman and Eric A. Suber, eds. Peterson's Guides, annual. hard and soft. 1 vol. approx 2,400 pp. illus. index. ISBN 0-87866-027-5 (hard); 0-87866-990-6 (soft). $33.95 (hard); $17.95 (soft). handbook. online.
L901.P463 378.73

Peterson's Guide to Four-Year Colleges provides information concerning undergraduate study at four-year institutions in the United States, its territories, Canada, and foreign countries. The book contains the usual material found in college guides, such as advice and suggestions on gathering information on colleges and universities, financial aid, and taking standardized tests. (This review is based on examination of 1989's 20th edition; the new edition was available as this book went to press.)

Peterson's Guide to Four-Year Colleges has several unique features. One of these is a section on majors and careers in which majors are grouped into 21 general areas or fields followed by a one- to three-paragraph discussion on the career possibilities in each area. Another special feature is a directory section that is set apart with blue pages. This section includes listings of institutions alphabetically by name and location according to entrance difficulty, cost ranges, and majors. The entrance difficulty levels (most difficult, very difficult, moderately difficult, minimally difficult, and noncompetitive) are based on freshmen admissions and set by the publishers. Entrance difficulty is comparable to the selectivity indicator found in other college guides, such as BARRON'S PROFILES OF AMERICAN COLLEGES and Cass and Birnbaum's COMPARATIVE GUIDE TO AMERICAN COLLEGES FOR STUDENTS, PARENTS AND COUNSELORS.

The directory of cost ranges is divided into eight categories and reflects the cost of tuition, mandatory fees, and room and board. Ranging from "less than $2,000" to "$14,000 and over," each cost range is subdivided by "colleges with no room and board or with room only" and "colleges with room and board." The directory of 450 undergraduate major fields of study reflects the majors most widely offered by institutions.

Another directory lists the names of colleges and universities within the alphabetical arrangement of state, territory, province, and country. This provides tables of comparative information on degrees awarded, institutional control or status (such as independent or proprietary), student body makeup (coed, women only, men only, and other possible configurations such as "coordinate men" or "coordinate women" in which there are separate colleges or campuses but shared facilities). The percentage of women at each institution is frequently given, along with the enrollment figures and standardized test score ranges for ACT and SAT.

With the exception of a section on the Army ROTC program, the remainder of the book presents profiles of colleges. Announcements, highlighting special features or current developments, appear at the end of the profiles. Entries in this section refer to fuller descriptions of the institution, if available, in the "In-Depth Descriptions of the Colleges." The announcements and two-page descriptions in this section are written and contributed voluntarily by college officials. An index to colleges and universities completes this volume.

With its unique features and abundance of information in one volume, *Peterson's Guide to Four-Year Colleges* belongs in all libraries. The Board recommends this work for the core collections of public, academic, and school libraries.

Peterson's Guide to Independent Secondary Schools. Peterson's Guides, annual. hard and soft. 1 vol. 1,312 pp. illus. index. ISBN 0-87866-970-1 (hard); 0-87866-969-8 (soft). $36.95 (hard); $20.95 (soft). handbook.
L900.P48 373.2′22′02573

Peterson's Guide to Independent Secondary Schools is a comprehensive and detailed authoritative annual guide to independent secondary schools. This work covers over 1,300 college preparatory schools in the United States, its territories, Canada, and foreign countries. Standard college preparatory schools and schools that focus on preparing students with special needs to enter standard college preparatory schools are included in this guide.

Typical of other Peterson's Guides, this publication begins with general information in tabular form and continues with profiles, announcements, and descriptions of the institutions. The section entitled "General Register" provides a basic overview of the schools, arranged alphabetically by name within an alphabetical state-by-state listing. Indications are given for grade levels served; enrollment; number of faculty; courses; advanced placement subjects; sports offered; type of school (boarding, day, coed, boys, or girls); availability of services to students with special academic needs; and availability of remedial work.

The "Profiles and Announcements" section, arranged alphabetically by school name, consists of concise factual and statistical information, such as type of school; grade levels; founding date; profile of student body; academic emphasis; number and type of facilities; number of faculty by gender and highest earned degree; admissions figures and college placement figures; athletic programs; and courses of study. This information is gathered from the responses to an annual survey distributed to the schools. The announcement portion—approximately 50 words—immediately follows the factual and statistical information and is written by officials from the schools to emphasize special aspects of the schools. The "Descriptions" section consists of fuller descriptions of schools, as contributed and written by school officials.

A unique and valuable feature of *Peterson's Guide* is the "Directories" section, consisting of approximately 30 directories organized into the broad categories of school types, curricula, financial data, special programs, and special needs, as well as four to eight specific subcategories. Under these subcategories schools are listed according to features such as academic accommodation for the gifted and talented, a guaranteed tuition plan, computer proficiency as a graduation requirement, accommodation for underachievers, programs for study abroad, and classes for deaf students. An additional directory in this section provides SSAT requirements and lists schools requiring or recommending the SSAT. Two additional sections are an independent lower and middle schools directory that lists "feeder" schools to those profiled in the guide, and "Special Needs Directories" that list schools for underachievers or students with special needs. An index and a list of "Resources for Further Information" complete this volume.

Although sources such as the HANDBOOK OF PRIVATE SCHOOLS include secondary schools, *Peterson's Guide to Independent Secondary Schools* focuses on them solely and in greater detail (including historical background information, which is not found in the HANDBOOK). The Board recommends this work for the core collections of public and school libraries.

Requirements for Certification of Teachers, Counselors, Librarians, Administrators for Elementary and Secondary Schools. Univ. of Chicago, annual (1935–). hard. 1 vol. 250 pp. appendix. ISBN 0-226-08107-9. $30. handbook.
LB1771.W842R 371.133

Published in a new edition each year since 1935, *Requirements for Certification of Teachers, Counselors, Librarians, Administrators for Elementary and Secondary Schools* is a classic work that provides current information on state certification requirements for professional school personnel in elementary and secondary schools.

The work is arranged alphabetically by state. Subdivisions within each section make specific information on type of certificates issued by each state, type of personnel, and educational level clear and easy to find. These subdivisions and the specificity of information vary depending on the certification arrangements and terminology established by each state department of education. For example, the subdivisions for New Hampshire are "Certified Educator" and "Levels of Professional Certification," whereas the subdivisions for Kentucky are "General Requirements," "Approved Programs," "Special Education," "Instructional Leadership," "Guidance Counselor," "Individual Intellectual Assessment," "Librarian and School Media Librarians," "School Psychologist," "Teaching of Music," and "Teacher for Gifted Education." Similarly, the length of entries varies from one and a half pages for the former to eight and a quarter pages for the latter. In addition to the state sections, there is a section on the recommendations of regional and national associations and on sources of information regarding teacher applications in U.S. possessions and territories.

Although this book provides general certification requirements that will satisfy the needs of many students and school personnel who are considering a move to another state, users may occasionally require more detailed certification information for specific categories or fields. Therefore, a list of the state offices of certification, with addresses and telephone numbers, is provided in the appendix.

Altogether, *Requirements for Certification of Teachers, Counselors, Librarians, Administrators for Elementary and Secondary Schools* is notable for its comprehensiveness, currency, and physical quality. The Board recommends this work for the core collections of public and academic libraries.

Supplementary Titles

Academic Year Abroad. Institute of International Education, annual. soft. 1 vol. ISBN 0-87206-174-4. $29.95. handbook.
LB2376.U46 370.1962

Board's recommendation: Public and academic libraries.

The College Money Handbook. Karen C. Hegener. Peterson's Guides, annual. hard and soft. 1 vol. ISBN 0-87866-688-7 (hard); 0-87866-888-8 (soft). $33.95 (hard); $18.95 (soft). handbook.
LB2337.4.C66 378.3097

The College Money Handbook "includes aid for which the student must show financial need as well as funds that colleges award on the basis of accomplishment, talent, or special characteristics. For each college the handbook prints a profile containing a summary of expenses . . . ; an undergraduate financial-aids summary; a need-based freshman aid profile; a non-need freshman awards profile; and a section giving money-saving options available at a given college." (*Choice,* June 1984, p. 1438)

"Like other Peterson guides, this one is current, easy to use, and, in its paperback edition, relatively inexpensive. The Profiles, arranged alphabetically by school name, make it easy to determine what employment opportunities exist and if accelerated degree programs to shorten study are possible. The reader also is introduced through detailed questions and answers to the application process. . . . The Cost Profiles then can be used for more detailed study." (*BL,* December 1, 1984, p. 494)

"[This book is] a good starting point to help students decide if they . . . [will be able to] afford a particular college or university." (*VOYA,* June 1984, p. 108)

Also reviewed in: *ARBA,* 1984, p. 285; *BL,* April 15, 1984, p. 1158; February 15, 1988, p. 981; March 1, 1988, p. 1127; *Kliatt,* Winter 1984, p. 39; January 1988, p. 34; *LATBR,* January 1, 1984, p. 5; *Money,* March 1984, p. 70.

Board's recommendation: Public and school libraries.

A Critical Dictionary of Educational Concepts. Robin Barrow and Geoffrey Milburn. St. Martin's, 1986. hard. 1 vol. 274 pp. ISBN 0-312-00229-7. $35. dictionary.
LB15.B29 370.321

"*A Critical Dictionary* [*of Educational Concepts*] is not a dictionary of definitions of terms but rather a dictionary of explanations of the significance of key concepts. . . . it explores the role in the educational process of ideas such as analogy, concept, curriculum, ethics, ideology, language, multiculturalism, . . . and values clarification." (*WLB,* April 1987, p. 65)

"Useful for students of education, this work not only defines terms but also discusses both sides of controversies, and it takes a critical stand on the worth of a particular concept to teaching and learning. . . . A reader would not find 'custodian' or 'semester' in Barrow and Milburn but would find an enlightening discussion of 'behaviorism,' 'research,' 'integrated studies,' or 'educanto.' The book is a valuable reference book for libraries serving both undergraduate and graduate students of sociology, psychology, and education. The bibliography serves as a useful introduction to the fields represented by the terms." (*Choice,* July/August, 1987, p. 1672)

Also reviewed in: *TES,* June 19, 1987, p. 23.

Board's recommendation: Academic libraries.

Digest of Educational Statistics. National Center for Education Statistics. U.S.G.P.O., annual. soft. 1 vol. ISBN 0-16-006773-1. $25. handbook.
L11.D48 370.212

The *Digest of Education Statistics* is "a general statistical source for all areas in education. This publication includes statistics on minority students enrolled at the elementary, secondary, college, and university level. It does not contain specific statistical information on bilingualism or bilingual programs. The data on minority students, however, may be useful for pinpointing large Spanish speaking groups and for comparison studies between ethnic groups." (*RSR,* Spring 1983, p. 42)

Also reviewed in: *ARBA,* 1976, p. 305; *BL,* June 15, 1974, p. 1138; January 15, 1981, p. 679; *JEL,* December 1974, p. 1438; *RSR,* October 1981, pp. 76, 103; *WLB,* May 1970, p. 975.

Board's recommendation: Public, academic, and school libraries.

The Educational Software Selector, 3d edition. Teachers College Pr., 1986. soft. 1 vol. 980 pp. appendixes. indexes. ISBN 0-8077-2829-2. $34.95. handbook.
LB1028.7.E38 370.2854

The Educational Software Selector is "a buying guide to computer programs . . . [which] contains more than 7,700 product descriptions from 625 suppliers of educational software, for microcomputers most commonly found in schools. . . . Section 1, the introduction, lists 'Seven Steps for Responsible Software Selection.' . . . Section 2 contains software descriptions arranged by curriculum area and within that area by subject. . . . Section 3 contains the 'Contents of Program Packages.' . . . Section 4 is 'Summary Listings by Hardware System.' . . . [Section 5] is a list of software suppliers and distributors. . . . Both a subject and product-name index are included.

"A brief glossary of terms is provided in Appendix A. Appendix B briefly describes EPIE's courseware evaluation process. Appendix C contains a variety of software evaluation forms that readers may use in evaluating software on their own. . . . This comprehensive source of information on educational software brings together product information that is published in numerous periodicals in the field. *TESS* is not only recommended for school, community college, and public library use but also for microcomputer enthusiasts." (*BL*, January 15, 1987, p. 770)

Also reviewed in: *SE*, January 1987, p. 55.

Board's recommendation: Public, academic, and school libraries.

El-Hi Textbooks and Serials in Print. Bowker, annual (1970–). hard. 1 vol. 1,224 pp. indexes. ISBN 0-8352-2815-0. $99.95. bibliography.
Z5813 016.371

"*El-Hi Textbooks and Serials in Print* . . . lists 27,418 elementary, junior, and senior high school texts and pedagogical books compiled from the catalogs of 471 el-hi publishers. It is designed to be a comprehensive, not a selective, list with emphasis on textbooks for the classroom. Some appropriate reference books, periodicals, maps, tests, teaching aids, and programmed materials are also included.

This work contains four indexes. The main index is by subject. . . . A table of contents lists the 21 broad subject areas covered: Art; Business; Dictionaries; Encyclopedias and Reference Education; Foreign Languages; Guidance; Health and Physical Education; Home Economics; Language Arts; Literature and Drama; Mathematics; Music, [etc.].

"The arrangement of the subject index is alphabetical by subject division, then by title within each subdivision. Teachers' Professional Books are listed at the end of the appropriate subdivisions.

[This book] "is a valuable bibliographic tool for school libraries as well as college and university libraries, especially those institutions with teacher education programs." (*RSR*, Summer 1984, p. 54)

Also reviewed in: *ARBA*, 1976, p. 335; 1981, p. 320; 1983, p. 274; 1987, p. 132; *BL*, November 1, 1974, p. 301; January 1, 1978, p. 771; October 15, 1980, p. 348; *CLW*, November 1971, p. 167; *Emerg Lib*, May 1983, p. 26; *LJ*, January 15, 1971, p. 248; *RQ*, Winter 1970, p. 167; *Sch L*, Summer 1971, p. 55; *Ser Lib 2nd*, 1985, p. 244.

Board's recommendation: Academic and school libraries.

The Insider's Guide to Foreign Study. Benedict Leerburger. Addison-Wesley, 1987. soft. 1 vol. 579 pp. index. ISBN 0-201-15745-4. $12.95. handbook.
LB1028.43.H55 370.19'62

The Insider's Guide to Foreign Study is "a guidebook that offers information on more than 400 programs available to American college and university students for study abroad. Program descriptions are arranged by geographic area, and include a brief description of the program, admittance requirements, teaching methods, methods of evaluation, credits offered, housing, dates, costs, the year the program was established, the number of students in the program in 1985, and information on applying for the particular program. Besides describing programs offered by US universities, the work mentions the possibility of studying at foreign universities, giving for each country brief lists of 'selected colleges and universities.' An extensive introduction, 'The How and Whys of Foreign Study,' discusses such considerations as finances, living arrangements, traveling, and receiving academic credit." (*Choice*, July/August 1988, p. 1675)

Board's recommendation: Public libraries.

The International Encyclopedia of Education. Torsten Husen and T. Neville Postlethwaite. Pergamon, 1985. hard. 12 vols. ISBN 0-08-028119-2 (set). $2,150 (set). encyclopedia.
LB15.1569 370.3'21

The International Encyclopedia of Education comprises "over 4,500 subject areas in 1,448 articles ranging from Abilities and Aptitudes from California to Zoology Educational Programmes from Jerusalem.

"The vast, cross-referenced index volume, running to 420 pages, is itself a major work which could well stand as a reference volume in its own right. . . . This is by far the most ambitious [educational encyclopedia] yet.

"The encyclopedia is designed to respond to the knowledge explosion in education. . . . The volumes try to do more than present information; they also endeavour . . . to evaluate it and identify future areas of research." (*TES*, May 17, 1985, p. 24)

Board's recommendation: Public and academic libraries.

Teaching Abroad 1988–1991. Institute of International Education, 1988. soft. 1 vol. 250 pp. index. ISBN 0-87206-158-2. $21.95. handbook.
LB2283.B42 370.19'63'024

Board's recommendation: Public and academic libraries.

New and Noteworthy

The Boarding School Guide. Kiliaen V. R. Townsend. Agee Pubs. 1989. soft. 1 vol. 282 pp. ISBN 0-935265-18-X. $16.50. handbook.
373.222

The Boarding School Guide is designed "for parents and students to focus on 'the information desired by clients in order to make intelligent preliminary choices.' Included are facts about 231 U.S. schools with more than 60 boarders, along with maps, comparative charts, and advice about choosing and attending the schools. One-page entries for the schools (144 coed, 35 for girls, 52 for boys) are arranged in alphabetical order." (*BL,* January 15, 1990, p. 1038)

College Majors: A Complete Guide from Accounting to Zoology. Ellen Lederman. McFarland, 1990. hard. 1 vol. 122 pp. index. ISBN 0-89950-462-0. $18.95. handbook.
LB2361 378.1'99

"Compiled from college catalogs, the NECS *Classification of Instructional Programs,* and the HEIGS *Taxonomy,* [*College Majors*] describes approximately 488 majors. Each description is about 100 words in length and includes a definition of the major, levels of degree offered (from associate through doctoral), typical courses given (usually four), related or complementary majors, needed abilities, and career possibilities." (*BL,* June 15, 1990, pp. 2026–2028)

Education: A Guide to Reference and Information Sources. Lois J. Buttlar. Libraries Unlimited, 1989. hard. 1 vol. 258 pp. index. ISBN 0-87287-619-5. $35. bibliography.
Z5811.B89 011.02

Education "covers more than 900 titles in the education field, including major guides, bibliographies, indexes, abstracts, online databases, and other reference sources. . . . Bibliographic entries follow the format of *American Reference Books Annual* and include price. For the most part, annotations are descriptive rather than evaluative. . . . The book has a classified arrangement. Under broad subjects (e.g., higher education, special education, career and vocational education), titles are arranged by type (bibliographies, directories, statistics sources, etc.)." (*BL,* November 15, 1989, p. 689)

The Educator's Desk Reference: A Sourcebook of Educational Information and Research. Melvyn N. Freed et al. Macmillan, 1989. hard. 1 vol. 536 pp. index. ISBN 0-02-910740-7. $49.95. handbook.
LB1028.26.F74 370.7

The Educator's Desk Reference "includes (1) an annotated list of major education reference books arranged by type . . . ; (2) leading publishers of books [etc.] . . . , arranged by field; (3) publishers' guidelines for authors; (4) profiles of major standardized tests; (5) a description of microcomputer software for statistics in educational research; (6) guidelines for the selection of the appropriate research design for the study of a research question; (7) a critical description of various research designs and statistical procedures; (8) an overview of sampling techniques; and (9) a directory of selected national and regional education organizations." (*BL,* November 15, 1989, p. 689)

Financial Aid Available Now for Research, Study, Travel, and Other Activities Abroad. Gail A. Schlachter and R. David Weber. Reference Service Pr., 1990. hard. 1 vol. 586 pp. ISBN 0-918276-12-8. $40. handbook.

Financial Aid Available Now for Research, Study, Travel, and Other Activities Abroad "contains more than 1,700 references and cross-references to international funding opportunities. . . . The listings cover every major field of study, are tenable in practically every country/region of the world, are sponsored by more than 500 different private and public agencies and organizations, and are open to all segments of the population. . . . Each entry . . . provides detailed information on program title, sponsoring organization address and telephone number, . . . purpose, eligibility, financial support, duration, special features and limitations, number of awards, and deadline date." (Excerpted from publisher's announcement)

Focus on School: A Reference Handbook. Beverly A. Haley. ABC-Clio, 1990. hard. 1 vol. approx. 250 pp. ISBN 0-87436-099-4. $29.50. handbook.
LB17 370

"*Focus on School* provides comprehensive background information along with a wide range of print and nonprint resources for understanding and succeeding in the educational system. Students will find it useful for locating information for research projects, getting help in solving school-related problems, or exploring options for further education. . . . Chapter topics include the role of the school, the role of the student, focusing for success, learning outside school, getting help, and planning for the future." (Excerpted from publisher's announcement)

Scholarships, Fellowships, and Grants for Programs Abroad: A Handbook of Awards to U.S. Nationals for Study or Research Abroad. American Collegiate Svc., 1989. soft. 1 vol. 299 pp. indexes. ISBN 0-940937-02-6. $29.75. handbook.
LB2338 378.34

"The fellowships, scholarships, and grants listed [in *Scholarships, Fellowships, and Grants for Programs Abroad*] are available at the undergraduate, graduate, or post-doctoral level. The information is arranged alphabetically under 374 institutions and includes the address, contact person, names and number of awards, value, duration, elegibility, field of study, application deadline, and country where the award may be utilized. Another section lists basic information on the host countries—area, population, language, religion, government, capital currency, academic year, general comments, and addresses for additional information." (*BL,* February 15, 1990, p. 1190)

Cynthia Stewart Kaag

Engineering

See also Science and Technology

Engineering is a fast-moving field where current, accurate, accessible information is of the essence. Therefore, much emphasis in the reviews that follow is placed on currency and ease of use. The rapidity of change in the engineering disciplines is demonstrated by the currency of the titles reviewed (all were published in the 1980s and nearly half since 1988) and the fact that new editions of three of the titles included came out after the original selections for this section were made. Literary style is not a consideration in these reviews unless the material is so abstruse as to be unusable. For the most part, large public and academic libraries will be interested in these titles because of the cost of these works and the clientele to which most of them are addressed.

Several of the core titles deal with electronics and electrical engineering, an indication of the importance of this field in contemporary science and technology. Other areas covered include civil, chemical, mechanical, aerospace, and materials engineering. Most titles considered are handbooks, dictionaries, or encyclopedias.

Librarians new to the field should make it a point to consult the bibliographic guides to the literature, as these provide a framework for building a good engineering reference collection. A number of fine bibliographic sources appear on the supplementary list. Another good source for further information is the *Scientific and Technical Organizations and Agencies Directory* (Margaret Lubash Young, ed., Gale, 1987). Whether you plan to fill gaps in your collection, weed and update to meet changing needs, or start from scratch, the titles included in this section will provide a good basis for access to engineering information.

Core Titles

General

Handbook of Engineering Fundamentals, 4th edition. Byron D. Tapley. John Wiley, 1990. hard. 1 vol. 2,368 pp. illus. index. ISBN 0-471-89084-7. $74.95. handbook.
TA151.S58 620.002

The *Handbook of Engineering Fundamentals* is a reference work that concentrates on the basics, not current information or practice. This is reflected in its publishing pattern: once every two decades. Thus, the handbook's scope and organization differ from other, more specific and up-to-date engineering reference works. This work is for the generalist, not the specialist, or alternately for the novice in the field rather than the professional. The *Handbook of Engineering Fundamentals* does a fine job of covering equations, tables, properties of materials, and basic laws and theories of engineering.

Core Titles

GENERAL	PUBLIC	ACADEMIC	SCHOOL
Handbook of Engineering Fundamentals, 4th edition Byron D. Tapley. John Wiley, 1990		✦	
IEEE Standard Dictionary of Electrical and Electronics Terms, 4th edition Jay, Frank, ed. Institute of Electrical and Electronics Engineers, 1988	✦	✦	
McGraw-Hill Encyclopedia of Engineering Parker, Sybil P., ed. McGraw-Hill, 1983	✦	✦	
Reference Data for Engineers: Radio, Electronics, Computer, and Communications, 7th edition Jordan, Edward C., ed. Sams, 1985		✦	
Who's Who in Engineering, 7th edition Davis, Gordon, ed. American Assn. of Engineering Societies, 1988		✦	
AERONAUTIC ENGINEERING			
Jane's Aerospace Dictionary, 3d edition Gunston, Bill, ed. Jane's Information Group, 1988	✦	✦	
CIVIL ENGINEERING			
Standard Handbook for Civil Engineers, 3d edition Merritt, Frederick S., ed. McGraw-Hill, 1983	✦	✦	
ELECTRICAL ENGINEERING			
Encyclopedia of Electronics, 2d edition Gibilisco, Stan, and Neil Sclater, eds. TAB Bks., 1990	✦	✦	
Illustrated Dictionary of Electronics, 4th edition Turner, Rufus P., and Stan Gibilisco, eds. TAB Bks., 1988	✦	✦	
Standard Handbook for Electrical Engineers, 12th edition Fink, Donald G., and H. Wayne Beaty, eds. McGraw-Hill, 1987	✦	✦	
MATERIALS ENGINEERING			
Encyclopedia of Materials Science and Engineering, 8 vols., 1 suppl. Bever, Michael B., ed. MIT Pr., 1986		✦	
MECHANICAL ENGINEERING			
Marks' Standard Handbook for Mechanical Engineers, 9th edition Avallone, Eugene A., and Theodore Baumeister III, eds. McGraw-Hill, 1987	✦	✦	

The section headings in the table of contents give a concise summary of the scope of the material included in this volume: "Mathematical and Physical Tables," "Mathematics," "Physical Units and Standards," "Mechanics of Rigid Bodies," "Mechanics of Deformable Bodies," "Mechanics of Incompressible Fluids," "Aeronautics and Astronautics," "Engineering Thermodynamics," "Electromagnetics and Circuits," "Electronics," "Radiation," "Light and Acoustics," "Heat Transfer," "Automatic Control," "Chemistry,"

"Engineering Economy," and "Properties of Materials." Each section is preceded by its own table of contents, and the index at the end of the volume is more than adequate.

The typeface is small, but legible, and the paper is of good quality, an important consideration for a work that will have to stand up to heavy use for perhaps 20 years. Graphs and tables are especially well designed for clarity and ease of use.

As a classic in its field, the *Handbook of Engineering Fundamentals* has proven its worth to libraries and practicing engineers. The Board recommends this work for the core collection of academic libraries.

IEEE Standard Dictionary of Electrical and Electronics Terms, 4th edition. Frank Jay, ed. Institute of Electrical and Electronics Engineers, 1988. hard. 1 vol. 1,270 pp. illus. appendix. ISBN 1-55937-000-9. $65. dictionary.
TK9.I35 621.303

The *IEEE Standard Dictionary of Electrical and Electronics Terms* is, without question, an essential reference work for the public library. When "standard" was included in the title, it meant exactly that: these definitions are based on the standards developed over the years by various committees and subcommittees of the Institute of Electrical and Electronics Engineers (IEEE). This dictionary is considered by the IEEE to be the definitive work on electrical and electronics terminology.

The entries are arranged alphabetically. A few formulas and tables are included, but most entries are defined solely by words. Terms that have different meanings in different fields are clearly labeled, and the IEEE standard from which the definition was derived is listed at the end of the entry. There is a listing of these source IEEE standards at the end of the main entry section.

The electrotechnology field uses an ever-increasing number of acronyms. Thus the inclusion of a list of over 15,000 acronyms will be particularly useful. You may think you know what *XMAS* is, but in electrical or electronic jargon it stands for "extended mission Apollo simulation." *ZODIAC* is not an astronomical term; it means "zone defense integrated active capability." While it is certainly useful to know what these acronyms stand for, the problem is that neither the acronyms nor the actual term for the preceding examples are defined in the text; the user may well be left hanging with a partial answer only.

This volume will not take the place of a good computer science dictionary. While some computer-related terms are included (such as *kernel* and *label* in their computer sense), others are not. This is not an omission, but an editorial decision made regarding the scope of this particular dictionary; indeed, no one volume could hope to cover every term that might have relevance to electrical or electronics subjects.

The quality of the paper, the physical layout, and the typeface are very good in this volume. It is easy to pick out the terms being defined, other important terms within the definition, and cross-references. Formulas are given in a large, easy-to-read type. Obsolete terms are marked with an asterisk and the term *deprecated.*

Many technical dictionaries would not have to be updated every four years or so as this one has been, but the rate of change in the field makes it necessary to keep up with the language currently in use, as well as earlier definitions which are "reaffirmed" here. Approximately 4,000 new and revised terms have been added since the 1984 edition of the *IEEE Standard Dictionary of Electrical and Electronics Terms.* The Board recommends this work for the core collections of public and academic libraries.

McGraw-Hill Encyclopedia of Engineering. Sybil P. Parker, ed. McGraw-Hill, 1983. hard. 1 vol. 1,264 pp. illus. index. ISBN 0-07-045486-8. $82.50. encyclopedia.
TA9.M36 620.003

Many engineering reference works are designed for specialists in one narrow discipline, and are, therefore, inaccessible to the nonscientist or even to engineers in other fields. The *McGraw-Hill Encyclopedia of Engineering* was designed to cover the whole field, giving information on what the editors considered to be the ten major branches of engineering: chemical, civil, electrical, industrial, manufacturing, marine, mechanical, methods, mining, and nuclear. The basic electrical, mechanical, and thermodynamic principles of engineering are also covered.

There are nearly 700 alphabetically arranged entries; all are signed, and some have bibliographies appended. It should be noted that all entries are taken from the 1982 edition of the McGRAW-HILL ENCYCLOPEDIA OF SCIENCE AND TECHNOLOGY (see Science and Technology), and libraries having that set, or the newer 1987 edition, would need this volume only in special circumstances. The *McGraw-Hill Encyclopedia of Engineering* is worth considering for the smaller collection serving a nonspecialized clientele.

The entries are written to be accessible to the user reading on a high school level. Main entry words and subheadings are clearly set off by boldface type. The index is adequate. There are 6,000 entries, but the index could have been prepared with more care. *Wankel engine* is indexed but does not appear under the entry *rotary engines,* which is the title of the main text entry in which it appears. However, the entry for *fretting corrosion* has an entry in the index and can be located as a subentry under *corrosion.* Thus, the user may find it necessary to try several approaches to locate all references to a related topic because of inconsistent indexing of related subjects.

Currency is a problem for some subjects. This material was first copyrighted in 1982, and the *superconductivity* entry, as one example, is not where you want to send users for current information. (Part of the entry states that "the conservative opinion is that superconductors will remain essentially in their present form.") The 1987 edition of the McGraw-Hill Encyclopedia of Science and Technology, for example, has an updated entry on this topic.

On the whole, however, the *McGraw-Hill Encyclopedia of Engineering* is a useful one-volume compendium of information on a whole spectrum of engineering topics. The Board recommends this work for the core collections of public and academic libraries.

Reference Data for Engineers: Radio, Electronics, Computer, and Communications, 7th edition. Edward C. Jordan, ed. Sams, 1985. hard. 1 vol. 1,370 pp. illus. index. ISBN 0-672-21563-2. $79.95. handbook.
TK6552 621.38

For a half-century *Reference Data for Engineers: Radio, Electronics, Computer, and Communications* has been a standard reference tool. The previous editions were all titled *Reference Data for Radio Engineers,* and the change in title for the seventh edition is significant. "The nature and extent of the remarkable changes that have occurred in this field in recent years are reflected in this new edition, and have necessitated the change of title. . . . Nothing in electronics has escaped the effect of the transistor and the computer chip that came from it. The result has been a major metamorphosis and expansion of the entire field far beyond informed predictions of only twenty years ago" (preface). And that is exactly why a good, current compendium of data is necessary.

The scope of this work, as the subtitle suggests, includes radio, electronics, electronic devices, computer engineering, and communications. The book is divided into 48 chapters, such as: "Properties of Materials," "Fundamentals of Networks," "Attenuators," "Analog Communications," "Scattering Matrices," "Computer Organization and Programming," "Probability and Statistics," and "Mathematical Equations." There were over 70 contributors to this edition; perhaps half of the material is new. Each chapter is preceded by a short table of contents.

Basically, the text explains the tables, graphs, charts, and so forth, rather than the other way around. Chapter 40, "Computer Organization and Programming," can be used as an example. The introduction explains figure 1, "Levels of Detail of a Computer." Chapter 40 includes sections on number systems and arithmetic, basic computer organization, processors and programming, and input-output. There is a cross-reference to chapter 20 for information on integrated-circuit technologies. Many of the chapters have appended lists of references to related articles, standards, and monographs, although chapter 40 does not.

The index is good, with a few exceptions. A user can look up either *slot lines* or *lines, slot* and get the page numbers without having to go through a "see" reference. However, BASIC and FORTRAN, although mentioned briefly in the text, are not in the index; nor are computer languages, although *language(s)* is. Acronyms are included in the index.

Some of the chapters ("Mathematical Equations," "Mathematical Tables") contain basic information, obtainable elsewhere but useful to have here (although one wonders whether "Materials and Finishes for Tropical and Marine Use" was really a necessary chapter, given the scope of the book). The problem arises not because extraneous information was included, but because some recent information was not included. There are no references in the text to compact, laser, or optical disks, all topics that users might logically expect to find in a book of this kind.

A new edition of *Reference Data for Engineers: Radio, Electronics, Computers, and Communications,* incorporating the advances of the past half decade, would be most welcome; meanwhile, this is still a useful basic tool. The Board recommends this work for the core collection of academic libraries.

Who's Who in Engineering, 7th edition. Gordon Davis, ed. American Assn. of Engineering Societies, 1988. hard. 1 vol. 937 pp. index. ISBN 0-87615-015-6. $200. biographical dictionary.
TA12

This latest edition of *Who's Who in Engineering,* the standard engineering biographical reference work, does not depart much from the format it has evolved over the years. The actual title, series numbering, and sponsoring organization have undergone various permutations over the years since the 1922–1923 *Who's Who in Engineering* came out. That series ran through nine editions, ending in 1964, overseen by the Engineers Joint Council. In 1970 that same group came out with the first edition of *Engineers of Distinction,* which—with the third edition in 1977—became *Who's Who in Engineering.* The current edition is published by the American Association of Engineering Societies, an umbrella group of professional societies that represent over a half-million engineers in government, industry, and academia. The intent of this work is to "promote greater public awareness of the importance of engineering" ("Criteria for Inclusion").

The criteria for inclusion are clearly set out at the beginning of the work. "An applicant for *Who's Who in Engineering* must conform to one of the following: a baccalaureate or higher degree in engineering; a registered engineer in one or more states; achieve more than the first professional membership grade of an engineering society; be living and meet the requirements or definitions in one of [*sic*] more of the following: Member of the National Academy of Engineering; National Engineering and Related Scientific Societies; Educators; Engineers in Industry; Consultants; Engineers in Government; Other Eminent Engineers." These broad criteria make this the most inclusive of the engineering biographical directories (of which there is a plethora).

Each entry gives the person's name, followed by an address, specialization, and society memberships. Sometimes family information, hobbies, and extracurricular interests are included. These entries form the bulk of the volume.

A very useful section is the listing of engineering societies, with addresses, top officers, and awards. Each award is briefly described, and recipients for the past two decades are listed. There are indexes for this section, by society and award.

At the end of the book are two more useful indexes: individuals by state and by specialization. The specialization listings also give the person's name and state.

With a price of $200, *Who's Who in Engineering* is not for everyone. This is a good source, though, for the library with a need for quick-reference biographical information on engineers in a wide range of fields. The Board recommends this work for the core collection of academic libraries.

Aeronautic Engineering

Jane's Aerospace Dictionary, 3d edition. Bill Gunston, ed. Jane's Information Group, 1988. hard. 1 vol. 605 pp. appendix. ISBN 0-7106-0580-3. $45. dictionary.
TL509.G86 629.1′03

Since the first edition came out in 1980, *Jane's Aerospace Dictionary* has been the source for current aerospace and aeronautics terminology. In a field that changes as rapidly as aerospace does, the third edition is a welcome update.

There are over 20,000 entries; a quarter of these are acronyms. Arrangement is alphabetical, letter by letter, which is the most useful approach because so many entries are acronyms, and the user may not know whether the "word" needed is really a word or not. Definitions are short, and it sometimes is helpful to look up terms within the original definition to get a better grasp on the meaning. There are cross-references that help lead the user through the jargon of the field.

Many entries have multiple meanings, but the terms included here are those that would not be found in a standard dictionary. They are specific to the aerospace field, which leads to such amusing entries as *"George* automatic pilot (colloq, arch). Let George do it!"

The introduction contains much information on the ins and outs of using the volume. It is hard to get users to read front matter when all they want is a quick answer, but this is one case where five minutes of reading can really help. The definitions themselves are terse, to say the least; any superficial wordage has been discarded. What is left is the core of a definition that could hardly be reduced. The practitioner in the field will be grateful for this approach, but average users may need to make a greater effort to fully understand the material. The editor has made a conscious decision to keep the work to a manageable size and price and has succeeded.

Librarians may find it difficult to justify the purchase of a new edition when the last *Jane's Aerospace Dictionary* was published only four years ago, but for large public and academic libraries, this is an important title. The Board recommends this work for the core collections of public and academic libraries.

Civil Engineering

Standard Handbook for Civil Engineers, 3d edition. Frederick S. Merritt, ed. McGraw-Hill, 1983. hard. 1 vol. 1,620 pp. illus. index. ISBN 0-07-041515-3. $102. handbook.
TA151.S8 624

The scope and intent of the *Standard Handbook for Civil Engineers* are well summed up in the preface: "to provide in a single volume a compendium of the best of current civil engineering practices" and to hope "that application of its information will stimulate greater production of cost-effective, energy-efficient and environmentally sound civil engineering works."

The expansion of the third edition to incorporate new trends in planning, design, and construction has meant some obsolete or peripheral material has been omitted. New sections have been added; these are "Systems Design, Construction Materials," "Geotechnical Engineering," "Concrete Design and Construction," "Structural-Steel Design and Construction," "Community and Regional Planning," and "Harbor Engineering."

Approximately half the book deals with engineering in general: systems design, specifications, management, construction, structural, and geotechnical engineering. The systems design section is new to this edition and presents an overview of performance criteria, systems and systems analysis, goals and objectives, standards, costs, models, and so on. The section is well written and of use to both practicing and student engineers.

An ample number of graphs, tables, and illustrations are included to augment the text. These are all clearly labeled. An appendix providing metric conversion factors is included in this edition. The index is well done and logically constructed; small typographic touches such as putting the section number in boldface type help the user to find needed information. However, there are omissions: an index entry *ejectors, sewage* is given, but not sewage ejectors, and the index entry for *sewage* tells the user to see *runoff* or *wastewater,* neither of which has a subentry for ejectors.

Although the *Standard Handbook for Civil Engineers* is an essential tool for engineers and engineering students, the omission of a section on computer applications in the field of civil engineering is a problem. Although uses for computers expand and change daily (so that no reference work can be fully up to date), leaving the subject out entirely is no answer. The scope of the third edition should certainly be expanded by the inclusion of a section on computer applications in the next edition. The Board recommends this work for the core collections of public and academic libraries.

Electrical Engineering

Encyclopedia of Electronics, 2d edition. Stan Gibilisco and Neil Sclater, eds. TAB Bks., 1990. hard. 1 vol. 1,024 pp. illus. index. ISBN 0-8306-3389-8. $69.50. dictionary.
TK7804.E47 621.381

The *Encyclopedia of Electronics* is a good, accessible and reasonably priced source of information on electricity, electronics, and communications. The first edition was chosen as one of *Booklist*'s "Best Reference Books of the '80's." The text is wide ranging, bringing in aspects of related subjects that are necessary for an understanding of the main topics of the volume, but the scope is not so broad as to be unwieldy. For example, computer sciences are treated as they relate to electronics, the intent being not to attempt to be a complete encyclopedia of computer sciences too.

Arrangement of the entries is alphabetical. Cross-references are used frequently. The list of subject categories which was included in the first edition has unfortunately been dropped, but there are enough "see" references in the main text to guide the user to related material. As an example, the entry for *gallium arsenide* explains quite clearly the structure and importance of gallium arsenide (GaAs) in semiconductor devices, and has seven "see" references for those who want more information.

The illustrations are plentiful; apparently the policy was "no less than one per page." Most are clear and useful, with a minimum of extraneous information. They match the text policy of presuming no technological expertise on the part of the user. There is a list of symbols for use in schematic diagrams in the front, which is helpful.

The index is easy to use; the reader can look up *horizontal polarization* or *polarization, horizontal* and get the page numbers of relevant entries without having to go through a "see" reference. Therefore, related subjects are brought together (for example, there are some three dozen entries for terms beginning *oscilla-*), while the user can still get direct access for a specific term (*Hertz oscillator* or *sweep-frequency filter oscillator.*) There are certain omissions in content and indexing: there is no entry for high definition television, although the descriptive copy on the jacket flap lists this as an entry. The acronym WORM is not in the index, although the term it represents, the less-frequently used *write-once read many,* is; the information on *CD-ROM optical disk drive* is not listed with the *compact disk* page numbers, although these entries are closely enough related that the latter would help the user understand the former.

In a field that changes as rapidly as electronics, it is good news that there is a new edition of the *Encyclopedia of Electronics.* The readability and coverage of this work, along with the reasonable price, make it worth considering for public as well as academic collections, even if the 1985 edition is already held. The Board recommends this work for the core collections of public and academic libraries.

Illustrated Dictionary of Electronics, 4th edition. Rufus P. Turner and Stan Gibilisco, eds. TAB Bks.,

1988. soft. 1 vol. 648 pp. illus. appendix. ISBN 0-8306-2900-9. $24.95. dictionary.
TK7804.T87 621.381

The intended audience for the *Illustrated Dictionary of Electronics,* a compilation of some 22,000 short definitions and 500 accompanying illustrations, is "the electronics hobbyist and professional." This is not a research-oriented or advanced-level tool, and tends more toward trade jargon than academic language in its definitions. Patrons' needs and abilities should be the governing factor in deciding between this and the IEEE STANDARD DICTIONARY OF ELECTRICAL AND ELECTRONICS TERMS, which was also published in 1988 and which costs nearly twice as much.

Entries in the *Illustrated Dictionary of Electronics* are arranged alphanumerically, with numbers spelled out. Illustrations are captioned with the term they are supposed to accompany, which is a useful feature. It should be mentioned that some of the illustrations seem to have been included because it was time for an illustration, while some definitions that really could use an accompanying illustration lack one.

Cross-references ("see," "see also," and "compare") help guide the user to related information. The definitions are short and basic; the definition of *aurora* mentions atmospheric electricity, but not sunspots or other possible causes. There is an entry for *ROM* as an abbreviation of "read only memory," but the definition of that phrase mentions only "computers or calculators" without going into optical applications, and the *compact disk* entry is defined only in terms of "modern stereo systems." Thus, this would not help the user who needed a quick definition of CD-ROM.

The format is good and the typeface clear. Errors in alphabetization *(coplanar* is listed before *complement)* will undoubtedly be corrected in future printings. There are several basic tables appended to the text. Among these are resistor color codes, factorials, electronic abbreviations, and conversion factors. There are "several hundred" new definitions in this edition of the *Illustrated Dictionary of Electronics,* and those who found the third edition of this work useful will likely want the updated one. The Board recommends this work for the core collections of public and academic libraries.

Standard Handbook for Electrical Engineers, 12th edition. Donald G. Fink and H. Wayne Beaty, eds. McGraw-Hill, 1987. hard. 1 vol. 2,416 pp. illus. appendix. index. ISBN 0-07-020975-8. $92. handbook.
TK151.S8 621.3

The stated scope of the *Standard Handbook for Electrical Engineers* includes traditional engineering topics such as generation, transmission, distribution, control, conservation, and application of electrical power. The aim is to "contain in a single volume all pertinent data within its scope, to be accurate and comprehensive in technical treatment, to be of use in engineering practice (as well as in study and in preparation for such practice) and, above all, to be oriented toward practical application, including the impact of economic considerations" (preface). As this is the twelfth edition of the handbook, one can assume students as well as practicing engineers have found it to live up to its aim. The current editors have impressive professional credits and are affiliated with the Institute of Electrical and Electronics Engineers and the National Academy of Engineering, among other organizations.

The previous edition of the *Standard Handbook for Electrical Engineers* was published in 1978. Since then there have been major changes in the political and social climate in which electrical engineers work. The significance of the Three Mile Island and Chernobyl incidents is brought out in the preface to this edition, and their impact on the future of nuclear power generation is reflected in the changes from earlier editions. More attention is given to wind, solar, and geothermal power; magnetohydrodynamics; nuclear fusion; storage systems; fuel cells; and the conservation of energy sources in general.

The volume is organized into 26 major sections, with numerous subsections for each. All sections have been updated or rewritten. The growth in computer applications in electrical engineering has resulted in a greatly expanded section on that topic. "Project Economics," a new section, was added, dealing with financial considerations.

The diagrams, tables, formulas, line drawings, and graphs scattered throughout are well done and clearly reproduced. One nice feature is the minibibliography appended to many of the sections. These listings usually provide standards and references for further research.

For some reason the editors have chosen to shorten the index in this edition. Because a number of pages are left blank at the end of the book, this cannot have been based solely on fitting the material into a limited number of pages. Given the subheadings under *agriculture* (for example, *brooders, electricity in, heating systems*), *farm structures* might logically have been included, yet it is given a separate entry. *Fluidized bed combustion of coal* is not listed under *coal,* and its section number is different from the one listed for *coal, combustion of.* A user might easily miss needed information because of this sort of inadequate indexing.

Despite the indexing problems and the sizable price, librarians will want this volume simply because it is so comprehensive and so handy. Similar works such as the *Handbook of Modern Electronics and Electrical Engineering* differ in focus and emphasis enough so that the *Standard Handbook for Electrical Engineers* will remain a necessary tool for the field. The Board recommends this work for the core collections of public and academic libraries.

Materials Engineering

Encyclopedia of Materials Science and Engineering. Michael B. Bever, ed. MIT Pr., 1986. hard. 8 vols. plus 1 suppl. 5,000 pp. illus. indexes. ISBN 0-262-02231-1 (set). $1,950 (set). encyclopedia.
TA402.E53 620.11.0321

The *Encyclopedia of Materials Science and Engineering* is several orders of magnitude larger—and more expensive—than most of those included in this category. The question then is: Is it worth it? For academic libraries concerned with the various disciplines and subjects encompassed by materials science and engineering, the answer is yes.

Materials science and engineering is a young field, hardly more than 50 years old in the sense that we know it now. The field encompasses everything from fundamental science to engineering applications, from the technicalities of developing, processing, and using new materials to the impact of these materials on the consumption of energy supplies, health and safety, and the environment. The broad scope of this eight-volume set reflects the nature of the subject. Entries include materials based on their nature (ceramics, fibers, polymers) and on their applications (industrial, superconducting, biomedical), as well as materials-related methods and phenomena and general subjects. Excluded are foodstuffs, drugs, and fuels (other than nuclear). What remains is more than enough to fill seven volumes of articles. A systematic outline of the encyclopedia appears in the indexes volume (8). A one-volume supplement to this set was published in 1988.

The nearly 1,500 entries are arranged alphabetically, with the entry word formulated so that the key concept precedes a qualifying phrase. The overall convention is for "aspects" to follow "materials" and for "processes" to precede "materials." In cases where this logic would have resulted in awkward-sounding phrases, these entry words have been arranged in the most natural-sounding order. These variations might have been more of a problem for the user to locate if the index contained in volume 8 were not as good as it is. Over 50,000 index entries ensure access to information no matter how the entries are arranged in the text. Also contained in volume 8 is the systematic outline, which sets out the conceptual organization for the work (although the "Guide to Use of the Encyclopedia" is in volume 1); the list of contributors; the author citation index (which leads to bibliographic entries for works by particular people); a list of acronyms; and a valuable chapter on "Materials Information Sources."

The numerous illustrations are generally well reproduced. There are cross-references to related entries both embedded in and appended to most articles, and all articles have bibliographies. Some of the bibliographies seem a bit dated for a 1986 publication. This may have occurred because the development process for the book took ten years.

There is some overlap between the *Encyclopedia of Materials Science and Engineering* and other works, but that is a result of the multidisciplinary nature of materials science and engineering. The Board recommends this work for the core collection of academic libraries.

Mechanical Engineering

Marks' Standard Handbook for Mechanical Engineers, 9th edition. Eugene A. Avallone and Theodore Baumeister III, eds. McGraw-Hill, 1987. hard. 1 vol. 1,936 pp. illus. appendix. index. ISBN 0-07-004127-X. $92. handbook.
TJ151.M37 621.02

Marks' Standard Handbook for Mechanical Engineers is the ninth edition of a work first published in 1916. In the preface to the first edition, Lionel Marks stated that the work was intended as an authoritative and comprehensive handbook for the "practicing engineer and the student." Three-quarters of a century later, it would be safe to say he has succeeded; the work known widely as *Marks* is the standard in its field.

There are 19 sections, ranging from "Mathematical Tables and Measuring Units" to "Strength of Materials" to "Power Generation" to "Shop Processes." Each section has a detailed table of contents for the chapters it contains. Contributors are listed in the front matter, as a group, and as individuals preceding the sections and chapters that they were responsible for revising. A short list of pertinent references accompanies each chapter.

The ninth edition is a major revision. Approximately 80 percent of the material included has been updated, especially in the areas of mathematics, machine elements, piping, environmental control and pollution, and use of personal computers in mechanical engineering practice. There is an entirely new chapter on robotics.

Care has been taken to make *Marks' Standard Handbook for Mechanical Engineers* a really practical, useful tool. Where symbols common in a field differ from those in engineering practice, as in cryogenics, a special listing is given. The list of "Commonly Used Piping Standards" is followed by a list of the addresses of the sources of the standards. The "Industrial Engineering" section contains a ten-page chapter, "The Costs of Electric Power," which could be useful to the nonengineer as well as to the practitioner. Because the use of International System (SI) units of measurement is not universal, U.S. Customary System (USCS) units are also given.

In order to keep the work to a manageable size, a thin paper has been used that is not completely opaque. This is a minor problem. The nearly 3,000 tables and illustrations are clear and well chosen to complement the text. There is a 61-page index that, even at that length, is not as comprehensive as the text requires: *Air chambers of pumps* is there, but not chambers or air chambers as a subheading of *pumps. Pumps, reciprocating* gives a "see" reference to *Reciprocating pumps.* The user needs to be persistent to find specific information in the index.

For libraries with a need for mechanical engineering information, *Marks' Standard Handbook for Mechanical Engineers* is likely to be the tool of choice. The Board recommends this work for the core collections of public and academic libraries.

Supplementary Titles

General

Information Sources in Engineering, 2d edition. L. J. Anthony, ed. Butterworth, 1985. hard. 1 vol. ISBN 0-408-11475-4. $95. handbook.
T10.7.J54 620.00719

Board's recommendation: Academic libraries.

Chemical Engineering

Perry's Chemical Engineers' Handbook, 6th edition. Robert H. Perry, late ed., and Don W. Green, ed. McGraw-Hill, 1984. hard. 1 vol. 2,336 pp. illus. index. ISBN 0-07-049479-7. $105. handbook.
TP151.C52 660.2'8

The sixth edition of *Perry's Chemical Engineers' Handbook* is "written by more than 100 experts [and it] . . . updates the fifth edition published in 1973. . . . The 25 sections of the previous edition have been revised and updated, with sections on economics, distillation, extraction, and absorption completely rewritten. Two new sections dealing with waste management and biochemical engineering have been added. Another significant addition is the use of both SI (International System of units) and U. S. customary systems of units. Indexing remains the same with a detailed table of contents preceding each section and an overall alphabetic index. The more than 1,800 illustrations are clear. . . . This easy-to-use handbook remains a useful addition to college and special library collections." (*ARBA,* 1985, p. 543)

Also reviewed in: *Choice,* May 1974, p. 410; *SB,* September 1974, p. 154; *SciTech,* August 1984, p. 26.

Board's recommendation: Public and academic libraries.

Electrical Engineering

American Electricians' Handbook, 11th edition. Terrell Croft. McGraw-Hill, 1987. hard. 1 vol. illus. index. ISBN 0-07-013932-6. $69.50. handbook.
TK151.C8 621.3

The *American Electricians' Handbook* is a "classic reference [book that] describes how to select, install, maintain, and operate all types of electrical equipment and wiring. It covers fundamentals, typical calculations, equipment considerations, wiring tables, and current electrical-code practices. New material has been included on electronic and solid-state circuits. All-new electric-lighting tables reflect current bulb technology, new types of area coverage lamps, and new types of energy-saving lighting." (Engineering Societies Library book review, July 1987)

"The most significant updates in this edition are divisions 6 and covering solid-state devices, circuits, and electric lighting. The general principles, terminology, and applications of each division's subject are thoroughly described and illustrated with the appropriate standards referenced. The extensive 44-page index in this volume allows the reader to access appropriate sections easily.

"[This book] maintains the standards of previous editions. It is a professional reference volume for the practicing electrician; useful to students studying electricity or related areas; and an excellent source for those who are curious about electrical principles or [are] seeking information on the subject." (*SciTech Annual Ref Rev,* 1989)

Also reviewed in: *ARBA,* 1988, p. 640; *New Tech Bks,* November 1987, p. 338; *SciTech,* October 1987, p. 38.

Board's recommendation: Public and academic libraries.

Dictionary of Electronics, 2d edition. S. W. Amos. Butterworth, 1987. hard. 1 vol. 324 pp. illus. ISBN 0-408-02750-9. $42.95. dictionary.
TK7804.A47 621.381.03

"The *Dictionary of Electronics* is intended primarily for engineers, technicians, students and amateurs. Some entries are short essays with diagrams. . . . Although it is British, North American technology is fully represented. [The] second edition includes updates on semiconductors, digital techniques, computers and microprocessors." (*New Tech Bks,* March/April 1988, p. 621)

This is a "needed revision of the 1981 edition. . . . Some 300 definitions have been added and about 200 have been reworded or expanded. The digital techniques and dictionary not only cover the computer terms currently in use in the UK and US, but also explain many terms in depth; illustrations and extensive cross-reference[s] are included. An appendix gives many commonly used abbreviations and acronyms." (*SciTech,* January 1988, p. 39)

Also reviewed in: *ARBA,* 1988, p. 639; *R&R Bk N,* February 1988, p. 21; *SciTech,* January 1988, p. 27.

Board's recommendation: Public and academic libraries.

Modern Dictionary of Electronics, 6th edition. Rudolf F. Graf. Howard W. Sams, 1984. hard. 1 vol. 1,152 pp. ISBN 0-672-22041-5. $39.95. dictionary.
TK7804.G67 621.381'03'21

The *Modern Dictionary of Electronics* "is a dictionary containing more than . . . [20,000] authoritative definitions of terms . . . used in the general field of electronics. Mr. Graf, who has a background of 20 years in the electronics field as instructor, consultant, and design and development engineer, covers the areas of radio, television, communications, radar, instrumentation, industrial and medical electronics, computers, data processing logic, lasers, fiber optics, semi-conductors, microelectronics, and reliability. This dictionary will be useful to engineers, technicians, technical writers, editors, students, and others affiliated with the electronics field." (*LJ,* April 15, 1968, p. 1618)

Also reviewed in: *ARBA,* 1979, p. 772; *RSR,* October 1979, p. 31; *SLJ,* February 1981, p. 37.

Board's recommendation: Public and academic libraries.

Modern Electronic Circuits Reference Manual. John Markus. McGraw-Hill, 1980. hard. 1 vol. 1,238 pp. illus. ISBN 0-07-040446-1. $89.95. handbook.
TK7867.M345 621.3815'3

The *Modern Electronic Circuits Reference Manual* is an "invaluable manual contain[ing] . . . an entire library shelf of data culled from important electronics applications journals and applications notes of the past several years. . . . Organized and indexed for convenient reference, it gives the values of all significant components to facilitate adaptation to another application and offers suggestions for making such revisions. Long articles and reports are condensed into concisely worded abstracts containing maximum information in the least possible space. Readable by a wide variety of users at many levels of complexity, this volume would be equally useful to electronic engineers, students of electronics at the high school level, electronics experimenters and hobbyists, and amateur radio operators." (*BL,* May 15, 1982, p. 1246)

Also reviewed in: *Choice,* February 1981, p. 820.

Board's recommendation: Public and academic libraries.

Portable Electronics Data Book. John Douglas-Young. Prentice-Hall, 1989. hard. 1 vol. ISBN 0-13-685827-9. $37.60. handbook.
TK7825.D68 621.381021

Board's recommendation: Academic libraries.

Mechanical Engineering

Dictionary of Mechanical Engineering, 3d edition. G. H. F. Nayler. Butterworth, 1985. hard. 1 vol. 394 pp. illus. ISBN 0-408-01505-5. $80. dictionary.
TJ9.N3 621.03

The *Dictionary of Mechanical Engineering* "provides . . . comprehensive coverage of terms currently used in mechanical and production engineering. Since the publication of the previous edition ten years ago[,] many new terms have been added to the engineer's vocabulary, particularly in the fields related to robotics, automation and computer applications.

"This new edition has been completely revised to cover a broader field of topics and contains many new illustrations and over 700 new entries. The appendices listing engineering symbols and abbreviations have also been revised and brought up-to-date." (Engineering Societies Library book review, April 1986)

The *Dictionary of Mechanical Engineering* is "an illustrated dictionary of value to engineers and students as well as technical writers, journalists, and others who need technically accurate information that is concise, straightforward, and accessible." (*R&R Bk N,* Spring 1986, p. 12)

Also reviewed in: *Appl Mech Rev,* August 1988, p. 1205; *ARBA,* 1987, p. 615; *New Tech Bks,* October 1986, p. 600; *SciTech,* May 1986, p. 31.

Board's recommendation: Academic libraries.

Machinery's Handbook: A Reference Book for the Mechanical Engineer, Draftsman, Toolmaker and Machinist, 23d edition. Eric Oberg, Franklin D. Jones, and Holbrook L. Horton. Industrial Pr., 1988. hard. 1 vol. 2,511 pp. illus. index. ISBN 0-8311-1200-X. $55. handbook.
TJ151.0245 621.8′0212

"From 1914 to the present, [*Machinery's Handbook*] has been the standard reference work on machines and mechanical products. Every possible aspect is included in the over 140 topics. Each topic is covered completely, with tables, standards, illustrations, brief text, definitions, formulae, and worked examples. The 140 topics are included under the broad areas of mathematical tables, logarithms, trigonometric functions, mechanics, strength of materials, gearing, screws, threads, fits, small tools, special feeds, steels, non-ferrous, and weights and measures. A detailed index is included." (*ARBA,* 1976, p. 779)

Board's recommendation: Public and academic libraries.

New and Noteworthy

Concise Encyclopedia of Building and Construction Materials. Fred Moavenzadeh. Pergamon, 1990; distrib. by MIT Pr. hard. 1 vol. 682 pp. illus. ISBN 0-08-034728-2. $175. encyclopedia.
TA402.C657 624

The *Concise Encyclopedia of Building and Construction Materials* contains "over 100 articles [that] cover general building materials, their mechanical properties, and economic and historical aspects, as well as dealing specifically with the use of materials such as clays, ceramics, cement, sand, gravels, glass, metals, wood, polymers, plastics, and composites. [The work is] extensively illustrated and indexed throughout, the articles introduce the reader to one topic in turn, giving sources for further reading in the concise and up-to-date bibliographies with which each concludes." (Excerpted from publisher's announcement)

Concise Encyclopedia of Composite Materials. Anthony Kelly. Pergamon, 1989; distrib. by MIT Pr. hard. 1 vol. 317 pp. illus. ISBN 0-08-034718-5. $135. encyclopedia.
TA418.9.C6C635 620.11803

"The 55 articles in . . . [the *Concise Encyclopedia of Composite Materials*] provide a full and up-to-date account of all aspects of composite materials, including fiber composites, particulate composites and naturally-occurring composite materials and their properties. Current coverage is also given to metal matrix composites and thermoplastic resins reinforced with fibers. . . . Each article is extensively cross-referenced to other related topics and has a bibliography referring readers to the appropriate current literature." (Excerpted from publisher's announcement)

Concise Encyclopedia of Mineral Resources. Donald D. Carr and Norman Herz. Pergamon, 1989; distrib. by MIT Pr. hard. 1 vol. 426 pp. illus. ISBN 0-08-034734-7. $145. encyclopedia.
TA402.C66 620.11

In the *Concise Encyclopedia of Mineral Resources,* "112 articles comprehensively address the problems of economic geology in a single volume. Industrial minerals are discussed according to their use, whilst metals and fuels (such as coal, petroleum and nuclear energy minerals) are dealt with on the basis of their properties, distribution, production history and future outlook. Recent developments in alternatives to the use of asbestos, computer models in mining and exploration and the world distribution of coal and petroleum are also covered." (Excerpted from publisher's announcement)

Concise Encyclopedia of Wood and Wood-Based Materials. Arno P. Schniewind. Pergamon, 1990; distrib. by MIT Pr. hard. 1 vol. 354 pp. illus. index. ISBN 0-262-19289-6. $125. encyclopedia.
TA419.C64 620.110321

The *Concise Encyclopedia of Wood and Wood-Based Materials* is "alphabetically organized, with 73 articles by over 60 leading authorities on wood. . . . This encyclopedia covers the whole range of knowledge and current research in wood science. Included are articles on the availability and economics of timber resources, wood products such as plywood and mineral-bonded wood composites, descriptions of the major commercial wood species of the world, fundamentals of wood properties and behavior, factors causing deterioration and their control and principal processing methods. . . . A comprehensive, three-level subject index is also provided." (Excerpted from publisher's announcement)

Handbook of Plastic Materials and Technology. John Wiley, 1990. hard. 1 vol. ISBN 0-471-09634-2. $115. handbook.
TP1130.H35 668.4

"The *Handbook of Plastic Materials and Technology* . . . answers the most often asked questions about 119 different plastics topics. . . . Every material is analyzed according to its: chemical name, category, history, polymerization, description of properties, applications, advantages/disadvantages, processing techniques, resin forms, specification of the properties, processing requirements, processing sensitive end properties, shrinkage, trade names and information sources." (Excerpted from publisher's announcement)

Television and Audio Handbook: For Technicians and Engineers. K. Blair Benson and Jerry C. Whitaker. McGraw-Hill, 1990. hard. 1 vol. 640 pp. illus. ISBN 0-07-004787-1. $39.95. handbook.
TK6642.B45 791.45

"Comprehensive in scope and highly practical in approach, the *Television and Audio Handbook: For Technicians and Engineers* projects all the basic data needed to maintain, troubleshoot, and service today's state-of-the-art systems. . . . The handbook not only explains the fundamental concepts of TV and audio circuit design and performance, but also offers detailed information on the operation, maintenance, and testing of both systems and components." (Excerpted from publisher's announcement)

Andrea Yang

Ethnic Studies

See also Genealogy

The field of ethnic studies is wide and varied, and specialists have yet to agree on a common definition of what constitutes an ethnic group. Frequently, ethnic groups are defined as any group of people sharing a common culture, who may or may not share racial characteristics. At other times, ethnic groups have been defined according to place of origin, religion, language, ancestry, or life ways. Therefore, a librarian compiling a collection on ethnic studies will inevitably select books that reflect different definitions of ethnicity.

A core reference collection should include historical and contemporary information on hundreds of ethnic groups. Because these groups may be studied from anthropological, sociological, economic, linguistic, and various other approaches, a core collection should also include works that allow users to analyze ethnic groups from all angles.

A wide variety of reference sources are available. For example, specialized biographical works can identify past and present leaders within ethnic communities. Directories, such as the *Directory of Services for Refugees and Immigrants* (Alan Edward Scharr, ed., Denali Pr., 1987), are helpful in locating ethnic organizations, interest groups, and ethnic presses. Specialized encyclopedias and dictionaries (for example, the ENCYCLOPEDIA OF NATIVE AMERICAN TRIBES) shed light on culture, history, and life ways of ethnic groups. There are atlases available that show the origins of ethnic groups, trace their migrations, and explain demographic trends. Bibliographies identify a wide variety of publications about individual ethnic groups as well as publications by ethnic organizations. MINORITIES IN AMERICA: THE ANNUAL BIBLIOGRAPHY is one example of this type of work.

Standard works, such as the HARVARD ENCYCLOPEDIA OF AMERICAN ETHNIC GROUPS, can provide basic descriptions and demographic data on hundreds of ethnic groups in a single volume. In addition, specialized works on each of the larger ethnic communities in the United States, such as the ENCYCLOPEDIA OF JEWISH HISTORY, will be needed to satisfy many patron inquiries. Frequently, specialized works on the local ethnic populations will be needed to supplement the core works reviewed in this volume. Works such as the *Index to Afro-American Reference Sources* (Rosemary Stevenson, comp., Greenwood, 1988) can be useful in identifying supplementary works that meet local needs for reference works on specific groups.

Core Titles

	PUBLIC	ACADEMIC	SCHOOL
Atlas of the North American Indian Waldman, Carl. Facts On File, 1985	✦	✦	✦
Encyclopedia of Native American Tribes Waldman, Carl. Facts On File, 1988	✦	✦	✦
Harvard Encyclopedia of American Ethnic Groups Thernstrom, Stephan, ed. Belknap/Harvard, 1980	✦	✦	
The State of Black America Dewart, Janet, ed. National Urban League, annual	✦	✦	
We the People: An Atlas of America's Ethnic Diversity Allen, James Paul, and Eugene James Turner. Macmillan, 1988	✦	✦	✦

Core Titles

Atlas of the North American Indian. Carl Waldman. Facts On File, 1985. hard and soft. 1 vol. 276 pp. illus. appendix. index. ISBN 0-87196-850-9 (hard); 0-8160-2136-8 (soft). $29.95 (hard); $16.95 (soft). atlas.
E77.B6 970.00.497

The *Atlas of the North American Indian* by Carl Waldman is as much an encyclopedia as an atlas. The text includes photos, illustrations, and 96 two-color maps, many of which are thematic and are used to illustrate migration and settlement patterns, cultural areas, land cessions, the sites of Indian wars, and much more. The maps, photographs, and illustrations are appropriate and well done, and Waldman's accompanying text also gives accurate, basic information on many other aspects of Indian life.

The *Atlas of the North American Indian* is divided into seven chapters that treat rather broad topics: "Ancient Indians," "Ancient Civilizations," "Indian Lifeways," "Indians and Explorers," "Indian Wars," "Indian Land Cessions," and "Contemporary Indians." Chapters are subdivided according to subject, geography, or tribe. The early chapters include sections on the Indians of Central America as well as those of North America. Of particular interest is the "Indians and Explorers" chapter, which presents a useful chronology of North American explorers' contacts with Native Americans. In addition, the final chapter, "Contemporary Indians," presents a brief overview of government policies, social conditions, and Indian activism up to the early 1980s.

Cross-references are used liberally throughout the text. Chapters are well written and provide good topical overviews. Readers who need to look for further details can consult the brief bibliography provided at the end of the book. Those interested in a particular tribe could also consult Waldman's 1988 publication, ENCYCLOPEDIA OF NATIVE AMERICAN TRIBES, for more specific discussion.

A good subject index adds to the value of the *Atlas of the North American Indian* as a core reference work. The appendix provides a number of useful features, including a chronology of significant historical events; a list of Indian tribes and their historical and contemporary locations in the United States and Canada; a register of reservations, trust areas, and native villages within the United States; a list of Indian bands in Canada; a glossary of Indian place names; and a list of relevant historical organizations and archaeological sites.

Waldman and cartographer and illustrator Molly Braun are a free-lance team with an abiding interest and extensive background in Native American studies. Also, the use of consultants such as Dr. John Trimbur of Boston University, a specialist in American studies, and Christopher Campbell, a cartographic analyst, adds to the authority of this reference.

The *Atlas of the North American Indian* will appeal to a broad audience. It is a sensitive, readable, and visual treatment of Native American experiences in North America. The atlas is also inexpensive and is available in both hardcover and paperback.

The *Atlas of the North American Indian* was named one of the "Outstanding Reference Books of 1985" by the American Library Association. The Board recommends this work for the core collections of public, academic, and school libraries.

Encyclopedia of Native American Tribes. Carl Waldman. Facts On File, 1988. hard. 1 vol. 293 pp. illus. appendix. index. ISBN 0-8160-1421-3. $40. encyclopedia.
E76.2.W35 970.004'97'00321

The *Encyclopedia of Native American Tribes* by Carl Waldman is comprised of brief, easy-to-read entries about Native American tribes (such as the *Navajo*), language families (for example, the *Athapascan*), and culture areas (such as the *Great Basin culture area*). In the introductory section entitled "How to Use This Book," Waldman defines a culture area as a "geographic region where the various Indian peoples had lifeways in common."

Space requirements limited the number of tribes in the encyclopedia to 150. Tribes were chosen for inclusion according to their historical significance or because of their representativeness of a particular way of life; South American tribes are not included. Readers will find essays on present-day tribes (such as the *Seminoles*) as well as those of the past. For example, the encyclopedia includes a short entry on the *Beothuk,* whose last known descendant died in 1829. Also included are entries on more general cultural themes, such as *prehistoric Indians,* and early civilizations, such as the *Aztec* and the *Maya.*

Entries are arranged alphabetically, and a chart is provided that shows the relationships among tribes, language families, and culture areas. In addition to the chart, cross-references are used extensively within most entries to connect related topics. Some entries are less than a page in length, while others range from one to seven pages long. The encyclopedia includes more than 250 color illustrations, and 11 maps by Molly Braun. The illustrations, which depict various artifacts, tools, costumes, and structures, complement the text very well.

The author and illustrator are a free-lance team who produced the ATLAS OF THE NORTH AMERICAN INDIAN. Consultants were used in their earlier work, but the *Encyclopedia of Native American Tribes* seems to rest completely on Waldman and Braun's expertise. Some entries appear to be better researched than others. For example, the coverage of subtopics such as religion, food, and social structure within the tribal entries is inconsistent, with the degree of detail varying from essay to essay. While these entries offer readers an overview based on generally accepted knowledge about each tribe, language group, or culture area, the brief essays on the lesser-known and seldom-studied tribes will probably be the most helpful. The more commonly studied tribes are frequently covered just as well by any general encyclopedia.

A good index, a valuable glossary, and a short bibliography conclude the work. The bibliography is organized into categories such as "Indian Art and Artifacts" and "Indian Wars." It includes some of the standard works as well as a list of books for young readers. Most of the titles listed should be readily available in public or school libraries.

While the *Encyclopedia of Native American Tribes* has a place in all libraries, the color illustrations and the reading level make it especially appropriate to school and public libraries. The brevity of the essays limits the book's usefulness to the academic patron. Nevertheless, the academic library user will find the concise essays helpful in many situations. The Board recommends this work for the core collections of public, academic, and school libraries.

Harvard Encyclopedia of American Ethnic Groups. Stephan Thernstrom, ed. Belknap/Harvard, 1980. hard. 1 vol. 1,076 pp. illus. appendix. ISBN 0-674-37512-2. $90. encyclopedia.
E184.A1H35 973.04

The *Harvard Encyclopedia of American Ethnic Groups* is a unique and useful reference source. The single-volume work is the result of a six-year project involving 120 contributors, a large editorial staff, and over 170 consultants. Although many of the consultants and contributors were historians, a number of others represented such academic disciplines as economics, linguistics, sociology, and political science. Not all contributors were academics; some cited no scholarly or organizational affiliations. The editors stress, however, that sometimes only a particular person—regardless of the lack of affiliation—had the knowledge to write the entry. Although most entries are signed, a few are not, either because the contributor requested anonymity or because the entry was written by a member of the editorial staff. Notable contributors who are represented by signed entries include Nathan Glazer, Michael Novak, and Michael Walzer.

Entries are arranged alphabetically by name of ethnic group or subject. One hundred six entries are on ethnic groups, and 29 are thematic essays with such titles as "Assimilation" and "Pluralism," "Folklore," "Prejudice," and "Survey Research." Also, because the editors' definition of ethnicity includes American regional groups, readers will find entries on *Appalachians, Southerners, Yankees,* and *Mormons,* as well as on the expected groups of foreign origin.

Eighty-seven black-and-white maps and numerous tables describing migration, population, and group characteristics enhance the text. Many of the tables and much of the statistical information in the entries are based on 1970 census data. Naturally, these figures no longer reflect the actual status of most ethnic groups. An appendix includes the essay "Methods of Estimating the Size of Groups" and sample tables from the U.S. Bureau of the Census.

The content and length of each entry varies. Contributors were provided with an outline (reprinted in the introduction) suggesting essay content, but few addressed every topic. Most essays range from 3,000 to 15,000 words. The length of an essay appears to be affected by the source material available and the size of the ethnic group. Short bibliographies follow entries, and the numerous cross-references are helpful.

In some cases, the *Harvard Encyclopedia of American Ethnic Groups* will be one of the best sources of information available on a particular ethnic group. The book offers material on groups about which there is very little in print (such as the entry for the *Carpatho-Rusyns*). For groups about which much has been published (such as the entry for *Afro-Americans*), the text offers accurate and concise summaries.

Occasionally, readers may question some of the categories or groupings used in the book. For example, the entry for *Central and South Americans* focuses primarily on Colombians. In another instance, Vietnamese, Laotians, and Cambodians are all discussed in an entry titled *Indochinese.* Far too little of this entry is devoted to the differences among the three ethnic groups.

A revised edition of the encyclopedia that incorporates more recent census information and focuses on the new or growing ethnic groups of the 1980s would be welcome. Nevertheless, the *Harvard Encyclopedia of American Ethnic Groups* is a one-of-a-kind source that retains its value and relevancy, even though it could be more current. The Board recommends this work for the core collections of public and academic libraries.

The State of Black America. Janet Dewart, ed. National Urban League, annual (1976–). soft. 1 vol. ISBN 0-914758-11-X. $19. yearbook.
E185.5 973.04.96073

The State of Black America is an annual publication (since 1976) of the National Urban League, a widely respected, nonprofit organization devoted to the achievement of equal opportunity for blacks and other minorities. The stated purpose of the publication is to promote "awareness of the reality of life within Black America and to influence the decision-making process."

This reference is an inexpensive source of up-to-date information on issues of concern to black Americans. Although the topics treated vary from year to year, each volume in the series follows the same general format. Each begins with a preface that provides a brief biographical sketch of the primary contributors. The first chapter, usually authored by the president of the National Urban League, offers a survey of significant trends or events that affected black Americans in the previous year. This chapter reflects the views of the National Urban League leadership and typically mentions the economy, law, and national policy. Recurrent themes include economic disparity, social welfare legislation, and racism.

The major part of each volume is comprised of essays written by distinguished, independent scholars and social leaders. These topical essays range from a few pages to over 30 pages in length and address a wide variety of issues that affect black Americans. Recent volumes have addressed subjects such as AIDS, the family, state and local government, the black church, and drugs. Notes and references as well as a chronology of the year's events based on news reports are located at the end of each volume. Within the chronology, there are brief entries for the following categories: *politics, civil rights, federal budget, affirmative action, education/desegregation,* and *race relations.*

The specific criteria used to select the articles are not revealed. However, the introduction states that the purpose of the topical articles is to inform and that the works "do not necessarily reflect the official position or policies of the National Urban League." Indeed, a separate chapter entitled "Conclusions and Recommendations" typically follows the main articles and serves as a forum for the policies, initiatives, and recommendations of the National Urban League.

The State of Black America series is appropriate for a general audience, and the wide range of topics covered in each issue adequately reflect contemporary social concerns of black Americans. The Board recommends this work for the core collections of public and academic libraries.

We the People: An Atlas of America's Ethnic Diversity. James Paul Allen and Eugene James Turner. Macmillan, 1988. hard. 1 vol. 315 pp. illus. appendixes. index. ISBN 0-02-901420-4. $125. atlas.
E184.A1A479 305.8′00973

We the People: An Atlas of America's Ethnic Diversity is the result of a seven-year project involving numerous consultants and cartographers. The authors, James Paul Allen, a professor of geography, and Eugene James Turner, a professor and specialist in computer mapping, have produced an exceptional reference work that "examines ethnic population patterns primarily in terms of counties and the major towns and cities of distinctive ethnic settlements" (preface). The atlas is based on data obtained from 1980 U.S. Bureau of the Census data tapes. The atlas includes 115 maps (44 are full page) and valuable text identifying the origins of ethnic groups, important subgroups within ethnic groups, and distribution and migration patterns. There are a few historical maps representing ethnic distributions as of 1920, but most maps are based on 1980 distributions.

According to the preface, *We the People* is intended for scholars, specialists, and those "millions of people who have an interest and pride in their own ethnic background." The atlas makes use of sophisticated statistical and mapping techniques. With some effort, however, the atlas will also provide the nonspecialist with a great deal of unique and useful data. Cartograms and choropleth maps are used to convey visually population statistics. Summary tables of statistics are also provided. Maps are large and utilize color effectively. The atlas is oversize. Although the book can be awkward to handle, the size facilitates the use of legible, detailed maps.

The atlas begins with three chapters that aid the reader in interpreting the maps and data provided in later chapters. The first chapter, "Quality of the 1980 Census Data on Ethnicity," is an excellent review essay about the design, problems, and appropriate uses of census data. Chapter 2, "Data Selection and Map Design," explains why the county is a satisfactory basic mapping unit for the study of ethnicity. The chapter also explains why the atlas is based on single-ancestry data rather than multiple-ancestry data from census tapes. The authors note the lack of census data on religion (because questions pertaining to religion cannot be asked in the decennial census) and explain how they compiled a map on the Jewish ethnic group. Finally, a third introductory chapter explains how to interpret the maps in the remainder of the atlas.

The atlas focuses on the distribution of ethnic groups. Therefore, migration of ethnic groups is discussed with attention to why places were chosen for settlement, work opportunities available to ethnic groups, and the phenomenon of chain migration. The ten core chapters of the atlas discuss ethnic groups according to place of origin (such as "People of Western European Origin"). In all, 67 racial and ethnic groups are discussed. In addition, many subgroups, such as the Swiss Amish and the Sephardic Jews, are included in the discussions of the major ethnic groups.

The atlas concludes with a lengthy bibliography and appendixes listing data on ancestries of state populations, ethnic population data, and reference maps of U.S. counties. A brief index is also provided.

We the People: An Atlas of America's Ethnic Diversity is a solid reference work based on the best data available. The authority, scope, detail, and visual attraction of this reference make it an excellent research tool. The Board recommends this work for the core collections of public, academic, and school libraries.

Supplementary Titles

American Jewish Year Book. Milton Himmelfarb and David Singer, eds. American Jewish Committee/Jewish Publication Society of America, annual. hard. 1 vol. 516 pp. ISBN 0-8276-0313-4. $28.50. yearbook.
E184.J546

This book is "an annual publication of inestimable value . . . *The American Jewish Year Book* contains the customary directories, lists, necrologies, calendars, demographic surveys and reports on Jewish communities in Europe, Israel, and elsewhere in North America. . . . [The volume should] be widely read." (*RSR,* April 1988, p. 171)

This volume "continues the tradition of presenting well-organized and pertinent data regarding the activities, developments, and major events occurring among the world's Jews. . . . Civic, political, communal, and demographic developments among Jews in the United States are presented. In addition, Jewish life in Canada, Western, Central, and Eastern Europe, Israel, South Africa, and Australia is also covered. New estimates of the Jewish population worldwide are provided. Directories of organizations, periodicals, federations, and welfare funds, as well as religious calendars and obituary notices complete this reference tool." (*ARBA,* 1983, p. 208)

Also reviewed in: *ARBA,* 1976, p. 212; 1980 p. 202; *RSR,* October 1974, p. 151; October 1982, p. 391; October 1983, p. 390; *Wil Q,* Autumn 1981, p. 149.

Board's recommendation: Public libraries.

Encyclopedia of Jewish History. Joseph Alpher, ed. Facts On File, 1986. hard. 1 vol. 287 pp. illus. index. ISBN 0-8160-1220-2. $35. encyclopedia.
DS114.E53 909.049240

The *Encyclopedia of Jewish History* is "a survey history in encyclopedia format of the Jewish people from their origins until modern times. Consisting of about 100 historical entries, the bulk of the work [seeks to] describe the major events and key figures in Jewish history in . . . essays of about 800 words written by Israeli scholars and writers. Arranged chronologically, each article contains: a main text, supplemented with illustrations, photographs, and maps; a list of cross-reference terms; and an illustrated key, which sums up the theme of each entry. A dozen appendixes [include] articles on the Hebrew alphabet, Jewish symbols and costume, and a synchronic chart comparing Jewish history with important events in world history.

"Lavishly illustrated, succinctly written, and well-indexed, this work serves as an excellent general reference work on the topic." (*Choice,* January 1987, p. 740)

"The emphasis . . . is on the modern period, with more than half of the book devoted to the 20th century. Each brief feature article is arranged on facing pages and is surrounded by related paintings, maps, photographs, woodcuts, and artifacts. . . . The book is eminently suitable for pleasurable browsing." (*LJ,* April 1, 1986, p. 149)

Also reviewed in: *A Lib,* May 1987, pp. 332, 337; *ARBA,* 1987, p. 163; *BL,* April 15, 1986, p. 1179; *B Rpt,* May 1987, p. 49; *R&R Bk N,* Summer 1986, p. 6.

Board's recommendation: Public and academic libraries.

Minorities in America: The Annual Bibliography. Wayne Charles Miller. Pennsylvania State Univ. Pr., annual. hard. 1 vol. 500 pp. index. ISBN 0-271-00380-4. $100. bibliography.

"Despite increasingly conservative social and governmental attitudes reflected on many campuses by movements to return to a 'traditional' curriculum, ethnicity persists as a significant force in American cultural life. Beginning in the 1960s, the publication of a substantial number of monographs demonstrates that ethnicity is an indissoluble sociopolitical reality. Bibliographies and other information sources that have appeared within the last ten years . . . belie that notion that academic concern with ethnic groups is transitory. Building on the foundation established by his earlier work, *A Comprehensive Bibliography for the Study of American Minorities* (*Choice,* February 1977), Miller . . . and his colleagues have now produced the most comprehensive resource on American ethnicity. Miller's first compilation included material published through 1975; *Minorities in America* resumes this coverage with the year 1976 as an annual bibliography. Unlike some [other] works, [this book] offers information on ethnic people of color, indigenous as well as immigrant, in addition to those of European background. A total of 41 groups are designated; each volume contains approximately 7,500 entries. The entries are drawn from more than 900 journals, from American university press and commercial press books, government publications, and relevant dissertations. Each entry is annotated, most with abstracts of from 75 to 100 words. The bibliography itself is arranged by ethnic group and subdivided by subject, e.g., bibliographies and guides, history, education, health, religion, literature. A final section, similarly subdivided, treats multigroup studies. There is also an author index in each volume. . . . This is an outstanding resource, destined to be even more heavily used than its predecessor. A necessary acquisition, not only for those interested in ethnicity, but for anyone interested in American life and culture." (*Choice,* November 1985, p. 426)

Also reviewed in: *ARBA,* 1988, p. 165.

Board's recommendation: Public libraries.

Reference Encyclopedia of the American Indian, 5th edition. Barry T. Klein, ed. Todd, 1990. hard. 1 vol. approx. 1,050 pp. index. ISBN 0-915344-16-5. $125. bibliography.
E76.2.R4 970.103

A review of the earlier two-volume edition called the *Reference Encyclopedia of the American Indian* "a resource directory listing individuals, organizations, and materials relating to Indians and Indian affairs. . . . Volume 1 consists of two parts. The first contains listings of organizations, national and state associations, government agencies, reservations and tribal councils, Canadian reserves, museums and libraries, Indian schools and health services, colleges offering courses on the American Indian, and annotated lists of Indian-related audiovisual aids, magazines, and periodicals. . . . The second part is a bibliography of approximately 3,500 in-print books about Indians of North America. . . . Volume 1 concludes with a list of publishers and their addresses. . . . The second volume is a who's who of American Indians prominent in Indian affairs, business, and arts and professions, as well as non-Indians active in Indian affairs, history, art, anthropology, archaeology, and . . . related fields.

"While there are other bibliographies and directories on native Americans, the value of this title is that it brings together information otherwise found in many other sources." (*BL,* May 15, 1987, p. 1492)

Also reviewed in: *ARBA,* 1987, p. 166; *Choice,* June 1987, p. 1429; *R&R Bk N,* Fall 1986, p. 5; Winter 1987, p. 5; *RSR,* Winter 1987, p. 94; *WLB,* September 1987, p. 67.

Board's recommendation: Public, academic, and school libraries.

New and Noteworthy

The Blackwell Companion to Jewish Culture: From the Eighteenth Century to the Present. Glenda Abramson, ed. Basil Blackwell, 1989. hard. 1 vol. 853 pp. illus. index. ISBN 0-631-15111-7. $65. encyclopedia.
DS102.8.B46 909.04924

The Blackwell Companion to Jewish Culture is a "one volume compendium [that] provides an analytical overview of the role played by Jews in literature, art, music, the social and natural sciences, and medicine during the past 200 years. . . . [This work] deals only with culture and limits itself to that of Ashkenazic (East European) Jews, whether they live in Europe, the U.S., South Africa, or Australia. . . . There are three types of entries in the book: biographies offering factual details about the subjects and brief evaluations of their work; essays on topics relating to Jewish culture . . . ; and survey articles that cover peripheral areas." (*BL,* February 15, 1990, p 1184)

East and Southeast Asian Material Culture in North America: Collections, Historical Sites, and Festivals. Patricia Haseltine, comp. Greenwood, 1989. hard. 1 vol. 185 pp. ISBN 0-313-25343-9. $39.95. directory.
E184.06H37 973.049500

East and Southeast Asian Material Culture in North America is a "directory . . . designed primarily to contribute to the study of Asian immigration, assimilation, and ethnic distinctiveness. . . . [This work] lists objects, as well as photographic and historical records, maintained in museums and historical societies . . . sites bearing significance to the lives of Asian immigrants [and] . . . the ways artistic and material culture traditions are maintained in Asian festivals." (Excerpted from publisher's announcement)

Hispanic-American Material Culture. Greenwood, 1989. hard. 1 vol. ISBN 0-313-24789-7. $42.95. directory.
E184.S75G69 306.408968

"*Hispanic-American Material Culture* lists collections, sites, archives, and festivals in 25 states and Puerto Rico. While Mexican, Mexican American, and Puerto Rican culture are most heavily represented, there are also listings for Cuban, Central and South American, and even Basque culture." (*BL,* September 15, 1989, p. 202)

Latinas of the Americas: A Source Book. K. Lynn Stoner. Garland, 1989. hard. 1 vol. 692 pp. indexes. ISBN 0-8240-8536-1. $94. bibliography.
HQ1460

Latinas of the Americas "is an invaluable aid for research on Latin American Women. . . . The work functions as both critical overview and bibliography, with short essays on the subjects covered along with a bibliography of printed materials for each subject." (*Choice,* October 1989, p. 294)

Women of Color in the United States: A Guide to the Literature. Bernice Redfern. Garland, 1989. hard. 1 vol. 156 pp. indexes. ISBN 0-8240-5849-6. $25. bibliography.
HQ1410 016.3054

Women of Color in the United States contains "more than 600 annotated references on African-American, Hispanic-American, Native American, and Asian-American women. . . . Every chapter . . . is preceded by an articulate description of the status of the literature on that group of women. That is, Redfern discusses the kinds of works (autobiographical, employment study, etc.) prevalent in each chapter as well as the amount of literature on each group and in which areas more research needs to be done. Entries are organized by broad subject within each chapter." (*Choice,* July/August 1989, p. 1818)

Tim J. Watts

European History

See also British History; World History

History is nothing less than the record of humanity's efforts, achievements, and failures. All intellectual progress, all political institutions and military activities, all great people, and the daily lives and circumstances of the mass of people are in history's province. Everything about human life itself is a part of history, either past, present, or future.

Because American culture and society are primarily a result of a European background, access to information on European history is vitally important. Since the Middle Ages, Europe has had a major influence on the rest of the world. The developments and changes in European culture, society, and government have had a pronounced effect on other nations.

Reference works in European history may be very specialized in time period or subject matter, or they may attempt to be very broad and universally authoritative in scope. A core and supplementary reference collection must ideally include all types. The ENCYCLOPEDIA OF THE RENAISSANCE and the DICTIONARY OF THE MIDDLE AGES are good examples of the more specialized, limited reference source. THE NEW CAM-

Core Titles

	PUBLIC	ACADEMIC	SCHOOL
Atlas of Medieval Europe Matthew, Donald, and Graham Speake, eds. Facts On File, 1983	✦	✦	✦
Dictionary of the Middle Ages, 13 vols. Strayer, Joseph R., ed. Scribner, 1982–1989	✦	✦	
Encyclopedia of the Renaissance Bergin, Thomas G., and Jennifer Speake, eds. Facts On File, 1987	✦	✦	
The New Cambridge Modern History, 14 vols. Potter, G. B., et al., eds. Cambridge, 1957–1979		✦	

BRIDGE MODERN HISTORY, on the other hand, provides broad overviews of European history.

The collection should include ready-reference sources, as well as those that can explain and detail issues, trends, and current theories in historiography (something that can only be done with relatively lengthy essays). The collection should be able to provide a biographical sketch of Karl Marx, as well as an explanation of his theory of historical materialism; these works should provide the reader with the date on which Martin Luther posted his 95 theses, as well as details of what Luther's theological teachings were. The patron should be able to read about the varying theories explaining the rise of the Nazi party and the outbreak of World War II. Ideally, the collection should also provide bibliographies that will allow a patron to pursue further information on a particular topic.

Additional related works can be found in the British History and World History categories. Librarians may also wish to consider purchasing the following titles, now out of print. *A Bibliography of Modern Europe* (1968) supplies bibliographies that were not included with THE NEW CAMBRIDGE MODERN HISTORY. *The Facts On File Dictionary of 20th Century History, 1900–1978, The Facts On File Dictionary of European History,* and *The Oxford History of Modern Europe* are also useful acquisitions if they can be obtained from an out-of-print book dealer.

Core Titles

Atlas of Medieval Europe. Donald Matthew and Graham Speake, eds. Facts On File, 1983. hard. 1 vol. 240 pp. illus. appendixes. index. ISBN 0-87196-133-4. $45. atlas.
G1791.M3 911.4

The *Atlas of Medieval Europe* combines the disciplines of history and geography with a profusion of illustrations to make the Middle Ages come alive for modern readers. The title is somewhat misleading; the book is much more than a simple collection of maps. The atlas attempts to illustrate how medieval humans viewed the world, focusing on the different levels of political and religious loyalties and sophistication, the complicated social structure, and the forms of art that were unique to particular locations.

The author, Donald Matthew, is known for his other works in medieval history, including *The Norman Monasteries and Their English Possessions* and *The Medieval European Community.* His very readable text complements the many maps and illustrations.

The arrangement of the first half of the book is a chronological one. After an introductory discussion of what the Middle Ages were and what major themes existed in medieval society, Matthew outlines the ancient Roman world and its decline, which provided the roots of medieval Europe (part 1). He continues the narration with the establishment of the Church and local rulers as the successors to Roman authority, and the creation of the stability of medieval society (part 2). The third part of the book provides a discussion of particular aspects of medieval life, divided into three parts: urban society, rural society (by far the shortest part), and the arts of the Middle Ages. The final section (part 4) deals with the breakdown of the medieval synthesis and the coming of the modern world.

The text of the *Atlas of Medieval Europe* is in the form of a series of short essays. Each essay is amply illustrated with a combination of maps and reproductions of medieval art or photographs of surviving artifacts of the Middle Ages. The section on "Urban Society," for example, begins with photographs of the medieval sections of La Couvertoirade, York, and Roth enburg in which there are still medieval homes and public buildings that exhibit typical characteristics of their time and are inhabited after hundreds of years. There are maps of Europe that indicate the production centers of different goods as well as the spread of the Black Death. A separate seven-page segment lists surviving urban centers of the Middle Ages, complete with modern photographs and one-paragraph descriptions. Other sections, such as the one on painted glass, are gloriously illustrated with color photographs of the best remaining examples.

The book contains a number of special features that will be of interest to librarians and patrons. One to two-page sidebars on particularly significant features of the Middle Ages are included; these range from one on castles to one on Alpine passes and one on Petrarch—the first humanist—whose philosophy of life can be seen as marking the end of the Middle Ages and the beginning of the Rennaissance.

Other useful features of this work include an index, a list of the many maps throughout the book, a glossary of terms (including *Guelf,* a term associated with the Middle Ages but not necessarily familiar to today's readers), and a list of illustrations arranged in the order in which they appear. A three-page bibliography, arranged by topic, is included for those wishing to undertake further research; nearly all the works are written in English, although a few foreign titles are also listed.

Perhaps the most unique feature, and one which reflects the "atlas" in this reference work, is a gazetteer that lists place names mentioned in the text.

Each place name (many of which are no longer used) is followed by its longitude and latitude, as well as the pages on which it is mentioned in the *Atlas of Medieval Europe.*

Overall, Matthew and the editorial team at Facts On File have done a wonderful job of bringing the medieval world to life in the *Atlas of Medieval Europe.* The blending of text, maps, and illustrations places medieval humans in the context in which they lived. The text is written in terms easily understandable for the layperson as well as the specialist, although the many popes, rulers, and nobles mentioned may lead some to wish for a cast of characters. The essay format does not lend itself to ready-reference use, but it does provide a starting place for those doing in-depth research or those who need only a short overview of a topic. The Board recommends this work for the core collections of public, academic, and school libraries.

Dictionary of the Middle Ages. Joseph R. Strayer, ed. Scribner, 1982–1989. hard. 13 vols. 8,726 pp. illus. index. ISBN 0-684-19073-7 (set). $1,025 (set); $85 per vol. dictionary.
D114.D5 909.07

The *Dictionary of the Middle Ages* was published in response to a perceived need for a work that would bring together information in all areas of research into the Middle Ages. The scope of the book includes not only political, legal, and institutional history, but also such fields as economics, literature, music, art, architecture, technology, and science. As stated in the preface, the dictionary "would not only be a practical guide for the novice and a useful reference work for the advanced student, but would also serve as a valuable tool for the professional scholar," allowing access to areas of specialty not the scholar's own.

The *Dictionary of the Middle Ages* was originated under the sponsorship of the American Council of Learned Societies, with Joseph R. Strayer acting as editor in chief. Among Strayer's other credits are numerous works on life, religion, and government in medieval Western Europe. Scholars were recruited to contribute short articles in their respective fields of research. Each volume contains a list of contributors, their educational affiliations, and the topics on which they have written. Each entry is signed.

The dictionary is published in 12 volumes with one index volume. Each textual volume is approximately 600 pages long and is composed of brief entries. Simple definitions and identifications usually are about 50 to 100 words in length, while more significant entries (such as that on *Judaism*) may receive up to 10,000 words. Chronological limits for subjects in the dictionary range from A.D. 500 to 1500. The geographical limits are Western Europe, Slavic areas, Asia Minor, and the Muslim regions of the Middle East and North Africa. The broad limits of time and space were believed necessary to reflect the interaction and influence of different cultures during the Middle Ages.

Entries are arranged in alphabetical order. Some are illustrated with black-and-white prints of artworks or line drawings of medieval buildings or artifacts. All entries that are more than brief identifications include a bibliography of a size appropriate to the entry. Most bibliographies list primary and secondary works, in both English and foreign languages; as such, these seem most useful to the advanced student wishing to study the topic further.

Subjects of entries range from individuals (such as *Geoffrey Chaucer*) and geographical entities to words and concepts important to the intellectual life of the Middle Ages (such as *chivalry*). "See" and "see also" entries are included to direct users to related articles.

To assist users in finding subjects that do not have a separate entry but which are included in broader entries, a comprehensive index volume is included. The index indicates the volume and page on which a subject may be found. (This system is necessary because each volume is individually paginated.)

Like all works which attempt to be comprehensive and authoritative, the *Dictionary of the Middle Ages* tends to include technical terms that may be unfamiliar to the layperson; definitions are available, but users may have to jump from volume to volume to find them. Nonetheless, the *Dictionary of the Middle Ages* is an excellent reference source. The dictionary's comprehensive treatment of all aspects of medieval life should supply the answers to nearly all questions asked by patrons and indicate where other answers may be found. The Board recommends this work for the core collections of public and academic libraries.

Encyclopedia of the Renaissance. Thomas G. Bergin and Jennifer Speake, eds. Facts On File, 1987. hard. 1 vol. 454 pp. illus. appendixes. ISBN 0-8160-1315-2. $45. encyclopedia.
CB361.B43 940.2′1′0321

The *Encyclopedia of the Renaissance* is intended as a quick and accurate guide to notable figures, movements, technologies, and geographical locales of the European Renaissance. As such, the encyclopedia is a collection of short, explanatory, unsigned entries, written by different authors under the aegis of Thomas G.

Bergin, the consulting editor. Bergin, who died in 1987, was Sterling Professor of Romance Languages at Yale University and is known for his works on authors of the Italian Renaissance.

The editors of the encyclopedia have interpreted the Renaissance in broad terms, seeing this period not only as a time of growth in arts and literature but also as a movement that touched on science, geography, politics, religion, and all other aspects of human endeavor between 1300 and 1600. As stated in the introduction, the Renaissance "brought a new sense of freedom and a new appreciation of man and his potential: a legacy that has been the precious patrimony of all succeeding generations."

With this all-encompassing view of the Renaissance, it is no surprise that the encyclopedia includes persons as varied as Petrarch, Gutenberg, Shakespeare, Columbus, Kepler, and Luther. People from all fields of human thought and activity are represented. Entries are not limited, however, to individuals alone. Significant Renaissance families, such as the Medici and the Fugger, rate their own articles. Representative and important Renaissance objects are also treated, ranging from the *cassoni* chests to the "new star" discovered by astronomer Tycho Brahe. Technologies and art forms such as printing and sculpture receive relatively lengthy entries, explaining their importance to the changing European society of the Renaissance. Even cities and regions that were centers of intellectual ferment and growth are given treatment.

All entries are arranged in alphabetical order. Information usually included for each subject are the birth and death dates (where appropriate), biographical information, and the significance of the subject to the Renaissance, according to the guidelines set forth in the preface. Of necessity with a work of this size, most entries are short (several hundred words), but a few very important or representative entries (such as *Michelangelo*) are given more extensive treatment.

No index is included, since the alphabetical arrangement is self-indexing. The encyclopedia, however, does include several valuable appendixes. A seven-page bibliography of primary and secondary sources may be useful to the student seeking further information on one of the topics included. A chronological table of significant events in different areas is also included, allowing users to set each in the context in which it occurred.

The *Encyclopedia of the Renaissance* is a very valuable resource for answering those ready-reference questions on any person or object in Western Europe between 1300 and 1600. The language used is nontechnical and easily understandable to the layperson unfamiliar with the Renaissance. The greatest shortcoming may be the geographical limitation to western Europe, because it does not take into consideration the interaction between the Christian West and the Slavic and Moslem East. The DICTIONARY OF THE MIDDLE AGES provides more comprehensive coverage of these areas and their influence on and contributions to the culture of this period.

Despite this flaw, the *Encyclopedia of the Renaissance* is a worthwhile purchase. The Board recommends this work for the core collections of public and academic libraries.

The New Cambridge Modern History. G. B. Potter et al., eds. Cambridge, 1957–1979. hard. 14 vols. index. ISBN 0-521-34536-7 (vol. 2). $49.50 (vol. 2). history.
D208.N4 940.2

The New Cambridge Modern History was planned as a successor to *The Cambridge Modern History* (published at the beginning of this century) to update the earlier work and include events through World War II. The goal of the original work, and one which the new edition embraces, is to tell objectively the history of the European world since the Middle Ages. Toward that end, noted historians (primarily English) were requested either to submit essays on their special areas of knowledge or to edit a number of essays that dealt with a particular time period. For example, G. R. Elton, known primarily for his writings on the Reformation, edited the volume on that subject.

The major portion of *The New Cambridge Modern History* consists of 12 volumes organized in chronological order. They reflect the traditional view of history as the record of great individuals, governments, institutions, politics, literature, and the arts. To bring the set into line with more modern theories of history, a volume 13 was added. Unlike the first 12, the contents of this volume are not limited to a particular time period; instead, its chapters examine recurring themes and topics, such as economics, industrial development, science, and social history. Emmanuel Le Roy Ladurie, for example, contributed the chapter on peasants, which discusses the life of the common people (the majority of the population, usually ignored by orthodox history) and their effect on European society. The inclusion of ideas and groups, without regard to time and geographic limitations, gives the reader an introduction to the new trends in historiography.

Each volume of *The New Cambridge Modern History* is approximately 300 to 500 pages long and consists of essays in the form of chapters, each about 25 pages in length. Each chapter is narrowly defined in scope and limited in the time frame it covers. The volume on the Renaissance, for example, has chapters whose topics range from the papacy and Catholic Church to the Ottoman Empire (1481–1520) and from France under Charles VIII and Louis XII to the arts in Western Europe.

Each chapter is usually without subdivisions and is unsigned. Users may only discover the identity of an author, and the authority with which he writes, by examining the table of contents at the front of each volume. The table of contents also provides a detailed breakdown of the contents of each chapter, making it a useful tool for ready-reference work with the set. In addition, a lengthy subject index at the end of each volume makes access easier. However, *The New Cambridge Modern History* is better suited for providing a general introduction to the orthodox historical views of a topic or time period than as a beginning place for advanced research, because footnotes are rare and no bibliography of works for further investigation is provided.

Volume 14 is an atlas containing a detailed collection of multicolored maps that trace the development of Europe. The map volume may easily stand on its own as a significant reference source, graphically portraying information that could not otherwise be shown.

The New Cambridge Modern History was intended, like its predecessor, as a universal history of postmedi eval times. Its focus is Europe and the effect of European expansion on the rest of the world; the encyclopedia also gives a traditional, chronological framework to history. The work is aimed at general audiences needing an introduction to the last 500 years, not at the specialist. With these limitations in mind, it can truthfully be stated that *The New Cambridge Modern History* sets the standard for a basic multivolume history of modern Europe. The Board recommends this work for the core collection of academic libraries.

Supplementary Titles

Dictionary of Medieval Civilization. Joseph Henry Dahmus. Macmillan, 1984. hard. 1 vol. 700 pp. ISBN 0-02-907870-9. $75. dictionary.
CB351.D24 909.07

The *Dictionary of Medieval Civilization* contains "6600 entries, covering ideas and institutions, battles, and significant religious, political, philosophical, scientific, theological, and artistic figures—for the Western Christian, Muslim, Judaic, Slavic, and Byzantine medieval cultures.

"This . . . work comes from one scholar. . . . It's a daunting undertaking; and, for what it sets out to do, a successful one. . . . Most entries are inevitably brief. The information is sound, though some definitions are so concise as to be misleading. Strong on England, the Dictionary is weak on Eastern Europe, women, and blacks, about which a great deal is now known. . . . Still, students and general readers, for whom the book is intended, will find it handy and useful." (*LJ,* October 1, 1984, p. 1840)

The work is "a fairly bare-bones dictionary of persons, places, and things medieval, covering 12 centuries (A.D. 300–1500), [and] is a useful volume which, according to its Preface, contains 'no original analyses' and in which the definitions will 'strike the informed reader as conventional.' Coverage of topics is good, based on a judicious balance between 'what would suffice for the majority of readers' and the limitations of space in a book of only 700 pages. . . . There are no pronunciations, and very few etymologies are given. The latter are likely to be sorely missed by scholars and others interested in word derivation. On the whole, *Dictionary of Medieval Civilization* is well done and will find ready acceptance in academic and public libraries, especially those with a readership oriented toward history." (*BL,* June 1, 1985, p. 1382)

The *Dictionary of Medieval Civilization* "will be attractive not only to educated dilettantes, which all experts are on occasions, but also to students. Nor will it be out of place on coffee tables." (*TLS,* July 19, 1985, p. 807)

Also reviewed in: *JHI,* October 1984, p. 626; *WLB,* October 1984, p. 145.

Board's recommendation: Academic libraries.

European Historical Statistics, 1750–1970. B. R. Mitchell. Columbia, 1975. soft. 1 vol. 827 pp. ISBN 0-231-03973-5. $34. encyclopedia.
HA1107.M5 314

"This work brings together major statistical governmental series for the purpose of documenting the growth and development of 26 European nations. . . . Seventy-six tables divided into 11 sections cover the following: climate, population and vital statistics, labor force, agriculture, industry, external trade, transport and communications, finances, prices, education, and national accounts. . . . The main introduction underlines some of the difficulties involved in the use of historical statistics, and emphasizes the factors which may affect the reliability and continuity.

"[The book is] . . . weighted toward economic analysis, while it omits important social parameters of development. But, on the whole, this clear, well-researched study will provide social scientists with a wide range of information and will alleviate the difficulty of identifying sources and the often frustrating task of extracting comparable data from disparate origins." (*LJ,* November 15, 1975, p. 2133)

"[Mitchell cautions] that though these collections [of statistics] are official, they are sometimes inaccurate. . . . He also warns of the unknown efficiency of compilers and imprecise terms used (does 'pig-iron' include or exclude ferro-alloys?) . . . In addition, he points out that nations as a whole may 'correct' and inflate statistics on wealth and population to impress or deter possible enemies. . . . This volume is attractively printed with small but easily readable type which stands out clearly on the page." (*BL,* March 15, 1976, p. 1063)

Also reviewed in: *ARBA,* 1976, p. 393; *Econ,* July 5, 1975, p. 155; *EHR,* January 1976, p. 135; *JEH,* June 1976, p. 498; *Kliatt,* Fall 1979, p. 54; *LJ,* April 15, 1976, p. 968; *RQ,* Winter 1975, p. 176; *RSR,* October 1976, p. 10; *WLB,* December 1975, p. 329.

Board's recommendation: Academic libraries.

The Soviet Union and Eastern Europe. George Schöpflin, ed. Facts On File, 1986. hard. 1 vol. 637 pp. index. ISBN 0-8160-1260-1. $45. encyclopedia.
DK17.564 947

The Soviet Union and Eastern Europe "is a political, social, and economic encyclopedia of the Soviet Union and the socialist states of Eastern Europe.

"[In this revised edition] the . . . essays have been rewritten and expanded, reflecting, in the main, the broader levels of understanding of the area and the increased amount of data that has become available over the past 16 years. . . . The 20-page index, along with the fine graphs, charts, and maps, make [this] an easy to use reference book. The contributors are of high caliber. Although not so detailed as such one-dimensional works as John Peter Cole's recent Geography of the Soviet Union (1984), this book nevertheless constitutes a truly indispensable reference work for all serious libraries, academic and public." (*Choice,* July 1986, p. 1661)

Also reviewed in: *ARBA,* 1987, p. 59; *BL,* August 1986, p. 1676; *Enc,* September 1986, p. 52; *LJ,* August 1986, p. 136.

Board's recommendation: Academic libraries.

Western Europe. Richard Mayne, ed. Facts On File, 1986. hard. 1 vol. 699 pp. index. ISBN 0-8160-1251-X. $45. encyclopedia.
D907.W47 946

Western Europe is "part of the 'Handbooks to the Modern World' series and is a . . . revised version of the 1967 edition. . . . The first part supplies information about each of the 27 independent, non-Communist countries of Europe, including the smaller ones like Liechtenstein and the Vatican. . . . The second part of the book contains [articles] . . . on political, economic, and social affairs and covers topics such as German disunity, parliamentarianism, energy and foreign labor in Western Europe. This is followed by a series of essays on European integration.

"There are 30 pages of comparative statistics showing everything from length of railway lines to the number of TV receivers in each nation (with the tiniest ones being omitted). . . . Despite an occasional minor error, the book is a reference work that belongs on the shelves of every academic and public library." (*Choice,* July 1986, p. 1662)

"[This work] possesses the characteristics of a general reference tool. . . . Chapters include recent statistics and give detailed information on topics such as national insurance programs, price and wage trends, and political parties. A map accompanies each country section. While much of this information repeats that given in other reference sources (through which it also can conveniently be updated), its presentation here provides a background for the issue-oriented essays that follow. . . . While the essays do not include full documentation, a substantial bibliography is appended to each one. . . . For the layperson who cares to be well informed, the student, the scholar, and those with a special interest in a particular country or region, [this book] will be useful. The careful analyses of current issues by experts [is its] most important attribute." (*BL,* August 1986, p. 1676)

Also reviewed in: *ARBA,* 1987, p. 58; *Enc,* September 1986, p. 52; *LJ,* August 1986, p. 136; *Ref Bk R,* 1986, p. 15; *R&R Bk N,* Summer 1986, p. 11.

Board's recommendation: Public and academic libraries.

New and Noteworthy

Encyclopedia of the Holocaust. Yisrael Gutman, ed. in chief. Macmillan, 1990. hard. 4 vols. 1,905 pp. illus. appendix. ISBN 0-02-896090-4. $285 (set). encyclopedia.
D804.3.E53 940.53

The *Encyclopedia of the Holocaust* covers "everything touching the Holocaust . . . : cities and towns, ghettos and prisons, books, dates, statistics, massacres, revolts, names and pseudonyms, victims, villains, heroes, martyrs. There are geographical and biographical entries, and many articles on the Third Reich and historical events. There are articles describing the prewar world of European Jews, maps, and descriptions of each concentration camp. . . . Entries are in alphabetical order with extensive cross-references directing the user to a specific topic." (*SLJ,* May 1990, p. 29)

Global Studies: Western Europe. Dr. Henri J. Warmenhoven. Dushkin, 1990. soft. 1st of 6 vols. 244 pp. illus. appendix. index. ISBN 0-87967-793-0. $10.95. handbook.

Global Studies: Western Europe "provides excellent regional essays, country reports, world press articles, a glossary, topic guide, bibliography, and index." (*SLJ,* May 1990, p. 30)

The Middle Ages: A Concise Encyclopedia. H. R. Loyn. Thames & Hudson, 1989. hard. 1 vol. 210 pp. illus. ISBN 0-500-25103-7. $39.95. encyclopedia.
CB351.M565 909.07

The Middle Ages "guides both novice and specialist through the complexities of this rich and rewarding subject, providing a wealth of information on the achievements of soldiers and statesmen, craftsmen and clergy, from Scandinavia to the Middle East, from the turbulent fifth century to the first flowering of the Renaissance. Nearly one thousand entries include: biographies of all important figures . . . discussion of vital themes, including chivalry, feudalism, heresy, science, war, and the role of women . . . [and] concise, factual assessments of the major battles, treaties, dynasties, councils, and countries." (Excerpted from publisher's announcement)

Phillip A. Smith

Film

Considering the dearth of reference books on film published during the "golden age" of filmmaking (the 1930s through the 1950s), the number and variety of sources made available in the last 25 years seems truly remarkable. Currently librarians can answer most reference inquiries readily through a well-stocked film reference section, and the interested filmgoer can, at little expense, assemble a useful home reference shelf.

Two phenomena account for most of the increased activity in film reference publishing: the wider public access to films on television, videotape, and videodisk; and the growing recognition of film research as a valid scholarly pursuit, exemplified by the establishment of film studies programs and new film schools on the nation's campuses during the 1960s and 1970s. Although these trends have also encouraged the publication of many shoddy or spurious reference books, the current choices for film reference collections are, for the most part, well researched and reliable. In keeping with the tenor of the industry they document, they are also frequently entertaining.

A broad variety of reference books exist, including those devoted to terms used in the industry (such as Konigsberg's THE COMPLETE FILM DICTIONARY), those emphasizing performers and other filmmakers, and those giving factual or critical data on specific films (HALLIWELL'S FILM AND VIDEO GUIDE, MAGILL'S SURVEY OF CINEMA series, and THE MOTION PICTURE GUIDE). All-purpose dictionaries include the one-volume HALLIWELL'S FILMGOER'S COMPANION and the five-volume set, THE INTERNATIONAL DICTIONARY OF FILMS AND FILMMAKERS. Specialized dictionaries for individual genres abound: the ENCYCLOPEDIA OF THE MUSICAL FILM is one notable example.

Two indexes that began publication in the early 1970s can aid the film researcher in finding articles on specific film topics: *Film Literature Index* (Filmdex, quarterly) and the scholarly *International Index to Film Periodicals. Film Review Index* (Oryx, 1987) is one of several special sources for locating reviews of specific films.

From the casual fan to the dedicated film scholar, those interested in film are well served by the broad array of reference sources listed in this section.

Core Titles

	PUBLIC	ACADEMIC	SCHOOL
The Complete Film Dictionary Konigsberg, Ira. NAL, 1987	✦	✦	
Filmed Books and Plays: A List of Books and Plays from Which Films Have Been Made, 1928–1986 Enser, A. G. S. Gower, 1989	✦	✦	
Halliwell's Film and Video Guide, 6th edition Halliwell, Leslie. Scribner, 1988	✦	✦	✦
Halliwell's Filmgoer's Companion, 9th edition Halliwell, Leslie. Scribner, 1988	✦	✦	✦
Magill's Survey of Cinema: English Language Films, first series, 4 vols. Magill, Frank N., ed. Salem, 1980	✦	✦	
Magill's Survey of Cinema: English Language Films, second series, 6 vols. Magill, Frank N., ed. Salem, 1981	✦	✦	

Core Titles

The Complete Film Dictionary. Ira Konigsberg. NAL, 1987. hard. 1 vol. 420 pp. illus. ISBN 0-453-00564-0. $24.95. dictionary.
PN1993.45.K661987 791.43'0321

The Complete Film Dictionary is an admirable glossary of the working vocabulary of the film industry, if not quite the comprehensive source suggested by the title. The emphasis in this volume is on movie technology, although the entries also provide information on other aspects of the film industry.

The author, Ira Konigsberg, includes the following categories of terms: (1) practical terminology, such as specific camera or lighting techniques; (2) technical terminology, such as photographic or sound equipment; (3) the language of the film business, film production, and the box office; (4) historical terms (such as the *Hays Office* and the *Hollywood Ten*); and (5) the language of criticism and theory. Konigsberg excludes entries on individual films or filmmakers, which can be found in HALLIWELL'S FILM AND VIDEO GUIDE and HALLIWELL'S FILMGOER'S COMPANION and in other film dictionaries.

On the whole, the definitions are well written and clear. Entries range in length from a one-line definition (for example, a *belly board* is defined as "a board on which the camera is mounted for low-angle shots") to a page or more for succinct surveys of film genres (such as the horror film and the musical) and entries on the role of the director, producer, and other key personnel involved in filmmaking. Especially valuable are the capsule histories of the studios and the citations within entries to specific films to illustrate a filmmaking technique or industry trend. The entry for *multi-image,* for example, notes its use in the classics *Birth of a Nation* and *Napoleon,* but also points out more recent uses of the technique in *The Thomas Crown Affair* and *Carrie.*

The black-and-white photographs and the many line drawings (by Adam Indyke) are attractive and instructive. Ample cross-references are used to direct the user from an alternate term to the main entry (for example, the entry for *location cart* is a "see" reference to the main entry *production cart*) and to link related terms (for example, the entry for *Panavision* advises the user to see the entries for *anamorphic lens* and *wide screen* for additional information).

The value of this kind of a dictionary for students enrolled in film courses or individuals involved in making films is obvious. Because nearly half of the entries are concerned with technical aspects, *The Complete Film Dictionary* may be less useful to others who have limited knowledge of the processes by which films are made. For example, the definition of *hanger* as "a mounting device which attaches to a grid or beam for supporting a luminaire" will not be self-explanatory for many users, who will have to further consult the entry for *luminaire* and, perhaps, the essay on lighting cross-referenced under that entry. A basic text on filmmaking might better serve the general reader.

With the increasing public appetite for films and interest in moviemaking terminology, resources such as *The Complete Film Directory* are in demand. The Board recommends this work for the core collections of public and academic libraries.

Filmed Books and Plays: A List of Books and Plays from Which Films Have Been Made, 1928–1986. A. G. S. Enser. Gower, 1989. hard. 1 vol. 770 pp. ISBN 0-566-03564-2. $59.95. bibliography (filmography).
Z5784.M9E563(PN1997.85) 016.8088

A. G. S. Enser's *Filmed Books and Plays* is the standard source for answering such questions as: What film(s), if any, was made from a particular novel or play? What was the original literary source for a film? Was the title changed in the transfer from print to screen? How many films have been made from a given author's works? This volume has been revised or supplemented frequently since its first appearance in 1968. The current edition was revised in 1987 and reprinted in 1989.

Each of the three parts of the text is printed in a two-column format and is arranged alphabetically. This straightforward presentation makes the work easily accessible to users. The first part, "Film Title Index," lists films alphabetically, followed by the name of the maker or production company (abbreviated) and the date of release. For each film title included, a second column gives the original author's last name and first initials; the original title, if different from the release title; an indication if the source is a play (those not so marked are assumed to be books); and the name of the publisher. The second part, "Author Index," reverses the access, listing authors and co-authors (with full names) and their works, with a second column giving data on film versions. Variant names for authors and co-authors are cross-referenced in the index. The final part, "Change of Original Title Index," refers the reader from the title of the source material to the title of the film when a change has occurred. For example, the entry for *King of Hearts* by Jean Kerr and Eleanor Brooke shows that the 1956 film version of this play was titled *That Certain Feeling.* Included for the first time in this edition are some made-for-television films and indications of the availability of films on videotape. A table of abbreviations, which contains mainly shortened names for studios, is also included.

Although *Filmed Books and Plays* is a first stop for information of this kind, the work is not without limitations. Enser includes only feature-length English-language films of the sound era. Readers must look elsewhere for information on silent and foreign-language versions of books and plays. Enser also generally excludes short stories (although most of Poe's tales *are* cited). Readers will, therefore, have to consult other sources for feature films and short-subject films based on short stories. Finally, for American users, Enser's British orientation presents some problems with title variations for U.S. and British releases of a film. As one example, Paramount's 1983 treatment of Graham Greene's *The Honorary Consul* was seen in England under that title but was released in the United States as *Beyond the Limit.* The British title is indexed but the American one is not.

Despite these shortcomings, *Filmed Books and Plays* will answer most questions posed by the film buff as well as by the casually curious. The Board recommends this work for the core collections of public and academic libraries.

Halliwell's Film and Video Guide, 6th edition. Leslie Halliwell. Scribner, 1988. hard. 1 vol. 1,186 pp. illus. indexes. ISBN 0-684-18928-3. $47.50. handbook.
PN1993.45.H27 791.43.H191

The sixth edition of *Halliwell's Film and Video Guide,* profiling some 16,000 motion pictures, provides film aficionados with a wealth of data. Leslie Halliwell, the author of this and other related guides to film and television, is a British author and film critic.

Entries are arranged alphabetically by film title and typically include: a rating symbol of general quality (zero to four stars); country of origin; year of release; running time; black-and-white or color indication; special process, if any (such as Cinemascope); production credits; brief plot synopsis; brief critical assessment; writer credit (and source, where applicable); director credit; music credit; principal members of the cast; excerpts from reviews (many of them from the trade publication *Variety*); and Academy Award winners and major nominees (if applicable). When Halliwell judges persons worthy of particular notice, he indicates this by placing their names in italics.

There are some variations in this model. Additional production credits, such as special effects and costume design, are sometimes indicated when they are important to the film's impact (for example, makeup for *The Seven Faces of Dr. Lao*). Several films have only acting, directing, and producing credits listed. Although no explanation is given for this practice, it appears that these entries are first-time inclusions of older films (mostly from the 1940s) and serials. Selected entries are prefaced by a promotional tag line. One notable example is from the publicity for the Bette Davis flop, *Beyond the Forest:* "A twelve o'clock girl in a nine o'clock town!" Finally, in a very few instances, some memorable lines from the script are also given.

To guide the user, the author includes an alphabetical index to alternative titles (mostly for variations in British and American release titles) and two indexes for foreign-language films, showing their placement in the guide: "English-Language Titles of Foreign Films" and "Original Titles of Foreign-Language Films Listed in English." Halliwell concludes the volume with a somberly witty essay entitled "The Decline and Fall of the Movie."

Although *Halliwell's Film and Video Guide* is unquestionably useful for answering many questions about specific motion pictures, it is somewhat limited as a guide to viewers. For example, the plot synopses are often too short to give a clear idea of content. The author states that he is concerned with brevity and accuracy, but a summary such as "Children train a horse to win the Grand National" (for *National Velvet*) seems a trifle slight. Although the rating system is, by its nature, subjective, many of the critical assessments also can be (and have been) faulted as being too cryptic and personal to serve the general viewer. In this regard, *Halliwell's Film and Video Guide* is similar to sources such as LEONARD MALTIN'S TV MOVIES AND VIDEO GUIDE in that plot details and critical evaluations are highly compressed so that more films can be included. In fairness, the reader who consults either work with some regularity soon becomes accustomed to the author's personal tastes and style and is able to make reasonable viewing judgments on the basis of the information supplied. Also, despite the compression of film summaries, Halliwell is often highly effective in cutting directly to the core, as his evaluation of the 1972 version of *Lost Horizon* shows: "Torpid remake with a good opening followed by slabs of philosophizing dialogue and an unbroken series of tedious songs." The volume contains numerous illustrations reproduced from stills and posters.

The British origin of *Halliwell's Film and Video Guide* accounts for two additional factors. First, the work includes a good many British films that are seldom cited in other reference sources. Second, the term *video* in the title refers only to indications of a film's availability in video format in Great Britain. Furthermore, the guide excludes listings of movies made for television and data on television programs.

Halliwell's Film and Video Guide is a reference notable for its breadth of coverage, depth of credit data, and charm of treatment. The Board recommends this work for the core collections of public, academic, and school libraries.

Halliwell's Filmgoer's Companion, 9th edition. Leslie Halliwell. Scribner, 1988. soft. 1 vol. 786 pp. illus. appendixes. ISBN 0-684-18410-X. $16.95. handbook.

PN1933.45.H3 791.43'03

Now in its ninth edition, *Halliwell's Filmgoer's Companion* continues to assert its claim to being the most valuable all-purpose reference book in the field. British author and film critic Leslie Halliwell has produced a volume that is bigger and more useful than ever.

The *Filmgoer's Companion* is basically a dictionary of film, consisting of the following types of entries: (1) performers; (2) other filmmakers, such as directors and writers; (3) significant films; (4) important terms; (5) fictional screen characters and series; (6) themes in films. Halliwell writes for the film buff and uses a fair amount of jargon, but his work is generally accessible to the average reader.

The biographical entries are typically brief, giving birth and death dates; a one- to two-line career summary (such as the entry for *Tony Curtis:* "Bouncy American leading man of fifties actioners who constantly sought a wider range"); a list of films (complete for major personalities, partial for minor ones), with the most important of their films highlighted in italics; and television series. Entries are provided for selected nonactors, such as directors and cinematographers. Halliwell devotes most of his attention to performers. All major (and a great many minor) American and British actors as well as the more notable stars of other countries are profiled. Film stars who have attained legendary status (such as Humphrey Bogart, Marilyn Monroe, and Bette Davis) have additional material appended to their entries. This material may incorporate quotes by them, about them, or from their films, as well as an assessment of their major career contributions.

The selection of films included is representative, if somewhat eclectic. Unlike HALLIWELL'S FILM AND VIDEO GUIDE, which provides capsule coverage of 16,000 motion pictures, the *Filmgoer's Companion* discusses only about 940 films. Rather than claiming that these are the "best" films, Halliwell advances the following criteria for their inclusion: "films which were significant to the industry, in that they started trends; films which were popular enough to be frequently remade; films which began series; films which were notable milestones in the history of censorship, or which uniquely held up a mirror to reality; and some films which are simply excellent of their kind."

Although relatively few entries for technological terms are included, the definitions are clear and concise. The chosen terms are those of most interest to the nonspecialist (for example, *tracking shot, close-up, dubbing*).

The long entries for specific fictional screen characters and series (such as *The Thin Man*) are useful, but perhaps the most valuable feature of the book is the inclusion of just over 300 short entries on themes in films. These serve as excellent guides to the treatment of such topics as *amnesia, birds, confidence tricksters, plastic surgery,* and *staircases.* Although Halliwell makes no pretense of being complete, his selection of films cited or discussed is remarkably inclusive, and even more valuable because no comprehensive index to film subjects is currently available.

Appended to this volume are alphabetical lists of films, fictional characters and series, themes, and British-American alternative titles. A brief list of recommended books concludes the volume.

A few quibbles remain, however, on some additions to this work: The numerous quizzes, while fun, are unnecessary and rather distracting, as are many of the quotations that accompany the entries. These could be safely eliminated in the next revision. Finally, the maddening tendency to place pictorial matter on a page other than that for the entry it accompanies (or on the facing page) persists in this edition. The value of the evocative stills and posters is thereby diminished.

The preceding are minor flaws, and *Halliwell's Filmgoer's Companion* remains a first-rate and indispensable source. The Board recommends this work for the core collections of public, academic, and school libraries.

Magill's Survey of Cinema: English Language Films, first series. Frank N. Magill, ed. Salem, 1980. hard. 4 vols. 1,989 pp. appendix. index. ISBN 0-89356-225-4 (set). $200 (set). criticism. on-line.
PN1993.45.M3 791.43'75'2'19

Magill's Survey of Cinema: English Language Films, second series. Frank N. Magill, ed. Salem, 1981. hard. 6 vols. 2,948 pp. appendix. index. ISBN 0-89356-230-0 (set). $300 (set). criticism. on-line.
PN1993.45.M32 791.43'75'2'19

Magill's Survey of Cinema attempts to provide basic data for and detailed critical evaluations of selected motion pictures. The format of the volumes is similar to Magill's MASTERPLOTS II sets (see American Literature; British Literature) in that a signed critical essay is provided for each motion picture included.

The two English Language Films series cover 1,266 films of the sound era, ranging from *The Jazz Singer* (1927) to *Raiders of the Lost Ark* (1981). Films were selected for inclusion by Magill and his associate editors in consultation with a number of film specialists, such as film historian Anthony Slide. According to the preface, "guidelines called for the inclusion of all important names, eras, trends, and genres, noting the 'firsts' as well as the 'best' for [these] years." Therefore, the choices are representative rather than exclusive. Films of the stature of *Citizen Kane* and *Gone with the Wind* are, of course, included, but the survey also accommodates relatively minor films, such as *Artists and Models* as an example of the work of Dean Martin and Jerry Lewis, and *The Southerner,* considered by some to be French director Jean Renoir's best American film.

Each set of volumes in the English Language Films series has its own alphabetical arrangement (by film title). The first series covers films from 1927 to 1980; the second series, from 1928 to 1981. This plan is somewhat awkward, as there is no way of predicting which of the two series might include a given film; a combined title index in volume 6 of the second series, however, indicates in which volume a film is entered.

There are six indexes in each volume in the series: title, director, screenwriter, cinematographer, editor, and performer. A chronological list of film titles follows the indexes. Factual information supplied for each film varies slightly but typically includes: release date; production credit; direction credit; screenplay credit (and source, if based on another work); cinematography credit; editing credit; running time; and principal characters, giving both character and performer names. For some titles other credits (such as music and special effects) may also be listed. An Academy Award recipient is noted by the symbol "AA" following his or her name.

The heart of each entry is the review essay, which consists of a plot summary, a critical appraisal, and, in most cases, a discussion of the film's importance in terms of the context in which it was made, its popular and critical reception, the part it played in the career of one of the participants, and so forth. The lengthy signed essays (typically three to four pages) were written by a panel of 138 contributors, most of them film scholars or critics. As always in this type of collaborative endeavor, the individual reviews vary in style, balance of summary to critical material, and viewpoint, but the overall quality of the writing is good, and there is a reasonable degree of consistency from essay to essay.

Magill has also edited a companion set called MAGILL'S SURVEY OF CINEMA: FOREIGN LANGUAGE FILMS. A five-volume set, MAGILL'S AMERICAN FILM GUIDE, is basically a recompilation of material from the two English-language series. The publisher also issues *Magill's Cinema Annual* (1982–), which covers about 85 films in depth and gives basic credits and a short plot summary for more than 300 additional movies released in the United States during the year being surveyed. The annual includes both English-language and foreign-language films. The "Retrospective Films" section, which functions as an addendum to the original sets, provides in-depth essays for selected older releases (five to ten per volume). An augmented, updated, on-line version of the *Magill's* data base is available through Dialog Information Services.

For libraries that can afford them, the various components of the *Magill's Survey of Cinema* offer good value. Libraries with limited funds should consider the two English-language films series as first choices. The Board recommends these works for the core collections of public and academic libraries.

Supplementary Titles

Encyclopedia of Horror Movies. Phil Hardy, ed. Harper & Row, 1986. hard and soft. 1 vol. 408 pp. illus. appendixes. index. ISBN 0-06-096146-5. $16.95. encyclopedia.
PN1995.9H6M5 791.430909

The *Encyclopedia of Horror Movies* presents information and commentary on 1,300 horror films. "Entries are grouped by decade and then alphabetically within each year. Film dates range from a two-minute French effort in 1896 to films produced in early 1985. An introductory essay traces the history of the horror genre, and each decade is also prefaced by a short overview. . . . Studio and running time are given, as are the director, producer, writer, cinematographer, and at least six leading actors. The [focus] of the work is the plot analysis and critical commentary by the authors, editors, and three other contributors. . . . An index gives film titles and production dates, and appendixes include a select bibliography, Oscar horror nominations and awards, top-ten lists from nine film critics, and a listing of horror films that surpassed more than $4 million in American and Canadian theater receipts.

"There are more than 450 well-chosen photographs, including a 16-page color insert [in the hardback edition]. . . . Comprehensive in scope, well written, and visually pleasing, this is the preferred guide to the horror film genre." (*BL,* July 1987, p. 1660)

Board's recommendation: Public libraries.

Encyclopedia of the Musical Film. Stanley Green. Oxford, 1988. soft. 1 vol. 344 pp. ISBN 0-19-505421-0. $13.95. encyclopedia.

"Which songs were sung in which movies? Who wrote them? Who first sang them? This handy guidebook [*Encyclopedia of the Musical Film*] alphabetically lists songs from films (including both musical films like 'Gigi' and 'Singin' in the Rain' and theme songs from such nonmusical films as 'Goldfinger' and 'The Days of Wine and Roses'), as well as composers, lyricists, singers, dancers, actors, directors, writers, and choreographers. Not only does the author provide lots of information, but he also has an adroit way with adjectives, making his descriptions of songs, films, and people a real pleasure to read." (*CSM,* July 1, 1988, p. B6)

Also reviewed in: *Kliatt,* September 1988, p. 57.

Board's recommendation: Public libraries.

The International Dictionary of Films and Filmmakers. Christopher Lyon and James Vinson. St. James, 1984–1987. hard. 5 vols. 560 pp. (vol. 5). index. ISBN 0-912289-86-4 (vol. 5). $250 (set). dictionary.
PN1997.8.F555 791.43092'1

"Published over a four-year period. . . . [*The International Dictionary of Films and Filmmakers* is a] guide to films and to individuals involved in the motion picture industry." (*BL,* August 1988, p. 1904)

Volume 1 is "an alphabetical arrangement of more than 600 film titles . . . [while] Volume 2 . . . deal[s] with more than 450 internationally acknowledged directors." (*Choice,* January 1985, p. 660)

In volume 3, *Actors and Actresses,* "biographees are listed alphabetically, with brief biographical data presented first. A chronological listing of movies follows, each with the director identified and—sometimes—the name of the character portrayed." (*BL,* December 1, 1986, p. 562)

"Volume 4 treats 484 writers and production artists. Among the latter are costume designers, makeup artists, composers, art directors, cinematographers, sound technicians, animators, etc. . . . Volume 5, Title Index, indexes all films cited in the previous volumes.

Especially valuable for its bibliographical citations and its extensive filmographies, . . . [*The International Dictionary of Films and Filmmakers*] is an excellent source for academic and large public libraries and for any other libraries that support in-depth film research." (*BL,* August 1988, p. 1904)

Also reviewed in: *Brit Bk N,* July 1987, p. 448; *Choice,* June 1988, p. 1536; *JQ,* Winter 1987, p. 897; *LJ,* November 1, 1984, p. 2057.

Board's recommendation: Public and academic libraries.

International Motion Picture Almanac. Quigley Pubs., annual. hard. 1 vol. 771 pp. ISBN 0-900610-42-5. $71. almanac.
PN1993.3.I55 791.43'05

The *International Motion Picture Almanac* is a "complete compendium of information on the motion picture industry. The 21 sections . . . include: statistics on theater grosses, expenses, attendance, admission prices, etc.; the Great Hundred, a list of outstanding films; information on awards and polls; a list of international film festivals; an extensive who's who listing; feature films released during the preceding year; film-related services, from animal trainers to film distributors; talent and literary agencies; advertising and publicity representatives; equipment; corporations; theater circuits; . . . a buying and booking guide; drive-in theaters; nontheatrical motion pictures; film related organizations; the press, covering trade publications, newspapers, and fan magazines; the classification and rating code; the advertising code; . . . and the world market. There is a subject index and an index to advertisers." (*Ser Lib 2nd,* 1985, p. 12)

Also reviewed in: *A Lib,* March 1981, p. 154; *ARBA,* 1985, p. 456; *LJ,* February 15, 1965, p. 859.

Board's recommendation: Public, academic, and school libraries.

Leonard Maltin's TV Movies and Video Guide. NAL, 1989. soft. 1 vol. 1,328 pp. ISBN 0-451-16238-2. $5.95. handbook.
PN1988.M277 016.79'43'7519

Board's recommendation: Public, academic, and school libraries.

Magill's American Film Guide. Frank N. Magill. Salem, 1983. soft. 5 vols. 3,879 pp. ISBN 0-89356-250-5. $135 (set). handbook. on-line.
PN1997.8.M24 791.437509

Board's recommendation: Public and academic libraries.

Magill's Survey of Cinema: Foreign Language Films. Frank N. Magill, ed. Salem, 1985. hard. 8 vols. 3,743 pp. ISBN 0-89356-243-2 (set). $350 (set). criticism.
PN1993.45.M34 791.43

Magill's Survey of Cinema "presents films alphabetically by title, using the name by which a film is best known. . . . For each, country of origin, credits, and principal characters/cast are provided followed by a signed, three- to four-page essay that provides a plot summary and critical comments. The time span covered is from the early 1930s through the early 1980s.

"Most of the 'standards' are here along with some not-so-familiar movies. . . . A definite strength is the excellent indexing—by title, director, screenwriter, cinematographer, editor, art director, composer, performer, and subject. The separate index volume ends with films by country and by year. All in all, *Foreign Language Films* provides good coverage of its topic and will be suitable for public and academic libraries." (*BL,* October 1, 1986, p. 210)

Also reviewed in: *Choice,* July/August 1986, p. 1658.

Board's recommendation: Academic libraries.

The Motion Picture Guide. Jay Robert Nash and Stanley Ralph Ross, eds. CineBooks, annual. hard. 12 vols. 726 pp. illus. indexes. ISBN 0-933997-29-9. $750 (set); $99.50 per vol. handbook.
PN1995.N3460 791.437.5

The Motion Picture Guide "describes in alphabetical order by title more than 28,000 films, with an additional 11,500 films briefly listed. Volumes 1–9 contain films released from 1927 to 1983; Volume 9 also has a separate alphabetical sequence of 1984 film releases with full entries, plus a list of brief entries for about 1,500 films the authors considered minor. Volume 10 is devoted to silent films, with detailed information on about 3,500 and a listing of 10,000 more. . . . Volumes 11 and 12 . . . contain the index.

"Running heads add to ease of access, and the 10-part division makes each volume relatively easy to handle." (*BL,* August 1987, p. 1724)

"The indexing has been improved in the second supplement. . . . [Also,] the 'Obituaries' section covers both the famous . . . and the relatively obscure character actors, film doubles, and the like. . . . Few other sources are comparable to [*The Motion Picture Guide*]." (*BL,* November 15, 1987, p. 549)

Also reviewed in: *AB,* December 14, 1987, p. 2361; *ARBA,* 1988, p. 539; *Choice,* January 1988, p. 750; *FQ,* Winter 1987, p. 59; *Punch,* February 18, 1987, p. 62; *R&R Bk N,* Fall 1987, p. 30; *WLB,* November 1987, p. 94.

Board's recommendation: Public and academic libraries.

Priscilla Drach

Folklore and Mythology

See also Ancient and Classical Literature

Is folklore a part of mythology or is mythology a part of folklore? Are they distinct disciplines with overlapping tendencies or are they indistinguishable? The debate roars on. Whatever the relationship between folklore and mythology, elements from these fields affect all of the scholarly disciplines. Literature, the fine arts, and history cannot be studied without encountering myths and legends. In the social sciences, various cultures are studied, and culture and civilization cannot exist without myths and stories. Certainly philosophy and religion have strong ties to mythology. Linguists study mythology's influence on the language, and science and technology are often more interesting when one is acquainted with the lore that was used to explain the unexplainable in ancient times.

Much of folklore and mythology has been preserved in bits and pieces. To patch the stories together, one needs information about what the words meant and to whom or what the names in the stories refer. Consequently, the core collection reviewed here is made up primarily of dictionaries and indexes. One exception, BULFINCH'S MYTHOLOGY, is like a handbook of exciting and suspenseful stories. Cotterell's A DICTIONARY OF WORLD MYTHOLOGY uses a regional approach to myths, while Bell, in his splendidly organized DICTIONARY OF CLASSICAL MYTHOLOGY, simply identifies characters and places (he alone consistently identifies original source material). The INDEX TO FAIRY TALES can provide a patron with listings of collections of myths and lore readily available in the United States. (Although indexes have not generally been reviewed in this buying guide, an exception has been made here, as the INDEX TO FAIRY TALES is central to the interpretation of symbols in folklore and mythology.)

A patron who needs to find the derivation of a literary allusion to "Jezebel" can turn to BREWER'S DICTIONARY OF PHRASE AND FABLE. The other core references will also help patrons to identify and understand various myths and legends.

Two other works, currently out of print, should also be considered for the core collection: *Man, Myth and Magic: The Illustrated Encyclopedia of Mythology, Religion, and the Unknown,* edited by Robert Cavendish, and the 1986 translation of Pierre Grimal's *Dictionnaire de la Mythologie Greque et Romaine, The Dictionary of Classical Mythology.* According to the publisher, Marshall Cavendish, *Man, Myth, and Magic* is scheduled to be revised in 1991 or 1992.

Core Titles

	PUBLIC	ACADEMIC	SCHOOL
Brewer's Dictionary of Phrase and Fable, 14th edition Evans, Ivor H., ed. Harper & Row, 1989	✦	✦	✦
Bulfinch's Mythology Bulfinch, Thomas. Crowell/Harper & Row, 1970	✦	✦	✦
Dictionary of Classical Mythology: Symbols, Attributes, and Associations Bell, Robert E. ABC-Clio, 1982	✦	✦	
Dictionary of Mythology, Folklore, and Symbols, 3 vols. Jobes, Gertrude. Scarecrow, 1962	✦	✦	
A Dictionary of World Mythology Cotterell, Arthur. Perigee/Putnam, 1982	✦	✦	✦
Funk & Wagnalls Standard Dictionary of Folklore, Mythology, and Legend Leach, Maria, ed. Harper & Row, 1984	✦	✦	✦
Index to Fairy Tales, 1949–1972, Including Folklore, Legends and Myths in Collections Ireland, Norma Olin, comp. Scarecrow, 1973	✦	✦	✦
Index to Fairy Tales, 1973–1977, Including Folklore, Legends and Myths in Collections, 4th suppl. Ireland, Norma Olin, comp. Scarecrow, 1985	✦	✦	✦

Core Titles

Brewer's Dictionary of Phrase and Fable, 14th edition. Ivor H. Evans, ed. Harper & Row, 1989. hard. 1 vol. 1,220 pp. index. ISBN 0-06-016200-7. $35. dictionary.
PN43.B65 803

Brewer's Dictionary of Phrase and Fable was originally published in 1870 as the *Dictionary of Phrase and Fable,* by Dr. Ebenezer Cobham Brewer. Brewer was an Anglican clergyman, a renowned educator, and the author of over 40 educational books. He wanted the dictionary to give "the derivation, source or origin of common phrases, allusions, and words that have a tale to tell" (preface). The expanding middle class of the time probably accounted for the work's early popularity. With this reference work the allusions found in literature became more comprehensible. Included were words and phrases from such sources as the Bible, Chaucer, Shakespeare, Milton, Scott, Pope, Byron, Thackery, Dickens, Longfellow, Tennyson, and many authors of classical antiquity. In short, Brewer drew material from ancient and contemporary works and authors that were known in the Victorian Age.

Over the years various editions began to expand the contents of the book beyond its original intent. However, beginning in 1963, Ivor H. Evans, editor of this edition and previous ones, undertook to return the reference to Brewer's concept of "tale to tell." The fourteenth edition has over 20,000 entries. Of these, 300 are new or amended entries, such as *glastnost, inner cities,* and *mole* from the modern world, and *Br'er Fox, he lay low, gaudeamus igitur,* and *Jezebel* from past ages.

Information is accessible through main entries arranged in standard dictionary format. Subentries are arranged according to the most important word in the phrase. It is important to note that in the subentries, the singular form of the word precedes the plural form; consequently, *city* precedes *cities,* and *inner cities* is found under the subentry *city.* Where more than one grammatical form of the word is cited, verbs are listed first, followed by adjectives and then nouns. Main entries and subentries are in boldface type. Subentries are indented. The introduction to the book does not explain arrangement and access.

The entries include explanations of ancient and modern origins and meanings. Quotations from literature are frequently presented to illustrate the actual use of the word or phrase. There are many cross-references, and, for the first time, the fourteenth edition provides a selective index of main entries and cross-references.

The philology of *Brewer's Dictionary of Phrase and*

Fable has long been highly respected. The dictionary's use as a wonderful armchair browsing book should not be overlooked. The Board recommends this work for the core collections of public, academic, and school libraries.

Bulfinch's Mythology. Thomas Bulfinch. Crowell/ Harper & Row, 1970. hard. 1 vol. 980 pp. illus. appendixes. index. ISBN 0-690-57260-3. $17.95. handbook.
BL310.B8 290

Bulfinch's Mythology, originally published in the mid-nineteenth century, has become a classic reference for the general study and understanding of mythology. The author, Thomas Bulfinch (1796–1867), whose avocation was the pursuit of classical studies, wanted to provide the general reader with an understanding of mythology, especially "mythology as connected with literature" (author's preface). As a result, he set out to tell mythological stories and legendary lore in an easy-to-understand prose format and to make them "a source of amusement . . . to teach mythology not as a study, but as a relaxation from study" (author's preface). And he did just that, filling the stories with romance and adventure, with courage and intrigue. He saw these stories as the "handmaid of literature" and makes many references to the use of myths and mythological allusions in literature. In addition to the prose text, Bulfinch made liberal use of poetical citations "to fix in memory the leading fact of each story" and to "enrich the memory with many gems of poetry" (author's preface).

This Crowell edition gathers together into one volume Bulfinch's complete retellings of myths and legends, which originally appeared as three separate volumes: *The Age of Fable* (1855), *The Age of Chivalry* (1858), and *Legends of Charlemagne, or Romans of the Middle Ages* (1863). While carefully following Bulfinch's original text, the publishers have taken the liberty to make some additions. For example, the section entitled "Northern Mythology" has been made more complete with a prose retelling of the Nibelungenlied, including a summary of the story as told through Wagner's operas. In "Hero Myths of the British Race" (primarily taken from the work of M. I. Ebbutt), the publishers have added several stories, such as that of Beowulf, in order to provide a more rounded history of Britain's heroes. Also added are about 30 verse extracts that appeared in literature after Bulfinch's death. The index has been completely reworked, changing it from a list of names into a small classical and mythological dictionary. Each entry contains a brief definition (from one line to a column in length) and page references to the text. It is now called "Dictionary and Index."

Material can be accessed through the table of contents as well as through the index. When searching for the title of the mythological lore, one uses the table of contents (which is divided into four main sections, with individual myths and legends as subsections). The index can be used independently of the text because it provides an alphabetical listing of all the proper names, places, and terminology used in the book.

A section entitled "Proverbial Expressions" is composed of quotations from Virgil and Ovid (in both Latin and English) that are used in the text; it appears at the back of the work. Also appended is a "List of Illustrative Passages Quoted from the Poets," which gives the last names of the poets and the pages on which their works appear in the text. However, no specific bibliographic sources or poem titles are given. Bulfinch acknowledges the general sources for the stories and the poetical citations in his preface, citing Ovid, Virgil, Mallet's *Northern Antiquities,* and some German collections of popular tales. Major archaeological sites revelant to this book are listed (current to 1968).

The strength of *Bulfinch's Mythology* lies in the stories themselves. Bulfinch retells the entire story, rather than putting bits and pieces together, and he ties the myths tightly to literature. The use of black-and-white photographs of both classical and contemporary artworks on classical themes, maps, and genealogical charts bring a sense of currency to the myths. The Board recommends this work for the core collections of public, academic, and school libraries.

Dictionary of Classical Mythology: Symbols, Attributes, and Associations. Robert E. Bell. ABC-Clio, 1982. hard. 1 vol. 390 pp. illus. appendixes. ISBN 0-87436-305-5. $49. dictionary.
BL715.B44 292.13'0321

Robert E. Bell, a reference librarian, had an intense interest in mythology for over 40 years and had long felt the need for a quick-access reference book on the personalities of Greek and Roman mythology. His *Dictionary of Classical Mythology: Symbols, Attributes, and Associations* reflects the orderly organization of a librarian and the enthusiasm of a devotee.

Information in the dictionary is limited to the mythological personae of Greece and Rome, except where Assyrian, Phoenician, Etruscan, or Egyptian mythologies have a special bearing. The work is an alphabetically arranged topical dictionary of symbols, attributes, and associations. About 1,000 subjects, from general *(bird, tree)* to specific *(woodpecker, cedar)*, and from abstract *(beauty, ugliness)* to concrete *(metal, twine)*, form the topic entries. Under each of these subjects are from 1 to 100 separate entries, which are restricted to proper names from Greek and Roman mythology. For each name entry, 1 to 40 lines of explanation are given, including identification of the person and, if appropriate, a brief summary of the myth involving the person or a short explanation of how the topic applies to him or her.

Adding to the usefulness and accessibility of this reference are the abundant cross-references. Most entry definitions also include citations to original sources, in the standard bibliographical format used in classical scholarship. "Guide to Citation Abbreviations" precedes the main text of the book. For convenience, the sources are restricted to the ones found in the Loeb Classical Library series. It should be noted that the *Dictionary of Classical Mythology* is the only work in the core collection that almost consistently refers the reader to the original source.

The format of the book is graphically pleasing. Each page of text has two columns of definitions. Subject headings are arranged alphabetically, set in boldface type, and centered in the column. The name entries are in capital letters and alphabetized underneath the subject heading. There is a good deal of white space on each page, clearly delineating the entries and topics. In addition, 16 full-page black-and-white illustrations are scattered throughout the work.

Three appendixes devoted to special topics add to the wealth of information provided in this dictionary. A valuable appendix titled "Surnames, Epithets, and Patronymics" presents "evidence of the persistence of surnames of deities after ancient migrations took place" (introduction). The author hopes that the gathering together of these names will help in archaeological and anthropological research as well as in clarifying the various names by which a mythological being may be known. For example, there are 87 separate surname entries for *Apollo.* "Heroic Expeditions" is an appendix that provides the names of those who were involved in various activities, from the passenger list of the *Argo* to the casualty list of the Trojan War. The "Guide to Personae" is a complete cross-index to the dictionary, listing the proper names in alphabetical order with the subject heading(s) (that is, the symbols, attributes, and associations of the person) indented under the appropriate names. No page numbers are given, but because access to the dictionary is alphabetical by subject heading, the reader should have no problem using this guide.

Because the *Dictionary of Classical Mythology* focuses on the personae of Greek and Roman mythology, those with a need to know more about a particular name or what it represents would do well to turn to this resource first. The reference will be most useful, however, to those who can quickly interpret the bibliographic format of classical scholarship. The Board recommends this work for the core collections of public and academic libraries.

Dictionary of Mythology, Folklore, and Symbols.
Gertrude Jobes. Scarecrow, 1962. hard. 3 vols. 2,241 pp. appendixes. index. ISBN 0-8108-2036-6 (set). $97.50 (set). dictionary.
GR35.J6 398.03

To better understand symbols found in literature and art as well as to improve her own creative writing, Gertrude Jobes began to delve into the meanings behind symbols, and from that research emerged the *Dictionary of Mythology, Folklore, and Symbols.* This work provides explanations already in existence plus a few original interpretations for a myriad of symbols and symbolic situations found in folktales and myths. The guiding principle of the dictionary is that symbolism "unites all peoples," that "it is a universal language, a means of wider communication" (introduction).

According to the author, a symbol is "anything that comes into existence, that which is or was" (introduction). In other words, almost anything can be a symbol. Through her research, Jobes has provided a key to the interpretation of common objects as symbols. Criteria for inclusion are broad but are not specified in the text. The scope ranges from *Downing Street* as the symbol of British government; to the *Jenny Wren* that was sacred to the Druids; to *Qolucotun,* the creator-god of the Washington State Indians; to the many symbolic meanings of *triangle.* Most entries pertain to the ancient and classical worlds. Because of the 1962 publication date, space-age symbolism is absent.

The first two volumes of the dictionary contain approximately 17,000 capitalized main entry words that are alphabetically arranged in two columns of text. Definitions range from one line to several columns and are often phrases rather than complete sentences. Any subentries appear underneath the primary entries and are underlined; brief descriptions show their relationship to the main entry. For example, under the main entry for *Charon* appear the secondary entries for *Charon's toll* and *Charon's staircase.*

Definitions focus on symbolic meaning. The format followed for entries on deities is to give "genealogy, function, explanation of activities and behavior, attributes or emblems, steeds, how depicted in art, and parallel deities" (introduction). Entries of a general nature follow a format that contains "universal and popular symbolism, dream significance, significance in Freemasonry, heraldic significance, occult significance, word explanation, cognates or comparisons, and mythological and religious significance listed alphabetically under the culture" (introduction). There are no cross-references in the entries. Surprisingly, there are no illustrations, although there are some charts, such as one on birthstones. Unfortunately, the bibliography appended to the second volume provides incomplete bibliographic information; neither the publisher nor the copyright date is cited.

The third volume, which is very useful for tracking down often-elusive answers to reference questions, especially in mythology, has 25,000 listings divided into a 392-page topical index pertaining to the fields of interest associated with deities, heroes, and personalities and a 69-page index dealing with supernatural forms, realms, and things. The two indexes are the essence of the third volume, and it is in them that "see" and "also see" references are found. These dual indexes give the patron much quicker access to the dictionary itself and provide useful and interesting information at a glance (such as the 103 personal names associated with music).

The Board recommends the *Dictionary of Mythology, Folklore, and Symbols* for the core collections of public and academic libraries.

A Dictionary of World Mythology. Arthur Cotterell. Perigee/Putnam, 1982. soft. 1 vol. 256 pp. illus. appendix. index. ISBN 0-399-50619-5. $8.95. dictionary.
BL303.C66 291.1'3

A Dictionary of World Mythology, by Arthur Cotterell, the author of several works on ancient civilizations, is a basic reference work. In the introduction Cotterell identifies some of the theories of the origins of myths, ranging from the beliefs that they were derived from rituals to the assumption that folklore and mythology are indistinguishable. For Cotterell, however, myths "possess an intensity of meaning that is akin to poetry," and they "appeal to the unconscious" mind (introduction).

His approach is to examine great geographical areas and the myths associated with these regions. Divided into groupings of the "seven great traditions of world mythology: namely, West Asia, South and Central Asia, East Asia, Europe, America, Africa and Oceania" (introduction), about 500 myths are very briefly told. Arranged alphabetically by mythological character (although occasionally a noun, such as *potlatch* or *relics,* sneaks in) within the geographical groupings, the entries generally range from 200 to 500 words. The character or word is briefly identified; then the myth is very briefly retold, stressing ancestry, characteristics, and deeds. Although quotations are frequently used in the entries, sources are not cited.

Each geographical grouping is preceded by a brief historical background of factors that influenced the people of the region and the creation of their myths. A map for each region is also included. Eighty black-and-white photographs of ancient artifacts and archaeological sites are scattered throughout.

Access to the material is made easier by a general index that has entry words printed in boldface type. References in the index are to material in the introductions to the various geographical groupings as well as to the entries themselves. A list giving a smattering of suggested readings for each geographical region is also included as an appendix.

This work will suffice as a quick and inexpensive reference to world myths. While the myths are so distilled in this reference that their flavor is sometimes lost, *A Dictionary of World Mythology* is useful in order to quickly identify the regional origin of a myth. The Board recommends this work for the core collections of public, academic, and school libraries.

Funk & Wagnalls Standard Dictionary of Folklore, Mythology, and Legend. Maria Leach, ed. Harper & Row, 1984. soft. 1 vol. 1,236 pp. illus. index. ISBN 0-06-250511-4. $39.95. dictionary.
GR35.F82 398.042'03

Funk & Wagnalls Standard Dictionary of Folklore, Mythology, and Legend is a wonderfully readable and scholarly work compiled by a fine array of consultants and contributors. Folklorists, anthropologists, musicologists, linguists, and a lexicographer—scholars all—make up the impressive list of those whose combined talents have produced this reference. First published in 1949 in a two-volume set, this dictionary is now available in a one-volume paperback edition.

As the title indicates, there is great diversity in the work. The scope is broad; over 8,000 entry words include samplings of folklore and mythology from all over the world: *gods* and *demons; heroes, tricksters,* and *numskulls; dance* and *song; festivals* and *rituals; plants* and *animals; charms* and *spells; fairies* and *zombies.* The material included is generally well balanced among the legends of many cultures and ethnic groups, with lighter emphasis on Greek and Roman mythology because it is so well known and well documented. A heavier emphasis is placed on Native American, African-American, and African material primarily because of the twentieth-century surge of interest in these cultures.

Arranged in alphabetical order, the entries range from one line to over 20 pages. Survey articles appear as part of the alphabetical order. The list of these articles at the beginning of the book provides quick access to them. Of particular interest is the inclusion of folklorist Ralph Steele Boggs's eight-page table of classification in the article entitled "Types and Classifications of Folklore." Boggs's much narrower approach is quite unlike library classification schemes and should be a boon to those who are trying to keep their research in order.

All of the survey articles and several of the entries are signed and have notes and bibliographies. The only illustration is on a double-page spread that explains the symbols and designs used in the cover art.

The index to this dictionary is of great importance because it brings the entries into subject-related groupings by providing references to "2,405 countries, regions, cultures, culture areas, peoples, tribes, and ethnic groups from 5 continents and many islands of the world."

According to the preface, this edition contains "several hundred" revisions, some deletions and additions that reflect the most recent scholarship, but remains true to the original work as much as possible. Undoubtedly there will be future editions, as the editor states that the book will never be completed until there is an end to "spontaneous song and creative symbol."

Funk & Wagnalls Standard Dictionary of Folklore, Mythology, and Legend is a fine reference work that can be used on many levels. The Board recommends this work for the core collections of public, academic, and school libraries.

Index to Fairy Tales, 1949–1972, Including Folklore, Legends and Myths in Collections. Norma Olin Ireland, comp. Scarecrow, 1973. hard. 1 vol. 741 pp. ISBN 0-87305-101-7. $45. index.
Z5983.F17I73 016.3982

Index to Fairy Tales, 1973–1977, Including Folklore, Legends and Myths in Collections, 4th suppl. Norma Olin Ireland, comp. Scarecrow, 1985. hard. 1 vol. 259 pp. ISBN 0-8108-1855-8. $29.50. index.
Z5983.F17I732 016.3982

In 1926 Mary Huse Eastman compiled the first *Index to Fairy Tales, Myths and Legends.* This reference was followed by two supplements, the last one indexed through 1948. These works have long been recognized as major reference tools in the fields of folklore and library science. In 1973 Norma Olin Ireland of Ireland Indexing Service compiled the *Index to Fairy Tales, 1949–1972,* a book that continues Eastman's work. These works were originally published by F. W. Faxon Company and are now being reprinted by Scarecrow Press.

Ireland's index covers a 33-year span and indexes 406 books that contain collections of fairy tales, folklore, legends, and myths from around the world. All indexed books are in English, and most were published in the United States. Her supplement of 1973–1977, called the fourth supplement because it is the fourth compilation since Eastman's first index, was first published in 1979 and indexes 130 collected works. In that supplement only, criteria for inclusion were based on "availability and favorable reviews in professional journals" (foreword). (No criteria are stated in the 1949–1972 index.) The latest supplement includes some books that were missed in the 1949–1972 volume, such as Jagendorf's *Noodlehead Stories from Around the World* (1957), and some reprints, such as Curtin's *Myths and Folk-Tales of the Russians, Western Slavs, and Magyars* (1890, 1971) and DeBosschere's *Christmas Tales of Flanders* (1917, 1972). All books in the supplement were published in the United States.

Both Ireland indexes include stories from around the world, but both also reflect the American publishing industry's tendency to place heavy emphasis on tales with European origins. In addition, only stories in collections are indexed; therefore, many fine single-story editions are excluded.

Access to the index and its supplement is by title and subject. Arrangement is alphabetical by word, with two columns per page. Authors and title variations are listed only if they are mentioned in the collections; therefore, the earlier editions of Eastman indexes should be referred to for the variants (assuming the library already has the three volumes or can acquire them through out-of-print sources). The title of the work is the main entry and refers the researcher, through a code, to the proper story collection. The code is simple and means that the bibliographic descriptions are given only once, in the "List of Collections Analyzed in the Work and Key to Symbols Used." The more than 2,050 subject entries appear in boldface type and are common ones rather than folklore motifs. Particularly useful are the many cross-references that are found throughout the works.

The *Index to Fairy Tales, 1949–1972* and the *Index to Fairy Tales, 1973–1977* are enormously valuable resources to those trying to locate a specific story and to those in search of a subject-related story to tell to children. The Board recommends these works for the core collections of public, academic, and school libraries.

Supplementary Titles

Dictionary of Gods and Goddesses, Devils and Demons. Manfred Lurker; G. L. Campbell, trans. Routledge, Chapman & Hall, 1987. hard and soft. 1 vol. 451 pp. illus. ISBN 0-7102-1106-6 (hard); 0-7102-0877-4 (soft). $45 (hard); $15.95 (soft). dictionary.
BL303.L8713 291

The *Dictionary of Gods and Goddesses, Devils and Demons,* originally published in German in 1984, "contains about 1,800 entries that include gods and other supernatural beings drawn from religions and mythologies of ancient, medieval, and contemporary cultures.

"Both familiar and obscure figures are included, and there are numerous cross-references. Especially helpful are [the] appendixes . . . and a selective bibliography." (*Choice,* January 1988, p. 748)

"[The supernatural beings included] come from many cultures, including Lithuanian, Moluccan, Hittite, Buddhist, Australian aboriginal, [etc.]. . . . Although the scope is wide, the classical mythologies of the Old World predominate. . . . Entries are one to five sentences in length and usually identify at least culture and function. Among other information that may be included are the evolution of the being, familial relationships, parallel divinities in other cultures, era/dates, alternate names, symbols, and original name and meaning. . . . [T]he wide scope of coverage, the scholarship reflected, the attractive format, the recency of publication, . . . and the continuing interest in the topic make this a desirable addition to most academic, public, and [even some] secondary school libraries." (*BL,* February 1, 1988, p. 94)

Also reviewed in: *ARBA,* 1988, p. 529; *Brit Bk N,* April 1987, p. 207; *WLB,* December 1987, p. 91.

Board's recommendation: Public and academic libraries.

The Facts On File Encyclopedia of World Mythology and Legend. Anthony S. Mercatante. Facts On File, 1988. hard. 1 vol. 807 pp. illus. indexes. ISBN 0-8160-1049-8. $95. dictionary.
BL303.M45 291.1'3'0321

The Facts On File Encyclopedia of World Mythology and Legend includes approximately 3,200 entries for "personal names, place-names, scriptural and literary works, legends and fables, and zoological and botanical symbols. . . . One can find entries . . . from classical civilization; . . . from Egyptian, Babylonian, Norse, and Celtic mythology; Australian, Japanese, Polynesian, and Siberian legends; ancient and medieval epics; Jewish, Muslim, and Hindu sacred texts; Christian hagiography; Aesopian fables; Grimms' fairy tales; and American folklore. . . . The introduction discusses the differences between myth, legend, fable, folktale, and fairy tale. [Special features included are] . . . a key to variant spellings, . . . [an] annotated bibliography, . . . a cultural and ethnic index, which classifies terms under more than 75 cultural groups, and a general index.

"A further enhancement to the text are the numerous black-and-white illustrations. . . . . Because of the way it gathers such a wealth of information into a single source, [this] is a useful ready-reference tool for most libraries." (*BL,* January 15, 1989, p. 849)

Also reviewed in: *B Rpt,* January 1989, p. 51; *WLB,* January 1989, p. 124.

Board's recommendation: Public, academic, and school libraries.

The Golden Bough. Sir James George Frazer. St. Martin's, 1969. hard. 13 vols. index. ISBN 0-312-33215-7 (set). $375 (set). handbook.
BL310.F72 291

The New Golden Bough, rev. edition. Theodore Gaster, ed. St. Martin's, 1975. hard and soft. 1 vol. 832 pp. index. ISBN 0-87599-036-3 (hard); 0-45162208-1 (soft). $33.95 (hard); $6.95 (soft). handbook.
BL310.F72 291

"In 1890, Sir James George Frazer published The Golden Bough in two volumes, [and] later expanded it to 12. For . . . [100] years it has been a classic in the interpretation and understanding of man's cultural origins and motivations." (*Chicago Sunday Tribune,* August 16, 1959, p. 2)

Over the years, the reference has gone through several printings and abridgments. This edition is the current reprint of the original 12 volumes plus the 1936 supplement titled *Aftermath,* which has become the thirteenth volume. The volumes cover such topics as "The Magic Art and the Evolution of Kings," "Taboo and the Perils of the Soul," and "The Scapegoat." The "supplementary volume contains new matter gathered from works published since 1915, and from some earlier sources not utilized in the basic work.

"[*The Golden Bough* is] not a reference book in the ordinary sense of the word, but a great storehouse of information about primitive religion. The very detailed general index makes it possible to use the set for ready reference, and the bibliography is extensive." (*Guide to Reference Books,* 10th ed., 1986, p. 749)

"Theodore Gaster has done a wonderful job of abridgment . . . [of the original 12 volumes plus the supplement of *The Golden Bough*]. More, however, he has reevaluated much of Frazer's basic data and interpreted them in the light of modern social anthropology. . . ." (*Chicago Sunday Tribune,* August 16, 1959, p. 2)

"[This abridgment is] recommended for all libraries, including those already possessing the complete set of . . . [Frazer's] earlier abridgment [1922], neither of which should be discarded." (*LJ,* August 1959, p. 2359)

Also reviewed in: *BL,* November 15, 1980, p. 475; *CR,* August 1975, p. 112; *Obs,* July 20, 1975, p. 21.

Board's recommendation: Public and academic libraries.

A Guide to Folktales in the English Language: Based on the Aarne-Thompson Classification System. D. L. Ashliman. Greenwood, 1987. hard. 1 vol. 368 pp. appendix. index. ISBN 0-313-25961-5. $55. handbook.
Z5983.F17A83 016.39820

"The purpose of . . . [*A Guide to Folktales in the English Language*] is 'to help readers find reliable texts of any given folktale (available in English), not only in its best-known version, but also in less familiar variants' (introd.). The author, an associate professor of German at the University of Pittsburgh, has arranged the book by Aarne-Thompson numbers, the standard folklore classification system. He provides brief plot summaries for the stories associated with each index number and then lists several collections in which versions of the story appear." (*CRL,* July 1988, p. 345)

"[The author] has 'revised Thompson's verbal descriptions of the types . . . to better describe the variants that are currently available in English,' has incorporated several new numbers proposed by other scholars and collectors for the Aarne-Thompson system, and has included two bibliographies, one of books about folklore and folktales, the other an up-to-date list of folktale collections. . . . There are cross-references from one tale type to another, a complete listing of Grimm's 200 tales with type classifications as an appendix, and an index of best-known titles and key words from typical plots." (*Choice,* February 1988, p. 881)

Also reviewed in: *CAY,* Winter 1987, p. 2; *R&R Bk N,* June 1988, p. 30.

Board's recommendation: Public and academic libraries.

Mythical and Fabulous Creatures. Malcolm South, ed. Greenwood, 1987. hard. 1 vol. 393 pp. illus. index. ISBN 0-313-24338-7. $14.95. handbook.
GR825.M87 398

Mythical and Fabulous Creatures is designed " 'as a reference and research guide that describes fabulous creatures and their appearances in history, literature, and art.' . . . [It] begins with an introduction by . . . [the author] that includes a bibliographic essay identifying bibliographies, anthologies, other reference sources, and general books. This is followed by . . . 20 chapters on individual creatures arranged in four sections, each reflecting the creatures' characteristics: 'Birds and Beasts,' . . . 'Human-Animal Composites,' . . . 'Creatures of the Night' . . . and 'Giants and Fairies.' . . . [Each chapter] is written as a descriptive and critical bibliographic essay . . . [and] ends with a selected bibliography. . . . The second part of the book [features] . . . 'creatures that have received little or no attention in the introduction and the previous entries' and . . . a chart classifying 125 of these creatures, along with the 20 covered by the chapters.

"The essays are not only thorough, scholarly, and comprehensive, but also are highly readable and will appeal to the interested layperson as well as the scholar. . . . [The volume also contains] a detailed index with see references . . . [and a] glossary [that] provides one- or two-line definitions of the 20 [major] creatures plus 43 others. . . . A small section of illustrations, . . . the art nouveau-inspired titles and chapter headings, and the gray and blue binding with embossed gold letters and dragon make this an exceptionally handsome volume." (*BL,* July 1987, p. 1662)

Also reviewed in: *Choice,* July 1987, p. 1678; *LJ,* June 15, 1987, p. 64; *R&R Bk N,* Summer 1987, p. 8.

Board's recommendation: Public, academic, and school libraries.

The Woman's Encyclopedia of Myths and Secrets. Barbara G. Walker. Harper & Row, 1983. soft. 1 vol. 1,124 pp. illus. ISBN 0-06-250925-X. $23.95. dictionary.
BL458.W34 291

The Woman's Encyclopedia of Myths and Secrets is a compilation of "information relating to religious scriptures, archaeological and anthropological findings, and myths into a volume of 1,350 entries all focused on the subject of femininity. Entries range from Koran to Aphrodite, Moses to Mary, Gnosticism to Witch." (*Choice,* March 1984, p. 960)

"It is clear that Walker has devoted considerable research and time to her well-written compendium of myth, lore, and scholarship on women and sexism.

. . . She draws on a variety of works from such disciplines as religion, mythology, psychology, anthropology, literature, and history. While scholars generally agree that some of these authors present fascinating hypotheses rather than established facts, the less-educated user could easily mistake speculation for truth, given the encyclopedia's factual style of presentation. [Therefore,] reference librarians need to approach some of this information with caution and pay attention to the source cited." (*LJ,* February 1, 1984, p. 174)

Also reviewed in: *AB,* March 5, 1984, p. 1732; *Atl,* February 1984, p. 105; *LATBR,* January 29, 1984, p. 8; *N Dir Wom,* March 1984, p. 14; *Parabola,* November 1984, p. 108; *WLB,* February 1984, p. 454.

Board's recommendation: Public and academic libraries.

New and Noteworthy

A Dictionary of Irish Mythology. Peter Berresford Ellis. ABC-Clio, 1989. hard. 1 vol. 240 pp. ISBN 0-87436-553-8. $39.50. dictionary.
BL980.I7E45 299.16

"The *Dictionary* [*of Irish Mythology*], 'essentially for the lay reader,' covers gods, human heroes, titles, sites, and objects, as well as subjects ranging from *divination* and *druid* to *fasting* and *medicine.* Entries vary in length from brief identification . . . to the three-page tale of King Diarmuid. . . . Entries . . . differentiate among various personages with the same name . . . by the cross-references necessitated by varied systems of Anglicized spellings, and by the listing of variant versions of the tales." (*BL,* November 1, 1989, p. 603)

A Dictionary of Superstitions. Iona Opie and Moira Tatem. Oxford, 1989. hard. 1 vol. 494 pp. index. ISBN 0-19-211597-9. $30. dictionary.
BF1775.D53 001.9′6

A Dictionary of Superstitions "consists of nearly 1,600 alphabetically arranged entries that treat superstitions of the British Isles—including divinations, spells, cures, charms, signs and omens, rituals, and taboos—that have survived into the nineteenth and twentieth centuries. . . . The quotations are from a wide range of published and unpublished sources—diaries, letters, local histories and glossaries, works of literature, folklore publications, journals . . . and newspapers. . . . The *Dictionary* concludes with an extensive select bibliography. . . ." (*BL,* December 1, 1989, pp. 764–766)

Valsa Varma

Food and Nutrition

The role of good nutrition in the maintenance of good health and prevention of disease is being increasingly recognized by the general public. Today the health-conscience consumer is interested in low-calorie diets, reducing the risk of such diseases as heart disease and cancer through dietary modifications, and the benefits that may be accrued from using vitamin and mineral supplements. Every day consumers are faced with an avalanche of food and nutrition information that is both factual and fictitious. The library patron will often consult the food and nutrition reference section to obtain reliable information and answers to questions. Because of this great diversity and public interest, a library should have a comprehensive core collection in the subject of food and nutrition. Such a collection should reflect the different aspects of the subject, ranging from the production, processing, and distribution of food to the assimilation of food in the human body.

Nutrition is the study of the interrelationships among food, bodily functions, and health. It is a highly interdisciplinary field. Nutritional information is sought and used by various biomedical and agricultural sciences. Nutrition is also concerned with the socioeconomic, cultural, and psychological aspects of food and eating.

In the United States nutrition labeling of packaged foods, although not mandatory in all cases, is being practiced by several well-known food-processing companies. Such practice certainly provides information, though library patrons often want background information to help them interpret these labels.

Intense research is now underway to unravel the biological functions of several newer trace minerals that can be found in certain foods. This can lead to exciting discoveries. Also, problems of vitamin and mineral overuse are being discovered, and consumers are becoming more aware of such problems and, more importantly, are learning how to avoid them.

With the rapid expansion of the elderly population in the United States, new interest is being generated in their nutritional needs and concerns. The development of adequate diets for the maintenance of optimal health in the elderly is a matter of high priority for health care providers.

While many technologically developed countries have solved the problem of nutritional deficiencies and are wrestling with the problem of overnutrition, deficiency diseases are still a major public health concern in many less technologically developed countries. The reasons are obvious. Uncontrolled population growth and lack of farming technology and food distribution results in decreased crop production and increased

Core Titles

	PUBLIC	ACADEMIC	SCHOOL
Bowes and Church's Food Values of Portions Commonly Used, 15th edition Pennington, Jean A. T. Harper & Row, 1989	✦	✦	
The Columbia Encyclopedia of Nutrition Winick, Myron, et al., comp. and ed. Putnam, 1988	✦		
A Consumer's Dictionary of Food Additives, 3d edition Winter, Ruth. Crown, 1989	✦		
Foods and Food Production Encyclopedia Considine, Douglas M., ed. Van Nostrand Reinhold, 1982		✦	
The Prentice-Hall Dictionary of Nutrition and Health Anderson, Kenneth, and Lois Harmon. Prentice-Hall, 1985	✦		

waste. The World Health Organization and national governments are involved in research activities to remedy such problems.

With the development of data bases and application of computer technology, diet analysis has become an easy task. The use of computers in nutrition is becoming more and more popular.

Some reliable sources of food and nutrition information will be discussed in this section. Others include publications from the U. S. Department of Agriculture and Department of Health and Human Services, the American Dietetic Association, the American Cancer Society, the National Dairy Council, and the World Health Organization. A very useful out-of-print source is *The World Encyclopedia of Food* (L. Patrick Coyle, Facts On File, 1982). In addition, there are numerous publications written by well-known authorities in the field of food and nutrition that are likely to appear in circulation rather than in the reference section.

—*V. V.*

With contributions by Jill H. Powell.

Core Titles

Bowes and Church's Food Values of Portions Commonly Used, 15th edition. Jean A. T. Pennington. Harper & Row, 1989. hard. 1 vol. 328 pp. index. ISBN 0-06-055157-7. $24.95. handbook.
TX551.B64 641.1

The first edition of *Bowes and Church's Food Values of Portions Commonly Used* was published in 1937; this title has since become a standard reference source of information on food composition. The current edition, the fifteenth, has been revised by Jean A. T. Pennington. There are two major additions in this edition. First, the values of dietary fiber are included in the main table, instead of being listed in a supplementary table. (This is a very timely revision since dietary fiber is currently of great public concern.) Second, the listing of recent literature on the composition of foods has been updated and extended.

The book supplies authoritative data on the nutritional value of foods in a quick-and-easy chart format. The book is divided into one main table and several smaller supplementary tables. The main table, entitled "Nutrient Contents of Foods," alphabetically lists 35 food groups such as beverages; cheese and cheese products; eggs, egg dishes, and egg substitutes; fast foods; meats; and milk, milk beverages, and milk beverage mixes. Fruits and vegetables are also included. Each group is further divided into subgroups as needed. For example, the section "Fast Foods" provides an alphabetical list of common fast food chains and the food items sold by each. The "Beverages" section includes the most commonly consumed alcoholic beverages in America. The average consumer will find these sections useful when calculating daily nutrient intake. Each food is identified by name, description, brand name (where applicable), and serving portion. Portions are given in familiar measurements such as cups, fluid ounces, pieces, and numbers. For calculation of diets from weighed portions, the actual weight of the food is given in grams. The nutritional information provided for each food includes calories, cholesterol, fiber, and several vitamins and minerals. The information is arranged in an easily readable columnar format.

In addition to the main table, there are supplementary tables that provide valuable information on amino acids, caffeine, trace minerals, and so on, that are found in various foods. Following the supplementary charts, the book lists the many different sources from which the data are taken.

There are many causes for nutrient variations in foods. Because of nutrient variation and the fact that the data are collected from various sources, some inconsistencies may be noticed. However, this in no way affects the quality of this excellent book.

To conserve space, each food is listed only once, although it may apply to several sections. The index will aid the reader when a food cannot be easily located. A list of abbreviations and symbols is provided. Footnotes to the tables help clarify the information.

Special features of the book include tables that appear in the front of the book. These tables present the "Recommended Daily Dietary Allowances," "Estimated Safe and Adequate Daily Dietary Intakes of Selected Vitamins and Minerals," "Mean Heights and Weights and Recommended Energy Intake," and "United States Recommended Daily Allowances." These provide a useful background to the other tables in this book.

The author of *Bowes and Church's Food Values of Portions Commonly Used* is a well-recognized authority in the field of food and nutrition. The Board recommends this work for the core collections of public and academic libraries. —*V. V.*

The Columbia Encyclopedia of Nutrition. Myron Winick et al., comps. and eds. Putnam, 1988. soft. 1 vol. 349 pp. index. ISBN 0-399-13298-8. $12.95. encyclopedia.
QP141.C69 613.2'03'21

The Columbia Encyclopedia of Nutrition is a scholarly contribution that attempts to fill the gap between the findings of the nutrition researcher and the application of such knowledge to solving everyday problems by the lay public. This reference tool is both timely and useful.

The editors of this book are competent professionals who specialize in nutrition. They have attempted to evaluate all available evidence before reaching a conclusion or recommending a change of diet. The chief editor and compiler of the book, Myron Winick, is the director of the prestigious Institute of Human Nutrition at Columbia University's College of Physicians and Surgeons and has published hundreds of articles and over 20 textbooks on nutrition.

The book contains over 100 alphabetically arranged entries and discusses topics from infant feeding to obesity. Some topics are covered in more depth than others, but all pertain to human health. The book does not offer "quick fixes" for chronic health problems that have, in fact, multiple causes, but rather attempts to broaden the reader's knowledge so that he or she can make informed decisions.

The book offers authoritative information on what is known and what is not known; which dietary changes are appropriate and which are not; and when supplements are beneficial and when they are harmful. The book does not attempt to cover all aspects of nutrition; rather, it focuses on current issues in diet, nutrition, and health with which the lay public is concerned. It is written in a simple, easy-to-read style.

The book makes scientifically sound dietary recommendations such as cutting down on fatty meats to reduce the intake of fat and cholesterol, restricting sodium intake to control hypertension, and increasing calcium intake to 1 gram per day to lower the risk of osteoporosis. In this era of "fad" diets, the book exposes the unbalanced nature of such popular diets as the Scarsdale Diet, the Stillman Quick Weight Loss Diet, and the Last Chance Diet. It also provides accurate information about problem nutrients and avoiding malnutrition when following a vegetarian diet.

The usefulness of the book is greatly enhanced by the inclusion of several tables such as "Vegetables Naturally High in Sodium," "Foods with Insignificant Amounts of Sodium (Permitted for All Diets)," and "Sources of Naturally Occurring Nutrients." Another valuable feature is four menus aimed at persons who want to improve their athletic performance.

This book contains an excellent index, which is encyclopedic in nature. However, a table of contents would have been helpful. *The Columbia Encyclopedia of Nutrition* presents nutritional information to the reader at an affordable cost. The Board recommends this work for the core collection of public libraries.

—*V. V.*

A Consumer's Dictionary of Food Additives, 3d edition. Ruth Winter. Crown, 1989. soft. 1 vol. 352 pp. ISBN 0-517-57262-1. $10.95. dictionary.
TX553.A3W55 664.06'0321

The first edition of *A Consumer's Dictionary of Food Additives* was published by Ruth Winter in 1972 and revised in 1978. The newly revised third edition of Winter's *A Consumer's Dictionary of Food Additives* contains very little change from the 1978 edition. Winter is the author of a number of titles aimed at providing consumers with information on science-related topics.

Food additives are chemicals intentionally added to foods. Although they serve a variety of purposes in modern food processing and food production, additives may also pose potential health problems to the public. As stated in the introduction, the purpose of the dictionary is to provide consumers with information about food additives which will enable them to make educated decisions about whether or not they should continue using certain food products.

In order to keep foods safe for consumption, the government regulates the use of food additives through legislation and administrative rulings. In fact, the government has prepared a list of food additives considered "Generally Recognized as Safe" (GRAS). This list includes about 1,750 additives that have been added to foods for a long time, such as salt, sugar, baking powder, spices, and flavorings, which, under conditions of their intended use, are not known to produce harmful side effects.

A Consumer's Dictionary of Food Additives defines food additives in simple, everyday language. The entries are arranged alphabetically by additive, providing information about its origin, its chemical composition, its appearance and taste, what it is used for, what it does, whether it is toxic or beneficial, and its GRAS status.

This dictionary does not contain a content listing or indexes, but the introduction is a helpful guide to using the book. There is also a brief bibliography at the end of the dictionary. The alphabetical arrangement with "see" references is helpful in locating information.

The Board recommends this work for the core collection of public libraries. —*V. V.*

Foods and Food Production Encyclopedia. Douglas M. Considine, ed. Van Nostrand Reinhold, 1982. hard. 1 vol. 2,305 pp. illus. appendix. index. ISBN 0-442-21612-2. $249.95. encyclopedia.
TX349.F58 664.03'21

The *Foods and Food Production Encyclopedia,* in the tradition of VAN NOSTRAND'S SCIENTIFIC ENCYCLOPEDIA (see Science and Technology), provides an extensive and thorough treatise of the highly interdisciplinary subject of foods and food production. The book covers three stages of food production: growth, harvesting, and processing. A work of this nature requires integration of numerous food-related disciplines such as botany, biochemistry, genetics, processing sciences, and nutrition.

This encyclopedia contains 1,201 alphabetically arranged entries, 2,950 cross-reference headings, 1,006 illustrations, 587 tables, and 7,500 items in the alphabetical index. The multitude of tables, flowcharts, maps, and chemical structures bear testimony to the work's emphasis on precise information.

The book is international in scope. It gives statistics on production of all crops and products for all countries producing over 1 percent of a given crop or product. However, it does not provide a country-by-country assessment of food-producing methods.

The entries in this volume vary widely in coverage and depth. Topics include cultivation of crops, raising of animals for food, diseases and pests of plants and animals, agricultural chemicals, food additives, flavoring agents, and sweeteners.

Another area well discussed in the book is biochemistry and nutrition. Topics are treated not only in terms of human nutrition but also from the standpoint of feeding livestock and poultry. An entry on dietary trends in the United States, United Kingdom, and other countries is included.

"See" and "see also" references are generous, and the index is excellent. The bibliography that is given at the end of each article is very useful for further research, although it may be somewhat dated given the 1982 publication of this edition. The appendix includes a list of food additives and chemicals and provides their principal characteristics, synonyms of the compounds, recommended daily dietary allowances, and conversion tables.

Douglas Considine has authored and edited many authoritative scientific and technical books. Some of his well-known works include VAN NOSTRAND'S SCIENTIFIC ENCYCLOPEDIA (see Science and Technology), and the Van Nostrand Reinhold ENCYCLOPEDIA OF CHEMISTRY (see Chemistry). The Board recommends this work for the core collection of academic libraries. —*V. V.*

The Prentice-Hall Dictionary of Nutrition and Health. Kenneth Anderson and Lois Harmon. Prentice-Hall, 1985. hard and soft. 1 vol. illus. ISBN 0-13-695610-6 (hard); 0-13-695602-5 (soft). $21.95 (hard); $9.95 (soft). dictionary.
TX349.A54 613.2'03

A core collection in any subject requires a good dictionary, and *The Prentice-Hall Dictionary of Nutrition and Health* is an excellent choice. This reference tool contains 1,236 separate entries on common and uncommon minerals, diets, vitamins, diseases, acronyms, and phrases used by dieticians. Definitions are clear and easy to understand. The audience, primarily health-conscious consumers, will find entries for *niacin, nutrification, carbohydrate loading, zen macrobiotic diet, saturated fats,* and phrases listed on food labels, such as *BHA, BHT, MSG, partially hydrogenated soy oil,* and *FD&C Red No. 40.* Each entry includes either a paragraph definition or a historical and medical discussion, which can run over a page in length.

There are a few problems with the book. First, it lacks a bibliography. Second, some of the definitions, although accurate, are incomplete, such as the definitions of *quinones* and *waxing of fruits and vegetables.* Quinone is the name for the chemical compound that causes fruit to turn brown after it is exposed to air. What the definition fails to convey is whether it is hazardous to eat the browned areas. As for waxing of produce, the definition explains why and how it is done, and that the practice is controversial, but makes no recommendation as to the safety of consuming waxed skins. The longer entries contain additional information that may prove helpful. For example, the article on cancer and diet includes a list of foods that might aid in cancer prevention. Other entries list specific doses of note for natural and artificially added ingredients. For instance, the lethal dose of caffeine is 10 grams, or 100 cups of coffee. Information about the chemical composition of natural foods and synthetic foods, food additives, food safety laws, and the physical effects of dietary deficiencies and excesses is covered as well.

A valuable part of the book is the "Appendix of Tables." It includes statistical charts listing the amount of calories burned by various physical activities, the caloric content of food, recommended dietary allowances required, and other information. The nutrient values (mineral, vitamin), cholesterol, and fat content of many foods are listed. *The Prentice-Hall Dictionary of Nutrition and Health* does not have an index, but items are fairly easy to find.

The Board recommends this work for the core collection of public libraries. —*J. H. P.*

Supplementary Titles

The Complete Book of Food: A Nutritional, Medical, & Culinary Guide. Carol Ann Rinzler. Pharos Bks., 1987; distrib. by Ballantine. soft. 1 vol. 488 pp. index. ISBN 0-88687-436-X. $14.95. encyclopedia.
TX353.R525 641

The Complete Book of Food provides readers with much useful information. For example, "tea is high in vitamin K. Lima beans are contraindicated in a low fiber diet. Yogurt makes tetracycline less effective. These facts are a sample of the kinds of information found in this encyclopedic volume. Basing her work on current research, Rinzler, author of popular treatments of health topics, has assembled a unique compendium of medical effects of food for the layperson. Arranged alphabetically, the 103 entries covering 277 foods give the nutritional composition for each food and suggest proper methods of storage and preparation. Chemical reactions that take place during cooking, medical uses, adverse effects, and drug interactions are also enumerated. [This book is] a worthwhile addition for public libraries." (*LJ,* October 1, 1987, p. 86)

"Reference librarians bombarded with questions about individual foods, their nutritional values, and their chemical makeups will welcome Rinzler's compendium of facts. Arranging food alphabetically, the book accessibly describes traits in the same order for each item. Rinzler tabulates each food's nutritional value, gives basic information on buying the best, storing properly, preparing, and cooking. Medical data include the food's uses in medicine, any adverse reactions associated with the food, and possible drug interactions. Because of the text's arrangement, much information gets repeated verbatim, but this ultimately saves the reader from having to page back and forth. Orderly arrangement and clear writing make this volume supremely useful for quick research on basic information." (*BL,* September 1, 1987, p. 17)

Also reviewed in: *ARBA,* 1988, p. 592; *Cha Ti,* March 1988, p. 121; *PW,* August 21, 1987, p. 64; *R & R Bk N,* February 1988, p. 21.

Board's recommendation: Public libraries.

The Nutrition Desk Reference, rev. edition. Robert H. Garrison, Jr., and Elizabeth Somer. Keats, 1990. hard and soft. 1 vol. 368 pp. illus. index. ISBN 0-87983-523-0 (hard); 0-87983-488-9 (soft). $34.95 (hard); $15.95 (soft). encyclopedia.
QP141.G83 613

"The original edition of *The Nutrition Desk Reference* . . . was hailed by the American Library Association's *Booklist* as one of the two best reference books of the year, and was one of the most successful Main Selections of the Prevention Book Club. . . .

"This new edition, expanded by two update chapters and a completely new section on diet and disease—covering nutritional aspects of 20 major health conditions—has been revised in detail throughout to include the latest information from a full review of current scientific literature.

"The revised and updated *Nutrition Desk Reference* is a vital information resource for both laymen and professionals—a one-volume library of the most up-to-the-minute information in the most crucial area of health, complete with hundreds of references and 34 informative tables." (Excerpted from publisher's announcement)

Also reviewed in: *ARBA,* 1986, p. 571; *Choice,* October 1985, p. 324; *LJ,* July 1985, p. 59; April 15, 1986, p. 36.

Board's recommendation: Public and academic libraries.

New and Noteworthy

1000 Cooking Substitutions. Debbie Khoee. Global Trade Co., 1989. hard and soft. 1 vol. 158 pp. index. ISBN 0-9622451-8-6 (hard); 0-9622451-7-8 (soft). $22.95 (hard); $15.95 (soft). manual.

641.5

1000 Cooking Substitutions lists "more than 1,200 cooking substitutions. . . . It is divided by type of food (butter and oil, dairy, meat, spices, etc.) and suggests all manner of substitutes. Some examples include the obvious . . . [while others] are not as obvious." (*BL,* January 1, 1990, p. 948)

Charla A. Coatoam

French Literature

See also World Literature

The study of French literature spans several centuries and includes many different genres, from the twelfth century *chansons de geste* to the post–World War II *nouveau roman.* It should be noted that French literature, the written language, is a distinct subject and is separate from French language as it is spoken. The works included in these collections of recommendations are primarily concerned with the body of written works, although some books may allude to the spoken language, its history, development, geography, and so forth. It is also necessary to remember that the French language is and has been the language of people in many different countries. French literature may pertain to writings of people living in Canada, Africa, the Caribbean, Switzerland, and Belgium. Although most of the works reviewed herein are primarily concerned with the literature of France, non-French authors are often mentioned, particularly in the more recent publications.

The librarian building a collection in French literature reference works has two audiences to keep in mind: the general reader and the student. The genuine scholar (usually, although not always, an academic) is served well by two or three titles reviewed here. *Modern French Literature* (Debra Popkin, Ungar, 1977), a compilation of critical excerpts on 168 French writers, was identified by the Board as a particularly useful title for academic libraries. Unfortunately, it is now out of print. In general, however, the core and supplementary books selected address the needs of students and interested readers. Two of the core titles in particular have long been acknowledged as standard encyclopedia/dictionary sources: the Oxford University Press publications THE OXFORD COMPANION TO FRENCH LITERATURE and THE CONCISE OXFORD DICTIONARY OF FRENCH LITERATURE. The Board identified these two works as appropriate for collections in all three types of libraries. These volumes have the breadth of coverage and ease of use appropriate for school and public library patrons and also provide the university student with a comprehensive first resource. The other three titles in the core collection are either more focused or are oriented to the needs of research.

Core Titles

The Concise Oxford Dictionary of French Literature.
Joyce M. H. Reid, ed. Clarendon/Oxford, 1976. hard and soft. 1 vol. 669 pp. ISBN 0-19-866118-5 (hard); 0-19-281200-9 (soft). $29.95 (hard); $12.95 (soft). dictionary.
PQ41.C6 840.03

Core Titles

	PUBLIC	ACADEMIC	SCHOOL
The Concise Oxford Dictionary of French Literature Reid, Joyce M. H., ed. Clarendon/Oxford, 1976	✦	✦	✦
A Critical Bibliography of French Literature, 6 vols. Cabeen, D. C., gen. ed. Syracuse Univ. Pr., 1947–		✦	
Dictionary of Modern French Literature: From the Age of Reason Through Realism Dolbow, Sandra W. Greenwood, 1986	✦	✦	✦
The Oxford Companion to French Literature Harvey, Paul, and J. E. Haseltine. Clarendon/Oxford, 1961	✦	✦	✦
Research and Reference Guide to French Studies, 2d edition Osburn, Charles C. Scarecrow, 1981		✦	

The Concise Oxford Dictionary of French Literature is a revision of THE OXFORD COMPANION TO FRENCH LITERATURE, which was published in 1959 and reprinted in 1961. The preface states that revision has been accomplished not by omission but by condensing some entries and combining others, and adding new ones to bring information up to date. The major omission was most of the article on French-Canadian literature, which is now covered more thoroughly in THE OXFORD COMPANION TO CANADIAN LITERATURE (see Canadian History and Literature).

Several major areas have been updated. "Critics and Criticism" has been augmented to take into account recent movements, and there are now separate entries for *structuralism* and *Roland Barthes.* Francophone authors are discussed in new entries. There is a separate entry for *Leopold Senghor; Simone de Beauvoir* now has her own substantial entry; and there is now a brief section on the Resistance and major authors and publications of that movement. (There were few entries after World War II in THE OXFORD COMPANION TO FRENCH LITERATURE.)

Although the format has remained the same as that of its predecessor—two columns per page, boldface type for entry headings—this *Concise Dictionary* is more compact, with thinner paper and smaller (though readable) print.

This work is a necessary companion to THE OXFORD COMPANION TO FRENCH LITERATURE because of the additional updated material it includes. *The Concise Oxford Dictionary of French Literature* can also stand alone as a sourcebook for reference in French literature. The Board recommends this work for the core collections of public, academic, and school libraries.

A Critical Bibliography of French Literature. D. C. Cabeen, gen. ed. Syracuse Univ. Pr., 1947– . hard. 6 vols. indexes. ISBN 0-8156-2204-X (vol. 6). $150 (vol. 6). bibliography.
Z2171.C74

A Critical Bibliography of French Literature is a massive, comprehensive work in six separate volumes. Volume 6 has three parts (each a separate book), and there are supplementary volumes to volumes 3 and 4. The supplements cover works published since the cutoff dates of the standard volumes. According to the introduction, this work is regarded as the standard bibliography of its type in the field of French studies, and indeed it is difficult to imagine a more thorough, detailed work. The bibliographic entries are arranged in alphabetical order, by author or by title, if no author is listed. Works in French, English, German, and Italian, among others, are included. These entries do not merely list relevant works; scholars are noted for their knowledge of the particular period of study. The annotations, which are the primary value of the entries, range from one sentence to one or two paragraphs, though the general length is a few sentences. The annotations tell briefly what the work is, its relevance, its authority, and special advantages or drawbacks to using it. Reviews are also cited at the end of the entry. Thus, this bibliography is extremely useful to students and scholars examining specific aspects of French literature.

The volumes in this work are: *The Medieval Period; The Sixteenth Century; The Seventeenth Century; The Eighteenth Century; The Nineteenth Century;* and *The Twentieth Century.* Of these, the sixth volume, *The Twentieth Century,* is the most voluminous. Part 1 concerns general subjects and the pre-1940 novel; part 2, poetry, theater, and essays for the period before 1940; and part 3, post-1940 literature, in all genres. There are extensive tables of contents and an index to each volume. The bibliographical forms used conform to those used in the H. W. Wilson periodical indexes and by the Library of Congress for books. Each citation has a reference number for cross-reference purposes; it is illustrative of the scope of this work that the last number cited in part 3 of volume 6 is 17,939.

A Critical Bibliography of French Literature is an exhaustive, standard work in the field of French studies. The Board recommends this work for the core collection of academic libraries.

Dictionary of Modern French Literature: From the Age of Reason Through Realism. Sandra W. Dolbow. Greenwood, 1986. hard. 1 vol. 365 pp. appendixes. index. ISBN 0-313-23784-0. $50.95. dictionary.
PQ41.D65 840.3

The title of this work, *Dictionary of Modern French Literature,* could be misleading if one did not note the subtitle, *From the Age of Reason Through Realism.* Readers hoping for an explanation of the "nouveau roman" will be disappointed, as this volume treats literature from about 1715 to 1880. The cutoff date conforms roughly to the end of romanticism and realism and the beginnings of naturalism and symbolism. (Lengthy definitions of *romanticism* and *realism* are provided in this volume.) According to the preface, a companion volume, *From Naturalism and Symbolism to Postmodernism,* is in preparation, and cross-references frequently refer to this as-yet-unpublished work.

The dictionary contains almost 300 entries, most of them authors, titles of works, and literary terms. The author entries are often extensive, especially for major figures. The entry for *Balzac* is more than six pages long. In many cases entries for titles are also extensive (*Madame Bovary*—four pages) and include not only a plot summary, but also critical opinion, information on the work's place in the author's general achievements, and a list of works for further study. Entries for literary terms are very useful and often not found elsewhere. Here, for example, are two such entries: *Bovarysme,* which ". . . describes a pessimistic romantic condition in which one seeks an ideal of unattainable perfection, . . ." and *Beylism,* in which " 'the happy few' find happiness." Both definitions include examples and explanations of the works of Flaubert and Stendhal respectively.

The author, a journalist and former French teacher, has made an effort to cite current articles (up to 1984) in the often-extensive lists of "further information" appended to many entries. For example, these recommendations for further reading run to one and a half pages of close print for both *Voltaire* and *J.-J. Rousseau*, an unexpected and welcome boon to teachers and students. These citations include both books and periodicals.

The book is well bound with easily readable print for the main text, and readable, though smaller, print for the "Further Information" sections. A useful appendix entitled "Historical and Literary Events" matches one column designated "History" with another labeled "Literature." From this, we can see at a glance, for example, that nothing of literary note was published during the revolutionary years between 1788 and 1800. The appendix of entries that is grouped by subject matter makes it easy to find authors by century and genre. There is also a 12-page index.

The *Dictionary of Modern French Literature* is an extremely useful work, and the forthcoming companion volume of post-1880 information will be a welcome addition to the field. The Board recommends this work for the core collections of public, academic, and school libraries.

The Oxford Companion to French Literature. Paul Harvey and J. E. Haseltine. Clarendon/Oxford, 1961. hard. 1 vol. 771 pp. ISBN 0-19-866104-5. $44.95. dictionary.
PQ41.H3 840.3

The Oxford Companion to French Literature is indispensable. That said, it should also be noted that the copyright date is 1959 (reprinted in 1961) and that the work encompasses, with a few exceptions, the literary life of France only up to the outbreak of World War II. Therefore, do not search here for information about Jean Genet, Marguerite Duras, Claude Simon, or Hélène Cixous, nor for plot summaries of *L'Amant* or *Le Voyeur.* Barthes, Derrida, and Lacan do not appear in the "Critics and Criticism" section. While THE CONCISE OXFORD DICTIONARY OF FRENCH LITERATURE is a revision of this work, a new edition of this standard volume is needed. Like the other *Oxford Companions*, this volume is a standard work because it is a model of clarity, comprehensiveness, and trustworthiness. One turns to it for advice, information, and stability.

This one-volume encyclopedia contains over 6,000 entries arranged in alphabetical order with extensive cross-references, so that the reader unfamiliar with French definite articles or prepositions may still find the pertinent entry. Entries are arranged two columns per page and are easily found by boldface entry headings and judicious spacing.

The editors chose to concentrate on authors, specific works, and allusions. Most works are entered by first main word of the title—for example, *Grand Meaulnes, Le.* An extensive plot summary and brief explanation of the work's importance follow. Chronological listings of titles and publication dates are also provided to assist readers wishing to read Zola's Rougon-Macquart series or Balzac's *La Comédie Humaine,* for example.

Author entries, generally extensive for major authors (the Victor Hugo entry runs to two and a half pages), are divided into numbered sections. These sections provide information on family and early childhood influences, early education and early career, adulthood and mature works, literary reputation, beliefs and philosophy, importance and reputation in the context of other works of the period, and a brief publication history. However, for twentieth-century entries, especially what is now thought of as postwar writing, a newer edition would undoubtedly be revised with a shift in emphasis, even on some subjects included in this edition. For example, though there is an extensive one-page entry on *existentialism*, the entry on *Sartre* is comparatively brief, and only passing mention is made of *Simone de Beauvoir* (found only by cross-reference), in reference to Sartre's literary review, *Les Temps Moderne.*

The allusions contain information on various topics pertaining to French literature and culture, such as titles of works, fictional characters, place names, and political and journalistic allusions. A quick check under *Thermidor* refers the reader to *republican calendar;* information about the French Revolution itself may be found under *revolutions,* which lists the four major ones between 1789 and 1870 with concise chronological information on major events. This entry is four pages long.

In summary, *The Oxford Companion to French Literature* is exhaustive and authoritative, despite the limitations imposed by its age, and this work remains a standard reference in the field. The Board recommends this work for the core collections of public, academic, and school libraries.

Research and Reference Guide to French Studies, 2d edition. Charles B. Osburn. Scarecrow, 1981. hard. 1 vol. 532 pp. indexes. ISBN 0-8108-1440-4. $39.50. bibliography.
Z2175.A208 016.44

The second edition of *Research and Reference Guide to French Studies* revises the 1968 original and its 1972 supplement. According to the introduction, this edition is "thoroughly revised." While the work does not entirely supersede the first two volumes, the 1981 edition does pay more attention to the literature of the twentieth century. There is also more emphasis on literature than on peripheral, though related, fields, such as cinema. The second edition contains approximately 6,000 citations of a variety of works, which include dictionaries, concordances, filmographies, encyclopedias, and bibliographies. Charles B. Osburn, the author, states that this is not intended as a definitive work and that his choice of works included was based on usefulness; he sometimes chose a work with a very old copyright if it could show development of ideas and put this information in perspective. This edition is intended as a bridge between the two previous editions and the new machine-readable data base of the MLA annual bibliography (now available).

Even with the advent of computer data bases, the *Research and Reference Guide* is still a useful title; it is a compact, relatively comprehensive, easy-to-use reference work for introducing students to the vast subject of French study research materials.

The work is divided into six parts: "French Literature," "French Language," "French Language and Literature Outside France," "Romance Philology and Occitan Studies," "General Background and Related Areas," and "Scholars and Critics." The largest portion of the book is taken up by part 1, which cites material available on French literature of various time periods, medieval through twentieth century, and by genre and movement within those time frames. The extensive and detailed table of contents facilitates browsing and also the locating of specific topics. There are also two extensive indexes, an author index, and a separate subject index. Names can appear in both, as the subject of a study and as the author of one. Materials cited are predominately in English, French, and German.

The *Research and Reference Guide to French Studies* is useful as an update to the previous editions and also where the MLA on-line bibliography is available, as its arrangement of sources gives an easy, instant frame of reference to a large field. The Board recommends this work for the core collection of academic libraries.

Supplementary Titles

Bibliography of 17th Century French Prose Fiction. Ralph Willis Baldner. Columbia, 1967. hard. 1 vol. 197 pp. ISBN 0-87352-016-5. $35. bibliography.
Z2174.F4B35

Board's recommendation: Public and academic libraries.

Dictionary of French Literature. Sidney D. Braun. Greenwood, 1971. hard. 1 vol. illus. ISBN 0-8371-5775-7. $35. dictionary.
PQ41.B7 840.9

Board's recommendation: Public and academic libraries.

A History of French Dramatic Literature in the Seventeenth Century. Henry Carrington Lancaster. Gordian Pr., 1966. hard. 9 vols. appendixes. indexes. ISBN 0-87752-060-7. $350 (set). handbook.
PQ526.C3 842.409

A History of French Dramatic Literature in the Seventeenth Century is "a detailed history with lists of plays, bibliographical footnotes, etc., v. 5 includes a subject index, a finding list of plays, and a general index to all 5 v." (*Guide to Reference Books,* Sheehy, p. 491)

Board's recommendation: Public, academic, and school libraries.

Plots and Characters in Classic French Fiction. Benjamin E. Hicks. Archon Bks./Shoe String, 1981. hard. 1 vol. 253 pp. index. ISBN 0-208-01703-8. $27.50. handbook.
PQ631.H5 843.009′24

"The purpose of [*Plots and Characters in Classic French Fiction*], according to its Preface is 'to provide plot summaries and character identification for a select group of significant French prose works.' Hicks covers 32 such pieces by 21 authors spanning the years 1678 to 1885. He limits coverage to: 'those works which have passed the test of time and which are traditionally regarded as major prose works by French authors.' . . . Most authors are represented by only one selection, but Voltaire, Chateaubriand, Stendhal, Balzac, Flaubert, and Zola are, because of their stature, represented by several." (*BL,* October 1, 1982, p. 264)

Also reviewed in: *ARBA,* 1983, p. 587; *FR,* October 1983, p. 103; *RQ,* Spring 1982, p. 304.

Board's recommendation: Public, academic, and school libraries.

Twentieth-Century French Literature. Germaine Brée; Louise Guiney, trans. Univ. of Chicago, 1983. hard. 1 vol. 390 pp. appendixes. index. ISBN 0-226-07195-2. $30. handbook.
PQ305.B64 840.9′0091

Twentieth-Century French Literature includes "such topics as literary trends, information theory, political movements, publishing preferences, and conflicting philosophies. . . . [Brée] examines the development of the novel, poetry, and theater from 1920 to 1970. She then studies two authors representative of each decade (e.g., Cocteau, Breton; Malraux, Céline; Beauvoir, Camus)." (*LJ,* May 15, 1983, p. 1003)

Also reviewed in: *BL,* May 15, 1983, p. 1182; *Choice,* December 1983, p. 577; *NYTBR,* July 31, 1983, p. 10; *VQR*, Winter 1984, p. 7.

Board's recommendation: Academic libraries.

Luren E. Dickinson

Genealogy

Genealogy is the study of the origins and history of persons, families, or groups. The nature of the books in this category can best be explained by examining briefly the historical background of this field. The word stems from the Greek words *genea,* "race," "generation," and *logos,* "word." Genealogies are commonly referred to as family trees or pedigrees and have existed since ancient times among civilized and uncivilized peoples throughout the world.

There are three stages of genealogical development: the period of oral tradition, the beginning of written records, and the modern period. In ancient times, family records were part of an oral tradition passed down through generations. The modern reader can find examples of these records in biblical passages such as "and Enoch lived sixty and five years, and begat Methuselah" found in the books of *Genesis, Chronicles,* and elsewhere.

In fact, genealogies were so important to the Jews that Christ's ancestry was traced twice—to Abraham in the book of Matthew and to Adam in the book of Luke. The scrolls in which the members of the priestly tribe traced their ancestry back to Aaron were considered sacred and were kept in the temple in Jerusalem until its final destruction in A.D. 70.

The beginning of written genealogy can be traced to various tribal forms of recording, such as the ropes and knots system of the Incas of Peru. The more advanced civilizations, such as the Greeks, the Egyptians, and the Romans, traced their descent from the gods themselves as royal and noble families attempted to glorify their pedigrees. In Egypt, for example, the pedigrees of pharoahs from various dynasties were often carved in stone, then inscribed on papyrus and later on parchment.

In Great Britain, the earliest written genealogies, though rudimentary and strictly from royal lines, were taken from oral tradition and today can be found in the transcription of the epic *Beowulf* and the *Anglo-Saxon Chronicle.* After the Norman Conquest of 1066, attempts were made to register land ownership (for example, the Domesday Book of 1086) for tax purposes. By 1484 a more sophisticated method of recording genealogies was instituted—the Heralds' College, which kept genealogical records as well as granted coats of arms. It is interesting to note that the use of surnames did not become prevalent until this period of the Middle Ages.

The modern period of genealogical development dates from the sixteenth century, when the governments of Western Europe attempted to keep records not only for the nobility and royalty but also for the commoners. In the early 1500s the English statesman Thomas Cromwell instituted parish registries for recording baptisms, marriages, and burials. Prior records are available, but sparse. The registration of births,

Core Titles

	PUBLIC	ACADEMIC	SCHOOL
Guide to Genealogical Research in the National Archives, rev. edition U.S. National Archives and Records Service, National Archives Trust Fund Board, 1985	✦		
The Oxford Dictionary of English Christian Names, 3d edition Withycombe, E. G., ed. Oxford, 1977	✦		
Passenger and Immigration Lists Index, 3 vols., annual suppls. Filby, P. William, and Mary K. Meyer, eds. Gale, 1981	✦		
Searching for Your Ancestors: The How and Why of Genealogy, 5th edition Doane, Gilbert H., and James B. Bell. Univ. of Minnesota Pr., 1980	✦		✦
The Source: A Guidebook of American Genealogy Eakle, Arlene, and Johni Cerny, eds. Ancestry, 1984	✦		

marriages, and deaths with the state was made compulsory in England in 1837. Core works, such as SEARCHING FOR YOUR ANCESTORS, explain the types of records that will be encountered in genealogical research in European countries. Supplements, such as ETHNIC GENEALOGY, offer further guidance in this area.

In the United States census records maintained by the National Archives, and also stored at regional centers throughout the country, go back to 1790. As in Great Britain, church records and legal records are very important. Passenger lists for various periods are also crucial to the tracing of the many immigrants who have come to America. GUIDE TO GENEALOGICAL RESEARCH IN THE NATIONAL ARCHIVES, part of the core collection, explains many of these records and provides excellent reproductions of these documents.

The study of genealogy in the United States has been bolstered by the Church of Jesus Christ of Latter Day Saints, headquartered in Salt Lake City, Utah. Mormon belief holds religious significance in the discovering of one's ancestors. As a result, some of the best genealogical collections and guides have been produced by the Mormons.

Recent interest in genealogy has also been generated by bicentennial observances in the United States. In addition, interest in national and ethnic backgrounds has been prompted by Alex Haley's book *Roots* and the subsequent television miniseries. Therefore, it has become increasingly necessary for the librarian to provide basic references for those patrons eager to search for their ancestors.

However, because of the international scope of genealogical research, the references reviewed here—geared as they are mostly to American research—can only begin to scratch the surface or give an overview of the myriad of resources available. Desirable supplements to this collection on a more international scale will be determined by the ethnic makeup of the community in which the library is situated. For example, *Biography and Genealogy Master Index,* edited by Barbara McNeil (Gale, 1986), though not reviewed here, is an important source for consultation.

Core Titles

Guide to Genealogical Research in the National Archives, rev. edition. U.S. National Archives and Records Service. National Archives Trust Fund Board, 1985. hard and soft. 1 vol. 304 pp. illus. appendixes. index. ISBN 0-911333-00-2 (hard); ISBN 0-911333-01-0 (soft). $35 (hard); $25 (soft). handbook.
Z5313.U5U54 016

The 1985 revised edition of the *Guide to Genealogical Research in the National Archives* is an attractively produced and well-organized volume introducing the lay reader to the records at the National Archives and the 11 National Archives field branches. It supersedes the 1964 *Guide to Genealogical Records in the National Archives* and contains new material, primarily records of genealogical value in the National Archives field branches.

The archival and editorial team brought together by the National Archives have done a superb job in making the *Guide to Genealogical Research in the National Archives* the premier authority for federal genealogical records in the United States.

The brief introduction gives a basic overview of federal records, along with guidance for new researchers and the names and addresses of regional Archives field branches throughout the United States. The book is divided into four sections. Section A deals with population and immigration, and includes chapters on census records, passenger arrival lists, and naturalization records. Samples of census records are given along with the types of questions asked in each census from 1790 through 1910. The availability of various records on a state-by-state basis is provided. Charts also show available passenger lists.

Section B covers military records from the regular army to volunteers, naval and Marine records, pension records, bounty land warrant records, and other records related to military service. Again, sample records are listed, and special consideration is given to aids for recovering American war records. Particular attention is paid to the time period from the Revolutionary War through the Spanish-American War. Modern records are covered more briefly due to limited accessibility.

Section C covers records relating to particular groups. Included are civilians during wartime, Native Americans, black Americans, merchant seamen, and civilian government employees. In addition, Bureau of Indian Affairs field office records are listed by school or agency.

Section D describes other useful records such as land, claims, and court records; records of the District of Columbia; miscellaneous records; and cartographic records. Samples of maps, passport records, and so on, are given.

Selective bibliographic references are sprinkled throughout the text, citing general reference aids and more specialized guides in the appropriate locations. In addition, there are two appendixes that cite record groups and microfilm publications. The guide concludes with an alphabetically arranged index keyed to subheading numbers within the text.

From its color frontispiece and wide margins to its numerous photographs, tables, maps, and other illustrations, the *Guide to Genealogical Research in the National Archives* is a model for any resource of its type. Furthermore, the large, easy-to-read typeface, the lists of illustrations and tables, the useful appendixes, and the excellent index make this reference easily accessible to all patrons. The Board recommends this work for the core collection of public libraries.

The Oxford Dictionary of English Christian Names, 3d edition. E. G. Withycombe, ed. Oxford, 1977. hard. 1 vol. 310 pp. appendix. ISBN 0-19-869124-6. $10.95. dictionary.
CS2375.G7W5 929.4

The Oxford Dictionary of English Christian Names was first compiled in 1945 and has been slightly revised in subsequent editions. For example, the third edition reviewed here contains 43 names not found in the first or second editions, and some "additions to existing articles, many of which reflect the changes in usage, frequency, and status of names that have occurred in the thirty years since the first edition was published" (preface to the third edition).

The compiler and editor, Elizabeth Gidley Withycombe, has produced the first scholarly account of English Christian names with the publication of this dictionary. This reference work is the result of her exhaustive research among census records, church registers, marriage licenses, and other sources dating back to the Domesday Book of 1086.

The main part of the work is an alphabetical listing of names from Aaron to Zoe. Each name is noted as being masculine or feminine (or both). The meaning and etymological derivation or ancient forebear of the name is given.

Each description is then followed by a history of the name as it relates to Great Britain and other English-speaking nations, such as the United States. Also given are variations of the name, variant spellings, and cross-references to related names. An appendix contains "some common words derived from Christian names."

Perhaps one of the most interesting aspects of this dictionary, especially from a genealogical standpoint, is its 35-page introduction. This contains factual information pertaining to the history of names from Semitic and Indo-European civilizations through Greek, Roman, Celtic, and Old English cultures. In addition, the effects of the Norman Conquest are considered along with the growing influence of the Church, political and social changes during the twelfth and thirteenth centuries, and the increasing use of surnames. Also addressed are the legal aspects of names, nicknames, masculine and feminine names, the impact of the Reformation, and other factors affecting the usage of various names. Of special interest to American audiences is the final section on the "modern eclecticism" of English names, especially in the United States.

As a source of linguistic and genealogical importance, *The Oxford Dictionary of English Christian Names* stands alone. The Board recommends this work for the core collection of public libraries.

Passenger and Immigration Lists Index. P. William Filby and Mary K. Meyer, eds. Gale, 1981. hard. 3 vols. plus annual suppls. (1982–). 2,339 pp. ISBN 0-8103-1099-6. $425 (set). index.
CS68.F537 929.373

Passenger and Immigration Lists Index is subtitled as "a guide to published arrival records of about 500,000 passengers who came to the United States and Canada in the seventeenth, eighteenth and nineteenth centuries." It was edited by the well-known genealogical writer P. William Filby with the assistance of Mary K. Meyer.

This work puts in alphabetical order a listing of names from available published passenger lists or naturalization records. As noted by the editors in their introduction: "such lists are of primary importance to genealogists, since almost all passengers arriving in the New World during the period covered were not casual travelers but immigrants intending to remain in America as permanent residents."

The original three-volume set contains over 480,000 names from more than 300 sources, which are listed at the beginning of the reference. A sample entry key explains how to read the name of the passenger (plus the names of accompanying family for heads of household), age, place of arrival, sourcebook code number, and the page number of the source where the particular name is found. For handy reference, sourcebook code numbers are also listed on the inside cover pages at the front and back of each volume.

Because new information has become regularly available, supplemental volumes to the *Passenger and Immigration Lists Index* have been issued annually since 1982. Up to 200,000 additional records have been added each year and are presented in the same format as that of the original set. As of 1989, 1 million new names were already available for indexing.

As in any indexing project of this magnitude, there are errors of duplication, entry, and outright omission. However, despite occasional mistakes, this source has proven to be particularly informative, and it will continue to be an essential part of any strong genealogical collection for years to come. The Board recommends this work for the core collection of public libraries.

Searching for Your Ancestors: The How and Why of Genealogy, 5th edition. Gilbert H. Doane and James B. Bell. Univ. of Minnesota Pr., 1980. hard. 1 vol. 270 pp. appendixes. index. ISBN 0-8166-0934-9. $16.95. handbook.
CS16.D6 929.1028

Searching for Your Ancestors is one of the best-known books on genealogy intended for a general audience. Originally published in 1937, this classic guide has been completely revised and updated for its current fifth edition. The scope has been broadened to include information for more than 35 ethnic groups.

The editors of the guide, Gilbert Doane, editor emeritus of the *New England Historical and Genealogical Register,* and James Bell, director of the New England Historic Genealogical Society and author of *Family History Record Book,* have produced a reference that is not only accurate, up to date, and packed with information, but also enjoyable to read.

The anecdotal and common-sense approach to the subject of genealogy gives *Searching for Your Ancestors* a folksy style all its own.

The work is divided into two parts: "How to Search for Your Ancestors" and "Special Searches." The opening chapter begins with the many interesting facets that may result from genealogical research. For example, the humorous first names of the Dewey family are given: Armenius Philadelphus, Almira Melpomena, Pleiades Arastarcus, Victor Millenius, Octavia Ammonia, and Encyclopedia Britannica (an 84-year-old spinster!). Also chronicled is Ebenezer Richardson's marital history. In 1799, at the age of 75, he married his seventh wife, having been widowed the previous six times. True stories like these are enough to capture anyone's imagination!

The editors have an entertaining way of making facts and information come alive in a practical way. This can easily be seen in chapters 2, 3, and 4, which give instructions on how to begin a genealogical search by interviewing living relatives. The authors also provide helpful hints for analyzing family traditions and investigating family papers. All of these chapters contain excerpts of stories from genealogical research (including a paraphrased version of Alex Haley's *Roots*) that make this book useful for research methods or even just for browsing.

Chapters 5 through 10 cover how to find information in books and libraries and town, cemetery, probate, church, and government records. Chapter 11 explains the writing of a genealogical history and includes several sample charts. Chapter 12 sorts out miscellaneous items of importance such as calendar changes and adoptions.

Part 2 deals with special searches and contains new material added to this edition. Chapter 13 covers searching for ethnic roots in the Western Hemisphere—Native American, Canadian, Mexican, Puerto Rican, and Cuban—while chapter 14 discusses genealogical searches in 28 countries overseas, with special sections devoted to black Americans and Jewish history.

Appendixes include a thorough bibliography, a list of state offices of vital statistics, addresses of the National Archives and its regional centers, and in-depth background on U.S. census records. In addition, *Searching for Your Ancestors* boasts a fine, alphabetically arranged index, easy-to-read typeface, and a conversational yet practical tone that make the reference very accessible to all patrons. What this book does best, however, is to open the world of genealogical research to newcomers, and for that reason alone it belongs in all libraries concerned at all with genealogy. The Board recommends this work for the core collections of public and school libraries.

The Source: A Guidebook of American Genealogy. Arlene Eakle and Johni Cerny, eds. Ancestry, 1984. hard. 1 vol. 786 pp. illus. appendixes. indexes. ISBN 0-916489-00-0. $39.95. handbook.
CS49.S65 929.3

The Source: A Guidebook of American Genealogy is one of the most comprehensive handbooks available for American genealogical research. It was edited by Arlene Eakle, who has been a professional genealogist for over 25 years and is president and founder of the Genealogical Institute, and Johni Cerny, who is the president and founder of LINEAGES, Inc., and has been involved in genealogical research for 30 years. In addition, each section of *The Source* was written by an authority on that particular topic. For example, William Thorndale contributed the article on census indexes and spelling variants, while Loretto Dennis Szucs contributed the article on newspapers. Many of the essays, however, were written by the editors themselves.

In the foreword, P. William Filby, the noted genealogical author, states that in this extensive volume "every problem is authoritatively examined and discussed, and in clear language researchers are told the solution—where records are, how to secure them, how to use them and how to do further research."

An excellent introduction examines types of genealogical records and techniques for first-time searchers, presents material on how-to books and periodical articles available on a regional or state-by-state basis, and provides valuable information on such legal aspects as rights of privacy and copyright. This section, as well as most chapters, concludes with bibliographic notes.

The core of the reference is divided into three main sections. Part 1 covers major record sources. Each chapter within part 1 begins with an information guide containing a matrix that illustrates the type of material covered and an analysis of whether a person will be able to use this chapter. Chapters included cover family sources, vital statistics and cemetery records, marriage and divorce records, census and church records in the United States, American court records, land and tax records, military records, institutional records, and business and employment records.

Part 2 deals with published genealogical sources, discussing city directories and other types of directories (for example, professional directories), newspapers, genealogical tools and indexes, and compiled biographies. Though less than 70 pages long, this section contains important sources for research.

The final section, part 3, covers special resources, such as immigrant origins, sources for urban ancestors, Native American research, sources in the Spanish and Mexican Southwest, black ancestry, Asian-American research, Jewish-American research, the use of computers, and society records.

One aspect of this comprehensive volume, however, may be considered a drawback by some and an asset by others. At times, the editors stray from the general purpose with the inclusion of too much technical detail or extraneous material that might be gathered elsewhere. For example, in the chapter on the use of computers in genealogical searches, the coverage of types of hardware, the inclusion of a computer glossary, and the introduction to on-line data base searching goes beyond the scope of this reference.

Illustrations, charts, photographs, and tables are used profusely throughout *The Source.* Sometimes, however, the use of these visual aids may be considered excessive. In the chapter on business records, for example, company listings take up over 20 pages.

The volume concludes with several appendixes covering federal, societal, and library record depositories, and a list of genealogical book publishers. A glossary, a bibliography, and subject indexes add to the accessibility of the volume. Although *The Source* often tries to cover too much material, it does a good job overall in presenting the wealth of sources available for genealogical research and the means to secure and use them. The Board recommends this work for the core collection of public libraries.

Supplementary Titles

Afro-American Genealogy Sourcebook. Tommie Morton Young. Garland, 1987. hard. 1 vol. 199 pp. illus. ISBN 0-8240-8684-8. $39. bibliography.
E185.96.167 929.1088996

"The *Sourcebook* identifies various types of materials used in Afro-American genealogical research, gives examples of these types, and lists locations of specific materials. Each of the four divisions of the guide begins with an introduction, and many of the sections have brief prefatory remarks.

"Part 1, Background Readings and Basic Reference Sources, principally treats secondary materials. Covered are works dealing with the historical background of Africa and the Africans, the slave trade and traders, the Underground Railroad, Afro-American basic references (biographical sources, bibliographies, guides, directories by and about Afro-Americans, newspapers, etc.), how-to-books, and oral histories. . . .

"The other three parts of the source book emphasize primary materials, repositories, and societies. Included are public records (federal, city, and country including North Carolina's interesting cohabitation records) and an impressive listing of private papers. According to the compiler a survey of over two hundred libraries and collections of genealogical and historical organizations and societies was undertaken to identify as many resources as possible that have not been treated in other genealogical publications. . . . The final part, Directory of Resources, gives addresses for vital-statistics offices in the fifty states, branch libraries of Salt Lake City's Family History Library, numerous state and institutional archives and libraries, historically black colleges and universities, and various societies.

"Users should be aware that many of the addresses were out-of-date at the time the book was issued. . . . [However] the *Afro-American Genealogy Sourcebook* is indispensable for anyone studying families of Afro-American origin." (*NGSQ,* Fall 1989, p. 227)

Also reviewed in: *ARBA,* 1988, p. 178; *FRT,* February 1988, p. 69.

Board's recommendation: Public and academic libraries.

American and British Genealogy and Heraldry: A Selected List of Books, 3d edition. P. William Filby, comp. New England Historic Genealogical Society, 1983. hard. 1 vol. 736 pp. index. ISBN 0-88082-004-7. $49.95. bibliography.
Z5311.F55 016.929107

American and British Genealogy and Heraldry "is an excellent aid to identification of about 9,800 genealogical sources, including original and reprinted government documents." (*RQ,* Winter 1983, p. 154)

"This classic bibliography has nearly doubled in size from the previous edition (1975) and is more valuable than ever. The majority of listings are general genealogical works and local histories that provide sources of genealogical information. Family genealogies are not included. A separate section covers heraldry. While the emphasis is still heavily American and British, there are more entries than in previous editions for Canadian and English-language books published worldwide. . . . Most [entries] are briefly annotated and describe both strengths and limitations. This volume includes new editions up to fall 1981." (*LJ,* October 1, 1983, p 1869)

Also reviewed in: *A Arch,* October 1970, p. 412; *AB,* July 11, 1977, p. 141; *A Lib,* June 1970, p. 620; *A Lib,* July 1970, p. 715; *ANQ,* November 1978, p. 49; *ARBA,* 1977, p. 232; *ARBA,* 1984, p. 206; *BL,* September 1, 1970, p. 5; *BL,* May 1, 1977, p. 1372; *Choice,* October 1970, p. 1014; *Choice,* November 1976, p. 1116; *CRL,* March 1971, p. 151; *LJ,* November 15, 1970, p. 3895; *LR,* Spring 1971, p. 61; *NGSQ,* June 1984, p. 150; *RQ,* Winter 1970, p. 174; *WLB,* October 1970, p. 183; *WLB,* September 1976, p. 92.

Board's recommendation: Public and academic libraries.

Burke's American Families with British Ancestry. John B. Burke. Genealogical Publishing, 1983; reprint of 1939 edition. hard. 1 vol. illus. ISBN 0-8063-0662-9. $30. biographical dictionary.

Burke's American Families with British Ancestry lists "the lineage of 1600 families of British origin now resident in the United States of America [and contains a section of color illustrations] of coats of arms." (*The Reader's Advisor,* p. 316)

Also reviewed in: *General Reference Books,* Sheehy, p. 316.

Board's recommendation: Public and academic libraries.

The Complete Peerage of England, Scotland, Ireland, Great Britain, and the United Kingdom: Extant, Extinct, or Dormant. Vicary Gibbs et al. St. Martin's, 1984. hard. 13 vols. ISBN 0-312-15836-X. $450 (set). biographical dictionary.

"Like the British peerages themselves, *The Complete Peerage* is a family enterprise. First published between 1887 and 1898 under the editorship of George Edward Cokayne, it was revised and reissued in 12 volumes between 1910 and 1959 under the editorship of Vicary Gibbs (Cokayne's nephew) and others. These editors enriched the original with a thirteenth volume (1940) covering peerages created between 1901 and 1938. All 13 volumes retain their value as tools for the study of Britain and its distinguished families. They give 'concisely and precisely so far as they have been obtainable, particulars of the parentage, birth, honors, orders, offices, public services, politics, marriage, death and burial, of every holder of a Peerage' extant, extinct, or dormant at the time of original publication. The work's title has remained constant through its various incarnations. Although in this compact reprint the original page size has been reduced by half, the print is legible even to unassisted eyes." (*Ref Bks Bul,* August 1985, p. 1642)

Also reviewed in: *ARBA,* 1986, p. 152; *Spec,* November 28, 1981, p. 21.

Board's recommendation: Public libraries.

Ethnic Genealogy: A Research Guide. Jessie Carney Smith, ed. Greenwood, 1983. hard. 1 vol. 440 pp. illus. index. ISBN 0-313-22593-1. $49.95. handbook.
CS49.E83 929.7

Ethnic Genealogy: A Research Guide "presents an introduction to the problems that confront those searching for ancestors who are American Indian, Asian-American, black-American, or Hispanic. The first half of the guide is devoted to general genealogical research; the second half contains extended chapters on each of the groups mentioned above." (*Choice,* April 1984, p. 1110)

"Each chapter has thorough documentation, annotated bibliographies and, in some cases, lists of periodicals, directories of societies and repositories. . . . Throughout, the style is one of helpfulness for both novices and advanced searchers. . . . A general index concludes the work." (*BL,* November 15, 1984, p. 430)

"[*Ethnic Genealogy* will be especially] useful in any academic or public library collection where genealogists and historians work." (*Choice,* April 1984, p. 1110)

Also reviewed in: *A Arch,* Summer 1984, p. 314; *A Lib,* April 1984, p. 222; *LQ,* October 1984, p. 429; *RQ,* Summer 1984, p. 473.

Board's recommendation: Public and academic libraries.

Genealogical Research and Resources: A Guide for Library Use. Lois C. Gilmer. ALA, 1988. soft. 1 vol. 64 pp. index. ISBN 0-8389-0482-3. $12.50. handbook.
Z688.G3654 026.9293

"Written to help the librarian who is *not* trained in genealogy, *Genealogical Research and Resources: A Guide for Library Use* is . . . . a 70-page booklet [which] combines an introduction to genealogical reference sources with insights into the special requirements of genealogical searching." (*LJ,* October 15, 1988, p. 63)

"[The author, a library director,] provides in five concise chapters basic information that she hopes will help the librarian to narrow the topic, guide the patron to locally available sources, and refer patrons to other libraries, archives, and organizations. . . . Since [the reference] is in the form of a bibliographic essay, it also makes a handy tool for collection development." (*LJ,* October 1, 1988, p. 81)

Also reviewed in: *BL,* May 1, 1988, p. 1460.

Board's recommendation: Public libraries.

Genealogies in the Library of Congress: A Bibliography. Marion J. Kaminkow, ed. Magna Carta, 1972, 1977. hard. 2 vols. plus supplement (vol. 3). 905 pp. (vol. 1); 961 pp. (vol. 2); 285 pp. (vol. 3). ISBN 0-910946-15-9 (first 2 vols.); 0-910946-19-1 (vol. 3). $175 (2-vol. set). bibliography.
Z5319.U53 016.921

Genealogies in the Library of Congress: A Bibliography is "the most comprehensive bibliography of family histories of America and Great Britain available. [The first two volumes, published in 1972,] treat over 20,000 items, including some published in [other countries]. Besides published materials, [the bibliography] also deals with family histories . . . in unpublished manuscripts, on microfilm, and in books that are not specifically genealogical in nature. . . . [The volumes are] arranged alphabetically by family surname, with [thousands of] cross references directing attention to variations in spelling and to some collateral family surnames. Each volume has an addendum." (*LJ,* July 1972, p. 2376)

"The third volume . . . lists books added to the Library's collections from 1972 to July 1976." (*LJ,* April 1, 1977, p. 789)

Also reviewed in: *ARBA,* 1978, p. 214; *BSA-P,* April 1973, p. 219; *LJ,* April 15, 1973, p. 1243; *RSR,* April 1979, p. 26.

Board's recommendation: Public and academic libraries.

New and Noteworthy

Ancestry's Red Book: American State, County, and Town Records. Alice Eichholz, ed. Ancestry, 1989. hard. 1 vol. 800 pp. index. ISBN 0-916489-47-7. $39.95. directory.
CS49.A55

Ancestry's Red Book "describes each type of resource: census records, maps, church records, archives, etc., and is followed by 10 regional overviews. There is a historical summary for each state followed by discussions, lists, and addresses for obtaining each type of record. An alphabetical list of counties gives each county seat address, date the county was formed, and years for which specific records are available." (*BL,* April 15, 1990, p. 1655)

Concise Genealogical Dictionary. Maurine Harris and Glen Harris. Ancestry, 1989. soft. 1 vol. 259 pp. ISBN 0-916489-06-X. $10.95. dictionary.
CS6.H37 929

The *Concise Genealogical Dictionary* provides "extremely concise definitions for a wide variety of words that genealogists might encounter in their research. . . . Derivations and variations are occasionally provided. The book begins with a brief guide to its use and a bibliography of dictionaries from which the authors selected words. The last 25 pages list definitions for abbreviations." (*BL,* April 15, 1990, p. 1655)

A Dictionary of Surnames. Patrick Hanks and Flavia Hodges. Oxford, 1989. hard. 1 vol. 840 pp. index. ISBN 0-19-211592-8. $75. dictionary.
CS2385.H27 929.4

"The 100,000 entries . . . [in *A Dictionary of Surnames*] cover Europe, Australia, North America, and the British Isles. Surnames are arranged alphabetically under most common spelling, with variant spellings in 'nested groups' under main entries. Easy access is provided through the index." (*LJ,* April 15, 1989, p. 40)

Family Diseases: Are You at Risk? Myra Vanderpool. Genealogical Publishing, 1989. hard. 1 vol. ISBN 0-8063-1254-8. $14.95. handbook.
RB155.5.G67 616.042

Family Diseases is an "easy-to-read guide [that] describes hereditary illnesses and provides assistance in researching family genetic or other medical disorders. Included are a basic medical pedigree chart, family health medical record form, questions checklist, list of helpful organizations, and glossary." (*BL,* April 15, 1990, p. 1658)

International Vital Records Handbook. Thomas J. Kemp. Genealogical Publishing, 1990. soft. 1 vol. ISBN 0-8063-1264-5. $24.95. handbook.
929

The *International Vital Records Handbook* "updates and broadens the scope of the earlier *Vital Records Handbook* . . . and provides addresses, costs, and special instructions for obtaining vital records from U.S. states and 67 foreign countries. Users can photocopy the application forms that are provided for all but the European countries." (*BL,* April 15, 1990, p. 1654)

The Library of Congress: A Guide to Genealogical and Historical Research. James C. Neagles and Mark C. Neagles. Ancestry, 1990. hard. 1 vol. index. ISBN 0-916489-48-5. $35.95. bibliography.
929

The Library of Congress: A Guide to Genealogical and Historical Research "describes significant materials in the Local History and Genealogy Reading Room as well as other areas of the Library of Congress. It is divided into three sections: Part 1 is an introduction to the Library, its divisions, services, and catalogs. Part 2 discusses categories of records and publications pertinent to genealogy, while Part 3 . . . describes key source materials by region and state." (*BL,* April 15, 1990, p. 1654)

Managing a Genealogical Project. William Dollarhide. Genealogical Publishing, 1990. soft. 1 vol. ISBN 0-8063-1222-X. $14.95. manual.
929

Managing a Genealogical Project "focuses on organizing research materials with explanations for beginning and experienced genealogists. Two different systems for numbering ancestors are also explained. Suggestions are given for creating a computer database and for using commercially prepared genealogy software. In addition to providing many sample forms, the author includes master forms that may be photocopied." (*BL,* April 15, 1990, p. 1652)

Christine Kollen

Geography

Geography is a broad and varied discipline that includes subdisciplines in economic, political, social, physical, and historical geography. All the reference books in this section are classified under a "general" category, although some of these books include specific information pertaining to the various geographical genres. When choosing a core collection in geography, it is important to assemble titles that will provide both general and specific information. The geography core collection should accommodate patrons who need to determine the location of Zimbabwe, as well as serve those interested in finding a survey of Zimbabwe's contemporary history. In addition, the geography core collection should be able to provide a patron with general maps of any continent, region, or country in the world.

Geographical dictionaries, or gazetteers, can be consulted for general information, such as the location and population of cities, area and population of administrative subdivisions, and location of natural features. Other geographic reference books should supply more details, such as the country's political, physical, social, historical, and economic attributes. A collection of maps, such as *Maps on File,* will give patrons easy access to basic maps, from which photocopying for educational purposes is permitted by the publisher. *Maps on File*—and all general atlases—is reviewed in the companion Buying Guide, *Reference Books for Young Readers.*

Depending on their patrons' main interests, librarians may wish to supplement the core collection with additional titles. Some of these supplementary titles, such as STATE MAPS ON FILE and THE WORLD FACTBOOK, may provide more detailed information or present the same information in a slightly different way. Other titles, such as the DICTIONARY OF HUMAN GEOGRAPHY, provide completely new information that may be of use to patrons specifically engaged in an in-depth study of geography.

Core Titles

Chambers World Gazetteer: An A–Z of Geographical Information, 5th edition. Dr. David Munro, ed. Chambers/Cambridge, 1988. hard. 1 vol. 733 pp. illus. ISBN 1-85296-200-3. $34.50. gazetteer. (next scheduled revision, 1991. The new title for the sixth edition will be *The Cambridge World Gazetteer: A Geographical Dictionary.)*
G103.5 910.3

First published in 1895 by Dr. David Munro, the *Chambers World Gazetteer* is still a very useful geo-

Core Titles

	PUBLIC	ACADEMIC	SCHOOL
Chambers World Gazetteer: An A–Z of Geographical Information, 5th edition Munro, Dr. David, ed. Chambers/Cambridge, 1988	✦	✦	✦
Places Rated Almanac: Your Guide to Finding the Best Places to Live in America, 2d edition Boyer, Richard, and David Savageau. Prentice-Hall Travel, 1989	✦		
The Statesman's Year-Book World Gazetteer, 3d edition Paxton, John. St. Martin's, 1986	✦		✦
Webster's New Geographical Dictionary Merriam-Webster, 1988	✦	✦	✦
Worldmark Encyclopedia of the Nations, 6th edition, 5 vols. Sachs, Moshe Y., ed. Worldmark, 1984; distrib. by John Wiley (See Current Events)	✦	✦	✦
Worldmark Encyclopedia of the States, 2d edition Sachs, Moshe Y., ed. Worldmark, 1986; distrib. by John Wiley (See American History)	✦	✦	✦

graphical dictionary. Throughout its successive editions, this reference work has remained both authoritative and comprehensive.

The gazetteer includes entries on regions, countries, administrative subdivisions, cities, and physical features. Also included are entries on national parks and international economic and cultural regions. As the subtitle implies, the work is set up in a dictionary format; the entries are arranged alphabetically. Each entry includes the following information (when appropriate): pronunciation, location (by latitude and longitude), official name, time zone, religion, language, currency, membership in international organizations, rainfall, climate, government and constitution, industry, economy, and agricultural and administrative divisions. Entries range from a few lines to two pages.

All countries and their states or provinces and capitals are included. County subdivisions are included when possible. Cities and towns are selected for their administrative function and by population. The population threshold differs for each country. Also included are places of special interest for historic, religious, industrial, or tourist reasons, as well as places important in a worldwide news event and places that have purely a curiosity value (for example, Okinawa, Brazil).

All countries have a map showing states or provinces and a table showing areas and populations of these administrative divisions.

Country entries use the English form of their name, but all other entries use the local form. Physical features that cross international boundaries are an exception to this rule. They are written in English.

The gazetteer includes numerous cross-references. For some entries, there are cross-references from the outdated English form of a word to its native spelling. For example, the English version of *Peking* directs the user to the pinyin, *Beijing.* There are also cross-references from former place names or geographical features (for example, the entry *Persia* directs the reader to see *Iran*). There is also a handy world atlas at the end of the book showing cities, countries, and physical features.

The information appears to be current; tables with statistical information are reasonably up to date (data are taken from 1980 to 1984). However, the typeface is fairly small and may be difficult to read, especially for long entries.

There are a few omissions in the cross-references. Some cross-references that should have been made were not. For example, *Istanbul* lists Constantinople and Byzantium as former names; however, neither is given as a cross-reference to *Istanbul.*

The *Chambers World Gazetteer* is an excellent, comprehensive one-volume reference work for geographical names. The Board recommends this work for the core collections of public, academic, and school libraries.

Places Rated Almanac: Your Guide to Finding the Best Places to Live in America, 2d edition. Richard Boyer and David Savageau. Prentice-Hall Travel, 1989. soft. 1 vol. 421 pp. illus. appendixes. ISBN 0-13-677006-1. $16.95. almanac.
HN60.B69 307.7

This is the second edition of the *Places Rated Almanac.* The first edition appeared in 1981. The authors, Richard Boyer and David Savageau, have also written *Retirement Places Rated.* Richard Boyer is a professional writer, and David Savageau is the "principal-in-charge" of a personal relocation consulting firm.

This reference book is designed to assist people in selecting a place to live. It ranks 333 officially defined metropolitan areas (determined by the U.S. Bureau of the Census). The book is arranged by chapters into subject areas such as cost of living, jobs, crime, health care, and environment. Each chapter begins with an explanatory text including various statistical tables, and continues on to rank metropolitan areas from best to worst. Sections entitled "Place Profiles" and "Et Cetera" give additional information.

The ranking of places to live is based on a score which is determined by using different criteria for each chapter. For example, in the chapter on jobs, the percentage increase in new jobs is multiplied by the number of new jobs between now and 1995 to produce a metropolitan area's score. The last chapter, "Putting It All Together," lists cities alphabetically with scores for each category previously discussed, a cumulative score, and an overall rank.

The statistical information presented is taken from U.S. government sources and reports by specialized agencies and associations, and surveys conducted by the "Places Rated Partnership." The statistical tables in the text portion of each chapter are up to date, as most are taken from 1988 and 1989 sources.

Most entries are arranged according to rank within each subject, but in the "Place Profiles" section, the entries are arranged alphabetically. The overall ranking chapter can be used as an index because these entries are also listed in alphabetical order. There are also several appendixes, consisting of a listing of "Metro Areas by State," a "Metropolitan Place Finder," and a "List of Tables, Maps, & Diagrams." Overall, the work appears to be very current and accurate.

This book is a paperback and may need to be rebound if used extensively. Some of the tables and listings are somewhat difficult to read since there is no extra space between lines.

Aside from the very practical information included in the almanac (climate, crime rate, cost of living, availability of jobs, and so forth), there is also a great deal of interesting trivia. For example, a chart in "The Arts" section, entitled "Touring Artists Bookings: The Top 20 Markets" lists the 20 most popular concert cities. For those interested in baseball trivia, the "Recreation" section has a chart showing how America's baseball teams have so frequently changed their names and the cities in which they play. For those who like the outdoors, there is a section on hay fever, and where one might live in order to avoid it. Interesting tidbits of information like these will please the browser and researcher alike. *Places Rated Almanac* is entertaining as well as useful.

The *Places Rated Almanac* is an authoritative, excellent reference source for people needing information about moving to another city or area. The Board recommends this work for the core collection of public libraries.

The Statesman's Year-Book World Gazetteer, 3d edition. John Paxton. St. Martin's, 1986. hard. 1 vol. 665 pp. ISBN 0-312-75725-5. $35. handbook.
G103.5.P38 910.321

This is the third edition of the *Statesman's Year-Book World Gazetteer.* This reference book was first published in 1975 as a supplement to THE STATESMAN'S YEAR-BOOK (see Political Science). The *World Gazetteer* is particularly versatile because it can function as a companion volume to THE STATESMAN'S YEAR-BOOK as well as stand alone as an independent publication. John Paxton is well known as the editor of THE STATESMAN'S YEAR-BOOK and has edited several other authoritative reference books.

The Statesman's Year-Book World Gazetteer provides short entries (from three lines to one and a half pages) on continents, countries, states or provinces, counties, cities, villages, and physical features. In the introduction, the author states that this gazetteer is not comprehensive; however, no mention is made of how these entries were selected. Each entry includes information on location, recent history (if relevant), industries, and population. In the back is a small glossary of geographical terms. The entries for continents, countries, and physical features are listed in English, and entries for cities and towns are usually listed in the language of the country in which they are situated.

The cross-references are adequate, although not abundant. There are cross-references from previous names, foreign names, and English language names.

Some of the statistics appear to be fairly outdated (mid-1970s). These older statistics may prove problematic and detract from the value of the book. Because the latest edition of this work was in 1986, users should consult the companion volume for more up-to-date facts and figures (the companion work is an annual).

No errors were found, but there were some inconsistencies. Some entries for major cities list the population of the city and its metropolitan area. Others list only the city's population. The introduction gives no explanation for this seeming inconsistency.

In summary, the problems with *The Statesman's Year-Book World Gazetteer* include inconsistencies, lack of current population statistics, and infrequent cross-references. For the public or school library that already receives or is planning to receive THE STATESMAN'S YEAR-BOOK, *The Statesman's Year-Book World Gazetteer* may be a good addition to the core collection. However, a public or school library in search of a good world gazetteer to add to its core collection can find other more comprehensive current consistent gazetteers, such as CHAMBERS WORLD GAZETTEER or WEBSTER'S NEW GEOGRAPHICAL DICTIONARY. The Board recommends this work for the core collections of public and school libraries.

Webster's New Geographical Dictionary. Merriam-Webster, 1988. hard. 1 vol. 1,376 pp. illus. ISBN 0-87779-446-4. $19.95. dictionary. (A limited number of pages revised every four years.)
G103.5 910.321

Webster's New Geographical Dictionary has been published for many years by Merriam-Webster Inc., which is well known for its other well-researched, authoritative dictionaries, such as *Webster's Third New International Dictionary* and *Webster's Ninth New Collegiate Dictionary.*

This geographical dictionary provides brief information on spelling, pronunciation, and (if appropriate) location, population, size, economy, and history of a given geographical area. There are more than 47,000 entries, with 218 maps prepared by Hammond International.

Entries, which are arranged alphabetically, are selected on the basis of usefulness and interest to the general reader. Included are entries on individual countries, dependencies, major administrative subdivisions, largest cities, significant natural features, and entries of historical interest. The preface explains that entries for the United States, Canada, and English-speaking countries are more prevalent than entries for other countries because the book's audience is in these aforementioned areas. All entries are in English. All continents, countries, U.S. states, and Canadian provinces include a map showing political boundaries, roads, rivers, mountains, cities, and other important features. Countries and U.S. states include tables that show the area, population, and capital of states or provinces.

There are more than 15,000 cross-references for alternative and former names and foreign-language variants. Many counties, dams, national parks, national monuments, and other points of interest are entered with cross-references to a table that can be found under the entry for the appropriate country. For example, under *Hoover Dam,* the entry reads: "See United States, Dams and Reservoirs." Upon referring to this table, the user can determine the year Hoover Dam was completed, its height, location, and purpose, and its architectural classification.

Included at the beginning of the work are tables of abbreviations, pronunciation symbols, geographical terms, a section on map projections, and a list of maps.

The dictionary appears to be current in terms of place names, although some statistical population data presented may be somewhat dated (1980 or earlier). However, as the publisher states, "population figures were taken from the most recent available official sources" (preface).

The dictionary is accurate; no errors were found in a survey of the entries and cross-references. One complaint is that the dictionary will sometimes list countries by their more generally accepted name. For example, Tuvalu is listed under *Ellice Islands* even though it formally became Tuvalu in 1976. The same is true with Burkina Faso, which still has its main entry under *Upper Volta.* However, cross-reference entries are given in both cases.

Although *Webster's New Geographical Dictionary* does emphasize English-speaking countries and is not as detailed as the CHAMBERS WORLD GAZETTEER, it is a good, fairly comprehensive geographical dictionary. The Board recommends this work for the core collections of public, academic, and school libraries.

Worldmark Encyclopedia of the Nations, 6th edition. Moshe Y. Sachs, ed. Worldmark, 1984; distrib. by John Wiley. hard. 5 vols. 1,746 pp. illus. index. ISBN 0-471-88622-X (set). $285 (set). encyclopedia.
G63.W67 910.3'21

See Current Events.

Worldmark Encyclopedia of the States, 2d edition. Moshe Y. Sachs, ed. Worldmark, 1986; distrib. by John Wiley. hard. 1 vol. 690 pp. ISBN 0-471-83213-8. $99.95. encyclopedia.
E156.W67 973.03'21

See American History.

Supplementary Titles

Cities of the World, 3d edition. Margaret Walsh Young and Susan L. Stetler, eds. Gale, 1988. hard. 4 vols. index. ISBN 0-8103-2528-4 (set). $255 (set). encyclopedia.
G153.4.C57 910.2

Cities of the World "is a compilation of information on the social, cultural, political, and industrial aspects of the nations and cities of six continents [based on] briefings prepared for diplomatic personnel and issued as Post Reports by the U.S. Department of State. . . . [These volumes] present not only geographical and historical facts, but also . . . data on local customs, community health services, political conditions, municipal services, and educational and commercial facilities . . . Each country's report provides notes on religious services available in the major cities . . . [and information] on the availability of fishing and hunting licenses in a number of countries. . . . [The volumes are] arranged alphabetically by country name." (introduction)

"[These volumes] delete information meant only for the diplomatic community and have added or expanded sections on history, government, economy, and education. . . . Coverage is comparable to the State Department's Background Notes, though *Cities of the World* has more information of use to travelers, and less of interest for general reference users." (*Choice,* July/August 1982, p. 1535)

Also reviewed in: *ARBA,* 1987, p. 175; *Gov Pub R,* November 1986, p. 795; *Ref Bk R,* 1986, p. 4.

Board's recommendation: Public and academic libraries.

Dictionary of Human Geography. R. J. Johnston et al., eds. Basil Blackwell, 1987. hard and soft. 1 vol. 592 pp. illus. index. ISBN 0-631-14655-5 (hard); 0-631-14656-3 (soft). $75 (hard); $15.95 (soft). dictionary.
GF4 304.2'03'21

"Intended 'for professional geographers, tertiary level students, other social scientists, and secondary school teachers,' the *Dictionary of Human Geography* includes more than 500 terms in current use. ('Human geography,' according to the *Dictionary,* is 'the geography of man-made world' and embraces cultural, economic, historical, political regional, social, and urban geography.)

"Entries range from single sentences to essays of up to six pages. The essay-length entries, of which there are about a dozen, cover the major divisions of geography and related fields and provide contexts within which definitions of specific terms can be more clearly understood.

"In keeping with the stated aim of the *Dictionary* to cover current vocabulary, newer terminology (e.g., gentrification, redlining) is well represented. Occasionally, English terminology is used in place of terms more likely to be familiar to American users (e.g., ribbon development instead of strip development). Twenty-four definitions are enhanced by black-and-white line drawings.

"The Introduction suggests that the *Dictionary* can serve in some measure as an encyclopedia of its field. This can be effected through the use of the cross-reference system, which will lead one to additional definitions . . . and the Index, which helps one locate other entries in which the term is used. Although there are no separate personal-name entries (the entry for Malthus appears to be an exception), the contributions of individuals to the development of human geography are discussed in the appropriate entries, and their names are included in the Index.

"Definitions are arranged two columns to a page. Guide words facilitate the location of entries. Entry words are printed in boldface [type] and definitions in small but clear type." (*BL,* August 1983, p. 1484)

The Dictionary of Human Geography "is an excellent piece of scholarship and is one of the finest subject dictionaries available for any discipline in the social sciences. The quality of the definitions is uniformly good, and the coverage of relevant terminology is strong. . . . [The work] is also recommended for collections in the fields of sociology, planning, demography, and transportation." (*RQ,* Spring 1982, p. 297)

Also reviewed in: *ARBA,* 1983, p. 340; *Brit Bk N,* July 1982, p. 450; *Choice,* July 1982, p. 1535; *GJ,* March 1983, p. 103; *J Hist G,* July 1983, p. 332; *Indexer,* April 1984, p. 74; *Sch L,* September 1982, p. 274; *TES,* August 1982, p. 20; May 1984, p. 35; *WLB,* April 1982, p. 622.

Board's recommendation: Academic libraries.

State Maps on File. Facts On File, 1984. looseleaf binder. 7 vols. 1,200 pp. index. ISBN 0-8160-0116-2 (set). $345 (set). atlas.
G1200.F3 912

State Maps on File consists of seven "large heavy-duty, three-ring looseleaf notebooks with clear black-and-white maps printed on heavy paper stock. The volumes are sold separately or as a set. Each state is first shown in a map of the United States, then in a regional map, allowing users to orient themselves to state locations. This is followed by about 20 full-page maps of the state: first an outline map, then maps of counties and county seats, state legislative districts, senatorial and congressional districts, topographical features, agricultural and mineral resources, industries, highways, population, boundary changes, railroads, and historical events. This is a similar format to *Maps on File* (reviewed in *SLJ* in 1983) and *Historical Maps on File* (reviewed in *SLJ* in 1985).

"*State Maps on File* is a boon to students, teachers, and librarians. The publishers encourage the photocopying of these maps for educational purposes. Because of the great clarity and simplicity of the maps, the set can be used by students from first grade through high school." (*SLJ,* May 1986, p. 27)

Also reviewed in: *ARBA,* 1985, pp. 147–148; 1986, p. 162; *CLW,* January 1986, p. 154; *LJ,* March 15, 1985, p. 54; *RQ,* Spring 1985, p. 365; WHQ, October 1985, p. 477; *WLB,* March 1985, p. 504.

Board's recommendation: Public and school libraries.

The World Factbook. Central Intelligence Agency, ed. U.S.G.P.O., 1983. soft. 1 vol. 265 pp. illus. ISSN 0277-1527. $23. encyclopedia.
G122.U56a

The World Factbook contains a "succinct listing of the essential facts of the world's countries. The following characteristics are included: land, water, people, government, economy, and communications. A small map showing a country's location in respect to its immediate neighbors accompanies each listing and is referenced to one of 11 larger maps. Membership in the United Nations and associated agencies and in other important international organizations is also noted. [This source is] very good for quick reference." (*Ser Lib,* 1985, p. 276)

"This paperbound reference book contains facts about 190 or more countries. . . . It includes a table of contents; a page of definitions, abbreviations, and explanatory notes; a list of international organizations; a conversion table of measures; and twelve colored outline maps of the world. One or more pages and a small outline map are devoted to each country. National information is provided on each country's land, water, people, government, economy, communication, and defense forces. These seven major headings are then separated into a total of 51 subdivisions, such as type of government, literacy level, per capita income, and party voting strength. The book is revised annually.

"[The volume] is a simple book and should be useful for quick reference work to provide a variety of current facts about a large number of countries." (*ARBA,* 1984, p. 153)

Also reviewed in: *BL,* January 1, 1975, p. 469; *Choice,* September 1974, p. 920; *JQ,* Spring 1986, p. 220; *RSR,* Fall 1982, p. 53; 1985, p. 36; *WLB,* September 1974, p. 92.

Board's recommendation: Academic libraries.

New and Noteworthy

Exploring Your World: The Adventure of Geography. National Geographic Society, 1989. hard. 1 vol. 608 pp. illus. index. ISBN 0-87044-727-0. $39.95. encyclopedia.
G63.E97 910.3

Exploring Your World is "arranged in dictionary form, . . . [and its] 334 encyclopedic entries cover a wide array of geographical topics and range in size from a paragraph . . . to as many as fifteen pages. . . . Virtually every entry is followed by a large number of cross-references which provide students with valuable paths to more information." (*SLJ,* May 1990, p. 21)

Facts About the States. Joseph Nathan Kane, ed. Wilson, 1989. hard. 1 vol. 556 pp. illus. ISBN 0-8242-0407-7. $55. encyclopedia.
E180.K4 973

"Arranged alphabetically, *Facts about the States* . . . includes information [on each of the fifty states as well as] on the District of Columbia and Puerto Rico. Each of the fifty-two articles contains information on geography and climate, national sites, history (in a chronological table), demography, government and politics, finances, economy, culture and education, literary references, guide to resources, and selected nonfiction sources. Holidays, nicknames, and museums are described in each information-packed entry, and there is even a description of license plates currently in use." (*SLJ,* May 1990, p. 21)

Rand McNally Children's World Atlas. Rand McNally, 1989. soft. 1 vol. 93 pp. illus. appendix. ISBN 0-528-83348-0. $12.95. atlas.
912

The *Rand McNally Children's World Atlas* includes "directions for using a bar scale, map keys, map symbols and legends, and an explanation of longitude and latitude, along with a one-paragraph description of each kind of map used in this atlas: terrain, political, physical-political, and thematic. Five double-page maps of the globe follow; each has a key and four paragraphs briefly interpreting the map illustrated. The main body is divided into seven parts, one for each of the major continental regions of the world." (*SLJ,* May 1990, p. 24)

The Third World Guide. Third World Editors, 1989; distrib. by Neal-Schuman. soft. 1 vol. 625 pp. illus. index. ISBN 950-99264-0-X. $59.95. encyclopedia. 310.9

The Third World Guide "includes overview articles on such topics as transnational corporations, nonalignment, AIDS, the Olympics, and hunger. Many of these essays are accompanied by graphs and charts. Biographies of Third World Leaders, 'men and women who made major contributions to the struggles of their peoples and nations,' include figures such as Salvador Allende, W. E. B. Dubois, Martin Luther King, and Eva Peron. The bulk of the volume contains profiles of every nation of the world, which include a narrative, a map, and statistical information." (*BL,* February 15, 1990, p. 1191)

US Atlas. Richard Saul Wurman. Access Pr., 1990; distrib. by Prentice-Hall. soft. 1 vol. 144 pp. index. ISBN 0-13-001760-4. $12.95. atlas. 912

"*US Atlas* divides the country into 70 maps, each 250 by 250 miles. . . . Map coverage begins in the Pacific Northwest and ends in southern Florida. The neighboring portions of Canada and Mexico are also included. This format is designed specifically for the traveler; the 48 contiguous states are mapped at one scale . . ., and the user can look at a map the way one would drive across the country—state by state, not alphabetically. . . . In addition to the 70 U.S. maps, there are 34 metropolitan center maps . . . and 8 downtown center maps. . . ." (*BL,* February 15, 1990, p. 1191)

Arla Lindgren

German and Scandinavian Literature

See also World Literature

With German and Scandinavian literature, three aspects need to be considered: geography, language, and history. Equal weight cannot be placed on all three aspects at the same time. In a kaleidoscopic fashion, history continuously changes the combinations, and it is hard to maintain a balance of information. Only the largest libraries or those serving specialized clientele may be able to acquire a collection equal in emphasis on linguistics as well as literature studies.

For example, look at Germany during the twentieth century. You will see a very mixed picture. Due to massive historical upheavals, Germany was split in two for almost half of the century. Each side subscribed to an opposing political ideology. The mass emigration of German authors, which had begun after Hitler seized power in 1933, had spread German language and culture to many other parts of the world. Until after the end of World War II, the bulk of significant German literature was produced outside the borders of Germany. Thomas Mann, Franz Werfel, and many other less-known authors published in the United States; Bertolt Brecht wrote plays in Finland; and Peter Weiss became a Swedish citizen. For those who were still in Germany, the task was to face the physical and spiritual ruin of Germany. Many people did so by denying the existence of the Nazi past. The depressed writers of post–World War II Germany created a literature of inner emigration or discontinued self. Others, like the Group 47, attempted to build a new literature and a new language free of the distortions of the earlier era. That is how distinct but contemporary literatures were created—parallel in development but linked only by language.

A core collection on German literature has to deal with all these variables and also include the literature of Austria and German-speaking Switzerland. The sources selected here bring together the bulk of the literature bound by its common language. Questions will need to be answered about modern drama, poetry, and fiction regardless of the author's political persuasion. The suggested core collection here is defined primarily by language and geography, with an emphasis on the twentieth century. The Scandinavian countries are well served since their culture is more limited geographically and united historically, even if the people do not all share the same linguistic roots.

The golden era of German literature from the 1770s on must be included in the collection since some of the greatest literary works of all time—the work of Goethe—date from this period. Significant literary periods such as the romantic period need to be treated with some depth.

Depending on the clientele the library serves, librarians may need to acquire several comprehensive dictio-

Core Titles

	PUBLIC	ACADEMIC	SCHOOL
Contemporary German Fiction Writers, first series Elfe, Wolfgang D., and James Hardin, eds. Gale, 1988		✦	
Contemporary German Fiction Writers, second series Elfe, Wolfgang D., and James Hardin, eds. Gale, 1988		✦	
German Fiction Writers, 1885–1913, 2 vols. Hardin, James, ed. Gale, 1988		✦	
German Fiction Writers, 1914–1945 Hardin, James, ed. Gale, 1987		✦	
A History of Scandinavian Literature, 1870–1980 Rossel, Sven H. Univ. of Minnesota Pr., 1982		✦	
Modern German Literature: A Library of Literary Criticism, 2 vols. Domandi, Agnes Körner, ed. Ungar, 1972	✦	✦	
The Oxford Companion to German Literature, 2d edition Garland, Henry, and Mary Garland. Oxford, 1986	✦	✦	✦

naries, lexicons, thesauruses, and phrase books as well as materials on the history of the languages and literatures, especially folklore. A well-rounded collection of language dictionaries is also essential to support this topic.

Libraries who own Use K. Faulhaber's *German Literature: An Annotated Reference Guide* (Garland, 1979), now out of print, are well equipped to answer questions on German literature in English translation, since this is the only comprehensive annotated bibliography on the subject. Another useful out-of-print title—more guide to research than mere bibliography—is Larry Richardson's *Introduction to Library Research in German Studies: Language, Literature, and Civilization* (Westview, 1984).

Core Titles

Contemporary German Fiction Writers, first series. (vol. 69 of the *Dictionary of Literary Biography.*) Wolfgang D. Elfe and James Hardin, eds. Gale, 1988. hard. 1 vol. 424 pp. index. ISBN 0-8103-1747-8. $103. bibliography.
PT772.C59 833.914

Contemporary German Fiction Writers, second series. (vol. 75 of the *Dictionary of Literary Biography.*) Wolfgang D. Elfe and James Hardin, eds. Gale, 1988. hard. 1 vol. 378 pp. index. ISBN 0-8103-4553-6. $103. bibliography.
PT772.C593 833.914

German Fiction Writers, 1885–1913. (vol. 66 of the *Dictionary of Literary Biography.)* James Hardin, ed. Gale, 1988. hard. 2 vols. 728 pp. ISBN 0-8103-1774-3 (set). $206 (set). bibliography.
PT771.G47 833.8

German Fiction Writers, 1914–1945. (vol. 56 of the *Dictionary of Literary Biography.)* James Hardin, ed. Gale, 1987. hard. 1 vol. 395 pp. index. ISBN 0-8103-1734-6. $103. bibliography.
PT772.G39 833.912'09

German Fiction Writers, 1914–1945, volume 56 of the *Dictionary of Literary Biography* (DLB), was the first volume of the series dealing with literature that was not in English. This marked the beginning of a new direction for the series, which had previously been devoted to North American and British writers. The goal of the publisher was to include all German literature from 1700 to the present in a number of topical books. The present four volumes (five books) cover German and Swiss-German prose writers from 1885 to the present. Separate volumes treat Austrian authors of the same period; see *Austrian Writers Since 1914* (DLB, vol. 85) and *Austrian Writers, 1875–1913* (DLB, vol. 81).

Each book is an independent work with its own group of contributors, all experts in German literature teaching at American universities. The general editor for the German literature set, James Hardin, is a baroque specialist at the University of South Carolina. He worked under the auspices of the DLB advisory board to uphold the series' high standards and to carry on its style. As with other volumes in this series, the excellent biobibliographical essays with lists of primary and secondary literature are arranged alphabetically by author. Information on translations of the literary works is also provided.

The unique organization of the titles in the *Dictionary of Literary Biography* series is also a source of problems. The literature is classified not only by language or nationality of the author but also by literary genre. Then the literature is placed into very specific historical time frames. This requires a superior balancing act. The organizational problems are made up for by the way the parts of the set complement each other, and also by the flexible editorial policy that allows the same author to be included in different volumes which emphasize the aspect of the author's career appropriate to each book. Authors who represent a different genre, and whom you would not expect to find in the present volumes, are included. For example, you will find entries in these titles for the dramatists Bertolt Brecht, Friedrich Dürrenmatt, Gerhart Hauptmann, and Peter Weiss, as well as the poets Johannes Bobrowski, Sarah Kirsch, and Günter Eich (who is barely known for more than one significant prose work). However, readers might wonder why the Romanian-born poet Paul Celan is included but not the Prague-born prosaist Franz Werfel. The other famous Prague-German writer, Franz Kafka, is classified as an Austrian and therefore is included in the set for Austrian writers.

These volumes give a broad view of German prose literature. For this reason, it is easier to pinpoint authors who are included rather than find many who are excluded. A substantial portion of the more than 150 writers covered could be considered obscure. However, many world-renowned literary figures, such as Thomas Mann, Hermann Hesse, Heinrich Böll, Erich Maria Remarque, Günter Grass, and Christa Wolf, do receive in-depth treatment that is appropriate to their stature. Of the authors in the most current volume, *Contemporary German Fiction Writers,* second series, all but four are still alive. This shows that the editors understand the need for up-to-date information and that they are bold enough to evaluate "living literature," knowing that these sketches will not be final assessments of authors' works.

The selection of authors reflects the editors' attempt to write cultural history and bring a more complete picture of German life and letters to American audiences. Several supplemental essays are included as appendixes to illuminate the historical and cultural premises of their time. The topics considered in these essays include: pre–World War I Germany (volume 66); the years between Germany's defeat in World War I and the rise of National Socialism (vol. 56); Nazi rule and World War II (vol. 69); and the divided Germanies (vol. 75).

No comparable reference work exists in English. The articles are written for nonspecialists, but scholars can also find important information here. Books for further reading are listed as well as references to manuscript sources. Excellent typography, fine paper, and interesting illustrations make these large books easy to handle and easy to read. A cumulative index to all published titles in the *Dictionary of Literary Biography* series is included in each volume. The completion of this series will be a major publishing event. The Board recommends these four works for the core collection of academic libraries.

A History of Scandinavian Literature, 1870–1980. (vol. 5 of the Nordic series.) Sven H. Rossel. Univ. of Minnesota Pr., 1982. hard and soft. 1 vol. 492 pp. appendix. index. ISBN 0-8166-0906-3 (hard); ISBN 0-8166-0909-8 (soft). $27.50. handbook.
PT7078.R6713 839.5

Scandinavian culture had its first peak during the Viking era 1,000 years ago. Sven H. Rossel's *A History of Scandinavian Literature* concentrates on the modern period from 1870 to 1980. This leaves out anything from the Icelandic ages to Hans Christian Andersen. However, in recognition of the common cultural background of the Scandinavian countries, the author has brought together the literatures of Denmark, Finland, Iceland, Norway, Sweden, and the Faroe Islands. These cultures involve six different languages, one of which (Finnish) is not even related to the other five. This is a considerable task for a volume of fewer than 500 pages. Even so, almost 200 Nordic authors of the period are covered, whether in a few cursory remarks or a full-length article.

The main interest in this book is the writers who are emerging now or who are waiting to be discovered by the English-speaking world. Writers such as Karen Blixen (Isak Dinesen), Ibsen, Strindberg, and Undset are well covered in many standard English language sources, but many other authors are not.

In this book, fine coverage is given to the Fenno-Swedish authors, whose literature is often overlooked. Both Märta Tikkanen and Christer Kihlman, two authors with recent English-language translations of their works, receive timely and meaningful commentary. See poems by Märta Tikkanen, *Love Story of the Century* (Borgo Press, 1988) and a novel by Kihlman, *The Blue Mother* (University of Nebraska Press, 1990).

Writers in the Finnish language do not get extensive

coverage, but a good selection is provided. However, the rather superficial treatment of Aleksis Kivi, Väino Linna, and Eeva Joenpelto is disappointing, particularly since their works (except for Joenpelto) are translated into many languages. The same is true of Ivar Lo-Johansson (only a few references are given) and the Norwegian Cora Sandel.

The 1982 edition is an updated translation of the original *Skandinavische Literatur,* 1870–1970 (1973). The updated version is primarily aimed at an English-speaking audience. The book is divided into five parts, each identifying a specific literary period from the late nineteenth century to "Recent Trends." Each part begins with a short outline of historical and political events that places the literature in its appropriate chronological context. However, the author is not a political historian, and some of his statements are arguable. The treatment of literary trends, writers, and their works, on the other hand, is encyclopedic, factual, and loaded with detail. Descriptions of authors' lives and works sometimes seem too similar. Readers get the impression that most Scandinavian poets are products of a bourgeoisie society revolting against its values, and that they deal endlessly with the chaos of life, loneliness, death, and eternity.

An index of authors and the titles of their works is included. It is somewhat cumbersome to use because writers who are selected for individual treatment are not always identified that way. Readers will find some spelling errors as well, though this may be a function of listing names and titles from six languages. An extensive bibliography of critical books and articles in English adds significantly to the value of *A History of Scandinavian Literature, 1870–1980.* A comparable work does not exist.

The Board recommends this work for the core collection of academic libraries.

Modern German Literature: A Library of Literary Criticism. Agnes Körner Domandi, ed. Ungar, 1972. hard. 2 vols. 836 pp. index. ISBN 0-8044-3075-6 (set). $130 (set). criticism.
PT401.D6 830.9'0091

This two-volume compendium of critical reviews on twentieth-century German literature is a title in the Library of Literary Criticism, a series by Frederick Ungar Publishing that continuously produces excellent sourcebooks on world literature. Gems in *Modern German Literature* include the first reviews of Thomas Mann's *Buddenbrooks* in 1901 as well as the distressed and somewhat conflicting reviews by two well-known New York drama critics on seeing *The Investigation,* Peter Weiss's 1966 documentary drama on Auschwitz. Readers are also treated to Albert Camus writing on Franz Kafka and Wolf Biermann declaring that he could not "choose freedom" and go west if the Wall were opened and the streets of welcoming West Berlin were covered with gold. *Modern German Literature* is a work of often superb writing, even if the authors themselves rarely speak except through the words of their critics.

Included are works by over 200 authors writing in German that have been published since 1900. Entries are arranged alphabetically by the authors' names. Those names appear in clear boldface type with birth and death dates. Volume 1 covers authors from Ilse Aichinger to Frederick G. Jünger; volume 2 contains Franz Kafka to Stefan Zweig. Each entry includes excerpts of reviews varying in length from 20 pages for Bertolt Brecht to an average of three and a half pages for most others. Works that are reviewed are listed at the end of each entry with dates for first publication and subsequent English translation (if applicable at the time of this publication). Details about the author's life and career are not included unless the critics have mentioned them. An index to critics increases the value of this work as a two-way source.

Reviews are selected from a list of about 130 literary magazines, book review journals, newspapers with book review sections, and scholarly books and periodicals. Almost half of the reviews were published in East and West Germany or Austria. All entries are either original in English or translated to English for this work. Emphasis is also given to British and American critics because, according to editor Agnes Körner Domandi, "their methods and style reflect the intellectual climate in which the English-speaking reader lives and works."

The authors who are included are, in the editor's view, the best and most representative of German literature—fiction, drama, and poetry. Such a selection is by nature subjective, and one can always argue about the inclusions and omissions. For example, why is Heinar Kipphardt, author of *In the Matter of J. Robert Oppenheimer* and well published in both Germany and the United States through the 1960s, not included? Readers will find that authors who were not well established by the early 1970s are not included in this sourcebook.

Regardless of its shortcomings, this is a treasury of fine writing and a source of information on some of the most important literary works that have shaped our world since the beginning of this century. Many of the excerpted reviews are still surprisingly up to date and in agreement with current critics. For example, Peter Handke's works still meet with controversy and conflicting critical views, as they did almost 20 years ago.

If the relatively high price for the two volumes is not an obstacle, *Modern German Literature* is a valuable addition to any core collection. There is more depth in this work than in either CONTEMPORARY LITERARY CRITICISM (see World Literature) or *Twentieth-Century Literary Criticism* (both published by Gale).

The Board recommends this work for the core collections of public and academic libraries.

The Oxford Companion to German Literature, 2d edition. Henry Garland and Mary Garland. Oxford, 1986. hard. 1 vol. 1,020 pp. ISBN 0-19-866139-8. $49.95. dictionary.
PT41.G3 830.03'2'19

If you can only afford to buy one book on German literary history, the book should be *The Oxford Companion to German Literature.* This handy one-volume dictionary covers nearly 12 centuries of literary developments in each of the German-speaking countries. The first edition, published in 1976, was acclaimed as a model of its kind, and the revised and updated second edition has received similarly favorable reviews.

An astonishing array of entries are included here. In addition to novelists, playwrights, poets, and their works, literary movements and poetical forms, plot summaries and fictional characters, medieval manuscripts, literary journals, and first lines of poems and songs, one can find historical figures and events, historians, philosophers, artists, and composers. The impact of the French Revolution on literature in Germany, Voltaire's friendship with King Friedrich II of Prussia, and the latter's life and character as a subject of plays and novels are described. Goethe's life, works, poems, and people in his life, including women he loved, all have their own entries with cross-references (such as one for his mother's nickname, Frau Aja). Shakespeare has a listing, and we learn that his plays were more frequently staged in Germany than in his native land during the nineteenth century. Governmental policies restricting literary expression in the twentieth century, such as *Bitterfelder Weg* (official writer's policy of East Germany) and *Entartete Kunst* (a National Socialist term for "degenerate art"), are explained. Ample cross-referencing facilitates access to this feast of topic coverage.

In this edition the editor, Mary Garland, has aimed to add "concise information about those trends which have left their mark since the 1960's, and which reflect the political and cultural climate of the period." Entries for living authors have been consistently updated. In 1976 Stephan Hermlin, Ernst Jandl, and Franz Fühmann (whose name was misprinted as Führmann) had about 8 to 12 lines each. Now a full column is devoted to each of them. Volker Braun, Franz Kroetz, and Günter Kunert, among others, were not even included in the first edition. The literature selection still reflects a rather conservative approach, and subsequently the interrelationship between German cinema and drama has been overlooked. Thus there is no entry for Rainer Werner Fassbinder. All titles of literary works are given in their German original. No information on English translations is provided. This is unfortunate, because it would have greatly enhanced the value of the work for students with limited German-language skills, potential translators, and others.

This dictionary concentrates on factual encyclopedic information. Only a few minor errors can be spotted. English alphabetical arrangement is used with ä as a, ö as o, and ü as u. Otherwise, German-language terminology and forms of names prevail, such as *Jedermann* (everyman), *Konkrete poesie* (concrete poetry), *Dritter Reich* (Third Reich), *Friedrich II* (Frederick the Great). However, *Le nozze di Figaro* is found under the original Italian title of the libretto rather than *Figaro's Hochzeit,* as it is known in Germany.

The Oxford Companion to German Literature is a delightful book for browsing, crossword puzzle enthusiasts (did you know who wrote *Bambi?),* and all students who wish to check on their facts and learn some more at the same time. The Board recommends this work for the core collections of public, academic, and school libraries.

Supplementary Titles

A Bibliography of Danish Literature in English Translation, 1950–1980. Carol L. Schroeder. Nordic Bks. 1982. hard. 1 vol. 197 pp. ISBN 87-7429-044-4. bibliography.
Z2574.T7537 016.8398'1'9

A Bibliography of Danish Literature in English Translation "is not only meticulously prepared, but also designed in such a way that it is a pleasure to use. . . . In addition to listing any major—or minor—Danish work of literature translated into English, the book contains references to critical studies on individual authors and genres and a special selective section of books on Denmark. . . . Thus, not only the student of Danish literature but the social scientist as well as the layperson will find this handsomely produced book very useful." (*Choice,* July–August 1983, p. 1578)

Board's recommendation: Academic libraries.

The Bibliography of German Literature: An Historical and Critical Survey. Michael S. Batts. Peter Lang, 1978. hard. 1 vol. 239 pp. appendixes. index. ISBN 3-261-03026-7. $36.80. bibliography.
Z2231.A1B37 016.83

The Bibliography of German Literature, authored by "Professor Batts, a medievalist with a recent master's degree in library science, . . . [is] an unusual book which traces the development of enumerative bibliography from the pre-printing era to the mid-1970s and makes proposals for improvements. The first half (to 1939) is historical and the second critical.

"Throughout, the author sets each compilation in its cultural context, skillfully weaving together the different strands of booktrade, private collections, institutional libraries, and scholarship. He [also] traces the evolution of the various bibliographical forms. . . . [as well as] the development . . . of personal, subject, national, and form bibliographies." (*MLR,* January 1981, p. 227)

"In any case, this is a sound and thorough work.

"Three appendixes, a valuable list of 520 'works cited and consulted,' and a serviceable index add to the value of this thought provoking . . . book." (*LQ,* October 1979, p. 479)

Also reviewed in: *JLH,* Summer 1979, p. 375.

Board's recommendation: Academic libraries.

Bibliography of Modern Icelandic Literature in Translation. Phillip Marshall Mitchell and Kenneth H. Ober. Cornell Univ. Pr., 1975. hard. 1 vol. 324 pp. index. ISBN 0-8014-2475-5. $35. bibliography.
Z2551.M57 016.839′6908

The *Bibliography of Modern Icelandic Literature in Translation,* "part of a series based on the Fiske Icelandic Collection at Cornell University [begun in 1908 with the publication of Halldor Hermanannsson's *Bibliography of the Icelandic Sagas and Minor Tales*], . . . contributes significantly to the study of modern Icelandic literature in translation. The bibliography attempts to record all translations of modern Icelandic literature during the last 100 years, making it a repository of useful and otherwise inaccessible information. Moreover, the volume creates a vivid impression of the widespread appeal of modern Icelandic literature." (*LJ,* April 15, 1975, p. 747)

"It goes without saying . . . that a bibliography like this, containing perhaps three or four thousand items, . . . is built upon a solid framework of standard translations into better-known languages.

"This bibliography will be coveted . . . by scholars and libraries on both sides of the Atlantic. Its format and quality [could not] have been achieved with [anything] less than a passion for accuracy and a ravenous appetite for work." (*JEGP,* July 1976, p. 392)

Also reviewed in: *ARBA,* 1977, p. 615.

Board's recommendation: Academic libraries.

A Bio-bibliography of German-American Writers, 1670–1970. Robert Elmer Ward. Kraus International, 1985. hard. 1 vol. 448 pp. ISBN 0-527-94444-0. $72. biobibliography.
Z1229.G3.W35 016.83′08′0973

In *A Bio-bibliography of German-American Writers,* "Ward includes a brief overview of the major bibliographies of German-American writers, sections on the major collections, anthologies, periodical articles, and anonymous works, and a 33-page bibliography of sources consulted. . . . The biobibliography itself consists of more than 3,000 alphabetical entries; they are succinct and thoroughly cross-referenced, [and] the bibliographies for individual authors are extensive. . . . The work is particularly strong in coverage of authors associated with the *Turnbewegung* (gymnastics movement) and the German-American social activists from 1880 to 1930. The text is clear and remarkably free of typographical error." (*Choice,* October 1985, p. 278)

"Ward has compiled the present volume from material collected for his [now discontinued] dictionary. [In the introduction he defines] German-American literature . . . as 'that body of creative writing composed in the German language by persons of any nationality who reside or have resided in the U.S.A.'. . . . The volume should be extremely useful to anyone working in this field, but unfortunately the high price may discourage purchase by libraries without strong collections of the relevant literature." (*CRL,* January 1986, p. 71)

Also reviewed in: *ARBA,* 1986, p. 474.

Board's recommendation: Academic libraries.

A History of Swedish Literature. Alrik Gustafson. Univ. of Minnesota Pr., 1961. hard. 1 vol. 708 pp. index. ISBN 0-8166-0236-0. $27.50. history.
PT9263.G8 839.709

A History of Swedish Literature "is the first comprehensive study of Swedish literature in English. This work enables Americans to put Swedish authors in their true cultural context. Professor Gustafson's volume is well-composed and well-balanced. . . . His intimate knowledge and his sincere love for his subject . . . [are] especially noticeable in the stimulating chapters about [August] Strindberg and Pär Lagerkvist.

"In his . . . volume Gustafson devotes two-thirds of the space to Swedish literature from August Strindberg to the present day. In the first third of the book Gustafson presents a survey of the highlights and trends of Swedish literature from the more than a century old rune stones up to Strindberg. . . . He deals with the individual authors by first presenting a rather short biography and then analyzing their more important works." (*CSM,* June 15, 1961, p. 11)

"Many Swedish writers and poets with their works unknown to the exclusively English-reading public are discussed in their national context with its provincial, Continental, and Anglo-American influences." (*LJ,* April 1, 1961, p. 1162)

"[The reference] includes a bibliography, a list of the more important translations of Swedish fiction, . . . a guide to the pronunciation of Swedish names, [and an] index." (*BRD,* 1961, p. 562)

Board's recommendation: Academic libraries.

Janet K. Wright

Graphic Arts

See also Art; Book Arts; Painting and Sculpture

Graphic artists and designers design the images we see and read, infusing the environment with purposefully directed messages. The graphic artist must understand what triggers mass response. Information gleaned from research scientists and psychologists on human reactions, vision, and the subconscious has helped graphic artists direct the appeal of the images they create.

Skillfully conveying the content and form of visual images requires a working knowledge of graphic production techniques and consumer psychology and marketing. The development of electronic technology and revolutionary methods of design—such as those involved in video production and computerized publishing—have made keeping up to date a challenge to those in the field.

The roots of graphic design are the fine arts, especially painting. Such fine artists as Toulouse-Lautrec, Bonnard, and Warhol enriched their paintings with elements from the graphic arts. The development of graphic design brought about an expansion of visual limits, with new techniques, materials, and printing processes coming into use. For providing perspective on and definition of these developments, encyclopedias and handbooks are essential to a core collection of reference books in this field.

Most graphic artists today work for a number of

Core Titles

	PUBLIC	ACADEMIC	SCHOOL
Artists' and Illustrators' Encyclopedia, 2d edition Quick, John. McGraw-Hill, 1977	✦	✦	
Artist's Market: Where and How to Sell Your Graphic Art Conner, Susan, ed. Writer's Digest Bks., annual	✦	✦	
Contemporary Graphic Artists, 3 vols. Horn, Maurice, ed. Gale, 1986–1988		✦	
Graphic Arts Encyclopedia, 2d edition Stevenson, George A. McGraw-Hill 1979	✦	✦	

clients, including politicians, corporations, advertising agencies, governments, and institutions. Library patrons who are interested in full-time employment or free-lance work in graphic design may wish to consult handbooks on where and how to publish and sell graphic art. Also, advice on portfolios and how to access markets can contribute to a designer's success. In most major cities, graphic design societies maintain lists with information on local designers. Such lists from an area's local association would augment a library's core reference collection.

The four encyclopedias and handbooks listed here provide a strong beginning for defining the graphic arts field and for identifying terms, techniques, processes, and markets. Despite the pervasiveness of graphic design in our society, there is not yet a large body of literature devoted to documenting designers or their work. The supplementary list contains a few titles (more specialized in scope than the core titles suggested) that can lead the graphic artist or interested reader in further exploration of the field. Although the *Print Index: A Guide to Reproductions* (Perry Jeffcott and Kathe Chipman, comps., Greenwood, 1983) is not reviewed herein, it does make accessible the work of over 2,000 graphic artists through the mid-1970s and is a worthwhile purchase.

Core Titles

Artists' and Illustrators' Encyclopedia, 2d edition. John Quick. McGraw-Hill, 1977. hard. 1 vol. 327 pp. illus. index. ISBN 0-07-051063-6. $46. encyclopedia.
N33.Q51977 703

The *Artists' and Illustrators' Encyclopedia* describes methods and materials used to produce a visual end product. The encyclopedia provides graphic designers with definitions of the tools and techniques necessary for the process of reproduction.

The author, John Quick, obviously knows the field well, and he has designed the encyclopedia as both a working tool and a survey of the arts and graphic arts. Terms are defined in detail, and although many entries are brief, the information is sufficient to answer questions or to guide the researcher to other sources. Some entries include all possible aspects of the definition; for example, the entry for *bookbinding* includes 49 descriptive terms. The entry for *brushes* has an alphabetical listing of 42 of the more common brushes. One impressive 21-page list provides the common names and descriptions of various pigments. The list also includes a color's history, source or composition, use, permanency, and reaction with other colors. Another informative list names familiar plastics commercially available, with water-based plastic materials cross-referenced to synthetic resin materials. When appropriate, definitions also explain techniques that do not work; for example, inks that cannot be mixed smoothly with other inks. Definitions also call attention to products that should be used with caution. For example, the entry for *benzene,* a substance used in rubber cement and as a paint varnish remover, notes that the chemical is believed to cause certain types of cancer when inhaled over long periods of time. (Because this work was published in 1977, information of this nature is not altogether up to date.)

The information in the *Artists' and Illustrators' Encyclopedia* is presented attractively. The book is a convenient size, and the layout, charts, and diagrams are graphically appealing. Easy-to-read entry words are printed in boldface type with definitions set off in lightface type. At the top of each numbered page the first and last entry words are listed as guide words, enabling the user to locate terms quickly and easily. An excellent index provides access to every term. Concluding the work is a bibliography containing relevant books, manuals, and catalogs.

Because most graphic artists today are involved in more than one medium, the scope of this encyclopedia will serve them well. Quick states in his preface, "This book succeeds if it provides the artist or artisan with a few choices or new ideas."

Although this book is in need of updating, librarians, art students, and practicing artists will still find the *Artists' and Illustrators' Encyclopedia* useful for identifying terms, obtaining information on techniques or materials, and verifying the best technique or material to use for a specific project. The Board recommends this work for the core collections of public and academic libraries.

Artist's Market: Where and How to Sell Your Graphic Art. Susan Connor, ed. Writer's Digest Bks., annual. hard. 1 vol. 608 pp. illus. appendix. index. ISBN 0-89879-426-9. $21.95. handbook.
N8600.A76 700.25

The *Artist's Market* is an annual sourcebook of requirements and contact information for companies all over the United States that buy art for ads, albums, cartoons, greeting cards, illustrations, prints, and posters. Writer's Digest Books publishes this guide, as well as the WRITER'S MARKET (see Publishing) and the POET'S MARKET (see Publishing)—all of which have similar formats. The major portion of the *Artist's Mar-*

ket consists of a list of firms. According to the publisher, 80 percent of this information is revised annually. Articles at the front of the book and in the appendix introduce job opportunities for free-lance illustrators and designers and give an overview of available markets and how to approach them. An artist's resource list includes addresses of publications that offer market news, and a glossary is also provided.

The series contains excellent advice on various trade concerns, as in the close-up feature by Seymour Chwast on portfolios and in the feature by Victoria Marshall, a greeting card illustrator, on tips for free-lancing. Unfortunately, the list of firms is limited and should be consulted with caution. For example, only nine places for selling work are given for Kansas City and St. Louis, Missouri; and there is a very short list of advertisers given for Chicago, even though Chicago has one of the largest groups of ad agencies in the country. Prominent firms are sometimes missing, while some extremely small businesses are listed. While there is a qualifying statement at the front of the book explaining why a market or a firm might not be listed, this statement should be displayed more prominently because it is important for the user to be aware of the work's limitations. The work has some inconsistencies, as well as some listings for firms who buy little or no artwork. A person new to the field might wish to refer to an area's local advertising directory or graphic artists' directory in addition to the *Artist's Market.*

Advertising, audiovisual, and public relations firms are conveniently arranged alphabetically by geographical area. Listings in other sections of the book are simply grouped together alphabetically.

In spite of these qualifications, the *Artist's Market* contains unique features that make the work valuable for a core reference collection for graphic arts. The volume contains many diverse categories; up-to-date advice on topics such as self-promotion, record keeping, and copyright; and interviews that feature respected designers. The book also defines current markets that are open to free-lance artists and designers and offers tips on selling in those markets.

Given the fast pace of change in the graphic arts field, the currency of the *Artist's Market* is to be appreciated. The Board recommends this work for the core collections of public and academic libraries.

Contemporary Graphic Artists. Maurice Horn, ed. Gale, 1986–1988. hard. 3 vols. illus. indexes. ISBN 0-8103-2189-0 (vol. 1); 0-8103-2190-4 (vol. 2); 0-8103-4230-4 (vol. 3). $95 per vol. biographical dictionary.

NC999.2.C66 760.092C761

Contemporary Graphic Artists is a "biographical, bibliographical, and critical guide that provides detailed information about the lives and accomplishments of graphic artists who have made a significant contribution to contemporary art" (preface, volume 1). The work includes information on illustrators of books, magazines, and other publications; graphic designers; editorial cartoonists; magazine and newspaper cartoonists; newspaper artists; comic book artists and animators; animation directors; and producers. Emphasis is primarily on North American artists, but other artists of international reputation are included.

Alphabetically arranged entries are presented in the same format as Gale's Contemporary Authors series, wherein each entry is divided into topical sections, such as personal information, awards and honors, career, biographical and critical sources, and writings. Each topical section is clearly delineated, and numerous illustrations give an idea of each artist's work. As with other Gale publications, size, typeface, paper, and binding are functionally designed for easy use.

These volumes are the first in an ongoing series that will offer approximately 125 entries in each biannual volume. The first volume contains a historical overview of the graphic arts and entries on individual artists. The overview provides background for placing the artists in context. The graphic arts have had a long history, but it is in the last few decades that they have come to dominate artistic expression. With future development of the field it will be even more important to provide access to information on practicing artists and designers who have been influential.

The second volume begins with a two-page feature on prominent graphic artists. This volume also includes a cumulative index of artists, an occupation index, and a subject index. The cumulative subject index is a welcome feature which can be used to find information pertaining to diverse key topics, such as "Bugs Bunny," "Campbell's Soup Kids," or "Gay Comix."

Entry information for the directories was obtained directly from biographies, if available, or from reliable sources such as biographical dictionaries and art encyclopedias. Entries vary from single-paragraph obituary notices, such as that for *Ken Ernst* (best known as the artist of the "Mary Worth" comic strip), to over five pages devoted to *Joe Barbera* of *Tom and Jerry* animated cartoon fame. No matter how brief the entry, the useful feature of "Biographical/Critical Sources" at the end of each entry makes further research possible. Entries do, of course, become outdated, and the editors plan to provide revisions in future volumes when significant change is required.

Contemporary Graphic Artists provides biographical and critical information on popular graphic artists that is often difficult to find. The volumes have been designed to assist a variety of users. For example, people entering the field may use this work to determine the steps that successful graphic artists have taken to get where they are.

The Board recommends this work for the core collection of academic libraries.

Graphic Arts Encyclopedia, 2d edition. George A. Stevenson. McGraw-Hill, 1979. hard. 1 vol. 483 pp. illus. appendixes. indexes. ISBN 0-07-061288-9. $52.95. encyclopedia.
Z118.S82 686.2′03

The *Graphic Arts Encyclopedia* serves as a guide to the various materials, tools, and techniques involved in the graphic reproduction of images. George A. Stevenson, who has had many years of practical experience in the graphic arts field, describes the work as a view of "subject matter in the light of actual working experience" and a presentation not only of "the 'what,' but also the 'why' and the 'how' " of the graphic arts (preface).

This encyclopedia contains more than 4,000 alphabetically arranged entries, from *AA* to *zinc halftone.* Products or materials mentioned in the entries are indexed separately, enabling the reader to locate that information with a minimum of effort. Names of manufacturers are also indexed as an aid to finding information when the name of a product or material is not known. (However, because of the publication date of 1979 the usefulness of these sections has surely diminished, as new products have emerged since then and manufacturers have come and gone.) The indexing system allows the researcher to generate study lists from pertinent topic headings. In this respect, the book serves as a textbook, providing extensive information gathered within fields of interest.

In addition to three indexes, the encyclopedia includes a bibliography of relevant general books and pamphlets (again, in need of some updating), including military standards and specifications. Useful tables in the appendix cover metric conversion; paper sizes; paper-cutting charts for booklets and blotters; the Greek alphabet; useful mathematical rules; constants and conversion factors; Arabic, Greek, and Roman numerals; mathematical symbols; decimal equivalents; elements and symbols; and even temperature conversion.

The encyclopedia contains numerous illustrations and photographs of graphic arts products and equipment. The diagrams and illustrative examples are reproduced well, the type is easy to read (main entry words stand out in boldface type), and the paper is of good quality.

The *Graphic Arts Encyclopedia* contains definitions of jargon terms, such as *widow, gatefold,* and *mouse,* as well as definitions of more commonly known terms. Although some of the technology covered in the work is dated (for example, because of the 1979 publication date, the latest computer graphics information is conspicuously absent), the encyclopedia still contains a significant body of basic information that has not changed over the years.

As Stevenson developed the *Graphic Arts Encyclopedia* he drew on the expertise of many consultants in order to make the encyclopedia a reliable reference work. This work is useful as a basic reference guide for graphic artists involved in the preparation of artwork for printing, for students at the secondary and college levels, and for anyone interested in attempting a graphic arts method or process for the first time. The Board recommends this work for the core collections of public and academic libraries.

Supplementary Titles

Encyclopedia of Design. Harold H. Hart, comp. Hart, 1983. hard and soft. 1 vol. 399 pp. illus. ISBN 0-8055-1276-4 (hard); 0-8055-0452-4 (soft). encyclopedia.
NK1530.E53 745

The *Encyclopedia of Design* "is a compilation of hundreds of black-and-white illustrations that may be copied without fee or permission. The 29 chapters are arranged by cultures, i.e., Assyrian, Celtic, Greek, Peruvian, Scandinavian, etc. . . . Many of the designs include one-line descriptions, and all have short source designations keyed to the Bibliography. The designs are from . . . pottery, masks, tapestry, tiles, columns, furniture, and stained glass . . . [and] range from folk motifs to ornate pieces of period art. The Bibliography lists 94 sources and consists chiefly of older books now in the public domain, foreign publications, and nineteenth-century magazines such as *Century* and *Harpers*. . . .

"[T]he large-scale reproductions and sturdy format should make *Encyclopedia of Design* a useful book, especially for artists, publishers, art directors, printers, craftspersons, and others wanting one source for a selection of designs from many cultures and historical periods." (*BL,* July 1984, p. 1532)

Also reviewed in: *Choice,* February 1984, p. 803; *LATBR,* October 23, 1983, p. 4.

Board's recommendation: Public and academic libraries.

Rookledge's International Type-Finder: The Essential Handbook of Typeface Recognition and Selection. Christopher Perfect and Gordon Rookledge. Beil, 1983. hard. 1 vol. 272 pp. illus. index. ISBN 0-913720-45-3. $50. handbook.
Z250.P42 686.2′24

In *Rookledge's International Type-Finder* "some seven hundred faces are shown, divided into text and decorative alphabets. These sections are divided again into eight subsections (oblique serif, straight serif, slab serif etc.). Each of these sections then further subdivides into alphabets with differing variations of specific letter construction, thus leading enquirers to the name of the type they could not place." (*Brit Bk N,* April 1984, p. 235)

"But that is not all. There are fifty pages of earmark tables. For example, over sixty variations of the letter 'u' alone are illustrated, and each is keyed to one or more of the text faces. The tables are an alternative companion to the earlier [sections and subsections]. They make it possible to begin the search to identify a typeface with only one letter at hand and to remain fairly confident in the prospect of success." (*ABC,* July 1984, p. 48)

Board's recommendation: Public and academic libraries.

Carol L. Ebener

Horticulture and Gardening

See also Agriculture; Botany

The field of horticulture attracts a widely diverse group of people, ranging from the botanical expert to the amateur vegetable gardener to the person interested in developing an award-winning flower for the local garden show. A library's core reference collection should meet the range of needs and interests of the varied patrons whose interests are focused on this field.

The most basic source of information to consider for a reference collection in horticulture is a standard dictionary of plants, such as HORTUS THIRD. This source should be accessible by botanical name for genera and species and should include an index or cross-referencing system for common names. A source of this type would serve both the patron looking for a particular species of rose, for example, as well as the one interested in identifying the characteristics of the genus *Prunus.* A practical encyclopedia with clear, colorful illustrations should also be considered as central to the reference collection. Such a work should be useful for plant identification and research on gardening practices. A standard set to consider for this type of information is the ten-volume NEW YORK BOTANICAL GARDEN ILLUSTRATED ENCYCLOPEDIA OF HORTICULTURE; however, the sizable price of this set may prove to be prohibitive for some libraries, so the work has been listed as a supplementary source in this section.

Core Titles

	PUBLIC	ACADEMIC	SCHOOL
The Complete Handbook of Garden Plants Wright, Michael. Facts On File, 1984	✦	✦	
Hortus Third: A Concise Dictionary of Plants Cultivated in the United States and Canada Bailey, Liberty Hyde, and Ethel Zoe Bailey, comps. Macmillan, 1976	✦	✦	
Wyman's Gardening Encyclopedia, 2d edition Wyman, Donald. Macmillan, 1986	✦	✦	

After acquiring such basic works, a library could add more specialized sources, depending on the scope of interests and needs of its patrons. For example, a library may consider sources offering information on control of plant pests and diseases, such as the thorough but high-priced ORTHO PROBLEM SOLVER. For patrons interested in organic gardening, THE ENCYCLOPEDIA OF ORGANIC GARDENING is a standard.

Another important category of work to consider in this field is the directory. This source should be as current as possible and include botanical and horticultural libraries and related organizations and associations. Additionally, the directory should contain information on the locations of flower shows, horticulture awards, specialty gardens, and so forth.

Older, out-of-print sources should be carefully evaluated before being discarded from a collection or refused from a donor. For example, L. H. Bailey's *Standard Cyclopedia of Horticulture* (1947; reprinted by Macmillan, 1963) is still considered an important work in the field.

Core Titles

The Complete Handbook of Garden Plants. Michael Wright. Facts On File, 1984. hard. 1 vol. 544 pp. illus. index. ISBN 0-87196-632-8. $24.95. handbook. SB407.W73 635.9′02′02

The Complete Handbook of Garden Plants is designed to be a comprehensive one-volume guide to decorative outdoor garden plants. The main body of the handbook contains material on over 9,000 species of plants, which are then divided into types of plants such as trees and shrubs, perennial climbers, and border and bedding perennials. Other useful sections include hardiness zones, a glossary, an article on pests and diseases, and considerations for choosing plants for a home garden. Plants chosen for inclusion are limited to those grown in temperate climates, excluding vegetables and fruits.

An exceptional feature of the handbook is the approximately 2,600 watercolor paintings provided as illustrations for the entries. These are most often conveniently located on the page directly opposite the related entry.

Entries in the handbook are listed first by genus, then by species. Some general information is given in the opening paragraph of each entry describing the characteristics of the genus and the methods of cultivation and propagation. The species are then described individually. Each description is followed by numbers referring to corresponding illustrations on the opposite page. Although the method of arrangement is by botanical name, common names are also given. If the user does not know the specific genus or broad category of plant as listed in the contents, the index provides further access to the entries by common name and genus.

To keep the volume small, the author has used a number of abbreviations within the text, as well as other space-saving measures. All these steps are clearly defined in the introduction.

Michael Wright has authored and edited other gardening books, and a host of consultants in the field of horticulture are acknowledged as having contributed to this project in some way. In addition to these horticultural experts, at least 23 illustrators are listed. This publication is by no means the work of an individual.

The Complete Handbook of Garden Plants, with its clear format, relative currency, extraordinary illustrations, and thorough indexing, is a valuable source of gardening information for the amateur gardener and botanical expert alike. This handbook is not to be underestimated because of its size. The Board recommends this work for the core collections of public and academic libraries.

Hortus Third: A Concise Dictionary of Plants Cultivated in the United States and Canada. Liberty Hyde Bailey and Ethel Zoe Bailey, comps.; revised and expanded by the staff of the Liberty Hyde Baily Hortorium. Macmillan, 1976. hard. 1 vol. 1,290 pp. illus. index. ISBN 0-02-505470-8. $135. dictionary. SB45.B22 582.06′1

Hortus Third: A Concise Dictionary of Plants Cultivated in the United States and Canada, the culmination of nearly a century of research and revision, is designed to provide basic information on plants cultivated in North America, north of Mexico. Unlike its predecessors, *Hortus* (1930) and *Hortus Second* (1941), *Hortus Third* includes plants cultivated in Puerto Rico and Hawaii, which expands the scope of the dictionary to represent more fully plants native to tropical climates.

Originally *Hortus Third* was projected to be an updated version of the previous editions; however, individual entries were eventually rewritten and expanded. Many plants no longer being cultivated were omitted, while many new plants were added.

L. H. Bailey, one of the original compilers of the *Hortus* dictionaries, had a very distinguished career in horticultural research. Bailey was also the founder and president of the American Society for Horticultural Science (1913) and the Botanical Society of America (1926). His horticultural manuals and encyclopedias (such as his *Standard Cyclopedia of Horticulture* [1947; reprinted by Macmillan, 1963; now out of print]) are classics in the field.

Entries in *Hortus Third* provide a general description of the taxonomic group and often include information on geographical distribution, economic importance, and propagation. For example, the entry for the genus *Eucalyptus* provides a general description, common names, and information about the economic importance of eucalyptus wood, essential oils, and tannins. Descriptions of specific species follow this general information and include the geographic regions where the species are most common.

Numerous cross-references are provided as well as a glossary of botanical terms. The index to common names is especially helpful, making the dictionary accessible to the amateur gardening enthusiast as well as to the botanical expert. (For the amateur gardener, however, THE NEW YORK BOTANICAL GARDEN ILLUSTRATED ENCYCLOPEDIA OF HORTICULTURE is a more practical and accessible source of information on general propagation techniques, hardiness zones, and so forth.)

Each main entry word of *Hortus Third* is set in uppercase boldface type, making entries easy to locate. The various components of the individual entries are distinguished by different sizes and styles of typefaces; however, some of the print is quite small and may be difficult to read. Also, for its size, considerable cost, and the amount of use this dictionary receives, the binding is extremely inadequate; the volume will need to be rebound after only minimal use.

Hortus Third is the most accurate, authoritative work available for names and descriptions of plants grown currently in North America. Although published in the mid-1970s, this dictionary is the most important single-volume work in the field and remains central to a core reference collection on horticulture. The Board recommends this work for the core collections of public and academic libraries.

Wyman's Gardening Encyclopedia, 2d edition. Donald Wyman. Macmillan, 1986. hard. 1 vol. 1,221 pp. illus. ISBN 0-02-632070-3. $50. encyclopedia.
SB450.95.W96 635.03'21

Wyman's Gardening Encyclopedia is written by Donald Wyman, horticulturist emeritus at Harvard University's Arnold Arboretum and recipient of numerous prestigious horticultural awards. Other works by Wyman include *Trees for American Gardens, Shrubs and Vines for American Gardens,* and the *Saturday Morning Gardener.* In addition to Wyman, many other specialists in the field acted as contributing authors for this work. Their names are listed in the front of the encyclopedia.

Wyman has designed this encyclopedia to provide access to information on approximately 9,500 plants, mainly those of ornamental or economic value. Wildflowers are excluded as well as rare species and varieties not available to the public. Retaining the same format as the two previous editions, the encyclopedia lists most plants by scientific name with cross-references to common names; however, fruits and vegetables are listed and described by their common names.

The primary purpose of each entry is to describe the plant's physical characteristics, native environment, hardiness zones, and propagation techniques. The table of contents lists major entries on horticultural practices such as *insecticides, compost, propagation,* and *pruning.* In this latest edition, the table of pesticides and laws pertaining to their use has been revised, as has the *plant quarantines* entry. A few black-and-white photographs and drawings are included with selected entries.

Although the volume is now several years old, most of the information contained in the text has been subject to little or no change. The information in entries on such topics as pesticides and plant quarantines, however, may be somewhat out of date.

The chosen audience for the well-researched *Wyman's Gardening Encyclopedia* is both the amateur gardener and the horticulture specialist, making this substantial volume a valuable resource. The Board recommends this work for the core collections of public and academic libraries.

Supplementary Titles

The Encyclopedia of Organic Gardening. Staff of *Organic Gardening,* eds. Rodale, 1978. hard. 1 vol. 1,236 pp. ISBN 0-87857-351-8. encyclopedia.
SB453.5.E5 631.58

"In this completely revised updated version . . . [of *The Encyclopedia of Organic Gardening* are] more than 1,500 entries devoted to the identification, cultivation, and use of specific fruits, grains, nuts, vegetables, and ornamentals. Also included are sections covering all the basic elements of organic gardening. The emphasis is on practical how-to's. For example:

"Companion planting—how to plant your garden so that flowers, vegetables, and herbs benefit from one another.

"Composting—how to make compost quickly by encouraging natural biological processes at work in soil and plant debris.

"Greenhouses—how to construct and maintain an energy-efficient greenhouse.

"Insect control—how to identify more than 75 garden pests and control them with organic materials.

"Special attention is given to recent developments in many areas, such as livestock, indoor and outdoor horticulture, ecological landscaping, urban gardening, and home food processing. Like the original edition, the new *Encyclopedia of Organic Gardening* shows its readers ways to restore the fertility of their land, grow more bountiful crops, and become more self-reliant." (*Your Life and Health,* August 1982, p. 30)

Board's recommendation: Public libraries.

The Gardener's Illustrated Encyclopedia of Trees and Shrubs. Brian Davis. Rodale, 1987. hard. 1 vol. 256 pp. illus. index. ISBN 0-87857-679-7. $24.95. encyclopedia.
SB435.D25 635.977032

The Gardener's Illustrated Encyclopedia of Trees and Shrubs is "a perfect shopper's guide to trees. It starts out with dictionary sections which contain alphabetical entries for more than [2,000] varieties of tree and shrub. [Approximately 650 color] photos illustrate the best features of each plant.

"The entries include details about the origin of the plant and its use in the landscape, plus a description of the plant and its cultural needs. The book ends with information about pruning and planting, a glossary of terms and a chapter containing lists to help the reader choose the right trees and shrubs for a variety of conditions." (*Baltimore Sun,* February 7, 1988)

This book "offers information on trees and shrubs together with color photographs illustrating many of these plants and highlighting their outstanding seasonal features. Entries include details on plants' origins, their use for particular sites and descriptions of foliage, flowers, fruit and bark. Practical details about soil conditions for growing, hardiness, height over a period of years, sun/shade and pruning requirements and propagation are also included. Both the botanical and common names are given and indexed for each tree and shrub. (*Science News,* August 8, 1987, p. C1)

Also reviewed in: *Chicago Sun-Times,* September 18, 1987, p. 10.

Board's recommendation: Public libraries.

The New York Botanical Garden Illustrated Encyclopedia of Horticulture. T. H. Everett, ed. Garland, 1980–1982. hard. 10 vols. 1,468 pp. illus. ISBN 0-8240-7222-7. $600 (set). encyclopedia.
SB317.58.E94 635.90321

"Although directed primarily at the serious horticulturist, this encyclopedia is written and organized in a style that makes it accessible to the beginning gardener as well. Some 20,000 plants are described, including background information, garden and landscaping uses, and cultivation. Most genera are also illustrated with photographs, some in color. Cross-references lead the reader from common to Latin names. In addition, excellent longer articles discuss a wide range of topics including propagation, gardening methods, greenhouses, garden pests, and particular types of gardens and plantings. This authoritative set should become the standard reference source in horticulture." (*LJ,* May 15, 1981, p. 1044)

Board's recommendation: Public and academic libraries.

Ortho Problem Solver, 3d edition. Michael D. Smith. Ortho Information Services, 1989. hard. 1 vol. 1,056 pp. illus. index. ISBN 0-89721-199-5. $225. handbook.
SB603.5.077

Board's recommendation: Public libraries.

The Oxford Companion to Gardens. Patrick Goode and Michael Lancaster, eds. Oxford, 1986. hard. 1 vol. 635 pp. illus. ISBN 0-19-866123-1. $49.95. bibliography.
SB469.25.095 712

"World-wide in scope, this work is an encyclopedia of the art of garden design from the earliest known gardens to the present. The 1500 entries by 170 specialists cover large, small, public, and private gardens of significance; ancient and modern design and designers; and landscape architects, plant collectors, and influential garden enthusiasts. All of this is in alphabetical order, meticulously cross-referenced. Although well illustrated, this is not a picture book but a reference for amateurs and professionals concerned with studying or visiting gardens and checking details of the evolution and development of gardens." (*LJ,* February 15, 1987, p. 139)

Also reviewed in: *ARBA,* 1987, p. 563; *B&B,* December 1986, p. 12; *BL,* April 15, 1987, p. 1265; *Brit Bk N,* January 1987, p. 40; *BW,* December 7, 1986, p. 16; *Choice,* April 1987, p. 1202; *CSM,* December 5, 1986, p. B6; *LATBR,* November 30, 1986, p. 7; *LJ,* February 15, 1987, p. 139; April 15, 1987, p. 37; *NY,* February 16, 1987, p. 110; *TLS,* February 27, 1987, p. 225.

Board's recommendation: Public and academic libraries.

New and Noteworthy

The American Horticultural Society Encyclopedia of Garden Plants. Christopher Brickell, ed. Macmillan, 1989. hard. 1 vol. 608 pp. illus. index. ISBN 02-557920-7. $49.95. encyclopedia.
SB403.2.A46 635.9′03

"This beautiful work was compiled and originally published in Great Britain. . . . The *Encyclopedia* is arranged in two major sections: the 'Plant Catalog' and the 'Plant Dictionary.' The catalog contains brief descriptions and color photographs of more than garden plants. . . . The 'Plant Dictionary' is a guide to the characteristics and cultivation of more than 8,000 plants—the 4,000 listed in the 'Plant Catalog' and an additional 4,000." (*BL,* March 15, 1990, p 1496)

Larousse Gardening and Gardens. Pierre Anglade, ed. Facts On File, 1990. hard. 1 vol. 624 pp. illus. index. ISBN 0-8160-2242-9. $35. handbook.
635.9

"*Larousse Gardening and Gardens* . . . [describes] shrubs, trees, ferns, and flowers. . . . Entries within the plant section give descriptions of the genus and one or a few species, common names, hardiness zones, and a brief section on cultivation. About one of every 10 species is illustrated with a color drawing. . . .

"The *A–Z* plant section makes up about half the book. There are very interesting narrative chapters on the history of the garden, types of gardens, gardening techniques, and people. . . ." (*BL,* September 15, 1990)

Sharon A. Huge

How-To and Self-Help

In recent years the fastest-growing categories of nonfiction books have been how-to and self-help. The trend seems to be a natural response to the fact that many Americans have greater amounts of leisure time and are using that time to pursue more activities that involve some kind of personal growth.

Self-help is actually an offshoot of the longstanding category of how-to. For years bookstores and libraries have stocked books on the repair, maintenance, and creation of various mechanical devices, gadgets, crafts, and domestic items. That do-it-yourself mentality has now spread to more personal concerns. Both categories have continued to grow, and publishers have responded to demand by printing more and more titles.

Decisions for publishers as to what to publish in these areas may be difficult enough, but choices for booksellers, librarians, and readers as to what to buy are equally, if not more, difficult. Fortunately for all concerned, the self-help and how-to categories have been around long enough that a consensus seems to have been reached concerning a short list of standard titles. In addition, there are now several reference sources that serve as evaluative guides and bibliographies that can be quite helpful in making a purchasing decision.

The core list must provide fact-finding tools and supply how-to-do-it information. For example, no library should be without a good book on etiquette or a

Core Titles

	PUBLIC	ACADEMIC	SCHOOL
The Amy Vanderbilt Complete Book of Etiquette: A Guide to Contemporary Living Baldrige, Letitia, ed. Doubleday, 1978	✦	✦	✦
How-To: 1,400 Best Books on Doing Almost Everything Katz, Bill, and Linda Sternberg Katz. Bowker, 1985	✦		
Robert's Rules of Order, rev. edition Robert, Henry M. Scott, Foresman, 1985	✦	✦	✦
Self-Help: 1,400 Best Books on Personal Growth Katz, Bill, and Linda Sternberg Katz. Bowker, 1985	✦		

source on rules and procedures for running meetings and organizations. Thus THE AMY VANDERBILT COMPLETE BOOK OF ETIQUETTE and ROBERT'S RULES OF ORDER should be part of the core collection. Supplementary titles that provide the basics on various legal matters are also welcome sourcebooks. But the wealth of titles available in self-help and how-to make finding tools important additions to the core list. Therefore, the two books by the Katzes have been included in this buying guide. The Board also voted Norman Lathrop's *Index to How to Do It Information* (Lathrop, annual, 1980–1986) to the core collection. This title, planned to be updated in 1991, provides patrons with access to how-to information in periodicals. Bruce Felknor's *How to Look Things Up and Find Things Out* (Morrow, 1988) was also voted onto the core list by the Board but has since gone out of print.

With the core and supplementary list at hand, librarians, booksellers, and readers alike can feel assured that they have the best and most widely used books in the area of how-to and self-help.

Core Titles

The Amy Vanderbilt Complete Book of Etiquette: A Guide to Contemporary Living. Letitia Baldrige, ed. Doubleday, 1978. hard. 1 vol. 879 pp. illus. index. ISBN 0-835-13375-8. $19.95. handbook.
BJ1853.V27 395

When the need to consult a book of etiquette arises, there is no better book to consult than *The Amy Vanderbilt Complete Book of Etiquette: A Guide to Contemporary Living.* Since Vanderbilt's death, the work of revising her guide to etiquette has been handled by Letitia Baldrige, who was chosen by both the publisher and Vanderbilt's heirs because of Baldrige's many years of experience in international diplomacy and public relations.

In her preface, Baldrige addresses the question of what etiquette is and how it works in our lives: Etiquette involves not only "when you wear white gloves and how you unfold the napkin on your lap" but also *"real manners,"* such as "being thoughtful toward others, being creative in doing nice things for others, or sympathizing with others' problems."

In revising a classic work Baldrige had a very big task, indeed, as mores and customs have changed considerably in our society since the book's last major revision (1972). However, Baldrige handled the changes skillfully and succinctly. Changes have been particularly apparent in the area of business, and the chapters related to corporate etiquette are particularly useful, especially as they relate to the lives of professional women. For example, there is an excellent discussion of the use of "Ms." when addressing a woman.

The sections on gift-giving and the various ceremonies of life will get considerable use, and the chapters on weddings will no doubt be finger-worn in a short time, as the marriage ceremony seems to prompt the most queries about proper behavior.

The book is divided into eight parts covering everything from behavior in the family to the etiquette of travel. Each part is further divided into chapters; for example, part 7, "You on Public View," contains chapters on such topics as wardrobe, dining in restaurants, sports etiquette, and public speaking. Particularly interesting is the discussion on "How to Eat a Maine Lobster," which is accompanied by black-and-white drawings. Within the chapters Baldrige often uses vignettes to illustrate her points.

Although etiquette books often have poor indexes, perhaps because the language and terms that are used fluctuate wildly according to geographic region and even ethnic origin, the index in *The Amy Vanderbilt Complete Book of Etiquette* is well organized, thorough, and easily accessible.

The Amy Vanderbilt Complete Book of Etiquette makes clear that etiquette is not a stuffy subject, despite its reputation. Amy Vanderbilt proved that point with her original editions of this work, and Letitia Baldrige continues the tradition. The Board recommends this work for the core collections of public, academic, and school libraries.

How-To: 1,400 Best Books on Doing Almost Everything. Bill Katz and Linda Sternberg Katz. Bowker, 1985. hard. 1 vol. 377 pp. indexes. ISBN 0-8352-1927-5. $39.95. bibliography.
Z6151.K38 011.7

A companion volume to SELF-HELP: 1,400 BEST BOOKS ON PERSONAL GROWTH, *How-To: 1,400 Best Books on Doing Almost Everything* follows the format and style of the former volume and exhibits the same high standards. The editors recommend in their preface that readers consult both books to get a full range of titles in the categories of self-help and how-to.

In the preface of this work, "how-to" books are defined as those that "help the individual carry out an action, usually with materials of one sort or another." The Dewey Decimal system was also employed to help define the scope of this work, so that books on indoor games of skill, games of chance, and athletic sports and games all find places in the how-to category. Such varied subjects as bowling, calligraphy, falconry, and taxidermy are included. Materials selected for inclusion were all published between 1980 and 1984.

A detailed table of contents lists subjects alphabetically; under each subject, titles are presented in boldface type and related subjects in regular type, also in an alphabetized arrangement. Within the body of the book, subject headings appear in small capitals followed by individual titles listed alphabetically by author's name. A bibliographic headnote for each entry lists author, title, publisher, year, page length, price, and Dewey number, after which the title is described in a brief annotation. Some white space separates each entry.

The excellent author, subject, and title indexes add to the accessibility of *How-To: 1,400 Best Books on Doing Almost Everything.* In addition, there is a generous supply of cross-references. Laypersons will find the book easy to use, and booksellers and librarians will find the volume to be a useful and important evaluating tool.

The Board recommends this work for the core collection of public libraries.

Robert's Rules of Order, rev. edition. Henry M. Robert. Scott, Foresman, 1985. hard. 1 vol. 594 pp. index. ISBN 0-6731-5472-6. $16.95. handbook.
JF515.R692 060.4

The first edition of *Robert's Rules of Order* (1876) was researched, written, and published by Major Henry M. Robert. The work was intended to serve as a uniform system of proceedings for political, literary, scientific, benevolent, and religious groups in the United States. In order to produce this work, Robert studied the rules of Congress and parliamentary law and applied their general principles while adapting their specifics to better serve the needs of ordinary societies and clubs. His intent was to give organizations methods for conducting business meetings that could be employed easily. The rules were also intended to provide guidelines for the duties of a group's officers, as well as the handling and disposition of documents.

Major Robert's success in creating uniform but adaptable procedures is shown dramatically by the eight editions and countless printings over the book's 100-plus-year history. Various revisions have worked to modernize spelling and punctuation, and occasional rule changes also have occurred. Even these changes, however, take their precedent from Robert, as he would interpret subtle changes in parliamentary law and then reflect those changes from printing to printing. Despite the changes made over the years, every edition has ensured the principles of certain rights: the right of the majority to prevail, the right of the minority to be listened to, and the right of the individual to contribute to the process of the group.

The reference is divided into 20 parts, which are in turn subdivided into chapters. For example, part 1, which deals with the deliberative assembly, contains one chapter that defines the nature and types of such assemblies and one that covers such aspects as constitutions and standing rules.

The clear and complete index should help even the novice user to find the appropriate section of the *Rules* to consult for a given situation. The language of the text is precise and updated for contemporary use so as to be easily interpreted for most situations.

Robert's Rules of Order should find a place in every organization's library because of the venerable work's use as ultimate arbiter of many procedural questions. The Board recommends this work for the core collections of public, academic, and school libraries.

Self-Help: 1,400 Best Books on Personal Growth. Bill Katz and Linda Sternberg Katz. Bowker, 1985. hard. 1 vol. 379 pp. indexes. ISBN 0-8352-1939-9. $39.95. bibliography.
Z7204.S44K38 011.7

The well-known and well-regarded reference experts Bill Katz and Linda Sternberg Katz have compiled and edited the annotated bibliography *Self-Help: 1,400 Best Books on Personal Growth.* In the preface of this work the Katzes provide a working definition for *self-help books:* those "guides, manuals, and general treatises that help an individual improve, modify, or otherwise understand his or her physical or personal characteristics."

Materials selected for inclusion in this work were published between 1980 and 1984, with only a few exceptions. Included are U.S. government documents, which are a neglected storehouse of useful and excellent information. The word *Best* in the title means materials written by authorities in the field, with an emphasis on ease of use. Therefore, titles in which the language is accessible to the layperson were generally chosen over highly technical works unless the latter stood out as the single or best representative for a topic. Titles that encompass a variety of interest levels in any given subject area were incorporated where possible.

The main part of the text is arranged alphabetically by subject. Within each subject category, titles are listed alphabetically by author or editor. The annotations themselves, ranging in length from 50 to 100 words, are clearly written and easy to understand. Annotations are preceded by full bibliographic information, including a Dewey number.

Three useful indexes are included: author, title, and subject. A detailed table of contents of the subject headings, alphabetically arranged, appears at the beginning of the reference. Helpful cross-references and "see also" references appear within the text.

While *Self-Help: 1,400 Best Books on Personal Growth* is designed primarily for the layperson, librarians who are asked to recommend self-help books or who need a good standard work that is also fairly current will welcome this guide in their collections. The Board recommends this work for the core collection of public libraries.

Supplementary Titles

Complete Guide to Prescription & Nonprescription Drugs. H. Winter Griffith. Price/Stern/Sloan, 1989. hard and soft. 1 vol. 1,232 pp. index. ISBN 0-317-66061-6 (hard); 0-89586-860-1 (soft). $25 (hard); $14.95 (soft). encyclopedia.
RM302.5.G75 615.1

See Consumer Health.

Family Law Dictionary: Marriage, Divorce, Children, and Living Together. Robin D. Leonard and Stephen R. Elias. Nolo Press, 1988. soft. 1 vol. 193 pp. illus. ISBN 0-87337-061-9. $13.95. dictionary.
346.015′03

"The *Family Law Dictionary* has "definitions for the layperson of over 500 legal terms and phrases used in the area of family law. Examples of family law issues are marriage, divorce, adoption, support, custody, guardianship, living together, paternity, and abortion. In addition to legal terms, nonlegal but related terms like *extended family* are defined. The authors of the [*Family Law*] *Dictionary* are both lawyers.

"The book is arranged alphabetically and the outside edges of pages are marked to show the beginning of each new letter. Each entry is easy to discern because it appears in slightly larger, boldface type. The definitions of words and phrases vary in length from one sentence to several paragraphs; most entries are a paragraph or two. The authors employ several features to make entries clear. The context in which terms are used is explained, there are boxed examples to illustrate meaning, numerous cross-references to related terms are provided, and charts are sometimes used when concepts that vary from state to state are discussed. However, many entries generalize about state law, and readers may have to consult other sources to find the law for their state. . . .

"This book presents clearer definitions than those found in *Black's Law Dictionary,* which is designed for the law student, lawyer, and judge, and libraries providing legal reference works for the general public will want to consider it." (*BL,* October 1, 1988, p. 240)

A new edition of this book is to be published in the fall of 1990.

Board's recommendation: Public libraries.

New and Noteworthy

The Crafts Supply Sourcebook. Margaret A. Boyd. Betterway Publications, 1989. soft. 1 vol. 286 pp. index. ISBN 1-55870-121-4. $14.95. handbook.
680.028

[*The Crafts Supply*] *Sourcebook* lists more than 2,600 suppliers of craft materials, videos, and books covering hobbies and needlecraft. . . . Typically, each entry includes name, address, telephone number, if a catalog is available, and a description of craft supplies available. It also notes if there is a charge for the catalog or if a self-addressed stamped envelope is required.

"Individuals wishing to broaden their crafts horizons will value all this title has to offer. Public libraries will welcome it as a compendium of catalogs and mail order suppliers of art and craft materials." (*BL,* February 15, 1990, p. 1184)

The Vogue/Butterick Step-by-Step Guide to Sewing Techniques. Prentice-Hall, 1989. hard. 1 vol. 415 pp. illus. index. ISBN 0-13-944125-5. $24.95. encyclopedia.

"More than 500 of the 2000 dressmaking procedures regularly used in Vogue and Butterick patterns are demonstrated in this visual encyclopedia of sewing. . . . The editors' goal [in *The Vogue/Butterick Step-by-Step Guide to Sewing Techniques*] was to illustrate [sewing] techniques so clearly that professional results could be achieved by all home sewers. Since the step-by-step illustrations focus on technique and not on today's fashion, this title has an enduring quality. The sole concern is dressmaking. . . . This bible of dressmaking techniques will appeal to both the novice and experienced home seamstress and belongs in all public libraries." (*LJ,* July 1989, p. 75)

Heidi Mercado

Human Sexuality

The topic of human sexuality as a subject for research and study is relatively new. Before Alfred Kinsey's publication of *Sexual Behavior in the Human Male* (Saunders, 1948) and *Sexual Behavior in the Human Female* (Saunders, 1953), works on sexuality were few. Since the 1950s, however, a growing number of scholars have begun to study the subject in great detail, causing an exponential growth of publications in the field both in the technical literature as well as in popular books and magazine articles. Even though our permissive society makes information on this controversial topic regularly available, ambivalence toward it and avoidance of it continue.

Unfortunately, few reference works are available on human sexuality. The subject has generally been treated from an interdisciplinary approach and is part of indexes and abstracts of such related areas as medicine, psychology, sociology, biology, as well as seemingly unrelated areas such as political science, law, literature, art, and music. Indexes and abstracts used to list most of this information are: *Index Medicus, Psychological Abstracts, Social Sciences Index,* and ISI's *Social Sciences Citation Index.*

STUDIES IN HUMAN SEXUALITY: A SELECTED GUIDE, reviewed in this section, is the most comprehensive bibliography available, although only of monographic works. It covers all aspects of sexuality and is outstanding in its selection of works and the quality of descriptive abstracts. All other available guides, bibliographies, and other works are on specific topics of human sexuality, such as sexual assault, sexual harassment, homosexuality, or incest. Some excellent works

Core Titles

	PUBLIC	ACADEMIC	SCHOOL
Homosexuality: A Research Guide Dynes, Wayne R. Garland, 1987		✦	
Studies in Human Sexuality: A Selected Guide Frayser, Suzanne G., and Thomas J. Whitby. Libraries Unlimited, 1987		✦	

on these specialized topics were identified as supplementary titles: Mary de Young's *Incest: An Annotated Bibliography* (McFarland,1985), currently out of print; William Parker's three bibliographies on homosexuality covering the English-language literature through 1982, the last one entitled, HOMOSEXUALITY BIBLIOGRAPHY: SECOND SUPPLEMENT, 1976–1982; and Ann W. Burgess's RAPE AND SEXUAL ASSAULT: A RESEARCH HANDBOOK. A particularly good core reference for public and school libraries, though currently out of print, is Patty Campbell's *Sex Guides: Books and Films About Sexuality for Young Adults* (Garland, 1986).

Core Titles

Homosexuality: A Research Guide. Wayne R. Dynes. Garland, 1987. hard. 1 vol. 853 pp. indexes. ISBN 0-8240-8692-9. $53. bibliography.
Z7164.S42D96 016.3067′6

In *Homosexuality: A Research Guide,* Wayne R. Dynes, who is also the editor of the recently published *Encyclopedia of Homosexuality* (Garland, 1990), "seeks not only to mirror the large number of existing publications, but also stimulate new work by pinpointing neglected themes and methods" (preface). This research guide is part of the Garland Reference Library of Social Science series.

This comprehensive bibliographic work of some 4,858 annotated sources contains journal articles, nonfiction monographs, and some dissertations. Its coverage is international; much research on homosexuality has been conducted in Europe. Therefore, works in Dutch, French, German, Italian, Portuguese, Spanish, and the Scandinavian languages are represented, as well as the many written in English. A significant number of references in Chinese and Japanese are also included.

To reflect the interdisciplinary character of research on homosexuality the author has selected references from the fields of anthropology, art, religion, language studies, education, business, sociology, biology, and many others. All views, whether popular or unpopular, are represented.

Such entries as "Business Boom of Gay Savings and Loan," *New York Native* (December 6, 1982), *The Male Homosexual in Literature* (Scarecrow, 1982), *Gertrude Stein in Pieces* (Oxford, 1970), and "Homosexuality in the Ten-Spined Stickleback," *Behaviorism* (1952), reflect the broad scope of the work.

When a subject or viewpoint is heavily covered in the literature, the guide presents it selectively, but Dynes fleshes out less-studied topics such as music and economics. Historical studies that go back to the time of the ancient Greeks are also included.

Each topic in the main body of the work is introduced with a headnote which gives an overview of the subject with cross-references to related subjects. Each entry contains a short annotation, which describes the work and often gives additional references or cross-references to other entries. For very descriptive titles, the corresponding annotations are very short.

Name and subject indexes conclude the reference. The name index, the more comprehensive of the two, lists author entries as well as entries for references about persons. On the other hand, the short subject index has no cross-references and refers to section and subsection numbers instead of page numbers. It is necessary to look these up in the contents in the front of the book to find the page numbers. This contents table, in fact, is much more useful than the subject index because it lists both broad topic headings and detailed subheadings, giving a good overview of the subjects in this work. For example, under the broad heading "Philosophy and Religion," the more specific subheadings such as "Religious Backlash," and "Gay Clergy" provide a handy guide to the subject of each section.

The entries for this very detailed bibliographic work, which was ten years in development, were compiled from many specialized sources such as the Canadian Gay Archives, Gay Academic Union, Homosexual Information Center, and the International Gay and Lesbian Archives, as well as several large academic libraries, including the Columbia University libraries, New York Public Library, and the University of California libraries at Berkeley and Los Angeles.

Homosexuality: A Research Guide is an accurate, comprehensive, and up-to-date reference designed primarily for professionals. The Board recommends this work for the core collection of academic libraries.

Studies in Human Sexuality: A Selected Guide. Suzanne G. Frayser and Thomas J. Whitby. Libraries Unlimited, 1987. hard. 1 vol. 442 pp. indexes. ISBN 0-87287-422-2. $47.50. bibliography.
Z7164.S42F73 016.612′6

Studies in Human Sexuality: A Selected Guide contains a list of 627 monographic titles in human sexuality designed primarily for professionals. The authors, Suzanne Frayser, an anthropologist and sexologist, and Thomas Whitby, a professor of librarianship and information management, are both affiliated with the University of Denver. Their aim is "to provide a selection of highly influential and informative sex books of our times and to prepare informative abstracts of those books in an unbiased manner" (preface).

This hardcover guide is one of the first attempts to cover the interdisciplinary field of human sexuality. Limited to technical, scholarly, and popular monographic works, the bibliographic guide consists of reference books, guides, studies, collections, surveys, and bibliographies. While 542 of the 627 listed titles were published after 1970, only 36 of the balance were printed before 1950, around the time when Alfred Kinsey first published his groundbreaking studies on human sexuality (1949, 1953). Criteria for inclusion were that the works be by pioneers in human sexuality or by experts in the field, and that they have an important effect on society or reflect some of its major concerns. Works by such well-known authors as Sigmund Freud, Havelock Ellis, William Masters and Virginia Johnson, Karen Horney, Richard von Krafft-Ebing, and Albert Ellis, among others, are included. The authors also selected well-written, informative, well-researched, and aesthetically pleasing books. Various viewpoints are represented, including liberal, conservative, feminist, traditional, popular, and scholarly. For example, entries range from Susan Brownmiller's *Feminity* and Helen Gurley Brown's *Sex and the Single Girl* to Mary G. Durkin's *Feast of Love: Pope John Paul II on Human Intimacy,* Ralph Slovenko's *Sexual Behavior and the Law,* and *The Report of the Commission on Obscenity and Pornography.*

The abstracts for each of the 627 titles average 300 words, although some take more than a page. A helpful feature is the indication of the reading level for each entry with a two-letter code (for instance, *PR* means professional and *YA*, young adult). The entries are easily found by using the detailed table of contents, which represents a classification system for human sexuality devised by the authors. A broad topic such as "Sexual Functioning and Disorders" has subtopics for "Biomedical Aspects" and "Behavioral Aspects," which are further divided into specific subjects such as "Pregnancy," "Jealousy," and "Kissing." A detailed subject index includes descriptive terms with numerous cross-references. Accessibility is increased with separate indexes for authors and titles listed. The indexing has been very well done, as have the detailed instructions on its use in the preface.

Studies in Human Sexuality is a primary source for good books on sexuality. It is a meticulously researched guide and is unique in its field. Many other guide books exist on specific topics such as rape, sexual harassment, assault, and homosexuality, among others; however, this guide covers all aspects of sexuality. The Board recommends this work for the core collection of academic libraries.

Supplementary Titles

Homosexuality Bibliography: Second Supplement, 1976–1982. William Parker. Scarecrow, 1985. hard. 1 vol. approx. 300 pp. index. ISBN 0-8108-1753-5. $35. bibliography.
Z7164.S42P34 016.30141

In *Homosexuality Bibliography* "the listing of books, pamphlets, dissertations, and scholarly articles is comprehensive; the listing of articles from newspapers, popular magazines, and homophile publications is selective. Although there are omissions, the bibliography is both comprehensive and timely. Appendixes list movies, television programs, and applicable American laws. The arrangement is somewhat unusual in that it is by type of publication. . . . Given the lack of either classified or subject arrangement in the bibliography, the Subject index is extremely important. . . . Entries are numbered consecutively and arranged by author within each of the 13 sections. Complete citations are given. The format and binding are acceptable. . . . [This volume] is a convenient, reliable guide to the expanding literature on homosexuality. It brings together material scattered in a variety of indexes and identifies a number of items not easily accessible elsewhere." (*BL,* June 1, 1978, p. 1575)

"There is an excellent index of subjects and an equally good index of authors. The print is highly readable. . . . [Parker] updates the 1,265 listings of writings from 1940 through 1968 that Martin S. Weinberg and Alan P. Bell covered in their *Homosexuality: An Annotated Bibliography.* . . . And it is more readable and systematically organized than *A Gay Bibliography,* ed. by Jonathan Katz (1975). An excellent reference book for researchers who want to know about recent writings on homosexuality by English-speaking authors." (*Choice,* November 1977, p. 1194)

Also reviewed in: *ARBA,* 1986, p. 318; *BL,* June 1, 1988, p. 1650; *CP,* 1986, p. 156; *LR,* Winter 1986, p. 270; *Ref Bk R,* 1985, p. 26; *RSR,* Spring 1985, p. 16; *WLB,* October 1977, p. 185.

Board's recommendation: Academic libraries.

Rape and Sexual Assault: A Research Handbook. Ann W. Burgess, ed. Garland, 1985. hard. 1 vol. 433 pp. index. ISBN 0-8240-9049-7. $60. handbook.
HV6561.R37 364.1

Rape and Sexual Assault: A Research Handbook has received the following comments: "Articles on dispelling rape mythologies, sexual assaults and the handicapped, and rape-prevention issues are particularly noteworthy [features of this reference tool]. . . . Feminist conceptualizations are appropriately developed throughout the book. The overriding focus . . . is on women and children as victims and males as aggressors. Male victimization is minimally considered. . . . Writing style and clarity varies [*sic*]. . . . The bibliographies, located at chapter ends, are comprehensive but occasionally redundant. [This work is] a superb edition appropriate for serious students and researchers in the upper-division undergraduate level and above." (*Choice,* June 1985, p. 1574)

"Essays cover the physical and emotional needs of victims, social attitudes and norms, and typologies of and treatment for abusers. Each chapter is followed by a bibliography. [This title is] highly recommended." (*LJ,* February 1, 1985, p. 109)

Board's recommendation: Academic libraries.

Sexual Abuse of Children: A Resource Guide and Annotated Bibliography. Benjamin Schlesinger. Univ. of Toronto, 1982. soft. 1 vol. 200 pp. index. ISBN 0-8020-6481-7. $11.95. bibliography.
HQ72.C3S35 016.362704

Sexual Abuse of Children: A Resource Guide and Annotated Bibliography "presents an overall review of research findings on child sexual abuse and recommends a basic library, including films, on sexual abuse of children. Also covered are interviewing techniques, investigation and evaluation guidelines, guidelines for physical examination, and models from Canada for social and legal services. . . . [The] annotated bibliography . . . covers all aspects of child sexual abuse, categories of offenders, ethics, counseling, management, etc.

"Schlesinger, who has written extensively on family life, has brought together in one volume all the research to date on a subject that is currently a focus of interest not only from professionals but also from the general public. This book is indispensable for academic library collections in health, medicine, nursing, and the social sciences, as well as for public libraries." (*Choice,* October 1982, p. 246)

The work "attempts to pull together the relevant material for program development in the treatment of sexually abused children and their families. . . . Contents are divided evenly between U.S. and Canadian sources. The annotated bibliography is comprehensive, including books, journal articles, and other bibliographies. The book also discusses the issues from a social and moral perspective." (*LJ,* July 1982, p. 1314)

Also reviewed in: *ARBA,* 1984, p. 324; *CT,* November 1982, p. 36; January 1983, p. 36.

Board's recommendation: Public and academic libraries.

New and Noteworthy

Sexuality Education: A Resource Book. Carol Cassell and Pamela M. Wilson. Garland, 1989. hard. 1 vol. 446 pp. index. ISBN 0-8240-7899-3. $60. bibliography.
HQ56.S38633 306.7′07

Sexuality Education: A Resource Book is "a compilation of articles contributed by 38 psychologists, planned-parenthood specialists, doctors, nurses, social workers, and educators. The purpose of the book is twofold: 'to describe a variety of ways to plan and implement sexuality education and to provide in-depth information on the current resources available.' [In this volume the] . . . essays are practically oriented. . . . Where appropriate, contributors have summarized the major research in an area. Careful editing is quite evident throughout. . . ." (*BL,* September 1, 1989, pp. 106–108)

Grove Koger

Italian Literature

See also World Literature

Italian literature flourished long before there was an Italian nation; until 1870 Italy was a loosely connected group of often antagonistic city-states with shifting boundaries and allegiances. The peninsula's writers, however, have produced works of international importance from the fourteenth century onward. Early figures such as Dante Alighieri, Francesco Petrarca (Petrarch), and Giovanni Boccaccio have exercised profound influence on future generations of other writers. The *commedia dell'arte,* which evolved in sixteenth-century Italy, established archetypal comic figures and situations familiar to us still. In later centuries Alessandro Manzoni and Giovanni Verga produced *The Betrothed* and *The House by the Medlar Tree,* respectively, two of the world's great novels.

Yet despite the variety and vitality of Italian literature, few American readers can readily name any figure between Dante and contemporary novelist Alberto Moravia. More remarkable still, there are few works in English that deal with the entire range of Italian literature.

Librarians will find that the core collection titles answer most basic questions. Their patrons may most appreciate Sergio Pacifici's lively survey of what is arguably one of the richest and certainly the most accessible of the country's literary achievements. His THE MODERN ITALIAN NOVEL (see supplementary list) appeared in three volumes: *From Manzoni to Svevo, From Capuana to Tozzi,* and *From Pea to Moravia.* Unfortunately, only volume 3, *From Pea to Moravia,* is still in

Core Titles

	PUBLIC	ACADEMIC	SCHOOL
Dictionary of Italian Literature Bondanella, Peter, and Julia Conaway Bondanella, eds. Greenwood, 1979	✦	✦	✦
A History of Italian Literature, rev. edition Wilkins, Ernest Hatch; rev. by Thomas G. Bergin. Harvard, 1974		✦	

print. Librarians who want a complete survey of this genre should try to obtain the other two volumes through an out-of-print book dealer. Another useful addition to the collection would be *Italian Renaissance Poetry: A First Line Index to Petrarch, Ariosto, Tasso, and Others,* by Maureen E. Biya (Garland, 1987).

Core Titles

Dictionary of Italian Literature. Peter Bondanella and Julia Conaway Bondanella, eds. Greenwood, 1979. hard. 1 vol. 621 pp. appendixes. index. ISBN 0-313-20421-7. $49.95. dictionary.
PQ4006.D45 850.3

Described as "the first short reference guide to Italian literature in the English language," the *Dictionary of Italian Literature* is an alphabetical arrangement of more than 350 entries. Most deal with individuals, but a handful are devoted to literary movements, societies, and forms (such as the entry *sonnet*). Broad genres such as the novel are not discussed individually. A wide range of individuals—politicians, saints, and artists as well as authors—is represented, including *Arrigo Boito, Giovanni Botero, Benvenuto Cellini, Catherine of Siena, Dario Fo, Giuseppi Garibaldi,* and *Giorgio Vasari.*

The length of entries varies from about 100 words for *caccia* (a poetic form) to more than four pages for *Dante,* with most entries running over a page. Every entry is followed by a bibliography. All entries are signed, either by an individual reviewer or by one of the editors, all of whom are noted scholars of Italian or comparative literature.

Almost without exception the entries are written clearly and accessibly, fulfilling the editors' stated aim of producing what will be the "initial reference tool" for the general reader and the specialist alike (editor's preface). No errors of fact are apparent, and the selection of subjects is balanced, with ample attention given to contemporary (and hence more familiar) figures.

"See" references in the table of contents—identifying persons who do not receive separate entries, but who are discussed elsewhere—are repeated within the body of the dictionary. The index includes "references to names or pseudonyms of writers, artists, musicians, and film directors; literary academies; literary prizes; and journals, newspapers, and periodicals." This system operates well in most cases, but readers of that most famous of modern Italian novels, *The Leopard,* are likely to conclude that its author is ignored. There is no entry under "Lampedusa, Giuseppe di" in the table of contents, body of the volume, or index. Only those who know to look under "Tomasi di Lampedusa" (the Italian form of the name) will find the entry in the table of contents.

The volume includes two appendixes: a detailed timeline linking developments in Italian literature with those in world literature, politics, science, and so on, and a grouping of entries by subject matter and period. A brief list of reference aids supplements the bibliographies accompanying the individual entries.

With the exception of the entry for Tomasi di Lampedusa, the *Dictionary of Italian Literature* is easy to consult and is sturdily bound. The Board recommends this work for the core collections of public, academic, and school libraries.

A History of Italian Literature, rev. edition. Ernest Hatch Wilkins; rev. by Thomas G. Bergin. Harvard, 1974. hard. 1 vol. 570 pp. appendix. index. ISBN 0-674-39701-0. $35. history.
PQ4038.W5 850.9

First published in 1954, *A History of Italian Literature* was revised 20 years later and remains virtually the only English-language survey of Italian literature in print. The author, Ernest Hatch Wilkins (1880–1966), achieved renown as a scholar of Italian literature and later served as the president of Oberlin College.

A History of Italian Literature is chronological in broad outline (beginning with "Early Folk Music and Minstrelsy"), but most of its 53 chapters are grouped around major figures—an eminently practical approach given Italy's fragmented political history. Though never less than lucid, Wilkins is at his very best in his three-chapter discussion of Dante, whose *Divine Comedy* is a unique summation of medieval theology and philosophy. He is less successful with Petrarch, whose Renaissance worldview is arguably closer to our own. Noteworthy is Wilkins's discussion of figures not commonly considered literary: the scientist Galileo, unclassifiables Giordano Bruno and Giambattista Vico, and that audacious autobiographer Benvenuto Cellini. Very brief biographical sketches abound; for example, there is Wilkins's description of Friar Bernardino da Siena (1380–1444) as one who preached to "thousands on thousands" in "the very idiom of their own daily speech," and whose "curiously sunken face still looks out patiently from scores of Italian frescoes and altarpieces of his century."

Wilkins's original survey concluded with a chapter on "Writers of the Twentieth Century." In preparing the revision of Wilkins's work in 1974, Thomas G. Bergin (1904–1987) of Yale University enlarged the "List of English Translations and Books in English Dealing with Italian Literature," added a simple map of Italy and a chronological chart, and appended another chapter dealing with Italian literature since World War II. Thus, most important contemporary writers are mentioned, although the enormous influence of the postwar Italian film industry on the literary world is neglected. A partial remedy to this omission will be found in the chapter "The New Cinema" in Sergio Pacifici's GUIDE TO CONTEMPORARY ITALIAN LITERATURE.

Although the index fails to include a number of terms and references encountered in the text, *A History of Italian Literature* is generally a balanced and reliable survey. The Board recommends this work for the core collection of academic libraries.

Supplementary Titles

Guide to Contemporary Italian Literature: From Futurism to Neorealism. Sergio Pacifici. Southern Illinois Univ. Pr., 1972. soft. 1 vol. 245 pp. ISBN 0-8093-0593-3. $9.95. criticism.
PQ4087.P23 850.90091

Board's recommendation: Academic libraries.

Italian Theatre. Joseph Spencer Kennard. Ayer, 1972; reprint, 1932 ed. hard. 2 vols. 556 pp. illus. ISBN 0-405-08692-X. $44. history.
PQ4134.K4 852.09

The volumes of *Italian Theatre* present "a prodigiously detailed study of the Italian theatre from its inception to the present day, a project which has never before received full treatment in any language. This survey will be of value to students of Italian literature and history, and to students of the drama in general.

"Dr. Kennard writes methodically, with the sober consciousness of the importance of reconstructing the social, economic and political fabric of a people through one phase of its national art. His style is genial, his presentation patient and unhurried; at the risk of producing an anthology of the 'stories' of representative plays, he has related entire plots when by so doing he could illustrate the influence of passing events. Since he has been able to include a number of very fine reproductions of contemporary engravings and paintings, these volumes, beautifully printed, present a thoroughly charming appearance." (*NYT,* April 17, 1932, p. 17)

Italian Theatre "will be useful to all those students of comparative literature, of the stage, and of Italian history who cannot read fluently Latin and Italian. It is based on a long continued and sympathetic study of the chief primary and secondary Italian authorities. . . . All this literary and theatrical material is related to the historical development of Italian society." (*Theat A,* November 1932, p. 492)

Also reviewed in: *Choice,* January 1965, p. 487; *New R* May 4, 1932, p. 325.

Board's recommendation: Academic libraries.

The Modern Italian Novel: Volume 3, From Pea to Moravia. Sergio Pacifici. Southern Illinois Univ. Pr., 1979. hard. 1 vol (of a 3-vol. set). 853 pp. ISBN 0-8093-0873-8. $16.95. history and criticism.
PQ4173.P28 853.03

"Pacifici . . . is thorough and assiduous in this book. . . . The material is presented for Americans with some literary background but no specific information on the subject. The titles are given in English, and there is a certain amount of plot summary—this is not a critical book in any precise sense, but a book of presentation and explanation. In this it fills an obvious need. . . . Pacifici's is a book every library and every reader of modern literature, should have." (*CSM,* January 3, 1968, p. 9)

"Perhaps not everyone will entirely agree with the selection of the writers examined or of the works chosen as best representing their literary output, but even in disagreeing one must be grateful to Pacifici for his objective and challenging discussion of them. Even from a cursory reading it will immediately become clear that this work rests not only on a careful first-hand reading and meticulous reassessment of the opus of the authors considered, but also on the familiarity of the writer with the most recent and relevant critical literature. . . . [This] is a most valuable book whose worth is increased by its readability, typographical format, and by the highly satisfactory annotated bibliography added at the end." (*MLJ,* April 1974, p. 217)

"Although billed as a history, this is really a collection of essays, each concentrating on a small portion (one novel, usually) of an author's work. . . . A welcome entry in a sparse field." (*LJ,* 1973, p. 1168)

Also reviewed in: *BL,* September 1, 1979, p. 17; *Choice,* June 1968, p. 492; November 1979, p. 1179; *CLW,* February 1968, p. 446; *CSM,* January 3, 1968, p. 9; *MFS,* Winter 1980, p. 701; *MLJ,* April 1969, p. 284; April 1974, p. 217; *WHR,* Spring 1968, p. 170; Summer 1980, p. 286; *WLT,* Autumn 1979, p. 663.

Board's recommendation: Academic libraries.

A Short History of Italian Literature. J. H. Whitfield. Manchester Univ. Pr., 1980. soft. 1 vol. 335 pp.

ISBN 0-8371-8890-3. $35. bibliography.
PQ4043.W5 850.9

A Short History of Italian Literature, "as its title indicates, is a short history of Italian literature from the lyric poetry of the Sicilian School to the present. . . . The author, an internationally recognized scholar, is best known for his studies on Dante, Petrarca, Valla, Machiavelli and Leopardi.

"It is an almost unsurmountable task to synthesize, summarize, and criticize the vast corpus of Italian literature. Given the extensiveness of the period and subject matter, Whitfield presents clear, straightforward, and understandable explanations. . . . For the most part, this volume is not a mere bibliographic compilation, but rather represents a conscious effort to limit biographical and bibliographical information. . . . Instead of the usual factual listings, the author discusses ideas, periods, genres, and movements. . . . Overall, sound judgments characterize this brief literary history of Italy.

"Whitfield's *forte* is his personal judgements and the many personal interventions. Obviously, this short history of Italian literature is a product of much deliberation and not a superficial anthologized reading list. Of the fifteen chapters, 'Petrarch and the New World of Learning,' 'Epic Poetry from Pulci to Tasso,' and 'The End of the Nineteenth Century,' . . . are the most detailed and comprehensive. Undoubtedly, these three chapters are his best. Moreover, each of these chapters could stand independently from this study.

"[This volume] . . . is a personal, comprehensive and scholarly study from the origins to the present. It is highly readable and it never borders on the pedantic. . . . The author has tended to include those Italian authors that are more sought-after or have some bearing on English and European authors.

"Whether scholars, students, or *dilettanti* in literature, all stand to gain from this volume." (*MLJ,* Spring 1982, p. 111)

Board's recommendation: Public and academic libraries.

Wendell Cochran

Journalism

Journalism consists primarily of reporting the news. Traditionally, it is the job of the journalist to report the five Ws and one H—Who, What, Where, Why, When, and How. But news can be more than just current events, the stuff of morning headlines and television news roundups. At the *New York Times,* for example, the definition of news has been condensed to this: telling readers how people live. By this definition, a report of scientific research is news, too, as is a book review, or an account of travels in Yucatán.

News is gathered and written by reporters, processed by editors, and then printed or broadcast. It is distributed in the form of newsletters, newspapers, magazines, film, radio and television broadcasts, and electronic bulletin boards. Some news organizations in each communications medium gather and report news to a general audience, while others are designed to serve special-interest groups or particular crafts and professions.

Thus, journalism involves writing, editing, the graphic arts, and multifarious ways of printing on paper, and—more recently—the technology of computers and broadcast electronics. Rules for writing remain much the same, as do the ways of turning facts

Core Titles

	PUBLIC	ACADEMIC	SCHOOL
The Associated Press Stylebook and Libel Manual, rev. edition French, Christopher W., ed. Addison-Wesley, 1987		✦	
The Encyclopedia of American Journalism Paneth, Donald. Facts On File, 1983	✦	✦	✦
The New York Times Manual of Style and Usage: A Desk Book of Guidelines for Writers and Editors, rev. edition Jordan, Lewis, ed. Quadrangle/New York Times, 1982	✦	✦	
World Press Encyclopedia, 2 vols. Kurian, George Thomas, ed. Facts On File, 1982	✦	✦	

into ink on paper or patterns on a cathode-ray tube.

In order to do their jobs effectively, journalists often require specialized reference works. For librarians, the problem becomes one of making selections that will serve a variety of users with many purposes and guide them to related fields.

A core collection in journalism may stress references that writers and editors frequently consult—for example, encyclopedic guides to the general field and style manuals for writers. Supplementary works may range from glossaries that define terminology to style guides for technical matters, to directories of special-interest publications and broadcast outlets, or finally, to annual surveys in marketing and demographics.

Collections of the sort considered here should help writers (including novices) find editors who can help make their work public—that is, publish it. Journalism is a practical field.

Core Titles

The Associated Press Stylebook and Libel Manual, rev. edition. Christopher W. French, ed. Addison-Wesley, 1987. soft. 1 vol. 330 pp. ISBN 0-201-10433-4. $10.95. handbook.
PN4783.A8 070.415

Nearly 90 percent of *The Associated Press Stylebook and Libel Manual* consists of an alphabetically arranged guide to capitalization, abbreviations, and punctuation—the things news editors usually mean by "style." The book is also a general reference source for working editors and writers. The work includes concise explanations of such matters as Celsius temperature and the Richter earthquake scale, and the guide shows the preferred form of many common words and proper names. The book also discusses the use of such words as *hopefully* and *like* (for *as*), although it is not a substitute for a good English usage dictionary. This work is revised annually or biannually, depending on policy changes which influence editorial style at the Associated Press. Revisions are also incorporated in new printings of the work which occur between announced editions. The next edition of *The Associated Press Stylebook* is scheduled for 1991.

The book opens with a one-page "Key" explaining the organization of the text and giving examples of typographic indications of entry words, usage (good or bad), and related topics.

Most entries are only a few lines long—the pages are arranged in a two-column format—but some topics require more space. For example, *Methodist churches* and *quotation marks* warrant entries that run a page, and the entry for *possessives* is even longer. The entry for *pooh-pooh* receives no definition; only spelling and hyphenation are shown. *Mercalli scale* refers readers to *earthquakes;* the *Sierra Nevada* entry cautions readers that *Sierra* means "mountains"; *Skid Road, Skid Row* observes that only the former is proper for Seattle. A metric conversion chart fills a half page.

A separate section (in single-column pages) outlines the principles of libel and deals with special problems of writing about public officials, public figures, and public issues, and the right of privacy. Other chapters discuss photo captions and how to code wire stories for fast transmission throughout the AP network.

The alphabetic arrangement of entries makes the book largely self-indexing. A bibliography lists principal references for special fields, such as foreign geographic names and government organizations, as well as other major style books and authorities on grammar and usage.

This work's authority, accuracy, and currency have been achieved with the assistance of numerous working journalists. Over the years, thousands of reporters and copy editors have contributed (actively and passively) to correct errors, submit new entries, and suggest changes. The same sort of revision by *The Associated Press Stylebook* users helps to make the guide current. Because language does change—new words appear and old words take on new meanings—newspapers reflect such changes, and journalists pass them on to the editors of *The Associated Press Stylebook* and so into future revisions.

The Associated Press Stylebook and Libel Manual has been adopted widely throughout the United States as a standard for newspapers and thus sets a style that millions of readers are accustomed to seeing. (Its strength is also its weakness: no one style guide can fit all publications perfectly.) One original intent was to set style that member publications of the Associated Press could use with a minimum of editing; certainly, a uniform style makes it easier for writers to concentrate on facts and their interpretation.

The Associated Press Stylebook and Libel Manual is an important work to include in collections in academic libraries, as most journalism students will use the book at some time in their careers. Because of its frequent revisions, *The Associated Press Stylebook* is a more reliable source for current names in the news and definitions of terminology than THE NEW YORK TIMES MANUAL OF STYLE AND USAGE, which has not been revised since 1976. Many other writers will find it useful as their own standard reference work in this field.

The Board recommends this work for the core collection of academic libraries.

The Encyclopedia of American Journalism. Donald Paneth. Facts On File, 1983. hard. 1 vol. 548 pp. index. ISBN 0-87196-427-9. $55. encyclopedia.
PN4728.P35 070.03

The scope of *The Encyclopedia of American Journalism* is comprehensive. Its readers may explore journalism by subject—news, information, fact, and opinion of current interest; by process—gathered, evaluated, and disseminated; or by form—newspapers, magazines, radio, television, and film. Entries also allow the user to examine the style, principles, issues, and technology of each communications medium; or to take a chronological approach and trace the development of journalism from the seventeenth up to the twentieth century. There are entries for important individuals in the field of journalism: *Benjamin Franklin, John Peter Zenger,* and *Edward R. Murrow,* among others.

Entries are arranged alphabetically, and the text is printed in a two-column format. Some entries are as short as one line, but perhaps the most typical is one for *John Gunther* (1901–1970), in which the biographical sketch occupies 4 ½ column inches and emphasizes Gunther's jobs and publications. Another, for *Harold Ross* (1892–1951), is slightly shorter but adds two references for further reading and a cross-reference to the *New Yorker* entry, which occupies about 15 column inches (and includes no cross-references). The entry for the *New York Times* has 11 cross-references and fills more than four pages.

The work includes entries on the first American newspaper (Boston's *Publick Occurrences* of 1690) and on many other prominent daily newspapers dating from the seventeenth century to the present day. The United States now has at least four times as many radio and television stations as daily newspapers; this encyclopedia notes the early news broadcasts in 1920 by stations KDKA of Pittsburgh and 8MK of Detroit and many later developments in radio and television. There are brief entries that simply give definitions of technical words, while longer entries discuss economics, management, labor relations, and prospects of the new technology. The information about computers is dated, however, because the use of microcomputers in journalism has grown markedly since the early 1980s. As the title indicates, there is little mention of journalism in its international aspects.

The author (who is a former newspaperman and was for four years the editor of Facts On File's *News Dictionary*) designed the book on the idea of freedom of the press "as a necessity and a principle, the most important issue in American journalism." Thus, there are articles on *censorship, privacy, libel,* and the *filthy words* banned from the airwaves by the Federal Communications Commission.

Bibliographic references abound. In some ways this work's best use may be as a starting point: a summing up of a given subject, with directions for digging deeper. The book's index is thorough and well organized, making it easy for the reader to access information within the volume.

The Encyclopedia of American Journalism may also be used as an indicator of future developments: the history of journalism can be an aid to integrating our handling of information and a way of identifying and covering problems important but still neglected. The Board recommends this work for the core collections of public, academic, and school libraries.

The New York Times Manual of Style and Usage: A Desk Book of Guidelines for Writers and Editors, rev. edition. Lewis Jordan, ed. Quadrangle/New York Times, 1976. 231 pp. hard and soft. 1 vol. ISBN 0-8129-0578-4 (hard); 0-8129-6316-4 (soft). $15.95 (hard); $7.95 (soft). handbook.
PN4783.J6 651.7'402

As its subtitle suggests, *The New York Times Manual of Style and Usage* is more than just a copyediting style guide. In addition to arbitrating on such matters as spelling, capitalization, abbreviation, punctuation, and numbers, it also answers many routine copydesk questions about the spelling of geographic, commercial, and personal names, although it is no longer an up-to-date source for these. The aforementioned items have not been revised since 1976. Entries concerning rules of grammar and word usage (for example, *plurals of common nouns; sequence of tenses;* and *rebut, refute*) are interspersed throughout. Also, many entries define terms that may require an explanation in news stories (for example, *Abstract Expressionism; Richter scale;* and *relativity, theories of*).

A great number of library users seek out this book because of the *Times*'s longstanding reputation for good writing and careful editing. It is a standard style guide, less widely used than THE ASSOCIATED PRESS STYLEBOOK AND LIBEL MANUAL but perhaps more highly esteemed in terms of grammar and usage. Its accuracy and authority reflect the broad experience of the *Times* staff.

The manual's entries are arranged alphabetically, in double-column text on a page; the only exceptions to this format are a page of standard proofreading marks and a sample of a marked proof. Cross-references enhance the book's accessibility and make it virtually self-indexing.

Entries, rules, and discussions reflect the demands of daily usage. Newspapers are records not only of historic events but of our changing language, and so we find four separate entries explaining the use of *China, Communist China, Nationalist China,* and *Taiwan.* Similarly, under *Chinese names* there is a short description of the rules for transliteration into the roman alphabet. However, the book's copyright date of 1976 now renders this information obsolete. The *Times* itself now uses the pinyin system of transliteration (THE ASSOCIATED PRESS STYLEBOOK AND LIBEL MANUAL does contain an explanation of the pinyin system). Other entries include *Commonwealth, the,* with a list of the member states; *cliches,* with examples and a caution; and *sources of news,* which gives guidance on how to handle confidential sources in print. Matters such as *apostrophe* and *split infinitive* are usually discussed rather than stated as rules. However, preferred use is always shown in examples. Many important entries are missing here, such as AIDS, supercomputer, and Tiananmen Square, due to the 1976 copyright date.

New material in this edition apparently grew out of an occasional publication of internal criticism at the *Times* called "Winners & Sinners," which praises good stories and headlines by *Times* writers and editors but also discusses their errors.

The New York Times Manual of Style and Usage is recommended because of its usefulness to journalists, students, and professional writers and editors of nonfiction in matters of style. However, for up-to-date terminology and names of persons and things in the news, THE ASSOCIATED PRESS STYLEBOOK AND LIBEL MANUAL must be considered the authority.

The Board recommends this work for the core collections of public and academic libraries.

World Press Encyclopedia. George Thomas Kurian, ed. Facts On File, 1982. hard. 2 vols. 1,248 pp. index. appendixes. ISBN 0-87196-392-2 (vol. 1); 0-87196-497-X (vol. 2); 0-87196-621-2 (set). $145 (set). encyclopedia.
PN4735.K87 070.893

The *World Press Encyclopedia* is a two-volume guide to basic facts about the state of the press (including broadcast news media) and their environments in 180 countries around the globe.

The focus, as the editor puts it, is on the quality of journalism, its "historical evolution, present structure, and future trends." Journalism is considered in all its aspects—economic, political, and professional.

The encyclopedia is systematic and thorough, as may be expected of both editor and publisher; Kurian also edited the Facts On File ENCYCLOPEDIA OF THE THIRD WORLD (see African History). In compiling the present work he was aided by an editorial board consisting of about 50 persons and roughly the same number of contributors, all professors of journalism or working journalists.

Section 1 contains six brief chapters that give a statistical profile of the world press; sum up the politics of international information; and discuss comparative press laws, the world's elite newspapers, and aspects of international advertising.

Section 2, which comprises the bulk of the *World Press Encyclopedia,* is devoted to individual countries, arranged alphabetically in three sections: "Developed Press Systems" (82 countries, from Albania to Zimbabwe), "Smaller and Developing Press Systems" (33 countries, Afghanistan to Zaire), and "Minimal and Underdeveloped Press Systems" (65 countries, Andorra to Yemen).

The text in these sections is printed in a two-column format. Entries are devoted to the political and economic climate of each country and the history and operation of the national press. The editor aimed to cover the presses in terms of performance and political and economic setting and to indicate in each case a national pattern. In each entry, basic data are first summarized in a box giving the area of the country, its gross national product, the literacy rate, the number of dailies (and nondailies, broadcasting stations, and receivers), the annual consumption of newsprint, and the total advertising receipts. The ensuing discussion concerns the country's economic framework, press laws, censorship, press-state relations, attitude toward foreign media, the news agencies, and electronic media. The material closes with a summary of trends, a chronology, and a bibliography. In certain instances (for example, in cases where the press is suppressed or strictly regulated), some information was of course not available to the editors. Political conditions have also changed markedly in a number of countries (for example, the Philippines, South Africa, and Eastern Europe and the Soviet Union) since 1982.

Newspapers discussed in *Word Press* are classified in this way: (1) newspapers of general interest that record current events; (2) daily newspapers of general interest published at least thrice a week; (3) nondaily newspapers—published less than three times weekly; (4) periodicals—other publications of general interest emphasizing news or specialized information.

The table of contents is full and clear; the index long and elaborate. These features make the *World Press Encyclopedia* more accessible to the average reader. The Board recommends this work for the core collections of public and academic libraries.

Supplementary Titles

A Broadcast News Manual of Style. R. H. MacDonald. Longman, 1987. soft. 202 pp. ISBN 0-582-99865-4. $16.95. manual.
PN4784.B75M24 808.02

"Actual newswriting examples, punctuation rules, correct spelling, accepted acronymns, abbreviations, and contractions are discussed [in *A Broadcast News Manual of Style*]. Standardization of script page format, weather reporting, and wire service material are covered. A special section contains a comprehensive usage guide featuring phonetic spelling and a list of words frequen[tly] mispronounced or misused." (*JQ,* Winter 1987, p. 911)

Board's recommendation: Public and academic libraries.

Editor and Publisher International Yearbook. Orlando Velez, ed. Editor and Publisher, annual (1959–). soft. 1 vol. approx. 700 pp. index. ISBN 9-993-7798-1. $70. yearbook.
PN4700.E42

The *Editor and Publisher International Yearbook* "includes lists of both United States and foreign newspapers, arranged in geographical sections. Newspaper listings include circulation totals, publication data, subscription and advertising costs, lists of supplements and special editions, names of corporate officials and editorial staff, mechanical specifications, and other relevant information. The book contains subject listings of specialized papers, such as black newspapers, college newspapers, and religious newspapers. Equipment directories, lists of associations, directories of clipping bureaus, lists of news and syndicate services, and a directory of organizations relating to newspaper journalism are also included. . . ." (*RSR,* Winter 1986, p. 109)

Board's recommendation: Public libraries.

Editor and Publisher Market Guide. Orlando Velez, ed. Editor and Publisher, annual (1924–). soft. 1 vol. approx. 600 pp. illus. approx. $60. guide.
HF5905.E38 380.122

"Each recent issue [of *Editor and Publisher Market Guide*] offers individual market surveys of some 1,500 United States and Canadian cities where a daily newspaper is published. Arranged by state and city, [the guide] gives for each city such information as: population, location, trade area, banks, principal industries, colleges and universities, largest department stores, chain stores, retail outlets, newspapers, etc." (*Guide to Reference Books,* 1986, Sheehy, p. 844)

Also reviewed in: *Ser Lib 2nd,* 1985, p. 58.

Board's recommendation: Public libraries.

The Elements of Editing: A Modern Guide for Editors and Journalists. Arthur Plotnik. Macmillan, 1982. soft. 1 vol. 156 pp. index. ISBN 0-02-047430-X. $4.95. handbook.
PN4778.P59 070.4′1

The Elements of Editing is "a tool for writers and editors, a reference book for all those concerned with publishing, a text-manual for students and teachers of journalism. . . . The special section called 'The Office Reference,' offering a publishing bibliography, further amplifies the thoroughly splendid body of knowledge." (*Choice,* February 1983, p. 823)

"This handbook . . . distills the essential components of an editor's job. Eminently readable, the book has many strengths: explanations of such concerns as copyright and libel; definitions of graphics terms used in production; a capsule view of the job of book editor; [and] a section on photography." (*LJ,* December 1, 1983, p. 823)

Board's recommendation: Public, academic, and school libraries.

Guidelines for Journal Editors and Contributors. Conference of Editors of Learned Journals. MLA, 1984. soft. 1 vol. 19 pp. ISBN 0-87352-117-X. $4.50. handbook.
PN146.68 070.5′1

Board's recommendation: Public and academic libraries.

The Language of Journalism: A Glossary of Print-Communications Terms. Ruth Kimball Kent. Kent State Univ. Pr., 1970. hard and soft. 1 vol. 186 pp. illus. ISBN 0-87338-091-6 (hard); 0-87338-092-4 (soft). $8 (hard); $4 (soft). dictionary.
PN4728.K4 070.418

The Language of Journalism is "a collection of terms arranged in alphabetical order. . . . There are the technical or semi-technical terms of journalism . . . [and a] selection of graphic arts terms . . . [as well as] terms having to do with paper, book production, the electronic media, statistical research, law of the press, and photography." (preface)

"The book can serve as an elementary compilation

for high school libraries. . . . Included are a 17-page section on origins of some terms . . . a 12-page section of abbreviations . . . two pages on proofreaders' marks and their use, and 18 pages of sources consulted." (*Choice,* September 1971, p. 811)

"This book . . . should be valuable to anyone who needs a glossary of the terminology used in journalism, publishing, and printing." (*CC,* March 24, 1971, p. 388)

Board's recommendation: Public, academic, and school libraries.

Magazine Writers Nonfiction Guidelines: Over 200 Periodicals Editors' Instructions Reproduced. Judy Mandell, ed. McFarland, 1987. hard. 1 vol. 392 pp. appendix. ISBN 0-89950-239-3. $22.50. handbook.
PN147.M33 070.572'09

Magazine Writers Nonfiction Guidelines "photoreproduces the writers guidelines for news stand magazines, popular periodicals sold by subscription only, and airline magazines. An additional 30 magazines that accept free-lance contributions but that do not have formal guidelines for writers are listed in an appendix. Much of the information in this book can also be found in *Writer's Market,* but Mandell includes some magazines not listed there." (*BL,* April 1, 1987, p. 1186)

Board's recommendation: Public and academic libraries.

Writer's Market. Glenda Tennant Neff, ed. Writer's Digest, annual (1968–). hard. 1 vol. 1,056 pp. indexes. ISBN 0-89879-442-6. $24.95. handbook.
PN161.W956 070.52097

See Publishing.

New and Noteworthy

Biographical Dictionary of American Journalism. Joseph P. McKerns, ed. Greenwood, 1989. hard. 1 vol. approx. 800 pp. index. ISBN 0-313-23819-7. $95. biographical dictionary.
PN4871.B56 070.922

"This is an excellent collection of . . . biographical sketches of 500 noteworthy journalists from 1690 to the present. . . . No previous work of this nature exists. . . . Each detailed yet readable sketch stresses the person's significance in shaping American journalism, including newspapers, magazines, broadcasting, news agencies, and news photography. . . . This book . . . may become the takeoff point for thousands of term papers and should be in reference collections, as well as in all serious media collections." (*LJ,* June 15, 1989, p. 50)

The Encyclopedia of Censorship. Jonathan Green. Facts On File, 1990. hard. 1 vol. 338 pp. index. ISBN 0-8160-1594-5. $45. encyclopedia.
Z657.G73 098.13

"This comprehensive ready-reference source covers the history and present status of censorship worldwide. The approximately 1,000 alphabetically arranged entries include the names of individuals (both censors and censored), works subjected to censorship (Shakespeare to *Lady Chatterley's Lover*), organizations that have advocated or opposed censorship, important legal cases, and many other types of entries relevant to the subject. . . . The U.S. and the United Kingdom receive the most extensive coverage, followed closely by other Western nations (including South Africa), Europe and the communist block, China and the Third World." (*BL,* March 15, 1990, p. 1498)

Donna L. Singer

Language and Linguistics

Life in the twentieth century has become increasingly complex due to the development of new technologies and the need for rapid information retrieval and dispersement. Sophisticated communications systems have diminished the distances not only between cities but also between continents. The concept of the "global village" is rapidly becoming a reality. The English language has been transformed by these advancements through the adoption of thousands of foreign terms and phrases, the proliferation of acronyms and abbreviations, and the infusion of slang and colloquialisms. Therefore, a core reference collection in the field of language and linguistics should contain standard reference works that reflect this broad scope.

There are some works that were excluded from the language and linguistics category because they were covered in earlier volumes of the Bowker Buying Guide series. For example, *The Oxford English Dictionary, The Oxford Guide to the English Language, Roget's Thesaurus,* and many other similar works have already been reviewed in *General Reference Books for Adults.* Included in this volume are works that provide definitions of acronyms, abbreviations, and foreign terms. Also included are a few additional usage and word books that were omitted from *General Reference Books for Adults* because they were too specialized in nature.

The core collection, therefore, should be flexible enough to provide information for the person who is looking for the meaning of the British colloquialism *argy-bargy* as well as for the patron who needs to find the definition and usage of the Latin phrase *tabula rasa.* It should satisfy the researcher's quest for details on *procedural grammar* and provide identification of the abbreviation *ISE* or the acronym *NABISCO* for the curious reader.

Most of the reference works reviewed here are dictionaries, each specializing in a particular area of language usage or linguistics. In addition to the conventional dictionaries dealing with slang or foreign phrases, AMERICAN SIGN LANGUAGE: A COMPREHENSIVE DICTIONARY should be an integral part of the core collection.

Many librarians may need to extend the core collection with some of the additional titles suggested, depending on patron interest. If available, *The Dictionary of Contemporary Slang* (Jonathan Green, Stein & Day, 1984) can be a useful adjunct to Partridge and Beale's DICTIONARY OF SLANG AND UNCONVENTIONAL ENGLISH. The scope of the collection can be further broadened by the inclusion of supplementary works, such as THE DICTIONARY OF CLICHES or PICTURESQUE EXPRESSIONS. The issue of sexism and language can be addressed through the inclusion of THE NONSEXIST WORD FINDER, a standard work in this area. Librarians compiling a collection in language and linguistics can and should explore many

Core Titles

	PUBLIC	ACADEMIC	SCHOOL
Acronyms, Initialisms & Abbreviations Dictionary, 15th edition Mossman, Jennifer, ed. Gale, 1990	✦	✦	✦
American Sign Language: A Comprehensive Dictionary Sternberg, Martin L. A. Harper & Row, 1981	✦	✦	✦
Dictionary of Foreign Phrases and Abbreviations, 3d edition Guinagh, Kevin, trans. and comp. Wilson, 1983			✦
A Dictionary of Linguistics and Phonetics, 2d edition Crystal, David. Basil Blackwell, 1985		✦	
A Dictionary of Slang and Unconventional English: Colloquialisms and Catch-phrases, Solecisms and Catachreses, Nicknames and Vulgarisms, 8th edition Partridge, Eric; Paul Beale, ed. Macmillan, 1984	✦	✦	✦
The Harper Dictionary of Foreign Terms, 3d edition Ehrlich, Eugene, ed. Harper & Row, 1987	✦		✦

additional topics, as these suggestions merely scratch the surface of the category.

Core Titles

Acronyms, Initialisms & Abbreviations Dictionary, 15th edition. Jennifer Mossman, ed. Gale, 1990. hard. 1 vol. 3,600 pp. ISBN 0-8103-5075-0. $208. dictionary.
P365.A28

The *Acronyms, Initialisms & Abbreviations Dictionary,* now in its fifteenth edition, was developed as a response to what the preface calls an explosion of "initialese" and "abbreviomania"—the convenient "linguistic shorthand"—brought about by rapidly expanding technology and the need to convey information quickly. This work is designed to make the "language" of abbreviations "manageable" for the public (preface). Divided alphabetically into three parts, the dictionary contains more than 480,000 entries, over 22,000 of which are new to this edition (such as *Flojo* for Florence Griffith-Joyner, American Olympic gold medalist). Extremely broad in scope, this reference work covers not only abbreviations used in fields such as banking, law, medicine, and aerospace, but also abbreviations for slang expressions (for example, *TGIF*—Thank God it's Friday) and alphabetical designations for musical groups (for example, *U2*—a popular music group), films (such as *GWTW—Gone with the Wind*), Shakespearean works (such as *R&J—Romeo and Juliet*), food (for example, *BLT*—bacon, lettuce, and tomato sandwich), and so on. Several thousand foreign abbreviations and acronyms are included, related primarily to the military, international association names, and print and broadcast media.

The dictionary remains extremely accurate and current, with extensive updating in this edition for radio and television station call letters and stock exchange symbols. The preface presents the scope, defines terms, lists major fields covered by entries, and discusses trends in the formation of acronyms, among other related topics. Included in the front matter are an explanation of editorial policies and a list of selected major sources for terms, arranged alphabetically by code abbreviation. The key to the source codes is printed on the endpapers. While some terms come from the major sources listed, the origin of a large number of terms is unknown; many of these come from miscellaneous newspaper or magazine references.

No entries have been deleted from the fourteenth edition. Even if an entry has become obsolete, it is included, with its status as an obsolete word noted. Only outdated stock exchange symbols and radio and television station call letters have been deleted, because they change frequently and because symbols or call letters abandoned by one firm or station can be adopted later by another.

The entries are arranged alphabetically in letter-by-letter sequence, regardless of spacing, punctuation, or capitalization. If an abbreviation has more than one meaning, the various meanings are arranged alphabetically in a word-by-word sequence (*ABC* has over 100 meanings, beginning with *Abacus*—a publication). A typical entry contains the meaning of the abbreviation or acronym, an English translation and language of origin for non-English entries, a sponsoring organization (if any), the subject area in which the term is used, and the source code (where applicable). Variant abbreviations for the same term are listed separately (for example, master of arts in teaching appears as *MA in T* and *MAT*).

This excellent reference contains common acronyms and initialisms, such as *SRO* (standing room only) as well as technical ones, such as *MABP* (mean arterial blood pressure).

The *Acronyms, Initialisms & Abbreviations Dictionary* is easily accessed by students, researchers, professional linguists, and casual readers alike. This volume is the classic reference work of its type. The Board recommends this work for the core collections of public, academic, and school libraries.

American Sign Language: A Comprehensive Dictionary. Martin L. A. Sternberg. Harper & Row, 1981. hard. 1 vol. 1,132 pp. illus. indexes. ISBN 0-06-014097-6. $49.50. dictionary.
HV2475.S77 419

American Sign Language: A Comprehensive Dictionary was hailed by the National Association of the Deaf as "by far the largest and most complete dictionary of sign language ever published." This comprehensive work contains over 5,000 entries accompanied by 8,000 drawings by Herbert Rogoff, drawn from thousands of rapid photographs of hand movements depicting the signs. The author of this superb reference is deaf and works with other deaf persons. In addition, a general editorial committee is listed, including a noted linguist, Dr. William F. Marquardt; special consultants for the different categories of signs (such as Catholic signs and vocational signs); and consultants for the foreign-language indexes.

The author states that some new signs or new applications for old signs may not have been included due to the broad scope of the work, and, conversely, some older signs, now largely unused, are included to serve as "historical benchmarks in sign development" (acknowledgments). The dictionary includes signs to denote countries, signs for such everyday expressions as "How are you?" and signs for the contemporary usage of some words (such as *dope* for narcotics).

When using the dictionary, the reader must remember that American Sign Language is a separate language with its own grammar and syntax; therefore, the entries represent phrases or sentences, not single words. The reference is in dictionary form, arranged alphabetically. A pronunciation guide, abbreviations list, explanatory notes, and the American Manual Alphabet are given as part of the front matter.

Each entry word, abbreviation, or compound word is capitalized and set in boldface type. If more than one sign exists for a word (for example, there are four entries for *sharp*), the entry word is repeated and becomes a separate entry with cross-references to similar entry words. Each entry has a code number appearing in brackets above it that is used in conjunction with the foreign-language indexes. Syllabification and pronunciation appear in parentheses. The part of speech is given in italics, followed by sign rationale [that is, explanatory material that enables the user "to remember how a sign is formed" (explanatory notes)]. Next the sign and its formation are described in writing that is clear enough to be followed by a novice. The written description is followed by an illustration that reinforces the description. Cross-references are indicated in small capitals at the end of the written description.

Supplementing the main text of the dictionary are an excellent introductory essay entitled "The Study and Use of Sign Language," a bibliography arranged alphabetically by author and numbered consecutively, and a subject index to the bibliography, which lists sources and gives the bibliography number. Of special interest in this reference are the appendixes containing seven foreign-language indexes, which are alphabetized in the particular language. The English-word equivalent appears beside each foreign word, followed by the code number of the entry in the main text of the dictionary. These indexes were "developed to make the book accessible to deaf people and hearing workers of other lands" (acknowledgments).

This authoritative and comprehensive dictionary is easily accessible to the deaf and the hearing reader. Deaf persons can be guided by this work to increase their signing vocabulary, while hearing readers will find the alphabetical word-sign order helpful in learning to communicate with deaf or hearing-impaired persons.

American Sign Language is the best available dictionary of its kind. The Board recommends this work for the core collections of public, academic, and school libraries.

Dictionary of Foreign Phrases and Abbreviations, 3d edition. Kevin Guinagh, trans. and comp. Wilson, 1983. hard. 1 vol. 261 pp. ISBN 0-8242-0675-4. $38. dictionary.
PE1670.G8 422.4'03

The third edition of the *Dictionary of Foreign Phrases and Abbreviations* contains about 5,250 entries, over 500 of which are new to this edition. In addition, the sources of numerous expressions that appeared in earlier editions have been added, and the number of languages represented has increased from 11 in the first edition to 15 in the current dictionary. This reference is designed to help the reader find the meaning of foreign expressions encountered in daily life (preface). For example, the reader may need to find the correct meaning of such frequently used phrases as *persona non grata* (Latin: "an unacceptable person") and *déjà vu* (French: "already seen"), or such abbreviations as *ca.* (Latin: *circa*—"about") and *ad. val.* (Latin: *ad valorem*—"according to the value"). Also, the user may need to decipher the many foreign phrases that are used primarily within a specific field of study. An example from art is *trompe-l'oeil* (French: "a still-life deception"); from law, *corpus delicti* (Latin: "basic facts necessary to prove the existence of a crime"); and from literature, *dramatis personae* (Latin: "list of characters in a play").

According to the preface, Kevin Guinagh, the compiler of this dictionary and the former head of a university department of languages, consulted many dictionaries and other references in preparing this reference work. Guinagh has omitted any phrase longer than a couplet, as well as single words (such as *voilà*), which can be found in foreign-language dictionaries. Also excluded are Latin and Greek phrases used in the biological sciences because they are found in technical manuals. Finally, Guinagh indicates that the material included has been selected partly because of its frequent usage and partly because it reflects his own tastes.

The expressions and abbreviations are arranged alphabetically and appear in upper- and lowercase letters in boldface type. A pronunciation guide (new to this edition) is given in parentheses, followed by the language of origin. The translation—often quite literal—and any explanations concerning meaning or historical context form the heart of the entry. At the end of many entries the source is given (for example, author's name, work in which the phrase is found, and chapter or verse, if applicable). Entries vary in length from 1 to 12 lines. The dictionary also contains a note on pronunciation, a list of abbreviations used, and a list of phrases arranged by language of origin to help those users who know the language from which an expression comes but are not quite sure of the spelling of the individual words.

The *Dictionary of Foreign Phrases and Abbreviations* is a convenient, easy-to-use reference that remains current because many of the phrases have been used without change for years. Its dual access by phrase or by language of origin adds to its usefulness. Further depth will be added to the collection if THE HARPER DICTIONARY OF FOREIGN TERMS, which provides access to single-word definitions, is included.

The Board recommends the *Dictionary of Foreign Phrases and Abbreviations* for the core collection of school libraries.

A Dictionary of Linguistics and Phonetics, 2d edition. David Crystal. Basil Blackwell, 1985. soft. 1 vol. 339 pp. ISBN 0-631-14081-6. $16.95. dictionary.
P29.C65 410.3'21

A Dictionary of Linguistics and Phonetics is designed to be an introductory reference that attempts "to meet the popular demand for information about linguistic terms" (preface to the first edition). Added to the 2,000 entries from the first edition (1980) are 125 new main entry words and over 100 new secondary terms. Also, over 100 entries have been expanded to encompass new senses for certain words. Nothing has been deleted. Most of the new entries come from more recently developed areas, such as transformational grammar (for example, *X-bar syntax*), pragmatics (such as *pragmalinguistics*), and discourse analysis (for example, *foregrounding*).

The author, David Crystal, is a prominent British linguist who has written and edited several books on language, including THE CAMBRIDGE ENCYCLOPEDIA OF LANGUAGE. The dictionary is not intended to cover the whole field of language, communications, linguistics, and phonetics; therefore, only "terms or senses which have arisen because of the influence of twentieth-century linguistics and phonetics" are included. Excluded, for example, are words such as those whose meaning can be found in a good dictionary, technical terms of traditional language studies, and grammatical terms. Overall, the selection criteria are based on Crystal's "rule" to include a term only "if it is still being talked about three years later" (preface).

An interesting aspect of this dictionary is that each entry is self-contained; there are no cross-reference entries, although terms defined elsewhere in the dictionary appear in small capitals within an entry. As a result, there is some repetition of common characteristics of one term under a related term, as with the interdependent terms *performance* and *competence.* The main entry word is in boldface type, as are any secondary terms being defined within the entry. The entries include detailed definitions, examples of usage, and often a discussion of the historical context. At the end of each entry is a bibliographical reference to a chapter from one of a select number of secondary reference sources. A list of these sources, with full citations, is given in the front matter. Entries vary in length from one line to one page and cover such commonly used terms as *structuralism* and *poetics* and such technical terms as *diglossia.* In addition, some schools of thought (such as *Firthian* and *Jakobsonian*) are included. Also, the abbreviations for certain terms (for example, *TG* for *transformational grammar*) appear as entries.

A Dictionary of Linguistics and Phonetics is a convenient, easily accessible standard reference for students and researchers alike. The Board recommends this work for the core collection of academic libraries.

A Dictionary of Slang and Unconventional English: Colloquialisms and Catch-phrases, Solecisms and Catachreses, Nicknames and Vulgarisms, 8th edition. Eric Partridge; Paul Beale, ed. Macmillan, 1984. hard. 1 vol. 1,400 pp. appendix. ISBN 0-02-594980-2. $75. dictionary.
PE3721.P3 427.09

The eighth edition of *A Dictionary of Slang and Unconventional English* was the first complete revision and update of this classic reference in 13 years. Almost half of the more than 100,000 entries are new or contain new information. All changes and additions made since the first edition have been integrated into the body of the dictionary, rather than put into a separate section, as in previous editions, thus making the volume much easier to consult. This dictionary is shaped by a historical perspective, citing original sources and giving derivational details as well as presenting concise definitions of all types of slang, colloquialisms, vulgarisms, and catch-phrases that have occurred in the English language over the past five centuries.

The author, Eric Partridge, was a renowned lexicographer. Paul Beale, who edited the current edition, collaborated with Partridge on the revision prior to Partridge's death in 1979. In the preface to the eighth edition, Beale indicates that this work places a conscious emphasis on unconventional British English. Language considered standard English and language associated with dialects, such as Cockney, are excluded. In addition, almost all solecisms and catachreses found in earlier editions have been omitted because they can be found in the *Oxford English Dictionary* or Partridge's *Usage and Abusage* (reviewed in *General Reference Books for Adults*). In his preface to the original edition, Partridge explains his policy to include all vulgarisms, dealing with them as briefly as possible.

The entries are arranged alphabetically in dictionary format, with the main entry word in boldface type followed by the part of speech in parentheses. Next are the definition or explanation, the type of unconventional term (that is, colloquial, slang, vulgarism, and so forth), and the main users of the term (for example, the military, politicians, prisoners, and so forth). The entry concludes with the historical data, including a dating of the term, the source, and an early example of the term's use in print. An appendix contains material that requires more explanation than the format in the main body of the text allows. Included is terminology for bird-watchers' slang and tavern terms.

The entries range from such expressions as *bubble and squeak* (a dish of fried potatoes, greens, and meat) to *sheila* (Australian term for a girl). Such frequently used colloquialisms as *ad lib* and *the fat is in the fire* and slang terms such as *skinhead* are discussed. Cross-cultural slang, such as vulgarisms, are included; however American "CB" slang is not.

Though its 1,400-page size is a bit unwieldy to handle and the typeface is small, this comprehensive and well-researched dictionary remains the standard reference work on slang. The copious cross-references, explanatory notes on arrangement and dating of expressions, and lists of various kinds of abbreviations add to the accessibility of the work. Although the material remains current, some updating is needed, such as the most recent use of the word *geek* by adolescents. However, *A Dictionary of Slang and Unconventional English* is an excellent reference for scholars, writers, and any persons who have an interest in the English language. The Board recommends this work for the core collections of public, academic, and school libraries.

The Harper Dictionary of Foreign Terms, 3d edition. Eugene Ehrlich, ed. Harper & Row, 1987. hard and soft. 1 vol. 423 pp. index. ISBN 0-06-181576-4 (hard); 0-06-091686-9 (soft). $20 (hard); $10.95 (soft). dictionary.
PE1670.M3 422.4

This third edition of *The Harper Dictionary of Foreign Terms* contains definitions for more than 15,000 common and uncommon foreign words and phrases, taken from over 50 languages, that are found in spoken and written English. According to the preface, as the English language is embellished through the "adoption of foreign words and phrases that give opportunities for colorful and precise expression," it was necessary to provide a single-volume source that explains these foreign additions to language usage. This well-researched dictionary succeeds admirably by providing an easy way for a reader quickly to locate the meaning of a foreign word or phrase without having to search through a foreign-language dictionary. All fields of study have been enriched by foreign words and phrases, such as *maestosamento* (majestically) in music, *mandat* (warrant) in law, *madeleine* (a rich cake) in cooking, and *serape* (Mexican blanket) in clothing.

This third edition of the dictionary is based on the first edition compiled by lexicographer C. O. Sylvester Mawson (in 1934) and the second edition prepared by foreign-language textbook author Charles Berlitz (in 1962). The current editor, Eugene Ehrlich, who is also the chief editor of *The Oxford American Dictionary,* has updated the volume by adding terms from languages that have become more prominent in spoken English since the second edition (such as Russian, Japanese, and Hebrew) and by correcting errors noted by reviewers in the previous editions. New to this edition is an excellent English index to the thousands of entries found in the main body of the dictionary. For example, a reader looking up the word *lover* in the index will be directed to seven foreign words that are entries in the dictionary proper.

Listed alphabetically, each main entry word or phrase appears in boldface type, followed by the language of origin printed in brackets. A translation is provided, and any plural forms or parts of speech or combinations using the word to form phrases are listed where applicable. Frequently a citation of the field in which the word is used most often appears in italics at the end of the entry. If the phrase is from a well-known figure or from the Bible, the name (for example, Virgil) or chapter and verse (Daniel 1:19) are also given. Entries vary in length from 1 line to over 20 lines (for a word such as *coup* and all of its phrase combinations).

Although many words and phrases in the dictionary are no longer part of the speech of their original language (for example, terms associated with the British *raj* in India), they are included because of their continuing literary importance in English (preface). Some words, such as *chic* and *graffiti,* are so much a part of everyday conversation and writing that they are not recognized as foreign in origin.

The Harper Dictionary of Foreign Terms is an invaluable reference for students, teachers, travelers, and anyone who reads or writes. Its accessibility is enhanced by the index, judicious use of cross-references, and the large print. For coverage of abbreviations of foreign terms and access to a greater list of foreign phrases, the collection should also include the DICTIONARY OF FOREIGN PHRASES AND ABBREVIATIONS. The Board recommends this work for the core collections of public and school libraries.

Supplementary Titles

Abbreviations Dictionary: Augmented International, 7th edition. Ralph De Sola, ed. Elsevier, 1986. hard. 1 vol. 1,240 pp. index. ISBN 0-444-00807-1. $95. dictionary.
PE1693.D4 423.1′19

The *Abbreviations Dictionary* "features over 23,000 new and augmented entries, along with expanded and updated treatment of many previous topics, including multilingual geographical equivalents, nicknames and pseudonyms, names of diseases, gemstones and common chemicals, nicknames of American states and their flowers, [etc.]. . . . New addenda cover the following topics: Bafflegab (euphemisms), British and Irish County Abbreviations, Citizen's Band Call Signs. . . . International Vehicle License Numbers, Numbered Abbreviations, Prisons of the World and Their Toponyms. . . . and much more." (*JAL,* March 1986, p. 52)

"Most of the new entries seem to be for acronyms and initialisms, as are many of the numerous new definitions for entries that were in earlier editions. . . . [T]here are many nicknames and eponyms (e.g., *Age of Anxiety* for Bernstein's Symphony No. 2, *Iron Lady* for Margaret Thatcher) and geographic equivalents (e.g., *Middle East, Pacific Northwest*). . . . [I]t will be a good addition for libraries . . . that get frequent requests for help in unraveling shortcut expressions." (*BL,* June 1, 1986, p. 1443)

Also reviewed in: *Econ Bks,* March 1986, p. 68; *New Tech Bks,* December 1986, p. 668.

Board's recommendation: Public, academic, and school libraries.

A Dictionary of Catch Phrases: American and British from the Sixteenth Century to the Present Day, rev. edition. Eric Partridge. Stein & Day, 1986. hard. 1 vol. 384 pp. ISBN 0-8128-3101-2. $24.95. dictionary.
PE1689.P297 427.09

"Despite the title, [*A Dictionary of Catch Phrases*] is not confined to 'catch phrases' . . . but also includes '. . . greetings, toasts, exclamations, exhortations, . . . invitations, jokes and puns, cliches, misquotations, modern proverbs, adages and maxims, euphemisms, and vulgar idioms.' . . . This revision of the 1977 edition continues 2,500 of the more than 4,000 original entries unchanged, while 1,200 have been augmented or amended. Nearly 1,800 are new entries, most of which are based on notes that Eric Partridge made before his death in 1979. Beale has greatly enhanced this volume with many more keyword cross-references than were included in the original edition. . . . [T]his dictionary can be recommended for most reference collections, especially in public libraries." (*Choice,* March 1987, p. 1034)

Also reviewed in: *GW,* January 19, 1986, p. 21; *LATBR,* December 14, 1986, p. 10; *NYT,* January 2, 1987, p. 18; *Sch Lib,* May 1987, p. 174.

Board's recommendation: Public libraries.

The Dictionary of Cliches. James Rogers. Facts On File, 1985. hard. 1 vol. 320 pp. index. ISBN 0-8160-1010-2. $24.95. dictionary.
PE1689.R65 423.1

The Dictionary of Cliches "looks at some 2,000 'over-used and under-appreciated expressions' . . . defining each in terms of contemporary use and exploring its origin and history. The cliches are arranged alphabetically by first keyword, and the discussions, ranging from two lines to a paragraph, are both informative and readable. They are followed by an Index of Cross References, e.g., from *pale, beyond the* to *beyond the pale.*

"The result [of Rogers's work] is an interesting, indeed illuminating, compilation that school, public, and academic libraries ought to consider." (*BL,* May 1, 1986, p. 1292)

Also reviewed in: *ARBA,* 1986, p. 411; *CSM,* May 2, 1986, p. 24; *JQ,* Summer 1986, p. 431; *Kliatt,* Spring 1987, p. 32; *Ref Bk R,* 1986, p. 21; *WLB,* January 1986, p. 63.

Board's recommendation: Public, academic, and school libraries.

The Nonsexist Word Finder: A Dictionary of Gender-Free Usage. Rosalie Maggio. Beacon Pr., 1989. soft. 1 vol. 224 pp. ISBN 0-8070-6001-1. $9.95. dictionary.
PE1689.M23 423

The Nonsexist Word Finder lists approximately "3,000 words and phrases alphabetically, stating why they are considered sexist or, in some instances (e.g., timothy grass, jackdaw, Manichaeism), that they are not . . . [and providing] suggestions for alternative usage.

"[Maggio has] compiled a dictionary and handbook that will help writers 'scrap outdated, stereotypical, and unrealistic sexist terminology.' . . . Appendix A, 'Writing Guidelines,' a 22-page article on writing in a nonsexist way . . . provides much practical advice along with specific examples, such as the awkward area of letters salutations. The main word list, with its multiple suggestions for alternative usage is a thought-provoking thesaurus. . . . The more controversial expressions are discussed at length, with cross-references either within the dictionary or to the essays in the appendix. . . . [this] is more than a practical tool: it is also a highly readable and excellent sociolinguistics text." (*BL,* February 15, 1988, p. 984)

Also reviewed in: *ARBA,* 1988, p. 429; *CC,* August 3, 1988, p. 712; *Choice,* January 1988, p. 748; *Emerg Lib,* January 1988, p. 42; *R & R Bk N,* February 1988, p. 14; *WLB,* December 1987, p. 95.

Board's recommendation: Public, academic, and school libraries.

Picturesque Expressions: A Thematic Dictionary, 2d edition. Laurence Urdang, Walter W. Hunsinger, and Nancy LaRoche, eds. Gale, 1985. hard. 1 vol. 770 pp. index. ISBN 0-8103-1606-4. $84. dictionary.
PE1689.P5 428.3′19

Picturesque Expressions "is thematic in the sense that it lists and describes locutions under topical or generic terms, alphabetically arranged.

"The second edition is greatly enlarged: it now covers some 7,000 expressions; hence the likelihood of a particular locution's being discussed is very much enhanced. In addition, there is now an opening display of headings used plus a great many cross-references, e.g., 'Mourning see Grieving'—a change that will facilitate searches, as will the fact that the revised index cites item numbers. . . . An informative . . . compilation, it should be considered for school, public, and academic libraries." (*BL,* June 15, 1986, p. 1520)

Also reviewed in: *ANQ,* January 1986, p. 86; *ARBA,* 1987, p. 402.

Board's recommendation: Public, academic, and school libraries.

The World's Major Languages. Bernard Comrie, ed. Oxford, 1987. soft. 1 vol. 1,025 pp. illus. ISBN 0-19-506511-5. $29.95. handbook.
P371.W6 409

The World's Major Languages is "an excellent survey of some of the world's languages . . . The book is well edited, and in general very clear and readable. Tables and diagrams are useful and straightforward. The index in such a reference book is all-important, and this one is quite good." (*Choice,* February 1988, p. 888)

"The articles illuminate members of the better-known families, including Uralic, Turkic, Dravidian and Indo-European, as well as a selection of lesser-known tongues such as Thai, Vietnamese, Tagalog, Swahili, and many others." (*TLS,* January 15–21, 1988, p. 67)

Also reviewed in: *ARBA,* 1988, p. 419; *LJ,* September 15, 1987, p. 75; *Lon R Bks,* January 7, 1988, p. 22; *R & R Bk N,* Summer 1987, p. 26; *TES,* May 22, 1987, p. 27.

Board's recommendation: Public and academic libraries.

New and Noteworthy

The Cambridge Encyclopedia of Language. David Crystal. Cambridge, 1990. hard. 1 vol. 472 pp. illus. ISBN 0-521-26438-3. $49.50. encyclopedia.
P29.C64 403

"*The Cambridge Encyclopedia of Language* gives a straight, narrative account of language variety, history, structure, and behavior. Where did language come from? How many languages are there? Are some languages better than others? How do we learn our first language, or a second language? *The Cambridge Encyclopedia of Language* is carefully designed to answer these and other questions about language. . . . This celebration of language is made lively by over 300 illustrations and 30 maps. . . ." (Excerpted from publisher's announcement)

Thesaurus of American Slang. Robert L. Chapman, ed. Harper & Row, 1989. hard. 1 vol. 489 pp. index. ISBN 0-06-016140-X. $22.50. thesaurus.
PE2846.C465 427.973

The *Thesaurus of American Slang* lists " 'over 17,000 zippy synonyms for thousands of alphabetically arranged slang words. . . .' Groups of semantically related words are gathered under one chosen as the lead or entry term. For example, *blooper, boo-boo, goof-up, snafu* and 28 other terms are listed under *boner,* defined as 'A blunder; an egregious mistake.' Parts of speech are indicated by abbreviations." (*BL,* February 15, 1990, p. 1190)

Joseph Holub

Latin American History

See also World History

Many of the reference works essential to Latin American history also cover other disciplines. Latin Americanists of all disciplines have long pooled their resources because Latin America has sometimes been viewed as marginal to the dominant focus of each discipline and, more importantly, because of the difficulty in obtaining information from and about Latin America. Thus, Latin Americanists since 1935 have produced the premier serial bibliography for all disciplines, the HANDBOOK OF LATIN AMERICAN STUDIES, and, since 1975, *HAPI, the Hispanic American Periodicals Index.* Indexes and bibliographies not specific to the region should not be ignored, however, especially *Historical Abstracts,* which has the two advantages of being available on-line and of having greater currency than *HAPI* or HANDBOOK OF LATIN AMERICAN STUDIES. These three titles, plus the standard humanities and social sciences indexes, provide wide bibliographic coverage adequate for most contemporary research needs.

In any case, all reference collections should have

Core Titles

	PUBLIC	ACADEMIC	SCHOOL
The Cambridge Encyclopedia of Latin America and the Caribbean Collier, Simon, Harold Blakemore, and Thomas E. Skidmore, eds. Cambridge, 1985	✦	✦	
The Cambridge History of Latin America, 6 vols. Bethell, Leslie, ed. Cambridge, 1984–1986		✦	
Handbook of Latin American Studies Martin, Dolores Moyano, ed. Univ. of Texas Pr., annual (1979–)		✦	
South America, Central America, and the Caribbean, 2d edition Europa, 1987	✦	✦	

some retrospective bibliographies, such as Charles C. Griffin, LATIN AMERICA: A GUIDE TO THE HISTORICAL LITERATURE, which is selective and annotated. There are also subject-specific and country-specific bibliographies, as well as bibliographies of bibliographies, most notably those produced by Arthur E. Gropp and published by Scarecrow Press that cover material up to 1979. Probably the best source for selective, annotated bibliographies is the multivolume CAMBRIDGE HISTORY OF LATIN AMERICA, in which every chapter is accompanied by a bibliographical essay.

Historical surveys other than those in general encyclopedias and one-volume histories on Latin America can be found in THE CAMBRIDGE ENCYCLOPEDIA OF LATIN AMERICA AND THE CARIBBEAN. THE CAMBRIDGE HISTORY OF LATIN AMERICA mentioned earlier, provides lengthier and more scholarly treatment of historical subjects, serving as a bridge to the specialized literature. An encyclopedia employing an alphabetical arrangement, which necessarily provides less of a historical overview than THE CAMBRIDGE ENCYCLOPEDIA but more names and facts, is Helen Delpar's *Encyclopedia of Latin America* (McGraw-Hill, 1974). Unfortunately, this title is currently out of print, but it should remain on the library shelves if it is already owned. Scarecrow Press publishes historical dictionaries of individual countries, most of which date from the early 1970s, that provide even more names and facts, and some append bibliographies or listings of heads of state. A new biographical dictionary that covers nineteenth- and twentieth-century figures is on the supplementary list (BIOGRAPHICAL DICTIONARY OF LATIN AMERICAN AND CARIBBEAN POLITICAL LEADERS).

Non-discipline-specific sources are essential to research in Latin American history, providing not only historical information but also additional data and context that inform historical understanding. A standard reference work, an annual that dates back to 1924, is the SOUTH AMERICAN HANDBOOK. An excellent source for statistics for individual countries that also provides historical, political, and economic background information is the annual two-volume EUROPA WORLD YEAR BOOK (see Current Events), or its one-volume version for Latin America that appears on the core list: SOUTH AMERICA, CENTRAL AMERICA, AND THE CARIBBEAN. The latter is probably the easiest source to use for demographic and economic data. More historical time-series data—though still emphasizing current data—can be found in a supplementary title, the STATISTICAL ABSTRACT OF LATIN AMERICA, published since 1955 by the Latin American Center at the University of California, Los Angeles. Volume 27 of the series was published in 1989.

Information on the history of Latin America is relatively accessible, in large part because of the innovative work in developing reference sources undertaken by Latin Americanists from all disciplines. Indeed, with the exception of Europe and the United States, no other region is so well served by its reference sources.

Core Titles

The Cambridge Encyclopedia of Latin America and the Caribbean. Simon Collier, Harold Blakemore, and Thomas E. Skidmore, eds. Cambridge, 1985. hard. 1 vol. 456 pp. illus. index. ISBN 0-521-26263-1. $49.50. encyclopedia.
F1406.C36 980.003.21

The Cambridge Encyclopedia of Latin America and the Caribbean serves admirably as a one-volume introduction to Latin America that generally does not compromise detail, analysis, or good writing. Indeed, there is no other book that covers so much material so effectively.

The encyclopedia is not unlike Cambridge's other major Latin American reference work, THE CAMBRIDGE HISTORY OF LATIN AMERICA, in that it aims at comprehensiveness and offers articles by a large number of contributors (68). Indeed, the encyclopedia treats more briefly many of the same topics that receive extended treatment in the history, though the history section is one of the longest in the encyclopedia.

That the encyclopedia is a British product is even clearer than in the case of THE CAMBRIDGE HISTORY; the preponderance of British contributors is far greater. Of the three general editors, two, Simon Collier and Harold Blakemore, are affiliated with British universities. The third, Thomas Skidmore, is American. All three are distinguished scholars. Most of the other contributors, however, do not enjoy the international stature characteristic of THE CAMBRIDGE HISTORY's contributors. There is little to criticize in their work, however.

The encyclopedia covers far more than history; it attempts to survey every conceivable topic, such as the press, cinema, literature, and language. The six main sections are "The Physical Environment," "The Economy," "The Peoples," "History," "Politics and Society," and "Culture." Each of these contains divisions and, often, subdivisions. For example, "History" is divided chronologically into such periods as "America Before Columbus," "The Colonial Period," and so on. The section "Latin America Since Independence" is further divided regionally, with essays on individual countries (as with Mexico, Chile, and Brazil) or on two or more countries considered together (as with Peru and Bolivia). Each of these individual articles is signed and followed by a bibliography of a few titles that are intended as a spur to further reading.

The articles are generally excellent. Especially impressive are those on the less traditional subjects, such as folk and popular music, Amerindian music, theater and cinema, radio and television, and science. Though some of these articles are too brief, the effort and the achievement are admirable. On the other hand, one might argue that some major topics, such as indigenous peoples, are not treated as extensively as others. Also, because the work lacks an introduction, the editors' intentions for this encyclopedia are not obvious to the user. For example, the fact that the work is not organized as an alphabetical listing may frustrate patrons accustomed to the traditional, alphabetically arranged encyclopedia. Therefore, if one is looking for a brief biography, the details of a treaty, or the historical role of a Latin American city, Helen Delpar's *Encyclopedia of Latin America* (McGraw-Hill, 1974), now out of print, may be a preferred source.

Both black-and-white and color photographs add to the attractiveness of the volume and provide significant illustrations of the text, especially with such subjects as geography. In addition, there are over 50 maps, some in color, which are clear, accurate, and useful. The fine index and a select glossary add to the accessibility of the reference. The layout of the work, plus the book's compact size, make it appealing and easy to use.

The Cambridge Encyclopedia of Latin America and the Caribbean is essential to academic and public reference collections. The sophisticated writing, however, would make it difficult for most younger readers. The Board recommends this work for the core collections of public and academic libraries.

The Cambridge History of Latin America. Leslie Bethell, ed. Cambridge, 1984–1986. hard. 5 vols. illus. index. ISBN 0-521-24517-6 (vol. 5). $87.50 (vol. 5). history.
F1410.C1834 980.2'19

Five of the projected eight volumes of *The Cambridge History of Latin America* have now appeared. Unlike other Cambridge histories, these volumes have appeared in chronological order. Thus volumes 1 and 2, which cover the conquest of Latin America and colonial period, appeared in 1984. (While the history of indigenous cultures is given some attention in these first volumes, another Cambridge series will focus exclusively on them.) Volume 3, covering independence to about 1870, was published in 1985; volumes 4 and 5, chronicling the years 1870 to 1930, were published in 1986. The remaining three volumes will carry the history from 1930 to the present.

The Cambridge histories as a whole attempt to survey their respective subjects as widely as possible by offering a large number of articles and companion bibliographical essays written by specialists. Each specialist presents a comprehensive view of a particular subject, which is intended to smoothly synthesize facts and the latest research. Inasmuch as Cambridge University Press enlists highly regarded scholars worldwide, the overall product is inevitably of high quality. The representation is truly international, although English-speaking, particularly British, historians predominate.

The history is a massive work. Each volume runs 600 to 1,000 pages and contains 15 to 20 articles. The text is followed by the bibliographical essays at the end of the volume, which could be the most important pieces in the book for students or researchers. The articles usually run 30 to 50 pages, the bibliographical essays about 5. Each volume has its own index, which does not reference citations in the bibliographical essays.

Each theme is treated within political and geographical boundaries, as well as chronological limits. For the preindependence period, the political division is between Spanish America on the one hand and Brazil on the other. Because of Brazil's importance and distinct historical experience, it receives considerable space. With the independence period, a number of articles develop the histories of the major states separately. Some states are considered together (Venezuela, Colombia, and Ecuador are one group, and the Central American countries another). Even smaller nations, such as Haiti, Santa Domingo, and Puerto Rico, are given attention.

Editor Leslie Bethell wanted to stress postindependence history, in part as a corrective to traditional emphases on the colonial and independence periods and in part to emphasize the research of the past 20 years. Thus, more than anything else, the history is a work by scholars for scholars. Bethell explains that it should serve as a "solid base for future research." While the novice or nonprofessional is not the primary audience for this *Cambridge History,* those new to the field can certainly read the work with profit. For example, David Rock's two articles about early twentieth-century Argentina are as easily and more quickly read than that author's own full-length history of the period. It makes sense for a student to read the appropriate *Cambridge History* chapters before moving to long monographs and specialized journal articles. Also, since each article stands on its own, it can be a pleasure for the casual reader with an interest in Latin America to read one or more chapters at random. The chapters, in fact, are so effective that Cambridge has repackaged some of them into paperback format.

It should be kept in mind that the text is the thing in *The Cambridge History.* There are not many maps, tables, or footnotes, and no photographs. The reference is not the first source a newcomer to the field would use, but it is essential for those who need to deepen their knowledge of some part of Latin American history. As a touchstone in historical scholarship, the work is essential for all academic and most public libraries.

The Board recommends this work for the core collection of academic libraries.

Handbook of Latin American Studies. Dolores Moyano Martin, ed. Univ. of Texas Pr., annual (1979–). hard. indexes. ISBN 0-292-73038-1. $65. handbook.
Z1605.H23 016.98

The *Handbook of Latin American Studies* is a selective, annotated, annual bibliography that was first published in 1935. Since 1964 separate volumes for the humanities and the social sciences have appeared in alternate years. A humanities volume (containing works on art, folklore, history, language, literature, music, and philosophy) comes out in even-numbered years; the social sciences volume (with works on anthropology, economics, education, geography, government and politics, international relations, and sociology) is published in odd-numbered years. This reference is the single most important bibliographic serial publication for Latin American studies; there is nothing comparable published anywhere else in the world.

The handbook was developed by Latin Americanists because older resources in their respective disciplines did not treat Latin American material adequately. First published under the auspices of the Committee on Latin American Studies for the American Council of Learned Societies, the work has been sponsored by the Library of Congress since 1943. The contributors are distinguished academicians, with the overwhelming majority of them affiliated with research institutions in the United States.

In recent years each issue of the handbook has contained between 750 and 900 pages that index and annotate between 7,500 and 8,500 publications. The editor's note (of about five pages) that follows the table of contents reviews new directions in the areas of scholarship examined in that issue, notes the state of publishing in various countries, and discusses new features of the handbook's format as well as changes in personnel.

The handbook proper begins with a section devoted to "Bibliography and General Works," which is followed by individual sections for each discipline. In some cases there will be an essay of one to four pages that highlights publication and research trends in the field as a whole. Yet, within every discipline there are essays for the major subfields and, often, for the subsequent divisions within the subfields. Thus, in volume 49 (1989), there is no introduction in the anthropology section to the annotations of articles and books of a general nature, but there are essays, each signed by one of the volume's approximately 50 contributing editors, that precede the annotations for the various subfields of anthropology: Mesoamerica, the Caribbean area, and South America. Within ethnology there are essays for Middle America, the West Indies, the South American highlands, and the South American lowlands.

Each field is divided differently, depending on the traditions of the discipline and the notions of the editor. Thus anthropology is subdivided first into disciplines, which are sometimes further divided geographically. On the other hand, the major divisions in economics are geographical. In any case, all fields receive some level of analysis with respect to research trends and the nature of the current literature.

The annotations to cited publications are concise, running from at least 40 words to over 100. The section for each discipline concludes with a list of journal abbreviations used. At the end of each volume is an "Indexes" section that includes abbreviations and acronyms, a title list of journals indexed, a subject index, and an author index.

Though this reference is a selective bibliography, a great number of journals are covered (between 400 and 600 in recent years). This thoroughness pervades every aspect of the work. The indexes are quite comprehensive and provide "see" references; the annotations are clearly written and helpful; and the essays can deepen one's understanding of a particular field.

The handbook's major weakness is its lack of currency, because of the alternate-year structure and the size and detail of each volume. Frequently, annotated articles date from five years before the volume's publication date. Since there is often no alternate source more current than the handbook (though on-line indexes are beginning to appear), the delay can be especially frustrating to researchers and can reduce the value of the analysis of scholarly trends. Nonetheless, the *Handbook of Latin American Studies* is essential for larger research libraries and for most smaller college libraries. The Board recommends this work for the core collection of academic libraries.

South America, Central America, and the Caribbean, 2d edition. Europa, 1987. hard. 1 vol. 683 pp. illus. ISBN 0-946653-39-9. $140. history.
F1406.5.S687 980.219

The second edition of *South America, Central America, and the Caribbean,* derived from the London-published EUROPA WORLD YEAR BOOK (see Current Events), provides an excellent introduction to the political economy of the region and its individual countries. The emphasis is on the contemporary situation within an international context. The book's essays provide historical background, but the level of detail concerning recent events is far greater. More importantly, the reference is filled with facts. The strength of the book lies in its statistical and directory sections, which list the political and economic names as well as data on all aspects of the region.

The first of the volume's three parts is "Background to the Region." The six essays that begin the section are by noted British scholars and specialists: Robin Chapman on the economy; Harold Blakemore on dictatorship and democracy; Kenneth N. Medhurst on the church and politics; George Philip on the role of petroleum and other minerals; P. A. R. Calvert on Central America; and Colin Clarke on the Caribbean. These are fine, succinct (about five pages each) essays that provide an overview on the state of Latin America, yet still offer considerable detail. An informative 24-page discussion of each of the region's major commodities follows, providing both scientific and commercial data on such items as coffee, sugar, and tin, plus tables with production figures for individual Latin American countries and other world producers. The next two sections list, respectively, institutes all over the world that focus wholly or in part on Latin America, and approximately 100 periodicals that deal with Latin American topics. Though obtainable elsewhere, such information is especially convenient and easy to access in this volume.

Part 2, "Regional Organizations," lists both United Nations agencies in Latin America and groups formed through regional accords, such as the Organization of American States, the Andean Group, and the Central American Common Market. A summary of the organization's purpose, its address, and the names of its top officials are provided for each group. Entries are no more than two pages in length; for some organizations only addresses are listed.

Part 3, "Country Surveys," constitutes more than 80 percent of *South America, Central America, and the Caribbean.* For all except the smallest countries, each country listing contains short essays on history and the economy (the essay on the economy is invariably longer, though never more than seven pages). Next, the "Statistical Survey" provides many tables with demographic data, including the population of each state or province; a breakdown of the workforce; figures on the production of farm, industrial, and mineral products; national finances; trade; transport; tourism; communications; and education. The "Directory" describes the constitution and government and gives the names and addresses of such people and organizations as ministers, political organizations, embassies, supreme court judges, newspapers and periodicals, publishers, radio and television stations, banks, insurance companies, chambers of commerce, and various governmental agencies involved in transportation, power, tourism, atomic energy, and defense. A short but sometimes inadequate bibliography concludes each essay.

South America, Central America, and the Caribbean is clearly a very useful work, although there are some minor drawbacks, such as the bulky size and the lack of an index. The latter is not essential in a work of this type, however. More significant is the fact that most of the critical statistical and directory information is already available and in more current form in the EUROPA WORLD YEAR BOOK. The first edition of *South America, Central America, and the Caribbean* appeared in 1986. The additional material in this second edition is attractive but hardly essential. In terms of quantity the material unique to this volume amounts to not much more than 15 percent of its nearly 700 pages. Thus, if a collection already receives EUROPA annually, it may be difficult to justify adding a work that duplicates it. For libraries wishing to focus on Latin America, however, this is a useful book. The Board recommends this work for the core collections of public and academic libraries.

Supplementary Titles

Biographical Dictionary of Latin American and Caribbean Political Leaders. Robert J. Alexander, ed. Greenwood, 1988. hard. 1 vol. 509 pp. index. ISBN 0-313-24353-0. $75. encyclopedia.
F1414.2.B48 972.9′009

The *Biographical Dictionary of Latin American and Caribbean Political Leaders* "contains approximately 450 signed biographical sketches covering . . . nineteenth- and twentieth-century political figures in 41 countries and territories of Latin America and the Caribbean. . . . The entries—varying in length from a few lines to three or four pages—emphasize the political significance of the biographees, giving . . . details on their political careers, family backgrounds, education, and . . . nonpolitical activities. These evaluative essays conclude with selected bibliographies citing . . . sources in English, Spanish, and Portuguese. . . . Appendix A is a chronology of . . . events in the region from 1804 to 1985. Appendix B lists entries by country or territory.

"All in all, [this work] . . . will serve scholars and students of Latin American and Caribbean affairs well, whether they are patrons of academic or large public libraries." (*BL,* November 1, 1988, p. 460)

"A subject/name index and a listing of names by country facilitate use of the book. Information about 19th-century figures from the better-known countries is readily found elsewhere, but biographies of 20th-century political leaders, particularly from the less-studied Caribbean and Central American nations, make the book worthwhile. Subsequent editions would benefit from having the name of the country included as part of the format. . . . Because it provides useful information in a convenient single volume, this title should be acquired by libraries that need more than rudimentary reference information about Latin America." (*Choice,* December 1988, p. 622)

Also reviewed in: *ARBA,* 1989, p. 250; *CRL,* January 1989, p. 84.

Board's recommendation: Academic libraries.

Cuba, 1953–1978: A Bibliographical Guide to the Literature. Ronald H. Chilcote, ed. and comp. UNIPUB-Kraus International, 1986. hard. 2 vols. 1,387 pp. illus. appendix. index. ISBN 0-527-16824-6. $295. bibliography.
Z1511.C48 016.97291'064

Cuba, 1953–1978: A Bibliographical Guide to the Literature is "an impressive compilation of more than 25,700 items focusing on the first 25 years of the Cuban Revolution. . . . The main focus is on materials relating to the revolution and to the revolutionary processes including the history, politics, economics, and contemporary social conditions of the period. . . . Entries include books, articles, pamphlets, letters, press conferences, and speeches.

"Following a lengthy and informative introduction the bibliography is conveniently divided into 68 separately numbered chapters in ten general sections. Some of the most extensive chapters describe: history and biography (2,296 citations), literature and the creative arts (1,233 citations), education and youth (1,178 citations), and Cuban relations with the US (769 citations). The final six chapters focus on the revolutionary leadership of Ernesto 'Che' Guevara and Fidel Castro. . . .

"The bibliography is an extremely rich guide to scarce materials on the revolution, including clandestine materials covering 1953–58 housed in Havana. A 47-page appendix gives an annotated list of Cuban newspapers and periodicals." (*Choice,* October 1986, p. 276)

Also reviewed in: *ARBA,* 1987, p. 65; *HAHR,* August 1987, p. 530.

Board's recommendation: Academic libraries.

Latin America: A Guide to the Historical Literature. Charles C. Griffin, ed. Univ. of Wisconsin Pr., 1971. hard. 1 vol. 700 pp. index. ISBN 0-299-08220-2. $35. bibliography.
Z1601.G75 016.98

Latin America: A Guide to the Historical Literature "is a selective annotated bibliography compiled by 37 qualified contributors, chiefly professors of Latin American history in North American universities. Seven broad sections include a valuable bibliography of bibliographies, guides to manuscripts, biographical, geographical, and statistical sources, and encyclopedias, followed by a general section further subdivided by individual countries. The other five parts cover the field chronologically. . . . The descriptive and often critical annotations are augmented by introductions to the various sections which set forth criteria for selection of titles, or note the characteristics of and outstanding contributors to the literature of a period or country." (*WLB,* June 1972, p. 928)

"A final chapter deals with materials on inter-Hispanic American relations since 1830. . . . Coverage is through 1966. . . . The detailed table of contents serves in lieu of a subject index; an author index is provided. This is a useful compilation for the researcher in Latin American history." (*CRL,* July 1972, p. 326)

Also reviewed in: *Choice,* September 1972, p. 791; *Choice,* June 1981, p. 1386.

Board's recommendation: Academic libraries.

South American Handbook. Howell Davies, ed. Wilson, annual. soft. 1 vol. 842 pp. index. ISBN 0-13-826249-7. $29.95. handbook.
F1401.S71 016.98

"[The] *South American Handbook* [is] an excellent guidebook intended for travelers but containing much information of interest to a more general audience. It is a notable source of information about small cities, as well as about the obvious larger cities and capitals. In addition to the usual listings of accommodations and tourist attractions, it includes information on geography, history, communications, holidays, local festivals, and similar topics. These features combined with sections devoted to exchange rates, climatic tables, distance tables, and maps of city centers and regions enhance the general reference potential of this publication." (*Choice,* June 1981, p. 1377)

"Current, compact and packed with reliable information, the *South American Handbook* . . . is a most valuable vademecum for travelers south of the border. The subtitle 'a traveller's guide to Latin America and the Caribbean' clarifies its scope. Earlier editions did not include the Caribbean area. 'South America' in British usage refers to all of the Western Hemisphere except Canada and the United States.

"[The book] . . . has a table of contents, general hints about valuable health information and a brief introduction to the history of Latin America and its people. . . . A mini index on the first page of each country's entry provides easy access to specific sections of information. A brief bibliography, a list of British-Latin American organizations, Diners Club, American Express, and Travellers Cheques Offices and an index of place names are worthwhile inclusions." (*RSR,* October/December 1980)

Also reviewed in *ARBA,* 1980, p. 275; *GW,* March 8, 1975, p. 22; *NY,* July 25, 1977, p. 80; *Obs,* May 12, 1974, p. 39; *TES,* September 4, 1981, p. 35.

Board's recommendation: Public, academic, and school libraries.

Statistical Abstract of Latin America. UCLA Latin America Center Publication, annual. soft. 1 vol. 639 pp. ISBN 0-87903-249-9. $150. bibliography.
HA931.C3

"The *Statistical Abstract of Latin America* is an annual publication summarizing the demographic, social, economic, and political statistics country by country. A bibliography cites the sources from which the data were derived, including the statistical publications of international, government, and private agencies, so that the user needing more detailed information can go to the source." (*Choice,* June 1981, p. 1376)

This volume is a comprehensive "listing of statistics from national and international sources, as well as statistics generated by UCLA researchers. [It contains approximately] 700 tables, vast coverage of subjects, including foreign trade, prices, balance of payments, national accounts, population data, religions (including Catholic and Jewish population), plus several essays on different topics." (*CLW,* November 1983, p. 178)

Also reviewed in: *APSR,* June 1967, p. 552.

Board's recommendation: Academic libraries.

New and Noteworthy

The Dictionary of Contemporary Politics of South America. Phil Gunson. Macmillan, 1989. hard. 1 vol. 314 pp. illus. index. ISBN 0-02-913145-6. $35. dictionary.
JL1851.A25G86 980.03

The Dictionary of Contemporary Politics of South America focuses "primarily on the period since 1950 in the 12 independent republics and one overseas department in South America. . . . [The work] includes almost 400 entries on virtually every important aspect of the political scene. Brazil draws the most attention with 55 entries, while French Guiana has the fewest with 5. An index of entries by country facilitates finding this information. Biographical sketches of most presidents since 1950 are included, as are discussions of major political parties and movements, important trade unions, guerrilla groups, and economic movements." (*BL,* November 1, 1989, pp. 602–603)

Peoples of the World: Latin Americans. Joyce Moss and George Wilson. Gale, 1989. hard. 1 vol. 323 pp. illus. index. ISBN 0-8103-7445-5. $39.95. bibliography.
F1408.3.M84 980

"The stated purpose of . . . [*Peoples of the World*] is to present descriptions of 'the different groups in this area of the world [not] currently available to the average reader.' Information for the 62 cultural groups represents 'a compilation of field studies, source material, and original research on peoples of South America, Central America, and the Caribbean.' Entries are arranged alphabetically by the name of the group. Each gives population, location, and languages spoken. This is followed by a brief essay of 5–9 pages that discusses geography, history, and the culture today—economy, food, religion, recreation, government, etc." (*BL,* January 15, 1990, pp. 1045–1046)

Rachelle Moore

Latin American Literature

See also Spanish and Portuguese Literature; World Literature

Latin American literature is an immense subject area that incorporates different geographic regions and their diverse histories, centuries of evolution, productivity in all literary genres, and a tradition of criticism and interpretation that today includes a cadre of international scholars. Appropriately, laypersons, students, researchers, and librarians have at their disposal a wide range of reference materials that have been published in English in the United States. These titles began to emerge around the mid-1970s, paralleling the event in Latin American literary history known as "The Boom." This term has been used to describe the rise in popularity of Latin American literature in the United States and Europe over a relatively short period of time.

Without question, David W. Foster, a scholar at Arizona State University, is the leader in the field of reference materials on this topic. Of the 13 core titles reviewed, Foster is responsible for almost two-thirds, including a handbook, two author references, and five bibliographies. Three other worthwhile titles by Foster, *Argentine Literature: A Bibliography of Secondary Sources* (Garland, 1989), *Chilean Literature: A Working Bibliography of Secondary Sources* (G. K. Hall, 1978), and *Dictionary of Contemporary Latin American Authors* (Center for Latin American Studies, 1975), were chosen by the Board as core titles but are no longer in print and, therefore, not reviewed. However, they are recommended for purchase if they ever become available through reprint or are issued as revised editions.

In addition to Foster's works, this core collection includes literary histories and general handbooks. They support all levels of research interest in South America, Central America, Mexico, and the Caribbean. The literary histories provide concise yet informative surveys of the unique national traditions. One additional such title, now out of print, was selected by the Board for the core collection: Leonard Klein's *Latin American Literature in the Twentieth Century: A Guide* (Ungar, 1985). Another work, focused on the Caribbean, was also voted to the core list but is also now out of print: Page and Roh's *Selected Black American, African, and Caribbean Authors: A Bio-Bibliography* (Libraries Unlimited, 1985).

Two more general supplementary titles are now out of print as well. The first is *Manual of Hispanic Bibliography,* second edition (Garland, 1977), prepared by Foster, the master bibliographer. The second is Enrique Anderson-Imbert's two-volume overview of the field, *Spanish American Literature: A History* (Wayne State Univ. Pr., 1963). Two other supplementary titles now out of print would provide greater depth for spe-

Core Titles

GENERAL	PUBLIC	ACADEMIC	SCHOOL
Handbook of Latin American Literature Foster, David W., comp. Garland, 1987	✦	✦	
Latin American Literary Authors: An Annotated Guide to Bibliographies Zubatsky, David. Scarecrow, 1986		✦	
Latin American Writers, 3 vols. Solé, Carlos A., ed. in chief. Scribner, 1989	✦	✦	
Modern Latin American Literature, 2 vols. Foster, David W., and Virginia Ramos Foster, comps. and eds. Ungar, 1975		✦	
A Sourcebook for Hispanic Literature and Language: A Selected Annotated Guide to Spanish, Spanish-American, and Chicano Bibliography, Literature, Linguistics, Journals, and Other Source Materials, 2d edition Bleznick, Donald W., comp. Scarecrow, 1983		✦	
The 20th Century Spanish-American Novel: A Bibliographic Guide Foster, David W., comp. Scarecrow, 1975		✦	
CENTRAL AND SOUTH AMERICA			
Dictionary of Brazilian Literature Stern, Irwin, ed. Greenwood, 1988	✦	✦	
A Dictionary of Contemporary Brazilian Authors Foster, David W., and Roberto Reis, comps. Center for Latin American Studies, Arizona State Univ., 1981		✦	
Mexican Literature: A Bibliography of Secondary Sources Foster, David W., comp. Scarecrow, 1981		✦	
Peruvian Literature: A Bibliography of Secondary Sources Foster, David W., comp. Greenwood, 1981		✦	
CARIBBEAN			
Cuban Literature: A Research Guide Foster, David W., comp. Garland, 1985		✦	
Fifty Caribbean Writers: A Bio-Bibliographical Critical Sourcebook Dance, Daryl Cumber, ed. Greenwood, 1986		✦	
Puerto Rican Literature: A Bibliography of Secondary Sources Foster, David W., comp. Greenwood, 1982		✦	

cific geographic areas. They are Carlos Pena's *History of Mexican Literature* (Southern Methodist Univ. Pr., 1968) and Brice King's *West Indian Literature* (Shoe String, 1980). An index to more general titles that would be accessible to the nonspecialist is now, unfortunately, out of print. Freudenthal and Katz's *Index to Anthologies of Latin American Literature in English Translation* (G. K. Hall, 1978) provides references to material that would appeal to patrons who cannot read Spanish but are interested in this growing body of world-class literature.

Patrons may also want to consult some reference tools that deal with the more specialized topics of Latin American literature. Herbert Hoffman has prepared two valuable indexes. The two-volume *Latin American Play Index* (Scarecrow, 1983, 1984) was voted to the core list. *Hoffman's Index to Poetry: European and Latin American Poetry in Anthology* (Scarecrow, 1985) was judged by the Board to be a valuable supplementary title. Good coverage of primary and secondary sources on drama can be further achieved by acquiring the BIBLIOGRAPHY OF LATIN AMERICAN THEATER CRITICISM, a supplementary title, or by obtaining a copy of *Spanish Theatre: An Annotated Bibliography* (G. K. Hall, 1987), now out of print.

Since many titles provide only superficial coverage of women authors, and this topic continues to attract scholarship, the supplementary title WOMEN WRITERS OF SPANISH AMERICA: AN ANNOTATED BIO-BIBLIOGRAPHIC GUIDE will become indispensable. Another often neglected group of writers is the subject of a title that has gone out of print: *Afro-Spanish American Authors: An Annotated Bibliography* (Garland, 1980).

As with so many reference titles representative of the categories mentioned earlier, currency of information poses a problem. Serial publications such as the *Modern Language Association Bibliography* and the *Hispanic American Periodical Index* can be used in conjunction with all these titles in order to ensure comprehensiveness. They are also helpful in locating material on the narrowly focused subject matter that does not receive in-depth coverage by the core titles.

Core Titles

General

Handbook of Latin American Literature. David W. Foster, comp. Garland, 1987. hard. 1 vol. 300 pp. index. ISBN 0-8240-8559-0. $50. handbook.
PQ7081A1.H36 809.898

The *Handbook of Latin American Literature* is a collection of national literary histories. The work is clearly a key resource for anyone with a beginning interest in an overview of Latin American literature, the development of the literary tradition of each Latin American country, or the role of particular authors in these traditions. While the handbook is primarily aimed at general readers and non-Hispanists, it is also useful for students and researchers in need of specific information.

The literary histories, unique contributions by different scholars, are arranged alphabetically by country and are followed by an author index. The compiler, David Foster, indicates in the preface that these histories aim to illustrate the national literatures as internally coherent traditions in order to counteract the tendency to view Latin American literature as a single entity.

All essays are rich in detail, yet concise and well written for easy reading. The contributing writers present the main literary trends of each country from early periods to the present and highlight the works of important writers in a social, cultural, and very often a political context. Because of this broad time frame, the strong traditions are discussed in a manner that promotes comparison to more contemporary topics. For example, the essay on Argentina written by Naomi Lindstrom traces issues from the early nineteenth century, when the concept of civilization preoccupied many writers, to the present day, with its focus on women writers. With regard to feminist criticism, Lindstrom discusses relatively new authors, such as the poet Alejandra Pizarnik, and how they can generate a new interest in the poets of the past, such as Maria Elena Walsh and Alfonsina Storni.

The handbook also reflects the increased attention that Cuban writers are currently receiving. Matías Montes Huidobro presents an excellent essay on their role in Cuban literary history. Students will find a great deal of information on postrevolution Cuban literature, as well as mention of recent writers associated with exile and dissidence.

The bibliographic information offered in this book gives the user an opportunity to pursue the literary traditions of a country or a particular author. Preceding the actual country histories is an excellent annotated bibliography of the seminal sources on Latin American literary history. Also, titles of the works of the individual authors mentioned within the essays are provided in their original language and in English translation, along with the dates of publication. In addition, each country history is followed by a brief annotated bibliography that covers introductory sources pertinent to that country.

The *Handbook of Latin American Literature* should be one of the first sources consulted in the search for concise overviews. The Board recommends this work for the core collections of public and academic libraries.

Latin American Literary Authors: An Annotated Guide to Bibliographies. David Zubatsky. Scarecrow, 1986. hard. 1 vol. 332 pp. ISBN 0-8108-1900-7. $35. bibliography.
Z1609.L7Z82 016.86'08'098

Latin American Literary Authors: An Annotated Guide to Bibliographies serves a variety of purposes for people working in the field of Latin American literature. For example, researchers and students interested in specific authors should consider using *Latin American Literary Authors* at the very beginning of their search strategy. As indicated in the preface, this is an annotated bibliography of personal bibliographies, which are defined as bibliographies of a writer's works, works about the writer, and works about the writer's works.

Approximately 1,300 authors who span the time period of colonial to contemporary literature are included in an alphabetical arrangement. The term *author* is broadly interpreted; users will find bibliographic information on essayists, journalists, linguists, and literary critics, as well as on writers of novels, short stories, poetry, and drama. Works of writers in exile in Latin America are excluded.

The alphabetical-by-author arrangement only assists users who have specific authors in mind and already possess some knowledge about them. This guide would be more useful if the compiler had either provided a brief biographical abstract for each author, or had arranged the authors by country or literary time period. Consequently, patrons new to Latin American literature should review other sources before using this one.

As for content, *Latin American Literary Authors* has citations for material that appears in periodicals, books, dissertations, and festschrift volumes. It also indexes some of the major bibliographies, such as David W. Foster's series, Angel Flores's *Bibliografia de escritores Hispanoamericanos (Bibliography of Hispanic Writers)* and Richard Jackson's *Afro-Spanish American Authors.* Other major bibliographies, such as Walter Rela's *Guía bibliographica de la literature Hispanoamericana (Bibliographic Guide to Hispanic Literature),* are not indexed. It is difficult, however, to make an assessment of the bibliographies that are indexed, since we are not given information on criteria employed for selection. In addition, the annotations for the bibliographic material are somewhat spotty, but they provide enough information to determine coverage and arrangement where appropriate.

In addition to personal bibliographies, this title has a section on general bibliographies that are relevant to Latin American literature. These are arranged alphabetically by author or by country where appropriate. The annotations for these titles are very good in directing users to a wealth of information.

As part of a core academic reference collection, librarians will find *Latin American Literary Authors* useful for evaluating their collection of access tools for Latin American literature. This reference should also be considered a primary source for those engaged in or thinking about compiling their own bibliographies on a subject related to Latin American literature. The Board recommends this work for the core collection of academic libraries.

Latin American Writers. Carlos A. Solé, ed. in chief. Scribner, 1989. hard. 3 vols. 1,497 pp. ISBN 0-684-18463-X. $250 (set). biographical dictionary.
PQ7081.A1L37 860.9′98

Latin American Writers is a three-volume collection of individual essays on 149 representative writers from Spanish America and 27 from Brazil. According to the editors, the primary goal in presenting these writers is to offer a panoramic view of Latin American literary history from the colonial era to the present. Intended for the English-speaking world, this work is useful for a broad audience that includes researchers, students, and the general public.

The authors are presented in chronological order according to their date of birth and represent a variety of literary genres—the chronicle, poetry, theater, prose fiction, and the essay. Since the editors have included only those considered to be the major voices of Spanish-American and Brazilian literature, users will find only one or two from Costa Rica, the Dominican Republic, Ecuador, El Salvador, Guatemala, Honduras, Nicaragua, Panama, and Paraguay.

Volume 1 begins with a lengthy and informative preface on the purpose and scope of *Latin American Writers.* The criteria used for selecting these writers are not discussed in detail. The editors merely mention that they considered the body of evaluation that literary critics have placed on the works of these writers. The preface is followed by a 42-page introduction that provides a solid background and context for the essays. It portrays the evolution of Spanish-American and Brazilian literature as a whole with analytical comments on specific themes and major literary movements. After the last essay in volume 3, there is an index, a list of the writers in alphabetical order by their native country, a list of the authors in alphabetical order with their birth and death dates, and a list of the contributors with their home institution and the name of the author or authors they wrote about.

The index is worth noting, as it is the key means for accessing information. The index is comprehensive and useful, containing a host of events, movements, titles, and influencing themes associated with the writers. The table of contents only contains the names of the writers in the order in which they appear in each volume.

The essays vary in length but tend to be consistent in format, tone, and style. They combine biographical details with an analysis of the writers' contribution to Latin American literature and the sociohistorical influences that motivated them. An author's works are discussed separately yet evaluated in their totality. To assist the English-speaking audience, parenthetical English translations follow the first mention of a Spanish or Portuguese title. If the English title appears in italics, the work exists in translation. The publication dates given are those of the original language titles.

Even though there is a wealth of evaluative and interpretative material on such writers as Carlos Fuentes, Gabriel García Márquez, and Julio Cortázar, the essays devoted to them are fresh and concise and provide good background material for those embarking on in-depth studies. For many other writers—such as Bartolomé de la Casas, José Mármol, Marco Denevi, and Severo Sarduy—this is a unique reference source for a discussion of their works with a sociohistorical focus. The essays on Rosario Castellanos, Griselda Gambaro, and Luisa Valenzuela are also highly recommended because they project these women writers into the mainstream of contemporary Latin American literature as opposed to giving them token treatment.

At the end of each essay are two select bibliographies. One contains the writer's work in chronological order grouped by genre, important editions, and notable translations into English. The other contains biographical and critical studies. In the citations for monographic material, the name of the publisher is omitted.

Latin American Writers provides wide-ranging coverage of Latin American literature with a unique focus. The Board recommends this work for the core collections of public and academic libraries.

Modern Latin American Literature. David W. Foster and Virginia Ramos Foster, comps. and eds. Ungar, 1975. hard. 2 vols. 1,047 pp. index. ISBN 0-8044-3139-6. $120 (set). criticism.
PQ7081.F63 860.9

Modern Latin American Literature is a collection of excerpts of critical and interpretive commentaries on the works of 137 twentieth-century authors. These commentaries were originally published in a variety of international sources and represent the core scholarship on Latin American literature to 1975. As with Foster's other reference works published in the mid-1970s, his purpose is to provide testimony to the growing importance of Latin American literature.

The commentaries are in two volumes, arranged alphabetically by author. Each volume begins with two lists of who is included: one list is alphabetical by name, and the other list is by country. The authors included have played a prominent role in the development of Latin American literature and have attracted serious research and scholarship. The latter criterion resulted in the omission of some famous authors such as Miguel Barnet, Reinaldo Arenas, and Ernesto Cardenal because they had not as yet received a body of criticism at the time of publication. Patrons interested in women authors will find commentaries on only eight; therefore, they should be directed to more current sources such as the HANDBOOK OF LATIN AMERICAN LITERATURE. Those who are interested in the giants such as José Donoso, Carlos Fuentes, Jorge Luis Borges, and Julio Cortázar will find several commentaries, though they may need to consult the *MLA Bibliography* if more current material is needed.

About one-half of the critical excerpts come from English-language sources (American and British), while most of the remainder are translations from the Spanish or Portuguese. There are also a few excerpts representing other European languages. All critics and their corresponding authors are listed in the index of critics at the end of volume 2.

Modern Latin American Literature remains a vital part of an academic library's reference collection in spite of its date of publication. It can save librarians and students a considerable amount of time in tracking down critical and interpretive material on the key authors of Latin America.

The Board recommends this work for the core collection of academic libraries.

A Sourcebook for Hispanic Literature and Language: A Selected Annotated Guide to Spanish, Spanish-American, and Chicano Bibliography, Literature, Linguistics, Journals, and Other Source Materials. 2d edition. Donald W. Bleznick, comp. Scarecrow, 1983. hard. 1 vol. 304 pp. indexes. ISBN 0-8108-1616-4. $27.50. bibliography.
Z2695.A2B55 016.86

With an increase of 384 entries for a total of 1,412, revised bibliographic data, and a new chapter covering Chicano bibliographic information and language, the second edition of *A Sourcebook for Hispanic Literature and Language* is an excellent annotated resource for the overall study of Hispanic literature. The coverage for Latin America is equally as good as that for Spain. Students and scholars can refer to the work for a variety of research needs. Librarians can use it as a tool for collection development and evaluation.

As the well-outlined table of contents indicates, the sourcebook includes a wide range of monographic material divided into 16 categories. The categories especially useful to students and scholars are: general bibliographic guides and references, bibliographies of Hispanic literature, literary dictionaries and encyclopedias, histories of Hispanic literatures, a Chicano bibliography, and a bibliography of literature in translation. The books chosen for inclusion are basic to the subject area and, therefore, would be important for most middle- and large-sized academic libraries.

The annotations, although brief, are very useful and provide information on the coverage of authors in bibliographies and anthologies where appropriate. Arrangement is enhanced by the comprehensive title and author indexes that follow the last section.

Librarians can use the sourcebook as a collection evaluation tool. The section on literary dictionaries and encyclopedias, as well as the one about bibliographies of Hispanic literature, is useful for evaluating reference collections. Titles in other relevant sections can be used for evaluating various areas of the circulating collection. The sections on scholarly periodicals and selected publishers and book dealers can be of assistance to acquisitions librarians and bibliographers.

Of course, there is always the problem of currency with reference tools of this nature, and the sourcebook is no exception. According to the preface, the cutoff date for inclusion of materials is 1982. Therefore, several titles may be out of print, journals may have ceased publication, and new journals may have emerged. Lack of currency may also be true of names listed in the section of publishers and book dealers, although the major ones are still going strong and have diversified their services.

However, the sourcebook continues to be a core title for academic libraries serious in their efforts to provide a comprehensive reference service and collection development in the area of Hispanic literature. The various categories in *A Sourcebook for Hispanic Literature and Language* establish a good overview of fundamental material for students, researchers, and librarians. The Board recommends this work for the core collection of academic libraries.

The 20th Century Spanish-American Novel: A Bibliographic Guide. David W. Foster, comp. Scarecrow, 1975. hard. 1 vol. 227 pp. index. ISBN 0-8108-0871-4. $20. bibliography.
Z1609.F4F68 016.863

The 20th Century Spanish-American Novel: A Bibliographic Guide is one of the many guides compiled by David Foster in the area of Latin American literature. The focus of this bibliography is the novel, perhaps the most important and popular genre of Latin American literature. The term *novel* is used in its broadest sense and includes, where appropriate, material on the novella.

The first section of *The 20th Century Spanish-American Novel* lists 18 general bibliographies on Latin American literature. The second section is devoted to general monographic studies on the novel and studies on the novel as associated with specific countries.

The main section of the bibliography lists critical and interpretative references for 56 novelists. According to Foster, the novelists covered are those most commonly studied in the United States. One can find such notables as Gabriel García Márquez, Carlos Fuentes, and Mario Vargas Llosa. With the exception of Rosario Castellanos and Beatriz Guido, however, women authors are not represented. If Foster had had the insight to broaden his criteria to include more women (who were already generating more interest at the time of this publication), this guide would have more value today.

The material listed for the authors that are included is classified according to bibliographies, books, and critical essays (journal articles). This format is similar to that employed in other bibliographies by David Foster and is suitable for browsing or specific inquiry. Material such as dissertations, journalistic and short reviews, and nonnovelistic studies of an author's works has been omitted.

David Foster's contributions to Latin American literature, as both a scholar and a bibliographer, have resulted in a rich collection of reference material for college and university libraries. *The 20th Century Spanish-American Novel* is more than 15 years old, yet it is an excellent place to begin the study of one of the most popular and respected genres of Latin American literature. The Board recommends this work for the core collection of academic libraries.

Central and South America

Dictionary of Brazilian Literature. Irwin Stern, ed. Greenwood, 1988. hard. 1 vol. 402 pp. index. ISBN 0-313-24932-6. $65. dictionary.
PQ9506.D53 869.09'981

The *Dictionary of Brazilian Literature* will no doubt become a classic reference for the field. It provides an excellent overview of the literature throughout the centuries within the necessary sociocultural context of the country. This latter coverage is so often missing in similar reference titles that users are not given the opportunity to view the literary tradition alongside other important national forces.

In compiling all the information and viewpoints provided in this dictionary, Stern has brought together a variety of well-known scholars who are amply identified in the "Contributors" section. The term *dictionary* hardly seems appropriate for all the material students, researchers, and librarians will find covered here. The reference is more like an encyclopedia since it includes a map of Brazil; chronologies of Brazilian literature,

Brazilian history, and foreign literature; bibliographical references; an introduction to Brazilian literature in a cultural perspective; and a glossary of frequently used Brazilian words.

The main body of the reference is a collection of 300 entries on Brazilian writers, literary schools, and related sociocultural movements in the literary history of Brazil, arranged in alphabetical order. The final section is a comprehensive index of authors, keywords, and phrases.

Before using the dictionary, readers are advised to read both the preface, for a comprehensive statement on coverage, arrangement, and methodology, and the introduction, which sets an excellent foundation for assessing the actual entries. The author entries contain a combination of biographical information with a discussion from a critical perspective. They also contain references to specific works, giving not only title and date of publication, but also the English translation. A very brief bibliography of critical sources with all bibliographic information is provided at the end of each entry.

The entries on literary schools and sociocultural literary movements are excellent. Readers new to Brazilian literature will find them especially useful as introductory and background material. Librarians will find them useful for collection development, selection, and evaluation as specific titles are discussed within the context of a particular theme. Some examples of these entries are: *dictatorship and literature, film and literature, modernism, new writers, slavery and literature,* and *travel literature.* Specific titles cited in these sections, however, do not mention the publishers, but they do have the date of publication and an English translation of the title. Many sources, such as journal titles and anthologies, whether mentioned in these entries or in the author entries, are in abbreviated format. Users must refer to the section on "Bibliographic References" for the explanation of the abbreviations.

Intended for the English-reading population, the *Dictionary of Brazilian Literature* is a vital tool for those at all levels of experience. The Board recommends this work for the core collections of public and academic libraries.

A Dictionary of Contemporary Brazilian Authors. David W. Foster and Roberto Reis, comps. Center for Latin American Studies, Arizona State Univ., 1981. hard and soft. 1 vol. 152 pp. ISBN 0-87918-051-X. $18.95 (hard); $11.95 (soft). dictionary.
PQ9506.F6 869

In contrast to the avid interest received by the literature of other South American countries, Brazilian literature has not been studied to any great extent in the United States. However, the rich literary tradition of Brazil cannot be ignored in the overall analysis of South American literature. To inspire a breakthrough, David W. Foster and Roberto Reis have compiled *A Dictionary of Contemporary Brazilian Authors.*

The authors included were alive at the time of publication. Two notable exceptions are Jõao Guimarães Rosa and Manuel Bandeira, who have made such significant contributions that they could not be ignored. For those living authors, individuals who had not received wide acclaim were nonetheless included if they had published at least one book of notable importance.

Arranged in alphabetical order by author, the entries were written by several well-known international literary scholars. Even though these entries are the work of many writers and may have been translated into English by Foster, they are consistent in quality and focus. Each entry provides general information about the author's role in the contemporary literature of Brazil, includes some discussion of individual works, and pinpoints the author's specific importance. At the end of each entry the principal works of the author are listed. These citations are incomplete, however, as the publisher is omitted.

Since this dictionary is ten years old, it does lack currency with respect to works published since 1981 and to the appearance of new authors on the Brazilian literary scene. Patrons may consult such current sources as the *Modern Language Association Bibliography* and *Hispanic American Bibliographic Index* for up-to-date information to supplement the dictionary.

The lack of currency and incomplete citations do not detract from the importance of this resource. *A Dictionary of Contemporary Brazilian Authors* is in the forefront of reference materials on Brazilian literature and is an excellent supplement to Foster's *Dictionary of Contemporary Latin American Authors* (now out of print).

The Board recommends this work for the core collection of academic libraries.

Mexican Literature: A Bibliography of Secondary Sources. David W. Foster, comp. Scarecrow, 1981. hard. 1 vol. 386 pp. index. ISBN 0-8108-1449-8. $32.50. bibliography.
Z1421.F63 016.860'9'972

Bibliographies that cover the critical and interpretative material of a Latin American country's literary traditions are vital components of a core reference collection. *Mexican Literature: A Bibliography of Secondary Sources* is still current enough to satisfy most academic research and study needs. However, patrons would need to be directed to the very up-to-date sources such as periodical indexes to make their investigation complete. (This is the case for all subject bibliographies in this category.)

The patron should approach this bibliography by reading the preface first. It is an excellent statement of the book's purpose and leaves no uncertainties as to its coverage. This coverage includes studies on a number of topics associated with Mexican literature and 50 authors of significant renown, such as poet Octavio Paz and novelist Carlos Fuentes. Novices to Mexican literature should consult Foster's HANDBOOK OF LATIN AMERICAN LITERATURE before using this bibliography in order to gain background information and develop a perspective. Users will notice that *Mexican Literature* gives adequate coverage to many themes and authors that are included in the HANDBOOK.

The first section of this bibliography, called "General References," organizes the material into various chapters with headings that represent historical periods, genres, or facets of Mexican literature. Examples of these headings are colonial prose fiction, general studies on poetry, women authors, and twentieth-century drama. However, they do not follow any immediately perceivable classification scheme, which causes some confusion, resulting in the user's relying heavily on the table of contents.

It is advisable to check the chapter on "Bibliographies" for titles that will be useful for in-depth research. This chapter contains over 100 bibliographies that cover a variety of general and specific categories associated with the publication output of Mexico, such as catalogs of archives and libraries, journals in the field of the humanities, and regional publications of a given time period.

The second section of *Mexican Literature* is devoted to critical and interpretive studies on Mexican authors. The authors are listed in alphabetical order. The citations are subdivided into bibliographies, critical monographs and dissertations, and critical essays (that is, journal articles). This division facilitates access for those who are looking for a particular kind of reference work. One drawback is that the journal titles are in abbreviated form; therefore, the user has to constantly refer to the abbreviation key. Also, several of these journals may not be part of a library's collection (especially those which are small or of medium size).

The last section of *Mexican Literature* is an alphabetically arranged index of the authors of all these studies.

The Board recommends this work for the core collection of academic libraries.

Peruvian Literature: A Bibliography of Secondary Sources. David W. Foster, comp. Greenwood, 1981. hard. 1 vol. 324 pp. index. ISBN 0-313-23097-8. $46.95. bibliography.
Z1861.F67 016.860'9'985

Peruvian Literature: A Bibliography of Secondary Sources contains critical and interpretive studies on many aspects of Peruvian literature and on 38 noted authors from Martin Adán to Mario Vargas Llosa. Although published in 1981, the work is still current enough to be a central resource for research and study. Indexes such as the *MLA Bibliography* can be used for publications since 1981. Patrons who are new to the field of Peruvian literature should consult the HANDBOOK OF LATIN AMERICAN LITERATURE for more recent background material.

The preface of *Peruvian Literature* is very useful and gives excellent details on coverage and methodology.

The first section of this bibliography is called "General References." The material included is organized into various chapters with headings that represent genres, facets, or historical periods of Peruvian literature. Examples of these headings are colonial drama, twentieth-century poetry, women authors, and special topics in prose fiction. However, they do not follow any immediately perceivable classification scheme, which causes confusion, resulting in a heavy reliance on the table of contents.

The first chapter, "Bibliographies," is especially useful for in-depth research as it contains 47 bibliographies that cover a variety of general and specific categories associated with the publication output of Peru, such as catalogs of libraries containing Peruvian material, regional publications of a given time period, and literature.

The second section of *Peruvian Literature* is devoted to critical and interpretive studies on Peruvian authors, listed in alphabetical order. The special feature here is that the citations are subdivided into bibliographies, critical monographs and dissertations, and critical essays (that is, journal articles). This division facilitates access for those who are looking for a particular kind of reference work. One drawback to this bibliography is that journal titles are cited in abbreviated form. This forces users to constantly refer to the abbreviation key. Also, several of these journals may not be part of a small or midsized library's collection.

The final section of the bibliography is an alphabetically arranged index of the authors of all these studies.

Peruvian Literature and the other Foster bibliographies have made major contributions to the bibliographic control of the literary history and interpretation of Latin American literature. The Board recommends this work for the core collection of academic libraries.

Caribbean

Cuban Literature: A Research Guide. David W. Foster, comp. Garland, 1985. hard. 522 pp. index. ISBN 0-8240-8903-0. $88. bibliography.
Z1521.F694 016.86′09′97291

Cuban Literature: A Research Guide is the last in a series of bibliographies on the literature of individual Latin American countries compiled by David W. Foster. Between 1978 and 1982, David Foster compiled bibliographies for Argentina, Chile, Mexico, Peru, and Puerto Rico. They all follow the same format and methodology; together they can be considered touchstones in bibliographic control. Many have found their way into the Board's recommended core collection.

The preface should be consulted before using the guide proper for it provides some background on Cuban literature as well as information on the characteristics of the bibliography itself.

The first section of *Cuban Literature,* called "General References," is devoted to citations on general topics such as twentieth-century prose fiction, relations with foreign literatures, and general literary histories. Even though Foster has accomplished a high degree of comprehensiveness on these topics, they do not seem to have an apparent order or classification scheme. Users should examine this section carefully to determine areas of relevance for particular research needs. As is pointed out in the preface, Foster includes material of an academic or critical nature but does not include journalistic presentations.

The second section contains material on 98 Cuban authors. The authors are arranged in alphabetical order; the resource material is arranged by the subdivisions of bibliographies, critical monographs and dissertations, and critical essays (journal articles).

In dealing with the situation of writers who are in exile, Foster wisely chose to include individuals who were born and raised on the island, such as novelist Reinaldo Arenas. However, these authors are included only if they have written in Spanish; therefore, users will not find José María de Heredia, considered a French-language author. The only exception here is María Mercedes Santa Cruz, who also wrote in French. Foster includes her because of the large amount of criticism in Spanish on her works and because of Foster's desire to represent key women authors. It is important to note that Foster has aimed for accurate and balanced representation with factors such as publisher, place of publication, and interpretation of social history considered irrelevant.

The last section is an alphabetical index of critics whose material is included in the bibliography. Even though this section is not vital, in combination with similar sections in the other Foster bibliographies, it gives students and researchers an opportunity to determine the major contributors to Latin American literary history and interpretation.

Cuban Literature: A Research Guide is rather expensive but worth the investment for academic libraries. As Communist countries continue to draw attention in the area of social and political change, interest in Cuba will no doubt continue. The Board recommends this work for the core collection of academic libraries.

Fifty Caribbean Writers: A Bio-Bibliographical Critical Sourcebook. Daryl Cumber Dance, ed. Greenwood, 1986. hard. 1 vol. 530 pp. index. ISBN 0-313-23939-8. $67.95. biobibliography.
PR9205.A52F54 810.9′9729

Fifty Caribbean Writers: A Bio-Bibliographical Critical Sourcebook covers 50 major Caribbean authors of the nineteenth and twentieth centuries, excluding those from the Spanish-speaking countries and Haiti. Therefore, the title is somewhat misleading. Nevertheless, the user can expect to find excellent essays on the authors included, written by a variety of international scholars in the field of Caribbean literature. Information on these scholars can be found in the last section of the book. Those new to this subject area should consult the preface as it provides a very good overview of Caribbean literature and an orientation to the role played by these authors.

Arranged in alphabetical order, the author essays are intended to introduce a wide range of important figures from the pioneers to those who have recently entered the literary scene. One useful feature of these essays is the subdivision or categorization of information. Each essay has a brief biography, a lengthy critical review of major works and themes, an evaluative survey of selected scholarship, and a bibliography of primary and secondary sources. This arrangement allows for an in-depth reading, brief review, or casual browsing.

The author essays are followed by a bibliography of general sources. Although this bibliography is small, it does cover some important survey material in monograph format. An index of names, subjects, and titles also adds to the accessibility of this reference.

No academic library reference collection that aims to provide resources on the literature of the English-speaking Caribbean should be without *Fifty Caribbean Writers.* It is useful for ready-reference questions as well as for introductory material on Caribbean literature. The Board recommends this work for the core collection of academic libraries.

Puerto Rican Literature: A Bibliography of Secondary Sources. David W. Foster, comp. Greenwood, 1982. hard. 1 vol. 232 pp. index. ISBN 0-313-23419-1. $40.95. bibliography.
Z1557.L56F67 016.860'09'97295

Puerto Rican Literature: A Bibliography of Secondary Sources is similar in format to the bibliographies on Peru, Mexico, and Cuba also compiled by David Foster. Even though Puerto Rican literature is one of the major literatures of the Caribbean, Foster's bibliography is the only one that provides coverage for critical and interpretive studies on many of its famous authors. It also gathers together studies on various topics associated with Puerto Rican literature. The preface of *Puerto Rican Literature,* as with that of all of Foster's bibliographies, is excellent and provides useful information on specific coverage and methodology.

The material included in the first section, "General References," is organized into chapters with headings that represent genres, facets, or historical periods of Puerto Rican literature. Examples of these headings are women authors, general studies on the essay, special topics in drama, and twentieth-century poetry. As with other Foster bibliographies, these chapters do not follow any immediately perceivable classification scheme. Thus users will need to rely a great deal on the table of contents for direction.

The chapter on "Bibliographies" is especially useful for in-depth research as it contains 36 bibliographies that cover a variety of general and specific categories associated with the publication output of Puerto Rico, such as journals and newspapers, materials on specific libraries, and literature.

The second section of *Puerto Rican Literature* is devoted to critical and interpretive studies on Puerto Rican authors. They are listed in alphabetical order; the citations are subdivided into bibliographies, critical monographs and dissertations, and critical essays (journal articles). This division enhances accessibility for those who are looking for a particular kind of reference work. One drawback to this bibliography is that journal titles are cited in abbreviated form. As a result, users must constantly refer to the abbreviation key. Also, several of these journals may not be part of a small or midsized library's collection.

The final section is an alphabetically arranged index of the authors of all these studies.

Although *Puerto Rican Literature* was published in 1982, the bibliography is still current enough to be a central resource for research and study. The work provides comprehensive coverage of Puerto Rican literature. The Board recommends this work for the core collection of academic libraries.

Supplementary Titles

General

A Bibliography of Latin American Theater Criticism, 1940–1974. Leon F. Lyday and George W. Woodyard, eds. Univ. of Texas Pr., 1976. soft. 1 vol. 243 pp. index. ISBN 0-292-70717-7. $5.95. bibliography.
Z1609.D7L9 016.862

"Covering a thirty-five-year period that 'corresponds to the establishment and development of a truly national theater movement in most areas of Latin America' (Introd.), this useful bibliography lists some 2,300 items of Latin American theater criticism. Books, periodical articles (including book reviews), and doctoral dissertations are entered in an alphabetical arrangement by critical authors. . . . Brief explanatory notes or contents notes are provided for some items. A separate listing of bibliographies of Latin American theater precedes the numbered entries." (*CRL,* January 1978, p. 37)

"A topic and author index is provided for readers interested in a particular subject or playwright. The regional and national references that accompany the entries (in the right-hand margin) are helpful, but force the reader to peruse the entire volume when compiling entries on the drama of a specific country or region." (*HAHR,* November 1977, p. 783)

Also reviewed in: *ARBA,* 1979, p. 494; *Choice,* April 1977, p. 180.

Board's recommendation: Academic libraries.

Latin American Writers: A Bibliography with Critical and Biographical Introductions. Alok Bhalla. Envoy, 1987; distrib. by Apt Bks. hard. 1 vol. 174 pp. index. ISBN 0-938719-20-3. $22.50. bibliography.
PQ7081.3.B4 016.86'09'98

Latin American Writers "covers eighteen major Spanish-American literary figures. . . . Brazilian writers are not included. . . . The entry for each author includes a biographical and critical introduction, and bibliographies of the author's original works, his works in English translation, and criticism in English.

"The introductions combine biographical data . . . with rather subjective discussions of the philosophical or ideological viewpoints which inform the writer's literary efforts, and summaries of or comments on major works. The cut-off date for the accompanying bibliographies is about 1985, although a very few 1986 imprints were noted." (*ARBA,* 1989, p. 464)

Board's recommendation: Academic libraries.

A New History of Spanish American Fiction. Kessel Schwartz. Univ. of Miami Pr., 1971. hard. 2 vols. 436 pp. (vol. 1); 445 pp. (vol. 2). indexes. ISBN 0-87024-228-8. $37.90 (set). history.
PQ7081.834 863.009

Kessel Schwartz "has authored a rather monumental historiography of the Spanish American narrative [titled *A New History of Spanish American Fiction*]. . . . [T]his two-volume work is . . . [quite] current . . . , contains abundant information on the short story, and is one of the most amply documented works published recently. The approximately one hundred pages of notes, bibliographies, and indexes in each volume provide . . . an excellent reference tool.

"The subtitles of the two volumes indicate the scope of this study: *From Colonial Times to the Mexican Revolution and Beyond,* and *Social Concern, Universalism, and the New Novel.* . . . The first volume contains chapters on [such topics as] . . . 'Realism, Naturalism, Modernism,' 'Criollismo,' and 'The Novel of the Mexican Revolution.' The second volume has two chapters on . . . 'Public Service Literature' and four chapters on 'The New Novel,' with subdivisions largely geographical. . . .

"[The author] incorporates varied critical viewpoints from a vast array of books and journal articles but he never hesitates to present his own opinions based on lengthy experience in Hispanic literature.

"[In addition, he] does not neglect the production of the smaller countries. For instance, Acevedo Díaz, Reyles and Amorim, of Uruguay, are covered in some detail, as are L. A. Martínez, Pareja Diezcanseco, and Aguilera Malta, of Ecuador." (*Hisp,* May 1974, p. 379)

Also reviewed in: *Choice,* September 1972, p. 822; *Ga R,* Summer 1973, p. 284.

Board's recommendation: Academic libraries.

Outline History of Spanish American Literature, 4th edition. John E. Englekirk et al., eds. Irvington, 1981. soft. 1 vol. illus. ISBN: 0-89197-326-5. $12.95. history.
PQ7081.I52 860.9

Reviews of the first edition of the *Outline History of Spanish American Literature* noted that "*Outline* is divided into [chronologically arranged] sections. . . . Each section has an Introductory Summary, an essay which gives an over-all picture of the background to the literature produced within that chronological period." (*MLJ,* February 1966, p. 114)

"Not the least valuable of the book's features is the Bibliography . . . listing [over 300] volumes. It is select, comprehensive, and can serve as an excellent checklist for libraries. . . . [There are also specific] bibliographies following each author's entry. The volume's format is attractive, it is clearly printed, there is an adequate number of maps in both color and black-and-white, and the price is reasonable." (*Hisp,* December 1965, p. 958)

Also reviewed in: *ABC,* May 1965, p. 32; *Choice,* July 1965, p. 303.

Board's recommendation: Academic libraries.

A Selective Bibliography of Bibliographies of Hispanic American Literature, 2d edition. Shasta M. Bryant, comp. Univ. of Texas Pr., 1976. soft. 1 vol. 100 pp. indexes. ISBN 0-292-77522-9. $4.95. bibliography.
Z1609.L7B77 016.92008

Board's recommendation: Academic libraries.

Spanish American Writing Since 1941: A Critical Survey. George R. McMurray. Ungar, 1987. hard. 1 vol. 340 pp. index. ISBN 0-8044-2623-6. $24.50. criticism.
PQ7081.M373 860

In *Spanish American Writing Since 1941: A Critical Survey,* "McMurray systematically traces the recent development of Spanish American prose, poetry, and drama, first providing an in-depth analysis of the major authors and then a comprehensive, almost encyclopedic country-by-country rundown of the less influential ones." (*LJ,* July 1986, p. 86)

"The author provides biographical information and plot summaries along with critical observations on style, structure, and thematic content.

"The general reader will find this study very readable as literary history and of inestimable value as a reference source for quick identification of authors and works. It is the most current and comprehensive single-volume survey of its kind available." (*Choice,* September 1987, p. 133)

Also reviewed in: *ARBA,* 1988, p. 501; *MFS,* Winter 1987, p. 705; *WLT,* Spring 1988, p. 256.

Board's recommendation: Public and academic libraries.

Women Writers of Spanish America: An Annotated Bio-Bibliographical Guide. Diane E. Martin, ed. Greenwood, 1987. hard. 1 vol. 448 pp. ISBN 0-313-24969-5. $57.95. biography.
Z1609.L7W63 016.86'09'9287

Women Writers of Spanish America: An Annotated Bio-Bibliographical Guide "lists approximately 3,000 authors. Designed to serve a wide readership and arranged in English alphabetical order, the guide uses the most complete form of the author's name. Seventy-two contributors supplied annotations, . . . [and] the initials of each contributor appear after each entry. The work features authors of creative literature who were born in or lived in Latin America, *Chicanas* or women of Spanish-American background born in the United States, and other Hispanic women writers who write mainly in Spanish. Women whose works have hitherto appeared only in anthologies or journals have not been included as well as journalists and non-fiction writers. . . .

"Each entry includes biographical information, a list of works, and commentary when available." (*Ams,* April 1988, p. 505)

Also reviewed in: *ARBA,* 1988, p. 501; *Choice,* January 1988, p. 752; *R & R Bk N,* February 1988, p. 16.

Board's recommendation: Academic libraries.

Central and South America

An Annotated Bibliography of the Novels of the Mexican Revolution of 1910–1917. John Rutherford. Whitston, 1972. hard. 1 vol. 180 pp. ISBN 0-87875-071-7 $10. bibliography.
Z1424.F4R88 016.863'081

"The author [of *An Annotated Bibliography of the Novels of the Mexican Revolution of 1910–1917*], after summarizing standard definitions of the novel and, specifically, the term 'novels of the Mexican Revolution,' gives an extended list of authors of this genre. The short essays on the novelists are partly biographical; for each novelist . . . information on editions, translations, and criticism is furnished as well as brief summary and analysis of the novels themselves.

"Included in this bibliography are 146 titles which seem to represent a comprehensive collection of the novels in question. . . . The entire book (introduction and notes) is done in two equal parts, the text in English followed by the identical Spanish version, a method which makes the reference work useful to readers of either language." (*Choice,* November 1972, p. 1115)

Also reviewed in: *Ams,* July 1978, p. 127; *BL,* June 15, 1975, p. 1052; *BSA-P,* January 1973, p. 98; *HAHR,* November 1977, p. 785; *TLS,* September 22, 1972, p. 1093.

Board's recommendation: Academic libraries.

Marvelous Journey: A Survey of Four Centuries of Brazilian Writing. Samuel Putnam et al. Hippocrene Bks., 1948. hard. 1 vol. 265 pp. index. ISBN 0-374-96703-2. $20.50. history.
PQ9511.P8 869.09

Marvelous Journey: A Survey of Four Centuries of Brazilian Writing is a "charmingly written and excellent analytical history of Brazilian literature. . . . No more rewarding criticism can be found in English of the works of Cunha, Ramos, Freyre, Nabuco, and Amado." (*LJ,* June 1, 1948, p. 877)

"[The survey is] a fine and stimulating book, which works in a generous historical and social background, and manages to kindle in the reader a strong curiosity about Brazil's literary riches." (*NY,* June 19, 1948, p. 92)

"For the general reader [the book] relates Brazilian literature to a warm, sympathetic interpretation of the national life. Its meaty notes and bibliography make it also by far the most serviceable book in English for anyone who feels special interest in the subject." (*Yale R,* Winter 1949, p. 369)

Also reviewed in: *BL,* July 15, 1948, p. 378; *KR,* April 15, 1948, p. 206; *Nat,* October 2, 1948, p. 379; *NY Herald Tribune,* July 4, 1948, p. 1; *NYT,* July 25, 1948, p. 18; *SR,* July 31, 1948, p. 23.

Board's recommendation: Public and academic libraries.

Mexican American Literature: A Preliminary Bibliography of Literary Criticism. Mike Anzaldúa. Univ. of Texas Pr., Institute of Latin American Studies, 1980. soft. 1 vol. 34 pp. ISBN: 0-86728-004-2. $3.95. bibliography.

Mexican American Literature: A Preliminary Bibliography of Literary Criticism "is a good beginning for those embarking upon a course of Chicano history and culture. The author mentions certain caveats and constraints in his introduction, but the overall quality of the material is evident." (*Ams,* April 1981, p. 530)

Board's recommendation: Academic libraries.

Research Guide to Argentine Literature. David W. Foster and Virginia Ramos Foster. Garland, 1982. hard. 1 vol. 146 pp. index. ISBN 0-8240-9397-6. $145. bibliography.
Z1621.F22 016.86′09′982

Research Guide to Argentine Literature "is an attempt at organizing a guide to the criticism of Argentine literature and literary figures. It is primarily intended as a tool for the student of the field.

"The work is divided into four parts. Part I lists general bibliographic sources; Part II, journals publishing research on Argentine literature; Part III, general works on Argentine literature; and Part IV, articles and books about Argentine literary figures. Each part has various subsections.

"The most valuable part of the book is undoubtedly Part IV, which deals with individual Argentine literary figures. . . . All major figures as well as many 'minor' authors are included. Under the name of each author are listed all relevant works about the author and his works." (*CRL,* January 1972, p. 64)

"This latter section, which comprises most of the book, includes . . . 18th-, . . . 19th-, and . . . 20th-century writers. . . . The average author entry contains about 25 citations. . . . When they exist, English-language sources are included; but otherwise this is basically a guide to sources in Spanish." (*LJ,* June 15, 1970, p. 2247)

Also reviewed in: *ANQ,* May 1971, p. 138; *Choice,* October 1970, p. 1014; *CRL,* January 1971, p. 41; *MLJ,* March 1971, p. 189; *WLB,* June 1970, p. 1067.

Board's recommendation: Academic libraries.

Caribbean

Cuban Exile Writers: A Biobibliographic Handbook (published as ***Escritores de la diaspora Cubana: manual bibliografica***). Daniel C. Maratos and Marnesba D. Hill. Scarecrow, 1986. hard. 1 vol. 391 pp. index. ISBN 0-8108-1878-7. $42.50. biobibliography.
Z1520.M37 016.97291′064

Cuban Exile Writers: A Biobibliographic Handbook "focuses on the exiles, particularly the literature and criticism they have published outside Cuba since 1959. Biographies and bibliographies of 420 writers are provided. Biographical information was compiled from questionnaires sent to authors, supplemented by research in the Otto Richter Library of the University of Miami. Included are date of birth, educational background, academic affiliations, and date of exile from Cuba. Bibliographies list books and major critical reviews from periodicals. . . . Two essays complete the volume . . . [which is] a worthy contribution to the bibliography of Latin American literature." (*Choice,* January 1987, p. 746)

Note: The text is in both Spanish and English.

Board's recommendation: Academic libraries.

Lois Cherepon

Law

Law is a highly specialized and somewhat technical field that can be organized into three primary areas: statutory or legislative law, judicial or case law, and administrative law. The study of legal issues requires a researcher to access numerous materials, including statutes, court cases, and rules or regulations. The primary and secondary sources that support legal studies are often voluminous and costly, and the maintenance of these sources also requires tremendous amounts of time and effort from librarians. A certain degree of subject expertise is required to access legal resources, and collections need constant updating to reflect current changes in the law. Given these parameters, it is not surprising that most legal research is conducted in law libraries at law schools, courthouses, and law firms and that, given the choice, most librarians would prefer to send patrons with legal reference queries to the nearest law library. Yet a core collection of legal materials can prove valuable and essential to public, academic, and school libraries because patrons may need basic information about a specific legal issue.

The core collection includes the basic sources that the library should acquire. With law, the special uses applied to certain terms is an important consideration; thus, two legal dictionaries are valuable parts of the list of core titles. Encyclopedias of the law, the Constitution, or the U.S. legal system are important components of the core list as well. Many patrons will wish to consult THE GUIDE TO AMERICAN LAW, a 12-volume work that presents legal issues in terms intelligible to the layperson. The core collection is rounded out by the inclusion of works that contain the federal code, or the body of national laws. These works are appropriate for larger academic and public libraries. A valuable bibliographic work was originally voted by the Board for inclusion in the core collection of academic libraries but is now out of print: *American Legal Literature: A Guide to Selected Legal Resources* (Bernard Reams, Jr. et al., Libraries Unlimited, 1985).

Although many of the core legal materials reviewed in this section contain citations to law review articles, patrons may also need a source that provides subject access to current legal periodicals. H. W. Wilson has published the *Index to Legal Periodicals* since 1908. Issued monthly with quarterly cumulations, this index contains citations to over 400 English-language periodicals.

Another useful source not listed with the core reviews is *Supreme Court of the United States 1789–1980: An Index to Opinions Arranged by Justice* (Kraus International, 1983), edited by Linda A. Blanford and Patricia Russell Evans. Organized into seven categories, this source lists all U.S. Supreme Court decisions from 1789 to 1980. Landmark Supreme Court decisions are

Core Titles

	PUBLIC	ACADEMIC	SCHOOL
Black's Law Dictionary, 5th edition Black, Henry Campbell, Joseph R. Nolan, and M. J. Connolly. West Publishing, 1979	✦	✦	✦
Code of Federal Regulations, 4 vols. Office of the Federal Register, National Archives and Records Administration. Bowker, annual	✦	✦	
Congressional Quarterly's Guide to the U.S. Constitution: History, Text, Index, and Glossary Mitchell, Ralph. Congressional Quarterly, 1986	✦	✦	✦
A Dictionary of Modern Legal Usage Garner, Bryan A. Oxford, 1987		✦	
Encyclopedia of the American Constitution, 4 vols. Levy, Leonard W., ed. in chief, Macmillan, 1986	✦	✦	
Encyclopedia of the American Judicial System: Studies of the Principal Institutions and Processes of Law, 3 vols. Janosik, Robert J., ed. Scribner, 1987	✦	✦	✦
Fundamentals of Legal Research, 3d edition Jacobstein, J. Myron, and Roy M. Mersky. Foundation Pr., 1985	✦	✦	
The Guide to American Law: Everyone's Legal Encyclopedia, 12 vols. West Publishing, 1985	✦	✦	✦
Martindale-Hubbell Law Directory, 8 vols. Martindale-Hubbell, annual	✦	✦	
United States Code, 23 vols., 18 suppls. U.S.G.P.O., 1988	✦	✦	
United States Code Annotated, 224 vols. West Publishing, annual	✦	✦	

also cited in various other publications, such as: CONGRESSIONAL QUARTERLY'S GUIDE TO THE U.S. SUPREME COURT, the ENCYCLOPEDIA OF CRIME AND JUSTICE, and the two major legal encyclopedias, CORPUS JURIS SECUNDUM and AMERICAN JURISPRUDENCE SECOND. These four works are all supplementary titles.

Many legal sources are also available on-line through the two major legal data bases, LEXIS and WESTLAW. Libraries subscribing to either system need to budget for initial hardware expenditures and on-going subscription fees, which are both very costly. A basic legal collection should be able to accommodate most legal reference queries; therefore, computer services such as LEXIS and WESTLAW are best left to the legal professionals in law libraries.

Because the study of law often spans other subject areas, such as accounting, labor, and medicine, users may want to consult reviews in related areas for interdisciplinary materials. In addition to building a core collection of legal materials, librarians should also take advantage of the materials collected in U.S. government depository libraries. These collections are located throughout the country and offer users free access to many of the primary legal sources necessary for research.

Most of the sources reviewed in this section focus on administrative law. The connection between administrative and judicial law is tenuous, joined by cross-referencing from court cases to statutes. Libraries may want to consider collecting judicial reference sources, such as case reporters and case digests. Note that case reporters and digests are updated on a regular basis and require a tremendous amount of maintenance. In addition to federal administrative materials, state statutes should also be part of a core legal collection. A local law school library or county law library should be able to provide a list of core legal materials for the home state.

Also omitted from the list of reviews are the many

commercial looseleaf services, which provide a topical approach to specific areas of the law. Looseleaf services are convenient because they provide compilations of current statutes and cases, but inexperienced users may find them difficult to access. Additionally, looseleaf services are costly, represent an on-going expense for updating, and are labor intensive because they require regular filing and weeding by library staff.

Core Titles

Black's Law Dictionary, 5th edition. Henry Campbell Black, Joseph R. Nolan, and M. J. Connolly. West Publishing, 1979. hard. 1 vol. 1,511 pp. appendixes. ISBN 0-8299-2041-2. $22.95. dictionary. online.
KF156.B53 340.03

Black's Law Dictionary is a classic among legal dictionaries. The fifth edition contains over 30,000 alphabetically arranged entries, 10,000 of which are either new or revised. Most of the new material reflects recent changes in the law, especially in the areas of constitutional law, civil and criminal procedures, taxes, finance and uniform laws, and federal legislation. In the preface, the publisher cites a "major new feature" of the fifth edition: "the inclusion of pronunciation guides after all entries which pose pronunciation difficulties." Most of the pronunciation guides follow Latin or foreign words. New appendixes and additional entries covering federal acts, agencies, departments, and officials were also added to the fifth edition. *Black's Law Dictionary* provides definitions and pronunciation guides for U.S. and English jurisprudence terms and phrases of both modern and ancient usage and is a standard legal dictionary for ready reference.

The first edition of *Black's Law Dictionary,* published in 1891, was compiled by Henry Campbell Black, M. A. Throughout the years, this dictionary has undergone numerous changes. The fourth edition added the "Code of Professional Responsibility," the "Code of Judicial Conduct," and "An Outline of the Minimum Requirements for Admission to Legal Practice in the U.S." The fifth edition omits all three of these features and instead offers three new appendixes: the "Constitution of the United States," a "U.S. Government Organizational Chart," and a "Time Chart of the U.S. Supreme Court," which identifies justices throughout American history. The fifth edition includes two appendixes from the fourth edition, a "Table of Abbreviations" and a "Table of British Regnal Years." The appendixes make the dictionary useful for ready-reference queries by providing additional information.

The dictionary also contains an "Outline of Latin Pronunciations" and a "Guide to Pronunciation Symbols" intended to assist users with the numerous Latin and foreign words found throughout the text. The outline and the guide precede the main entries and are accompanied by a brief explanation of the three major systems of Latin pronunciation: reformed philological, Italianate, and Anglo-Latin. The publisher reminds the reader that "any attempt at 'correct' pronunciations of foreign terms can at best be only weak approximations," especially since the Latin and foreign phrases in the dictionary are drawn from a variety of sources spanning many centuries.

Many entries contain updated citations to judicial opinions or legislation. These citations substantiate the meaning of a given word or phrase by providing the user with additional legal references. For example, the entry for *abortion* cites the landmark U.S. Supreme Court case of *Roe* v. *Wade,* 410 U.S. 113, 93 S.Ct. 705, 35 L.Ed.2d 147. Readers unfamiliar with legal citations such as this could refer to the "Table of Abbreviations," which provides full titles of law reporters; law reviews; and federal agencies, departments, and officials. *Black's Law Dictionary* also includes explanations of legal maxims that are otherwise difficult to locate, such as "Equity follows the law."

Libraries anticipating heavy usage may want to invest in the higher-priced deluxe edition of *Black's Law Dictionary,* which is thumb-indexed and has sturdier binding than the standard hardcover edition. An online version of *Black's Law Dictionary,* fifth edition, is available through WESTLAW, West Publishing's legal data base. Libraries subscribing to WESTLAW should also own a print copy of the dictionary.

Black's Law Dictionary is a standard legal reference tool in most law libraries. The large print and numerous appendixes make this dictionary both convenient and useful for ready-reference collections. The Board recommends this work for the core collections of public, academic, and school libraries.

Code of Federal Regulations. Office of the Federal Register, National Archives and Records Administration. Bowker, annual. soft. 4 vols. appendixes. indexes. ISBN 0-8352-2808-8 (set). $550 (set). online. microfiche.
J1.A21

The *Code of Federal Regulations* (CFR), a federal document published by the U.S. Government Printing Office, is a voluminous set that compiles all the regulations adopted by federal agencies as printed in the daily edition of the *Federal Register* (U.S. Government

Printing Office). The codified version of the regulations arranges the information by title or broad subject area. Subjects range from "Health and Human Services" to "Transportation," and they change indiscriminately. Each of the 50 titles is further subdivided into chapters, subchapters, parts, and sections. Because the CFR is kept current by references to new, amended, or proposed rules and regulations in the *Federal Register,* one must subscribe to both publications. Without the *Federal Register,* the *Code of Federal Regulations* is an inadequate legal research tool, giving the user only part of the information needed.

The CFR is published in separate pamphlets, and each of the 50 titles is replaced annually according to a quarterly distribution schedule. In the "Explanation" prefacing each title of the CFR, the director of the Office of the Federal Register states that the CFR is "prima facie evidence of the text of the original documents." *Prima facie evidence* here indicates that when the language of the CFR differs from that of the official rule or regulation adopted by the agency, the original rule or regulation takes precedence. Therefore, the CFR is not a duplication of the original documents published in the *Federal Register.* Access to both of these sources is facilitated through the coordination of indexing terms. An in-house thesaurus developed by the Office of the Federal Register is used for indexing both publications.

The CFR's general index presents all 50 titles in the set by subject and agency. The index also includes various "Finding Aids," such as the "Parallel Table of Statutory Authorities and Agency Rules" and a list of CFR titles, chapters, and parts. Several commercially published subject indexes to the CFR are also available, and libraries with heavy usage may consider subscribing to additional indexes for the patron's convenience. The CFR also contains some agency-produced indexes for individual titles throughout the set. A cumulative list of these agency indexes is in the general index. The subject index refers the user to the specific title and part of the CFR needed to locate a regulation. The indexing terms are somewhat broad. For example, definitions an agency might list in a subchapter are not necessarily indexed in the CFR's subject index. For this reason alone, the easiest approach to locating specific rules and regulations is through the on-line version of the CFR available through LEXIS or WESTLAW.

An integral part of using the CFR is coordinating the 50 titles in the set with the new, amended, or proposed rules and regulations found in the *Federal Register.* The *List of CFR Sections Affected* (LSA) helps coordinate efforts between the code and the *Federal Register.* This monthly pamphlet informs the user which sections of the code have been changed by referring to new or amended rules and regulations. The *Federal Register* page numbers are listed to help the user quickly locate these changes. Proposed regulations appear at the end of the LSA.

The *Code of Federal Regulations* is an important tool for conducting federal legal research. However, only a library with adequate space and a staff able to coordinate the cross-references between the *Code of Federal Regulations* and the *Federal Register* should subscribe to this publication. An alternative to the print format of the code is on-line access through LEXIS or WESTLAW. The on-line version of the CFR is much easier to research, but the cost and training requirements are major considerations when deciding between on-line and print access. The Board recommends this work for the core collections of public and academic libraries.

Congressional Quarterly's Guide to the U.S. Constitution: History, Text, Index, and Glossary (formerly *An Index to the Constitution of the United States, with Glossary*). Ralph Mitchell. Congressional Quarterly, 1986. soft. 1 vol. 108 pp. index. ISBN 0-87187-392-3. $11.95. handbook.
KF4528.5.M57 342.73′023

CQ's Guide to the U.S. Constitution: History, Text, Index, and Glossary provides students and general readers with a concise and useful reference guide to the fundamental law of the United States. As the author states in the book's preface, he attempts to fill the need for a reference tool that would make all the Constitution's "provisions and concepts easily located by those who want to know." The guide, written in this spirit, makes a conscious effort to keep the information succinct and comprehensible to a wide range of readers.

The book is arranged in two sections. The first section contains a brief history of the Constitution followed by an overview of the document's organization and the text of the Constitution and amendments. The second section includes a subject index and glossary of terms. A one-page "Organization of the Constitution of the United States" helps readers view the historical progression of the document, from ratification in 1788 to the latest amendment in 1971.

The historical material is titled "Writing the Constitution." This section takes the reader from the beginnings up to amendment and ratification of documents. The material is well written and aimed at a general audience, providing enough information in this section to satisfy more advanced students without overwhelming younger ones. The material in the first half of the book is actually "drawn from other CQ publications."

Anyone familiar with Congressional Quarterly, a major publisher of congressional and governmental information, would expect the high-quality material that is presented here. Summaries of various events and concepts occur throughout the text. For example, under the "Executive Branch" heading, there is a one-page description of the cabinet. This format makes the information more accessible to inexperienced researchers.

Ralph Mitchell, a high school teacher, compiled the second main section of the book, which includes the subject index and glossary. The subject index presents "groupings of provisions under main headings," such as "States," "Congress," and "House of Representatives." Since the subject index does not contain cross-references, the approach of using main headings may seem cumbersome. However, because the index is relatively small, the lack of cross-references is not a problem. In a few instances, the reader is referred to a series of notes following the subject index. Otherwise, the index leads directly to a particular article, amendment, section, or paragraph of the Constitution. The glossary provides clear and concise definitions of words with historical connotations and Latin phrases such as *pro tempore* (for the time being).

With the bicentennial of the U.S. Constitution recently behind us, this book should prove a useful and handy guide for most reference collections. Few publications provide a concise and highly readable history of the U.S. Constitution, except perhaps other CQ publications or general encyclopedias. Since this is one of the few subject indexes to the Constitution (barring the volumes on the Constitution in the UNITED STATES CODE ANNOTATED), this guide is worth having on the reference shelves. The fact that *Congressional Quarterly's Guide to the U.S. Constitution* is inexpensive, well written, and concise makes it even more valuable. The Board recommends this work for the core collections of public, academic, and school libraries.

A Dictionary of Modern Legal Usage. Bryan A. Garner. Oxford, 1987. hard. 1 vol. 587 pp. ISBN 0-19-504377-4. $35. dictionary.
KF156.G367 340.03

A Dictionary of Modern Legal Usage is actually a writing skills guide for the legal profession. In the introduction, the author discusses three primary functions of the dictionary: to help "lawyers chart their way through the bogs of legal language"; to address the "many problems of usage that do not ordinarily arise in the writing of persons untrained in the law"; and to serve "as an instrument of reform." Although the work is intended for attorneys and "legal writers," the dictionary is nonetheless a useful source for those outside the legal profession because the book offers assistance with the type of legal jargon found in statutes and court opinions. The guide, written in dictionary format, presents topical essays that cite correct or standard usage. Case or statute citations are listed within entries to substantiate the author's explanations. The author's prose style and humorous asides in many of the entries make the dictionary highly readable and entertaining, while serving as a pathfinder through the language of the legal profession.

A majority of the topical essays focus on the difference between good and bad legal writing. The emphasis is on avoiding legalese, a verbose and overly complicated style of writing and speaking adopted by many legal professionals. The dictionary cites standard usage as the preferred writing style and labels legalese "a scourge of the legal profession." Bryan A. Garner, a practicing attorney who has written numerous articles on legal writing, gives the reader an insider's view of the usage problems prevalent in the legal profession.

The entries are arranged alphabetically; topical essays appear in the same listing as basic definitions. A "Classified Guide," listing all the topical essays, precedes the text and arranges the entries by broad groups: usage; word formation, spelling, and inflections; pronunciation; and punctuation and typography. This guide excludes definitions and entries reflecting "idiomatic use," which are listed throughout the text in lowercase letters. (The entry words for topical essays are in all capitals.) The format clarifies the distinction between the topical essays and other types of entries, such as definitions.

Almost 400 topical essays and basic definitions, aided by numerous cross-references, are presented in the dictionary. The entries range in length from a few short sentences for many of the definitions to nearly three pages of text for entries such as *doublets and triplets of legal idiom.* Many entries refer the user to the preferred or standard word usage, with special emphasis on the distinction between U.S. and British styles, such as "Learnt is a BrE [British English] variant of the past tense *learned.*"

The topical essays often blend usage explanations with humorous asides. For example, the entry *lawyers, derogatory names for* lists colloquial negative titles for attorneys (including "ambulance chaser," "pettifogger," and "shyster"). Garner, while presenting a wide spectrum of legal usage problems, acknowledges the somber nature of the legal profession and offers the reader some comic relief.

A "Pronunciation Guide," based on the system employed in the *Oxford American Dictionary* (Oxford, 1980), precedes the text and offers readers assistance with the Latin and foreign words found in the dictionary. Those less familiar with legal terms will find this feature useful. A "List of Abbreviations" also precedes the text and presents over 50 abbreviations to references cited throughout the dictionary, such as "Black's" for BLACK'S LAW DICTIONARY. The abbreviations list excludes abbreviations for most of the common legislative and case citations, a definite disadvantage for people who are not familiar with legal research and who may not know, for example, that "F.2d" means *Federal Reporter, 2nd Series.*

A "Select Bibliography" that is arranged by subject follows the text. The bibliography lists additional sources in eight categories, including "English Dictionaries," "Usage," and "Legal Language and Writing." Some of these sources are standard writing guides, whereas others focus specifically on legal writing and its unique characteristics. The author notes that additional references are also cited in some of the topical essays, such as "Plain English."

Users of *A Dictionary of Modern Legal Usage* will find the topical essays on word usage particularly helpful. However, a standard law dictionary, such as BLACK'S LAW DICTIONARY, should be consulted for authoritative and complete definitions of legal words. *A Dictionary of Modern Legal Usage* should be considered not a replacement for a standard law dictionary but a guide to better legal writing. The Board recommends this work for the core collection of academic libraries.

Encyclopedia of the American Constitution. Leonard W. Levy, ed. in chief. Macmillan, 1986. hard. 4 vols. 2,196 pp. appendixes. indexes. ISBN 0-02-918610-2 (set). $400 (set). encyclopedia.
KF4548.E53 342.73′023′03

The American Library Association's Reference Sources Committee chose the *Encyclopedia of the American Constitution* as one of the "Outstanding Reference Sources of 1986," and this work lives up to that distinction. The encyclopedia is the only source of its kind. Over seven years of effort went into the publication of this work, with 262 authors contributing. The editors of the encyclopedia saw the need for "a single comprehensive reference work treating the subject in a multi-disciplinary way . . . to bridge the disciplines of history, law, and political science." Therefore, the work appeals to readers seeking basic information about the Constitution as well as those looking for scholarly research on certain constitutional concepts.

The articles in this four-volume set fall into five groups: constitutional law, people, judicial decisions, public acts, and historical periods. Some of the entries, such as *flag desecration,* contain only a few paragraphs. However, entries on major topics are typically 6,000 words. For example, the entries listed under *constitutional history* comprise nearly 100 pages of text and contain details about each phase of constitutional history, ranging from the period before 1776 to events as recent as 1985. Entries are arranged alphabetically by article title and, as the editors state, they are "liberally cross-referenced" (preface), with related articles and short bibliographies cited at the end of many entries.

The majority of articles are understandable to the general reader. However, given the nature of the law, some of the syntax is lengthy and complex. Often, the authors cite concrete examples and judicial decisions to substantiate their information or opinions. The glossary of terms in volume 4 helps the reader through some of the unfamiliar language, but younger students who are inexperienced with legal research may encounter some difficulties deciphering the longer entries.

The last volume concludes with seven appendixes, the glossary, and three indexes. The appendixes include the text of the U.S. Constitution, the Articles of Confederation, and a chronology of events. The glossary's short entries generally define legal or Latin phrases. The case, name, and subject indexes are extensive. The subject index is the longest and probably the most useful of the three indexes. Thirty pages long, the subject index highlights main entries in the encyclopedia with boldface page numbers. Subject terms are clear and accurate, with cross-references cited where needed. The case index lists the full, official citation of judicial decisions and the page number in this work of corresponding entries. All three indexes cite page references only; information at the bottom of each index page reveals which pages appear in which volume.

Every article in the encyclopedia is signed. The impressive list of contributors has been categorized into three groups: historians, lawyers, and political scientists, with lawyers having "produced about half of the words in the Encyclopedia" (preface). In an effort to compile a balanced list of contributors and thereby a balanced overview of the subject, authors from every region of the United States and every academic environment are represented. The editors "sought to include a range of views," which is evident from the expansive list of contributors, whose titles range from law school faculty to Supreme Court justices.

With over 2,000 articles written by some of the best legal and political science scholars in the country, the *Encyclopedia of the American Constitution* is a truly comprehensive legal reference tool on the U.S. Constitution. The articles are comprehensible to a wide range of audiences from advanced high school students to scholars. Unlike Ralph Mitchell's CQ's GUIDE TO THE U.S. CONSTITUTION, this set goes beyond simply guiding a reader through the document; rather, the encyclopedia offers detailed analysis of both major and minor constitutional issues.

In the *American Reference Books Annual, 1987* (Libraries Unlimited), Thomas A. Karel notes that "The National Endowment for the Humanities . . . designated this as one of the four core reference sources for a 'Bicentennial Bookshelf.' " This praise for the *Encyclopedia of the American Constitution,* along with the ALA's endorsement, is well deserved. The Board recommends this work for the core collections of public and academic libraries.

Encyclopedia of the American Judicial System: Studies of the Principal Institutions and Processes of Law. Robert J. Janosik, ed. Scribner, 1987. hard. 3 vols. 1,420 pp. illus. appendixes. index. ISBN 0-684-17807-9 (set). $250 (set). encyclopedia.
KF154.E53 347.300321

The *Encyclopedia of the American Judicial System: Studies of the Principal Institutions and Processes of Law* is the fourth work in Scribner's American Civilization series. This three-volume set provides detailed analysis of issues in both constitutional and nonconstitutional law. The editor has organized a wide spectrum of topics into the following six categories: "Legal History," "Substantive Law," "Institutions and Personnel," "Process and Behavior," "Constitutional Law and Issues," and "Methodology." Each volume contains two of the six categories, and the last volume also contains a subject index to the entire set. Although this encyclopedia covers many of the same constitutional issues in the ENCYCLOPEDIA OF THE AMERICAN CONSTITUTION, the *Encyclopedia of the American Judicial System* provides a broader selection of topics, including information about legal institutions and, as the editor states in the preface, "selections about the personnel who inhabit and use those institutions."

The encyclopedia's 88 essays were contributed by an impressive list of legal scholars, including professors from universities across the country as well as federal and state judges. A "List of Contributors" and their affiliations precedes the subject index in volume 3. As stated in the preface, all the essays "were written as self-contained units" so that they can be read independently. The writing is aimed at a general audience, including, as Janosik states, "the reader without legal training." Cross-references, court cases, and a selected bibliography are cited at the end of most entries.

The essays are arranged alphabetically within five of the six categories. The exception is "Legal History," which presents the essays in a chronological scheme from the colonial period through the 1980s. A broad range of topics is covered, with some articles as short as 9 pages and others as long as 32. The average length is about 12 pages. Ideas seem to progress logically throughout the set. In volume 2, "The Criminal Justice System" presents a general discussion of the legal system, emphasizing criminal justice personnel. More details on some components of that system appear in separate essays entitled "The Police" and "The Judiciary," which appear in the same category and provide detailed discussions about these two groups. Many issues are presented in this way, first as part of broad subject areas and later in separate analytical essays.

The issues discussed within each of the six categories are varied and range from such topics as "Tax Law" to "Religious Liberty," an essay that discusses the use of nativity scenes in public Christmas displays. General legal issues are covered in many of the entries. In "The Federal Court System," the structure of our judicial system is discussed and a chart is presented outlining the federal judicial process from criminal arrest to sentencing. Some of the entries contain specific information about current issues. For example, "Law and the Media" discusses cable television regulations.

Legal terms and phrases are used throughout the encyclopedia. As a result, a glossary of legal terms and phrases would have been helpful to the inexperienced legal researcher. The encyclopedia also lacks a separate case index. However, cited cases are listed by official reporter citation at the end of each essay and are cited in the subject index, where they are italicized and filed among the various subject terms. These are minor criticisms of an otherwise excellent legal research tool.

The subject index includes page references to major essays in boldface type. The indexing seems accurate, and the editor has exercised careful use of "see" and "see also" references. Volume and page correspondence is listed at the bottom of each index page. The format of the index lists subheadings in paragraph style instead of on separate lines within the subject heading. This type of listing makes finding subtopics within a heading difficult, especially under longer entries such as "Supreme Court of the United States." A "List of Contributors" and an "Alphabetical Listing of Articles" precede the subject index.

The articles throughout the *Encyclopedia of the American Judicial System* are well written and informative and present many viewpoints. In the preface, Janosik states that the contributors were asked "to express a personal voice in their essay . . . a range of postures concerning American law and the legal system." This blend of fact and opinion makes the encyclopedia very readable, especially for users who do not have backgrounds in law. Broader in scope than other specialized encyclopedias and aimed at an audience unfamiliar with the law, this reference tool fills the need for information on the U.S. legal system and its institutions. Libraries with limited resources may choose a resource such as THE GUIDE TO AMERICAN LAW: EVERYONE'S LEGAL ENCYCLOPEDIA, which encompasses most of the topics presented in the *Encyclopedia of the American Judicial System* but presents briefer discussions focusing primarily on factual information. The *Encyclopedia of the American Judicial System* includes detailed information and a range of opinions about the U.S. legal system, its processes, and the people who are part of its institutions. The Board recommends this work for the core collections of public, academic, and school libraries.

Fundamentals of Legal Research, 3d edition. J. Myron Jacobstein and Roy M. Mersky. Foundation Pr., 1985. hard. 1 vol. 705 pp. appendixes. index. ISBN 0-88277-554-5. $29.50. guide.
KF240.J3 340.072073

The preface of *Fundamentals of Legal Research* describes the book as "a basic text for students who are learning to do legal research." This is one of the many guides available on legal research. A list of similar sources is available in the now out-of-print *American Legal Literature: A Guide to Selected Legal Resources* (Libraries Unlimited, 1985). In *Fundamentals of Legal Research,* authors Jacobstein and Mersky, professors of law at Stanford University and the University of Texas, respectively, focus on the procedures necessary to conduct legal research. The text discusses the primary and secondary sources of judicial, legislative, and administrative law at the federal, state, and municipal levels. Research in international law and the English legal system are also covered briefly in this volume. The third edition presents expanded and additional references to computer-assisted legal research (CALR). In fact, an entire chapter is devoted to CALR, with discussions of the two major on-line legal systems, LEXIS and WESTLAW. Although this work was published in 1985, the basic research strategies and descriptions of primary and secondary legal sources presented in the text are just as relevant today.

This guide is required reading for people learning legal research and those assisting novice researchers. Although the text is organized for use in a legal research course, the guide is useful in a more general collection because the sources and processes analyzed are relevant to anyone conducting legal research. Each of the 24 chapters contains a summary detailing the contents of the chapter. The summaries are excellent study aids for students and quick-access sources for information within each chapter. Because the index is very general and arranged primarily by broad subject headings, the chapter summaries are useful for locating specific sources.

Also included in this guide are numerous illustrations, such as sample cases from court reporters and organization charts of the American Digest System. Entire pages are reproduced from official and unofficial court reporters. Court reports or opinions are published by official agencies on the federal and state levels and in unofficial, annotated versions by private publishers. The parallel illustrations of official and unofficial reporters might appear distracting; however, the illustrations assist the user in comprehending the various forms of publication available for each judicial opinion. Examples of printed sources, such as legislative materials, and computer printouts displaying on-line versions of sources are shown to illustrate differences in form.

A "Glossary of Terms Used in Legal Research" precedes the first chapter. The glossary and the appendix explaining legal abbreviations are both useful for the legal research novice. Definitions of words and phrases are concise, unlike the longer definitions found in sources such as BLACK'S LAW DICTIONARY. Chapters range from general to specific areas of law. The first five chapters cover the legal process and the judicial reporting system. The remaining chapters, 6 through 24, focus on specific legal areas such as digests and the key number system; legislative histories; looseleaf services; Shepard's citations; and legal encyclopedias, periodicals, and indexes. There's also a lengthy chapter on federal tax research.

This guide presents a wide range of topics, from general explanations of the U.S. court system to specific accounts of the CODE OF FEDERAL REGULATIONS. Thus this book is useful to a wide range of users. The comprehensive coverage of the legal research process and the tools necessary for research makes *Fundamentals of Legal Research* valuable to all librarians and patrons who need legal information and related materials.

The Board recommends this work for the core collections of public and academic libraries.

The Guide to American Law: Everyone's Legal Encyclopedia. West Publishing, 1985. hard. 12 vols. 3,000 pp. illus. appendixes. indexes. ISBN 0-314-73224-1 (set). $990 (set). encyclopedia.
KF156.E83 348.73′6

Until the publication of *The Guide to American Law: Everyone's Legal Encyclopedia,* researchers outside of the legal profession lacked a reference tool that organized and explained the vast amount of information relating to the U.S. legal system. Attorneys and other legal professionals often consult one of the two legal encyclopedias that restate U.S. substantive and procedural law—AMERICAN JURISPRUDENCE, SECOND or CORPUS JURIS SECUNDUM. Both encyclopedias are useful research tools for those well versed in legal literature, but these books are not accessible to the average researcher. West Publishing Company produced *The Guide to American Law* to fill the gap in legal research between the legal professionals and the general population. West is a reputable publisher with long experience in the legal field.

In the preface, the editors summarize the encyclopedia: "This unique multivolume work brings together diverse features and accurate text written in plain English that transcend the traditional format of legal encyclopedias and other secondary sources." This highly readable introduction to U.S. jurisprudence offers a concise compilation of the issues, theories, people, and institutions comprising U.S. administrative and case law. The encyclopedia is updated by annual yearbooks that present current case and statutory citations and discuss recent legal issues.

Spanning 12 volumes, the encyclopedia is arranged by subject in alphabetical order and contains over 5,000 entries with over 400 signed articles. Entries range in length from one sentence for basic definitions to over 20 pages for detailed discussions, such as the entry *civil rights.* As stated in the preface, the entries explain "the legal significance of a phrase, concept, topic, legal organization, individual, historical movement, or government agency." Entries appear in volumes 1 through 10. Volume 11 is an appendix volume; volume 12 contains indexes.

Signed entries appear on rose-colored pages to distinguish them from the basic entries. Contributors of signed articles consist primarily of leaders in the legal profession, although some are scholars from other disciplines such as philosophy, history, anthropology, and libraries. Volumes 1 to 10 contain lists of all contributors, authors of signed articles, and their affiliations. A cumulative list of contributors and authors appears in the index volume. Each volume also presents a contents list of the articles and authors in that volume. General entries and signed articles include the following information: complete case and statutory citations to official and West publications; references to bibliographic materials, such as law review articles, hornbooks, and treatises; and definitions. Signed articles also contain a selective bibliography of additional sources.

A list of the West publications cited in that volume follows the text of each volume. Preceding the main entries in each volume are the following tables: abbreviations that list references to items, such as reporters, statutes, and law reviews; cases cited; and popular name acts. The index volume contains cumulative versions of the West publications lists and all tables in volumes 1 to 10.

The encyclopedia's format enhances its accessibility. Entries are printed on double-column pages with boxes used to mark definitions within entries. Entries containing multiple definitions use such boxes to highlight each definition and mark the last definition in the entry. Cross-references, generously used throughout the encyclopedia, function in two capacities. Small capital letters are used in an entry to signify other, related entries, and "see also" references direct readers to additional entries (often signed articles).

Historical and contemporary illustrations and photographs are presented throughout the set. For example, the entry *American law book publishing* contains interesting photographs of early twentieth-century book production. Each volume also contains two sets of color plates. Therefore, in addition to providing useful legal information, the encyclopedia is visually appealing.

The appendix, volume 11, contains four appendixes and a subject index to the appendixes. Appendix A presents over 100 sample legal forms. The general preface in volume 1 reminds users that sample forms are included "not to replace consultation with an attorney, but to illustrate the application of law to everyday life." Sample forms are presented for procedures, such as adoption, divorce, and search warrants. Appendix B contains historical documents arranged chronologically by general topic. This section is a valuable ready-reference tool, compiling the text of over 50 documents, including the Ten Commandments, the Bill of Rights, and the U.N. Charter.

Appendix C cites important legal developments throughout U.S. history in a timeline. Major legal events are listed by year, followed by a brief summary of their importance. Related events are listed after the summaries. Appendix D contains miscellaneous information, running the gamut from a concise discussion of legal symbols, such as the gavel, to a metric conversion table.

Subject access to the encyclopedia is provided in two ways: through the general subject index in volume 12 and through separate subject indexes in each of the 10 main volumes. The general subject index is based on the individual indexes in volumes 1 to 10. However, the general subject index does not duplicate the information in the individual indexes. Subject terms are accessible to both lawyers and laypersons, but the indexing seems to focus on general accessibility for the user who does not have a law background. The preface to the index volume describes the indexing as "information listed under both the precise legal terms that are familiar to attorneys and under the more general legal terms that nonlawyers would be likely to use." As an example of this dual indexing, an attorney looking for specific information on the liability of drinking establishments would more than likely search under the subject heading "Dram shop acts," whereas the general researcher would access this information under the headings "Alcoholic beverages" or "Drinking establishments." References to "Dram shop acts" are listed under all three subject headings.

The index volume also contains the following specific indexes: "Quotations by Topic," "Quotations by Author," "Illustrations," and "Name." Researchers looking for all the entries on a general legal topic can consult a section in the index volume entitled "Special Topics Lists." This section lists major entries and articles in six areas of the law, such as "British Legal History," "International Law," and "Legal Education."

The Guide to American Law is a great introduction to the extensive and highly specialized area of U.S. law. Definitions, citations, and historical documents are all presented in a concise, accessible, and attractive format. The contributors made a conscious effort to avoid legalese in their writing, which makes the encyclopedia useful for a general audience. One minor criticism is the lack of a pronunciation guide, which would have been a useful tool for the Latin and foreign phrases common in the language of the law. However, given the accessible format, skillful indexing, and useful tables and appendixes, the Board recommends this work for the core collections of public, academic, and school libraries.

Martindale-Hubbell Law Directory. Martindale-Hubbell, annual. hard. 8 vols. appendix. index. ISBN 1-56160-001-6 (set). $255 (set). directory. CD-ROM.
KF190.M37 340.025

A truly comprehensive list of all practicing attorneys in the United States does not exist. The publication that comes closest to providing such a list is the *Martindale-Hubbell Law Directory.* This multivolume set is published annually and lists all attorneys admitted to the U.S. bar. The directory also provides legal information not readily available elsewhere.

The directory has been published in its current format since 1931. This work is actually a consolidated version of what was once two separate publications: *Martindale's American Law Directory* (1868–1930) and *Hubbell's Legal Directory* (1870–1930). The current edition consists of eight volumes arranged alphabetically by state and within each state by city.

Attorneys and law firms are listed by state and city in volumes 1 to 7. Each volume presents two lists. The first list contains brief biographical profiles and rating information about individual attorneys. The biographical information, presented in an abbreviated format, lists information such as date of birth, college and law school attended, date of admission to the bar, and area of legal expertise. The rating information on the list of attorneys is based on confidential recommendations received by the publisher from attorneys and judges in the jurisdiction where the attorney practices. Abbreviations and symbols are explained in the "Confidential Key" and "Notes and Symbols" paragraphs that appear on the inside cover of each volume. The rating information does not serve as an endorsement of a particular attorney or law firm. Similarly, as the publisher states in the foreword, absence of a rating should not be construed as an "unfavorable inference" because in some instances the information was simply not available. Attorneys are not charged for inclusion on this list.

The second list in each volume is of law firms and is also arranged alphabetically by state and city. This list contains basic information about firms, such as addresses, telephone numbers, office locations, and types of law practiced. Biographical profiles of the firm's partners and associates are also presented in this section. Firms are charged for this listing; therefore, some entries contain detailed biographical information whereas others provide only standard information.

Each volume contains an "Index of Special Services for Lawyers" that lists legal services available to attorneys. Included are the names and addresses of services, such as banking; investigators; and court, shorthand, and stenotype reporters. These services are listed by state and city throughout volumes 1 to 7.

Volume 7 also includes special lists, such as attorneys in foreign countries whose legal practices are international in scope and international patent lawyers and agents; U.S. government attorneys are listed under "Washington, D.C.," whereas patent attorneys are listed in separate sections throughout volumes 1 to 7.

The usefulness of the directory is perhaps most apparent in volume 8, the digests volume, which presents digests of statutory law for the 50 states, Canada, and over 50 foreign countries. The U.S. law digest is arranged alphabetically by state, and the foreign digests are arranged alphabetically by country. The digests, written by prominent law firms, organize and summarize current statutory law by general topic. This section also contains a digest for U.S. copyright, patent, and trademark laws. Although the digests are not comprehensive in scope, they offer users a current overview of state and foreign statutes that is not readily available in other publications.

By consulting the digest, researchers discover basic legal information about each state, such as whether a state allows individuals to have living wills and which states have no-fault insurance for motor vehicles. The state digests summarize statutory law by broad subject areas under topics, such as *dissolution of marriage and legal separation, holidays, motor vehicles,* and *taxation.* In the digests for other countries, the researcher can discover general legal information such as the country's government structure and rate of currency. The topics in the foreign country digests are also arranged by broad subject areas that focus on information such as *constitution and government, currency,* and *wills.* Preceding the digests is a topical index that offers users subject access to both the state or country digests. This subject index links subjects with digest topics, through general and legal subject terms, making the directory accessible to users without a law background as well as legal professionals.

In addition to the law digests, volume 8 also contains information about the U.S. court system such as lists of justices and judges from the Supreme Court to the tax courts. Special sections on "Uniform and Model Acts" and the "American Bar Association" are also included in volume 8.

The *Martindale-Hubbell Law Directory* is quite large. Each volume consumes over 3 inches of library shelf space. The sheer size of each volume makes it unwieldy and somewhat cumbersome to handle. However, the convenience of offering multiple state listings in each volume compensates for its massive size. Libraries that have the hardware for CD-ROMs may want to consider the CD-ROM version of the directory, scheduled for release in 1990.

Other types of law directories are available from state bar associations and from other commercial publishers. The American Bar Association (ABA) developed rules and standards pertaining to the publication of law lists and directories. To ensure reliability and credibility, researchers should consult only those directories that are certified by the ABA, such as the *Martindale-Hubbell Law Directory.*

A minor criticism of the directory is the lack of a consolidated list of all the attorneys listed in the set. The directory is arranged geographically. Therefore, the reader cannot locate information simply by knowing an attorney's name. A user who does not know both the name and the location of an attorney must search through the listings of each individual state.

The *Martindale-Hubbell Law Directory* is the most comprehensive directory of its kind. The directory not only provides a current list of practicing attorneys in the United States and in some foreign countries but also contains an invaluable volume of law digests for states and other countries. Although the directory focuses on the United States, the digests also offer useful international information. The Board recommends this work for the core collections of public and academic libraries.

United States Code. U.S.G.P.O., annual (1926–). hard. 23 vols. plus 18 suppls. appendix. indexes. ISBN 0-16-020514-X. $50. code. on-line.
KF62 348.73

United States Code Annotated. West Publishing, annual. hard. 224 vols. appendix. indexes. $315 (set); $322 (1990 cumulative pocket parts); $28 per vol.; $7 per single pocket part. code.
KF62.bU6 345.21

The *United States Code* is a codification and consolidation of all general and permanent U.S. laws currently in force. The code does not contain private laws or those of a temporary or emergency nature. The first edition of the code was published in 1926 by the U.S. Government Printing Office, with West Publishing Company serving as consultants. The 50 titles that comprise the set arrange general U.S. statutory law by subject. Researchers looking for federal laws by topic would generally choose to access the *United States Code* instead of sources that list the statutes or session laws chronologically and arranged by statute number. The code does not duplicate the session laws but instead presents a restatement of the law, organizing the information in the statutes by subject and arranging the various subjects into groups called "titles." The U.S. Government Printing Office, which publishes the official version of the code, produces a new version approximately every six years. Bound supplements are published annually to update the code during the interim.

An unofficial, annotated version of the code is produced by West, a commercial publisher. The annotated version offers researchers many advantages over the official version, including separate volumes for each title in the code; frequent updates through annual pocket parts and special supplementary pamphlets; detailed general indexes with separate indexes for each title; and, most important, annotations and commentaries on relevant federal and state court decisions. When only the text of the code is needed, the *United States Code* is adequate. However, those conducting legal research usually need additional information and may prefer consulting the annotated version.

Twenty-five titles of the code have been enacted into "positive law," which means they can be cited as legal evidence in a court of law. Two of the 25 titles have received only partial enactments. The remaining titles of the code are considered "prima facie evidence," so that wherever a discrepancy exists between the language in statutes and the *United States Code,* the statutes take precedence. The Office of the Law Revision Counsel of the U.S. House of Representatives is involved in an ongoing project to have all the titles of the code revised, codified, and enacted into positive law.

The code contains many divisions within its various titles. Each title is divided into chapters and then into sections. A list of all code titles appears at the beginning of each volume of the code. Titles enacted into positive law are noted with asterisks on the list. The code contains 49 titles, numbered 1 through 50. Title 34 (navy) was eliminated by the enactment of Title 10 (armed forces). Some of the lengthy titles are divided into parts and then subparts to assist in organizing the information. The numerous divisions of the code sometimes cause difficulties in locating specific sections. In addition, because the code is derived from statutes spanning many years, conversion and parallel tables are provided to assist users in various ways, such as listing statute numbers with corresponding U.S. code citations.

Preceding the text of the code is a section entitled "Organic Laws of the United States." This section contains historical documents such as the Declaration of Independence, the Articles of Confederation, and the U.S. Constitution. An "Analytical Index to the Constitution of the United States and Amendments" follows the text of these documents. The annotated version of the code also contains these historical documents.

The subject and popular name indexes to the code are not as detailed or as current as the indexes in the annotated version. Researchers can access the code through the general subject index by topic or by government agency name. Infrequent use of cross-references and lack of detailed indexing makes the subject index difficult to use, especially for inexperienced researchers. The nine tables following the subject index offer additional access to the code and compensate for some of the limitations of the subject index. Another problem encountered when using the official version of the code is the lack of frequent updates. New laws are passed throughout the year, yet the code is only updated on an annual basis and consolidated only once every six years. Researchers looking for a composite list of a current code section thus need to look in both the annual supplements and the latest cumulative version.

The *United States Code Annotated (U.S.C.A.)* contains over 100 volumes, with each title consisting of one or more volumes. This is a tremendous amount of information compared to the official version of the code. The language, titles, chapters, and section numbers are identical to the official version. The annotations, such as citations to judicial opinions, historical notes, and practice commentaries, are invaluable to legal researchers. In addition to citing relevant federal and state court cases, *U.S.C.A.* also cites by West topic and key number to other West publications such as the legal encyclopedia CORPUS JURIS SECUNDUM. Law review articles and agency regulations, such as the CODE OF FEDERAL REGULATIONS, are also cited.

The annotations following the text of the code consist of historical and statutory notes, cross-references, editorial notes, and notes of decisions. The historical notes present a brief chronology of relevant statutory citations such as statute sources, relevant public laws, amendments, and effective dates. The cross-references provide citations to relevant code titles and sections. Editorial notes consist of "library references" or citations to other West publications, such as their digest system, encyclopedia, and forms volumes. Current volumes and pocket parts also contain references to the "Westlaw Electronic Research Guide" located at the beginning of the volume or pocket part. Electronic research refers to West's on-line legal system, WESTLAW, which contains an on-line version of the code.

Some code sections are followed by "Practice Commentaries." These editorial notes, which are written by practicing attorneys, summarize and explain a code section. "Notes of Decisions" contain brief summaries of court cases relevant to that code section and citations to decisions published in other West volumes. The notes are organized by subject area, a particularly useful format for locating relevant decisions in longer code sections such as those in Title 26, internal revenue.

A multivolume general subject index, containing a popular name table, is published annually and provides access to the entire set. In addition, each title of the set contains its own subject index. Researchers seeking information in a specific area of the law can access the code title directly through the title's index, a great advantage for advanced researchers who prefer to use a title-specific subject index instead of the voluminous general subject index.

The *U.S.C.A.* is updated by annual pocket parts or when necessary by special supplementary pamphlets. New bound volumes are issued when the size of a pocket part or supplementary pamphlet becomes unwieldy. An interim pamphlet service is published monthly to cover new material between the annual updates provided by the pocket parts.

The code is available on-line, in WESTLAW,

LEXIS, and in current use through TYMNET. The on-line versions offer users greater flexibility of subject searching for relevant code sections. However, the cost of on-line searching is a major consideration when deciding between print and computer access.

The *United States Code* and the *United States Code Annotated* provide legal researchers with a topical approach to the general and permanent laws of the United States. Each publication offers different features, with the annotated version offering greater subject access, current case citations, and valuable notes and commentaries. A basic legal collection should include at least one version of the code. Most U.S. government depository collections contain the *United States Code.* In addition, nearly every law library subscribes to the annotated version. Smaller libraries may choose to refer patrons to a U.S. government depository collection or a law library. The Board recommends these works for the core collections of public and academic libraries.

Supplementary Titles

American Jurisprudence Second. Lawyers Cooperative Publishing, 1962–1976, with annual suppls. hard. 82 vols. indexes. $49.50 per vol.; $305 (subscription to annual suppls.). encyclopedia.
KF154.A42 340.0973 (1962); 348.73′6 (1977)

Corpus Juris Secundum. American Law Book, 1963–1983, with annual suppls. hard. 158 vols. indexes. $3,689.50 (set); $284.50 (1990 cumulative pocket parts); $47 per vol.; $6 per single pocket part. encyclopedia.
KF154.C56 345.5

"Two competitive general legal encyclopedias, *American Jurisprudence Second* [*(Am. Jur. 2d)*] [82-volume set] and *Corpus Juris Secundum* [*(C.J.S.)*] [158-volume set], . . . are excellent starting points for a search in the law.

"[Each strives] to include a complete and integrated narrative statement of applicable American law with references to reliable authority, good indexes, and [annual cumulative] supplements.

"In *C.J.S.* the publisher attempts to restate the entire body of American case law [both state and federal] from the first reported case to date. . . . *Am. Jur. 2d* differs from *C.J.S.* in that its editors . . . cite [only] selected case decisions. Both encyclopedia sets contain over 400 alphabetically arranged topics or titles designed to cover the entire field of American law. Each title resembles an individual treatise which summarizes the rules of law and makes references to supporting authorities. Additionally, both encyclopedias provide dictionary definitions and judicial interpretations of words, phrases, and legal maxims.

"The narrative text of each encyclopedia occupies the upper portion of a page. This text, which is the secondary authority, is supported by copious footnotes on the bottom portion of the page that lead to primary sources such as legal cases and statutes.

"The indexes to both sets deserve special attention. . . . *Am. Jur. 2d* has three distinct index units. The general index [8 vols.] is an access point to all the articles in the . . . set.

"Another index unit is the individual index to each volume . . . [and] the third index unit . . . is the recompiled or republished volume index.

"The *C.J.S.* general index [5 vols.] is similar to the *Am. Jur. 2d* general index in that it has annual cumulative supplements, it indexes all the volumes of the set, and it also lists words and phrases. However, the *C.J.S.* general index serves more as a title or subject finder, . . . [and provides] many cross-references which aid the researcher.

"A group of expert writers prepares the narrative texts for both encyclopedias. More recent *Am. Jur. 2d* titles are signed by the authors, while the individual titles in *C.J.S.* are not signed.

"Both encyclopedias are kept up-to-date primarily by annual cumulative pocket supplements which fit in the back covers of the bound volumes.

"New titles and major revisions are introduced by both encyclopedia publishers in an interim format.

"Academic libraries . . . will want to consider purchasing one of these competitive sets." (*RSR,* Spring 1984, p. 36)

Also reviewed in: *SL,* January 1979, p. 10.

Board's recommendation: Academic libraries.

Congressional Quarterly's Guide to the U.S. Supreme Court, 2d edition. Elder Witt. Congressional Quarterly, 1990. hard. 1 vol. 1,060 pp. illus. index. ISBN 0-87187-502-0. $149. encyclopedia.
JK1571.C65 347.73

"[The] U.S. Supreme Court is 'the most powerful court of justice the world has ever known,' and since 1979, when the first edition of *Congressional Quarterly's Guide to the U.S. Supreme Court* . . . [was published,] it has been a court of both continuity and change.

"[This book] . . . is timely, coinciding with the Court's bicentennial.

"[The book's] . . . organization remains the same. Parts 1 and 5 provide detailed information on the history, organization, operations, and traditions of the Court, the justices, and supporting personnel. Part 4, 'Pressures on the Court,' looks at external forces (Congress, the president, the press, and the public) that attempt to influence the court. Parts 2 and 3, which comprise 55 percent of the book, provide extensive discussion of the Supreme Court's decisions as they relate to the federal government and the individual.

"[The revisions in this book] . . . are significant, incorporating a decade of court decisions and changes. Those libraries owning the first edition will want to purchase the second. Public and academic libraries will find this title a useful reference purchase." (*BL,* May 1, 1990, p. 1728)

Board's recommendation: Public and academic libraries.

Encyclopedia of Crime and Justice. Sanford K. Kadish, ed. in chief. Free Pr. 1983. hard. 4 vols. 1,790 pp. index. ISBN 0-02-918110-0 (set). $375 (set). encyclopedia.
HV6017.E52 364

The *Encyclopedia of Crime and Justice* is an "interdisciplinary study of the field of criminal justice. The 287 articles . . . cover the legal, political, and historical relationships of crime to society. Ranging in length from 1000 to 10,000 words . . . the entries provide . . . information about often complex concepts. Each article is accompanied by a bibliography and cross references to related articles." (*LJ,* January 1984, p. 74)

"It is a mark of distinction that [this] work is as close to totally objective as possible in a field that is filled with emotionally laden issues. Various topics, ranging from the custom and history of law to the latest case material on capital punishment, are treated in articles that present all sides of the cogent arguments without becoming oppressive or pedantic. . . . Among several unique and positive features, most impressive is the excellent index. . . . The explanatory 'Guide to Legal Citations' is especially noteworthy, making this work one of the few that translates legal citations into references usable by [the layperson]." (*Choice,* March 1984, p. 950)

"[In addition, the articles] were written . . . by noted specialists in the field. These include primarily law professors, but well-known psychologists, judges, sociologists, and consultants in criminal justice have also contributed. . . . The volumes are sturdily bound; both print and paper are of high quality, and the format is arranged to facilitate ease of reading and use. . . . The interdisciplinary scope of this work enhances its usefulness to informed general readers, students, and teachers . . . as well as to criminal justice and court personnel." (*BL,* October 1, 1984, p. 202)

Also reviewed in: *A Lib,* May 1984, p. 299; *ARBA,* 1984, p. 252; *RQ,* Spring 1984, p. 362; *WLB,* February 1984, p. 451.

Board's recommendation: Public, academic, and school libraries.

The International Law Dictionary. Robert L. Bledsoe and Boleslaw A. Boczek. ABC-Clio, 1987. hard and soft. 1 vol. 422 pp. index. ISBN 0-87436-406-X (hard); 0-87436-489-2 (soft). $49 (hard); $24 (soft). dictionary.
JX1226.B57 341.03'21

The International Law Dictionary "of 368 key terms in international law—concepts, major treaties, international conventions, and theories—offers needed clarity [on issues of international law] to a broad range of readers. . . . [The dictionary] is organized thematically. Its twelve chapters bring together terms on topics such as jurisdiction and jurisdictional immunities, treatment of aliens, the law of the sea, and laws of war and neutrality. The two-part entries first define the term and then explain its significance and implications through historic and current examples. Most of the *see also* references within the definitions refer to other terms within the same chapter. Because most entries, particularly their interpretive sections, are brief essays, the strong index not only identifies entry terms, but also analyzes the essays' contents, allowing thorough retrieval on any topic." (*WLB,* November 1987, p. 94)

Also reviewed in: *ARBA,* 1988, p. 221; *R & R Bk N,* Fall 1987, p. 21.

Board's recommendation: Academic libraries.

New and Noteworthy

National Directory of Legal Services. Robert L. Davidson, ed. Prentice-Hall, 1989. hard. 1 vol. 589 pp. ISBN 0-13-609397-3. $79.95. directory.
KF190.N33 349.73'025

The *National Directory of Legal Services* provides "attorneys and law offices with listings of individuals and organizations that can serve important needs of a law practice, for instance, expert witnesses, investigators, model makers, and photographers. The book is arranged in four sections. The first is a glossary of abbreviations and acronyms used. The second section is the 'Discovery Key Indexing,' which lists by subject the individuals and/or organizations that provide services for attorneys. . . . After locating a name in the subject section the reader must refer to the third and fourth sections to find more information on the individual or business. The third section is the 'General Services Listing' and the fourth is the 'Computer Services Listing,' both arranged alphabetically by the name of the business. [This book] . . . provides access to more than 700 businesses serving the legal profession." (*BL,* November 1, 1989, p. 610)

Public Interest Law Groups: Institutional Profiles. Karen O'Connor and Lee Epstein. Greenwood, 1989. hard. 1 vol. 261 pp. index. ISBN 0-313-24787-0. $45. bibliography.
KF299.P8025 349.73′025

"*Public Interest Law Groups* 'describes the many and varied organizations that litigate on behalf of the public interest and/or use the courts to achieve policy ends.' It provides detailed institutional profiles for more than 170 U.S. public interest groups that focus on the protection of civil rights, legal aid, conservation, consumer interest, abortion, and capital punishment. [The book contains a] . . . brief introduction [that] provides an overview of how public interest law has evolved over the years. The institutional profiles and descriptions follow. Each profile provides a brief historical description of the organization and is often accompanied by a discussion of significant legal cases with which it has been associated. More than 350 cases are cited in the main body of the book and are indexed in a table of cases following the appendixes." (*BL,* November 15, 1989, p. 698)

World Encyclopedia of Police Forces and Penal Systems. George Thomas Kurian. Facts On File, 1989. hard. 1 vol. 582 pp. index. ISBN 0-8160-1019-6. $95. bibliography.
HV7901.K87 363.2′03

The "*World Encyclopedia of Police Forces and Penal Systems* provides information on the law enforcement and corrections systems of 183 countries. The entry for each country begins with a basic fact sheet, giving data on area, population, type of government, population per police officer, and police expenditures per 1,000 inhabitants. For large countries the information on law enforcement and corrections is organized under four headings: History & Background; Structure & Organization; Recruitment, Education & Training; and The Penal System. [The entries] . . . for smaller countries follow those for large countries and consist primarily of the basic fact sheet and a short descriptive paragraph." (*BL,* September 15, 1989, p. 211)

Steven J. Schmidt

Library Science

See also Book Arts; Publishing

The word *librarian* comes from Latin and means the "keeper of the books." The titles on the following list represent the nucleus of the library science trade. They are the fundamental tools we require to select, organize, and utilize fully a library's collection.

Each library is a unique reflection of its environment, so no blanket recommendation is possible. Thus this list for core collections is not comprehensive. Many other titles are worthy of consideration as core titles. The *American Library Directory* (Bowker, annual), for example, is a valuable source for information about other libraries, library schools, and organizations across the country. Other distinctive directories exist that fill more specialized needs, for example, the *Directory of Special Libraries and Information Centers* (Brigette I. Darney, Gale, 1988) or the *Interlibrary Loan Policies Directory* (Leslie R. Morris and Patsy Brautigam, ALA, 1984). For keeping track of current trends in the field, there are monthly periodical indexes, such as *Library Literature* (Wilson, annual), as well.

Another basic resource for any library would be a classification index. Two major systems are used in this country: One is the Dewey decimal system, which is popular in school and public library settings. The second, the Library of Congress classification system, is more often found in academic settings. Several titles included on this core list utilize the current twentieth edition of the *Dewey Decimal Classification and Relative Index* (Melvil Dewey, Forest Pr., 1989).

With these directories and indexes and the core titles reviewed here, the librarian will have a solid body of work to use for reference.

Core Titles

ALA Filing Rules. ALA, 1980. soft. 1 vol. 50 pp. appendixes. index. ISBN 0-8389-3255-X. $8. guide.
Z695.95.A52 025.3′17

ALA Filing Rules is a brief but comprehensive guide to the arrangement of bibliographic records. This edition was produced by the Resources and Technical Services Division (RTSD) Filing Committee of the ALA and supplants the 1942 and 1968 editions of the *ALA Rules for Filing Catalog Cards.* The committee included librarians from the Library of Congress and several divisions of the ALA; the committee worked in close cooperation with the British Library Filing Rules Committee and the ALA/RTSD committee responsible for compiling *Anglo-American Cataloguing Rules,* second edition.

ALA Filing Rules translates a very complex set of

Core Titles

	PUBLIC	ACADEMIC	SCHOOL
ALA Filing Rules ALA, 1980			✦
The ALA Glossary of Library and Information Science Young, Heartsill, ed. ALA, 1983	✦	✦	
ALA Handbook of Organization and Membership Directory ALA, annual		✦	
ALA World Encyclopedia of Library and Information Sciences, 2d edition Wedgeworth, Robert, ed. ALA, 1986		✦	
Bowker Annual: Library and Book Trade Almanac Simora, Filomena, ed. Bowker, annual	✦	✦	
Elementary School Library Collection: A Guide to Books and Other Media, 16th edition Winkel, Lois, ed. Brodart, 1988			✦
General Reference Books for Adults: Authoritative Evaluations of Encyclopedias, Atlases, and Dictionaries Sader, Marion, ed. Bowker, 1988	✦		
Guide to Reference Books, 10th edition Sheehy, Eugene P., ed. ALA, 1986	✦	✦	✦
Sears List of Subject Headings, 13th edition Rovira, Carmen, and Caroline Reyes, eds. Wilson, 1986	✦	✦	✦

rules into guidelines that are easy to understand and simple to follow. The 1980 edition is based on the principle of "file-as-is" for records, including catalog cards as well as other formats. These rules are intended to operate independently of the precepts that were in effect when the records were created. This practice resolves the problem of datedness. The basic rule of order is to file records word by word. This produces a nonhierarchical set of records that is structured on bibliographic information. For example, when filing using this system, punctuation is not considered. This makes access simpler and more direct.

The *ALA Filing Rules* contain only a few succinct rules, yet the scope of the work is all-encompassing. Only a few exceptions are outlined, and, for the most part, the optional rules of the past have been eliminated. The rules have been divided into two classes—general rules and special rules. The special rules are extensions of the regular rules to deal with unusual problems that arise occasionally, such as how to file roman numerals. Modified letters, unusual characters, and foreign articles are treated in the appendixes. A brief glossary of special terms used in the rules as well as a detailed index are included in *ALA Filing Rules.*

The Board recommends this work for the core collection of school libraries.

The ALA Glossary of Library and Information Science. Heartsill Young, ed. ALA, 1983. hard. 1 vol. 245 pp. ISBN 0-8389-0371-1. $50. glossary.
Z1006.A48 020.3

Because library and information science can reach into almost any field of endeavor, *The ALA Glossary of Library and Information Science* draws terms from a multitude of fields: printing and publishing, photography, reprography, education, computer science, telecommunications, and administration. Specifically, the glossary includes terms related to the production, reproduction, collection, organization, retrieval, and conservation of documents. The theme of the *ALA Glossary of Library and Information Science* is the access to information.

The definitions in the book are intended to be utilitarian, reflecting current practices in the field of library science. The editor is not suggesting that these definitions carry the official endorsement of the ALA. The editor's goal is simply to standardize meanings to promote the exchange of information and ideas between librarians and experts in related fields.

The glossary is arranged letter by letter. The names of persons and corporate bodies are excluded, so popular and commercial terms, such as OCLC or SSCI, are not listed. Most terms are located where expected in the alphabet, but some are alphabeticized differently. *Library of Congress classification* is listed under that heading, for instance, but the Dewey decimal system is entered under *Decimal classification.* Although the latest edition of *The ALA Glossary of Library and Information Science* ventures into the realm of computers, recent phenomena, such as CD-ROM and WORM (write once, read many times), are not included.

Despite these minor shortcomings, the work is valuable. The Board recommends this work for the core collections of public and academic libraries.

ALA Handbook of Organization and Membership Directory. ALA, annual. soft. 1 vol. 1,048 pp. appendixes. indexes. ISBN 0-8389-5730-7. $20. handbook.
Z673.A5H37 020.622

As the name implies, the *ALA Handbook of Organization and Membership Directory* is really two books in one. One-third of this annual compilation is a guide to the organization and structure of the ALA. This portion functions as a directory of the current officers, councilors, committee members, and representatives of the myriad divisions, roundtables, chapters, and affiliated organizations. Brief descriptions are given of the focus, goals, publications, and membership of each division. The officers of each of the 1,200 committees are listed, as are those for the roundtables and discussion groups supported by the ALA.

Also included in the handbook are a number of valuable features, such as documents detailing the constitution and bylaws of the organization, a select list of ALANET electronic mail addresses, and a list of library-related awards and honors.

The final two-thirds of the volume consists of an alphabetical list of members of the ALA. The list gives the names and addresses of the more than 45,000 people and organizations that belong to the ALA. The list is broken down into the following categories: "Special Members," "Personal Members," and "Organization Members." A special section at the beginning of the directory lists honorary and other special members. Access to the handbook is through two indexes; one lists persons named in the directory proper, and the other indexes topics in the text.

The *ALA Handbook of Organization and Membership Directory* has been published annually by the ALA since the early 1970s and is distributed free to organizations and life members of the ALA. This paperback volume closely resembles the *U.S. Government Manual* in size and layout. Like most field-specific handbooks, its format makes the book quick and easy to use; however, the text is riddled with acronyms and abbreviations that are meaningless to people outside the library world. Mindful of this potential problem, one of the appendixes is a glossary of abbreviations and acronyms. The other appendixes include ALA documents, calendars, forms, other organizations, insurance addresses, and general information about ALA. The *ALA Handbook of Organization and Membership Directory* is an excellent tool for helping librarians interact with others in their profession.

The Board recommends this work for the core collection of academic libraries.

ALA World Encyclopedia of Library and Information Sciences, 2d edition. Robert Wedgeworth, ed. ALA, 1986. hard. 1 vol. 895 pp. illus. index. ISBN 0-8389-0427-0. $165. encyclopedia.
Z1006.A18 020.3

The first edition of the *ALA World Encyclopedia* appeared in 1980 and provided a global overview of the history and development of library science as well as a ready-reference source for information about major institutions and names in the field. The second edition builds upon this foundation with almost double the scope and coverage of its predecessor.

The layout of the *ALA World Encyclopedia of Library and Information Sciences* is similar to that of other single-volume encyclopedias on the market. The articles are arranged alphabetically by subject. The editors draw together the concepts using an "Outline of Contents." This outline categorizes all the entries into one of the following five areas: "Library in Society," "Library as an Institution," "Theory and Practice of Librarianship," "Education and Research," and "International Library, Information and Bibliographical Organizations." "Library in Society" looks at the role of libraries from ancient times to the present. "Library as an Institution" discusses the different types of libraries, mainly from a North American point of view. "Theory and Practice of Librarianship" examines the broad principles underlying the policies and practices of the profession. The section on "Education and Research" includes the major articles dealing with fundamentals of library education. The fifth section, "International Library, Information and Bibliographical Organizations," describes 30 major library organizations in the world.

Over 400 people contributed to this resource. The signed articles in the *ALA World Encyclopedia of Library and Information Sciences* are, for the most part, short and to the point. For example, one provides a quick description of the state of libraries in Bahrain, and another supplies an overview of copyright problems in libraries. Whenever possible, a brief set of references is included at the end of articles. Most entries are illustrated with black-and-white photographs, and a large number of charts and statistical tables appear throughout the volume. For further information, the index refers the user to the annual *ALA Yearbook for Library and Information Services* for the latest information on certain topics.

Biographies, most of which are accompanied by a portrait of the subject, make up another important part of the encyclopedia. They include people who made significant contributions to the field or had a primary influence on a major library. Although the *ALA World Encyclopedia of Library and Information Sciences* is international in scope, the biographical coverage is slightly biased in favor of English-speaking people.

The Board recommends this work for the core collection of academic libraries.

Bowker Annual: Library and Book Trade Almanac. Filomena Simora, ed. Bowker, annual. hard. 1 vol. index. ISBN 0-8352-2943-2. $119.95. almanac.
Z731.A47 020.58

For over 30 years, *The Bowker Annual,* recently renamed *Bowker Annual: Library and Book Trade Almanac,* has been the bible for librarians seeking information in the fields of librarianship, publishing, or the book trade. Each annual edition carries a retrospective look at the year's events, including an in-depth discussion of recent events and legislation that affect libraries. In recent years, problems such as copyright and the right of patron confidentiality have been examined.

The *Bowker Annual* contains more information on the library and book trade than almost any other source. Acquisitions expenditures, book and periodical prices, library scholarships, book awards, and much more are standard features of the volume. For example, one regular department, the "Librarian's Bookshelf," lists recent professional development titles for most types of libraries. Other regular features include a list of best-sellers for the previous year; a summary of book production; average book and periodical prices; and a list of toll-free telephone numbers of publishers and distributors. The almanac also includes a look at the trends in placements and salaries for recent library school graduates on a state-by-state basis along with a comprehensive list of placement services.

Recent editions have some new features, such as a quick-find index and a buyer's guide for library-related products and services. Another new feature, the "High Technology Bibliography," discusses technology in the library world.

The index and the detailed table of contents provide easy access to information in the almanac. The long tradition of accuracy and currency make the *Bowker Annual* one of the basic sources in the field. The Board recommends this work for the core collections of public and academic libraries.

Elementary School Library Collection: A Guide to Books and Other Media, 16th edition. Lois Winkel, ed. Brodart, 1988. hard. 1 vol. 1,028 pp. appendixes. indexes. ISBN 0-87272-092-6. $99.95. guide.
Z1037.E4 011.62

Elementary School Library Collection: A Guide to Books and Other Media is a valuable tool for maintaining and developing school library media centers. The guide contains over 7,000 annotated entries for books, periodicals, filmstrips, sound recordings, kits, prints, videocassettes, and microcomputer software for preschoolers through sixth graders. Reference and professional development sources for the library media specialist are included as well. The sixteenth edition of the guide covers new titles published primarily between 1985 and 1987. Older titles that the editors feel are especially useful in a school library setting are included as well.

One strength of the *Elementary School Library Collection* is the way that the criteria for selection and evaluation are explained in detail in the introduction. These criteria keep the guide in tune with the rapidly changing technological needs of the library media center. The work is an annotated bibliography of works classified by type: reference, nonfiction, fiction, easy, periodicals, and professional collection. Entries are arranged in alphabetical order by author. In addition to the basic citation and a brief descriptive note about the work, entries include Dewey decimal classification, type of material, interest level, readability estimate, price, ISBN, and subject headings. A special code is used to indicate a combined entry, such as when one title has a book and audiocassette version. Phase indicators are used to suggest the priority for acquiring each title. These indicators are based on the quality of the title compared to other works on the same topic.

Access to the materials covered in the *Elementary School Library Collection* is through a series of indexes—author, title, and subject. There is also a directory of publishers, producers, and distributors in the back of the book. A couple of special features make the guide an extremely valuable selection tool for school libraries: the appendixes, which draw together the materials according to interest level, and a list of books and audiovisual titles that made unusual or unique contributions to the special needs of children.

The Board recommends this work for the core collection of school libraries.

General Reference Books for Adults: Authoritative Evaluations of Encyclopedias, Atlases, and Dictionaries. Marion Sader, ed. Bowker, 1988. hard. 1 vol. 614 pp. illus. index. ISBN 0-8352-2393-0. $69.95. guide.
Z1035.1.G45 028.1′2

General Reference Books for Adults: Authoritative Evaluations of Encyclopedias, Atlases, and Dictionaries is the second volume in the Bowker Buying Guide series. Like its predecessor, *General Reference Books for Young Readers,* this guide provides authoritative, objective evaluations of over 200 encyclopedias, atlases, dictionaries, and thesauruses. The editors limited the scope of the *General Reference Books for Adults* to sources in print as of April 1, 1988.

The introduction begins with a brief but informative history of general reference books. Following that is a guide to the selection of reference materials, which includes the results of a survey of librarians across the country. In that survey, librarians rated some basic reference sources. The introductory chapters end with a series of quick-reference charts comparing the titles in the evaluations.

The remainder of the work is divided into classes—encyclopedias, atlases, dictionaries and word books, and large-print reference books. The first three parts open with an informative "What to look for" discussion covering the unique features and key points related to the genre. These include format, currency, layout, accessibility, and other issues. The chapter on atlases, for instance, includes a discussion of scale and projections. Each of these chapters ends with a glossary of terms. These guides are invaluable sources of information for collection development or beginning reference students.

Each title receives a comprehensive evaluation and review that covers authority, scope, format, accuracy, currency, legibility, and accessibility. The evaluations cover the reviewed works in considerable depth (*The World Book Encyclopedia* receives more than seven pages; the new unabridged *Random House Dictionary* receives more than six). Reviews take a detailed look at sample entries, focusing on common entries for a comparable class of reference works. Comments throughout the reviews compare references works, making the evaluations useful to librarian or patron. Most entries include a reproduction of a typical page demonstrating the layout and sample entries. Price and ordering information is included, as is the schedule for revision. The volume ends with a bibliography, a list of publishers, a list of titles reviewed, and an index.

General Reference Books for Adults is designed as an aid to collection development. However, the bright and polished layout and easy-to-read style of *General Reference Books for Adults* are destined to make the book a standard tool in library science classrooms as well. The Board recommends this work for the core collection of public libraries.

Guide to Reference Books, 10th edition. Eugene P. Sheehy, ed. ALA, 1986. hard. 1 vol. 1,560 pp. index. ISBN 0-8389-0390-8. $65. guide.
Z1035.1.S43 011.02

The *Guide to Reference Books* has been known and respected by librarians and library science students for nearly a century. This work was first published in 1902. Most commonly referred to as *Sheehy,* the guide was originally intended as a training tool for library school students. Over the years, however, the emphasis of the text shifted. Today the work is directed toward the needs of the practicing librarian.

The tenth edition, Sheehy's last one as editor, offers brief and descriptive annotations of over 15,000 reference titles published in the United States and Canada. English-language and foreign-language titles are listed. The *Guide to Reference Books* is frequently criticized for not offering an evaluation of the sources the book covers, but no other reference guide approaches the comprehensive and well-balanced coverage or the respect that Sheehy has garnered over the years. The greatest limitation of the *Guide to Reference Books* is that the book is descriptive and makes few, if any, evaluative comments.

This one-volume work is divided into five major disciplines: "General Reference Works," "Humanities," "Social and Behavioral Sciences," "History and Area Studies," and "Science, Technology and Medicine." Each discipline is subdivided into more specific subjects. Major reference works for each topic are then listed according to format, such as dictionaries, handbooks, and directories. Although subject coverage is more balanced than in most other reference guides, there are still some gaps, and treatment is not always equal.

On-line data bases were first included as part of a

supplement to the ninth edition. In the current edition, coverage of on-line resources is limited to just a few standard guides and directories. Sources that are available in a machine-readable form are marked with a bullet.

The index includes authors, editors, compilers, sponsoring organizations, titles, and subjects. Rather than giving the page number on which these citations fall, the index lists the citation's entry number. Because the first and last entry numbers on two facing pages are printed at the tops of those pages, accessing entries using this system is relatively straightforward.

When the eleventh edition appears some years from now, it is safe to assume that there will be some changes in format and in the way electronic and other nonprint resources will be handled. The criteria of *usefulness,* which was applied to every title in the first edition, is still valid today. The *Guide to Reference Books* will continue to be an indispensable resource for the library student and the public, school, or academic librarian who is looking for help in an unfamiliar area. The Board recommends this work for the core collections of public, academic, and school libraries.

Sears List of Subject Headings, 13th edition. Carmen Rovira and Caroline Reyes, eds. Wilson, 1986. hard. 1 vol. 681 pp. ISBN 0-8242-0730-0. $34. handbook.
Z695.S43 025.4′9

Minnie Sears brought out the first *List of Subject Headings for Small Libraries* in 1923 to fill the critical need for uniform subject headings in libraries where the ALA and Library of Congress lists did not work. Then, as now, the Sears headings are presented in a format that is similar to the Library of Congress subject headings. This allows libraries to "graduate" to the Library of Congress headings when they outgrow more limited lists.

The front of the book contains a detailed explanation of the underlying principles behind the *Sears List of Subject Headings,* including guidelines on format, special rules of grammar, a glossary, a bibliography, and a sample page for checking and adding entries. The bulk of this one-volume book is made up of an alphabetical list of subject headings. A typical entry gives the proper subject heading in boldface type, along with the relevant Dewey decimal classification numbers. Appropriate "see," "see also," and "refer from" references accompany each entry, as do notes on the creation and clarification of subject headings. The traditional "x" and "xx" symbols are used in much the same manner as the "UF" and "RT" indicators in the Library of Congress subject headings.

In the preface to the thirteenth edition, the editors maintain that "No list can hope to keep completely abreast of the information explosion, nor can it provide for every idea, object, process, and relationship." However, by providing a basis for consistency, catalogers will be able to add new headings that will be consistent with the rest of the list. One criticism of the *Sears List of Subject Headings* is that the work was designed for use with a manual card catalog. The list has made no concession to the computer age except to add new terminology.

The Board recommends this work for the core collections of public, academic, and school libraries.

Supplementary Titles

Harrod's Librarians' Glossary of Terms Used in Librarianship, Documentation and the Book Crafts, and Reference Book, 6th edition. Ray Prytherch, comp. and ed. Gower, 1987. hard. 1 vol. 880 pp. ISBN 0-566-03538-3. $79.50. dictionary.
Z1006.H32 020.319

In the preface of *Harrod's Librarians' Glossary* "the editor details the work's publishing history and cites revisions of . . . entries and the addition of . . . new terms, primarily in the fields of automation, telecommunications, and information technology.

"Because the glossary goes far beyond explanations of professional terminology and includes historical descriptions of institutions and programs, it serves as a valuable handbook as well. It is particularly strong on developments in Great Britain, the U.S., Canada, and Australia. . . . Despite its price, Harrod's is a worthwhile addition to any professional collection worthy of the name." (*BL,* April 1985, p. 1108)

Also reviewed in: *AB,* September 8, 1980, p. 1328; *ARBA,* 1979, p. 82; 1985, p. 189; 1988, p. 238; *BL,* March 1, 1980, p. 1002; *Brit Bk N,* May 1987, p. 305; *CLW,* April 1972, p. 475; *Indexer,* October 1987, p. 250; *IRLA,* October 1984, p. 1; June 1987, p. 10; *JAL,* July 1987, p. 177; *JLH,* Summer 1979, p. 403; *Lib Sci Ann,* 1985, p. 55; *LJ,* November 1, 1971, p. 3579; June 15, 1978, p. 1238; *LQ,* January 1972, p. 167; *LR,* Winter 1971, p. 153; Summer 1987, p. 153; *TES,* June 2, 1978, p. 49; *WLB,* May 1972, p. 841.

Board's recommendation: Academic libraries.

Library and Information Science Annual. Libraries Unlimited, 1988. hard. 1 vol. indexes. ISBN 0-87287-683-7. $37.50. handbook.
Z666 011.02

Library and Information Science Annual "is an interesting, informative annual. Each volume is divided into four parts: a section of essays on the 'production and distribution of knowledge in library and information science,' which includes an article about a library publisher; a long section . . . of reviews of books in the field; a section of reviews of library periodicals; and a section of selected [doctoral] dissertation abstracts." (*JAL,* May 1988, p. 108)

"[The reference covers] materials from the United States, Canada, Great Britain and Ireland. . . . Part II features in excess of 380 reviews of publications in library and information science. These are grouped by subject with reviewer and source cited.

"Acquisitions librarians, library science librarians, and anyone needing to purchase a book or periodical in the field of information science would find this book helpful. An author/title index and a subject index are included." (*IRLA,* November 1987, p. 10)

Also reviewed in: *ARBA,* 1988, p. 241; *B Rpt,* November 1987, p. 48; *Indexer,* October 1988, p. 136; *LJ,* November 15, 1988, p. 52; *R & R Bk N,* Fall 1987, p. 41.

Board's recommendation: Public and academic libraries.

New and Noteworthy

The New York Public Library Desk Reference. Stonesong Pr., 1989; distrib. by Prentice-Hall. hard. 1 vol. 836 pp. illus. index. ISBN 0-13-620444-9. $29.95. encyclopedia.
AG6.N49 031

"Subtitled 'The Ultimate One Volume Collection of the Most Frequently Sought Information,' *The New York Public Library Desk Reference* is a massive compilation of facts, figures, charts, tables, and illustrations which reference librarians in all kinds and sizes of libraries will find indispensable. Divided into twenty-six chapters, the book covers such wide-ranging subjects as symbols and signs, philosophy, religions, etiquette, words, inventions and scientific discoveries, sports and games, literature, and travel." (*SLJ,* May 1990, p. 22)

The School Librarian's Sourcebook. Claire Rudin. Bowker, 1990. hard. 1 vol. 504 pp. indexes. ISBN 0-8352-2711-1. $34.95. bibliography.
Z675.S3R79 016.0278'223

"This unique annotated bibliography [*The School Librarian's Sourcebook*] is designed to provide a convenient guide for school librarians to further their own independent learning. It is divided into five sections covering administration, collections, services, user education, and technology and other current issues. . . . More than 300 books are given lengthy annotations, often more than a page long, that discuss their purpose, contents, usefulness, and the authority of the authors." (*BL,* May 1990, p. 1745)

Wendell Cochran

Marine Science

See also Science and Technology

Marine science is the study of the parts of the Earth covered by salt water—the seas and oceans. However, the hydrosphere cannot exist independently of the lithosphere and atmosphere. In fact, the water cycle (the continuous cycle of evaporation, condensation, and precipitation) depends upon the interrelationship of land, sea, and air. Thus the boundaries of marine science cannot be drawn definitively, and the reference collection should include information from various scientific disciplines.

Because the subject of marine science is large and complex, so are the references required. First, every collection needs an atlas focusing on the water-covered areas of the Earth. The best atlases show place names, coastlines, shapes, and distances. They should also show resources (food and minerals). A good historical atlas will show how humans have exploited waterways not only for their natural resources but also as routes for commerce and war. No one atlas may meet all demands, so it may be necessary to purchase more than one. The core collection includes two admirable titles.

Also of great importance are dictionaries and encyclopedias that define terms; name and describe animals, minerals, vegetables, and natural phenomena; and ex-

Core Titles

	PUBLIC	ACADEMIC	SCHOOL
The Facts On File Dictionary of Marine Science Charton, Barbara. Facts On File, 1988	✦	✦	✦
McGraw-Hill Encyclopedia of Ocean and Atmospheric Sciences Parker, Sybil P., ed. in chief. McGraw-Hill, 1980	✦	✦	✦
The Rand McNally Atlas of the Oceans Bramwell, Martyn, ed. Rand McNally, 1977	✦	✦	✦
The Times Atlas and Encyclopedia of the Sea, 2d edition Couper, Alastair, ed. HarperCollins, 1990		✦	✦

plain the physics, chemistry, and biology of the marine world.

Unfortunately, works such as those described tend to be large (posing problems in shelving) and expensive. Their selection requires a balance between breadth of coverage and depth of explanation. Also, important works may have gone out of print. For example, the *Ocean World Encyclopedia* (Donald G. Groves and Lee M. Hunt, McGraw-Hill, 1980) and *Seawatch: The Seafarer's Guide to Marine Life* (Paul V. Horsman, Facts On File, 1985) may only be obtained through out-of-print book dealers. Finally, the library's marine science references should complement those in other categories, such as earth science, geology, geography, and biology.

Core Titles

The Facts On File Dictionary of Marine Science. Barbara Charton. Facts On File, 1988. hard. 1 vol. 336 pp. appendixes. ISBN 0-8160-1031-5. $24.95. dictionary.
GC9.F28 551.46003

The authority of *The Facts On File Dictionary of Marine Science* reflects the dictionary's place in the well-respected Facts On File Dictionaries series. Barbara Charton's credentials are also impressive, as she has been library director at Hunter College and has worked as a science reference librarian at Hofstra University.

The Facts On File Dictionary of Marine Science includes nearly 2,000 entries covering a wide range of marine phenomena, including water chemistry, marine ecosystems, physical features of the oceans, currents and their effects, and fauna and flora of the ocean.

The arrangement is alphabetical, word by word, for example, *sea turtle, sea urchin, seal, Sealab, seamount, seawater.* Definitions range from one line (*sea lily,* cross-referenced to *Crinoidea*) to one and a half columns (for *tide*). Other examples further illustrate the range: the definition of *Arabian Plate* occupies six lines, *diving* requires about two columns, and *pollution* occupies more than a page.

The work is written for the nonspecialist, so some readers will need to consult more specialized references. Cross-references are prevalent. Each page has two columns and a guide word at the top of the page to aid in access. Terms are set in boldface. Definitions are separated by blank lines.

The discussion of *Brachiopoda* seems representative of a typical entry in this book. *Brachiopoda* (occupying nearly a column plus a cross-section sketch) is defined as "a phylum of bivalves in which the two valves or shells (dorsal and ventral) are asymmetric, with the ventral shell the larger of the two." The author goes on to say that about 300 living species are known, that the phylum first appeared in the Cambrian period, and that more than 30,000 species have been identified. Current species are from 2 to 115 centimeters long (fossil forms up to 35 centimeters have been discovered). The phylum has been divided into Articulata and Inarticulata, and a widely known genus, *Lingula,* is found in the Hawaiian Islands. Finally, the reader is referred to the entry for *Mollusca.*

This work is also useful for its historical information, such as the brief biographical sketch of Baron Ferdinand Petrovich von Wrangell (1796–1870), governor of Russian America (1829–1835). An appendix provides a chronology of significant events in marine history, from the seventh century B.C. (when Koelus sailed through the Strait of Gibraltar) to 1977 (when vent communities were discovered on the seafloor).

Other useful appendixes in the *Facts On File Dictionary of Marine Science* are a geologic time scale, a taxonomic classification of living organisms (often with the number of known species), and a list of major research projects including the Deep Sea Drilling Project. The Board recommends this work for the core collections of public, academic, and school libraries.

McGraw-Hill Encyclopedia of Ocean and Atmospheric Sciences. Sybil P. Parker, ed. in chief. McGraw-Hill, 1980. hard. 1 vol. 580 pp. ISBN 0-07-045267-9. $76. encyclopedia.
GC9.M32 551.4′6′003

The authority of the *McGraw-Hill Encyclopedia of Ocean and Atmospheric Sciences* depends largely on that of its parent volumes in the McGraw-Hill Encyclopedia of Science and Technology (see Science and Technology) and on its consulting editors, John C. Drake of the University of Vermont, Ralph Shapiro of the U.S. Air Force, and Donald J. P. Swift of the National Oceanic and Atmospheric Administration. Ultimately, of course, the credit belongs to the 209 specialists who wrote the 236 articles.

The work is large but not unwieldy. The work covers most of the Earth's lithosphere and all its atmosphere. Articles are arranged alphabetically *(sea ice, sea-level fluctuation, sea water, seamount).*

The range of topics and length of discussion vary widely, as indicated by the following random samples: the entry for *delta* occupies three and a half pages, *marine mining* continues for seven pages, but *meteorological solenoid* requires only a few lines.

The reading level seems as nearly suitable for general readers as possible, considering the technical complexity of some entries. For the most part, nonspecialists should have little trouble, although keeping a dictionary handy is advisable.

Each page has two columns and a guide word at the top. Frequent boldface subheads aid skimming and searching, as do sideheads in boldface and italic typeface. Helpful devices include tables, bibliographies, and frequent cross-references to other articles. An illustrative example is the entry for *sea water,* which runs to about 23 pages with 16 figures, 9 tables, 5 bibliographies, and about 25 cross-references. This particular entry was written by more than 20 people.

The book lacks discussion of recent research satellites such as Landsat and mentions the Deep Sea Drilling Project only once (there are photos of the principal drilling vessel, the *Glomar Challenger*). Plate tectonics is discussed (under *oceans*), but plumes, hot spots, and subduction receive little or no coverage. The latest bibliographic entries are for 1978, but most of the information is current enough to be useful. The price of the *McGraw-Hill Encyclopedia of Ocean and Atmospheric Sciences* is the highest for books in this category, but no other title discusses water and air and their interaction to the same degree. The Board recommends this work for the core collections of public, academic, and school libraries.

The Rand McNally Atlas of the Oceans. Martyn Bramwell, ed. Rand McNally, 1977. hard. 1 vol. 208 pp. index. ISBN 0-528-83295-6. $40. atlas.
G2800.R3 551.46

The Rand McNally Atlas of the Oceans has 35 contributing authors and editorial consultants, led by William A. Nierenberg, director of the Scripps Institution of Oceanography, and Henry Charnock and George Deacon of the Institution of Oceanographic Sciences. Most of the authors are from the East and West coasts of the United States and from England. This international assembly has also published variations of this work (under slightly different titles) in other countries.

The atlas is large, as any serious research atlas requires large pages to display maps and other illustrations. The work is not cumbersome, however.

As stated in the introduction, this atlas focuses on the "component parts of the ocean—its life, its surface, its depths, its islands and archipelagos, and its interface with the continents we live on. . . . [I]t also pertains to man's interaction with, and intervention, in the oceans."

The atlas uses the theory of plate tectonics as the unifying theme of the book: the "physical features of the oceans and their relationships with the continents can all now be rationalized in the new concept of plate tectonics and continental drift" (introduction). Other themes include the ocean as a source of food and minerals, an aid to commerce, an important factor in weather and climate, and an object of research and applied science. If any one subject is especially prominent, it is the ocean as a realm of life and a source of food.

The organization of this work facilitates either reading from beginning to end or using the index for efficient research. The reader may also wish to consult the contents page, where the following chapter titles are listed: "The Ocean Realm," "Man's Oceanic Quest," "Life in the Oceans," "The Great Resource," "The Face of the Deep," and "Encyclopedia of Marine Life."

The contents of each chapter are briefly described on the contents page. For example, under "Life in the Oceans," the explanation reads, "The pyramid of marine life; from plankton to dolphins—the structure of sea creatures; vertebrates and invertebrates—living fossils—mammals and reptiles—birdlife and the shoreline—creatures of the shallows and the deep ocean." These brief analyses, used in conjunction with the index of nearly 7,000 entries, should suffice for most ordinary information searches.

Throughout *The Rand McNally Atlas,* the data appear to be as recent as can be expected. The reading level is suitable for nonspecialists, although some of the more technical terms may require the use of the glossary of about 85 terms. Librarians may wish to compare *The Rand McNally Atlas of the Oceans* with THE TIMES ATLAS AND ENCYLCOPEDIA OF THE SEA; coverage is much the same, but the organization differs markedly. The Board recommends this work for the core collections of public, academic, and school libraries.

The Times Atlas and Encyclopedia of the Sea, 2d edition. Alastair Couper, ed. HarperCollins, 1990. hard. 1 vol. 272 pp. appendixes. index. ISBN 0-06-016287-2. $59.95. atlas.
G2800.T5 551.46002

The Times Atlas and Encyclopedia of the Sea has been called "the finest reference book of the year" by the American Library Association. The reputations of the first edition, the original publisher, the editor, and the 27 contributors justify confidence in the work's authority. The editor and most contributors are either British or from the eastern seaboard of the United States, suggesting an Atlantic point of view, but no factual bias is evident in content.

The pages are large, permitting sizable maps and more than 600 detailed, color illustrations. As indicated by the recent publication date, the information is very current.

This work serves several purposes; it is an inventory of total ocean resources, an explication of physical and biological interactions, and a history of seafaring, including the reasons for merchant routes and the deployment of navies. Other topics covered are the research and management of resources and the international laws of the sea.

The reading level of this reference tool is appropriate for both experts and general readers, although nonspecialists may consult the glossary more frequently.

The organization of the book enables readers to begin anywhere without having prior knowledge of the material. The index, which is 15 pages long and includes about 7,000 entries, speeds searching, and numerous cross-references facilitate access to related matter.

Also helpful are the two tables of contents. The shorter of the two lists only the main sections—"The Ocean Environment," "Resources of the Ocean," "Ocean Trade," and "The World Ocean," with several major topics under each.

The longer listing of contents (of eight pages) expands on these topics. Each main section is listed and then outlined in detail on facing pages. For example, "The Ocean Environment" is further divided into: "The Geography of the Oceans and Seas," "The Ocean Basins," "The Ocean-Atmosphere System," and "The Oceans and Life." Reading from left to right across the two pages, each topic is summed up in about 200 words, illustrated with a photograph, and then subdivided into about six subtopics, each with a short description and its page number.

Finally, the book concludes with a glossary of about 680 terms, a bibliography, an index, and appendixes on units of measurements, oceanic geography, oceans and life, living resources, oil and gas, ships and cargoes, shipping routes (with distance and sailing times between ports), naval operations, major research programs, the problem of managing oceans (including pollution control), and a list of endangered species.

The price of *The Times Atlas* will undoubtedly lead to comparisons with THE RAND MCNALLY ATLAS OF THE OCEANS. Although *The Times Atlas* is considerably more expensive, the choice should be made according to organizational preference. The Rand McNally work is more traditional, and suited to extended reading; *The Times Atlas and Encyclopedia of the Sea* is less conventional and suited to searching and sampling.

The Board recommends this work for the core collections of academic and school libraries.

Supplementary Titles

The Ocean Almanac. Robert Hendrickson. Doubleday, 1984. soft. 1 vol. 446 pp. index. ISBN 0-385-14077-0. $15.95. encyclopedia.
GC21.H4 551.46

"Marine life, sea stories and legends, famous ships and sea battles, pirates and mutineers, and a variety of . . . sea lore are contained in [*The Ocean Almanac*]." (*SB,* November 1984, p. 81)

"[Reading this book] is a bit like being at sea in a rudderless boat, adrift among anecdotes, short essays, and random entries, some quite fascinating and exciting. . . . What this volume lacks in coherence, however, it makes up in variety of topics. It is a browser's delight. . . . Only good marine jokes are missing." (*LJ,* January 1984, p. 75)

Also reviewed in: *BL,* February 1, 1984, p. 773; *CG,* June 1984, p. 78; *PW,* January 13, 1984, p. 67.

Board's recommendation: Public and academic libraries.

Dr. Lesley S. J. Farmer

Mathematics

Mathematics, though it is a vital subject, is often overlooked in reference collection development. While the traditional concepts have not changed measurably, recent developments in mathematics and its applications necessitate that librarians keep current on what is available in new reference editions.

Besides the foundation concepts of algebra, geometry, and calculus, mathematics information entails statistics, measurement, recreational mathematics, history, biography, and applications in an increasing number of related fields. Reference material should also exhibit an international perspective, particularly in terms of conversion factors and standards.

User information needs range from quick definitions for young students to research reviews for scholars. Users may consult mathematical reference tools to help them review for examinations, convert units for machine repair, calculate annuities, or determine levels of significance in testing hypotheses.

In developing the mathematical reference collection, the librarian should look for these qualities: authority and reputation, accuracy, currency, completeness, and ease of use. Knowledge of potential user needs will help determine whether a general or a specialized reference is required. The librarian should examine frequently used terms and formulas when selecting mathematical tools. Few high-quality reference works in mathematics exist, so "brand name" reference book publishers become a safe way to develop the collection.

At the minimum, though, a reference collection should include a mathematical dictionary, a handbook of formulas and tables, and a guide to international units of measurement. Both pure and applied mathematics should be covered in reference sources. The titles chosen for the core and supplementary lists adequately address these needs. The academic collection also should include, of course, journals and periodicals, such as the *Mathematical Review,* the principal source for information about current mathematical research.

Core Titles

CRC Handbook of Mathematical Sciences, 6th edition. William H. Beyer, ed. CRC Pr., 1987. hard. 1 vol. 860 pp. illus. appendix. index. ISBN 0-8493-0656-6. $79.95. handbook.
QA47.H324 510.21′2

CRC Press is well known for its authoritative technical handbooks for the sciences. The *CRC Handbook of Mathematical Sciences* exemplifies the high stan-

Core Titles

	PUBLIC	ACADEMIC	SCHOOL
CRC Handbook of Mathematical Sciences, 6th edition Beyer, William H., ed. CRC Pr., 1987		✦	
Dictionary of Mathematics Terms Downing, Douglas. Barron's, 1987	✦	✦	
Handbook of Mathematical Tables and Formulas, 5th edition Burington, Richard S. McGraw-Hill, 1973	✦	✦	
Mathematics Dictionary, 4th edition James, Glenn, Robert C. James, and Armen A. Alchian. Van Nostrand Reinhold, 1976	✦	✦	✦
Quantities and Units of Measurement: A Dictionary and Handbook Drazil, J. V. Mansell, 1983; distrib. by Wilson	✦	✦	

dards set by the publisher. Probably the most comprehensive reference source for both traditional and modern mathematical concepts, this handbook may be used by the serious student as well as by the mathematics and science professional.

The *CRC Handbook of Mathematical Sciences* has been published for over 20 years. The editors carefully review the contents of each edition for continued accuracy and relevance. The sixth edition has been expanded in the area of statistics, which reflects the impact of computer technology. This work, however, will be equally useful to physicists, engineers, and others seeking mathematical solutions.

Thirteen sections deal with various mathematical topics. Each section groups major concepts together, providing full explanations of formulas and including some examples and diagrams. Tables of values are integrated with the presentation of the accompanying formula.

The first section contains units of measure and their conversions, along with common fractions and constants. The second section covers algebra: basic concepts through matrices and determinants. The third section covers combinatorial analysis: powers of numbers, probability, number bases, and factors and primes.

The fourth section briefly summarizes geometric figures and formulas. The fifth section covers trigonometry in more detail, and the sixth section covers logarithmic, exponential, and hyperbolic functions. The seventh section notes formulas for solid geometry.

Sections 8 through 11 explain calculus topics: integations, differential equations, special formulas, and numerical methods.

Section 12 treats probability and statistics, including various distribution tables. The final section covers basic equations used in astrodynamics.

An extensive list of mathematical symbols and abbreviations for each field concludes the handbook. A simple subject index provides some access, although there are few subheads to aid the user.

Although substantial in bulk, the volume is well bound. The only visual drawback is the uneven quality and size of typeface.

The treatment of various topics throughout the *CRC Handbook of Mathematical Sciences* is balanced, with the understanding that the user has a basic knowledge of elementary mathematics. Academic students can learn the fundamentals of most concepts by using this reference work, and the advanced professional will value CRC for its clear, short review of basic principles. The Board recommends this work for the core collection of academic libraries.

Dictionary of Mathematics Terms. Douglas Downing. Barron's, 1987. soft. 1 vol. 241 pp. illus. appendix. ISBN 0-8120-2641-1. $8.95. dictionary.
QA5.D69 510.3'21

For a compact guide to mathematical terms and statistical tables, Downing's *Dictionary of Mathematics Terms* is a cost-effective purchase for reference collections.

Author Douglas Downing, who is affiliated with the School of Economics at Seattle Pacific University, provides a practical list of over 600 mathematical terms used in basic mathematics, statistics, and computer technology. Although he assumes that the user has a basic knowledge of mathematics, Downing offers definitions that the high school student can grasp. In fact, his explanations for simpler concepts seem clearer and more detailed than those for more advanced terms.

A brief list of mathematical symbols begins the text. Next, a selected list of terms grouped by mathematical category (for example, algebra or calculus) provides the user with an idea of the scope of material included.

The main body of the text consists of a dictionary of definitions for mathematical terms. Entries tend to be a few lines long, although the *simultaneous equations* entry continues for three pages. Some entries include cross-references that refer the reader to other entries for background information or more advanced terminology. This feature somewhat compensates for the lack of an index. Some entries include examples and application information. The writing style is clear and simple, and clear line drawings augment the text.

While traditional mathematical material is the primary focus, some terms from applied sciences, such as physics, are included. Computer terms are few.

An inexpensive, current paperback, this volume offers information about common mathematical terms that is easily accessible. The Board recommends this work for the core collections of public and academic libraries.

Handbook of Mathematical Tables and Formulas, 5th edition. Richard S. Burington. McGraw-Hill, 1973. soft. 1 vol. 500 pp. illus. appendix. indexes. ISBN 0-07-009015-7. $37.95. handbook.
QA47.B8 510.21′2

Since 1933, the *Handbook of Mathematical Tables and Formulas* has been a basic reference tool for students and professionals in the applied sciences. A companion to Burington's *Handbook of Probability and Statistics with Tables,* this source concentrates on pure and applied mathematics. As the author notes in the preface, the use of computer technology does not negate the use of tables that compile figures. Rather, the need for such compilations has grown for the academic and public population.

Part 1 of the book contains basic formulas, definitions, and theorems found in elementary mathematics. Basically, information is arranged in order of complexity, from the most basic concepts and terms to the most advanced. Topics include algebra, elementary and analytic geometry, trigonometry, the calculus, vector analysis, set and group theory, logic, number systems, matrix and linear algebra, numerical analysis, special functions and equations, series, transforms, and statistics. Some introductory explanations and examples complement the list of formulas.

Part 2 consists of tables: logarithmic, trigonometric, exponential and hyperbolic functions, simple powers and roots, basic circle-based figures, factorials, basic statistical distributions, interest and actuarial tables, constants and fractions, and basic measurement conversion factors.

To augment the main text of the *Handbook of Mathematical Tables and Formulas,* the author has appended a bibliography of related treatises, textbooks, tables, and general guides to tables. A glossary of symbols, grouped by mathematical category, provides an overview of common signs encountered in the text. Two indexes are included: an index of numerical tables and a subject index with lengthy subentries, which further assist the user in accessing the text.

The Board recommends this work for the core collections of public and academic libraries.

Mathematics Dictionary, 4th edition. Glenn James, Robert C. James, and Armen A. Alchian. Van Nostrand Reinhold, 1976. hard. 1 vol. 509 pp. illus. indexes. ISBN 0-442-24091-0. $39.95. dictionary.
QA5.J32 510.3

First published in 1949, the *Mathematics Dictionary* continues to provide authoritative definitions for a broad range of mathematics taught at the secondary and undergraduate levels, although professionals as well as students can make good use of the information provided in the text.

This fourth edition includes three significant improvements over past editions: updated information on probability and statistics, short biographies of mathematicians, and foreign-language translations of common mathematical terms.

The main text of the dictionary is an alphabetical arrangement of definitions of mathematical terms. The main entry words for each term are followed by the definition, different usages of the term, subentries, and associated terms. Extensive cross-references offer additional access to related terms.

The definitions are written in a condensed style, but the user gains a perspective on associated terms, as can be seen in the entry for *differential.* Besides a brief definition and pronunciation guide, applicable entries also include formulas and occasional diagrams.

Additional features include conversion tables for international measurements, mathematical symbols associated with different mathematical topics (each category is arranged alphabetically), differentiation formulas, integral tables, and four separate indexes that translate terms from French, German, Russian, and Spanish into their English equivalents.

Compared to other standard reference tools, the *Mathematics Dictionary* covers more topics than the DICTIONARY OF MATHEMATICS TERMS, including recreational mathematics. However, the *Mathematics Dictionary* assumes a greater mathematical knowledge base on the part of the user and does not deal with application of the terms in other fields.

The Board recommends this work for the core collections of public, academic, and school libraries.

Quantities and Units of Measurement: A Dictionary and Handbook. J. V. Drazil. Mansell, 1983; distrib. by Wilson. soft. 1 vol. 313 pp. appendixes. indexes. ISBN 0-7201-1665-1. $29.95. handbook.
QC82.D73 530.8'03'21

Finding comprehensive lists of international standards and units of measurements poses a problem for the librarian and researcher. Recognizing these limitations, Drazil's *Quantities and Units of Measurement* offers help in this area.

Drazil bases the data on SI standards, U.S. and British standards, and those of other national groups. The values for constants are derived from the *Report of the CODATA Task Group in Fundamental Concepts* (published by the National Bureau of Standards).

With an emphasis on applied sciences and technology, Drazil provides guides for the correct use and definition of this terminology. Part 1 covers units of measurement for international systems and provides conversion factors. Part 2 notes quantities and constants used in applied sciences as well as standard units. Part 3 lists symbols for quantities and constants.

Entries are brief, ranging from a few lines to a half page, and are arranged alphabetically. Each entry includes the term, its symbol, the equivalent French and German term, the system or country where the term is used, the relationship between units and systems and quantity and systems, dimension (such as time or temperature), conversion factors, and appropriate tables. Many entries contain cross-references to reinforce quantitative relationships. A guide at the front of the book ("Symbols and Abbreviations Used") helps decipher the concise format of the entries. It should be noted that British spelling is used throughout.

Four appendixes follow the main text: definitions of base SI units, a comparison between British and U.S. units, and recommended consistent values of fundamental constants (such as ergs). The fourth appendix lists national and international standards—information that is usually difficult to find in other sources. Indexes for the French and German terms conclude the volume and provide further evidence of its international scope and use. Another valuable feature, found at the beginning of the book, is a list of common prefixes and expressions used in measurement.

The paperback binding is poor, and some of the type is small, which limits the book's usefulness. However, because of the international scope of this valuable information, *Quantities and Units of Measurement* will be most helpful, particularly for the professional user in the applied sciences. The Board recommends this work for the core collections of public and academic libraries.

Supplementary Titles

Encyclopedia of Statistical Sciences. Samuel Kotz, Norman L. Johnson, and Campbell B. Read, eds. John Wiley, 1982–1988. hard. 8 vols. ISBN 0-471-05556-5 (vol. 8). $121 (vol. 8). encyclopedia.
QA276.14E5 519.5'03'21

The *Encyclopedia of Statistical Sciences*, ". . . an eight-volume compendium of statistics, will be the most comprehensive encyclopedia in its subject yet published. . . . [The reference] is intended for the reader who wants an introduction to a statistical concept or application and who has some general understanding of mathematics. Among the kinds of topics covered are concepts and theorems (analysis of covariance, Bayesian inference), formulas and models (concentration ratio . . .), applications (anthropology . . .), biographical articles, and articles on major statistical journals and organizations. Each article includes a list of bibliographic references. There are numerous cross-references to related articles and terms as well as the usual see references. The text is extremely well written and edited, and the volumes are well bound and typographically pleasing." (*ARBA,* 1984, p. 340)

"According to the preface, the set attempts to be comprehensive and to 'mirror the state of the art in the last quarter of the twentieth century.' . . . All entries except those written by the editors are signed. A list of contributors and affiliations is included in each volume.

"Kotz, Johnson, and Read have produced an outstanding encyclopedia, a soon-to-be-recognized 'standard work.' " (*ARBA,* 1987, p. 324)

Board's recommendation: Academic libraries.

Encyclopedic Dictionary of Mathematics, 2d edition. Mathematical Society of Japan. MIT Pr., 1977. hard. 4 vols. 1,750 pp. appendixes. indexes. ISBN 0-262-09016-3. $350. dictionary.
QA5.N513 510.3

The *Encyclopedic Dictionary of Mathematics* "is the English translation of the second (1968) edition of a Japanese work whose first edition appeared in 1954. . . . The body of the dictionary consists of an alphabetically ordered collection of 436 articles of mathematical subjects from 'Abel, Niels Henrik' to 'Zeta functions.'

"Two long appendixes supply the most important mathematical tables and formulas that are not readily available in standard books. The name and subject indexes are both thorough and very helpful. Other useful reference features are lists of mathematical journals, mathematical publishers, and special mathematical notation." (*Choice,* March 1978, p. 46)

"Each [main article] is prefaced with general remarks or a history, [and] subdivided into appropriate (cross-referenced!) sections." (*LJ,* December 15, 1977, p. 2492)

Also reviewed in: *ARBA,* 1978, p. 628; *RSR,* July 1978, p. 19; *SA,* April 1981, p. 31; *WLB,* March 1978, p. 587.

Board's recommendation: Academic libraries.

Handbook of Applied Mathematics: Selected Results and Methods. Carl E. Pearson, ed. Van Nostrand Reinhold, 1983. soft. 1 vol. 1,304 pp. illus. index. ISBN 0-442-00521-0. $39.95. handbook.
QA40.H34 510.2'02

The *Handbook of Applied Mathematics* "contains 21 chapters on various techniques in applied mathematics, such as vector analysis, differential equations, transform methods, asymptotic methods, oscillations and wave propagation. References and bibliography follow each chapter." (*RSR,* January/March 1975, p. 125)

Also reviewed in: Choice, May 1975, p. 422; *SB,* January 1984, p. 136.

Board's recommendation: Academic libraries.

McGraw-Hill Dictionary of Physics and Mathematics. Daniel N. Lapedes, ed. in chief. McGraw-Hill, 1978. hard. 1 vol. 1,074 pp. illus. appendix. ISBN 0-07-045480-9. $46.50. dictionary.
QC5.M23 530.03

The *McGraw-Hill Dictionary of Physics and Mathematics* "is intended 'to provide the high school and college student, librarian, teacher, engineer, researcher, and the general public with the vocabulary of physics, mathematics, and related disciplines such as statistics, astronomy, electronics, and geophysics.' The more than 20,000 terms . . . are those that the editor considered fundamental to the understanding of physics and mathematics.

"Relevant synonyms and acronyms are cited [in this volume], and cross-references abound. . . . The definitions average about three to four lines each." (*BL,* March 15, 1980, p. 1083)

"There are roughly 4 illustrations for every 100 items. . . . In addition, an extensive appendix provides useful tables of fundamental constants, conversion factors, semiconductor symbols, elementary particles, chemical elements, crystal structure, mathematical notation, and astronomical information." (*Choice,* March 1979, p. 56)

Also reviewed in: *ARBA,* 1979, p. 660; *Cur R,* May 1979, p. 138; *RSR,* July 1982, p. 17; *SB,* September 1979, p. 82; *WLB,* January 1979, p. 409.

Board's recommendation: Public, academic, and school libraries.

Women of Mathematics: A Biobibliographic Sourcebook. Louise S. Grinstein and Paul J. Campbell, eds. Greenwood, 1987. hard. 1 vol. 292 pp. appendixes. indexes. ISBN 0-313-24849-4. $55. bibliography.
QA28.W66 510.92'2

"Each of the forty-three articles in [*Women of Mathematics*] 'contains a biography, a summary of achievements, and a bibliography of works by and about the woman mathematician.' Numerous appendixes and indexes enhance the value of this bibliography." (*Choice,* November 1987, p. 512)

"With its thoughtful essays, . . . bibliographies, and summary of sources of biographical information, the volume should prove useful both as a reference work and as a stimulus for further investigations of the history of women in mathematics." (*Sci,* November 20, 1987, p. 1153)

Also reviewed in: *ARBA,* 1988, p. 700; *CRL,* January 1988, p. 71; *LJ,* September 1, 1987, p. 175; *R&R Bk N,* Fall 1987, p. 34; *SB,* January 1988, p. 159; *SciTech,* October 1987, p. 7.

Board's recommendation: Academic libraries.

New and Noteworthy

Webster's New World Dictionary of Mathematics. William Karush. Webster's New World, 1989; distrib. by Prentice-Hall. soft. 1 vol. 317 pp. ISBN 0-13-192667-5. $11.95. dictionary.
QA5.K27 510.3

"*Webster's New World Dictionary of Mathematics* is the latest addition to the growing number of dictionaries in the field of mathematics. Through its 1,422 alphabetically arranged entries, this work provides definitions of terms from all of the various subfields of mathematics. . . . This work is designed for high school and college students, and the definitions are written at the appropriate reading level. It provides an effective overview of the field for students of mathematics and other readers with some technical background." (*BL*, December 15, 1989, pp. 860–861)

Barbara C. Beattie

Medicine and Dentistry

See also Consumer Health; Nursing; Psychology and Psychiatry

The field of medical reference works is both diverse and complex. It reflects the changing state of medical practice. In less than a century the medical profession has changed from one in which the general practitioner was the dominant force to one in which there are 24 recognized medical specialties, many of which have subspecialties. The proliferation of medical publishing reflects this growth. Numerous texts, handbooks, and journals exist for each branch of medicine. It is beyond the scope of this core collection, of course, to include references that provide specialized information such as the details of surgical techniques or the staging of a particular form of cancer. Instead, the core collection offered here consists of generalized works that address the field of medicine as a whole. These are basic, standard resources that any layperson or student might need to consult from time to time.

Medicine is also a field in which consumerism has come to play an active role. Laypersons and patients are encouraged and motivated to be informed about their health, illness, and treatment. This collection includes resources that lay consumers would also find helpful.

A few dictionaries and a fact book of medicine are included, as well as some references about drugs, chemicals, and poisons. Two texts, one professional and one lay oriented, provide information about the whole range of medical problems and their treatment. An anatomy text, a health care facility guide, and miscellaneous other reference books complete the collection.

In addition to the main text, many of these references contain appendixes with handy ready-reference information. Weight and measure equivalents, medical etymology, medical symbols and abbreviations, and normal laboratory values are some of the data available in many of these books. Historical, biographical, and statistical information on the medical field can also be found by consulting these resources.

This should not be considered an all-encompassing medical reference collection. Rather, this should be regarded as a basis upon which to build according to the needs of each set of users. Academic libraries will need to add to this collection by acquiring standard textbooks in the different medical specialties. Public libraries may also wish to acquire a few select professional texts as well as consumer-level books on various topics according to demand. Fortunately, the references recommended here are reasonably priced, with one or two exceptions. Medical books can be quite costly, and librarians will probably have to choose their additions very carefully.

Three other resources not considered here should also be considered part of a core medical collection.

Core Titles

	PUBLIC	ACADEMIC	SCHOOL
Admission Requirements of U.S. and Canadian Dental Schools American Assn. of Dental Schools, annual (1974–)	✦	✦	
American Hospital Association Guide to the Health Care Field American Hospital Assn., annual (1972–)	✦	✦	
American Medical Association Family Medical Guide, rev. edition Kunz, Jeffrey, R. M., and Asher J. Finkel, eds. Random House, 1987 (See Consumer Health)	✦	✦	✦
Dangerous Properties of Industrial Materials, 7th edition Sax, N. Irving, and Richard J. Lewis, Sr. Van Nostrand Reinhold, 1988	✦	✦	
Dorland's Illustrated Medical Dictionary, 27th edition Saunders, 1988	✦	✦	✦
Handbook of Poisoning: Prevention, Diagnosis and Treatment, 12th edition Dreisbach, Robert H., and William O. Robertson. Appleton & Lange, 1987	✦	✦	
Medical School Admission Requirements Assn. of American Medical Colleges, annual (1978–)	✦	✦	
The Merck Index: An Encyclopedia of Chemicals, Drugs, and Biologicals, 11th edition (See Chemistry)	✦	✦	
The Merck Manual of Diagnosis and Therapy, 15th edition Berkow, Robert, ed. Merck, Sharp & Dohme, 1987	✦	✦	
The Oxford Companion to Medicine, 2 vols. Walton, John, Paul B. Beeson, and Ronald B. Scott, eds. Oxford, 1986	✦	✦	
Physicians' Desk Reference Barnhart, Edward R., pub. Medical Economics, annual (1947–)	✦	✦	
Webster's Medical Desk Dictionary Pease, Roger W., Jr., ed. Merriam-Webster, 1986	✦		

The *American Medical Directory* (American Medical Association, biennial) lists all licensed physicians in the United States and is the most comprehensive directory of physicians available. *Index Medicus* (National Library of Medicine, U.S.G.P.O., monthly) is the single most important index to biomedical periodical literature published in the United States and is a valuable source for physicians, writers, and editors. Last, the *American Dental Directory* (American Dental Association, annual) is the American Dental Association's authoritative listing of dentists in the United States.

Core Titles

Admission Requirements of U.S. and Canadian Dental Schools. American Assn. of Dental Schools, annual (1974–). soft. 1 vol. 205 pp. illus. appendix. ISSN 0091-729X. $20. guidebook.
RK91.A5822 617.6'0023

Admission Requirements of U.S. and Canadian Dental Schools is a complete compendium of information and data relating to dental education. Published in its

26th edition in 1988 by the American Association of Dental Schools (AADS), this book is an authoritative guide to all 58 U.S. and 10 Canadian schools. The book is revised annually.

The first chapter of the book briefly describes dentistry as a career, discussing types of opportunities and giving sources of further information. Chapter 2 provides general information about dental education. Admission tests, admission procedures, and costs are covered. Of particular interest is the section on financial aid, in which 14 programs are described. The Guaranteed Student Loan Program, Perkins Loans, work-study programs, the Health Professions Student Loan Program, and a package of loans endorsed by the AADS and the American Student Dental Association are among the programs listed.

Chapter 3 forms the main body of the work and profiles each of the dental schools. The information contained in the profiles is supplied by the schools themselves to ensure accuracy. The profiles are arranged alphabetically by state or province. Each four-page entry follows a standard format that includes sections on general information, dental program descriptions, admission requirements, selection factors, application timetable, financial aid, and information for special applicants.

The dental program section explains in detail the structure of the curriculum, clinical experience and research opportunities, and student evaluation. Admission requirements include the number of predental college years, Dental Admission Test (DAT) scores, GPA, and residency. The selection factors section describes additional attributes considered in candidates as well as interviewing policy. The timetable supplies dates and deadlines for the filing of applications, notification of acceptance, applicant response to acceptance, and the start of the program. Each profile also includes a chart of estimated expenses for each year of the program for both resident and nonresident students, excluding living expenses. Each profile also provides a description of the characteristics of the most recent entering class. Statistics shown include number of applicants and number enrolled (both broken down into sex and race), number of residents and nonresidents, years of predental education, and mean test scores.

Admission Requirements of U.S. and Canadian Dental Schools is a primary resource for students considering a dental career. By consulting this reference, a student can obtain a reliable picture of potential schools and a reasonable idea of the cost of a dental education. The Board recommends this work for the core collections of public and academic libraries.

American Hospital Association Guide to the Health Care Field. American Hospital Assn., annual (1972–). soft. 1 vol. 956 pp. illus. index. ISBN 0-87258-544-1. $195. handbook. abridged version on disk.
RA977.A1H6 362

The *American Hospital Association Guide to the Health Care Field* serves as both a directory and a factbook for all health-related facilities and organizations in the United States and associated territories. Published annually by the American Hospital Association (AHA), it is based upon data gathered in the AHA Annual Survey of Hospitals. While the AHA states in the introduction that it does not guarantee the accuracy of data voluntarily reported by institutions, the *AHA Guide* is nonetheless considered an essential, authoritative sourcebook.

The book is divided into sections, which are on differently colored pages and easily identifiable. In addition to the main contents page, each section has its own detailed table of contents, which allows readers to find their way smoothly through the guide.

The first section, the largest, contains a complete listing of U.S. hospitals. Osteopathic hospitals are included as well as government hospitals outside the United States. Arrangement is alphabetical by state, then city, then hospital. For each hospital a wealth of information is provided in a concise format, including the hospital address, phone number, administrator, type of hospital, specific services and facilities available, accreditations, and whether it is affiliated with a multihospital system. Brief statistical information concerning inpatient data, expense, and personnel is also provided. In order to keep the entries concise, some of the information is coded, which means that the reader must flip back and forth between the key and the page being consulted. This is a minor inconvenience, however, compared to the detail of information this arrangement allows. Using the facility codes for a given hospital, for example, the reader can refer to the key to ascertain whether it has an open heart surgery facility, a burn care unit, a psychiatric inpatient unit, and so on, as well as an explanation of exactly what services that type of facility encompasses. The last part of this section is an alphabetical listing of all the hospitals, and thus serves as an index to the main geographical listing.

The second section provides directory and brief statistical data on multihospital systems and their member hospitals. Access is provided alphabetically, geographically, and by system code.

Another very useful section in the *AHA Guide* lists various types of health organizations and agencies. These include international, national, regional, state, and local organizations; U.S., state, and local government agencies; and health care providers other than hospitals. The state and local listings include hospital associations; hospital, medical, and nursing licensing agencies; peer review organizations; and state health planning agencies. The health care providers category conveniently lists long-term-care facilities, HMOs, ambulatory surgery centers, hospices, and psychiatric services. Thus, the reader can find the address for the Florida Blue Cross–Blue Shield plan, a listing of hospices in New Jersey, or the North Carolina state health planning agency.

A brief index is provided, although it is hardly necessary given the detailed contents pages mentioned earlier.

The *American Hospital Association Guide to the Health Care Field* is a comprehensive sourcebook covering all facets of the health care delivery system and is the only publication of its kind. It is a first-stop reference that brings together much information that the reader would otherwise have to search out through numerous sources. The compact format of the guide allows it to remain a manageable size. Because it is softcover, however, repeated handling may cause pages to become unglued. Although it is rather costly, the Board recommends this work for the core collections of public and academic libraries.

American Medical Association Family Medical Guide, rev. edition. Jeffrey R. M. Kunz and Asher J. Finkel, eds. Random House, 1987. hard. 1 vol. 832 pp. illus. appendix. index. ISBN 0-394-55582-1. $29.95. handbook.
RC81.A543 616

See Consumer Health.

Dangerous Properties of Industrial Materials, 7th edition. N. Irving Sax and Richard J. Lewis, Sr. Van Nostrand Reinhold, 1988. hard. 3 vols. 4,000 pp. illus. index. ISBN 0-442-28020-3 (set). $395 (set). handbook.
T55.3.H353 604.7

Dangerous Properties of Industrial Materials is an extensive compendium of toxicology data for more than 19,000 substances. It is designed to be a reference regarding hazard information for laboratory chemicals and industrial materials with the aim of promoting safety in the workplace.

The volume, which claims to be "the classic book in the field," includes "drugs, food additives, preservatives, ores, pesticides, dyes, detergents, lubricants, soaps, plastics, extracts from plant and animal sources, plants and animals which are toxic by contact or consumption, and industrial intermediates and waste products from production processes." Trade name commercial products are for the most part excluded, since they are compounded mixtures of more than one substance.

The main body of the work is the alphabetical listing of substances, consisting of approximately 2,200 pages. Various types of toxicology data are supplied, including mutation data, skin and eye irritation data, toxic dose data, aquatic toxicity ratings, and the American Conference of Government Industrial Hygienists (ACGIH) Threshold Limit Values. The ACGIH value refers to the average concentration of a substance to which a person can be exposed without any adverse effects. Most of the aforementioned data are accompanied by cited references. In addition to the detailed toxicological data, each entry includes synonyms, Chemical Abstracts Service number, National Institute for Occupational Safety and Health (NIOSH) number, and molecular weight and formula. Finally, entries provide citations to literature reviews, government standards and regulations, and a statement regarding potential fire, explosion, and disaster hazards.

Entries are in an abbreviated format, and much of the data are coded. The information is thus not readily accessible to the uninitiated user. The 13-page introduction provides very detailed explanations of each data line, and a thorough reading of these pages is necessary to ably interpret the information supplied in the entries.

Literature references are supplied through the use of a code: source titles are identified by a six-letter designation followed by three numbers representing the volume number, page number, and year of publication. The reader must then refer to the last section of the book, which lists all of the designations and the source titles they represent.

Immediately following the substance description section is a synonym index that lists almost 55,000 synonyms and cross-references them to the main entry name.

The front matter of this volume consists of five essays related to various aspects of safety in the workplace. The first explains the general principles of toxicology. The second concerns industrial air contaminant control. The third essay discusses risks imposed by industrial and environmental carcinogens. The fourth essay, entitled "Occupational Biohazards," is a discussion of allergenic, toxic, or infectious effects of animal and plant products. The last essay concerns the application, benefits, and risks of nuclear medicine. Each section is written by experts in the respective fields.

Dangerous Properties of Industrial Materials is an exhaustive toxicology reference. The seventh edition is a huge volume, weighing approximately ten pounds. Its high price reflects its detailed content. It is an essential resource for all personnel concerned with the effects of chemical substances. Academic and public libraries will need a copy in order to serve students, medical workers, medical personnel, and researchers. The Board recommends this work for the core collections of public and academic libraries.

Dorland's Illustrated Medical Dictionary, 27th edition. Saunders, 1988. hard. 1 vol. 1,888 pp. illus. appendixes. ISBN 0-7216-3154-1. $39.95. dictionary.
R121.D73 610.321

Dorland's Illustrated Medical Dictionary has served as a reputable source of medical and scientific terminology for 88 years. Its consistency of quality over time has established it as the "standard" unabridged medical dictionary.

Dorland's is revised regularly (there are three years between the previous and current editions), and this is important in the medical arena, where advances and new discoveries are occurring constantly.

The purpose of *Dorland's* is twofold: to be a record of medical vocabulary currently in use and to establish proper usage. The editors have attempted to strike a balance between these two objectives by including all terms in everyday use, but by indicating preference for the more correct forms. The preface states: "We have in some cases yielded entirely to usage, however, when to ignore a term that has become entrenched among a community of users would leave our collection suspect as to currency and completeness." The result is a compendium that is both comprehensive and authoritative.

A front section entitled "Notes on the Use of This Dictionary" provides detailed explanations concerning sequence of entries, pronunciation, cross-references, symbols, and so on. The dictionary employs the convention of main entries and subentries in its arrangement of terms. Main entries are for the most part single terms. Terms of two or more words in length are generally included as subentries under the noun. For instance, *Meniere's disease* is listed as a subentry under the main entry *disease,* and *break-off phenomenon* is listed under *phenomenon.* This concept is important for the novice user to remember, since the first inclination might be to look under the first word of the term. Fortunately, many of the compound terms that are subentries are eponyms, all of which are listed twice in the dictionary. Biographical information is provided at the personal name, with a cross-reference to the noun where the term appears as a subentry with a definition. This aid to locating information does not help with compounds that do not include names, however. While the benefit of this arrangement is that related terms are grouped together, it does create some rather lengthy listings. The main entry for *syndrome* is 18 pages long, and the subentries are not necessarily related other than that they are all syndromes.

One unique feature of *Dorland's* is the section "Fundamentals of Medical Etymology," which explains the derivation of medical vocabulary from the Greek and Latin languages. A list of roots, prefixes, and suffixes is included, which serves as an aid in analyzing the meaning of existing medical terminology.

The dictionary has 53 plates and 29 tables that reinforce or expand upon the text. Various appendixes provide handy reference information: temperature conversion chart, tables of weights and measures, laboratory values, and so forth.

Dorland's Illustrated Medical Dictionary is recommended without qualification as a dictionary of the first rank. All libraries should have this reference to assist in medical queries and to aid in research. The Board recommends this work for the core collections of public, academic, and school libraries.

Handbook of Poisoning: Prevention, Diagnosis and Treatment, 12th edition. Robert H. Dreisbach and William O. Robertson. Appleton & Lange, 1987. soft. 1 vol. 589 pp. illus. index. ISBN 0-8385-3643-3. $18. handbook.
RA1215.D73 615.9'002'02

The *Handbook of Poisoning* is a concise guide to the prevention, diagnosis, and treatment of poisoning. It is a ready-reference handbook that also lists appropriate sources for further reading. Although the preface states that the book is written for medical students and physicians, it is also useful for allied health students and concerned laypersons.

Chapter 1 concerns the prevention of poisoning and includes discussions of household, agricultural, and industrial hazards. Air pollution and environmental contamination, suicidal poisoning, and exposure to substances during pregnancy are also covered.

Chapters 2 through 4 deal with the diagnosis, evaluation, and management of poisoning. Both acute and chronic (that is, from long-term exposure) poisonings are addressed. Procedures are clearly outlined for all the treatments that may be necessary in a given situation. In addition to measures aimed at eliminating the poison itself, the text explains measures for handling resulting symptoms such as fluid imbalance, convulsions, delirium, and shock.

Chapter 5 briefly addresses the various legal aspects of poisoning as these affect the medical profession, such as written records, preservation of evidence, and the reporting of cases to appropriate authorities.

The remainder of the the handbook (chapters 6 to 36) covers poisoning by specific agents. It is divided into five major sections: "Agricultural Poisons," "Industrial Hazards," "Household Hazards," "Medicinal Poisons," and "Animal and Plant Hazards." Each section consists of a number of chapters representing different categories of substances. For example, the section on industrial hazards has nine chapters covering nitrogen compounds, halogenated hydrocarbons, alcohols and glycols, corrosives, and so on.

Specific substances are discussed individually within each chapter, although occasionally similar substances are grouped together. A description is given of each substance, indicating its commercial and industrial uses and in what products it is likely to appear. Formulas are shown for chemical substances, and data such as melting point, boiling point, and vapor pressure are provided where relevant. The entry then discusses clinical findings (divided into signs and symptoms and laboratory findings), prevention, treatment (for both acute and chronic poisoning), and prognosis. These headings appear in boldface type for easy identification. References to selected current articles complete the entry.

A detailed index at the back of the book leads the reader quickly to individual substances. Many tables are interspersed throughout the text, providing useful listings of data for quick reference. An index to these tables appears in the front of the book.

A summary of emergency first aid measures that can be carried out by laypersons is provided on the inside front and back covers of the handbook in an effort to increase its emergency utility.

The *Handbook of Poisoning* covers an extensive number of poisons in spite of its small size. The fact that it is available in its twelfth edition attests to its success. Its compact format, modest price, and accessible language make it a good choice as a primary resource on poisoning. The Board recommends this work for the core collections of public and academic libraries.

Medical School Admission Requirements. Assn. of American Medical Colleges, annual (1978–). soft. 1 vol. 400 pp. $10. handbook.
R745.M4 610.711

Medical School Admission Requirements is a compilation of admissions information for 127 accredited medical schools in the United States and Puerto Rico and 16 accredited schools in Canada. It is published annually to ensure the accuracy and timeliness of the information provided. Data are updated as of January of each year, and the book is issued in April. The book does warn that tuition and expenses are subject to change at any time and that individual schools should be contacted for more complete information.

The reference is published by the Association of American Medical Colleges (AAMC), whose primary purpose is "the advancement of medical education and the nation's health." Its membership includes all American and Canadian medical schools as well as many teaching hospitals, academic societies, and individuals. The AAMC is also responsible for the Medical College Admission Test (MCAT) and the American Medical College Application Service (AMCAS).

U.S. schools are listed in order by state and Canadian schools by province. The front of the book contains separate alphabetical and geographical listings of schools with page numbers to assist in the easy location of particular institutions. Each medical school entry follows a standard two-page format with the following headings in boldface type: "General Information," "Curriculum," "Requirements for Entrance," "Selection Factors," "Financial Aid," "Information for Minorities," "Application and Acceptance Policies," and "Tuition and Student Fees." Statistics on the number of applicants, interviewed applicants, and new entrants to the most recent first-year class are also included. Many of the entries include additional statistics on the current first-year class, such as average grade point average; MCAT scores; and male-female, resident-nonresident, and minority percentages. The "Application and Acceptance Policies" section gives deadline and notification dates for the coming academic year.

The book serves as an overall handbook for an individual interested in pursuing a medical career. Nine chapters explain various facets of applying to and attending medical school. Two chapters discuss the nature of medical education in general and how to decide whether and where to apply. Another chapter discusses premedical educational planning. Two more chapters describe in detail the MCAT exam, the AMCAS, and the overall medical school application and selection process. Still other chapters provide financial information and information for minority groups, for high school students, and even for those applicants not accepted to medical school. The last chapter of the book gives information on medical schools which offer combined college-M.D. programs for high school graduates. Many of the chapters finish with a bibliography of additional information sources. Several tables are included throughout the text, providing illustrative data on the topic under discussion.

Medical School Admission Requirements is an essential reference for academic and public libraries. The book serves as the authoritative guide to medical careers and education and is one of the first sources a potential medical student should consult. The extremely affordable price of this reference makes for an easy annual purchase. The Board recommends this work for the core collections of public and academic libraries.

The Merck Index: An Encyclopedia of Chemicals, Drugs, and Biologicals, 11th edition. Susan Budavari, ed. Merck, 1989. hard. 1 vol. 1,463 pp. illus. appendix. indexes. ISBN 0-911910-27-1. $28.50. encyclopedia. on-line.
RS356.M524 615.103

See Chemistry.

The Merck Manual of Diagnosis and Therapy, 15th edition. Robert Berkow, ed. Merck, Sharp & Dohme, 1987. hard. 1 vol. 2,696 pp. illus. index. ISBN 0-911910-08-5. $21.50. handbook.
RC55.M4 616

When the *The Merck Manual of Diagnosis and Therapy* was first published in 1899, it was 262 pages long, and its purpose was to assist general practitioners in formulating therapy decisions for the whole range of medical ailments. Now, almost a century later, the knowledge base of medicine has expanded exponentially, and the field is marked by increasing specialization. *The Merck Manual* has grown with the times; the current edition contains 2,696 pages. It has retained its original purpose, however, of providing information covering the entire field of medicine to all physicians and health professionals.

The Merck Manual remains the ideal reference work for busy specialists to consult for reliable information on matters outside their areas of expertise. The entries in *The Merck Manual* are written by distinguished authors, and the entire work is peer reviewed. Extensive editorial revision results in a work that is comprehensive in scope but to the point. However, because of its brevity and the increased number of more thorough texts, *The Merck Manual* is no longer a primary reference for physicians. It does, however, remain an excellent ready-reference manual for all levels of health professionals, as well as laypersons. The clarity of writing makes the manual accessible to most lay readers.

The manual claims to cover "all but the most obscure disorders of mankind." Diseases of infants, children, and adults are all included. In addition to the discourse that defines the disease itself, signs and symptoms are discussed, as well as clinical procedures and laboratory tests. Medical and pharmacologic treatment is discussed in detail, as well as prophylaxis. Surgical procedures are not in the scope of this volume and are not discussed.

The text is arranged mainly by organ system (such as genitourinary disorders) and by medical discipline (for example, pediatrics). Each section is marked with a thumb tab that has an identifying abbreviation. The main table of contents lists each section, and each section has its own in-depth table of contents that outlines chapters and subdivisions within them. These detailed contents pages aid greatly in the ease of use of the manual. In addition, an extensive index leads the reader directly to specific topics.

The final sections of the manual address topics not specifically mentioned elsewhere. The section entitled "Special Subjects" includes geriatric medicine, aids for the disabled patient, nuclear medicine, hyperbaric oxygen therapy, and laboratory medicine. Of particular note are the chapters that contain "ready-reference guides," which conveniently provide tables, dosage calculation guides, weight and measure equivalencies, and normal laboratory values.

The section "Clinical Pharmacology" provides an overview of the principles of drug administration and has separate chapters covering the various classes of drugs.

The last section of the manual deals with poisoning and venomous bites and stings. A 19-page table lists specific poisons and their symptoms and treatment, serving as a quick-reference aid.

The Merck Manual of Diagnosis and Therapy manages to provide a broad spectrum of medical information in an extremely compact format. The use of lightweight bible paper allows it to retain its handbook size, and its quality binding makes it quite durable. Its comprehensiveness, ready-reference quality, and reputation make it an important core text for academic libraries. It serves all levels of health professionals and students. It is also recommended as a valuable addition to public library collections, since most consumer-level books do not address the less common medical disorders. The Board recommends this work for the core collections of public and academic libraries.

The Oxford Companion to Medicine. John Walton, Paul B. Beeson, and Ronald B. Scott, eds. Oxford, 1986. hard. 2 vols. 1,524 pp. illus. appendix. ISBN

0-19-261191-7 (set). $125 (set). dictionary.
R121.088 610.3'21

The Oxford Companion to Medicine professes to be a "comprehensive reference book concerned with the theory, practice and profession of medicine." It addresses a wide range of subjects relating to the provision of health care in the United States and the United Kingdom. It is intended to be a resource utilized by physicians and allied health practitioners, as well as students and laypersons.

Entries are arranged alphabetically and treated in an encyclopedic format. Coverage varies from brief definitions of medical terms, diseases, and drugs (*patella* receives three lines) to 150 lengthy essays on major topics. Each medical specialty is treated as a major topic, as are several allied disciplines, such as nursing, psychology, and dentistry. Broad subjects important to the field of health care are also afforded major essays. Examples are "Death, Dying and the Hospice Movement," "Ethics of Medical Experimentation on Human Subjects," and "Herbal Remedies and Physic Gardens." Institutional aspects of health care are covered, such as medical jurisprudence, medical education, and government and medicine. *The Companion* also provides over 1,000 biographical sketches of notable men and women in medicine, excluding those still living. Many important British and American statutes are also given coverage. In many cases separate essays are devoted to explanations of the same topic as it relates to the United States and the United Kingdom. The essays generally include a historical discussion of the topic in addition to addressing the present-day situation.

Most of the essays list references, and many entries have a bibliography for further reading. This is useful for the researcher wishing to locate more information on the subject, although it sometimes seems that the citations are spotty and could be more current. The entry on *acupuncture,* for instance, lists a sole 1973 journal article citation.

A few peripheral subjects are also covered as major topics and help the book live up to its title as a "companion" to medicine. Twenty-six pages are devoted to the subject of "Art and Medicine." Other human interest topics are "Illnesses of the Famous" and "Doctors in Other Walks of Life."

The main entries are listed in the front of the book as an aid to the reader. Perusal of this list will help the reader identify topics of interest immediately instead of having to search blindly through the two-volume set. "See" and "see also" references are used to guide the reader to related entries. Within entries, terms that have their own entries are preceded by an asterisk. Two appendixes list abbreviations for medical qualifications, degrees, and terms.

The Companion seems to give equal attention to the British and American scenes, although an occasional British slant may be noticed. Spellings tend to be British *(paediatrics, programme, naevus).* Writers from both countries are contributors to the book, and they also have distinguished credentials.

The Oxford Companion to Medicine serves as a useful first reference on health care subjects. Its broad, slightly eclectic coverage makes it attractive to a variety of users and gives it a serendipitous quality for those interested in browsing. One small drawback is the fact that it was published in 1986; with each passing year the perspective that it provides of the current medical scene will become a little more dated. A second edition would obviously solve this problem. Still, *The Companion* provides much well-researched information and is a beneficial resource. The Board recommends this work for the core collections of public and academic libraries.

Physicians' Desk Reference. Edward R. Barnhart, pub. Medical Economics, annual (1947–). hard. 1 vol. 2,418 pp. indexes. ISBN 0-87489-716-5. $49.95. handbook. on-line. CD-ROM.
RS75.P5 615

The *Physicians' Desk Reference* is one of the most widely known medical titles, both inside and outside the medical community. It is the first source most health care practitioners and consumers consult to obtain information about prescription medications. It is commonly referred to as the *PDR.*

The *PDR* is published annually with periodic supplements. It is produced with the cooperation of the product manufacturers. This is a key point that readers should be aware of when consulting this source. The book states that "[t]he information concerning each product has been prepared, edited and approved by the medical department, medical director, and/or medical counsel of each manufacturer." Because the *PDR* functions as both a marketing tool and a disclaimer for the manufacturers, it is important to remember that the wording of entries will reflect their interest. On the other hand, FDA regulations require that the information supplied in the *PDR* must be identical both in language and emphasis to the approved labeling for the product. The result is that the *PDR* is for the most part a compilation of the official package inserts. The patient, however, does not receive these official inserts from his or her physician. Hence the lay user often consults the *PDR* to obtain such information. Because manufacturers supply the information, identical products from different manufacturers may not get equal treatment.

The forty-third edition contains descriptions of over 2,500 prescription drugs and diagnostic products. It is arranged alphabetically by manufacturer. Descriptions include chemical name, clinical pharmacology, indications and usage, dosage and administration, contraindications, warnings, precautions, adverse reactions, overdosage, and how supplied. The descriptions are lengthy and detailed. For example, every possible adverse reaction to a drug is listed regardless of incidence, and the incidence figure is not always supplied. Thus it may sometimes be difficult for the reader to gain a clear perspective of the potential benefits and risks of the drug.

One special feature of the *PDR* is the "Product Identification Section." Arranged alphabetically by manufacturer, it consists of color illustrations of capsules, tablets, and containers.

Several color-coded indexes assist in the location of information. A manufacturers' index lists all companies that have products listed in the *PDR* with their address, emergency phone number, and list of described products. The product name index is an alphabetical listing by brand name of all products included. The product category index lists the drugs according to their classifications (for example, antibiotics and diuretics). The generic and chemical name index lists drugs according to their principal ingredients. Each index gives page numbers to the main text. Finally, at the back of the book, there is a list of poison control centers, a section that gives guidelines to the management of overdose, and a section on weights and measures.

The *Physicians' Desk Reference* is a standard, well-known drug reference, which, despite the caveats mentioned earlier, belongs in all library collections serving health professionals and the public. The *PDR* states that its primary audience is physicians. Even so, because of the volume's comprehensiveness and familiarity, the work is a necessary part of the core collections of both academic and public libraries. Patrons will ask for this book by name. The Board recommends this work for the core collections of public and academic libraries.

Webster's Medical Desk Dictionary. Roger W. Pease, Jr., ed. Merriam-Webster, 1986. hard. 1 vol. 790 pp. appendixes. ISBN 0-87779-025-6. $21.95. dictionary.

R121.W357 610.3′21

Webster's Medical Desk Dictionary follows the traditional style of other Merriam-Webster dictionaries. Thus it differs from most medical dictionaries, which have come to focus more on supplying encyclopedic medical information than on features of the terminology itself. *Webster's Medical Desk Dictionary* adheres to the practice of providing only information on the medical vocabulary. Entries include pronunciation, end-of-line division, functional labels, derivatives, and inflected forms. This emphasis justifies its appellation as a desk dictionary and makes it a useful reference for questions concerning proper word usage.

Webster's focuses on current and actual usage as a basis for determining which words appear in the dictionary. The editorial staff of Merriam-Webster's accomplishes this through a reading program in which over a million current medical citations are reviewed. Archaic words and outmoded definitions of currently used words are not included. The dictionary can thus be considered a reliable source of appropriate modern medical vocabulary.

Entries are arranged alphabetically, letter by letter, and include British spelling variations. The dictionary does not invert compound terms, which makes it more straightforward to use. For instance, *carpal tunnel syndrome* will be found under *carpal* rather than in a long list of subentries under the term *syndrome* (the latter being the format used by most other medical dictionaries). Spelling and pronunciation variants are indicated, showing which are more frequently used. Definitions are clear and concise. The straightforward language used in the definitions makes this work accessible to laypersons. It is interesting to note that the defining vocabulary is controlled so that every word used in a definition is defined itself in either this dictionary or in *Webster's Ninth New Collegiate Dictionary.*

Two types of cross-references are employed. The first is simply a referral to a synonymous term under which the definition appears. The second is a comparative referral, in which the reader is referred to other terms with related meanings in order to gain better understanding of the original word. For example, the word *congenital* refers the reader to the related terms *familial, hereditary,* and *acquired.*

Eponyms include a brief biographical sketch indented under the main entry for the disease.

Additional material commonly found in nonmedical dictionaries is included in this work. An essay on the history and etymology of medical vocabulary appears in the front of the book. A list of prefixes, suffixes, and combining forms used in medical writing is also provided, with pronunciations, definitions, and examples. An appendix supplies a list of signs and symbols used in medical and related sciences. Another appendix is an abbreviated but very useful handbook of writing style, which provides clear pointers on punctuation, italicization, capitalization, and reference citations.

In all, *Webster's Medical Desk Dictionary* is attractively produced. Entries are clearly laid out, and the use of boldface type makes for easy browsing. Guide words at the top of each page also assist in ease of use. The features and format of this dictionary make it a good standard reference on contemporary medical vocabulary. The Board recommends this work for the core collection of public libraries.

Supplementary Titles

AIDS Bibliography. David O. Tyckoson. Oryx, biennial. soft. 2 vols. index. ISBN 0-89774-578-7. $21.50 per vol. bibliography.
RA644.A25A.342 016.61697′92

The *AIDS Bibliography* "breaks from tradition by covering only a six-month period rather than a complete year.

"Prefaced by a research review, the bibliography is arranged under thirty-one classed headings, each treating a narrow aspect of the larger subject. Tyckoson provides a complete bibliographic citation, accompanied by a fifty to one-hundred-word annotation, for each entry. The author index is coded to entry number. Among the many subtopics included are AIDS in minorities; AIDS in correctional facilities; patent disputes over the AIDS virus; international aspects of AIDS; testing and the blood supply; heterosexual transmission; moral and religious aspects; legal, political, and social aspects; victims, caregivers, and friends; and employment and workplace issues.

"As a reference tool, this work should be in most libraries. It is invaluable for its selection of key articles on the subject of AIDS, and will provide the user with a handy guide to the literature. . . . This work is well worth the investment." (*ARBA,* 1989, p. 616)

Also reviewed in: *ARBA,* 1986, p. 647; *BL,* December 1, 1985, p. 546; *SB,* January 1986, p. 157; *VOYA,* April 1988, p. 52; *WLB,* September 1985, p. 75.

Board's recommendation: Public and academic libraries.

AIDS Information Sourcebook, 2d edition. H. Robert Malinowski and Gerald T. Perry, eds. Oryx, 1988. soft. 1 vol. 85 pp. index. ISBN 0-89774-544-2. $32.50. bibliography.
RC607.A26A3475 616.97′1

"For libraries with limited funds, . . . [the *AIDS Information Sourcebook*] should be useful as a single-volume handbook on AIDS. Other libraries will want to consider it for purchase as a supplement to monographs and articles. The work has three major divisions. The first is a useful chronology of AIDS from June 1981 to November 1987. The second is a directory of organizations concerned with AIDS. This is arranged alphabetically by state, then by name of organization. Directory information is provided, followed by organizational profile indicating staffing, budget, funding source, library, outreach, network affiliation, additional information, available literature, and languages spoken. An alphabetical index to organizations is provided. The final section of this work is an enumerative and partially annotated bibliography of articles, bibliographies, books, films, periodicals, and plays on the subject of AIDS. A separate subject index is provided.

"[This work is] highly recommended for all public, academic, and medical libraries, and for all collections emphasizing AIDS education." (*ARBA,* 1989, p. 616)

Also reviewed in: *BL,* June 15, 1988, p. 1715; *Choice,* July/August, 1988, p. 1671; *LJ,* April 15, 1989, p. 38; *Ref Bks Bul,* June 1, 1988, p. 1648; *SB,* January 1989, p. 159; *WLB,* May 1988, pp. 103–104.

Board's recommendation: Public and academic libraries.

The Illustrated Dictionary of Dentistry. Stanley Jablonski. Saunders, 1982. hard. 1 vol. 919 pp. illus. ISBN 0-7216-5055-4. $61. dictionary.
RK27.J3 617.600321

The Illustrated Dictionary of Dentistry "is a comprehensive dictionary that covers all specialties of dentistry and allied fields. It includes some terms of historical or etymological interest." (*BL,* September 1, 1984, p. 38)

The book is "written by an expert in the field of medical terminology" and "defines terms in all specialties of dentistry and allied fields of science and technology and health care (including dental practice management and health insurance) as well as some terms of historical or etymological interest. The format . . . includes for each entry the preferred term, a phonetic respelling, an etymological source, a descriptive definition, synonyms, trademarks (where applicable), and cross-references. Many illustrations and tables are included that augment the definitions.

"Supplemental information includes: an introduction to the language of medicine and dentistry, an explanation of the organization and functions of the

American Dental Association and the Canadian Dental Association, directories of schools of dentistry in the United States and Canada, and a table of laboratory reference values of clinical importance.

"The content was reviewed for accuracy, completeness, and currency by a large number of consultants. This dictionary should prove indispensable to the reference collections of most health sciences libraries." (*ARBA,* 1984, p. 708)

Board's recommendation: Academic libraries.

Industrial Medicine Desk Reference. David F. Tver and Kenneth A. Anderson. Routledge, Chapman & Hall, 1986. hard. 1 vol. 307 pp. ISBN 0-412-01101-8. $39.95. dictionary.
RC963.3.T9 616.9'803

The *Industrial Medicine Desk Reference* "describes 900 diseases and chemicals that can arise from the industrial environment. Entries for chemicals include the formula, definition, health hazards, and standards in place by various agencies.

"Entries for diseases provide clear definitions and list exposed groups, symptoms, etc. This work is also useful because it has entries for certain occupations." (*Choice,* December 1986, p. 611)

"Entries are arranged alphabetically and are usually one-half page or less except for entries for major health disorders that may go on for two or more pages. These entries, such as the ones for cancer, asthma, and cardiovascular diseases, may have associated tables. . . .

"Entries for chemicals cite current worker exposure limits provided by the Occupational Safety and Health Administration (OSHA), the National Institute for Occupational Safety and Health (NIOSH), and other government agencies. . . .

"The *Industrial Medicine Desk Reference,* as was intended, is a source of accurate and concise information for health practitioners, business and plant managers, engineers, and others who are likely to come across hazardous substances in the workplace." (*BL,* January 15, 1987, p. 769)

Also reviewed in: *ARBA* 1987, p. 627; *New Tech Bks,* November 1986, p. 639; *R&R Bk N,* Winter 1987, p. 24; *SciTech,* November 1986, p. 26; February 1987, p. 26.

Board's recommendation: Public and academic libraries.

Medical Word Finder: A Reverse Medical Dictionary. Betty Hamilton and Barbara Guidos. Neal-Schuman, 1987. hard. 1 vol. 177 pp. ISBN 1-555-70011-X. $45. dictionary.
R121.H232 610.1

The *Medical Word Finder* is "a tool for identifying technical medical terminology from common words and phrases. . . . According to the authors, approximately 10,000 terms are included. . . . Entries are arranged alphabetically, letter by letter up to the first punctuation mark. Terms under entries, which include synonyms and closely related terms, are listed alphabetically. Where appropriate, medical prefixes and suffixes are included in entries. . . . The preface points out that sometimes one word or phrase . . . may refer to several medical terms or conditions unrelated to one another.

"[This book] is most appropriate for students and researchers . . . or as an aid for the layperson in finding the correct technical terms.

"In most cases, the *Medical Word Finder* can be used to find appropriate synonymous medical terminology. It is therefore recommended because of its currency." (*BL,* October 15, 1987, p. 379)

Also reviewed in: *ARBA,* 1988, p. 657; *Choice,* January 1988, p. 746; *R&R Bk N,* February 1988, p. 19; *SciTech,* December 1987, p. 19; *WLB,* September 1987, p. 106.

Board's recommendation: Public and academic libraries.

Modern Nutrition in Health and Disease, 7th edition. Maurice E. Shils and Vernon R. Young, eds. Lea & Febiger, 1988. hard. 1 vol. 1,694 pp. appendix. ISBN 0-8121-0984-8. $79.50. handbook.
QP141.N776 613.2'19

Modern Nutrition in Health and Disease, "first published in 1955 . . . , is a massive, fully referenced nutrition text and reference book covering basic nutritional science, safety and adequacy of food supply, interrelationship of nutrients, metabolism, diagnosis of nutritional deficiency and role of nutrition in prevention and treatment of disease.

"[It] contains new chapters on food faddism, diet hyperlipidemia, and atherosclerosis, anatomy and physiology of the gastrointestinal tract, malnutrition in the hospitalized patient; effect of processing on the nutritional value of food. The chapter on criteria for an adequate diet has been expanded to include vegetarian diets, dietary fiber and current faddist non-vitamin 'supplements.'

"The appendix is expanded to present information about diet supplements to implement recommendations in the text; guidelines for use of liquid formulae; and detailed composition of commercially available products." (*RSR,* April 1982, p. 21)

Also reviewed in: *Sci Tech,* March 1988, p. 14.

Board's recommendation: Academic libraries.

Taber's Cyclopedic Medical Dictionary, 15th edition. Clayton L. Thomas. Davis, 1985. hard. 1 vol. 2,170 pp. illus. appendixes. ISBN 0-8036-8308-1. $25.95. dictionary.
R121.T144 610.3′21

Taber's Cyclopedic Medical Dictionary is a "guide to the language of the health professions. Promotional material claims 56,136 definitions (7,000 of them new) and more than 200 illustrations.

"[The work] is mainly addressed to persons providing health care, but sophisticated laypersons can certainly use it. Although, as one might expect in a dictionary, emphasis is on terms, there is—as its title suggests—much 'cyclopedic' material on symptoms, causes, treatments, etc. Fifteen appendixes provide information on a variety of topics, including prescription writing, drug interactions, dietetics, and poison control centers. . . ." (*BL,* January 15, 1986, p. 746)

"Unlike the large standard medical dictionaries available on today's market, *Taber's* not only provides coverage of the basic medical terminology but also includes material specific to nursing and many allied health disciplines. This reference tool presents the most thorough treatment available among the leading health-related dictionaries on the special vocabularies used in fields such as respiratory therapy, dental hygiene, physical therapy, and radiologic technology.

"Complete definitions are provided for each major term, as well as phonetic spelling for 90 percent of the entries and, when available, standard abbreviations. . . . In addition, this volume also provides translations of basic health-related questions into English from French, Spanish, Italian, and German." (*ARBA,* 1986, p. 638)

Board's recommendation: Public and academic libraries.

New and Noteworthy

The American Medical Association Encyclopedia of Medicine. Charles B. Clayman, ed. Random House, 1989. hard. 1 vol. 1,183 pp. illus. index. ISBN 0-394-56528-2. $44.95. encyclopedia.
RC81.A2A52 610.321

"This wide-ranging, up-to-date dictionary [*The American Medical Association Encyclopedia of Medicine*] describes diseases, conditions, symptoms, medications, tests, procedures, and surgical operations for the layperson. Its authority, broad coverage, and excellent diagnostic charts distinguish it from similar works. . . . A short list of self-help organizations (with phone numbers and addresses) emphasizes the limited usefulness of any work of this type. Nonetheless, for quick explanations, this book is among the best." (*LJ,* June 15, 1989, p. 50)

Atlas of Human Anatomy. Frank H. Netter, M.D. CIBA-Geigy, 1989. hard and soft. 1 vol. 592 pp. illus. index. ISBN 0-914168-18-5 (hard); 0-914168-19-3 (soft). $120 (hard); $49.95 (soft). atlas.
QM25.N46 611.0022

"Detailed, lavish plates are just the beginning of this exquisite book [*Atlas of Human Anatomy*]. The work of a medical illustrator accounts for the high degree of integrity and accuracy. The content is divided into seven broad sections: Head and Neck, Back and Spinal Cord, Thorax, Abdomen, Pelvis and Perineum, Upper Limb, and Lower Limb. [In the book's Introduction] . . . Dr. Netter states the importance of achieving a balance between 'complexity and simplification'—if too complex, pictures may prove confusing; if too simple, they may prove inadequate. He strove, therefore 'for a middle course of realism without the clutter of confusing minutiae.' He succeeds admirably. A comprehensive index aids in making this an extremely usable reference well worth the price." (*SLJ,* May 1990, p. 28)

Brenda M. Zimmerman

Middle Eastern History

See also African History; Asian History

The mere physical description of the Middle East is a much-debated topic among those in the field of area studies. Furthermore, substantive comprehension of any other aspect of this region and its inhabitants is a daunting prospect to most in the West.

Geographically, the Middle East not only comprises the commonly recognized countries, such as Iran and Saudi Arabia, but also can include such disparate areas as China, Cyprus, and North Africa. The inclusion of such disparate areas is a result of the sphere of influence of Islam, the dominant religion of the Middle East. Today 20 percent of the world's population is Muslim, largely confined to areas that are only recently becoming "developed." This fact, coupled with the area's relatively high birthrates and frequent political unrest, yields much potential for change.

When taken together the reference books examined herein offer a comprehensive view of the Middle East. Countries that are treated in all works are Bahrain, Egypt, Iran, Iraq, Israel, Jordan, Kuwait, Lebanon, Libya, Oman, Qatar, Saudi Arabia, Sudan, Syria, Turkey, the United Arab Emirates, Yemen Arab Republic, and the People's Democratic Republic of Yemen. In addition, there is some coverage of Cyprus, Afghanistan, Algeria, Djibouti, Mauritania, Morocco, Somalia, Tunisia, and Western Sahara, as well as Southeast Asia, Central Asia, and China.

Works range from exhaustive, almost entirely textual handbooks to resplendently illustrated encyclopedias and atlases of the Middle East, North Africa, and the Islamic world. In general, an atlas will provide a more graphic representation than a handbook, while an encyclopedia will contain elements of both.

If the clientele warrants it, the core collection might be suplemented by the MIDDLE EAST CONTEMPORARY SURVEY and A MIDDLE EAST STUDIES HANDBOOK. The *Middle East Political Dictionary* (ABC-Clio, 1984) is a useful addition to the collection that is now out of print.

Core Titles

Atlas of the Islamic World since 1500. Francis Robinson. Facts On File, 1982. hard. 1 vol. 238 pp. illus. appendix. index. ISBN 0-87196-629-8. $45. atlas.
G1786.S1R5 911.17671

As stated in the preface, the purposes of the *Atlas of the Islamic World since 1500* are: (1) to provide a framework within which the last 500 years of Muslim history can be understood; (2) to introduce the reader to the lives that Muslims live; and (3) to provide a basis for a broader vision of the Islamic world. The author,

Core Titles

	PUBLIC	ACADEMIC	SCHOOL
Atlas of the Islamic World since 1500 Robinson, Francis. Facts On File, 1982	✦	✦	
Atlas of the Middle East Brawer, Moshe, ed. Macmillan, 1988		✦	
The Cambridge Encyclopedia of the Middle East and North Africa Mostyn, Trevor, exec. ed., and Albert Hourani, adv. ed. Cambridge, 1988	✦	✦	
Encyclopedia of the Third World, 3d edition Kurian, George Thomas. Facts On File, 1987 (See African History)	✦	✦	✦
The Middle East Adams, Michael, ed. Facts On File, 1988	✦	✦	✦
The Middle East and North Africa Europa, annual; distrib. by Gale	✦	✦	

Francis Robinson, former prize fellow of Trinity College, Cambridge University, and now lecturer in history at Royal Holloway College, University of London, has pursued the study of the subject of Islam in India for many years. The advisory editor, Peter Brown, formerly fellow of All Souls College, Oxford, is professor of ancient history and Mediterranean archaeology at the University of California at Berkeley.

The atlas is a work of art. Printed on heavy stock paper, it is lavishly illustrated with over 300 photos, drawings, and historic artworks, two-thirds of which are in color, and 50 maps. There is an introductory section comprising a chronological table, a chart of the rulers of the Islamic world, a preface, and an introduction that discusses Western attitudes to Islam. This section is followed by two parts: "Revelation and Muslim History" and "To Be a Muslim." In addition to the historical narrative, part 1 also includes special features on the Mughal world, the Ottoman world, Javanese culture and Islam, the Madrasas of central Asia, mosques of the further Islamic lands, modern Arab art, and Islam in the West, among others. The feature on the Mughal world reveals a richness and diversity of art and architecture under these rulers that will enlighten most Western readers. Part 2 is subdivided into three sections: "Religious Life," "Arts of Islam," and "Society and the Modern World." Of particular interest to Western readers will be the chapter on the position of women in society. This material is sensitively written and explores the religious, philosophical, and political factors that shape the treatment of women in Islamic countries.

Maps tell an important part of the story; most of the 50 maps herein are drawn on a Mercator projection. This enables the shape of an area to remain accurate at distances from the equator.

Transliteration of the sounds of the Islamic languages into roman script is based on the *Encyclopedia of Islam* (first edition), with minor variations that are clearly noted in the preface.

The reference concludes with a glossary, list of illustrations, bibliography, gazetteer, and index. Subject matter in illustration captions is not included in the index. The organization of the atlas should make the work quite accessible to a general audience. This reviewer found the separation of the gazetteer from the index to be somewhat cumbersome. However, few errors or inconsistencies were found in this volume.

The publication date of 1982 affects the scope of the work only very slightly. Nonetheless, recent events throughout the Arab world could make a revised edition of the *Atlas of the Islamic World since 1500* necessary in the near future.

The Board recommends this work for the core collections of public and academic libraries.

Atlas of the Middle East. Moshe Brawer, ed. Macmillan, 1988. hard. 1 vol. 140 pp. illus. appendix. index. ISBN 0-02-905271-8. $60. atlas.
G2205.K33 912.56

The *Atlas of the Middle East* is edited by Moshe Brawer, who holds a Ph.D. in geography from the University of London, has had a long and distinguished university career at the University of Tel Aviv, and is a "prolific author of articles and books on the geography of the Middle East" (about the author). Printed on a heavyweight, durable paper, the book is mainly a visual one—maps, charts, and other visual elements are reproduced throughout in two colors.

The atlas is divided into two parts titled "The Region" and "The Countries." Part 1 is a general overview of the Middle East. A map of the Middle East—including all the countries within the scope defined by the book—opens the section. This is followed by maps and text on the region's geology, climate, fauna and flora, population, oil fields, and political history. Part 2 examines each country. This list of countries includes Libya, Egypt, Sudan, Yemen, South Yemen, Saudi Arabia, Oman, United Arab Emirates, Qatar, Bahrain, Kuwait, Iraq, Iran, Turkey, Cyprus, Syria, Lebanon, Israel, and Jordan. Each country is then examined in detail through uniform headings on such topics as topography, climate, population, economy, agriculture, minerals, industry, history, and government and politics, among others. These standard headings can be further amplified by additional headings of special interest, such as the "Suez Canal" (for Egypt) and the "Euphrates and Tigris Rivers" (for Iraq), and special headings for countries whose populations are divided politically. In the section on Cyprus, for example, there are separate headings for the economy of Greek and Turkish zones.

Part 1 has a section on fauna and flora that is an outstanding encapsulation of information from 24 million years ago to the present. The text also includes maps on geobotanical regions and bird migration.

There is a tremendous amount of information packed into all of the charts in this atlas. For example, the section entitled "Military Balance in the Middle East, 1986" (also in part 1) gives a country-by-country reckoning of numbers of soldiers, tanks, fighter planes, warships, and the rate of defense cost as part of the gross domestic product.

The index, bibliography, and suggested reading list of the *Atlas of the Middle East* are adequate for the general audience of nonspecialists for whom this work was written. Also, no errors were noted. Most of the visual representations are current as of 1986, which is comparable with other sources reviewed in this category for the text or cartography. Population estimates are from 1984.

The Board recommends this work for the core collection of academic libraries.

The Cambridge Encyclopedia of the Middle East and North Africa. Trevor Mostyn, exec. ed., and Albert Hourani, adv. ed. Cambridge, 1988. hard. 1 vol. 504 pp. illus. index. ISBN 0-521-32190-5. $49.50. encyclopedia.
DS44.C37 956

A companion volume to THE CAMBRIDGE ENCYCLOPEDIA OF AFRICA (see African History), *The Cambridge Encyclopedia of the Middle East and North Africa* was published in 1988. This encyclopedia offers far better organization and more current information than the earlier work. This volume is easy to handle and read, with liberal use of maps and photographs, many of them in color. *The Cambridge Encyclopedia of the Middle East and North Africa* utilizes somewhat fewer tables than THE CAMBRIDGE ENCYCLOPEDIA OF AFRICA, but it is written in the same easy-to-read style. This 1988 volume is more accessible to the young student or the casual reader than, for example, THE MIDDLE EAST AND NORTH AFRICA, the annual that covers the same area.

The Cambridge Encyclopedia of the Middle East and North Africa contains the contributions of approximately 75 academics and journalists who are international experts in their fields. Professional affiliations of the contributors are listed at the beginning of the volume and the initials of the author appear at the end of each essay. Trevor Mostyn, a British writer and journalist, is the executive editor; Albert Hourani, St. Antony's College, Oxford, is the advisory editor.

The volume is divided into six parts: "Lands and People," "History," "Societies and Economies," "Culture," "The Countries," and "Interstate Relations." Each part is usually divided into sections on related topics. Sections range from 2 to 11 pages in length. Part 1 is a general treatment of the physical environment, the people, and their languages and religions. In part 2 the history of Africa is broadly treated in eight chapters covering ancient history through 1939. (African history since 1939 is covered in the introduction to part 5, "The Countries.") Part 3 deals with economic and social change, again from a regional perspective. Culture is covered in part 4 and includes sections on religion, literature, the arts, music, and Islamic science.

Twenty-seven Middle Eastern and North African countries are included in part 5, "Countries." Information here is fairly up to date. Part 5 also includes a final section titled "Peoples Without a Country," covering Armenians, Kurds, and Palestinians.

The sections on individual countries are very informative; for many readers these will be the part of the book consulted most often. Each country section includes a map as well as subsections on geography and topography, peoples, religion, history since the Second World War, and modern economy and society. A useful system of cross-referencing within the text is employed for greater accessibility. An asterisk indicates topics covered in other essays, which can be found by consulting the index.

The editors have endeavored to follow the system of

transliteration used by the *Encyclopaedia Judaica* (Macmillan, 1972—now out of print) for Hebrew and the system (here, somewhat simplified) used by the *International Journal of Middle East Studies* for Arabic, Persian, and Turkish.

The volume concludes with part 6, "Inter-State Relations," which treats relations among the Arab states, the Iran-Iraq war, the Arab-Israeli war, and the Lebanese civil war, among other topics. The bibliography of further reading at the end of each section is more convenient for the user than the comprehensive bibliography at the end of the volume.

Although much has happened in the Middle East in the four years since the 1986 publication of this reference work, the need for up-to-the-minute facts is a minor consideration within the scope of *The Cambridge Encyclopedia of the Middle East and North Africa.* Users needing more current information would do well to consult a yearbook such as the annual THE MIDDLE EAST AND NORTH AFRICA.

The Board recommends this work for the core collections of public and academic libraries.

Encyclopedia of the Third World, 3d edition. George Thomas Kurian. Facts On File, 1987. hard. 3 vols. 2,384 pp. appendixes. ISBN 0-8160-1118-4 (set). $195 (set). encyclopedia.
HC59.7 909.09724

See African History.

The Middle East. Michael Adams, ed. Facts On File, 1988. hard. 1 vol. 865 pp. illus. index. ISBN 0-8160-1268-7. $45. handbook.
DS44.M495 956

The Middle East, part of Facts On File's Handbooks to the Modern World series, provides statistics and comprehensive essays by experts on current Middle Eastern topics. The editor, Michael Adams, was a correspondent in the Middle East for 25 years for a major British newspaper and is the author of several books on the Middle East. Countries covered in this volume are Bahrain, Egypt, Iran, Iraq, Israel, Jordan, Kuwait, Lebanon, Libya, Oman, Qatar, Saudi Arabia, Sudan, Syria, Turkey, United Arab Emirates, Yemen Arab Republic, and People's Democratic Republic of Yemen. Such topics as geography, population, constitutional system, recent history, economy, and some biographical sketches on important people are covered for each country (in 1 to 12 paragraphs).

The 41 contributors and their professional affiliations and works written are listed in great detail at the beginning of the volume. Most have long and varied associations with the Middle East, and many have impressive academic credentials.

There are five parts in this volume. Part 1, "General Background," contains 5 essays of approximately 15 pages each on such topics as the Jews and the Middle East and Arabic language and culture. Part 2, "The Countries of the Middle East," contains 20 essays of the same length. Part 3, "Political Affairs," contains 7 essays of 10 to 20 pages in length on such topics as the Palestinian problem, Arab nationalism, and Zionism. Economic affairs, such as industrialization, foreign aid, and travel, are discussed in part 4. Education, Westernization, and the position of women are three of the topics covered in the 6 essays of part 5, "Social Affairs." Readers will find the factual information in parts 1 and 2 to be very useful and informative. However, the essays in parts 3 and 4, written by proven experts, will assist the reader in gaining much insight into the complexities of this region. These essays cover the full range of topics, from the Palestinian problem to future implications for Arab oil to the position of women in Arab society.

The reading level is suitable for a general audience. The work is well indexed. There is a list of maps as well as a list of comparative statistics in tabular form. Each table presents statistics for all the countries in the volume, culled from a variety of sources, including national government statistics, the various U.N. publications, and *Lloyd's Bank Economic Reports* for various countries. The book is as current as a compilation of this kind can possibly be. The binding, printing, and paper are of good quality, and the size affords great ease of use.

If a core collection is to contain only one book on the general area, it should be *The Middle East,* as its modest price should allow it to be acquired by almost all types of libraries. The Board recommends this work for the core collections of public, academic, and school libraries.

The Middle East and North Africa. Europa, annual; distrib. by Gale. hard. 1 vol. 949 pp. illus. appendix. index. ISBN 0-946653-52-6. $210. handbook.
DT160 961.04805

The thirty-sixth edition of *The Middle East and North Africa* has been expanded and updated. Europa, the publisher, is highly regarded for the yearbooks that it produces. Among other works in the series are AFRICA SOUTH OF THE SAHARA (see African History) and THE EUROPA WORLD YEAR BOOK (see Current Events). This yearbook identifies the authors of the various essays but does not provide their credentials.

The arrangement is a tripartite one: part 1 is a general survey with essays on such topics as the Suez Canal and the controversy over Jerusalem; part 2 deals with regional organizatons, such as the League of Arab States; and part 3 focuses on surveys of individual countries. There are 23 essays in part 1 plus a selected bibliography. Part 2 comprises 250 pages. The essays on the countries average 25 pages each. Each essay on a country is subdivided into sections covering physical and social geography, history, economy, a statistical survey, a directory, and a bibliography. The directory section is of special interest because it contains (where applicable) material on the constitution, the government and legislature, political organizations, diplomatic representation, the judicial system, religion, the press and publishers, radio and television, finance, trade and industry, transport, tourism, atomic energy, defense, and education. New to this edition are telephone and telex numbers in the country directories, which make this listing of contacts all the more useful.

The reading level should accommodate the general reader, although much of the tabular information is highly complex. Often a background in a particular field would be useful to fully understand the data. The index is adequate, as is the currency of the volume. For example, part 1, "General Survey," has been fully revised and updated, including a new article on the Iran-Iraq conflict, which is current with the August 1988 cease-fire.

The Middle East and North Africa is printed on very lightweight paper; otherwise the sheer number of pages would make the bulk cumbersome. However, the text is easy enough to read with its layout of two columns per page.

The Board recommends this work for the core collections of public and academic libraries.

Supplementary Titles

Middle East Contemporary Survey. Itamar Rabinovich et al. Westview, 1989. hard. 11 vols. illus. index. ISBN 0-8133-0925-5 (vol. 11). $89.50 (vol. 11). encyclopedia.
DS62.8.M53 956

Middle East Contemporary Survey is "a planned annual record and analysis of political, economic, military[,] and international development[s] in the Middle East. . . . [It] is divided into two parts; the first includes current issues such as the Arab-Israeli conflict, the Palestinians, . . . and economic affairs; the second includes individual articles on Arab countries from Libya east to Iraq and the Gulf, Israel, Iran, and Turkey.

"Most, but not all the authors are leading Israeli Middle-East scholars. They have approached their task with a high level of scholarship and relatively great objectivity. Only rare nuances of personal political predilections are evident. Sources used include the most significant international relations references, a wide array of the Arabic-language press, [and] major news and radio broadcasting monitoring services. Articles such as those on the Palestinians, Israeli[s], Egypt, and the West Bank are not only timely and information laden, but show exceptional insights. . . . [The *Middle East Contemporary Survey*] is a recommended investment for institutions with up-to-date reference collections." (*Choice,* January 1979, p. 1500)

Also reviewed in: *ARBA,* 1979, p. 177; 1982, p. 198; *BF,* April 4, 1979, p. 582; *Cu H,* January 1980, p. 30; *LJ,* April 15, 1980, p. 919; *MEJ,* Autumn 1982, p. 623; Winter 1984, p. 169; *Obs,* May 27, 1979, p. 36; *WLB,* March 1989, p. 527; *WSJ,* February 1, 1980, p. 16.

Board's recommendation: Academic libraries.

A Middle East Studies Handbook. Jere L. Bacharach. Univ. of Washington Pr., 1984. soft. 1 vol. 160 pp. illus. index. ISBN 0-295-96144-9. $15. handbook.
DS61.B3 956

A Middle East Studies Handbook "is intended to provide a one-volume 'ready reference' collection of maps, tables, and other expository data concerning Southwest Asia and Egypt. Chapters cover: transliteration systems and Islamic names; abbreviations for periodicals and reference works; Islamic calendar and conversion table; tables of relevant dynasties, rulers, and administrators; a chronology of events (by Western calendar); acronyms of 20th-century organizations; historical atlases; [a] gazetteer; [and a] glossary. (*LJ,* December 1984, p. 2263)

[This is] "a most welcome [volume]. . . . Substantial additions have been made to the abbreviations of reference works and periodicals, acronyms of organizations, and to the glossary. Sections on Islamic names and Muslim holidays and a gazetteer are new to this edition. Revisions and additions account for the approximately one-fifth increase in length of the handbook. . . . [The author] provides in one neat package all the odds and ends needed for ready reference in Middle East studies. . . . The work is invaluable to all levels of users, from those who have a simple . . . question to the advanced researcher. Bacharach is to be highly commended for providing this new revision." (*Choice,* April 1985, p. 1135)

Also reviewed in: *AB*, June 10, 1985, p. 4488; *ARBA*, 1985, p. 50; *MEJ*, Winter 1985, p. 198.

Board's recommendation: Academic libraries.

New and Noteworthy

Political Leaders of the Contemporary Middle East and North Africa: A Biographical Dictionary. Bernard Reich, ed. Greenwood, 1990. hard. 1 vol. 570 pp. ISBN 0-313-26213-6. $79.95. biographical dictionary.

DS61.5.P65 920.056

Political Leaders of the Contemporary Middle East and North Africa is a "masterful compilation of biographical essays on prominent Middle East and North African political leaders [that] fills a void in the current reference literature. The essays, of substantial length and written by experts, cover 70 persons who have made an impact on world events since World War II. . . . A detailed chronology of events is included, and each entry is followed by a list of works by and about the person. . . . [T]his valuable work is highly recommended for large general collections as well as for scholarly libraries." (*LJ*, February 15, 1990, p. 180)

Paul Sprachman

Middle Eastern Literature

See also World Literature

The rubric *Middle Eastern literature* is of such broad temporal and geographic scope as to defy the true test of sound classification: meaningful inclusiveness and useful exclusivity. The reference works described here represent a narrowing of that rubric based on the commercial availability of the item and the modern readers' expectations. The core collection deals with literature in and on Arabic, a language read by the majority of literate populations in North Africa and on the southwest edge of Asia. The supplements include two works on Hebrew literature and three on Persian literature. Therefore, although Arabic and Persian are well served by the selection, works on literature written in Turkish and Armenian—to name the most obvious omissions—are treated only peripherally. E. J. W. Gibb's six-volume *A History of Ottoman Poetry* (London, 1900–1909), which is similar to the supplementary work A LITERARY HISTORY OF PERSIA by E. G. Browne, is, unfortunately, now out of print. Also out of print is Salih Altoma's *Modern Arabic Literature* (Indiana Univ. Pr., 1975). These works would be valuable to the librarian seeking a collection of greater depth.

One complicating feature common to both biographical and bibliographical work on Middle Eastern literatures is the problem of romanization. The difficulty of establishing the accepted forms of the names

Core Titles

	PUBLIC	ACADEMIC	SCHOOL
'Abbasid Belles-Lettres, Cambridge History of Arabic Literature series Ashtiany, Julia, et al., eds. Cambridge, 1990		✦	
Arabic Literature to the End of the Umayyad Period, Cambridge History of Arabic Literature series Beeston, A. F. L., ed. Cambridge, 1983		✦	
Modern Arabic Literature, A Library of Literary Criticism series Allen, Roger, comp. and ed. Ungar, 1987		✦	

of authors and works becomes more complex when transliteration is involved. The establishing of a name by the Library of Congress by no means eliminates the ghosts conjured up by ignorance or by not consulting name authority files. Although the reference works listed here go a long way to exorcise such ghosts, more and more authors and works are entering bibliographic data bases in a variety of spellings and configurations. Those who lack the specialist's knowledge of the original languages should be mindful of the field's lack of uniformity when it comes to naming names.

Another challenge to the researcher—by no means unique to Middle Eastern literature—is the rapidity with which works become obsolete. The rate at which Middle Eastern works are studied and translated into English is increasing, while the resources necessary for adequate bibliographic control are shrinking. It is not hard to predict the foreseeable bibliographic future of these materials. Two worthwhile works that have already gone out of print are Margaret Anderson's *Arabic Materials in English Translation* (G. K. Hall, 1980) and Charles Storey's *Persian Literature: A Bio-bibliographical Survey* (Luzac, 1927–1971).

Despite the misgivings mentioned above, the works listed here are more than sufficient to answer most of the questions about Middle Eastern literatures posed by populations served by both large community and college libraries. The core and supplementary works are not only forthcoming about the literatures but also provide the historical and social contexts of the works they survey. In this way both the core collection and the supplements are guides to the cultural, political, and social history of many parts of the Middle East. Librarians should keep in mind the extended scopes of Middle Eastern biobibliography and literary history when searching for answers to their patrons' needs for information that does not pertain to literature.

Core Titles

'Abbasid Belles-Lettres, Cambridge History of Arabic Literature series. Julia Ashtiany et al., eds. Cambridge, 1990. 517 pp. index. ISBN 0-521-24016-6. $90. history.
PJ7530.A18 892.7'090034

'Abbasid Belles-Lettres is the second volume in the Cambridge History of Arabic Literature series and, like its predecessor, ARABIC LITERATURE TO THE END OF THE UMAYYAD PERIOD, amirably supersedes other reference books in the field. Unlike its predecessor in the series, the work focuses on belles lettres, or *adab.* After an introductory chapter that sets the historical setting, this work explores the concept of *adab* in illuminating detail.

'Abbasid Belles-Lettres approaches literary history in two basic ways: literary personalities and genres. Separate chapters are devoted to the lives and works of Ibn al-Muqaffa', al-Jāḥiẓ, al-Mutanabbī, and Abu'l-Alā'al-Ma'arrī, among others; other chapters examine hunting, love, political, wine, mystical, and acetic poetry; still others explore the conventions of 'Abbasid prose works. This design provides readers with two types of access to information; the design also necessitates a measure of factual redundancy (for example, readers learn in both chapter 13 and chapter 16 that Jews, Christians, and Zoroastrians were permitted to make wine). Penetrating analyses of the canons of literary taste and criticism and surveys of regional literature in Egypt and Yemen make this volume a valuable addition to any general reference collection.

'Abbasid Belles-Lettres is also a volume for our times. Chapter 17, on al-Mutanabbī, voices concern about "increasing the distance between us and the poet." The study of Abū'l-'Alā'al-Ma'arri in chapter 19 speaks of his "great contemporary appeal," and the theorist al-Qādī 'l-Jurjāni is praised for anticipating the linguistic and literary constructs of Ferdinand de Saussure and Roman Jakobson (chapter 20). Despite its explicit awareness of a modern audience, this volume of the Cambridge History of Arabic Literature—like its predecessor—uses dated or literal translations of some of the greatest achievements in Arabic writing. Abū Nuwās' famous line, cited to illustrate the imagery of love poems, is hammered flat by the literal translation and commentary "O moon, whom I glimpsed at a funeral, lamenting amid her companions, weeping, and shedding pearls [tears]" (chapter 17). Such translations increase the distance between the modern reader and the 'Abbasid writer. More modern translations might have served the verse better, and remarks on the literary devices could have been consigned to subsequent paraphrase and commentary. This minor criticism in no way detracts from *'Abbasid Belles-Lettres'* status as the standard volume on the subject for many years to come. The Board recommends this work for the core collection of academic libraries.

Arabic Literature to the End of the Umayyad Period, Cambridge History of Arabic Literature series. A. F. L. Beeston, ed. Cambridge, 1983. 547 pp. index. ISBN 0-521-24015-8. $90. history.
PJ7510 892.7'09

Arabic Literature to the End of the Umayyad Period

is the opening volume in the Cambridge History of Arabic Literature series, which is intended to supersede such standard English-language histories as Nicholson's *The Literary History of the Arabs* (Books on Demand UMI) and H. A. R. Gibb's *Arabic Literature*. The present volume performs this function admirably, embracing much of the significant scholarship on Arabic literature carried out since the earlier histories were completed. However, much of the source material that informs the chapter on pre-Islamic poetry remains the same works consulted by Nicholson and Gibb: namely, Isfahani's *Aghani* and Lyall's version of the *Mufaddaliyyat.* Considerable work on classical literature has been published in European-language and Arabic journals since the appearance of those standard sourcebooks. The volume appears to have had a prolonged gestation period. Although published in 1983, the date of the most recent citation in the bibliography and notes found throughout is 1981.

Defining *literature* in its broadest sense, *Arabic Literature to the End of the Umayyad Period* includes studies of pre-Islamic poetry, the Qur'ān (both its traditional exegesis and influence and its modern ramifications), *Ḥadīth,* fables and legends, music and verse, and the various non-Arabic literatures that were influential in Arabic literary traditions. The wealth of detail in this volume is offered chronologically. The work begins with essays on the linguistic and geopolitical background of the Arabic language. In the next three chapters the narrative bridges the artificial gap imposed by previous histories between the pre-Islamic and the Islamic; these chapters show how Islamic literary practice evolved naturally from pre-Islamic codes and conventions. The work then devotes four separate chapters to the genesis, style, and influence of Koranic prose. Allied genres of religious literature are examined in detail: *Ḥadīth,* or reports of the sayings and behavior of Muhammad, the Prophet; *Maghāzī* literature, the accounts of the wars of faith waged by Muhammad and his followers; and Sīrah literature, biography of the Prophet and his early followers. The volume's treatment of secular literature and allied arts is equally well documented.

The work offers a balanced view of the genesis of Umayyad literature, arguing against assertions of a guiding Greek or Persian genius behind literary achievement in Arabic. For example, in chapter 13, "The Persian Impact on Arabic Literature," the author, C. E. Bosworth, cautions, "In evaluating the contribution of Persian culture to early Arabic literature, one needs to avoid an over-enthusiastic, neo-Shu'ūbīẓ attitude by attributing too much to Persian influence, when we possess so little of the literature directly emanating from translators."

Appended to the volume are an annotated bibliography of Qur'ān and a comprehensive glossary of Arabic technical terms.

Though novel in many ways, *Arabic Literature to the End of the Umayyad Period,* in minor respects, shares the faults of its predecessors in this field. Throughout the volume there is a tendency to use dated translations or very literal renderings to represent the artistry of the greatest Arab poets. Hence the first hemistych of a crucial ode by al-Shanfarā is: "Mount your riding beasts, sons of my mother, and be off with you" (chapter 2), a translation that throws the author's assertion of the poet's greatness into question. Al-Shanfarā might have been better served by a poetic paraphrase of his famous line followed by the literal version in parentheses or a footnote. This fidelity to the literal in no way hampers access to the wealth of information found in *Arabic Literature to the End of the Umayyad Period.* The level of detail found in this volume makes it more than adequate to meet the general reference needs of college and university libraries.

The Board recommends this work for the core collection of academic libraries.

Modern Arabic Literature, A Library of Literary Criticism series. Roger Allen, comp. and ed. Ungar, 1987. hard. 1 vol. 400 pp. index. ISBN 0-8044-3024-1. $75. criticism.
PJ7538.M58

Modern Arabic Literature is a collection of excerpts from the writings of critics on plays, poems, and novels written in Arabic. The book is part of Ungar's series A Library of Literary Criticism, which aims at wide geographical representation in its literary surveys. Roger Allen, the compiler and editor, has assembled a geographically representative group of Arabic authors; he includes critical literature on some 27 Egyptians, 16 Lebanese, 7 Palestinians, 8 Syrians, and 10 Iraqis. To broaden the literary map, he has also chosen 2 Tunisians, a Saudi, a Sudanese, and an Algerian. Hence the collection reflects the relative sizes of the publishing industries in the major Middle Eastern literary capitals: Cairo, Beirut, Damascus, and Baghdad.

The compiler includes entries for authors who have achieved fame outside of the Arab world through the translation of their works. Nobel Prize winner Najib Mahfuz and other noted Egyptian writers, such as Yusuf Idris and Tawfig al-Hakim, are treated in detail. However, missing from the collection are critical reviews of the works of such Lebanese emigrants to New York as poet Rashid Ayyub (1872–1941) and prose writer Mikhail Naimy (b. 1889) and members of the

Arab diaspora in South America such as the poet Ilyas Faraḥāt (b. 1893) and journalist and poet Shukr Allah al-Jurr (b. 1900). The publication date of *Modern Arabic Literature* probably precluded the inclusion of Peter Theroux's 1989 excellent English translation of ʿAbd al-Rahman Munif's 1984 novel *Cities of Salt (Mudun al-milh).*

Its fair sampling of Middle Eastern literature not withstanding, *Modern Arabic Literature* is not the place to go for literary biography or cultural history. The collection reflects, rather, some of the critical standards used by Middle Eastern and Western writers. For example, Ahmad Muhammad ʿAtiyya in his review of ʾAbd al-Hakim Shawqī's *The Blood of Yaʿqūb's Son* identifies a true "Egyptian novel" as one that uses the Egyptian colloquial language. *Modern Arabic Literature* also abounds in such generalizations as Iliyya al-Hawi's comment on Salah Labakī poetry: "His romantic bent gives his poetry a particular stamp in its subject matter, style, and imagery, but he keeps a firm control on his sentiments and attitudes, and does not allow them to take over or be the subject of improvised compositions." These generalizations, which are neither supported nor exemplified by citations from the works under review, may mystify the reader who is unfamiliar with the standard debates of modern Arabic literary criticism. In his own excerpted criticism, the compiler, moreover, judges works for their subtlety or lack thereof.

Modern Arabic Literature provides a useful bibliography of the works of the authors mentioned, some of which have been translated into English, and an index of critics is cited. There is no general index, however. Despite the criticisms, *Modern Arabic Literature* is a welcome addition to the growing body of reference works on Middle Eastern languages and literatures. It is a partial supplement to the modern literary component of Margaret Anderson's *Arabic Materials in English Translation* (G. K. Hall, 1980), which is now out of print.

The Board recommends this work for the core collection of academic libraries.

Supplementary Titles

History of Iranian Literature. Jan Rypka, in collaboration with Otakar Klima et al.; Karl Jahn, ed. Reidel Publishing, 1968; distrib. by Kluwer Academic. hard. 1 vol. 929 pp. illus. index. ISBN 90-277-0143-1. $110. handbook.
PK6097.R913 891.5

The *History of Iranian Literature* "examines . . . the entire span of the history of Iranian literature from the very first traces of evidence bearing on the subject up to the present. . . . [It is] a masterpiece of scholarship which . . . is by virtue of infinite literacy, elegance of style, and interpretation, the best of its kind in the field." (*Choice,* February 1969, p. 1588)

"The chronological and geographical coverage of Jan Rypka and his collaborators is awe-inspiring. . . . Particularly valuable are the references to the works of Russian scholars . . . [and] the . . . interesting . . . section . . . [on] folk literature." (*TLS,* December 5, 1968, p. 1388)

"[T]his English [-language] version, far from being but a translation, is in many ways a completely new work and surpasses in quantity, scope, and subject matter its predecessors and any other previous works on the topic. . . . Many of the sections have been revised and brought up to date and have taken into account literary discoveries and divergent views of scholars from both East and West. Two entirely new chapters have been incorporated. . . . [This work] will prove to be indispensable to Orientalist and layman alike." (*AHR,* December 1968, p. 678)

Also reviewed in: *MEJ,* Winter 1969, p. 91.

Board's recommendation: Academic libraries.

A Literary History of Persia. Edward G. Browne. Cambridge, 1969. hard. 4 vols. 2,205 pp. illus. ISBN 0-521-04344-1 (vol. 1); 0-521-04345-X (vol. 2); 0-521-04346-8 (vol. 3). $75 per vol. handbook.
PK6097.B7 801.502

A Literary History of Persia "is among the most valuable works in English on the subject. Browne's love of Iran and its people make him a sensitive interpreter of Persian life and literature. He includes numerous texts and translations, and carries his narrative down to 1924. The Islamic era receives the most attention." (*The Reader's Advisor,* 1986, p. 718)

A review of the first edition stated: "The Persian scholar will find . . . [this reference] a stout staff to lean on in all matters of biography, bibliography, and textual apparatus." (*London Times,* October 12, 1906, p. 34)

Also reviewed in: *Acad,* January 5, 1907, p. 9; *Dial,* December 1, 1906, p. 400; *Enc,* August 1972, p. 61; *Lit D,* December 1, 1906, p. 813; *SR,* January 26, 1907, p. 114; *Spec,* January 5, 1907, p. 19.

Board's recommendation: Academic libraries.

Modern Hebrew Literature in English Translation. Leon I. Yudkin and Brian Chayette. Weiner Pub.,

1987. soft. 1 vol. 296 pp. IBSN 0-910129-80-0. $16.95. bibliography.
PJ5021.C66 892.407117

Board's recommendation: Academic libraries.

Persian Literature. Ehsan Yarshater, ed. Bibliotheca Persica, 1987; dist. by State Univ. of New York Pr. hard and soft. 1 vol. 562 pp. appendix. index. ISBN 0-88706-263-6 (hard); 0-88706-264-4 (soft). $59.50 (hard); $19.50 (soft). handbook.
PK6097 891.55'09

Persian Literature is a "collection of 25 essays by major scholars of Persian studies [which] focuses on 'imaginative literature' and presents both analyses of individual writers and generic or thematic treatments. The volume covers the pre-Islamic, classical, and contemporary periods of Persian literature and discusses Persian cultural developments outside Iran . . . and includes an article on Persian literature in translation for the nonspecialist. . . . Avestan and Manichaean literature focus the representation of the pre-Islamic period, while the essays on the classical age cover epic, lyric and court poetry, satire, romance and tragedy, as well as readings of such figures as Omar Khayyam, Rumi, and Nezami. The coverage of contemporary literature is equally diverse, looking at poetry, prose, drama, and the works of Hedayat and Farrokhzad. The bibliography of translations from Persian literature, both classical and modern, is a useful supplement to this volume, which should serve as an important resource for both scholars in the field and more general readers." (*Choice,* January 1989, p. 813)

Also reviewed in: *ARBA,* 1981, p. 171; *Choice,* April 1981, p. 1067.

Board's recommendation: Academic and school libraries.

John F. Drexel

Music

See also Popular Music

Music is an extraordinarily wide field. It includes not only classical or serious genres (both terms are somewhat inaccurate and misleading), but also ethnic, folk, jazz, opera, and popular categories. The majority of the reference works treated here fall under the broad rubric "general music," but more often than not they deal with music from more than one specialized category. Clearly, choosing works for a core reference collection in this field is largely a matter of assembling a given number of works that, in the sum of their diverse parts, will cover a broad spectrum. Ideally, the music reference collection should accommodate the patron who wants information on the debut of Beethoven's Ninth Symphony as well as the one who wants information on the seventeenth-century organist and composer Dietrich Buxtehude. It should provide background on Japanese music as well as a synopsis of *Madama Butterfly,* and satisfy the curiosity of the researcher who wants to learn about the inner workings of the piano and also needs a brief definition of the 12-tone system. In short, this collection should contain works that deal with the cultural, historical, biographical, and technical aspects of music from the earliest times to the present day.

Biographical dictionaries will be consulted frequently for information about the lives and works of composers, performers, and others who have influenced the course of music. Some of these dictionaries deal exclusively with performers in a particular category, while others include only entries for composers. In other, more general music dictionaries, biographical entries may be merely incidental, or they may not be included at all. Such general dictionaries may concentrate instead on technical terms, specific compositions, historical movements and periods, and so forth.

Other general music reference works are narrower and more specialized in their focus, but they are no less useful in answering certain patron queries. Directories list names and addresses of living musicians and of musical organizations. Discographies list recordings; in many cases, these lists are annotated with critical, evaluative comments.

Depending upon their patrons' main interests, librarians may wish to supplement the core works reviewed here with additional titles in any of the specialized categories. On the other hand, many librarians will find that some of the core works in the general category are sufficiently comprehensive to provide answers to questions about jazz, pop, rock, and other musical categories; in some libraries, expanding the collection by including the titles listed in the section on Popular Music will be necessary.

Core Titles

GENERAL	PUBLIC	ACADEMIC	SCHOOL
The Concise Oxford History of Music Abraham, Gerald. Oxford, 1979; reprinted, 1988	✦	✦	✦
Musical Instruments of the World: An Illustrated Encyclopedia The Diagram Group, comp. Facts On File, 1978	✦	✦	✦
Musicians since 1900: Performers in Concert and Opera Ewen, David. Wilson, 1978	✦		✦
National Anthems of the World, 7th edition Reed, W. L., and M. J. Bristow, eds. Blandford, 1988; distrib. by Sterling	✦	✦	✦
The New Grove Dictionary of American Music, 4 vols. Hitchcock, H. Wiley, and Stanley Sadie, eds. Grove's Dictionaries of Music/Macmillan, 1986	✦	✦	
The New Grove Dictionary of Musical Instruments, 3 vols. Sadie, Stanley, ed. Grove's Dictionaries of Music/Macmillan, 1984	✦	✦	
The New Grove Dictionary of Music and Musicians, 20 vols. Sadie, Stanley, ed., Grove's Dictionaries of Music/Macmillan, 1980	✦	✦	
The New Harvard Dictionary of Music Randel, Don Michael, ed. Belknap/Harvard, 1986	✦	✦	✦
The New Oxford Companion to Music, 2 vols. Arnold, Denis, gen. ed. Oxford, 1983	✦	✦	✦
The New Oxford History of Music, 11 vols. Abraham, Gerald, et al. Oxford, 1954–1983		✦	
The Oxford Dictionary of Music Kennedy, Michael. Oxford, 1985	✦		✦
Supplement to Music since 1900 Slonimsky, Nicholas. Scribner, 1986	✦		
OPERA			
The Concise Oxford Dictionary of Opera Rosenthal, Harold, and John Warrack. Oxford, 1979; reprinted, 1986	✦	✦	✦
The Definitive Kobbé's Opera Book Kobbé, Gustav; Earl of Harewood, ed. and rev. Putnam, 1987	✦	✦	✦

In addition to the works discussed in these reviews, certain standard titles outside the scope of this buying guide ought to be considered part of a core music reference collection. The annual *Schwann Record and Tape Guide* is a valuable aid, as are the well-respected titles of the *ASCAP Biographical Dictionary* (Bowker), *Baker's Biographical Dictionary* (Schirmer Bks., 1978), *The International Cyclopedia of Music and Musicians* (Dodd, Mead, 1985), and *Who's Who in American Music* (Jacques Cattell Pr./Bowker), which are now out of print. Finally, libraries that serve patrons of the performing arts will want to add POPULAR MUSIC: AN ANNOTATED GUIDE TO AMERICAN POPULAR SONGS (see Popular Music) and *Popular Song Index* to their collections.

—*J. F. D.*

With contributions by Donna L. Singer.

Core Titles

General

The Concise Oxford History of Music. Gerald Abraham. Oxford, 1979; repr. 1988. soft. 1 vol. 968 pp. illus. index. ISBN 0-19-284010-X. $21.95. history.
ML160 780.9

The Concise Oxford History of Music, authored by a respected writer on music, spans the history of music from its earliest recorded appearance to the death of Stravinsky. It is not based on THE NEW OXFORD HISTORY OF MUSIC in any way. In the preface, the author explains his arbitrary selection of material for inclusion; for example, he has deliberately chosen less familiar examples of music to illustrate historical development except for the nineteenth century, where he has emphasized the familiar masterpieces. The reference covers the development of church music, orchestral music, and opera. Generally "popular or folk music" is omitted with the exception of a section on the music of black Africa and America, which discusses jazz, blues, and ragtime. While the major focus is on the development of Western music, coverage is also given to non-Western music (eastern Asia, India, Islam, Africa). Finally, the author's overall approach to music history is to view it as a "continuum" in which individual composers are discussed insofar as they contributed to the evolution of music.

The reference is divided into five major parts, which unfold the history of music chronologically, from "The Rise of West Asian and East Mediterranean Music" to "The Fragmentation of Tradition" in the twentieth century. Each part is further divided into chapters, which are in turn divided into sections—indicated by all capital letters. Interspersed between the parts are three chapters called "Interludes," which deal with ethnic music ("Music in the Islamic World," "Music of India," "Music of Black Africa and America"). Numerous black-and-white plates with captions, as well as musical examples, add to the usefulness of the history. Three maps detail areas covered in the text. In addition, there is a copious use of footnotes, which appear at the bottom of the relevant page, numbered consecutively within each chapter.

A section containing sources for further reading and recommended editions, arranged alphabetically under chapter titles, follows the main text. Accessibility is enhanced by a comprehensive index in alphabetical order, with boldface figures indicating the most important references and italic figures denoting illustrations or their captions. Lists of black-and-white plates and acknowledgments appear in the front matter.

This excellent history can provide information on such different aspects of music as the Lutheran *geistliche Lieder* during the Counter-Reformation; the influence of John Blow's "miniature opera," *Venus and Adonis,* on the music of Henry Purcell in Restoration England; or the emergence of a new type of musical theater, *ching-hsi* ("Peking opera"), in the late Manchu period. The large typeface, use of illustrations and musical examples, and the fine index make this reference easy to use by the general reader as well as by the serious student. However, a lot has happened in music since Stravinsky died in 1971, and this reference should be updated to reflect this recent musical history. Nevertheless, *The Concise Oxford History of Music* is a convenient and authoritative reference. The Board recommends this work for the core collections of public, academic, and school libraries. —*D. L. S.*

Musical Instruments of the World: An Illustrated Encyclopedia. The Diagram Group, comp. Facts On File, 1978. hard and soft. 1 vol. 320 pp. index. ISBN 0-87196-320-5 (hard); 0-8160-1309-8 (soft). $40 (hard); $18.95 (soft). encyclopedia.
ML102.15D5 781.9'1'03

Musical Instruments of the World is a comprehensive, beautifully illustrated reference that covers a wide range of instruments, from the bull-roarers of the Stone Age to sophisticated electronic equipment like the vibraphone of the twentieth century. With an emphasis on visual presentation, the reference contains over 4,000 original, color-highlighted drawings that illustrate the structure, function, and decoration of thousands of instruments. These detailed representations were drawn from authentic sources such as monographs, actual instruments, or pictures of instruments in major collections. While there are brief introductory paragraphs for each main category of instruments and subsequent subsections, the major use of text is in descriptive and identifying paragraphs that complement the drawings.

This excellent reference was compiled by the Diagram Group, who assembled a team of 40 researchers, writers, and illustrators to gather and prepare the material. Scholars, museums, and private collections from more than 20 countries were consulted. As a result, this history of world instruments is authoritative, accurate, and the best-illustrated reference among comparable works (the *History of Musical Instruments* by Curt Sachs is another title on this subject).

The reference is organized according to the widely accepted system of instrument classification established in 1914 by Erich von Hornbostel and Curt Sachs, which categorizes instruments by how the sound is produced. These categories are aerophones (bagpipe, saxophone), idiophones (church bells, xylophone), membranophones (kettledrums), and chordophones (violin, piano). A fifth category, mechanical and electrical instruments such as music boxes and electric guitars, has been added to update the classification system. Following these sections are four additional ones that regroup the instruments into historical and geographical categories, discuss musical ensembles, and present illustrated biographical entries on personalities important in instrumental history, such as the Neuschel family, who were German brass instrument makers. Category headings ("Aerophones: Introduction") are indicated by large-print boldface type, as are subsection headings ("Vessel Flutes and Whistles"). Caption headings are in smaller boldface type.

Each section explains the nature of a single group or category of instruments, including historical, musical, and technical explanations of the characteristics of each member of the group. Where appropriate there are boxes showing a diagram of the position of an instrument in the modern orchestra, a section of a score for that instrument, a list of compositions featuring the instrument, and a figure demonstrating the correct playing position. Museums or private collections that have a particular instrument are identified in parentheses in the text dealing with that instrument. In addition the patron will find an extensive index, a bibliography that includes publishers, and a list of museums throughout the world that have collections of musical instruments.

The attractive, largely pictorial format, the index and bibliography, as well as the dual approach to the instruments through classification by sound production and the more traditional historical-geographical approach make *Musical Instruments of the World* an easily accessible reference for any reader. The Board recommends this work for the core collections of public, academic, and school libraries. —*D. L. S.*

Musicians since 1900: Performers in Concert and Opera. David Ewen. Wilson, 1978. hard. 1 vol. 974 pp. illus. ISBN 0-8242-0565-0. $70. biographical dictionary.
ML105.E97 780.922

Musicians since 1900: Performers in Concert and Opera is a biographical dictionary that "covers performers, living or dead, whose art has left a permanent impress upon the musical culture of the twentieth century" (introduction). It contains entries on more than 430 performing musicians—conductors, concert soloists, and opera singers. The articles are well written, interesting, and contain much pertinent information on their subjects in 1,500 to 3,000 words. As he does in other biographical dictionaries he has edited, Ewen makes especially telling use of excerpts from concert reviews and biographical articles to create well-rounded portraits. However, the choice of musicians included does not always meet Ewen's own selection criteria as quoted above. For example, there are no entries for such major figures as conductors Eugen Jochum and Hans Schmidt-Isserstedt, pianists Dinu Lipatti, Ivan Moravec, and Solomon, and tenor Fritz Wunderlich, while some personalities of dubious merit (such as the mezzosoprano *Gladys Swarthout*) are included. Moreover, a large percentage of the entries could use updating to reflect the recent accomplishments of some performers and the passing of others. New entries are also needed for important musicians, such as Leonard Slatkin, Kathleen Battle, and Simon Rattle, whose reputations have been established since the late 1970s. Nevertheless, until a revised edition or a supplement is issued, *Musicians since 1900* will remain a core selection on the music reference shelf of public and school libraries. Its virtues are numerous and outweigh its defects (as long as the user is aware of them).

The Board recommends this work for the core collections of public and school libraries. —*J. F. D.*

National Anthems of the World, 7th edition. W. L. Reed and M. J. Bristow, eds. Blandford, 1988; distrib. by Sterling. hard. 1 vol. 513 pp. appendix. ISBN 0-7137-1962-1. $70. handbook.
M1627.N269

This seventh edition of *National Anthems of the World* contains the piano scores and vocal parts for the anthems of 173 independent countries, including Vatican City. The number of entries has not changed since the 1985 edition because no new independent countries with their own national anthems have emerged. However, this edition does have new versions of the anthems of Burkina Faso, Yemen Arab Republic, and Yemen People's Republic, as well as newly revised anthems for Brunei Darussalam, Irish Republic, Libya, Norway, Portugal, Saudi Arabia, and Venzuela. Additionally, words have been fitted to music for the anthems of Afghanistan, Burundi, Equatorial Guinea, Iraq, Maldives Republic, and Morocco. The correct wording for the anthems of Belgium, China, and Switzerland has also been established. As stated in the preface, "in most cases the version of the melody and accompaniment is that officially authorized by the state."

A very useful appendix provides a list of national days, organized alphabetically by country; it has been revised and updated for this edition. It is designed in an easily accessible three-column format; the first column presents the country's name in all capitals, the second lists the day and month of the national day, and the third shows the title of the day and year of inauguration.

The national anthems are arranged alphabetically by country, with the country's name centered and in boldface capitals. Underneath the country on the left side is the lyricist's name with birth and death dates in parentheses; on the right side is the composer's name with birth and death dates in parentheses. The name of the arranger, or the person who wrote the band score, is placed under the composer's name, where applicable. An asterisk next to a name sends the reader to a footnote, which usually explains that the same melody is used by another country, or that the same person wrote another country's anthem. Next, the musical score with the words in the language of the country is reproduced. At the foot of the score is information covering when the anthem was composed or adopted; it also lists copyright acknowledgments when ownership is known. Unlike earlier editions, English translations are printed separately at the end of the anthems to which they refer, instead of under the vocal lines. The exceptions are countries where English is an "official alternative language," such as Botswana and Zambia. In these cases the English words are printed with the primary language in the score. The translator or person who verified the translation is listed. If an anthem has a second and third verse, these are often given, but additional verses are excluded (for example, Greece has 158 verses to its anthem).

The large typeface, sturdy binding, clearly reproduced scores, as well as the currency and accuracy, make *National Anthems of the World* a useful reference for those who need to play or sing a particular anthem or for readers interested in general information on the anthem for a relatively new country such as Vanuatu (anthem adopted 1980), or the two parts of the Czechoslovakian anthem (one in Czech, the other in Slovak). The Board recommends this work for the core collections of public, academic, and school libraries.

—D. L. S.

The New Grove Dictionary of American Music. H. Wiley Hitchcock and Stanley Sadie, eds. Grove's Dictionaries of Music/Macmillan, 1986. hard. 4 vols. illus. ISBN 0-943818-36-2 (set). $695 (set). dictionary.

ML101.U6N48 781.773'03'21

The New Grove Dictionary of American Music attempts to do for music in America what THE NEW GROVE DICTIONARY OF MUSIC AND MUSICIANS does for all music. Indeed, some of its entries were first published in the latter work; others also appear in THE NEW GROVE DICTIONARY OF MUSICAL INSTRUMENTS. Nonetheless, this four-volume set is sufficiently distinct from the other Grove titles to warrant consideration on its own merits.

This *New Grove* is mainly, though not exclusively, a biographical dictionary, concentrating on composers and performers. It also includes entries on U.S. cities, musical organizations, festivals, instrument manufacturers, and movements. It covers subjects in the rock, pop, country-western, folk, jazz, and gospel genres, as well as classical music. Like the other works in the *New Grove* series, this may be a "dictionary" in title, but the range of entries and breadth of coverage is encyclopedic. The treatment of peculiarly American genres—jazz and country-western, for example—is extensive, as is the coverage of the many aspects of rock and popular music.

In fact, this work perhaps errs a little on the side of being overly inclusive—but this is by no means a grave fault. Foreign-born performers and composers who spent a significant portion of their careers in America and made contributions to American musical culture are included, even if (as in the case of Rachmaninoff, for example) the figure cannot be considered American by any stretch of the imagination.

Nearly 1,000 contributors are listed at the back of volume 4; their entries are also identified. Among these contributors are leading musicologists, music critics, and biographers. Two dozen advisors also assisted the editors in shaping this work. The entries themselves (most of which are signed) are models of clarity—intelligent, straightforward, and critical in the best sense. Most importantly, each entry places its subject in context. Excellent bibliographies include not only books but also newspaper and magazine articles. Partial discographies, listing important recordings, are given at the end of biographical entries on performers. Outstanding graphic design—a good, clear, readable typeface—also adds to the appeal of this work. Moreover, many entries are illustrated by large, well-chosen black-and-white photos that will enhance the reader's understanding of the subject.

The New Grove Dictionary of American Music gives as complete and composite a picture of American musical life as is possible in a four-volume work. This is a most valuable and welcome addition to the outstanding Grove series of musical dictionaries.

The question arises, does a library need this set if it already has THE NEW GROVE DICTIONARY OF

MUSIC AND MUSICIANS? If there is a high patron demand for reference sources on American musical culture, *The New Grove Dictionary of American Music* will be a core selection; otherwise, it may be a supplementary choice.

The Board recommends this work for the core collections of public and academic libraries. —*J. F. D.*

The New Grove Dictionary of Musical Instruments. Stanley Sadie, ed. Grove's Dictionaries of Music/ Macmillan, 1984. hard. 3 vols. illus. ISBN 0-943818-05-2 (set). $495 (set). dictionary.
ML102.15N48 781.91'03'21

The New Grove Dictionary of Musical Instruments is encyclopedic in scope. It contains entries in five broad subject categories: instruments of classical Western music; instrument makers; modern Western instruments; performance practice; and non-Western, folk, and traditional instruments. There are nearly 10,000 entries in this last category alone. Most of the articles on Western classical instruments are derived or adapted from THE NEW GROVE DICTIONARY OF MUSIC AND MUSICIANS, but the entries in virtually all other subject areas are new and were not included in *Music and Musicians;* thus, the degree of overlap between the two works is minimal.

Like the other works in the *New Grove* series, this dictionary displays evidence of the highest and most thorough scholarship. Most articles are signed; a list of 400 contributors and their articles appear at the back of volume 3.

Entries range in length from a few lines to several dozen pages. The extended articles are highly structured. For example, the 36-page article *pianoforte* is divided into two broad sections, history and piano playing. The history of the piano is further divided into nine sections (introduction and eight historical periods); piano playing is divided into four sections (classical, romantic, twentieth-century, and jazz playing). Archaic instruments (for example, *aulos*, 3 pages) and folk or national instruments (for example, *bagpipe,* 12 pages) receive extensive attention. The scholarly attention given to obscure or minor subjects is indicated, for example, by the entries for *arckwa, arengas, arghanon,* and *arghul,* among others, on page 72, volume 1, or the entries for *tepsija, tepuzquiquiztli, tepqing,* and *teran* on page 568, volume 3.

The reader is aided by generous cross-references. Other scholarly apparatus includes a list of general biblographical abbreviations at the front of each volume. End-of-article bibliographies are thorough, and the illustrations are most useful in helping the reader visualize the instrument being described.

As with other *New Grove* works, the graphic design in this set is attractive, and the bindings appear to be extremely durable.

The New Grove Dictionary of Musical Instruments will be most useful for the professional musicologist or the graduate-level researcher. The Board recommends this work for the core collections of public and academic libraries. —*J. F. D.*

The New Grove Dictionary of Music and Musicians. Stanley Sadie, ed. Grove's Dictionaries of Music/ Macmillan, 1980. hard. 20 vols. illus. ISBN 0-333-23111-2 (set). $2,300 (set). dictionary.
ML100.N48 780.3

The Grove name, perhaps the most famous single name in the music reference field, goes back more than 100 years. The first edition of *The Grove Dictionary of Music* was issued in four volumes, from 1878 to 1890, prepared by the British musicologist Sir George Grove, and won immediate acclaim for its comprehensive scholarship and authority. The work was subsequently revised on several occasions by other editors. The fifth edition, edited by Eric Blom, was published in nine volumes in 1954, with a supplementary volume issued in 1961. The present work, conceived in 1969, was originally planned as the sixth edition, but it soon became apparent to the editors that an entirely new work was needed; thus the title change to *The New Grove Dictionary of Music and Musicians.*

According to editor Stanley Sadie, *The New Grove* "seeks to discuss everything that can be reckoned to bear on music in history and on present-day musical life." This work is intended as "a critically organized repository of historically significant information." More than half the entries deal with composers. Performers, theorists, administrators, dancers, choreographers, librettists, patrons, publishers, instrument makers, musicologists—anyone, in short, who has had some influence on the history of music—are also included. *The New Grove* also contains entries for musical terms, instruments, institutions, cities with significant musical traditions, and genres, as well as entries on bibliographical and reference material.

Unlike previous editions, *The New Grove* gives considerable attention to non-Western and folk music. For example, there is a six-page article on music in Mozambique, discussing history and ethnography, music areas, instruments and instrumental music, and vocal music. Jazz, pop, and rock music are well covered in numerous other entries. For example, *Jelly Roll Morton, the Beatles,* and *Chuck Berry* each have substantial entries. The 34-page entry on *pop music* covers the subject up through and including punk rock and rap music. At the opposite end of the spectrum, *The New Grove Dictionary of Music and Musicians* covers early music thoroughly and with impeccable scholarship.

Long articles on complex subjects are well structured. For example, the entry on *Robert Schumann* is divided into 25 sections. The first 20 are a chronological account of his life and work; the last 5 discuss specific compositions (and his critical writings). A complete table of his works (indexed) and a comprehensive bibliography follow the article itself. In fact, similar tables are given in entries on other major composers: the 55-page entry on *J. S. Bach* includes an 18-page table of his 1,087 cataloged works (arranged by genre). The subentry on other Bach family members lists 78 musical Bachs (with dates and other pertinent information) and presents a two-page family tree tracing eight generations of musical Bachs. Among the impressive illustrations throughout the work are facsimiles of autograph scores.

No other music reference work begins to match the breadth and depth of detail contained in *The New Grove Dictionary of Music and Musicians.* The product of 2,500 expert contributors, this is unquestionably the most comprehensive and authoritative music reference work on the market today and should remain so for some time. The Board recommends this work for the core collections of public and academic libraries.

—*J. F. D.*

The New Harvard Dictionary of Music. Don Michael Randel, ed. Belknap/Harvard, 1986. hard. 1 vol. 966 pp. illus. ISBN 0-674-61525-5. $35. dictionary.
ML100.R3 780.3'21

The impressive *New Harvard Dictionary of Music* is, according to the editor, "based on" the earlier *Harvard Dictionary of Music,* but it includes only a handful of articles reproduced from that work. The great majority of the entries in this book are new and were written specifically for this work. *The New Harvard Dictionary of Music* aims "to serve as a convenient reference work for laymen, students, performers, composers, scholars, and teachers" (preface).

Unlike THE OXFORD DICTIONARY OF MUSIC, *The New Harvard* does not include biographical entries, but it does include entries for specific works of music as well as for musical terms. The entries—over 6,000 in all—range in length from a few lines (e.g., for the terms *shift, sho, short,* and *score*) to a brief paragraph (e.g., for *Sheherazade, sheng, shofar,* and *Siegfried Idyll*), to a page or more for broader subjects (e.g., *piano,* six pages; *pitch,* one and a half pages; *Poland,* one page; and *popular music,* two and a half pages). The majority of entries are of the brief, dictionary type. Cross-reference entries are included when appropriate (e.g., *signature* refers to the reader to entries on *key signature, time signature,* and *conflicting signatures*). Main entry words are printed in boldface type; throughout, the typeface is easy to read. Guide words at the top of each page enhance accessibility.

The editor is quite accurate in claiming that "within the tradition of Western art music, which remains its central concern, the [*New Harvard Dictionary of Music*] reflects recent scholarship on all periods and the growing proportion of scholarship and criticism devoted to more recent music." The work also covers non-Western music, popular music, and musical instruments of all cultures. The text is supported by 220 drawings of musical instruments and 250 musical examples.

Articles are signed with the contributor's initials; a key to contributors (of whom there are 70) at the front of the book identifies their professional affiliations and subject specialties. The reader is also aided by an 11-page list of abbreviations in the front of the book.

The New Harvard Dictionary of Music is as near a definitive music dictionary as we shall ever likely have in one volume. On the whole, this work is probably more useful overall than THE OXFORD DICTIONARY OF MUSIC, its main rival, but it is not quite as comprehensive as THE NEW OXFORD COMPANION TO MUSIC. The Board recommends this work for the core collections of public, academic, and school libraries.

—*J. F. D.*

The New Oxford Companion to Music. Denis Arnold, gen. ed. Oxford, 1983. hard. 2 vols. illus. ISBN 0-19-311316-3. $125. dictionary.
ML100 780.3'21

The successor to *The Oxford Companion to Music,* which was first published in 1938, *The New Oxford Companion to Music* is an entirely new work. Its contents have been expanded beyond those covered in the old *Oxford Companion* to include aspects of popular music and non-Western music. Oriented toward the general reader, this two-volume work is designed to be complete in itself. It includes 6,000 entries on all aspects of music—composers, individual works, music of specific periods and countries, jazz, popular music, acoustics, musical instruments for all parts of the world, and plot synopses of 100 operas. There are also articles on musical theory and forms. An additional 2,000 entries define musical terms.

As an example of the breadth and depth of coverage, consider the following entries from a dozen pages under *C. Cello* take up five pages, includes five illustrations and a musical example, and is divided into six sections. The entry on *Central Asian and Siberian music* is five pages, with seven photos, and is also structured in several sections. Following this entry is a cross-reference entry for *Central Tutorial School for Young Musicians,* a three-sentence entry on the term *cents,* a short paragraph on the composition *Ce qu'on entend sur la montagne* by Liszt, two sentences on the term *Cercar la nota,* single paragraphs on Britten's *A Ceremony of Carols, Joan Cererols, Bohuslav Matej Cernohorsky,* and *Pierre Certon,* with one line on *Ces,* the German word for the note C-flat.

The excellent black-and-white illustrations throughout the work are central, not merely incidental, to this work. The bibliographies that accompany some of the entries are intended as suggestions for further reading in the subject; they are not comprehensive, but they are useful. The work's 90 contributors are listed in the front of volume 1, with their areas of expertise. Most entries, except for those that are definitions, plot summaries, or identifications of musical compositions, are signed. The lack of an index may be a drawback in some circumstances, but it does not render the work inaccessible; it will take some patience and persistence on the reader's part, however, to determine if there is an entry on a given subject.

The New Oxford Companion to Music may well be the most comprehensive and authoritative all-around small-volume musical reference work available today; the work is an essential work for public, academic, and school libraries. For smaller libraries that cannot afford the 20-volume THE NEW GROVE DICTIONARY OF MUSIC AND MUSICIANS, this 2-volume work makes a good alternative. The Board recommends this work for the core collections of public, academic, and school libraries. —*J. F. D.*

The New Oxford History of Music. Gerald Abraham et al. Oxford, 1954–1983. hard. 11 vols. illus. index. ISBN 0-19-316310-1 (vol. 11). $95 (vol. 11). history. ML160.N44 780

The 11-volume *The New Oxford History of Music* is not a revision of the older *The Oxford History of Music* but, as the general introduction states, "an entirely new survey of music from the earliest times down to comparatively recent years. . . . [The] object has been to present music, not as an isolated phenomenon or the work of outstanding composers, but as an art developing in constant association with every form of human culture and activity. . . . No hard and fast system of division into chapters has been attempted. The treatment is sometimes by forms, sometimes by periods, sometimes also by countries, according to the importance which one element or another may assume."

This set is perhaps the most comprehensive survey of music history available. The books, devised as a series, are independent of one another (although volumes 5 and 6 are complementary). The chapters within each volume are actually self-contained essays by different authors. The contents of each volume are delineated at the beginning of the respective volume; the individual chapters or essays are divided into separate sections for easy reference, and this is also shown in the table of contents. The contents of volume 10 may be considered typical of the organization of each book in the series. Here, Gerald Abraham has separate essays on "The Apogee and Decline of Romanticism: 1890–1914" and "The Reaction Against Romanticism: 1890–1914"; Martin Cooper contributes an essay on "Stage Works: 1890–1918"; Mosco Carner writes about "Music in the Mainland of Europe: 1918–1939"; Peter Evans assays "Music of the European Mainstream: 1940–1960"; Arthur Hutchins discusses "Music in Britain: 1918–1960." "American Music: 1918–1960," including both the United States and Latin America, is covered by Richard Franko Goldman and Gerard Behague, while Gerald Abraham also writes on "Music in the Soviet Union."

Throughout the set, the text is supported by generous musical examples. Each volume includes several multipage black-and-white photo inserts on glossy stock. In most cases, these are reproductions of works of art; photos of composers are reproduced in *The Modern Age.* Each of the first ten volumes includes an extensive (though not comprehensive) bibliography and an index; a complete bibliography and index for the entire set, along with chronological tables, makes up volume 11.

The books in THE NEW OXFORD HISTORY OF MUSIC can be used in a variety of ways: they can be consulted for ready reference, the essays can be read individually for background, single books can be read cover to cover as a survey of a particular period, or the entire series can be read for a course in the history of music. The essays are not only thoughtful, but often subtle and engaging.

While *The New Oxford History of Music* is not flawless—this work is only a survey, despite its length—the series is ambitious and sophisticated. The Board recommends this work for the core collection of academic libraries. —*J. F. D.*

The Oxford Dictionary of Music. Michael Kennedy. Oxford, 1985. hard. 1 vol. 824 pp. ISBN 0-19-311333-3. $45.

780.3′21

The Oxford Dictionary of Music is a revision and enlargement of the third edition of *The Concise Oxford Dictionary of Music,* published in 1980. Kennedy, a noted British critic and biographer who is the sole author of this work, claims to have added 500 new entries, revised 100 existing ones, and amended or corrected the majority of others from that work. The entries are concise and lexicographic rather than encyclopedic, factual rather than critical. To conserve space in the text, Kennedy makes extensive use of abbreviations—for example, *bar.* for "baritone," *cl.* for "clarinet," *pf.* for "pianoforte," *RPO* for "Royal Philharmonic Orchestra," and so on.

The majority of all the 11,000 entries are biographical, but musical terms and specific works are also included. There is especially good coverage of living composers and performers. Entries for composers include abridged lists of major works. Entries are arranged alphabetically; entry words are set in boldface type for easy accessibility, but the very small typeface and thin paper (both necessary in order to accommodate the large number of entries in one volume) make reading difficult.

The Oxford Dictionary of Music is intended for "the concert- and opera-goer, the radio listener (and television viewer), and anyone involved in any musical pursuit." For ready reference it is a good work of its kind, although MUSICIANS SINCE 1900, the NEW GROVE titles, and the out-of-print *Baker's Biographical Dictionary* (Schirmer Bks., 1978) offer deeper, more detailed insight into many of the subjects covered here. The Board recommends this work for the core collections of public and school libraries. —*J. F. D.*

Supplement to Music since 1900. Nicholas Slonimsky. Scribner, 1986. hard. 1 vol. 398 pp. index. ISBN 0-684-18438-9. $30. history.
ML197.S634 780.904

In *Supplement to Music since 1900,* Slonimsky continues his life-long task of chronicling the activities of musicians. As its title implies, this work is intended to supplement the author's massive 1,500-page *Music since 1900* (4th edition, Scribner, 1971, now out of print), which gave a descriptive chronology of music events worldwide through 1969. In its first section, this *Supplement* takes up that chronology in 1970 and brings it up to date through June 1985 in some 230 pages. It primarily notes premieres of new works, as well as the deaths of notable performers. In the next section of the book, Slonimsky provides additions, amplifications, and corrections to the chronology of 1900 to 1969.

Throughout, Slonimsky proves a scrupulous historian, but leavens his writing with wit, irony, and acerbity. For example, reporting the premiere of *Polinteracões* by the Brazilian composer Jocy de Oliveira in St. Louis on April 7, 1970, he remarks that the performance "was interrupted in midcourse by the loud protest of the building superintendent as a noisy and noisome nuisance."

Supplement to Music since 1900 will be a valuable addition to academic and performing arts libraries, which should already have Slonimsky's *Music since 1900* in their reference collections. The Board recommends this work for the core collection of public libraries. —*J. F. D.*

Opera

The Concise Oxford Dictionary of Opera, 2d edition. Harold Rosenthal and John Warrack. Oxford, 1979; repr. 1986. soft. 1 vol. 561 pp. ISBN 0-19-311321-X. $13.95. dictionary.
ML102.06 R67 782.103

This is a paperback reprint of the 1979 second edition of *The Concise Oxford Dictionary of Opera* and provides concise but comprehensive coverage of all aspects of opera, including composers, librettists, singers, conductors, technical terms, and opera companies. Also included are entries on operettas (such as *The Merry Widow*), individual operas (such as *Aida*), and characters from well-known operas (for example, *Tatyana,* heroine of Tchaikovsky's *Eugene Onegin*). There are numerous in-depth entries on opera in different countries and cities, and several literary references upon which operas have been based (such as plays of Shakespeare, the subject of Faust, poems of W. B. Yeats). This paperback edition has all the additions and revisions incorporated in the 1979 hardcover, which itself was a complete revision of the first edition (1964). Entries for singers who came into prominence since the first edition (such as *Frederica von Stade*) were added, and the number of entries for singers of the past (for example, French soprano *Delphine Ugalde*) were also increased. Though the reference has a basically British slant, its coverage of the international opera scene is quite thorough.

The authors are respected authorities on opera. Harold Rosenthal has written several opera guides and is an editor of *Opera* magazine and a former archivist at the Royal Opera House, Covent Garden, while John Warrack has written books on Tchaikovsky and Carl Maria von Weber and is an editor for THE NEW GROVE DICTIONARY OF MUSIC AND MUSICIANS.

Entries are alphabetical in a two-column format with the main entry in boldface, immediately followed by birth and death dates (where applicable) in parentheses. The core of each entry contains either a brief description, definition, identification, historical overview, or biographical data, which includes major contributions or career highlights. Some entries conclude with a bibliographical reference to the standard work on the subject. Numerous cross-references are indicated by italic type. Operas are entered under their original-language titles as well as their English translations, but information is only given under the original-language entry; cross-references send the reader to that entry. Asterisks are used before a reference within an entry to indicate another entry that is relevant to the one being discussed. Entries vary in length from two lines for character identification, such as Sharpless from *Madama Butterfly,* to over three columns for a prolific composer like Verdi.

This broad-based reference provides information on lesser-known operas such as *La Wally,* as well as material on popular operas such as *Carmen.* A reader can find a succinct definition of a *covered tone,* a detailed discussion of the *aria,* or information on the use of ballet in opera.

Though the print is small, the binding is sturdy. The dictionary also contains brief lists of books covering synopses and/or analyses of operas, as well as catalogs of operas; all of which enhance the book's usefulness. The librarian should be aware, however, that this reference needs updating. Singers such as Jessye Norman, Kiri Te Kanawa, and Samuel Ramey, and contemporary composers such as Phillip Glass have established their reputations in the ten years since the last major revision of this dictionary and should be included. Other entries, such as those for *José Carreras* and *Herbert van Karajan,* need to be updated. Overall, *The Concise Oxford Dictionary of Opera* is a convenient and authoritative reference for all opera enthusiasts. The Board recommends this work for the core collections of public, academic, and school libraries. —*D. L. S.*

The Definitive Kobbé's Opera Book. Gustav Kobbé; Earl of Harewood, ed. and rev. Putnam, 1987. hard. 1 vol. 1,404 pp. illus. index. ISBN 0-399-13180-9. $35. handbook.
MT95.K52 782.1

The Definitive Kobbé's Opera Book is the first major revision in 10 years of this highly regarded, authoritative, and internationally oriented opera guide that was first published in 1919 as *The Complete Opera Book,* authored by opera connoisseur and music critic Gustav Kobbé. This current edition has been completely revised, expanded, and updated by Lord Harewood, former director of the Royal Opera House, Covent Garden, and the English National Opera, who has been the editor for the various revisions and editions of the *Kobbé's* for more than 30 years.

The reference is divided into three major sections ("1600–1800," "The Nineteenth Century," "The Twentieth Century"), which are in turn divided into chapters representing countries, such as German opera, Russian opera, or specific composers, such as Giuseppe Verdi. Each of the more than 300 entries begins with the composer's name in large capitals and boldface type followed by the opera title, generally given in its original language with the English translation underneath. Next comes a headnote containing dates, places, and casts of significant premieres and revivals, followed by a list of characters with their vocal parts. The major portion of each entry is the detailed synopsis of the plot, often including analysis of important aspects of that particular opera, such as the Siegmund motif and the Sword motif in Richard Wagner's *Die Walküre,* or critical commentary, such as Stendhal's remarks on Rossini's *L'Italiana in Algeri.* The length of entries ranges from 4 pages for Richard Strauss' *The Woman Without a Shadow* to 12 pages for *Aida.* There are some brief explanatory footnotes and a general, alphabetically arranged index containing opera titles, composers, librettists, opera companies, and other aspects related to opera.

The reference reflects the author's/editor's responsiveness to opera of all eras and from all countries and to the current trends of revivals, new works, and the standard repertory. Operas selected for inclusion are those a "travelling opera-goer is likely to meet . . . during his peregrinations," as well as those of historical importance (preface). As a result, 29 new operas have been added to this edition, some expanding the entries for a composer previously included (for example, the number of operas for Handel have doubled—eight—since the 1976 edition), and some representing a composer for the first time, such as Philip Glass and his opera *Akhnaten.* Such contemporary composers as Argentinian Alberto Ginastera *(Bomarzo),* Australian Richard Meale *(Voss),* and American Oliver Knussen *(Where the Wild Things Are)* have been added, as well as composers from an earlier era, such as Gabriel Fauré, whose works are enjoying renewed interest. Twenty titles that appeared in the 1976 edition have been dropped, while entries for other operas have been expanded or revised, such as the entry for Leoš Janáček's *Jenufa.*

The Definitive Kobbé's Opera Book, with its sturdy binding, easy-to-read typeface, clearly presented material, and fine index is highly accessible to all users. In addition, the liberal reproduction of parts of musical scores enhances the understanding of each opera. Furthermore, the accuracy, currency, international scope, and judicious selectivity make this reference a must. The Board recommends this work for the core collections of public, academic, and school libraries.

—D. L. S.

Supplementary Titles

General

The Choral Singer's Companion. Ronald Corp. Facts On File, 1987. hard. 1 vol. 192 pp. illus. index. ISBN 0-8160-1776-X. $24.95. dictionary/handbook.
MT875.C68 784.9′6

"Although [*The Choral Singer's Companion*] gives short shrift to American music, which is mostly relegated to a brief list, 'Choral Works by American Composers,' this British handbook for singers and directors will prove useful. It first proffers advice on singing, fitting into a choir, running a choral society, conducting, rehearsing, program planning, and obtaining music. Brief dictionaries of classical choral composers and major compositions follow, affording an overview of the repertoire. An admirably expansive glossary of terms from *a capella* to *voice,* a set of Latin and English texts for the most frequently set liturgy, and a collection of reference lists ('Easter Music,' 'Works for Female Voices,' 'Useful Addresses,' etc.) conclude. Select bibliography and index." (*BL,* October 1, 1987, p. 202)

Also reviewed in: *ARBA,* 1988, p. 519; *B Rept,* March 1988, p. 45; *Choice,* February 1988, p. 916; *M Ed J,* March 1988, p. 22.

Board's recommendation: Public libraries.

Heritage of Music (series). Michael Raeburn and Alan Kendall, eds. Oxford, 1989. hard. 4 vols. illus. ISBN 0-19-520493-X. $195. history.
ML160.H527 780

The *Heritage of Music* series is a "history of Western music, lavishly presented with hundreds of color plates and illustrations. . . . Its various chapters are independently written by 55 scholars (a format used successfully by the ten-volume *New Oxford History of Music,* 1953), and stories of composers' lives are limited to the major figures (Bach, Beethoven, etc.), with biographical material about others consigned to short sketches at the end of each volume. This allows the authors to dwell on important compositions, placing music in its historical and social setting.

"The copious illustrations have detailed captions and are tightly integrated into the text, providing a part of the essential story rather than merely serving as ornaments. Historical information is, for the most part, up to date. There is considerable variety in the writing styles and approaches of the different authors. . . . In most . . . essays, . . . the quantity of material and pace of the writing [are] quite comfortable. On the whole, then, this is a solid accomplishment." (*LJ,* October 1989, p. 76)

Board's recommendation: Public and school libraries.

Music Reference and Research Materials: An Annotated Bibliography, 4th edition. Vincent H. Duckless and Michael A. Keller. Schirmer Bks./Macmillan, 1988. hard. 1 vol. 729 pp. indexes. ISBN 0-02-870390-1. $34.95. bibliography.
ML113.D83 016.78

"The fourth edition [of *Music Reference and Research Materials*] continues in much expanded form the high standards established in previous editions. . . . the work is arguably the best single guide to reference sources in the field of music.

"Like the earlier editions. . . . [this book] is an annotated bibliography of numbered entries arranged alphabetically by author within broad categories (dictionaries and encyclopedias, bibliographies of music, catalogs of music libraries, discographies, etc.), which in turn are subdivided into narrower subjects. There are more than 3,200 entries.

"Coverage is international and includes Asian materials. Non-Roman titles are transliterated. The clearly written annotations are descriptive with occasional critical comment.

"The fourth edition reflects current interest with a 'Women in Music' section and inclusion of computer-based reference sources. Duckless concludes with indexes totaling 160 pages.

"*Music Reference and Research Materials* is highly recommended for all reference collections where users are seriously interested in music; it will receive repeated use from both librarians and researchers." (*BL,* May 1, 1989, pp. 1520–1522)

Also reviewed in: *Choice,* June 1989; *M Ed J,* May, 1989, p. 55.

Board's recommendation: Public and academic libraries.

The New York Philharmonic Guide to the Symphony. Edward Downes. Walker, 1976. hard. 1 vol. 1,058 pp. illus. ISBN 0-8027-0540-5. $50. guide.
MT125.D68 785.01'519

The New York Philharmonic Guide to the Symphony "is based on the program notes Downes wrote for the concerts of the Philharmonic Symphony Society of New York. Each of the more than 450 works described has information about the circumstances in which it was written, historical background, quotations from composers' letters, or other pertinent biographical material. Additionally, each work is described analytically, with appropriate thematic quotations. The notes also include texts of vocal works." (*LJ,* February 15, 1977, p. 497)

"The volume is rich not only in musical examples but in illustrations: e. g., photographs of composers and conductors, scenes of first productions of works." (*Am,* April 30, 1977, p. 402)

"The mixture of data gathered in this one volume is not to be encountered in any other anthology: works by Varèse, Webern, Rochberg, Crumb, Ruggles, Sessions, Lutoslawski, Kirchner, Cage, and Carter, for instance, are discussed at great length. Often Downes includes statements from the composers—these frequently are most enlightening. This rich mine for the student of contemporary music is recommended for all types and levels of libraries." (*Choice,* September 1977, p. 872)

Also reviewed in: *ARBA,* 1978, p. 470; *RSR,* April 1978, p. 27.

Board's recommendation: Public and academic libraries.

The Penguin Guide to Compact Discs, Cassettes and LPs. Edward Greenfield et al., eds. Penguin, 1986. soft. 1 vol. 608 pp. ISBN 0-14-046754-8. $14.95. handbook.
ML156.9G76 789.913

"The latest edition of [*The Penguin Guide to Compact Discs, Cassettes and LPs*] emphasizes the technological revolution brought about by the compact disc. The prominence of compact discs is underscored in these listings of recommended recordings not just by the sheer number included but also by the boldface type of the CD references themselves. While cassettes and LPs are also listed, they are clearly relegated to inferior positions. Otherwise, the musical approach . . . remains standard in this exemplary evaluation of centuries of music. This compilation updates the series' previous three volumes and is thus an important addition to most music collections." (*BL,* January 15, 1987, p. 741)

Also reviewed in: *Choice,* March 1987, p. 1030; *ON,* December 6, 1986, p. 68; *TES,* December 5, 1986, p. 29.

Board's recommendation: Public, academic, and school libraries.

Short History of Opera, 2d edition. Donald Jay Grout, ed. Columbia, 1987. soft. 1 vol. 1,120 pp. ISBN 0-231-06192-7. $39. history.
ML1700.G83 782.1'09

Board's recommendation: Public and academic libraries.

New and Noteworthy

The Art of the Piano: Its Performers, Literature, and Recordings. David Dubal. Summit, 1989. hard. 1 vol. 476 pp. index. ISBN 0-671-49238-1. $40. encyclopedia.
ML105.D8 786.4'041

"The first section of this two-part reference work [*The Art of the Piano*] is a biographical dictionary of more than 500 concert pianists from the eighteenth century to the present. . . . [Essays may characterize] . . . the artists' style, describe the music they were best known for performing, or list their students. [The second part of the book presents] . . . a guide to the literature of piano music, with descriptive notes on several hundred works by major keyboard composers, along with suggested recordings. [The book's strength] . . . lies in its evaluative commentary on both the pianists and the music. . . . Critical appraisal is pervasive and stated frankly and briefly; while it is distinctly personal and clearly opinionated, it is also credible and reflects a consensus that is broad, if inevitably arguable." (*BL,* March 1, 1990, pp. 1378–1379)

An Eighteenth-Century Musical Chronicle: Events 1750–1799. Charles J. Hall, comp. Greenwood, 1990. hard. 1 vol. 176 pp. index. ISBN 0-313-26576-3. $35. history.
ML195.H28 780.903′3

"This final volume [*An Eighteenth-Century Musical Chronicle*] in a trilogy of reference works that chronicle musical history from the present to 1750 presents . . . a plethora of information that centers on music . . . [,] important world events, cultural activities, and distinguished contributions in both art and music. Musical events are presented year-by-year in their social, political, and general contexts and while the emphasis is on 'art' music, some popular genres have been highlighted." (Excerpted from publisher's announcement)

Gänzl's Book of the Musical Theatre. Kurt Gänzl and Andrew Lamb. Schirmer Bks., 1989. hard. 1 vol. 1,353 pp. index. ISBN 0-02-871941-7. $75. encyclopedia.
MT95.62 782.81

"Ganzl and Lamb propose [*Gänzl's Book of the Musical Theater*] as a companion to Gustav Kobbe's *Kobbe's Complete Opera Book*. . . . In format, size, and organization, Ganzl and Kobbe are similar; but Ganzl includes no music, and Kobbe has no illustrations. Ganzl features several sections of photographs. The volume lists more than 300 shows, arranged by country or region. . . . Each section begins with a historical introduction to the musical theater in that area. . . . For each title, basic production information is given. . . . Characters are listed and a relatively detailed plot synopsis follows. . . . The authors admit their listing is selective, announce their criteria, and recognize that their choices will not please everyone. . . . In spite of the several omissions, this volume will prove a reference tool equally as valuable as Kobbe in public and academic libraries." (*Choice,* June 1989, p. 61)

Great Composers. Piero Ventura. Putnam, 1989. hard. 1 vol. 124 pp. illus. index. ISBN 0-399-21746-0. $20.95. biographical source.
ML3929.V4613 780.922

"[*Great Composers* invites readers] . . . to understand the works of the most famous musicians in the context of time and place. There is a relatively brief discussion of each composer and his contribution to the field of music in the one to two pages devoted to each. Major works are noted. . . . The format . . . encourages browsing among the entertaining illustrations and concise descriptions. . . . Brief biographies of each musician in the same chronological order end the book. [Ventura] shows what influenced each artist and how each musician contributed to the overall development of music. Librarians should be aware, however, that the binding is not of the highest quality." (*SLJ,* May 1990, p. 26)

Instrumental Virtuosi: A Bibliography of Biographical Materials. Robert H. Cowden, comp. Greenwood, 1989. hard. 1 vol. 366 pp. indexes. appendixes. ISBN 0-313-26075-3. $49.95. biobibliography.
ML128.B3C73 016.780922

"With *Instrumental Virtuosi,* Robert Cowden has completed his comprehensive three volume bibliography of musical performers. [The work is] a compilation of resources drawn from dictionaries, encyclopedias, periodicals, and published materials by and about individual musicians. . . . The first two sections of the book list some 300 works on various types of virtuosi. . . . The final section contains alphabetical entries for more than 1,200 artists." (Excerpted from publisher's announcement)

Lectionary of Music. Nicholas Slonimsky. McGraw-Hill, 1989. soft. 1 vol. 528 pp. ISBN 0-07-058222-X. $22.95. dictionary.
ML100.S637 780.3

Lectionary of Music "sparkles with Slonimskian fact and fun . . . all music lovers can be enlightened and amused by this 'reading' lectionary. Set out from A to Z, the entries range from music terms, styles, and major concepts to opera synopses and musical trivia. . . . [The author] treats all entries with an inimitable authority mixed with wit and telling anecdote. . . . Recommended, especially for public libraries." (*LJ,* June 1, 1989, p. 100)

Musical Terms, Symbols and Theory: An Illustrated Dictionary. Michael C. Thomsett, comp. McFarland, 1989. hard. 1 vol. 277 pp. illus. ISBN 0-89950-392-6. $39.95. dictionary.
ML108.T46 780.3

"Thomsett, a composer and prolific author, [in *Musical Terms, Symbols and Theory*] provides short, usually clear definitions of more than 1,400 musical terms and symbols in a pleasing format (relatively large, clear print, well set off). . . . [Most music] . . . students and teachers, as well as other musicians will find this a handy volume to use for a quick review. Its ease of use, pleasing format, and definitions make this suitable for the consideration of school libraries as well as academic and public libraries." (*BL,* March 1, 1990, p. 1386)

The New Everyman Dictionary of Music. Eric Blom, comp. Weidenfeld & Nicolson, 1989. hard. 1 vol. 876 pp. ISBN 1-55584-336-0. $34.95. dictionary.
ML100.B47 780.3

"[*The New Everyman Dictionary of Music*] . . . has evolved into an authoritative and comprehensive source of information for a broad range of readers . . . [of great] usefulness with 1500 new and 1000 updated entries, a list of operatic roles and composers, dates of significant compositions, and coverage of many performers. . . . [T]he only apparent weakness of the work is its lack of bibliographic references, for which the reader may wish to consult a comparable volume, i.e., J. A. Westrup and F. L. Harrison's *The New College Encyclopedia of Music.* . . . [This book] is [recommended] for many public and other libraries." (*LJ,* July 1989, p. 68)

A Twentieth-Century Musical Chronicle: Events, 1900–1988. Charles J. Hall, comp. Greenwood, 1989. hard. 1 vol. 347 pp. index. ISBN 0-313-26577-1. $45. encyclopedia.
ML197.H15 780.9

"[The author] . . . presents the first of a trilogy of volumes that will chronicle music history from 1750 through the present. [*A Twentieth-Century Musical Chronical*] . . . relates year by year, important happenings in the field of music in the context of world and other cultural events. With three pages for each year, events are presented in tabular or other brief format. Each year begins with about a half-page chronicling world and cultural events. [Next, musical] . . . events are listed under [various] headings: Births; Deaths; Debuts . . . ; New Positions . . . ; Prizes and Honors; Biographical Highlights . . . ; Musical Literature . . . ; and Musical Compositions. [In this book] . . . the greatest detail is provided for classical music, but some jazz and pop musicians are included as well. (*BL,* December 15, 1989, p. 860)

Mimi King

Nursing

See also Careers and Occupations; Medicine and Dentistry

Like other medical and health-related fields, nursing is in a state of flux. In the 1950s, nurses began to reexamine their role in the healing process. The result was a movement that developed a holistic, wellness-based nursing model distinct from the traditional, illness-based medical model. A scientific, structural framework for the nurse-patient relationship was formulated and called "the nursing process." When, in 1984, Congress adopted the Diagnosis Related Groups reimbursement system for Medicare, hospitalization patterns changed and nurses moved into more nontraditional settings. Technological advances have required additional specialization and training. HIV, the AIDS virus, has provided challenges in patient care and preventative education as well as presenting health risks to attending nurses.

All these factors have had tremendous impact on nursing literature. For example, the three dictionaries in the list of core titles deal successfully in individual ways with some aspects of the speed and scope of change in nursing, but none manages to cover all the bases. For that reason, all three may be necessary for an effective reference core collection.

One can conceptualize nursing as having four axes of content: structure, details, history, and new developments. A library's nursing core collection should contain tools for each area. The core titles help with the structure, the details, and, to a fair extent, the history of nursing. In addition, copies of "The Patient's Bill of Rights," medical and nursing law guides, biographical dictionaries on nurses, general histories of hospitals and nursing, and information on nurses' uniforms, caps, and pins will be requested. References providing nursing care plans and common drug interactions will be useful for libraries serving student populations. Psychology, behavioral science, and social science dictionaries and works on health maintenance and patient education can round out the collection.

Libraries serving nursing schools should expect requests for videotaped or filmed materials that demonstrate various processes, methods, and equipment. Modules are also being created that will allow students to practice using equipment that may be too expensive for hands-on training.

Periodical literature can be accessed using the *Cumulative Index to Nursing and Allied Health Literature* (CINAHL) (Glendale Adventist Medical Center, annual). This index uses subject headings that were developed by the National Library of Medicine and includes nursing-specific terms. CINAHL monitors national and international nursing and related journals in English.

Core Titles

	PUBLIC	ACADEMIC	SCHOOL
Duncan's Dictionary for Nurses, 2d edition Duncan, Helen A. Springer, 1989	✦	✦	
Encyclopedia and Dictionary of Medicine, Nursing, and Allied Health, 4th edition Miller, Benjamin F., and Claire Brackman Keane. Saunders, 1987	✦	✦	
Guide to Schools of Nursing in Four-Year Colleges and Universities: Baccalaureate and Graduate Programs in the United States and Canada Redman, Barbara K., and Linda K. Amos, eds. Macmillan, 1987	✦		✦
The Lippincott Manual of Nursing Practice, 4th edition Brunner, Lillian, and Doris Smith Suddarth. Lippincott, 1986	✦	✦	
Mosby's Medical, Nursing, and Allied Health Dictionary, 3d edition Glanze, Walter D., ed. Mosby, 1990	✦	✦	
State-Approved Schools of Nursing L.P.N./L.V.N. National League for Nursing, annual	✦		
State-Approved Schools of Nursing R.N. National League for Nursing, annual	✦		

Core Titles

Duncan's Dictionary for Nurses, 2d edition. Helen A. Duncan. Springer, 1989. hard and soft. 1 vol. 802 pp. illus. appendixes. ISBN 0-8261-6201-0 (hard); 0-8261-6200-2 (soft). $38.95 (hard); $24.95 (soft). dictionary.
RT21.D85 610.3'21

Duncan's Dictionary for Nurses was created by a nurse for other nurses. That is its most striking feature. This book is not a medical dictionary with some of the terms left out but a compilation of words that nurses use and encounter regularly. *Duncan's* is a simple but more than adequate reference. The black-and-white line drawings are not fancy but are clear. The language is very accessible, even for novices. The sources of new terms are credited in the definition. To say that *Duncan's* is practical is not to say that the information is spare. The definitions reach remarkable depth. For example, under the word *reflex* are 58 different terms explained as synonyms, special categories, or specific types. Although the list is not definitive, it puts most of the useful terms in one place. In other dictionaries, users might find only simple definitions.

Vocabulary for professional nursing processes and responsibilities that are evolving receives special emphasis. Here, unfortunately, some flaws are noted. For example, the definition for *nursing orders* reads: "Written instructions for the nurse . . . written and signed by a professional nurse . . . not to be confused with medical orders." However, *medical orders* are never defined. This omission poses a problem, especially for students. Users will have to seek other sources for elucidation on that particular point.

For librarians who are building a collection, the appendixes more than compensate for other minor flaws. The appendixes contain a nine-page list of nursing and related periodicals that includes the frequency of publication and publisher. There are also lists of state nurses' associations and boards, nursing or related organizations and agencies, and health-care related organizations. Nursing students will also find handy information in the appendixes. Found along with standard prescription abbreviations, conversion tables, and normal laboratory test values are two assessment aids: the NANDA-approved nursing diagnostic categories with their taxonomic codes and the *Diagnostic Statistical Manual,* third edition disorders diagnostic categories, axes I and II. Finally, *Duncan's Dictionary for Nurses* includes the "Code for Nurses" and the "Nightingale Pledge," both of which are frequently requested by students but hard to find in one place.

The Board recommends this work for the core collections of public and academic libraries.

Encyclopedia and Dictionary of Medicine, Nursing, and Allied Health, 4th edition. Benjamin F. Miller and Claire Brackman Keane. Saunders, 1987. hard and soft. 1 vol. 1,427 pp. illus. appendixes. ISBN 0-7261-1815-4 (hard); 0-03-011507-8 (soft). $25.95 (hard); $21.95 (soft). encyclopedia and dictionary.
R121.M65 610.3′21

Combining an encyclopedia and dictionary provides users with background on medical terms that would not be easily available elsewhere. Keeping entries current and choosing new topics and terms in such a rapidly changing environment as medicine and health care presents a tremendous challenge to editors. Saunders's fourth edition of the *Encyclopedia and Dictionary of Medicine, Nursing, and Allied Health* admirably responds to that challenge.

Building on the many good features of earlier editions, this edition has expanded to include both technological and philosophical developments. All the members of the editorial board are nurses. In addition, physician consultants have reviewed each section dealing with treatment to ensure that procedures are accurate and current. Therefore, the articles employ both the nursing process and client-centered approach to patient care when presenting principles of medical and nursing management. Medical and nursing diagnoses are compared, and careful distinctions are drawn between the two. The new emphasis on patient education is demonstrated by a four-page directory of sources for patient education materials. Because such a plethora of new terms exists, including or defining every word in current use is impossible. Supplemental dictionaries would be desirable in most nursing collections.

This is a handsome and accessible work. The language meets the needs of both students and experienced practitioners. Longer tables have been relegated to the appendixes to make the text more readable. Sixteen color plates highlight structures and functions of the human body. Elsewhere, the text is illustrated by black-and-white or two-color drawings. An economical softcover version and a deluxe hardcover version are available. The soft binding is sturdy enough for individual use, but libraries purchasing a copy for reference will need the deluxe version to withstand the heavy use the *Encyclopedia and Dictionary of Medicine, Nursing, and Allied Health* is certain to receive.

The Board recommends this work for the core collections of public and academic libraries.

Guide to Schools of Nursing in Four-Year Colleges and Universities: Baccalaureate and Graduate Programs in the United States and Canada. Barbara K. Redman and Linda K. Amos, eds. Macmillan, 1987. hard. 1 vol. 472 pp. indexes. ISBN 0-02-901490-5. approx. $30. guide.
RT79.G85 610.73′07′117

The Guide to Sçhools of Nursing in Four-Year Colleges and Universities: Baccalaureate and Graduate Programs in the United States and Canada fills the need for a single, comprehensive source of information on nursing education. This guide is the best source of focused information on upper-level educational opportunities available in nursing. With 592 institutions listed, this work is superior to the National League of Nursing's (NLN) annual survey of registered nurse (RN) programs, which provides only skeletal data on 145 programs.

The NLN survey publications, the American Association of Colleges of Nursing membership roster, and various college guides were used to identify nursing programs in the United States and Canada. Those institutions were then asked to provide pertinent information. All but four of the institutions that were contacted responded with more data. Thus this work can be relied on to be comprehensive and accurate.

Three introductory chapters discuss the background, rationale, and nature of university-based education for nurses, the types of baccalaureate programs available, and graduate-level research. A summary table, arranged by state, lists institutions and degrees offered, providing quick access to specific programs available in a geographic area. Each institutional entry first gives an overview that includes the institution's address, history, size, locale, type, and campus. Special accommodations for minority, non-English-speaking, and disadvantaged students are also listed. The next section focuses on the nursing school, its faculty, tuition, special admission requirements and procedures, and transfer policies for generic baccalaureate, degree completion, or second-degree programs. Finally, each entry has specific information on master's, doctoral, postdoctoral, continuing education, and special programs.

The sturdy hardcover binding should stand up even under heavy use, which the editors predict will be from a wide and diverse audience. There are only 38 doctoral and 11 postdoctoral programs in the United States and Canada combined; therefore, guidance counselors, potential students, and nursing scholars will need this guide to locate advanced degree opportunities. Nursing school heads or health care agency personnel officers will also find *Guide to Schools of Nursing in Four-Year Colleges and Universities* a valuable tool for recruiting faculty or professional staff.

The Board recommends this work for the core collections of public and school libraries.

The Lippincott Manual of Nursing Practice, 4th edition. Lillian Brunner and Doris Smith Suddarth. Lippincott, 1986. hard. 1 vol. 1,562 pp. illus. appendixes. indexes. ISBN 0-397-54499-5. $46.95. manual.
RT51.B78 610.73

Although published in 1986, the *Lippincott Manual of Nursing Practice* is based on an older order of nurses' training. The nursing process is incorporated throughout this edition; however, this work is organized using the "medical and illness" paradigm and it focuses on functions within nursing specializations rather than on the patient. In the list of contributors, specific sections are attributed to authors who are doctors, practicing nurses, or nurse educators. The list of acknowledgments credits more general contributions from doctors, nurses, nurse educators, and librarians.

The work is divided into three sections: "Medical-Surgical Nursing," "Maternity Nursing," and "Pediatric Nursing." The information in each section is arranged by disorders of anatomical systems, such as respiratory tract and cardiovascular system. Special sections are also included to address special circumstances, such as "Care of the Aging Person" and "Nursing the Person with Cancer."

The editors assume that the readers are novices who need instruction even for basic nursing skills. Each chapter ends with a lengthy bibliography. The appendixes give thorough explanations of diagnostic tests and their meanings, standard conversion tables, and the widely accepted normal values for pediatric tests. Charts, diagrams, and photographs are used liberally to illustrate a wealth of information.

Unfortunately, the high degree of detail and variety of formats, though suited to their immediate purposes, make the work as a whole seem disorganized and overwhelming. The nursing process is presented clearly only in the first chapter. Thereafter, though its outline headings are retained, this basic structure becomes hard to follow because it is superimposed on a confusing array of other formats and outline headings. For example, a discussion of each disease or condition begins with a short summary of the problem. Then headings for etiology, incidence, and detailed nursing instructions are interspersed with other headings for the nursing process. The typography is further complicated by occasional "Nursing Alerts" (in red), which are intended to highlight health risks that are involved when attending patients with infectious diseases, awareness of conditions that should arouse "suspicions," and warnings against unprofessional behavior, such as unguarded comments in the presence of certain patients. Under the entry *assessment procedures,* the section on the adult physical examination begins with a paragraph of general principles, then outlines techniques, lists and illustrates equipment needed, and shifts into tabular format to give "Technique" and "Findings." Also interspersed throughout the text are 147 "guidelines" to illustrate procedures for using special equipment, assisting in specific procedures, and conducting various tests. All these things make the presentation too dense.

The Lippincott Manual of Nursing Practice is extremely valuable in all nursing collections, even though the book requires a lot of guidance for effective use. Its editors have provided some of that guidance in four indexes: the general index, an emergency index inside the front cover, an index to the guidelines, and an index to health and patient education material.

The Board recommends this work for the core collections of public and academic libraries.

Mosby's Medical, Nursing, and Allied Health Dictionary, 3d edition. Walter D. Glanze, ed. Mosby, 1990. hard. 1 vol. 1,608 pp. illus. appendixes. ISBN 0-8016-3227-7. $25.95. dictionary.
R121.M89 610.3'21

Mosby's Medical, Nursing, and Allied Health Dictionary has been considered the standard for nursing dictionaries. In this edition, the editors have expanded their consultant board to include international nursing authorities and specialists from diverse subject areas. The editors are forward-looking in several ways. The entire edition has been computerized for ongoing revision. More fundamentally, even though automated searching is not discussed, this edition squarely faces a future that will include computers. Beyond the fact that many entries explain computer jargon, the editor's stated rationale for a medical dictionary is in accord with the objectives of automated data base developers. The editor sees access to precise language as the indispensable key to sorting out what is relevant from the mass of information in medical literature.

In this edition such features as attention to patient's rights and the nursing process are retained. There are 3,000 new entries and three new entry categories that broaden Mosby's audience to include allied health professionals as well as nurses. The editors focus on physical therapy, occupational therapy, and respiratory care—fields in which nurses, physicians, and other health professionals currently have significant interaction. The 21 appendixes contain several unique and timely items: drug names and interactions; a table of communicable diseases; the Center for Disease Control's precautions for prevention of HIV transmission (HIV is the virus which causes AIDS); a list of poison control and burn centers and skin banks; and Spanish translations for common medical terms with clinical interaction phrases.

The format of *Mosby's Medical, Nursing, and Allied Health Dictionary* is simple, the type is easy to read, and the line drawings and photographs are appropriate. There is a 44-page, full-color atlas of the human anatomy placed in the front of the book for easy access. The binding is sturdy and should hold up well.

The Board recommends this work for the core collections of public and academic libraries.

State-Approved Schools of Nursing L.P.N./L.V.N. National League for Nursing, annual. soft. 1 vol. 72 pp. illus. ISBN 0-88737-481-6. $21.95. directory.
RT81.U6N28 610.73'071173

State-Approved Schools of Nursing R.N. National League for Nursing, annual. soft. 1 vol. 98 pp. illus. ISBN 0-88737-480-8. $21.95. directory.
RT81.U6N3 610.73'071173

State-Approved Schools of Nursing L.P.N./L.V.N. and *State-Approved Schools of Nursing R.N.* are quite similar except for some additional data given on the RN level. Both books reflect data gathered in the National League of Nursing's annual survey of nursing schools. Because the questionnaires are distributed to each state's board of nursing, all programs listed have been approved (unless indicated by a footnote). A 100 percent response rate is reported, but omissions occur in programs that admit RNs only and do not require state approval. Therefore, only 145 programs are represented. American Samoa, Puerto Rico, and the Virgin Islands are surveyed for both publications. Guam is added to the list in the RN version. Several schools withheld permission to publish statistical information on students; this is noted in the entries.

Both publications have four main sections: a list of states within each region; the main entry section; summary tables; and a directory of boards of nursing. The RN version also provides a directory of schools offering the baccalaureate exclusively for RNs.

The main entry section is tabular. Each school is listed by state and includes the following: address, telephone number, director, accreditation status, funding source, administrative control, length of program, minimum educational level for entering students, and statistics on admissions, enrollments, and graduations. Standard footnotes, abbreviations, and symbols are given at the beginning of the main entry section. The summary tables highlight new and recently closed programs by state. Complete information on these programs is located in the main entries.

The format is straightforward and easy to read. The binding is stapled and the cover is a slightly heavier stock. Since *State-Approved Schools of Nursing L.P.N./L.V.N.* and *State-Approved Schools of Nursing R.N.* will be replaced regularly to maintain currency, binding reinforcement will not be required unless heavy use is anticipated.

The Board recommends these works for the core collection of public libraries.

Supplementary Titles

Dictionary of American Nursing Biography. Martin Kaufman et al., eds. Greenwood, 1988. hard. 1 vol. 462 pp. appendixes. ISBN 0-313-24520-7. $49.95. biographical dictionary.
RT34.D53 610.730922

"The purpose of the [*Dictionary of American Nursing Biography*] is to provide, in one location, concise biographical sketches of persons important to American nursing. It is intended as a companion volume to the *Dictionary of American Medical Biography* (Greenwood, 1984) and utilizes a similar layout: biographical information, annotations concerning the subject's contribution to American nursing, a maximum of five important or representative works, and several selective references.

"The editors selected 196 persons for inclusion after researching the subjects' importance to American nursing as well as the availability of sufficient information to form a complete biographical sketch. The work is arranged alphabetically by name, including cross-references for birth names. There are three appendixes: listings by place of birth, state where prominent, and specialty or occupation. States and specialties are not duplicated in the index.

"An appendix or index by date would have been useful to users attempting to obtain information from a specific time period. According to the preface, the subjects range from the 'early pioneers of the mid-nineteenth century to those who entered the scene after the process of professionalization had clearly begun and who carried on the work of their foremothers in transforming nursing from a trade to a profession based on scientific research and formal education in a college or university setting.' Any important figures who died after the cutoff—January 31, 1987—were not included. Subsequent editions are planned by the editors as updated biographical information is obtained.

"The consolidation of biographical information and suggested references for detailed historical data makes this a useful tool for graduate and undergraduate students who are developing a paper or presentation." (*RQ,* Fall 1988, p. 113)

Also reviewed in: *ARBA,* 1989, p. 622; *Isis,* June 1989, p. 358; *LJ,* April 15, 1989, p. 38; *R&R Bk N,* August 1988, p. 28.

Board's recommendation: Academic libraries.

Facts About Nursing. American Journal of Nursing, 1987. soft. 1 vol. 217 pp. illus. index. ISSN 0071-3651. $18.95. encyclopedia.
RT1.A67 610.73'08

Facts About Nursing is "the authoritative collection of fundamental data on the nursing profession and its practitioners. It provides information on trends in nurse distribution and characteristics which are useful in understanding the role of nursing in the nation's health care delivery system. There is a subject index." (*Ser Lib,* 1985, p. 199)

Board's recommendation: Public libraries.

New and Noteworthy

Core Collection in Nursing and the Allied Health Sciences: Books, Journals, Media. Annette Peretz et al. Oryx, 1990. soft. 1 vol. 236 pp. indexes. ISBN 0-89774-464-0. $39.50. bibliography.
RT41.P44 016.61073

"Libraries will find this bibliography useful for identifying potential reference sources and for collection development in nursing and the allied health sciences. . . . [*Core Collection in Nursing and the Allied Health Sciences*] also emphasizes materials suitable for larger collections and for laypersons and includes a great deal of nonprint media. Approximately 1,000 books and nonprint materials published between 1980 and 1988 are listed with annotations. Materials are divided into broad subject sections such as 'AIDS,' 'Computers,' 'Emergency Nursing,' and 'Nutrition.' . . . Following the subject sections is a periodicals section." (*BL,* August 1990, p. 2201)

Scholarships and Loans for Nursing Education 1989–1990. National League for Nursing, 1990. soft. 1 vol. approx. 100 pp. ISBN 0-88737-477-8. $10.95. bibliography.
RT79.S36 610.73'07'9

Scholarships and Loans for Nursing Education 1989–1990 "describes scholarships that are available to those pursuing a nursing education. Information ranges from choosing a school and applying for financial aid to obtaining special awards, pursuing postdoctoral study, and applying for research grants." (editor's note)

Judith Herschman *M. Dorcas Hand*

Painting and Sculpture

See also Art

Not surprisingly, much information about painting and sculpture can be found in general sources identified in the Art category. Titles specifically about these art-forms fall roughly into four categories: dictionaries or encyclopedias of artists and their works, indexes to reproductions of specific works found in published sources, works on the techniques and materials of painting and sculpture, and sources on themes and subjects. Of the sources on painting, the LAROUSSE DICTIONARY OF PAINTERS, THE LIVES OF THE PAINTERS, NINETEENTH-CENTURY PAINTERS AND PAINTING, the CYCLOPEDIA OF PAINTERS AND PAINTINGS, and the NEW YORK HISTORICAL SOCIETY'S DICTIONARY OF ARTISTS IN AMERICA, 1564–1860 all fall into the first category. *The Encyclopedia of Painting* (Crown, 1979) also falls into this category, but unfortunately the work is now out of print. Although there is a great deal of overlapping coverage, the titles often differ sufficiently in scope, orientation, and treatment to warrant having all these titles in a good art reference collection.

The painting indexes, *Index to Reproductions of American Paintings* (Wilson, 1964) and *World Painting*

Core Titles

	PUBLIC	ACADEMIC	SCHOOL
Dictionary of American Sculptors: 18th Century to the Present Opitz, Glenn B., ed. Apollo, 1984	✦	✦	
Larousse Dictionary of Painters Laclotte, Michel, and Alistair Smith, eds. Larousse, 1981	✦		✦
The Lives of the Painters, 4 vols. Canaday, John. Norton, 1969	✦	✦	
Nineteenth-Century Painters and Painting: A Dictionary Norman, Geraldine. Thames & Hudson, 1977		✦	

Index (Scarecrow, 1982), are indispensable sources for locating and identifying reproductions that have been published in books, catalogs, and monographs. Similar indexes should be considered for reference collections as well. Librarians, however, should not forget the value of periodical indexes in locating published reproductions, even though they are more tedious to use.

The *Encyclopedia of Oil Painting: Materials and Techniques* (North Light/Writer's Digest, 1984) falls into the category of technical works. This particular work is no longer in print, but Ralph Mayer's A DICTIONARY OF ART TERMS AND TECHINQUES (see Art) incorporates much of the same information and is a reasonable substitute.

The *Encyclopedia of Themes and Subjects in Painting* belongs in the final category. Although it is out of print, this book (as well as other iconographic sources such as the *Dictionary of Subjects and Symbols in Art*) is important for the interpretation of the content and meaning of particular paintings and should be kept on the shelves if it is currently owned. The advantage of this source is the inclusion of a large number of illustrations that provide examples of the historical subjects.

Ideally, a sculpture reference collection would provide biographical, technical, and thematic access to both historical and current artists, their work, and their schools. While general art history references may contain a chapter on sculpture and sculptors, it is essential that a core collection contain works devoted to sculpture exclusively. A good dictionary, such as the DICTIONARY OF AMERICAN SCULPTORS, will provide ready-reference information for a patron looking for characteristics of the sculpture of Canada or the style of American sculptor Walter Hancock. The *Sculpture Index* (Jane Clapp, Scarecrow, 1970–1971) is an important work because of its wide range of information. Although it is currently out of print, copies of this work should remain on the library shelves because it provides extensive listings for sculptors and their works. *American Sculpture: A Guide to Information Sources* (Janis Eckdahl, Gale, 1977) is also out of print, but is a very comprehensive bibliography for patrons doing research.

Some librarians, especially those in academic libraries, may wish to supplement these basic core references with more specialized references, such as CONTEMPORARY AMERICAN WOMEN SCULPTORS.

Librarians should be aware that most of the painting and sculpture references reviewed here are current only to the mid-to-late 1970s. Although these works are standards in the field, the inclusion of some up-to-date supplements will make for a richer and more complete collection. —*J. H. and M. D. H.*

Core Titles

Dictionary of American Sculptors: 18th Century to the Present. Glenn B. Opitz, ed. Apollo, 1984. hard. 1 vol. 656 pp. illus. ISBN 0-938290-03-7. $85. dictionary.
NB236.064 730.92

The *Dictionary of American Sculptors* is intended as an alphabetical compendium of basic information on 5,000 sculptors, primarily from the nineteenth and twentieth centuries. About 2,000 of these are contemporary artists, and a few are from the eighteenth century. Opitz has used Charles Caffin's *American Masters of Sculpture* (1903), Lorado Taft's *The History of American Sculpture* (1924), Wayne Craven's *Sculpture in America* and *American Art Annuals, 1898–1933,* and résumés solicited from current artists, as well as a variety of other available and out-of-print sources in compiling the dictionary. Artists with an international reputation as well as those who specialize in specific styles or regions, such as the American West, are covered. Nearly all art trends, including media ranging from traditional marble and clay to neon tubing, are represented.

Artists were selected for inclusion partly because of the presence of their work in exhibitions or major cultural centers of the United States. However, as with any work of this nature, not everyone is included, and the selection criteria are not always clear. Mark di Suvero is not included, while little-known *Leo Mielziner* receives an entry. But Opitz has managed a balance between the conservative academic tradition and the avant-garde, providing the former more coverage than many other works. This is no doubt the direct result of the extensive cooperation of the National Sculpture Society, in which many of the academicians hold membership.

The use of so much material submitted by artists themselves, either through solicited résumés or autobiographical material from the *American Art Annuals,* has led to some disproportionate coverage. For example, the entry for *Walter Hancock* rates 30 lines, while *Harriet Clark Hanley* (Minneapolis, active in the 1930s) rates only 3. However, a researcher from the Corcoran Gallery of Art reported that the reference to Hanley was the first she had found outside the Corcoran's files.

The format of the dictionary closely resembles that of the *American Art Annuals,* which is no surprise given that many entries seem to be taken almost verbatim from that source. While some may complain that modern scholarship requires a different approach,

Opitz has provided a wealth of biographical data not easily available elsewhere. He lists date and place of birth (and death), association memberships, place of work, awards, important pieces, museums holding pieces in their collections, and last known address. This is more than enough to get researchers started. Opitz also includes over 200 glossy black-and-white photographs from the collections of the National Sculpture Society and the Vassar College Art Gallery, among others.

Interestingly, with a 1984 copyright, there is little information on contemporary sculptors after 1970, such as Gwen Lox and James Rosati. Perhaps it was too difficult to determine who was worthy of inclusion, but we can hope that the planned update will correct this 14-year gap.

There have also been some criticisms of Opitz's accuracy, such as the missing but available death date for Tony Smith and an erroneous date for Hiram Powers's *Fisherboy.* Others have criticized the absence of bibliographical citations, even significant treatises by artists about their own works, such as that by Donald Judd. However, these lapses are infrequent and do not mar the work, which researchers will appreciate. The dictionary is easy to use, with a clear layout and sturdy binding. No other title exists that comes close to its comprehensive coverage and ambitious scope.

The Board recommends this work for public and academic libraries. —*M. D. H.*

Larousse Dictionary of Painters. Michel Laclotte and Alistair Smith, eds. Larousse, 1981. hard. 1 vol. 467 pp. illus. index. ISBN 0-88332-265-X. $39.98. biographical dictionary.
ND35L3713 759.19

Like John Canaday's THE LIVES OF THE PAINTERS, the *Larousse Dictionary of Painters* attempts to give an overview of art history from a biographical perspective. The difference in approach between the two is the format. The *Larousse Dictionary of Painters* is arranged alphabetically by artist, whereas THE LIVES OF THE PAINTERS is organized by historical period. Another major difference is that like many encyclopedic works, the signed articles in this volume have been written by a collection of international scholars and authorities rather than by one person. A list of contributors appears in the front of the volume. The work covers Western painting, largely European and American, from the medieval period through the contemporary period. Although no actual number is given, there are approximately 500 artists listed. Major living painters such as *Jasper Johns* and *Frank Stella* are included. Although one may have certain reservations about some of the inclusions and omissions (Berthe Morisot, Helen Frankenthaler, and Diego Rivera are not listed), it is a relatively comprehensive source. Perhaps it would have been helpful to discuss selection criteria and methodology in the introduction.

Entries vary in length, depending to some degree on the importance of the subject in the context of the history of painting. They generally range from one column (of a three-column page) to four pages for a major figure such as *Rembrandt.* Each article, highly informative and scholarly in tone, contains biographical data and discussions of the artists' work and influence. Articles are usually accompanied by either a black-and-white or color reproduction illustrative of the painters' work. Generally, these reproductions are of reasonably good quality.

Following the text is an eight-page bibliography, which lists some general historical works and many works of geographical orientation, arranged by country, but is most important for the listing of monographic works on individual painters. The works listed include English as well as foreign-language publications. Publishers are not given in the citations.

The bibliography is followed by a name index that refers the reader to entries indicated by page numbers in boldface type and to discussions or mentions of painters imbedded in other entries. Although alternative names of the artists are given in the entries themselves, unfortunately there are no cross-references in the index to different forms of their names. Similarly, the absence of index entries for titles of particular paintings somewhat impairs accessibility. However, a list of abbreviations of museums and common terms does appear in the front of the *Larousse Dictionary of Painters.*

The Board recommends this work for the core collections of public and school libraries. —*J. H.*

The Lives of the Painters. John Canaday. Norton, 1969. hard. 4 vols. 1,124 pp. illus. index. ISBN 0-393-04231-6. $75. biographical dictionary.
ND35.C35 759

John Canaday, a respected art critic for the *New York Times,* is the author of the four-volume *The Lives of the Painters,* a highly readable, charming, and useful history of Western painting from the end of the Middle Ages to the twentieth century (or more precisely, from Giotto to Cezanne). In the tradition of his illustrious Renaissance predecessor, Vasari, Canaday writes his history as a series of biographies that document the artists' lives and work. Although the work can be read from cover to cover, *The Lives of the Painters* is also a reference work of some importance.

The actual biographies, several hundred in all, appear in the first three volumes: volume 1 covers late Gothic to high Renaissance; volume 2 covers the Baroque period; and volume 3 covers Neoclassicism to post-Impressionism. Volume 4 contains more than 352 plates, in color and black and white, arranged in roughly the same order as the text of the first three volumes. In actuality there are more than 352 examples of paintings because, oddly enough, many plates are unnumbered. The reproductions are small, but of high quality, and are preceded by an alphabetical list of the artists and works represented. Finally, the last volume ends with an extensive index that lists the titles of works discussed and illustrated. Most of the index entries are for names and titles; movements and styles are listed inconsistently. "International Style," for example, appears in the index, as does "Impressionism," which also has a separate chapter. "Mannerism," however, does not appear, in spite of a lengthy discussion of this style embedded in the chapter entitled "Sixteenth-Century Crisis in Italy, Spain, France" (volume 1).

Because the individual biographies are presented in the context of the period of art being discussed, it is necessary to use the index to find the essay in which a particular figure appears. Canaday has included all of the major and minor painters of historical significance and some who might not be included except for their particular interest to him. The length of the discussion is not necessarily governed by importance, but is sometimes dictated by the inherent interest of the painters' lives or their exemplification of a particular time. By placing the painters in the context of the times in which they lived, Canaday has provided the kind of perspective lacking in more traditionally formatted biographical sources.

Not aimed particularly at a scholarly audience, *The Lives of the Painters* is a rich and delightful source of information about painting, painters, and the history of Western art. The Board recommends this work for the core collections of public and academic libraries. —*J. H.*

Nineteenth-Century Painters and Painting: A Dictionary. Geraldine Norman. Thames & Hudson, 1977. hard. 1 vol. 240 pp. illus. index. ISBN 65-20-03328-0. $77.50. biographical dictionary.
ND190.N67 759.05

Geraldine Norman's *Nineteenth-Century Painters and Painting* distinguishes itself from similar works in the scope of its coverage; the book includes styles, movements, and institutions in addition to artists' biographies. More than 700 painters are listed, arranged in dictionary format. Entries include major figures of all the national schools, lesser-known artists, and members of the avant-garde. The particular strength of this dictionary is its coverage of minor figures because many of the important ones (such as Cezanne, Gauguin, or Delacroix) are treated extensively in other sources. Eighteenth-century painters who lived only a few years into the nineteenth century but whose works were especially influential in that period (such as *William Blake* and *Jacques Louis David*) are also included. The dictionary puts particular emphasis on European artists.

Entries are relatively brief, none covering a full page, and are often accompanied by a small black-and-white illustration. The entries on painters are largely biographical in nature, with some discussion of the artists' importance, reputation, subject matter, and style. Cross-references to other entries are indicated within the text by capital letters. A brief bibliography completes most entries. Entries for schools and movements (such as the *French art establishment* or *neoclassicism*) tend to be somewhat longer than individual artist entries. However, less emphasis is put on later developments such as art nouveau or the arts and crafts movement.

The introduction to *Nineteenth-Century Painters and Painting* contains a general discussion of the conflicting traditions and genres of painting that characterized the period and a summary of its artistic history. The introduction contains the only color reproductions in the volume.

A six-page bibliography cites general works, treatments of styles, and geographically oriented works in all European languages. Publishers are not included in the bibliographic entries. Those sources that were of particular importance to the author in computing the work are indicated by an asterisk.

At the end of the book there is a list of illustrations, alphabetically arranged, which includes the dimensions, medium, and location of the works. This list provides a quick reference for particular paintings. There is no general index.

Although not a professional art historian, Norman has put together a prodigiously researched, important reference source for this period of painting. The narrow scope of *Nineteenth-Century Painters and Paintings* allows for in-depth coverage of the era. The Board recommends this work for the core collection of academic libraries. —*J. H.*

Supplementary Titles

Contemporary American Women Sculptors. Virginia Watson-Jones. Oryx, 1986. hard. 1 vol. 665 pp. illus. index. ISBN 0-89774-139-0. $135. biographical dictionary.
NB212.W37 730.92

Contemporary American Women Sculptors is a biographical dictionary which covers "328 living American women sculptors . . . selected from 1,500 questionnaires sent to art galleries, museums, art societies, and professionals in the art world. . . . [A page] of biographical information includes education, exhibitions, collections, awards, preferred media, related professions, a selected bibliography, and a mailing address. Each entry is accompanied by a . . . black-and-white photograph of . . . [an art] work and a signed statement by the artist." (*Choice,* October 1986, p. 288)

"The term sculpture is used very broadly. . . . Thus are included, along with pieces that laypersons might be expected to call 'statues,' a garden gate, a series of banners, and even a work requiring the presence of live persons. This broad scope is a reflection of this rapidly changing area of visual art." (*BL,* December 15, 1986, p. 632)

"All 50 states are represented as is a cross-section of styles and media. . . . The book is accurate, attractively arranged, sturdy, and well made on glossy paper. There is no comparable work devoted to contemporary American women sculptors." (*Choice,* October 1986, p. 288)

Also reviewed in: *AB,* September 22, 1986, p. 1053; *Am Craft,* April 1987, p. 87; *ARBA,* 1987, p. 396; *RQ,* Fall 1986, p. 111; *R & R Bk N,* Summer 1986, p. 13; *WLB,* September 1986, p. 79; *Wom R Bks,* November 1986, p. 9.

Board's recommendation: Academic libraries.

Cyclopedia of Painters and Paintings. John Champlin, Jr., and Charles C. Perkins. Irvington, 1978. soft. 4 vols. illus. ISBN 0-8046-1824-0. $77. encyclopedia.
ND30.C4 759

"Champlin's *Cyclopedia of Painters and Paintings.* . . . a product of the late nineteenth century, was reprinted in 1927 and now in 1969, evidence that there is still a demand for its alphabetically arranged biographies of painters and descriptions of individual paintings. It is also a useful source for monograms and signatures of painters, many of which are reproduced. The entries are usually provided with abbreviated citations to sources, which are fully listed in volume one. [There are] outline drawings and a few black-and-white plates. . . . [Overall] the *Cyclopedia* is a source . . . which stands the test of time because of its broad coverage and convenient arrangement." (*WLB,* February 1970, p. 661)

Board's recommendation: Public and academic libraries.

New York Historical Society's Dictionary of Artists in America, 1564–1860. George C. Groce and David H. Wallace. Apollo, 1979. hard. 1 vol. 759 pp. ISBN 0-686-43145-6. $80. dictionary.
N6536.W4 927.5

The *Dictionary of Artists in America* is "a documented biographical dictionary of painters, draftsmen, sculptors, engravers, lithographers, and allied artists, either amateur or professional, native or foreign-born, who worked within the present continental limits of the United States between the years 1564 and 1860 inclusive (intro). [The reference] includes almost 11,000 names, [and has] a bibliography." (*Guide to Reference Books,* Sheehy, p. 541)

Board's recommendation: Public and academic libraries.

New and Noteworthy

American Women Sculptors: A History of Women Working in Three Dimensions. Charlotte Stretfer Rubinstein. G. K. Hall, 1990. hard. 1 vol. 600 pp. ISBN 0-8161-8732-0. $50. history and criticism.
NB236.R8 730.82

"As the first comprehensive chronological survey of the subject, [*American Women Sculptors*] presents a remarkable, previously unrecognized history of sculpture by American women. It offers detailed background on more than 200 female sculptors, from precolonial times to the present, as well as critical assessment of each sculptor's contribution to artistic movements of her era.

"[Information in the book is easy to access]. . . . Each chapter begins with an introduction that places women sculptors in their historical settings, outlines major movements and discusses women's roles as participants and innovators. Following are artist entries arranged by movement or genre, each containing a brief biography and discussion of the sculptor's training, development and work. Entries include titles, dates and locations of individual works." (Excerpted from publisher's announcement)

Lorraine A. Jean

Philosophy

See also Religion

Philosophy in medieval times embraced the sum of all knowledge, arts as well as sciences. Today the system of philosophy has narrowed to a consideration of concepts and methods of knowledge. Philosophers seek to answer such fundamental questions as "What is real?" "What is being?" "What is beauty?" They probe the nature of belief, experience, and knowledge. They examine the process of reasoning and the determination of right and wrong. In other words, philosophers concern themselves with metaphysics, aesthetics, epistemology, logic, and ethics. They may do so from the perspective of different traditions, movements, or schools of thought, either Western (for example, existentialism, Marxism, neo-Scholasticism) or non-Western (for example, Buddhism, Taoism, or Islam). A core collection in philosophy must represent at least the major traditions or approaches. Librarians should be aware, however, that it is not always readily apparent from the title what approach a reference work will take. Many works based in the Anglo-American tradition either ignore or pay lip service to Eastern philosophy, sometimes deliberately, sometimes unconsciously, with resulting inaccuracies or a lack of balance.

The basic texts of philosophy are the writings of individual philosophers. Critical evaluations form the secondary literature. Bibliographies, indexes, and other reference books form the third tier. The reference collection in philosophy should accommodate the user who needs information about individual philosophers, about special branches of philosophy, or about the interrelationships among various systems of thought.

All of the usual categories of reference works exist in philosophy, with an additional category—concordances—that it shares in common with literature and religion. Although this buying guide does not review any books of this type, there are concordances for several major philosophers (such as Plato, Aristotle, and Thomas Aquinas), which academic libraries, in particular, will want to buy. Controversial issues generate their own reference works: both the BIBLIOGRAPHY OF BIOETHICS and the ENCYCLOPEDIA OF BIOETHICS address the moral and ethical concerns raised by human experimentation, in vitro fertilization, euthanasia, and mass screening for AIDS.

Academic libraries will want to purchase one or more directories of living philosophers and scholars, such as the *Directory of American Philosophers,* or its companion volume, the *International Directory of Philosophy and Philosophers,* as well as a major English-language index of books and journal articles such as the *Philosopher's Index.* All three titles are produced by the Philosophy Documentation Center at Bowling Green State University.

The *Dictionary of the History of Ideas* (Philip P.

Core Titles

	PUBLIC	ACADEMIC	SCHOOL
Bibliography of Bioethics, 15 vols. Walters, LeRoy, and Tamar Joy Kahn, eds. Kennedy Institute of Ethics, annual		✦	
A Dictionary of Philosophy, 2d edition Lacey, A. R. Routledge & Kegan Paul, 1986	✦	✦	
A Dictionary of Philosophy, 2d edition Flew, Antony, ed. consultant. St. Martin's, 1984		✦	
The Encyclopedia of Philosophy, 4 vols. Edwards, Paul, ed. in chief. Free Pr./Macmillan, 1967; reprinted, 1972	✦	✦	
Philosophy: A Guide to the Reference Literature Bynagle, Hans E. Libraries Unlimited, 1986		✦	
World Philosophy: Essay-Reviews of 225 Major Works, 5 vols. Magill, Frank N., ed. Salem, 1982	✦	✦	

Wiener, ed., Scribner, 1973), a five-volume compilation of multidisciplinary and multicultural articles in the history of ideas, has recently gone out of print. The broad scope of this work makes it a worthwhile purchase to pursue through out-of-print sources.

Core Titles

Bibliography of Bioethics. LeRoy Walters and Tamar Joy Kahn, eds. Kennedy Institute of Ethics, annual. hard. 15 vols. appendixes. indexes. ISSN 0363-0161. $45 (vol. 15). bibliography. on-line.
Z6675.E8W34 016.1742

Published for the Kennedy Institute of Ethics, Georgetown University, first by Gale (vols. 1 to 6), then by The Free Press (vols. 7 to 9), and now by the institute itself (vols. 10 to 15), the *Bibliography of Bioethics* is the printed product of a data system established "to identify the central issues of bioethics, to develop an indexing language appropriate to the field, and to provide comprehensive, cross-disciplinary coverage of current English-language materials on bioethical topics" (introduction).

Bioethics is defined in the introduction as "the systematic study of value questions that arise in the biomedical and behavioral fields." While the topics covered are oriented toward health care, it is their treatment as ethical concerns that make this a useful source for the philosopher. Thirteen reference tools, 13 data bases (including the *Philosopher's Index* on DIALOG), and 84 journals and newspapers are examined for substantive articles, monographs, essays, court decisions, bills, laws, audiovisual materials, and unpublished documents in English.

Main entries are arranged alphabetically by author within subject entry sections. The material is arranged in two columns per page. A typical entry consists of the subject heading, bibliographic citation, keywords, and an abstract (if the item is from one of 16 journals identified as major sources in the field or if it is a court decision). The abstracts are brief and nonevaluative. From 10 to 12 keywords are assigned to each document; asterisks mark the most important of these. While the large number of keywords may be a boon for on-line searching, they do not increase accessibility in print. For example, the entry *AIDS: screening of possible carriers and human rights* has five asterisked descriptors: acquired immunodeficiency syndrome, HIV seropositivity, mass screening, public policy, and Netherlands. Of these, only *acquired immunodeficiency syndrome* and *mass screening* are entries in the print bibliography.

Accessibility is increased by cross-references ("see," "see also," and "see under"), by title and author indexes, and by the "Bioethics Thesaurus" (the thesaurus is included in this work). The title index is somewhat cumbersome. This index provides a page number (individual entries are not numbered), but not the author of the article; the user must scan the entire page to find the title. There is not even an "a" or a "b" to indicate in which column the entry occurs. The author index is more useful in that it gives author's name, titles, and page numbers. Co-authors are also indexed, with "see" references to the primary author.

The "Bioethics Thesaurus" (44 pages long in the 1989 volume) contains keywords for searching the BIOETHICSLINE data base, which cumulates the printed volumes of the bibliography. The thesaurus identifies narrower, broader, and related terms as well as terms used instead of a given term; it also includes scope notes. Two additional symbols indicate that a more specific term exists or that a phrase is represented by two terms rather than one. There are two appendixes: a selected list of "major issue" keywords and a list of subject captions for very broad areas or types of approach.

The *Bibliography of Bioethics* is most up to date in its on-line version, although the printed volume is more current than many annual bibliographies. Volume 15, published in 1989, contains 2,400 documents, 1,145 of which were published in 1988, 819 in 1987, 218 in 1986, 75 in 1989, and the rest between 1978 and 1985. The bibliography is sturdily bound with sewn signatures.

The Board recommends this work for the core collection of academic libraries.

A Dictionary of Philosophy, 2d edition. A. R. Lacey. Routledge & Kegan Paul, 1986. hard. 1 vol. 266 pp. ISBN 0-7102-0991-6. $13.95. dictionary.
B41.L32 103.21

A Dictionary of Philosophy is one individual's attempt to bring order to the terminology of philosophy in language a student or a layperson can understand. The author is a member of the Department of Philosophy, King's College, University of London. Lacey's aim is not to explain in depth but to try to convey "the general character of the term." His emphasis is on the Anglo-American tradition, with more space devoted to logic and epistemology than to aesthetics, ethics, or politics. The dictionary also includes biographical entries for approximately 80 philosophers, among them the important international figures from across the centuries, such as *Immanuel Kant* and *Søren Kierkegaard.* However, there are no Eastern philosophers represented.

Arranged alphabetically from *Abelard* to *zombie,* the dictionary entries range in length from the one-line entry for *Cartesian* to the more than three-page entry for *perception.* What distinguishes the dictionary is its bibliographies. Not every entry receives one (for example, *genetic fallacy* and *behaviorism* do not have bibliographies); those entries that do can have anywhere from one citation to almost a full page of articles and books that may include the work that originally introduced the term, some basic discussions of the idea, or more recent items. The bibliography for the entry *space and time,* for example, includes sources ranging in publication date from 1910 to 1984.

The second edition of the dictionary (the first was published in 1976) adds 25 new entries and 24 new cross-references, with two deletions from the first edition. There are corrections to older entries (although some typographical errors were introduced) as well as additions to some bibliographies. It is in the new terms and bibliographic entries that the dictionary's currency can be most easily demonstrated. *Cambridge change* has one bibliographic citation dated 1984, while *Heap (paradox of)* includes citations dated 1985 and 1986.

Though the work is purportedly written for the nonspecialist, some definitions succeed only in mystifying in their attempt to pare a discussion down to its bare bones. What is the layperson to think of the following passage taken from the entry on *explanation:* "Nomological explanations are DEDUCTIVE. The explanandum is deduced from the premises. Statistical explanations are usually (not always: see Hempel) INDUCTIVE. For reasons given under CONFIRMATION statistical explanations must be supplemented by Carnap's *requirement of total evidence* (or Hempel's weaker form, the *requirement of maximum specificity*)."

Generally, however, the dictionary is clear and understandable. British spellings such as *behaviour* should pose no difficulties for American readers, although some British references (for example, "pillar box" in the entry on *seeing*) may.

Cross-references guide the reader to discussion of related terms; "see" references lead to a preferred term from a term not used. Lacey's rule-of-thumb for cross-references within entries is to provide them only when they seem useful.

The paper on which the dictionary is printed is not quite heavy enough to prevent type from showing through, but this is visible only in white spaces and does not interfere with reading. The typeface is legible, with bold type used for main entry words, italics for book and periodical titles as well as for emphasis within the text, and all capital letters to show cross-references. The dictionary is sturdily bound and will hold up well under normal use.

Both public and academic libraries will find *A Dictionary of Philosophy* a good, basic dictionary on the topic. But its declared Anglo-American bias means that they will need to supplement the work with other titles in order to achieve a rounded, world view of the discipline as a whole. The Board recommends this work for the core collections of public and academic libraries.

A Dictionary of Philosophy, 2d edition. Antony Flew, ed. consultant. St. Martin's, 1984. soft. 1 vol. 380 pp. illus. appendixes. ISBN 0-312-20924-X. $10.95. dictionary.
B41.D42 103.21

A Dictionary of Philosophy is the work of 33 contributors based in Britain, most with advanced degrees in philosophy. With entries ranging from *abandonment* to *Zeno's paradoxes,* the work defines key terms and concepts, including biographies of up to 4,000 words for the most important philosophers. While A. R. Lacey imposes a nearly uniform length on biographical entries in his A DICTIONARY OF PHILOSOPHY, Flew lets the subject's importance determine the length. For example, Plato gets a 10-line entry in Lacey's work and just over 4 pages in Flew.

There are no bibliographies, although entries for persons list major works authored. Flew includes terms from non-Western philosophy such as *yin yang, vijnanavada,* and *Mencius,* which are absent from Lacey's dictionary. Entries range in length from one line for *unit class* to just over four pages for *Platonism.* Entries also include nicknames for famous philosophers (such as *Universal Doctor* for Albertus Magnus), schools of thought, and Latin phrases.

The dictionary is characterized by clear writing with an occasionally delightful turn of phrase. Lewis Carroll's *Alice in Wonderland,* for example, is praised as "a logical-philosophical causerie, garnished with innumerable examples of elegant and unforgettable absurdity." There are cross-references within the text, with asterisks to indicate text words that have separate entries, and "see" and "see also" references leading to related headings. "See" references lead from terms not used to terms used: for example, "*Avicebron.* See *Ibn Gabirol.*"

The entries do not have bibliographies, making it difficult to assess the dictionary's currency. Flew claims that this edition has cleaned up typographical errors (he missed a few: "Plantonism" for "Platoism" in a running head; "Spengler" as a running head above the entry on *Spinoza* for two consecutive pages) and that it has made "many substantial additions and changes," though these are neither quantified nor identified.

A special feature of the dictionary is the five tables of symbols and abbreviations that precede the definitions. Several entries contain truth tables; in addition, there are line drawings to illustrate *Venn diagrams* and *square of opposition.*

A Dictionary of Philosophy is printed on good-quality paper with a good, clear, rather small typeface. Main entry words are printed in boldface type. Though the asterisks that precede cross-references are less visible than cross-references in capital letters would be, the alert reader will see them. The binding on the hardcover edition is adequate; libraries buying the paper edition should have it bound before use.

Because of the non-Western coverage, academic libraries will want to add Flew's *A Dictionary of Philosophy* to the reference shelf beside Lacey's. Not only does Flew define more terms, but he also pays greater attention to world philosophers.

The Board recommends this work for the core collection of academic libraries.

The Encyclopedia of Philosophy. Paul Edwards, ed. in chief. Free Pr./Macmillan, 1967; repr. 1972. hard. 4 vols. 4,206 pp. index. ISBN 0-02-894950-1 (set). $400 (set). encyclopedia.
B41.E5 103

Over 500 individuals around the world contributed nearly 1,500 entries to *The Encyclopedia of Philosophy* in an attempt to cover the whole field: East and West; ancient, medieval, and modern. More than 900 entries focus on individual thinkers, including those outside the field if their theories have had an impact on philosophy. Some biographical entries (for example, *Marx* or *Engels*) are intentionally short because separate articles focus on their theories. All entries are signed, and all have bibliographies, some of which are extensive. These may be simply enumerative, or they may take the form of annotated bibliographies or bibliographic essays.

The entries in the encyclopedia are well written, readable, informative, and can be understood by a varied audience from informed laypersons to specialists. Cross-references occur at the point of lookup *(conservation principles* see *energy)*, within the entries, and in the index (both as "see" and "see also" references). Most entries are divided by subheadings for ease in locating information on a given aspect of a topic.

Users of the reprint edition must pay particular attention to volumes and pagination, for while the text is exactly the same as that of the original edition (1967), the reprint compresses the original eight volumes into four. Therefore, each physical volume contains two sets of pages beginning with the page number 1.

The index volume provides a numerical reference to volume and page; however, no range of pages is given to indicate the length of the discussion. One interesting feature of the index is its classification of people by category; for example, "The encyclopedia contains articles on the following persons frequently classified as idealists," followed by a list of names. (There are no page references, however; individuals must be looked up again in alphabetical order in the index.) The index contains 23 such lists. In addition, one will find individuals listed under concepts and schools of thought; for example, there are major subentries for "philosophers" under the main headings for "Truth" and "Russian philosophy."

The reprint edition retains the entire text of the original, although the print is smaller, the paper is thinner (but of good quality), and the margins are less generous. The book is sturdily bound and will withstand repeated use.

Because *The Encyclopedia of Philosophy* is a reprint, however, the user must be aware that the material in it was assembled in 1965, so that newer concepts do not appear. Bioethics, for example, does not exist as a separate entry, although there are entries for both *biology* and *ethics.* Likewise euthanasia has no separate entry but is discussed within the entry for *suicide.* After 25 years, the encyclopedia is showing its age and should be due for a complete overhaul, including updating bibliographies and biographical entries for modern figures who have died in the intervening years. The set is still valuable for the theories and the figures it does treat, however, and should find continued use until a new edition is made available. The Board recommends this work for the core collections of public and academic libraries.

Philosophy: A Guide to the Reference Literature. Hans E. Bynagle. Libraries Unlimited, 1986. hard. 1 vol. 170 pp. indexes. ISBN 0-87287-464-8. $35. bibliography.
Z7125.B97 016.1

Philosophy: A Guide to the Reference Literature is intended for use in academic settings by teachers, librarians, professional philosophers, and students. Bynagle's bibliography attempts to cover reference works on philosophy "dealing with any period, movement, school, branch, major figure, or geographical-cultural subdivision, non-Western as well as Western" (preface). The arrangement reflects the author's background; he is library director at Whitworth College in Spokane, Washington. Titles are organized by format: bibliographies, guides, dictionaries, encyclopedias, indexes, review journals, directories, biographical sources, concordances, and so forth. Of the 421 entries, 337 are for reference works. A few are interdisciplinary (for example, the *New Catholic Encyclopedia*) and most are in English, although non-English works appear if they are not restrictively specialized.

The annotations are what gives this bibliographic guide its value, for they are evaluative as well as descriptive. They range in length from the two-line annotation to the *Index Aristotelicus* (one of the few titles the author notes he did not physically examine), to nearly a full page for such seminal works as Baldwin's *Dictionary of Philosophy and Psychology.* An Anglo-American bias appears in his coverage of individuals: none of the 59 thinkers treated represent Eastern philosophies, and only two are Islamic.

Although this bibliography is geared to the scholar and the student of philosophy, the text should be intelligible to the educated layperson. Accessibility is enhanced by separate subject and author-title indexes. The subject index includes persons, schools of thought, ideas, types of materials (periodicals, quotations), and some titles. For example, to find a concordance to Thomas Aquinas's *Summa Theologica,* look in the subject index under "Thomas Aquinas, Saint—*Summa Theologica*—word index," or look in the author-title index under "Complete Index of the *Summa Theologica* of St. Thomas Aquinas." Schools or branches of philosophy in the subject index have cross-references to individuals associated with that school (for example, "Catholic philosophy. See also Gilson, Etienne; Marcel, Gabriel"). "See" references lead to the preferred form of the entry word. The author-title index contains authors and titles of the reference works evaluated in the text.

Incomplete cross-references occasionally hamper the book's usefulness. There are three entries under "Computer databases" in the subject index: "bioethics," "humanities," and "philosophy (general)," so that one can find them all. On the other hand, users locating the index entry for the print version of *Philosopher's Index* will not find a "see also" reference to the separate entry for the on-line version at the end of the chapter. In addition, the subject index has no heading for book reviews. Looking under "Reviewing journals" one finds *Philosophical Books* and *Philosophischer Literaturanzeiger.* However, there is no reference to the *Repertoire Bibliographique de la Philosophie,* even though that title reserves its November issue annually for book reviews.

Although Bynagle cites an August 1985 cutoff date for inclusion of titles, only three titles carry that date. However, the emphasis is on books published in recent decades; older works (pre-1945) are included only if they have been reprinted or are still in print.

Philosophy: A Guide to the Reference Literature is a sturdily bound volume printed on good-quality paper, using a readable typeface. Each bibliographic entry is numbered clearly.

All in all, *Philosophy: A Guide to the Reference Literature* is a handsome and useful guide to the literature. The Board recommends this work for the core collections of academic libraries.

World Philosophy: Essay-Reviews of 225 Major Works. Frank N. Magill, ed. Salem, 1982. hard. 5 vols. 2,533 pp. indexes. ISBN 0-89356-325-0. $250 (set). encyclopedia.
B29.W68 100

Written by 50 scholars with advanced degrees in philosophy, *World Philosophy* enlarges on the two-volume *Masterpieces of World Philosophy in Summary Form* (1961) and aims to provide "substantial scholarly examinations of most of the key works needed to examine the major trends in world philosophy" (introduction). The five-volume set is organized by time period, beginning with the sixth century B.C. and concluding in 1971.

Entries (which average ten pages in length) follow a standard format. A headnote identifies the title, author, type of work, and date of first transcription. This is followed by a list of "Principal Ideas Advanced," then the long, signed essay that summarizes and evaluates the work. Of particular interest are the two or more shorter reviews that follow. These are reviews not of the major work but of critical writings that relate to it; they are contributed by a different scholar than the reviewer of the basic work. A list of "Additional Recommended Reading," as well as a brief annotated bibliography of books and articles, rounds out the entry.

The essays are clearly written, with concepts defined within the text. Volume 1 has a 12-page "Glossary of Common Philosophical Terms" that briefly defines major philosophies (Buddhism), as well as concepts (absolute idealism, deontological ethics, essence). There is an "Alphabetical List of Titles" for the entire set in volume 1, while the beginning of each volume contains a "Chronological List of Titles" for that volume only. Volume 5 includes an author index for the authors of the 225 major works, then separate indexes, arranged alphabetically by author, for the critical works discussed and additional recommended reading sections. Because no one author index ties the whole together, the user will find three works by Bertrand Russell in the author index; four additional works by Russell in the "Pertinent Literature" index; and two more works, plus references to different parts of two works from the previous list and a co-authored work in the "Additional Recommended Reading" index. Other authors are similarly scattered. There are no cross-references from one part of the set to another.

For all their shortcomings the indexes are easy to read and use. All page references include volume and page (for example, III-1031), even though the work is consecutively numbered through all five volumes. However, a subject index pulling together common themes would have been useful.

The philosophical works discussed in *World Philosophy* continue to be read and studied in a variety of college curricula. A revised edition could update the critical works and the reading lists with new scholarship. The set is arranged so that a new volume could be added covering primary literature written after 1971.

The short, squat Magill format allows the volumes to stand on a shelf without falling. They are produced on good-quality paper, using a typeface that is easy on the eyes. The sturdy, hardcover bindings will stand up to use.

For academic and public libraries whose patrons need a concise, critical overview of works such as the *Bhagavad Gita, I Ching,* Plato's *Republic,* Machiavelli's *The Prince,* Sir Thomas More's *Utopia,* and other time-tested works of philosophy, Magill's *World Philosophy* provides a handy, efficient place to start. The Board recommends this work for the core collections of public and academic libraries.

Supplementary Titles

Dictionary of Philosophy. Peter A. Angeles. Barnes & Noble, 1981. soft. 1 vol. 326 pp. index. ISBN 0-06-463461-2. $8.95. dictionary.
B41.A53 103.21

Dictionary of Philosophy "is a dictionary of some 2,000 terms used in beginning philosophy courses (epistemology, metaphysics, ethics, aesthetics, logic, and the philosophies of religion and politics). . . . Multiple . . . [meanings] and brief etymologies are given for . . . English, Latin, Greek, and French words and phrases.

"[Angeles] is the author of several books and many articles in the field. . . . [Definitions] are often identified with individual philosophers, e.g., *pour soi* (Sartre). Cross-references are extensively used. . . . In selection of entries and clarity of definitions, [the] *Dictionary of Philosophy* augments English-language unabridged dictionaries and can be recommended for student use. . . . It is beneficial for quick reference and for those who want less information than that found in the more exhaustive *Encyclopedia of Philosophy.* . . . Issued only in paperback, it may soon need rebinding, and its margins are, fortunately, adequate for the purpose." (*BL,* April 15, 1982, p. 1115)

Also reviewed in: *ARBA,* 1982, p. 574; 1983, p. 492.

Board's recommendation: School libraries.

Dictionary of Philosophy and Religion: Eastern and Western Thought. William L. Reese. Humanities Pr., 1980. soft. 1 vol. 644 pp. ISBN 0-391-00941-9. $25. dictionary.
B41.R43 103

The *Dictionary of Philosophy and Religion* "contains 3,500 entries on philosophical and religious concepts, terms, personalities[,] and movements. Cross-references 'lead to the explanation of key terms within the contexts of the conceptual systems of those who have introduced and developed such terms. . . . Long entries under philosophers' names are divided into main points or concepts and numbered for reference.'

"The articles run from as little as one or two lines to as much as nine columns and include references to primary material. . . . One-third of the entries are cross-references. Philosophy entries outnumber religion entries two to one. Some key Christian words like Annunciation, Ascension, and Crucifixion are not listed. . . . Only 10 percent of the entries pertain to Eastern philosophy and religion. The article on Zen is short, but it is a good beginning, covering some very essential points. . . . The *Dictionary of Philosophy and Religion* will be helpful in providing an insight into interrelationships in Western philosophical thought by means of short, well-written articles and copious cross-references." (*BL,* September 15, 1981, p. 131)

"The dictionary entries in this . . . volume contain an excellent cross-reference system. There is good biographical coverage, . . . but bibliographical information is severely limited to the titles of major primary sources. The author meets his stated goal of providing reliable . . . information on the topics presented. For more extensive treatments he directs the reader to the standard dictionaries and encyclopedias. . . . The book is very clearly written, instructive in its arrangement, and useful for quick reference information in both Eastern and Western philosophy and religion." [Many libraries will find it useful.] (*Choice,* July/August 1980, p. 656)

Also reviewed in: *ANQ,* November 1981, p. 55; *ARBA,* 1981, p. 506; *CLW,* May 1982, p. 439; *Col Lit,* Spring 1983, p. 184; *Ethics,* January 1981, p. 349; *Hum,* May 1980, p. 44; *LJ,* May 15, 1981, p. 1041; *Obs,* December 7, 1980, p. 29; *Rel St Rev,* January 1984, p. 64; *RSR,* January 1982, p. 10; *TES,* May 18, 1984, p. 33.

Board's recommendation: Academic libraries.

Encyclopedia of Bioethics. Warren T. Reich, ed. in chief. Free Pr./Macmillan, 1978. hard. 2 vols. index. ISBN 0-02-926060-4 (set). $250 (set). encyclopedia.
QH322.E53 174.2

The *Encyclopedia of Bioethics* includes 315 articles by 285 contributors under review by a 60-member international advisory board. The articles range from 800 to 12,000 words, with some entries composed of several articles to achieve greater systematic coherence. Bibliographies are given after each article, and the articles are . . . cross-referenced. . . . [Included are] articles on abortion, contraception, ethics, gene therapy, . . . the person and . . . the philosophy of biology.

"On the whole, the articles are well written and informative, and the bibliographies are relatively up-to-date and useful. Major subjects are presented fully and fairly. There is little duplication, since overlap falls to authors with different expertise. The volumes are well bound, the paper is strong, and the print easy to read. Scientific research that makes some factual parts of the work obsolete can conveniently be dealt with in periodic supplements. The encyclopedia can be used profitably by both laypersons and researchers who venture into fields outside their expertise." (*LJ,* March 1979, p. 616)

"Contributors were required to summarize the significant different ethical viewpoints on topics, and to explain the justification offered for each viewpoint. The result is that articles are remarkably (though of course not entirely) free of personal bias. . . . There is throughout an emphasis on major positions and schemes of analysis, rather than attempts to make definitive statements in fixed categories." (*Choice* November 1979, p. 1150)

Also reviewed in: *ARBA,* 1980, p. 490; *BL,* March 15, 1983, p. 988; *CLW,* December 1979, p. 237; *Cng,* February 1979, p. 49; *CRL,* January 1980, p. 62; *PSQ,* Winter 1980, p. 708; *PT,* March 1979, p. 104; *Rel St Rev,* January 1981, p. 5; *RSR,* October 1979, p. 13; July 1981, p. 9; Fall 1983, p. 10; *Soc,* March/April 1980, p. 95; *TT,* July 1980, p. 221; *WLB,* September 1979, p. 66.

Board's recommendation: Public and academic libraries.

The Philosopher's Guide to Sources, Research Tools, Professional Life, and Related Fields. Richard T. DeGeorge. Regents, 1980. hard. 1 vol. 261 pp. index. ISBN 0-7006-0020-3. $25. bibliography.
Z7125.D44 016.1

The Philosopher's Guide to Sources, Research Tools, Professional Life, and Related Fields is a "classified, annotated bibliography, designed for philosophy students and researchers, [that] contains approximately 1,600 entries dealing with philosophy and 400 citations to reference works in other disciplines. The philosophy portion is divided into four major parts: general histories and reference works; sources for the history of philosophy (by period, and including sections on leading individual philosophers); divisions of the field, movements and national or regional trends; serials, publishing, and professional activities. Annotations are concise and sometimes evaluative as well as descriptive. There are numerous cross references. The forty-page index includes author, subject, and many (but not all) title entries.

"Originally planned as a ten-year supplement to De George's *A Guide to Philosophical Bibliography and Research* (Appleton, 1971), the work under review incorporates, updates, supplements, and supersedes the earlier titles. The compiler is University Distinguished Professor of Philosophy, University of Kansas. . . . De George has produced the most authoritative, current, and comprehensive work available. . . . One might quarrel with certain omissions in the humanities and fine arts sections, but such criticism would miss the point. In the field of philosophy, this book is superb. [Many libraries will find *The Philosopher's Guide* invaluable in their collections.]" (*RQ,* Winter 1980, p. 214)

Also reviewed in: *ARBA,* 1982, p. 569; *CRL,* July 1981, p. 357; *Choice,* November 1983, p. 391; *Ethics,* July 1982, p. 788; *RSR,* July 1982, p. 277.

Board's recommendation: Academic libraries.

Symbolism: A Comprehensive Dictionary. Steven Olderr, comp. McFarland, 1986. hard. 1 vol. 153 pp. ISBN 0-89950-187-7. $25.95. dictionary.
CB475.038 001.51

Symbolism: A Comprehensive Dictionary "will be a welcome addition to reference collections. . . . It provides short definitions for many of the vast array of symbols that may have meanings in philosophy, art, literature, dreams, and the like. It serves as a complement to the standard work, Juan E. Cirlot's *Dictionary of Symbols.* . . . Unlike Cirlot, Olderr does not provide references within the definitions or a bibliography of sources. Some may find this a major shortcoming. The Olderr work lists brief definitions that provide minimal context and often seem to be culled directly from Cirlot's longer definitions. The Olderr dictionary has the advantage of many more direct entries with fewer cross-references to broad areas. . . . In sum, Olderr's book belongs in . . . [public and academic] libraries as a complement to, not a substitute for, Cirlot's *Dictionary of Symbols.*" (*Choice,* November 1986, p. 460)

Also reviewed in: *ARBA,* 1987, p. 340; *JQ,* Winter, 1987, p. 900; *R & R Bk N,* Summer 1986, p. 4.

Board's recommendation: Public and academic libraries.

Thinkers of the Twentieth Century: A Biographical, Bibliographical, and Critical Dictionary, 2d edition. Roland Turner, ed. St. James, 1987. hard. 1 vol. approx. 650 pp. ISBN 0-912289-83-X. $85. bibliography.
CT120.T45 920.00904

Thinkers of the Twentieth Century "is a compilation of bio-bibliographies and articles on 413 'thinkers' by 127 academics. Articles, averaging 1500 words, describe the subject's work, development, [and] significance. People covered. . . . include humanists, social scientists, jurists, scientists, and a handful of writers, composers, architects, and political revolutionaries." (*LJ,* June 1, 1984, p. 1122)

Also reviewed in: *ARBA,* 1985, p. 465; *BL,* April 1, 1985, p. 1109; *Choice,* February 1985, p. 800; *Ref Bk R,* 1984, p. 1; *RQ,* Winter 1984, p. 235.

Board's recommendation: Public and academic libraries.

Diana Hanaor

Photography

See also Art

Photography reference works fall into three broad categories: technical books that explain "how," marketing books that explain "where," and biographical books that explain "who." The technical books provide information on photographic equipment, techniques, and processes. This category includes dictionaries and encyclopedias, which form a large part of any photography collection.

The marketing books are reference tools for photographers wishing to sell their works and researchers wishing to locate them. Into this category we can fit *Photography Books Index: A Subject Guide to Photo Anthologies,* compiled by Martha Moss (Scarecrow, 1985), and *Photography Index: A Guide to Reproductions,* by Pamela Parry (Greenwood, 1979). Because they facilitate access to published photographs by subject, title, and photographer, these indexes are valuable guides for librarians and users alike.

The third category, biographical books, provides a guide to the world of photography—the curators and critics, the inventors and photographers. The two leading biographical works in this field are reviewed herein.

Core Titles

	PUBLIC	ACADEMIC	SCHOOL
Contemporary Photographers Walsh, George, Colin Naylor, and Michael Hold, eds. St. Martin's, 1988	✦	✦	
Dictionary of Contemporary Photography Stroebel, Leslie, and Hollis N. Todd. Morgan & Morgan, 1974	✦	✦	✦
Focal Encyclopedia of Photography, 2 vols. Kraszna-Krauz, A., ed. Focal Pr., 1982	✦		✦
Photographer's Market: Where and How to Sell Your Photographs Marshall, Sam, ed. Writer's Digest, annual	✦	✦	✦

Unfortunately, all too many fine photographic reference works go out of print after just three or four years. One such work is *The International Center of Photography Encyclopedia of Photography,* edited by Cornell Capa, Jerry Mason, and William Broeker (Crown, 1984). This encyclopedia straddled all three categories. Its 1,300 entries described the current state of aesthetic and technical applications of photography, provided full information about agencies and picture libraries, and identified inventors and photographers. Another useful out-of-print aid is the *Index to American Photographic Collections,* edited by James McQuaid (G. K. Hall, 1982). This work is a directory of American photographic collections arranged by state, city, and institution. Also out of print are the *Macmillan Biographical Encyclopedia of Photographic Artists and Innovators* (1983) and *The Photographer's Bible* (Bruce Pinkard, Arco, 1982). Librarians may wish to supplement their collections by obtaining these works through an out-of-print book dealer.

The basic buying criteria for all reference works—usefulness, authority, and accessibility—apply to photographic reference works. However, the quality and choice of photographs used in such works is especially important. Many of the books mentioned in the core and supplementary lists are relatively high in price; the costs of producing these works and securing reproduction rights may account for this.

Librarians should be aware that the rapid advances in photographic technology require that photography reference books be revised and updated regularly.

Core Titles

Contemporary Photographers. George Walsh, Colin Naylor, and Michael Hold, eds. St. Martin's, 1988. hard. 1 vol. 837 pp. illus. ISBN 0-312-16791-1. $120. biographical dictionary.
TR139.C66 770.922

Contemporary Photographers, a fine biographical work, is proof positive that reference books can be both visually beautiful and textually useful. A board of distinguished advisors, including Cornell Capa and Helmut Gernsheim, selected 650 prominent contemporary photographers for inclusion. "Contemporary" is broadly defined to cover those who are living or who died in the recent past, photographers from earlier generations whose reputations are essentially contemporary, and photographers from the 1920s and after who continue to be important influences.

Each biographical entry provides the following information: biography, exhibitions, galleries and museums holding the entrant's works, and a bibliography of books and articles by and about the entrant. The entry ends with a signed critical essay by one of 155 contributors. Almost every entry has a sample of the photographer's work, some filling an entire page.

The critical essays help to fit the photographer into a wider context. They draw attention to aspects of the photographer's work that may not show up in bare biographical outlines. The essay on sports photographer *Gerry Cranham,* by Sue Davies, notes how he has overcome the relentless repetition of subject that is an occupational hazard of sports photography. Vladimir Renes looks at the cycles of ballet photographs by *Alexandr Makarov* and shows how he has brought out the backstage life of the dancers, capturing those moments of supreme mental and physical concentration.

Contemporary Photographers contains current information and splendid photographic reproductions. The Board recommends this work for the core collections of public and academic libraries.

Dictionary of Contemporary Photography. Leslie Stroebel and Hollis N. Todd. Morgan & Morgan, 1974. soft. 1 vol. illus. ISBN 0-87100-065-2. $15. dictionary.
TR9.S88 770.3

The *Dictionary of Contemporary Photography* is an illustrated dictionary that records recent usage in photography, cinematography (including animation), and photographic engineering. The 4,500 definitions and explanations also encompass terms from other disciplines as they relate to photography—for example, *regression* and *element.*

The authors have culled words from a variety of journals and professional materials, excluding trade and personal names and chemical terms. In their preface, Stroebel and Todd acknowledge that the photographic vocabulary is expanding, and they promise an update. To date, however, none has been forthcoming, and for terms that have come into use more recently than the early 1970s, the photographer must turn to Pinkard's *Photographer's Bible* (now out of print).

The definitions are clear and unencumbered by jargon. For example, *reseau* is defined as a "fine grid formerly used in screen color processes (now obsolete). The term is now used to identify a similar grid used for measurement purposes."

Many definitions are accompanied by drawings and photographs that provide further clarification. *Arrow illusion* and *bayonet mount,* for example, are immediately recognizable from the line drawings alongside their definitions. Likewise, *side lighting* and *halation effects* are illustrated by excellent photographs.

Spelling and usage in photography are not yet standardized. Where two or more words are in use for the same concept, the authors' preference is indicated clearly. Thus, they prefer *electronic flash* to *strobe* or *speedlight; luminance meter* to *brightness meter* or *reflectance meter.* Cross-references are provided. The book has large (10-by-10-inch) glossy pages, and the print is readable, with generous space between columns and definitions.

Despite the 1974 copyright date of the *Dictionary of Contemporary Photography,* this work is still quite a useful reference. The Board recommends this work for the core collections of public, academic, and school libraries.

Focal Encyclopedia of Photography. A. Kraszna-Krauz, ed. Focal Pr., 1982. hard. 2 vols. 1-vol. desk edition. 1,690 pp. illus. ISBN 0-240-50631-6 (set); 0-240-50680-4 (desk edition). $150 (set); $39.95 (desk edition). encyclopedia.
TR.15 770.3

The *Focal Encyclopedia of Photography* has been a standard reference tool for more than 30 years. Some nine revisions have appeared since 1956, each recognizing new technologies and their corresponding terminologies. The text has grown from 1.3 million words to 1.7 million words and the number of illustrations from 1,500 to 1,750. More than mere bulk, however, the revisions reflect the shift of balance in the field, and new contributors have joined the already impressive *Focal Encyclopedia* team from such disciplines as economics, education, and science. This encyclopedia was produced in England. The spellings and some of the entries have a British slant, but this does not detract from the work's general usefulness to an American audience.

Signed essays by such experts as H. Gernsheim and C. B. Neblette give the *Focal Encyclopedia* both scholarly authority and personal style. Sometimes this personal style is meandering and discursive. For example, L. A. Mannheim, writing on slide lectures, recommends (among other things) that the lecturer arrive early and keep his or her head up while speaking. Other essays are more scientific in nature, although the text is never too technical for the average reader. A definition for *while-you-wait-photography* is followed by succinct descriptions of *ferrotype method, paper negative method,* and *diffusion transfer,* all used in this kind of photography.

Entries appear in dictionary order and vary in length from five lines for *potassium iodide* to 60 pages for *colour.* Major articles are divided into manageable sections. *Big game* has sections on type of subject (buffalos, zebras, giraffes, and so forth), technique, photographing animals from a car, and the equipment required for successful big-game photography. The entry for *hands* discusses lighting and shadows, gives bibliographic references, and supplies a cross-reference to portraiture.

Biographies of photographic innovators and stylists mention key collections of their work. Illustrations and tables are given sufficient space for display. The entry *depth of field,* for instance, includes a full-page table of hyperfocal distances.

Because *The International Center of Photography Encyclopedia of Photography* is no longer in print, the *Focal Encyclopedia of Photography* has claimed the title as the best one-volume dictionary and encyclopedia of photography. The Board recommends this work for the core collections of public and school libraries.

Photographer's Market: Where and How to Sell Your Photographs. Sam Marshall, ed. Writer's Digest, annual. hard. 1 vol. 608 pp. illus. index. ISBN 0-89879-424-2. $21.95. handbook.
TR690.P4 770.23

For complete marketing and business advice, the commercial free-lance photographer need look no further than the *Photographer's Market: Where and How to Sell Your Photographs.* This work, revised annually, has a reputation for accuracy and creative ideas on how a photographer can carve a niche in this huge and often bewildering marketplace.

The book is divided into three sections. Introductory essays include keys to selling (technical proficiency, knowledge of markets, ruthless portfolio editing, understanding of the law, and professional presentation), ownership rights, and tax law as it affects photographers. The second section offers exhaustive coverage of the American market for photographs. Approximately 2,500 photo buyers are divided into advertising, business, and trade publishers; stock photo agencies; and audiovisual firms. Each of these divisions opens with a readable introductory essay describing the particular type of market, and subsequent listings include information on whom to contact, the kind of photos needed, payment rates, and useful tips on the type of work usually accepted by the publication or organization. For example, the journal *Nature Conservancy News,* as might be expected, looks for photographs of rare species. The *AOPA Pilot* wants 2¼-by-2¼-inch transparencies, and *Balloon Life* requires all photographs to be accompanied by a story.

A fifth of the listings, many of which appear in the stock photo agencies section, are totally new. Annual changes update addresses, contact names, and pay rates for all listings, as required. The stock photography market continues to expand, and both domestic and foreign agencies are listed.

The third section of the book is broadly titled "Services and Opportunities." It covers contests (with warnings to entrants not to agree to give up all rights when they win) and workshops on subjects ranging from special-effects work to portfolio review sessions. A glossary of terms and an exhaustive index appear at the end of the book.

Two features make *Photographer's Market* more than a dry resource directory. There are fine reproductions of photographs with informative captions detailing the sale of the originals—who purchased them and for what price. Even more interesting are close-up interviews with a variety of free-lance photographers and photo buyers whose skills are unique to the section in which the interview appears. Among those interviewed are the commercial photographer Cosimo, who discusses how to make the transition from still to film photography; Dick Frank, a New York photographer, who talks about the techniques involved in photographing food; and Anita Douthat, curator of the Photography Resource Center in Boston, who explains how to get a gallery exhibit.

Photographer's Market is a unique and important sourcebook, and its information is vital to free lancers who wish to make contacts and sell their work in the photographic marketplace. Librarians should add the most recent edition to their reference shelves to ensure that their patrons have access to the most recent names, addresses, and pay rates in this field. Earlier editions, which are still somewhat useful after a new edition has been published, may be saved and circulated. The Board recommends this work for the core collections of public, academic, and school libraries.

Supplementary Titles

The History of Photography from 1839 to the Present, 5th edition. Beaumont Newhall. Museum of Modern Art, 1982; distrib. by Bullfinch Pr. hard and soft. 1 vol. 320 pp. illus. index. ISBN 0-87070-380-3 (hard); 0-87070-381-1 (soft). $40 (hard); $23.50 (soft). history.
TR15.N47 770.9

"Beaumont Newhall has done an excellent job of telescoping what is really a very large subject into a complete and compact volume. . . . [*The History of Photography from 1839 to the Present*] gives the esthetic as well as the factual side of photography's development." (*NYT,* July 10, 1949, p. 1)

The "newly refined *History of Photography* provides a solid introduction for the newcomer, a flexible and interesting textbook for the classroom, and a familiar yet challenging trusted reference for the scholar embarking on more specialized studies. It is arguably the highest degree of refinement possible in a reasonably-sized volume, given the current state of scholarship in this field." (*Hst of Photo,* October–December, 1983, p. 330)

"So much beauty, so much solid (as well as curious) information, so much intelligence in the arrangement of essential facts have gone into the making of this book that it would be difficult to praise it too highly. It takes its place at once as the best compact history of photography in existence." (*SR,* September 3, 1949, p. 30)

Also reviewed in: *Afterimage,* April 1986, p. 4; *Artweek,* November 6, 1982, p. 12; *Brit Bk N,* October 1982, p. 599.

Board's recommendation: Public and academic libraries.

Sarojini Balachandran

Physics

See also Science and Technology

The science of physics makes inquiries into the structure of matter. Physicists study interactions between natural elements and conduct experiments that allow formulation of theories about our world and our universe. Physics serves as a building block for all the natural sciences. At one time physicists considered their discipline the center of all natural knowledge, encompassing astronomy, chemistry, metallurgy, meteorology, and geology. Although these fields have since become separate disciplines, they are still fundamentally linked to physics. This link is manifested in the recent development of sciences such as physical chemistry, chemical physics, meteorological physics, astrophysics, biophysics, plasma physics, semiconductor physics, and geophysics. Therefore, both librarians and physics patrons need to be aware of the considerable overlap of the natural and physical sciences.

There are two types of physics: theoretical and experimental. These two divisions encompass a wide range of topics such as classical and quantum mechanics, thermodynamics, heat, electricity, magnetism, optics, solid-state physics, sound, nuclear physics, atomic physics, particle physics, relativistic mechanics, laws of conservation, and fundamental forces and fields. The theoretical practitioners must publish their work quite often to remain active in the field. Although experimental physicists do publish their findings, much of their time is spent in the laboratory.

In recent decades, specialization in all the sciences has exploded. Those involved in research have had to keep current by reading and participating in what might be called invisible colleges maintained through primary and secondary journals, letters, review articles, treatises and texts, dissertations, seminars, and conference proceedings. Despite the explosion of knowledge in the field, students and professional librarians have been helped tremendously by the availability of many abstracting and indexing services, handbooks, manuals, biographical and terminological dictionaries, and guidebooks and sourcebooks, some of which are reviewed in this category. These sources have helped provide bibliographic control and easy access to needed information in physics. The recent development of online products has further accelerated the availability of up-to-date scientific data. Therefore, developing a physics reference collection is not a question of availability but rather a matter to be limited by the librarian's needs, expertise, and, of course, library funds.

Core Titles

	PUBLIC	ACADEMIC	SCHOOL
CRC Handbook of Chemistry and Physics Weast, Robert C., ed. CRC Pr., annual	✦	✦	✦
A Dictionary of Scientific Units: Including Dimensionless Numbers and Scales, 5th edition Jerrard, H. G., and D. B. McNeill. Routledge, Chapman & Hall, 1986		✦	
The Encyclopedia of Physics, 3d edition Besançon, Robert M., ed. Van Nostrand Reinhold, 1985	✦	✦	
Information Sources in Physics, 2d edition Shaw, Dennis F., ed. Saur, 1985		✦	
McGraw-Hill Dictionary of Physics Parker, Sybil P., ed. in chief. McGraw-Hill, 1984	✦	✦	
McGraw-Hill Encyclopedia of Physics Parker, Sybil P., ed. in chief. McGraw-Hill, 1983	✦	✦	

Core Titles

CRC Handbook of Chemistry and Physics. Robert C. Weast, ed. CRC Pr., annual. hard. 1 vol. 2,528 pp. illus. index. ISBN 0-8493-0470-9. $97.50. handbook.
QD65.C911 540.212'12'19

For a number of years, the CRC Press has been publishing numerous ready-reference books designed to provide scientists, engineers, and librarians with timely information on a variety of topics in one convenient volume. Although tremendous strides have been made in the different branches of science and technology, the publishers have managed to preserve the original format of the *CRC Handbook* established in the 1920s. This has been achieved by judiciously selecting topics better suited for inclusion in a lengthy work. This edition is the last (of 37) to be edited by Robert C. Weast. His successor, David R. Lide, will be called on to continue a valuable legacy.

The latest edition of the *CRC Handbook of Chemistry and Physics,* as in the past, covers basic tables in physics, chemistry, and mathematics, with a section devoted to the interpretation and use of the tables. The sections of the book include mathematical tables, elements and inorganic compounds, general chemical constants, general physical constants, and a section of miscellaneous data that were not suitable for inclusion in other parts of the book. Chapters and subchapters are interspersed with numerous sources and references. A subject index is thoughtfully provided to make access easier for the novice.

The dynamic nature of the field necessitates constant revision of this work. Therefore, each edition includes information on current research topics. The topics highlighted in this seventieth edition are transistor-accelerated studies of chemistry and physics of solid state, semiconductor properties, and superconductivity under both low and high temperatures. Also, the 1988 publication includes new atomic weights. New tables include diffusivities of metallic solutes in molten metals, metallic tracers in mercury, particle size conversion, thermal conductivity of organic compounds, reduction and oxidation potentials for ion radicals, and diffusion coefficients of liquids at infinite dilution.

The *CRC Handbook of Chemistry and Physics* is not an easy reference to use, but those who have familiarized themselves with its format over the period of years know what a gold mine of information it is. This valuable one-volume reference source is a necessary purchase for all libraries, especially those with large science collections. The Board recommends this work for the core collections of public, academic, and school libraries.

A Dictionary of Scientific Units: Including Dimensionless Numbers and Scales, 5th edition. H. G. Jerrard and D. B. McNeill. Routledge, Chapman & Hall, 1986. hard and soft. 1 vol. 222 pp. appendixes. index. ISBN 0-412-28096-6 (hard); 0-412-28100-7 (soft). $39.95 (hard); $19.95 (soft). dictionary.
QC82.J4 530.8'03'21

A Dictionary of Scientific Units is a guide to the many different types of sophisticated scientific measurement. This reference tool describes such concepts as the three fundamental mechanical units, mass, length, and time, which define all nonelectrical physical quantities. In addition, the work mentions a fourth unit that is needed to define electric and magnetic qualities. Such a unit can be electrical current, permeability, or permittivity. Some of the units of measure are almost arbitrary in origin—the yard, for instance. Others can be precisely linked to natural phenomena. For instance, the meter can be defined in terms of the wavelength of the orange light emitted when krypton gas is excited in an electrical discharge.

Although most scientific units have been in use for centuries, electrical and magnetic quantities were not used until the middle of the nineteenth century. The intense specialization of the different branches of science and technology has often resulted in confusion and discrepancies in the nomenclature of the various fields. Currently, quite a few units, scales, and dimensionless numbers are used throughout the world as measurements or expressions of any quantity. Since the advent of the Gaussian system toward the middle of the nineteenth century, a number of publications have dealt with the definition of various measurements. The most recent include Stephen Dresner's *Units of Measurement: An Encyclopedic Dictionary of Units, Both Scientific and Popular* (1971, now Books on Demand), David Goldman's *International System of Units* (5th edition, National Bureau of Standards Special Publication No. 330, 1986), B. S. Massey's *Measures in Science and Engineering; Their Expression, Relation and Interpretation* (Halsted Pr., 1986), and J. V. Drazil's *Quantities and Units of Measurement: A Dictionary and Handbook* (Mansell, 1983).

Obviously, library users will find this one-volume publication covering most, if not all, measurements very convenient. The dictionary presents a comprehensive and clearly defined listing of all units used in science, technology, and medicine. The dictionary reflects over 850 technical advances made as of the time of the fifth edition (an increase of 50 entries since the fourth edition). The reference includes not only metric and SI units but also the value of fundamental physical constants based on atomic constants. All the definitions provided have been approved by the appropriate international committees.

The appendixes contain significant amounts of useful information such as standardization committees and conferences, tables of weights and measures, conversion tables, and conversion factors for SI and CGS units. The comprehensive bibliography following the appendixes will help supplement the already considerable information provided in the entries. The index is also very good.

No matter how readily available the information in other sources, such as multivolume encyclopedias and dictionaries, the convenience of the single-volume *A Dictionary of Scientific Units* makes it a most attractive purchase. The Board recommends this work for the core collection of academic libraries.

The Encyclopedia of Physics, 3d edition. Robert M. Besançon, ed. Van Nostrand Reinhold, 1985. soft. 1 vol. illus. 1,378 pp. ISBN 0-442-00522-9. $49.95. encyclopedia.
QC5.E546 530.03'21

The purpose of any encyclopedia is to provide the lay reader with an overview of the fundamentals of the subject it covers and to help sophisticated scholars find the intricacies of related topics when they need more specialized information. Judged by this standard, all editions of the Van Nostrand Reinhold *Encyclopedia of Physics* have achieved their purpose. The authority of the encyclopedia is further enhanced through its many learned authors. The work was compiled by more than 300 experts from the United States and abroad. The list of contributors not only includes names and academic affiliations, it also stipulates the content area to which each contributed.

Readers using the encyclopedia will be well served by consulting the article entitled "Physics," followed by the review of other articles dealing with major areas of physics. Articles cover topics such as the history of the subject, measurement, symbols, units, and nomenclature. Comprehensive coverage has been provided for the fields of astrophysics, geophysics, biophysics, and mathematical and experimental physics. The latest volume contains articles on gauge theories, quantum electrodynamics, weak electrons, and grand unified theories. Revisions have been made to the earlier treatment of elementary particles, weak interactions, strong interactions, parity, and quantum theory. Increased emphasis has been given to the role of physics in medicine and biology by the additional treatment of molecular biology, biomedical instrumentation, biophysics, health physics, and bionics. Other fields receiving similar coverage include optics and energy storage.

The entries contain not only the definition of the technical terms but also an adequate explanation. For obvious reasons, the technical levels of the articles are not uniform. More specialized or complex definitions are provided when the concept is difficult, and, although not all topics in physics can be described without using mathematical formulas, the volumes do avoid it where possible. The result is that both the lay reader with a limited mathematical background and the experienced physicist will get plenty of useful information from this encyclopedia. Numerous references to articles and books provide additional sources of information, should this be required. This reference work also includes many well-planned cross-references.

The current edition of *The Encyclopedia of Physics* will be of great use to students, librarians, physicists, and engineers. The convenience of a single-volume ready reference at a reasonable price makes it quite attractive to academic and large public libraries. However, with the continuing explosion of knowledge in physics, the single-volume format of *The Encyclopedia of Physics* may not be feasible in future editions without sacrificing important material. Nevertheless, the Board recommends this work for the core collections of public and academic libraries.

Information Sources in Physics, 2d edition. Dennis F. Shaw, ed. Saur, 1985. hard. 1 vol. 456 pp. appendixes. ISBN 0-408-01474-1. $80. bibliography.
Z7141.I54 016.53′2′19

Information Sources in Physics is a definitive review of reference material in all major branches of the field, including atomic and molecular physics, chemical physics, statistical physics, thermodynamics, crystallography, electricity, magnetism, electromagnetism, electronics and computer technology, experimental heat and low-temperature physics, geophysics, astrophysics and meteorological physics, nuclear and particle physics, mechanics, acoustics, optics, spectroscopy, semiconductors, and theoretical physics.

According to Dr. John Ziman, who wrote the introduction to both editions of *Information Sources in Physics,* the official literature of physics is of perplexing diversity. The change in the title of this enlarged and completely rewritten version (originally published as *Uses of Physics Literature*) conveys its true scope and dimension as a valuable reference source for physicists and librarians. Two decades ago, users were well served by helpful guides such as Byron Yates's *How to Find Out About Physics* (Pergamon, 1965) and Robert Whitford's *Physics Literature* (Scarecrow, 1968). This volume provides valuable coverage that is more up to date. Dennis Shaw, the Keeper of Scientific Books of the Radcliffe Science Library at Oxford and a physicist himself, has done a commendable job of getting together a very knowledgeable group of people to cover the information transfer process in physics.

In an introductory guide of this nature, it is impractical to treat peripheral areas of cross-disciplinary and applied physics, which are better suited to books dealing with engineering literature. Therefore, the user of this book is not likely to find information on topics such as nuclear engineering, rheology, materials science, energy research, environmental science, biophysics, medical physics, and biomedical engineering.

The treatment of over 2,000 physics-related references is quite authoritative, and the bibliographic citations to information sources are complete. The book covers the history of physics literature, abstracting and indexing services, on-line sources, and general treatises and patents (a new feature of this edition). This source also talks extensively about grey literature, although its British definition may not agree with U.S. users' views. The appendixes provide valuable information in terms of acronyms, initialisms, important core journals and organizations such as the IEEE, and vendors such as INSPEC.

Although international in its coverage, *Information Sources in Physics* does reflect a British bias. The slant notwithstanding, the volume lives up to the standard established by Butterworth's Guides to Information Sources series. The Board recommends this work for the core collection of academic libraries.

McGraw-Hill Dictionary of Physics. Sybil P. Parker, ed. in chief. McGraw-Hill, 1984. soft. 1 vol. 646 pp. ISBN 0-07-045418-3. $21.95. dictionary.
QC5.M424 530.03′21

The *McGraw-Hill Dictionary of Physics* was developed from the material published in the 1984 third edition of the McGraw-Hill Dictionary of Scientific and Technical Terms (see Science and Technology for the fourth edition). The new edition includes terms reflecting the advances in the discipline in the early 1980s. A total of over 11,000 physics terms, as well as terms from related areas such as mathematics and metallurgy, were excerpted from the main volume to produce an inexpensive paperback reference book devoted exclusively to those users who need definitions of physics-related terminology. This shortened version is no less authoritative. It encompasses some 18 areas of classical and modern physics, including acoustics, astrophysics, atomic and nuclear physics, biophysics, electromagnetism, geophysics, fluid mechanics, plasma physics, optics, quantum mechanics, cryogenics, crystallography, materials science, particle physics, physical chemistry, relativity, solid-state physics, and thermodynamics.

The dictionary is arranged in the following format: Each entry is printed in boldface type, followed by a label indicating the branch of physics to which it belongs. A concise and technical definition immediately follows. The length of the definition depends on the nature of the topic. As is usually the case with technical dictionaries, most definitions are comprehensible to the educated layperson, but others require some technical background. Useful aspects of the book include extensive cross-references, explanations of the abbreviations and acronyms, variant spellings, and symbols and synonyms.

McGraw-Hill dictionaries have generally enjoyed wide acceptance in academic libraries because of their thoroughness and authoritativeness. The *Dictionary of Physics* is no exception. The dictionary's value lies in the inclusion of terms covering up-to-date research and theory. Although users may find this dictionary a convenient reference source, it must be pointed out that the publishers have recently completed the fourth edition of the parent volume, the MCGRAW-HILL DICTIONARY OF SCIENTIFIC AND TECHNICAL TERMS (see Science and Technology). The most recent physics terms can thus be found in this revised, enlarged edition.

The *McGraw-Hill Dictionary of Physics* is a useful publication that will be used by both experienced and novice patrons. The Board recommends this work for the core collections of public and academic libraries.

McGraw-Hill Encyclopedia of Physics. Sybil P. Parker, ed. in chief. McGraw-Hill, 1983. hard. 1 vol. 1,343 pp. appendix. index. ISBN 0-07-045253-9. $54.50. dictionary.
QC5.M425 530.03′21

All the material in the *McGraw-Hill Encyclopedia of Physics* has been previously published as part of the fifth edition of the MCGRAW-HILL ENCYCLOPEDIA OF SCIENCE AND TECHNOLOGY (see Science and Technology for the sixth edition). However, this separate edition has been completely revised and updated. Leading international experts have participated in the preparation of over 700 alphabetically arranged articles dealing with classical and modern physics.

The encyclopedia covers not only the historical developments in the field of physics (for example, Einstein's development of the theory of relativity) but also more recent advances, including theoretical and elementary particle physics and such technical applications as lasers and superconductivity. Detailed information is given on acoustics, atomic physics, particle physics, molecular physics, nuclear physics, classical mechanics, electricity, electromagnetism, fluid mechanics, heat and thermodynamics, low-temperature physics, optics, relativity, solid-state physics, and selected topics in mathematics.

The text is supplemented by more than 1,000 drawings, graphs, charts, and photographs. A detailed analytical index and cross-references make access to information easier. A list of further readings is suggested in the bibliographies. The appendix includes international system conversion tables, a list of mathematical notation, a table of fundamental constants, and a periodic table of elements.

The encyclopedia is an important source of information for scientists, engineers, students, librarians, and others interested in understanding the natural phenomena of the physical world. It is clear, however, that students and laypersons may find the book somewhat confusing, due, in part, to the difficult nature of the subject matter itself. Comprehending and absorbing information, equations, and cross-references may take some doing for the beginner. In spite of this drawback, this single-volume encyclopedia is a significant accomplishment. Readers should be aware that McGraw-Hill has recently published a one-volume *Concise Encyclopedia of Science and Technology* (1989), which may be referred to for more recent advances in physics.

The *McGraw-Hill Encyclopedia of Physics* is affordable for those libraries whose clientele has a need for physics-related information. The Board recommends this work for the core collections of public and academic libraries.

Supplementary Titles

The Biographical Dictionary of Scientists. David Abbott, gen. ed. Bedrick Bks., 1984–1986. hard. 6 vols. 1,208 pp. illus. index. ISBN 0-87226-009-7 (vol.6). $28 per vol. biographical dictionary.
QC15.B56 530.092′2

See Science and Technology.

New and Noteworthy

A Companion to the Physical Sciences. David Knight. Routledge, Chapman & Hall, 1989. hard. 1 vol. 177 pp. index. ISBN 0-415-00901-4. $25. dictionary.
Q123 500.2′03

"[This volume includes] . . . 225 terms in the physical sciences. Entries vary from one-quarter to two pages. Objective topics like *atom, magnetism, energy,* and *work* are covered as well as more subjective topics (e.g., *hypothesis, paradigm, God*). . . . Despite some redundancy, *A Companion to the Physical Sciences* is an excellent complement to [Medawar's *Aristotle to Zoos*] and a good supplement to [Bynum's *The Dictionary of the History of Science*]. Because of the level at which it is written, it is not suitable for school libraries but is appropriate for academic and public libraries with collections in the history of science." (*BL,* October 1, 1989, p. 389)

The Nobel Prize Winners: Physics. Frank N. Magill, ed. Salem, 1989. hard. 3 vols. 1,364 pp. illus. indexes. ISBN 0-89356-557-1. $210. biographical dictionary.
QC25.N63 530.092

The Nobel Prize Winners: Physics "provides chronological coverage of all physics laureates from 1901 through 1988. Each award-winner is given separate coverage. . . . Each entry is divided into three sections: the award, biography, and scientific career. . . . [S]cientific terms are not defined and a knowledge of physics is required to fully understand the entries." (*BL,* November 15, 1989, p. 698)

Mary Jane Brustman
Dorothy J. Coakley
Lois Cherepon
Richard Irving

Political Science

See also American History; Current Events; Economics; Public Administration

To Plato, Aristotle, and Thucydides, political science was the queen of the sciences and the most important field of endeavor from which all other disciplines emanated. Philosophy, history, sociology, public administration, law, and international relations were all contained within its domain. Religion, household management, and arguably even the roots of feminism were contained within political thought. For example, Plato entertained the possibility that females could be raised to be philosopher-kings in *The Republic.*

Today, political science includes all the aforementioned categories plus the works of Machiavelli, the civic humanist; Marx, the seminal communist; and Locke, Hobbes, Calvin, and Luther. Formal or positive theory, methodology, urban studies, economics, and political psychology are often included within the subject. Primarily, however, political science today is identified with the study of international and national government.

The core library collection should focus on the U.S. political system, its underlying political philosophy, and its officeholders. A general encyclopedia of political thought will give access to the history of political science. Additional encyclopedias provide a broad treatment of the movements and ideas which generated the formation of the federal government and the U.S. Constitution. Terms unique to U.S. government and politics are readily accessible through subject dictionaries.

The U.S. government comprises three distinct branches: the judicial, the legislative, and the executive. The legislative branch has two houses: the Senate and the House of Representatives. Congressional committees operate under the jurisdiction of Congress. The *Official Congressional Directory* (U.S.G.P.O., annual) is an essential reference tool for a political science collection. This directory contains changes that have occurred in the membership after each election and "historically . . . has been one of the most comprehensive and detailed resources for identifying the components of the three branches of the federal government" (foreword, *1989–1990 Official Congressional Directory*).

Biographies and lists of officeholders, with addresses, are an important part of the political science reference collection. They should be updated frequently. Therefore, the political science core collection should include addresses of state and local officials as well as names of ambassadors and addresses of consulates and embassies.

The field of international relations is very complex and often involves materials that must be updated daily through reputable international newspapers. However,

Core Titles

GENERAL	PUBLIC	ACADEMIC	SCHOOL
The Blackwell Encyclopaedia of Political Thought Miller, David, ed. Basil Blackwell, 1987		✦	
The International Year Book and Statesman's Who's Who Reed Information Svcs., annual (1953–)		✦	
Political Handbook of the World Banks, Arthur S., ed. CSA Publications, annual	✦	✦	
The Statesman's Year-Book: Statistical and Historical Annual of the States of the World Paxton, John, ed. St. Martin's, annual	✦	✦	✦
World Encyclopedia of Political Systems & Parties, 2d edition, 2 vols. Delury, George E., ed. Facts On File, 1987		✦	

UNITED STATES	PUBLIC	ACADEMIC	SCHOOL
The Almanac of American Politics 1990 Barone, Michael, and Grant Ujifusa. National Journal, 1989	✦	✦	
America Votes 18: A Handbook of Contemporary American Election Statistics Scammon, Richard M., and Alice V. McGillivray, eds. Congressional Quarterly, 1989	✦	✦	
American Leaders 1789–1987: A Biographical Summary McGuiness, Colleen, and Maria J. Sayers, eds. Congressional Quarterly, 1987	✦	✦	
The American Political Dictionary, 8th edition Plano, Jack C., and Milton Greenberg. Holt, Rinehart & Winston, 1989	✦	✦	✦
Congress and the Nation, 6 vols. Congressional Quarterly, 1965–1985	✦	✦	✦
Congressional Quarterly Almanac Lawrence, Christine C., ed. Congressional Quarterly, annual	✦	✦	
Congressional Quarterly's Guide to U.S. Elections, 2d edition Congressional Quarterly, 1985	✦	✦	
The Dorsey Dictionary of American Government and Politics Shafritz, Jay M. Brooks/Cole, 1988; distrib. by Wadsworth		✦	
Encyclopedia of American Political History: Studies of the Principal Movements and Ideas, 3 vols. Greene, Jack P., ed. Scribner, 1984	✦	✦	✦
Encyclopedia of the American Constitution, 4 vols. Levy, Leonard W., ed. in chief. Macmillan, 1986 (See Law)	✦	✦	✦
Politics in America: 1990, the 101st Congress Duncan, Phil, ed. Congressional Quarterly, 1989		✦	
The United States Government Manual U.S.G.P.O., annual	✦	✦	✦
Who's Who in American Politics, 1989–1990, 12th edition Bowker, 1989		✦	

an encyclopedia of the basic political systems and parties will be useful in a political science reference collection. —*D. J. C.*

With contributions by Susan C. Awe.

Core Titles

General

The Blackwell Encyclopaedia of Political Thought. David Miller, ed. Basil Blackwell, 1987. hard. 1 vol. 570 pp. index. ISBN 0-631-14011-5. $75. encyclopedia.
JA61.B57 320.03′21

The preface to *The Blackwell Encyclopaedia of Political Thought* describes the book as a "guide to the major ideas and doctrines that influence the contemporary world." This book includes important theories, concepts, schools of thought, and thinkers in political science as well as selected entries in the related disciplines of law, sociology, and economics. The 400 entries are primarily limited to Western political thought. Non-Western ideas, such as those from China or the Muslim world, are outlined in survey articles. Lengthy entries are devoted to political thinking of major historical periods such as the *Reformation* and major traditions such as *Liberalism* and *Conservatism.*

The editor, David Miller of Oxford University, is the author of a number of books on political theory and philosophy. Approximately 130 academics, mostly from British and U.S. universities, contributed signed articles to this encyclopedia.

Entries range from 15 to 2,500 words. The entries typically run about 500 words. Most entries have a brief bibliography appended. An excellent name and subject index is thorough and clear. Cross-references within the text are frequent and useful.

Most entries go beyond mere definitions. These are essays that discuss ideas and concepts and mention important literature on the topic. The many biographical entries are often evaluative and conclude with an assessment of the person's place in the history of political thought. Users will have difficulty finding such a range and depth of information on political thought elsewhere. Comments are, at times, highly opinionated. This makes for interesting and provocative reading. For example, under the entry *Immanual Kant,* we read "Kant is a political philosopher of the very first rank whose evolutionary political goals would, if actually realized, constitute a valuable revolution in history." Miller's preface notes that in the encyclopedia the "policy has been to select the best contributor regardless of academic or political allegiance and to place no restrictions on choice of approach."

The Blackwell Encyclopaedia of Political Thought is geared to a sophisticated audience. The language is dense and challenging, the material often complex. The work handles this material well. The Board recommends this work for the core collection of academic libraries. —*M. J. B.*

The International Year Book and Statesman's Who's Who. Reed Information Svcs., annual. (1953–). hard. 1 vol. 637 pp. appendix. ISBN 0-611-00738-X. $230. yearbook.
JA51.I57 320.05

The International Year Book and Statesman's Who's Who has been published annually since 1953. This British reference source contains current political, statistical, and directory data for each country of the world as well as information on international organizations. The researcher listed for the "Countries Section" is Mervyn O. Pragnell and for the "Biographies Section" is Helga Castle; no further background information is given, but the long history of the publication supports a feeling of reliability. Indeed, the contents page states that "every care has been taken to check the information supplied for the preparation of the articles in this volume."

Part 1 of the book covers the "United Nations," "Intergovernmental Organisations," and "Other International and National Organisations." Part 2, after some preliminary tables and charts, consists of three sections: "States of the World in Alphabetical Order," "Dependent States and Territories," and the "Biographical Section." The typeface used is small and somewhat difficult to read, and the first 114 pages have page numbers written in roman numerals. These two formatting flaws may detract from the readability of this book.

Entries are arranged alphabetically under the main subject divisions. As there is no index, the table of contents provides the only access to the information, sometimes causing difficulties. Nations are listed alphabetically within sections, which means locating a specific country is not impossible but will require a time-consuming search through the pages because the contents page does not give page numbers for individual countries. (Dependent states and territories are listed individually in the contents; because they are treated in the text under the nation with sovereignty over them, they would otherwise be impossible to locate.) THE EUROPA WORLD YEAR BOOK (see Current Events) covers similar information, as does the POLITIcal Handbook of the World; both these sources are generally easier to use.

The "Biographical Section" is unique among books of this type, giving sketches of world leaders in government, church, business, industry, and education. These brief biographies make the volume valuable long after the year is finished. The country and biographical information is both accurate and current; the book is a well-known source for political science research.

Because of the occasional stylistic problems and the relatively high purchase price, *The International Year Book and Statesman's Who's Who* may not be an ideal reference source for all libraries. The Board recommends this work for the core collection of academic libraries. —*S. C. A.*

Political Handbook of the World. Arthur S. Banks, ed. CSA Publications, annual. hard. 1 vol. 910 pp. illus. appendixes. indexes. ISBN 0-933199-05-8. $89.95. handbook.
JF37.P6 320.3

The *Political Handbook of the World* was first published in 1928 as *A Political Handbook of the World.* The book was edited by Malcolm W. Davis and Walter H. Mallory and was published by the Harvard and Yale University Presses for the Council on Foreign Relations. The years since have seen numerous changes in publishers and editors; CSA Publications took over in 1985. The current editor, Arthur S. Banks, is on the faculty of the political science department at the State University of New York at Binghamton. In addition to Banks and other editors mentioned on the title page, members of a panel of "area consultants" reviewed portions of the manuscript. Individual articles are unsigned.

The main portion of this annual handbook consists of an alphabetical arrangement of over 180 countries. This encompasses, with disclaimers, some less than fully independent nations, such as San Marino and the black homelands of South Africa, as well as entities without territory, such as the Palestine Liberation Organization. Under each country you will find the following listed: political status, area, population, urban centers, languages, money, and head of government. This list is followed by a general description of each country's government and political background, foreign affairs, political parties, legislature, news media, and intergovernmental and governmental representation.

Entries generally run 2,000 to 4,000 words. The descriptive sections are dense with factual information. For example, provided under "Government and Politics" is very detailed coverage of political events, leaders, and elections. Data on political parties consist of a general history of the nation's parties followed by history, leaders, and political stance. Some interpretation and discussion accompany the facts in each entry.

The second section of the book describes 110 world intergovernmental organizations that have permanent "means for implementing collective decisions." Founding date, purpose, location, officers, and recent activities are noted. Indexes to the handbook are for geographical and organizational names as well as personal names. Appendixes offer a chronology of world events, UN conferences, and memberships in UN agencies. A useful feature is the explanation in the preface that helps sort out the confusing array of transliterated and de-Westernized personal and place names.

The currency of this handbook is excellent. The 1989 edition is, with a few exceptions, updated to March 1989. Political developments through June 15, 1989, are included. For example, the May and June 1989 events in China and Tienanmen Square are reported. Every entry has changes since the 1988 edition. The content and scope of the handbook overlaps considerably with the World Encyclopedia of Political Systems & Parties. The latter covers electoral systems and individual parties more thoroughly but offers less background and currency.

The *Political Handbook of the World* is impressive for its collection of factual information and the well-written and interesting manner in which that information is presented. The handbook is geared to an academic and an educated public library audience. The Board recommends this work for the core collections of public and academic libraries. —*M. J. B.*

The Statesman's Year-Book: Statistical and Historical Annual of the States of the World. John Paxton, ed. St. Martin's, annual. hard. 1 vol. 1,691 pp. indexes. ISBN 0-312-03235-8. $65. yearbook.
JA51.S7 310.58

The Statesman's Year-Book is a compact, highly reliable manual describing each nation of the world and containing information on its history; area and population; climate; constitution and government; defense; economy, energy, and natural resources; industry and trade; communications; religion, education, and welfare; and diplomatic representatives. Macmillan (the British publisher) and St. Martin's Press (the U.S. publisher) are well-established companies with a reputation for accuracy and authority. The reliability of this work is further demonstrated by its lineage of one and a quarter centuries. The book itself is small, about

5-by-8 inches, with good-quality binding and small but clear print. A minor distraction is the very thin paper, which allows type on other pages to show through.

The *Year-Book* begins with 15 pages of tables and a chronology for the prior year; these are followed by "Part I: International Organizations" and "Part II: Countries of the World A–Z." Entries in the first part range from several paragraphs to several pages. In the second part, entries range from one-half page for Antarctic Territory to nearly 200 pages for the United States of America.

The text of the handbook is written in a terse but readable prose that is full of facts, names, places, and statistics. The bibliographies of statistical and other reference sources listed for each country are very useful. *The Statesman's Year-Book* is very easy to use and makes information on governments quick to locate. Three indexes—"Place and International Organizations Index," "Product Index," and "Name Index"—add to the easy accessibility of the information. Annual publication ensures the currency of the data, and accuracy is always a priority.

The Statesman's Year-Book is a one-of-a-kind source, the best-known, most frequently used reference source on countries and their governments. The Board recommends this work for the core collections of public, academic, and school libraries. —*S. C. A.*

World Encyclopedia of Political Systems & Parties, 2d edition. George E. Delury, ed. Facts On File, 1987. hard. 2 vols. 1,410 pp. illus. index. ISBN 0-8160-1539-2. $175. encyclopedia.
JF2011.67 324.2'02'02

George E. Delury of Stanford University edited not only the *World Encyclopedia of Political Systems & Parties* but also *Deadline Data on World Affairs* (1969–1972) and, from 1972 to 1980, THE WORLD ALMANAC AND BOOK OF FACTS (see Current Events). This is the second edition of the encyclopedia; the first edition was also edited by Delury and published by Facts On File in 1983. One hundred and forty-two contributors have signed entries in this edition.

The encyclopedia covers 170 countries and 8 dependent territories. Delury sees certain aspects of political systems as the important interacting elements. Each entry describes these elements—institutions of government (executive, legislative, and judicial branches; forms of regional and local government) and electoral systems (elections and their integrity, how winners are determined, party systems, opposition groups and other political forces). Individual parties are described in detail with history, organization, policy, membership, support, finances, and leadership. Each article concludes with a discussion of future political prospects and trends. Factual information and analysis and interpretation are presented.

Countries are arranged alphabetically; entries range from 500 to 15,000 words, but they typically run 2,000 to 4,000 words. Each entry includes a brief bibliography of further reading on the politics of the country. An index lists personal and organizational names plus a very limited number of subjects. A list of acronyms (mostly parties) completes the volumes.

This encyclopedia is written for a fairly sophisticated audience. The content level is most appropriate to university students, particularly graduate students. For instance, the introduction includes a lengthy and complex explanation of proportional representation. Its application in particular countries comes up under entries for several Western European democracies.

A major drawback of this source is its lack of currency. Information in the 1987 edition is, according to the introduction, current only as of summer to fall 1985. There were four years between the first two editions, but it is not clear if future editions are planned.

Although the *World Encyclopedia of Political Systems & Parties* and the POLITICAL HANDBOOK OF THE WORLD cover much of the same material, the encyclopedia does not include as much general background on countries or information on international organizations as the handbook does. Instead, the encyclopedia devotes greater space to covering issues and mechanisms in electoral systems and more thorough coverage of individual parties. Another source that concentrates solely on political parties is *Political Parties of the World,* edited by Alan J. Day (St. James, 1988). The Day title is now out-of-print.

The *World Encyclopedia of Political Systems & Parties* is an impressive collection of interesting information. The book is particularly noteworthy for its detail on parties and its commentary on electoral systems. The Board recommends this work for the core collection of academic libraries. —*M. J. B.*

United States

The Almanac of American Politics 1990. Michael Barone and Grant Ujifusa. National Journal, 1989. hard and soft. 1 vol. 1,500 pp. illus. index. ISBN 0-89234-043-6 (hard); 0-89234-044-4 (soft). $56.95 (hard); $44.95 (soft). almanac.
JK271.B343 328.73

Michael Barone, the principal author of *The Alma-*

nac of American Politics 1990, is a senior editorial writer for the *Washington Post* and a respected political analyst. For 20 years, he and Grant Ujifusa have been writing this perceptive and informative reference to the players, issues, and trends in national politics. Published in the years between congressional elections, *The Almanac* provides an overview of the national political scene, as determined by the most recent elections, and a forecast of political trends.

The basic format has remained intact over the years. This almanac's real strength rests in its authors' pithy analyses and commentaries on the political issues and trends in each state and congressional district. Each governor, representative, and senator is subjected to a nonpartisan analysis of his or her record, political background, and political interests. Information used to support the analysis of senators and representatives includes election results (primary and general), votes on recent key issues, ratings by interest groups, campaign contributions and expenditures, and the ratings by the *National Journal* itself.

The state and congressional district information is arranged in alphabetical order by state, with the congressional districts within each state arranged in numerical order by district. This arrangement facilitates use of the almanac, as does the index, which includes both subject and proper name entries.

The commentaries on the states are several pages long and are written in an engaging style, summarizing the economic, social, and cultural history of the state as well as its political background, issues, and trends. The writing, although nonpartisan, can be opinionated and hard-hitting. For example, New York Senator Alfonse D'Amato is described as "shrewd to the point of shamelessness in taking practically any position, espousing any cause, and lobbying for any project that could be popular with even the smallest segment of the New York electorate." The articles on each congressional district are considerably shorter but written in the same style. Demographic information is included for each state and congressional district.

Additional commentaries at the front of the volume describe and analyze the political climate for the nation, its regions, the House, the Senate, and the presidency. The almanac also includes valuable information on the changing demographics in the states and congressional districts and campaign finance information on each congressional member. *The Almanac of American Politics 1990* includes a listing of the governors and state congressional delegations for each state, rosters of congressional committees, and maps of the congressional districts. The Board recommends this work for the core collections of public and academic libraries. —*R. I.*

America Votes 18: A Handbook of Contemporary American Election Statistics. Richard M. Scammon and Alice V. McGillivray, eds. Congressional Quarterly, 1989. hard. 1 vol. 506 pp. illus. ISBN 0-87187-522-5. $95. handbook.
JK1967.A8 324.973

The *America Votes* series provides statistical information for U.S. presidential, gubernatorial, and congressional elections held in all 50 states and the District of Columbia. The data presented are not analyzed or discussed in a narrative format. As stated in the introduction, "The *America Votes* series draws from official state sources the raw material of American elections behavior." The aim is to build "a set of national reference volumes on American politics," and by presenting the "raw material" of election statistics in a simple format, the publisher has accomplished this goal.

This biennial publication presents tables of basic election statistics in a "state chapter system." This makes indexes and cross-references unnecessary. The contents list preceding the text guides the reader to page references for each state. Fifty-seven pages of tables precede the state profiles with national election information such as past election changes, special elections to Congress, presidential results from 1920 to 1988, the 1988 presidential primaries, and the presidential primaries from 1968 to 1984.

Statistics for each presidential election are listed in reverse chronological order (most recent to oldest). Electoral vote, total vote, and percentages for each major party are included among the various statistics. Brief summary votes precede the tables of presidential election statistics. The notes section, which accompanies the tables for each presidential election, contains relevant information about the election. For example, the notes for "President 1972" state that "In August 1974 President Nixon resigned and was succeeded by Vice President Ford." However, the notes are very brief and selective. They fail to cite important events, such as Vice-President Lyndon B. Johnson's succeeding the assassinated President John F. Kennedy, or Vice-President Harry S Truman's becoming president following the death of President Franklin D. Roosevelt.

The state chapters comprise over three-quarters of the text. Maps of congressional districts precede the tables in each state section. The maps incorporate changes implemented since the 1980 census, and the editors note in the general introduction that previous editions of *America Votes* should be consulted for earlier district boundaries and retrospective election results. (A future edition will reflect redistricting in response to the 1990 census.) The tables following the district maps arrange the data by county within each state. Tables of the statewide vote for president, governor, and senator since World War II precede general statistics in each state chapter. The notes at the end of each state chapter highlight the state's political environment and special elections. Large voting areas, such as New York City, Chicago, and Los Angeles, have separate data tables and individual district or ward maps that appear under the appropriate state chapter.

Although *America Votes* lacks information such as election results by gender, race, religion, or income, the timely publication of basic election statistics provides researchers with the raw data needed for further statistical analysis. The postwar statistics reprinted in each new volume of *America Votes* prove useful because the retrospective data as well as current election results are compiled in one volume. *America Votes* is a basic handbook containing the raw material of U.S. elections and therefore is very useful for ready-reference queries or patrons needing simple election statistics. The Board recommends this work for the core collections of public and academic libraries. —*L. C.*

American Leaders 1789–1987: A Biographical Summary. Colleen McGuiness and Maria J. Sayers, eds. Congressional Quarterly, 1987. hard. 1 vol. 427 pp. appendix. index. ISBN 0-87187-413-X. $22.95. handbook.
E176.A495 973.092′2

Congressional Quarterly is a prolific and respected publishing company and editorial research service. *American Leaders 1789–1987: A Biographical Summary* contains an amazingly broad collection of ephemera about U.S. presidents, vice-presidents, Supreme Court justices, members of Congress, and state governors. Although the material lends itself to browsing, the organization of the table of contents and the excellent index make its use as a ready-reference tool possible. Within this volume, leaders are organized according to office. Each leader is given a very brief entry that includes only the most rudimentary information.

In addition to biographies, interesting material abounds throughout the volume. For example, it is noted that the only time the Twenty-fifth Amendment was invoked was when Ronald Reagan underwent surgery to remove a cancerous polyp. George Bush (then the vice-president) served as acting president for seven hours. Other facts include the following: All presidents have been Caucasian males, and all but one have been married. Ronald Reagan has been the only divorced president. The president is generally of English, Scots, or Irish descent (Eisenhower was Swiss-German.) Only 16 chief justices have served in the history of the Supreme Court. Thirty vice-presidents served in Congress.

Elected officials do not remain in office beyond the length of their statutory tenure, so volumes of this type need to be supplemented with current data. For example, George Bush is now president, some of the state governors are no longer in office, and some members of Congress are new. Although several years have passed since the publication of this book, the material remains fresh and vital because of the depth and variety of the anecdotes and statistical analyses. The material in *American Leaders 1789–1987* is easily accessible to the general reader, and professional political scientists and students will have the skills to make minor statistical adjustments and amendments to the data to extract completely current material. The Board recommends this work for the core collections of public and academic libraries. —*D. J. C.*

The American Political Dictionary, 8th edition. Jack C. Plano and Milton Greenberg. Holt, Rinehart & Winston, 1989. soft. 1 vol. 608 pp. index. ISBN 0-03-022932-4. $20.75. dictionary.
JK9.P55 320.973′03′21

Jack C. Plano of Western Michigan University is a prolific and well-respected lexicographer in political science and public administration. Among his works are four editions of THE INTERNATIONAL RELATIONS DICTIONARY (a supplementary title) and two editions of THE PUBLIC ADMINISTRATION DICTIONARY (see Public Administration) as well as other dictionaries and monographs. Milton Greenberg, of American University, has been coauthor of all the editions of *The American Political Dictionary* (since the work first appeared in 1962). This book is sold only in paperback, and its binding is of marginal strength for reference use.

The American Political Dictionary "defines and discusses the significance of more than 1,200 terms, agencies, court cases and statutes that the authors consider most relevent for a basic comprehension of American government" (preface). The dictionary is selective, choosing those terms that are fundamental for beginning study in U.S. government and for an understanding of current events. Terms are organized into 14 broad topics, such as the "U.S. Constitution and Federal Union," "Legislative Process," "Public Administration," "Organization and Personnel," "Business and Labor," and "Foreign Policy and National Defense." Each category lists about 80 to 90 terms. These are further arranged, where applicable, into four groups: basic terminology, agencies, cases, and statutes.

Entries range from 100 to 400 words, with the text divided into two sections—definition and significance. The former is a concise, careful definition; the latter discusses terms "in the context of their relevance to historical events and to the contemporary political scene" (preface).

This dictionary was designed to be a study guide and a reference for political science definitions. As a study guide, the preface indicates that the dictionary reflects the organization of many U.S. political science texts. For this purpose, access is very direct and efficient. As a reference dictionary, the fairly complex subject arrangement (which requires a two-step process to look up a term) makes the book cumbersome. This disadvantage is offset by plentiful cross-references and a clear index to terms, names, organizations, cases, and statutes.

The American Political Dictionary maintains good currency. Although the seventh edition (1985) and eighth edition (1989) are virtually identical in organization and length, the preface notes the revision and updating of numerous entries and the addition of many newer terms. Updates are easy to spot while scanning the text; for example, a 1988 Supreme Court decision on federal taxation of state employees is discussed, as is the 1987 Iran-Contra investigation.

THE DORSEY DICTIONARY OF AMERICAN GOVERNMENT AND POLITICS offers many more definitions (more than 4,000) and up-to-date bibliographic references than does *The American Political Dictionary.* However, Plano and Greenberg cover their 1,200 selected terms with more depth than THE DORSEY DICTIONARY. The inclusion of "Significance" sections adds greatly to the value of *The American Political Dictionary,* particularly for undergraduate college students and high school students, who are its primary audience. The Board recommends this work for the core collections of public, academic, and school libraries.

—*M. J. B.*

Congress and the Nation. Congressional Quarterly, 1965–1985. hard. 6 vols. illus. appendix. index. ISBN 0-87187-334-6 (vol. 6). $120 per vol. handbook.
JK1051.C56 320.973

Congress and the Nation is a six-volume work spanning 40 years of reporting on public policy. Congressional Quarterly published the first volume of the series in 1965 with a 2,000-page reference book. Each succeeding volume covers a period that coincides with a four-year presidential term. (A new volume, covering 1985 to 1988, should be published soon.) The result is an encyclopedic but not pedantic chronicle of the actions of the members of the House of Representatives and the Senate and of the reigning administration.

Readers are given an overview of the four-year period, including its significant events. Detailed chronologies of government action appear in every major subject area. A summary table of contents is provided for overall organization, but a more detailed table of contents follows each chapter, with a listing of all stories contained within that chapter. There is a legislative summary of each session of Congress. For example, volume 6 begins with a summary of the period that is informative for both the lay reader and professional researcher. "The 97th and 98th Congresses" may mean little to the reader, but the editor's summary reminds us that they "chronicle an upheaval in governmental policy as dramatic as any since the great Depression of the 30s." This period saw Reagan call for deep cuts in federal domestic spending, an unprecedented peacetime military buildup, and measures taken to ensure the financial stability of the ailing Social Security system. There is a discussion of the 1982 and 1984 elections and a final chapter on Reagan's relations with Congress. An appendix follows.

Good formatting and featured discussions have made the legislative actions of Congress come alive. The format lends itself to easy access, and the material is discussed in topical essays, such as "El Salvador Aid" and "U.S.-Vatican Relations." There is also a discussion of the Korean airliner that allegedly went down over Soviet airspace and of the Grenada invasion.

Each volume contains special reports on topics of particular concern as well as tables with the key votes in both Senate and House. There are no apparent errors or inconsistencies in the material. Congressional Quarterly has produced an accurate and extensive listing. *Congress and the Nation* lists the members of Congress and governors of each state. The Board recommends this work for the core collections of public, academic, and school libraries. —*D. J. C.*

Congressional Quarterly Alamanac. Christine C. Lawrence, ed. Congressional Quarterly, annual. hard. 1 vol. 1,000 pp. illus. appendixes. indexes. ISBN 0-87187-507-1. $195. almanac.
JK1.C66 328.73

Congressional Quarterly is a distinguished publisher of information on the U.S. government. Its reference works are noted for their accuracy and objectivity. The *Congressional Quarterly Almanac* is an annual compendium of information on the most recently completed congressional session. This almanac is complemented by other Congressional Quarterly publications, several of which are reviewed in this guide. Libraries wanting information on the current congressional session should consider subscribing to the periodical, *CQ Weekly Report.*

The first chapter of the almanac is devoted to congressional organization, such as the selection of congressional leaders, campaign finance reform, congressional ethics, and trends in congressional membership. The rest of the chapters are devoted to legislative activity within different subject areas, such as "Agriculture Policy," "Economic Policy," and "Foreign Policy." Under each subject, specific legislation is followed through the legislative process with reference made to key players in the process. Included with the legislative summaries and analysis are sidebars and charts that provide background information on the issue. For example, in the 1988 volume, the text on savings and loan legislation is accompanied by two sidebars. One explains the nature of the problems confronting the industry; the other, a chart, indicates the number of savings and loan failures over the past several years.

The appendixes are loaded with information, including a complete record of all roll call votes for the session and an analysis of each member's voting pattern as determined by party loyalty, support of presidential position, and the ratings of interest groups. The appendixes also include the text of presidential messages to Congress, including veto messages, as well as short summaries of all the public laws enacted during the session. Other information included in the appendixes varies from year to year but includes things such as federal election results, the text of presidential debates, and summaries of U.S. Supreme Court decisions.

The table of contents provides a detailed listing of the subject matter included within each chapter. A general index includes subject and proper name entries and covers information in the appendixes as well as the text chapters. The legislative activities of members can be traced using the index. A separate subject index is inserted for the roll call vote appendix.

Scholars may find the voting data and the complete text of major documents of more value than the legislative summaries, but *Congressional Quarterly Almanac* is a useful addition to the collection. The Board recommends this work for the core collections of public and academic libraries. *—R. I.*

Congressional Quarterly's Guide to U.S. Elections, 2d edition. Congressional Quarterly, 1985. hard. 1 vol. 1,308 pp. illus. appendixes. indexes. ISBN 0-87187-339-7. $110. guide.
JK1967.C662 324.973

Congressional Quarterly's Guide to U.S. Elections is a massive compilation of presidential, gubernatorial, and congressional election returns from 1789 through 1984. All election data, unless otherwise noted in the text, are taken from the Inter-University Consortium for Political and Social Research (ICPSR), located in Ann Arbor, Michigan. Basic voting statistics are presented for each candidate. The election data are not analyzed or interpreted for the reader, and the election results are not tabulated by race, gender, age, or income. The editors improved the second edition of the guide by offering additional appendixes and expanding the indexes. Various maps and charts assist in the interpretation of the data. The visual aids and the narrative discussions make this reference tool more than just a compilation of useful election statistics.

The data are organized into six parts; each part contains narrative discussions of the data as well as extensive bibliographies. The six parts are as follows: "Political Parties," "Presidential Elections," "Gubernatorial Elections," "Senate Elections," "House Elections," and "Southern Primaries." "Political Parties" is a narrative that traces the development of the U.S. political party system from 1789 through the evolution of national party conventions. Parts 2 through 6 also contain narrative descriptions of the U.S. electoral process; however, the election data are the main focus throughout these sections.

"Presidential Elections" presents explanations of the electoral college and presidential primaries. Maps outline the electoral votes for all U.S. presidential elections from 1789 through 1984, and visual aids, such as a chart listing all the presidents and vice-presidents, are also included in this section.

Parts 3 through 6 follow a similar format. The first section begins with a narrative introduction tracing historical developments and concludes with an extensive bibliography. In addition to the basic election statistics, each part also contains chapters listing the popular vote returns. Maps of congressional districts are conspicuously missing from the guide. Although part 5 does list election returns numerically by district, without the aid of a district map, determining the size or location of a voting district within any given state is impossible. A narrative explanation of the redistricting procedures is presented in this section, but district maps would have been a welcome addition for many researchers.

Twelve appendixes follow the main text of the guide and provide useful information, such as "Sessions of Congress, 1789–1985," "Summary of American Presidential Elections, 1860–1984," "United States Census of Population, 1790–1980," and "Political Party Abbreviations." An interesting appendix entitled "Immigrants by Country, 1820–1980" lists statistics of annual immigration to the United States from major countries throughout the world.

The indexes are divided into two basic categories: candidate indexes and a general index. The eight candidate indexes list the names and years of candidacy for each candidate; each of these indexes is devoted to a specific type of office. The general index contains listings by subject and by candidate, except for the popular vote returns that are listed separately in the candidate indexes. This is a useful format for those seeking information about a candidate who participated in multiple elections throughout his or her lifetime. For example, Ronald Reagan's candidacy in California's gubernatorial race and later in the presidential race are both listed in the general index under his name as well as in the presidential and gubernatorial candidate indexes.

One feature that separates this guide from other election statistics sources such as AMERICA VOTES 18: A HANDBOOK OF CONTEMPORARY AMERICAN ELECTION STATISTICS is the comprehensive nature of the data. Whereas AMERICA VOTES is a biennial publication containing postwar election statistics, *Congressional Quarterly's Guide to U.S. Elections* contains both current and historical election statistics. All election statistics in *Congressional Quarterly's Guide to U.S. Elections*—including the presidential electoral votes and the popular returns for all presidential, gubernatorial, and congressional elections—are presented in an organized format. The narrative explanations and the comprehensive treatment of U.S. election returns are useful. The Board recommends this work for the core collections of public and academic libraries.

—L. C.

The Dorsey Dictionary of American Government and Politics. Jay M. Shafritz. Brooks/Cole, 1988; distrib. by Wadsworth. hard and soft. 1 vol. 661 pp. illus. appendixes. index. ISBN 0-256-05639-0 (hard); 0-256-05589-0 (soft). $40 (hard); $21.75 (soft). dictionary.
JK9.S42 320.973′03

The Dorsey Dictionary of American Government and Politics is a single-volume work that is republished frequently to reflect the most recent terms and concepts of the U.S. government. Libraries that have older versions will find most of the material accurate and timely; however, recent cases and political terms may be lacking. The presidency, Congress, and the court system are represented, as are terms used in foreign policy, public administration, political economy, and taxation.

Jay M. Shafritz has written a number of other texts including THE FACTS ON FILE DICTIONARY OF PUBLIC ADMINISTRATION (see Public Administration). Shafritz was the director of the Executive Development Program at the Johnson Space Center from 1980 to 1986. In *The Dorsey Dictionary of American Government and Politics,* he has written an easily understood reference work for those who seek information on national, state, or local government and politics.

The dictionary is well organized, with a detailed section on "How to Use This Book" that explains ways of finding information depending on the facts the reader knows. The entries are arranged in alphabetical order that, as the editor notes, allows quick comparisons of terms with the same root. A list of key concepts in one of the five appendixes can also be used to locate important ideas or terms.

There is good cross-referencing, and citations of bibliographic sources are given for further study of individual entries. The actual case citations are given for legal decisions, which makes looking up the original case much easier; many lay texts neglect to give these legal details. Addresses are provided with the entries where appropriate. For example, the entry for the *American Political Science Association* includes both a current address and the journals published under the auspices of the association.

An interesting feature of this dictionary is the addition of black-and-white political cartoons and photographs that add visual interest and edify the reader. Inset quotations also add interest and make the dictionary a pleasure to browse. For example, readers will find Henry David Thoreau's defense of anarchism from "On the Duty of Civil Disobedience" on page 25.

Entries are written to be accessible to readers of differing political sophistication. Some entries have short definitions, whereas others require more elaboration. Regardless of the length, all entries are appropriate in style and accurate. Therefore, a simple entry such as *paper tiger* contains only a brief definition with no citations: "A Chinese expression for someone or some institution that is not as strong or powerful as appearances or reputation would suggest." More complicated concepts are defined at greater length, and definitions contain enough bibliographic annotations that the reader can explore additional avenues of scholarship. For example, the entry for *Pareto optimality* in *The Dorsey Dictionary of American Government and Politics* provides the definition "an equilibrium point in a society when resource allocation is most efficient; that is, no further changes in resource allocation can be made that will increase the welfare of one person without decreasing the welfare of other persons." Two journal references follow the definition.

The Board recommends this work for the core collection of academic libraries. —*D. J. C.*

Encyclopedia of American Political History: Studies of the Principal Movements and Ideas. Jack P. Greene, ed. Scribner, 1984. hard. 3 vols. index. ISBN 0-684-17003-5 (set). $250 (set). encyclopedia.
E183.E5 320.973′03′21

The *Encyclopedia of American Political History: Studies of the Principal Movements and Ideas* provides a broad overview of U.S. political philosophy, its movements and thoughts. The encyclopedia contains 90 articles of topical interest on subjects ranging from the American Revolution to the women's rights movement. Although several of the essays focus on documents of historical interest such as the Federalist Papers, the Constitution, and the Declaration of Independence, most center on major issues or themes. "Church and State," "Civil Disobedience," and "Ethnic Movements" are a few of the topics covered.

The authors represent a broad range of ideological and historical points of view; this was the deliberate intent of the editor. Each author is identified as a scholar within his or her field and is affiliated with a major academic institution. Each one has been encouraged to apply a personal interpretation to the assigned subject. The result is an eminently readable series of pithy articles, which should provide both students and lay readers with material for further discussion and thought. For example, Roderick Nash from the University of California at Santa Barbara comments in his article on conservation that, although the first settlers found billions of passenger pigeons in the Ohio Valley, "in 1914 the nation received the almost unbelievable news that the last passenger pigeon, a female dubbed Martha, had died quietly in the Cincinnati zoo." Writing on the subject of women's rights, Carol Ruth Berkin of Baruch College comments that an early crusader argued that "the only real basis for female emancipation was financial independence, not political suffrage."

The list of contents is contained only in the first volume of the three-volume set, which occasionally makes for difficult use of the other two volumes. This drawback should not discourage most users. The bibliography after each multipage article contains convenient cross-referencing to related articles within the encyclopedia.

The encyclopedia is appropriate for those who are familiar with political science as well as those who are taking introductory courses in political thought. The topics in *Encyclopedia of American Political History* have been selected by the editor and are remarkably germane to students of current affairs. For instance, a newspaper article on the boycott of the International AIDS Conference by those protesting the immigration policy for people who test positive for HIV will be placed in historical context by reading Victor Greene's text on immigration policy. The Board recommends this work for the core collections of public, academic, and school libraries. —*D. J. C.*

Encyclopedia of the American Constitution. Leonard W. Levy, ed. in chief. Macmillan, 1986. hard. 4 vols. 2,196 pp. appendixes. indexes. ISBN 0-02-918610-2. $400 (set). encyclopedia.
KF4548.E53 342.73′023′03

See Law.

Politics in America: 1990, the 101st Congress. Phil Duncan, ed. Congressional Quarterly, 1989. hard. 1 vol. 1,700 pp. illus. index. ISBN 0-87187-508-X. $59.95. handbook.
JK1010.P64 328.73′073′025

As its name suggests, Congressional Quarterly is one of the primary publishers of materials about the U.S. Congress and government. *Politics in America: 1990, the 101st Congress* is its most recent compilation of profiles of the men and women of Congress. The single volume also includes information about the governor of each state, statistics relevant to each state, and a map of congressional districts within each state. The material is written by the staff of *Congressional Quarterly,* led by a seasoned editor from four previous editions.

Although the book is adequately bound for service over the intended life of the volume, the heavy cloth covers of larger (and perhaps more venerable) encyclopedia sets are more serviceable. The handbook is attractively covered and almost jaunty, as if to suggest that politics need not be exclusively the province of academicians.

The text also reflects this almost-populist attitude. The profiles of politicians are accurate but are full of colorful incidents rather than being terse biographies. "This book is chock full of stories about headstrong members who never met a clash of wills they didn't like," says editor Phil Duncan in the introduction. The book reveals the human dimension of politics. In describing New Jersey Senator Bill Bradley's fight for his tax reform idea in the mid-1980s, the text supplements descriptions of Bradley's plan and his efforts at coalition building with a note on the more personal approach he took to selling his plan: "Bradley backed up his tireless public advocacy with some private persuasion of the good-old-boy sort that is rare for him—playing basketball with House members."

Black-and-white photographs of some of the senators and governors are included. The statistics are presented accurately and interestingly. The reading level of the book is lively and acceptable for a general audience, and information, which is arranged by state, is easy to find.

Two special features also make *Politics in America: 1990, the 101st Congress* a valuable asset to the reference collection. The first is a pronunciation guide for Congress to help the reader with "some of the most-often-mispronounced names of members of Congress." The other is a table revealing the few House elections in 1988 that were close calls. The Board recommends this work for the core collection of academic libraries.
—*D. J. C.*

The United States Government Manual. U.S. G.P.O., annual. (1935–). soft. 1 vol. 914 pp. illus. appendixes. indexes. SuDoc. GS 4.109 1989/90. $21. manual.
JK421.A3

The United States Government Manual, the official handbook of the federal government, is published annually by the Office of the Federal Register as a special edition of its daily publication, the *Federal Register.* The manual serves as both a directory to government officials and as a brief guide to the three main branches of the government and its many departments, agencies, and quasi-official agencies. In addition to guiding users through the complex maze of the federal government, the manual also contains other useful information such as the text of the Declaration of Independence, plus the U.S. Constitution and its amendments. This is a basic reference tool providing information not readily available from other commercially published directories.

The manual presents basic information about the structure and organization of the government and the elected officials and personnel who keep the federal wheels turning. The legislative, judicial, and executive branches are listed near the beginning of the manual. Charts outlining the organizational structure of the Senate, House of Representatives, and the Executive Office of the President assist readers in comprehending the interrelationships among the various committees and offices.

The sections for the three branches of the government are followed by listings for agencies; departments; independent establishments and government corporations; boards, committees, and commissions; quasi-official agencies; and selected multilateral and bilateral organizations. In addition to including telephone numbers and addresses, "a typical agency description includes a list of principal officials, a summary statement of the agency's purpose and role in the Federal Government, a brief history of the agency, including its legislative or executive authority, a description of its programs and activities, and a 'Sources of Information' section" (preface). Many entries also contain organizational charts depicting the hierarchy of the agency or department.

The summary statements and condensed histories are very useful to students who need background information about a department or agency for a research paper. Most useful to the general public, perhaps, are the "Sources of Information" entries. These provide information about consumer-related activities. For example, telephone numbers are listed for citizens interested in bidding on government contracts. Additional listings in these entries include information about employee recruitment for the agency, major publications issued by the agency, and the availability of reading rooms for the public.

The length of each entry varies depending on the size and activities of the department, agency, or administration. Most entries average about one or two text pages, with department descriptions generally longer than descriptions of divisions within departments. Each description includes the Washington, D.C., address and telephone number. Wherever possible, local, district, or regional offices are also listed. For example, the entry for the Department of Veterans Affairs includes a listing of the national office and the facilities and offices located throughout the 50 states.

The manual contains four appendixes: "Standard Federal Regions," "Commonly Used Abbreviations and Acronyms," "Terminated and Transferred Agencies," and an alphabetical listing of "Agencies Appearing in the *Code of Federal Regulations.*" A list of "Recent Changes" follows the indexes. This list cites personnel amendments to the main text of the manual.

The two indexes are useful but somewhat limited. The "Name Index" provides access to all officials listed throughout the manual. The "Agency/Subject Index" is a general index to the entire manual except the appendixes. The major flaw with the "Agency/Subject Index" is its limited use of cross-references. For example, a user looking for information about the Federal Bureau of Investigation will not find listings under "FBI" or under "Federal." Instead, the FBI is indexed solely under *Investigation, Federal Bureau of.* A more liberal use of "see" and "see also" references would greatly enhance the accessibility of this index.

The United States Government Manual is a handy reference tool for users seeking information about the federal government and its many affiliated agencies. This U.S. Government Printing Office publication not only acts as a directory of government officials but also serves as a pathfinder through the increasingly complex hierarchy of federal government agencies. The Board recommends this work for the core collections of public, academic, and school libraries. —*L. C.*

Who's Who in American Politics: 1989–1990, 12th edition. Bowker, 1989. hard. 1 vol. 1,936 pp. index. ISBN 0-8352-2577-1. $174.95. handbook.
E176.W6424 920

Who's Who in American Politics contains brief bibliographic sketches of individuals currently participating in politics at local, state, and national levels. The book is updated frequently, and biographees who were included in previous editions may update their profiles by adding current data. Information, therefore, is continually revised and can be presumed to be both current and accurate. In this edition, 1,787 new individuals were listed out of a total of 24,561 bibliographic entries.

Students and researchers seeking home addresses, political or religious affiliations, names of children, or birth dates of prominent political figures will find them within this single, compact volume, although each entry may have some of the categories deleted. For instance, Michael Dukakis has not listed his religion but has listed his legal and mailing addresses, whereas Ronald Reagan lists himself as "Christian" but has not included his legal address and may be contacted through Fox Plaza in Los Angeles. Length of entry is likewise variable. Dukakis has only a brief entry, but lesser political figures such as March Fong Eu (secretary of state of California) and Guy Havard Raner, Jr. (a member of the San Fernando Valley Democratic Executive Committee), have provided a much fuller account of their respective accomplishments.

The volume also contains current lists of governmental officials. Members of the presidential cabinet, state delegations to Congress, governors of the states, and state party chairpersons are all included in lists for ready reference. An index provides access to bibliographical listings, which are organized by state. *Who's Who in American Politics* is accessible for the general reader, although to understand profiles users will probably need to refer to the list of abbrevations, which appears before the entries.

The possibility of misstatement of facts is always a problem in books of this type, which rely to a great extent on information provided by the biographees themselves. Readers can presume that the information in *Who's Who in American Politics* is primarily accurate but possibly self-serving. Reporters and others seeking to document individual statements may want to consult several sources. The publishers have made every attempt to be accurate with the materials given to them. The Board recommends this work for the core collection of academic libraries. —*D. J. C.*

Supplementary Titles

General

The Facts On File World Political Almanac. Chris Cook, comp. Facts On File, 1989. hard. 1 vol. 453 pp. index. ISBN 0-8160-1377-2. $40. handbook.
D843 909.82

"The author's aim [in *The Facts On File World Political Almanac*], as stated in the preface, is to 'assemble . . . as many of the key facts and figures as possible on the major political developments of the postwar world.' Since it was impossible to be comprehensive, he concentrates on 'countries and events for which the reader is most likely to require information.' Countries that the author did not consider important enough to get separate entries include Guyana, Iceland, Kenya, and Lebanon, but some information can be found on them using the index. For the countries he deems important, Cook lists in separate chapters the heads of state since 1945, a description of the legislatures and constitutions, treaties and other diplomatic agreements, political parties, elections, population, and urbanization statistics and trends. If all this information had been grouped together by country, the *Almanac* would have been more useful as a ready-reference source.

"Other chapters cover international political organizations and civil conflicts. Also included are a chronology of the nuclear age, a dictionary of political events, and a biographical dictionary.

"The chapter on wars and civil strife is a good summary of . . . [the] world since 1945. For each event the combatants, key dates, and casualties are included. In addition, the chronology on the nuclear age is an important aspect of the book. There is a table comparing the U.S. and Soviet nuclear arsenals and the number of nuclear explosions by country and year since 1945. Included also are lists of bilateral and multilateral agreements, with a table of countries and whether they adhere to a particular multilateral agreement." (*BL,* June 1, 1989, p. 1705)

"This handbook conveniently consolidates many useful facts into one volume at a very reasonable price. . . . It is unique in its specialized chronologies of international and civil conflicts, acts of terrorism, nuclear events, and heads of state." (*LJ,* April 15, 1989, p. 66)

Also reviewed in: *Choice,* July 1989, p. 1809; *R & R Bk N,* April 1989, p. 4.

Board's recommendation: Public and academic libraries.

Information Sources of Political Science, 4th edition. Frederick L. Holler. ABC-Clio, 1986. hard. 1 vol. 417 pp. indexes. ISBN 0-87436-375-6. $79. bibliography.
Z7161.H64 016.32

"Updating the 1981 edition of this detailed, descriptive inventory of reference sources, this fourth edition [of *Information Sources of Political Science*] contains 2,423 annotated citations. . . . This represents an increase of almost 700 citations from the previous edition. . . . The typology index is completely new to this edition; it identifies reference sources by their genre (abstracts, bibliographies, directories, encyclopedias, etc.). . . . [This] is an essential purchase for academic libraries supporting graduate studies in political science and high level undergraduate work in the field; it is also indispensable for large public library research collections. Libraries serving graduate students in librarianship/information science will also find this a very useful reference tool. Because of the increased coverage in this latest edition and the inclusion of a typology index, those libraries owning previous editions of the guide should replace them with the fourth edition." (*BL,* December 15, 1986, p. 634)

Also reviewed in: *ARBA,* 1987, p. 266; *CRL,* January 1987, p. 69.

Board's recommendation: Academic libraries.

The International Relations Dictionary, 4th edition. Jack C. Plano and Roy Olton. ABC-Clio, 1988. hard and soft. 1 vol. 446 pp. index. ISBN 0-87436-477-9 (hard); 0-87436-478-7 (soft). $49 (hard); $24 (soft). dictionary.
JX1226.P55 327.0321

"The arrangement of the fourth edition of [*The International Relations Dictionary*] is the same as the earlier edition. Within subject chapters (e.g., 'International Law,' 'Diplomacy'), the 570 numbered entries are arranged alphabetically. Each has a definition paragraph, followed by a paragraph headed Significance. . . . The preface notes that the fourth edition has 34 new entries, the definitions and Significance paragraphs have been expanded and updated, and a number of national (as distinct from international) political system entries have been deleted. [There is] a new alphabetical 'Guide to Major Concepts' at the beginning of the book. . . . [The index lists] concepts, personalities, documents, activities, and nations or regions.

"The fourth edition of this important work has clear definitions of Gorbachevism, New International Economic Order, and New World Information and Communication Order. Although the work contains separate entries on the League of Nations and Central Treaty Organization (both of historical interest only), there are no entries on the Islamic Revolution, Iran's role in world terrorism, or the international arms trade, although information on these topics can be found within other entries. Neither South Africa nor the Republic of South Africa are in the index of the 'Guide to Major Concepts,' although there is the entry *Apartheid.* Despite these shortcomings, the latest edition of this standard work will again prove useful in [many] libraries." (*BL,* October 1, 1988, p. 241)

Also reviewed in: *ARBA,* 1989, p. 273.

Board's recommendation: Academic libraries.

United States

The Book of the States. Jack L. Gardner, ed. Council of State Governments, biennial. hard. 1 vol. 734 pp. index. ISBN 0-87292-955-8. $42.50. yearbook.
JK2403.B7243 353.9

"This biennial publication [*The Book of the States*] of the Council of State Governments, which conducts research on state programs and problems, presents information on the structures, working methods, financing, and functional activities of state governments.

"Social welfare researchers will find useful data on human services such as aid to families with dependent children, general assistance, public health, education, housing, and development." (*RSR,* Spring 1986, p. 45)

"The material is arranged in nine sections: Intergovernmental Affairs; Legislation, Elections and Constitutions; The Governors and the Executive Branch; the Legislatures; The Judiciary; Administration; Finances; Major State Services; and the State Pages. This final section presents select information on each of the states and territories: chief officials, a few key statistics, state motto, etc.; directories of state officials are published as separate supplements.

"Typically, each section is subdivided by specific topic; each subdivision has an introductory article followed by tables. Many of the articles, such as those on state-local relations, the legal status of women, postsecondary education, and consumer protection, are recurring features. Special feature articles in this edition include discussions of reapportionment, state aid for victims of mental illness and developmental disabilities, and 50-year reviews of constitutional revisions and state government finances. Contributors include council staff, staff of such kindred organizations as the Advisory Commission on Intergovernmental Relations, and officials from various state governments. The volume ends with a short Author Index and a Subject Index.

"*The Book of the States* provide[s] a wealth of data and timely analysis regarding the other 50 partners in our federal system of government. Few collections of any size can afford to be without this unique information source." (*BL,* September 15, 1983, p. 148)

Also reviewed in: *ARBA,* 1977, p. 256; 1979, p. 262; 1988, p. 286; *RSR,* January 1981, p. 89; *Ser Lib 2nd,* 1985, p. 263.

Board's recommendation: Public and academic libraries.

Congressional Quarterly's Guide to the U.S. Supreme Court, 2d edition. Elder Witt. Congressional Quarterly, 1990. hard. 1 vol. 1,060 pp. illus. indexes. ISBN 0-87187-502-0. $149. encyclopedia.
JK1571.C65 347.73

See Law.

Current American Government. Congressional Quarterly, biennial. soft. 1 vol. illus. ISBN 0-87187-551-9. $11.95. yearbook.
JK1.C14 320.9'73'092

Current American Government provides "the standard information on who holds which federal position [and] also numerous articles on various issues before Congress and the nation. . . . The Electoral College is described as it operates today and the suggested reforms of the system are analyzed.

"In addition to the sections on politics, there is discussion of the presidency, the Congress and the judiciary lobbies (with various of the more powerful ones thoroughly probed), and articles on federal-state relations.

"Handy as a research tool, it also has a lot of fascinating 'inside'-type information." (*NCR,* June 1971, p. 355)

Articles discuss "various attempts [by Congress] to reform the seniority system and change the practice of committee secrecy as well as of congressional proposals regarding the federal budget. Decisions handed down by the Supreme Court are assessed and the role of lobbyists is also described. A glossary of congressional terms, the U.S. Constitution, and related materials [are] appended." (*BL,* December 1, 1973, p. 356)

Board's recommendation: Academic libraries.

The State and Local Government Political Dictionary. Jeffrey M. Elliot and Sheikh R. Ali. ABC-Clio, 1988. hard and soft. 1 vol. 325 pp. index. ISBN 0-87436-417-5 (hard); 0-87436-512-0 (soft). $49 (hard); $19.95 (soft). dictionary.
JK2408.E44 353.9'03

"This new title [*The State and Local Government Political Dictionary*] in the ABC-Clio Dictionaries in Political Science series is arranged in the same format as previous titles, i.e., with definition and significance paragraphs for each term. The authors (members of the faculty of North Carolina Central University) have a combined total of 20 years of study, research, and teaching of state and local government.

"The work is divided into 11 subject chapters, with the 290 entries arranged alphabetically within them. Representative chapter headings are 'The Judicial Branch,' 'Cities and Metropolitan Areas,' and 'Financing State and Local Government.' *See Also* references are noted at the end of each entry. Five pages of notes at the end of the volume document direct quotations in the entries and serve as a bibliography. Works cited are current through 1987. A 14-page index provides further access for users.

"The entries provide clear explanations that will be helpful for a wide range of users. In some instances, examples of the term or the pros and cons of the topic are explored, thus providing the user with a good perspective beyond a straight definition. However, some of the topics covered are also in another recent ABC-Clio title . . . although the text is unique in each book.

"For libraries where users need special access to state and local government terms, this new work will be helpful." (*BL,* January 15, 1989, p. 852)

"Arrangement by chapters (intergovernmental relations, constitutions, finance, cities) allows . . . [this book] to serve as a reference/study guide. Lengthy entries are supported by a clear index. Comparison with Jack Plano and Milton Greenberg's *American Political Dictionary* (Holt, 1985) reveals extensive overlap, but this book explains terms at more length and provides some unique information. [This work is recommended] for . . . libraries with a political science or public administration concentration." (*LJ,* February 15, 1988)

Also reviewed in: *ARBA,* 1989, p. 258; *Choice,* January 1989, p. 780; *R & R Bk N,* June 1988, p. 14.

Board's recommendation: Academic libraries.

New and Noteworthy

American National Election Studies Data Sourcebook, 1952–1986. Warren E. Miller and Santa Traugott. Harvard, 1989. hard. 1 vol. 375 pp. ISBN 0-674-02636-5. $35. bibliography.
JK1967.M54 324.973′092

"[*American National Election Studies Data Sourcebook, 1952–1986*] is a revised and updated edition of a book first published in 1980. . . . The authors state in the introduction that 'elections are best understood in a historical context,' and the statistics have been compiled 'to enhance the understanding of individual elections and . . . to provide a basis for broader generalizations about post-World War II American politics.' This volume, with more than 550 tables of statistics, will aid political scientists in understanding American elections and the electorate.

"The first six chapters cover . . . social characteristics of the electorate, party identification, positions on public policy issues, support of the political system, involvement and turnout, and the vote. The seventh chapter . . . contains data on citizens' reactions to Congress and their representatives. The statistics for this chapter cover the last five congressional election years, 1978–86." (*BL,* December 15, 1989, p. 851)

The Arms Control, Disarmament, and Military Security Dictionary. ABC-Clio, 1989. hard and soft. 1 vol. ISBN 0-87436-430-2 (hard); 0-87436-532-5 (soft). $49 (hard); $19.95 (soft). dictionary.
JX1974.E45 327.174032

The Arms Control, Disarmament, and Military Security Dictionary "contains 268 definitions for treaties, laws, organizations, and terms like *domino theory* and *stealth aircraft.* Each entry is in two parts: a definition and a significance paragraph. [This book] is recommended for many libraries." (*BL,* September 15, 1989, p. 202)

Beacham's Guide to Key Lobbyists: An Analysis of Their Issues and Impact. Walton Beacham et al., eds. Beacham Publishing, 1989. hard. 1 vol. 632 pp. illus. index. ISBN 0-933833-13-X. $95. directory.
JK1118.B3924 328.73′078

"The judicial, executive, and legislative branches of our government are elected or appointed to interpret, create, and amend the laws of our land. However, there is an unofficial, yet very influential, and often invisible fourth branch of government: lobbyists.

"[In *Beacham's Guide to Key Lobbyists*] . . . Beacham has selected 125 men and women whom he considers to be the most effective and influential lobbyists on Capitol Hill. Each profile is accompanied by a black-and-white photograph and begins with address, telephone and fax numbers, issue specialties, clients, party affiliation, and when applicable, political action committee (PAC) name for the organization the individual represents. . . . This information is followed by a three- to four-page narrative that provides a history of the lobbying activities of the person and his or her association, an association/organization/firm profile, and background and personal information on the lobbyist. . . . Coverage is balanced. For example, lobbyists representing both sides of abortion and gun control are included.

"[This book] shows how one part of our political system works." (*BL,* October 1, 1989, pp. 387–388)

Biographical Directory of the United States Congress, 1774–1989, 15th edition. U.S.G.P.O., 1989. hard. 1 vol. 2,104 pp. ISBN 052-071-00699-1. $82. biographical source.
JK1010.U5 973.3′12

"This bicentennial edition [of the *Biographical Directory of the United States Congress, 1774–1989*] is the most complete and up-to-date source for biographical information on the more than 11,000 men and women who have served in Congress.

"[This book] . . . is in two sections: a preliminary and a biographical section. The preliminary section includes a complete listing of all the members of each presidential cabinet through Reagan's second administration, the membership and leadership of the Continental Congress and the first 100 congresses, and a one-page table showing congressional apportionment for the first 20 censuses. The tabular information is preceded by an excellent introduction on the history and publication of this work. . . . The biographical section, which comprises about three-quarters of the book is arranged alphabetically by the individual's surname. . . .

"All GPO depository libraries have received a copy of this title whether they selected it or not. The *Biographical Directory of the United States Congress, 1774–1989* is a one-of-a-kind biographical reference source, and all public and academic libraries will want it in their reference collections." (*BL,* October 1, 1989, pp. 388–389)

Congressional Quarterly's Guide to the Presidency.

Michael Nelson, ed. Congressional Quarterly, 1989. hard. 1 vol. 1,521 pp. illus. index. ISBN 0-87187-500-4. $145. encyclopedia.
JK516.C57 353.0313

"The publication of *Congressional Quarterly's Guide to the Presidency* completes CQ's in-depth coverage of the three branches of the U.S. government. . . . [This book] explains 'the origins, evolution, and contemporary workings of the most important office of the U.S. political system' and is written with the average reader in mind.

"The *Guide* presents in seven parts all aspects of the presidency and its relationship to other individuals, departments, agencies, and branches of government, covering such topics as the origins of the presidency, selection and removal of the president, and presidential powers. . . . [Those] libraries wanting the most complete and authoritative publication on the office of the presidency will want to purchase [this book]." (*BL*, May 1, 1990, p. 1727)

The Electoral Politics Dictionary. ABC-Clio, 1989. hard and soft. 1 vol. ISBN 0-87436-517-1 (hard); 0-87436-518-X (soft). $49 (hard); $19.95 (soft). dictionary.
JK1971.R46 324.70973

"[*The Electoral Politics Dictionary*] . . . contains definitions for more than 400 terms, court cases, and associations arranged in seven topical chapters covering the mass media, political campaigns, interest groups, etc. [The book is recommended for many libraries.]" (*BL*, September 15, 1989, p. 202)

Political Resource Directory. Carol Hess Assoc., 1989. soft. 1 vol. 496 pp. illus. index. ISBN 0-944320-01-5. $95. directory.
JK2283.P65

"The official directory of the American Association of Political Consultants, this 1989 edition [of the *Political Resource Directory*] is the organization's first nationwide listing of its 250 members and 2,950 other individuals and organizations who specialize in political campaign management, media production, telemarketing, fundraising, direct mail, legal services, and other related services. . . . No other directory covers all the various services listed here. . . . This would be an excellent one-stop source for political candidates and their campaign staffs, but . . . probably is only affordable to large public libraries or those with a specific need." (*LJ*, July 1989, p. 73)

U.S. Government: A Resource Book for Secondary Schools. Mary Jane Turner and Sara Lake. ABC-Clio, 1989. hard. 1 vol. 317 pp. index. ISBN 0-87436-535-X. $35. encyclopedia.
JK38.T87 320.473'07

"[*U.S. Government*] is part of a new series of social studies reference books and contains a potpourri of information useful to teachers and librarians. . . . The first two chapters, 'The Purposes and Principles of U.S. Government' and 'The Philosophers,' discuss government in general, the U.S. system of government, the Constitution, political parties, and philosophers (e.g., Plato and Locke) whose writings influenced the founders of the republic. Next is a 'Chronology of Important Documents, Decisions, and Events.' . . . This is followed by the texts of the Mayflower Compact, the Declaration of Independence, the Constitution, and the Preamble to the Charter of the United Nations. Another chapter lists members of the 100th Congress, current Supreme Court justices, all presidents and chief justices, and a variety of statistical information. . . . The remaining third of the book contains two bibliographies, one of reference works and the other of classroom materials." (*BL*, September 15, 1989, p. 210)

Washington Representatives, 1989: Who Does What for Whom in the Nation's Capital, 13th edition. Arthur C. Close et al., eds. Columbia Bks., 1989. soft. 1 vol. 723 pp. index. ISBN 0-910416-78-8. $55. directory.
JK1118.D58 328.73'078

"The judicial, executive, and legislative branches of our government are elected or appointed to interpret, create, and amend the laws of our land. However, there is an unofficial, yet very influential, and often invisible fourth branch of government: lobbyists.

"[*Washington Representatives, 1989*] . . . aims to be all-inclusive. More than 12,000 individuals and 11,000 companies, interest groups, and public relations firms are listed. . . . It is a 'compilation of Washington representatives of the major national associations, labor unions and U.S. companies, registered foreign agents, lobbyists, lawyers, law firms and special interest groups, together with their clients.' The information is divided into four sections: an alphabetical list of individuals, an alphabetical list of companies and organizations, an index of companies and organizations grouped by subject or industry group, and a country-by-country listing of foreign governments with representation in Washington.

"[The book] . . . is, as stated in the introduction

'basically a list of people.' It provides the user with extensive directory information and does it well." (*BL,* October 1, 1989, p. 387)

The World Almanac of U.S. Politics. Sharilyn Jee, ed. World Almanac, 1989; distrib. by St. Martin's. hard and soft. 1 vol. 414 pp. index. ISBN 0-88687-432-7 (hard); 0-88687-431-9 (soft). $29.95 (hard); $14.95 (soft). encyclopedia.

"Designed to contain 'everything every citizen should know about who and what governs this country,' [*The World Almanac of U.S. Politics*] covers topics such as the 1988 elections, political terminology (e.g., incumbent, lame duck, left wing), the legislative process, the budget process, how to contact government officials, the electoral college, political parties, voter registration, and campaign financing. . . . *The World Almanac of U.S. Politics* is a handy, inexpensive, ready-reference guide to U.S. government. It will be useful in small high school and public libraries that don't own the more comprehensive and more expensive titles from CQ and National Journal." (*LJ,* August 1989, p. 128)

Worldwide Government Directory, with International Organizations, 1990. JoAnne DuChez et al., eds. Cambridge Information Group Directories, 1989. hard and soft. 1 vol. 912 pp. ISBN 0-942189-53-1 (hard); 0-942189-54-X (soft). $325 (hard); $275 (soft). directory.

351.2

"Locating the names and addresses of foreign officials and government agencies has always been a labor-intensive process. Adequate and accessible information is available for countries like Canada, France, and the Soviet Union, but not always for places like Guinea-Bissau, Nepal, and the Seychelles. . . . [*Worldwide Government Directory, with International Organizations, 1990*] continues to be the most comprehensive source for foreign directory information. Names, titles, addresses, telephone numbers, and, when applicable, telex and cable numbers are provided for principal government officials of the legislative, executive, and judicial branches of 175 countries. Similar information for state-run agencies and corporations and the central bank are also provided.

"[In the directory timeliness] . . . is a key factor. . . . [The directory] . . . includes information 'as late as November 1989.' As a result, the recent changes in many Eastern European governments are not reflected.

"[The book's] . . . stated purpose, to provide 'access to government officials of 175 countries,' is straightforward and is definitely met." (*BL,* July 1990, p. 2118)

Joan Stahl

Popular Music

See also Dance; Music; Theater

The definition of popular music is elusive. Obviously, popular music is not classical music, but what is it? Broadly speaking, popular music is everything but classical music. It is folk, country, jazz, rock and roll, blues, gospel, easy listening, heavy metal, movie and show music—and the list goes on. Popular music is composed of many categories. The lines between categories, particularly in recent years, have become blurred. No one reference source, therefore, can adequately cover all the manifestations of popular music. Librarians developing a core collection will need to rely on several sources that specialize in one or more different categories. The contemporary categories in popular music—generally considered to be rock and roll, heavy metal, jazz, and blues—are constantly changing in both content and performance. New artists appear and disappear; new styles of music develop and become fused with other styles. Librarians will appreciate having the most current sources that are available, and yet they will be painfully aware that these works will become dated very quickly.

A core collection in popular music should provide the librarian with basic information about the history of popular music, its people, events, and songs. An index such as *Popular Music 1920–1979: An Annotated Index* (Nat Shapiro and Bruce Pollack, eds., Gale, 1985), is a useful title that librarians should consider for core collections. Biographical dictionaries and encyclopedias, which focus primarily on people and events and only secondarily examine song titles, offer the broadest access to the field. This recommended list is weighted in favor of such sources and includes biographical dictionaries and encyclopedias for jazz, rock and roll, and theater music. One excellent source that is out of print is the *Encyclopedia of Folk, Country, and Western Music* (Irwin Stambler and Grelun Landon, St. Martin's, 1982).

In addition to requests for biographical and historical information about musicians and their work, the reference librarian receives a large number of questions about the words and music to popular songs. *Popular Song Index* (Scarecrow, 1984) and its supplements, compiled by Patricia Havlice, lists songs in songbook collections. It is a most useful title, and librarians will wish to consider it for a core collection. Another valuable index is *Songs of the Theater: Definitive Index to the Songs of the Musical Stage* (Wilson, 1984). Terry Hounsome's *Rock Record* (Facts On File, 1987) provides a good discography of rock performers and songs.

Although book-length bibliographies and discogra-

Core Titles

	PUBLIC	ACADEMIC	SCHOOL
American Musical Theatre: A Chronicle Bordman, Gerald. Oxford, 1978	✦		
American Songwriters: One Hundred Forty-Six Biographies of America's Greatest Popular Composers & Lyricists Ewen, David. Wilson, 1986	✦		✦
Encyclopaedia of the Musical Theatre Green, Stanley. Da Capo, 1980	✦		
Encyclopedia of Jazz Feather, Leonard. Da Capo, 1984	✦		
Encyclopedia of Jazz in the Sixties Feather, Leonard. Da Capo, 1986	✦		
Encyclopedia of Jazz in the Seventies Feather, Leonard, and Ira Gitler. Da Capo, 1987	✦		
Encyclopedia of Pop, Rock and Soul, rev. edition Stambler, Irwin. St. Martin's, 1989	✦	✦	
The Great Song Thesaurus Lax, Roger, and Frederick Smith. Oxford, 1984	✦		
The Harmony Illustrated Encyclopedia of Rock, 6th edition Clifford, Mike. Harmony, 1988	✦		✦
Popular Music: An Annotated Guide to American Popular Songs, 14 vols. Pollack, Bruce, and Nat Shapiro, eds. Gale, 1964–(now annual)	✦	✦	
Rock On: The Illustrated Encyclopedia of Rock n' Roll Nite, Norm N. Harper & Row, 1974–1985	✦	✦	✦
The Rolling Stone Encyclopedia of Rock & Roll Pareles, Jon, and Patricia Romanowski, eds. Rolling Stone Pr./Summit, 1983	✦	✦	✦

phies have not been selected as part of this core listing, many of the recommended sources include such abbreviated lists in their appendixes. Patrons can begin more specialized work there. In addition, there are many specialized sources in the field of popular music. Rock and roll groups and solo artists are one area, for example, in which a considerable number of reference works are available. The decision on which of these titles should supplement a collection will largely depend on the interests of the library's patrons. —*J. S. With contributions by Donna L. Singer.*

Core Titles

American Musical Theatre: A Chronicle. Gerald Bordman. Oxford, 1978. hard. 1 vol. 749 pp. appendix. indexes. ISBN 0-19-502356-0. $49.95. history.
ML1711.B67 782.8′1′0973

The title—*American Musical Theatre: A Chronicle*—accurately reflects the contents of this work. Author Gerald Bordman elucidates his goal in a concise and clearly written introduction. It was his intention to create a thorough and unerring history of the U.S. musical, starting with the first musical done in this country and continuing through 1978, when the book was published.

Bordman's task, though formidable, was one he was well equipped to handle. He has written a great deal on the musical theater, including books on composers Jerome Kern and Vincent Youmans. The research on this volume was conducted in 22 libraries and theater collections throughout the country.

The arrangement of chapters—prologue, acts one through four, intermission, and epilogue—is in keeping with the subject. Seasons before 1866 are covered in a summary chapter. The book then moves season by season, show by show, to cover every musical done on Broadway and, occasionally, musicals performed in

Boston, Philadelphia, and Chicago. Bordman excludes shows that opened out of town and then closed before reaching Broadway.

An incredible amount of information is packed into these pages. Bordman documents each show with dates, theater personnel, leading songs, length of run, theater, characters' names, and touring companies. He also provides story outlines, but is careful to state that if the musical originated in another country, the summary of the U.S. production may differ greatly from that of the original. Biographical information on actors and other people in the theater is included, and the critical comments on the shows represent a consensus among reviewers. Finally, Bordman adds some social and economic history for good measure.

One is not likely to read this chronology from cover to cover. Therefore, the editorial decision to highlight names in boldface type is a help to the user in locating specific information. The appendix is useful, and the indexes are essential to the volume. The appendix of people links them to their major accomplishments. At a glance, one can get an overview of a career in the musical theater. For example, George Abbott's name is followed by a listing of his shows and their dates. The index includes three parts: shows and sources for those shows, songs cited in the text, and a name index.

This reference work is accurate, well planned, well organized, and very complete. Librarians will find it an excellent source for ready-reference information on the musical theater. The comprehensiveness and detail of *American Musical Theatre* will be a bit overwhelming for the school-age user, but the general adult patron in the public will be well served by this book. The Board recommends this work for the core collection of public libraries. —*J. S.*

American Songwriters: One Hundred Forty-Six Biographies of America's Greatest Popular Composers & Lyricists. David Ewen. Wilson, 1986. hard. 1 vol. 489 pp. index. ISBN 0-8242-0744-0. $56. biographical dictionary.
ML390.E825 784.5′0092′2

American Songwriters, which supersedes the earlier works *Popular American Composers* (1962) and *Popular American Composers: First Supplement* (1972), contains biographical sketches of 146 composers and lyricists from the nineteenth and twentieth centuries. The scope of the work has been broadened to include biographies of lyricists, giving them, according to the introduction, the "same in-depth treatment as composers." Performance history and critical reception of individual songs or musical shows, and performers associated with them, receive added attention. In this dictionary, biography receives more emphasis than criticism, and the entries are peppered with information on musical revivals, awards, and statistics on performance runs.

According to the selection criteria given in the introduction, only those songwriters who "have a durable place in the history of the American popular song through sustained creative achievement over an extended period of time" and those whose "most memorable numbers" have become part of the "permanent repertory of American popular music" are included. The reader can find information on such varied songwriters as country music writer *Hank Williams,* folk writer *Stephen Foster,* operetta composer *Rudolf Friml,* Broadway musical great *Stephen Sondheim,* and popular singer-songwriters *Billy Joel* and *Carly Simon.*

The author, David Ewen, is one of the most prolific and respected writers of music references, with works on classical, modern, and opera music as well as books on individual musicians such as Leonard Bernstein and Richard Rodgers. To ensure accuracy of material, he asked living songwriters to review the first draft of their biographies. The only errors seem to be typographical ones, such as the misspelling of names: Jan Pearce instead of Jan Peerce.

The two-column reference is organized in alphabetical order by last name, which appears in boldface capital letters. Birth and death dates are in parentheses followed by the biographical sketch, which discusses major songs, awards, and achievements. Each entry is accompanied by a photograph of the songwriter and concludes with selected bibliographies. Within the entries, song titles are in quotation marks and titles of musicals are in italics. The careers of lyricists identified primarily with one composer, such as Alan Jay Lerner (with Frederick Loewe), are discussed within the entry on that composer. Lyricists are in the alphabetical listing, but they are cross-referenced to the relevant composer. Only those lyricists who worked with many composers have separate entries, but the performance history of their songs is in entries of relevant composers, as indicated by cross-references.

An excellent feature of the book is an alphabetical song index, which lists about 5,600 compositions mentioned in the biographical sketches. This enables a reader to look up the Everly Brothers pop hit "Bye, Bye Love" and be directed to the entry on composer and lyricist team *Boudleaux Bryant* and *Felice Bryant.* The author could have made the book even easier to use by including a performers' index as another way of accessing composers and lyricists, since many songwriters' compositions are indelibly linked with a particular performer. For example, songs of Jimmy van Heusen were linked with Bing Crosby in the 1940s and with Frank Sinatra in the 1950s.

Despite these minor flaws, *American Songwriters* is well done and quite useful. The Board recommends this work for the core collections of public and school libraries. —*D. L. S.*

Encyclopaedia of the Musical Theatre. Stanley Green. Da Capo, 1980. soft. 1 vol. 488 pp. appendixes. ISBN 0-306-80113-2. $14.95. encyclopedia.
ML102.M88G7 782.8

The *Encyclopaedia of the Musical Theatre* is a reprint of the 1976 edition. The purpose of the work is straightforward: Author Stanley Green writes, "This is a ready-reference book containing succinct information regarding the most prominent people, productions, and songs of the musical theatre, both in New York (including off-Broadway) and London." Ready-reference books are ideally easy to use, and the *A* to *Z* arrangement of this volume makes the book fit that criterion.

The only question in the user's mind might be, "What does the author define as 'musical theater?' " Green considers musical theater to be musical comedies, musical plays, musical farces, spectacles, revues, operettas, and, when offered for a commercial run, operas. Excluded from the scope of this encyclopedia are vaudeville, Gilbert and Sullivan, limited engagements, cabaret entertainments, plays with one or two songs, foreign-language musicals, one-man or one-woman shows, one-act plays, minstrel shows, concert parties, children's musicals, benefits, amateur productions, and ice shows.

Green, author of several books on the musical theater (*Broadway Musicals: Show by Show* [H. Leonard Publishing, 1980], *Broadway Musicals of the 30s* [Da Capo, 1982]), includes entries for people, productions, and songs. The entries are concise, rarely exceeding three paragraphs in length. The entries on people include actors, composers, lyricists, directors, choreographers, producers, and librettists; the subject's full name or nickname is included. Musical productions with which the individual was associated are listed by year. In the case of actor entries, Green has included the role the actor played following the title of the show. In the case of a composer or lyricist, Green has included the name of the collaborator following the title of the show.

The production entries include listings of only the best-known songs and the leading cast members. The number of performances at each theater is also given in the entry; the absence of such a number indicates that the show was still running as of January 1, 1976. Green notes if the musical was adapted to film. The song entries include a brief summary of each song, discussing the circumstances under which it was written and the context in which it appeared in the musical. Song entries also include the name of the performer who first introduced the song and the date of its premiere.

The appendix has four sections. The first is a list of awards and prizes. The second section is a list of long runs—those shows that ran over 1,000 performances. A 6-page selected bibliography forms the third section. The appendix concludes with an 11-page discography. Since the book is ten years old, some of the information in the appendixes has decreased in usefulness.

The length of entries, clear layout and arrangement, and the author's emphasis on essential information combine to make the *Encyclopaedia of the Musical Theatre* a highly desirable addition. The Board recommends this work for the core collection of public libraries. —*J. S.*

Encyclopedia of Jazz. Leonard Feather. Da Capo, 1984. soft. 1 vol. 527 pp. ISBN 0-306-80214-7. $19.95. biographical dictionary.
ML102.J3F4 785.42'03'21

Encyclopedia of Jazz in the Sixties. Leonard Feather. Da Capo, 1986. soft. 1 vol. approx. 400–500 pp. ISBN 0-306-80263-5. $14.95. biographical dictionary.
ML105.F35 785.42'09'046

Encyclopedia of Jazz in the Seventies. Leonard Feather and Ira Gitler. Da Capo, 1987. soft. 1 vol. approx. 400–500 pp. illus. ISBN 0-306-80290-2. $16.95. biographical dictionary.
ML105.F36 785.42'092'2

Jazz history and Leonard Feather go hand in hand. He has written extensively on jazz, and the *Encyclopedia of Jazz* series is certainly a seminal one for any popular music collection in which jazz is represented. The volume includes *Encyclopedia of Jazz* (reprint of 1955 edition), *Encyclopedia of Jazz in the Sixties* (reprint of 1966 edition), and *Encyclopedia of Jazz in the Seventies* (reprint of 1976 edition).

The volumes are biographical dictionaries. The first volume covers from the beginnings of jazz until 1955, the second volume covers 1956 through 1966, and the third volume covers 1967 through 1975. A name may appear in all three volumes if the artist was active throughout those years. The three volumes comprise a series covering 75 years of jazz history, but the volumes also function autonomously.

The author includes the following information for each artist: name (nickname), instrument(s), birth date, chronology of school and career, compositions, albums (compact discs were not yet available when the books were published), influences, favorite performers and recordings, address (if somewhat permanent), and a few critical comments. The user must keep in mind that this information is dated due to the original copyright dates of these volumes.

The definition of *jazz* is problematic at best. In the first volume, Feather includes an excellent, detailed essay entitled "What Is Jazz?" The essay analyzes the elements that identify a performance as jazz. Critics often disagree about these criteria, and what was considered jazz some years ago, if created today, might no longer be considered jazz. Who, then, should be included in these volumes? Feather writes, "One of the most complex problems involved in the compilation of biographies was the question of where to draw the lines—the thin often invisible line between jazz and popular music." If the lines were blurred when Feather produced the first volume, they were even fuzzier by the time he completed *Encyclopedia of Jazz in the Seventies:* "Even more than during the compilation of the earlier books, the lines between jazz and other idioms became vague and arbitrary."

The volumes contain similar features with only a few modifications. Ira Gitler, who was an associate of Feather's from the beginning, is a full-fledged co-author of the third volume. Each volume has an introduction by a renowned musician. The introductions to volumes 1 to 3 are written by Duke Ellington, John Lewis, and Quincy Jones, respectively. These introductions are not fillers but thoughtful remarks on the state of the art. Among other features included in all three volumes are over 350 black-and-white photographs; listings of jazz organizations and record companies; poll results from *Downbeat, Metronome, Esquire,* or *Record Changer;* filmographies, discographies, and bibliographies.

The writing is accessible to high school level and above. The entries are written in a shorthand style. For example, the entry on *Gus Johnson* says, "Colleague of Ch. Parker in Jay McShann band in early '40's. Later played with Earl Hines; Count Basie 1948–54."

The information in the *Encyclopedia of Jazz* series with regard to musicians who are still performing is, of course, incomplete. (It is well past time for *Encyclopedia of Jazz in the Eighties.*) The Board recommends these works for the core collection of public libraries.

—*J. S.*

Encyclopedia of Pop, Rock and Soul, rev. edition. Irwin Stambler. St. Martin's, 1989. hard. 1 vol. 864 pp. illus. appendixes. ISBN 0-312-02573-4. $19.95. encyclopedia.

ML102.P66S8 784.5'0092'2

Irwin Stambler, the author of the *Encyclopedia of Pop, Rock and Soul,* is well credentialed. He was a popular songwriter and radio commentator in the field of pop music. His writing and research touches all types of popular music. He authored *The Encyclopedia of Popular Music,* covering the years 1925–1965 (Reprint Svcs., 1965), and coauthored *The Encyclopedia of Folk, Country, and Western Music* with Grelun Landon (St. Martin's, 1982).

This project is described by Stambler as a comprehensive but not all-inclusive one-volume encyclopedia. Most of the contents are devoted to alphabetically arranged biographical entries on artists, promoters, and songwriters. The entries are well written in narrative form, as opposed to an abbreviated listing of dates and facts, and in general they are lengthier than those in either THE HARMONY ILLUSTRATED ENCYCLOPEDIA OF ROCK or THE ROLLING STONE ENCYCLOPEDIA OF ROCK & ROLL. The entries often include quotes from the personality. The many cross-references from individuals to bands and groups are helpful. There are 157 black-and-white photographs in groupings throughout the book; most personalities are not in photographs.

By definition, an encyclopedia is more expansive than a dictionary. This encyclopedia is expansive but also contains definitions of terms. For example, one can find entries for *acid rock, feedback, fuzz, fuzztone, groupies, surfer music,* and *wah-wah.* These definitions, useful as they are, comprise a small part of the whole. Stambler provides no criteria for the selection and inclusion of terms, and librarians or patrons are unlikely to use this book as a dictionary.

The inclusion of Broadway musicals is a somewhat quirky feature. The user can find entries, comparable in length to the biographical entries, on such shows as *Promises, Promises; Company; Godspell;* and *Applause.* Again, this book will be an unlikely first source for a librarian to locate such information. A fourth type of entry is devoted to places and events important in the history of pop, rock, and soul, such as *Apollo Theater, Fillmore Theaters, Watkins Glen,* and *Woodstock Festival.*

The book has a few welcome, though not essential, features. The introductory essays by John Otis on "R & B," Michael Ochs on the history of pop music, and Stambler on the general history of rock and soul are entertaining. The appendixes include a listing of gold record awards, Grammy awards by category, and Oscar nominations and winners in music. Of note, and absent from other similar encyclopedias, is the bibliography, which documents Stambler's research and provides the user with more source material.

The *Encyclopedia of Pop, Rock and Soul* will be

heavily used in public and academic libraries. The recent revision, which brings the information up to date, increases the title's desirability for core collections. The Board recommends this work for the core collections of public and academic libraries. —*J. S.*

The Great Song Thesaurus. Roger Lax and Frederick Smith. Oxford, 1984. hard. 1 vol. 792 pp. ISBN 0-19-503222-5. $75. thesaurus.
ML128.S3L4 784.5'0016

A unique musical thesaurus, *The Great Song Thesaurus* gives a historical context for more than 10,000 songs written over the last 700 years. According to its compilers, "The original intent of this book was to select, from all divisions of song literature, the 10,000 best-known popular and/or significant songs in English-speaking countries and to cross-index the pertinent data associated with each for immediate and accessible reference." Entries include popular songs, such as commercial hits from the days of Tin Pan Alley through the present; folk songs; nursery rhymes; sea chanteys; works from musical theater, film, radio, and television; school songs; advertising jingles; and bugle calls. "Also included were classical, ballet, and symphonic themes that are today world standards."

The book is divided into nine sections. Part 1, "The Greatest Songs," is a chronological list of song titles. In headnotes, the editors give historical background and anecdotes, both musical and social. For example, we learn that in 1907 royalties on Irving Berlin's first published song amounted to 37 cents.

Part 2, "The Award Winners," lists by year all songs receiving major U.S. awards since 1932 and all songs to win major British awards since 1955. Part 3 identifies theme songs, trademark songs, and "signature tunes." Part 4 lists "Elegant Plagiarisms." We learn, for example, that the 1942 World War II song "When the Lights Go on Again" was based on Beethoven's Minuet in G.

Part 5 lists song titles alphabetically, identifying composers and lyricists and giving pertinent information about song origins. Part 6 lists titles of British songs, grouped by year. Part 7 lists 5,500 lyricists and composers, along with each one's principal songs. Part 8 categorizes songs from the musical theater, film, television, and radio. Among other things, 838 musicals are listed, with such information as number of Broadway performances, year of premiere, and major songs. Part 9 is a "Thesaurus of Song Titles by Subject, Key Word, and Category." This part includes 2,293 subject, keyword, and category headings, each followed by relevant song titles.

This well-designed book benefits from a clear typeface and easy accessibility. *The Great Song Thesaurus* provides answers to thousands of questions, such as: What were the top hits of 1968? How did the song "We Shall Overcome" originate? What is the earliest reference to "Greensleeves"? This thesaurus will provide endless fascination for the curious and will be especially valuable for musical directors, arrangers, performers, and radio and television programmers who are preparing shows, revues, concerts, and recordings. The Board recommends this work for the core collection of public libraries. —*J. S.*

The Harmony Illustrated Encyclopedia of Rock, 6th edition. Mike Clifford. Harmony, 1988. soft. 1 vol. 208 pp. illus. appendix. ISBN 0-517-57164-1. $14.95. biographical dictionary.
ML102.R6C6 784.5'4'00321

Originally published in Great Britain as *The New Illustrated Rock Handbook, The Harmony Illustrated Encyclopedia of Rock* is a biographical dictionary of today's leading rock musicians. Author Mike Clifford, a former musician with a soul band, a publicist for Aretha Franklin and James Brown, and a journalist, was assisted by ten contributors who have years of experience performing and writing about rock music.

The book includes more than 700 entries, each accompanied by a color photo. Most of the entries in earlier editions have been updated. "Selection," Clifford writes, was "fairly subjective, with more than a few 'borderline' cases included because of their originality, influence on other artists, or contributions to rock, rather than popularity or chart success." The appendix has brief notes on 500 additional personalities, who, the compilers felt, deserved recognition.

The entries are brief, averaging 700 to 1,000 words. The headings for artists include country of origin, date and place of birth, and real name (if applicable). The biographical data outline the career of the artist or group, and in the case of the latter include the original and current line-up of personnel. A discography of hot singles currently in print follows the entries. Entries include referrals to related entries. Twelve family trees are scattered throughout to show the links between major rock groups.

The writing style is conversational and subjective in tone. For example, the entry on *Bryan Adams* reads: "All-round journeyman rocker who takes craftsmanlike approach to his profession, Adams may well outlast some of the flashier and more gimmicky artists currently on offer."

This book is geared to a young adult audience. Librarians will appreciate the currency of information since the cutoff date for the compilation of information was May 1988. Currency is this volume's strong point. The user will find information on musicians not included in other encyclopedias. For example, *Bryan Ferry* and *Fine Young Cannibals* appear here, but not in other books. On the minus side, the work contains no bibliography, and the binding will probably not hold up to the wear and tear the book will receive.

The editorial staff at Harmony Books has clearly come up with a marketable product. School and public librarians will want to purchase *The Harmony Illustrated Encyclopedia of Rock* and subsequent editions to meet the demand for such information from the young adult and juvenile audience. The Board recommends this work for the core collections of public and school libraries. —*J. S.*

Popular Music: An Annotated Guide to American Popular Song. Nat Shapiro, ed. (vols. 1–8); Bruce Pollock, ed. (vols. 9–13). Gale, 1964 (now annual). hard. 14 vols. illus. appendixes. indexes. ISBN 0-8103-4946-9 (vol. 14). $675 (set); $55 (vol. 14). guide. ML210.U5S5 784.5

The publishing history of *Popular Music: An Annotated Guide to American Popular Song* is complicated. This title has undergone a series of editorial changes since its inception in 1964. Today, in its entirety, the series covers the history of popular song from 1920 to 1988.

Volume 1, published by Adrian Press in 1964 and edited by Nat Shapiro, covered the years 1950 to 1959 and was conceived as a series that would accurately document significant popular songs of the twentieth century. Shapiro justified the need for the project in the preface: "Galloping chaos has been a classic and chronic symptom of the artistic as well as the commercial state of American popular music throughout its entire history. The very special, inbred community of music publishers, song writers, and performers of popular music is peopled by a remarkable collection of artists and hacks, craftsmen and hoodlums, geniuses and mountebanks. Considering this marvelous and varied group, it is no wonder that a reliable record of the accomplishments—and follies—of these colorful souls is virtually non-existent."

Shapiro used many sources, including trade organizations, trade journals, and more, to compile this index to songs. This work is a selective listing of "significant" songs that meet the following criteria: They achieved a substantial degree of popular acceptance, they were exposed to the public in especially notable circumstances, and they were accepted by and performed by influential musical and dramatic artists. Jazz, theater, film, country and western, and folk songs are included. Since labels are arbitrary and sometimes relate more to the history and performance of a song than its origin, Shapiro chose not to classify the inclusions.

Songs are arranged alphabetically under the year of original copyright. The list of titles at the end of the volume refers the user to the appropriate year. The title entry includes the full title of the song, any alternate titles, the lyricist and composer, and the *current* publisher (as of the volume's publication). The listing also includes the first and best-selling record associated with the title, the performers, the record company, the production (movie or theater) in which the song was introduced, and other relevant performers. If a song relates to a year other than the year in which it was copyrighted, the editor includes cross-references.

The appendixes include the aforementioned list of titles and a list of publishers. The latter includes the current address of each publisher and the performing rights affiliation.

Subsequent volumes in the series, still under the editorship of Shapiro, followed the same format and covered the following years: volume 2: 1940–1949; volume 3: 1960–1964; volume 4: 1930–1939; volume 5: 1920–1929; volume 6: 1965–1969. In 1984, Gale reissued the Adrian Press series (c. 1964–1973) and added two new volumes: volume 7 covered 1970–1974, and volume 8 covered 1975–1979. Gale also published a revised three-volume cumulation of volumes 1–8. The cumulation, entitled *Popular Music, 1920–1979,* was edited by Shapiro and Pollock (Gale, 1985) and includes all 18,000 songs in volumes 1–8. The revised cumulation reflects an adjustment in arrangement. Songs are consolidated into one alphabetical list. The addition of an index of composers, lyricists, and performers makes this set easier to use than the eight separate volumes. The revision also includes an awards index, listing nominees for Academy Awards and Grammy Awards.

Volumes 9–13, under the editorship of Pollock and published by Gale, follow the improved format of the revised cumulation. One index was added which groups songs under the year of copyright registration. By volume 10 still another editorial adjustment made the series an annual, with each volume spanning one year of song history. The advantage of this publishing schedule is that song information is available as soon as possible after the song gains prominence, and the depth of coverage has been extended from an average of 300 songs to 400 songs per year.

To round out coverage of the popular music of this century, Gale has published a volume entitled *Popular Music 1900–1919* edited by Barbara Cohen-Stratyner (Gale, 1988). That work is described as a "companion" volume to the series. The book is an annotated list of 2,600 significant songs, and its format follows that of the three-volume revised cumulation and subsequent volumes in the series.

Popular Music: An Annotated Guide to American Popular Song is an invaluable compilation of hard-to-locate information. Librarians will use the work in many ways—to verify titles, to identify performers who popularized titles, to locate publishers' addresses, to trace the popularity of a title, and to connect songs with theater, film, and television productions. The Board recommends this work for the core collections of public and academic libraries. —*J. S.*

Rock On: The Illustrated Encyclopedia of Rock n' Roll. Norm N. Nite. Harper & Row, 1974–1985. hard. 3 vols. illus. appendix. index. ISBN 0-06-181642-6 (vol. 1); 0-06-181643-4 (vol. 2); 0-06-181644-2 (vol. 3). $34.95 (vol. 1); $29.95 (vol. 2); $25 (vol. 3). encyclopedia.
ML105.N49 784.092

The compiler of the data in *Rock On: The Illustrated Encyclopedia of Rock n' Roll* is Norm N. Nite, "Mr. Music," who hosted the popular radio show *Nite Train* in Cleveland. He was encouraged by his listeners to do this definitive work on rock and roll.

The scope of these titles has changed slightly with each volume as the music has changed. Volume 1 *(The Solid Gold Years)* contains "any artist who was in the Charts during the fifties and early sixties with a hit record." Anyone who made the Top 100 in the weekly magazines was included. Consequently, one can see how different strains of popular music such as blues and country were integrated with rock and roll. In addition to the obvious hit singers, one can locate *Bubber Johnson,* a ballad singer who had one hit, "Come Home" in 1955.

Albums, as opposed to singles, were of major importance to the careers of rock artists in the 1960s. Therefore, in volume 2 *(The Years of Change: 1964–1978)* Nite included artists with hit albums as well as those with hit singles. The burgeoning of rock groups in the 1960s forced Nite to exclude some groups. A section entitled "These Too Made It" is a five-page listing of top hits by lesser-knowns who Nite felt did not warrant a complete entry. Together, volumes 1 and 2 include information on 2,500 musicians. Volume 3 *(The Video Revolution: 1978–Present)* reflects another trend in rock music—the video revolution. Seventy percent of the artists in volume 1 are no longer performing and 50 percent of those in volume 2 are no longer performing, but fully 90 percent of those in volume 3 are still active.

This biographical dictionary is arranged alphabetically. Entries are very brief, yet in many cases the artist or group is not likely to be included in any other similar reference source. In one or two paragraphs, Nite cites the artist's real name, birth date and place, death date where applicable, and hit recordings with each one's date of release and record label. Many black-and-white photographs provide further documentation.

Like compilers of other rock encyclopedias, Nite strove for accuracy. However, he met resistance from some performers who would not supply information. Nite had a team of people in the United States and Great Britain whom he called upon to assemble the data. He also culled information from record trade publications as well as interviews.

The combination of many illustrations, brief and conversational text, and lots of white space per page reflect the popular orientation of the set. Nevertheless, librarians will find *Rock On: The Illustrated Encyclopedia of Rock n' Roll* used by all age levels, since Nite has ably documented the early years of rock and roll, an era of music history still in need of a great deal of study. The Board recommends this work for the core collections of public, academic, and school libraries.

—*D. L. S.*

The Rolling Stone Encyclopedia of Rock & Roll. Jon Pareles and Patricia Romanowski, eds. Rolling Stone Pr./Summit, 1983. soft. 1 vol. 614 pp. illus. 0-671-44071-3. $14.95. encyclopedia.
ML102.R6R64 784.5'4'00321

Rolling Stone, the premiere rock music publication, takes rock music seriously. The intent of the editors of *The Rolling Stone Encyclopedia of Rock & Roll* was to impart the same authority and serious approach to this reference.

Finding the existing rock encyclopedias wanting in depth and accuracy, Pareles (former editor of *Rolling Stone*) and Romanowski (current editor of the magazine) sought to correct this deficiency with this reference. The encyclopedia was a collaborative effort, containing contributions from critics and journalists whose credits include articles in *Rolling Stone,* the *Village Voice,* the *New York Times, Crawdaddy,* and *Billboard.* The book is a chronology of events, current through May 1983.

In explaining the scope of the volume, Pareles acknowledges the tangled history of rock and roll: "It is a music that just can't be pinned down, a contradiction any old way you choose it." The book documents the music of the 1950s, 1960s, and 1970s—folk, rock, soul, psychedelic rock, heavy metal, funk, blues, disco, reggae—through its practitioners. The book is primarily a biographical encyclopedia, arranged from *A* to *Z*. In this reference, musicians were given priority for inclusion over disc jockeys, businesspeople, and related occupations. As compared with previous rock dictionaries and encyclopedias, this volume includes more black performers. This encyclopedia also includes definitions of terms, such as *a cappella, cover,* and *the blues,* but such entries play a secondary role.

The editors found that previous books on rock music were rife with inaccuracies, since the history of this music is so intertwined with myth and legend. Documentation was a goal for this volume; it was not easy to achieve. Romanowski gathered and corroborated information from record companies, artists, their representatives, writers, collectors, and fans. Even simple facts were elusive, however. Romanowski states that 70 to 80 percent of her requests for a performer's birth date were "either refused, answered incompletely, or answered in a way that was—either deliberately or accidentally—inaccurate."

Each entry begins with a selective discography of releases preceded by the release date of the album. Because this is not a critical encyclopedia but a biographical one, the length of the entries is determined by the complexity of the artist's life history. The editors' sleuthing is evident in the inclusion of such information as a performer's cause of death, which may have previously been surrounded by rumor.

An interesting though not completely successful feature is the inclusion of bits of rock history, such as listings of rock festivals, examples of film documentation of rock music, Grammy Award winners, and an explanation of the phenomenon "death rock." This information appears in outlined boxes throughout the volume. However, in order to locate them, one must know to look under the proper heading—"Clubs," "Comedy," or "Dances." The sprinkling of black-and-white photographs is a plus.

The entries are clearly written and accessible for high school level and above. The editors' commitment to reliable information makes *The Rolling Stone Encyclopedia of Rock & Roll* an important volume in any popular music collection.

The Board recommends this work for the core collections of public, academic, and school libraries.

—*J. S.*

Supplementary Titles

Folk Music in America: A Reference Guide (Reference Library of the Humanities, vol. 496). Terry E. Miller. Garland, 1987. hard. 1 vol. 424 pp. index. ISBN 0-8240-8935-9. $45. bibliography.
ML128.F74M5 016.781773

Folk Music in America is a "much-needed guide to the literature of American folk music [which] encompasses not only Anglo-American forms, traditional and recent, but [also] Afro-American (including gospel and blues), Native American, and various ethnic musics as well. It provides annotated listings of books, dissertations, scholarly articles, and other materials published in English since 1900, with an emphasis on recent items.

"The 1,927 entries are arranged in nine chapters (each introduced by a very brief essay). . . . Separate author and subject indexes refer the user to the unique number assigned to each entry. Entries give author, title, publisher or journal, date, and pages; brief annotations describe the nature and scope of the item.

"The in-depth nature of *Folk Music in America* commends it to special collections in music, popular culture, folklore, and anthropology and to academic libraries supporting curricula in these areas; large public libraries may also find use for the list, particularly since popular titles are included." (*BL,* May 15, 1985, p. 1428)

Also reviewed in: *Choice,* June 1987, p. 1536; *LJ,* March 1, 1987, p. 68.

Board's recommendation: Public and academic libraries.

The New Grove Dictionary of Jazz. Barry Kernfeld and Stanley Sadie, eds. Grove's Dictionaries of Music, 1988. hard. 2 vols. 1,360 pp. ISBN 0-935859-39-X (set). $350 (set). biobibliography.
ML102.J3N48 785.42′1

The New Grove Dictionary of Jazz covers "[such aspects of jazz as] theory, instrumentation, performers, composers, bands, films, and institutions associated with this music. . . . Of the over 4,500 entries in the Dictionary, more than 3,000 are biographies, most for performers, but also for composers, arrangers, record producers, writers, editors, and discographers. . . . Each musical instrument commonly used in the performance of jazz has received an entry in the Dictionary. This two-volume set is the first comprehensive, scholarly reference work on jazz. . . . Most of the 250 contributors are academics and represent 25 nations." (*BL,* April 15, 1989, p. 1438)

"This massive work deserves highest praise for bringing to jazz music the breadth and rigorous methodology that characterizes Grove projects. Supplementing and updating all extant jazz reference works, this set will prove important for a variety of collections and will not likely be superseded in the near future." (*LJ,* February 1, 1989, p. 61)

Also reviewed in: *BW,* December 4, 1988, p. 17; *Econ,* January 21, 1989, p. 91; *NL,* January 23, 1989, p. 20; *NYT,* December 30, 1988, p. C20; *TLS,* February 3, 1989, p. 105; *WCRB,* 1989, p. 61; *WLB,* January 1989, p. 131.

Board's recommendation: Public and academic libraries.

New and Noteworthy

The Blues: A Bibliographical Guide. Mary L. Hart et al. Garland, 1989. hard. 1 vol. 636 pp. indexes. ISBN 0-8240-8506-X. $66. bibliography.
ML128.B49H3 016.781643

The Blues "is the first book-length compilation of information sources related to blues. Materials selected for inclusion include books, journals, newspapers, reports, theses, book reviews, films, and liner notes from record albums. . . . Dates range from the origin of blues in the nineteenth century through 1985. . . . Despite the problems of two alphabetical sequences within each chapter and some very obscure citations, this work begins to bring some bibliographic control to the literature of this neglected genre of American music." (*BL,* March 1, 1990, pp. 1379–1380)

Contemporary Musicians: Profiles of the People in Music. Michael L. LaBlanc, ed. Gale, semiannual (1989–). hard. 1 vol. 253 pp. illus. indexes. ISBN 0-8103-2211-0. $49.95. biobibliography.
ML385.C65 780.92

Contemporary Musicians "contains biographical and critical information on people in the music industry, including lyricists, composers, and performers. It will be published twice a year, and each volume will include 80–100 artists. Volume 1 details the accomplishments of 82 individuals and groups. Most of them represent popular music—rock, country, blues, etc.—but a few classical performers like Placido Domingo, who have achieved success with the general public, are also included. . . . Each biography ranges from 1½ to 5 pages, with most 3–4 pages in length. . . . Details of the biographee's life are briefly discussed, and a few compositions by the artist are mentioned (if appropriate)." (*BL,* November 1, 1989, p. 602)

The Penguin Encyclopedia of Popular Music. Donald Clark, ed. Viking/Penguin, 1989. hard. 1 vol. 1,376 pp. index. ISBN 0-670-80349-9. $40. encyclopedia.
ML102 782.8′1

"There has long been a need for a comprehensive reference tool for popular music. . . . [*The Penguin Encyclopedia of Popular Music*] fills the void nicely, offering basic information on rock, country, jazz, gospel, heavy metal, reggae, rap, ragtime, new age, folk, zydeco, funk, punk, and the blues. The nearly 3000 extremely readable entries describe artists, albums, labels, and genres, weaving an intricate web. . . . A 90-page index pulls together most of the loose threads. . . ." (*LJ,* September 1, 1989, p. 184)

Rock Movers and Shakers. Barry Lazell. Watson-Guptill/Billboard Bks., 1989. soft. 1 vol. 560 pp. illus. ISBN 0-8230-7608-3. $16.95. biographical dictionary.
ML385.R736 784.5′4

"*Rock Movers and Shakers* provides chronologies for over 700 individual and group rock performers. These cover the past 30 years, with the most recent events listed as December 1988. Entries include peak chart positions for recordings. There are cross-references from individual entries to group entries; the lineup for group entries is either the original one or the one best known." (*BL,* October 1, 1989, p. 396)

Diane Zabel

Psychology and Psychiatry

Psychology, the scientific study of the mind and behavior, was developed as a discipline in the late nineteenth century. Prior to that time, psychology was regarded as an extension of philosophy. Psychology is classified as a social science, and like other social sciences, it uses empirical research methods. The discipline has ties to sociology, social work, education, anthropology, political science, and business. Psychology also has close relationships to the natural sciences, particularly biology, physiology, zoology, and mathematics. This link to the sciences is reflected in the types of publications prevalent in psychology. For example, journal literature is more heavily used than monographic literature, and current literature is emphasized over retrospective material. Consequently, periodical indexes and corresponding data bases are far more important than books and bibliographies. These characteristics parallel the dissemination of information in the sciences.

Psychiatry, the diagnosis and treatment of mental disorders, is regarded as a medical field. Although this chapter includes only a few books on psychiatry, several of the general psychology sources include psychiatry and mental health in their scope.

Psychology is a profession as well as an academic discipline. In fact, applied psychology has experienced tremendous growth during the period since World War II. Psychologists are employed in education, industry, government, human services, and private practice. Activities range from studying infants to administering standardized tests to measuring variables such as aptitude and intelligence. PSYCHOLOGICAL ABSTRACTS, the leading periodical index in the field, organizes psychology into 17 broad subfields, including personality, treatment and prevention, developmental psychology, and social psychology.

When compared to other social sciences, the bibliographic access to journal literature in this field is outstanding. The American Psychological Association has been largely responsible for this achievement. The Association produces PSYCHOLOGICAL ABSTRACTS, the corresponding data base, and the THESAURUS OF PSYCHOLOGICAL INDEX TERMS, which is a companion to both. This professional association also performs an important role in the dissemination of information because it publishes numerous research journals.

The proliferation of journal literature makes it difficult for individuals to keep up with the most recent developments in their areas of interest. For this reason, secondary sources should be consulted for overview articles on topics. Psychology and psychiatry have sev-

Core Titles

	PUBLIC	ACADEMIC	SCHOOL
American Handbook of Psychiatry, 2d edition, 8 vols. Arieti, Silvano, ed. Basic Bks., 1974 – 1986		✦	
Concise Encyclopedia of Psychology Corsini, Raymond J., ed. John Wiley, 1987	✦	✦	✦
Diagnostic and Statistical Manual of Mental Disorders, 3d edition rev. American Psychiatric Assn., 1987	✦	✦	
Dictionary of Behavioral Science, 2d edition Wolman, Benjamin B., comp. and ed. Krieger, 1989		✦	
Encyclopedia of Psychology, 4 vols. Corsini, Raymond J., ed. John Wiley, 1984	✦	✦	
The Encyclopedic Dictionary of Psychology Harré, Rom, and Roger Lamb, eds. MIT Pr., 1983	✦	✦	
International Encyclopedia of Psychiatry, Psychology, Psychoanalysis, & Neurology, 12 vols., 1 suppl. Wolman, Benjamin, B., ed. Van Nostrand Reinhold, 1977		✦	
The Oxford Companion to the Mind Gregory, Richard L., ed. Oxford, 1987	✦	✦	✦
Psychiatric Dictionary, 6th edition Campbell, Robert Jean. Oxford, 1989		✦	
Psychological Abstracts American Psychological Assn., monthly (1927–)		✦	
Publication Manual of the American Psychological Association, 3d edition American Psychological Assn., 1983		✦	
The Tenth Mental Measurements Yearbook Conoley, Jane Close, and Jack J. Kramer, eds. Buros Institute of Mental Measurements, 1989; distrib. by Univ. of Nebraska Pr.	✦	✦	
Tests: A Comprehensive Reference for Assessments in Psychology, Education, and Business, 2d edition Sweetland, Richard C., and Daniel J. Keyser, eds. PRO-ED, 1990		✦	
Thesaurus of Psychological Index Terms, 5th edition American Psychological Assn., 1988		✦	

eral excellent handbooks and encyclopedias that trace previous research relating to a topic. One such work selected by the Board for the core list but now out of print, is Robert Goldenson's *Encyclopedia of Human Behavior* (Doubleday, 1970).

Several reference works on psychological tests and measurements are exemplary. Psychologists, educators, and personnel specialists frequently need information on tests. Although many heavily used tests are available from test publishers, a large number of tests are unpublished, devised primarily for research purposes. Although tests are not widely collected by libraries, librarians in academic settings often need to locate descriptions or reviews of tests. Libraries serving programs in clinical, educational, and industrial psychology will probably want to supplement these core works on tests and measurements with the supplementary title TEST CRITIQUES.

Core Titles

American Handbook of Psychiatry, 2d edition. Silvano Arieti, ed. Basic Bks., 1974 – 1986. hard. 8 vols. illus. indexes. ISBN 0-465-00159-9 (vol. 8). $85 (vol. 8). handbook.
RC435.A562 616.89

The first edition of the *American Handbook of Psychiatry* consisted of three volumes published between 1959 and 1966. This handbook was the first of its kind for U.S. psychiatry, and its goal was to represent the current state of psychiatry in this country. From its first printing in 1974, the series was well received here and abroad. Psychiatry has experienced rapid growth and change since the mid-1960s. The second edition was produced to incorporate these new developments.

To date, eight volumes have been published in this series. The first three volumes, *The Foundations of Psychiatry; Child and Adolescent Psychiatry, Sociocultural and Community Psychiatry;* and *Adult Clinical Psychiatry*, were published in 1974. Volume 4, *Organic Disorders and Psychosomatic Medicine,* volume 5, *Treatment,* and volume 6, *New Psychiatric Frontiers* were all published in 1975. In 1981 Basic Books published volume 7, *Advances and New Directions;* volume 8, *Biological Psychiatry,* was produced in 1986.

The first volume examines the historical, theoretical, and methodological foundations of psychiatry. One section discusses the contributions made to psychiatry by such other disciplines as philosophy, literature, history, religion, mathematics, and language. This section will be particularly interesting to graduate students in these fields. Volume 2 includes child, adolescent, and community psychiatry, in addition to the psychosocial aspects of psychiatry. Chapters cover a wide range of topics including adolescent eating disorders, learning disabilities, and mental health programs in colleges. This volume will be useful to educators, social workers, health planners, pediatricians, and other mental health professionals. As the title indicates, volume 3 focuses on adults in the clinical setting. Volume 4 treats the psychosocial aspects of medicine, and volume 5 focuses on treatment. The new psychiatric frontiers explored in volume 6 include genetic research and the development of new drug therapies. Volume 7 looks at issues emerging in the 1980s: computer applications in psychiatry, ethics in psychiatry, and new research on child abuse and neglect. Volume 8 examines the relationship between neurobiology and behavior.

Arieti, a clinical professor of psychiatry, is the overall editor; he has been ably assisted by several other editors. Although volumes focus on different topics, each volume includes diverse points of view regarding psychiatric theories and treatments. Traditional ideas and the results of recent research are presented simultaneously.

Volumes range in length from 856 to 1,270 pages. Each volume is divided into parts, which are subdivided into chapters. Each chapter is written by a subject expert and concludes with a substantial set of references. Illustrations, charts, and photos are plentiful and aid the reader in comprehending the text. Separate author and subject indexes exist for each volume.

The *American Handbook of Psychiatry* serves as a textbook for U.S. psychiatry. This reference tool is a fundamental source for libraries serving psychiatry and clinical psychology students. Furthermore, the handbook's usefulness extends to students in other behavioral and health sciences. The Board recommends this work for the core collection of academic libraries.

Concise Encyclopedia of Psychology. Raymond J. Corsini, ed. John Wiley, 1987. hard. 1 vol. 1,242 pp. illus. index. ISBN 0-471-01068-5. $99.95. encyclopedia.
BF31.C67 150.3′21

The excellence of the original four-volume set of ENCYCLOPEDIA OF PSYCHOLOGY has not been compromised in the *Concise Encyclopedia of Psychology,* an adept, one-volume condensation. This abridgment retains 80 percent of the material published in the original set with only 55 percent of the original's bulk. This abbreviated edition was produced to make the work affordable for even the smallest libraries.

Corsini states in the preface that this version includes every entry found in the multivolume work. Although some of the original articles have been updated, several entries relating to new developments have been added. One important addition is the entry *artificial intelligence.*

There are 2,150 entries: 1,500 treat topics; 650 are biographical. Entries, which are arranged alphabetically, are signed. Articles are clearly written and generally conclude with a list of one to three references for further reading. These references are listed in the bibliography at the end of the book. An adequate subject index and abundant cross-references lead readers to related entries.

The technical production of this book is superior. The layout is attractive as well as functional: The double-column format makes entries easy to read. Headings, subheadings, and cross-references are printed in boldface type. Although this version is substantially shorter than its parent, the alterations have not detracted from the book's quality and usefulness.

Corsini's careful distillation has created the best existing single-volume encyclopedia of psychology. At less than one-third the price of the original, this work is within the means of most libraries. Most libraries owning the original encyclopedia will probably decide not to purchase the *Concise Encyclopedia of Psychology* since the work duplicates material found in the four-volume set. However, the new work's updates make it useful, and the work is quite valuable for libraries that could not afford the parent work. The Board recommends this work for the core collections of public, academic, and school libraries.

Diagnostic and Statistical Manual of Mental Disorders, 3d edition rev. American Psychiatric Assn., 1987. hard and soft. 1 vol. 567 pp. appendixes. indexes. ISBN 0-89042-018-1 (hard); 0-89042-019-X (soft). $43.95 (hard); $32.95 (soft). manual.
RC455.2.C4D54 616.89′075

The *Diagnostic and Statistical Manual of Mental Disorders,* 3d edition, revised (called *DSM-III-R*), is the standard handbook used by mental health professionals and researchers in the United States to define and diagnose mental disorders. The work is a revision of the third edition, which was published in 1980. Almost four years in the making, *DSM-III-R* updates, clarifies, and corrects some of the diagnostic criteria contained in the 1980 manual. The fourth edition is scheduled for publication sometime in the 1990s.

The American Psychiatric Association appointed 26 advisory committees made up of more than 200 members to work on the revision. Committee members were carefully selected to achieve a balance between clinicians and researchers. Drafts of the manual were made available to interested professionals in an effort to obtain feedback; for some disorders, diagnostic criteria were tested in national field trials.

A lengthy introduction traces the manual's history, the process used to revise the third edition, and the basic features of this edition. Following the introduction, a cautionary statement warns that the proper application of these guidelines requires clinical training. Three chapters, eight appendixes, and two indexes make up the remainder of the book.

The first chapter outlines the classification scheme used to categorize more than 200 illnesses and disorders. Because of the complexity of this tool, an entire chapter is devoted to instructions on using the manual. Chapter 3 defines disorders and describes their symptoms. A standardized format allows for comparison between disorders. The following characteristics are generally identified for each disorder: associated features, age at onset, course, impairment, complications, predisposing factors, prevalence, sex ratio, familial pattern, and differential diagnosis. Diagnostic criteria are listed in boxes and set off from the text. Disorders are grouped by broad categories (mood disorders, sleep disorders, personality disorders, and so on).

The most useful appendixes of the eight provided are appendix B, which diagrams decision trees to assist clinicians in diagnosis; appendix C, which is a glossary of technical terms; and appendix D, which compares *DSM-III* and *DSM-III-R.* Other appendixes included are appendix A, "Proposed Diagnostic Categories Needing Further Study"; appendix E, "Historical Review, ICD-9 Glossary and Classification, and ICD-9-CM Classification"; appendix F, "DSM-III-R Field Trial Participants"; appendix G, "Alphabetic Listing of DSM-III-R Diagnoses and Codes"; and appendix H, "Numeric Listing of DSM-III-R Diagnoses and Codes." There are two separate indexes: symptom and diagnostic.

The guidelines in this manual are widely accepted in the mental health fields. This manual is an essential purchase for any library serving programs in psychology, psychiatry, counseling, social work, and medicine. The *Diagnostic and Statistical Manual of Mental Disorders* also aids patrons in understanding professional terminology and diagnoses. The Board recommends this work for the core collections of public and academic libraries.

Dictionary of Behavioral Science, 2d edition. Benjamin B. Wolman, comp. and ed. Krieger, 1989. hard. 1 vol. 370 pp. ISBN 0-12-762455-4. $39.95. dictionary.
BF31.D48 150.3

The first edition of the *Dictionary of Behavioral Science,* published by Van Nostrand Reinhold, was chosen as one of the outstanding reference books of 1973 by the American Library Association. Since then the dictionary has become a standard source for locating brief and precise definitions of terminology in the psychosciences. The second edition is more current than the *Longman Dictionary of Psychology and Psychiatry* and broader in scope than the ENCYCLOPEDIC DICTIONARY OF PSYCHOLOGY or Campbell's PSYCHIATRIC DICTIONARY.

Each of the 20,000 terms included in the first edition was evaluated for accuracy and currency. If a revision was necessary, an entry was rewritten by the original contributor. Ninety distinguished researchers and clinicians contributed to the 1973 edition. These contributors included such major figures as Jerome Bruner, Raymond Cattel, H. J. Eysenck, Anna Freud, Erich Fromm, Carl Rogers, and B. F. Skinner. The preface states that the second edition revised or added scores of entries.

All subfields of psychology are included: experimental, developmental, applied, social, industrial, and educational. Psychiatry, clinical practice, biochemistry, and psychopharmacology are also part of the broad scope, and neurology, neurosurgery, genetics, endocrinology, and psychoanalysis have some coverage. A few of the entries are biographical. In conceptual entries, the originator of a concept, idea, or technique is identified in parentheses after the term. For example, Adler is named as the author of the *inferiority complex.*

Entries are unsigned and listed in alphabetical order. Definitions range in length from one line to almost three pages, the longest entry being a condensation of the classification of mental disorders. Many entries are a single sentence, and most do not exceed a paragraph in length. No pronunciations are given, but cross-references are provided. Language is geared to the undergraduate.

Excellent graphics help make the book easy to use. Terms appear in clear boldface type, and a spacious layout and double-column format allow for easy scanning of entries. Cross-references are distinguished by italic type. The paper is high-quality stock, and the binding is designed to withstand heavy use.

No other dictionary in the field is as up to date, concise, comprehensive, and readable as the *Dictionary of Behavioral Science.* Libraries with a psychology reference section should consider this an essential purchase. The Board recommends this work for the core collection of academic libraries.

Encyclopedia of Psychology. Raymond J. Corsini, ed. John Wiley, 1984. hard. 4 vols. illus. index. ISBN 0-471-86594-X (set). $345 (set). encyclopedia. BF31.E52 150.3'21

All areas of psychology are equitably covered in this exceptional multivolume *Encyclopedia of Psychology.* A total of 2,100 articles fill three volumes. The fourth volume is an extensive bibliography, listing 15,000 references.

Many factors contribute to the authority of this work. Corsini has edited numerous books in psychology and education and is also a psychologist specializing in psychotherapy. He has assembled an impressive group of editorial consultants and contributors. The foreword is written by Rollo May, the distinguished psychoanalyst. All 16 consulting editors are past presidents of the American Psychological Association, the leading professional association for psychologists in this country. The 14 associate editors and the 21 foreign editors are recognized authorities in their subfields of psychology. May refers to the list of 486 contributors as a "Who's Who" in psychology. A quick scan of the roster reveals the names of well-known experts such as Louise Bates Ames and Thomas Szasz.

Corsini consulted reference books, textbooks, *Psychological Abstracts,* and the THESAURUS OF PSYCHOLOGICAL INDEX TERMS to develop a balanced list of topics. These subjects encompass aspects of general, experimental, developmental, social, educational, applied, and clinical psychology. Biographical entries include living and deceased psychologists.

Entries are in alphabetical order, and the author of each article is identified. The length of items ranges from fewer than 200 words to more than 900 words. Many articles are subdivided and include a list of references for further reading. The complete bibliographic information for each reference is contained in volume 4. Ample cross-references are given to link concepts. The final volume also includes a name index and a subject index. Although the encyclopedia has slightly more than 2,000 entries, the indexes provide access to more than 24,000 subjects.

Jargon is kept to a minimum, so articles are understandable to the educated lay reader as well as the specialist. Students, researchers, and professionals in the mental health professions will find this work to be a reliable source of information. The work has a few drawbacks, however. Some may consider the bibliography in volume 4 cumbersome and unwieldy. Corsini justifies the bulk of this volume in the introduction, maintaining that complete bibliographic information was necessary in order to avert duplication and ensure accuracy. Unfortunately, the boldface type used for headings, subheadings, and cross-references is indistinguishable from the rest of the type. These flaws, although irksome, do not significantly hamper the work's usefulness.

No other psychological encyclopedia is as comprehensive, reputable, and current as the *Encyclopedia of Psychology.* This encyclopedia will be a clear choice for libraries where high cost is not an obstacle. (Fortunately, libraries unable to afford the *Encyclopedia of Psychology* have the option of purchasing Corsini's excellent and affordable abridgment, the CONCISE ENCYCLOPEDIA OF PSYCHOLOGY.) The Board recommends this work for the core collections of public and academic libraries.

The Encyclopedic Dictionary of Psychology. Rom Harré and Roger Lamb, eds. MIT Pr., 1983. hard. 1 vol. 718 pp. illus. index. ISBN 0-262-08135-0. $95. dictionary.
BF31.E555 150.3′21

The Encyclopedic Dictionary of Psychology serves as a handbook to traditional and peripheral topics in psychology. The inclusion of "fringe psychologies" differentiates this title from similar sources. One example of the coverage of nontraditional areas is the entry on *transpersonal psychology.* When defining the volume's scope, the editors organized psychology into three categories: cognitive psychology, psycholinguistics, and neuropsychology. These major divisions were broadened to encompass developmental, educational, social, physiological, clinical, and comparative psychology. Sixteen prominent psychologists, philosophers, and physiologists acted as consultants in determining topics for inclusion. Entries were authored by more than 300 researchers and practitioners. Editors Rom Harré and Roger Lamb are both affiliated with Oxford University, but contributors were drawn from various institutions in North America and Europe. Initials identify the author of each article.

Although the majority of articles relate to subjects, biographical articles are included. Many of the biographies are not the standard ones found in dictionaries or encyclopedias of psychology. For example, several lesser-known philosophers are included. In fact, the incorporation of philosophy greatly enhances this volume, since psychology has been traditionally viewed as a branch of philosophy. Another distinct feature of this dictionary is its substantial coverage of subjects relating to animal behavior and animal learning.

Many concepts are concisely defined in one or two paragraphs, and other entries average a page in length. General readers, students, researchers, and professionals can benefit from these well-written survey articles. Authors adeptly use examples and rhetorical questioning to clarify concepts. A few black-and-white illustrations add to the text. Articles frequently trace the chain of research relating to an idea. References to key publications are made in the text, and full citations to these sources are provided in the bibliography that accompanies most articles. A quick glance at these sources for further reading gives the user a sense of the historical development of a subfield or theory. Extensive cross-referencing directs readers to related articles. In addition, a detailed index and glossary are supplied, which will aid the student or lay reader who may be unfamiliar with the more technical language. The design of the book contributes to its ease of use. Different typefaces are effectively used, and entries are spaciously laid out in a double-column format.

When compared to other reference books in psychology, *The Encyclopedic Dictionary of Psychology* offers a broader and unique perspective. The Board recommends this work for the core collections of public and academic libraries.

International Encyclopedia of Psychiatry, Psychology, Psychoanalysis, & Neurology. Benjamin B. Wolman, ed. Van Nostrand Reinhold, 1977. hard. 12 vols. plus 1 suppl. illus. indexes. ISBN 0-918228-01-8. $675. encyclopedia.
RC334.I57 616.8′9′003

The *International Encyclopedia of Psychiatry, Psychology, Psychoanalysis, & Neurology* is an award-winning set that took eight years to produce and involved 1,500 contributors and almost 300 editors and consultants. Comprised of 12 volumes, the work contains approximately 5 million words. The book's authority was confirmed when it received the Dartmouth Medal in 1978, the American Library Association's tribute to the year's outstanding reference work.

Editor Benjamin Wolman has authored and edited numerous books in psychology, psychiatry, and psychoanalysis, including the DICTIONARY OF BEHAVIORAL SCIENCE, which was first published in 1973. He is also a clinical psychologist of considerable eminence. Both researchers and clinicians were enlisted as contributors and consultants for the encyclopedia. The foreword is written by Jean Piaget. The roster of participants is impressive, including well-known national and international scholars.

This encyclopedia provides comprehensive coverage of topics in psychology, psychiatry, psychoanalysis, and neurology. Coverage also extends to related areas such as biochemistry, genetics, ergonomics, and psychosomatic medicine. While designed primarily for graduate students and researchers in the four fields identified in the title, the work is also an excellent reference source for professionals working in medicine, mental health, and social work.

Approximately 2,000 signed articles are printed in alphabetical order in the first 11 volumes. Volume 12, over 400 pages in length, contains an alphabetical list of articles, a name index, and an extensive subject index. Topical articles are wide ranging, including *biorhythms, child abuse, consumer psychology, genius, obesity* and its treatment, *retirement, school phobia, shyness, testing the mentally retarded,* and *women psychiatrists.* There are also separate entries on the state of psychology and psychiatry in foreign countries.

Most biographies recount the lives and accomplishments of deceased persons, although a few living individuals are included. Articles generally conclude with a selective list of sources, and full bibliographic information is provided for each source. The source lists are minor weaknesses; very few references date later than 1974, and sources are restricted to English-language material.

Topics do not always receive even coverage. This is probably unavoidable given the encyclopedia's magnitude. Fortunately, generous cross-references and the detailed subject index lead readers to related topics. Overall, articles are well written, authoritative, and provide a good overview. The text is readable and appropriate for the undergraduate student as well as upper-level students and scholars. Line drawings, charts, and graphs illustrate the text. Ease of use is enhanced by the double-column format and various typefaces.

Progress Volume I, a supplement updating the 12-volume set, was published in 1983 by Aesculapius. This volume follows the format established in the set and makes numerous references to articles in volumes 1 through 11. This volume reports on developments that have emerged since 1977. The publisher plans additional supplements as needed. Libraries owning the set will find this supplementary volume essential.

Although the set is more than a decade old, the work remains a standard source for academic libraries, even at its somewhat hefty price. Broader in scope than Corsini's ENCYCLOPEDIA OF PSYCHOLOGY and more comprehensive than Wolman's DICTIONARY OF BEHAVIORAL SCIENCE, the *International Encyclopedia of Psychiatry, Psychology, Psychoanalysis, & Neurology* is a worthy addition to collections serving students in the behavioral and health sciences. The Board recommends this work for the core collection of academic libraries.

The Oxford Companion to the Mind. Richard L. Gregory ed. Oxford, 1987. hard. 1 vol. 856 pp. illus. index. ISBN 0-19-866124-X. $49.95. dictionary.
BF31.094 128.2

The Oxford Companion to the Mind brings together definitions of concepts, theories, and processes relating to the psychology, physiology, and philosophy of the mind. More than 100 eminent contributors have written for this one-volume reference work, which distinguishes itself from numerous other dictionaries and encyclopedias in psychology by incorporating entries for diverse and distinct subjects related to the main topic. The wide-ranging scope is reflected by the following entries: *artificial intelligence, bilingualism, child abuse, Egyptian concepts of mind, ergonomics, evolution, hearing, Leonardo Da Vinci,* the *psychology of music,* and *Spinoza.* The reader is also tempted to browse, given the work's inclusion of interesting topics such as *biological clock, blushing* (which Darwin studied extensively), *computer chess, déjà vu, dreaming, jet lag,* and *taste.*

The editor is well qualified to assemble articles about the operations of the mind. Richard Gregory is a professor of neuropsychology as well as the director of Britain's Brain and Perception Laboratory at the University of Bristol. There is a noticeable British slant to this work: Most of the contributors are British, and no attempt is made to include the U.S. spelling of terms. Regardless of this bias, Gregory is to be applauded for his success in obtaining the participation of several distinguished British and U.S. theorists. The late B. F. Skinner contributed an entry on *behaviorism,* and Noam Chomsky discussed his ideas about *language.* H. J. Eysenck authored the entry on *behavior therapy,* an ideal choice because Eysenck originated the term in the 1950s.

Approximately 1,000 entries are arranged in alphabetical order and range in length from a few lines to more than 20 pages. The entry exceeding 20 pages is in fact a tutorial on the nervous system. Biographical entries are included but limited to deceased individuals. Lengthier articles are signed and conclude with short bibliographies listing the most fundamental and often primary sources on a subject. Access to entries is enhanced by abundant cross-references and an index to subjects, the authors of entries, and the authors of cited references. Illustrations include black-and-white photographs and line drawings.

The Oxford Companion to the Mind was selected by the American Library Association as one of the 26 outstanding reference books of 1987. The Board recommends this work for the core collections of public, academic, and school libraries.

Psychiatric Dictionary, 6th edition. Robert Jean Campbell. Oxford, 1989. hard. 1 vol. 811 pp. ISBN 0-19-505293-5. $45. dictionary.
RC437.H5 616.89′003′21

The *Psychiatric Dictionary* is a standard work in its field that was first published in 1940. Although the primary goal of this reference tool remains the definition of psychiatric terminology, the sixth edition incorporates the language of other professions, such as law. Author Robert Campbell recognizes the necessity for psychiatrists to understand terms used by lawyers, legislators, public officials, health care managers, journalists, and other physicians. The change in medical care delivery over the past decade is reflected in the inclusion of terms such as *HMO, PPO,* and *cost shifting.* This edition also mirrors the recent expansion of information in the neurological sciences and in certain areas of clinical psychiatry (including but not limited to the treatment of sleep and eating disorders, speech disorders, and depression). The terminology of the third edition (revised) of the DIAGNOSTIC AND STATISTICAL MANUAL OF MENTAL DISORDERS is also introduced in this edition.

The size of the dictionary has increased with this update. Although the number of entries is not identified, this edition is approximately 100 pages longer than the fifth edition (published in 1981). The number of deletions, additions, or revisions is not stated; however, the length of entries is consistent with the previous edition. Although some terms are adequately defined in a sentence or two, many terms receive encyclopedic treatment. Ease of use is facilitated through the use of abundant cross-references and the pronunciations that are provided for many terms. Obsolete terms are labeled as such. The writing is comprehensible to practitioners as well as students and professionals in related areas. The preface indicates Campbell's intent to make the work more understandable and more useful to a wider range of readers.

This volume has been expertly produced. Terms appear in boldface type, and cross-references are identified by italic type. Scanning is made easy by the double column format, adequate spacing, and large typeface. The binding is designed for heavy use.

This work is unquestionably the best psychiatric dictionary on the market. Oxford's *Psychiatric Dictionary* would benefit the core collection in an academic library serving students and professionals in psychiatry and clinical psychology. Students in nursing, social work, and other allied health fields will also find this reference work useful. The Board recommends this work for the core collection of academic libraries.

Psychological Abstracts. American Psychological Assn., monthly (1927–). soft. indexes. ISSN 0033-2887. $995 (per year). on-line.
BF1.P65 150.5

Empirical research findings in psychology are generally reported in scholarly journals rather than books. In fact, one could effectively argue that journal articles in psychology are primary rather than secondary sources of information. This emphasis on journal literature has contributed to the development of *Psychological Abstracts,* an excellent indexing and abstracting service providing bibliographic access to the world's journal literature in psychology and related areas.

Although core journals in psychology are also indexed in the *Social Sciences Index* and the *Social Sciences Citation Index, Psychological Abstracts* is considered to be the single most comprehensive index to the serial literature in psychology. Indexers scan approximately 1,400 journals annually for coverage. All areas of psychology are represented as well as the allied disciplines of psychiatry, sociology, social work, anthropology, education, linguistics, marketing, and management.

Psychological Abstracts began in 1927 as the successor to *Psychological Index.* Numerous changes have been made since the first edition; for example, dissertations, books, and book chapters had been included in the printed index but were omitted in 1980. Foreign-language journals were removed from the printed index in January of 1988. (Access to dissertations and foreign-language articles is still available through PsycINFO, the corresponding data base.) Book coverage has ceased in both the print and on-line version of *Psychological Abstracts* and has only recently been made accessible through *Psycbooks 1988: Books & Chapters in Psychology,* a 1989 publication of the American Psychological Association.

Since 1984 *Psychological Abstracts* has been published monthly. Citations to articles and accompanying abstracts are organized under 17 broad categories ("Developmental Psychology" and "Treatment and Prevention" are two). Most categories are further divided by subsections. This arrangement essentially allows users to browse through abstracts in their areas of interest. Abstracts are consecutively numbered. More than 37,000 articles were indexed in 1988. Monthly issues include author and subject indexes. The subject index alphabetically lists subject headings established by the THESAURUS OF PSYCHOLOGICAL INDEX TERMS. Separate author and subject indexes are produced annually. Cumulative author and subject indexes are available for the period 1927 through 1983.

A record in the printed index contains the following elements: record numbers; name(s) of author(s) or editor(s); institutional affiliation of the first named author or editor; article title; journal name, date, volume, and pages; a descriptive summary of the article; and the number of cited references. The exclusion of foreign-language material in the printed source has been effective in dramatically reducing the backlog in indexing. The average time lag between article publication and indexing is now only five months.

The data base and compact disc product were as carefully constructed as the printed index. PsycINFO, the on-line version, covers 1967 to the present. PsycLIT, the compact disc counterpart, covers from 1974 to the present and indexes journal literature only.

Psychological Abstracts, both in printed and computerized form, has set the standard by which other indexes and abstracts can be judged. This superb index is an indispensable tool in any library where users need articles relating to the behavioral sciences. The Board recommends this work for the core collection of academic libraries.

Publication Manual of the American Psychological Association, 3d edition. American Psychological Assn., 1983. soft. 1 vol. 208 pp. appendix. index. ISBN 0-912704-57-8. $19.50. manual. on-line.
BF76.7.P83 808.02

The American Psychological Association's (APA) guidelines for the preparation and writing of journal articles were first published in a short article in the February 1929 issue of the *Psychological Bulletin,* a prestigious journal published by the Association. Although the APA produced only four journals in those years, even then it envisioned the need to prepare manuscripts in a uniform style. This third edition details the present standards for the submission of articles for publication consideration in the more than 25 research journals sponsored by the APA. This bibliographic format is used in psychology as a whole as well as in many of the other social sciences. Most psychology departments in the United States require that students use this format for papers, theses, and dissertations.

This edition of the *Publication Manual* represents an expansion, reorganization, and revision of the previous edition, published in 1974. Information is organized into seven chapters. An appendix outlines the preparation requirements for material other than journal articles (student papers, oral presentations, brief reports, theses, dissertations), contrasting the differences between requirements. The index refers users to the appropriate page number rather than to the section number, as was the case in the second edition. This arrangement is more understandable and easier to use.

Several improvements have been made in this edition. An increase in the number of examples overall greatly adds to the guide's clarity.

Chapters are arranged in a logical sequence. The first chapter covers the content and organization of manuscripts, comparing review articles, theoretical articles, and reports of empirical studies. Chapter 2 gives authors guidelines on writing clearly and without grammatical errors. This edition is the first to include a section on avoiding sexist language. The core of the manual is Chapter 3, which describes in detail APA editorial style. This chapter dictates the rules concerning punctuation, abbreviations, illustrative materials, headings, and references to citations in the text and the bibliography of a manuscript. Rules are clarified with examples. Chapter 4 gives instructions on typing a paper, followed by a sample that incorporates those guidelines. The procedures for submitting an article for publication consideration are explained in the following chapter, as are instructions on proofreading galleys of articles accepted for publication. Chapter 6 is restricted to a discussion of the policies of the individual journals published by the APA. The final chapter is a bibliography listing sources about the history of the manual, sources referenced in the third edition, and sources for further reading on topics covered in the manual.

Most academic libraries will need to acquire multiple copies of the *Publication Manual of the American Psychological Association.* The soft binding will not withstand the heavy use that this volume will receive. The Board recommends this work for the core collection of academic libraries.

The Tenth Mental Measurements Yearbook. Jane Close Conoley and Jack J. Kramer, eds. Buros Institute of Mental Measurements, 1989; distrib. by Univ. of Nebraska Pr. hard. 1 vol. 1,014 pp. indexes. ISBN 0-910674-31-0. $125. yearbook. on-line.
Z5814.P8B932 371.26

The Tenth Mental Measurement Yearbook is recognized as the standard source for factual and evaluative information on commercially available English-language tests used in psychological and educational assessments. The series was initiated by Oscar Krisen Buros in 1938. Although Buros is deceased and his editorial work has been carried on by others, patrons continue to ask for "Buros" when they need test information.

Each yearbook supplements previous volumes. Although the first nine yearbooks were published irregularly, the Buros Institute of the University of Nebraska at Lincoln has established a regular publishing schedule with this edition. The plan calls for a yearbook to be published every two years and a supplement to be published in the alternate years. *The Mental Measurements Yearbook (MMY)* is also available on-line, covering the period from 1977 to the present, with selective retrospective coverage for the year 1972.

The Tenth MMY describes 396 tests that have been devised or substantially revised since the publication of *The Ninth MMY* in 1985. Three hundred fifty-one of the tests have been critiqued by knowledgeable reviewers. More than 60 percent of the tests included have been reviewed by two individuals. Most reviews conclude with a list of references. Tests cover 16 broad categories including achievement, intelligence and scholastic aptitude, personality, reading, speech and hearing, and vocations.

The yearbook has an encyclopedic format; entries are arranged in alphabetical order by test title and are numbered. Test descriptions include information relating to purpose, population, timing, scoring, cost, and publisher. Cross-references refer to earlier editions of *MMY* and *Tests in Print,* a series functioning as an index to *MMY.* Descriptive data are followed by critical reviews written by specialists working in a wide range of settings including universities, public schools, industry, and private practice.

Six separate indexes are provided. Citations are to test numbers, not pages. This feature may confuse some users even though test numbers and test titles are printed at the top of each page. The title index provides cross-references to superseded and alternative titles. Each title is coded to indicate whether the test is new or revised. An acronyms index allows users to locate information on tests that are more likely to be known by their acronym than by their full title. The classified subject index groups tests into 16 broad categories. Address information for publishers is listed in the publisher's directory and index. Test entry numbers are included for each publisher, a feature that allows users to examine the range of tests sold by a particular publisher. The index of names includes the names of test reviewers, test authors, or cited references. Finally, the score index alphabetically lists all the scores for tests included in the yearbook, effectively serving as a detailed subject index.

No other reference work on tests and measurements is as evaluative and thorough as *The Mental Measurements Yearbook* series. This reference tool can be used as a test selection aid by psychologists, educators, guidance counselors, personnel examiners, and speech pathologists. *The Tenth Mental Measurements Yearbook* is a basic source for users who need information on standardized tests. The Board recommends this work for the core collections of public and academic libraries.

Tests: A Comprehensive Reference for Assessments in Psychology, Education, and Business, 2d edition. Richard C. Sweetland and Daniel J. Keyser, eds. PRO-ED, 1990. hard and soft. 1 vol. 1,122 pp. indexes. ISBN 0-89079-255-0 (hard); 0-89079-256-9 (soft). $59 (hard); $34 (soft). handbook.
BF176.T43 153.9′3

Tests: A Comprehensive Reference for Assessments in Psychology, Education, and Business is a compendium briefly describing more than 4,000 published English-language tests frequently used in psychology, education, and business. Reviews or critiques of tests are not included. All tests were in print at the time of publication. This edition revises and updates the first edition published in 1983 and the 1984 *Supplement.* The original edition was printed three times within its first year of publication because it was so well received.

Sweetland and Keyser, clinical psychologists, edit TEST CRITIQUES, a series containing evaluations of commercially available tests used for assessments in psychology, education, and industry. Their familiarity with this field lends authority to this work.

The book is divided into three broad sections: psychology, education, and business and industry. These categories are further subdivided into a total of 73 subsections. Each test is assigned to only one subsection of a major category, although a test may be cross-referenced in up to two subsections. Tests are listed alphabetically by title.

The following information is provided for each test: the test title and author; the population for which the test is designed (child, adolescent, adult, age or grade range); a visual code that indicates whether the test is administered by the testee or by an examiner; one or two lines defining the test's purpose; a paragraph summary of the test; and an outline of the number of test items, test format, variables measured, materials used, manner in which the test is administered, foreign-language availability, and special features. Following the description, data are given on timing, scoring, cost, and publisher. Information about tests was verified by contacting the 437 publishers represented in the volume. Boldface type and the double-column format make the information easy to read.

Eight indexes are provided to assist users in locating tests. The title index allows users to locate tests by title, if known. Individuals needing information about tests for special populations may find the hearing-impaired, visually impaired, physically impaired, and foreign-language availability indexes helpful. Users who know a test's author or popular name may consult the author index. Address information for publishers is included in the publisher and distributor index; tests that have gone out of print since the first edition are listed in the out-of-print index.

Tests: A Comprehensive Reference for Assessments in Psychology, Education, and Business is a good starting point for individuals wanting basic information on tests. It is an essential item for a reference collection focusing on tests and measurements. However, persons needing evaluative material on tests will still have to use THE TENTH MENTAL MEASUREMENTS YEARBOOK or the editors' TEST CRITIQUES in addition to *Tests.* The Board recommends this work for the core collection of academic libraries.

Thesaurus of Psychological Index Terms, 5th edition. American Psychological Assn., 1988. spiralbound. 1 vol. 291 pp. appendixes. ISBN 0-912704-67-5. $65. thesaurus.
Z695.1.P7 025.4′915

Since the publication of the first edition in 1974, the *Thesaurus of Psychological Index Terms* has been regarded by librarians as an exemplary thesaurus. Essential for users of PSYCHOLOGICAL ABSTRACTS and the corresponding PsycINFO data base, the thesaurus lists the terms used to index documents in the printed index, on-line data base, and compact disc product.

A controlled vocabulary is a must in psychology because of the interdisciplinary nature of the field. Specificity in language is even more important because psychology involves both animal and human populations. In this thesaurus, the American Psychological Association has established descriptors, or subject headings, for topics in order to organize the expansive vocabulary. Indexers who assign descriptors to items have been careful to select the most precise thesaurus terms available.

This work is organized into two divisions: the "Relationship" section and the "Rotated Alphabetical Terms" section. In the former section, terms are listed alphabetically in boldface type. A two-digit number after the term indicates the year that the term was designated as a descriptor. The postings note, identified as PN, shows how frequently a term is used in the indexing of PsycINFO records. The subject code relating to the term is represented by a five-digit number. The definition of a term may be stated in a scope note (SN) if it is unique to the data base, ambiguous in meaning, or the meaning has changed over time. The code UF indicates that the thesaurus term is used instead of a similar term and that the UF term is not searchable (for example, "women" would be the common term, but "human females" would be the searchable term). The hierarchical relationship of terms is demonstrated by a listing of broader (B) and narrower (N) terms. Related terms (R) may also be noted. Users are referred to the appropriate descriptor by the "use" reference.

The rotated alphabetical terms section lists searchable and cross-reference terms in alphabetical order. Nonsearchable terms are printed in italics and starred with an asterisk. This edition is the first to include nonpostable terms in this section.

There are three appendixes. Appendix A records the 250 descriptors that have been added since the publication of the fourth edition of the thesaurus in 1983. Appendix B lists 100 new nonsearchable terms. The third appendix outlines the content classification system used by PsycINFO.

In each edition of the *Thesaurus of Psychological Index Terms,* changes have been made to improve the guide's usefulness. The fifth edition is enriched by the addition of 100 new scope notes and the revision of 75 existing scope notes. Unfortunately, the guide is still published in a spiralbound format. Most libraries will have to substitute library binding given the heavy usage of this source. Nevertheless, for any library subscribing to PSYCHOLOGICAL ABSTRACTS or searching the data base, the *Thesaurus of Psychological Index Terms* remains a basic acquisition. The Board recommends this work for the core collection of academic libraries.

Supplementary Titles

Biographical Dictionary of Psychology, 2d edition. Leonard Zusne. Greenwood, 1984. hard. 1 vol. 563 pp. appendixes. index. ISBN 0-313-24027-2. $79.95. dictionary.
BF109.A1Z85 150.92′2

"Reviewed favorably when the first edition [titled *History of Psychology*] appeared in 1975, the second edition [retitled *Biographical Dictionary of Psychology*] . . . should also have broad appeal to academic libraries. . . . [One hundred and one] new biographies have been added. The chronological arrangement of the earlier edition has given way to a more useful alphabetical one. . . . Many of the original biographies have been revised, and the list of biographical sources that follow each biography has been greatly expanded. . . . The index, a strong feature of the earlier edition, is even more useful in the present work." (*Choice,* March 1985, p. 972)

"Each of [some] 600 . . . deceased biographees has an entry stressing contributions and listing place and date of birth and death, highest degree, and major positions held, followed by a selective list of accessible sources for further biographical data, and a . . . narrative section averaging 23 lines. Sources and death dates extend up to 1982." (*LJ,* August 1984, p. 1438)

"There are three Appendixes: a chronological listing by birth date; a ranking by relative eminence, and groups of names by academic and research institutions." (*BL,* May 15, 1985, p. 1314)

Also reviewed in: *A Lib,* May 1986, p. 318; *ARBA,* 1985, p. 241; *Nature,* December 13, 1984, p. 672; *RQ,*

Spring 1985, p. 352; *Ref Bk R,* 1985, p. 27; *WLB,* February 1985, p. 420.

Board's recommendation: Academic libraries.

Library Research Guide to Psychology. Nancy E. Douglas and Nathan Baum. Pierian Pr., 1984. soft. 1 vol. 65 pp. 0-87650-175-7 $15. handbook.
BF76.5.D63 150.72

Library Research Guide to Psychology explains "the use of fundamental reference tools such as *Psychological Abstracts* in the context of the library search strategy. The *Research Guide,* [a selective, basic reference] . . . covers the *Social Sciences Index* . . . but not [O.K.] Buros's [*Mental Measurements Yearbooks*] or numerous other specialized tools. . . . [In short,] the *Research Guide* treats [a few] titles in [great] detail." (*WLB,* November 1984, p. 227)

Also reviewed in: *ARBA,* 1985, p. 243.

Board's recommendation: Academic libraries.

Test Critiques. Daniel J. Keyser and Richard C. Sweetland, eds. PRO-ED, 1990. hard. 8 vols. indexes. ISBN 0-89079-254-2 (vol. 8). $498 (set); $79 per vol. handbook.
BF176.T419 150.28′7

"*Test Critiques* contain a set of reviews by measurement specialists of widely used psychological tests. . . . The selection of tests to be reviewed and critiqued was based on 'polling' of psychologists, educators, and members of various professional organizations.

"The reviews in each volume are presented alphabetically by title of test. Each volume contains an index of test publishers. [There are also] an index of test titles and an index of test authors and reviewers.

"Each review . . . follows a standard format. There is (1) an introductory section which generally gives the reader a detailed description of the test and the history of its development. This is followed by (2) a section dealing in practical applications, (3) a section on technical aspects of the test dealing with validity, reliability, etc., (4) a critique of the instrument, and (5) a listing of the references used by the reviewers." (*ARBA,* 1986, p. 286)

Also reviewed in: *ARBA,* 1987, p. 293.

Board's recommendation: Academic libraries.

New and Noteworthy

The Concise Dictionary of Psychology, 2d edition. David A. Statt. Routledge, Chapman & Hall 1990. soft. 1 vol. 136 pp. illus. ISBN 0-415-02662-8. $9.95. dictionary.
BF31.S62 150.3

"This revision of *The Dictionary of Psychology* (1981) defines many more words than a glossary in a psychology textbook. . . . An eclectic compilation of terms from virtually all schools of psychology (Freudian, behavioral, humanistic, Gestalt, etc.), [this book] also includes entries on people. All 1,300 entries whether biographical or general, are brief and written for the nonspecialist.

"[Many] . . . dictionaries of psychological terms [are] available. . . . [However, this book] is a good purchase for public and high school libraries that need a psychology dictionary aimed at laypeople." (*BL,* August 1990, p. 220)

The International Dictionary of Psychology. Stuart Sutherland. Continuum, 1989. hard. 1 vol. 500 pp. ISBN 0-8264-0440-5. $49.95. dictionary.
BF31.S83 150.321

"At long last, psychologists and lay readers have a legitimate dictonary (rather than an encyclopedia masquerading as one) that briefly defines technical psychological language and jargon borrowed from other disciplines. [This] easy-to-use, up-to-date reference source supplies explanations (and sometimes examples) for traditional psychological terms. . . . But more importantly, [it] includes phrases from related subject areas, e.g., *propositional attitude* (philosophy). . . . [The book's] entries, which contain ample cross-references, are usually no more than a paragraph and occasionally inject some humor. . . . This is an essential reference tool." (*LJ,* June 1, 1989, p. 102)

A Student's Dictionary of Psychology. Peter Stratton and Nicky Hayes. Arnold, 1989. hard and soft. 1 vol. 216 pp. illus. ISBN 0-7131-6501-4 (hard). $49.50 (hard); $13.95 (soft). dictionary.
BF31.S69 150.3′21

"[This book] defines psychological terms for the layperson. Basic terms and concepts in clinical and experimental psychology such as *schizophrenia* . . . and *play* receive short definitions in language an introductory college student can understand. There are no biographical entries. Dictionary information on pronunciation and usage [has] been omitted. . . . The layperson or student of introductory psychology is well served by this *Dictionary* of basic psychological terms." (*BL,* January 15, 1990, p. 1046)

Mary Jane Brustman

Public Administration

See also Political Science

Librarians purchasing reference materials in public administration must contend with the problem of defining the scope of public administration as a field of study. Over the course of American public administration's 100-year history, there has been no consensus as to its focus and boundaries. Narrowly defined, this field is the study of management in government. Broadly defined, public administration encompasses all of the study of social organization. Gerald Caiden, in his chapter "The Scope of American Public Administration" in *American Public Administration: A Bibliographical Guide to the Literature,* offers his definition, which he believes reflects current mainstream thought. Public administration is the "formulation and implementation of policies through the public bureaucracy." Some of the areas of study subsumed under this would be public management, human resources, public finance, policy analysis, public law and regulation, and comparative public administration. The last reflects the fact that public administration differs markedly from one country to another.

The boundaries of the literature of public administration are not easily defined. A look at standard textbooks suggests a core literature that consists partly of public administration journals and texts and partly of materials drawn from closely related fields. In reality, however, scholars and practitioners in public administration routinely reach far beyond this suggested core literature and into political science, law, economics, sociology, psychology, mathematics, management, history, and labor and industrial relations.

Providing access to the segment of this diverse and wide-ranging literature that is appropriate to the library's clientele is a major challenge to the collection-

Core Titles

	PUBLIC	ACADEMIC	SCHOOL
The Facts On File Dictionary of Public Administration Shafritz, Jay M. Facts On File, 1985	✦	✦	
The Public Administration Dictionary, 2d edition Chandler, Ralph C., and Jack C. Plano. ABC-Clio, 1988		✦	

development librarian. Users of public administration reference materials may include practitioners, scholars, students, or the general public.

The two core titles in public administration, both general dictionaries, complement each other. THE PUBLIC ADMINISTRATION DICTIONARY focuses on those terms "essential to understanding the field of public administration." THE FACTS ON FILE DICTIONARY OF PUBLIC ADMINISTRATION is comprehensive (covering over ten times as many terms as the previously mentioned title) and includes many terms in related fields. Many specialized dictionaries are available as well.

There are several excellent guides to the literature, including Frederick L. Holler's THE INFORMATION SOURCES OF POLITICAL SCIENCE, selected as a supplementary title.

Two indexes provide coverage of the journals, books, and government publications relevant to public administration. *PAIS Bulletin* (Public Affairs Information Service, 1915–) covers the wider public affairs and policy fields. This would be the basic source for most public and academic libraries. *Sage Public Administration Abstracts* (Sage Publications, 1974–) is an important purchase that would support academic programs in public administration.

A comprehensive collection would require additional specialized public administration indexes, the major political science indexes, and a cross-section of indexes from other related disciplines as well. Statistical sources, directories of government agencies, officials, research organizations, and individuals in public administration and affairs as well as handbooks and dictionaries would be necessary as well. Although most of these sources are not overly expensive, cross-disciplinary coverage would be required for academic programs.

The Facts On File Dictionary of Public Administration. Jay M. Shafritz. Facts On File, 1985. hard. 1 vol. 610 pp. illus. appendixes. ISBN 0-8160-1266-0. $40. dictionary.
JA61.S54 350.000321

The Facts On File Dictionary of Public Administration contains entries for theories, concepts, and practice in public administration, as well as selected biographical entries, court cases, journals, laws, and organizations. With over 4,000 entries, its aim is to be comprehensive. The dictionary aims to include all "words, terms, phrases and processes with which a student or practitioner of public administration should be familiar, and then some" (preface). The preface indicates that terms were selected if they appeared in any of the standard texts on public administration. The selection process necessitated constant judgment calls on the part of the author on how far to go into other disciplines.

Jay M. Shafritz, now a professor at the Graduate School of Public and International Affairs, University of Pittsburgh, is a well-known author in the public administration field. He has published several books as well as numerous well-respected dictionaries on public administration or closely related fields. These include THE DORSEY DICTIONARY OF AMERICAN GOVERNMENT AND POLITICS (see Political Science) and *The Facts On File Dictionary of Personnel Management and Labor Relations.*

Terms are presented in two types of entries: brief glossary-type definitions and longer comprehensive entries. Shorter definitions run as few as 3 words; longer ones run up to 1,500 words. The author notes that they vary in length according to the importance of the term to the field. For example, *task* is defined simply as a "unit of work," whereas the entry for *grant* is 750 words long and has 20 bibliographic reference citations.

Access to this dictionary is excellent. Entries are arranged alphabetically. Although there is no index, useful cross-references abound. The design of the volume is visually pleasing, and the different segments of each entry (definitions, cross-references, bibliographic notes) are easy to follow. Boldface type highlights terms defined or cross-referenced.

In addition, the preface gives an excellent introduction, which succinctly defines the scope of the dictionary and explains the various types of entries. Two appendixes provide additional information, and a judicious use of charts and diagrams adds to the understanding of certain entries.

This dictionary is targeted at the student or practitioner. The terms covered and the reading level make this a good source for a well-educated general adult audience also. Its currency still remains good. Many of the bibliographic notes cited date from the 1980s.

The Facts On File Dictionary of Public Administration nicely complements THE PUBLIC ADMINISTRATION DICTIONARY. Aside from the comprehensiveness of the former and selectivity of the latter, content of entries serves as the major point of contrast. Taking as an example the entry on *comparable worth,* Shafritz provides an approximately 100-word, nonevaluative definition, followed by ten useful references to other sources. THE PUBLIC ADMINISTRATION DICTIONARY provides a definition of roughly the same length followed by 150 words on its significance. This puts the term in context and introduces some of the issues involved.

The Facts On File Dictionary of Public Administration is a basic source for all academic and most public libraries. The dictionary is recommended because of its comprehensive coverage, accurate and clear definitions, and useful bibliographical notes. These bibliographic notes provide valuable access to other sources and are an exceptionally useful feature for student papers. The Board recommends this work for the core collections of public and academic libraries.

The Public Administration Dictionary, 2d edition. Ralph C. Chandler and Jack C. Plano. ABC-Clio, 1988. hard and soft. 1 vol. 430 pp. indexes. ISBN 0-87436-498-1 (hard); 0-87436-499-X (soft). $49 (hard); $24 (soft). dictionary.
JA61.C47 350.000321

The preface to *The Public Administration Dictionary* states that it is a selective dictionary focusing on terms that are "fundamental to an understanding of the field." The 330 entries include concepts, events, strategies, theories, institutions, and leading thinkers. These entries are arranged into seven broad subject areas: fundamentals of public administration; public policy; public management; bureaucracy and administrative organization; financial administration; and public law and regulation. These subject divisions are intended to correspond roughly to the arrangement of some of the major texts in the public administration field. The arrangement was also meant to facilitate the use of the volume as either a study guide *or* a dictionary of terms.

The entry for each term has a definition of approximately 150 to 175 words, followed by a statement of its significance, which runs about the same length. The "Significance" section comments on historical or current relevance of the term. References are listed frequently within the text or at the end of the entry. (Full bibliographic information on the 125 references cited is found at the end of the book.)

The accuracy and authoritativeness of this dictionary are excellent. The authors, Chandler and Plano, both of Western Michigan University, are experienced and well-respected lexicographers. Ralph C. Chandler is author of the *Constitutional Law Dictionary* (ABC-Clio, 1985–1987). Jack C. Plano's THE AMERICAN POLITICAL DICTIONARY and THE INTERNATIONAL RELATIONS DICTIONARY (see Political Science for both titles) have been through numerous editions. Plano is also the author or editor of several other political science dictionaries.

The intellectual level of this dictionary is best suited to the college student. It is also this user group that might utilize it as a study guide and for which the subject division arrangement works best. For dictionary users, this type of access is more complicated. This is offset by the alphabetical arrangement of entries within broad subject divisions. Terms are also numbered. An excellent index uses these numbers to provide access to both entries and to terms embedded in entries. Cross-references are also plentiful.

The currency of this dictionary is excellent. Over half of the items in the bibliography date to the 1980s. According to the preface, 25 new entries have been included and numerous listings have been "revised and updated" for this second edition.

There are several points of contrast between *The Public Administration Dictionary* and THE FACTS ON FILE DICTIONARY OF PUBLIC ADMINISTRATION. The first is a selective dictionary, arranged by subject division and created for the dual purpose of serving as a study guide and dictionary, while the second is a straightforward dictionary of public administration terms. Chandler and Plano augment their definitions with comments on the significance of concepts, while THE FACTS ON FILE DICTIONARY OF PUBLIC ADMINISTRATION offers further sources of information.

The Public Administration Dictionary is notable for its careful, accurate, and detailed coverage of concepts and the usefulness of its notes on significance. The dictionary is an excellent starting point for further research.

Libraries will want to purchase *The Public Administration Dictionary.* The Board recommends this work for the core collection of academic libraries.

Supplementary Titles

American Public Administration: Past, Present, Future. Frederick C. Mosher, ed. Univ. of Alabama Pr., 1975. hard and soft. 1 vol. 298 pp. ISBN 0-8173-4828-X (hard); 0-8173-4829-8 (soft). $9.50 (soft). encyclopedia.
JF1338.A2A67 350.0007′1173

"[This book is the result of a conference that the] . . . National Association of Schools of Public Affairs and Administration (NASPAA) [held at the Maxwell School of Citizenship and Public Affairs at Syracuse University]. . . . NASPAA arranged for a series of seven lectures by the 'leading lights' of public administration, and *American Public Administration* is the compilation of those lectures. The contents include subjective reminiscences, efforts to analyze present problems associated with efforts to train for public service careers, and serious attempts to develop theory for a discipline of public administration. There is no other book on public administration comparable in scope and quality. Its availability in paperback should lead to widespread use as supplementary reading in public administration courses, and every library at any college offering even one course in public administration should have this book in its collection." (*Choice,* March 1976, p. 138)

"This collection of seven essays by some of the most eminent scholars and practitioners in the field of public administration is unmatched in its scope and quality. Each essay examines public administration thought and education during a given time period, but the volume is far more than a chronology of events." (*J Pol,* 1977, p. 270)

Board's recommendation: Academic libraries.

Information Sources of Political Science, 4th edition. Frederick L. Holler. ABC-Clio, 1986. hard. 1 vol. 417 pp. indexes. ISBN 0-87436-375-6. $79. bibliography.
Z7161.H64 016.32

See Political Science.

The Public Policy Dictionary. Earl R. Kruschke and Byron M. Jackson. ABC-Clio, 1987. hard and soft. 1 vol. 158 pp. index. ISBN 0-87436-443-4 (hard); 0-87436-460-4 (soft). $49 (hard); $19.95 (soft). dictionary.
H97.K78

"[In the *Public Policy Dictionary* the]. . . . purposes of the authors . . . are (1) to assist students to understand public policy and (2) 'to supplement the basic texts in public policy, political science, public administration, business, human resources, and the helping professions.' . . .

"Using expertly written definitions, the authors provide the meaning of a given term, in some instances the major authorities associated with the term, and finally the significance of the term. The 'significance' is a special feature designed to minimize the semantic confusion by indicating the term's relevance to modern politics or current trends in social science thinking.

"While the definitions are clear, the arrangement of the book is confusing. The term *public policy* is defined in chapter 1, "The Nature of Public Policy." Without the assistance of the index, it is difficult to find this term. A conventional single alphabetical dictionary arrangement would be more valuable to the reader.

"A second difficulty with the book is the 'significance' special feature. *Public policy* is frequently used as a rationale in many judicial decisions; however, the authors mention that the concept is 'based on law and authority' without ever discussing its application in case law. A similar problem emerges when trying to understand *affirmative action policy.* The definition mentions a 1961 executive order, but the significance section does not mention the related public laws or court cases that expand or clarify the concept of affirmative action. . . .

"[However,] *The Public Policy Dictionary* does clarify many terms, [and] it would be useful in large academic libraries with public administration doctoral programs or large public libraries with a clientele oriented toward cities and their governance." (*RQ,* Fall 1987, p. 143)

Also reviewed in: *ARBA,* 1988, p. 300; *Choice,* December 1987, p. 602; *R & R Bk N,* Summer 1987, p. 8.

Board's recommendation: Academic libraries.

Barbara A. Burg

Publishing

See also Book Arts; Graphic Arts

The publishing process involves an extraordinary array of activities in order to "get the word out" in final book form. The reviews that follow identify a core of reference books that serve some aspect of the publishing process, from preparing manuscripts (such as THE CHICAGO MANUAL OF STYLE or the MLA HANDBOOK FOR WRITERS OF RESEARCH PAPERS) to identifying awards for literary excellence (LITERARY AND LIBRARY PRIZES). Works that list markets for a writer's works—such as POET'S MARKET and WRITER'S MARKET—occupy a significant place in any publishing collection. These works are often published annually, and last year's edition will be useful on the circulating shelves. Useful supplements to this category will be additional style guides and dictionaries. Most of these sources are major tools of the trade for librarians, so patrons may have to vie with librarians for their use.

The scope of this volume precludes reviews of directories, but a brief discussion of the following titles—which have proven over time to be essential to a collection of works on publishing—is useful in defining the nature of this category.

The *American Book Trade Directory* (Bowker), a biennial publication, is the foremost guide to retailers and wholesalers in the United States and Canada. Included are listings for literary auctioneers, collection appraisers, foreign-language book dealers, and wholesale importers and exporters.

Most academic and public libraries will rely on the annual *Literary Market Place* (Bowker), for locating book publishers; editorial services; advertising, marketing, and publicity agencies; book manufacturing companies; and trade associations in the United States and Canada. *LMP*'s counterpart, *International Literary Market Place* (Bowker), provides access to publishers and book trade information in 160 foreign countries.

Finally, the indispensable *Books in Print* (Bowker) continues to be improved and expanded. As a necessary component of the publishing category, this valuable annual should be discussed briefly. Beginning with the 1989–1990 edition, this work now includes a separate volume listing some 50,000 titles that are out of print or out of stock indefinitely, in addition to a directory of search services and out-of-print bookstores. The four-volume *Subject Guide to Books in Print* (Bowker) is recommended for locating nonfiction titles using Library of Congress subject headings. This is the volume that writers seek out when trying to avoid duplicating material that has already been published and that librarians and their patrons use to locate additional titles in a specific subject area. The entire collection of Bowker's *Books in Print* volumes, including *Forthcom-*

Core Titles

	PUBLIC	ACADEMIC	SCHOOL
The Chicago Manual of Style, 13th edition, rev. and expanded Univ. of Chicago, 1982	✦	✦	✦
Literary and Library Prizes, 10th edition Weber, Olga S., and Stephen J. Calvert, eds. Bowker, 1980	✦	✦	
MLA Handbook for Writers of Research Papers, 3d edition Gibaldi, Joseph, and Walter S. Achtert. MLA, 1988	✦	✦	✦
Poet's Market: Where & How to Publish Your Poetry Jerome, Judson, ed. Writer's Digest, annual	✦	✦	
Writer's Market Neff, Glenda Tennant, ed. Writer's Digest, annual	✦	✦	

ing Books and the *Books in Print Supplement*, is now available on CD-ROM.

Core Titles

The Chicago Manual of Style, 13th edition, rev. and expanded. Univ. of Chicago, 1982. hard. 1 vol. 738 pp. index. ISBN 0-226-10390-0. $37.50. handbook.
Z253.U69 686.2'24

The Chicago Manual of Style is an institution in the field of publishing. For over 80 years it has guided countless writers and editors through the tortuous tangle of processes for preparing manuscripts for publication.

The Chicago Manual, first published in 1906, began humbly as the personal style sheet of a University of Chicago Press proofreader. Because style manuals were originally used by printers, the first 12 editions of *The Chicago Manual* included type specimens. These are omitted in this latest edition, which has become, in the words of the editorial staff, "more of a 'how-to' book for authors and editors than was its predecessor."

The thirteenth edition has been thoroughly updated and enlarged to reflect many of the technological and procedural changes that have occurred in publishing over the last 13 years. The new edition contains 738 pages—194 pages more than the twelfth edition.

Like the previous edition, the text is divided into three parts: "Bookmaking," "Style," and "Production and Printing." The chapters in each part are divided into numbered paragraphs. The index consists of main entries and subentries that are taken directly from the numbered paragraphs in the main text. The paragraph numbers that follow the subentries enable users to locate easily the information they want. For the most part, the manual's index meets its own criteria for a superior index by its "choice of good subheadings, both logical and useful to the reader."

Throughout the book, chapter headings and subheadings have been revised to provide greater accessibility to the reader. This is particularly noticeable in an examination of the table of contents that precedes each chapter. Further highlights of this edition include several new "how-to" sections. "How to Mark a Manuscript" describes and illustrates the standard editorial markings used for making changes on copy. Also included is a detailed set of instructions on how to mark a manuscript for a typesetter, which replaces the "Marking for a Printer" portion of the previous edition. The rewritten chapter on tables has new material that discusses in great detail how to make statistical tables from raw data. The section on making an index has been reorganized and now includes a step-by-step guide to this process. Another special addition is the Chinese Romanization table, which converts the Wade-Giles system to pinyin, and vice versa.

In the "Rights and Permissions" chapter, there is a thorough treatment of the Copyright Act of 1976, with suggestions for further reading at the end of the chapter. The three chapters on documentation, bibliographic forms, and note forms have been greatly enhanced with more examples and the inclusion of nonprint formats.

The "Production and Printing" chapter at the end

is worthwhile in itself for its thorough overview of how books are made. The glossary of technical terms used in printing is inclusive, as is the annotated bibliography, which includes other style manuals, usage and writing guides, dictionaries and glossaries, and other useful reference works.

Other important topics include spelling and distinctive treatment of words; foreign languages in type; illustrations, captions, and legends; and mathematics in type. Throughout the manual the editors explain why they favor a particular format or style. Most of their recommendations result from experience—with an eye toward economy, consistency, and common sense.

The Chicago Manual of Style is successful at being all things to all people. It serves as a style manual for major publishers of books, journals, and magazines, yet is accessible enough to serve as a how-to manual for persons who want to acquire proofreading and copyediting skills. The Board recommends this work for the core collections of public, academic, and school libraries.

Literary and Library Prizes, 10th edition. Olga S. Weber and Stephen J. Calvert, eds. Bowker, 1980. hard. 1 vol. 651 pp. index. ISBN 0-8352-1249-1. $26.95. handbook.
PN171.P75L5 807.9

Literary and Library Prizes originated in 1935 as *Famous Literary Prizes and Their Winners.* Library prizes were added to the fourth edition in 1959. According to the editors, approximately 675 literary and library prizes with more than 10,000 winners have been featured since the beginning of the series.

The tenth edition of *Literary and Library Prizes* lists 454 awards, 97 of which are new to this edition. Obscure prizes are excluded from the scope of this work, as are those that have only local importance. Most journalism awards are omitted. The criteria for inclusion are based on the subject of the award, recognition of regional talent, and the prominence of the sponsoring organization. Awards that have been discontinued since the last edition are still listed, with all winners, up to final ones, recorded. These awards, however, do not have descriptive entries in the tenth edition.

Literary and Library Prizes is divided into four parts: "International Prizes," "American Prizes," "British Prizes," and "Canadian Prizes." The American prizes are subdivided into the categories for general prizes, publishers' prizes, juvenile prizes, poetry prizes, drama prizes, short story prizes, and library prizes. There is one index, which lists the names of award sponsors and winners. Awards that have been discontinued since 1959 are also entered in the index with the edition date of the last *Literary and Library Prizes* in which a full descriptive entry appeared. The accessibility of future editions would be facilitated greatly by the addition of a subject index to the types of awards. In the present edition readers have to read through the alphabetically arranged entries in each section to find the purpose of each prize.

Each entry includes the full name of the award, the sponsoring agency, the date it was established, the award offered, award criteria and requirements, submission deadlines, and the address for information and applications. Following the entry are the names of the prize's recipients (arranged chronologically), the publications for which they received the award, and the names of the publishers.

Literary and Library Prizes can be used by librarians and patrons for a variety of reference purposes, including developing collections, creating recommended reading lists, and identifying notable as well as little-known authors. Writers will use it as a source of competitions for which their works may be eligible. However, they will have to consult the WRITER'S MARKET or POET'S MARKET for the most up-to-date addresses of these competitions. The book's major drawback as a reference source is that it is now 11 years old. There is no coverage of recent literary activity. At this time there is no word about plans for an eleventh edition.

Although currency is a drawback, *Literary and Library Prizes* is still the most effective resource of its type. The Board recommends this work for the core collections of public and academic libraries.

MLA Handbook for Writers of Research Papers, 3d edition. Joseph Gibaldi and Walter S. Achtert. MLA, 1988. soft. 1 vol. 248 pp. index. ISBN 0-87352-379-2. $8.95. handbook.
LB2369.G53 808.02

Since 1951, the Modern Language Association of America has been publishing style sheets setting forth the guidelines for humanities scholars to follow in preparing manuscripts for publication. The *MLA Handbook for Writers of Research Papers,* first published in 1977, incorporates the MLA style into a manual that primarily describes how to prepare a research paper and is geared toward undergraduate students.

The latest edition of the handbook has six chapters: "Research and Writing," "The Mechanics of Writing," "The Format of the Research Paper," "Preparing the List of Works Cited," "Documenting Sources," and "Abbreviations and Reference Words." Chapter 1, "Research and Writing," begins with a succinct overview of what a research paper is, how to choose a topic, and how to organize an approach to writing. Many students can be saved from the potential pitfalls of preparing a research paper by carefully considering the sage advice offered in this section.

Chapter 1 also includes a section on using the library, which is remarkably brief, yet comprehensive. A very clear and concise description of on-line searching has been added to this section. Students are also advised as to how they can gain access to on-line data bases if they have a computer equipped with a modem. The chapter goes on to mention some of the standard reference works and bibliographic sources used in most academic disciplines.

Chapter 1 includes new material on the advantages of using a word processor and provides a detailed discussion on how to use one most effectively. Although instructing students on how to write is beyond the scope of this handbook, the first chapter ends with an updated, unannotated bibliography of guides to writing. Included are handbooks of composition, dictionaries of usage, books on style, and a new section listing guides to nonsexist language.

Chapter 2, "The Mechanics of Writing," covers spelling, punctuation, names of persons, numbers, titles of works, quotations, capitalization, etc. This chapter is followed by advice on typing or printing the research paper, margins, spacing, headings, page numbers, and corrections and insertions. The MLA documentation style is covered in the chapters on "Preparing the List of Works Cited" and "Documenting Sources." These chapters provide many examples of entries showing proper citation forms for books and articles, as well as an array of nonprint sources, such as computer software, full-text material from data base vendors, TV and radio programs, videotapes, works of art, and cartoons. At the end of the chapter is a list of other style manuals used by publications in the fields of biology, chemistry, geology, linguistics, mathematics, medicine, physics, and psychology. The last chapter, "Abbreviations and Reference Words," provides information on geographical names, common scholarly abbreviations, publishers' names, and abbreviations for proofreading and correction symbols.

The legibility of the text has been greatly improved by changing the typeface for the main text. The new typeface emphasizes the difference between what is text and what is an example.

Locating specific passages within the handbook has been simplified by the index, which consists of headings with numbered subentries corresponding to sections in each chapter.

The *MLA Handbook for Writers of Research Papers* is an important reference source that will be consulted by users of all ages and educational levels. Students may use the manual to prepare their first term papers and continue to consult the volume through their post-graduate writing efforts. The Board recommends this work for the core collections of public, academic, and school libraries.

Poet's Market: Where & How to Publish Your Poetry. Judson Jerome, ed. Writer's Digest, annual. hard. 1 vol. 515 pp. illus. indexes. ISBN 0-89879-423-4. $19.95. manual.
PN1059.M3P59 808.1

The 1991 *Poet's Market* is the sixth edition of this essential reference work. Created and edited by Judson Jerome, former professor of literature at Antioch College and former poetry editor of the *Antioch Review,* this edition includes approximately 1,700 listings of publishing companies, magazines, journals, and reviews that buy poetry, including magazines, books, newsletters, audio cassettes, and radio and television programs. These listings are annually verified and updated for accuracy by the publisher of this volume. Jerome has added 350 new markets in this edition and seems to delight in finding unlikely markets for writers, such as *Juggler's World* magazine or *Superintendent's Profile & Pocket Equipment Directory.*

The volume begins with several informative preliminary chapters: "How to Use Poet's Market," "Building a Poetic Career," and "The Business of Poetry." The major portion of the *Poet's Market* is divided into two sections: "Markets" and "Resources." The listing for each source in the "Markets" section includes the names and addresses of all listed magazines and publishers; contests and awards sponsored by the publication; phone number; date of founding; contact person; submission policies; frequency of publication; several lines of poetry indicative of the quality of the publication; submission requirements; reporting time; query letter required; and, usually, editorial comments by a representative of the publication regarding the kind of poetry they publish. Judson also assigns a market category designation to each listing. These designations range from I through V and indicate whether a publication is: open to submissions from beginners (I); a general market (II); a prestige market (III); a specialized publication (IV); or does not accept unsolicited manuscripts (V).

Page-length profiles of 14 poets, editors, and publishers—a very welcome special feature of the "Markets" section—appear throughout the market listings. Poets, such as Tess Gallagher, Frederick Turner, and Herbert Martin, speak engagingly about their careers and offer their experience-honed advice and encouragement. The editors included in these "Close-Ups"—representing a wide range of publications—offer their criteria for the selection of poetry for publication. The "Markets" section also includes listings for contests and awards, everything from the Pulitzer Prize to small contests with entry fees. The section concludes with a selection of greeting card markets.

In the "Resources" section readers will find descriptive listings of various writing colonies; organizations that support poets and writers, such as foundations and arts councils; and an annotated guide to some publications useful to poets. There is no bibliography per se, although throughout the directory Judson does recommend other Writer's Digest publications, including his own. A glossary of publishing terms appears at the end of the volume.

Poet's Market has several indexes. Particularly interesting is an index to chapbook publishers, that is, those who produce pamphlets (30 or fewer pages) of a poet's work. The subject index divides publications, contests, and awards by topics, themes, and form and style. A geographical index includes publications about specific states or countries and those that publish works by poets residing in a specific area. The general index includes all titles and names and refers the reader to page numbers in the "Markets" section.

The *Poet's Market* is a remarkable reference source. The Board recommends this work for the core collections of public and academic libraries.

Writer's Market. Glenda Tennant Neff, ed. Writer's Digest, annual. hard. 1 vol. 1,046 pp. illus. indexes. ISBN 0-89879-422-6. $24.95. directory.
PN161.W956 070.52097

Since 1929 *Writer's Market* has been the prime compilation of a vast number of markets in the United States and Canada where writers can sell their work. As were the previous 61 editions, the 1991 *Writer's Market* was produced by Writer's Digest Books (an imprint of F&W Publications), the publisher of many "how-to-write" titles and of the popular *Writer's Digest* magazine. The 1991 edition includes approximately 800 new markets and lists some 4,000 places where writers can sell their articles, nonfiction manuscripts, fillers, greeting card messages, plays, novels, scripts, and short stories. In recent years Writer's Digest Books has produced separate editions of *Writer's Market* for children's authors, novelists, short story writers, and poets.

According to the "From the Editors" introductory note, listings were initially gathered by sending out questionnaires and letters to approximately 15,000 prospective markets. These listings are verified annually by mail or by telephone contact. The primary reason for exclusion of a listing from *Writer's Market* is the lack of response to these inquiries. The "How to Use the Writer's Market" section lists additional reasons for the exclusion of publications—from the nonpayment of free-lance fees to lack of a market for free-lance work.

The *Writer's Market* is divided into three sections: "The Writing Profession," "Markets," and "Services & Opportunities." The first section includes a valuable chapter on "The Business of Writing," which addresses pragmatic topics such as approaches to marketing, bookkeeping, tax information, and copyright procedures. The chapter ends with a useful guide to the payment rates that free-lance writers generally charge for a variety of different jobs, such as speechwriting or translating. This chapter is followed by the "Writers' Roundtable," which features the response of three full-time writers to questions, such as how they handle late payment problems or editing disagreements.

The "Markets" section divides its listings into book publishers; small presses; consumer publications; trade, technical, and professional journals; scriptwriting; syndicates; and greeting card publishers. Each entry includes name and address; phone and fax numbers; contact names; size of market; emphasis and readership; submission requirements; word length; payment rates; and tips and suggestions. Interspersed throughout these listings are "Close-Ups," one-page interviews with a variety of editors and authors.

The last section, "Services & Opportunities," includes a discussion about authors' agents. The topics covered are choosing an agent, how a literary agent works, understanding commissions and fees, and evaluating an agent. Following this chapter are alphabetical listings of literary agents, which also include their fees and the publications they have most recently sold. The last section, "Contests & Awards," lists awards for writing in a variety of forms and styles—from Shakespearean sonnets to works about bowling. *Writer's Market* ends with a helpful glossary of terms used in the entries, such as "kill fee" or "slush pile."

Two indexes provide subject access to the entries; one for book publishers, the other for literary agents. Each of these indexes is further divided into fiction and nonfiction specialists. An all-inclusive name and title index completes the volume.

The *Writer's Market* addresses the needs of a variety of users. In addition to its great appeal to writers and readers, librarians will find the *Writer's Market* useful for identifying the specialities of many publishers. The Board recommends this work for the core collections of public and academic libraries.

Supplementary Titles

A Manual for Writers of Term Papers. 5th edition. Kate L. Turabian; Bonnie Birtwistle Honigsblum, ed. Univ. of Chicago, 1987. hard and soft. 1 vol. 300 pp. ISBN 0-226-81624-9 (hard); 0-226-81625-7 (soft). $20 (hard); $7.95 (soft). handbook.
LB2369.T8 808.02'19

This edition of *A Manual for Writers of Term Papers* "is the fifth edition of a classic style guide for authors of research papers, revised and expanded by Bonnie Birtwistle Honigsblum. In addition to treating matters such as spelling, punctuation, and distinctive word usage, the manual outlines correct format for parenthetical references and reference notes, footnotes, endnotes, and bibliographies. There are also chapters on abbreviations, tables, illustrations, layout, and physical appearance. The manual has been updated to include guidelines for computer users, including advice on what to look for in hardware and software. . . . [This is] a must purchase for libraries serving students from high school up." (*BL,* October 1, 1987, p. 209)

Also reviewed in: *ARBA,* 1988, p. 369; *Choice,* November 1987, p. 460; *Kliatt,* September 1987, p. 35; *PW,* May 8, 1967, p. 66; *R & R Bk N,* Fall 1987, p. 24; *TES,* July 23, 1982, p. 22; *WLB,* September 1987, p. 88.

Board's recommendation: Public, academic, and school libraries.

The MLA Style Manual. Walter S. Achtert and Joseph Gibaldi. MLA, 1985. hard. 1 vol. 271 pp. ISBN 0-87352-136-6. $19. handbook.
PN147.A28 808.02

"[*The MLA*] *Style Manual* describes the Modern Language Association's current procedures for citing and documenting sources in scholarly writing.

"The book does give scholars a thorough explanation of one of the major styles of documentation used in the humanities. There is also information about publication, the mechanics of writing, manuscript preparation, and the use of abbreviations and proofreading symbols." (*LJ,* January 1986, p. 70)

"Coverage ranges from plagiarism and copyright to preparing manuscripts in machine-readable form, and includes more than 100 pages on documentation. . . . The prose is exact, and the organization, index, and examples are most helpful. . . . The bibliographical references for further consultation are excellent." (*Choice,* February 1986, p. 845)

Also reviewed in: *ANQ,* May 1985, p. 181; *BL,* December 15, 1985, p. 604; *CHE,* September 25, 1985, p. 5.

Board's recommendation: Public, academic, and school libraries.

Oxford Dictionary for Writers and Editors. Oxford, 1981. soft. 1 vol. 448 pp. ISBN 0-19-212970-8. $15.95. handbook.
PE1628.C54 423

The *Oxford Dictionary for Writers and Editors* is "a pocket-sized handbook . . . described by the publishers as 'primarily a dictionary of style for written English.' The scope of entries includes foreign phrases, abbreviations, preferred spellings, and in longer entries . . . conventions of usage for specific fields, e. g., dates. The book is actually a small encyclopedic dictionary with a focus on literary items." (*LJ,* July 1981, p. 1405)

"[This work] covers an astonishing range of personal and place names and is commonsensical. . . . In almost all cases . . . it comes off the fence and leaves the reader with a single solution." (*Econ,* May 30, 1981, p. 86)

Also reviewed in: *ARBA,* 1982, p. 608; *BL,* January 15, 1982, p. 676; *Lis,* April 16, 1981, p. 514; *LR,* Autumn 1981, p. 202; *TES,* May 15, 1981, p. 41.

Board's recommendation: Public and academic libraries.

Mary Ellen Collins

Recreation and Hobbies

The recreation and hobbies category embraces both outdoor and indoor pursuits. It includes family and individual activities, sports, games, collecting, and crafts. It is a diverse category that includes rules of sports and games; information on the collecting of stamps, coins, paper money, china, dolls, and so on; and instructions for arts and crafts. The recreation and hobbies collection may also include listings of recreational parks and other locations that are suitable for activities such as hiking and camping.

A reference collection in recreation should be descriptive enough to meet the needs of a wide variety of patrons. Readers interested in stamp collecting (philately) will require reference titles that provide definitions and explanations of the basic principles of this hobby. Such titles must include the international aspects of stamp collecting and also provide examples of rare and common specimens. Reference books on crafts should reflect a wide variety of craft types, such as weaving, quilting, lace making, and so on. For games,

Core Titles

	PUBLIC	ACADEMIC	SCHOOL
A Guide Book of United States Coins Yeoman, R. S.; Kenneth Bresset, ed. Western, annual (1946–)	✦		
Standard Catalog of World Coins, 17th edition Krause, Chester L., and Clifford Mishler. Krause, 1990	✦		
Standard Catalog of World Paper Money, 6th edition Pick, Albert; Bruce, Colin R., II, and Neil Shafer, eds. Krause, 1990	✦		
Standard Postage Stamp Catalogue, 4 vols. Cummings, William W., ed. Scott, Foresman, annual; distrib. by Harper & Row	✦		✦

both the rules and the history should be available. Useful game books include coverage of card games, board games, and singing games for children and adults. Outdoor recreation sources should include activities that appeal to both the amateur and the specialist.

The types of books that belong in the general reference recreation category are numerous. Dictionaries are necessary for people at all levels of expertise. Histories of games prove interesting to some patrons, while directories are useful for patrons who seek addresses and characteristics of campground sites or of associations connected with various hobbies. Catalogs are particularly valuable to coin, stamp, rock, and gem collectors. These sources estimate prices that are commonly determined by market conditions. They may also explain how to ascertain the condition and value of an item. The degree of specialization of these works will depend on the size of the library and the popularity of a particular hobby in the community.

Besides the works included in this section, several other titles would be useful in a recreation and hobbies reference collection, including the following: *The Way to Play: The Illustrated Encyclopedia of Games of the World* (Paddington Pr., 1975); *Contemporary Games* (Gale, 1973–1974); *Woodall's Trailering Parks and Campground Directory* (Woodall, 1967–); *Recreation and Outdoor Life Directory* (Gale, 1979). Two valuable titles chosen by the Board as part of the core list have since gone out of print: Laura Torbet's 3-volume *Encyclopedia of Crafts* (Scribner, 1980) and the *Allstate Motor Club RV Park & Campground Directory* (Catherine H. Fay, Prentice-Hall, 1989). Other topics that might be included in a reference section on recreation and hobbies are photography, jewelry making, pottery and ceramics, antiques (collecting and refinishing), making musical instruments, and toy making.

Core Titles

A Guide Book of United States Coins. R. S. Yeoman; Kenneth Bresset, ed. Western, annual (1946–) soft. 1 vol. 272 pp. illus. index. ISBN 0-307-19892-8. $8.95. handbook.
CJ1826.G785 737.4

A Guide Book of United States Coins is a standard source that is revised each year. The authority of the work is increased by editor Kenneth Bresset, who has been a professional coin photographer and has edited the *Whitman Numismatic Journal.* He is a member of the American Numismatic Society and the American Numismatic Association and has written several books on numismatics and collecting money.

This work serves as a price catalog for U.S. coins. Prices are averaged from information given by contributors who have estimated what dealers would pay for certain coins. As the title page proclaims, the work also serves as a "brief history of American coinage." The publisher does not deal in coins; therefore, this handbook is not a catalog of any supply of coins. Information in the book is intended to help coin collectors identify coins dating from the late 1700s to the present. The editor and contributors stress that this book is to be used primarily by hobbyists interested in coin collection and for educational and pleasurable purposes. Any usefulness the work has for investors is only secondary.

Coins are pictured in black and white (both obverse and reverse sides), with features and worn parts clearly displayed. Both the classification and the condition of the coins are given. For example, a coin may be classified as "proof," which means it is "distinguished by sharpness of detail and usually with a brilliant, mirrorlike surface." "Proof" refers to the method of manufacture, not the condition of the coin. The condition is reflected in the grade a coin has received: uncirculated, mint state, extremely fine, very fine, and so on, in decreasing order of value. Early coins from Great Britain and the American colonies are categorized separately as very fine, fine, very good, and good.

The handbook is arranged chronologically by time category; for example, British coins of the colonies and coins of the early states are in the same category. The listing is further divided into denominations beginning with cents and continuing up through dollars, from the earliest mintings of each denomination to the latest. The introduction to this work discusses mint marks and identifies the location of mints and their dates.

Following the section on regular coinage is a section on commemorative coins. This section discusses a number of companies that struck special coins.

This handbook appears to be very current; some of the most recent coins are represented. Illustrations are clear, and the binding and paper are of good quality.

A Guide Book of United States Coins has been a standard for years. The Board recommends this work for the core collection of public libraries.

Standard Catalog of World Coins, 17th edition. Chester L. Krause and Clifford Mishler. Krause, 1990. soft. 1 vol. 1,920 pp. illus. index. ISBN 0-87341-136-6. $36.95 handbook.
CJ1755.K72 737.4

The *Standard Catalog of World Coins* is aimed at both the experienced and the amateur numismatist. A user of this handbook will find that a basic knowledge of nineteenth- and twentieth-century world history is helpful, as coverage includes coins from the last 190 years. The catalog is very current, as new issues of coins can be included just a few days prior to printing. The *Standard Catalog* staff monitors world coinage minting via a communications network that includes collectors, dealers, and authorized agents, as well as national banks and treasuries.

Apart from the listings, the *Standard Catalog* includes such features as the "Hejira Date Conversion Chart," which shows the difference in dates between the Christian and Muslim calendars; the Standard International Numerical System; a foreign exchange table; and an index by country.

Coins are listed alphabetically according to the current name of the issuing nation. Old names of a country or area are cross-referenced to the current name; for example, coins of Persia can be located by consulting the listings for Iran, and coins for Russia are found under the Union of Soviet Socialist Republics. Coins are then arranged by denomination from lowest to highest, except for cases in which an arrangement according to historical events, such as a particular ruler or special period of time, makes more sense.

Dating of coins was often subject to the idiosyncrasies of numeric styling and calendar variations. For example, coins of Oriental origin—those of Japan, Korea, China, Tibet, and some modern gold issues of Turkey—are dated according to the year of the calendar used by the issuing government when the coins were issued. However, these dates have alternately been determined using locally observed and Christian calendars.

Each entry includes a map of the area where the coin was minted; a description of the government, population, main industries, and products; and a short history of the country or region. Black-and-white photographs depict the actual size of the coins. The catalog number is included, along with the date and quantity of coins minted. Also provided are the grade of the coin and the price valuation as governed by prevailing market conditions. Prices are determined by top numismatists around the world.

The *Standard Catalog of World Coins* is a paperback work with somewhat translucent pages. Occasionally, this format makes the book hard to read. However, despite this minor drawback, the catalog is a standard source and a current guide for hobbyists. The Board recommends this work for the core collection of public libraries.

Standard Catalog of World Paper Money, 6th edition. Albert Pick; Colin R. Bruce II and Neil Shafer, eds. Krause, 1990. soft. 1 vol. 1,087 pp. illus. indexes. ISBN 0-87341-128-5. $49. handbook.
HG353.P543 769.55

Albert Pick wrote the first edition of the *Standard Catalog of World Paper Money* in 1985. Pick is noted as an authority in the area of paper money, having served on the staff of the Bayerische-Hypotheken-und-Wechsel-Bank in Munich from 1964 to 1985. He was a curator of the bank's collection of paper money, which he had been building since 1930. Editor Neil Shafer has served as numismatic editor for Western Publishing Company and also as a contributor and associate editor of the *Whitman Numismatic Journal.* He has several books on numismatics to his credit and is a life member of the American Numismatic Association and other groups.

With catalogs and price lists hard to come by in this hobby, this effort to catalog paper money from around the world proves to be very useful. This handbook attempts to bring together earlier efforts to cover American and European paper money. This fifth edition, comprised of two volumes, fully documents paper money and legal tender from nearly 300 past and present world governments, including countries of Europe, Asia, Africa, and the Americas. Volume 1 concentrates on "Specialized Issues"; volume 2 covers "General Issues."

This work illustrates general issues of money that are circulated by recognized national governments and banking agencies. The catalog is arranged alphabetically by country of origin of the money; the arrangement is then chronological by issue, followed by denomination, lowest to highest. Illustrations are profuse; each entry provides an illustration of the specimen, obverse and reverse. Also given are the catalog entry number, denomination, date of printing, description (color, what is illustrated, who is portrayed), and condition. Condition is described as very fine, extra fine, and uncirculated. The last item given is the price.

The *Standard Catalog of World Paper Money* includes an introduction that explains the collecting of paper money, what people need to understand in order to be effective collectors, the difference between paper money and bank notes, and the problem of counterfeiting.

Other features of the book include a chart listing Western numerals and their non-Western counterparts; a list of abbreviations; information on caring for a collection; the Standard International Grading Terminology; and a world paper money glossary. Most helpful is an extensive multilingual bibliography of sources about money. The charts in this book include the months in various languages, foreign exchange fixed rates, and the "Hejira Date Conversion Chart," which illustrates the differences between the Muslim and the Christian calendars.

The *Standard Catalog of World Paper Money* would provide a good introduction to the world of paper money for the hobbyist interested in collecting paper money or for the person interested in the history of paper money in recent centuries. The Board recommends this work for the core collection of public libraries.

Standard Postage Stamp Catalogue. William W. Cummings, ed. Scott, Foresman, annual; distrib. by Harper & Row. hard and soft. 4 vols. 4,988 pp. illus. index. ISBN 0-89487-125-0 (hard, vol. 1); 0-89487-120-X (soft, vol. 1). $49.95 per vol. (hard); $25 per vol. (soft). handbook.
HE6226.S48 382.2

Now in its 146th edition, the *Standard Postage Stamp Catalogue* is a classic reference tool for philatelists, both amateur and advanced. This annual publication is now edited by William W. Cummings.

The 1990 edition is comprised of four volumes, which cover stamps issued around the world. Volume 1 covers the United States, which includes territories such as the Canal Zone, Danish West Indies, Guam, Marshall Islands, Federated States of Micronesia, Republic of Palau, and others. Also included here are stamps of the United Nations, Great Britain, and countries associated with the British Commonwealth (such as Grenada, Kuwait, Kenya, Uganda, Tanzania, Jamaica, Ireland, and Seychelles). Volumes 2, 3, and 4 cover the European countries and colonies and the independent nations of Africa, Asia, and Latin America.

In each volume, there is an introduction by Richard L. Sine, the editorial director, who discusses recent changes and additions to the work. The arrangement of entries is alphabetical by country, and within each country, by function and date of issue of the stamp. Each entry gives the Scott number, used to identify stamps in trading, buying, and collecting. Also given are the illustration number and a notation on paper color. Stamps are indicated as "majors"—primary issues—or "minors"—stamps of a different coloration or watermark. Date of printing, denomination, color, year of issue, value of used or unused issues, and total value of a set are also listed.

The prices given for the stamps included are determined by consultation with stamp dealers, auction prices, and advertisements in the philatelic media. These prices are an accurate estimate of what one would have to pay for a given grade of stamp.

The catalog includes a "Special Notices Section," which is a detailed description of the classification of stamps, their grades, and conditions; also included in this section is a discussion of valuing notations. A list of abbreviations follows.

In the section called "Basic Stamp Information," the physical aspects of stamps are defined, as are the basic concepts concerning the identification of stamps, forgeries, and reprints. The "Terminology" section, which is a glossary for stamp collectors, will be very useful to those less familiar with this hobby.

"Catalog Information" is a section that gives data on how stamp prices are determined. It outlines the meanings of "grade" and "condition" as they relate to stamps. "Understanding the Listings" presents an illustration of what information in the listings means.

The *Standard Postage Stamp Catalogue* is intended for philatelists and persons new to the field of stamp collecting and is the basic and authoritative source of information in this area. The Board recommends this work for the core collection of public and school libraries.

Supplementary Titles

Make It—II: An Index to Projects and Materials, 1974–1987. Mary Ellen Heim. Scarecrow, 1989. hard. 1 vol. 552 pp. ISBN 0-8108-2125-7. $42.50 handbook.
Z7911 016.7455

A review of the first edition said *Make It: An Index to Projects and Materials* "is an index to 475 books on projects and materials involving needlework, weaving, plastics, ceramics, electronics, leather, metal, wood, and natural materials. . . . Part I, Index to Projects (pages 29–366), is an alphabetical listing of the subject headings with references indented beneath. Chapter titles, code name of the book, and paging are given. . . . Part II, Index to Material (pages 367–477), is an alphabetical listing of all types of raw materials with references listed below of projects utilizing these materials. Egg cartons, plastic lemons, dry cleaning bags, pine cones, [etc.]—are among the raw materials listed.

"[The] book has numerous cross-references. . . . Its layout is attractive and functional. However, the subject headings are this book's most striking feature. They are those used in the dictionary catalogs of the Library of Congress and *Readers' Guide,* but original headings have also been devised that are in the crafts vernacular. . . ." (*BL,* October 15, 1976, p. 342)

"No magazine articles are included, and the emphasis is on appealing to craft hobbyists, teachers, day-campers, occupational therapists, and church bazaar workers. . . . *Make It* is enthusiastically recommended for public libraries." (*Choice,* October 1976, p. 958)

Also reviewed in: *ARBA,* 1976, p. 453; *Hob,* November 1975, p. 158; *LJ,* June 1, 1975, p. 1112; *RSR,* January 1975, p. 133; *TN,* November 1975, p. 82; *WLB,* June 1975, p. 751.

Board's recommendation: Public libraries.

National Park Guide. Michael Frome. Prentice-Hall, 1989. soft. 1 vol. 256 pp. illus. index. ISBN 0-13-609819-3. $12.95. atlas.

"Completely revised in its [current] annual edition, . . . [*National Park Guide*] is a guide to all areas of the National Park System. . . . [It is] copiously illustrated with handsome color photographs and clear maps. . . . The author is an authority on travel, and his practical and specific advice and identification stress responsibility." (*RSR,* October/December 1974, p. 31)

"[The *Guide*] . . . 'has been designed since the first edition in 1967 to give practical guidance—a clear picture of all the facilities in the parks and how to use and enjoy them fully—in the hope that appreciation will follow.' . . . Features include sections on archaeological, historical, natural and recreational areas." (*RSR,* October/December 1974, p. 149)

Board's recommendation: Public libraries.

The Official Overstreet Comic Book Price Guide, 19th edition. Robert M. Overstreet. House of Collectibles/Ballantine, 1989. soft. 1 vol. 740 pp. illus. ISBN 0-87637-791-6. $12.95. guide.

The Official Overstreet Comic Book Price Guide is a "price list cum catalog of exclusively American comic books from 1900 to the present. The greater part of the guide is an alphabetical title listing of comic books with cross-references to series, former titles, or succeeding titles. . . . Consecutive numerical issues of comic book titles are listed beside three cash values for each issue . . . [which] correspond to good, fine, and mint condition grades for each comic book. . . . [The prices] are derived from 'convention sales, dealers' lists, adzines, and by special contact with dealers from coast to coast.' Consequently, the prices listed in the guide are real figures, representing an average of the prices paid for each comic book. . . ." (*BL,* March 15, 1978, p. 1218)

"Since its inception, the Overstreet guide has been the most comprehensive, accurate, and authoritative price guide for American comic books. . . . This latest annual revision [not only] supplies the current market prices for hundreds of . . . American comic books, [but also] discusses all aspects of the buying, storing, and selling of comic books, and contains a variety of interesting articles . . . and useful reference features (including lists of comic book conventions, comic book clubs and fan publications, and a directory of comic book and nostalgia shops). In addition, there are . . . color portfolios of comic book covers and many black-and-white photographs of comic book covers distributed throughout the price guide section." (*ARBA,* 1988, p. 387)

Also reviewed in: *ARBA,* 1984, p. 425.

Board's recommendation: Public libraries.

New and Noteworthy

Access America: An Atlas and Guide to the National Parks for Visitors with Disabilities. Northern Cartographic, 1988. spiralbound. 1 vol. 444 pp. illus. maps. ISBN 0-944187-00-5. $89.95. atlas.

"Aimed at making the outdoors 'not only accessible, but usable, to people who represent the full spectrum of human abilities,' this unprecedented guide [*Access America*] evaluates the accessibility of our national parks to the disabled. A team of geographer/cartographers, ably assisted by over 60 disability specialists, has prepared detailed maps, charts, and commentary on such specifics as climate, medical services, and transportation—all specially keyed to show features of interest to disabled visitors. This valuable information, not readily available elsewhere, is highlighted by the personal accounts of those who have enjoyed our parks despite handicaps." (*LJ,* April 15, 1989, p. 38)

The Coin World Comprehensive Catalog & Encyclopedia of United States Coins. David T. Alexander, ed. Pharos Bks./World Almanac, 1990. hard and soft. 1 vol. 456 pp. illus. index. ISBN 0-88687-484-X (hard); 0-88687-483-1 (soft). $29.95 (hard); $16.95 (soft). encyclopedia.

CJ1826 737.4973

"[*The Coin World Comprehensive Catalog & Encyclopedia of United States Coins*] gives an overview of [our] nation's use of coins. . . . Users will appreciate these features: the essay on coin collecting in the U.S., well-researched introductions to the work's major sections, and comprehensive indexing. . . . The editors have included all colonial and early state coins, associated coins, and tokens traditionally collected as part of the U.S. series." (*BL,* August 1990, p. 2198)

An Educational Guide to the National Park System.

Carol Smallwood. Scarecrow, 1989. hard. 1 vol. 403 pp. ISBN 0-8108-2137-0. $39.50. bibliography.
E160.S63 016.363680

"[*An Educational Guide to the National Park System*] is a guide for teachers, librarians, curriculum directors, and others to unique resources available free or for sale from the national park system facilities. It is aimed at visitors to sites as well as at those who can obtain resources only by mail.

"Student/teacher visiting guides, films, books, curriculum guides, posters, videos, games, pamphlets, maps, bibliographies, and slides are just some of the materials available. Many other items—from coal tar soap and prairie seed mix to a miniplanisphere—are sold. Many printed materials are free; many audiovisuals are loaned without charge. . . . Each entry lists name, type of facility, address, telephone, acreage, year authorized or established, location, purpose, features of interest, visitor accommodations, free print material annotations, bibliography . . . suggested curriculum application, and suggested Sears subject heading. [The book] also includes a brief history of the National Park Service and a title index." (Excerpted from publisher's announcement)

Hobbyist Sourcebook. Denise M. Allard, ed. Gale, 1990. hard. 1 vol. 459 pp. index. ISBN 0-8103-4748-2. $49.95. encyclopedia.
GV1201 790.1016

Hobbyist Sourcebook "was developed specifically to serve as a resource guide to sources of background information for new and experienced hobbyists. Forty-three broad-based, high-interest hobbies that are currently popular have been profiled alphabetically. . . . A brief introduction to the field, containing such information as the estimated number of hobbyists, record setters, famous personalities, trends, and statistics, precedes each profile. The profile is then divided into as many as 15 subcategories of information geared to varying levels of expertise, ranging from juvenile material for the elementary school grades to advanced learning programs, and professional opportunities. . . . The list of adult beginner guides includes basic general books and periodicals useful for a sound introduction to the hobby.

"[This book] will . . . interest collectors of all sorts, amateur magicians, animal lovers, gardeners, military history buffs, and other enthusiasts." (*BL,* August 1990, p. 2203)

Walter Breen's Complete Encyclopedia of U.S. and Colonial Coins. Walter Breen. Doubleday, 1989. hard. 1 vol. 754 pp. illus. index. ISBN 0-385-14207-2. $75. encyclopedia.
CJ1830.B69 737.4'973

"A new approach in coin collecting—an encyclopedia, not a catalog of values—this meticulously documented work [*Walter Breen's Complete Encyclopedia of U.S. and Colonial Coins*] . . . has nearly 8000 coins arranged chronologically, with some 4000 excellent photo reproductions. Each entry provides physical and metallic specifications, historical background, degree of rarity, quantity minted, and more." (*LJ,* April 15, 1989)

The World of Games: Their Origins and History, How to Play Games, and How to Make Them. Jack Botermans et al. Facts On File, 1989. hard. 1 vol. 240 pp. illus. ISBN 0-8160-2184-8. $29.95. encyclopedia.
GV1200.W4713 796.09

"[*The World of Games*] is divided into five broad categories of games: board, dice, card, dominoes, and activity games, including a small number of children's games. Two classes of board games are discussed—ancient and modern. . . . How-to instructions for making 40 of the lost or obscure games are featured in the text. . . . The value of this book is in its historical and cross-cultural information (e.g., native American games) and its handsome illustrations." (*BL,* February 1, 1990, p. 1118)

Craig W. Beard *M. Patrick Graham* *Gary Holloway*

Religion

See also Philosophy

The study of religion, broadly conceived, encompasses sacred texts, history, and theology. Reference collections in religion in most U.S. libraries focus primarily on the Judeo-Christian tradition. These collections contain works dealing with Hebrew and Christian scriptures such as the Old and New Testaments, the background and history of these two traditions, and their religious teachings. The titles in this category reflect this emphasis, although they also include other major religions and some minor ones.

As with other disciplines, a major problem for librarians is fitting the collection to the clientele. Library users come from a wide range of religious backgrounds and have different levels of sophistication. Public and academic collections often need to serve lay and professional religious workers, fact finders, and researchers. School library collections should serve the needs of students and teachers.

Dictionaries and encyclopedias form the backbone of any disciplinary or general reference collection by introducing readers to topics, ideas, people, terminology, and so on. Therefore, a core reference collection in religion should provide comprehensive coverage of the discipline of religion with its major streams of tradition, doctrines and dogmas, and leading figures. Eliade's THE ENCYCLOPEDIA OF RELIGION is an excellent choice, although school libraries also could be well served by the less extensive FACTS ON FILE DICTIONARY OF RELIGIONS. A good out-of-print encyclopedia is James Hastings's 13-volume *Encyclopaedia of Religion and Ethics* (Scribner, 1926). In addition, specialized encyclopedic works, such as the *Encyclopaedia Judaica* (Macmillan, 1972—now out of print) and the NEW CATHOLIC ENCYCLOPEDIA, and other resources such as atlases, commentaries, and concordances add depth and breadth to the collection. One excellent resource that is out of print is *Nelson's Complete Concordance of the Revised Standard Version of the Bible* (edited by John Ellison, Thomas Nelson, 1985).

Reference collections of sacred texts can fill user needs by providing a few standard translations of the Bible that include the Apocrypha or deuterocanonical books, such as the King James Version, the New Revised Standard Version, and the New International Version. Some other library communities may require additional texts, such as the Koran. When available, annotated editions or commentaries on the texts should be a high priority.

To meet the needs of library users, a collection must provide access to current information, even in humanities disciplines such as religion. For that reason, libraries should purchase supplementary volumes, new edi-

Core Titles

	PUBLIC	ACADEMIC	SCHOOL
Atlas of the Bible Rogerson, John. Facts On File, 1985	✦		✦
Butler's Lives of the Saints, 2d edition, 4 vols. Thurston, Herbert, and Donald Attwater, eds. Christian Classics, 1956; repr. by Harper & Row, 1985	✦	✦	
A Dictionary of Comparative Religion Brandon, S. G. F., gen. ed. Scribner, 1970	✦		
The Eerdmans Analytical Concordance to the Revised Standard Version of the Bible Whitaker, Richard E., and James E. Goehring, comps. Eerdmans, 1988	✦	✦	
The Encyclopedia of American Religions, 3d edition Melton, J. Gordon. Gale, 1989	✦	✦	
The Encyclopedia of Religion, 16 vols. Eliade, Mircea, ed. in chief. Macmillan, 1987	✦	✦	✦
Encyclopedic Handbook of Cults in America Melton, J. Gordon. Garland, 1986	✦	✦	
The Facts On File Dictionary of Religions Hinnells, John R., ed. Facts On File, 1984	✦		✦
Harper's Bible Dictionary Achtemeier, Paul, gen. ed. Harper & Row, 1985	✦	✦	✦
The International Standard Bible Encyclopedia, rev. edition, 4 vols. Bromiley, Geoffrey W., ed. Eerdmans, 1979–1988	✦		
The Interpreter's Bible, 12 vols. Buttrick, George Arthur, ed. Abingdon, 1951–1957	✦	✦	
The Macmillan Bible Atlas, rev. edition Aharoni, Yohanan, and Michael Avi-Yonah. Macmillan, 1977	✦	✦	
New Catholic Encyclopedia, 18 vols. McDonald, William J., ed. in chief. McGraw-Hill, 1967–1989	✦	✦	
Oxford Bible Atlas, 3d edition May, Herbert G., ed. Oxford, 1984			✦
The Oxford Dictionary of Saints, 2d edition Farmer, David Hugh. Oxford, 1987	✦	✦	
The Oxford Dictionary of the Christian Church, 2d edition Cross, F. L., and E. A. Livingstone, eds. Oxford, 1974	✦	✦	
The Perennial Dictionary of World Religions Crim, Keith, ed. Harper & Row, 1989	✦	✦	
Yearbook of American and Canadian Churches Jacquet, Constant H., Jr., ed. Abingdon, annual	✦	✦	✦

tions, and other up-to-date works to complement present holdings.

Another source of current information is periodicals. Although periodicals are beyond the scope of this guide, certain periodical indexes should round out a religion reference collection. School libraries probably will not have a place in the budget for these. However, academic and larger public libraries can provide the *Humanities Index* (Wilson, 1974) and, if the clientele justifies it, *Religion Index One: Periodicals* (American Theological Library Assn.). Both of these are also available on-line and in CD-ROM format.

Additional recommendations for developing a core reference collection can be found in Blazek and Aversa's *The Humanities: A Selective Guide to Information Sources,* 3d edition (Libraries Unlimited, 1988).
—*C. W. B.*

Core Titles

Atlas of the Bible. John Rogerson. Facts On File, 1985. hard. 1 vol. 237 pp. illus. index. ISBN 0-8160-1207-5. $45. atlas.
BS630.R6 912.122

The *Atlas of the Bible,* by John Rogerson, takes a divergent approach to the study of the Bible. Traditionally, Bible atlases have treated their subject historically. In those atlases, the maps and other illustrative material are arranged chronologically according to Judeo-Christian history. The other atlases evaluated here—THE MACMILLAN BIBLE ATLAS and the OXFORD BIBLE ATLAS—are representative of this approach. In contrast, Rogerson's *Atlas of the Bible* does not present a reconstruction of biblical history supported by maps and pictures. Instead, the major portion of this volume is organized geographically.

The atlas is divided into three parts. The first part briefly surveys the composition and transmission of the Bible through the Revised Standard Version. The second part takes the historical view, presenting a brief, more or less traditional overview of biblical history from the call of Abraham to the missionary journeys of Paul. This overview is accompanied by the usual assortment of atlas maps: the route of the Exodus; the movements of Israelite troops in the conquest of Canaan; the division of the land into tribal territories; the empires of David and Solomon and of the divided kingdom; the neighboring empires of Assyria, Babylon, and Persia; Palestine and the surrounding world of intertestamental times; and the missionary journeys of Paul. In addition, there are artistic representations of biblical episodes.

The third part is the focal point and by far the largest part of the atlas (nearly 170 of its 237 pages). It is this division of the *Atlas of the Bible,* "The Bible and Geography," that sets this work apart from other Bible atlases. The part begins with a general discussion of biblical geography in which Rogerson identifies the major regions of the land that will be treated in more detail and describes features of the biblical landscape, such as geography, geology, climate, and vegetation. One important point is made here and worked out in the following pages: The Holy Land of biblical times is quite different from that of today. For example, Rogerson claims that at the time of the Israelite settlement of the land, there was more wooded area than is present today. If so, a different perception of the world in which early biblical characters existed is possible, including factors that complicated migration and daily life.

In the remainder of the third part, the lands of the Bible are divided into 12 regions. Each section begins with a map of the region. The text then treats the major biblical events associated with the region. The maps provide legends and keys for locating ancient and modern sites. Plentiful photographs and drawings help the reader form a vivid image of the region under discussion.

If there is a drawback to this work, it is the geographical arrangement. Those who are used to the traditional historical arrangement may not feel well served by this atlas. However, if used in conjunction with another atlas using that format, the *Atlas of the Bible* can provide a complementary perspective on the biblical stories by presenting a comprehensive view of important biblical sites. The Board recommends this work for the core collections of public and school libraries.
—*C. W. B.*

Butler's Lives of the Saints, 2d edition. Herbert Thurston and Donald Attwater, eds. Christian Classics, 1956; repr. by Harper & Row, 1985. hard and soft. 4 vols. appendix. index. ISBN 0-88479-045-7 (hard); 0-88479-137-2 (soft). $140 (hard); $95 (soft). biographical dictionary.
BX4654.B8 922.22B

This work is a good example of how a valuable reference tool can be kept alive for centuries through the work of competent editors who update its content. Alban Butler produced his *Lives of the Saints* between 1756 and 1759. The work was significantly revised by Herbert Thurston between 1932 and 1938. This second, revised edition, edited by Donald Attwater, expands Butler's original 1,486 entries to 2,565 while significantly reducing the number of pages by omitting Butler's daily homilies on the saints, exhortations that to Attwater now seem "repetitious and monotonous."

What is left is an edition that lets the saints' lives speak for themselves. The saints are not arranged alphabetically but chronologically under their respective feast days. This makes the work useful as a devotional tool; Butler intended his readers to follow the calendar and venerate each saint. For this reason, the work contains entries on religious feasts, such as *All Saints' Day* (November 1), as well as on specific saints.

The usefulness of this work as a reference tool depends on the index in volume 4. One must use it to look up the saint by name, find the saint's day, and then look under that day in the appropriate volume. Each volume's table of contents also lists the saints covered in it.

The articles are well written, in single columns, and generally of moderate length. Few are longer than the six pages for *Gregory the Great,* but few are less than half a page. Western saints predominate, but a few Eastern ones are included. Each entry contains a helpful bibliography updated to 1956. The work would be enhanced by illustrations but contains none, perhaps due to space limitations or the lack of illustrations in Butler's original version. The readable type is printed on good stock, with a high-quality, attractive binding.

Although Butler's original work idealized the saints, the successive revisions have attempted to be more objective in their treatment of the history of the saints without losing the personal quality found in Butler's articles. Consequently, this edition of *Butler's Lives of the Saints* is a valuable source of information. The Board recommends this work for the core collections of public and academic libraries. —*G. H.*

A Dictionary of Comparative Religion. S. G. F. Brandon, gen. ed. Scribner, 1970. hard. 1 vol. 704 pp. indexes. ISBN 0-684-15561-3 $60. dictionary.
BL31.D54 291.03

Unlike THE PERENNIAL DICTIONARY OF WORLD RELIGIONS and THE FACTS ON FILE DICTIONARY OF RELIGIONS, the primary focus of *A Dictionary of Comparative Religion* is not on living religions. This dictionary deals equally with ancient and modern faiths and related topics. The arrangement is alphabetical, with articles varying in length from a few lines to several pages according to the importance or the complexity of the subject. Each article has a bibliography for those who wish to pursue more comprehensive study.

Religions that are less significant in terms of distribution or influence are allotted single comprehensive articles; examples are *Australian aborigine religion* and *shamanism.* Major religious traditions, such as *Buddhism* and *Christianity,* have a general survey article accompanied by cross-references. However, the editors considered these topics to be so extensive that this approach in itself was insufficient, so a synoptic index also is provided. In this index, all articles that are pertinent to a major religious tradition are listed alphabetically under that heading. For example, articles under *Buddhism* fill three pages; those under *Christianity* fill two pages; and those related to *Judaism* fill one. An especially helpful feature of the synoptic listings is that they include blank headings, such as those with only a cross-reference, as well as substantive headings, such as those attached to articles. For example, a person using the synoptic index to study Buddhism who wants to read about its canon is directed to *canon of scripture, Buddhist.* There the reader finds a cross-reference to *Tipitaka.* Unfortunately, some of the listed terms are not given in the same form as the entry headings.

A general index of terms and names lists those that are not given a separate entry but treated within another article. For each item listed, the appropriate substantive heading is indicated.

Though this work is by no means as comprehensive as James Hastings's now out-of-print 13-volume *Encyclopaedia of Religion and Ethics* (Scribner, 1926) or Eliade's THE ENCYCLOPEDIA OF RELIGION, nor as current as the latter, *A Dictionary of Comparative Religion* has stood the test of time and has a definite place in a strong religion collection. This dictionary provides authoritative introductory information on comparative religion, which can be supplemented by Hastings and Eliade and by sources listed in the bibliographies.

The Board recommends this work for the core collection of public libraries. —*C. W. B.*

The Eerdmans Analytical Concordance to the Revised Standard Version of the Bible. Richard E. Whitaker and James E. Goehring, comps. Eerdmans, 1988. hard. 1 vol. 1,548 pp. indexes. ISBN 0-8028-2403-X. $59.95. concordance.
BS425.W48 220.5'20423

The Revised Standard Version of the Bible (Old and New Testaments and Apocrypha) was completed in 1952, and from 1957 *Nelson's Complete Concordance of the Revised Standard Version of the Bible* has been available to use with it. *Eerdmans Analytical Concordance,* though a bit tardy in appearing, takes the place of the now out-of-print *Nelson's Concordance.* This concordance is a substantial reference tool in size—over 1,500 pages of triple-column text—and capability. In addition, *Eerdmans* offers the student a significant advantage over other concordances to the entire Revised Standard Version (RSV) by keying the English to the Hebrew, Aramaic, Greek, and Latin texts that the RSV translates. This permits more serious study of the Bible.

The concordance consists of an alphabetical listing of the dictionary forms of words that occur in the RSV. The treatment of each term consists of three parts. First the dictionary form of the word appears as a boldface main entry. Next comes a numbered listing of the various Hebrew, Aramaic, Greek, or Latin terms that are translated in the Revised Standard Version by the English forms of the main entry word. Finally, there is a list of occurrences of the English word in question. Each occurrence is printed as part of the phrase in which it occurs, accompanied by the citation of the book, chapter, and verse in which it occurs. Each is also assigned a number corresponding to the foreign-language term that it translates. Therefore, if a single English word translates three different Greek words in as many different biblical passages, one is able to determine in each case which Greek word lies behind the English term. Proper nouns and numbers above 20 are grouped separately after the main section of the concordance.

The work concludes with a series of four indexes that list in alphabetical order Hebrew, Aramaic, Greek, and Latin words with their English counterparts in the RSV. The indexes allow one to begin with the original language of a term and, by tracking down all the English terms that were used to translate it, to trace all the occurrences of the ancient-language term. The user should bear in mind, however, that many conjunctions, prepositions, articles, adverbs, and auxiliary verbs were omitted from the concordance to reduce its size. It seems unlikely, though, that these omissions will inconvenience or hinder those who use the concordance.

The editors intended their work for the "person with a lively interest in the Bible but limited knowledge of the original languages" and believed that it would prove useful for "preachers, students, and scholars." Although the biblical scholar will prefer Greek or Hebrew concordances, the present work will undoubtedly serve preachers and students who have grown up hearing and reading the RSV. When used judiciously, this concordance may enhance their study of the Bible.

The editors and their staff are to be congratulated on the accomplishment of this concordance, which holds great potential for assisting users in the study of the Bible. However, the book's effectiveness will require serious effort and genuine dedication to the research enterprise. *Eerdmans Analytical Concordance* will guide one's study with the pre-1990 RSV but will not function adequately with the new edition—the first attempt to revise it in light of the latest developments in research and translation techniques. The Board recommends this work for the core collections of public and academic libraries. —*M. P. G.*

The Encyclopedia of American Religions, 3d edition. J. Gordon Melton. Gale, 1989. hard. 1 vol. 1,102 pp. illus. indexes. ISBN 0-8103-2841-0. $165. encyclopedia.
BL2525.M449 200

In 1978, the first edition of *The Encyclopedia of American Religions* appeared and quickly established Melton as a leading authority on U.S. religious groups. That edition classified and described some 1,200 churches and other religious bodies. In the second edition, that number rose to more than 1,300. Coverage in the third edition has been expanded by some 250 groups, bringing the total number of groups to 1,588. This increase includes, for the first time, Canadian churches and religious groups. The decision to include Canadian churches reflects an awareness of the strong doctrinal and historical interrelationship between the religious traditions of that country and the United States. Also new in this edition are two introductory essays, "An Interpretive View of the Development of American Religions" and "A Historical Survey of Religion in Canada, 1500 to the Present," which trace the development of religion and religions in North America and make some projections for the near future.

Melton's selection of religious groups is based on three criteria. First, the group must require the primary devotion of its members. Second, the group must meet particular size requirements, measured by the number of congregations or of members. In a few instances this requirement was waived to include certain groups, such as some Satanic and communal groups, in the encyclopedia. Third, the group should be involved in the promotion of its distinguishing doctrines. Melton classifies the religious bodies into 19 families, including Liturgical, Reformed-Presbyterian, Baptist, Pentecostal, and Middle Eastern. Instead of depending on traditional categories, he has devised his own simple formula for classification: "The member bodies of each family share a common heritage, thought world (theology in its broadest sense), and lifestyle" (introduction to the first edition).

Information on the religious families and on the individual bodies—some of them defunct but most still active—is presented in two sections. In the first part, essay chapters survey the historical development of each of the families, focusing first on the family as a whole and then on its constituent members. At the end of each chapter is a classified bibliography. Most of these bibliographies contain at least a few titles from recent years. In the second part, directory listings chapters correspond to the chapters in the first part. For example, chapter 11 in each part deals with the Adventist family. Two additional chapters in part 2 list 48 unclassified Christian churches and other religious groups. Most of the directory entries contain the following items: name and address of the organization; description of history, beliefs, and organization; current membership, including number of congregations and ministers; affiliated or approved colleges, universities, and seminaries; official periodicals; and lists of source materials. Access to the information contained in the essays and directory listings is enhanced by six indexes: educational institutions, periodicals, geographic locations, personal names, subjects, and organization or institution name.

Melton's research is quite thorough. This is especially obvious regarding the less well known groups, for whom information is not readily available. Melton is also objective in his presentation, even with groups whose claims and teachings may seem ridiculous or dangerous.

Occasional inaccuracies occur in the *The Encyclopedia of American Religions,* which is not surprising in a work of this scope. A supplement is planned to correct these, to update information on groups in this edition, and to provide coverage of new and newly discovered religious bodies.

The Board recommends this work for the core collections of public and academic libraries. —*C. W. B.*

The Encyclopedia of Religion. Mircea Eliade, ed. in chief. Macmillan, 1987. hard. 16 vols. illus. index. ISBN 0-02-909480-1 (set). $1,300 (set). encyclopedia.
BL31.E46 200.3′21

This is the latest and most ambitious work of its kind to appear in English since Hastings's *Encyclopaedia of Religion and Ethics* (Scribner, 1926). Mircea Eliade, who exerted enormous influence on twentieth-century research in the field of religion, assembled an international body of scholars to produce a "concise, clear and objective description of the totality of human experience of the sacred" for "educated, nonspecialist readers." The product is a 16-volume work, attractively bound, with double-column pages and ample margins.

There are three major kinds of entries in the work. The first are those that describe individual religious communities and traditions, such as *Islam, Hinduism, Christianity, Slavic religions, Oceanic religions,* and *Australian aboriginal religions.* Some of the larger categories include treatments of the religion within certain geographical regions, such as Islam in North Africa, Judaism in southern Europe, or Christianity in the Pacific Islands. The second kind of entry treats certain topics in the history of religions, such as *afterlife, angels, evil, myths, purification, sexuality,* and *visions.* Finally, essays sketch the "relationships between religion and other areas of culture," such as art, law, music, science, and philosophy. A number of the larger articles are subdivided and contain contributions from several specialists. For example, *iconography* has 14 parts. In addition to the foregoing three categories of entries, there are 143 articles about scholars who have made significant contributions to the study of religion, including *Auguste Comte, Friedrich Delitzsch, Mircea Eliade, Alfred Loisy, F. Max Mueller,* and *Victor Turner.* A bibliographical list or essay concludes each entry. The last volume in the encyclopedia consists of a directory of contributors and their contributions, an alphabetical list of entries, a synoptic outline of contents (articles are grouped according to subject), an extensive index, and corrigenda.

Although the articles are by no means uniform in approach or treatment, the encyclopedia as a whole—and in many particulars—is informed by its editor's assumption that "nothing is a purely religious phenomenon" but everything—including religion—is human phenomena. Consequently, explanations of religious communities, beliefs, and practices are provided in their larger human contexts and in relation to all other aspects of life, including philosophy, economics, and politics. Similarly, the influence of Eliade's own interests in archaic religion, symbols, and myths are also apparent.

The Encyclopedia of Religion will provide its readers with hours of stimulating, delightful, and informative reading. Although the specialist will find some articles mediocre or flawed and perhaps wonder why a particular contributor was selected when better authorities have written on the topic, many entries were written by internationally renowned experts and offer valuable summaries for the nonspecialist, such as Hoffner on *Hittite religion. The Encyclopedia of Religion* is long overdue and is a fitting, posthumous tribute to its editor.

The Board recommends this work for the core collections of public, academic, and school libraries.
—*M. P. G.*

Encyclopedic Handbook of Cults in America. J. Gordon Melton. Garland, 1986. hard. 1 vol. 272 pp. index. ISBN 0-8240-9036-5. $30. handbook.
BL2525.M45 291.0973

J. Gordon Melton of the Institute for the Study of American Religion has become one of the most prolific writers of reference books on religion. His well-researched and well-written *Encyclopedic Handbook of Cults in America* serves as a companion volume to THE ENCYCLOPEDIA OF AMERICAN RELIGIONS. The *Encyclopedic Handbook* is brief (272 pages) but gives detailed information on cults, particularly newer cults, in America.

The *Encyclopedic Handbook* is divided into six sections. The first section, "What Is a Cult?", is a balanced introduction to the subject. The next section discusses "twenty of the older, more established nonconventional religions" in America, such as the Church of Jesus Christ of Latter Day Saints (Mormons), the Jehovah's Witnesses, and even Satanism. The third section ably distills information on the diverse New Age movement. The heart of the *Encyclopedic Handbook* is the fifth section, which deals with 16 newer cults in America, including The Church of Scientology and The Unification Church. The fifth section is called "Counter-Cult Groups," and the sixth is an illuminating essay titled "Violence and the Cults."

Melton, an evangelical Christian, is quite even-handed and accurate in his treatment of the cults. He writes on a fairly simple level but ends each cult article with a current bibliography for further study. The index increases accessibility. The *Encyclopedic Handbook* is printed on high-quality paper with good-sized type and is bound well.

The danger with a reference book on such a timely subject is that its information goes out of date quickly. Melton is current in his research, but since this book was published in 1986, many changes have occurred within these cults, and new cults have arisen. It would be interesting, for example, to see what effect Melton believes the recent death of L. Ron Hubbard will have on The Church of Scientology that he founded. To remain current, Melton will have to produce revised editions of the *Encyclopedic Handbook of Cults in America.*

Right now, though, the handbook is the most current source available. The Board recommends this work for the core collections of public and academic libraries. —*G. H.*

The Facts On File Dictionary of Religions. John R. Hinnells, ed. Facts On File, 1984. hard. 1 vol. 560 pp. illus. indexes. ISBN 0-87196-862-2. $35. dictionary.
BL31.F33 291.03′21

The Facts On File Dictionary of Religions is a compact handbook of "the specialized vocabulary used by those who practice a religion and by those who write about it" (introduction). The alphabetical listing consists of 1,150 entries contributed by 29 scholars specializing in anthropology, archaeology, art history, classics, history, linguistics, Oriental studies, philosophy, sociology, and theology. Most of the scholars are British, giving the volume an overall British perspective. Entries range from a few lines to nearly a full page. Emphasis in this dictionary is placed on "living" religions, especially those that have large followings—Buddhism, Christianity, Hinduism, Islam, and Judaism—and secular alternatives. However, some space is given to Eastern and Western ancient religions and to the study of religion.

In addition to the dictionary proper, there are three other sections that comprise about one-third of the book: maps, bibliography, and indexes. Eleven maps show the locations of all important places—ancient and modern—mentioned in the text. An extensive bibliography divided according to subject headings provides direction for readers who wish to pursue a topic in greater depth. Each subject heading receives a roman numeral, and the entries that follow are numbered in arabic numerals. The dictionary entries are keyed to the bibliography using these numerals. References to the bibliography appear throughout the text. There are two indexes: synoptic and general. The synoptic index arranges all the terms found in the dictionary under the same subject headings used in the bibliography. The general index provides access to important terms, concepts, and persons treated within entries but not listed as main entry words. For example, *Martin Luther* is listed under *Lutheranism* and does not receive a separate entry. The general index also provides access to equivalent terms and concepts, such as *Muslim* and *Islam,* and to variant spellings, such as *Koran* and *Qur'an.*

What makes *The Facts On File Dictionary of Religions* a standout is the breadth of information presented. Although most of the terms defined here can be found elsewhere—for example, in THE PERENNIAL DICTIONARY OF WORLD RELIGIONS or THE OXFORD DICTIONARY OF THE CHRISTIAN CHURCH—written by authorities equal in stature to the contributors to this dictionary, one would have to consult several sources to find *all* the terms treated here, and a few of them—such as *anti-cult movement* and *White Eagle Lodge*—appear nowhere else. The interrelationship of the entries, cross-references, bibliography, and indexes makes this a particularly user-friendly tool, allowing multiple approaches to the text. For example, the place of funerary rites and practices in different religions can be traced by locating that main entry word in the general index. Or the user could locate major concepts of Buddhism by using the synoptic index.

As is usually the case with Facts On File publications, this one is well produced. The binding should stand up to reasonable use, the book is printed on nonglare paper, and the small trim size makes it a handy volume. The volume is already somewhat dated (preparation for publication began in 1981), and this is reflected in the bibliography entries. Therefore, some current concepts, such as the New Age movement and channeling, are not included. However, *The Facts On File Dictionary of Religions* is quite useful for the reader who is seeking ready-reference information on religion and religions.

The Board recommends this work for the core collections of public and school libraries. —*C. W. B.*

Harper's Bible Dictionary. Paul J. Achtemeier, gen. ed. Harper & Row, 1985. hard. 1 vol. 1,778 pp. illus. index. ISBN 0-06-069862-4. $31.95. dictionary.
BS440.H237 220.3

There have been eight predecessors to the *Harper's Bible Dictionary,* the last being the *New Harper's Bible Dictionary* published in 1973. The new edition is, in reality, a completely new work. All the articles are newly written by 179 biblical scholars from various religious traditions within the Judeo-Christian heritage and from several geographic locations. All contributors are members of the Society of Biblical Literature and are involved—some of them intimately—with cutting-edge biblical scholarship.

A broad range of topics is presented alphabetically covering the Bible and related matters. Biblical writings, including the books of the Apocrypha, receive standard introductory treatment: authorship, occasion, background, genre, summary of contents or theology, and outline. Many articles are devoted to aspects of the physical and social world of the Bible: cities and towns *(Jericho, Caesarea, Philippi),* nations and peoples *(Assyria, Babylonia,* the *Philistines),* mountains and mountain ranges *(Ararat,* the *Lebanon range),* rivers *(Jordan, Euphrates),* geographic regions (the *Negeb,* the *Shephelah*), geographic features *(forest, wilderness),* and daily life *(weights and measures, trade and transportation).* Place and personal names merit entries if they appear at least three times in the Bible or if they are otherwise important to the biblical story, including those not mentioned in the text, such as *Hammurabi* and *Qumran.* Coverage is thorough, but there are some gaps. For example, the article *Manasseh* is exclusively about the seventh century B.C.E. Judean king and does not mention the son of Jacob or the Israelite tribe that both bear that name. Important theological concepts, such as *baptism, holiness,* and *justice,* are treated as they occur in the Bible, excluding later developments. Several articles deal with facets of the study of the Bible: archaeology, biblical criticism, historical geography, sociology, and theology. Particularly important are the contributions in the area of archaeology. *Harper's Bible Dictionary* incorporates the latest possible archaeological data in articles on archaeology itself *(archaeology, methods of),* sites *(Amarna, Tell el-),* and periods *(Bronze Age).* Many other articles also include information of current discoveries.

The majority of the articles are set in a double-column format. In addition, there are 17 single-column articles, which include *Jesus Christ; Jerusalem; David;* and *texts, versions, manuscripts, editions.* The reader is not told why these articles are presented this way, but presumably it is to draw special attention to them or emphasize their importance. If this is so, it is difficult to understand why some of these subjects—such as *the Bible and Western art; money;* and *music*—merited special treatment above many other subjects in the dictionary.

Most of the single-column entries and several of the double-column ones include brief bibliographies. There is, however, an overall lack of bibliographies, which is disappointing in a scholarly work such as this. Illustrations, on the other hand, are not disappointing. Many illustrations of various types (drawings, photographs, maps, and charts) are located throughout the text. All are black and white and most are one column or less in size, although a full-page black-and-white picture appears at the beginning of each chapter. Two sections of color plates and 16 pages of color maps are included at the end of the volume.

Harper's Bible Dictionary generally represents the mainstream of contemporary critical biblical scholarship. This is easiest to identify in articles dealing with or reflecting controversial topics. For example, articles on the *Pentateuch* and its parts assume some form of documentary or source hypothesis of composition. Articles on *Paul* and his letters assume a limited authentic Pauline canon—Ephesians, Colossians, 2 Thessalonians, 1 and 2 Timothy, and Titus are considered post-Pauline.

Harper's Bible Dictionary is the most authoritative and current one-volume Bible dictionary available, and it is well-written, attractive, and reasonably sturdy. The Board recommends this work for the core collections of public, academic, and school libraries. —*C. W. B.*

The International Standard Bible Encyclopedia, rev. edition. Geoffrey W. Bromiley, ed. Eerdmans, 1979–1988. hard. 4 vols. illus. ISBN 0-80288-160-2 (set). $39.95 per vol. encyclopedia.
BS440.I6 220.329

This four-volume set is the second revision of *The International Standard Bible Encyclopedia.* Since 1915, this title has been one of the most respected Bible reference tools, particularly in conservative circles. This major revision by an international and ecumenical panel of scholars strives to continue the approach of what they call "a reasonable conservatism."

The encyclopedia is quite broad in scope, covering

every person and place in the Bible, biblical terms with theological and ethical meaning, and even significant terms from the Apocrypha. This work is best when discussing particular books of the Bible, such as the illuminating 14-page article on the "Acts of the Apostles." Intended as an exegetical tool, the encyclopedia discusses troublesome passages under the particular Bible books in which they are found. Articles on the production and transmission of the Bible, such as "Writing," are also in this work. Many articles contain helpful, up-to-date bibliographies at the end.

Most articles are written for a college-trained audience but are not too technical, in keeping with the editor's aim to serve "both the advanced student and yet also the average pastor and Bible student."

Entries are arranged alphabetically, using the spelling of the Revised Standard Version of the Bible. The only exception to this arrangement is the logical placement of certain Old Testament topics before New Testament ones, such as "Canon of the Old Testament" before "Canon of the New Testament." Most articles provide cross-references to other pertinent articles.

High-quality black-and-white and color illustrations enhance the presentation. The maps scattered throughout the volumes are quite helpful. The type, in double columns, is quite small, but bold and readable. The binding, paper, and layout are attractive and of high quality.

Though conservative in outlook, *The International Standard Bible Encyclopedia* is quite evenhanded in its treatment of controversial topics in Bible study, such as in the article "Criticism." The encyclopedia uses current information to illuminate longstanding arguments. For example, in "Daniel," arguments are presented for an early date for the composition of the book (a traditionally conservative argument), but making the case mainly on the basis of recent material from the Dead Sea Scrolls.

The Board recommends this work for the core collection of public libraries. —*G. H.*

The Interpreter's Bible. George Arthur Buttrick, ed. Abingdon, 1951–1957. hard. 12 vols. illus. indexes. ISBN 0-687-19206-4. $299.95 (set). commentary. BS491.2.I55 220.7

This 12-volume set of commentaries was produced in the 1950s by 125 authors who offered "the best exegetical and expository skill" of the day and intended to make the latest information related to biblical scholarship available to "preachers, teachers, and other students." The work includes general articles on a variety of topics, such as the "English Bible," the "Canon of the Old Testament," the "Study of the Bible," the "Life and Ministry of Jesus," and the "History of the Early Church." Articles range in length from about 10 to 30 pages. The work also includes the text of the King James and Revised Standard Versions of the Bible, printed in parallel columns. Another feature of this work is an introduction and a verse-by-verse exegesis and exposition of each book of the Old and New Testaments. Genesis, for example, receives 400 pages of treatment. A number of maps and scripture and subject indexes round out the commentary.

The introduction and exegesis for each book were done by a biblical scholar, and the exposition was done by an accomplished preacher; in some cases the same writer did both. There are substantial bibliographies and ample cross-references. The volumes are hefty; each ranges in size from about 650 to 1,150 pages. The paper and binding are durable, and the print is clear.

The Interpreter's Bible was received with great acclaim when it was issued, and it has won a respected place in the history of twentieth-century biblical interpretation. Nevertheless, users need to keep several points in mind. At the time that the commentary appeared, the work met the critical need among preachers, students, and educated laity for a commentary on the English Bible that reflected the great advances in scholarship during the first half of the twentieth century. The scholars and preachers who participated were among the finest in the United States and Britain. Moreover, the work represented a serious attempt to assist preachers and teachers in their efforts not only to understand the Bible but also to make it relevant for life.

In spite of these accomplishments, readers today must realize that the work is essentially the product of mid-twentieth century U.S. and British Protestantism. Jewish scholars, Roman Catholics, and specialists from other religious traditions were not contributors. Hence, the Bible of this commentary is the Protestant Bible, or the Old Testament without the Apocrypha, and it is the Old and New Testaments (Christian terminology) rather than the Hebrew Bible and the Christian New Testament. Consequently, the user should not turn to *The Interpreter's Bible* for the views of non-Protestants. Moreover, the Protestantism that the writers reflect is that of the biblical theology movement, which flourished in the 1950s but withered in the late 1960s.

A second problem with the commentary arises when one compares the exegesis with the exposition sections. Ideally, the latter should be based on the former, but in fact, the two often take different paths, and on some occasions (such as Matthew 6–9) the two contradict one another. Such incongruities only confuse the reader.

Finally, due to the great strides that have been made during the last generation in archaeology, biblical studies, and a host of other disciplines, *The Interpreter's Bible* is dated and has been eclipsed by a number of more recent commentary series. Nevertheless, some of the general articles may still be read with profit, and the commentary is a milestone in the history of biblical interpretation. In this regard, therefore, the commentary is an important resource for seminary and university libraries that intend to support the study of the Bible.

The Board recommends this work for the core collections of public and academic libraries. —*M. P. G.*

The Macmillan Bible Atlas, rev. edition. Yohanan Aharoni and Michael Avi-Yonah. Macmillan, 1977. hard. 1 vol. 184 pp. illus. appendix. index. ISBN 0-02-500590-1. $29.95. atlas.
G2230.A2 912.56

The first edition of this large, sturdily bound atlas appeared in 1968, although earlier forms of it had been published by Carta (an Israeli map publisher) several years before. The late authors were professors of archaeology at Hebrew University in Jerusalem and well known for their contributions in archaeology. Aharoni was responsible for maps numbered 1 to 171 and Avi-Yonah for the rest. The atlas is concerned primarily with Palestine but treats surrounding areas as necessary. The chronological span covered is circa 3000 B.C.E. to 200 C.E.

The atlas consists of 262 two-color maps, each accompanied by a narrative that explains the events or circumstances depicted. The large number of maps, each with a restricted purpose, such as the depiction of a single battle or journey, and the simplicity of presentation make the maps clear and easy to use. Similarly, the symbols used on the maps are explained well, and boldface type distinguishes the cities that are more important. The representational ability of the maps is enhanced by the use of shading, but elevations are difficult to show. In this respect, Macmillan's atlas is inferior to the OXFORD BIBLE ATLAS and others that use a variety of colors to indicate elevation.

The maps differ in size and scale. Scale is indicated with a bar marked according to miles and kilometers. Longitude and latitude are not specified, and the atlas lacks grids or other techniques that allow precise location. In spite of this, places are not difficult to locate, since each map plots a relatively few sites. Therefore, the index keys each place name to the number of the map on which it appears.

The atlas concludes with a list of books of the Bible and the maps that treat their contents, chronological charts that are exceptionally useful, and an extensive index that gives ancient and modern names with map references. There is no gazetteer, however, to provide information about pronunciation and other important matters.

The chief value of the Macmillan atlas is the large number of detailed maps that it provides. This is enhanced by the multitude of drawings and charts (there are virtually no photographs) and by the explanatory narrative. The narrative is reasonably current and in tune with contemporary scholarship. It is noted, for example, that there are archaeological problems with the biblical accounts of the conquest of Jericho and Ai, and the complexity of establishing boundary lines is also pointed out. However, the arrows and lines that represent the authors' reconstructions of the movements of people and armies tend to convey a greater degree of certainty about such things than is warranted. The structure and method of presentation distinguish this atlas from many comparable works and make it an invaluable tool for serious study of the Bible.

The Macmillan atlas is now over a decade old, however, and the publisher should give serious consideration to the preparation of a third edition that would reflect the most recent advances in archaeological and biblical studies. Nevertheless, *The Macmillan Bible Atlas* is an inexpensive and extremely useful resource. The Board recommends this work for the core collections of public and academic libraries. —*M. P. G.*

New Catholic Encyclopedia. William J. McDonald, ed. in chief. McGraw-Hill, 1967–1989. hard. 18 vols. illus. index. ISBN 0-07-010235-X. $750 (set). encyclopedia.
BX841.N44 282.03

The *New Catholic Encyclopedia,* comprising 17,000 signed articles by 4,800 scholars, is the standard English work on world Catholicism. The articles cover all aspects of the doctrine, organization, and history of the Catholic Church as well as significant ideas and movements that have affected the Church from without. This broad scope is illustrated by such lengthy articles as "American Literature," "Hinduism," and "Population."

The alphabetically arranged entries are well illustrated with photographs (including a few color plates), maps, and charts. A short bibliography follows each entry. Accessibility is increased by the 978-page index volume, which contains thousands of headings and subheadings. As expected in a work with this many contributors, the writing level differs considerably from article to article. Most, however, are written for a college-level audience.

The weakness of the *New Catholic Encyclopedia* is its lack of currency, since it was published in 1967. The publishers have sought to remedy this by publishing three supplements to the set—volumes 16 to 18—in 1974, 1979, and 1989. The supplements follow the same alphabetical arrangement as the main encyclopedia with bibliographies, illustrations, and an index. Articles in the supplements update articles in the main encyclopedia or introduce new topics significant to the contemporary world. The high quality of research and writing found in the main set is continued in the supplements.

In spite of their high quality, the use of supplements instead of a complete revision of the encyclopedia does pose problems. Since the articles in the supplements do not always supersede the articles in the main set, readers may have to examine four different volumes to receive a full discussion of a particular topic.

The paper, binding, and layout of the encyclopedia are of high quality and quite attractive. Even though the entries are in double columns, the type is quite readable.

The broad scope and objective stance in most articles make the *New Catholic Encyclopedia* valuable not only as a window into Catholic thought, but also as a tool for understanding Christianity and culture as a whole. The Board recommends this work for the core collections of public and academic libraries. —*G. H.*

Oxford Bible Atlas, 3d edition. Herbert G. May, ed. Oxford, 1984. hard and soft. 1 vol. 144 pp. illus. ISBN 0-19-143452-3 (hard); 0-19-143451-5 (soft). $24.95 (hard); $14.95 (soft). atlas.
BS630.096 220.9

The *Oxford Bible Atlas* first appeared in 1962. The second edition was published in 1974 and the third in 1984. This latest edition includes recent developments in site identification and historical reconstruction and continues the high standards and solid reputation of the publisher and editors.

The atlas begins with a substantial (38 pages) introduction that surveys the climate, geography, and history of Palestine and the ancient Near East. This section is profusely illustrated with black-and-white photos, drawings, and chronological charts. The discussion in this section focuses on the Palestine of the Bible and neighboring areas as they impinge on the biblical narrative.

The central part of the atlas consists of 26 maps with explanatory text, set in chronological order from the time before the Exodus from Egypt and extending to the time of the early Christian church. Four maps that treat archaeological matters round out this section.

Finally, an essay and a gazetteer conclude the work. The former, "Archaeology and the Bible," takes up a number of important topics, such as the patriarchs, Exodus and settlement, and divine images, to show what archaeology has contributed to contemporary biblical interpretation. The gazetteer lists the name of each site mentioned in the atlas, providing both ancient and modern forms of the names, sometimes a brief description of the site, and the page numbers and grid location of its occurrences. Cross-references enable the reader to find the appropriate map when the site is known by a variety of names.

Most of the maps were prepared in six colors to illustrate elevation. Although the colors are clear and attractive, there are some minor problems with their registration, and a color key for each map is lacking. The scale of the maps varies and is typically noted in miles and kilometers. One pattern of grids is used for all maps, though, so that a site has the same coordinates on each map. The symbols that are used on the maps are usually clear and useful but are not always adequately explained. On a few occasions, boundary lines are difficult to follow. A wide variety of typefaces is used to designate cities and regions of different sizes and significance. The binding is adequate, but in the softcover edition, some details are difficult to find on maps that extend beyond a single page.

The *Oxford Bible Atlas* was written for the student and, as such, has proven useful. Although the archaeological or topographical specialist will find the work too brief and will quarrel with some of its conclusions, on the whole, the *Oxford Bible Atlas* is an improvement on earlier works because it introduces the reader to some of the latest developments in archaeological and historical research on the Bible and its setting. The Board recommends this work for the core collection of school libraries. —*M. P. G.*

The Oxford Dictionary of Saints, 2d edition. David Hugh Farmer. Oxford, 1987. hard and soft. 1 vol. 478 pp. appendixes. index. ISBN 0-19-869149-1 (hard); 0-19-282038-9 (soft). $11.95. dictionary.
BR1710.F34 270.092′2

David Hugh Farmer has written 79 new or substantially revised articles for this second edition of his ambitious *Oxford Dictionary of Saints.* Although his qualifications for writing are unquestionable, a reference work of this magnitude written by one person is unusual.

Farmer's purpose is to cover all English saints; the most notable saints from Ireland, Scotland, and Wales; all saints with notable cults in Great Britain; and other important Western and Eastern saints. Coverage of Eastern saints has been expanded in this edition to a total of almost 1,100 entries.

Most entries are brief, ranging from two and a half pages on well-known figures such as *Patrick* and *Thomas More,* down to five lines on obscure saints such as the eleventh-century abbess *Cuthfelda.* It is precisely in these extremes that the dictionary is weakest. Information on the more famous saints is readily available elsewhere, and the entries on minor saints are too brief to be helpful. The work's best points are the page-long entries on personalities such as *Simeon Stylites.*

These articles are arranged alphabetically under Christian names up to the end of the fifteenth century but under surnames after that time. This arrangement is confusing to readers who are unfamiliar with the chronology of a particular saint. The dictionary tries to remedy this through the use of "see" citations under alternate names; however, there are not enough of these cross-references. The brief bibliographical notes at the end of each entry refer the reader primarily to older works on each saint.

The vocabulary of the entries contains few British words but may be too advanced for high school students. More distressing to U.S. readers is the detailed knowledge of British geography that most articles assume. An index of British places associated with particular saints is included to assist readers with this difficulty. Other appendixes include a list of unsuccessful British candidates for canonization, lists of the principal patronages and iconographic emblems of each saint, and a feast day calendar.

The paper quality and binding of the paperback edition are quite poor for a reference book. The hardback edition is preferred, but the type is quite small and thus may be unsuitable for many readers.

Although *Butler's Lives of the Saints* should be a library's first choice for a reference work on the saints, *The Oxford Dictionary of Saints* still provides a good deal of information at a reasonable price. The Board recommends this work for the core collections of public and academic libraries. —*G. H.*

The Oxford Dictionary of the Christian Church, 2d edition. F. L. Cross and E. A. Livingstone, eds. Oxford, 1974. hard. 1 vol. 1,520 pp. ISBN 0-19-211545-6. $65. dictionary.
BR95.08 203

Cross first issued this dictionary in 1958 and was working on the revision at the time of his death in 1968. Elizabeth A. Livingstone completed the work, and the dictionary was published in 1974. Since then, the volume has been reprinted several times with corrections.

Cross was an accomplished church historian, and his work has been well received. One of the chief criticisms of the first edition, however, was that the selection and treatment of topics had an Anglican bias, and consequently, inadequate attention was paid to the Roman Catholic and Orthodox churches. The effects of Vatican II on Roman Catholic faith and practice made the revision of the dictionary even more necessary. Therefore, as Cross set about preparing a second edition of the dictionary, he made a serious and somewhat successful attempt to address the concerns of his critics.

The product of Cross's labor is a work of 1,520 two-column pages that are bound well and easy to use. The entries are arranged in alphabetical order and consist of: (1) a brief definition or characterization of the subject, (2) an elaboration of its antecedents and historical development, and (3) a brief bibliography. The text is written for "the educated public as a whole"—whether Christian or not—and the entries assume no specialized training or knowledge. A wide variety of topics are treated, ranging from persons (clerics, scholars, and saints) and religious bodies (churches, monastic orders, and councils) to doctrines (orthodox and heretical) and practices (the sacraments, for example). A chronological list of popes and antipopes, as well as other addenda, is attached at the end of the volume. Cross-references guide the reader from alternative spellings of terms to the form under which the entry appears; within articles, asterisks mark topics for which additional information is provided.

In spite of the editors' efforts, though, the work still has some deficiencies. The articles continue to address subjects with special reference to the Church of England. Furthermore, U.S. readers will probably be less than satisfied with the length and clarity of some entries on U.S. churches, including *Baptists* and *Disciples of Christ.* Most readers will disagree with the amount of space allotted to certain subjects. For example, the essay on Paul Tillich is relatively brief.

Nevertheless, *The Oxford Dictionary of the Christian Church* represents a monumental accomplishment and is superior to other such works, including *The New International Dictionary of the Christian Church* (edited by J. D. Douglas and Earle E. Cairns, Zondervan, 1978). Consequently, *The Oxford Dictionary* remains one of the most useful reference tools for answering basic historical or theological questions about Christianity. The Board recommends this work for the core collections of public and academic libraries.

—*M. P. G.*

The Perennial Dictionary of World Religions. Keith Crim, ed. Harper & Row, 1989. soft. 1 vol. 830 pp. illus. ISBN 0-06-061613-X. $19.95. dictionary.
BL31.A24 291.03

The Perennial Dictionary of World Religions, originally released in 1981 as the *Abingdon Dictionary of Living Religions,* focuses on religions and religious movements that are currently practiced. Ancient religions and movements whose practice has ceased, such as Donatism and Manichaeism, are included where they figure in the development of a living religion. Each major current religion is assigned a lengthy primary article (*Buddhism,* 12 pages; *Christianity,* 8 pages; *Hinduism,* 12 pages; *Islam,* 13 pages; *Judaism,* 7 pages). These articles follow no set pattern; however, they usually inform the reader about the origin, development, and beliefs of each tradition. In addition to these articles, other entries deal with specific and related topics. These include terminology, persons (historical and mythological), places (shrines and other holy places), doctrines and theological concepts *(reincarnation* and *revelation),* minor religions and movements (the *Little Flock Movement*), sacred writings (the *Bible* and the *Bhagavad Gita*), and feasts, festivals, and holy days *(Passover, Purim,* and *Sabbath).* Although concepts associated with Middle Eastern and Asian religious thought are notoriously difficult for the Western mind to comprehend, in most cases, the contributors to this work have rendered them somewhat less mysterious.

Articles are set in a two-column format. Many articles are identified by an abbreviation with the religious tradition they relate to (for example, *H* for *Hinduism*). Also, for terms, the language of derivation and meaning are often included along with the pronunciation. Most of the articles have bibliographies ranging from one item to about two dozen items. Items in the bibliographies are not limited to those in English, which will limit their usefulness for nonspecialists.

More illustrations would have improved the appeal of this volume. In a dictionary of 830 pages, 150 black-and-white illustrations seem sparse, especially since most are rather small. A few illustrations are so small that the details described in the captions are almost impossible to discern (see the picture of the Heian Shrine on page 373). Eight color plates included in the original edition are missing from this one. In addition to the illustrations, eight pages of color maps are placed, somewhat oddly, within the article on *yoga.*

Managing a comprehensive volume such as this is difficult for both editors and users. Editors must decide how to provide proper access to related articles so that readers can get a complete picture of a topic of interest. *The Perennial Dictionary of World Religions* accomplishes this with cross-references and a classified guide—arranged by major religious tradition—to selected entries. Cross-references are used extensively, and this can be annoying. Occasionally, the user must consult several references to understand a single brief entry. This is often a hazard of one-volume dictionaries, in which duplication is kept to a minimum. Even so, there are omissions in cross-referencing. For example, neither Pentecost nor Merkabah mysticism can be found as references in the article on *Judaism.* There are fewer entries in the classified guide than in the synoptic index of the briefer FACTS ON FILE DICTIONARY OF RELIGIONS. In addition, *The Perennial Dictionary of World Religions* lacks a thorough index, which would have greatly increased its usefulness.

Librarians will be disappointed that the publisher chose to issue this reference book in softcover rather than hardcover, another deviation from the original edition. With much use, *The Perennial Dictionary of World Religions* may be ready for the bindery. This is unfortunate because the inner margin is not generous.

The Board recommends this work for the core collections of public and academic libraries. —*C. W. B.*

Yearbook of American and Canadian Churches. Constant H. Jacquet, Jr., ed. Abingdon, annual. soft. 1 vol. 304 pp. illus. index. ISBN 0-687-46642-3. $18.95. yearbook.
BR513.Y4 280.39

The *Yearbook of American and Canadian Churches* is the standard source for annual statistical information on religious bodies in the United States and Canada. This work was first published as the *Federal Council Yearbook* in 1916. Since 1973, it has included information on Canadian as well as U.S. churches. Constant H. Jacquet has served as its editor for over 20 years.

The bulk of each annual volume consists of alphabetically arranged entries on particular churches, briefly detailing their history and beliefs and listing the addresses of their organizations, officers, and periodicals. Size constraints allow for the inclusion of major religious groups as measured by the number of their adherents. Entries range in length from six pages for the *Roman Catholic Church,* to half a page for the *Reformed Church in America,* to only 20 lines on *primitive Baptists.*

This information on churches is augmented by a church calendar, a statistical and historical section dealing with religious trends in the two countries, a listing of regional church agencies, and lists of seminaries, church-related colleges, and other religious agencies.

The accuracy of the data in the yearbook depends on the reporting religious bodies. Not all churches report each year, and some churches rely on "educated guesses" in some statistical areas. For these reasons, the statistical data in the yearbook are incomplete and cannot be used to accurately compare churches. As the yearbook clearly admits, these statistics "vary greatly in quality and reliability."

Keeping this caveat in mind, the yearbook is still the most helpful, accurate, and current source of information on U.S. and Canadian churches. The clear and detailed table of contents and detailed index make information easy to access. The language is simple, but the small print in double columns is difficult to read. The paper used in the *Yearbook of American and Canadian Churches* is of high quality, and the paperback binding seems sturdy enough to last a year of heavy use.

The Board recommends this work for the core collections of public, academic, and school libraries.

—G. H.

Supplementary Titles

Biblical Quotations. Jennifer Speake, ed. Facts On File, 1983. hard. 1 vol. 208 pp. index. ISBN 0-87196-241-1. $27.95. handbook.
B5391.2.563 220.5'2036

Biblical Quotations "functions as a limited concordance, with approximately 1900 biblical passages ranging in length from single sentences to the Ten Commandments, and with approximately 10,000 index entries. . . . The text used is the King James translation, except for occasional verses from the Vulgate, and, betraying the work's British origin, the 1539 Coverdale translation of the Psalms from the Book of Common Prayer." (*LJ,* December 1, 1983, p. 2242)

"[The reference] is intended as an aid to 'readers seeking a specific passage or a text appropriate to a particular occasion' or in selecting a text for meditation. . . . Arranged by the traditional order of books, then chapter and verse, notable passages of the O.T., Apocrypha, and N.T. are presented, each with a unique accession number which is then used in the keyword Index to order entries under each keyword." (*BL,* April 15, 1984, p. 1168)

Also reviewed in: *ARBA,* 1984, p. 494; *RQ,* February 1984, p. 98.

Board's recommendation: Public libraries.

Biographical Dictionary of American Cult and Sect Leaders. J. Gordon Melton. Garland, 1986. hard. 1 vol. 354 pp. appendixes. index. ISBN 0-8240-9037-3. $45. dictionary.
BL2525.M448 920

"To be included in the *Biographical Dictionary* [*of American Cult and Sect Leaders*], a person must have been an outstanding leader or the founder of an alternative religious group and must have died prior to January 1, 1983. The sketches average around two pages in length. Each includes who's who-type data, along with information on major events in the person's life (emphasizing religious background), key religious experiences, and his or her role in founding or developing a religious group or movement. At the end of each sketch Melton lists works by the biographee . . . and secondary sources for further information about the person. Appendixes group biographees by the religious tradition of the religion they founded, by birthplace, and by their religious backgrounds." (*BL,* December 15, 1986, p. 633)

"The sketches are well written, giving clear and absorbing summaries of each leader's life and career. . . . [This reference] is highly recommended as the standard work on American cult and sect leaders." (*Choice,* October 1986, p. 284)

Also reviewed in: *A Lib,* May 1987, p. 344; *ARBA,* 1987, p. 527; *LJ,* February 15, 1986, p. 174.

Board's recommendation: Public and academic libraries.

Dictionary of American Religious Biography. Henry Warner Bowden. Greenwood, 1977. hard. 1 vol. 572 pp. index. ISBN 0-8371-8906-3. $45. biographical dictionary.
BL72.B68 209.2'2

In the *Dictionary of American Religious Biography,* "Bowden provides the user with 425 biographies (no living persons are included) drawn from more than three centuries of American religious life. . . . [Each] entry provides essential biographical information: birth and death dates, education and career positions, summary of a person's life work . . . , and a brief bibliography.

"There is a wide range of coverage: we find Cardinal Cushing, Madame Blavatzky, and Malcolm X; religious leaders, philosophers, reformers, dreamers, and charlatans. Ordained male white clergymen predominate, but there is also ample coverage of lay persons, women, and members of black, Indian, and Asian minorities." (*LJ,* May 15, 1977, p. 1167)

"Bowden has been remarkably balanced in both his inclusions and his characterizations. Bibliographical references at the end of each entry include a selected maximum of six works by the biographee and six works about the person, the latter providing citations to more exhaustive reference works when appropriate." (*Choice,* September 1977, p. 826)

Also reviewed in: *ARBA,* 1978, p. 511; *CC,* June 1, 1977, p. 547; *CH,* December 1978, p. 461; *CLW,* December 1977, p. 200; *JR,* July 1978, p. 334; *JR,* January 1982, p. 100; *LJ,* April 15, 1978, p. 817; *RQ,* Fall 1977, p. 70; *RSR,* April 1978, p. 16; *TT,* January 1978, p. 447; *WLB,* September 1977, p. 89.

Board's recommendation: Public and academic libraries.

Encyclopedia of the American Religious Experience. Charles H. Lippy and Peter W. Williams, eds. Scribner, 1987. hard. 3 vols. 1,872 pp. index. ISBN 0-684-18062-6 (set). $2,500 (set). encyclopedia.
BL2525.E53 291.0973

The *Encyclopedia of the American Religious Experience* "addresses the traditions, movements, and cultural influences underlying religious belief and practice in North America. [It] contains 105 specially commissioned essay." (publisher's note)

"Subject matter is broad in scope, covering backgrounds, history, and statistics of major denominations and important religious movements. . . . Subjects covered include the influence of religion on literature, art, architecture, and socio-political issues." (*LJ,* April 1, 1988)

"The essays are scholarly, yet not too abstruse; they are self-documented, with brief indications within the text of sources cited or quoted. The essays . . . generally run about 17 pages; each is usually divided into sections captioned with brief headings, and each ends with a summary paragraph and a bibliography of approximately 20 books and journal articles. . . . Similar to several other well-received encyclopedias, . . . [this reference] is not meant for ready reference, but for extended perusal. . . . The work deserves the highest praise for its scholarly approach, its varied yet uniform development of a wide range of topics, and the outstanding level of its editing and physical production." (*BL,* May 15, 1988, p. 1578)

Board's recommendation: Public and academic libraries.

Interpreter's Dictionary of the Bible. George Buttrick and Keith R. Crim, eds. Abingdon, 1976. hard. 5 vols. illus. ISBN 0-687-19269-2. $119. dictionary.
BS440.I63 220.3

The *Interpreter's Dictionary of the Bible,* in five volumes, covers "the different books of the Bible, [and is] edited by world-renowned Jewish, Catholic, and Protestant scholars. [The reference] brings together the best manuscripts, texts, and critical lore behind each text." (*A Lib,* February 1974, p. 72)

Board's recommendation: Public libraries.

New Bible Atlas. J. J. Bimson et. al., eds. Tyndale House, 1985. hard. 1 vol. 128 pp. illus. index. ISBN 0-8423-4675-9. $16.95. atlas.
912

"Geography (in its widest sense) and archaeology are essential background to the understanding of the Bible. This new *Bible Atlas* is probably the most comprehensive handbook to this background currently available. Maps fully illustrate every aspect of biblical history, there are sections on climate and vegetation, and an introduction to the main archaeological aspects, particularly of the Old Testament period. All is supported by text summarising the main historical outlines and closely related to the visual material; and there is an excellent supplement of pictures of Palestine today." (*Sch Lib,* December 1985, p. 378)

"Cartographically, the *New Bible Atlas* is as good as or better than any current rival.

"The maps, more than two-thirds of which are in color, illustrate [such expected features as] . . . topography, geological features, [as well as such aspects of biblical history as] . . . economy [and] trade routes. . . . Not only the Holy Land but also the surrounding region and its empires and peoples are amply covered.

"A product of highly competent scholarship (the editors are all associated with major British universities), the *New Bible Atlas* will serve well both casual and serious students of the Bible." (*ARBA,* 1986, p. 540)

Board's recommendation: Public and academic libraries.

A Popular Dictionary of Buddhism. Christmas Humphries. Merrimack Publishers, 1988; distrib. by State Mutual Bks. soft. 1 vol. 224 pp. ISBN 0-317-89780-2. $39. dictionary.
BQ130.H85 294.3'0'321

A Popular Dictionary of Buddhism "provides a brief description of some twelve hundred entries in an alphabetical arrangement. Most terms appear in either Sanskrit or Pali spellings, although Chinese, Japanese, and Tibetan terms appear as well as Western concepts (*asceticism, consciousness, motive,* for example), geographic entries, and Eastern and Western figures prominent in Buddhism and its study." (*ARBA,* 1986, p. 550)

Board's recommendation: Academic libraries.

New and Noteworthy

Critical Guide to Catholic Reference Books, 3d edition. James Patrick McCabe. Libraries Unlimited, 1989. hard. 1 vol. 323 pp. index. ISBN 0-87287-621-7. $47. bibliography.
Z674.R4 020

"Now in its third edition, [*Critical Guide to Catholic Reference Books*] includes more than 1,500 main entries, 243 of them new to this edition. As with the two prior editions . . . the works cited fall into two classes, (1) those dealing with topics peculiar to the Church, such as liturgy and other theological disciplines; and (2) those dealing with the social sciences, literature, the arts, and similar subjects. . . . The *Guide* is divided into five sections: 'General Works,' 'Theology,' 'The Humanities,' 'Social Sciences,' and 'History.' " (*BL,* April 15, 1990, p. 1660)

The Dictionary of Biblical Literacy. Ceil B. Murphey, comp. Oliver-Nelson, 1989. hard. 1 vol. 600 pp. illus. index. ISBN 0-8407-9105-4. $39.95. dictionary.
BS440.M87 209

"[*The Dictionary of Biblical Literacy*] attempts to epitomize what Christians should know about the Bible. It includes material that is 'basic to an understanding of . . . Christian faith; significant enough to be worth knowing; helpful in its overview of the life, culture, and times covered by the Bible; [and] enjoyable for readers who are interested in the Bible.'

"[This book] . . . is organized into 21 alphabetically arranged sections which are divided into a total of 66 chapters. While the major branches of the western Church are covered fairly adequately, information on the eastern churches is quite minimal. . . . [It] represents the viewpoint of conservative evangelical Protestantism. (*BL,* April 1, 1990, p. 1574)

The Encyclopedia of Judaism. Geoffrey Wigoder, ed. Macmillan, 1989. hard. 1 vol. 768 pp. illus. index. ISBN 0-02-628410-3. $75. encyclopedia.
BM50.E63 269.03

"[*The Encyclopedia of Judaism represents*] . . . the first new one-volume encyclopedia on Judaism in more than 20 years. . . . A brief preface defines the focus of the work as Jewish religious life and development, excluding secular concerns. . . . The entries are alphabetically arranged, with running heads at the top of each page. Articles vary in length . . . *Torah* is approximately two pages followed by briefer articles *Torah Blessings* and *Torah Ornaments.* Most biographical articles are a few paragraphs in length. . . . [This book] is greatly enriched by about 300 illustrations from all ages." (*BL,* March 1, 1990, p. 1384)

The Harper Religious and Inspirational Quotation Companion. Margaret Pepper, ed. Harper, 1989. hard. 496 pp. index. ISBN 0-06-016179-5. $22.50. dictionary.
082

"[*The Harper Religious and Inspirational Quotation Companion*] is a personal collection of more than 4,000 religious and inspirational quotations. . . . Arranged in alphabetical order by subject, from *Abandonment* to *Zeal,* the [book] has a subject index that just repeats these subject headings. . . . The quotations are from a wide variety of authors. . . . At least half of the quotations included . . . cannot be found in standard quotation reference sources. . . . This book serves well for occasions when an unusual quotation is needed or just for browsing." (*BL,* January 15, 1990, p. 1044)

The New Jerome Biblical Commentary. Raymond E. Brown et al. Prentice-Hall, 1989. hard. 1 vol. ISBN 0-13-614934-0. $69.95. bibliography.
BS491.2 220.7

"Written by U.S. Roman Catholic scholars, [*The New Jerome Biblical Commentary*] reflects the increased emphasis on biblical scholarship in the Catholic Church. In addition to the book-by-book commentary, about one-third of the text is devoted to topical articles on biblical subjects.

"The chapters for each book or topic have been compiled by specialists, many of whom present other points of view in addition to Roman Catholic interpretations. Bibliographies are provided for each chapter as well as for major divisions within chapters." (*BL,* December 1, 1989, p. 761)

Religions on File. Diagram Group. Facts On File, 1990. hard. 1 vol. 200 pp. ISBN 0-8160-2224-0. $145. encyclopedia.
BL82.R45 291.022

"[A] compilation of time lines, diagrams, drawings, and maps, [*Religions on File*] is designed to lead to understanding of the world's great religions, past and present, through the visual format. It is appropriate for junior high or high school students beginning their study of world religions, and for teachers of these students looking for visual material on the subject.

"The five major world religions (Hinduism, Buddhism, Judaism, Christianity, and Islam) are covered, as well as ancient religions (Greek, Zoroastrian, Aztec) and other Asian religions (Shinto, Taoism, Sikhism, etc.). Basic facets of each religion are presented.

"[The book] . . . achieves its purpose: a basic presentation of the world's great religions in visual format. It is not an exciting or provocative work and would certainly need to be used in conjunction with the rich primary materials of scripture, art, and culture from these religions in order to convey an accurate basic understanding of the subjects." (*BL,* August 1990, p. 2205)

Religious Writer's Market-Place, 3d edition. William H. Gentz, ed. Running Pr., 1989. hard. 1 vol. 223 pp. index. ISBN 0-89471-695-6. $19.95. directory.
Z479.G46 070.5'0973

"This new edition [of *Religious Writer's Market-Place*] . . . is designed to guide authors of Christian and Jewish religious material to potential publishers. The core sections consist of alphabetical listings of Christian-oriented periodicals, publishers of Christian-oriented books, and similar . . . lists of Jewish-oriented periodicals and book publishers. . . . Together these lists describe more than 400 U.S. and Canadian periodicals and nearly 274 publishing organizations. . . . The aim of the compiler . . . was to create a comprehensive handbook for the religious writer. He has accomplished this." (*BL,* February 1, 1990, p. 1116)

This Day in Religion. Ernie Gross. Neal-Schuman, 1990. hard. 1 vol. 294 pp. index. ISBN 1-55570-045-4. $39.95 bibliography.
209

"Taking data about 'the people that shaped contemporary religion' from encyclopedias, dictionaries, and biographies, the compiler [of *This Day in Religion*] has rearranged them by date, creating an almanac designed for daily reading. . . . The great majority of entries relate to persons, their births, deaths, and major events in between. . . . 'The book is devoted primarily to Christianity, with lesser emphasis on Judaism and Eastern religions . . . and does not have any denominational leanings. . . . [This book] will be useful for discovering events that happened on a particular day.' " (*BL,* April 1, 1990, p. 1582)

Twentieth-Century Shapers of American Popular Religion. Charles H. Lippy, ed. Greenwood, 1989. hard. 519 pp. ISBN 0-313-25356-0. $65. biographical source.
BL2525.T84 291.092

"The title [of *Twentieth-Century Shapers of American Popular Religion*] . . . indicates this text's distinctive temporal and topical scope. The 69 people profiled by 25 contributors were selected for their influence on audiences that 'cut across denominations and faith traditions to include ordinary men and women of every religious affiliation and no affiliation at all.' . . . The result is a collection of insightful essays, each highlighting the most significant, formative experiences in its subject's life and analyzing his or her influence on religious institutions and sentiments." (*BL,* June 15, 1989, p. 1807)

Susan W. Price

Russian Literature

See also Eastern European Literature; World Literature

The literature of czarist Russia and the modern Soviet Union is one of the most complex and fascinating literatures of the world. Russian literature begins with the literary language of Old Russia, which is known as Old Church Slavonic. Old Church Slavonic dates from the ninth century and is based on an old Bulgarian dialect infused with a strong Byzantine influence. Early Russian literature centers around Kiev, the political and cultural center of Russia in medieval times. Russian vernacular became the literary language of Muscovite Russia as the cultural center moved north from Kiev in the sixteenth century. What is referred to as Russian literature was the literary production of unified Russia in prerevolutionary times. After the 1917 Bolshevik revolution, the literature became that of the Russian Soviet Federated Socialist Republic (the largest of the 15 union republics that make up the Soviet Union) and of the Russians in exile. In other words, the history and assortment of Russian literature is clearly complex. A reference librarian needs to have resources available to provide bibliographic control of a literature that is a thousand years old and has evolved through many variations of language and two totally different political systems.

The librarian should know where to turn to answer such questions as: "What written records do we have

Core Titles

	PUBLIC	ACADEMIC	SCHOOL
Handbook of Russian Literature Terras, Victor, ed. Yale Univ. Pr., 1985	✦	✦	✦
The Modern Encyclopedia of Russian and Soviet Literatures, 9 vols. Weber, Harry B., and George J. Gutsche, eds. Academic International, 1977–		✦	
Plots and Characters in Major Russian Fiction Berry, Thomas E. Shoe String, 1977		✦	

of this thousand-year-old civilization?" "Who wrote them?" "Why did a given author write what he or she did?" "What were his or her qualifications for writing it?" "Just what was the author trying to tell us anyway?"

A requisite fundamental source to help address these questions is a good history of Russian literature. A highly readable survey that can scarcely contain the enthusiasm of the author, Dmitry Mirsky, is the HISTORY OF RUSSIAN LITERATURE FROM ITS BEGINNINGS TO 1900 and its supplement, CONTEMPORARY RUSSIAN LITERATURE, 1881–1925. The core list provides another history with more detailed references as well as an essential bibliography of Russian literature translated into English. The core list also contains an excellent encyclopedia of Russian literature, an ongoing project whose completion will be welcomed. The suggested handbook, HANDBOOK OF RUSSIAN LITERATURE, is essential for ready-reference questions.

Events in Eastern Europe in recent years have stimulated interest in contemporary Russian literature. The acquisition of RUSSIAN LITERATURE SINCE THE REVOLUTION will make a librarian's collection adequately up to date. Because Russian drama has long been famous among English-speaking peoples, a librarian would do well to supplement the collection with TWENTIETH CENTURY RUSSIAN DRAMA: FROM GORKY TO THE PRESENT and HISTORY OF RUSSIAN THEATRE. Several out-of-print works that librarians may wish to seek out are *Russian Literature: An Introduction* (Robert Lord, Taplinger, 1980), *An Introduction to Russian Language and Literature* (Robert Auty and Dimitri Obolensky, eds., Cambridge, 1977), and *The Slavic Literatures* (Richard C. Lewanski, comp., Ungar, 1971).

Core Titles

Handbook of Russian Literature. Victor Terras, ed. Yale Univ. Pr., 1985. hard. 1 vol. 558 pp. appendix. index. ISBN 0-300-03155-6. $55. dictionary.
PG2940.H29 891.3'03'21

The *Handbook of Russian Literature* contains a wealth of information about people, events, places, titles, and allusions that have influenced and generated Russian literature from the earliest writings in Russian to the literature published in 1983. The signed articles are supplemented by bibliographies containing Russian-language publications as well as more substantial specialized publications in English that lead to further research.

The information presented in this handbook is duplicated in other sources. However, the ability to find essential information on such a huge scope of literature under one cover and in English is an answer to a long-felt need among Russian enthusiasts in the English-speaking world. The project that compiled this reference was granted funding by the National Endowment for the Humanities in response to that expressed need. The *Handbook* is the only such reference tool in the English language.

Upon the suggestion of Yale University Press, the production of this work was organized by a committee of four scholars: Robert L. Jackson (Yale), Robert A. Maguire (Columbia), Frank R. Silbajoris (Ohio State), and the editor, Victor Terras (Brown). They gathered a larger group of 106 scholars, each of whom contributed major articles as well as a group of supplemental articles in the general area of his or her specialization.

The handbook is primarily aimed at students of Russian literature; however, those engaged in other branches of Russian studies and in various types of comparative studies are also finding the book useful.

The entries are presented in dictionary form. Entries vary in length from an article of several pages, such as the one on *old Russian literature,* to very brief "who's who"–type entries. Author entries give biographical notes; circumstances surrounding the writing of the works; and bibliographies of standard editions in Russian, translations into English, and selected secondary sources. Highly readable essays in the volume provide enlightening and instructive overviews of broad topics relating to Russian literature, such as the influence of the Russian Orthodox Church.

Numerous cross-references in the text of the *Handbook of Russian Literature* direct the reader to the term under which the desired information is presented. At the back of the volume is an extensive index referring to each page where a subject or person is mentioned. Also useful is a general bibliography at the end of the reference.

The Board recommends this work for the core collections of public, academic, and school libraries.

The Modern Encyclopedia of Russian and Soviet Literatures. Harry B. Weber (vols. 1–8) and George J. Gutsche (vol. 9–), eds. Academic International, 1977– . hard. 9 vols. 2,304 pp. $37 per vol. encyclopedia.
PG2940 M6 891.7

The Modern Encyclopedia of Russian and Soviet Literatures (MERSL) is a multivolume encyclopedia (9 volumes, *A* through *Ho,* of a projected 50-volume set) of Russian and Soviet literary figures, literatures of national groups within the Soviet Union and of émigrés, and aspects of cultural life which affect the literature. Many of the articles are adapted from the *Kratkaia Literaturnaia Entsiklopedia* (1962–1975) and from other standard reference sources on these subjects in the Russian language. Some entries are derived from Imperial Russian sources, while others are from sources dealing with Russian writers who have emigrated. The encyclopedia has up-to-date information and includes a broad range of sources when they are available. The set is being published at the rate of about one volume per year, so it is easily affordable by interested libraries.

MERSL is the most comprehensive and authoritative reference tool in the English language on the literature of Russia and the Soviet Union. The work gives unprecedented access to the basic Russian sources for the non-Russian reader.

The contributors are international scholars writing in their areas of specialization. The scope of this work includes entries pertaining to uniquely nationalistic Slavic literary characteristics, to émigré literature, and to non-Russian literature, as well as entries on Russian and Soviet literary production.

Each volume of the set contains about 250 pages and is made up of signed articles of varying length arranged in alphabetical order. Appended to each article are bibliographies of works (when appropriate) and references used in preparing the article. Each volume has a list of contributors at the front and a table of contents at the back.

A full index volume to the completed set would be a very useful tool. It would also be helpful if a preliminary index to existing volumes could be published with each new volume. Only a good index (or machine readable text with keyword searching) will make the treasures in this set completely accessible.

The appearance of each volume of *The Modern Encyclopedia of Russian and Soviet Literatures* is greeted with cheers in the reviews and expressed impatience for the next. Volumes 10 and 11 were scheduled for publication as this review was being prepared. This enthusiastic response is well deserved. The Board recommends this set for the core collection of academic libraries.

Plots and Characters in Major Russian Fiction. Thomas E. Berry. Shoe String, 1977. hard. 1 vol. 226 pp. index. ISBN 0-208-01584-6. $25. handbook.
PG3095.B4 891.7'3'03

Plots and Characters in Major Russian Fiction is a reader's companion that provides plot summaries to the works of nineteenth-century Russian literature most often read in translation by undergraduates. The volume also provides identification of characters, both historical and fictional, who appear in the selected titles.

The compiler and editor, Professor Berry, is on the faculty of the Slavic Department at the University of Maryland. This book evolved out of a number of semesters of his teaching nineteenth-century Russian fiction in translation. This reference work is especially useful for clarifying character names that are particularly troublesome to non-Russian readers (a given character can traditionally be referred to by several different names). Also, plot summaries can give a student an overview before he or she delves into the text; can help the student stay on track while reading rather than being hopelessly distracted by the voluminous details; and can help a student review the literature in preparation for an exam.

The volume includes plot summaries covering the best-known works of Pushkin, Lermontov, Turgenev, and Tolstoy. A companion volume now out of print contained material from the works of Gogol, Goncharov, and Dostoevsky. These writers represent the period from 1820 to 1900, the so-called golden and silver ages of Russian literature. Each volume is composed of two parts: plot summaries and an index of characters. The summaries vary in length from one page for a short story to six pages for *War and Peace.* Each plot summary is followed by an alphabetical list of characters in the piece of fiction.

Part 2 of each volume is an index of all the characters encountered in the works summarized; cross-references are provided for an entry if necessary, and then a line or two of identification is given. Part 2 also contains names of historical figures and characters of literary allusion, specifically citing where these references occur.

Characters in the index are listed alphabetically by the character's surname, with copious cross-references to the full name from variants that appear in the text. Another helpful feature is a chronological table of events pertaining to the lives of the authors. This chronology enables the student to gain a quick perspective on the historical events surrounding the writing of a novel or short story.

The Library of Congress transliteration table has been used to produce the spelling used in this work. *Tolstoi* and *Dostoevskii* are two examples of this spelling.

Plots and Characters in Major Russian Fiction is a highly useful reference tool, particularly for students. The Board recommends this work for the core collection of academic libraries.

Supplementary Titles

Contemporary Russian Literature, 1881–1925. Dmitry Mirsky. Krause, repr. 1972. hard. 1 vol. 372 pp. ISBN 0-527-64000-X. $29. encyclopedia.
PG2951.M52 891.7'09

"[*Contemporary Russian Literature, 1881–1925*], which takes up the history of Russian literature since Dostoyevski's death, is intended as a complement to another volume which Prince Mirsky has in preparation, covering the preceding period. The author, as he tells us in his preface, aimed to produce nothing more ambitious than a 'Baedecker or a Murray's Guide to Recent Russian Literature.' He gives attention generously to the important, the less important and the unimportant. He takes in every one, from those whom he calls 'feuilletonists' to futurists, and finds room for critics, sociologists and philosophers as well. He gives as much space to the biographies of his authors as he does to their works, with the result that one has here a comprehensive who's who in Russian letters." (*NY Herald Tribune,* July 11, 1926, p. 11)

"For the most part, Prince Mirsky writes of figures of whom his readers know nothing. Yet even with this enormous handicap he makes the development of Russian literature from 1881 to the present day comprehensible, and, indeed, intensely interesting. This is partly due to the consummate structure of the book." (*Nation and Ath,* August 7, 1926, p. 533)

"His definitions are precise, concise and clear, his narrative witty, entertaining and well constructed. Moreover, in the history of Russian literature he is certainly at home. His knowledge, authority and erudition cannot be challenged." (*NYT,* February 21, 1926, p. 2)

Also reviewed in: *Lit R,* April 24, 1926, p. 5; *SR,* September 4, 1926, p. 105; *Spec,* July 17, 1926, p. 105.

Board's recommendation: Academic libraries.

History of Nineteenth-Century Russian Literature. Dmitrij Tschizewskij. Vanderbilt Univ. Pr., 1974. soft. 2 vols. 454 pp. index. ISBN 0-8265-1187-2 (vol. 1); 0-8265-1190-2 (vol. 2). $9.95 per vol. history.
PG3012.C513 891.7'09'003

"Each volume of this [*History of Nineteenth-Century Russian Literature*] contains a foreword by Serge A. Zenkovsky, who is also the editor. The volume on Romanticism was first published in 1964 in German and was translated from that language by Richard Porter, who, like Zenkovsky, is a professor at Vanderbilt. The two volumes are actually v.2 and 3 of a three-part series starting with *History of Russian literature from the eleventh century to the end of the Baroque,* which appeared in 1960. A bibliography on Russian Romanticism (shorter than that in the German edition) is included, but not one on Realism, because there is actually yet to come another (fourth) volume which will treat late Realism, Symbolism, and Futurism, and to which a bibliography will be affixed." [Many libraries, undergraduate and graduate, will benefit from owning this set.] (*Choice,* December 1974, p. 1483)

"Since there is no really adequate study of 19th-Century Russian literature in English—a work that would do more than inform, survey, and criticize generally—Čiževskij's [transliterated to Tschizewskij] books will, for the time being, become the basic texts in the English-speaking world. Such studies are perhaps most helpful to people outside of the field who may be familiar with the literature of Russia's greats but may not have heard of A. K. Tolstoj, Fedor Tjutčev, Nikolaj Nekrasov, and a host of others." (*LJ,* November 15, 1974, p. 2965)

Board's recommendation: Academic libraries.

History of Russian Literature from Its Beginnings to 1900. Dmitry Mirsky. Random House repr. soft. 1 vol. index. ISBN 0-394-70720-6. $5.95. history.
PG2951.M49 891.7'09

This new edition of the *History of Russian Literature* "summarizes the development of Russian literature from the earliest times through 1925. . . . Biographical information is included on the major, and many of the minor figures, and there is much useful critical interpretation. In the abridgement, the editor has cut the biographical material throughout, omitting some sections on contemporary writers which were necessarily incomplete, and has added a brief review of the general development of Soviet literature. A bibliography of general studies in English and of anthologies in English translation is included." (*LJ,* August 1949, p. 1090)

"The present volume presents the two original works in a slightly abridged form. But the editor has approached his task with scrupulous care, leaving the original text in the main unaltered, and merely adding some useful footnotes in the later period to complete the picture. His postscript is necessarily very brief, and the reader who desired a broader view of developments in contemporary Soviet writing will still have to turn to such books as Mr. George Reavey's *Soviet Literature Today.* But for the whole period up to 1925, Prince Mirsky's work still has no rival, and might serve as a model for any aspiring literary historian." (*TLS,* February 17, 1950, p. 106)

Also reviewed in: *BL,* October 15, 1949, p. 66; *Nat,* March 4, 1950, p. 207; *NY,* January 28, 1950, p. 88; *SR,* April 8, 1950, p. 33; *YR,* Spring 1950, p. 548.

Board's recommendation: Public and academic libraries.

History of the Russian Theatre: Seventeenth Through Nineteenth Century. Boris V. Varneke. Hafner repr. soft. 1 vol. 459 pp. index. ISBN 0-02-854150-2. $23.95. history.

PN2721.V431h 792.0947

"Varneke's book is written in a surprisingly sprightly style for a scholarly textbook. . . . This edition [of *History of the Russian Theatre*], unlike the Russian original, includes an index of persons and an index of the plays mentioned; regrettably, pictures of actors and actresses and the bibliography have been omitted." (*SR,* August 11, 1951, p. 10)

"The standard work on the Russian Theatre published in 1908, . . . [has now been] made available in English. [It] is a basic work and as such is an essential volume for any theatre or Slavonic collection." (*LJ,* November 15, 1950, p. 2014)

Also reviewed in: *TLS,* October 5, 1951, p. 631.

Board's recommendation: Academic libraries.

Poets of Modern Russia. Peter France. Cambridge, 1982. hard and soft. 1 vol. 256 pp. index. ISBN 0-521-23490-5 (hard); 0-521-28000-1 (soft). $42.50 (hard); $18.95 (soft). history; criticism.

PG3056.F7 891.71409

"[The author's] method [in *Poets of Modern Russia*] is quite special for a survey: instead of going through the usual recitation of facts and summaries, he goes through each poet via a close textual analysis of a handful of poems. . . . [Since] France's prose is straightforward and his grasp of the material sure, the book is, in the end, both satisfying and deep. . . . France'[s] . . . presentation of the work of Aygi [is] a strikingly original cross between a modern surrealist and a quiet nineteenth-century lyricist like Fet. . . . The one shortcoming is a common one among surveys: why are we given this group of poets? What are the connections other than that they are all twentieth-century writers? . . . [France] has, nonetheless, given us a solid and deep presentation of his subjects." (*WLT,* Winter 1984, p. 125)

Also reviewed in: *Lon R Books,* September 15, 1983, p. 10; *MLR,* July 1984, p. 764; *TLS,* July 1, 1983, p. 703; *VQR,* Autumn 1983, p. 135.

Board's recommendation: Academic libraries.

Russian Literature Since the Revolution. Edward James Brown. Harvard, 1982. hard and soft. 1 vol. 413 pp. index. ISBN 0-674-78203-8 (hard); 0-674-78204-6 (soft). $35 (hard); $12.95 (soft). history; criticism.

PG3022.B7 891.709004

"The first two editions of [*Russian Literature Since the Revolution*] appeared in 1963 and 1969. 'The present edition is approximately one-third larger, partly because of the longer time period covered (to 1980) and partly because of the inclusion of exiled writers, especially those of the third wave.

"The new sections display the same encyclopedic knowledge, unerring literary judgment, and sense of proportion that characterized the previously written sections, which are now updated in matters of detail. . . . Although other volumes, such as Deming Brown's *Soviet Russian Literature Since Stalin* [*BRD,* 1978], cover various topics and periods in greater detail, the new edition of Edward Brown's gracefully written critical history is unsurpassed." (*Choice,* April 1983, p. 1145)

"Representing scholarship at its best, Brown is not only knowledgeable and lucid, but above all fair-minded in his judgments. . . . In spite of the centrality of his excellent treatment of Mayakovsky, Brown tends to favor prose over poetry; among literary critics, Shklovsky over Tynyanov and Voronsky over Bakhtin—who is, however, dealt with at some length. Rightly and resolutely, Brown insists on the political importance of Russian literature as literature, and it is the story of that importance that he has chosen to tell. What . . . is most impressive about the present volume is its inclusion of writers still in midcareer. . . . No doubt, future revisions will be needed, but Brown's story would not have been complete without them." (*WLT,* Autumn 1983, p. 657)

Also reviewed in: *Col Lit,* Winter 1983, p. 95; *Lon R Bks,* September 15, 1983, p. 10.

Board's recommendation: Academic libraries.

Russian Romantic Fiction. John Mersereau. Ardis, 1983. hard and soft. 1 vol. 336 pp. illus. index. ISBN 0-88233-739-4 (hard); 0-88233-740-8 (soft). $29.80 (hard); $10 (soft). history; criticism.

PG3098.3.M47 891.73309

"[In *Russian Romantic Fiction*] Mersereau does much to rescue from undeserved oblivion some writers of interest (Somov, Perovsky-Pogorelsky, Veltman, Odoevsky), but in the process—and perhaps for the sake of the 'complete picture'—he devotes too much space to writers and works that he himself dismisses as undistinguished. . . . Mersereau's consistent wit and eminently readable style serve in part to mitigate some problematic aspects of the book: plot summaries that are not always useful, very sparse footnoting, and no bibliography (a few scholarly works are mentioned in passing in the text). The book will be of greatest use as a reference text rather than as a study to be read 'cover to cover.' [This work is] appropriate for students of upper-division undergraduate and graduate levels." (*Choice,* January 1984, p. 711)

Russian Romantic Fiction "as a whole deserves warm praise. It is the only comprehensive study in English of this neglected period of Russian prose fiction and makes a most welcome contribution to the fuller understanding of European Romanticism." (*TLS,* June 8, 1984, p. 635)

Board's recommendation: Academic libraries.

Twentieth-Century Russian Drama: From Gorky to the Present. Harold B. Segel. Columbia, 1979. hard and soft. 1 vol. 502 pp. illus. index. ISBN 0-231-04576-X (hard); 0-231-04577-8 (soft). $132.50. bibliography.
PG3086.S44 891.72509

This survey "of Russian drama after Chekhov includes synopses of dramas by Gorky, Blok, Bulgakov, Sologub, and Mayakovsky as well as those by lesser-known playwrights.

"Moving easily through a maze of major and minor works [in *Twentieth-Century Russian Drama*], Segal cogently discusses various trends in the development of Soviet drama and evaluates the individual plays in terms of both their contemporary and historical significance. . . . This book is essential for any drama or Russian literature collection." (*LJ,* December 1, 1979, p. 2573)

"Segal gives us the first compendium of the Russian drama, and his book is useful both for reference and for reading. The illustrations are all from American collections, and some are of U.S. productions (more conservatively realistic in the twenties in their staging than the Russian ones); thus they supplement Herbert Marshall's *Pictorial History of the Russian Theatre* [BRD 1978]. . . . The plot summaries are readable and the artistic judgments sound. Segal's aim is to classify and describe. His quotes of dialogue or stage directions provide immediacy, and occasionally analogies are made to Western drama. . . . Segal rightly concentrates his attention on plays which have been translated into English. . . . The discussion is brought up to the present with the new plays of older dramatists, who began writing during the Thaw." (*WLT,* Summer 1980, p 452).

Also reviewed in: *Ant R,* Summer 1980, p. 390; *Comp Dr,* Spring 1981, p. 90; *Dr,* July 1980, p. 16; *SAQ,* Winter 1981, p. 110; *Theat J,* December 1980, p. 538.

Board's recommendation: Academic libraries.

Erna Beiser Chamberlain

Science and Technology

See also Computers and Artificial Intelligence; Engineering; specific sciences

A core collection of reference works in science and technology should cover a broad range of topics. Specific items chosen for such a collection will depend on the audience level that is to be accommodated. All libraries, however, should contain material that deals with biographical and technical information. Equally important are the tools that provide access to articles and monographs in a very specific field of study.

Indexes provide the user with access to periodical materials as well as selected and monographic series. The *General Science Index* (James Kochones, ed., Wilson, 1988) and the *Applied Science and Technology Index* (Joyce M. Howard, ed., Wilson, 1988) provide coverage of a broad range of topics and for a broad range of user populations. The *General Science Index* provides access to articles in over 100 science journals, ranging from *Science* to *Scientific American* to the *New England Journal of Medicine.* This index is ideal for high school libraries as well as academic and public libraries. *Applied Science and Technology Index* covers a broader range of topics and emphasizes a more in-depth coverage of topics than the *General Science Index.*

In addition, consider another type of index, such as the *Science Fair Project Index* (Scarecrow, 1973–1980). These indexes will provide the patron with access to the most timely information available on scientific and technical topics of current interest. Another useful work is a bibliography selected by the Board as a supplementary title but now out of print: C. D. Hurt's *Information Sources in Science and Technology* (Libraries Unlimited, 1988).

The field of science and technology depends on a variety of data, including numerical and graphical information. Handbooks, tables, and general and subject-specific dictionaries are necessary to provide these basic data elements. Encyclopedias help users start their information search by providing entries, of varying length and difficulty, containing background information and a baseline from which they can explore further. A bibliography of suggested readings will often be a part of the entry.

The items reviewed in this section will provide the answers to many ready-reference questions. They cover a broad range of topics on science and technology. Some patrons will need to pursue a subject or research question in greater detail than can be managed with these more general sources. Reference to the categories for specific fields will produce a list of titles that will be useful in such cases. *—E. B. C.*

With contributions by Doreen J. McCullough.

Core Titles

	PUBLIC	ACADEMIC	SCHOOL
The American Heritage Dictionary of Science Barnhart, Robert K. Houghton Mifflin, 1986	✦		
American Men and Women of Science 1989–90, 17th edition, 8 vols. Bowker, 1989	✦	✦	
Dictionary of Scientific Biography, 16 vols. plus suppl. Gillispie, Charles Coulston, ed. in chief. Scribner, 1970–1980	✦	✦	
Dictionary of the Physical Sciences: Terms, Formulas, Data Emiliani, Cesare. Oxford, 1987		✦	
Encyclopedia of Physical Science and Technology, 15 vols. Meyers, Robert A., ed. Academic, 1987		✦	
Encyclopedia of Telecommunications Meyers, Robert A., ed. Academic, 1989		✦	
The Facts On File Dictionary of Science, 6th edition Uvarov, E. B., and Alan Isaacs. Facts On File, 1986	✦		✦
Handbooks and Tables in Science and Technology, 2d edition Powell, Russell H., ed. Oryx, 1983		✦	
Lange's Handbook of Chemistry, 13th edition Dean, John A., ed. McGraw-Hill, 1985 (See Chemistry)	✦	✦	✦
McGraw-Hill Dictionary of Scientific and Technical Terms, 4th edition Parker, Sybil P., ed. in chief. McGraw-Hill, 1989	✦	✦	✦
McGraw-Hill Encyclopedia of Science and Technology, 6th edition, 20 vols. McGraw-Hill, 1987	✦	✦	✦
McGraw-Hill Yearbook of Science and Technology McGraw-Hill, annual	✦	✦	✦
Milestones in Science and Technology: The Ready Reference Guide to Discoveries, Inventions, and Facts Mount, Ellis, and Barbara A. List. Oryx, 1987			✦
The Museum of Science and Industry Basic List of Children's Science Books 1988 Richter, Bernice, and Duane Wenzel. ALA, 1988			✦
The New Illustrated Science and Invention Encyclopedia: How it Works, 26 vols. Stuttman, 1989	✦		✦
Van Nostrand's Scientific Encyclopedia, 7th edition, 2 vols. Considine, Douglas M., ed. Van Nostrand Reinhold, 1989	✦	✦	✦

Core Titles

The American Heritage Dictionary of Science (formerly *Hammond Barnhart Dictionary of Science*). Robert K. Barnhart. Houghton Mifflin, 1986. hard. 1 vol. 740 pp. illus. ISBN 0-395-48367-0. $21.95. dictionary.
Q123.B35 503.21

The American Heritage Dictionary of Science, by Robert K. Barnhart, is a 1988 reprint by Houghton

Mifflin of the *Hammond Barnhart Dictionary of Science,* originally published in 1986. The dictionary covers the basic terminology of the sciences, both physical and biological, and is intended for the layperson or beginning student.

The alphabetically arranged entry words appear in boldface type. If the entry is a difficult or unusual word, it is followed by a pronunciation in parentheses. A sample key of the vowel sounds is listed at the bottom right of each two-page spread. After the pronunciation, variant spellings, derivative words, prefixes, suffixes, and combining forms are listed.

The definitions contain many features that help the reader understand the entries. For example, if an entry has several definitions, the definitions are separated by subject labels. Homographs (different words with the same spelling) are entered separately. Within the definition, cross-reference terms and terms related to the entry are listed in boldface type.

At the end of the definition, the reader will find associated and related terms, usage notes that indicate how the entry is applied, and citations from a wide variety of scientific articles and textbooks that provide the reader with additional information sources. Many definitions are accompanied by small, clearly drawn illustrations. The legends link the illustrations to the definitions and provide greater depth to the definitions. Some definitions include tables and measurement scales to ensure clarity.

Standard abbreviations and etymologies are given throughout the dictionary. The metric system is used for all measurements. The prefatory pages include a listing of the physical constants and the signs and symbols used throughout the dictionary.

The dictionary is well formatted and easy to use. Future editions would benefit from having finger tabs for faster access to entries.

The American Heritage Dictionary of Science contains a larger number of general science terms with more comprehensive definitions than THE FACTS ON FILE DICTIONARY OF SCIENCE. In addition, its extensive usage notes, citations, and associated terms make this dictionary more suitable for a general audience than the MCGRAW-HILL DICTIONARY OF SCIENTIFIC AND TECHNICAL TERMS. The Board recommends this work for the core collection of public libraries.

—*E. B. C.*

American Men and Women of Science 1989–90, 17th edition. Bowker, 1989. hard. 8 vols. 7,700 pp. index. ISBN 0-8352-2568-2 (set). $617 (set). biographical dictionary. on-line. CD-ROM.
Q141.A47 509.2′2

American Men and Women of Science 1989–90, published by Bowker, is the 17th edition of what is now an eight-volume set containing biographical summaries of 3,831 currently active American scientists. (Scientists who are not citizens are included if they have been working in the United States for a reasonable period of time.)

Entrants have been selected from lists of names provided by academic, government, and private research programs. An advisory committee of peers aids in the final selection, using the criteria of distinguished achievement based on experience, accomplishments, and continuing activity in a scientific field.

The scientific fields represented include agricultural and forest sciences; biological sciences; chemistry; computer sciences; engineering; environmental, earth, and marine sciences; mathematics; medical and health sciences; physics; and astronomy, as well as some related disciplines, such as research administration, resource management, and science education.

The first seven volumes of the set contain biographical information supplied by each entrant and lists of abbreviations used within the body of the text. The entries are arranged alphabetically and contain data on birth date, birthplace, marital status, number of children, education and degrees, current position, honors and awards, professional memberships, area of research, and current mailing address. If an entrant has appeared in a previous edition but is not included in this edition, his or her name is listed in correct alphabetical sequence with a cross-reference to the appropriate edition and volume. If an entrant from a previous edition is no longer living, an appropriate statement is included in the entry.

The eighth volume of the set contains the index, which is organized by disciplines based on the National Science Foundation's taxonomy of degree and employment specialties.

American Men and Women of Science 1989–90 is a useful reference tool. The work is updated regularly, so the information is reasonably current. The encyclopedia is also available in an on-line version. The Board recommends this work for the core collections of public and academic libraries.

—*E. B. C.*

Dictionary of Scientific Biography. Charles Coulston Gillispie, ed. in chief. Scribner, 1970–1980. hard. 16 vols. plus suppl. appendix. indexes. ISBN 0-684-16962-2 (set); 0-684-18294-7 (suppl.). $1,080 (set); $160 (suppl.). biographical dictionary.
Q141.D5 920.03

The *Dictionary of Scientific Biography,* edited by

Charles C. Gillispie, consists of 16 volumes published between 1970 and 1980 by Charles Scribner's Sons under the auspices of the American Council of Learned Societies. This work provides a historical perspective of the development of science from classical antiquity to modern times.

The dictionary comprises signed, biographical essays on deceased scientists who made significant contributions in the fields of astronomy, mathematics, physics, biology, chemistry, and the earth sciences. Scientists who worked in the fields of philosophy, behavioral sciences, medicine, and technology are included only if their work was related to the physical, biological, and earth sciences.

The essays focus on the careers and accomplishments of the scientists. Each essay concludes with a bibliography containing citations on the original work as well as the personal life of the scientist. If the scientist published a great deal of material, citations to the most important papers or to other pertinent bibliographies are also included.

The sixteenth volume of the dictionary is the index volume, and it contains a large amount of useful information. The index contains a list of contributors along with their professional affiliations and the names of the entries they worked on, a list of all the societies mentioned in the essays, a list of periodicals mentioned in the essays, and lists of scientists arranged by field.

The *Dictionary of Scientific Biography* is a series of scholarly vignettes about the major scientific contributors throughout history. The Board recommends this work for the core collections of public and academic libraries. —*E. B. C.*

Dictionary of the Physical Sciences: Terms, Formulas, Data. Cesare Emiliani. Oxford, 1987. hard and soft. 1 vol. 384 pp. illus. appendix. indexes. ISBN 0-19-503651-4 (hard); 0-19-503652-2 (soft). $35 (hard); $19.95 (soft). dictionary.
Q123.E46 503.21

The *Dictionary of the Physical Sciences,* published in 1987 by Oxford University Press, is intended for use by students and professionals in the physical sciences. Author Cesare Emiliani is an eminent geoscientist, educator, and researcher. Unlike the other dictionaries in this section, the terms in this dictionary are limited to physics, chemistry, geological sciences, and cosmology; life sciences are not included. The terms are arranged alphabetically. The definitions are brief and supported by many graphs, diagrams, tables, and formulas for further clarification.

Where possible, the information sources are cited at the bottom of the tables and illustrations. If no source is identified, the material was provided by the author. A complete list of sources appears at the end of the volume.

Appropriate cross-referencing of terms is provided. Abbreviations and acronyms are used throughout the dictionary. Such terms appear alphabetically under their unabbreviated forms.

Terms that can be defined by a tabular format are located in a separate section. This arrangement aids in the rapid retrieval of data. Approximately one-third of this volume is devoted to tabular information. The tables include a listing of cosmic-ray-induced radionuclides, the relative abundance of nonvolatile rock-forming elements, the chemical composition of seawater, and the energy production of the stars.

The dictionary contains a brief table of contents and two separate alphabetical indexes for the illustrations and the tables. These features are useful and facilitate rapid retrieval of information.

The *Dictionary of the Physical Sciences* is briefer than the other dictionaries in this category, but this does not detract from its usefulness. This reference tool is an important addition to home and office libraries of students and professionals. The Board recommends this work for the core collection of academic libraries. —*E. B. C.*

Encyclopedia of Physical Science and Technology. Robert A. Meyers, ed. Academic, 1987. hard. 15 vols. 11,607 pp. illus. indexes. ISBN 0-317-58440-5 (set). $2,500 (set). $185 (vol. 15). encyclopedia.
Q123.E497 503.21

The *Encyclopedia of Physical Science and Technology,* edited by Robert A. Meyers and published in 1987 by Academic Press, provides in-depth coverage of the physical sciences, engineering, and mathematics for the scientific and engineering community. A 57-member advisory board, representing the major scientific disciplines that make up the physical sciences and technology, established 18 major topic areas and 200 subtopics. Then the board selected the articles to be included in the encyclopedia.

The encyclopedia consists of 15 volumes containing 550 articles and covering topics such as *defense technology, earthquake prediction, wave phenomena,* and *weather modification.* Each article is written by a specialist in the particular field. The articles average 20 pages in length. Each one contains a table of contents followed by a glossary of terms specific to the discipline covered, an introductory definition of the subject, detailed text, and a bibliography. This format is not found in any other encyclopedia. Detailed diagrams and mathematical analyses are used where appropriate. All the articles have undergone an extensive multilevel peer review process to ensure quality and accuracy.

Each of the 15 volumes contains a table of contents and a "Guide to Using the Encyclopedia." The fifteenth volume contains an alphabetical listing of all contributors with their professional affiliations and the titles of their entries, a relational index, and a subject index. The relational index groups related articles under specific subject headings. This enables the reader either to obtain a broad view of a subject or to focus on one specific aspect. The subject index contains alphabetically arranged cross-references to specific materials and processes. Volume numbers are in boldface type, followed by the page numbers. The indexes are easy to use and supplement the alphabetical arrangement of topics covered in the entire encyclopedia.

The *Encyclopedia of Physical Science and Technology* is devoted exclusively to the physical sciences. This book assumes that readers have a basic knowledge of elementary chemistry, physics, and calculus. The work serves a specialized audience: practicing scientists and engineers. Information media, legal, and management personnel in industry, government, and research institutes will also find the encyclopedia useful. A 1990 supplementary yearbook is also available. The Board recommends this work for the core collection of academic libraries. —*E. B. C.*

Encyclopedia of Telecommunications. Robert A. Meyers, ed. Academic, 1989. hard. 1 vol. 575 pp. illus. index. ISBN 0-12-226691-9. $59. dictionary. TK5102.E645 621.38

The *Encyclopedia of Telecommunications* is edited by Dr. Robert A. Meyers, a noted authority in the field of telecommunications. Information on the book jacket notes his affiliation with TRW, his educational background, and the fact that he has published "seven books and more than thirty articles reporting original research." Members of the Executive and Editorial Advisory Board are listed in the front of the book, along with the respective company or academic institution with which they are affiliated. A list of contributors and their affiliations also appears in this section.

This encyclopedia is broken down into 28 subject areas, which are alphabetically listed on the contents page. Each subject area covers the main disciplines within the field of telecommunications and is written by noted experts. These experts are associated with such leading firms as AT&T Bell Laboratories, Bell Communications Research, COMSAT Laboratories, Motorola, and RCA Laboratories, as well as a number of universities and government laboratories.

Each article begins with an outline and an introductory definition of the subject. This opening, coupled with a glossary within each article, is a special feature that will help readers access the material. The only shortcoming is the fact that the glossaries do not appear to be as extensive as they possibly could be, thus limiting their benefit to a minor degree.

The articles average 20 pages in length and are arranged alphabetically by title. Some articles address complete communications systems; examples are the articles titled "Communication Systems, Civilian"; "Computer Networks"; and "Microwave Communications." Others address the three major components of telecommunications: the transmitter, the communications channel, and the receiver. Transmission and reception are covered in such articles as "Antennas"; "Antennas, Reflector"; and "Digital Speech Processing." The communications channel is discussed in articles titled "Data Transmission Media"; "Optical Circuitry"; and "Optical Fiber Communications."

Within each article the reader will find a discussion that includes basic theory, derivations of mathematical relationships, hardware, history, and a forecast of future directions in telecommunications. Supplementing the text are numerous illustrations, which include photographs of devices presented as well as relational diagrams and sketches of electrical circuitry. In all, the work contains more than 400 illustrations, 50 tables, 200 bibliographic entries, and 300 glossary entries. To take just one example, the 23-page article on "Acoustic Signal Processing" contains a glossary of 14 words, 18 figures, 78 mathematical equations, and a bibliography of 13 sources. The reading level of this reference source is appropiate to both the informed specialist and the interested layperson.

Numerous cross-references facilitate access to additional information on a specific topic. The subject entry format used in the table of contents and the detailed index in the back of the book also contribute to easy accessibility of information. At 575 pages, the book itself is of manageable size, and is appropriate for the depth of information that is covered inside. Important subject headings are in boldface type, with the regular text a legible size. The text is on sturdy alkaline paper, with an excellent binding that should easily stand up to the heavy use that this source should receive.

The timeliness of this resource (1989) is exceptional considering the numerous changes that occur within this developing field. Indeed, this timeliness makes this book a must for the core collection. The *Encyclopedia of Telecommunications* keeps the reader on the cutting edge of the latest current developments in this field. Telecommunications books currently in print either are outdated or lack the depth and readability of this particular source. There also are no apparent inconsistencies or errors that detract from this encyclopedia's value.

The *Encyclopedia of Telecommunications* is the authoritative reference source in telecommunications. Any special library whose business deals with telecommunications should certainly not be without this reference source on its shelves. The Board recommends this work for the core collection of academic libraries.

—D. J. M.

The Facts On File Dictionary of Science, 6th edition (formerly *Penguin Dictionary of Science*). E. B. Uvarov and Alan Isaacs. Facts On File, 1986. hard. 1 vol. 468 pp. illus. appendix. ISBN 0-8160-1386-1. $24.95. dictionary.

Q123.U8 503.21

The Facts On File Dictionary of Science by E. B. Uvarov and Alan Isaacs was known as the *Penguin Dictionary of Science* in its five previous editions. E. B. Uvarov originated the dictionary in 1943, and both editors have been involved in subsequent revisions and editions.

The newly titled sixth edition, published in 1986, covers much of the exploration, change, and discovery that the sciences have undergone since the fifth edition was published in 1979. This is a general reference work, so its currency is not significantly affected by the 1986 copyright date. In this edition, as in previous editions, the editors included scientific terms and omitted technological terms.

There are over 7,500 entries, including new terms and updated and expanded versions of earlier definitions. The alphabetically arranged entries cover a broad range of scientific disciplines, including biological and medical sciences, chemistry, mathematics, and physics. Definitions are usually three or four lines long. More complex concepts, such as *fire extinguishers, radioactivity, nuclear reactor,* and *earth* receive more detailed explanations. Italicized terms within an entry are cross-references to related entries in the dictionary. Asterisks are used to denote trade names. The main body of text is preceded by a list of abbreviations and followed by an appendix of 11 tables. These tables include conversion factors, fundamental constants, elementary particles, electron configurations, differential coefficients, integrals, and so forth.

Limited use is made of diagrams; there are only 47. A greater use of diagrams might help promote the understanding of more complex concepts and instruments. The MCGRAW-HILL DICTIONARY OF SCIENTIFIC AND TECHNICAL TERMS is an example of a reference work that has been successful in clarifying terms through the liberal use of diagrams and illustrations.

Patrons of school and public libraries will find the brevity of the definitions and the extensive cross-references very helpful. This dictionary is a publication with British origins; however, that origin is only discerned through spelling differences *(fibre)* and subtle differences in phraseology. Overall, the slightly British slant does not detract from the usefulness of this book as a reference tool in the United States.

The Facts On File Dictionary of Science is suitable for a general audience. The Board recommends this work for the core collections of public and school libraries.

—E. B. C.

Handbooks and Tables in Science and Technology, 2d edition. Russell H. Powell, ed. Oryx, 1983. hard. 1 vol. 297 pp. indexes. ISBN 0-89774-039-4. $35.50. bibliography.

Z7405.T3P68 016.5'02'02

Handbooks and Tables in Science and Technology, edited by Russell H. Powell, is an annotated bibliography of over 3,000 titles that emphasizes compilations of physical and chemical values in diverse areas, such as mathematical formulas, conversion factors, physical constants, physical properties of materials, chemical reactions, and drug information.

Handbooks and Tables in Science and Technology is a useful information source for individuals working in these areas. The book is intended to help the user find the handbook or table that will supply necessary information or an answer to a ready-reference question. The book is also useful to the librarian selecting titles to be included in a reference collection.

This bibliography is arranged alphabetically by main entry and contains a subject index, an author or editor index, and a publisher index. Each main entry consists of the title, author or editor, publisher, edition, copyright date, pages, Library of Congress card number, ISBN, and price. If the title is a government document, the Superintendent of Documents (SuDoc) number, National Technical Information Service (NTIS) number, or accession number is noted. Following this information is a brief description of the contents. The reference number precedes each main entry. Reference numbers are listed in the author and subject indexes.

As stated in the preface, this bibliography emphasizes the physical sciences, such as physics, chemistry, engineering, mathematics, geology, medicine, and dentistry. Indexes, abstracts, dictionaries, encyclopedias, and so forth have been excluded. Popular sources, such as auto repair manuals, have also been excluded. Most of the titles are in the English language. Some notable exceptions are German-language treatises, which contain a large amount of important, tabulated information.

Many of the entries in this volume are over 15 years old. The user is advised to do a literature search or to consult library and information science reference texts for more recent editions. Much of the mathematical and formula tables have not changed since the time of Leibnitz, but rapidly changing technology and measurement techniques have made obsolete medical, drug, and chemical data, as just a few examples. For example, new compounds and new construction techniques are constantly being developed. In addition, price information is quickly outdated and is of limited value. Library of Congress card numbers and ISBNs are also of little value because the editions cited would rarely be used.

Because much of the information is obsolete, *Handbooks and Tables in Science and Technology* is most useful as a guide to the types of information that might be available. Ideally, works such as this should be updated a minimum of every five years. The Board recommends this work for the core collection of academic libraries. —*E. B. C.*

Lange's Handbook of Chemistry, 13th edition. John A. Dean, ed. McGraw-Hill, 1985. hard. 1 vol. 1,856 pp. illus. index. ISBN 0-07-016192-5. $73. handbook.
QD65.L36 540

See Chemistry.

McGraw-Hill Dictionary of Scientific and Technical Terms, 4th edition. Sybil P. Parker, ed. in chief. McGraw-Hill, 1989. hard. 1 vol. 2,137 pp. illus. appendix. ISBN 0-07-045270-9. $95. dictionary.
Q123.M34 503.21

The *McGraw-Hill Dictionary of Scientific and Technical Terms* specializes in providing definitions of scientific and technical terms for the general public as well as the professional community. The fourth edition, edited by Sybil P. Parker and published by McGraw-Hill in 1989, contains 100,100 terms (7,600 more than the previous edition), 117,500 definitions, and 3,000 detailed illustrations to support the definitions.

Each term is identified by the field with which it is associated. There are 102 scientific fields represented, such as atomic physics, building construction, computer science, evolution, food engineering, geology, invertebrate zoology, molecular biology, naval architecture, paleontology, quantum mechanics, statistics, textiles, and virology. The fields are described in a list contained in the front matter of the dictionary. The front matter also includes an alphabetical list of field abbreviations, notes on pronunciation, a pronunciation key, and a section on how to use the dictionary.

The terms appear in alphabetical order in boldface type. Each term is followed by a field identifier, a definition, and a pronunciation. A term may have several definitions, each introduced by a boldface number, or a term may have definitions in two or more fields. The definitions are written clearly and concisely. A definition may include synonyms, acronyms, abbreviations, symbols, and variant spellings. These also appear in the alphabetical sequence and are cross-referenced to the main entry. Definitions for chemical terms include formulas when appropriate. The pronunciation of each definition is a feature new to this edition.

The dictionary features an appendix full of useful and previously hard-to-find information. It includes a full explanation of the International System of Units, with conversion tables for the U.S. customary and metric systems; a table of chemical elements; a periodic table; lists of mathematical notation; tables of mathematical signs and symbols, fundamental constants, and elementary particles; semiconductor symbols and abbreviations; schematic electronic symbols; a list of abbreviations for scientific and technical organizations; a biographical listing of noted scientists; and an outline of the classification of living organisms, from kingdom to ordinary level.

The *McGraw-Hill Dictionary of Scientific and Technical Terms* is an excellent, comprehensive source, which is kept current by a five-year updating cycle. The book's relatively high price may be a selection factor for small public and school libraries; however, the dictionary is an essential purchase for all academic libraries. The Board recommends this work for the core collections of public, academic, and school libraries.

—*E. B. C.*

McGraw-Hill Encyclopedia of Science and Technology, 6th edition. McGraw-Hill, 1987. hard. 20 vols. 12,916 pp. illus. appendixes. indexes. ISBN 0-07-079292-5. $1,700 (set). encyclopedia. CD-ROM.
Q121.M3 503.21

The sixth edition of the *McGraw-Hill Encyclopedia of Science and Technology* continues a 30-year tradition of providing ready-reference information in all areas of modern science and technology, such as artificial intelligence, food manufacturing, and stereophonic sound.

This edition consists of 20 volumes containing 7,700 alphabetically arranged entries. The entries are broad survey articles written for the nonspecialist by an authority in the field. Each article contains a definition of the subject, background material, and a detailed description. The author's full name appears at the end of each entry.

Many features make this encyclopedia easy to use, including an effective combination of layout and typeface and extensive use of tables, line illustrations, and black-and-white and color photographs. Approximately 50,000 cross-references enable the reader to access additional information quickly. In addition, most of the articles contain bibliographies.

The last volume of this encyclopedia contains much valuable information, such as an alphabetical "Contributor's List" identifying all the authors and their professional affiliations along with the titles of the articles they wrote, contributed to, co-authored, or validated. This volume also contains a "Scientific Notation" section that clarifies the symbols, abbreviations, and nomenclature used in the encyclopedia and provides tables and conversion information for International System, U.S. customary, and metric measurements. Topical and analytical indexes complete the volume.

The "Topical Index" groups all the articles in the encyclopedia under 77 general headings. Using this index, the reader can find every article concerning a particular subject area, such as geophysics or medicine and pathology. This arrangement is similar to the relational index structure in the ENCYCLOPEDIA OF PHYSICAL SCIENCE AND TECHNOLOGY. The "Analytical Index" contains 150,000 entries that cover every important term, concept, and person mentioned throughout the 19 text volumes. The entries are arranged alphabetically on a word-by-word basis with references to volume and page numbers. To use this index efficiently, the reader should look for as specific a term as possible.

A new edition of this encyclopedia is published every five years. Recently, it has become available on CD-ROM. Supplemental information and updates are published annually in a yearbook. Librarians on a strict budget can buy sourcebooks that have been derived from this encyclopedia, such as the *Physical Chemistry Source Book,* the *Spectroscopy Source Book,* and the *Optics Source Book.*

The *McGraw-Hill Encyclopedia of Science and Technology* offers the most comprehensive selection of accurate scientific information for a broad, general audience. The Board recommends this work for the core collections of public, academic, and school libraries.

—*E. B. C.*

McGraw-Hill Yearbook of Science and Technology. McGraw-Hill, annual. hard. 1 vol. 464 pp. illus. index. ISBN 0-07-045501-5. $75. yearbook.
Q1.M13 505.8

The *McGraw-Hill Yearbook of Science and Technology* covers the key advances, developments, and discoveries in science and technology during the year of its publication. This volume is designed to be an annual review as well as a supplement to the McGRAW-HILL ENCYCLOPEDIA OF SCIENCE AND TECHNOLOGY.

The yearbook contains articles on broad topics that were judged by the editorial staff and a board of consulting editors to be the most significant developments of the previous year. In the 1990 yearbook, there are articles on acquired immune deficiency syndrome (AIDS), biotelemetry, genetics, printing, software engineering, and transplantation biology.

The yearbook follows the format of the encyclopedia. The alphabetically arranged articles are written by subject-matter specialists. The articles usually contain several levels of headings that allow the reader to find specific information quickly.

A list of cross-references to articles in the encyclopedia appears at the end of each article along with a short bibliography to provide further up-to-date information on the topic being discussed. The articles contain many two-tone charts, graphs, and diagrams as well as photographs. When possible, results are summarized and presented in tabular form. The two-column layout is easy to read and enables the reader to find information quickly.

At the end of the yearbook, there is an alphabetical list of contributors that identifies the authors, their professional affiliations, and the titles of the articles they wrote, contributed to, co-authored, or validated. A detailed subject index completes the yearbook.

The *McGraw-Hill Yearbook of Science and Technology,* like the encyclopedia, is intended for a general audience of all levels. The Board recommends this work for the core collections of public, academic, and school libraries. —*E. B. C.*

Milestones in Science and Technology: The Ready Reference Guide to Discoveries, Inventions, and

Facts. Ellis Mount and Barbara A. List. Oryx, 1987. hard. 1 vol. 141 pp. indexes. ISBN 0-89774-260-5. $35. guide.
Q199.M68 509

Milestones in Science and Technology: The Ready Reference Guide to Discoveries, Inventions, and Facts, by Ellis Mount and Barbara A. List, provides information on 1,000 significant events, discoveries, and facts in science and technology. The selection of these entries represents the compilers' estimation of their significance and importance in history from prehistoric times until 1987. As such, this work is not meant to be comprehensive.

The lack of stated criteria for the selection of the entries may be a minor drawback. Ellis Mount is a noted library and information science educator and science editor, and he and Barbara List state in the preface, "Obviously no two compilers would make the same selections. We tried to strike a balance among the many fields in which science and technology are significant." This has led to an excellent diversity of entries, but the general user may have a problem researching a particular topic. The entries range from basic discoveries, such as nuclear fission and relativity, to practical inventions, such as the lawn mower and the typewriter.

Each entry is assigned a broad category, such as anatomy, communications, computer science, mathematics, microbiology, oceanography, physics, and textiles. Most of the categories are the same as those used in the 1984 edition of the McGRAW-HILL DICTIONARY OF SCIENTIFIC AND TECHNICAL TERMS. The categories appear in capital letters to the extreme right of the entry terms.

Entries are arranged alphabetically by the name of the invention or discovery. Each entry contains a brief description of the topic, the names and the nationalities of the people involved, and the dates the events occurred. Cross-references to any related entries are provided at the end of the descriptions, along with the name of one additional book or reference source for more information. Cross-references within the entries are shown in boldface type.

The book has four indexes: personal name, chronological, geographical, and subject area. In each index, the name of the event and page number are cited. These indexes enable the reader to look at a particular year to see what events occurred, to locate the names of individuals involved in the discovery, to ascertain events that were discovered by people of a particular nationality, and to find out which events fall under one of the broad categories used in this work. These indexes increase the usefulness of this volume.

The book also contains two lists of references. The "Listing of Cited References" is an annotated list of the references that appear at the end of each entry. The "Listing of References of Interest" is an annotated list of references that the authors used in preparing this volume. These items provide further depth of information for the interested reader.

The major user of *Milestones in Science and Technology* will be the patron of a school library. This volume is an excellent starting point for a term paper. The Board recommends this work for the core collection of school libraries. —*E. B. C.*

The Museum of Science and Industry Basic List of Children's Science Books 1988. Bernice Richter and Duane Wenzel, comps. ALA, 1988. soft. 1 vol. 80 pp. appendixes. indexes. ISBN 0-8389-2499-8. $11.95. bibliography.
Z7401.M87 016.5

The Museum of Science and Industry Basic List of Children's Science Books 1988, published by the American Library Association, is a useful tool for developing a collection of science books for children in kindergarten through twelfth grade. The titles in this edition, which were compiled by Bernice Richter and Duane Wenzel, have not appeared in previous editions of the book.

All the entries in this book have been evaluated by Museum of Science and Industry reviewers. The factors considered in the review process included accuracy, currency, use of illustrations, advocacy of scientific training, and so forth. After the evaluation, each entry was assigned a reading level, which was based on the publisher's information.

The entries are arranged alphabetically under broad subject groupings, such as animals, astronomy, biography, earth sciences, fiction, life sciences, mathematics, computer science, physics, chemistry, plant life, and technology and engineering. Each entry includes a complete bibliographic citation, summary of content, the assigned reading level, and citations for additional reviews of the title.

The work includes several appendixes containing valuable information for librarians, teachers, and parents. There is a directory of publishers, with ordering information; a list of sourcebooks for adults that also contains information on science activities and projects; a list of children's science magazines with bibliographic and ordering information as well as appropriate audience information; and a list of review journals and science education journals also with ordering information. In addition to the appendixes, the work contains author and title indexes.

The Museum of Science and Industry Basic List of Children's Science Books 1988 is an easy-to-use and authoritative reference listing. The Board recommends this work for the core collection of school libraries.

—*E. B. C.*

The New Illustrated Science and Invention Encyclopedia: How It Works. Stuttman, 1989. soft. 26 vols. 3,628 pp. illus. appendix. indexes. ISBN 0-87475-450-X (set). $207.48 (set). encyclopedia.
Q123.I43 503.21

The New Illustrated Science and Invention Encyclopedia, published by H. S. Stuttman in 1987 and revised in 1989, consists of 26 volumes containing the latest scientific concepts and developments. The encyclopedia's contributors are from educational and research institutions, industry, and the media. The entries are written in authoritative and easily understood prose designed to be read by the nonspecialist.

Volumes 1 through 23 of the encyclopedia contain over 1,000 alphabetically arranged subject headings, ranging from artificial intelligence, coins and minting, genetic engineering, and hydroponics to nuclear waste disposal, paleontology, solar energy, and the zipper. The length of the entries varies from one to eight pages. Entries are profusely illustrated with color photographs and drawings. Detailed legends accompany the illustrations and provide additional explanations. Some entries contain a section entitled "Frontiers of Science." This section presents a comprehensive review of one aspect of the main entry. For example, in the entry for *ammunition,* the "Frontiers of Science" section discusses chemical weapons. In addition, many of the entries contain boxes entitled "Fact File." These boxes contain little-known historical information about the main entry.

Volume 24 contains biographies of 100 noted scientists and inventors. Individuals included in this volume range from Archimedes and Tycho Brahe to Rosalyn Yalow and Hans Bethe. Volume 25 is devoted to short articles about more than 70 scientific inventions and discoveries, ranging from the clock and the plow to the laser and the microchip. The final volume, volume 26, contains a chronological listing of scientific milestones, a glossary of technical terms, and separate thematic and general indexes.

The New Illustrated Science and Invention Encyclopedia provides broad, up-to-date coverage of science and technology. Its attractive layout and simple language will appeal to a wide audience. In content and style, *The New Illustrated Science and Invention Encyclopedia* lies at the layperson's end of a spectrum of science and technology encyclopedias. At the more technical end is the ENCYCLOPEDIA OF PHYSICAL SCIENCE AND TECHNOLOGY, and the MCGRAW-HILL ENCYCLOPEDIA OF SCIENCE AND TECHNOLOGY is in the middle. The Board recommends this work for the core collections of public and school libraries.

—*E. B. C.*

Van Nostrand's Scientific Encyclopedia, 7th edition. Douglas M. Considine, ed. Van Nostrand Reinhold, 1989. hard. 2 vols. 3,180 pp. illus. index. ISBN 0-442-21750-1 (set). $195 (set). encyclopedia.
Q121.V3 503.21

Van Nostrand's Scientific Encyclopedia, first published in 1938, is the oldest encyclopedia devoted solely to the sciences. Prior editions of this work appeared in a one-volume format. However, the scientific and technical data base has grown so rapidly that the current seventh edition, edited by Douglas M. Considine and published in 1989, has been expanded to two volumes to accommodate the information. Over 250 individuals and organizations provided information, graphics, and editorial input for this edition. The individuals (and their affiliations) and the organizations are listed in a separate acknowledgments section.

The encyclopedia covers a wide range of scientific and technical subjects including animal life; biosciences; chemistry; earth and atmospheric sciences; energy sources and power technology; mathematics and information sciences; materials and engineering sciences; medicine, anatomy, and physiology; physics; plant sciences; and space and planetary sciences. Each of the subjects covers a variety of topics. For example, the topics covered under earth and atmospheric sciences include climatology, ecology, geochemistry, geodynamics, geology, geophysics, hydrology, meteorology, oceanography, tectonics, seismology, and volcanology. Generally, topics are presented from a practical viewpoint. However, some theoretical topics are presented on a higher plane based on the assumption that readers who are interested in complex topics will also have a high level of scientific expertise.

Most of the entries include concise tutorial reviews in the first few paragraphs, followed by specific detailed information that becomes increasingly complex. For example, the entry *robot and robotics* starts with a definition and a historical perspective. The entry then covers such topics as classifications of robots, robot control systems, programming level for robots, load capacity and power requirements, hydraulic actuators for robots, and dynamic properties of robots.

Entries are arranged alphabetically. Cross-references to related entries in this work appear in boldface type both within the body of the entry and at the end. Where applicable, the author of the entry is noted at the conclusion, followed by a list of additional reading references. Over 3,000 illustrations and approximately 500 tabular summaries supplement the entries with additional information.

For the first time in its history, the encyclopedia includes an extensive (over 100-page long) index. This addition provides the reader with a speedy and convenient way to retrieve information.

The publishing history of the encyclopedia reflects a seven- to nine-year revision cycle. In this era of rapid change and discovery, such a lengthy cycle greatly affects the accuracy of entries dealing with the leading edge of scientific and technical exploration. However, the great majority of the entries can provide information to satisfy ready-reference questions.

Van Nostrand's Scientific Encyclopedia is designed for the general audience. This work is an invaluable source of concise, ready-reference information. The Board recommends this work for the core collections of public, academic, and school libraries. —*E. B. C.*

Supplementary Titles

The Biographical Dictionary of Scientists. David Abbott, gen. ed. Bedrick Bks., 1984–1986. hard. 6 vols. 1,208 pp. illus. index. ISBN 0-87226-009-7 (vol. 6). $28 per vol. biographical dictionary.
QC15.B56 530.092′2

"The [first] four volumes of [*The Biographical Dictionary of Scientists*] cover [over] 775 scientists. . . . [The fifth and sixth volumes were published subsequent to this review.] Each volume begins with a brief chronological review of the important milestones in the field. The biographical entries follow in alphabetical order.

"Each entry briefly mentions the early life of the individual and then concentrates on the scientific discoveries and contributions. The biographies are well written. . . . [This is] an excellent historical reference [set] that will be useful in public, . . . and college libraries." (*BL,* June 1, 1985)

Also reviewed in: *Choice,* February 1985, p. 791; *LATBR,* December 16, 1984, p. 7; *LJ,* March 15, 1985, p. 52; *SB,* September 1985, p. 31; *TES,* September 20, 1985, p. 57.

Board's recommendation: Public and academic libraries.

Cambridge Guide to the Material World. Rodney Cotterill. Cambridge, 1985. soft. 1 vol. 352 pp. illus. index. ISBN 0-521-37932-6. $27.95. handbook.
QC173.3.C66 500

"Describing the material world—from electrons to supernovae—in 350 pages is no easy undertaking, but Rodney Cotterill has done it in [*Cambridge Guide to the Material World*]." (*SA,* September 1985, p. 35)

"The nonmathematical account provides access for people of many backgrounds to a wonderful picture of the world at the molecular level. This marvelous book should become a reference standard." (*Choice,* July/August 1985, p. 1650)

"[T]he author's conversational style and the copious and excellent illustrations make the ideas [easy] to grasp. The organization—from single atoms through minerals to animals—makes sense." (*LJ,* September 15, 1984, p. 1748)

Also reviewed in: *Brit Bk N,* June 1985, p. 349; *Nature,* April 25, 1985, p. 686; *NYTBR,* April 21, 1985, p. 38; *Sch Lib,* September 1985, p. 288; *TES,* May 17, 1985, p. 50.

Board's recommendation: Public and academic libraries.

Women in Science: Antiquity Through the Nineteenth Century—A Biographical Dictionary with Annotated Bibliography. Marilyn Bailey Ogilvie. MIT Pr., 1986. hard. 1 vol. 254 pp. appendix. index. ISBN 0-262-15031-X. $29.95. biographical dictionary.
Q141.034 509.2

Women in Science contains "profiles of 186 women born before 1885. . . . At the conclusion of each [biographical] account is a list of . . . works by the subject and a list of items in the bibliography that will provide further information on the biographee. Twenty-six nineteenth-century women for whom there were very limited data are listed in an appendix. . . . [The book also includes an] . . . annotated bibliography, an alphabetical list of subjects of biographical accounts, and a name index. . . . An appendix presents each subject alphabetically in a four-column table with the subject's historical period, scientific field, and nationality.

"Ogilvie, a professor, author, and historian of science, has created an informative, well-organized reference source that will support research in both science and women's studies collections." (*BL,* June 1, 1987, p. 1509)

"[The book's] emphasis is on American women scientists—80 are listed—but representatives from nine European countries and from the Greek, Alexandrian, and Roman periods are also included. . . . Noteworthy is Ogilvie's introductory essay, 'Science and women: a historical view,' in which she examines chronologically Western science and the relation of women to it." (*Sci,* May 22, 1987, p. 989)

Also reviewed in: *A Lib,* March 1987, p. 229; *Choice,* May 1987, p. 1382; *Nature,* April 2, 1987, p. 452; *New Tech Bks,* February 1987, p. 58; *RQ,* Summer 1987, p. 527; *R & R Bk N,* Spring, 1987, p. 26; *SciTech,* March 1987, p. 5; *WLB,* April 1987, p. 69.

Board's recommendation: Public and academic libraries.

New and Noteworthy

Asimov's Chronology of Science and Discovery. Isaac Asimov. Harper, 1989. hard. 1 vol. 707 pp. indexes. ISBN 0-06-015612-0. $29.95. encyclopedia.
Q125.A765 509

"The approximately 1,450 entries in [*Asimov's Chronology of Science and Discovery*] are listed in chronological order starting with *Bipedality* in 4,000,000 B.C. and ending in 1988 with *Shroud of Turin, Distant Galaxies,* and *Greenhouse Effect.* In between is a wide range of discoveries in science and technology. . . . The entries . . . provide a description of the discovery and its operation, credit the discoverer(s) and give his or her nationality and dates of birth and death, and give a description of the process used in the discovery. . . . The number of entries in a year ranges from 1 to 15. . . . There is no introduction or table of contents to explain the work's coverage. . . . However, subject and name indexes are provided." (*BL,* February 15, 1990, p. 1183)

Dictionary of Science and Creationism. Ronald L. Ecker. Prometheus, 1990. hard. 1 vol. 263 pp. index. ISBN 0-87975-549-0. $32.95. dictionary.
BS652.E64 575

"This *Dictionary* [*of Science and Creationism*] is described by its author as 'a concise, nontechnical, ready-reference source of information, providing overviews of all major scientific areas that relate to evolutionary theory and using that information to show the pseudoscientific nature of "scientific" creationism.' Of use to defenders of the integrity of science education, the book is particularly designed to assist teachers and school board members who must deal with creationist pressure.

"Alphabetical entries, with many *see* references, include scientific terms . . . terms used by creationists . . . and court cases." (*BL,* May 1, 1990, p. 1736)

The History of Science and Technology: A Narrative Chronology. Edgardo Macorini, ed. Facts On File, 1989. hard. 2 vols. 889 pp. index. ISBN 0-87196-477-5. $160. history.
Q125

"[In *The History of Science and Technology,* material] . . . is arranged by centuries through 1100, by half centuries from 1200 to 1900 [vol. 1], and by decades from 1900 to 1970 [vol. 2]. . . . The work is perhaps best suited for providing a snapshot of the state of science and technology in a given time period." (*Choice,* July/August 1989, p. 1813)

McGraw-Hill Concise Encyclopedia of Science & Technology, 2d edition. Sybil P. Parker, ed. in chief. McGraw-Hill, 1989. hard. 1 vol. 2,222 pp. illus. index. ISBN 0-07-045512-0. $110. encyclopedia.
Q121.M29 503.21

"To create [the *McGraw-Hill Concise Encyclopedia of Science & Technology*] the editors 'extracted the essential text from each article in the parent work while retaining the same proportionality between subjects." [This new edition is] . . . larger by 157 pages . . . and has 400 articles. The parent work is the 20-volume *McGraw-Hill Encyclopedia of Science & Technology.* [The articles in that volume were favorably reviewed.] . . . All of the material in [this book] is essentially the same, only in condensed form." (*BL,* September 15, 1989, p. 207)

Science & Technology in Fact and Fiction: A Guide to Children's Books. DayAnn M. Kennedy et al. Bowker, 1990. hard. 1 vol. 319 pp. index. ISBN 0-8352-2708-1. $35. bibliography.
Z7401.R46 016.5

"Annotated [in *Science & Technology in Fact and Fiction*] are more than 350 fiction and nonfiction books for children, preschool to upper elementary, 'that will satisfy their curiosity as well as build a broader scientific and technological knowledge base.' . . . The physical and earth sciences are the principal focus. . . . All entries include a lengthy summary and an authoritative evaluation that addresses literary quality, attention to scientific and technological detail and accuracy, style and language, illustrations, appropriateness for intended audience, reference value (e.g., glossary), and format." (*BL,* April 1, 1990, p. 1581)

Charlene Kennedy

Sociology

Sociology is the scientific study of the individual in society. This study employs the process of scientific observation and the analysis of social data to determine the nature of human behavior in groups.

A person who is seeking knowledge or doing research in the field of sociology needs to have basic resources that will provide: (1) the major concepts of sociology; (2) access to the literature of sociology; (3) the methodologies of research, such as conducting surveys and statistical analysis; and (4) access to professional applications in the related fields of social work, social psychology, criminology, and so forth.

Public libraries should provide the basic tools for beginning students in sociology, such as the INTERNATIONAL ENCYCLOPEDIA OF THE SOCIAL SCIENCES and A NEW DICTIONARY OF THE SOCIAL SCIENCES. Both are resources that define basic concepts in sociology and its related disciplines and list influential thinkers and theorists, such as Max Weber and Karl Marx.

Academic libraries, which serve both student and faculty researchers in sociology, need to provide current, efficient, and accurate methods to access the worldwide literature of the field. Since 1953 SOCIOLOGICAL ABSTRACTS has fulfilled this need by indexing and systematizing information about the specialized works published in the field.

Bibliographies, such as SOCIOLOGY: A GUIDE TO REFERENCE AND INFORMATION SOURCES, are helpful to librarians who are selecting works for collection development and researchers who are seeking source materials to support their observations.

In addition to the titles reviewed, standard works that should supplement a core sociology collection include books with professional applications, such as the ENCYCLOPEDIA OF SOCIAL WORK and A GUIDE TO INFORMATION SOURCES FOR SOCIAL WORK AND THE HUMAN SERVICES.

Other supplementary resources that have proven to be of assistance to beginning students of sociology are the ENCYCLOPEDIA OF SOCIOLOGY and FINDING THE SOURCE IN SOCIOLOGY AND ANTHROPOLOGY.

Unfortunately, *The International Encyclopedia of Sociology* (Michael Mann, ed., Continuum, 1984) is a very useful work that has recently gone out of print. Librarians may wish to obtain this source through an out-of-print book dealer.

Core Titles

	PUBLIC	ACADEMIC	SCHOOL
International Encyclopedia of the Social Sciences, 8 vols. Sills, David L., ed. Free Pr./Macmillan, 1968–1979	✦	✦	
A New Dictionary of the Social Sciences, 2d edition Mitchell, G. Duncan, ed. Aldine/Routledge & Kegan Paul, 1979	✦	✦	
Sociological Abstracts, 5 vols. per year Chall, Leo P., ed. Sociological Abstracts, 1953–		✦	
Sociology: A Guide to Reference and Information Sources Aby, Stephen H., comp. Libraries Unlimited, 1987		✦	
Sources of Information in the Social Sciences: A Guide to the Literature, 3d edition Webb, William H., et al., eds. ALA, 1986	✦	✦	
Thesaurus of Sociological Indexing Terms, 2d edition Booth, Barbara, and Michael Blair, eds. Sociological Abstracts, 1989		✦	

Core Titles

International Encyclopedia of the Social Sciences. David L. Sills, ed. Free Pr./Macmillan, 1968–1979. hard. 8 vols. index. ISBN 0-02-895700-8 (set). $325 (set). encyclopedia.
H40.A2.I5 300.3

The *International Encyclopedia of the Social Sciences* is an 8-volume version of a 17-volume encyclopedia published by Macmillan from 1930 to 1935.

The original work, titled *Encyclopaedia of the Social Sciences,* was the first comprehensive encyclopedia to recognize the interdependence of the social sciences. Editors Edwin R. A. Seligman and Alvin Johnson set three basic goals for the encyclopedia: (1) to provide the scholar with a synopsis of the international progress that had been made in the various fields of social science; (2) to appeal to a broad international audience of intellectuals and enable them to keep abreast of recent investigations and achievements; and (3) to constitute a repository of authoritative knowledge for the creation of a sounder and more informed public opinion.

The format of the encyclopedia was alphabetical. This volume contained not only short articles but also longer, original contributions to the subject fields. Over 4,000 biographies were included of deceased persons whose work had been significant in the various fields of social science. Other special features included a lengthy introduction on the meaning of the social sciences, a history of the development of the field throughout the world, and a rigorous annotated bibliography covering the works of primary importance to the development of the social sciences.

The *International Encyclopedia of the Social Sciences,* published from 1968 to 1979, is not a revision of the earlier work, but attempts to pick up where the 17-volume set left off. The articles and bibliographies in each field of social science are designed to keep teachers and students informed of new developments in many hundreds of topics. The majority of the articles are devoted to concepts, theories, and methods in the following disciplines: anthropology, economics, geography, history, law, political science, psychiatry, psychology, sociology, and for the first time, statistics. The *International Encyclopedia* also includes articles about major world societies and religions, about the professions related to social science, and about modern social thought on the arts.

Like its predecessor, the *International Encyclopedia* is arranged alphabetically. However, specific articles that share a general subject are grouped under one heading. An extensive listing of cross-references, both of entries and those topics within the articles that do not receive entries, serves to guide the reader to the appropriate topic. The addition of an exhaustive index enables the reader to quickly locate a specific subject.

This work includes biographies of 600 persons whose research and writings have made major contributions to the social sciences. For the first time, biographies of living persons are included. However, in order to ensure that the person should have completed most of his or her scientific work, a rule was established not to include any living person born after 1890.

The *International Encyclopedia of the Social Sciences* should be found in all academic libraries. Those libraries who are not fortunate enough to have a print copy of the parent work, *Encyclopaedia of Social Sciences,* may wish to purchase the original edition in microfiche, the only version available at the present time.

The Board recommends this work for the core collections of public and academic libraries.

A New Dictionary of the Social Sciences, 2d edition. G. Duncan Mitchell, ed. Aldine/Routledge & Kegan Paul, 1979. hard. 1 vol. 244 pp. ISBN 0-202-30285-7. $37.95. dictionary.
HM17.M562 301.03

A New Dictionary of the Social Sciences, second edition, is a revision of *A Dictionary of Sociology,* which was first published in 1968. G. Duncan Mitchell, a professor of sociology at the University of Exeter, was the chief editor of both editions. This one-volume dictionary provides the beginning sociology student with a broad definition of sociology by including words used in the related disciplines of cultural and social anthropology, social psychology, and political science, in addition to entries about sociological concepts.

The length of the entry is determined by the complexity of the concept. For example, a short, four-line definition is sufficient for the term *situs,* while longer articles are provided for broader concepts, such as *role, authority,* and *social stratification* (at four pages). Cross-references are given.

Approximately 350 entries are included; many of these are signed. A few entries contain bibliographic references. Many biographical profiles are included for persons no longer living.

Because *A New Dictionary of the Social Sciences* is 10 years old, entries on current research and newly developed concepts are not included. However, this volume will give the reader a foundation in the primary concepts of the social sciences.

A New Dictionary of the Social Sciences will be useful to patrons of both public and academic libraries. The Board recommends this work for the core collections of public and academic libraries.

Sociological Abstracts. Leo P. Chall, ed. Sociological Abstracts, 1953– (published 5 times a year). soft. 5 vols (per year). annual index. ISSN 0038-0202. $120 (per year). on-line. CD-ROM.
HM1.S67 301.016

Since 1953, *Sociological Abstracts* has indexed and abstracted the world's professional literature in the field of sociology and its related disciplines. Co-sponsored by the International Sociological Association, *Sociological Abstracts* has an international orientation, (22 percent of its abstracts are in languages other than English) and brings its users the broadest possible range of sociological information.

From its inception, Leo P. Chall has served as *Sociological Abstracts'* editor and has established an editorial policy based on two criteria: (1) inclusiveness: "to abstract fully all core sociology journals (type I) and to select from journals in related disciplines (type II) those articles published by sociologists or those that are pertinent to sociology," and (2) continuity: "to abstract journals in chronological sequence of their publication whenever possible."

In 1953, *Sociological Abstracts* became available in a printed version, and it was updated quarterly. It now comes out five times per year (April, June, August, October, and December). Each year, the editorial staff screens approximately 1,600 journals worldwide for relevant material. Conference papers have been indexed from 1968 to 1972 and from 1977 to the present. Dissertations were added in 1986, along with book abstracts and bibliographic citations for book reviews appearing in the journals abstracted. Approximately 9,000 journal articles and association paper abstracts are added yearly.

The on-line version of *Sociological Abstracts* is searchable from 1963 to the present through four data base vendors: BRS, Dialog, Data-Star, and DIMDI. Accompanying the electronic format is a THESAURUS OF SOCIOLOGICAL INDEXING TERMS, which enables the researcher to use precise subject descriptors within Boolean search strategies.

With the advent of compact disc–read only memory (CD-ROM) technology, *Sociofile,* or *Sociological Abstracts* on CD-ROM, has become available. SilverPlatter Information Services has created state-of-the-art search and retrieval software, which enables rapid, inexpensive access to a vast repository of sociological research, through an annual subscription fee instead of on-line costs.

Whether in print, on-line, or in the CD-ROM version, *Sociological Abstracts* is the primary research tool in its discipline for students, faculty, and other persons concerned with research or report preparation. The Board recommends this work for the core collection of academic libraries.

Sociology: A Guide to Reference and Information Sources. Stephen H. Aby, comp. Libraries Unlim-

ited, 1987. hard. 1 vol. 231 pp. indexes. ISBN 0-87287-496-2. $36. bibliography.
Z7164.S68.A24 016.301

Sociology: A Guide to Reference and Information Sources is an annotated bibliography that provides undergraduate and graduate students, librarians, and researchers with descriptions of over 600 of the major reference sources in sociology, its subdisciplines, and related fields in the social sciences. *Sociology* is part of a series called Reference Sources in the Social Sciences, published by Libraries Unlimited. Each volume in the series focuses on a major discipline in the social sciences and recommends reference sources, data bases, and other useful tools for research.

Sociology is set up into three main parts: (1) general social science reference sources; (2) social science disciplines (such as education, economics, and psychology); (3) sociology: general reference sources and sociolocial fields (including clinical sociology, criminology, law and deviance, and gerontology).

Each part lists major guides, bibliographies, indexes and abstracts, handbooks and yearbooks, dictionaries and encyclopedias, statistical sources, directories, online data bases, journals, research centers, and organizations and publishers, if they exist for the category.

All entries are arranged alphabetically by author or editor, or, if none, by title. Entries follow *American Reference Books Annual* bibliographic format and are descriptively or critically annotated in approximately 60 to 200 words.

The selections cited are as up to date as possible at the time of publication, and references are made to earlier editions in many cases. Reference sources published from 1970 to early 1986 are included. Works that precede this period are listed if they are classics in the field or if more recent works do not exist. Helpful to the user are author/title and subject indexes.

This book is essential for libraries that are building their research collections in the social sciences and sociology. This work is also an excellent checklist of resources for students. *Sociology: A Guide to Reference and Information Sources* is recommended for all academic libraries, but would be useful in public libraries as well. The Board recommends this work for the core collection of academic libraries.

Sources of Information in the Social Sciences: A Guide to the Literature, 3d edition. William H. Webb et al., eds. ALA, 1986. hard. 1 vol. 777 pp. index. ISBN 0-83890-405-X. $70. bibliography.
Z7161.W49 016.3

The first edition of *Sources of Information in the Social Sciences* evolved as a result of the study of subject bibliography by library science students at Columbia University during the 1950s. The work that resulted proved to be helpful beyond the scope of library science. Social scientists discovered that subject bibliographies made it easier for them to locate knowledge not only in their field but also in related disciplines.

Because the purpose of the book is to provide a systematic guide to the literature of the behavior of people in relationship to one another and their environment, the following traditional fields were selected for inclusion: geography, economics, sociology, anthropology, psychology, and political science. Because of the trend toward interdisciplinary research, the scope of *Sources of Information in the Social Sciences* also includes fields of knowledge that are not always considered to be within the social sciences, such as education, business administration, and history.

Under the auspices of the American Library Association, each subject specialist selected, organized, and reviewed core works that were representative of the literature of the previously mentioned fields. Additional supplementary reference works were added to round out each category.

The physical organization of the book (the indexing and cross-referencing in particular) has also been influenced by the interdisciplinary nature of research. For those books that are inseparably related to works described in other chapters, it is recommended that the index be consulted to link related subjects. The first chapter, "Social Science Literature," supplements all the others. Cross-references have been used as much as possible, but multiple entries for the same title have been necessary to achieve a balanced picture of information resources on a particular subject. For example, *Research Methods in the Social Sciences* can be found under social science literature and political science.

Sources of Information in the Social Sciences has proven to be a classic social science subject bibliography. The Board recommends this work for the core collections of public and academic libraries.

Thesaurus of Sociological Indexing Terms, 2d edition. Barbara Booth and Michael Blair, eds. Sociological Abstracts, 1989. soft. 1 vol. ISBN 0-930710-06-1. $60. thesaurus.
Z691.1.S6.T44 301.016

Since the appearance of the first edition of the *Thesaurus of Sociological Indexing Terms* in 1986, many new terms and concepts have been added to the literature of sociology. Co-edited by Barbara Booth (principal lexicographer) and Michael Blair (thesaurus developing and indexing), the second edition of the thesaurus has been expanded to include over 175 new main-term descriptors, 300 scope notes, many new cross-references, and a new feature, the rotated term display, which "allows users to find multiword descriptors alphabetically by each meaningful component."

The thesaurus has a spiral binding that makes it easy to keep open when looking up terms to set up a search strategy.

The structure of the *Thesaurus of Sociological Indexing Terms* consists of an alphabetical listing of "main term" descriptors used for indexing and searching the SOCIOLOGICAL ABSTRACTS data bases and printed indexes, beginning with the April 1986 issue. It also references "discontinued terms" from the former Descriptor Authority File, which can be used to retrieve information prior to 1986. Main term descriptors appear in boldface type and are limited to 60 characters. Each main term has also been assigned a specific alphanumeric code, called the "descriptor code" (DC), that can be used in on-line searching to represent the main term itself, as shown in the following example:

Latin American Cultural Groups (MT) = (DC) D448500

Each main term entry may also include a "scope note" (SN), which is a brief statement of the intended meaning of a main term, such as *self-actualization.*

(SN) Process of realizing one's potentialities, capacities, and talents; of accepting oneself; and of integrating or harmonizing one's motives.

Likewise, a "history note" (HN) may be listed under a main term or a discontinued term, to link it with the Descriptor Authority File terms used prior to 1986, such as *American Indian reservations.*

(HN) Formerly (1963–1985) DC 385730, Reservation

Terms may also be referenced by the "used for" (UF) designation, indicating that it is a nonpreferred term. In the case of the term *films,* a search would show the following:

(UF) Cinema (1963–1985)

Motion Pictures

Movie/Movies (1963–1985)

Other designations for terms include "broader terms" (BT), "narrower terms" (NT), and "related terms" (RT).

The *Thesaurus of Sociological Indexing Terms* can serve as an aid to achieve effective literature searches with all the various formats of SOCIOLOGICAL ABSTRACTS (print, on-line, and CD-ROM). This work can be used in conjunction with the annual cumulative indexes of the SOCIOLOGICAL ABSTRACTS from 1986 on. Prior to 1986, the annual indexes can be used in conjunction with terms referenced in the "history notes" and discontinued "used for" terms.

For on-line or CD-ROM searching, it may be easier to use the respective descriptor codes rather than the index terms. Both old and new index terms can be combined with words in titles, identifier phrases, and abstracts in formulating search strategies.

Because of its versatility, the *Thesaurus of Sociological Indexing Terms* should be found in all libraries owning SOCIOLOGICAL ABSTRACTS in one or more of its available formats. The Board recommends this work for the core collection of academic libraries.

Supplementary Titles

Encyclopedia of Social Work, 18th edition. Anne Minahan. National Assn. of Social Workers, 1987. hard. 2 vols. plus 1 suppl. 2,172 pp. ISBN 0-87101-141-7. $85. encyclopedia.
HV35.S6 361.003

The *Encyclopedia of Social Work* "has been produced under the sponsorship of the National Association of Social Workers (NASW). . . . The NASW group charged with planning this new edition identified eight major categories to be covered: fields of practice, populations, social issues and problems, social work practice, social institutions and human development, research, profession, and miscellaneous. . . . [The] 124-page supplement [to this edition] consists of 'comprehensive statistical and demographic tables to illustrate and highlight social and economic trends and developments.' . . . Each group of tables, charts, and graphs is introduced by a one- to three-page essay. . . . [This supplement is included with the two-volume set.]

"Full bibliographic citations for items referenced follow each article. Many also include a bibliography of additional readings. . . . The eighteenth edition of the *Encyclopedia of Social Work* can be recommended highly. It is an essential part . . . of any academic library's social work reference collection." (*BL,* April 1, 1987, p. 1188)

Also reviewed in: *ARBA,* 1978, p. 336; 1988, p. 336; *BL,* July 1984, p. 1527; *Choice,* January 1978, p. 1478; *RSR,* 1989, p. 74; *SC,* April 1966, p. 242; *Ser Lib 2nd,* 1985, p. 302.

Board's recommendation: Public and academic libraries.

Encyclopedia of Sociology. Gayle Johnson and Peter

J. O'Connell, eds. DPG, 1981. soft. 1 vol. 330 pp. illus. bibliography. ISBN 0-87967-329-X. $11.95. encyclopedia.
HM17.E5 301.03'21

Reviews of the 1974 edition of the *Encyclopedia of Sociology* stated that it was a "dictionary of some 1,300 articles cover[ing] terminology, sociological theories, institutions of society, concepts, historical material, biographies of social scientists of the past and present, and research findings in the related social sciences of psychology, economics, anthropology, political science and history.

"Entries are short (up to 2,500 words), specific, and arranged in one alphabet; all but the briefest are signed. . . . Graphs, charts, tables, and photographs are used to advantage throughout on a three-column page, two devoted to text and one to illustration." (*CRL,* July 1975, p. 313)

"The *Encyclopedia of Sociology* follows a particular format: "(1) a list of contributors and expository preface; (2) the articles themselves . . . ; and (3) a classified bibliography. Alphabetically interspersed with the articles are both 'see' and 'see also' references. In addition, 'subject maps' show in a single display the interrelationships among the major areas of study within a field.

"[It is] recommended for all academic libraries." (*Choice,* July 1974, p. 734)

Also reviewed in: *BL,* September 15, 1974, p. 105; *SS,* January 1976, p. 43.

Board's recommendation: Academic libraries.

Finding the Source in Sociology and Anthropology: A Thesaurus-Index to the Reference Collection. Samuel R. Brown, comp. Greenwood, 1987. hard. 1 vol. 269 pp. index. ISBN 0-313-25263-7. $45. bibliography.
Z7164.S68B75 016.301

"The purpose of . . . [*Finding the Source in Sociology and Anthropology*] is to provide a subject index that can be used as a finding list for reference works and books dealing with subject content in the fields of sociology and anthropology. . . .

"Brown's work is organized into two major sections. The first is the list of citations to the core collection of books selected for inclusion. The second section consists of the indexes. The citations are subdivided into categories (such as general sources, anthropology, sociology, sexuality, and social issues); each of these categories is further subdivided, either by type of publication or by subject area. . . .

"The detailed thesaurus-type index makes a valuable contribution; there is no comparable work. [It is] recommended for purchase in large and medium-sized academic library reference departments, . . . [and] large public libraries." (*RQ,* Spring 1988, p. 428)

Also reviewed in: *ARBA,* 1988, p. 321; *Choice,* July 1987, p. 1672; *R & R Bk N,* Summer 1987, p. 15; *SF,* June 1988, p. 1161; *WLB,* June 1987, p. 83.

Board's recommendation: Academic libraries.

A Guide to Information Sources for Social Work and the Human Services. Henry Neil Mendelsohn. Oryx, 1987. soft. 1 vol. 136 pp. index. bibliography. ISBN 0-89774-338-5. $33. guide.
HV91.M43 026.36

A Guide to Information Sources is designed to "present sources that social practitioners, educators, and students can use to locate information in libraries. . . . [The introduction] outlines the work's 11 chapters and their use. After a . . . chapter on how libraries are organized, the guide . . . [discusses] information found in reference books, journal and newspaper articles, professional journals, computerized literature searches and databases, books, public documents, sources for statistics, legal sources, historical information, and current review and awareness media.

"This well-conceived bibliographic guide fills a gap in the literature of a profession that thrives on current information for its practice. . . . Each chapter is in narrative format with subheadings that explicate the value and use of each source. However, each chapter concludes with references to all sources discussed, with complete citation and annotation . . . in classified order. Thus, the best of both approaches is preserved. The complete title, organization, and subject index rounds out the ease of accessibility. . . . The guide will appeal to academic, larger public, and specialized libraries, as well as individual researchers." (*BL,* March 1, 1988, p. 1120)

Also reviewed in: *ARBA,* 1988, p. 336; *Choice,* March 1988, p. 1068; *R & R Bk N,* April 1988, p. 12; *SciTech,* November 1987, p. 5; *WLB,* December 1987, p. 93.

Board's recommendation: Academic libraries.

New and Noteworthy

A Critical Dictionary of Sociology. Raymond Boudon and François Bourricaud. Univ. of Chicago, 1989. hard. 1 vol. approx. 624 pp. index. ISBN 0-226-06728-9. $49.95. dictionary.
HM17.B6813 301.03

A Critical Dictionary of Sociology "offers very selective coverage of currently used terms which deal with the 'fundamental questions' of sociology. The authors' stated goal, 'to present a critical analysis of the sociological tradition,' is carried out in long essay-type entries averaging about 1700 words and including bibliographies.... No other current sociology dictionary takes on the theoretical, philosophical, and/or empirical aspects of topics in such depth." (*LJ,* October 15, 1989, p. 74)

The Encyclopedia of Marriage, Divorce and the Family. Margaret DiCanio. Facts On File, 1989. hard. 1 vol. 607 pp. index. ISBN 0-8160-1695-X. $45. encyclopedia.
HQ9.D38 306.8′03

"*The Encyclopedia of Marriage, Divorce and the Family* is billed by its publisher as [the] 'first single-volume all-in-one reference devoted to contemporary family lifestyles. . . . [I]ts coverage reflects today's unprecedented lifestyle options created by . . . changes over the last twenty-five years.' Subject matter varies from the expected long reports on marriage, family, and divorce to discussion of issues like dual-career marriages, the elderly, alcoholics, and cohabitation. Even some fairly peripheral topics are covered, for instance, *Gifted Children, Setpoint Theory of Weight Control,* and *Eating Disorders.* [The subject] . . . coverage is quite thorough within the parameters of the title and, depending on the issue, includes historical, legal, psychological, and sociological aspects." (*BL,* January 1, 1990, pp. 946–948)

The Social Sciences: A Cross-Disciplinary Guide to Selected Sources. Nancy L. Herron, ed. Libraries Unlimited, 1989. hard and soft. 1 vol. 287 pp. indexes. ISBN 0-87287-725-6 (hard); 0-87287-777-9 (soft). $36 (hard); $27.50 (soft). bibliography.
Z7161.S648 016.3

The Social Sciences presents 790 citations "in four main parts: 'General Literature,' 'Literature of the Established Disciplines,' 'Literature of the Emerging Disciplines,' and 'Literature of the Disciplines Related to the Social Sciences.' Individual chapters cover political science, economics and business, history, law, anthropology, sociology, education, psychology, communication, geography, and statistics and demographics." (*BL,* March 1, 1990, pp. 1387–1388)

Lawrence Olszewski

Spanish and Portuguese Literature

See also Latin American Literature; World Literature

As a reference category, Spanish and Portuguese literature poses several intriguing problems for the librarian, not the least of which is dealing with the dearth of adequate reference sources currently available in English. The sources included in a collection must accommodate not only novices who need basic introductory resources or access to works in translation but also students and scholars who need more advanced bibliographical tools. The time span in consideration is extensive—nearly 2,000 years for the Iberian peninsula. Also, the range of authors runs the gamut from the popular Miguel de Cervantes and poet-dramatist Federico García Lorca to authors known only to Hispanic scholars. In addition, Portuguese authors are for the most part unfamiliar to American audiences.

There are other challenges to the librarian assembling references for this category. Translations do not always convey the original intent or idea of the author faithfully and may even be inaccurate, and selecting works based on the merits or demerits of the translator's art requires a set of skills that most librarians have not acquired. Furthermore, access to the secondary material often assumes—unfairly—at least a reading knowledge of the original language, and quality critical studies in English may be limited for certain authors.

For both the Spanish and Portuguese elements, libraries are dealing in essence with two distinct literary worlds—that of the European homeland and that of the Western Hemisphere. The geographical unit called Spain is itself composed of linguistic minorities that have sizeable independent literatures; Galician and Catalan are the two most prominent.

Another point of concern is the treatment of Spanish surnames. Technically, Spaniards are often known by a combination of a paternal and maternal last name, in that order; however, they may be more commonly known to English and Spanish-speakers alike by the maternal surname, as is the case with Lorca.

The most commonly used reference tools in this area are bibliographies, dictionaries, and histories; biographical information that will lead to sound critical arguments and interpretations is also important. A good all-purpose bibliography, David Foster's *Manual of Hispanic Bibliography* (Garland, 1977), is unfortunately out of print. Maxim Newmark's *Dictionary of Spanish Literature* (Greenwood, 1952), available as a reprint (1972), is dated and should be used with caution. One of the standard histories, Guillermo Díaz-Plaja's *History of Spanish Literature* (New York University Press, 1971), is also out of print. One other excellent work now out of print, a bibliography, was chosen by the Board as a core title and may be worth

Core Titles

	PUBLIC	ACADEMIC	SCHOOL
Guide to Reference Works for the Study of the Spanish Language and Literature and Spanish American Literature Woodbridge, Hemsley C. Modern Language Assn., 1987	✦		
The Literature of Spain in English Translation: A Bibliography Rudder, Robert S., comp. and ed. Ungar, 1975		✦	
Modern Spanish and Portuguese Literature Schneider, Marshall J., and Irwin Stern, eds. Ungar, 1988		✦	
The Oxford Companion to Spanish Literature Ward, Philip, ed. Clarendon/Oxford, 1978	✦	✦	✦
A Sourcebook for Hispanic Literature and Language: A Selected, Annotated Guide to Spanish, Spanish-American, and Chicano Bibliography, Literature, Linguistics, Journals, and Other Source Materials, 2d edition Bleznick, Donald W. Scarecrow, 1983 (See Latin American Literature)		✦	

pursuing: George Parks and Ruth Temple's *Romance Literatures,* vol. 2 (Ungar, 1970).

Core Titles

Guide to Reference Works for the Study of the Spanish Language and Literature and Spanish American Literature. Hemsley C. Woodbridge. MLA, 1987. hard and soft. 1 vol. 183 pp. indexes. ISBN 0-87352-958-8 (hard); 0-87352-959-6 (soft). $37.50 (hard); $14.50 (soft). bibliography.
Z2695.A2.W66 016.86

The *Guide to Reference Works for the Study of the Spanish Language and Literature and Spanish American Literature* contains 908 extremely brief, descriptive annotations to works in both Spanish and English, which have often been extracted verbatim from the texts themselves. The first part, which contains citations for bibliographies and dictionaries, comprises 147 entries concerning the Spanish language (first in Spain, then in Spanish America). There is surprisingly little duplication here with the section on linguistics in A SOURCEBOOK FOR HISPANIC LITERATURE AND LANGUAGE.

The second and considerably larger part of this bibliographical work cites references in literature from about 1950 to early 1986. The geographical dichotomy in the language section is repeated here—works pertaining to Spain, arranged chronologically, precede those referring to Spanish America, the entries of which are arranged by country. Like the SOURCEBOOK, this work does not cover Portuguese or Brazilian literature.

Author Hemsley Woodbridge is no stranger to bibliography; his earlier compilations of secondary sources on Pérez Galdós and Rubén Darío constitute significant contributions to Hispanic scholarship. In addition, the publisher, the Modern Language Association, is the paramount language association in the country.

A unique and extremely useful feature of this work is the listings of bibliographies about specific authors published separately, either as monographs or as full-scale journal articles. Although they are embodied within each chronological or geographical section, as the case may be, they are accessible through a separate index. An additional index contains authors, editors, and compilers. Both indexes refer to item numbers. Unfortunately, there is no index to titles; however, the table of contents is extremely detailed and can serve as an index.

In short, Woodbridge's compilation constitutes a fine bibliographical overview for both Spanish language and literature. The availability of a paperback format as well as a fairly recent publication date make the *Guide to Reference Works for the Study of the Spanish Language and Literature and Spanish American Literature* an attractive choice for librarians concerned with acquiring authoritative information at a good price. The Board recommends this work for the core collection of academic libraries.

The Literature of Spain in English Translation: A Bibliography. Robert S. Rudder, comp. and ed. Ungar, 1975. hard. 1 vol. 637 pp. index. ISBN 0-8044-3261-9. $55. bibliography.
Z2694.T7R83 016.86′08

The Literature of Spain in English Translation represents a singular effort by Ungar (the publisher) to provide access to a wide corpus of Spanish literature in English for a variety of users interested in the literature of Spain but unable to read Spanish. The geographical scope is limited to the physical boundaries of Spain; early Latin authors and the lesser-known efforts of the Catalan, Galician, Valencian, and Basque minorities are included, but Portugal and all of Latin America are not. The liberal definition of literature includes philosophers *(Ortega y Gasset),* critics *(Menéndez Pidal),* and explorers *(Christopher Columbus).*

The length of the listings for the almost 600 named authors ranges from only a brief entry to 30 pages for *García Lorca.* The listing of authors' complete works overlaps the coverage in *The Romance Literatures* (now out of print); however, the separate entries for individually published poems, short stories, and significant excerpts, many in private printings, limited editions, and "little magazines," provide a unique and valuable resource.

The bibliography is broken down into six chronological periods: the medieval period, the Renaissance, the golden age, the eighteenth century, the nineteenth century, and the twentieth century, which contains the most entries. Within each chronological division, arrangement is alphabetical by author (after a section of anonymous works). Titles are listed alphabetically by the Spanish title; if the editor was unable to verify the corresponding Spanish title of a work, he alphabetized it under the English title. All translations are included, no matter how many there are. Although the citations include page references for journals, such references are omitted for collections and anthologies, forcing users to consult the referenced volume separately. Furthermore, since references to collections are indicated by code, users must consult the list of frequently cited anthologies at the end of the volume to obtain the full title of the indexed collection.

A 24-page addendum, arranged alphabetically by author (regardless of epoch), contains no cross-references to entries in the main text, although references to the addendum are included in the main index. However, the author index does not cross-reference consistently; there are no cross-references from *Lorca* to *García Lorca* nor from *Galdós* to *Pérez Galdós.* The Arcipreste de Hita can be found only under *Ruiz, Juan;* there is no cross-reference from either Arcipreste or Hita, both valid access points. San Juan de la Cruz is under *Cruz* only (with a "see" reference under *San*); Santa Teresa is found only under *Teresa.* Furthermore, there is no index by title; therefore, one cannot locate references to a translated title without determining the author first. In addition, the date of publication of the original Spanish version of a work is not provided.

Obviously and unfortunately, a work with a 1975 publication date will not be useful for locating recently translated titles. In some instances, users will be shortchanged; for example users will have to settle for the only named translation of Galdós's *Fortunata y Jacinta,* that of Lester Clark (Penguin, 1974), instead of the vastly superior but more recent one by Agnes Guillón (Univ. of Georgia Pr., 1986). The splendid translations in the Twentieth-Century Continental Fiction series by Columbia University Press are also too recent for this volume. Other shortcomings include the physical aspects of the volume: the unattractive typewritten text and the unstable binding detract from the work's overall effectiveness.

Despite the limitations, *The Literature of Spain in English Translation* is a useful resource, especially for academic collections, which are likely to have the complete works themselves or either access to or substantial holdings of periodicals and anthologies for the shorter works. The Board recommends this work for the core collection of academic libraries.

Modern Spanish and Portuguese Literature. Marshall J. Schneider and Irwin Stern, eds. Ungar, 1988. hard. 1 vol. 900 pp. index. ISBN 0-8044-3280-5. $85. handbook.
PQ6072.M57 860

Modern Spanish and Portuguese Literature is the newest member of the Ungar Library of Literary Criticism family. In fact, of the reference volumes included in this part of the Buying Guide, this is the most recent—yet the one in which currency matters least. The volume has three purposes: to provide an overview of critical opinions since the beginning of each author's career; to reproduce representative excerpts of critical opinion of selected works; and to serve indirectly as a core bibliography. An interesting sidelight is the inclusion of opinions of famous writers commenting on other writers; for example, Jorge Luis Borges's conversational critique of Miguel de Unamuno.

Galician and Catalan writers are included here, but Brazilian and Spanish-American writers are not, as they are covered elsewhere (in MODERN LATIN AMERICAN LITERATURE; see Latin American Literature). Lack of sufficient criticism eliminated writers whose careers began during the past ten years. Although selections date from the turn of the century to the present, uncertainty surrounds the editors' definition of "modern." *Angel Ganivet,* who died in 1898 but who influenced an entire later generation, is included, as is *Pérez Galdós,* who died in 1920 but whose best creative work lay behind him by 1900. However, two other nineteenth-century novelists who were contemporaries of both Ganivet and Galdós are conspicuously absent: Juan Valera, who, though he died in 1905, still enjoys popularity through the dissemination of his *Pepita Jiménez,* and Emilia Pardo Bazán, who died in 1921 and wrote into the twentieth century.

The 80 authors, only one-fourth of whom are Portuguese, are arranged alphabetically by country. Each of the 800 excerpts extracted from a wide variety of sources averages about one-half of a page. (Some users may find these snatches of criticism of limited value out of context.) A dagger indicates excerpts that appear here in English for the first time. Each author entry concludes with a listing of that author's works.

A useful introduction to the volume surveys the aspects of modern literature in each region. A bibliographical appendix arranged alphabetically by author lists all original works mentioned with appropriate English titles. The index, however, refers to critics only; there is no separate index to names "hidden" in the excerpts or to titles mentioned, except in the bibliography of each author's work, which presupposes knowledge of authorship.

Minor inconsistencies rather than full-blown errors detract from the book's general reliability. For example, the death of J. V. Foix in 1987 is accurately recorded, but that of Gerardo Diego, who died later that same year, is not. Also somewhat disconcerting is the lack of standard English titles; Benet's *Volverás a Región,* for example, is variously called *You Will Return to Region* and *Return to Region;* the latter is the official title of the 1985 translation.

The critical overview that *Modern Spanish and Portuguese Literature* synthesizes will find its most comfortable niche in an academic arena. The Board recommends this work for the core collection of academic libraries.

The Oxford Companion to Spanish Literature. Philip Ward, ed. Clarendon/Oxford, 1978. hard. 1 vol. 629 pp. ISBN 0-19-866114-2. $49.95. handbook.
PQ6006.O95 860.3

The Oxford Companion to Spanish Literature has the distinguished pedigree of the Oxford Companion series. The editor, Philip Ward, is a librarian and author of other works, though none as ambitious as this. This *Oxford Companion* covers authors, literary works, and movements from Roman times to 1977 from both peninsular Spain and Spanish America. The editor rightly claims equal treatment of all periods and genres. The definition of "author" in this work extends to critics, essayists, theologians, and philosophers; "Spanish" includes Basque, Catalan, and Galician. Selected non-Hispanic writers connected with Spanish themes are included, such as *Alain-René LeSage, W. H. Hudson, Henry Wadsworth Longfellow, Washington Irving,* and *George Ticknor.* A lack of references to political and historical events and characters as compared with other companions in the series is compensated for by the provision of more bibliographical information than can be found in the other companions.

All entries—works, authors, and movements—are in one sequence in English alphabetical order. Authors comprise over half of the listings. Length varies from the extreme of four pages (for *Lope de Vega*) to mere one-sentence descriptions (the entry for *Camino de perfección* says simply "the second novel in the trilogy *La vida fantástica* by Pio Baroja," repeating information more fully explained under both *Baroja* and *La vida fantástica*). Although the amount of information provided varies greatly from one entry to another, author entries generally consist of biographical, bibliographical, and critical elements, with varying degrees of emphasis. The utility of the volume would have been enhanced had bibliographical references been applied consistently and more fully to more entries.

Cross-references are either indicated in the alphabetical main listing or designated in the text with *q.v.;* for example, the referral to *García Lorca* from *Lorca* assists the novice who may be unfamiliar with Spanish patronymic protocol. The extensive network of cross-references ameliorates, but does not totally make up for, the lack of a general index; for example, the user is utterly unable to locate names of persons or works embedded within entries that are not separately cross-referenced.

Now over a decade old, this *Oxford Companion* is obviously deficient in current biographical and bibliographical data; for example, the treatment of *Camilo José Cela* does not reflect the renewed interest in Cela since he received the 1989 Nobel Prize. Incorrect birth dates (for *Julio Cortázar* and *Miguel de Unamuno,* for example) and relatively negligible bibliographical errors (Pérez Galdós's *La familiar de León Roch* was originally published in three volumes, not two) detract from an otherwise reliable source. In addition, the editor does not cite sources of individual articles that he claims to have verified, and he provides no information as to which of the several hundred consultants contributed what.

Despite its few shortcomings, *The Oxford Companion to Spanish Literature* is a well-respected one-volume handbook valuable for the wealth of bibliographical information collected in one source and for the references to classic studies provided. The handbook is one of the few reference books in this area that appeal to specialists and generalists alike. The Board recommends this work for the core collections of public, academic, and school libraries.

A Sourcebook for Hispanic Literature and Language: A Selected, Annotated Guide to Spanish, Spanish-American, and Chicano Bibliography, Literature, Linguistics, Journals, and Other Source Materials, 2d edition. Donald W. Bleznick, comp. Scarecrow, 1983. hard. 1 vol. 304 pp. indexes. ISBN 0-8108-1616-4. $27.50. bibliography.
Z2695.A2B55 016.86

See Latin American Literature.

Supplementary Titles

Brazil, Portugal and Other Portuguese-Speaking Lands: A List of Books Primarily in English. Francis M. Rogers and David T. Haberly. Harvard, 1968. soft. 1 vol. 75 pp. ISBN 0-674-08050-5. $1.95. bibliography.

Board's recommendation: Academic libraries.

Dictionary of Spanish Literature. Maxim Newmark. Greenwood, 1972. hard. 1 vol. 352 pp. ISBN 0-8371-5859-1. $35. dictionary.
PQ6006.W4 860.3

The *Dictionary of Spanish Literature* is "a reference book for students of Spanish and Spanish-American literature, containing biographies, chief works and critical evaluations of major writers, as well as articles on significant movements, schools and literary genres." (*Theat A,* August 1956, p. 10)

"The brevity of treatment necessary in a one-volume handbook such as this, . . . limits [its] reference use . . . to some extent. . . . But since there is no other dictionary of Spanish literature in English and since the compiler has consulted reputable sources, it brings together information on authors and titles not so readily available elsewhere in English. Because of this the *Dictionary of Spanish Literature* is recommended . . . as a convenient starting point for investigation in the field of Spanish and Spanish-American literature." (*BL & SBB,* June 15, 1957, p. 511)

Also reviewed in: *LJ,* May 1, 1956, p. 1190; *SR,* March 23, 1957, p. 30.

Board's recommendation: Public and academic libraries.

Origins of Spanish Romanticism: A Selective Annotated Bibliography. Margaret D. Jacobson. Society of Spanish and Spanish American Studies, 1985. soft. 1 vol. 93 pp. index. ISBN 0-89295-033-1. $25. bibliography.

Board's recommendation: Academic libraries.

Spanish Drama of the Golden Age. Jose M. Regueiro and A. G. Riechenberger. Hispanic Society of America, 1984. hard. 2 vols. 960 pp. illus. index. appendix. ISBN 0-87535-137-9. $85. handbook.
Z2694.D7R37 016.862′4

Board's recommendation: Academic libraries.

Spanish Literature, 1500–1700: A Bibliography of Golden Age Studies in Spanish and English, 1925–1980. William W. Moseley, Glenroy Emmons, and Marilyn C. Emmons, comps. Greenwood, 1984. hard. 1 vol. 765 pp. ISBN 0-313-21491-3. $79.95. bibliography.
PQ6063.M67 016.86

Spanish Literature, 1500–1700 "lists 11,181 unannotated items of secondary literature in English and Spanish. Citing books, dissertations, and articles, entries are arranged under the following headings: Festschriften, General, General Bibliography, Drama, Picaresque, Poetry, Prose, Romancero, and Individual Authors and Anonymous Works." (*BL,* August 1985, p. 1650)

"This is a nicely prepared work, virtually indispensable for collections serving advanced students and scholars in the field and highly recommended for undergraduate libraries that emphasize comprehensiveness and excellence in Hispanic studies." (*Choice,* April 1985, p. 1146)

Also reviewed in: *Hisp,* September 1985, p. 523; *Ref Bk R,* 1985, p. 21.

Board's recommendation: Academic libraries.

Women Writers of Spain: An Annotated Bio-Bibliographical Guide. Carolyn L. Galerstein and Kathleen McNerney, eds. Greenwood, 1986. hard. 1 vol. 410 pp. appendixes. index. ISBN 0-313-24965-2. $46.95. biobibliography.
Z2693.5.W6W65 016.86'09'9287

"Three-hundred authors are listed in alphabetical order [in *Women Writers of Spain*], and most have written poetry, fiction, and drama, though a few biographers, essayists, and journalists have been included if they treat literary subjects. Each entry provides a short biography followed by an alphabetical list of works. English annotations are provided for many of the works. . . . In addition to a title index, appendixes provide lists of authors by birthdate and language, and a selective list of translations in English, French, German, Italian, and Portuguese. . . .

"*Women Writers of Spain* . . . spans seven centuries, with thirty authors born before 1800, forty-two born in the nineteenth century, and more than two hundred born in the twentieth century." (*CRL,* July 1987, p. 351)

Also reviewed in: *ARBA,* 1987, p. 477; *Choice,* October 1986, p. 289; *R & R Bk N,* Summer 1986, p. 27.

Board's recommendation: Academic libraries.

New and Noteworthy

Biographical Dictionary of Hispanic Literature in the United States: The Literature of Puerto Ricans, Cuban Americans, and Other Hispanic Writers. Nicolas Kanellos, ed. Greenwood, 1989. hard. 1 vol. 374 pp. ISBN 0-313-24465-0. $49.95. biographical source.
PQ7420.2.K3 016.86'09

"[*Biographical Dictionary of Hispanic Literature in the United States*] provides an exhaustive reference guide to representative figures in Hispanic literature within the geographic, political, and cultural boundaries of the United States. [The book] is designed to make accessible to the English-language reader a literary world that has until now been articulated primarily in Spanish. Focusing mainly on Puerto Rican and Cuban writers, each entry summarizes the importance of the subject and indicates the literary genres and themes cultivated. There is a brief biography of each author, an analysis of major works and themes, and a survey of the criticism of the author's works.

"The first and most comprehensive volume on the subject, this extraordinarily detailed sourcebook is a compilation of bio-bibliographical essays on leading Hispanic novelists, poets, and dramatists, and includes secondary bibliographies for each entry as well as a general bibliography on Hispanic literature." (Excerpted from publisher's announcement)

Hispanic Writers. Bryan Ryan, ed. Gale, 1990. hard. 1 vol. approx. 500 pp. index. ISBN 0-8103-7688-1. $75. biographical source.

"[*Hispanic Writers* presents] . . . over four hundred of today's most significant Hispanic authors . . . [It] provides biographical sketches of influential literary, political, and scholarly authors from the U.S., Spain, Cuba, Puerto Rico, Mexico, and Spanish-speaking countries of South and Central America. Literary greats like Benito Perez Galdos, Ruben Dario, and Gabriel García Márquez are included, along with political figures such as Nicaraguan priest Ernesto Cardenal, former Costa Rican President Oscar Areas Sanchez, and Marxist revolutionary Che Guevara. . . . [The book] . . . provides informative biographies on the author's work and personal life including such details as: family background, address, honors, writings, works in progress, biographical/critical sources and more." (Excerpted from publisher's announcement)

Daniel Barkley *Michael Miranda*

Sports

Because a fascination with sports permeates all strata of our society, a tidal wave of information on the subject floods the librarian. Sports encyclopedias, biographical dictionaries, directories, rule books, and other compendiums appear with mounting numbers and seasonal regularity.

Some core publications chosen for inclusion here cover in detail several different sports topics—including baseball, football, and the Olympics—and others provide a good overview of a broad spectrum of sports. Together, these titles provide a solid collection of reference materials on the general topic of sports. Of course, no single publication is comprehensive, even when its coverage is focused on one specific sport. Because most sporting activities are team-oriented, requiring numerous individual participants, any work attempting to include every individual who participated in a given sport would require a large multivolume set, thereby probably exempting itself from a core collection on the basis of cost alone. Also, researchers attempting to document accurately those who played in the early days of sports such as baseball have had a great deal of difficulty verifying individual records and accomplishments because the methods used to record these statistics were not standardized.

Fortunately, today's modern researcher—as skilled as a detective and utilizing earlier compendiums as well as modern technology to compensate for earlier inaccuracies—has been increasingly able to cull statistical information from a variety of sources and arrange it into a logical, standardized format to allow for valid comparisons between past and present stars. Nonetheless, no work is complete, and *caveat emptor* is the rule when purchasing a title billed as such.

Each work has biases, of course, due either to the editor, compiler, or author; in some cases, certain criteria required for inclusion in a work were not met by an individual participant in a sport, and the criteria themselves represent a certain bias.

Ideally, the core reference collection will include a variety of resources covering all aspects of sports, from rulebooks to statistical compendiums. Encyclopedias and directories should comprise the main portion of a core collection as their coverage is the most broad. Such works provide basic explanations of each sport's rules, history, and development. They provide a useful service by addressing "nonmajor" sports—those that have not undergone the mixed blessing of professionalization. One such work voted by the Board to the core collection is now out of print. John Arlott's *Oxford Companion to World Sports and Games* (Oxford, 1975) describes sports from archery to yachting. A valuable selection for the sports collection is Alan Green's *Directory of Athletic Scholarships* (Facts On File, 1987).

Core Titles

	PUBLIC	ACADEMIC	SCHOOL
The Baseball Encyclopedia: The Complete and Official Record of Major League Baseball, 8th edition Wolff, Rick, ed. director. Macmillan, 1990	✦	✦	✦
Biographical Dictionary of American Sports: Baseball Porter, David L., ed. Greenwood, 1987	✦	✦	✦
The Complete Book of the Olympics Wallechinsky, David, ed. Viking-Penguin, 1988	✦	✦	✦
Encyclopedia of Physical Education, Fitness, and Sports, 4 vols. Cureton, Thomas K., Jr., ed. Brighton (vols. 1 and 2), Addison-Wesley (vol. 3), American Alliance for Health, Physical Education, Recreation, and Dance (vol. 4), 1977–1985		✦	
The Rule Book: The Authoritative, Up-to-Date, Illustrated Guide to the Regulations, History, and Object of All Major Sports The Diagram Group. St. Martin's, 1983	✦	✦	✦
The Sports Encyclopedia: Baseball, 1990 Neft, David S., and Richard M. Cohen. St. Martin's, 1990	✦		
The Sports Encyclopedia: Pro Basketball, 2d edition Neft, David S., and Richard M. Cohen. St. Martin's, 1989	✦		
The Sports Encyclopedia: Pro Football—The Modern Era, 1960–1990, 8th edition Neft, David S., and Richard M. Cohen. St. Martin's, 1990	✦		
Sports Rules Encyclopedia, 2d edition White, Jess R., ed. Leisure Pr., 1990	✦	✦	✦

Perhaps most patron interest focuses on player information; hence, the second most important part of a core collection should be statistical compendiums and biographical dictionaries. The former works provide important information on a player's achievements in his or her sport. Compendiums comparing and contrasting current and historical players are most important to today's research, and statistical works should include this information. Sterling's *Olympic Games: The Records* (Stan Greenberg, 1988) provided such a collection for the quadrennial showcase but is now out of print. Nevertheless, it is likely that this or another book will appear each time the Olympics approach—a good thing, since patrons will be looking for such a work. Also out of print is *The Official NFL Encyclopedia* (New American Library, 1988). Since football is also a popular topic, this work will no doubt be replaced shortly. Biographical dictionaries provide a more qualitative picture of performers' careers, often focusing on those who had a strong impact on the game or achieved star status. These works will also cover the behind-the-scene participants (developers, organizers, commissioners, journalists, and broadcasters) as well as players in defunct leagues.

Rulebooks, guides to game techniques and strategies, and other general miscellaneous publications round out the core collection. These important works offer the novice as well as the knowledgeable patron information necessary to understand and interpret the foundation of sports. *—D. B. and M. M.*

Core Titles

The Baseball Encyclopedia: The Complete and Official Record of Major League Baseball, 8th edition. Rick Wolff, ed. director. Macmillan, 1990. hard. 1 vol. 2,781 pp. appendixes. ISBN 0-02-579040-4. $49.95. encyclopedia.
GV877.B27 796.357′0973′021

While watching Nolan Ryan's first attempt to win his 300th victory (and thus achieve another milestone in a stellar career), many fans may have been curious as to his marks in other statistical categories in the major leagues and may have wondered how his accomplishments compare to other legends of the game. A copy of *The Baseball Encyclopedia* will surely satisfy their curiosity.

Pure and simple, *The Baseball Encyclopedia* is the authoritative compendium on baseball statistical information; no other work is more thorough, complete, or detailed.

This particular edition, the eighth, is a major revision of earlier editions, the first of which was published in 1969. Minor improvements have been made over the years, with categories being added in some cases and deleted in others when cost considerations were a factor, but the original intent—to provide the most comprehensive statistical compendium available on America's national pastime—has been honored. The new edition includes such additions as complete fielding statistics for all players and, significantly, lifetime records of 130 stars from the Negro Leagues.

Divided into 13 parts plus three appendixes, the encyclopedia begins with a detailed history of the development of the game and ends with the line scores and game highlights of each all-star game played since 1933. Chapters in between are devoted to award winners; tables of all-time leaders in batting, fielding, and pitching; teams and their players (1876–1987); home and road performance by teams; records of every manager, player, and pitcher who played in the major leagues; trades; records from the National Association Register (baseball's first professional league) and the Negro Leagues; and World Series and championship playoff line scores, highlights, and lifetime leaders.

Each chapter has been meticulously researched for accuracy, with no source left unturned. Considerable time was spent researching newspaper clippings; interviewing players, their relatives, and baseball historians; and poring through baseball official records not only to compile a complete historical statistical work but also to verify the accuracy of the statistics. Indeed, much publicity surrounded the book's release when it was revealed that careful checking of years of records had forced the editors to reduce the career hit total of Pittsburgh Pirate great Honus Wagner from 3,430 to 3,418. (Though the higher figure had been engraved on Wagner's bronze Hall of Fame plaque, the record had to change.) An exhaustive effort has been made to include anyone and everyone who has participated in the game, if only in a single appearance as a pinch-hitter or -runner.

The former guiding light of the encyclopedia—the late Joseph Reichler—was a well-known baseball historian who participated in this compilation from the first edition to the seventh. His successors seem to continue his tradition of scrupulous attention to detail.

The new edition employs a larger trim size that, despite the inclusion of even more statistics, keeps the text quite readable. Type size is legible, and certain typographic treatments enhance the users access to information; for instance, the highest total in the league in a given statistical category and a particular year is printed in boldface type. Thus, Babe Ruth's achievement stands out clearly: in one recorded stretch of 14 years, 12 of his home run totals are printed in boldface type.

This work is a must for any collection, large or small. The book is a classic, one around which a library of sports information should be built. *The Baseball Encyclopedia* is the baseball aficionado's summertime friend and wintertime consolation. The Board recommends this work for the core collections of public, academic, and school libraries. —*D. B.*

Biographical Dictionary of American Sports: Baseball. David L. Porter, ed. Greenwood, 1987. hard. 1 vol. 713 pp. appendixes. index. ISBN 0-313-23771-9. $75. biographical dictionary.
GV865.A1b55 796.357'092'2

The *Biographical Dictionary of American Sports* consists of four volumes that provide biographical coverage of more than 2,000 sports notables. This volume, published in 1987, covers baseball figures. Editor David L. Porter has compiled the volume with contributions from 100 noted baseball biographers, most belonging to the Society for American Baseball Research or the North American Society for Sport History. The biographers are primarily college and university professors who are authorities on baseball history. The remainder are drawn from other professions that cover baseball, such as publishers, editors, and journalists, as well as school teachers, librarians, and biographers who have earned reputations for compiling concise and accurate histories. Each biography is signed.

Over 500 alphabetically arranged entries comprise this volume. Each entry ranges from 200 to 900 words and cites the players's full name, date and place of birth, date and place of death (as applicable), parental background, formal education, wife and children if known, and major personal characteristics.

The entries contain a wealth of personal and statistical information on players, managers, commissioners, and others who have influenced the game. Using criteria for inclusion established by the editor, the reader can be assured of gaining insight into the best that baseball has produced since its inauguration as America's favorite pastime. No professional league has been excluded; therefore, black players from the Negro Leagues receive adequate treatment. Each entry also contains a list of additional biographical sources. Citations include articles appearing in periodicals such as the *Sporting News* or *Sport Magazine,* biographies, and other scholarly and general reading publications.

To supplement the alphabetical arrangement, entries are arranged into six appendixes: main category (player, pitcher, and so on), main position played, place of birth, Negro League players covered, dates of formation of Major and Negro Leagues, and players elected to the National Baseball Hall of Fame. The book is well indexed and contains a list of contributors. The book is hardcover and is produced on permanent paper.

The one minor criticism that can be made of the *Biographical Dictionary of American Sports: Baseball* concerns the biographical information. As objective as a biographer might wish to be, personal biases are difficult to exclude. The entry on Steve Garvey, for example, contains opinions of his personal character ("Garvey is a handsome, stalwart player considered to be as upright in character as in batting stance") that would best be omitted. Likewise, unnecessary attempts are made to explain why "Shoeless" Joe Jackson participated in the 1919 World Series scandal and what contributed to Ty Cobb's irascible personality and drive to win.

The information is current through 1987; therefore, new stars such as Will Clark and Roger Clemens are not covered. Their absence is not much of a drawback, however, because the aim of the work is to provide information on players who have made an impact on the game through their achievements over a number of years.

The *Biographical Dictionary of American Sports: Baseball* is an outstanding, authoritative reference work despite these minor flaws. The Board recommends this work for the core collections of public, academic, and school libraries. —*D. B.*

The Complete Book of the Olympics. David Wallechinsky, ed. Viking—Penguin, 1988. soft. 1 vol. 768 pp. illus. ISBN 0-14-010771-1. $12.95. handbook. GV721.5.W25 796.4'8

The Complete Book of the Olympics, compiled by David Wallechinsky, is a comprehensive collection of the events, records, and results of the Olympics from 1896 through the 1984 games. Regrettably, the volume does not include the 1988 games. While that staple of reference rooms everywhere, the almanac, will provide the names of winners of each event in 1988, as will *The World of Winners* (Gita Siegman, ed., Gale, 1989), an updating of *The Complete Book of the Olympics* to include the 1988 games is nevertheless desirable.

The book opens with an extensive introduction providing a listing of the locations and dates of the winter and summer games and a medal count for each of the games. A "Brief History of the Modern Olympics" follows and is basically a recap of significant events surrounding the games themselves. Next is an "Issues" section, which consists of short essays on Olympic politics and amateurism. While these essays are interesting, they have not aged particularly well.

Few sports fans will purchase or borrow this work for the essays, however. Virtually the entire book is a summary of the various events contested in each of the Olympic games, including the competitors, results, winners, and losers. As could be expected, the majority of this summarizing is devoted to the summer games, which have both a longer history and a greater number of events. Each of the 238 Olympic events is represented, providing the name, country, and score or time for the major finishers in each. There is also a brief narrative that summarizes the results, mentions any controversies or noteworthy circumstances, and recounts the contest itself. Page after page, sports from synchronized swimming to boxing to race walking are described. Also included are discontinued events (such as the standing long jump in track and field) and discontinued sports (such as lacrosse). The same detailed accounting is provided for the cold-weather sports that make up the winter games.

The book is easy to read and easy to use. Scattered throughout are a variety of photographs showing the great athletes and important moments of the games.

Being brought up to date to include the Seoul and Calgary games of 1988 would restore *The Complete Book of the Olympic*'s status as a landmark work. Even without such revision, the title remains valuable as a retrospective work. The Board recommends the work for the core collections of public, academic, and school libraries. —*M. M.*

Encyclopedia of Physical Education, Fitness, and Sports. Thomas K. Cureton, Jr., ed. Brighton (vols. 1 and 2); Addison-Wesley (vol. 3); American Alliance for Health, Physical Education, Recreation, and Dance (vol. 4); 1977–1985. hard. 4 vols. ISBN 0-89832-017-8 (vol. 1). $49.95 per vol. encyclopedia. GV567.E49 796.03

Published over the course of eight years, the four-volume *Encyclopedia of Physical Education, Fitness, and Sports* is a comprehensive, scholarly work that provides depth and structure to an often diffuse field. Each volume is dedicated to a particular aspect of the discipline: volume 1 is entitled *Philosophy, Programs, and History;* volume 2, *Training, Environment, Nutrition, and Fitness;* volume 3, *Sports, Dance, and Related Activities;* and volume 4, *Human Performance: Efficiency and Improvements in Sports, Exercise, and Fitness.* (Curiously, volume 3 was published first, in 1977, followed by volume 2 in 1980, volume 1 in 1981, and volume 4 in 1985.) The encyclopedia's editor is Dr. Thomas K. Cureton, Jr., a respected and prolific scholar in the field of physical education. The project was sponsored by the American Alliance for Health, Physical Education, Recreation, and Dance, the premier professional organization for physical educators. All of the entries are signed by the authors, who are generally professionals and scholars in areas related to their contributions. A biographical appendix to each volume provides the credentials for each of the contributors. Each section of the encyclopedia has an editor, whose credentials are presented at the beginning of that section.

As may be expected in a work that employs over 100 contributors (either authors of articles, or section editors), there is considerable variation in style and content, even within a single volume. With its volumes arranged by broad topic, this encyclopedia is very much like four separate, complementary works. Volume 1 attempts to "identify the scope and breadth of physical education in the United States" (preface) and accomplishes this rather ambitious task reasonably well, with a clear emphasis on physical education as opposed to sports. The topics are covered in a considered, scholarly manner; in fact, several entries are articles reprinted from scholarly journals. In addition to entries covering the history and philosophy of physical education in the United States, there are interesting discussions comparing sports in the United States to sports in Europe, a section on physical education for the handicapped, and a descriptive list of 29 physical education organizations. The articles in this volume have held up well through the years.

Volume 2, on training, the environment, nutrition, and fitness, was published in 1980. As in the previous volume, a number of the entries are previously published articles, which unfortunately dates this work. This volume is much more technical in subject matter than volume 1, and the authors assume considerable knowledge on the part of the readers. Articles generally provide solid background to the field, though at an advanced level.

Volume 3, the oldest of the series, covers individual sports, dance, and other movement-related activities. The major portion of the volume consists of detailed, alphabetically arranged descriptions of the nature of play, rules, and tactics of 47 sports. These include the major sports (baseball and basketball), some popular minor sports (handball and lacrosse), and some truly obscure sports (flickerball, gatorball, and quoits). In some cases the detail provided can be overwhelming, and the language used to describe simple actions can be a bit overblown. For example, in the basketball section *dribbling* is defined as "a skill in which a player gives impetus to the ball one or more times causing it to rebound from the floor . . . moving the ball to various locations on the court." Would not "bouncing the ball while walking or running" have sufficed? As in the other volumes, a number of the articles are reprints. The articles presented provide a thorough overview of significant sports. The section on dance is brief but informative. It explains the rationale for including dance in a work on physical education and provides a solid background for those interested in movement beautified. The final section of this volume is an introduction to such recreational activities as fishing, backpacking, and surfing and to athletics that for the purposes of the editors were not classed as sports (judo, karate, cycling).

Volume 4, the most recent of the set, aims to emphasize "the improvements which accrue as the result of consistent participation" in the various sports and activities described in the previous volumes. This volume is the most technically challenging and academically rigorous of the encyclopedia. As in the previous volumes, a number of the articles are reprints from scholarly journals; in fact, this volume is more like the annals of a physical education association than it is like an encyclopedia. The articles are of a consistently high quality, but the intense analysis of specific topics ("The Second Knee-bend in Olympic Weightlifting" or "A Biomechanical Analysis of Beamon, Williams, and an Average College Jumper," for example) is not what one expects to find in an encyclopedia. Still, the majority of articles are suited for encyclopedic research.

In all, the *Encyclopedia of Physical Education, Fitness, and Sports* is a valuable, impressive accomplishment. The Board recommends this work for the core collection of academic libraries. —*M. M.*

The Rule Book: The Authoritative, Up-to-Date, Illus-

trated Guide to the Regulations, History, and Object of All Major Sports. The Diagram Group. St. Martin's, 1983. soft. 1 vol. 431 pp. illus. ISBN 0-312-69576-4. $9.95. rulebook.
GV731.R75 796

In a single volume, *The Rule Book* provides the reader with an easily accessible and up-to-date reference to the rules and regulations of major sports. Although primarily concerned with Olympic sports and events, *The Rule Book* also provides coverage of more than 50 major world sports, from *archery* to *yacht racing.* This broad coverage provides an international flavor and gives the reader a view of competition in events that are not American in origin.

The entries are arranged alphabetically by major sport rather than by common name. Thus, one would find the entry on *rugby* under the general heading of "Football (Rugby League)." Each entry includes a brief developmental history and synopsis of the sport, the playing area and necessary equipment, the minimum and maximum number of allowed players, the number of officials, the duration of the event, scoring, starting and playing procedures, and major fouls and penalties. All of this information has been compiled through the cooperation of the various national and international sport governing bodies.

One of the most striking features of this compilation is the inclusion of over 5,000 illustrations. The illustrations provide in good detail the dimensions of the playing surfaces and the array and sizes of equipment needed to participate in the various sports. Most important, the illustrations demonstrate the proper techniques used in performing each sport.

There are several criticisms to offer about this work. One concerns the currency of material. *The Rule Book* was published in 1983 to ensure that new 1984 Olympic events, such as baseball, would be covered. Since its publication, however, rules and regulations have changed, particularly in amateur basketball. This fact somewhat limits the usefulness of the work.

Another criticism concerns the book's coverage of rules and regulations. Although major rules, regulations, violations, and penalties are covered, these are offered as an overview and should not be considered authoritative or definitive, as the title may lead one to believe.

Despite these limitations, *The Rule Book* is certainly a worthwhile addition to the general sports section of any library. What makes this publication most valuable for a reference collection in an American library is the coverage of sports that are unfamiliar to most Americans. Most knowledgeable sport enthusiasts can overlook the flaws of *The Rule Book,* and the novice will certainly find this work useful as an introduction to unfamiliar international sporting events. The Board recommends this work for the core collections of public, academic, and school libraries. *—D. B.*

The Sports Encyclopedia: Baseball, 1990 David S. Neft and Richard M. Cohen. St. Martin's, 1990. soft. 1 vol. 656 pp. ISBN 0-312-03938-7. $17.95. encyclopedia.
GV877.S78 796.357

The Sports Encyclopedia: Pro Basketball, 2d edition. David S. Neft and Richard M. Cohen. St. Martin's, 1989. soft. 1 vol. 592 pp. ISBN 0-312-03432-6. $16.95. encyclopedia.
GV885.5.N44 796.323'64'0973

The Sports Encyclopedia: Pro Football—The Modern Era, 1960–1990, 8th edition. David S. Neft and Richard M. Cohen. St. Martin's, 1990. soft. 1 vol. 688 pp. ISBN 0-312-04429-1. $17.95. encyclopedia.
GV955.N43 796.332'0973'021

The Sports Encyclopedia is a largely statistical compendium on the sports covered within the series. The *Baseball* and *Pro Football—The Modern Era* volumes are updated annually. Neft and Cohen, prolific compilers of statistics, have, with this series, provided the means by which to "go look it up," their stated intention in the preface. The authors have taken pains to work with the most authoritative figures and institutions in compiling these volumes. By drawing on the resources of the baseball and football halls of fame, the Society for Baseball Research (SABR), *Pro Football Weekly,* and the Elias Sports Bureau, among others, the authors have ensured an admirable level of consistency and accuracy.

Each work in the series follows the same basic format. The volumes are arranged in a series of logical divisions (generally by decade), which place the statistics in a context. An introductory essay establishes the significance of the period and the major changes or events that had an effect on the games. Complete statistics for teams and individuals follow, along with brief narratives on each team's performance for each year. These narratives, and those that recount postseason action, are well-written, frequently wry commentaries that add life to the statistics that are the backbone of the series. And statistics abound in this series. There are season and career numbers for each individual and season statistics for each team. Season and career leaders in the many statistical categories are identified. A comprehensive roster of all players to reach the major league level is included, with their career statistics. There are also special sections on the Hall of Famers in each sport, rules changes, team and individual award winners, and so on.

Keeping these figures up to date is, of course, quite a challenge. It also can get to be rather expensive as each year an entirely new volume is published to revise the figures based on the previous year's performances. However, given the immense popularity of both baseball and football, the updates are worthwhile. Possibly at some point the current volumes on football and baseball will have to spin off the most recent year's figures into a separate volume, if for no other reason than to cut down on the size of the volumes.

In all, *The Sports Encyclopedia* series is a thorough, comprehensive record of the sports covered. The Board recommends these works for the core collection of public libraries. —*M. M.*

Sports Rules Encyclopedia, 2d edition. Jess R. White, ed. Leisure Pr., 1990. hard. 1 vol. 732 pp. appendixes. ISBN 0-88011-363-4. $42. encyclopedia.
GV731.S75 796

The second edition of the *Sports Rules Encyclopedia* should be a welcome addition to the shelves of any library. Jess R. White, professor of physical education at Arkansas State University, has compiled an accurate, easy-to-use guide to the rules of 51 major sports, from *archery* to *wrestling.* The second edition expands considerably on the first, which was published in 1961. The new edition is published by Leisure Press, one of the more active publishers in the field of sports.

Each of the alphabetically arranged entries follows a standard format. The rules for the particular sport are given, followed by the name, the address, and, in some instances, a brief description of the governing body of the sport. Occasionally, if there is more than one recognized governing body, others will be listed. Finally, the names of the top two magazines that cover the sport are provided, including the name and address of the publisher.

The rules for a sport that are published in the encyclopedia are, whenever possible, the official rules as published by the sport's governing body. When exact reproduction is not possible, due to the length or complexity of the rules or to situations in which different levels of competition operate under varying rules, the editor has summarized the rules to present the most common elements. Rules presented directly from the governing board, however, have not been edited, and in all cases the work clearly states whether or not the rules have been summarized. Each entry includes illustrations or diagrams where appropriate. These illustrations are uniformly clear and well labeled.

Generally, the rules are presented in a straightforward manner. However, because the majority of the entries are the actual texts of rules written by the committee of a governing body, they tend to read like the quasi-legal documents that they are. A common impression is that arguments or questions can be immediately resolved by looking up a rule. This is not the case, however; virtually all sports rules must be interpreted before they can be applied to a particular set of circumstances. Interpretation is further complicated by the variations mentioned earlier in the application of rules to sports governed by a variety of boards. In most cases the rules included in this volume are those of the amateur governing body. It is important for the users of this volume, or any compilation of rules, to be aware that this variability exists. The editor has taken note of the situation and clearly states whose rules are being provided. Further, in those sports with a number of competing boards, addresses are given for all.

The inclusion of major magazines that cover each sport is an interesting—albeit somewhat arbitrary—attempt to provide access to further information on the field. Two appendixes round out the volume. The first is an alphabetic listing of 32 organizations devoted to promoting sports for people with handicaps. Names and addresses of the organizations are provided. The second supplies the names and addresses of governing bodies for 22 sports not covered in the encyclopedia.

Since it would be impractical for any library to acquire the official rules of this number of sports from the individual governing boards, the *Sports Rules Encyclopedia* is an excellent purchase. The Board recommends this work for the core collections of public, academic, and school libraries. —*M. M.*

Supplementary Titles

The Bill James Historical Baseball Abstract. Bill James. Villard Bks., 1985. hard. 1 vol. 721 pp. illus. index. ISBN 0-394-53713-0. $29.95. encyclopedia.
GV863.A1J36 796.357

"[*The Bill James Historical Baseball Abstract*] is divided into three parts. The first surveys various aspects of the game, decade by decade, from the 1870's through the 1970's. The second is devoted to the relative merits of the game's best players: Who are the 100 greatest players of all time? Is George Brett a better third baseman than Pie Traynor? How do Mickey Mantle and Willie Mays compare? The third part contains extensive data on many of the game's most famous players, past and present." (*NYTBR,* December 8, 1985, p. 20)

"By virtue of his annual reports, James has acquired a well-deserved reputation as the game's premier statistical analyst, and this work will only enhance that reputation. The book is essential reading for any fan, primarily because James goes beyond his usual number crunching to give us anecdotal, historical, and trivial glimpses at the way the game has been played since its inception. Perhaps of most interest are his rankings of players by position and his assigning of peak year and career values." (*LJ,* January 1986, p. 72)

Also reviewed in: *B Rpt,* November 1988, p. 53; *BW,* April 17, 1988, p. 12; *LATBR,* May 8, 1988, p. 14; *MQR,* Spring 1989, p. 283; *NYTBR,* May 4, 1986, p. 41; *SLJ,* August 1988, p. 117; *Time,* June 9, 1986, p. 70; *VOYA,* December 1988, p. 251.

Board's recommendation: Public libraries.

Dictionary of Sports Quotations. Barry Liddle, ed. Routledge & Kegan Paul, 1987. hard. 1 vol. 210 pp. indexes. ISBN 0-7102-0785-9. $24.95. dictionary.
GV706.8.D53 796

"The *Dictionary of Sports Quotations* attempts to 'select quotations for their bearing on the human condition, for their profundity and for the way in which they provide a balanced insight into individual sports and related issues' (pref.). Done primarily from the British perspective, the volume tries to include quotations from the sports literature in all sports as well as quotations on related topics such as Fitness/Health, Journalism/Television, and Winning. The arrangement is by sport and then alphabetically by author. If more than one quote is chosen from a particular author, the quotes are arranged alphabetically according to the source of the quote and then by date.

"The subject index is arranged by keyword and within each subject the entries are alphabetical by sport/topic. A similar arrangement is used in the author index. Because there are no cross-references (i.e., 'Real Tennis see Lawn Tennis' or 'Tennis see Lawn Tennis'), it is necessary to scan the complete 'List of Sports and Topics' to find some entries (e.g., bowling is under 'Bowls' and 'Tenpin Bowling')." (*CRL,* July 1988, p. 348)

This volume comprises "ninety-plus sections, some devoted to particular sports (angling, cricket, parachuting, surfing), others devoted to general topics (fitness, law, politics, women). Within each section quotations are arranged by their speakers' surnames; sources are cited adequately. Unusual for a specialized quotation dictionary but praiseworthy as an example, the *Dictionary of Sports Quotations* includes both keyword and author indexes." (*WLB,* November 1987, p. 89)

Also reviewed in: *ARBA,* 1988, p. 314; *LJ,* August 1987, p. 137; *LR,* 1988, p. 63; *R & R Bk N,* Fall 1987, p. 12.

Board's recommendation: Public libraries.

Sports Quotations: Maxims, Quips and Pronouncements for Writers and Fans. Andrew J. Maikovich. McFarland, 1984. soft. 1 vol. 168 pp. indexes. ISBN 0-89950-100-1. $18.95. bibliography.
GV706.8.M34 796.0321

Sports Quotations "is an excellent volume. . . . The 1,782 quotes are broken down into 23 sport categories, including brief but interesting sections on less prominent sports such as chess, crew, and mountain climbing. A name index provides easy access to the utterers of the quotes, and a useful subject index is also provided. . . . The volume exhibits an enjoyable balance between contemporary and older quotes, famous and obscure quotes, and quotes from individuals within and outside of sports. All in all, a fun volume that should prove useful in libraries at all levels where an interest in sports exists." (*Choice,* November 1984, p. 404)

" 'You can't win them all,' said Connie Mack, Philadelphia A's manager, after his team lost 117 games in one season. That is the brand of sardonic, pithy humor that shows up often in this first-ever compendium of aphorisms and sayings from the . . . sports world. The sayings in this small book, when read as philosophy, will quickly place sports in its correct niche in the relative scheme of things.

"The arrangement is by major category . . . Within a category, quotations have been ordered alphabetically as an aid in finding when the first word is known. Largest categories belong to football and baseball, while bridge, chess, crew, rodeo, and yachting are among the lesser-known sports and games. For writers and broadcasters, the name index and subject index provide a means to find the *bon mot* needed to enliven a story. Offering 1,782 quotes, with brief notes on utterer and context, the book will be of use to the librarian . . . when the quotation that is wanted does not quite measure up to *Bartlett's* standards, where baseball and other games are mentioned incidentally, if at all." (*ARBA,* 1985, p. 249)

Also reviewed in: *SLJ,* May 1985, p. 38.

Board's recommendation: Public and school libraries.

rare exceptions a photograph of the player accompanies his report." (*BL,* February 15, 1990, p. 1188)

New and Noteworthy

American Women in Sport, 1887–1987: A 100-Year Chronology. Ruth M. Sparhawk et al. Scarecrow, 1989. hard. 1 vol. 149 pp. illus. ISBN 0-8108-2205-9. $20. history.
GV583.A64 796.0194

"[*American Women in Sport, 1887–1987*] was compiled by a number of people concerned about the difficulty of locating information on American women athletes. . . . The chronology is divided into four chapters: 'The Pre-Organizational Era, 1887–1916,' 'The Organizational Years, 1917–1956,' 'The Competitive Period, 1957–1971,' and 'The Title IX Era, 1972–1987.' The year-by-year arrangement recognizes individuals and their accomplishments. . . . Since the work is a chronology, its lists provide only a minimum of explanation. However, by using the indexes one can trace an athlete's career, place her accomplishments in a historical framework, or trace the history of women in sports." (*BL,* January 1, 1990, p. 940)

Hockey Scouting Report. Michael A. Berger and Jiggs McDonald. Summerhill Pr., 1989. soft. 1 vol. 472 pp. illus. index. ISBN 0-920197-89-2. $9.95. encyclopedia.
796.96′26

"[*Hockey Scouting Report* provides] . . . each player's vital statistics, career statistics, and 1988–89 statistics. . . . [It also provides] an excellent narrative about each player's ability. . . . [The] narrative is divided into three sections: 'The Finesse Game,' 'The Physical Game,' and 'The Intangibles.' . . . With very rare exceptions a photograph of the player accompanies his report." (*BL,* February 15, 1990, p. 1188)

The Official NBA Basketball Encyclopedia: The Complete History and Statistics of Professional Basketball. Zander Hollander and Alex Sachare, eds. Random/Villard Bks. 1989. hard. 766 pp. illus. index. ISBN 0-394-58-039-7. $29.95. encyclopedia.
GV885.7.044 796.323′64

"[*The Official NBA Basketball Encyclopedia*] traces the sport's history 'from the early years of barnstorming teams who played their games in dance halls to the modern era of internationally known superstars who play in luxurious arenas.' The years before the NBA was formed are described in two short chapters followed by a 140-page history of the NBA through the 1988–89 season. . . . Almost half the book consists of an 'All-Time Player Directory' of more than 2,600 players including nickname, birth date, height, weight, college, season(s) and team(s), complete statistics in several categories for each season, and statistics for playoffs and all-star games." (*BL,* March 1, 1990, pp. 1386–1387)

Timetables of Sports History: Basketball. William S. Jarrett. Facts On File, 1990. hard. 1 vol. 96 pp. illus. index. ISBN 0-8160-1920-7. $17.95. history.
GV885.1.J37 796.323′0973

"[*Timetables of Sports History*] . . . presents the highlights of college and professional basketball from 1891 through the 1988–89 season. . . . [In the book the] . . . narrative highlights are fun to read and reveal rule changes, unusual facts and firsts, and outstanding performances." (*BL,* December 15, 1989, p. 859)

Phillip A. Smith

Theater

Theater involves not only plays and playwrights but also every aspect of the live performances of plays. When assembling a core reference collection on theater the librarian must include a variety of sources that can provide information on such aspects as actors, performance data for a given play, and plays available for high school or amateur productions. A patron should be able to locate the name of the actor who first played Willy Loman in *Death of a Salesman* on Broadway or be able find a definition of *arena staging.* Information on the Steppenwolf Theatre Company or the plays of Eugene Ionesco should be readily available.

For library users who are engaged in complex research on a theater topic, as well as those who occasionally want brief factual information on an actor or a play, there are ample reference sources available to satisfy most needs.

Of the many dictionaries reviewed, THE OXFORD COMPANION TO THE THEATRE is the most highly regarded for compactness and general utility. The MCGRAW-HILL ENCYCLOPEDIA OF WORLD DRAMA excels at providing information on plays and playwrights, and AN INTERNATIONAL DICTIONARY OF THEATRE LANGUAGE offers an in-depth approach to theater terminology. Specialized dictionaries of genres and ethnic contributions are represented by the supplementary work, the DICTIONARY OF THE BLACK THEATRE. *The Encyclopedia of the American Theater* was also chosen by the Board as a supplementary title, but has since gone out of print. Librarians may wish to obtain this work through an out-of-print book dealer.

Sources for locating playscripts include the essential *Play Index,* as well as *The Drama Scholars' Index to Plays and Filmscripts* and *Musicals! A Directory of Musical Properties Available for Production.* Reviews of performances can be found by consulting sets of reprinted reviews, such as the NEW YORK TIMES THEATER REVIEWS, or by tracking down citations indexed in sources such as A GUIDE TO CRITICAL REVIEWS. Biographical handbooks include the series *Who's Who in the Theatre,* which is, unfortunately, also out of print. The annual THEATRE WORLD provides an illustrated overview of the American professional theater scene. Some librarians may also wish to include the *National Playwright's Directory* and *Recorded Plays: Indexes to Dramatists, Plays, and Actors* in their theater reference collections. Jill Charles's *Dictionary of Theater Training Programs,* second edition (Theatre Directories, 1989), is another useful directory.

Since the term *theater* can refer both to the theatrical performance and to the dramatic text that serves as the basis for the performance, there are other sources of value for research on dramatic literature, such as CONTEMPORARY AUTHORS (see American

Core Titles

	PUBLIC	ACADEMIC	SCHOOL
The Concise Oxford Companion to American Theatre Bordman, Gerald. Oxford, 1987	✦		
The Concise Oxford Companion to the Theatre Hartnoll, Phyllis, ed. Oxford, 1986	✦		
Drury's Guide to Best Plays, 4th edition Salem, James M., comp. Scarecrow, 1987	✦	✦	✦
A Guide to Critical Reviews, 3d edition, 4 vols. Salem, James M. Scarecrow, 1979–		✦	
An International Dictionary of Theatre Language Trapido, Joel, gen. ed. Greenwood, 1985		✦	
McGraw-Hill Encyclopedia of World Drama: An International Reference Work in 5 Volumes, 2d edition, 5 vols. Hochman, Stanley, ed. in chief. McGraw-Hill, 1984	✦	✦	✦
The Oxford Companion to American Theatre Bordman, Gerald. Oxford, 1984	✦	✦	✦
The Oxford Companion to the Theatre, 4th edition Hartnoll, Phyllis, ed. Oxford, 1983	✦	✦	✦
Theatre World Willis, John. Crown, annual	✦		

Literature; Biography) and the MLA INTERNATIONAL BIBLIOGRAPHY OF BOOKS & ARTICLES ON THE MODERN LANGUAGES AND LITERATURES (see World Literature).

Core Titles

The Concise Oxford Companion to American Theatre. Gerald Bordman. Oxford, 1987. hard. 1 vol. 451 pp. ISBN 0-19-505121-1. $24.95. dictionary.
PN2220.B6 792.0973

An abridgement of Gerald Bordman's THE OXFORD COMPANION TO AMERICAN THEATRE, with some new material added, *The Concise Oxford Companion to American Theatre* contains entries for actors, directors, set designers, playwrights, individual theaters, theater companies, and a wide range of American plays and musicals. The work is both a valuable guide to theatrical production in the United States and a reliable handbook of American drama.

The condensation has been achieved by several means: cutting entries on lesser-known individuals and plays; eliminating topical articles, such as those on ethnic contributions to American theater; excising most entries on foreign playwrights (although *Shakespeare* and *Shaw* are still included); and reducing the ample typefaces and margins of the original. Although the preface indicates that about 40 percent of the text has been cut, the entries that remain have generally been left intact, and the choices for omission seem judicious. For example, the minor 1929 Maxwell Anderson drama *Gypsy* has been eliminated, but the 1959 musical *Gypsy* has been retained. The biographical sketch of contemporary playwright *Lanford Wilson* is included, but that of Harry Leon Wilson, a minor early-twentieth-century dramatist, has been omitted.

The new material consists of entries for "some important figures and organizations of contemporary significance" (preface), such as the avant-garde ensemble *Mabou Mines* and the founder of the Open Theatre, actor-director *Joseph Chaikin.* Some updating is also evident in a few of the entries, such as those for *David Mamet* and *Stephen Sondheim.*

Considering that the price of *The Concise Oxford Companion to American Theatre* is about half that of the original, the shorter version will be of interest to individuals for their home libraries and should be considered for purchase by public libraries, especially branches. (Libraries that need fuller coverage of American theater and drama will probably opt for the original.) The Board recommends this work for the core collection of public libraries.

The Concise Oxford Companion to the Theatre. Phyllis Hartnoll, ed. Oxford, 1986. soft. 1 vol. 640 pp. appendix. ISBN 0-19-281102-9. $10.95. dictionary.
PN2035.C63 792.03

This concise version of the renowned OXFORD COMPANION TO THE THEATRE is based on the text of the 1967 third edition of that work. Although *The Concise Oxford Companion to the Theatre* does not cover the many significant developments in world theater that have taken place over the last two decades, the dictionary remains a dependable, well-written guide for the theatergoer and a handy source for the reference librarian.

Like the parent work, *The Concise Oxford Companion to the Theatre* includes data on actors, playwrights, directors, set designers, theater companies and spaces, and genres. Surveys of national theater history for various countries have been omitted in this abridgment, and the amount of information on technical theater has been reduced. Other entries have either been dropped or shortened, and the illustrations have been eliminated. At the same time, some material not present in the first three editions of the larger work has been added. As the editor notes in the preface, "the scaffolding of the original work has been retained; only the ornamentation has been removed, a streamlining which should appeal particularly to those whose need is for easily accessible information rather than academic discussion."

Other features that made the original outstanding and that remain in the *Concise Companion* are the clarity and readability of the entries, as edited by Phyllis Hartnoll from contributions made by a panel of 50; the extensive cross-references to preferred terms, as well as to information in related entries; and "A Guide to Further Reading on Drama and the Theatre," a useful, albeit dated, list of English-language books.

The fresher and more complete content of the fourth edition of THE OXFORD COMPANION TO THE THEATRE will make that work the dictionary of choice for most libraries. However, cost-conscious public libraries (and theater lovers) will find *The Concise Oxford Companion to the Theatre* to be a reasonable, high-quality substitute. The Board recommends this work for the core collection of public libraries.

Drury's Guide to Best Plays, 4th edition. James M. Salem, comp. Scarecrow, 1987. hard. 1 vol. 488 pp. indexes. ISBN 0-8108-1980-5. $35. bibliography.
Z5781.D8 016.8

The fourth edition of *Drury's Guide to Best Plays* gives essential bibliographic data, information of interest to theatrical groups, and plot summaries for approximately 1,500 nonmusical, full-length plays written in (or translated into) English. This bibliographical work covers all periods of world drama, from the plays of ancient Greece to the works of contemporary American dramatists. "Best" plays in the title refers not only to established classics (by Sophocles, Shakespeare, O'Neill, and so forth) and Pulitzer and other prize-winning plays but also to commercial successes, to plays popular with amateur groups, and to those most frequently produced by high schools affiliated with the International Thespian Society.

Originally conceived by librarian Francis K. W. Drury and first published in 1953, the subsequent editions of *Drury's Guide* have been compiled by James M. Salem, who is also responsible for the multivolume set A GUIDE TO CRITICAL REVIEWS.

The plays are listed under the names of the playwrights, alphabetically arranged from *Rick Abbot* to *Stefan Zweig.* Each entry includes the date written; the translator's name (for foreign plays); inclusion in the Best Plays series, where applicable; the script publisher (or appearance in anthologies, if not currently available from a standard script source such as Samuel French); a one-paragraph plot synopsis; the number of acts; the cast composition; an indication of set requirements (for example, one interior, one exterior); and royalty terms, as indicated in 1986 editions of play publishers' catalogs.

The synopses are serviceable, if not particularly well written. In general they give enough plot detail to indicate the basic content of the play, but they often oversimplify the play's action and themes. The descriptions are sometimes inconsistent. Although normally uncritical, some contain evaluative comments, such as "a powerful and often brutal play" in the entry for John Osborne's *Look Back in Anger.* Oddly, except for these occasional comments, there is little effort to indicate whether the play is serious or comic, or for what type of audience it is intended. For example, the brief summary of Mary Chase's *Harvey* might tip off the reader that it is a comedy by the description of the lead character as an "amiable bibulous hero," but the synopsis for Shelagh Delaney's *A Taste of Honey,* although indicating adult themes, gives no clue that is a very funny slice-of-life drama. The entry for David Mamet's *American Buffalo* notes that the dialogue contains "shocking language to many," but there is no mention of equally coarse (or coarser) language in the entry for the same playwright's *Glengarry Glen Ross.*

The volume concludes with various indexes and lists. The indexes of cast composition and selected subjects are helpful. The cast index lists plays by number of characters and includes separate listings for all-male and all-female casts. Subject categories of plays include biographical (by name of individual), the black experience, courtroom, fantasy, and marriage, among others. There are lists of prize-winning plays and popular plays for high school and amateur productions. A title index for the play description section is also included.

Although the summaries of the plays leave something to be desired, *Drury's Guide to Best Plays* is useful for supplying basic information on the plays covered and for aiding groups seeking plays to produce. In this last regard, it is best used in conjunction with *Play Index,* with which it shares some common features. Most libraries that provide information on plays will want to have *Drury's Guide* on their reference shelves. The Board recommends this work for the core collections of public, academic, and school libraries.

A Guide to Critical Reviews, 3d edition. James M. Salem. Scarecrow, 1979– . hard. 4 vols. appendixes. indexes. ISBN 0-8108-0367-4 (vol. 4). $69.50 (vol. 4). handbook.
Z5781.S16 016.809′2

The major value of James M. Salem's *A Guide to Critical Reviews* is convenience. The various parts of this set identify reviews of American productions published over a period of 70 years. The reviews cited are from general-interest magazines such as *Time, Newsweek,* and *The New Republic,* or newspapers like the *New York Times,* all of which will be easily found in many libraries; or from theater periodicals such as *Theatre Arts,* which may be available in academic or larger public libraries.

The most current composition of parts consists of volumes published in the second and third editions. The individual parts reviewed here are part 1, *American Drama, 1909–1982* (third edition), and part 3, *Foreign Drama, 1909–1977* (second edition). Because part 4, *The Screenplay,* was not completed by the publication date of this buying guide, it is not reviewed. Part 2, which covers musicals, is currently out of print.

American Drama, 1909–1982 is arranged by playwright, then by play title. For each play, a brief production history is provided, followed by a list of review citations, indicating periodical or newspaper title, volume, pages, and date. If a play has been revived, reviews are cited for the revival, and the production history reflects information on the revival(s). Appendixes include: "About the Dramatists," which shows the birthplace and birth dates and death dates (if appropriate) for each playwright; a list of long-running American plays (200 or more performances), arranged by number of performances in descending order; and lists of plays that won the Tony Award, the New York Drama Critics' Circle Award, and the Pulitzer Prize. There are two indexes, one for co-authors, adaptors, and original authors of sources used for plays and one for play titles.

Foreign Drama, 1909–1977 closely follows the structure of part 1. Plays produced in New York are listed by playwright and play title, followed by production history and cited reviews. Appendixes are "About the Dramatists," with the playwright's nationality and birth dates and death dates (if appropriate) given; tables of prolific and frequently produced foreign dramatists (based on number of plays and performances noted in the volume); successful productions (those with 100 performances or more); and winners of the New York Drama Critics' Circle Award for best foreign play. An index of co-authors, adaptors, and translators, and a play title index are also included.

For all the convenience the work offers, *A Guide to Critical Reviews* has some limitations. The handbook is not, and does not claim to be, a complete guide to critical evaluations of American theatrical productions. There are, for example, no references to criticism in scholarly journals or books. With the exception of citations to the reference work *New York Theatre Critics' Reviews,* which primarily covers criticism in the New York dailies, most of the reviews cited could readily be located by consulting appropriate years of the *Readers' Guide to Periodical Literature.* There is some inconsistency in the treatment of co-authors. While references from a co-author to the main author are often given within the main list (for example, *Moss Hart* to *George S. Kaufman,* and vice versa, for their many collaborations), these individuals are not listed in the co-author indexes for parts 1 and 3. The appendixes, which duplicate information readily found in other sources, are largely superfluous.

These aspects aside, *A Guide to Critical Reviews* is a boon to academic library users. The work is an excellent timesaver and, if used in conjunction with indexes to literary criticism on drama, provides the researcher with a solid starting point for locating drama criticism. Because the sources cited are often available in larger public libraries, the guide might also be considered for acquisition by those libraries. The Board recommends this work for the core collection of academic libraries.

An International Dictionary of Theatre Language. Joel Trapido, gen. ed. Greenwood, 1985. hard. 1 vol. 1,032 pp. ISBN 0-313-22980-5. $99.50. dictionary.
PN2035.I5 792.03′21

An ambitious undertaking, *An International Dictionary of Theatre Language* identifies and defines English- and foreign-language terms relating to the theater. Theater scholar and general editor Joel Trapido, assisted by a distinguished panel of specialists, has produced by far the largest glossary of theater terminology available to American scholars.

The preliminary pages list the various editors, contributing editors, consultants, and contributors, giving their credentials and areas of expertise. These lists are followed by the general editor's preface, which outlines the concept and origins of the glossary; a guide to the dictionary, explaining its scope, limitations, and arrangement; and an informative article written by Trapido entitled "A Brief History of Theatre Glossaries and Dictionaries." Concluding the volume is a bibliography of sources consulted.

The heart of the work is the 983-page dictionary, containing 10,000 English terms, 5,000 foreign terms representing more than 60 languages, and numerous cross-references. The terms selected are words and phrases used to express theatrical and dramatic concepts *(heroic acting, naturalism),* functions *(understudy),* and devices *(proscenium arch).* According to the introductory guide, the various aspects covered include "acting, aesthetics, burlesque, children's theatre, costume, creative drama, criticism, dance, design, directing, dramatic literature, dramaturgy, lighting, musical theatre, opera, playwriting, puppetry, readers theatre, scenery, scenography, stage management, stage technology, theatre management, theatre architecture, theatre theory, variety, and vaudeville." There are no entries for individuals or play titles. Non-English terms are printed in italics.

The majority of entries consist of a term and its definition, which is clear and sometimes amusing (for example: *green-room actor* is defined as "a performer who boasts of his talent in the actors' lounge but who is unsuccessful on stage"). Nearly one-half of the entries also provide authority for the definition by listing a source in the bibliography (either generally or with reference to a specific page number). In some cases, if a term has more than one meaning (for example, the word *footlights,* which is treated both literally and figuratively), multiple definitions are supplied.

The large number of non-English entries are of special interest. As expected, all foreign terms that have gained some currency in this country (the German *Sturm und Drang,* the Italian *commedia dell'arte*) are included. More surprising are the many words and phrases drawn from the Asian theater, especially the Chinese. Terms from Russian, Spanish, French, and other Western languages are also in evidence, reflecting the international scope of the dictionary.

Despite the breadth of approach, there are some omissions, mostly having to do with trade names and standard technical implements with applications that extend beyond those of the theater. Other exclusions are the language of the mass media and certain forms of popular entertainment (such as the circus and magic acts), which are covered in more specialized dictionaries.

An International Dictionary of Theatre Language is an impressive achievement. The Board recommends this work for the core collection of academic libraries.

McGraw-Hill Encyclopedia of World Drama: An International Reference Work in 5 Volumes, 2d edition. Stanley Hochman, ed. in chief. McGraw-Hill, 1984. hard. 5 vols. 2,828 pp. illus. appendixes. indexes. ISBN 0-07-079169-4. $380 (set). encyclopedia.
PN1625.M3 809.2

Among its many virtues, the *McGraw-Hill Encyclopedia of World Drama* has three that stand out: long, excellent articles on world playwrights, featuring plot summaries of their works; extensive surveys of national and regional drama and theater; and an attractive format, highlighted by numerous illustrations of plays in production.

An expansion and revision of the first edition (1972), the current edition represents the work of the publisher's editorial staff and a panel of 55 scholarly advisors and contributors. All entries are signed, and the credentials and areas of specialization of the contributors are listed in the preliminary matter. Both the preface and the introduction emphasize the goal of providing new or expanded coverage of non-Western and Third World theater in this edition.

The first four and a half volumes of the set are arranged alphabetically and include the following types of entries: playwrights; "seminal" directors, such as *Stanislavsky* and *Peter Brook;* important theater companies *(Berliner Ensemble);* surveys of national or regional dramas and theatrical forms *(Canadian drama, Latin American drama, Chinese theater);* and selected special topics *(musical comedy, Kabuki, Shakespeare on film).*

The last half of volume 5 is devoted to a glossary and two indexes. The glossary defines terms relating to dramatic history and theory, such as *protagonist* and *naturalism.* Consistent with the scope of the encyclopedia, most terms that pertain primarily to theatrical production and practice are excluded. The first index lists all play titles noted in the lists that appear with entries for major playwrights, whether or not they are also discussed in the text, and gives playwrights' names. The second (general) index cites volume and page numbers for all individuals, companies, terms, national dramas, and plays discussed in the text.

The most important feature of the encyclopedia is the information on playwrights and their works. The range of authors profiled is broad, including many lesser-known writers, such as the eighteenth-century French dramatist *Edme Boursault* and the twentieth-century Paraguayan playwright *José María Rivarola Matto,* as well as the more familiar *(Plautus, Harold Pinter)* and the world-acclaimed *(Shakespeare, Molière).*

Length and detail of the entries vary according to the significance of the playwright, but even the most minor dramatists are accorded at least half a column of biographical and critical commentary. Entries include a biographical and critical overview; a narrative survey of the playwright's output; summaries of the plots of major or representative plays; a chronological list of all plays; a list of important editions of collected works and individual texts; and a bibliography of major criticism. The plot summaries are of special interest to drama students in that they give sufficient detail for students to sample a number of works that they might have difficulty encountering in production or even in print (at least in English translation).

The survey articles for countries and world regions are also valuable. The entry for *American drama* is the most extensive, running nearly 80 pages and being divided into five more or less chronological sections. Surprisingly, the survey of *Latin American drama* (including all Latin American countries except Brazil, Cuba, and Puerto Rico, which are entered separately) extends to more than 50 pages. The lesser-known dramas of such countries as Poland and Switzerland are amply covered, as are the indigenous theaters of India and Iran. Only the brief (nine-page) survey of African theater seems scant, in terms of the expressed goal of enhanced coverage of Third World drama.

The layout of the text and the selection and quality of the accompanying illustrations are excellent. Text is set in two columns, with a large, attractive typeface used for the basic text and a variety of contrasting typefaces employed for headings, subheadings, cross-references, play lists, bibliographies, and contributor names. Although the encyclopedia includes many photographs and line drawings of playwrights, most of the illustrations are photographs from actual stage productions. Of special interest are the many photographs of foreign productions, which lend variety and perspective to the visual presentation. However, the quality is somewhat uneven, with some photographs being too dark and others reproduced with excessive contrast. In other areas of editing and production and in the numerous bibliographic notes, the achievement is uniformly excellent.

The *McGraw-Hill Encyclopedia of World Drama* is a valuable addition to theater reference shelves, with special utility for those serving students of drama and theater. The Board recommends this work for the core collections of public, academic, and school libraries.

The Oxford Companion to American Theatre. Gerald Bordman. Oxford, 1984. hard. 1 vol. 740 pp. ISBN 0-19-503443-0. $49.95. handbook.
PN2220.B6 792.0973

Gerald Bordman's excellent handbook, *The Oxford Companion to American Theatre,* is modeled after Phyllis Hartnoll's THE OXFORD COMPANION TO THE THEATRE, which covers theater in all parts of the world. Although the Bordman work serves as a worthy adjunct to the parent work, the two differ significantly in approach and coverage.

Like Hartnoll's compilation, *The Oxford Companion to American Theatre* contains entries for actors, directors, set designers, playwrights (including foreign playwrights, such as *Ibsen,* whose works are frequently performed in this country), individual theaters, and theater companies. In addition, Bordman includes several long entries of topical interest, such as *censorship in American theatre* and *blacks in American theatre and drama.* Excluded in the American work are technical terms, genres, and surveys of non-American theater history. The major difference between the two books is the treatment of plays. Whereas THE OXFORD COMPANION TO THE THEATRE has no entries for individual plays, fully half of the Bordman *Companion* is devoted to essays on specific plays and musicals.

Criteria for inclusion of plays and musicals, as detailed in the preface, are rather complex. However, most plays of major playwrights, other plays and musicals of genuine merit, and long-running productions of all kinds are included. Off-Broadway and regional productions are entered very selectively. A typical entry contains the name of the playwright (or composer, lyricist, and author of the book for musicals), the name of the producer, the theater at which the work premiered, the opening date, the number of performances in the play's first run, a plot summary (with names of major performers given), and a critical and historical note. Although brief, the summaries competently capture the essence of each play or musical, and the notes do an excellent job of placing each work in its own context, in terms of background and reception.

One inconsistency must be noted. Although the number of performances required for inclusion of musicals is not explicitly stated, there are some inexplicable omissions, such as the long-running *Barnum, L'il*

Abner, and *I Love My Wife.* Thus, while the sketch on Judy Holliday points to her role in *Bells Are Ringing* as one of her two most memorable, that hit musical does not receive its own entry.

The format of two columns per page and the large, clear typeface make the text easy to read. Entries average one-half column in length, but those on major personalities (the Barrymores, Tennessee Williams) and topics are considerably longer. In addition to direct cross-references to a preferred entry term, the use of a small diamond symbol next to a name or term within an entry alerts the user to related entries of interest. There are no illustrations, indexes, or bibliographies included in the book.

Gerald Bordman, who has written many books on the American musical theater, has done an admirable job of providing a great deal of factual information in a compact and readable fashion in *The Oxford Companion to American Theatre.* The Board recommends this work for the core collections of public, academic, and school libraries.

The Oxford Companion to the Theatre, 4th edition. Phyllis Hartnoll, ed. Oxford, 1983. hard. 1 vol. 944 pp. ISBN 0-19-211546-4. $49.95. handbook.
PN2035.H3 792.03'21

Since the first edition in 1951, *The Oxford Companion to the Theatre* has generally been regarded as the indispensable one-volume dictionary of theater. The editor, theater historian and poet Phyllis Hartnoll, assisted by a panel of contributors, ranges broadly to include data on actors, playwrights, directors, set designers, national theater history, individual companies, important theaters, specific genres (such as *melodrama*), and technical production details (such as *lighting* and *flying effects*). There are no individual entries for plays.

The entries are arranged alphabetically in two columns per page and are typically quite brief (half a column or less), except for those covering national theaters (seven and a half pages are used for *German theater*) and some of the more important performers *(Laurence Olivier)* and genres *(musical comedy).* Cross-references are used to refer the reader from a variant entry to the location of the actual entry (for example, the entry for the *Fulton Theatre, New York* refers to the *Helen Hayes Theatre*) and from terms with their own entries mentioned in the body of another entry (for example, *Moscow Art Theatre* and *Chekhov* are cross-referenced in the article on *Stanislavsky*).

An attractive and useful feature is the inclusion of 96 black-and-white plates, grouped by the following subjects: Greece; Rome; early European drama; Shakespearean production; theatrical development, 1643–1978 (divided into three broad periods); popular theater; costume; China; Japan; and India. "A Guide to Further Reading," which concludes the volume, is also useful, identifying standard English-language books on various aspects of world theater.

Although succinct, the entries are packed with information and are impeccably written. A panel of 87 contributors is listed, and some individual contributions are acknowledged in the preface, but entries are not signed. The consistency and readability of the work as a whole show the hand of a master editor at work.

There are some limitations noted in the preface, most of them attributed to considerations of space. Recent developments in the technology of theater and in critical analysis of texts are barely covered, and related arts (such as ballet and opera) are essentially excluded. Although popular forms of entertainment such as music hall and vaudeville are surveyed as genres, they and their practitioners are not treated in detail. Thus, *The Oxford Companion to the Theatre* takes a somewhat conservative approach, focusing on legitimate theater and its history.

During the last four decades, many theater dictionaries have challenged the supremacy of *The Oxford Companion to the Theatre* or have provided valuable complementary coverage. Nevertheless, this work has rightfully held its place as the theater dictionary of first choice. The Board recommends this work for the core collections of public, academic, and school libraries.

Theatre World. John Willis, ed. Crown, annual. hard. illus. appendix. index. ISBN 0-517-57715-1 (vol. 45). $35. yearbook.
PN2277.N5.A17 792

For more than four decades, *Theatre World* has proved to be a valuable annual survey of American theatrical activity. With a wealth of illustrations and production credits, the yearbook is of interest both as a convenient overview of a particular season and as a permanent record of theatrical achievement from World War II to the present.

Theatre World was conceived by the original editor, theater and film historian Daniel Blum, as a chronicle of the New York theater season. In recent years, under the editorship of John Willis, expanded coverage has increasingly been given to off-Broadway and professional regional and repertory productions.

The following organizational approach has been used in recent volumes. Each annual is dedicated to an individual (Bernadette Peters in the 1987–1988 volume), who is honored by a page of photographs and a dedication statement. "The Season in Review" provides a one-page profile of highlights (and lowlights) for the year and is limited almost exclusively to the New York scene. Following these preliminary sections is the listing of productions, divided into five parts: "Broadway Calendar"; "Off-Broadway Calendar"; "National Touring Companies"; "Professional Regional Companies"; and "Annual Shakespeare Festivals." Rounding out the volume are lists of awards, biographical sketches, obituaries, and an index.

"Broadway Calendar" consists of two principal sections: productions that opened during the season in question (from June 1 of one year through May 31 of the following year), arranged in chronological order; and productions from past seasons that played through the current season, arranged alphabetically. One page is normally allotted to each production, and the entry includes the following: full production and technical credits; theater and date of opening; full cast; a brief summary of content; performance history; and major awards received. Two to four photographs from the production complement these data. A third section, for closing of plays held over from previous seasons, is also included in some volumes.

The "Off-Broadway Calendar" section differs in arrangement and detail. The first section, for productions that opened during the current season, lists productions chronologically and supplies data on theater, credits, and number of performances, but in a more compact format and with fewer illustrations. The "Company Series" section lists off-Broadway companies (for example, the American Place Theatre) alphabetically, devoting a page or two to each group's season.

"National Touring Companies" parallels the current Broadway season pattern, with one page and two or more photographs allotted to each show. "Professional Regional Companies" and "Annual Shakespeare Festivals" resemble the off-Broadway company section: an alphabetical arrangement by company or festival name (for example, *Long Wharf Theatre* and *Oregon Shakespeare Festival*), a detailing of company managerial credits, and a selection of photographs from the company's production season.

The usefulness of a systematically recorded presentation of a vast array of American productions and the extensive cast and production credits alone would render these volumes invaluable for theater research, but the illustrations, biographical material, and index are special bonuses. Although the black-and-white photographs of productions tended to be somewhat muddy in the earlier years, they are considerably crisper and better focused in recent volumes. Usually too small to provide set and costume detail, the illustrations nevertheless give a reasonable impression of the look of the show and its performers. In addition, *Theatre World* is the only readily available source for information on many of the individuals covered. As an essential key to the mass of data included each year, the index gives quick access to play titles, performers, and production staff and is also useful for identifying productions of particular playwrights and their works, such as performances of Chekhov's plays or stagings of *The Glass Menagerie.*

The Board recommends this work for the core collection of public libraries.

Supplementary Titles

Dictionary of the Black Theatre: Broadway, Off-Broadway, and Selected Harlem Theatre. Allen Woll. Greenwood, 1983. hard. 1 vol. 359 pp. indexes. ISBN 0-313-22561-3. $42.95. dictionary.
PN2270.A35W64 792.089960

"To the substantial shelf of recent books on black drama can now be added . . . *Dictionary of the Black Theatre.* . . . Taking as his subject Douglas Turner Ward's definition of black theater [as] 'by, about, with, for and related to blacks' from 1898 to 1981, Woll enters approximately 300 shows in his dictionary. The first part, arranged alphabetically by title, provides the name of the theater for first production, date, number of performances, the creative personnel, cast, songs, a sketch of the reviews, and plot summary. In the second part, Woll confirms his book's orientation toward history of theatrical production rather than texts by presenting brief sketches of the lives of major performers, writers, directors, and histories of theatrical organizations. For each of the major figures these entries also include a list of credits, and all entries, whether by Woll himself or signed by other contributors, include a listing of reference sources. Adding to the value of the excellent notes in these two parts of the book is apparatus that includes a chronology of the black theater; a discography; a selected bibliography including published versions of shows, books, articles, and dissertations; and indexes to proper names, plays and films, and songs. Greenwood is on the mark in touting the book as an important tool." (*Am. Literary Scholarship,* 1984, p. 405)

"A well-researched reference work devoted to the black contribution to [the] 20th century American stage, Allen Woll's [book] covers Broadway, Off Broadway, and selected Harlem shows, personalities and organizations. Some 300 productions are thoroughly documented and over 300 individuals profiled in comprehensive credits." (*Back Stage,* February 1984)

Also reviewed in: *Am Theatre,* November 1984, p. 35; *ARBA,* 1984, p. 463; *Choice,* April 1984, p. 119; *Freedomways,* 1984, p. 75; *Show Music,* June 1985, p. 32; *TLS,* December 30, 1983, p. 1461.

Board's recommendation: Public and academic libraries.

Encyclopaedia of the Musical Theatre. Stanley Green. Dodd, Mead, 1976. hard. 1 vol. 492 pp. illus. ISBN 0-396-07221-6. $14.95. encyclopedia.
ML102.M88G7 782.8

Encyclopaedia of the Musical Theatre presents "backgrounds, plots, casts and credits of over 200 musicals, descriptions and anecdotes of over 1000 songs, including who sang them in what, brief biographies of over 600 composers, lyricists, librettists, performers, directors, choreographers and producers, along with complete listings of all their Broadway and West End productions. . . . The period covered is from the late 19th century to 1975." (publisher's note)

"The book is sturdily bound in gray buckram and opens easily. The two-column pages are not crowded, and various typefaces are utilized so that the different kinds of information are readily located within entries. Inner margins, while not generous, should be adequate if rebinding is needed. Altogether, [this] is a fascinating fund of factual information which should delight any librarian who has ever been asked, 'Was there a character named Marcus, or something like that, in "The Music Man"?' " (*BL,* July 15, 1977, p. 1747)

"[This is] a bright and informative guide—well worth its space on any self-respecting theatrical reference shelf." (*CSM,* March 9, 1977, p. 23)

Also reviewed in: *ARBA,* 1977, p. 478; *Choice,* December 1983, p. 540; *Notes,* June 1977, p. 848; *Rp B Bk R,* 1980, p. 14; *WLB,* March 1977, p. 603.

Board's recommendation: Public and academic libraries.

A Guide to Reference and Bibliography for Theatre Research, 2d edition. Claudia Jean Bailey. Ohio State Univ. Pr., 1983. soft. 1 vol. 149 pp. index. ISBN 0-88215-049-9. $20. bibliography.
Z5781.B15 016.792

"The first part of [*A Guide to Reference and Bibliography for Theatre Research*] introduces users to basic library sources of information, e.g., national and trade bibliographies, biographical sources, and government publications. The final 400-plus entries focus on theater and drama sources by type (bibliographies, theses, directories) and subject (theory and criticism, costumes, theater architecture). Excluded are material on Shakespeare, techniques of acting and directing, and books published after fall 1979.

"Bailey . . . has compiled an annotated bibliographic guide to research in theater arts and drama that should prove very useful to students in those areas. . . . All items are consecutively numbered and include adequate bibliographic data." (*BL,* December 1, 1984, p. 503)

Also reviewed in: *A Lib,* May 1972, p. 558; *ARBA,* 1984, p. 456; *Choice,* November 1983, p. 391.

Board's recommendation: Academic libraries.

Musicals: A Directory of Musical Properties Available for Production. Richard Chigley Lynch. ALA, 1984. soft. 1 vol. 197 pp. appendixes. index. ISBN 0-8389-0404-1. $19.50 directory.
ML19.L9 782.81'029'473

"Lynch, assistant curator in the New York Public Library's Billy Rose Theatre Collection, presents [in *Musicals*] a . . . guide to 395 musical shows available for production. Designed to aid amateur groups in selecting a show, the work lists the shows in alphabetical order, providing a synopsis and brief comments (e.g., audience suitability) for each. It also gives names of librettists, composers, and lyricists; some of the show's plot; availability of libretto, piano-vocal score and sound recordings; and licensing agent." (*Choice,* December 1984, p. 540)

"Coverage [in *Musicals*] is more up to date here than in other books, making this useful for both the reference desk and the user deciding on what musical to stage next." (*LJ,* June 15, 1984, p. 1232)

Board's recommendation: Public and academic libraries.

New York Times Theater Reviews 1870–1919. Random House, 1976. hard. 5 vols. plus 1-vol. index. ISBN 0-405-06664-3 (set). $975 (set). guide.
PN2266.N48 792.015

New York Times Theater Reviews 1920–1980. Random House, 1981. hard. 13 vols. plus 2-vol. index. ISBN 0-405-00696-9 (set). $1,580 (set). guide.
PN2266.N48 792.015

"The glamour of . . . years of New York's legitimate theater is recaptured in the . . . volumes of *The New York Times* reprinting of theater critics' reviews. [In

New York Times Theater Reviews,] Brooks Atkinson sets the stage for the procession of reviews with a fascinating Introduction recalling the days when 15 New York daily newspapers were actively reviewing stage productions. During the first year of coverage (1920–1921) there were 157 New York productions; they reached an all-time high in 1927–1928 with 264 productions.

"The roster of *New York Times* reviewer/critics almost chronicles the story of twentieth-century theater in New York: Alexander Woollcott (critic 1914–1922), John Corbin (critic 1902, 1917–1919, 1928), Stark Young (critic 1924–1925), Brooks Atkinson (critic 1925–1942, 1946–1960), Lewis Nichols (critic 1942–1946), Howard Taubman (critic 1960–1965), Stanley Kauffman (critic 1966), Walter Kerr (critic 1966–1967), and Clive Barnes (critic 1967 to present). The first volume contains a brief biography of each.

"Printed four columns to a page, the volumes lie flat when open. Reproduction, of course, varies with the lightness or darkness of the original print. These sturdily bound volumes are a 'must' purchase for large theater collections." (*BL,* October 15, 1974, p. 255)

Board's recommendation: Public and academic libraries.

Theatre Language: A Dictionary of Terms in English of the Drama and Stage from Medieval to Modern Times. Walter Parker Bowman and Robert Hamilton Ball. Theatre Arts (div. of Routledge, Chapman & Hall), 1961. soft. 1 vol. 428 pp. ISBN 0-87830-561-3. $8.95. dictionary.
PN2035.B6 792.03

Theatre Language is organized according to "three principal classes of words and phrases: . . . technical terms, standard nontechnical terms, and slang, jargon, or cant; foreign terms are included if there is good evidence that they have been more or less absorbed into English." (*BL,* May 1, 1961, p. 539)

"In the English language, no more important volume of theater terminology has been written. . . . The authors of this volume have included every conceivable technical term. . . . Highly recommended not only for theater and drama collections but for the reference collections of middle-to-large public and university libraries." (*Theat A,* July 1961, p. 6)

Board's recommendation: Academic libraries.

Twentieth Century American Dramatists, Dictionary of Literary Biography series. John MacNicholas, ed. Gale, 1981. hard. 2 vols. 1,841 pp. illus. index. ISBN 0-8103-0928-9 (set). $103 (set). biographical dictionary.
PS129.D5.XV7 812.509

See American Literature.

New and Noteworthy

American Theatre Companies, 1931–1986. Weldon B. Durham, ed. Greenwood, 1989. hard. 1 vol. 596 pp. index. ISBN 0-313-25360-9. $95. encyclopedia.
PN2266.A54 792.0973

"With [*American Theatre Companies, 1931–1986,*] Durham . . . completes a monumental survey of American theater companies. The first two volumes covered the period 1749–1887 and 1888–1930; this volume includes companies through 1986.

"The decentralization of American culture is occurring at an increasing rate, and the growth in regional theater companies is a good example of this phenomenon. . . . Durham traces this history in general in the preface and then provides biographies of 78 theater companies, 48 of which were still in existence in 1986." (*BL,* December 15, 1989, p. 852)

The Book of 1000 Plays: A Comprehensive Guide to the Most Frequently Performed Plays. Steve Fletcher and Norman Jopling. Facts On File, 1989. hard. 1 vol. 352 pp. index. ISBN 0-8160-2133-8. $24.95. encyclopedia.
PN6112.5.F54 809.2

"[*The Book of 1000 Plays*] is a guide to what its authors claim have been the most popular plays in Britain and the U.S. during this century. . . . The work is arranged alphabetically by play title. Each entry provides title, author, category (comedy, tragedy, musical, etc.), date and place of first production, a descriptive plot synopsis of 150–400 words, and a list of characters. . . . [This book] . . . will be valuable to play-goers who wish to know a bit of the plot ahead of time." (*BL,* November 1, 1989, pp. 600–602)

The Cambridge Guide to World Theatre. Martin Banham, ed. Cambridge, 1989. hard. 1 vol. 1,104 pp. ISBN 0-521-26595-9. $49.50. encyclopedia.
PN2035 792.0321

"[*The Cambridge Guide to World Theatre*] . . . presents much valuable information in one alphabetical listing about theater—historical, present day, stage, and television—and theater people. Bibliographies extend the substance of most general and national entries; cross-references . . . name entries . . . seem to encompass any and all names of merit. The introduction states that the work purports to offer 'a comprehensive view of the history and present practice of theatre in all parts of the world.' It appears to succeed." (*Choice,* June 1989, p. 1654)

The Facts On File Dictionary of the Theatre. William Packard, David Pickering, and Charlotte Savidge, eds. Facts On File, 1989. hard and soft. 1 vol. 556 pp. ISBN 0-8160-1841-3 (hard); 0-8160-1945-2 (soft). $35 (hard); $15.95 (soft). dictionary.
PN2035 792.03

"This useful [*Facts On File Dictionary of the Theatre*] contains 5,000 brief (35–150 word) articles on 'actors, actresses, playwrights, directors and producers, plays, venues, genres, technical terms, organizations,' and related theatrical topics. Entries were selected to emphasize the contemporary stage and include important plays in the history of Western drama. A British and American emphasis is evident, but there are entries for major European dramatists. The arrangement is alphabetical, and extensive cross-references are included. [This book] provides superior coverage of contemporary theater ('off-off Broadway'), individual plays, critics, and technical terms. It is therefore more useful for brief, factual queries." (*Choice,* June 1989, p. 1660)

Notable Women in the American Theatre: A Biographical Dictionary. Alice M. Robinson et al., eds. Greenwood, 1989. hard. 1 vol. 993 pp. index. ISBN 0-313-27217-4. $99.50. biographical source.
PN2285.N65 792.082

"[*Notable Women in the American Theatre*] treats approximately 300 women (both living and dead) whose achievements were 'important and sigifniciant in the American theatre' and whose contributions were characterized as 'having a pioneering or innovative quality . . . actresses, producers, playwrights, directors, designers, critics, theatrical agents, managers, patrons, variety entertainers, dancers/choreographers . . . are included. . . . The contributors have tried . . . to convey a sense of the biographee's personal outlook on life.' . . . While more actresses are represented than any other profession, it is the biographies of agents, educators, patrons, and producers that should prove most useful." (*BL,* February 1, 1990, p. 1116)

Wendell Cochran

Transportation

Transportation concerns our society's dependence on moving people and goods—moving them, variously, by automobile, airplane, railroad, and ship.

For many library patrons, the dominating transportation concern is their own private means of transportation. Such people may wish to compare makes and models before buying a car, motorcycle, truck, or van. Those patrons want an up-to-date reference for the most recent model year. Alternatively, many patrons are interested in buying used vehicles or maintaining the vehicles they already own. Such patrons may seek repair manuals covering many model years into the past.

The sheer number of motor vehicles and their models can cause problems in shelving manuals; however, the number also means high print runs, holding down the price of these manuals and allowing libraries to update their collections frequently. The high demand for this information is reflected in the core collection, in which six of nine titles are related to cars, motorcycles, and trucks.

News stories may lead readers to libraries for identification of airplanes—say a Boeing 747 involved in a highjacking or an F16 fighter plane that the government proposes to sell to another country. Ships, too, are often in the news, as when an American aircraft carrier is sent to the eastern Mediterranean. Information about railways is increasingly important to voters interested in ways to relieve highway congestion or to reduce the cost of long-range freight. Basic references are available to fill the needs of these patrons, rounding out the core collection.

Typically, a reference source in the transportation category covers many models by many manufacturers, and the work must be revised every year. A new edition may appear first as a single-subject issue of a periodical and later—with or without revision—in book form. (Often publishers do not make the distinction apparent.) Cumulative volumes often appear, too. In any case, the older references remain useful (as to someone repairing a vintage Volkswagen or reading about Spitfires in the Battle of Britain). For this reason a librarian must consider each new reference carefully, compare it with last year's edition, and anticipate demand for both old and new.

Core Titles

Chilton's Auto Repair Manual 1983–90. Chilton, 1989. hard. 1 vol. 1,536 pp. illus. index. ISBN 0-8019-6914-X. $24.95. manual.
TL152.C5226 629.28722

Core Titles

	PUBLIC	ACADEMIC	SCHOOL
Chilton's Auto Repair Manual 1983–90 Chilton, 1989	✦		
Chilton's Import Car Repair Manual 1983–90 Chilton, 1989	✦		
Chilton's Motorcycle and ATV Repair Manual 1945–85 Chilton, 1986	✦		
Chilton's Truck and Van Repair Manual 1979–86 Chilton, 1986	✦		
Consumer Guide Automobile Book Signet, annual	✦		
Jane's All the World's Aircraft, 1989–90, 80th edition Taylor, John W. R., ed. in chief. Jane's Information Group, 1989	✦	✦	
Jane's Fighting Ships Sharpe, Richard, ed. Jane's Information Group, annual	✦	✦	
Jane's World Railways, 1989–90, 31st edition Allen, Geoffrey Freeman, ed. Jane's Information Group, 1989	✦	✦	
Used Cars Rating Guide, 1990 Edition, Consumer Guide Auto Series Signet, 1990	✦		

One of the most popular of a longstanding series is *Chilton's Auto Repair Manual,* with feedback from its many users over the years adding to the reliability of information presented by Chilton. (This review is based on an examination of the 1986 edition. A new edition includes cars through the 1990 model year.)

The book is thick and heavy, as may be expected of any source of so much information about so many cars. The material is densely packed.

The arrangement is systematic, comprising the "Car Section" (824 pages) and the "Unit Repair Section" (512 pages). In the first section, cars are grouped by manufacturer—American Motors, Chrysler, Ford, General Motors. An alphabetical list guides the reader to approximately 140 models, including AMX, Apollo, Comet, Dart, LeBaron, and Sunbird. Within those sections, detailed information is given on the manufacturer's models. The section on Ford Motor Company (as one example) opens with four pages of line drawings that identify models of Ford, Lincoln, and Mercury cars with rear-wheel drive. Next come several pages of mechanical specifications for those cars, with identification numbers to be used in obtaining parts. The last section provides detailed instructions for servicing systems and components, in the following sequence: charging, starting, ignition, fuel and cooling systems, emission controls, engine, clutch, transmissions (automatic and manual), driveshaft and U-joints, rear axle, jacking and hoisting, suspensions (front and rear), brakes, steering, instrument panel, wipers, radio, and heater. This information is followed by comparable material on front-wheel-drive models. The Chrysler section follows the pattern described here for Ford cars. The General Motors section, however, while including all of this information, organizes the information according to model or body type.

The "Unit Repair Section" concerns troubleshooting and overhaul procedures for the major components and systems, which are for the most part arranged by brand, manufacturer, or type of component rather than by car model. The specific categories are general maintenance, diesel engines, tools, air conditioning, gauges, charging and starting, carburetors, fuel injection, turbocharging, electronic ignition, emission controls, engine rebuilding, transmissions, transfer cases, drive axles, universal and constant-velocity joints, struts, brakes, and front-end alignment. Troubleshooting procedures and various data for mechanics are included at the end of the section.

As a how-to page explains, if your car's engine is misfiring, you may begin with "Troubleshooting" and determine that the problem is defective piston rings and the remedy is engine overhaul. Then you go to the indicated page in the "Car Section" to find how to pull the engine from the car and, finally, turn to "Engine Rebuilding" and follow the step-by-step procedure for completing the repair.

Even for a person not mechanically inclined, the book is easy to read and use. Finding a specific procedure is facilitated by an index arranged in a grid: across its top row are listed the model names (such as Bobcat and Thunderbird); in a side column are listed the procedures for unit repair.

The Board recommends *Chilton's Auto Repair Manual 1983–90* for the core collection of public libraries.

Chilton's Import Car Repair Manual 1983–90. Chilton, 1989. hard. 1 vol. 1,536 pp. illus. ISBN 0-8019-7672-3. $28.95 manual.
TL152.C529 629.28722

Chilton's Import Car Repair Manual is a companion to a Chilton's authoritative manual for repair of motor cars made in the United States and Canada (CHILTON'S AUTO REPAIR MANUAL). The work has been refined through successive editions and has a considerable size and weight, appropriate to the extensive information contained. (This review is based on an examination of the 1986 edition. A new edition covers autos through the 1990 model year.)

The book consists of two main parts, a "Car Section" (1,062 pages) and a "Unit Repair Section" (418 pages). The "Car Section" covers Audi, BMW, Chrysler, Datsun/Nissan, Fiat, Honda, Isuzu, Mazda, Mercedes-Benz, Merkur, Mitsubishi, Porsche (two series), Renault, Saab, Subaru, Toyota, Volkswagen (two series), and Volvo.

The "Unit Repair Section" comprises troubleshooting and overhaul and repair procedures for major systems and components. Specifically, the section covers tools and equipment, basic maintenance, gauges and indicators, air conditioning, diesel engines, carburetors, fuel injection and electronic controls, electronic ignition systems, turbocharging, engine rebuilding, brakes, universal and constant-velocity joints, transmissions (manual and automatic), transaxles, and struts.

A grid, which the editors refer to as the index, guides the user in this way: Along the top row is an alphabetical list of manufacturers of imports; down a side column are listed alphabetically components and systems that may need repair—alternator, automatic transmission, axle shaft, ball joints, brake adjustment, brakes, camshaft, and so on. Where row and column cross is listed a page number that leads to a description of a system or procedure for repair.

As a discussion of how to use the book explains, the user will commonly begin with a problem (for example, an engine that is not firing properly) and refer to the "Troubleshooting" section to determine the cause (for example, worn piston rings allowing oil to foul the sparkplugs, a finding that indicates that the engine must be overhauled). The reader then consults the proper section for detailed instructions for first pulling the engine out of the car and then completing the repair.

Descriptions, discussions, and procedures are simple, logical, and easy to read and apply (given proper equipment, mechanical ability, and some knowledge of part names). Numerous halftones and line drawings, including exploded views, supplement the text and do much to help identify parts with their names.

The Board recommends *Chilton's Import Car Repair Manual* for the core collection of public libraries.

Chilton's Motorcycle and ATV Repair Manual 1945–85. Chilton, 1986. hard. 1 vol. 1,422 pp. appendix. index. ISBN 0-8019-7635-9. $28.95. manual.
TL440.C457 629.28775

Chilton's Motorcycle and ATV Repair Manual covers motorcycles and all-terrain vehicles (ATV), the latter category including off-the-road and limited-production cycles and similar machines.

Despite commendable and efficient editorial compression, this is a big and heavy book—weighing just over 5 pounds. The manual includes information concerning machines manufactured by Harley-Davidson (92 pages), Honda (461), Kawasaki (239), Moto Guzzi (50), Norton (44), Suzuki (147), Triumph (76), and Yamaha (217). Generally speaking, the number of pages for each maker reflects the number of models or groups of models. For Harley, the main contents page lists only "V-Twins"; for Honda there are 10 categories; for Kawasaki, 5; for Suzuki, 4; and for Yamaha, 5. However, the list of contents for each make specifies models, and repair procedures often distinguish among model names and numbers.

After a short note on how to use the manual, the editors plunge right into the maintenance of Harley-Davidson machines. However, anyone who is not a repair expert should begin near the end of the book with the section of general information (75 pages). This section includes an introduction to using the manual, followed by safety precautions and a description of tools necessary for motorcycle repair. Also included in this section are discussions of maintenance, routine adjustments, tune-up, engine rebuilding, the fuel system, the chassis, and the battery. Finally there is a section on troubleshooting (17 pages), conversion tables, a glossary (about 130 terms), and a miscellany of data for mechanics (consisting mainly of more conversion tables).

Finding information in this manual is easy. First (as the text says) one must make sure the machine under study really is among those discussed. If a specific problem must be solved, the topic may be found most quickly under "General Information"; as examples, "Engine Rebuilding" first discusses the question "Is rebuilding necessary?" and "Maintenance" moves systematically from oils and additives to oil changes, transmission and drive boxes, chassis, cables and controls, drum brakes, moving parts, and drive-chain lubrication.

Applying the information found in this manual requires mechanical familiarity and dexterity, but even a novice should find the discussions and procedures presented readable and straightforward. For example, under the topic of clutch disassembly for the Triumph machine are nine detailed steps in clear and simple language ("4. Drain the oil from the chaincase, then remove the chain tension adjuster"), with two related line drawings available for study, one of which is an exploded view. Here, as elsewhere, helpful artwork abounds.

The Board recommends *Chilton's Motorcycle and ATV Repair Manual* for the core collection of public libraries.

Chilton's Truck and Van Repair Manual 1979–86. Chilton, 1986. hard. 1 vol. 1,456 pp. illus. ISBN 0-8019-7655-3. $28.95. manual.
TL230.5.C45C472 629.2874

Chilton's Truck and Van Repair Manual extends Chilton's automotive repair series to cover trucks and vans for model years 1979 through 1986. Like the other titles on the Chilton list, this series enjoys widespread use by do-it-yourself owners.

In this manual, "every mass-produced American or import truck is broken down into its component parts—engine, brakes, drivetrain, suspension, etc.—by make, model, and year" (cover copy). The extensiveness of coverage translates into 1,426 pages of repair information.

Like other Chilton manuals, this one is arranged in two parts. The first is called the "Truck Section," with 626 pages devoted to Chevrolet/GMC, Datsun/Nissan, Ford, International, Isuzu/LUV, Jeep, Mazda/Courier, Mitsubishi/D-50/Arrow, Toyota, and Volkswagen. The second, called the "Unit Repair Section" (800 pages), concerns tools, maintenance, air conditioning, electrical, emissions, carburetors, fuel injection/turbocharging, engine rebuilding, steering, wheel alignment, manual transmissions, transfer cases, drive axles, universal and constant-velocity joints, brakes, struts, diesel engines, troubleshooting, and mechanic's data.

A two-page grid (Chilton calls it an index) guides the reader from the manufacturer's name in the top row and the component involved in a side column to the appropriate page at the intersection of row and column for discussions, descriptions, specifications, and procedures concerning the required repair or servicing.

Assuming only that the reader can identify parts with their names, reading and using this book is easy. The language is plain and the numbered steps logical; for example, in the section on adjusting the shift lever on the Mazda/Courier, the most complicated instruction reads: "From this point, shift through the various positions, confirming that the shifter works as shown in the illustration." The illustration referenced is one of the many helpful line drawings—including exploded views—provided in this manual.

Often the most efficient way to approach a repair is to begin with the section on troubleshooting, which falls near the end of the book (in the "Unit Repair Section"). The reader merely looks for the part or system that is causing mechanical or electrical trouble, determines from the systematic list the most probable cause, and from there goes to the grid-like index to find the number of the page that describes the appropriate cure.

The Board recommends *Chilton's Truck and Van Repair Manual* for the core collection of public libraries.

Consumer Guide Automobile Book. Signet, annual. soft. 1 vol. 240 pp. illus. ISBN 0-451-82214-5. $8.95. handbook.
629.2222

For years, Consumer Guide has been noted for its up-to-date and factual discussions of motor cars; the *Consumer Guide Automobile Book* provides such discussions for new car models. The format is primarily that of a catalog, consisting mainly of entries with a rigidly parallel arrangement that facilitates comparison.

The book is primarily a compilation of profiles of new cars. The cover copy proclaims that "more than 170" cars are included. Any potential buyer should first read the three dozen pages of advice on shopping before proceeding to the main section ("Buying Guide"). In the "Buying Guide," finding specific information is virtually foolproof: models are listed alphabetically on the contents page and in the text, so that the page titled "How to Use This Book" is hardly needed.

The language is clear and uses a minimum of jargon terms. Even so, the three-page glossary of terms and the key to abbreviations may be helpful at times. Information on prices and specifications is as recent as printing and publication allow, and of course is subject to change by the manufacturers—the original source—without notice. Consumer Guide issues a new book each year.

The listing for the Dodge Caravan is representative of the other listings. A black-and-white photo is followed by "What's New," a run-in description of the vehicle that stresses changes since the previous model year (in this case a new V8 engine). Positive and negative features (labeled "For" and "Against") precede a "Summary," in which an anonymous author tells how the vehicle performed on the road and in everyday driving conditions. Summaries compare the vehicle with its competitors (in this case Mitsubishi and General Motors minivans) and comments on power, sound, appearance, and feel. Next come "Specifications," which provide tables of dimensions, engine characteristics, and EPA mileage estimates. The final section, "Prices," includes retail, dealer invoice, and low prices for basic models; a list of standard equipment; and extensive lists of optional equipment, each item with a price.

For first-time buyers especially, the introductory advice will be most helpful. It tells how to choose a dealer, read window stickers, negotiate a price, find a loan, read a contract, and decide whether to buy or lease and whether to sell an old car or trade it in. A chart, arranged by make and model, makes for easy comparison of warranties and service contracts. Four pages are devoted to consumer complaints, with checklists concerning getting references from friends and neighbors, actions to take before accepting delivery, service visits, coping with a lemon (real or suspected), mediation services, government agencies and consumer groups, and safety measures and equipment. The shopping section closes with six pages of "Best Buys"—39 cars recommended by the editors.

The Board recommends the *Consumer Guide Automobile Book* for the core collection of public libraries.

Jane's All the World's Aircraft, 1989–90, 80th edition. John W. R. Taylor, ed. in chief. Jane's Information Group, 1989. hard. 1 vol. 808 pp. illus. appendix. indexes. ISBN 0-7106-0896-9. $170. handbook.

TL509 533.6

Jane's annuals are universally accepted as authoritative, and *Jane's All the World's Aircraft* may lead the pack. The work's large size, high price, and frequent revision—to remain authoritative—seem to be unavoidable consequences of the currency and range of information contained.

The edition described here covers these main categories: "Aircraft" (a general class including military and commercial craft), "Sport Aircraft," "Microlights," "Sailplanes," "Hang Gliders," "Lighter than Air: Balloons" (including airships), and "Aero Engines." Under each category the arrangement is alphabetical by country and, under country, alphabetical by manufacturer.

A typical entry is the one for the *Lockheed Corporation* (under the heading "United States of America"). A profile of the company is given first (and a reference to its history in earlier editions of Jane's), with address and telephone number, principal officers, number of employees, and location of various facilities. Then the text discusses Lockheed-built planes, model by model. The first model discussed is the *F-117A*—the Stealth fighter—which had been unveiled by the U.S. Department of Defense only in the November preceding publication. In nearly a page devoted to the plane, Jane's sums up the history of development (including crashes of three test planes, plans for delivery of 52 by the end of the year, and the Air Force's plans for deployment). Next comes a detailed description of the aircraft and its dimensions (so far as known), accompanied by a photograph from the Air Force and line drawings of side and nose views.

Amidst the country headings is the heading "International Programmes," covering (among others) *Airbus Industrie,* a joint venture supported by England, France, and a few other European nations. This section is 36 pages long, as compared with 12 for the People's Republic of China, 64 for the U.S.S.R., 42 for the United Kingdom, and 190 for the United States.

Separate indexes cover the main categories noted earlier; entries in italic type refer the reader to ten previous editions of Jane's.

A feature not to be overlooked is the foreword, in which the editor discusses the global state of aircraft and gives commentary on political, commercial, and strategic concerns. In the edition described here, the editor reported "a strange lack" of new combat aircraft for many months at Ramenskoye, a military test-flight field southeast of Moscow, and suggested that the Soviet economy was far weaker than is generally known in the West. This comment was written more than a year before the unexpected political and economic changes of late 1989 in Eastern Europe.

The reading level is satisfactorily low, though the necessary technical terms may drive readers to the glossary of three 3-column pages.

Other features include a list of "first flights" in the previous year and a page of official records for speed, height, and so on.

The Board recommends *Jane's All the World's Aircraft* for the core collections of public and academic libraries.

Jane's Fighting Ships. Richard Sharpe, ed. Jane's Information Group, annual. hard. 1 vol. 849 pp. illus. indexes. ISBN 0-7106-0904-3. $170. handbook.
VA40.J35 359.5468

When any naval vessel anywhere makes the news, journalists consult the ship-reference section of *Jane's Fighting Ships,* a work large (and expensive) but likely to depict and describe in detail the ship in question or at least its naval class.

The ship-reference section makes up the bulk of this annual (in this edition, 830 pages of the 849 total). The arrangement is first by country, from *Albania* (through *Switzerland!*) to *Zanzibar.*

The entry for *Canada* is representative. It begins with organizational notes for the Ministry of National Defence and the Royal Canadian Navy and then goes on to state the strength of the fleet—in number of submarines, destroyers, frigates, yachts, and so on—and report the deployment of these vessels in various oceans. Next is Canada's pennant list, or the names of major ships. Then come detailed descriptions of ships, as in this pattern for frigates: class (City class), names (the *Halifax,* the *Vancouver,* and so on; with the name of the builder and dates that the ship was laid down, launched, and commissioned), displacement, dimensions, speed, weapons, and much more. Then for the *Halifax,* for example, supplementing all that information are half-tone photographs of the vessel and a line drawing keyed to a list of its weaponry, helicopter pad, and the like. At the end of the section are discussions of Canada's Coast Guard and its Department of Fisheries and Oceans.

Another section, the "Pennant List of Major Surface Ships," lists vessels (in order of pennant number) with ship name, type (such as submarine tender), and country. The listing includes about 1,650 ships in all.

Editor Richard Sharpe's foreword is more useful than its name suggests, consisting as it does of 22 pages of news and comment (dated April, with publication in May). Sharpe, a Royal Navy captain, discourses editorially and factually on the state of navies and especially on the economic and political decline of the Soviet bloc and its effect on weaponry at sea and on merchant shipping. The editor goes on to survey, in turn, the state of navies of the Soviet Union, Northern Europe, the United Kingdom, Western Europe, the Mediterranean, central and southern Africa, the Indian Ocean, the China Seas, Australasia, central and south America, North America, and the United States. (In other sections, the book also sums up naval strengths by nation and discusses naval equipment, including aircraft, antisubmarine weapons, electronic warfare, guns, missiles, radar, sonar, and torpedoes.)

The Board recommends *Jane's Fighting Ships* for the core collections of public and academic libraries.

Jane's World Railways, 1989–90, 31st edition. Geoffrey Freeman Allen, ed. Jane's Information Group, 1989. hard. 1 vol. 1,027 pp. illus. index. ISBN 0-7106-0891-8. $170. handbook.
TF1.J35 385

The soundness of *Jane's World Railways* rests on the work's own reputation through 30 earlier editions and also the reputations of Jane's other authoritative guides. Like other titles in the publisher's list, this volume includes extensive information, densely packed, and is large and relatively expensive. Of this edition, 345 pages of 1,027 are devoted to descriptions of railway systems, arranged alphabetically by country, from Afghanistan through Zimbabwe (113 in all). The reading level is easy, except in the most technical material.

The entry for Australia's railway systems occupies 24 pages (incidentally reporting 3,063 kilometers of gauge 1,435-millimeter track; 1,733 kilometers of gauge 1,067-millimeter track; and 1,849 kilometers of gauge 1,600-millimeter track). For Mexico the numbers are 2 pages and 21,032 kilometers; for the United States 49 pages, with route miles listed by individual railroad company; and for the U.S.S.R., 6 pages and 146,702 kilometers.

Typically, under each country name is a note about the pertinent government agency. This section includes the agency's address, officers, and a brief description. Similar information is given for manufacturers of equipment and then for railroad companies or regional systems.

The entry on the United Kingdom (as an example) has a note about the Department of Transportation and then the national company British Rail (BritRail). For the latter, after an organizational summary, the text provides such facts as the gauge (1,435 millimeter), total track (16,595 kilometers), and electrification specifications. Then comes a discussion of current status, government objectives, and reports on finances and various operational aspects (InterCity, Network SouthEast, the cross-London scheme, provincial service, freight, traction and rolling stock, the Channel Tunnel, and a new terminal at Kings Cross). Tables give trackage, sum up traffic and budget, and provide in great detail the number and specifications for BritRail's electric and diesel locomotives. Here, as throughout the book, photographs of track and trains abound.

The index to this volume runs to more than eight 3-column pages. The page-long foreword discusses the status and prospects of railways around the globe, especially in the United Kingdom, the United States, Germany, France, and Europe in general.

One section concerns rapid transit and underground railway systems in 56 countries, arranged alphabetically by city. Other sections cover manufacturers of railway equipment (about 475 pages, with multitudinous technical details), private freight-car leasing companies, international rail services in Europe, international railway associations and agencies, and consultants.

The Board recommends *Jane's World Railways* for the core collections of public and academic libraries.

Used Cars Rating Guide, 1990 Edition, Consumer Guide Auto series. Signet, 1990. soft. 1 vol. 160 pp. illus. ISBN 0-451-16551-9. $4.95. handbook.
629.2222

In *Used Cars Rating Guide,* Consumer Guide reports on used domestic and imported cars. The work's reputation is based on a long record of describing a notoriously difficult market. Coverage is for the model years since 1980.

The format is that of a catalog: two-column text, numerous black-and-white photos, and tables for comparing specifications on various models.

Putting first things first, this guide opens with a discussion of how to shop for used cars, covering such points as advertisements, prices, warranties, checking a used car, negotiating with the seller, contracts, and consumer protection. The work then provides 150 pages or so of discussions about specific models. This book discusses about 200 models, from Acura through Volvo. Perhaps typical is Buick (14 pages) and its models—Century, Electra, LeSabre, Reatta, Regal, Riviera, Skyhawk, Skylark, and Somerset. This listing oversimplifies matters somewhat. In fact, Electras are listed as 1980–84 and 1985–90, indicating a significant change in the model that will affect ratings.

With the entry for each car is a photograph (or several) accompanied by general remarks and tables giving price ranges (for cars in good, average, and poor condition), dimensions, and engine specifications.

As one example, most of a page is allotted to the Oldsmobile Delta 88/Eighty Eight Royale 1986–90. Photos show four models. The text notes that this model is smaller than its forerunners; remarks that the basic engine is "anemic"; approves air conditioning as standard equipment; discusses the suspension, passenger room, and trunk space; and notes a change in name for 1989. A table lists prices, dimensions (wheelbase, length, weight, fuel capacity, and so on), and engine (displacement, horsepower, and miles per gallon by EPA estimates).

A notably useful feature is inclusion of the recall history for each car: a potential buyer can reduce personal risk by finding whether or not the problems have been corrected.

Occasional technical terms aside, reading is easy, and the information provided is convenient to locate and compare.

The Board recommends the *Used Cars Rating Guide* for the core collection of public libraries.

Supplementary Titles

Classic Old Car Value Guide 1990, 24th edition. Quentin Craft, comp. Motorbooks International, 1990. soft. 1 vol. 200 pp. illus. ISBN 0-911473-37-8. $14.95. encyclopedia.
629.28

Board's recommendation: Public libraries.

The Encyclopedia of Classic Cars. Chris Harvey. Octopus Books, 1987; distrib. by Doubleday Canada. hard. 1 vol. 160 pp. illus. ISBN 0-7064-2874-9. $15. encyclopedia.

Board's recommendation: Public libraries.

Jane's Aerospace Dictionary, 3d edition. Bill Gunston, ed. Jane's Information Group, 1989. hard. 1 vol. approx. 550 pp. appendixes. ISBN 0-7106-0580-3. $45. dictionary.
TL509.G86 629.1'03

"From A0A1 to ZYGLO, [*Jane's Aerospace Dictionary*] provides definitions and explanations of the terminology of aerospace and aeronautics. Because of the fast-changing nature of these fields, the editor has added more than 4,000 new terms to his original 1980 work and has revised many of the previous definitions. Just as in the first edition, the main body of this work consists of more than 20,000 concise definitions without illustrations or pronunciation guides. Only specialized aerospace terms are included—any terms commonly found in an ordinary English-language dictionary are excluded. Because of the extensive use of acronyms in both military and civil aviation, almost one-fourth of all of the entries are for acronyms. All terms that have a distinct national or organizational origin are so indicated by a suffix following the definition.

"Each entry is written in the jargon of the aerospace industry, so a novice may need to look at more than one entry to understand the meaning of a single term fully. Some of the definitions are taken from other published sources, but most have been written by the editor. Fortunately, the editor is dedicated to simplifying and preventing the misuse of aerospace terms. In order to be as up-to-date as possible, the newest terms are listed as addenda at the end of the book. While this allowed the editor to include new terms after the main body went to press, it also creates a problem for the user in remembering to check both alphabets when searching for a term. A few other appendixes are provided, including a list of Greek symbols and their meanings, NATO and U.S. aircraft designations, and civil aircraft registrations from around the world. Overall, this work should become the standard source for definitions and acronyms in the aerospace industry." (*BL,* January 1, 1987, p. 699)

"If the nation is concerned about the quality of science and engineering education, books such as this should be added to every library serving adolescents. . . . The alphabetical listing and terse but instructional introduction make this a valuable volume both for general science students confused about terms used in the newspaper and AP physics students with projects." (*SLJ,* April 1987, p. 118)

Also reviewed in: *ARBA,* 1987, p. 674; *R & R Bk N,* Winter 1987, p. 26; *SciTech,* December 1986, p. 36; February 1987, p. 36.

Board's recommendation: Academic libraries.

New and Noteworthy

Dictionary of Automotive Engineering. Don Goodsell. Society of Automotive Engineers, 1989. hard. 1 vol. 182 pp. illus. ISBN 0-408-00783-4. $48. dictionary.

TL9 629.2′03

The *Dictionary of Automotive Engineering* "include[s] some 2,500 technical terms that engineers use plus some slang and common usage terms. The definitions are brief but accurate. . . . This is a small dictionary both in size and number of pages, as compared with another dictionary of automotive terminology, *Automotive Reference.* . . . [However there] . . . are many unique terms in each dictionary. . . . The two dictionaries complement each other. *Automotive Reference* has far more terms but is printed in an unattractive format with little or no white space. *Dictionary of Automotive Engineering,* on the other hand, is well designed." (*BL,* July 1990, p. 2114)

Terri J. Robar

Travel

Travel books have been popular since the days of Marco Polo. In recent years, with long-distance travel becoming more common, there has been a great proliferation of these materials.

Basically, there are two types of travel books: accounts of someone else's trip and accumulations of data for use in planning someone's own trip. It is the latter type that should be included in a core reference collection.

However, no librarian should start a travel collection without careful planning and deliberate restraint. Because there are so many travel guides available, only the largest public libraries can make any attempt to be comprehensive. Most librarians will design a customized collection tailored to the needs of their patrons.

This design should be based on both the geographic representation needed and the types of patrons served. Guide books—such as the Fodor or Michelin series—provide basic worldwide geographic coverage with each volume covering one city (Paris), a region (New England), a country (Germany), or an entire continent (South America). Each librarian must decide how much detail the collection requires and which series can best provide it.

There are also many special-interest groups among travelers, and their needs must also be considered. For example, if the library has many patrons who own recreational vehicles, then the annual *Rand McNally RV Park & Campground Directory* (Rand McNally, annual) should be included. On the other hand, if the average patrons are professional and business people, then the INTERNATIONAL BUSINESS TRAVEL AND RELOCATION DIRECTORY would be a better choice.

The most important thing to keep in mind, however, is currency. Despite the deceptively low price of many of these materials, a travel collection is expensive because so many items need to be updated each year to keep the material current. One acceptable solution is a three-year rotation plan—that is, to update one-third of the titles each year.

The titles that are reviewed in this section include both geographic and specialized travel information. Some titles actually represent a series that includes many travel books (such as FODOR, MICHELIN, MOBIL). A librarian may choose to purchase all volumes in a series, or some volumes from one series and some from another, or selected titles from each series in order to best serve the needs of the patrons. (Note that the bibliographic profiles for these series do not include Library of Congress or Dewey numbers because these numbers vary with the subject of individual volumes.)

Core Titles

	PUBLIC	ACADEMIC	SCHOOL
Fodor's Travel Guides (series) Fodor's Travel Publications/Random House, annual	✦		
International Youth Hostel Handbook, 2 vols. International Youth Hostel Federation, annual	✦	✦	
Michelin Hotel and Restaurant Guides (series); Michelin Tourist Guides (series); Michelin Maps (series) Michelin, annual	✦		
Mobil Travel Guides (series), 8 vols. Prentice-Hall, annual	✦		
OAG Travel Planner Hotel and Motel Redbook, 3 vols. Official Airline Guides, quarterly	✦		
Rand McNally Interstate Road Atlas: United States, Canada, Mexico Rand McNally, annual	✦	✦	✦
Work, Study, Travel Abroad: The Whole World Handbook, 9th edition Cohen, Marjorie Adoff, ed. St. Martin's, 1987	✦	✦	

Fodor's Travel Guides (series). Fodor's Travel Publications/Random House, annual. soft. 140 vols. illus. index. $6.95–$16.95 per vol. handbook.

In 1989 Fodor's began the ambitious project of rewriting all of their travel guides (of which there are some 140 different titles). These new editions of *Fodor's Travel Guides* are better than the earlier editions in their scope, detail, and map quality but not as good in the quality of paper used or the readability of the type because of its size.

The domestic Fodor's guides cover a particular city, state, or geographic area, while the foreign guides focus on a specific country, region of a country, major city, or an entire continent. Each guide describes those businesses or activities that are of interest to travelers, including such things as dining, lodging, transportation, tours, shopping, and special events. The new, revised guides now include such practical information as addresses and phone numbers as well as reviews and ratings of hotels and restaurants and more detailed background essays that create a portrait of each destination.

Each guide usually includes several maps, which have been computer-generated for clarity and accuracy. Points of interest are marked by numbers that correspond to the index on the same page. A nice feature in the new editions is that these numbers are also used within the text where these points of interest are discussed. There is an index in each volume, which makes it easier to access information on specific places or events. The accuracy and currency of *Fodor's Travel Guides* are generally excellent. For example, *Fodor's 90 London* alerts tourists to the fact that the historic restaurant Ye Olde Cheshire Cheese will be closed for most of the year for renovations, and that they may encounter inconvenience using the London subway system because some stations will be closed and others will have their escalators immobilized due to replacement of the old wooden escalators. Also included is information on excursions from London to Bath, Oxford, Stratford, Windsor, and Cambridge, including the best way to get to each town and up-to-date opening hours and admission fees for places of interest.

Equally strong in content are the Fodor's domestic travel guides, as seen in an examination of *Fodor's Florida (1990).* New to this edition is material on the location of welcome centers sponsored by the Florida Division of Tourism and a section called "Highlights '90" that presents discussions of important events, such as the opening of industrialist Henry Ford's winter home in Ft. Myers. Of particular note is a detailed discussion of the new Disney-MGM Studios and Universal Studios in Orlando. One important oversight, however, is the omission of historic Spanish Point in Osprey under points of interest, since it is considered one of the premiere archaeological-historical sites on the west coast of Florida. Hopefully, this omission will be corrected for the next edition of this excellent guide.

Finally, a librarian considering purchasing any of the *Fodor's Travel Guides* should remember that these guides are designed for travelers, not for libraries. As a result, each guide is small, compact, and inexpensive.

The titles are only available in softcover, so the somewhat unsturdy binding may start to deteriorate with even moderate use. The typeface used is as small as possible. The old versions had white pages so that there was a strong contrast with the typeface; the new versions use a darker, lower grade of paper that makes the text much harder to read. Some of the volumes are over 1,000 pages long, occasionally making them hard to handle.

The *Fodor's Travel Guides* series is recommended for public libraries where people might come to actually plan a trip. The information in the *Fodor's Travel Guides* is also better suited to American tourists than European-produced guides such as the MICHELIN series. The Board recommends this work for the core collection of public libraries.

International Youth Hostel Handbook. International Youth Hostel Federation, annual. soft. 2 vols. ISBN 0-901496-26-0. handbook.
TX907.I59 647.944

The *International Youth Hostel Handbook* consists of two volumes which are updated annually. The first volume covers Europe and the Mediterranean; the second covers the rest of the world.

This book lists *only* hostels; that is, lodges that provide basic accommodations for a nominal price. These usually include communal sleeping rooms and kitchens where the lodgers are expected to help clean and cook. The true concept of youth hostels originated in Europe; a whole network of them now crosses the continent, and the concept has been expanded to other areas of the world as well.

Each volume is small and compact and is designed primarily for use by people who are traveling through an area, usually on foot or by bicycle. The text is written in three major European languages as well as in English. The binding is roughly equivalent to the average, thin paperback. Because the reference only includes information about hostels, a traveler would need to consult a tourist guide such as FODOR'S or MICHELIN for a list of things to do or places of interest in each area.

There are maps included in these volumes, but they tend to be very small and cluttered. The books really need to be used with a separate, detailed map of the area in order to be truly useful.

This reference work is an authoritative and up-to-date source of information. The publisher, the International Youth Hostel Federation, not only encourages the use and proliferation of these hostels but also works to ensure that they meet the criteria of reasonable accommodation for which the hostel program has become known.

The idea of a "walking tour" of Europe (or other areas) has always been popular with young adults, especially college students, who travel on a limited budget. Staying in hostels contributes to the low cost of such a vacation.

Any library that has a large number of high school or college students among its patrons should have a copy of this title available for them to use. The Board recommends this work for the core collections of public and academic libraries.

Michelin Hotel and Restaurant Guides (series); ***Michelin Tourist Guides*** (series); ***Michelin Maps*** (series). Michelin, annual. hard and soft. illus. index. $6.95 and up per vol. handbook.

Michelin is a French tire company that has been publishing its "motoring guides" since the early part of the twentieth century, when recreational car travel became common. Today, the renowned *Michelin Guides* are actually composed of three different series.

The Michelin map series consists of detailed road maps for various regions, mostly in Europe. The "green guides" (so called for their traditionally green covers) are detailed tourist guides for cities or specific regions in the United States and foreign countries, with guides for European countries predominating. These guides give practical information on sightseeing, entertainment, and transportation, as well as some historical background. For specific information on hotels and restaurants, the traveler needs to consult the Michelin "red guides."

The red guides are the hotel and restaurant guides. Each hardcover guide covers one or two European countries (such as *France 1990* or *Great Britain and Ireland, 1990*), while the softcover volumes focus on a city or small area (such as *Greater London, 1989*).

The biggest problem with the *Michelin Guides* is language. Each volume is written in the native language of the country being reviewed. However, the front matter of each volume, which explains the symbols and abbreviations used and the basic format, is written in four languages: English, French, Italian, and German. This makes it possible to decipher much of the information in the main part of the guide without being fluent in the language. Europeans are not likely to consider this a problem; many Americans, however, will prefer a travel guide in English such as one from the FODOR'S TRAVEL GUIDES series. However, since *Michelin* has begun to offer guides to cities and regions of the United States, it is also offering more guides to foreign destinations written entirely in English. Currently, there are 21 "green guides" in English for such places as Austria, Rome, and Brittany.

There are many maps scattered throughout each book positioned near the pertinent text, with clear cross-references between the text and the maps. Indexes also make the guides more accessible.

The red guides, like *Great Britain and Ireland, 1990,* list towns alphabetically with a selection of restaurants and hotels evaluated underneath each place. Also included for each entry are the address for the local tourist office and a listing of selected places of interest. The entry for the Grosvenor Hotel in Shaftesbury, England, for example, gives up-to-date information on facilities and prices, while the most important historical sites are listed under the town entry.

The fifth edition of *Michelin London, 1990* (green guide) was also examined for this review. Three excellent foldout maps of central London, the city of London, and outer London are at the front of the volume, while detailed local maps are placed throughout the text. Particularly useful are the floor plans for the major museums and a calendar of events. The London sights are listed alphabetically, with brief descriptions of each plus accurate opening times and admission fees.

Also reviewed was the fourth edition of *Michelin New England* (green guide), which contains a fine introduction to the area, including the landscape, history, art, and legend. Cities, towns, and sights are arranged alphabetically under each state. The entry for Boston even provides a map of the subway system, exact fares, and schedules for subways and street cars.

Overall, the Michelin guides are quite thorough, accurate, and current. The green guides may prove to be more useful since they give detailed information on tourist activities, and there are a number of them available in English. However, the red guides on hotels and restaurants are meant to complement the green guides; they do so quite effectively, in spite of any language barrier. The *Michelin Tourist Guides* (green guides) and the *Michelin Hotel and Restaurant Guides* (red guides) are a useful addition to a library's travel collection. The Board recommends this work for the core collection of public libraries.

Mobil Travel Guides (series). Prentice-Hall, annual. soft. 8 vols. ISBN 0-13-587171-9 (set). $5.95 per vol. handbook.

Originally the *Mobil Travel Guides* were a set of seven volumes, each of which covered one region of the country. Since the first publication in 1984, however, each volume has been revised and published independently. Also, an additional volume has been added covering major cities. This allows a library to purchase only those books that are needed within its own travel collection.

These guides are definitely geared toward the casual tourist and are best suited for public libraries. The entries cover most of the cities in each state and list things to do, places to visit, where to eat, and where to sleep. If anything, there is too much emphasis on lodgings and restaurants, which are rated on a one- to five-star system.

At the beginning of each *Mobil Travel Guide* can be found useful information on handicapped access, money-saving travel programs, border-crossing regulations with Canada and Mexico, and toll-free "800" numbers for hotel and motel chains and car rental agencies.

Accuracy, currency, and thoroughness were certainly apparent in the *Middle Atlantic Mobil Travel Guide, 1989* evaluated for this review. For example, the entry for Kennett Square, Pennsylvania, listed not only the famous Longwood Gardens and Brandywine River Museum but also the lesser-known Phillips Mushroom Place among the places of interest. Likewise, the entry for Beaufort, South Carolina, presented a listing of all historic sites with up-to-date information, beaches, and resorts in and around the town, and gave an accurate address for obtaining more information on the annual tours of homes and gardens.

By the publisher's own admission, this sort of information becomes outdated very quickly. To offset this problem, each volume is revised annually. In order to keep the cost down, the books are printed on thin paper and bound in less-than-sturdy covers; therefore, they do not wear particularly well under heavy use.

There are additional drawbacks to these production methods, namely the poor quality of the printing. The entries for lodgings, for example, often include a variety of symbols to indicate facilities that are available, but the printing is so poor that these symbols are sometimes too dark to identify.

One serious access problem with these books is the location of the maps. All of the large color maps are at the front of the book, while the entries for cities, hotels, restaurants, and places of interest give only map coordinates. This results in a lot of flipping back and forth and could cause frustration for users who are trying to find the right map. The only maps included within the body of the text of each volume are very dark, very small, black-and-white maps, usually showing the route of an "auto tour" of the area.

The editors of each volume are not identified, but they claim to work with numerous field representatives who continuously update the information that is included.

The *Mobile Travel Guides* provide sound basic information for travelers, stressing hotel and motel and restaurant reviews. For a more detailed background of any given city or region and the places of interest, a reader will need to supplement these guides with more inclusive ones, such as the FODOR'S TRAVEL GUIDES. The Board recommends this work for the core collection of public libraries.

OAG Travel Planner Hotel and Motel Redbook. Official Airline Guides, quarterly. soft. 3 vols. ISSN 0894-1726. $88 (per year). guide.
TX907.034 647.94701

The *OAG Travel Planner Hotel and Motel Redbook* is published quarterly in three separate editions: North American, European, and Pacific/Asian. Each edition deals exclusively with lodgings and transportation. The coverage for lodgings does seem to be extensive, but the emphasis appears to be on chain hotels. The information on transportation is limited to which airlines service each city or country. There are some problems, however, with access to this reference work. For example, in the North American edition all of the cities are arranged in one alphabetical list; they are not divided by state. This arrangement can cause frustration when looking up several different cities.

The most cumbersome thing about this reference work, though, is the physical format. The North American edition, for example, is over three inches thick yet has a soft cover and weak binding. The text is printed on very thin, glossy paper and can tear easily. Pages are also slick, which makes them hard to turn.

There is almost too much information in each single-volume issue. First of all, there is a great deal of advertising by various businesses. While such advertisements might keep the costs down, they also tend to clutter the page and add to the size of the volume.

Another example of excess data is the inclusion of unnecessary information (such as the location of a flower shop) found on the airport maps that are included for all major cities. While these maps can be very useful, many of them are too cluttered with information and, therefore, difficult to read.

As with many other travel publishers, OAG uses its own complicated set of symbols and abbreviations to indicate the facilities available at each location. A person must use this title frequently to become accustomed to these symbols. The average library "tourist" patron might be better satisfied using a standard tourist guide such as one of the FODOR'S TRAVEL GUIDES series.

Although often considered a standard for a library travel collection, the *OAG Travel Planner Hotel and Motel Redbook* is better suited for a business office or travel agency where actual travel plans are made. However, it is prudent to include at least the North American edition in a public library collection because many patrons are likely to ask for it. The Board recommends this work for the core collection of public libraries.

Rand McNally Interstate Road Atlas: United States, Canada, Mexico. Rand McNally, annual. soft. 1 vol. 80 pp. ISBN 0-528-89923-6. $3.95. atlas.
G1201.P2R22 912.73

Rand McNally has an excellent and longstanding reputation as a publisher of clear, accurate, readable maps, and that is what the *Rand McNally Interstate Road Atlas* contains. Every American state and Canadian province is represented. A few of the smaller states are shown together on a single page. Each map has its own index on the same page as the map, which allows easy accessibility. There are also smaller maps of major cities showing greater detail.

The map of Mexico, however, is rather disappointing. In spite of its size, the entire country is shown on one page with a smaller map of Mexico City inserted in one corner. The atlas would be more useful if at least some of the Mexican states and other major cities were shown in greater detail.

One of the most surprising things about these maps is the amount of detail that shows up on close inspection. This is due to Rand McNally's masterful use of color. At first glance, there appears to be almost nothing on the map except roads (drawn in bold colors) and cities (shown in black ink). A closer examination will reveal a large number of tourist sites, parks, and other attractions whose names are written in fine red letters. Since these red labels tend to fade into the background when looking at the whole picture, they allow a great deal of information to be included on the map without making it look cluttered.

The atlas is updated annually. For example, the 1990 edition contains 19,536 changes from the 1989 edition. Of particular importance in each edition is the list of improvements to major routes, which are also reflected on the individual maps. In addition to the maps, each edition contains such items as a list of hotel and motel toll-free numbers for the major chains, tourist information centers, a calendar of major events for that year, a telephone area code map, and a section on the opening of new attractions during that year. For example, the 1990 edition lists such events as the opening of the Living World at the St. Louis Zoo and the opening of the Asolo Performing Arts Center in Sarasota, Florida.

As with most travel materials, however, this book is designed for travelers, not libraries. The cover is very thin and damages easily. The binding is done with staples and will come apart with heavy use. Therefore, a librarian should plan on purchasing a new edition each year not only for up-to-date road improvements but also to ensure that a usable copy is available.

Rand McNally publishes several small road atlases that are almost identical; most libraries would be better off to simply buy the *Rand McNally Interstate Road Atlas* (which contains only the basic set of maps) and supplement this volume with some detailed travel guides such as the FODOR'S TRAVEL GUIDES series.

The Board recommends this work for the core collections of public, academic, and school libraries.

Work, Study, Travel Abroad: The Whole World Handbook, 9th edition. Marjorie Adoff Cohen, ed. St. Martin's, 1987. soft. 1 vol. 445 pp. illus. appendix. index. ISBN 0-312-01539-9. $8.95. handbook. LB2376.W48 910.2

The emphasis of *Work, Study, Travel Abroad: The Whole World Handbook* is rather different from most other travel books, because this guide is designed for Americans who want to study or work abroad for either short or long periods of time. The guide is prepared under the auspices of the Council on International Educational Exchange, which sponsors undergraduate foreign study programs, high school exchange programs, work-abroad programs, and special travel services for students and teachers. The focus of this book, therefore, is on providing sources of information both in the United States and in each foreign country on unskilled and skilled jobs, special work projects or volunteer projects available, work regulations, study programs, and tours designed for students.

The volume does not include world coverage, but the amount of information for each country varies from a single address to several pages. The most complete information is for Western European countries that are most often frequented by Americans studying or working abroad.

For example, the section on Great Britain lists many fine books on accommodations and touring by BritRail and even discusses some weekly magazines, such as *Time Out,* which gives up-to-date information on anything happening in London. Also, such useful information as the availability of student discounts (with an International Student Identity Card) at London theaters is included.

The first chapter is particularly useful because it discusses such basic but important items as how to evaluate a foreign study program; how to find the scholarships, loans, and fellowships available; and how to obtain passports, visas, insurance, and international driving permits. Of special interest is the material on the International Student Identity Cards, Teacher Identity Cards, and Youth Hostel Membership Cards. The final chapter, which deals with university-level study programs, is also most helpful because it lists not only the names and addresses of participating colleges and universities but also the contact person for each institution. One drawback is that the travel portion for each country or geographical region tends to deal with the types of transportation that are available rather than prices or schedules.

This title is not revised on a regular basis and, indeed, the updating is done in a rather unusual fashion. Most of the changes are made at the suggestion of the users of the book who write to the publisher. As a matter of fact, the book contains many italicized quotes from past readers that detail their firsthand experiences in traveling, working, and studying abroad. Some checking is done to verify this information before inclusion. However, it would be helpful if the editor did some additional research, especially into the countries with brief coverage, in order to expand these entries. Also, the users will need to consult other travel guides for more up-to-date and specific information concerning prices, schedules, and points of interest.

Only a name index that contains the proper names of organizations, programs, and other entities is included. There are times when a subject index would be very helpful.

Work, Study, Travel Abroad would be useful to any library that includes among its clientele students, teachers, and others interested in foreign study or work programs. The Board recommends this work for the core collections of public and academic libraries.

Supplementary Titles

Baedecker's Guides (series). Prentice-Hall, frequently revised. soft. illus. approx. $17.95 per vol. handbook.

"From the middle of the last century until World War II, the German *Baedekers* were the preeminent guidebooks: in fact the name itself came to mean the genre. While no longer dominant, the series is still very good, and growing. Twenty-six countries, including the United States, are now covered, and there are 28 city guides as well. Prentice-Hall handles American distribution." (*LJ,* May 1, 1988, p. 36)

"*Baedeker's* was the first travel series, initiated in 1894. Smaller in size than the *Blue Guides*... in order to fit the pocket, *Baedeker's* contains somewhat less historical detail. There are many color maps of cities, floor plans of architectural landmarks, and pull-out country maps. Most guides have been revised since 1980. An advantage of the Baedeker series is the coverage of more than 20 major cities, mostly European, but also including Hong Kong and Jerusalem." (*BL,* January 1, 1988, 756)

Also reviewed in: *ARBA,* 1976, p. 282; *Books,* March 1988, p. 12; *GJ,* October 1974, p. 496; *Ms,* July 1984, p. 104.

Board's recommendation: Public libraries.

Blue Guides (series). Norton, annual. soft. illus. index. $14.95 and up per vol. handbook.

"Initiated in 1918 by Ernest Benn, the *Blue Guide* series now includes approximately 30 guides, mostly covering European countries and cities (exceptions include *Boston and Cambridge, New York, Cathedrals and Abbeys of England and Wales,* and *Literary Britain*). They offer the greatest detail of any general travel guide series on history, architecture, and natural history (e.g., diagrams of snakebite marks in *Egypt*), while also including color atlases of countries and cities plus a few pages per volume on practical matters such as transportation, currency, hotels, and restaurants. Their detailed indexes enhance the *Blue Guides'* usefulness as reference tools." (*BL,* January 1, 1988, p. 756).

Also reviewed in: *Books,* March 1988, p. 12; *Conn,* January 1979, p. 66; *CSM,* May 6, 1983, p. 824; *LJ,* May 1, 1988, p. 36; *RSR,* April 1980, p. 15; *TES,* July 27, 1984, p. 20; *Trav,* September 1982, p. 74.

Board's recommendation: Public libraries.

Eurail Guide: How to Travel Europe and All the World by Train. Kathryn Saltzman Turpin and Marvin L. Saltzman. Eurail Guides, annual. soft. 1 vol. ISBN 0-912442-20-4. $12.95. handbook.

385.22

Eurail Guide contains information "on train routes, excursions, Eurailpass bonuses, time-tables, and sightseeing arranged by country and city. [The guide] includes Europe, the Middle East, Africa, Asia, Australia, New Zealand, and North, Central, and South America." (*BL,* January 1, 1988, p. 758)

"The *Eurail Guide*... is the book for anyone who is persuaded by record-breaking statistics. It describes every rail journey in 115 countries which tourists might take, with details of 99 cheap passes and discounts offered by 36 much-travelled countries. It also gives information on 628 one-day train trips from 151 European cities. However, it is written by Americans for Americans: all the prices are in US dollars, and useful addresses are mainly in North America and Canada. ... [The book gives] indispensable advice on planning itineraries and on the problems and other aspects of rail travel, and is extremely comprehensive." (*TES,* May 13, 1983, p. 58)

Board's recommendation: Public libraries.

International Business Travel and Relocation Directory, 5th edition. Gale, 1985. hard. 1 vol. 995 pp. illus. ISBN 0-8103-2040-1. handbook.

910.21

"Though this impressive compilation on selected countries has been prepared specifically for organizations doing business abroad, [*International Business Travel and Relocation Directory*'s] country characteristics, financial information, communications, working hours, and extensive sources of further information will be helpful to anyone investigating present conditions in a country. Drawn from the Overseas Assignment Directory Service and prepared by the editors of Knowledge Industry Publications, this ... [title] is distinguished for its currency and detail. ... Small black-and-white maps of each country are undistinguished but serve as locators.... The directory will be most useful in business libraries and in institutions with international studies programs." (*BL,* June 1, 1986, p. 1447)

"The directory has been divided into two parts. Part One contains background information for personnel officers and for employees going abroad.... Part Two has been subdivided into five areas of the world: Africa, Asia, Europe, Mid East/North Africa, and the Western Hemisphere. ... Within each area, countries are arranged alphabetically." ("Nature of This Directory")

Also reviewed in: *ARBA,* 1988, p. 78.

Board's recommendation: Public libraries.

Let's Go Guides. Harvard Student Agencies. St. Martin's, annual. soft. index. $9.95 and up per vol. ISBN 0-312-03385-0 (1990-U.S.A.). handbook.

"Begun in 1961 by Harvard and Radcliffe students offering budget tips to other youthful travelers, *Let's Go Guides* now include 10 titles covering Europe, the U.S.,

Israel, and Egypt, updated annually by student researchers assigned to travel for two months on a shoestring budget. Each guide contains practical information on planning, transportation, shopping, accommodations, and food, but the bulk of each volume consists of detailed background information (e.g., on prehistoric and Roman remains in the Cotswolds in *Let's Go Britain and Ireland*). Unfortunately for reference collections, the index is to places only and does not include subjects." (*BL,* January 1, 1988, p. 756)

Also reviewed in: *ARBA,* 1984, p. 268; *Books,* March 1988, p. 12; *BW,* January 17, 1982, p. 12; *CSM,* May 1983, p. 824; *Kliatt,* Spring 1984, p. 55; *LJ,* May 1, 1988, p. 36; *SLJ,* March 1983, p. 121.

Board's recommendation: Public, academic, and school libraries.

Pamela J. Peters

Women's Studies

See also Biography

A relatively new field of scholarship, women's studies has a core of excellent resources. The number of universities and other institutions of higher education that recognize women's studies as a discipline and that grant four-year degrees has increased significantly over the last 15 years. Over 400 such institutions now exist.

The reference works reviewed in this section are important for any basic collection. Three titles supply information and guidance for further collection building, such as BUILDING WOMEN'S STUDIES COLLECTIONS; INTRODUCTION TO LIBRARY RESEARCH IN WOMEN'S STUDIES; and WOMEN'S STUDIES: A RECOMMENDED CORE BIBLIOGRAPHY 1980–1985. Many of the other core titles provide lists and evaluations of specialized sources, from fiction anthologies to dissertations and curriculum guides.

The three atlases are valuable because they offer statistics and overviews on the status of women. The biographical dictionaries offer concise data on celebrated women both past and present. Another excellent biographical source is NOTABLE AMERICAN WOMEN (see Biography). Readers are advised to consult reference works within subject areas for data on important women not covered in the sources listed in this category.

More than 60 women's studies journals are now published, from book reviews and scholarly research quarterlies to current issues newspapers. The listings of these important journals are scattered over several indexes; however, access to them remains concentrated in *Women's Studies Abstracts* (Rush, quarterly).

To update and enhance women's studies collections, readers should continue to consult traditional review materials. Readers who are interested in women's studies should also consult the reference RAPE AND SEXUAL ASSAULT: A RESEARCH HANDBOOK (see Human Sexuality).

In addition, an out-of-print book that is worth referring to is *Sexual Harassment: A Guide to Resources* (Dawn M. McGaghy; G. K. Hall, 1985). *—P. J. P.*
With contributions by Leslie L. Gale and Abby Yasgur.

Core Titles

Atlas of American Women. Barbara Gimla Shortridge. Macmillan, 1987. hard. 1 vol. 164 pp. illus. index. ISBN 0-02-929120-8. $85. atlas.
G1201.E1S5 912.13054′0973

The *Atlas of American Women* by Barbara Gimla Shortridge answers many social, political, and eco-

Core Titles

	PUBLIC	ACADEMIC	SCHOOL
Atlas of American Women Shortridge, Barbara Gimla. Macmillan, 1987	✦	✦	
Building Women's Studies Collections: A Resource Guide, Choice Bibliographical Essay series Ariel, Joan, ed. Choice, 1987	✦	✦	
The Continuum Dictionary of Women's Biography, exp. edition Uglow, Jennifer S., comp. and ed. Continuum, 1989		✦	
Introduction to Library Research in Women's Studies Searing, Susan E. Westview, 1985		✦	
Notable American Women 1607–1950, 3 vols. James, Edward T., ed. Belknap/Harvard, 1974 (See Biography)	✦	✦	✦
Notable American Women, the Modern Period Sicherman, Barbara, and Carol Hurd Green, eds. Belknap/Harvard, 1980 (See Biography)	✦	✦	✦
Who's Who of American Women, 16th edition Marquis, 1988	✦	✦	
Women in the World: An International Atlas Seager, Joni, and Ann Olson. Simon & Schuster, 1986	✦	✦	
Women in the World: Annotated History Resources for the Secondary Student Reese, Lyn, and Jean Wilkinson, comps. and eds. Scarecrow, 1987			✦
The Women's Atlas of the United States Gibson, Anne, and Timothy Fast. Facts On File, 1986	✦	✦	✦
Women's Studies: A Recommended Core Bibliography 1980–1985 Loeb, Catherine R., Susan E. Searing, and Esther F. Stineman. Libraries Unlimited, 1987		✦	

nomic questions by using tables, maps, and graphs to illustrate a variety of women's issues.

Shortridge is a geographer who uses data from the 1980 census and from many private and governmental statistical sources up to 1985 to show variations in the status of women on topics such as education, occupations, sports, pregnancy, crime, politics, relationships, and health. Maps show state-by-state and regional differences in the statistical data for the topics. The maps are not full color (brown, beige, and gray are used to show differences), but they are clearly marked and colored. The accompanying text analyzes the data and explains the regional variations.

This atlas gives users the words and the illustrations to view objectively the status and achievements of women in the United States. Shortridge explains in the preface: "If you see more female doctors and lawyers in your city, perhaps you assume that women are doing all right in your state. But your sample is limited and so is your knowledge about conditions in the neighboring state, let alone a state a thousand miles away."

The first chapter concentrates on basic population information, such as distribution, male and female ratios, rural and urban distinctions, age, race, and religious affiliation. The rest of the chapters comprehensively explore data on habits, life styles, and women's progress.

The graphs and color-coded maps are not as useful as the well-written, detailed, and interpretive text that is based on the compiled data. For example, in the information on girls in sports across the country, the insightful explanation of Title IX gives the map meaning. Shortridge's section on suffrage gives dates of state passage of women's suffrage, but the text gives the background material users need to understand the campaign for the vote.

The *Atlas of American Women* is useful for reports and for anyone needing regional comparisons or statistics. The statistics are understandable; Shortridge relies on percentages and proportions. She is honest about the errors that may occur, and she discusses how women's conditions are measured. For example, illiteracy among women was measured by the percentage of women who completed four or fewer years of elementary school. Shortridge admits that the measure works for conventional literacy but does not account for functional literacy or self-educated women.

The Board recommends this work for the core collections of public and academic libraries. —*A. Y.*

Building Women's Studies Collections: A Resource Guide, CHOICE Bibliographical Essay series. Joan Ariel, ed. Choice, 1987. soft. 1 vol. 48 pp. index. ISBN 0-914492-07-1. $120. bibliography.
Z7964.U49B844 016.3054

Building Women's Studies Collections: A Resource Guide has its roots in the women's studies section within the academic division of the American Library Association. This guide was developed to assist librarians and others who wish to develop women's studies collections. The book meets that goal admirably. As the women's studies librarian at the University of California at Irvine, Joan Ariel is in a position to recommend the sources in this guide.

This slim softcover volume contains 284 annotated entries divided into 18 categories of resources, such as publishers, data bases, and microforms. A title index is provided, but there is no access to information by author and subject. Given the length of this guide and the limited number of entries per category, the latter indexes are not essential.

Each category is prefaced by a short paragraph or two explaining the editor's rationale for selection and exclusion. Cross-references to other sections of the guide add to the thoroughness of this work. For each entry, there is complete address, phone number, and, where appropriate, price and subscription. The emphasis is on published English-language resources available primarily in the United States. However, the review sources, publishers, and book dealers listed throughout this guide would easily lead users to distributors and materials outside the United States.

The first section of *Building Women's Studies Collections* introduces basic bibliographies and guides that are essential for tracking publications. Related to this section is "Review Media," a list of review journals and other regularly published sources that connect readers with the small and alternative presses as well as standard review tools. A list of two dozen journals that regularly review books and other media of interest to women's studies concludes this section. These might be considered the core journals in the field of women's studies.

Feminist publishers and mainstream publishers who issue lists, catalogs, or series of women's studies titles as well as children's and young adult book publishers comprise three sections, followed by nongovernment organizations that met the editor's criterion of issuing "publications on a regular basis on women and women's issues." Organizations represent a wide range of interests and geographic areas, such as Girls Club of America, Older Women's League, and Women's International Resource Exchange. One notable omission is the Coalition of Labor Union Women.

Ariel's chapter on audiovisual materials is impressive. In it she highlights special features or publications by or about women for each entry. Another category lists data base vendors with selected files pertinent to women's studies research and data files available on computer tape or disk that may be searched or purchased.

To assist teachers in designing and integrating women's studies into the curriculum, sources of materials suitable for users from preschool to adult are found under "Curriculum and Program Materials." Ariel concludes her volume with a selected bibliography of articles published from 1976 to 1986 on women's collections, guides to specialized sources, feminist periodicals, and more.

Price, size, and, above all, thoroughness make *Building Women's Studies Collections* a must for any library or individual interested in women's studies. The Board recommends this work for the core collections of public and academic libraries. —*P. J. P.*

The Continuum Dictionary of Women's Biography, exp. edition (formerly *International Dictionary of Women's Biography*). Jennifer S. Uglow, comp. and ed. Continuum, 1989. hard. 1 vol. 621 pp. illus. index. ISBN 0-8264-0417-0. $39.50. biographical dictionary.
CT3202.C66 920.72

The Continuum Dictionary of Women's Biography provides concise biographical information on over 1,700 women in various fields from various places and times. This is the new expanded edition of the 1982 *International Dictionary of Women's Biography,* also edited by Jennifer Uglow. Uglow, a biographer and teacher, added and amended over 250 names for this 1989 edition.

How did Uglow select from half of the world's population for inclusion in this biographical dictionary? "Selection is necessarily idiosyncratic. . . . Women whose role in history, or whose contribution to society or use of talent would be remarkable regardless of their sex are included" (foreword).

Entries are concise—they include names, dates, and nationalities followed by short biographies. Most entries are followed by a reference to an autobiography or biography. Cross-references to women with their own entries are in capital letters. There are a few black-and-white photographs scattered throughout the text.

The subject index is indispensable to users who want to know names of women pioneers, nurses, witches, spies, and more. Women may be entered under two or three subject categories. For example, Bella Abzug appears under both "women's rights activists" and "elected officials." Evita Peron is listed under "elected officials" as well as under "beauties, lovers and society leaders." The subject categories also include professions, such as architecture and planning or commerce and industry. Birth and death dates and nationality follow the subject's name in the index.

There are misprints and errors in this work that should be corrected in future editions. For instance, the last paragraph of the foreword to the first edition is missing, and Katharine Hepburn is described as having starred in the film *The Whales of August,* which is not the case (it was Bette Davis).

The entries are written in a conversational tone that seems appropriate for high school students. Subjects are often referred to by their first names.

This dictionary brings together information about many women from diverse backgrounds. The book can be used to answer such simple questions as: Who is she? When did she live? What did she do? However, this dictionary is only a starting point for studying women's history.

The biographies are necessarily brief (a paragraph or two for obscure women and a column for famous women). Some important facts are left out. For instance, the fact that Angela Davis ran for vice-president on the Communist party ticket in 1980 is not included. One of the most useful features of *The Continuum Dictionary of Women's Biography* is its comprehensive list of other reference and research sources about women.

The Board recommends this work for the core collection of academic libraries. —*A. Y.*

Introduction to Library Research in Women's Studies. Susan E. Searing. Westview, 1985. soft. 1 vol. 257 pp. appendixes. ISBN 0-86531-267-2. $31.50. guide.
Z7961.S42 016.3054

In *Introduction to Library Research in Women's Studies,* Susan E. Searing targets the student researcher as well as the professor and scholar. In this comprehensive work, Searing, the women's studies librarian for the University of Wisconsin, puts together not only sources but also strategies for research. She makes this work indispensable for the novice as well as the experienced library user.

This work is organized by type of research tool, proceeding from general to specialized bibliographies and indexes. Part I introduces the reader to women's studies, then follows with a well-defined research strategy and a discussion of library organization and services. Searing explains the built-in biases and complexities of finding information on women's issues. Additional chapters address the use of biographical sources, directories of organizations, relevant women's studies periodicals, on-line data bases, and selected guides to special collections in women's studies (for example, the Schlesinger Library at Radcliffe).

Each chapter dealing with subject bibliographies and indexes includes a two- to four-paragraph overview of the scholarship and research in that particular field and suggests appropriate subject headings for use in the library catalog. Annotations are provided for each entry; they are well written and substantial, generally two to five sentences long. The annotations point out portions of the work or the best way to access material on women's studies. Dewey Decimal and Library of Congress numbers are provided for each title, and schedules for the two systems are in appendixes.

Many of the sources in this guide are periodicals, annuals, or other candidates for updates. Searing also edits *Feminist Collections: A Quarterly of Women's Studies Resources* and *New Books on Women and Feminism,* both of which are periodicals that are published by the University of Wisconsin Library. They alert readers to new reference materials in the field.

The weakest area in this guide is the international sources, possibly because there were few materials until the last four or five years. Other ways to improve *Introduction to Library Research* might include numbering the entries and having a more varied layout.

The interdisciplinary nature of women's studies comes through in every chapter of *Introduction to Library Research in Women's Studies,* from the sources mentioned to the suggested approaches for research. This book is a model for teaching critical thinking and library research.

The Board recommends this work for the core collection of academic libraries. —*P. J. P.*

Notable American Women 1607–1950. Edward T. James, ed. Belknap/Harvard, 1974. soft. 3 vols. 2,141 pp. appendix. ISBN 0-674-62734-2 (set). $40 (set). biographical dictionary.
CT3260N57 920.7N843

See Biography.

Notable American Women, the Modern Period. Barbara Sicherman and Carol Hurd Green, eds. Belknap/Harvard, 1980. hard and soft. 1 vol. 795 pp. appendix. ISBN 0-674-62732-6 (hard); 0-674-62733-4 (soft). $48 (hard); $12.95 (soft). biographical dictionary.
CT3260.N573 920.720973

See Biography.

Who's Who of American Women, 16th edition. Marquis, 1988. hard. 1 vol. ISBN 0-8379-0416-1. $170. biographical directory.
CT3260.W5 920.7

Once a directory of notable female civic and religious leaders and writers, *Who's Who of American Women* is now a standard source for biographical sketches of living American women. The directory adheres to the format of other Marquis publications, selecting biographees based on the position they have attained or their accomplishments.

Information is provided for each entry in the following order: name, occupation, vital statistics, parents, marriage, children, education, professional certification, career history, written or creative works, civic and political activities, military service, awards and fellowships, professional and association membersips, political affiliation, religion, clubs, lodges, avocations, and home and office addresses.

This most recent edition, published in 1988, lists over 25,000 sketches of notable women. Omissions are unavoidable since biographees' permission is required for inclusion. However, users might wonder what happened to Joan Armatrading, Meredith Monk, and even Susan Searing, whose work in the field of women's studies research and librarianship is noteworthy. Several national names, such as Alice Walker, Pat Schroeder, and Nancy Teeters, are listed in this work.

Many of the women in *Who's Who of American Women* are prominent executives, business owners, writers, performers, and educators. It seems that all of the women could be found in a myriad of individual directories, trade association membership lists, citation directories and data bases, and congressional biographical dictionaries. Academic libraries and organizations that target women will find it convenient to have one place to look for the standardized information. However, subject and geographical indexes would have greatly enhanced *Who's Who of American Women.* Nevertheless, this is a valuable work.

The Board recommends this work for the core collections of public and academic libraries. —*P. J. P.*

Women in the World: An International Atlas. Joni Seager and Ann Olson. Simon & Schuster, 1986. soft. 1 vol. 130 pp. illus. index. ISBN 0-671-63070-9. $12.95. atlas.
HQ1154.03965 912

In *Women in the World: An International Atlas,* geographers and feminists Joni Seager and Ann Olson show the world of women in economic, political, and social terms. The task of finding international data on women was difficult and suggests the "official invisibility of women."

Most information was gathered from feminists' writing in small presses, women's organizations, newsletters, and various journals throughout the world as well as from United Nations agency publications. Official U. S. and European statistical sources were also tapped. The most recent information is from 1985.

The book is divided into the following broad topics: "The Second Sex," "Marriage," "Motherhood," "Work," "Resources," "Welfare," "Authority," "Body Politics," "Change," and "Statistical Politics." Each topic is broken down into issues that are covered in one or more maps or charts. For example, the subject of rape is in the chapter "Body Politics." Rape is described in a world map of reported rapes per 100,000 population; another world map shows the status of wife rape laws; a chart describes percentage increases in rape in the United States, Canada, and France; and another chart shows the increase in rape crisis centers in the United States and United Kingdom.

Basic inequalities between men and women are illustrated throughout the book. The first part of the atlas uses maps and graphs to show that while women outnumber men, the status of women all over the world—based on literacy, contraceptive use, and paid work—is extraordinarily low. Each illustration is accompanied by a short description.

The graphs are visual and concise, but sometimes they require deciphering. Some graphs are crowded with data and symbols, such as the one with ladders showing women as a proportion of all teachers.

The back of the atlas consists of tables that list world countries in alphabetical order and give data on the following: population, rural population, population over 60 years, marriage, children, contraceptive use by women, maternal mortality, proportion of women in labor force, agricultural labor force, proportion of girls in secondary education, illiteracy, life expectancy at birth, anemia during pregnancy, and the year the right to vote was won by women.

The maps should not be used alone. Readers should refer to the back notes for explanations and discussion of the data. One of the most interesting maps, "Mapping the Patriarchy," is the last one in the book. It shows parts of women's lives that are not recorded in standard sources—the missing data that are found in this book.

The notes section of *Women in the World* consists of clearly written, interesting explanations of the maps and graphs. Users will find comments on the availability and reliability of the data. These notes are very helpful in understanding the complicated ideas. Both the notes and the bibliography list the sources for all data.

The index is located at the end of *Women in the World: An International Atlas.* It is sufficient for the atlas: it directs the user to the appropriate map or note on a topic.

The Board recommends this work for the core collections of public and academic libraries. —*A. Y.*

Women in the World: Annotated History Resources for the Secondary Student. Lyn Reese and Jean Wilkinson, comps. and eds. Scarecrow, 1987. hard. 1 vol. 228 pp. illus. appendix. indexes. ISBN 0-8108-2050-1. $22.50. bibliography.
Z7961.R44 016.3054

Women in the World: Annotated History Resources for the Secondary Student is a bibliography of over 430 print and audiovisual sources. This book is intended for teachers who want to stimulate their students' interest in women's history and in the contemporary problems and conditions of women. Topics range from women leaders in the anti-apartheid movement in South Africa to images of women in ancient Rome to poetry by Jamaican women to the stories of female survivors of the Holocaust. Well-known and respected writers, such as Ellen Kuzayawo, Nawal El Saadawi, Margaret Randall, and Paule Marshall, are represented. However, most of the first-person accounts, biographies, autobiographies, and social histories reflect the accomplishments of less famous women.

The compilers, Lyn Reese and Jean Wilkinson, are classroom teachers who recognized that good world history materials about women were not easily available. Reese and Wilkinson have developed a curriculum about women for world history classes and are the editors of a cross-cultural anthology titled *I'm on My Way Running: Women Speak on Coming of Age.* The research for *Women in the World* was financed by a Women's Education Equity Act Grant from the U.S. Department of Education.

Most of the listed works have been published since 1980, simply because women's studies as a cross-cultural discipline is a recent development. In the introduction, Reese and Wilkinson acknowledge that some sources may have been overlooked, and they ask for suggestions from other educators.

The book is organized by geographic area. The sections are "Africa," "Asia," "Cross-Cultural" (works drawn from more than one country), "Europe," "Latin America," and "The Middle East/North Africa." North America is not included. The introduction to each section discusses prevalent themes in the literature about the region, the stereotypes held about women there, difficulties in finding works, and areas in which more research is needed. Within each section, the titles are grouped into the following categories: background/reference, anthology, autobiography/biography, first-person accounts, fiction, and curriculum. Audiovisual materials are usually listed with curriculum.

Each annotation describes the time period, place, and themes of the work. Also provided are thorough descriptions of the books' content. The reading level is geared toward junior and senior high school students. The compilers give top rating to books that are "unique, substantive, well written, and notably relevant to the secondary student" ("How to Use the Bibliography"). The authors also suggest topics for classroom discussion, exercises, and research projects.

Reese and Wilkinson selected materials that would attract young adult readers. They did not include titles that require background knowledge beyond the secondary school level. "We tried to select only those pieces that most closely met the criteria of historical and cultural context, appropriate reading and maturity level, emotional impact, and, where possible, allowed women to speak for themselves," they comment in "How to Use the Bibliography."

There is a title index, but it is of limited use to teachers who do not have knowledge of the literature.

To find information on women and unpaid labor in sub-Saharan Africa, for instance, one would have to read the "Themes" section of each annotation in the Africa section and then check the "Cross-Cultural" section for relevant titles. It is easier to look up titles about a specific country, because there is a place index that lists the page numbers of such titles. Each section of the bibliography can be read easily and quickly, but a subject index should be considered for future editions. There is an appendix giving the names and addresses of the publishers and distributors of the resources mentioned.

Reese and Wilkinson have covered diverse topics with depth and balance. *Women in the World: Annotated History Resources for the Secondary Student* is an important step in providing a "more realistic history" to young adults, a history that recognizes the accomplishments of all women without regard to race or class.

The Board recommends this work for the core collection of school libraries. —*L. L. G.*

The Women's Atlas of the United States. Anne Gibson and Timothy Fast. Facts On File, 1986. hard. 1 vol. 248 pp. illus. appendixes. index. ISBN 0-8160-1170-2. $60. atlas.
G1201.E1G 912.13046

The Women's Atlas of the United States depicts the status of women in the United States in a wide variety of color maps. State-by-state and regional comparisons are supplemented by text. Categories include basic demographics, race and age distribution, educational attainment, occupations, marital status, vital statistics, contraception and abortion laws, and crime and politics.

The maps are generally a full page or half a page, and they are multicolor or shades of one color. The authors provide an explanation of the different maps used, such as chloropleth, symbol, prism, dot, and cartograms. A dozen or more maps are difficult to read. They would be clearer if a range of colors had been used. Most maps use color effectively.

Data are generally broken down into quintiles. Where appropriate, statistics are given for women as a percentage of the population being considered. For example, one map shows the percentage of all correctional officers that are female rather than just the number of female correctional officers. However, the authors are inconsistent here. For instance, a map showing that 2 percent of women in Oregon are black would be more useful if it included a racial breakdown of the population as a whole. Another map identifies the percentage of women living in rural versus urban areas—but what is the total population in these areas and how does it compare with men living in the same areas?

Although the main source of data is the 1980 census, a check of the well-documented "bibliography for maps" at the end of this atlas indicates extensive use of other government and private sources of statistics, making some of the data current as of 1983 or 1984. A few maps show data from 1977 and 1979. Life expectancy information is inexcusably from 1969 to 1971. Readers could update data in these maps with later editions of sources in the bibliography.

The subject index leads readers to the maps and the information in the text. A more detailed table of contents with explanatory, less catchy titles would improve the access in this work. For example, under the chapter heading "Family," we find "The Tie That Binds," "Kid Stuff," and "Breaking Up Is Hard to Do." An appendix in this work consolidates the information from almost every map in the book into columnar charts; each state marks the columns, and an *H* or *L* plots the data from each map (this presumably stands for the highest or lowest values—no key is provided).

Both *The Women's Atlas of the United States* and ATLAS OF AMERICAN WOMEN are of high quality. The major differences are as follows: Gibson and Fast have 145 maps versus Shortridge's 118. Gibson and Fast summarize the map data, whereas Shortridge analyzes the data in depth, citing scholarly journal studies. Gibson and Fast's full-page color maps are generally grouped together, such as three maps with one page of text, whereas Shortridge covers the same information with smaller maps surrounded by five pages of analysis. Each atlas has unique data: Maps unique to Gibson and Fast include marital rape laws, women on death row, number of female state officials, and number of women in Republican and Democratic committees. Shortridge's work shows literacy rates; work disability; high school, collegiate, and Olympic sports participation; and lack of seat belt use.

While many of the data in *The Women's Atlas of the United States* are found in standard, separately published works, there is great utility and convenience in having the data in one book, especially one that is so visually accessible and appealing.

The Board recommends this work for the core collections of public, academic, and school libraries.

—*P. J. P.*

Women's Studies: A Recommended Core Bibliography 1980–1985. Catherine R. Loeb, Susan E. Searing, and Esther F. Stineman. Libraries Unlimited,

1987. hard. 1 vol. 538 pp. appendix. indexes. ISBN 0-87287-472-9. $55. bibliography.
Z7963.F44L63 016.3054′2

Women's Studies: A Recommended Core Bibliography 1980–1985 is a continuation of Esther F. Stineman's 1982 work by the same name. This comprehensive work serves as a checklist for large research collections and as a springboard for research in most areas pertaining to women's studies. Stineman collaborated with Catherine R. Loeb and Susan E. Searing, both of the University of Wisconsin women's studies librarian's office, to compile this bibliography. This book contains 1,211 entries that evaluate English-language or translated titles in 19 broad categories, such as anthropology, art, business, education, history, law, literature, politics, psychology, sports, and the women's movement.

The first volume included some works published before the volume's beginning date of 1975; however, this supplement carries only works issued from 1979 to 1985. Both mainstream publishers and women's presses are found in this excellent work. A close look at the titles and the subject index reflects the authors' awareness of societal changes and the new concerns of feminist scholarship in the 1980s. For example, some titles address Latinas, minority women in literature, sports, international women's movements, discrimination, and disability.

Each section includes an introduction that explains the criteria for including books in that section and also refers the reader to general surveys in the particular field. This feature of citing other, sometimes peripheral or less pivotal, works is carried out in the annotations, practically doubling the number of works mentioned in this volume. Annotations are evaluative, authoritative, and extremely lucid. The number of works in each category varies substantially. "Literature" is the largest section with 332 titles, followed by "Reference Works," which has 100 titles. The smallest sections are "Science/Technology," "Sports," and "Language/Linguistics," each with 16 or fewer titles. All works cited or referred to are found in the author and title indexes.

Duplication between this book and other works is found mainly in chapters on reference works and periodicals. Both of those lists are similar to works in Joan Ariel's BUILDING WOMEN'S STUDIES COLLECTIONS: A RESOURCE GUIDE and Susan E. Searing's INTRODUCTION TO LIBRARY RESEARCH IN WOMEN'S STUDIES. Neither Ariel nor Searing annotate their lists of periodicals, and none of these three sources indicate where the titles are indexed.

There are seven or eight misplaced titles and one ghost reference in this work's index. Other than that, however, the indexing of *Women's Studies* is thorough and well thought out. For example, title and author indexes differentiate between main entries and references by using boldface and italic type, and main entries are subdivided in the subject index.

Whether this bibliography is used to verify works, to chronicle the trends in scholarship and publishing in women's studies, or to locate materials for research, both this volume and its predecessor are invaluable for any serious women's studies collection.

The Board recommends this work for the core collection of academic libraries. —*P. J. P.*

Supplementary Titles

Almanac of American Women in the 20th Century. Judith Freeman Clark. Prentice-Hall, 1987. soft. 1 vol. 320 pp. index. ISBN 0-13-022641-6. $15.95. encyclopedia.
HQ1420.C55 305.4

"[*Almanac of American Women in the 20th Century*] attempts to give readers a 'broad overview of women's history' by describing the achievements of the 'many women whose hard work, intelligence, courage, and talent transformed our nation during this century.' The Almanac, with coverage from January 1900 to March 15, 1987, is divided into nine chapters covering a decade each and an index. Within each chapter, a chronological listing of . . . events (each labeled with headings, such as Women's Issues, Popular Culture, Politics, Science, Ideas/Beliefs and followed by a one-sentence description) is interspersed with one-half- to one-page biographies and topical essays." (*BL,* October 15, 1987, p. 374)

"This work offers vignettes of significant issues and selected events marking women's achievements in recent U.S. history. . . . Although the essays are cursory and the criteria for inclusion . . . unclear, the Almanac can serve as a beginning research tool or as a general-interest source. The book's real value is in the chronology of events, which includes items as recent as March 1987. The Almanac complements the earlier *Good Housekeeping Woman's Almanac* (1977)." (*LJ,* August 1987, p. 115)

Also reviewed in: *Kliatt,* January 1988, p. 37; *RQ,* Winter 1987, p. 269.

Board's recommendation: Public and academic libraries.

Encyclopedia of Feminism. Lisa Tuttle. Facts On File, 1986. hard. 1 vol. 400 pp. ISBN 0-8160-1424-8.

$24.95. encyclopedia.
HQ1115.T87 305.4

"This one-volume [*Encyclopedia of Feminism*] seeks to define feminism by examining . . . figures, events, movements, slogans, works, ideas, and terminologies that have contributed to the development of feminist thought. In alphabetical sequence, the book contains explanations of such topics as the Women's Social and Political Union and the Equal Rights Amendment, . . . biographies of people, living and dead, who have influenced the cause; and definitions of concepts and terms specific to feminism: *gynergy, he/man language, individualist feminism.* It also discusses more familiar concepts, such as housework, marriage, and pornography, from a feminist perspective." (*BL,* March 1, 1987, p. 1000)

"[This encyclopedia is] an excellent reference guide to a vast body of information. Truly the first work of its kind, it goes far toward its stated goal of providing in one volume ready access to major events, people, ideas, organizations, and publications in the contemporary and past women's movements. . . . Extremely useful are the definitions of various concepts from the women's movement. . . . There are very few minor inaccuracies or omissions. The good cross-reference structure leads from one entry to another, making the book difficult to put down. An extensive, timely bibliography further enhances the value of this encyclopedia." (*Choice,* April 1987, p. 1204)

Also reviewed in: *A Lib,* March 1987, p. 229; *ARBA,* 1987, p. 334; *Brit Bk N,* January 1987, p. 13; *B Rpt,* March 1987, p. 49; *Obs,* March 22, 1987, p. 26; *R & R Bk N,* Winter 1987, p. 11; *TES,* May 22, 1987, p. 11; *WLB,* December 1986, p. 64.

Board's recommendation: Academic libraries.

The Equal Rights Amendment: An Annotated Bibliography of the Issues, 1976–1985. Renee Feinberg. Greenwood, 1986. hard. 1 vol. 164 pp. index. ISBN 0-313-24762-5. $35. bibliography.
KF4758.A1F45 342.73

"The eleven chapters in [*The Equal Rights Amendment*], organized by subject, cover public opinion and party politics; federal and state interpretations of ERA; employment; education; family and religion; the military; ratification efforts; boycott, extension, and rescission; defeat; television news coverage; and the period after the ERA's defeat in 1982. . . . The bibliography lists some 700 books, newspapers and journal articles, government publications and ERIC documents. Articles have been selected from both scholarly journals, such as law reviews, and popular magazines. . . . In addition to author and subject indexes, the book . . . includes a chronology of the Equal Rights Amendment, a list of states whose constitutions include an equal rights amendment or provisions along with year of adoption, a list of organizations that responded to requests for items for inclusion in the bibliography, and lists of organizations that in 1978 were on record as supporters of the ERA or in opposition to it." (*BL,* May 15, 1987, p. 1425)

"Few are better prepared to compile this comprehensive bibliography than Feinberg, who brings to the task a professional and long-term commitment to women's rights issues. . . . Access to bibliographic data bases and to the Vanderbilt Television News Archive assisted Feinberg in locating some elusive citations and in providing access to nonprint sources. It also enabled her to analyze the impact of mass TV coverage on the nonratification of the ERA. The introduction contains a well-written 20-page history of the nearly 60-year effort to pass the ERA and renders the book especially valuable." (*Choice,* May 1987, p. 1376)

Also reviewed in: *R & R Bk N,* Spring 1987, p. 18.

Board's recommendation: Academic libraries.

Feminist Resources for Schools and Colleges: A Guide to Curricular Materials, 3d edition. Anne Chapman, comp. Feminist Pr., 1986. soft. 1 vol. 208 pp. indexes. ISBN 0-935312-35-8. $12.95. bibliography.
Z5817.C48 016.375

"This revised edition of a work first published in 1973 describes 310 print (books, articles, pamphlets, periodicals) and 135 audiovisual (films, filmstrips, records, cassettes, and slides) resources published between 1975 and 1984. The entries [in *Feminist Resources for Schools and Colleges*] 'are organized by academic subject areas. Textbooks and biographies, novels, poetry, and drama by individual authors are excluded. Selection was based on "nonsexist outlook" (which Chapman did not find in all selections), multicultural perspective, sensitivity to gender or other forms of discrimination, sound scholarship, and reader appeal. Nonprint annotations are based on copy from distributor catalogs.' " (*Choice,* March 1987, p. 1026)

"The expansion of [this guide] from 67 pages in the second edition (1977) to 190 pages in this third edition reflects the growth and availability of literature and media about women. . . . [The work contains] descriptive, evaluative annotations. . . . The length of the annotations has been increased from one sentence to 50- to 200-word paragraphs and may include comparisons with other entries as well as estimations of age and reading levels. The most outstanding additions to the third edition are the author/title and subject indexes, which provide greater access to materials cited. . . . Refined by Chapman's editorial and subject expertise, the guide has evolved into a serviceable bibliography of textbook and supplemental materials for educators creating or revising nonsexist or feminist curricula." (*BL,* May 15, 1987, p. 1427)

Also reviewed in: *Kliatt,* Spring 1987, p. 38; *SLJ,* March 1987, p. 90.

Board's recommendation: Academic libraries.

The New Our Bodies, Ourselves; A Book by and for Women, rev. edition. Boston Women's Health Book Collective. Touchstone/Simon & Schuster, 1985. soft. 1 vol. 647 pp. illus. 0-671-46088-9. $16.95. handbook.
RA778.N67 613.04244

The New Our Bodies, Ourselves "is a collection of information and commentary on the physiology and psychology of women. . . . There has been an expansion of most of the original sections and . . . [there are] new chapters on such topics as new reproductive technologies, growing older, and environmental and occupational health." (*LJ,* March 15, 1985, p. 66)

"To simply call this a medical or health sourcebook is too limiting. With more than 600 pages of intense textual matter, enhanced with notable illustrations and enlightening personal quotations, it is a tour de force . . . [which] transcends its bodily beginnings into a series of compassionate expressions on the complete and potential human female." (*Choice,* June 1985, p. 1478)

Also reviewed in: *A Lib,* April 1985, p. 270; *BL,* November 15, 1984, p. 402; *BW,* January 20, 1985, p. 4; *Kliatt,* Spring 1985, p. 42; *KR,* November 15, 1984, p. 1077; *Ms,* May 1985, p. 96; *Nat,* April 20, 1985, p. 473; *N Dir Wom,* March 1985, p. 6; *NW,* February 4, 1985, p. 9; *NYTBR,* January 13, 1985, p. 16; *USA T,* January 4, 1985, p. 20; *VQR,* Summer 1985, p. 101; *WCRB,* March 1985, p. 19.

Board's recommendation: Public and academic libraries.

Women and Work, Paid and Unpaid: A Selected, Annotated Bibliography. Marianne A. Ferber. Garland, 1987. hard. 1 vol. 408 pp. index. ISBN 0-8240-8690-2. $35. bibliography.
Z7963.E7F47 016.3314

Women and Work, Paid and Unpaid is "an annotated index of 1,031 articles and books, mainly written since the 1960s, dealing with women's work in the labor market and at home. Though emphasis is on the United States, one section deals with research in other countries. In addition to the full bibliographic citation, annotations use a key to indicate whether the item emphasizes primarily theory, methodology, empirical evidence, or policy issues and whether considerable background in econometrics or mathematics is required. Where authors wrote very similar papers on the same topic, they generally are summarized under one heading. Comments and rebuttals are added to the original summary. Editorial comments that may be 'laudatory, explanatory, or critical' are appended to many of the summaries, and the entries frequently include cross references to investigations that obtained similar or conflicting results. Selections are arranged alphabetically under the following nine headings: general works, the family, labor force participation, occupational distribution, earnings and female-male pay gap, discrimination, unemployment, women in individual occupations, and women throughout the world. Each section is preceded by an introduction by the author. Ferber is Professor of Economics at the University of Illinois, Urbana." (*JEL,* March 1988, p. 213)

"The focus is on the literature of economics, but important references from other social science fields are also included. Although significant early works are listed, most of the books and articles date from the 1960s forward, since increased interest in women's economic roles dates from this time.

"[In this volume] the items chosen for inclusion are primarily important, original, scholarly works, often requiring some technical knowledge on the part of the reader. However, brief references to more popular or derivative works are also included. The summaries themselves also give useful information about research and conclusions even if the source may be difficult. This bibliography will be used in [specialized] . . . library settings." (*BL,* February 1, 1988 p. 920)

Also reviewed in: *ARBA,* 1988, p. 351; *Choice,* January 1988, p. 744; *Econ Bks,* March 1988, p. 95; *R & R Bk N,* February 1988, p. 8.

Board's recommendation: Academic libraries.

Women's Studies: A Bibliography of Dissertations 1870–1982. V. F. Gilbert and D. S. Tatla, comps. Basil Blackwell, 1985. hard. 1 vol. 496 pp. index. ISBN 0-631-13714-9. $55. bibliography.
Z7961.G55 016.3054

In *Women's Studies,* "Gilbert and Tatla have identified over twelve thousand dissertations on topics in the arts, criminology, demography, education, employment, family dynamics, feminism, health, history, language, law, literature, media, philosophy, physiology, politics, psychology, religion, reproduction, sexuality, sociology, sport, and women in the Third World—by author, title, university, and year of submission.

"The dissertations . . . are mainly in English. . . . [The authors] have given . . . a fairly comprehensive listing of dissertations about women—individuals, groups, movements, women-related issues and rights. The volume is exceptionally well organized with each of the topics analyzed closely. Under literature, for example, we find comparative studies, African, American, Asian, English, French, Islamic and so on; these also are subdivided into general studies and those on individual writers. . . . This volume makes a substantial contribution to scholarship about women by the number of works cited and its admirable chapter organization and subject index." (*ARBA,* 1986, p. 385)

Also reviewed in: *Choice,* April 1986, p. 1194.

Board's recommendation: Academic libraries.

New and Noteworthy

The Dictionary of Feminist Theory. Maggie Humm. Ohio State Univ. Pr., 1990. hard. 278 pp. ISBN 0-8142-0506-2 (hard); 0-8142-0507-0 (soft). $39.95 (hard); $14.95 (soft). dictionary.
HQ1115.H86 305.42'01

The Dictionary of Feminist Theory outlines "historical changes in, and [provides] multiple definitions of, major concepts in feminist writing in order to highlight the diversity of feminist throught. Both theories and theorists are found among the approximately 600 entries. [Theories include] *Christian Feminism, Consciousness-Raising, Family Wage* . . . and *Sexual Politics.* Theorists include . . . Susan B. Anthony . . . Germaine Greer . . . and Nancy Chodorow. . . . There are no cross-references between entries." (*BL,* April 1, 1990, p. 1575)

Handbook of American Women's History. Angela Howard Zophy, ed. Garland, 1990. hard. 1 vol. 763 pp. index. ISBN 0-8240-8744-5. $75. dictionary.
HQ1410.H36 305.4'0973

"Of the more than 1,000 entries in [*Handbook of American Women's History*], over a third are biographies of women, living and deceased. . . . There are also entries for associations and institutions *(Girl Scouts of America),* terms . . . laws and court cases . . . health issues . . . aspects of popular culture . . . social movements . . . novels . . . and very broad subjects like *Education, Business,* and *Music.* . . . There is an extensive system of cross references." (*BL,* March 15, 1990, p. 1500)

T.A.P.P. Sources: A National Directory of Teenage Pregnancy Prevention Programs. Dominique Treboux. Scarecrow, 1989. hard. 1 vol. 557 pp. ISBN 0-8108-2277-6. $42.50. directory.
363.9'6

The goal of *T.A.P.P. Sources* is to "'enable new and existing programs to easily access the work and wisdom of others in the field, to facilitate coordination of services, and to promote statewide networking.'

"[The book] includes a chapter that describes the various types of programs presently in existence. . . . Another chapter discusses teenage sexual behavior and the prevalent sex-role stereotypes that influence and govern it. . . . Information in each listing includes address and telephone number; contact person; type of agency; scope of program; years in operation; size of staff; target population; fees; whether parental notification is required; goals; direct, indirect, and special services; and funding sources. The book concludes with a list of six T.A.P.P. resource organizations . . . an annotated bibliography of 12 relevant publications . . . and a copy of the survey used to collect the information for the book." (*BL,* May 15, 1990, pp. 1844–1845)

Women's Studies Encyclopedia, vol. 1: ***Views from the Sciences.*** Helen Tierney, ed. Greenwood, 1989. hard. 417 pp. index. ISBN 0-313-26725-1. $59.95. encyclopedia.
305.4'03

"This first volume of a proposed three-volume [*Women's Studies Encyclopedia* brings] together feminist research in scientific disciplines, including medicine, psychology, sociology, anthropology, economics, and political science. . . . The 250 . . . entries are arranged alphabetically, beginning with *Abortion* and ending with *Working Women.* . . . Extensive cross-references link related articles." (*BL,* January 1, 1990, p. 949)

Donald E. Collins

World History

See also African History; American History; Ancient History; Biography; British History; European History

World history is essentially the story of humankind. As such, it concerns the entire span of time, from prehistory to the present, and all fields of human interest and activity. Thus it may include any or all of the following: the ancient, medieval, and modern periods; the world as a whole, Europe, Asia, Africa, or any other multinational geographic region; and the social, political, intellectual, economic, or other interests and activities of humanity. The field is very popular and has a large readership that includes young and old, the general public, students, and scholars. There is a large body of reference literature from which librarians may select appropriate material to satisfy the information needs of this far-ranging group.

Because history includes so many fields, librarians may rely on many of the standard dictionaries, encyclopedias, atlases, and other reference works for answering questions. However, these works must be supplemented with a variety of other subject-area materials. History texts, while not technically reference books, nevertheless provide answers that may be difficult to locate in other sources. The core and supplementary lists also reflect the frequent requests of users for maps. THE TIMES ATLAS OF WORLD HISTORY and THE HARPER ATLAS OF WORLD HISTORY offer affordable choices for libraries. Dates and other information concerning chronology are provided in several titles.

At the college and professional level, the need for identifying significant books and articles is great. *Historical Abstracts,* which is also available as an on-line data base, is an excellent guide to current periodical literature, while Frank Magill's GREAT EVENTS FROM HISTORY series not only treats major books but is also an important source of brief factual data on historical events. Biographical information, another common need among library patrons, may be provided through any number of national and general biographical sources, discussed in full in the Biography category of this buying guide.

The need for primary source materials is a major concern of scholars researching in history. While there are many guides to special collections in libraries and archives, perhaps the most useful is the *National Union Catalog of Manuscript Collections* (NUCMC), which identifies manuscript materials available throughout the United States. News coverage, which is a concern of patrons at all levels, is discussed in the Current Events category; however, past events are adequately represented here in the Facts On File DAY BY DAY series.

Finally, it should be noted that there are many valu-

Core Titles

	PUBLIC	ACADEMIC	SCHOOL
The Cambridge Ancient History Series, 1st, 2d, and 3d editions Cambridge, 1930–1988 (See Ancient History)		✦	
Day by Day Facts On File, 1977–1988	✦		✦
Dictionary of the Middle Ages, 13 vols. Strayer, Joseph R., ed. Scribner, 1982–1989 (See European History)	✦	✦	
An Encyclopedia of World History: Ancient, Medieval and Modern, Chronologically Arranged, 5th edition Langer, William L., comp. and ed. Houghton Mifflin, 1972	✦	✦	✦
Great Events from History Magill, Frank N., ed. Salem, 1973–1980	✦	✦	
The Harper Atlas of World History Vidal-Naquet, Pierre, ed. Harper & Row, 1987			✦
The Times Atlas of World History, 5th edition, rev. Barraclough, Geoffrey, ed. Hammond, 1985	✦	✦	✦

able works not treated in this section which, though out of print, may be found in a good core collection. Of particular interest is the American Historical Association's *Guide to Historical Literature* (1961), which provides students and librarians with an exceptionally good introduction to reference and nonreference materials in world history. Similarly, the 12-volume *New Larned History for Ready Reference, Reading, and Research* (1922–1924) still serves as an excellent source of quick facts and encyclopedic information.

Core Titles

The Cambridge Ancient History Series, 1st, 2d, and 3d editions. Cambridge, 1930–1988. hard. 12 vols. plus 7 vols. of plates. illus. appendixes. history.
D57.C25 913.32

See Ancient History.

Day by Day. Facts On File, 1977–1988. hard. 5 vols. illus. index. ISBN 0-87196-375-2 (*The Forties*); 0-87196-383-3 (*The Fifties*); 0-87196-648-1 (*The Sixties*); 0-8160-1020-X (*The Seventies*). approx. $125–$145 per vol. history.
D848.L4 909.82

The *Day by Day* series is designed to provide both quick reference to specific events and a broad overview of the years during and after World War II. To date, the series has covered the decades of the 1940s through the 1970s. The 1940s, 1950s, and 1960s occupy one volume each; the 1970s take two. Most of the material in the volumes comes from the Facts On File yearbooks, supplemented by major newspapers and reference books. The emphasis is on events reported in the news media. However, secret agreements and other nonpublic events are included when they were of critical importance.

Facts On File has long been a standard source for librarians and researchers in need of a quick fact or a brief digest of the news. In recent years, the publisher has expanded with a broad range of related reference works. The *Day by Day* series is a natural outgrowth of the Facts On File yearbooks.

A main objective of *Day by Day* is to provide a sense of what it was like to live during the decade under consideration. This objective is successfully accomplished through the layout of news events to present a broad overview of all aspects of life on any given date; black-and-white photographs; and the use of the terminology of the period. For example, the volume covering the decade of the 1940s follows the then-current newspaper practice of using *German* and *Nazi* interchangeably and uses *Negro* in preference to *black.*

The news of the decade is presented in several formats. Readers are introduced to the period through a well-written narrative essay. The essay is followed by year-by-year, month-by-month, and day-by-day surveys that provide both broad and specific chronological treatments of the events of a period of interest.

The arrangement is designed for ease of use. Oversize pages permit the easy display of material in ten columns on two facing pages; each column represents various geographic and subject categories. At a glance, the reader can trace a series of similar occurrences over a period of days or contrast the events of a single day without turning a page. Five columns on the left-hand page deal with international affairs and regions outside the United States. The columns on the right-hand page are devoted to U.S. politics and social issues; foreign policy and defense; economy and environment; science, technology, and nature; and culture, leisure, and life style. The general content of each column is identified by subject headings at the top, while notes at the bottom elaborate on a column's subject content. Subject headings and notes are repeated on each page for the benefit of the reader. Entries are brief but are sufficient to describe events. Readers are encouraged to follow up with other reference books when additional information is needed.

Access is excellent through the chronological and tabular format of the volumes and through the comprehensive indexes.

The *Day by Day* series is the most comprehensive of the calendar-type reference books on the market. The Board recommends this series for the core collections of public and school libraries.

Dictionary of the Middle Ages. Joseph R. Strayer, ed. Scribner, 1982–1989. hard. 13 vols. 8,726 pp. illus. index. ISBN 0-684-19073-7 (set). $1,025 (set); $85 per vol. dictionary.

D114.D5 909.07

See European History.

An Encyclopedia of World History: Ancient, Medieval, and Modern, Chronologically Arranged, 5th edition. William L. Langer, comp. and ed. Houghton Mifflin, 1972. hard. 1 vol. 1,569 pp. illus. appendixes. indexes. ISBN 0-395-13592-3. $400. encyclopedia.

902

A historical chronology rather than an encyclopedia, William L. Langer's *An Encyclopedia of World History: Ancient, Medieval, and Modern, Chronologically Arranged* was originally inspired by an old standard, Karl Ploetz's *Auszug aus der alten, mittleren und neuren Geschichte,* published in 1874 "as a factual handbook for students and for the convenience of the general reader" (preface to first edition). In 1883, it was translated into English and enlarged by William H. Tillinghast for Houghton Mifflin, the present publisher. The work's popularity was such that 24 printings were necessary before 1905. Because of the German orientation of the older work, the publisher employed Langer, a Harvard professor of history, to undertake a complete rewriting of the entire book.

Langer continued Ploetz's original conception of a handbook of historical facts, arranged so that the dates stand out while textual material flows in a reasonably smooth narrative. As in the past, emphasis is placed on political, military, and diplomatic history, with lesser attention given to literature, art, science, and economics. Historical coverage extends from prehistory to 1970.

Langer's attempt to provide a narrative treatment within a chronological framework is uneven. At times, narratives are used to introduce or connect entries; when practical, the textual flow is maintained through several or more entries. This format noticeably decreases in the second half of the book, with the final chapter consisting almost entirely of dates and brief facts.

An Encyclopedia of World History is organized with an emphasis on chronology first and geographical area or country second. National chronologies are divided into segments and integrated into appropriate historical periods. Accordingly, the history of France is spaced throughout the volume in eight separate segments, ranging from the years 987 to 1314 on pages 240 through 249 to 1939 to 1969 on pages 1180 through 1184. Even though national histories are segmented, information can be found with relative ease through the 22-page table of contents and extensive 190-page index. For example, the index entry for *France* pulls together widely scattered information under 53 subentries.

Fifty-seven maps, ranging in chronological subject order from the city-states of ancient Greece to Southeast Asia in 1970, are spaced throughout the volume to complement chronological entries. Similarly, 104 genealogical charts illustrate connections between families, dynasties, rulers, and so forth, including the house of Herod the Great, the Macedonian emperors, the Medici family, the descendants of Queen Victoria, the Manchu dynasty, and the Pahlavi dynasty of Iran. An appendix provides 12 additional lists of emperors, kings, caliphs, popes, U.S. presidents, member states of the United Nations, and founding dates of American and European universities.

Although the book was compiled and edited by Langer, 31 colleagues collaborated with him. Unfortunately, their credentials and responsibilities within the text are not provided.

An Encyclopedia of World History is frequently cited as a standard in the field. The narrative format provides a depth of treatment to historical events seldom found in chronological handbooks. However, because coverage ceases with events in 1970, libraries may wish to supplement this encyclopedia with more recent works. The Board recommends this work for the core collections of public, academic, and school libraries.

Great Events from History. Frank N. Magill, ed. Salem, 1973–1980. hard. 12 vols. indexes. ISBN 0-89356-116-9 (set). $115 per 3-vol. set. history. 909.09

Frank N. Magill is a familiar name to librarians and students, who have long relied on his MASTERPLOTS series for literary reference. (see American Literature, British Literature, and World Literature.) *Great Events from History* is, in effect, a "masterplots" of history. Like the MASTERPLOTS series, this effort should become a standard for student research.

Great Events from History consists of four separate but coordinated series of three volumes each that taken together provide a wealth of information on approximately 1,200 of the most significant events in world history. The first three series treat 1,000 topics in ancient, medieval, modern European, and American history. The fourth adds nearly 200 events that occurred worldwide between 1900 and 1979 and fell beyond the scope of, or were omitted from, the previous series.

The treatments of events in each series range from four to six pages in length and are arranged in chronological order. Each entry consists of four sections: a quick-reference listing of type of event, date, locale, and principal persons involved; a summary of the event presenting basic facts with some causes and effects; "Pertinent Literature," presenting two essay-reviews of scholarly works written about the event; and "Additional Recommended Reading," which lists and annotates other works on the topic. This approach enables the needs of users for either brief facts or in-depth research to be met in each article.

"Events" in the title is used in the broadest sense to include short-term and long-term movements and developments. This broad definition permits the inclusion of such topics as the demise of the Protestant ethic in America and the domestication of the horse (around 4000 B.C.). Users will be pleasantly surprised to find that in addition to the expected political, military, economic, and religious subjects normally treated in such works, *Great Events* includes entries for numerous other areas, such as books—including *The Grapes of Wrath,* the *Book of the Dead,* and Machiavelli's *The Prince.* There are also entries for inventions, including the wheel, gunpowder, the transistor, and diesel and jet engines; and discoveries, such as those of pulsars, quasars, and the structure of DNA. The total number of events and topics included makes it difficult to give a truly representative sampling in a brief review.

Access to information is excellent. Entries are chronologically arranged. Each series contains several lists and indexes to aid users, including an alphabetical list of events; a keyword index for events; a category index for type of event; an index to principal persons; and author indexes to works cited in the literature and additional readings sections. In addition, volume 3 of the *Worldwide Twentieth Century Series* includes the indexes for all four series that make up *Great Events from History.*

The articles and the reviews of historical literature were written by more than 200 history professors and scholars from over 50 campuses throughout the United States. A list of contributors and their academic affiliations is included at the beginning of each series, and the authorship of each entry is indicated by the writer's initials.

Great Events from History is an excellent resource that is within the price range of most small- to medium-size libraries. The Board recommends this series for the core collections of public and academic libraries.

The Harper Atlas of World History. Pierre Vidal-Naquet, ed. Harper & Row, 1987. hard. 1 vol. 340 pp. illus. index. ISBN 0-06-181884-4. $29.95. atlas. G1021.H5983 912

Originally published in 1986 under the title *Le Grand Livre de l'histoire du monde,* this French atlas appeared in the present English translation as *The Harper Atlas of World History* in 1987.

The volume spans time from prehistory (70,000,000 to 90,000 B.C.) to 1985. The subject matter covered is broad, including entries relating to music, art, religious, political, economic, and intellectual history. While nominally an atlas, the work is much more—the approximately 320 maps comprise less than one-third of the total space in the book. Each of the 160 topics is treated in a two-page spread that includes text, a timeline, a chronology of significant dates, color and black-and-white illustrations, and one or more maps. For example, "The Development of Printing 11th–16th Centuries" contains a five-paragraph discussion; a timeline (A.D. 1000 to 1590); a chronology (11th century to 1592); colored illustrations of a fifteenth-century printing shop and a page from a Gutenberg Bible; black-and-white pictures of Gutenberg, a twelfth-century Buddhist treatise printed using movable type, an early Chinese xylograph, and an illustrated page from a book printed in 1599; graphs showing the subject specializations of printing centers from 1445 to 1500; and two maps that illustrate the location of printing shops before 1471 and the spread of printing by 1500. *The Harper Atlas* was written by 62 people identified by name only, with no indication concerning areas of expertise or responsibilities within the text. The editor is Pierre Vidal-Naquet, and the cartography is by Jacques Bertin. The brilliant use of color makes this one of the most beautifully illustrated atlases on the market. The color is not only aesthetically pleasing but also aids in the interpretation of the maps and makes the illustrations more meaningful. The layout, which combines text, timelines, maps, and illustrations, provides a much better understanding of a topic than would maps or text alone.

The book suffers from one lack: there is no table of contents. This omission prevents an easy overview of the arrangement of the work and its substance by users who consult the book for the first time. Similarly, the failure to include a preface means that readers must scan the volume to learn the scope, purpose, format, and other features normally discussed in introductory material. Nevertheless, access to information is reasonably good through the index, which permits pertinent maps and topics to be located with relative ease.

Libraries with modest budgets that cannot afford the much more expensive TIMES ATLAS OF WORLD HISTORY may wish to consider *The Harper Atlas of World History* for their collections. The Board recommends this work for the core collection of school libraries.

The Times Atlas of World History, 5th edition, rev. Geoffrey Barraclough, ed. Hammond, 1985. hard. 1 vol. 360 pp. illus. index. ISBN 0-7230-0304-1. $85. atlas.
G1030.T54 911

At the time the first edition of *The Times Atlas of World History* appeared in 1978, atlases of world history tended to overemphasize European history. Other regions and nations were generally included only where Europe impinged upon them. *The Times Atlas* was one of the first to break with this Eurocentric view of atlas construction and to become a true "world" history atlas. Now in its fifth edition, *The Times Atlas* has been translated into nine languages and is regarded by many as a standard in its field.

The stated aim of *The Times Atlas* is "to present a view of history which is worldwide . . . and which does justice . . . to the achievements of all peoples in all ages and in all quarters of the globe" (introduction). Based on the belief that the histories of India, China, Japan, and other countries of Asia and Africa are as relevant as the history of Europe, the atlas is comprehensive and ecumenical in terms of geography and time. The work is, however, limited in terms of subject content, with emphasis placed on political, military, religious, and economic events, and changes in political geography. Little attention is devoted to cultural and intellectual history (though these are not topics that require spatial treatment, which is the purpose of an atlas).

The Times Atlas treats 126 topics that range from the prehistoric "Origins of Man" to a view of the "Rich Nations and Poor Nations: The World in the 1980s." A representative sampling of topics includes the development of the first cities; America before A.D. 900; Australia and Oceania before the Europeans arrived; the beginnings of Chinese civilization; the first empires of India; the rise of Christianity; the Jewish diaspora to 1497; the emergence of states in Africa; colonial America; the Industrial Revolution; and the Cold War. Each topic is presented with colored maps and commentary in a two-page spread. Many maps are accompanied by color and black-and-white illustrations. Graphs are frequently used with modern entries. Arrangement is chronological with some topical subgrouping.

The text begins with a 12-page chronology of world history dating from the domestication of animals and crops (about 9000 to 8000 B.C.) to the 1984 British-Chinese agreement on the return of Hong Kong to China. Entries are presented in five columns, the first four divided by continent and the fifth devoted to cultural and technological events. A 64-page glossary provides supplementary information about some of the individuals, peoples, and events mentioned in the atlas.

The text was written by an international group of contributors (91 in all) who are primarily academic specialists in such areas as history, archaeology, anthropology, and political science. Unfortunately, areas of responsibility are not noted, and the articles are not signed. The atlas was edited by a former president of the (British) Historical Association and professor of international and modern history, Geoffrey Barraclough.

Access to information is somewhat limited. The index excludes subject entries and includes place names only "where something happens" (that is, which carry a date or symbol or color explained in the key, or which are mentioned in the text).

Overall, *The Times Atlas of World History* is excellent. The use of color is good, and the maps are large enough to avoid the cluttered look of many atlases. The paper is sturdy and will withstand heavy use. A less expensive alternative, however, is THE HARPER ATLAS OF WORLD HISTORY. Both are similar in approach and content; however, THE HARPER ATLAS includes social and intellectual areas that are excluded from *The Times Atlas of World History.* The Board recommends this work for the core collections of public, academic, and school libraries.

Supplementary Titles

Dictionary of Wars. George C. Kohn. Facts On File, 1986. hard. 1 vol. 586 pp. indexes. ISBN 0-8160-1005-6. $35. dictionary.
D25.A2K63 904.7

The *Dictionary of Wars* "attempts to list and describe the major human conflicts from 2000 B.C. to the present. Claiming more than 1,700 entries, [the work] lists for each entry the name(s) of the conflict, the date(s), how it began, the opposing sides, a brief summary of events, and the outcome or significance of the conflict. . . . The arrangement is alphabetical by keyword (e.g., Jenkin's Ear, War of), and there are . . . cross-references to guide the user to the entry from variant and alternate names.

"The scope is worldwide and Kohn treats the Third World fairly, describing conflicts little known to the average U.S. citizen. To further set things in context, the birth, death, or activity dates of major individuals are also noted in the text.

"The geographical index has the wars arranged chronologically under the country names. [There is also a name index.]

"In sum, *Dictionary of Wars* is a very good single-volume work chronicling the major conflicts of the world. It is up-to-date and has concise but informative entries." (*BL,* December 1, 1986, p. 561)

Also reviewed in: *ARBA,* 1987, p. 258; *Choice,* December 1986, p. 608; *R & R Bk N,* Winter 1987, p. 3; *Sch Lib,* May 1987, p. 188; *WLB,* October 1986, p. 64.

Board's recommendation: Public, academic, and school libraries.

The Encyclopedia of Historic Places. Courtlandt Canby. Facts On File, 1984. hard. 2 vols. 1,052 pp. illus. ISBN 0-87196-126-1 (set). $175 (set). encyclopedia.
D9.C29 903

The Encyclopedia of Historic Places "is a two-volume gazetteer of locations having historical interest. Entries for political entities, regions, geographical features (lakes, rivers, and mountains), sites of battles and forts, shrines, and archaeological digs are arranged in one alphabetical sequence. Coverage is global and ranges from the 'remains of human beginnings' to the present. . . . For each of the places included, a brief description of the historical significance is given. Entries are identified by regional location in the current country and then by distance/direction from a nearby large city.

"The Encyclopedia is readily usable in its straightforward two-columns-per-page format. . . . [Also,] some entries are illustrated with black-and-white photographs." (*BL,* January 15, 1985, p. 698)

"Cross-references from each of the variants as well as from earlier names provide additional access points for the reader. 'See also' references lead the reader to additional sources of information. . . . Users from students to reference librarians to general readers will find in this work a convenient source of quick, accurate answers." (*Choice,* July/August 1984, p. 1582)

Also reviewed in: *A Lib,* May 1985, p. 339; *ARBA,* 1985, p. 141; *CRL,* January 1985, p. 63; *LR,* Spring 1985, p. 54; *RQ,* Spring 1985, p. 355; *SLJ,* May 1985, p. 41.

Board's recommendation: Public and school libraries.

Historical Maps on File. Martin Greenwald Associates. Facts On File, 1984. hard. 1 vol. 345 pp. ISBN 0-87196-708-1. $145. atlas.
G1033.M128 911

Historical Maps on File is a one-color atlas with maps printed on heavy stock and collected in a looseleaf binder for easy photocopying. "The approximately 300 maps are grouped into nine sections; following the first (Ancient Civilizations), the arrangement is by continent: Europe (to 1500, 1500–1815, 1815 to the present); the United States; Western Hemisphere (Canada and Latin America); Africa and the Middle East; Asia; and Australia.

"The sequence within each section is generally chronological. . . . [While] coverage of U.S. history is ample, . . . The Hundred Years' War gets no map, and . . . the French and Russian revolutions are not [covered].

"To insure that clear reproductions can be obtained on standard copiers, not only is the use of color ruled out, but text is restricted to the absolute minimum. . . . No interpretive commentary is supplied. . . . This set of maps does not pretend to be a substitute for a standard historical atlas, but . . . [in] situations where legally reproducible maps are needed, . . . this set could prove useful." (*BL,* January 1, 1985, p. 631)

Also reviewed in: *ARBA,* 1985, p. 175; *SLJ,* May 1985, p. 43.

Board's recommendation: School libraries.

Rand McNally Atlas of World History, rev. and updated edition. R. I. Moore, gen. ed. Rand McNally, 1987. soft. 1 vol. 192 pp. ISBN 0-528-83288-3. $18.95. atlas.
G1030.R3 911

"This new edition . . . [of the *Rand McNally Atlas of World History*] is almost identical to previous editions. . . . [The] maps show economic, social, and cultural as well as political developments. Though . . . the emphasis is on Western civilization, an attempt has been made to create a balanced view of world history by including maps that illustrate the emergence of cultures in Africa, Asia, and the Middle East.

"[The atlas] is divided into two sections. The first is a world historical section, with maps and text originally published in Great Britain. . . . The second is a U.S. historical section. . . . There are 87 maps in the world section under four main headings: 'The Ancient World,' 'Heirs to the Ancient World,' 'The Age of European Supremacy,' and 'The Emergence of the Modern World.' " (*BL,* June 15, 1988, p. 1722)

Also reviewed in: *ARBA,* 1989, p. 194.

Board's recommendation: Public and academic libraries.

New and Noteworthy

Battles and Battlescenes of World War Two. David G. Chandler. Macmillan, 1989. hard. 1 vol. 160 pp. illus. index. ISBN 0-02-897175-2. $19.95. encyclopedia.
D740.C45 940.54′1′03

"An impressive amount of information is packed into [*Battles and Battlescenes of World War Two.* It is a] relatively slim volume covering 52 of the most significant battles of World War II. [The book contains readable] . . . text [that] condenses a great deal of military history into an accessible format. This is an excellent ready reference: enough is included here for use as a single source, or it can be used as a starting point to lead one further into the subject." (*SLJ,* May 1990, p. 28)

The Month-by-Month Atlas of World War II. Barrie Pitt and Frances Pitt. Summit, 1989. hard. 1 vol. 178 pp. indexes. ISBN 0-671-68880-4. $35. atlas.
940.53′0223

"Taking a largely geopolitical approach, this latest [*Month-by-Month*] *Atlas of World War II* attempts to provide an overall historical picture of the war. To accomplish this, each month of the war appears as a double-page spread, a Mercator projection of the world, on which are superimposed the areas held at the end of the month by Germany and Japan. . . . This is a quality product with good maps, a detailed commentary, and an adequate though fragmented index. The unique approach used here will help the student or researcher gain a global perspective of what was really the first global war." (*BL,* May 1, 1990, p. 1749)

The Times Atlas of the Second World War. John Keegan, ed. Harper & Row, 1989. hard. 1 vol. 254 pp. illus. index. ISBN 0-06-016178-7. $50. atlas.
G1038.T6 911

The Times Atlas of the Second World War "includes 450 full-color maps, 150 photographs and illustrations, a 120,000-word narrative, and a 14-page month-by-month chronology. The format is oversize (11 by 14 inches) with sewn bindings. . . . Following the detailed chronology (arranged by region) of the events both prior to and during the war, the maps with accompanying text are arranged chronologically and regionally. There is also notable coverage of many obscure backwaters of the war, such as eastern Africa, the north Pacific, and the Arctic Circle. . . . [T]here is extensive coverage of the political, economic, and social costs of the war." (*BL,* February 15, 1990, p. 1191)

Martin E. Gingerich

World Literature

See also Children's Literature; literatures of specific countries

The category of world literature encompasses a wide range of reference works to serve the varying needs of library patrons.

The core collection has been divided into three subcategories: general works on literature, genre-oriented works, and guides. Selections reflect the many types of reference works available (such as dictionaries, handbooks, and encyclopedias). General references explore the many facets of world literature. These include the ENCYCLOPEDIA OF WORLD LITERATURE IN THE 20TH CENTURY and the DICTIONARY OF LITERARY BIOGRAPHY. (Though reviewed in this section, these general references also pertain to the British Literature and American Literature categories.) Genre-oriented references, such as CONTEMPORARY NOVELISTS and the POETRY HANDBOOK, provide access to information on authors and on the salient characteristics of a particular type of literature. Guides focus on the technical aspects of literature, such as form, structure, or literary terms (such as A HANDBOOK TO LITERATURE or the supplementary work, A DICTIONARY OF MODERN CRITICAL TERMS) or are collections of brief excerpts from literary works, such as the OXFORD DICTIONARY OF QUOTATIONS and Bartlett's FAMILIAR QUOTATIONS.

Essential to the study of literature are a number of indexes. The *Essay and General Literature Index* (Wilson) and the *Short Story Index* (Wilson) are particularly valuable. Two important broad-based indexes are *Granger's Index to Poetry* (Columbia) and the *Literary Criticism Index* (Scarecrow). If patron usage patterns warrant it, the librarian may wish to acquire the *Mystery Index* (ALA) and the *Science Fiction and Fantasy Reference Index, 1878–1985* (Gale).

A number of works selected by the Board have since gone out of print. These workers have value and may be worth acquiring. *Benet's Reader's Encyclopedia* (Harper & Row, 1987) provides an alphabetical listing of authors, works, characters, movements, and themes from world literature (mostly Western); it is a useful source for answers to ready-reference questions. Gale's *International Authors and Writers Who's Who* provides a useful ready-reference source on active writers. *The Crown Guide to the World's Great Plays: From Ancient Greeks to Modern Times,* second edition, by Joseph T. Shipley (Crown, 1984), includes summaries and performance histories of hundreds of plays, arranged alphabetically under the author's name. Another genre-related work now out of print is the *Reader's Guide to Fantasy* (Facts On File, 1982).

Some guides selected by the Board are now out of print as well. Three titles originally voted as supple-

Core Titles

GENERAL	PUBLIC	ACADEMIC	SCHOOL
Columbia Dictionary of Modern European Literature, 2d edition Bédé, Jean-Albert, and William B. Edgerton, gen. eds. Columbia, 1980	✦		
Contemporary Authors: A Bio-Bibliographical Guide to Current Writers in Fiction, General Nonfiction, Poetry, Journalism, Drama, Motion Pictures, Television, and Other Fields, 129 vols. May, Hal, and Susan M. Trosky, eds. Gale, 1962– (See Biography)	✦	✦	
Contemporary Authors, New Revision series, 30 vols. May, Hal, and James J. Lesniak, eds. Gale, 1990 (See American Literature)	✦	✦	
Contemporary Literary Criticism: Excerpts from Criticism of the Works of Today's Novelists, Poets, Playwrights, and Other Creative Writers, 58 vols. Gale, annual (1973–)	✦	✦	✦
Contemporary Novelists, 4th edition Kirkpatrick, D. L., ed. St. Martin's, 1986	✦	✦	
Dictionary of Literary Biography, 83 vols. Bruccoli, Matthew J., and Richard Layman, ed. directors. Gale, 1978–1989		✦	
Encyclopedia of World Literature in the 20th Century, rev. edition Klein, Leonard S., gen. ed., Ungar, 1981–1984	✦	✦	✦
GENRE			
Critical Survey of Short Fiction, 7 vols., 1 suppl. Magill. Frank N. Salem, 1981	✦	✦	✦
McGraw-Hill Encyclopedia of World Drama: An International Reference Work in 5 Volumes, 2d edition Hochman, Stanley, ed. in chief. McGraw-Hill, 1984 (See Theater)	✦	✦	✦
Poetry Handbook: A Dictionary of Terms, 4th edition Deutsch, Babette. Barnes & Noble, 1981	✦	✦	✦
Twentieth-Century Crime and Mystery Writers, 2d edition Reilly, John M., ed. St. Martin's, 1985	✦		
GUIDES			
Brewer's Dictionary of Phrase and Fable, 14th edition Evans, Ivor H., ed. Harper & Row, 1989 (See Folklore and Mythology)	✦	✦	✦
Familiar Quotations: A Collection of Passages, Phrases, and Proverbs Traced to Their Sources in Ancient and Modern Literature, 15th edition Bartlett, John, and Emily Morison Beck, eds. Little, Brown, 1980	✦	✦	✦
A Handbook to Literature, 5th edition Holman, C. Hugh, and William Harmon. Macmillan, 1986	✦	✦	✦
Oxford Dictionary of Quotations, 3d edition Oxford, 1979	✦	✦	✦

ments were the *Harper Handbook to Literature* (Northrop Frye, Sheridan Baker, and George Perkins, Harper & Row, 1985); Frank S. Mead's *Encyclopedia of Religious Quotations* (Revell, 1985); and B. Stevenson's *Home Book of Proverbs, Maxims, and Familiar Phrases* (Macmillan, 1987).

Other literature categories (especially American Literature and British Literature) contain valuable works that could be included as part of the world literature collection. The CRITICAL SURVEY OF DRAMA and CRITICAL SURVEY OF POETRY (both multivolume works edited by Frank Magill and published by Salem Press), reviewed in British Literature, are two examples.

Additionally, librarians at academic institutions may be particularly interested in acquiring references designed as research tools, such as the MLA INTERNATIONAL BIBLIOGRAPHY OF BOOKS & ARTICLES ON THE MODERN LANGUAGES AND LITERATURES.

—D. L. S.

With contributions by John F. Drexel, Celia Hales-Mabry, and Donna L. Singer.

Core Titles

General

Columbia Dictionary of Modern European Literature, 2d edition. Jean-Albert Bédé and William B. Edgerton, gen. eds. Columbia, 1980. hard. 1 vol. 895 pp. illus. ISBN 0-231-03771-1. $125. dictionary.
PN771.C575 803

The *Columbia Dictionary of Modern European Literature* is designed for students of comparative literature as well as general readers of European literature in English translation. This second edition was co-edited by Jean-Albert Bédé, who died in 1977, and completed under the general editorship of William B. Edgerton, who also served as editor of the Russian and Slavic sections. Twenty-seven other editors (not identified by name) were responsible for particular sections of the work or for entries relating to a particular national literature or language. Approximately 500 other contributors wrote individual articles. The contributors are listed by college, university, or country; while most work in the United States, they represent many countries. The reasons for the reputation of the Columbia University Press as a scholarly and authoritative reference publisher are evident throughout the work.

"Modern" in this case begins at the end of the nineteenth century with writers who are relevant to the literature of the twentieth century. For example, Baudelaire (1821–1867) and Becquer (1836–1870) are included because of their great influence on writers of subsequent generations. Indeed, French symbolism and Spanish poetry of the twentieth century can scarcely be imagined without their seminal influence. Dostoyevsky (1821–1881) is also found. The selection of writers to be included was left to the collective judgment of the 5 section editors and the 20 or so individual language editors.

The format essentially follows that of the first edition. Entries are arranged alphabetically. The number of authors entered has increased to 1,853, from 1,167 in the first edition. Author entries begin with a basic biography, followed by a critical discussion of principal works and a brief bibliography of secondary sources. Cross-references to other authors appear in small caps in the text when appropriate. Dates listed for literary works are for translations to English or for first publication. In addition to author entries, the *Columbia Dictionary of Modern European Literature* contains survey articles on each of 28 national languages.

The entries appear to be accurate, up-to-date (in terms of the publication date), and accessible to adult readers who are interested in the subject. The following short entry illustrates the general style and tone of the author entries:

> Drach, Ivan (1936–), Ukrainian Poet, was born of peasant stock in the village of Telizhentsi, Kiev province and studied in Kiev and Moscow. A member of the Communist Party, Drach belonged to an unofficial group known as the *skestydesyatnyky* (the Generation of the 1960s), young poets in search of new values during Nikita Khrushchev's "thaw." In 1961, Drach published a controversial philosophical poem, "Nizh u sontsi" (Knife in the Sun). His collections of poetry, marked by striking imagery, include *Sonyashnyk* (1962; Sunflower), *Protuberantsi sertsya* (1965; Protuberances of the Heart), *Balada budniv* (1967; The Ballad of Everyday), and *Do dzherel* (1972; To the Sources). He has also written film scenarios. A selection of his poetry appeared in English under the title Orchard Lamps (1978). G.S.N.L. [George S. N. Luckyj, University of Toronto]

The *Columbia Dictionary of Modern European Literature,* second edition, was designed for use by those interested in comparative literature, but the volume will also prove useful to those who study a particular European national literature in the context of other literatures and to specialists in European literature, who will find this work a supplement to more detailed reference works on single national literatures. And, of course, the *Columbia Dictionary of Modern European Literature* is useful for readers of European literature in English translations all over the world. The Board recommends this work for the core collection of public libraries. —*M. E. G.*

Contemporary Authors: A Bio-Bibliographical Guide to Current Writers in Fiction, General Nonfiction, Poetry, Journalism, Drama, Motion Pictures, Television, and Other Fields. Hal May and Susan M. Trosky, eds. Gale, 1962–. hard. 129 vols. 503 pp. index in even-numbered vols. ISBN 0-8103-1954-3 (vol. 129). $99 (vol. 129). biobibliography.
PN771.C66X 928.1

See Biography.

Contemporary Authors, New Revision series. Hal May and James J. Lesniak, eds. Gale, 1990. hard. 30 vols. index in even-numbered vols. ISBN 0-8103-1984-5 (vol. 30). $99 per vol. biobibliography.
Z1224.C62X 803

See American Literature.

Contemporary Literary Criticism: Excerpts from Criticism of the Works of Today's Novelists, Poets, Playwrights, and Other Creative Writers. Gale, annual (1973–). hard. 58 vols. illus. appendix. indexes. ISBN 0-8103-4432-7 (vol. 58). $99 (vol. 58). criticism.
PN771.C59 809

Published by Gale Research, one of the largest American reference book publishers, *Contemporary Literary Criticism* is a multivolume compilation of excerpts from critical essays and reviews of the works of noteworthy authors. Approximately five volumes are issued each year. Each volume contains approximately 600 excerpts covering approximately 35 authors who were living at the time of publication or who have died since December 31, 1959. Authors who have appeared in earlier volumes may receive new entries in later volumes as the facts of their careers change, but none of the criticism from previous volumes is reprinted.

Entries in each volume follow a standard format. Each entry includes an author heading, a black-and-white photograph (when available, beginning with 1982's volume 21), a biographical and critical introduction (with cross-references to CONTEMPORARY AUTHORS—see American Literature and Biography—and other Gale reference works, where appropriate), and the critical excerpts. The biographical and critical introductions sometimes focus on a specific work, especially if the author is well known. Faulkner's entry in volume 52, for example, is devoted solely to *Absalom, Absalom!* Faulkner also has entries in nine other volumes, each addressing a different novel or a particular aspect of his work. In most cases, however, the criticism deals with several of the author's works.

The critical excerpts that make up the bulk of *Contemporary Literary Criticism* are drawn from articles and reviews that originally appeared in books and in such distinguished journals as *Partisan Review, Encounter,* the *Times Literary Supplement,* and *Salmagundi.* Critics of the caliber of Helen Vendler, Hugh Kenner, and John Updike appear frequently in these pages. The reader is in fact given an illuminating overview of how major authors respond to the work of their peers. Each excerpt is reprinted in sufficient length to convey the main thrust of the original essay. The excerpts represent a fair and generous sampling of available contemporary criticism on the author under consideration, although negative reviews are not slighted.

The critical excerpts range from several paragraphs to several pages in length—a generous sampling indeed. There are generally upwards of a half-dozen selections for each author, although, of course, the number of excerpts and their length depends largely on the volume of critical response that an author's work has stimulated.

As an example of the variety of authors included in the work, and the coverage given to each, volume 48 devotes 11 pages to *Agatha Christie* and 20 to *Ezra Pound,* among the celebrated; 6 pages are given over to *Medbh McGuckian* and 11 to *R. S. Thomas,* among the less universally acknowledged. Among the 35 authors whose works are the subject of criticism in volume 52, *Conrad Aiken, William Faulkner, Lillian Hellman,* and *Jean-Paul Sartre* are selected from the deceased. *Woody Allen, Thomas Flanagan,* and *Joyce Carol Oates* are among the more popular living authors included, while *Gloria Naylor* (born 1950) and *Clive Barker* (born 1952) are the youngest.

Judging from the cumulative indexes as a whole, American authors seem to make up a plurality of entries. However, writers in all major languages and from all parts of the world are included, making *Contemporary Literary Criticism* truly a world reference resource.

Despite the mass of material in *Contemporary Literary Criticism,* access to criticism on individual authors is quite easy. Beginning with volume 41, each volume has four useful indexes: "Cumulative Author," "Cumulative Critic," "Nationality," and "Title." These are handy when a user cannot think of an author's name but can remember a title or a critic's name. Title indexes, however, list only titles reviewed in the current volume, not all of an author's published works. A paperbound edition of the title index, listing all titles reviewed in the series, is now issued each year. Each volume also has an appendix listing the sources of its excerpts, and at the front of every volume a page directs users to other Gale literary criticism series for authors who are not included in *Contemporary Literary Criticism.*

The Board recommends this work for the core collections of public, academic, and school libraries.

—*J. F. D.*

Contemporary Novelists, 4th edition. D. L. Kirkpatrick, ed. St. Martin's, 1986. hard. 1 vol. 1,003 pp. appendix. index. ISBN 0-312-16731-8. $79.95. biographical dictionary.
PR883.C64 823.9

In England *Contemporary Novelists* is published by Macmillan and is exactly the same work as that published by St. Martin's Press in the United States. Since the first edition, editor James Vinson has had an associate editor, D. L. Kirkpatrick, who took over the main editing duties in this fourth edition, which lists Vinson as consulting editor.

Contemporary Novelists, fourth edition, includes novelists writing in English no matter what their country. Thus, here are listed novelists from most of the British Commonwealth countries—India, Australia, Canada, and African nations—as well as British and U. S. writers. Entries have a standard format in this series. After a brief biographical note comes a list of published books by the author, followed by a list of critical studies. At this point in some entries appear comments by the author—all the authors, according to the editor, were invited to submit comments on their own work. These usually express the author's present interests, manner of working, or plans for new work. The bulk of the entry, however, is a signed critical and interpretive essay, which by and large for most of the authors is judicious, fair, and succinct. The bibliographies list the best-known works that are fairly easy to find and are therefore a good place to start in one's deeper study of the selected authors. These bibliographies are accurate and informative.

It should be pointed out that despite the more than 1,000 pages in this book, some novelists have been left out. If a favorite novelist cannot be found in the volume, however, it is not the fault of the editor. The novelists entered have all been recommended for inclusion by a panel of advisors, who are mostly themselves novelists.

A title index concludes the volume. Such an index is useful since one frequently remembers a title but cannot recall the author's name. There is also an appendix of writers who have died since the previous edition. Of the eleven writers entered in the appendix, eight are from the United States and three are from Britain.

The Board recommends this work for the core collections of public and academic libraries. —*C. H.-M.*

Dictionary of Literary Biography. Matthew J. Bruccoli and Richard Layman, ed. directors. Gale, 1978–1989. hard. 83 vols. illus. appendix. index. ISBN 0-8103-2781-3 (vol. 83). $103 per vol. biographical dictionary.
PQ671.F69 843.9

The *Dictionary of Literary Biography* is a work of enormous scope. As of this writing, 83 volumes have been published (along with more than a dozen related yearbooks and Documentary series titles). Each self-contained volume covers a different period in a particular country, and each is individually titled. The completed series is anticipated to include all authors of all periods and countries who have made substantial contributions to the literature of their time. Thus, in the full series the reader should be able to locate biographical information on ancient Greek dramatists, Italian Renaissance authors, poets of Russia's Silver Age, and recent Latin American novelists.

Of the 83 volumes of the *Dictionary of Literary Biography* (not counting the yearbooks and the Documentary series titles), only 11 concern writers who are not American and British. When first conceived in 1975, the series was intended to cover North American writers only. In 1982 its scope was enlarged to include British and European writers as well.

The project was commissioned by Frederick Ruffner of Gale Research, but is produced under the imprint of Bruccoli Clark Layman, an editorial consulting firm in Columbia, South Carolina. Matthew J. Bruccoli and Richard Layman are the editorial directors, with C. E. Frazer Clark serving as managing editor for the series. Each volume is overseen by an editor who is an expert in the period covered by that volume. The individual essays within each volume are written by subject specialists, most of whom are academics.

With volume 10 attention shifted from an exclusively North American point of view to include *Modern British Dramatists, 1900–1945,* in two parts, edited by Stanley Weintraub. The following year (1983) came another shift to include historians as well as creative writers, and hard upon that came volumes devoted to journalists, publishers, critics and scholars, and authors and illustrators of children's books.

Not until volume 53, though, was any attention paid to North American writers other than those of the United States, when *Canadian Writers Since 1960,* first series, appeared in 1986. The late 1980s brought the first volumes on writers of Germany, France, and Austria as well as additional volumes on Canadian, American, and British writers. In fact, with yearbooks and a Documentary series (concerned entirely with U. S. writers) the *Dictionary* has 98 volumes as of this writing—and counting. Some authors, it is true, appear in more than one volume; but in each they receive a different treatment because of the different emphasis. Hemingway, for example, figures in *American Writers in Paris, 1920–1939* and also in *American Novelists, 1910–1945.* Dylan Thomas, on the strength of *Under Milk Wood,* appears in *British Dramatists Since World War II* as well as in *British Poets, 1914–1945.*

There have been some changes in the format of the entries as the series has proceeded, but generally each entry includes an essay on the writer's life and career, a fairly full primary bibliography, and a selected secondary bibliography. Each volume includes an appendix of books for further reading and is lavishly illustrated with black-and-white photographs of not only authors, but also their families, homes, book jackets, manuscript pages, and the like.

The volumes follow one another neither alphabetically nor chronologically. They are numbered consecutively as they are published. To assist the reader in finding his or her way through this series, a cumulative index is printed in each volume. These indexes are essential for using the full resources of the dictionary effectively.

The *Dictionary of Literary Biography* is an expensive set of books, but that is probably the only deterrent to acquiring it. Public and high school libraries may not need the set—the Documentary series was published for them. The Board recommends this work for the core collection of academic libraries. —*M. E. G.*

Encyclopedia of World Literature in the 20th Century, rev. edition. Leonard S. Klein, gen. ed. Ungar, 1981–1984. hard. 5 vols. illus. index. ISBN 0-8044-3148-5. $545 (set). encyclopedia.
PN771.E5 803

The *Encyclopedia of World Literature in the 20th Century* is an authoritative and comprehensive multivolume guide to writers of all nations in this century and to individual national literatures. This edition of the work was edited by Leonard S. Klein. The many advisors and contributors are all rising scholars; they are listed in the front matter of each volume. Many are themselves distinguished authors.

Whereas in the first edition some literatures, such as that of Spanish America, had been treated under a single heading, these are now each treated separately, for the most part. Some of the more obscure European literatures—Albanian, Byelorussian, Luxembourgian—are included in this edition. Literatures of 85 African and Asian groups (including Asian republics of the Soviet Union) also receive survey articles in this new edition. Although topical articles on such subjects as *cubism* and *imagism* also appear, genre articles (the novel, drama, and so forth) are not included.

The core of the second edition comprises the separate articles on major and representative writers who were both living and producing after 1900. Each author receives an essay covering life and career and a bibliography. The entries are not merely factual but also present thoughtful evaluations of the author in question, placing his or her work in a historical and critical context. Some of the writers who are important in the less familiar literatures include the Byelorussian *Natalla Arsiennieva,* the Tanzanian *Shaban Robert,* the Tajik *Sodriddin Ayni,* the Burmese *Thawda Swe,* the Indian (Marathi-language) *V. S. Khandekar,* the Syrian *Nizar Qabbani,* the Kirgiz *Chingiz Aytmatov,* the Vietnamese *Nhat-Linh,* the Maltese *Carmelo Psaila,* and the Ugandan *Okot P'Bitek.* Of course, the reader will also find ample articles on such acknowledged masters as *Yeats, Tsvetayeva, Mann,* and *Milosz,* among others.

Author and topical entries are arranged in alphabetical order, with the entry word printed in boldface type for easy accessibility. Cross-references are extensive in the survey articles but are not elaborate in the articles on authors. For example, *Alain,* pseudonym of Emile-Auguste Chartier, is an entry; but there is no entry for Chartier. Titles of books are given either in their published English translations or, when no published translation exists, in a literal translation. American titles are preferred over British where these are different. Bibliographical sources are limited to articles in English, French, German, and Spanish. Articles on major writers also include excerpts from published critical essays illustrating differing or supporting opinions. Black-and-white photographs of most authors are included.

The fifth volume of the set is an index that enables readers to do most of their own cross-referencing and analysis of national literatures and literary languages. The subheading "Major Writers of" under the heading for each national literature lists all the authors treated in separate articles. Additional subheadings list literary critics within each literature and also writers whose literary language differs from their nationality.

All libraries will find the *Encyclopedia of World Literature in the 20th Century,* revised edition, a useful tool for their patrons. Although researchers will need to consult other sources for more up-to-date information on living authors who are still active, this is an especially good source for beginning work on the lesser-known literatures of the world. The Board recommends this work for the core collections of public, academic, and school libraries. —*M. E. G.*

Genre

Critical Survey of Short Fiction. Frank N. Magill, ed. Salem, 1981, 1987. hard. 7 vols. plus 1 suppl. index. ISBN 0-89356-210-7 (set); 0-89356-218-1 (suppl.). $375 (set); $80 (suppl.). criticism.
PN3321.C7. 809.31

According to the publisher's note, *Critical Survey of Short Fiction* is intended as "an exhaustive examination of the history, characteristics, structure, and prime examples" of the short story. This work does fairly well in fulfilling its intention. Some excellent essays in the first two volumes cover various aspects of the genre: its history and roots, its development in various countries, its special forms (such as detective fiction and science fiction), its language and techniques, and its criticism. Four volumes (3 through 6) contain articles on authors, arranged alphabetically. Each entry follows the standard format in Magill-edited series: principal short fiction, other literary forms (most authors have written novels as well), influences on and by the author, story characteristics, biography, analysis, major publications other than short stories (includes other literary forms in standard bibliographical form), and bibliography of secondary works. A good idea of the range of authors may be seen in the first entry, *Chinua Achebe,* and the second, *Joseph Addison* (this article treats Addison's essays as short fiction).

Volume 7, *Current Authors,* is a collection of one-page articles written by the authors themselves. Presumably all the unsigned articles are by the authors, which means at least 90 percent of them. They describe background, style, thematic concerns, and so on. Unfortunately, they are all written in the third person and sound arrogant and self-aggrandizing; that is, they say things others should say about the authors and come off like the blurbs on book covers. "Blending sophisticated and self-conscious storytelling with a folk mode found in the oral tradition of Appalachian America [this author's] stories are clear and well ordered, carefully crafted, yet the antitheses of dense and difficult fiction in the arabesque mode." Even the better ones participate in this self-advertising tone: "In these lyric fictions [this author's] interest in the prose poem, a form which appears frequently in his collection of poetry [book and publisher] is evident."

The final volume, a supplement, covers short fiction writers not included in the previous volumes. Selections range from *Ann Beattie* to *Vladimir Nabokov* to horror story specialist *Stephen King.*

An index of authors and titles is included in each of the volumes on authors. The two essay volumes are not indexed.

In summary, volumes 1 through 6 of *Critical Survey of Short Fiction* are very good, the other volumes not bad. *Current Authors* (volume 7) seems an unnecessary addition, especially in light of the style in which the articles are presented. The supplemental volume is adequate. The Board recommends this work for the core collections of public, academic, and school libraries. —*M. E. G.*

McGraw-Hill Encyclopedia of World Drama: An International Reference Work in 5 Volumes, 2d edition. Stanley Hochman, ed. in chief. McGraw-Hill, 1984. hard. 5 vols. 2,828 pp. illus. appendixes. indexes. ISBN 0-07-079169-4. $380 (set). encyclopedia.
PN1625.M3 809.2

See Theater.

Poetry Handbook: A Dictionary of Terms, 4th edition. Babette Deutsch. Barnes & Noble, 1981. soft. 1 vol. 203 pp. index. ISBN 0-06-4633548-1. $8.95. dictionary.
PN44.5.D4 808.1

Babette Deutsch's *Poetry Handbook,* first published in 1957, is "a dictionary of terms used in discussing verse techniques and some of the largest aspects of poetry, together with aspects of poetic practice" (preface). Designed for both the student and the working poet, it does not merely define terms but shows how they apply to particular poems. Deutsch is clearly concerned with practice, not merely with theory. She deals with such technical aspects as form, structure, and meter, lacing her entries with examples from the work of more than 180 poets.

The reader will find entries on such poetic forms as the *ballade, haiku, rondeau, sestina, sonnet,* and *villanelle.* There are explanations of such devices as *free verse, blank verse, iambic pentameter, masculine* and *feminine rhyme, sprung rhythm,* and *recessive accents,* and discussions of more general literary concerns such as *irony* and *metaphor.* Among the poets cited are

Homer, Horace, Ovid, and Sappho; Dante and Petrarch; Sidney, Donne, and Herbert; Coleridge and Keats; Hopkins and Swinburne; and Yeats, Eliot, Pound, Stevens, Moore, Auden, and Wilbur. Entries range from one sentence to several pages in length, with one-paragraph entries being most common. Excerpts from poems are from one line to several stanzas in length, depending upon the term or concept they are intended to illustrate. Cross-reference entries are frequent and useful. Main entry words are arranged alphabetically. However, some terms are treated as subentries within a main entry.

In this fourth edition there are a couple of small but helpful changes from the previous editions. In cross-referencing, for example, the exact page number is given for the subentry rather than the page number for the general article. For instance, *allegory* will be found on page 88, well into the article on *metaphor,* the entry for which begins on page 84. Another change of this kind that seems useful is that guide words on each page refer to the first entry on that page. In previous editions, the guide word of the right-hand page signaled the last entry on the page.

Among the new entries that appear in this edition are *bouts-rimes* and *crown of sonnets.* New material has been inserted into articles. For example, there is almost a full page of new material in the entry of *sonnets.*

Some users, especially the less experienced, will find the lack of an index to be a drawback. However, there is a "List of Poets Cited" that will allow readers to locate examples of superior versifying by their favorite poets.

Deutsch's *Poetry Handbook* became an immediate classic upon its publication, garnering accolades not only from teachers of English but also from many distinguished poets and critics, including William Carlos Williams, Marianne Moore, John Crowe Ransom, and Richard Wilbur. In this fourth edition it remains extremely valuable. The Board recommends this work for the core collections of public, academic, and school libraries. —*J. F. D.*

Twentieth-Century Crime and Mystery Writers, 2d edition. John M. Reilly, ed. St. Martin's, 1985. hard. 1 vol. 1,094 pp. appendixes. index. ISBN 0-312-82418-1. $95. biographical dictionary.
PR888.D4.T8 809.3

For this second edition of *Twentieth-Century Crime and Mystery Writers,* editor John M. Reilly used a board of advisers to select which of the many such authors should be included, as he had done for the first edition. To the original board were added a university professor and two writers who had received entries in the first edition. These join a group made up of knowledgeable persons in the field of crime fiction who are as good an authority as those on any such panel. Most of the contributors, a few of whom are also writers in the genre, are members of the faculties in various academic disciplines at colleges and universities in America. Britain, too, is well represented among the contributors. Reilly is himself professor of English at SUNY (Albany) and has written a book on the critical reception of Richard Wright and essays on black literature.

While most of the entries are twentieth-century British and American writers, two appendixes list nineteenth-century writers and foreign-language writers. This second edition gives no notice of what is new in it or omitted from the previous edition. The preface and the editor's notes are nearly the same in both editions. The second edition is a physically larger book than the first, but then this edition has much larger print. A few of the writers who had entries in the first edition do not appear anywhere in the second. This practice is mildly regrettable since information about these authors is not easy to find.

The work contains 640 entries. Writers represented include such classic writers in the genre as *Dorothy L. Sayers, Marjery Allingham, Ngaio Marsh, Raymond Chandler,* and *Dashiell Hammett.* Contemporary writers include *P. D. James, Martha Grimes,* and *Tony Hillerman.* Entries also include such writers as *William Faulkner* and *William F. Buckley,* better known for work outside this genre. Faulkner's claim to crime fiction rests apparently on *Sanctuary, Light in August, Absalam, Absalom!, Intruder in the Dust,* and *Knight's Gambit.* While Faulkner's inclusion could be questioned—it seems unlikely that a reader would look here for an account of Faulkner and his work, nor can he reasonably be accounted a "crime and mystery" writer—covering him in this work allows an unusual perspective on his novels.

Each entry consists of a biographic sketch, a bibliography, and a signed critical essay. Living authors were invited to comment on their own work; when they have done so, these comments are included. The essayists do a good job of summarizing the work of these prolific writers and usually strike right at the heart of their contribution (or lack thereof) to the field. Errors are all minor misprints that readers will read past. The bibliographies list both crime fiction and other publications. The crime fiction is subdivided by pseudonym. Uncollected stories are also listed, and for stories collected into an anthology, the anthology is listed.

The front matter includes a reading list of critical books on the subject and also a list of crime and mystery fiction writers. Some interesting names, like Ray

Bradbury and Max Brand, in the list in the first edition have been omitted from that in the second, with no explanation. Not all of these writers on this list, incidentally, are included as entries in the main part of the dictionary. This list cannot be used, therefore, as a quick alphabetical listing of the authors who have essays written about them.

Twentieth-Century Crime and Mystery Writers is a useful book, particularly for public libraries, where much of this fiction is found. It is even better to have both editions so that information on many of the less famous writers in this genre will remain available for interested readers. The Board recommends this work for the core collection of public libraries. —*M. E. G.*

Guides

Brewer's Dictionary of Phrase and Fable, 14th edition. Ivor H. Evans, ed. Harper & Row, 1989. hard. 1 vol. 1,220 pp. index. ISBN 0-06-016200-7 $35. dictionary.
PN43.B65 803

See Folklore and Mythology.

Familiar Quotations: A Collection of Passages, Phrases, and Proverbs Traced to Their Sources in Ancient and Modern Literature, 15th edition. John Bartlett and Emily Morison Beck, eds. Little, Brown, 1980. hard. 1 vol. 1,540 pp. index. ISBN 0-316-08275-9. handbook.
PN6081.B27 808.88

Bartlett's *Familiar Quotations* has been around so long now—this 15th edition marks its 125th anniversary—that "Bartlett's" itself has become a household word. "Look it up in Bartlett's" is probably an expression used by people who do not even know the title of the work.

Emily Morison Beck, the present editor, has written a preface and also a historical note for the front matter; and Mary Rackliffe of Little, Brown's editorial staff has prepared the user's guide, which one really ought to read for easiest access to the material. Also part of the front matter is an "Index of Authors," with each author listed alphabetically with dates and page numbers of quotations, including mentions in the footnotes. The Bible has its own alphabetical listing of books, as do Shakespeare's plays and the various divisions of anonymous works. Anonymous works are listed separately and divided by geographical and generic groups entered alphabetically: African, ballad, and so forth. The books of the Bible, however, are listed canonically, with the Apocrypha between the Old and New Testaments. Shakespeare's plays follow to the standard canon.

After the main section of quotations there is a keyword index, which enables users to find quotations that they may only partially remember. Such an index is, of course, invaluable. Numbers at the end of the index entries direct readers to the page number and to the number of the quotation on the page.

The quotations that make up the main body of the work range from ancient times (Queen Hatshepsut) to the present day (Steve Biko). Authors here are arranged chronologically by year of birth, and alphabetically within each year. Actual birthdays and deathdays are not given. For each author, quotations are listed chronologically by date of first publication.

Quotation entries include a source or identification line following the quotation to enable readers to find the complete work. Footnotes contain such information as translator, the original title of the translated text, historical data, and cross-references. For this edition, the editor has added 400 new quotations over previous editions, including famous quotations from the Bible ("Inherit the wind"), Dickens ("Bah! Humbug!"), Marshall McLuhan ("The medium is the message"), and Alan Jay Lerner ("I could have danced all night"), among many others. One wonders that they had not been in before. The editors, in fact, went out of their way to bring this edition up to date, for one finds the Beatles and Helen Reddy along with Muhammed Ali's "float like a butterfly, sting like a bee" and Stevie Wonder's "You are the sunshine of my life."

It is hard to fault the editors for their selections; after all, they are trying for a book of favorite personal quotations. There seem to be no inaccuracies, but of course from one's own personal viewpoint there are many omissions. For example, Dylan Thomas's "Before the children green and golden" is not included, even though other parts of "Fern Hill," in which this phrase occurs, are included. Naturally, one can always quibble, but it is difficult to imagine a more comprehensive or judicious selection of quotations.

This is a large book and needs to be laid on a desk or table for prolonged use. Print for the main entries is large and clear, but users with less-than-perfect vision will have difficulty with the small print of the footnotes. The paper is of sufficiently good stock to allow only minimal show-through.

Bartlett's *Familiar Quotations* is a standard reference work. The Board recommends this work for the core collections of public, academic, and school libraries.

—*M. E. G.*

A Handbook to Literature, 5th edition. C. Hugh Holman and William Harmon. Macmillan, 1986.

hard and soft. 1 vol. 647 pp. appendixes. index. ISBN 0-02-553430-0 (hard); 0-02-356410-5 (soft). $27.50 (hard); $20 (soft). handbook.
PN41.H6 803

A Handbook to Literature is a collection of essays of various lengths on words and phrases related to literature. The first edition was published in 1936 under the editorship of William Flint Thrall and Addison Hibbard. This fifth edition, revised and updated for readers in the 1980s by the late C. Hugh Holman and William Harmon, is a respectable successor.

Entries are arranged alphabetically. Some entries, such as *nocturne* or *pun,* are only a sentence or two. Others, on particular periods of literary history and on broad topics such as *myth,* run to a page and a half or so. Indeed, *criticism* has more than nine pages.

Entry words are printed in boldface type. Within an entry the term defined (and occasionally its synonyms) is printed in italics; terms that are defined in other entries are printed in small capitals. At the end of some entries a "see also" reference directs readers to related or otherwise helpful articles in the *Handbook.* Thus various kinds of cross-references supply a reader with an extended definition of a term. The article on *complication* illustrates the features appearing in most entries:

> That part of a PLOT in which the entanglement caused by the CONFLICT of opposing forces is developed. It is the tying of the knot to be untied in the RESOLUTION. In the five-part idea of DRAMATIC STRUCTURE, it is synonymous with RISING ACTION. The second ACT of a five-act TRAGEDY has been called the "act of *complication.*" See DRAMATIC STRUCTURE, ACT.

A new feature in the fifth edition is an "Index of Proper Names" of persons named in articles in the body of the handbook. Readers are referred to the title or short title of articles in which the person is mentioned, rather than to a specific page number. Perhaps it should be pointed out that these references are not articles about the persons. They serve only to illustrate a style in fiction, or a verse form, or a period in literary history marked by a particular temper or mood.

In addition to the "Index of Proper Names" are four interesting appendixes listing the winners of the Nobel Prize for Literature and the various Pulitzer Prizes (in fiction, poetry, and drama) from the first awards to 1985. For some reason birth and death dates are given for Nobel Prize winners but not for Pulitzer Prize winners, a curious omission.

There are many literary handbooks, and libraries should perhaps include more than one in their collections. *A Handbook to Literature* has been in print through various editions for more than 50 years and has proved its worth and authority. Its entries afford detailed yet accessible explanations of literary terms. The Board recommends this work for the core collections of public, academic, and school libraries.

—*M. E. G.*

Oxford Dictionary of Quotations, 3d edition. Oxford, 1979. hard. 1 vol. 907 pp. indexes. ISBN 0-19-211560-X. $45. handbook.
PN6081.09 808.88

The *Oxford Dictionary of Quotations* is a comprehensive compendium of some 70,000 quotations. In compiling this edition, Oxford's editors asked a panel of writers, scholars, members of Parliament, and other learned authorities to review the previous edition and delete whatever quotations they chose and list new ones they thought should be added. For the new edition the claim of *familiar* quotations was dropped as one of the criteria for inclusion and *popular* adopted in its stead.

Quotations are grouped by author or source. Authors' names are arranged alphabetically in the book, as are other sources (anonymous, ballads, the Bible, the Book of Common Prayer, and so forth). The different books of the Bible are in canonical order, with the Apocrypha included between the Old and New Testaments. An essential keyword index and a Greek index end the work. The present editors have decreased the number of keywords in the index for this edition, believing that the index in the previous edition was too cluttered.

The *Oxford Dictionary of Quotations* is somewhat more literary than Bartlett's *Familiar Quotations.* It does not include Bob Dylan, Edgar Guest, and writers of that ilk, for example. It also attempts to give more extended quotations than it had in previous editions; in this regard, it is superior to Bartlett's. For example, Bartlett's quotes only "It is spring, moonless night in the small town, starless and bible-black" from Dylan Thomas's *Under Milk Wood.* Oxford continues the sentence: "the cobblestreets silent and the hunched, courters'-and-rabbits' wood limping invisible down to the sloeblack, slow, black, crowblack, fishingboat-bobbing sea," followed by five more passages.

Although the dictionary is very up to date, it does not quote many living authors. A few exceptions are Solzhenitsyn and Sartre (who died in 1980, but was still living at the time of publication), Stephen Spender, Tom Stoppard, Marshall McLuhan, Harold Pinter, Ivan Illich, and Edward Heath. It quotes lots of Auden and Eliot and some Robert Lowell, but no Ted Hughes, the current poet laureate. Readers should, however, find most of the popular literary quotations and many of the nonliterary ones they are looking for.

The book is very easy to use. The print is smaller than had been used in previous editions, but still readable, and there is no show-through to speak of. The keyword index is indispensable. Probably the most frequent use for such dictionaries is to find the source of a remembered quotation or to check its accuracy, and without the name of the author one has to turn to the index. Even if one does recall the author, it is easier to use the index to find the quotation, particularly for much-quoted authors.

Librarians should consider adding the *Oxford Dictionary of Quotations,* third edition, to their world literature collections, but not as a replacement for the second edition. After all, some of those quotations deleted from the earlier work may still be sought from time to time. If a library does not own the second edition, by all means it should acquire this new one. It is a very useful reference work. The Board recommends this work for the core collections of public, academic, and school libraries. —*M. E. G.*

Supplementary Titles

General

Cyclopedia of World Authors. Frank N. Magill, ed. Salem, 1974. hard. 3 vols. 1,973 pp. index. ISBN 0-89356-125-8 (set). $100 (set). encyclopedia.
PN41.M26 803

"The *Cyclopedia of World Authors* is a collection of biographies, from 200 to 1,000 words in length, of 753 authors from Homer to James Gould Cozzens. The principal works of each writer are given, as is also a grouping of bibliographic references." (*Chicago Sunday Tribune,* January 4, 1959, p. 6)

"Each author's work is discussed critically, and the bibliographical references following each entry have value for the student wishing to read further. The articles vary in length according to the importance of the subject, and the data are conveniently arranged." (*WLB,* March 1959, p. 192)

Also reviewed in: *LJ,* February 1, 1959, p. 523; *SR,* March 21, 1959, p. 43.

Board's recommendation: Public, academic, and school libraries.

Dictionary of Literary Pseudonyms: A Selection of Modern Popular Writers in English. Frank Atkinson. ALA, 1987. hard. 1 vol. 304 pp. ISBN 0-8389-2045-4. $20. dictionary.
Z1065.A83 808.03'21

The *Dictionary of Literary Pseudonyms* "is based in large part on contributions from authors, publishers, librarians, literary agents, and readers. Atkinson has added some two thousand new entries to this fourth [1987] edition, and continues to use the same alphabetical format as in previous versions. His scope remains limited to twentieth-century English-language writers, with a strong emphasis on British authors. More and more American writers are being included, however, as are many Latin American authors whose works have appeared in English translation." (*ARBA,* 1988, p. 446)

"As in the past, this dictionary consists of two sections, each an index to the other. The first lists authors by their real names followed by pseudonyms; the second reverses the process, listing the pseudonyms and identifying the author behind each one. This continues to be a standard for academic and public library reference collections." (*WLB,* September 1987, pp. 89–90)

Also reviewed in: *CLW,* May 1987, p. 249.

Board's recommendation: Public and academic libraries.

A Dictionary of Modern Critical Terms, rev. edition. Roger Fowler, ed. Routledge, Chapman & Hall, 1987. hard and soft. 1 vol. 288 pp. index. ISBN 0-7102-1021-3 (hard); 0-7102-1022-1 (soft). $35 (hard); $12.95 (soft). dictionary.
PN41.D4794 801.95

A Dictionary of Modern Critical Terms "is a compilation of short essays on contemporary critical terms. . . . [The entries] explore the development of critical terminology and the variety of ways in which it is applied in contemporary writing. The present edition expands and updates the [first edition] . . . offering more than 200 explanations of terms. . . . The articles are arranged alphabetically.

"Citations to helpful references are numerous, either within a text or in a bibliography at the end of an essay. The style of the writing is unquestionably scholarly, requiring the reader to have a grasp of literature, literary terms, and a good understanding of genres and movements. As described by Fowler in his preface, this dictionary is intended to broaden approaches to criticism by providing 'a cross-section of critical attitudes and . . . a dramatic representation of the richness of contemporary criticism.' [This work] would add depth and a contemporary perspective to collections serving serious students of literature." (*BL,* December 1, 1987, p. 614)

Also reviewed in: *ARBA,* 1988, p. 446; *CR,* March 1987, p. 168; *CRL,* January 1988, p. 65; *WLB,* October 1987, p. 81.

Board's recommendation: Academic libraries.

European Writers series [*The Age of Reason and the Enlightenment, The Middle Ages and the Renaissance, The Romantic Century, Twentieth Century*]. George Strade, ed. Scribner, 1990 (vol. 13). hard. 13 vols. ISBN 0-684-19159-8 (vol. 13). $65 (vol. 13). handbook.
PN501.E9 809

[From a review of the three volumes titled *The Romantic Century.*] "Consisting of articles that can at once inform the beginner and interest the specialist, these . . . volumes [of *European Writers*] begin [a 13] volume work that will provide coverage of major European authors from the Middle Ages to the present. British authors, because they are covered in the publisher's *British Writers* series . . . are excluded. Averaging 15,000 words in length, the articles in these first volumes treat individual authors as well as genres, reflecting the fact that authorship was considered secondary to the work, especially in the medieval period. If the length of the articles intimidates some readers, their style should not, for they are facile and clear despite having been crafted by many hands." (*WLB,* February 1984, p. 451)

"[The work] contains essays by specialists on important European genres and writers from Prudentius (died ca. 410) to Calderon (died 1681). . . . The chapters are clear and enlightening, easily accessible to educated readers. Specialists will find the bibliographies well selected and essential." (*LJ,* October 1984, p. 478)

Also reviewed in: *AL,* October 1984, p. 463; *ANQ,* May 1983, p. 165; *ARBA,* 1986, p. 422; *Choice,* June 1984, p. 1460; *CLW,* May 1987, p. 280; *JHI,* October 1984, p. 626; *Ref Bk R,* 1984, p. 17; 1986, p. 18; *RQ,* Summer 1984, p. 475; *WLB,* January 1986, p. 64.

Board's recommendation: Public and academic libraries.

Great Treasury of Western Thought: A Compendium of Important Statements on Man & His Institutions by the Great Thinkers in Western History. Mortimer Adler and Charles Van Doren, eds. Bowker, 1977. hard. 1 vol. 1,771 pp. ISBN 0-8352-0833-8. $49.50. handbook.
PN6331.G675 080

The *Great Treasury of Western Thought* is "grouped in 20 chapters, each with several subsections. . . . Passages on subjects ranging from man to language, to law and justice, to art and aesthetics, to religion are included. The selections, from one line to over a page . . . are arranged chronologically with citations to their sources, works by some 200 . . . Western writers, including poets, historians, philosophers, scientists, novelists, and theologians [are also included].

"Adler and Van Doren have given us a large book in which pleasure and instruction are well combined. . . . The range of authors on any subject is surprising—on taxation, for example, are statements from the Bible, Plato, Tacitus, Shakespeare, Swift, Adam Smith, Gibbon, Kant, Hegel, Hill, and others. . . . The Treasury is a delightful book to browse in, with enough depth and variety to hold the reader's interest." (*LJ,* October 15, 1977, p. 2149)

Also reviewed in: *Am,* November 12, 1977, p. 335; *ARBA,* 1978, p. 51; *BL,* November 15, 1978, p. 572; *BS,* November 1977, p. 254; *BW,* December 11, 1977, p. E11; *Bus W,* November 21, 1977, p. 17; *Choice,* January 1978, p. 1480; *CLW,* February 1978, p. 310; *LJ,* April 15, 1978, p. 817; *PW,* August 1, 1977, p. 109; *RQ,* Spring 1978, p. 268; *SR,* September 3, 1977, p. 26; *WLB,* December 1977, p. 344; *WSJ,* October 17, 1977, p. 30.

Board's recommendation: Public and academic libraries.

Key Sources in Comparative and World Literature: An Annotated Guide to Reference Materials. George A. Thompson, comp. Ungar, 1982. hard. 1 vol. 383 pp. indexes. ISBN 0-8044-3281-3. $40. bibliography.
Z6511.T47 016.809

"The sources listed in . . . [*Key Sources in Comparative and World Literature*] cover comparative, general and European or world literature; literature in Greek and Latin; . . . the Romance literatures, with separate sections on French, Italian and Hispanic literatures; German literature; and literature in English. In addition, there is a section on the other literatures of Europe, with Russian being treated in most detail, and one on the literatures of the Orient. The final section of the book covers the related disciplines, chiefly in the arts and humanities. . . . Sources listed include bibliographies and reviews of research; handbooks and encyclopedias, including biographical collections; dictionaries of critical terms; guides and indexes to themes and plots; histories and other surveys. (introduction)

"Entry numbers used as running heads make finding a page easy. . . . The selection of sources is judicious." (*BL,* December 15, 1983, p. 619)

"Graduate students and scholars of comparative literature and the literatures written in Western European languages should find this [volume] . . . especially useful. . . . Approximately one-third of the entries are bibliographies published as books or as regular features in journals. . . . The 60 pages devoted to literature in English largely duplicates Margaret Pattersons's Literary Research Guide. . . . Despite these duplications, academic libraries with graduate programs in comparative and Western European literatures will find this source a worthwhile purchase." (*LJ,* April 15, 1983, p. 817)

Also reviewed in: *ARBA,* 1984, p. 541; *Choice,* May 1983, p. 1270; *RQ,* Fall 1983, p. 106; *WLB,* April 1983, p. 707.

Board's recommendation: Academic libraries.

Literary Research Guide, 3d edition. James L. Harner. MLA, 1989. hard and soft. 1 vol. 748 pp. ISBN 0-87352-182-X (hard); 0-87352-183-8 (soft). $35 (hard); $17.50 (soft). bibliography.
Z2011.H34 016.8209

The *Literary Research Guide* "includes an evaluative, annotated bibliography of . . . reference books and periodicals on English, Irish, Scottish, Welsh, Commonwealth, American, Afro-American, American Indian, Continental, Classical, and World literatures, and sixty literature-related subject areas including: Bibliography; Biography; Book Collecting; Film; Folklore; Linguistics; Little Magazines; Prosody; Reviews; Teaching Resources; Textual Criticism; [and] Women's Studies." (publisher's note)

"Some categories have been greatly expanded, among them sections on Commonwealth, classical, and world literatures, film, folklore, women's studies, and little magazines. A detailed search strategy on Flannery O'Connor has been added to the one on Byron found in the first edition. Access to the titles, all of them well annotated, and some of them quite lengthy, is supplied by a good Index and an analytical Table of Contents, which lists short titles for all numbered items under 19 categories. Appended are an explanation of classification systems and a Glossary of about 200 bibliographical terms, clearly and fully defined. The Modern Language Association, as publisher, lends added authority to this useful guide prepared by a college English teacher for graduate students in literature and related subjects." (*BL,* January 15, 1984, p. 734)

Also reviewed in: *ARBA,* 1977, p. 546; 1984, p. 540; *BK,* September 1, 1976, p. 57; *Choice,* May 1977, p. 346; November 1983, p. 392; *LJ,* April 1, 1976, p. 880; April 15, 1978, p. 817; *LR,* Spring 1981, p. 55; *RQ,* Winter 1976, p. 184; *RSR,* April 1979, p. 48; Winter 1983, p. 10; *WLB,* May 1976, p. 744.

Board's recommendation: Academic libraries.

MLA International Bibliography of Books & Articles on the Modern Languages and Literatures. MLA, annual (1921–). hard and soft. 5 vols. 2,713 pp. indexes. ISBN 0-87352-612-0. $850 (set). bibliography.
Z6511.M62 016.0168

The *MLA International Bibliography of Books & Articles on the Modern Languages and Literatures* is a "check list sponsored by the Modern Language Association. . . . It is the eighth in the series with 'international' coverage—based on a master list of approximately 1,150 periodicals and a variety of book sources, including Dissertation Abstracts. The principal books and articles on English, American, Canadian, French, Spanish, German, Italian, and other European literatures published in 1963 are listed, along with selected general studies, including those dealing with the Orient and Africa.

"The section on American literature . . . is, of course, one of the principal tools for the researcher in the field. Its availability in the separate volume is a welcome addition to the services to scholarship performed by the [Modern Language] Association." (*A Lit,* January 1965, p. 547)

Also reviewed in: *Mag Lib,* 1982, p. 23; *RSR,* October 1979, p. 22; Spring 1983, p. 36.

Board's recommendation: Academic libraries.

Reader's Adviser, 13th edition. Barbara A. Chernow and George A. Vallase. Bowker, 1986–1988. 6 vols. indexes. ISBN 0-8352-2428-7. $399.95. handbook.
Z1035.B7 016

The *Reader's Adviser* is "the thirteenth edition of a reference work which began in 1921 as The Bookman's Manual. . . . Each of the text volumes contains its own name, title, and subject indexes. Volume 6 merges all these indexes and includes a directory of publishers. . . . [Each chapter] begins with a three- to four-page introduction followed by listings of general treatises and reference books, works tracing historical or critical trends, and anthologies. The general sections are then usually followed by listings of works by and about individuals, . . . arranged alphabetically. . . . Bibliographic entries cite author, title, publisher, date of publication, and price. . . . Many entries also contain [annotations].

"The *Reader's Adviser* continues its main goal of identifying the 'best' books appropriate for the English-speaking layperson. . . . Least changed in the new edition, volumes 1 and 2 are principally updates to the twelfth edition. . . . The new volume 3 contains thoroughly revised and expanded chapters on general reference, biography, history, and social-science disciplines. . . . The new volume 4 expands coverage of philosophy and world religions by over 500 pages. . . . In addition to the expected chapters on subjects like chemistry, physics, and earth sciences, the editors [of volume 5] treat information and computer science, statistics and probability and energy. . . . Two chapters have been added covering philosophical and ethical aspects of science as well as pseudo-science. . . . This well-crafted and greatly expanded set is worthy of consideration by libraries of all sizes that provide reference and readers' advisory service to an adult population or that need to build general adult collections." (*BL,* February 1, 1989, p. 918)

Also reviewed in: *AB,* November 7, 1988, p. 1811; *ARBA,* 1988, p. 5; *CLW,* March 1988, p. 232; *LJ,* May 1, 1988, p. 34; *LRTS,* July 1988, p. 269; *SciTech,* January 1989, p. 35.

Board's recommendation: Public and academic libraries.

Research Guide to Biography and Criticism. Walton Beacham ed. Beacham Publishing, 1985. hard. 2 vols. plus suppl. 1,362 pp. indexes. ISBN 0-933833-00-8. $129 (set); $69 (suppl.). biobibliography.
Z2011.R47 016.8209

The *Research Guide to Biography and Criticism* "consists of three- to five-page signed articles on approximately 300 British and American poets, novelists, and prose writers from the Middle Ages to the present. . . . Each article includes a brief chronology of the writer's life, a selected bibliography of his or her works, overviews and evaluations of biographical and critical works, and references to dictionaries and encyclopedias. . . . Articles are arranged alphabetically by writers' names, but charts in the front of each volume list the writers by literary period, ranging from early English authors . . . and colonial American authors . . . to contemporary British and North American authors. An index of authors and major sources reviewed is included at the end of the second volume." (*BL,* February 15, 1986, p. 856)

"An excellent example of a kind of reference tool that is much needed in English literature, this will be especially useful to the beginning undergraduate student. . . . This is a good addition for all reference collections, public and academic, high school and up." (*Choice,* December 1985, p. 586)

Also reviewed in: *A Lib,* May 1986, p. 318; *WLB,* November 1985, p. 60.

Board's recommendation: Public and academic libraries.

Genre

Critical Survey of Long Fiction, Foreign Language series. Frank N. Magill, ed. Salem, 1984. hard. 5 vols. 2,396 pp. index. ISBN 0-89356-369-2. $275 (set). criticism.
PN3451.C74 823.009

Critical Survey of Long Fiction, Foreign Language series, "is the fifth in the *Critical Survey* sets by Salem Press.

"The first four volumes provide information about the lives and works of 182 writers important to the development of long fiction around the world. ('Long fiction' usually means novels or novel-like prose forms.) Each of these articles contains seven sections: (1) a list of principal long fiction, (2) a discussion of the writer's contributions to other literary forms, (3) an assessment of the writer's major achievements, (4) a brief biography, (5) an analysis of the writer's major works of long fiction, (6) a selective list of major publications other than long fiction, and (7) a brief, unannotated, selective bibliography of biographical and critical sources about the writer. The fifth volume contains sixteen substantial essays mainly devoted to the history of the novel in various areas of the world where English is not the native language. Volume 5 also includes an author-title index.

"The analyses of individual works are specific, concrete, and free of literary critical jargon, making them accessible to a beginner without insulting the intelligence of a more advanced reader needing background on an unfamiliar writer.

"This set is a useful addition to the *Critical Survey* set." (*ARBA,* 1986, pp. 423–424).

Also reviewed in: *Choice,* July 1985, p. 1610; *WLB,* May 1985, p. 624.

Board's recommendation: Public and academic libraries.

Major Modern Dramatists. Rita Stein and Friedhelm Rickert (vol. 1); Blandine M. Rickert et al. (vol. 2). Ungar, 1984, 1986. hard. 2 vols. 1,040 pp. indexes. ISBN 0-8044-3267-8 (vol. 1); 0-8044-3268-6 (vol. 2). $150 (set). criticism.
PN1861.M271983 809.2′04

"The principal aim of . . . [*Major Modern Dramatists*] 'is to give an overview of the critical reception of the dramatist from the beginning of his career up to the present time by presenting excerpts from reviews, articles, and books.' . . . 'Modern' begins with Ibsen and late-nineteenth-century realism. 'Major' means chiefly an international reputation and 'the existence of a substantial body of serious criticism.' Dramatists are grouped by language and, within those categories, are alphabetical by name.

"The excerpts are given in chronological order and generally represent a wide span of years. . . . Critical commentary was selected from a considerable number of books and periodicals; some English translations were done specifically for this work. Major drama critics are represented . . . as well as dramatists writing on the work of others. An adequate bibliographic citation is provided with each excerpt, and further information can be gathered from the extensive copyright acknowledgements. The length of excerpts ranges from one paragraph to one-and-one-half pages." (*BL,* October 15, 1986, p. 338)

Also reviewed in: *CRL,* January 1986, p. 71.

Board's recommendation: Public and academic libraries.

Princeton Encyclopedia of Poetry and Poetics. Alex Preminger. Princeton, 1974. hard and soft. 1 vol. 992 pp. illus. ISBN 0-691-06280-3 (hard); 0-691-01317-9 (soft). $24.95 (soft). encyclopedia.
PN1021.E5 808.1

The *Princeton Encyclopedia of Poetry and Poetics* "consists of about 1,000 individual entries ranging from twenty to more than 20,000 words, dealing with the history, theory, technique, and criticism of poetry from earliest times to the present. The entries are designed to be useful to the general reader, the student, and the professional scholar. They are supplemented by . . . bibliographies and . . . cross references. . . . The entries in the Encyclopedia are arranged in alphabetical order." (preface)

"[The] overall effect [of this encyclopedia] is to separate and classify every conceivable aspect of its subject from the earliest times to the present with reference to poetry throughout the world, including even Javanese and Vietnamese poetry. . . . This is in fact, as the editors claim, 'the most comprehensive treatment of its field yet attempted,' and it is next to inconceivable that any reference department could get along without it." (*LJ,* May 15, 1965, p. 2251)

Also reviewed in: *BL,* December 15, 1965, p. 376; *BW,* September 19, 1965, p. 23; *CRL,* July 1965, p. 332; *Enc,* March 1966, p. 53; *MLJ,* April 1966, p. 226; *SR,* March 19, 1966, p. 36; *TLS,* February 10, 1966, p. 94.

Board's recommendation: Public and academic libraries.

Science Fiction Writers: Critical Studies of the Major Authors from the Early Nineteenth Century to the Present Day. E. F. Bleiler. Scribner, 1982. hard. 1 vol. 623 pp. illus. index. ISBN 0-684-16740-9. $85. criticism.
PS374.S35S36 823.08

"*Science Fiction Writers* contains studies of the life and works of . . . (seventy-six) science fiction writers, ranging from the early nineteenth century to the present day. . . . Every article, specially commissioned for [this book] provides basic biographical information, commentary on major works, historical background, and a selected bibliography." (publisher's note)

"[The work] . . . has created a historical 'frame' by arranging the essays according to 'writing generations.' . . . This is a solid balanced overview of writers who have influenced the field in one way or another. Many of the writers are given their first extended coverage here, and the studies constitute a valuable contribution to science scholarship. . . . The . . . collection represents a variety of critical approaches, which the editor sees as an advantage, for science fiction is 'a varied, complex field.' . . . [This is] an important reference work." (*Choice,* September 1982, p. 78)

Also reviewed in: *Analog,* December 1982, p. 161; *ARBA,* 1983, p. 544; *BL,* April 15, 1983, p. 1113; *LJ,* May 15, 1982, p. 983; *RSR,* Winter 1983, p. 86; *SF&FBR,* June 1982, p. 6; *S Fict R,* August 1982, p. 38; *TN,* Fall 1982, p. 97; *WLB,* June 1982, p. 786.

Board's recommendation: Public and school libraries.

Survey of Modern Fantasy Literature. Frank N. Magill, ed. Salem, 1983. hard. 5 vols. 2,538 pp. illus. index. ISBN 0-89356-450-8 (set). $275 (set). criticism.
PN56.F34.S97 808.8

The *Survey of Modern Fantasy Literature* is "arranged by title. . . . The 500 'essay-reviews' treat individual works or groups of books [and] . . . there are also 10 topical or genre essays. . . . Essays range from 1000 to 10,000 words." (*LJ,* February 1, 1984, p. 174)

"The scope is impressive; the working definition includes both high and low fantasy, fairy tales, folklore, and horror ranging in time from the Victorians to very current authors. Influential Continental (Hesse, Hermann) and children's (Alexander, LeGuin) fantasists are included." (*Choice,* March 1984, p. 958)

"[This survey] will be consulted, studied, and enjoyed by a wide range of readers, from adolescent-fantasy buffs to venerable literary scholars; and for librarians engaged in collection development it is a potential gold mine." (*BL,* August 1984, p. 1618)

Also reviewed in: *ARBA,* 1984, p. 559; *Fant R,* March 1984, p. 15, June 1984, p. 34; *MFSF,* June 1984, p. 49; *WLB,* February 1984, p. 452.

Board's recommendation: Public, academic, and school libraries.

Twentieth-Century Science Fiction Writers, 2d edition. Curtis C. Smith. St. James, 1986. hard. 1 vol. 933 pp. illus. index. appendixes. ISBN 0-912289-27-9. $85. biobibliography.
PR830.S5 823

"This second edition of . . . [*Twentieth-Century Science Fiction Writers,* which is] devoted to English-language writers of science fiction since 1895[,] includes revisions and updates of the original entries as well as entries for fifty additional authors. Each entry consists of a biography, a bibliography, and a signed critical essay. Entries include manuscript collections, book-length critical studies and published bibliographies. Works about the genre as a whole appear in a 'reading list.' An appendix contains sections on thirty-eight foreign-language writers and five British fantasy writers.

"Each entrant's bibliography is intended to be as complete as possible, and it lists original British and U.S. editions. Bibliographies are divided into 'Science-Fiction Publications' and 'Other Publications.' . . . As a rule, all uncollected science-fiction short stories published since the writer's last collection have been listed. . . . Living authors were invited to offer comments on their oeuvres. . . . [This work] is distinguished by its scope and thoroughness. . . . Libraries owning these other titles will need to decide if they want the extended coverage and superior bibliographies of Twentieth-Century Science Fiction Writers." (*BL,* March 15, 1987, p. 1111)

Also reviewed in: *AB,* October 28, 1985, p. 3066; *Fant R,* October 1986, p. 32; *R & R Bk N,* Fall 1986, p. 18.

Board's recommendation: Public and academic libraries.

Guides

Dictionary of Fictional Characters. William Freeman; rev. by Fred Urquhart. The Writer, 1985. soft. 1 vol. 579 pp. illus. indexes. ISBN 0-87116-147-8. $15. dictionary.
PR19.F7 820.3

"In revising . . . [the *Dictionary of Fictional Characters*], which originally appeared . . . in 1963 and contained over 20,000 fictitious characters, Urquhart has eliminated about 400 characters, which 'reflected Freeman's devotion to the works of late Victorian novelists now unread and forgotten.' He has replaced them with . . . new references, which 'give the names and details of . . . characters taken from some 360 novels and plays. This includes about 180 works by 90 contemporary authors . . . and 180 new works by 88 authors already represented.' Each entry provides both a short descriptive phrase about the character and the author, title, and date of the work in which he appears. . . . Alphabetical indexes of authors and titles covered by the dictionary complete the volume. . . . [T]he *Dictionary of Fictional Characters* remains the most complete source available for the identification of fictitious characters classic and modern." (*BL,* November 15, 1974, p. 350)

Also reviewed in: *AB,* June 3, 1968; *J Hi E,* May 1965, p. 298; *RSR,* January 1975, p. 22.

Board's recommendation: Public, academic, and school libraries.

The International Thesaurus of Quotations. Rhoda Thomas Tripp. Crowell, 1970. hard. 1 vol. 1,088 pp. index. ISBN 0-690-44585-7. $19.95. handbook.
PN6081.T77 808.82

The International Thesaurus of Quotations is arranged in "sentences instead of words. The arrangement is alphabetical by idea-category. . . . In text headings, as well as in the index, the thousand-odd categories are accompanied by . . . cross-references, giving the subject index a total of more than 12,000 entries. This is supplemented by a 300-page key-word index similar to the detailed ones in standard compilations, and by a full index to the authors and sources." (*CC,* October 14, 1970, p. 1227)

"The cross referencing is very thorough (under the category habit one is referred also to custom and routine. . . . The concept of a thesaurus based on quotations rather than simply anonymous words and phrases is exciting and original; the work is clearly scholarly in execution; while it does not replace, say Roget and Bartlett, it belongs on the shelf beside them." (*LJ,* January 1, 1971, p. 64)

"Since more than a third of the quotations are from twentieth-century sources, and since older writers in other languages are often represented in recent translations and by material chosen for its usefulness to writers and speakers today, the big new treasury is as fresh as it is unique." (*SR,* December 5, 1970, p. 34)

Also reviewed in: *LJ,* April 15, 1971, p. 1328; *Obs,*

December 22, 1974, p. 22; *PW,* July 13, 1970, p. 142; August 3, 1970, p. 56; *RQ,* Spring 1971, p. 282; *TLS,* November 2, 1973, p. 1352; *WLB,* December 1970, p. 409.

Board's recommendation: Public and academic libraries.

Magill's Quotations in Context, second series. Frank N. Magill, ed. Salem, 1969. hard. 2 vols. 1,329 pp. indexes. ISBN 0-89356-136-3. $75. handbook.
PN6081.M29 808.882

"Each of the . . . quotations in . . . [*Magill's Quotations in Context*] is quoted in the context of the statement from which it was taken. In addition, a brief descriptive background note helps clarify the original meaning of the expression. Quotations are arranged alphabetically with access provided by a key word index." (*LJ,* April 15, 1971, p. 1327)

"*Magill's Quotations in Context* . . . is much more than a collection of 2,020 quotations 'drawn from more than 2,000 years of world literature.' For, in addition to giving source, author with dates, first publication or transcription, and type of work, it describes the setting of the quotation, and in some cases explains the meaning of a poem, e.g., Eliot's *Gerontion,* or cites its source, e. g., Tennyson's *Tithonus.* Quotations from plays are accompanied by brief resumes. Biblical quotations, of which there are about 200, are described in terms of characters and dogma. Alphabetically arranged by quotation preceded by an alphabetical list and key-word index and with an appended author index, it is easy to use though the key-word index does not attempt to index all the words in the quotations. . . . On the whole the selection is well balanced, and the volume is recommended to all libraries." (*WLB,* May 1966, p. 861)

Also reviewed in: *BL,* July 1, 1966, p. 1026; *Choice,* June 1966, p. 292; *LJ,* April 15, 1966, p. 2042; *SR,* November 19, 1966, p. 52.

Board's recommendation: Academic libraries.

The Originals: An A–Z of Fiction's Real-Life Characters. William Amos. Little, Brown, 1986. hard. 1 vol. 614 pp. illus. index. ISBN 0-316-03741-9. $19.95. handbook.
PN56.4.A4 809.3

"Novelists, playwrights, and poets from Shakespeare to Kerouac, have used friends, acquaintances, and contemporary figures as models for their characters. . . . William Amos spent 10 years compiling [. . . *The Originals.* It is a] list of close to 3,000 'originals,' [assembled by] combing through biographies, autobiographies, interviews, correspondence, and other leads. Entries are alphabetically arranged by the name of the fictional character. He attempts to indicate the strength of the identification—whether it is admitted by the author or assumed—and whether the character is wholly or partially inspired by the original."

"There are forty photographs of 'originals.' . . . This is a fascinating and entertaining book, suitable for browsing and for answering literary questions." (*BL,* September 15, 1986, p. 116)

"[Amos] handles an engaging topic in an engaging manner, offering his identifications with a touch of skepticism and cushioning the baldness of fiction-fact equations with apt, amusing anecdotes. Although some of the identifications are well known, a good deal of ingenious detective work has gone into tracking down others." (*CSM,* July 18, 1986, p. 22)

Also reviewed in: *BW,* May 25, 1986, p. 15; *Choice,* September 1986, p. 77; *LATBR,* May 11, 1986, p. 14; *SAQ,* Autumn 1986, p. 414; *Time,* May 26, 1986, p. 79; *TLS,* November 29, 1985, p. 1349.

Board's recommendation: Public libraries.

Penguin Dictionary of Quotations. J. M. Cohen and M. J. Cohen. Viking, 1977. soft. 1 vol. ISBN 0-14-051016-8. $8.95. dictionary.
PN6081 808

Board's recommendation: Public and academic libraries.

The Quotable Woman, From Eve to the Present. Elaine Partnow. Facts On File, 1991. hard. 1 vol. 608 pp. indexes. ISBN 0-8160-2134-1. $35. handbook.
PN6081 082

"Completely revised and updated, this is the definitive treasury of notable quotations by women—the source that *Library Journal* recommended as 'the only book available dedicated totally to quotations by women . . . no other source approaches its representation.'

"This new, expanded edition gathers over 20,000 quotations by more than 2,500 women from Biblical times to the Space Age. Now including entries from the 1980s, this comprehensive coverage spans the world as well as the ages.

"Herein you'll be reacquainted with some of the world's most outspoken women—and be introduced to many others nearly forgotten by history. Their words are as timely and salient today as when first uttered or written.

"Designed for fast, easy reference, *The Quotable Woman* is as accessible as it is comprehensive. Entries are arranged chronologically by contributor's birth dates and are conveniently accessed by any of four indices, a biographical index, a subject index, a nationality/ethnicity index and a career/occupation index." (Excerpted from publisher's announcement)

Also reviewed in: *ARBA,* 1984, p. 329; *Kliatt,* Fall 1986, p. 54; *LATBR,* May 11, 1986, p. 12; *LJ,* June 1, 1983, p. 1128; *RSR,* Winter 1982, p. 15; *WSJ,* March 28, 1983, p. 22.

Board's recommendation: Public and academic libraries.

New and Noteworthy

Black Writers: A Selection of Sketches from Contemporary Authors. Linda Metzger, ed. Gale, 1989. hard. 1 vol. 619 pp. ISBN 0-8103-2774. $80. biographical source.
PN490.B53 810.9′896

"Biographical and bibliographical information on more than 400 black authors active during the 20th century are found in [*Black Writers*] . . . Arranged alphabetically by author, this volume includes black writers active during the Harlem Renaissance as well as contemporary American, African and Caribbean writers. . . . Typical entries include personal data, an address, career information, membership in organizations, a listing of awards and honors, a chronological bibliography of the author's writings by genre, and descriptions of works in progress." (*SLJ,* May 1990, p. 28)

Characters in 20th-Century Literature. Laurie Lanzen Harris. Gale, 1990. hard. 1 vol. 480 pp. index. ISBN 0-8103-1847-4. $49.95. bibliography.
PN56.4.C4 809.927

"[*Characters in 20th-Century Literature*] treats works created by 250 of the century's major novelists, dramatists, and short story writers. 'Twentieth century' . . . includes living authors and those who have died since 1899. . . . The book is arranged alphabetically by author. After listing the author's dates, nationality, and principal genres, the main body of each entry is composed of brief essays on one or several of the author's works, which contain a brief plot synopsis as well as commentary on themes and the way in which characters illustrate these themes." (*BL,* March 1, 1990, p. 1381)

Dictionary of American Literary Characters. Benjamin V. Franklin, Facts On File, 1989. hard. 1 vol. 512 pp. appendix. index. ISBN 0-8160-1917-7. $60. dictionary.
PS374.C4305 813.009230

"[The *Dictionary of American Literary Characters*] gives brief identification (author and title) for over 11,000 characters from American novels published between 1789 and 1980. The author [has included] well-known characters such as Holden Caulfield, Simon Legree . . . and Lorelei Lee, as well as many characters who are fairly obscure. . . . The main alphabetical list of characters is supplemented by an appendix that lists famous series characters such as Tarzan and Charlie Chan." (*BL,* March 1, 1990, p. 1381)

Literary Terms: A Dictionary, 3d edition. Karl Beckson and Arthur Ganz. Farrar/Noonday, 1989. soft. 1 vol. 308 pp. ISBN 0-374-52177-8. $8.95. dictionary
PN44.5.B334 803

"Intended for writers and teachers as well as students and general readers, [*Literary Terms*] defines terms, concepts, and theories pertaining to various aspects of literature, such as techniques, forms, history, analysis, and criticism. . . . [Terms in the book] . . . are arranged alphabetically. . . . In some cases [the authors] use bibliographic references to sources of additional information." (*BL,* December 1, 1989, p. 766)

Masterpieces of World Literature. Frank N. Magill. Harper & Row, 1989. hard. 1 vol. 957 pp. index. ISBN 0-06-016144-2. $35. history and criticism.
PN44.M3448 809

"[This volume gives] . . . plot information, character descriptions, and critical evaluation of 204 works (novels, plays, stories, and poems), plus analysis of 66 others (mostly essays). . . . As in the parent sets [*Critical Surveys* series, *Masterplots* series, and the *Cyclopedia of Literary Characters*], the unsigned articles are clearly written, objective, accurate, and informative. Arrangement is alphabetical by the best-known English title. . . . This volume is an attractive purchase for home use." (*BL,* February 1, 1990, p. 1115)

Masterplots II: Nonfiction Series. Frank N. Magill. Salem, 1989. hard. 4 vols. 1,745 pp. index. ISBN 0-89356-478-8. $325. bibliography.
PN44.M345 080.2

"[*Masterplots II*] . . . covers currently faddish 'literary nonfiction,' some 300 autobiographies, memoirs, and . . . a 'broad selection of nonfiction works that the culturally literate person will encounter.' The selections are mostly 20th-century writings in English, though some 19th-century works in other languages, mainly European, are included. Each work is summarized, analyzed, and placed in a critical context: *Eichmann in Jerusalem, Blue Highways, The Double Helix* and *Small Is Beautiful* are typical selections." (*LJ,* September 1, 1989, p. 182)

Nobel Laureates in Literature: A Biographical Dictionary. Rado Pribic. Garland, 1990. hard. 1 vol. 473 pp. index. ISBN 0-8240-574-4. $75. dictionary.
PN452.P7 809.04

"[*Nobel Laureates in Literature*] . . . covers literature prize recipients up through the 1988 winner, Jajib Mahfuz. . . . The book begins with a chronological list of laureates; the essays about them are arranged in alphabetical order. . . . The biographical and critical information in the entries duplicates that in most standard biographical dictionaries of contemporary authors. The book concludes with an index of personal names." (*BL,* May 1, 1990, p. 1748)

Science Fiction, Fantasy and Horror Reference: An Annotated Bibliography of Works About Literature and Film. Keith L. Justice, comp. McFarland, 1989. hard. 1 vol. index. ISBN 0-89950-406-X. $27.50. bibliography.
Z5917.S36J86 016.8093'876

"[*Science Fiction, Fantasy and Horror Reference*] was compiled 'to help librarians, collectors, researchers, and others with an interest in SF/fantasy/horror reference materials determine what books might be of use or interest to them.

"[The book] . . . is divided into nine chapters with titles like 'General Bibliographies'; 'Biography, Autobiography, Letters & Interviews'; 'Encyclopedias, Dictionaries, Indexes & Checklists.' . . . The 304 books are arranged by the author's last name. . . . Each entry contains full bibliographic data and a long evaluative annotation that is particularly helpful. . . . *Science Fiction, Fantasy and Horror Reference* is an important contribution to science fiction literature." (*BL,* October 1, 1989, p. 396)

Short Story Criticism: Excerpts from Criticism of the Works of Short Fiction Writers, vol. 1. Laurie Lanzen Harris and Sheila Fitzgerald, eds. Gale, 1988. hard. illus. index. ISBN 0-8103-2550-0. $75. criticism.
PN3373.S56 809.3

"[*Short Story Criticism* was created] in response to librarians reporting an increase in requests for critical material on short stories. This first volume includes 14 major writers in the genre. . . . Each author entry includes a portrait, biographical and critical introduction, a list of principal works, and additional bibliography. Criticism . . . takes up a large portion of each entry, indicating the initial response to the work, the rise or decline in the author's reputation, and current analysis to show today's opinion. (*SLJ,* May 1989, p. 30)

Lori Bronars *Janet Chisman*

Zoology

See also Biology

Zoology, the study of animal life, has been a focus of interest for hundreds of years. This interest is shared by specialists in the field as well as by the general public. The earliest known writings on the natural history of animals may be those left by the philosopher Aristotle (384–322 B.C.): *Historia Animalium, De Partibus Animalium,* and *De Generatione Animalium.*

Carolus Linnaeus (1707–1778), Louis Agassiz (1807–1873), John James Audubon (1785–1851), Charles Darwin (1809–1882), and Theodosius Dobzhansky (1900–1975) are just a few of the other pioneers of zoological investigation and reporting. Works of these scientists and works about them are not included in the scope of the present guide, but should be considered for well-rounded science collections. The same holds true for many present-day zoologists as well, among them Konrad Lorenz, Karl von Frisch, G. Evelyn Hutchinson, George B. Schaller, and Jane van Lawick Goodall.

Checklists and field guides, lab manuals, periodical indexes, and classification or identification keys are other important sources of reference data not reviewed here, as are the many popular accounts of animal observation and adventures. In building a zoology collection it is imperative to have taxonomic sources of common and scientific names covering a range of time periods, since scientific consensus is rarely met. Having older and current name sources enables researchers to trace a given species between time periods. *Systema Naturae* (tenth edition, 1758) by Linnaeus introduced into common use the binomial, or two-name (genus and species), system for animals. Neave's *Nomenclator Zoologicus* and its supplementary volumes, covering 1758 to 1965, Sherborne's *Index Animalium,* covering 1801 to 1850, and, for current classification, *Synopsis and Classification of Living Organisms* (McGraw-Hill, 1982), edited by Sybil P. Parker, are suggested.

Titles for these types of sources may be readily identified through the use of *Walford's Guide to Reference Material* (ALA, various editions), Roger C. Smith's *Guide to Literature of the Zoological Sciences* (seventh edition, 1966), the American Library Association's *Guide to Reference Books* (various editions), *Pure & Applied Science Books 1876–1982* (Bowker, 1982), and *Guide to Sources for Agricultural and Biological Research* (Univ. of California Pr., 1981). The following sources are useful for identifying older works: C. A. Wood's *An Introduction to the Literature of Vertebrate Zoology* (1931) and R. E. Blackwelder's *Books on Zoology* (1963).

Among indexes to periodical literature, the venerable *Zoological Record* (1864 to present) is eminent,

Core Titles

	PUBLIC	ACADEMIC	SCHOOL
Black's Veterinary Dictionary, 16th edition West, Geoffrey P., ed. A & C Black, 1988		✦	
The Encyclopedia of Animal Behavior Slater, Peter J. B., ed. Facts On File, 1987	✦	✦	✦
The Encyclopedia of Animal Biology Alexander, R. McNeill, ed. Facts On File, 1987	✦	✦	✦
The Encyclopedia of Animal Evolution Berry, R. J., and A. Hallam, eds. Facts On File, 1987			✦
The Encyclopedia of Aquatic Life Banister, Keith, and Andrew Campbell, eds. Facts On File, 1985			✦
The Encyclopedia of Birds Perrins, Christopher M., and Alex L. A. Middleton, eds. Facts On File, 1985	✦	✦	✦
The Encyclopedia of Insects O'Toole, Christopher, ed. Facts On File, 1986	✦	✦	✦
The Encyclopedia of Mammals Macdonald, David W., ed. Facts On File, 1984	✦	✦	✦
The Encyclopedia of Reptiles and Amphibians Halliday, Tim R., and Kraig Adler, eds. Facts On File, 1986	✦	✦	✦
Grzimek's Encyclopedia of Mammals, 5 vols. Parker, Sybil P., ed. McGraw-Hill, 1990	✦	✦	
Macmillan Illustrated Animal Encyclopedia Whitfield, Phillip, ed. Macmillan, 1984	✦		✦
The Merck Veterinary Manual: A Handbook of Diagnosis, Therapy, and Disease Prevention and Control for the Veterinarian, 6th edition Fraser, Clarence M., ed. Merck, 1986		✦	
Oxford Companion to Animal Behavior McFarland, David, ed. Oxford, 1987		✦	
Walker's Mammals of the World, 4th edition, 2 vols. Nowak, Ronald M., and John L. Paradiso. Johns Hopkins Univ. Pr., 1983	✦	✦	

although not simple for all to use. *Biological Abstracts, General Science Index, Life Sciences Collection* (available on CD-ROM and as an on-line data base), *Wildlife Review,* and *Fisheries Review* are also useful.

The literature of zoology is vast, varied, and has a long history; therefore, in building a collection of reference materials, selection must often be prudent. The titles reviewed here and recommended for the core collection constitute a set of authoritative and scholarly works that provide facts and discussion of all major groups within the animal kingdom and that provide basic coverage for a core of the subfields of zoology: animal behavior, veterinary medicine, and evolution. An overview source, such as *Five Kingdoms: An Illustrated Guide to the Phyla of Life on Earth* (1988) by Lynn Margulis and Karlene V. Schwartz, would serve to balance the collection and place the recommended titles in a broader context. As is noted in some of the following reviews, a scientific or unabridged English-language dictionary will be necessary in conjunction with use of some of these sources. *—L. B. and J. C. With contributions by Mary Ann McFarland.*

Core Titles

Black's Veterinary Dictionary, 16th edition. Geoffrey P. West, ed. A & C Black, 1988. hard. 1 vol. 703 pp. illus. ISBN 0-7136-3004-3. $35. dictionary.
SF609.B53 636.089

Black's Veterinary Dictionary is a standard reference source first published in 1928 and now in its sixteenth edition. (This review was written from the fifteenth edition, since the sixteenth was unavailable from the publisher for review.)

The work follows a typical dictionary format, although entries range from one or two sentences to eight pages, with some general articles of encyclopedic length. For instance, the article on parasites and diseases is 40 pages long. Besides definitions, entries often include reports of actual cases, with references to the original articles given. "See also" references lead to definitions of related terms in the dictionary. Over 200 black-and-white illustrations, both drawings and photographs, supplement the text.

The dictionary is written for the practicing veterinarian and animal owners. The language is relatively nontechnical, with a focus on causes, symptoms, and treatment of diseases.

In 1988, two other veterinary dictionaries were also published. The *Concise Veterinary Dictionary* (Oxford, 1988) has an intended audience ranging from researchers to pet owners. Entries are shorter than those in *Black's* and tend more to definition than to practical information and case reports. The second, *Bailliere's Comprehensive Veterinary Dictionary* (Bailliere Tindall, London), contains definitions of over 52,000 terms and 18 tables dealing with laboratory services, biochemical and hematological reference values, and anatomical information. The definitions in this work are quite technical; the dictionary was written for veterinary students, practicing veterinarians, and biologists.

These three dictionaries are all comparably priced. However, *Black's Veterinary Dictionary* is still the recommended first purchase because of its focus on the practical and the readability of its entries. The Board recommends this work for the core collection of academic libraries. —*J. C.*

The Encyclopedia of Animal Behavior. Peter J. B. Slater, ed. Facts On File, 1987. hard. 1 vol. 144 pp. appendix. illus. index. ISBN 0-8160-1816-2. $29.95. encyclopedia.
QL751.E614 591.51

The Encyclopedia of Animal Behavior is a descriptive, highly readable account of the major topics in the field of animal behavior. It is an interesting blend of science and history, composed of signed articles written by 25 scientists. The editor, Peter J. B. Slater, is a professor at the University of St. Andrews in Scotland. He is also a former editor of the journal *Animal Behaviour* and is currently one of the editors of *Advances in the Study of Behavior.*

The work begins with an introductory section on the field of animal behavior—what it is, why it is studied, how it can be applied, and how it relates to humans. This is followed by the main entry articles, which are grouped into four broad areas: behavior of individual animals, animal relationships, the origins of behavior, and social organizations. Articles frequently begin with a series of questions, often about behavior familiar to all. For instance, the article on vertebrate societies begins with the following paragraph:

> It is easy to take for granted the fact that many animals live in social groups. A herd of cows, a school of fishes, a flock of birds are commonplace, but why should so many kinds of fishes, amphibians, reptiles, birds, and mammals live in groups? What kinds of groups do they live in? How do they manage to stay together, particularly if they live in dense undergrowth or murky water, where communication may be difficult? It is only in recent years that some of the answers to these questions have begun to emerge.

This questioning approach stimulates thought and emphasizes that there is still much to learn. Included within articles are boxed descriptions that highlight specific behavioral features such as memory, bonds between parents and young, and alarm pheromones. Over 120 color photographs and 50 diagrams and drawings complement the text.

The back of the book contains a bibliography of 46 references to key works on animal behavior and suggestions for further reading. A four-page glossary briefly defines some of the more technical terminology found in the text. There is also an alphabetical index of terms and concepts, which adds to the accessibility of the book.

The articles in *The Encyclopedia of Animal Behavior* cover topics that would be found in an introductory text on the subject. However, the language and style of writing make this more readable than most textbooks and increase the volume's usefulness as an introductory reference work for high school and undergraduate students as well as for the public. A comparable reference, the OXFORD COMPANION TO ANIMAL BEHAVIOR, will be more useful in meeting the needs of upper-level college students and scientists. The Board recommends this work for the core collections of public, academic, and school libraries. —*J. C.*

The Encyclopedia of Animal Biology. R. McNeill Alexander, ed. Facts On File, 1987. hard. 1 vol. 144 pp. appendix. illus. index. ISBN 0-8160-1817-0. $29.95. encyclopedia.
QL45.2.E53 591

Most of the other encyclopedias in this Facts On File series—birds, insects, reptiles and amphibia, aquatic life—emphasize the diversity of life. In contrast, *The Encyclopedia of Animal Biology* emphasizes the similarities among animals in their requirements for life, in their cellular and subcellular components, and in the physiological processes needed to sustain life.

The eight contributors to this work have succeeded in integrating ecology and cell biology into a unique view of the animal world. R. McNeill Alexander, the editor, is a professor of zoology at the University of Leeds and is the author of nine books and many scientific papers. The other seven contributors are also recognized experts in their fields of study. Each has emphasized the underlying principles of animal similarities, which gives the book a unifying theme.

This integration is reinforced by well-designed illustrations that often combine diagrammatic representations of different biological systems with color photographs of the animal in its natural setting. Thus the reader never loses sight of the animal while learning about its biology. There is also a refreshing view of the classification of animals. The first chapter presents a 17-page overview of the animal kingdom organized along a classification scheme preferred by the author of this section. However, it is also noted that "classification is a matter of opinion, and the differences of detail will often be found between schemes in different books." This will come as quite a relief to those who have probably been confused when comparing classification schemes among various books and have noted how rarely two are the same.

Following the overview of the animal kingdom are chapters on molecules and cells; feeding and digestion; gas exchange and circulation; the internal environment (regulatory mechanisms); the senses, movement, coordination, and control (the nervous system); and reproduction and development. Each chapter begins with a one- or two-paragraph introduction against the background of a two-page color photograph. For instance, the feeding and digestion introduction is accompanied by a photograph of a snake swallowing an egg four-and-a-half times its own head diameter. The artwork throughout the book—consisting of photographs, drawings of animals, and diagrams—is a beautiful complement to the text, clarifying concepts and instilling a sense of wonder.

High school students, college undergraduates, and the general public will find in *The Encyclopedia of Animal Biology* a solid, understandable introduction to animal biology. A bibliography of books for further reading is included and arranged under the same chapter headings as the text. Although brief, it includes key works by noted authors such as J. Maynard-Smith for evolution, M. Hildebrand for functional anatomy, and K. Schmidt-Nielsen for animal physiology. A glossary with about 300 briefly defined terms and an index increase the usefulness of this encyclopedia. The Board recommends this work for the core collections of public, academic, and school libraries. *—J. C.*

The Encyclopedia of Animal Evolution. R. J. Berry and A. Hallam, eds. Facts On File, 1987. hard. 1 vol. 144 pp. appendix. illus. index. ISBN 0-8160-1819-7. $29.95. encyclopedia.
QH366.2.E54 591.38

The Encyclopedia of Animal Evolution presents a balanced view of this frequently controversial topic. The 21 contributors are scientists associated with academic institutions or the British Museum of Natural History. The majority have written books and scientific articles on the topics they write about in this volume. Seven artists also collaborated to produce informative artwork panels, diagrams, and maps, which enhance and explain the text.

The book is arranged in six sections with one or more signed entries per section. The broad topics include the prehistoric world; the history, course, results, and mechanisms of evolution; and humans and evolution. The first section presents an overview of the different geological ages, their attendant animal populations, and environmental conditions. The historical section reviews Darwin's theory, pre-Darwinian evolutionary theories, and post-Darwinian controversies. The fossil record, extinction, and evolutionary trends are some of the topics discussed in the section on the course of evolution. The section on the consequences of evolution covers the origin of life, homology, and adaptation. In the section on the mechanisms of evolution, genetics and the origin of species are explained. The last section deals with the probable evolution of humans and briefly reviews the various controversies dealing with evolution.

The text is well written and should be understandable to students and adults alike. An example is the description of the difference between homology and analogy, a concept that often confuses students:

> Thus the forelimbs of humans, horses, whales, and birds are homologous: they are all constructed on the same pattern, and include similar bones in the same relative

> positions because these are all derived from the same ancestral bones. The wings of birds and insects, on the other hand are analogous: they serve the same purpose, but do not constitute modified versions of a structure present in a common ancestor.

This explanation is accompanied by an excellent diagram with color-coded bones showing the adaptations of the five-fingered hand for swimming, running, and flying.

"See" references allow the reader to move freely from one part of the text to another while pursuing additional information on a topic. There is also an excellent, though highly selective, bibliography of 124 books "compiled with the aim of including historically important books and the more significant modern ones. It should be regarded as a guide to further reading" (bibliography). Fifteen of the books in the bibliography, which is divided according to topics, are authored or edited by the contributors. A glossary and index complete the volume and increase the usefulness as well as the accessibility of the work.

The Board recommends this work for the core collection of school libraries. —*J. C.*

The Encyclopedia of Aquatic Life. Keith Banister and Andrew Campbell, eds. Facts On File, 1985. hard. 1 vol. 349 pp. illus. appendix. index. ISBN 0-8160-1257-1. $45. encyclopedia.
QL120.E53 591.92

Seventy percent of the earth's surface is covered with water. *The Encyclopedia of Aquatic Life* focuses on extant forms inhabiting this medium for their complete life cycle. "It thus excludes such amphibious animals as frogs and newts, which return to water to breed, and seals and sea lions which leave the sea to breed on land" (preface). Coverage is limited to animal life; plants are not included.

A group of 28 scientists, associated with major universities, museums, or governmental agencies, contributed articles to the volume. Although this is a large number of contributors, the articles have a consistency in their coverage: all include taxonomy, the relation of the animals to humans, and basic as well as unusual features of physiology or habit. As in the other Facts On File encyclopedias, the text is supplemented by numerous color photographs. Diagrams and drawings complete the illustrations.

The articles are arranged in three main sections: fishes, aquatic invertebrates, and sea mammals. Each section begins with an overview of the animals to be discussed, then individual taxonomic groups are covered. The articles about the groups include insets with information on classification and a small distribution map. There are also numerous two-page articles covering broader aspects of aquatic life, such a bioluminescence, ecology of zooplankton, and the songs of the humpback whale. Also included are a bibliography of key references used in writing the text and a glossary, which is divided into the same three sections as the text. An index of the entire contents completes the encyclopedia.

This book is written for the student or layperson interested in aquatic animals. The text is very readable, with most scientific terms explained within the text or in the glossary. Simple statements can arouse curiosity.

> There is no such thing as a fish. Fish is simply a shorthand notation for an aquatic vertebrate that is not a mammal, a turtle or anything else. There are four quite separate groups of fish, not closely related to one another. Lumping these four groups together under the heading fish is like lumping all flying vertebrates, i.e. bats (mammals), birds and even the flying lizard under the heading "birds" just because they all fly. The relationship between a lamprey and a shark is no closer than that between a salamander and a camel.

There are also frequent references to unexplained phenomena, which emphasize the need for more research and reinforce the idea that science has not found all the answers.

The Board recommends this work for the core collection of school libraries. —*J. C.*

The Encyclopedia of Birds. Christopher M. Perrins and Alex L. A. Middleton, eds. Facts On File, 1985. hard. 1 vol. 450 pp. illus. appendix. index. ISBN 0-8160-1150-8. $45. encyclopedia.
QL673.E53 598

The Encyclopedia of Birds presents an overview of the world's living bird groups accompanied by many attractive illustrations. Few books attempt to cover as wide a geographic range both for general identification purposes and for explanations of each family's characteristics. The 66 articles present information on plumage, bills, eggs, nests, foraging, diet, distribution, habitat, and feeding behavior for flightless birds, waders, game birds, waterfowl, birds of prey, and perching birds. Extinct species are not covered. The overall order of presentation closely follows the Wetmore order, used in many field guides, encyclopedias, and dictionaries of birds.

There is a noticeable bias in viewpoint; a strong conservation message appears in the preface and elsewhere. For any species recognized as being at least "threatened" by the International Council for Bird

Preservation, an indication of that status is given in the opening inset for the family.

This work's strength lies in the descriptions of physical features and in the interesting reading provided in the insets, which cover selected topics such as cooperative breeding in babblers, survival in cold weather, owl pellets, and penguin diving. More subjective topics such as behavior, evolution, natural history, flight, and migration warrant more in-depth treatment. Also, more obvious discussion of scientific controversies and research issues would have been beneficial. The authors do often remind the reader of scientists' limited knowledge of some groups or of specific characteristics of a group such as its breeding habits, range, or the function of a certain trait; this helps to give a sense of ornithology as a research discipline.

The 87 contributors represent a range of institutions and organizations, including Oxford University, the British Museum (Natural History), New York Zoological Society, Field Museum of Natural History, Brown University, and some Canadian, Australian, Scottish, Swedish, and South African institutions. The authority of this work is unquestionable; however, the quality of writing is quite uneven. The articles on cranes, rails, terns, limpkins, toucans, and honeyguides are a pleasure to read, but some of the others too eagerly present facts and description without discussion, personal observation, or explanation; consequently, these essays leave the reader uninspired.

It is surprising that at least a few taxonomic changes are not reflected. The ibisbill is still included in the article on avocets and stilts, and the Magellanic plover and ground-roller are not accorded articles although they are described as distinct families in the British Ornithologists' Union's A DICTIONARY OF BIRDS, also published in 1985.

Illustrations are great in number. The full-color drawings are nicely presented, as are the range maps and drawings showing general size compared to humans. There are many full-color photos.

This work is published in an 8½-by-11-inch format. The binding for its 450 pages is insufficient to stand up to the use it could be expected to see in most general science collections. Overall the work is a useful compilation; the lack of fuller textual examination of bird topics is the major weakness.

The index and glossary are useful, although somewhat inadequate for the scope of the book. The subject matter of the insets is not outlined in the contents pages and appears not to be indexed either. The glossary and bibliography should be expanded to better serve this popular field and present the rich literature that interests students, undergraduates, and hobbyists, the anticipated audience. Despite these minor flaws, *The Encyclopedia of Birds* is a valuable book. The Board recommends this work for the core collections of public, academic, and school libraries. —*L. B.*

The Encyclopedia of Insects. Christopher O'Toole, ed. Facts On File, 1986. hard. 1 vol. 143 pp. illus. appendix. index. ISBN 0-8160-1358-6. $24.95. encyclopedia.
QL462.2.086 595.7'003'21

The Encyclopedia of Insects is actually an introductory overview of the arthropods with an emphasis on insects. The editor, Christopher O'Toole, is an entomologist with several other books to his credit. Of the 20 other contributors, most hold Ph.D.'s and are associated with prestigious British institutions.

The signed articles follow a biosystematic arrangement. The book begins with an explanation of what an arthropod is, then presents a discussion of the myriapods (in four pages) and finally moves on to a discussion of insects in general. Subsequent entries treat each order of insect. The final section of 18 pages briefly discusses the arachnids.

Each entry is a visually attractive blend of text, insets, and color photographs. For each order, an introductory inset gives some or all of the following information: order, class, phylum, number of species and families, distributions, morphological features, and a list of some if not all family names, both common and scientific. Additional insets cover general topics such as courtship and nuptial gifts, flying with legs, or the song of the cicada. This main text is well written and entertaining, giving ecological and life habit information. For instance, one learns that the female earwig "guards her batch [of eggs] against predators. Such parental care is unusual among insects. For a week or two [after hatching] the female continues to guard her young. After this time she encourages them to leave by developing a marked tendency to eat them" (p. 41).

The only complaint is that this volume on the most numerous animals on earth is too short. A longer book could have prevented unfortunate omissions (there is no mention of the free-living forms of caddisflies or the rhyacophila) and overly condensed descriptions (in some cases, three or four orders appear on two pages). However, in spite of its brevity, this slender volume presents a good summary of the insect world. Information presented here can be supplemented by the volume on insects in the *Grzimek's Animal Life Encyclopedia* (Van Nostrand Reinhold, 1972–1975), now out of print.

The Encyclopedia of Insects will be accessible to the layperson. The text is not too technical. For more technical terms, there is a glossary of over 175 entries, which gives brief definitions and also signifies which words used in the definitions also are themselves defined in the glossary. An index increases access to the information in the text. There is also a bibliography of books used in writing the text and recommended for further reading. This could serve as a good resource for devising a circulating collection on insects. The Board recommends this work for the core collections of public, academic, and school libraries. —*J. C.*

The Encyclopedia of Mammals. David W. Macdonald, ed. Facts On File. 1984. hard. 1 vol. 920 pp. illus. appendix. index. ISBN 0-87196-871-1. $65. encyclopedia.
QL703.E53 599

Living mammals of the world are attractively featured and well described in the very readable *The Encyclopedia of Mammals,* edited by David Macdonald of Oxford University's Department of Zoology. The articles are arranged by taxonomic order, with carnivores discussed first, followed by sea mammals, primates (excluding humans), large herbivores, small herbivores, and, lastly, insect-eaters and marsupials. (Humans are not discussed.) These orders cover many very familiar animals such as cats, dogs, bears, raccoons, giant pandas, monkeys, apes, whales, dolphins, seals and sea lions, hoofed mammals, rodents, bats, and oppossums. A complete systematic listing of all mammals and their distribution constitutes the appendix. The class of mammals numbers approximately 4,000 species, represented by 125 family-, subfamily-, or genus-level articles and a handful of introductory articles in *The Encyclopedia of Mammals.*

Including the editor, there are 176 contributors listed, most of whom are P.h.D's. Individual articles are signed. In spite of the numerous writers, the text is clear and well-written throughout. The writers represent institutions in the United States (the majority), England, France, West Germany, Australia, Canada, Italy, and elsewhere.

The text is often fashioned in a standardized structure from article to article, touching on early accounts of a species, physical characteristics (weight, coloration, dentition), diet, breeding, evolution, interactions with other species, foraging and hunting, vocalizations, and skull anatomy. The treatment of behavior is notable. Comparisons of common and distinguishing features are made between species of the same genus or between those of different orders or families. The articles usually end with mention of major causes of mortality and factors affecting the animal's survival.

The side box on the opening page of each article carries a distribution map and basic facts, such as typical body dimensions, coat, habitat, gestation, and longevity. Additional insets on a variety of interesting topics also appear; for example, the size of a lion pride, the classification of the fox, hunting technique of the tiger, mass strandings of whales, evolution of large body size, and aggressiveness in bears.

Altogether this volume has an attractive layout and an inviting text. *The Encyclopedia of Mammals* is more pleasurable to read and to look through, with its captivating and detailed color photographs and drawings, than WALKER'S MAMMALS OF THE WORLD. This work reaches a wider audience and is easier to use than GRZIMEK'S ENCYCLOPEDIA OF MAMMALS because of its glossary, uniform presentation, and more complete index. However, for readers requiring more precise, scientific detail or pictures and descriptions of the lesser-known small mammals, WALKER'S should be consulted, as should GRZIMEK'S for a more leisurely yet lively discussion and for a broader range of references.

The Board recommends this work for the core collections of public, academic, and school libraries.

—*L. B.*

The Encyclopedia of Reptiles and Amphibians. Tim R. Halliday and Kraig Adler, eds. Facts On File, 1986. hard. 1 vol. 150 pp. illus. appendix. index. ISBN 0-8160-1359-4. $24.95. encyclopedia.
QL641.H35 597.6

Overall *The Encyclopedia of Reptiles and Amphibians* presents a surprising amount of information in a slim volume. The informal style of writing makes for a book less practical for quick fact finding than for interesting reading.

The 19 contributors are identified along with their professional affiliations, and the individual articles are signed. These researchers were drawn from major universities and museums, including Cornell University, University of California at Berkeley, University of Michigan, the Smithsonian Institution's National Museum of Natural History, and the British Museum (Natural History).

Salamanders, frogs, turtles, lizards, snakes, and crocodiles are among the groups covered, with a special article on the ever-popular dinosaurs. The information presented for each class and order includes the number of species, genera, and families recognized; habitat; distribution, size, and color; and courtship, reproduction, and life span. General behavior and physiology, diet, growth, and feeding behavior are discussed. Notes on the species' status are also included. Especially helpful is the special attention to representations of scale. For example, some organisms are shown in a simple block drawing that is sized with respect to the human form. Often, too, organisms are pictured full-length and close-up.

A clear typeface makes the layout of text, insets, and illustrations pleasant for reading. A keener eye on editing would have been beneficial, however. At times the highly informal and oversimplified writing detracts from the work's authority, and some articles suffer from questionable sentences, poor wording, and excessive brevity. Sometimes statements are oversimplified to the point of being misleading for the less knowledgeable reader. For example, the statement that "A very substantial number of lizards and snakes have forsaken egg-laying and gone over to live-bearing" suggests that this is an individual organism's decision rather than a result of evolution.

By contrast, however, the brief glossary is effective and useful. The presence of a bibliography is a bonus, but it would be more useful if footnoted or referred to at appropriate places in the main text. The index begs for simple improvement; for example, there should be a complementary entry *tongues—lizards* listed also as *lizards—tongues* for the inset on page 87. Compounding the weakness of the index is the occasional succession of unpaginated leaves due to illustrations or other material laid out in the page number space. This understandable problem is an inconvenience to the reader when it occurs often or in the extreme, as here where pages 12 through 20 are unnumbered.

In its 8½-by-11-inch format, this work makes good use of color photos, line drawings, paintings, and maps to enhance explanations. The illustrations are informative and interesting. The "Temperature Control by Sun and Shade" article provides an especially striking pair of illustrations showing skin darkening in a chameleon. There are a number of other exceptional photos, among them a 13-foot Oenpelli python caught in motion, an African python "subduing a crocodile," and a pair of wrestling Bengal monitors.

For heavily used collections, expect to spend an additional sum on rebinding; the original binding is rather weak. Academic libraries may need other sources (such as the out-of-print *Grzimek's Animal Life Encyclopedia,* Van Nostrand Reinhold, 1972–1975) that are more comprehensive, especially with regard to historical and evolutionary treatment. Otherwise, *The Encyclopedia of Reptiles and Amphibians* is an economical and sound choice.

The Board recommends this work for the core collections of public, academic, and school libraries.

—L. B.

Grzimek's Encyclopedia of Mammals. Sybil P. Parker, ed. McGraw-Hill, 1990. hard. 5 vols. illus. appendix. index. ISBN 0-07-909508-9 (set). $500 (set). encyclopedia.
QL201.G7913 599

It is tempting to indulge in hours of browsing through *Grzimek's Encyclopedia of Mammals* without even a need to find specific information. This five-volume set is the newest large-scale treatment of the class of mammals to appear in recent years and is one of the few to include a section on humans, as does WALKER'S MAMMALS OF THE WORLD. This work is the translation of the 1989 German *Grzimeks Enzyklopädie Säugetiere.*

Just over 100 authorities from a handful of countries contributed the 300 or so articles that are arranged in 50 main sections. There are specific articles that include coverage of whales, seals, rodents, carnivores, deer, camels, and other mammal groups, and other articles designed to explain more general aspects of mammal biology and behavior (evolution, ecology, ethology, conservation, and life in captivity). The text is interesting and informative. The background information is broad based. Liberal discussions of historical and mythological accounts and anecdotes, present-day concerns, and commercial questions involving mammals enliven the more standard presentation of factual information. The text extends the knowledge of mammals provided in the four volumes of *Grzimek's Animal Life Encyclopedia,* (Van Nostrand Reinhold, 1972–1975), which is now out of print, but it does not replicate that work. Information routinely covered includes distribution, diet, habitat, size and weight, dentition, reproductive biology, behavior, and other facts as known. Areas that are yet not well understood are indicated.

The photos have been improved over the previous Grzimek work in terms of color and clarity; they have also increased in number. Handsome two-page photo spreads are not uncommon. The "Comparison of Species" tables are a useful new feature.

Many readers will notice the unfortunate abundance of spelling, typographical, and grammatical errors, which even include misspelling the name of contributor George B. Schaller. Readers who are unfamiliar with this field may be led astray by such inaccuracies or hampered when seeking further information.

However, there does tend to be a longer text, more pictures, and particularly more on anatomy and physiology than is found in Macdonald's THE ENCYCLOPEDIA OF MAMMALS, although Macdonald's text is more clearly written. On the other hand, the purely scientific treatment of data is stronger and more easily located in WALKER'S MAMMALS OF THE WORLD. A glossary to accompany *Grzimek's* would be necessary in library settings for younger or more general audiences, because such specialized terms as *myrmecologist, philters,* and *symplesiomorphous* are uncommon.

Each volume contains a partial list of references and brief biographical data on authors in an appendix. Each volume contains a comprehensive index as well. Users may sometimes end up looking not only in the index but also in the contents pages for a particular group, as with simians and pangolins. Sometimes the common names of mammals are not found in the index or in the contents, as in the case of voles. The section can be found by looking under the generic name for voles *(Microtus)* in the index and then finding that it is in the "Burrowing Rodents" section of the larger chapter on "Mice and Dormice."

Grzimek's Encyclopedia of Mammals is highly commendable in its physical form. The binding, cloth cover, and paper are of high quality and look to be designed for durability. The Board recommends this work for the core collections of public and academic libraries. —*L. B.*

Macmillan Illustrated Animal Encyclopedia. Philip Whitfield, ed. Macmillan, 1984. hard. 1 vol. 600 pp. illus. appendix. index. ISBN 0-02-627680-1. $35.65. encyclopedia.
QL7.M33 591.0321

The animal kingdom's diverse vertebrates, a subphylum of the phylum Chordata, are the focus of the *Macmillan Illustrated Animal Encyclopedia.* Although only 2 or 3 percent of all known animal species are vertebrates, it is these that seem most popular and that people most often associate with the term *animal.*

Nearly 2,000 members of the approximately 43,500 known living species are described and pictured in this work. The selection of species is intended to highlight diversity. Neither extinct species nor domesticated species are covered. The human species is also excluded. Nearly 220 families or orders are represented, approximately half of those known for each of the groups included: mammals, birds, reptiles, amphibians, and fishes. Examples of those animal types not included are sponges, jellyfishes, corals, certain types of worms, mollusks (snails, octopuses, clams), insects (grasshoppers, wasps, butterflies, beetles, bees, ants), spiders, and crustaceans (shrimp, crabs, lobsters).

The layout is consistent: two pages are allotted to each family, with the text on the left-hand page and color drawings of the featured species on the right-hand one. The drawings are beautiful in their color and detail; the only fault is the lack of a common scale throughout or any scale at all on each illustrated page. Of great convenience to the reader is the printing of the animal's common name beside each drawing. The information presented for each family consists of common and scientific names, range, habitat, size, breeding habits, diet, general behavior, physical description, and conservation status.

The reference provides a great deal of information in a concise and easily accessible manner. The opening article, "Mammals—The Peak of Vertebrate Adaptability," reviews mammalian characteristics and is clearly written, as are the others that begin each group. Since some terms are explained in the text, but others are not (for example, resorbed, gestation, prehensile, epiphytic, and spawn), a glossary would have been a useful inclusion.

The text is factual, although a bias toward conservation is apparent in the foreword. There is little nonfactual discussion. Evolutionary transitions (reptile to mammal, amphibian to reptile, fish to amphibian) are touched on in the articles introducing each section, but only broadly. Areas of research are not pointed out, a weakness of the introductory articles.

The book's appearance and the quality of its materials are commendable. The paper and binding are quite durable and the typeface pleasant for reading.

The index entries consist of common and scientific names, but no subjects. A classification table for all vertebrate groups appears among the ending pages. It is odd that the classes of mammals, birds, and amphibians are broken down in this table into their orders and constituent families, but fishes are not detailed beyond the order level.

Although there are plenty of more comprehensive works on individual animal classes, the succinct, informative, and attractive presentation of this work distinguish it. No spelling, grammatical, or typographical errors were noticed. With its basic approach and primarily factual content, the *Macmillan Illustrated Animal Encyclopedia* should be useful for all but specialized research-level science collections. The Board recommends this work for the collections of public and school libraries. —*L. B.*

The Merck Veterinary Manual: A Handbook of Diagnosis, Therapy, and Disease Prevention and Control for the Veterinarian, 6th edition. Clarence M. Fraser, ed. Merck, 1986. soft. 1 vol. 1,677 pp. illus. index. ISBN 0-911910-53-0. $19. handbook.
SF748.M47 636.089

The Merck Veterinary Manual is intended "to supply a concise but authoritative reference for the veterinarian and his colleagues in the animal sciences" (foreword). The subtitle describes the scope and audience. Over 300 veterinarians and scientists made contributions. The sixth edition of this valuable reference is completely revised and updated, with much material that is new. According to the foreword, the emphasis in this edition is on diagnosis and treatment, with increased attention on prevention and control.

The information is presented in nine parts. Part 1 contains sections on diseases affecting different body systems or organs, conditions affecting the whole animal, plus physical causes of injury such as accidents or fire. Each section has its own detailed table of contents and begins with a review of the subject under consideration followed by discussion of the diseased condition. This first part constitutes about half the book. The remaining eight sections cover behavior; clinical values and procedures; fur, laboratory, and zoo animals; management, husbandry, and nutrition; poultry; toxicology; pharmacology; and zoonoses (diseases transmitted from animals to humans). The section on fur, laboratory, and zoo animals includes reviews of the management, husbandry, and diseases in fish, reptiles, and amphibians as well as mink, foxes, rabbits, and caged birds. The nutrition section contains information adapted from the National Research Council's "Nutrient Requirements of" series for small and large domestic animals. There are also instructions on what to feed your captive bat.

The text is supplemented with over 120 tables and includes "see" references that lead to additional information. There is a 66-page index, which further increases access to the information.

The language is technical, as expected given the intended audience. For example, the description of the origin and development of canine parvoviral infection reads: "After ingestion, tonsillar crypts and Peyer's patches are infected first. Infection of lymphatic tissues initiates viremia and later, infection of intestinal crypts. Loss of intestinal villi is the result of crypt cell necrosis. Death may follow as a result of dehydration, electrolyte imbalance, endotoxic shock, or secondary septicemia."

The Merck Veterinary Manual is an excellent work for university reference collections, although, even at this level, there should be a medical or veterinary dictionary handy for those outside the veterinary or animal science professions to consult. The Board recommends this work for the core collection of academic libraries. —*J. C.*

The Oxford Companion to Animal Behavior. David McFarland, ed. Oxford, 1987. hard and soft. 1 vol. 685 pp. illus. index. ISBN 0-19-866120-7 (hard); 0-19-281990-9 (soft). $49.95 (hard); $19.95 (soft). handbook.
QL750.3 591.51'03'21

The Oxford Companion to Animal Behavior is a handbook written for the layperson that contains entries dealing with all aspects of animal behavior as well as some explaining such basic biological phenomena as evolution, parasitism, and niche. There is also an 18-page entry on the history of ethology, plus separate entries on individuals of historical importance in the founding of the discipline. The main focus, however, is on the basic concepts of animal behavior. Specific animals are only discussed as they illustrate these ideas. The *Companion* was first published in 1981. A second printing with corrections to the text, an updated bibliography, and a subject index was published in 1987.

The editor, David McFarland, is a professor at Oxford University and the author of several other books. The other 69 contributors are scientists; over 30 of them have authored or edited entire books on behavioral topics. Several were also contributors to THE ENCYCLOPEDIA OF ANIMAL BEHAVIOR. The foreword is by Niko Tinbergen, one of the founders of modern ethology.

The signed entries are generally from 1 to 11 pages long and are arranged alphabetically. The language is nontechnical, as may be seen in the following excerpt:

> FIXED ACTION PATTERNS are activities which have a relatively fixed pattern of COORDINATION. Such patterns appear to be stereotyped, although they may show variability in ORIENTATION. A good example is the egg-retrieving behaviour of the greylag goose (Anser anser). These birds nest upon the ground, and when an egg has been displaced a short distance from the nest, the incubating bird attempts to roll it back with its bill, as illustrated in Fig. A. If the egg rolls slightly to one side during retrieval, the bill is moved sideways to correct for the displacement. However, if the bill loses contact with the egg, the bird does not immediately seek to re-establish contact, but first completes the retrieval movement.

There are numerous cross-references within the text (indicated by a word in all capital letters as seen in the quote above). In addition, many entries have numbered references at the end; these lead to further reading listed in the bibliography. Black-and-white drawings are included where a picture more effectively describes the concept under discussion.

Although it has been nine years since the first publication of this reference, the material is still quite current. This is primarily due to the emphasis on basic principles of ethology, to the exclusion of most concepts of modern sociobiology. Bearing this in mind, this is still an excellent source of basic information on animal behavior.

The bibliography in the 1987 printing contains 162 entries, increased from 146 in the 1981 publication. Most of the references are to books published before 1980. The subject index is a welcome addition, providing help in locating minor concepts contained in the articles, such as anting behavior in birds. *The Oxford Companion to Animal Behavior* is a must-have book. The Board recommends this work for the core collection of academic libraries. —*M. A. M.*

Walker's Mammals of the World, 4th edition. Ronald M. Nowak and John L. Paradiso. Johns Hopkins Univ. Pr., 1983. hard. 2 vols. illus. appendix. index. ISBN 0-8018-2525-3 (set). $75 (set). handbook.
QL703.W222 599

Walker's Mammals of the World has been a highly recognized, authoritative source on the mammal class since its first edition, *Mammals of the World,* appeared in 1964. This two-volume set may be considered more of a primary source than other mammal surveys written by experts, due to the many references that cite personal communications and to the frequent presentation of facts from direct observation.

The fourth edition, written by mammalogists Ronald Nowak and John Paradiso, continues the tradition of worldwide coverage of living and recently extinct mammals in the format established in earlier editions. Notes on physical description, taxonomic placement, habitat, diet, vocalizations, gestation, locomotion, litter size, causes of mortality and endangered status, and effects of interactions with humans are presented for 1,018 genera. All but about 300 are pictured.

The illustrations chosen are intended to show the characteristic form and attributes of a species. In comparison to those in GRZIMEK'S ENCYCLOPEDIA OF MAMMALS and THE ENCYCLOPEDIA OF MAMMALS, the photos are less attractive and enjoyable. All of the photos and drawings in *Walker's* are in black and white, and many are of museum specimens rather than animals in the wild.

The aim to provide a text understandable by general readers but also serving the professional community is nearly achieved. However, a dictionary will be needed for readers not familiar with this field. Terms such as *crepuscular, monestrous,* and *blastocyst* are not well known; in addition, the nonscientific vocabulary tends to be advanced. The text is more purely scientific and succinct than in the other sources previously mentioned.

The articles are on the order, family, and genus level. An effort was made to introduce both what is known and what is not known about the many subjects covered and to note alternative points of view. Distribution is indicated in the text and in the "World Distribution of Genera" table that appears at the beginning of the first volume, rather than in the more common and visually appealing map form typical of other sources. Name and range data are provided for every species, making this a landmark resource. Also, *Walker's* seems to be a more complete source for references than other sources on the subject. All of the references made to published literature are cited in full at the end of volume 2. For some groups references up to 1981 are found. This work, as well as the bibliography from the first edition, provides a good key to the older literature on mammals.

Each volume has its own index of common and scientific names (order, family, and genus), which makes location of the appropriate entry simple and straightforward. Inside the covers are length, weight, temperature, and area scales in metric and U.S. measurements.

In its physical form *Walker's* holds up well to frequent use. The binding, heavy cover, and glossy paper are durable. Although the type is small and the pages rather crowded, users already accustomed to nearly microscopic-sized print in *Science Citation Index* and the collective indexes to *Chemical Abstracts* will find this an endurable and somewhat unavoidable inconvenience.

Walker's Mammals of the World is an essential source. The Board recommends this work for the core collections of public and academic libraries. —*L. B.*

Supplementary Titles

The Audubon Society Encyclopedia of North American Birds. John K. Terres. Knopf, 1980. hard. 1 vol. 1,109 pp. illus. ISBN 0-394-46651-9. $75. encyclopedia.
QL681.T43 598.297032

"[*The Audubon Society Encyclopedia of North American Birds*] is a work of wider scope than its title suggests: it does include detailed, authoritative descriptive accounts of all 847 species of birds (including accidentals) recorded in the United States and Canada, grouped by family, but it also includes 625 articles on important aspects of avian biology, brief definitions of hundreds of terms, biographical sketches of prominent American ornithologists of the past, and histories of the national ornithological societies of the United States. All this information is tied together with comprehensive cross references, illustrated with first-rate black-and-white drawings and color photos, and capped by a bibliography of over 4000 entries. This massive work is an essential reference for all libraries serving professional or amateur ornithologists." (*LJ,* January 15, 1981, p. 137)

"Terres, former editor of Audubon magazine, . . . hopes 'to make the fruits of the science of ornithology available to the millions of North Americans who are interested in birds.' In his excellent introduction and how-to-use sections he says that the heart of his nearly 6,000 alphabetically-arranged entries and cross-references are descriptions of 847 birds that live in or have been sighted in North America. For each species Terres provides common name, scientific name (along with pronunciation, derivation, and meaning), physical description, differences between the sexes, characteristic behavior, calls or songs, feeding habits, nest and eggs, life span, range, and other details. . . . Terres' style and vocabulary will be interesting and understandable to nonspecialists. . . . Every library whose patrons are interested in birds should have this volume on the reference shelf. It makes such nice browsing that patrons will appreciate circulating copies as well." (*WLB,* June 1981, p. 782)

Also reviewed in: *ARBA,* 1982, p. 735; *Aud,* March 1981, p. 14; *BL,* June 1, 1982, p. 1325; *BOT,* February 1981, p. 69; *Bus W,* December 22, 1980, p. 9; *BW,* December 7, 1980, p. 10; *CC,* April 15, 1981, p. 428; *Choice,* April 1981, p. 1078; *CSM,* December 8, 1980, p. B11; *NH,* September 1983, p. 96; *NW,* December 8, 1980, p. 98; *NYTBR,* January 11, 1981, p. 35; *RSR,* Fall 1982, p. 32; *Sports Ill,* April 20, 1981, p. 24; *Time,* May 18, 1981, p. 88; *VV,* December 10, 1980, p. 55; *WSJ,* December 1, 1980, p. 26.

Board's recommendation: Public, academic, and school libraries.

The Audubon Society Field Guide to North American Birds: Eastern Region. John Bull and John Farrand, Jr. Knopf, 1977. soft. 1 vol. 775 pp. illus. index. ISBN 0-394-41405-5. $15.95. encyclopedia.
QL681.B775 598.2

The Audubon Society Field Guide to North American Birds: Eastern Region is "divided into two major sections: a 'Color Key' providing color photographs of species found east of the Rockies, grouped by color for songbirds, by shape for the others; and a 'Habitat Key' giving detailed descriptions for each species found in a particular habitat, e.g., the seashore. The two sections are cross-indexed, and there is a general index to common and scientific names.

"This . . . field guide, by ornithologists from the American Museum of Natural History, should be considered for purchase by all libraries holding any of the standard guides. It is as revolutionary as it claims to be, and it is obvious that the most careful thought and attention has been given to its planning and execution. . . . Although it's intended for beginning birders, those with experience will also find much of value and interest." (*LJ,* September 1, 1977, p. 1746)

"The photographs, by many different hands, are excellent, and avoid the high style and too brilliant color so often indulged in by ornithological artists. The test of the individual listings is properly lucid, and covers all the conventional points: description, voice, habitat, range, and nesting. The cross-indexing is flawless and foolproof. The result is a truly and fully practical guide—a delight to have and to use." (*NY,* September 12, 1977, p. 163)

Also reviewed in: *ARBA,* 1978, p. 671; *BL,* October 15, 1978, p. 403; *BW,* October 16, 1977, p. E1; *Choice,* June 1978, p. 523; *GW,* November 13, 1977, p. 18; *LJ,* April 15, 1978, p. 818; *NH,* February 1978, p. 98; *NYRB,* December 20, 1979, p. 10; *NYT,* August 26, 1977, p. C18; *NYTBR,* December 18, 1977, p. 38; *Prog,* October 1977, p. 60; *RSR,* Summer, 1984, p. 28; *SB,* September 1978, p. 95.

Board's recommendation: Public, academic, and school libraries.

The Audubon Society Field Guide to North American Birds: Western Region. Miklos D. F. Udvardy. Knopf, 1977. soft. 1 vol. 855 pp. illus. index. ISBN 0-394-41410-1. $14.95. encyclopedia.
QL681.U33 598.2

The Audubon Society Field Guide to North American Birds: Western Region is "good to excellent, and a nice touch has been added. Each entry ends with a chatty note, which contributes to the enjoyment of the birds. . . . The photographs are generally good, and some are truly fine. [The book is] nice to look at and can be helpful, particularly to the beginning and casual birder." (*NH,* February 1978, p. 98)

"Udvardy's work must be compared to the standard field guide for birders: Roger Tory Peterson's *A Field Guide to Western Birds.* . . . [The photographs] are outstanding in quality. . . . Peterson's uses pointers to indicate quickly the key characteristics; Udvardy's photographs are not handled this way. However, the photographs place the bird closer to the actual situation that one is apt to see in the field. . . . The volume under review contains more information on the use of silhouettes and also has a convenient way of relating those to the photographs. . . . In summation this is a completely different book than Peterson's and one would use both books in identifying western birds." (*Choice*, March 1978, p. 51)

Also reviewed in: *ARBA*, 1978, p. 675; *BL*, October 15, 1978, p. 403; *BW*, October 16, 1977, p. E1; *GW*, November 13, 1977, p. 18; *LJ*, April 15, 1978, p. 818; *NY*, September 12, 1977, p. 163; *NYRB*, December 20, 1979, p. 10; *RSR*, Summer 1984, p. 28.

Board's recommendation: Public, academic, and school libraries.

A Dictionary of Birds. Bruce Campbell and Elizabeth Lack, eds. Buteo Bks., 1985. hard. 1 vol. 670 pp. illus. ISBN 0-931130-12-3. $75. dictionary.
QL672.2.D53 598.1

"[*A Dictionary of Birds*] should remain a valuable reference work for decades. . . . [It] has a British/European bias but, since the phenomena discussed are of international relevance, this bias is not very limiting. . . . Nicely covered are biological subjects, bird families, anatomy, and physiology, as well as broad subjects such as behavior, migration, and plumage. Biographical information lies outside the dictionary's scope. . . . The format is good and the illustrative material is excellent and always germane." (*Choice*, January 1986, p. 725)

"The editors, by carefully choosing appropriate authors, have produced a superb book, full of clear, precise, and informative definitions. . . . The illustrations, drawn especially for the dictionary, are excellent, as are most of the photographs" (*LJ*, July 1985, p. 58)

Also reviewed in: *ARBA*, 1986, p. 595; *SciTech*, August 1985, p. 10.

Board's recommendation: Public and academic libraries.

The Encyclopedia of Animal Ecology. Peter D. Moore, ed. Facts On File, 1987. hard. 1 vol. 144 pp. illus. index. ISBN 0-8160-1818-9. $29.95. encyclopedia.
QH541.E46 591.51

"[*The Encyclopedia of Animal Ecology*] discusses 'basic concepts [of animal ecology] (cycles, species interaction, environmental influence, ecosystem), regions of the world . . . and the ecological role of humankind.'

"At times the amount of space devoted to illustrations seems excessive, and the need for some illustrations questionable but, on the whole, the illustrations enhance and complement the presentation of the information. . . . [The content] is reliable and very up to date, reflecting some of the current debates in scientific research. . . . [The volume] is written at a level appropriate for beginning undergraduate students and therefore would be useful in community and four-year colleges and public libraries." (*Choice*, December 1987, p. 598)

"While a few minor errors occur in the text relating to northern regions, the coverage of the field of ecology is remarkably comprehensive and clear. The detailed index makes this a useful reference, and the glossary will help the novice. . . . The value of this . . . [research tool] is its broad, accurate coverage, readability, and usefulness as a reference. No good library should be without it." (*SB*, March/April 1988, p. 246)

Also reviewed in: *BL*, November 15, 1987, p. 520; *CSM*, November 30, 1987, p. 26.

Board's recommendation: Public, academic, and school libraries.

New and Noteworthy

All about Tropical Fish, 4th edition. Derek McInemy and Geoffrey Gerard. Facts On File, 1989. hard. 1 vol. 480 pp. illus. appendixes. index. ISBN 0-8160-2168-6. $29.95. encyclopedia.
SF457.M375 639.3'4

"[*All about Tropical Fish*], which has been a standard for 30 years, has been updated. . . . This revision builds on the strengths of the old and updates information with the latest technology in terms of heaters, filters, medicine, etc. A new section has been added on marine fish and fish breeding.

"The book is divided into 23 chapters, 2 appendixes, and a reading list. The first 10 chapters cover setting up aquariums, selecting plants, and dealing with problems. . . . Chapters 11 through 23 cover types of fish and recommend easy-to-raise and breed species. The final two chapters include fish that favor brackish water and marine species.

"[In this book] . . . the text is easy to understand and the directions are especially clear and precise." (*BL*, March 1, 1990, p. 1378)

A Dictionary of Ethology. Klaus Immelmann and Colin Beer. Harvard, 1989. hard. 1 vol. 352 pp. ISBN 0-674-20506-5. $35. dictionary.
QL750.3.I4513 591.510321

"[*A Dictionary of Ethology*] clearly and accurately defines more than 600 terms used in ethology, the science of animal behavior, in entries of one or two paragraphs. While there are several reference books dealing with ethology, the only real rival to this title is *The Oxford Companion to Animal Behavior*. . . which covers half as many terms in twice as many pages, has hundreds of illustrations, and an index to the animals mentioned in the text." (*LJ*, June 15, 1989, p. 52)

Encyclopedia of the Animal World (series). Facts On File, 1989. hard. 12 vols. 96 pp. illus. index. ISBN 0-8160-1957-6 (set). $170 (set). $17.95 per vol.

Birds: The Aerial Hunters. Martyn Bramwell. ISBN 0-8160-1963-0.

Birds: The Plant- and Seed-Eaters. Jill Bailey and Steve Parker. ISBN 0-8160-1964-9.

Birds: The Waterbirds. Robin Kerrod with Jill Bailey. ISBN 0-8160-1962-2.

Fish. Linda Losito et al. ISBN 0-8160-1966-5.

Insects and Spiders. Linda Losito et al. ISBN 0-8160-1967-3.

Mammals: Primates, Insect-Eaters and Baleen Whales. Robin Kerrod. ISBN 0-8160-1961-4.

Mammals: The Hunters. Christopher O'Toole and John Stidworthy. ISBN 0-8160-1959-2.

Mammals: The Large Plant-Eaters. John Stidworthy. ISBN 0-8160-1960-6.

Mammals: The Small Plant-Eaters. Martyn Bramwell et al. ISBN 0-8160-1958-4.

Pets and Farm Animals. Linda Losito et al. ISBN 0-8160-1969-X.

Reptiles and Amphibians. John Stidworthy with Jill Bailey. ISBN 0-8160-1965-7.

Simple Animals. Linda Losito et al. ISBN 0-8160-1968-1.

"Animals virtually leap off the pages of these new volumes [of the *Encyclopedia of the Animal World*]. . . . Outstanding action photographs and drawings of animals at work and play in their habitats complement an easy-to-read text. . . . Coverage is provided not only of basics such as anatomy, development, behavior, ecology, conservation, and relationships with people, but also of the lesser-known, intriguing, and hard-to-forget 'specialties' of animals which developed in response to a particular diet, climate and habitat. The information on each animal is brief . . . but the discussion of behaviors will complement information found in a general encyclopedia. . . . This is tantalizing fare for researchers and browsers. . . . Attractive animal portraits on glossy, paper-covered boards invite heavy-duty use." (*SLJ*, May 1990, p. 26)

Predators and Predation: The Struggle for Life in the Animal World. Pierre Pfeffer, ed. Facts On File, 1989. hard. 1 vol. 419 pp. index. ISBN 0-8160-1618-6. $40. encyclopedia.
QL758.P735 591.53

"[The purpose of *Predators and Predation*] . . . is to demonstrate that there is nothing sinister about predators since they are simply part of the natural food chain in the animal world.

[This book] . . . is organized alphabetically by the common name of the animal. [Entries present] . . . information on classification (genus, species) and the animal's physical description, habitat, life cycle, mating, young, what it preys upon and how, and, in turn, what preys upon it. . . . All units of measurement throughout the text are metric. . . . A 17-page index provides cross references to prey and habitat locations. . . . [This book] is unique as a general survey." (*BL*, February 15, 1990, p. 1188)

Appendixes

Appendix A

Bibliography

Books

American Library Association. *ALA Yearbook of Library and Information Services.* Chicago: American Library Association, 1976–.

Association of College and Research Libraries. *Academic Libraries: Myths and Realities.* National Conference. Chicago: Association of College and Research Libraries, 1984.

Association of College and Research Libraries. *Books for College Libraries: A Core Collection of 50,000 Titles.* 3d edition. Chicago: American Library Association, 1988.

Bryant, David. *Finding Information the Library Way: A Guide to Information Sources.* Hamden, Conn.: Library Professional Publications, 1987.

Cheney, Frances Neel. *Reference Services and Library Education.* Lexington, Mass.: Lexington Books, 1983.

Cheney, Frances Neel, and Wiley J. Williams. *Fundamental Reference Sources.* 2d edition. Chicago: American Library Association, 1980.

Durrance, Joan C. *Armed for Action: Library Response to Citizen Information Needs.* New York: Neal-Schuman, 1984.

Evans, G. E. *Developing Library and Information Center Collections.* 2d edition. Littleton, Colo.: Libraries Unlimited, 1987.

Fetzer, M. K. "Reference and Information Work." In *International Information: Documents, Publications, and Information Systems of International Governmental Organizations,* edited by Peter J. Hajnal, pp. 147–177. Littleton, Colo.: Libraries Unlimited, 1988.

Galin, Saul, and Peter Spielberg. *Reference Books: How to Select and Use Them.* New York: Random House, 1969.

Grogan, Denis J. *Grogan's Case Studies in Reference Work.* 6 vols. Chicago: American Library Association, 1988.

Higgens, Gavin. *Printed Reference Material.* Chicago: American Library Association, 1980.

Hillard, James M. *Where to Find What: A Handbook to Reference Service.* Metuchen, N.J.: Scarecrow Press, 1984.

Jackaman, P. *Basic Reference and Information Work.* Knoxville, Tenn.: Elm Publications, 1985.

Katz, Bill, comp. *Reference and Information Services: A Reader for Today.* Metuchen, N.J.: Scarecrow Press, 1986.

Katz, Bill, and Anne Clifford. *Reference and Information Services: A New Reader.* Metuchen, N.J.: Scarecrow Press, 1982.

Katz, William A. *Introduction to Reference Work.* 2 vols. 5th edition. New York: McGraw-Hill, 1987.

Kent, Allen, and Harold Lancour, eds.; William Z. Nasri, assistant ed. *Encyclopedia of Library and Information Science.* New York: Marcel Dekker, 1968–.

Kohl, David F. *Reference Services and Library Instruction.* Santa Barbara, Calif.: ABC-Clio, 1985.

McCormick, Mona. *The New York Times Guide to Reference Materials.* rev. edition. New York: Times Books, 1985.

Murfin, Marjorie E., and Lubomyr R. Wynar. *Reference Service: An Annotated Bibliographic Guide.* Littleton, Colo.: Libraries Unlimited, 1977.

Murfin, Marjorie E., and Lubomyr R. Wynar. *Reference Service: An Annotated Bibliographic Guide; supplement 1976–82.* 2d edition. Littleton, Colo.: Libraries Unlimited, 1984.

Nichols, M. I. *Selecting and Using a Core-Reference Collection.* Austin, Tex.: Texas State Library (Library Development Division), 1986.

Prytherch, Raymond J. *Sources of Information in Librarianship and Information Science.* 2d edition. Brookfield, Vt.: Gower, 1987.

Robinson, T. S. *Subject Guide to U.S. Government Reference Sources.* rev. edition. Littleton, Colo.: Libraries Unlimited, 1985.

Rothstein, Samuel. *The Development of Reference Services Through Academic Traditions, Public Library Practice and Special Librarianship.* Chicago: Association of College and Research Libraries, 1955.

Schwarzkopf, Leroy C., comp. *Government Reference Books 1986–87: A Biennial Guide to U.S. Government Publications.* Littleton, Colo.: Libraries Unlimited, 1988.

Sheehy, Eugene P., comp. *Guide to Reference Books.* 10th edition. Chicago: American Library Association, 1986.

Slavens, Thomas P., ed. *Reference Interviews, Questions, and Materials.* 2d edition. Metuchen, N.J.: Scarecrow Press, 1985.

Stanley, S. "Information Sources." In *Handbook of Library Training Practice,* edited by Ray Prytherch, pp. 207–276. Brookfield, Vt.: Gower, 1986.

Stevens, Rolland E., and Joan M. Walton. *Reference Work in the Public Library.* Littleton, Colo.: Libraries Unlimited, 1983.

Stewart, Linda, and Peter Harvard-Williams, eds. *Reference Library Services: Function, Finance, and the Future.* Centre for Library and Information Management, Loughborough, Leicestershire, England, 1983.

Taylor, M., and R. R. Powell. *Basic Reference Sources: A Self-Study Manual.* 3d edition. Metuchen, N.J.: Scarecrow Press, 1985.

Tebbel, John William. *A History of Book Publishing in the United States.* 4 vols. New York: R. R. Bowker, 1981.

Walford, Albert J. *Reviews and Reviewing: A Guide.* Phoenix, Ariz.: Oryx Press, 1986.

Walford, Albert J. *Walford's Guide to Reference Material.* 3 vols. 4th edition. London: Library Association, 1980–1987.

Wedgeworth, Robert, ed. *ALA World Encyclopedia of Library and Information Services.* 2d edition. Chicago: American Library Association, 1986.

Wynar, Bohdan S., ed. *American Reference Books Annual (ARBA).* Littleton, Colo.: Libraries Unlimited, 1970–.

Wynar, Bohdan S., ed. *ARBA Guide to Biographical Dictionaries.* Littleton, Colo.: Libraries Unlimited, 1986.

Wynar, Bohdan S., ed. *ARBA Guide to Subject Encyclopedias and Dictionaries.* Littleton, Colo.: Libraries Unlimited, 1986.

Wynar, Bohdan S., ed. *Recommended Reference Books for Small and Medium-Sized Libraries and Media Centers.* Littleton, Colo.: Libraries Unlimited, 1981–.

Wynar, Christine Gehrt. *Guide to Reference Books for School Media Centers.* 3d edition. Littleton, Colo.: Libraries Unlimited, 1986.

Periodicals

Adalian, P. T., and I. F. Rockman. "Title-by-Title Review in Reference Collection Development." *Reference Services Review* 12 (Winter 1984): 85–88.

Alloway, C. S., et al. "Field-Tested Reference Books: A Survey of What Has Worked Best." *Wilson Library Bulletin* 63 (Jan. 1989): 37–38.

Ball, D. J. "Current Issues in Reference and Adult Services." See issues of *RQ* beginning Winter 1986.

Bates, M. J. "What Is a Reference Book? A Theoretical and Empirical Analysis." *RQ* 26 (Fall 1986): 37–57.

Berman, J. "Reference Serials." See issues of *Reference Services Review* beginning Fall 1987.

Biggs, Mary, and Victor Biggs. "Reference Collection Development in Academic Libraries." *RQ* 27, no. 1 (Fall 1987): 67–79.

Biggs, Mary, et al. "Replacing the Fast Fact Drop in Libraries with Gourmet Information Service." *Journal of Academic Librarianship* (May 1985): 68–78.

Booklist: Including Reference Books Bulletin (formerly *Booklist and Reference and Subscription Books Reviews).* Chicago: American Library Association, 1905–. Semimonthly.

Boylan, P. "Young Adult Reference Services in the Public Library." *Top of the News* (Summer 1984): 415–17. (The title of this journal changed to *Journal of Youth Services in Libraries* in 1987.)

Bryon, J. F. W. "Comprehensive and Efficient? Reference Service." *New Library World* 86, no. 1018 (April 1985): 70–71.

Bundy, Mary Lee, and Amy Bridgman. "A Community Based Approach to Evaluation of Public Library Reference Service." *Reference Librarian* no. 11 (Fall/Winter 1984): 159–174.

Bunge, Charles A. "Strategies for Updating Knowledge of Reference Resources and Techniques." *RQ* 21, no. 3 (Spring 1982): 228–232.

Burkhart, Gayle, and Joan Somerville. "A Reference Librarian Explains the Job." *Unabashed Librarian* no. 61 (1986): 19.

Childers, T. "A Generic Reference Collection." *Reference Services Review* 15 (Spring 1987): 5–6.

Choice. Association of College and Research Libraries, a division of the American Library Association, 1964–. Monthly.

College and Research Libraries. Chicago: Association of College and Research Libraries, a division of the American Library Association, 1939–. Bimonthly.

Craver, K. W. "The Changing Instructional Role of the High School Library Media Specialist." *School Library Media Quarterly* (Summer 1986): 183–191.

Dalrymple, P. W. "Closing the Gap: The Role of the Librarian in Online Searching." *RQ* 24 (Winter 1984): 177.

Davis, S. A. "Professional Materials." *RQ* 25 (Fall 1985): 150–152.

Dawson, Keith, and Laura Nixon. "Looking It Up." *Publishers Weekly* (July 14, 1989): 18–34.

Demo, Teresa L., and Charles R. McClure. "Information and Referral in the Academic Library: Lessons in Attitude and Service from the Public Library." *Reference Librarian* no. 21 (1988): 95–108.

Emmick, Nancy J., and Luella B. Davis. "A Survey of Academic Library Reference Service Practices." *RQ* 24, no. 1 (Fall 1984): 67–81.

Flinner, Beatrice E. "A Scenario of the Reference Librarian in a Small University Library." *Reference Librarian* no. 19 (1987): 341–358.

Ford, B. J. "Reference Beyond (and Without) the Reference Desk." *College and Research Libraries* 47 (Sept. 1986): 491–494.

Gleaves, Edwin S. "Carter and Bonk Revisited: A Review of Recent Collection Development Literature." *Collection Management* 9 (Spring 1987): 79–85.

Griffin, Mary Ann. "Collection Development to Information Access: The Role of Public Services Librarians." *RQ* 24, no. 3 (Spring 1985): 285–289.

Grover, R. J., and M. L. Hale. "The Role of the Librarian in Faculty Research." *College and Research Libraries* (Jan. 1988): 9–15.

Haycock, K. "Strengthening the Foundation for Teacher-Librarianship." *School Library Media Quarterly* (Spring 1985): 102–109.

Hellemans, A. "New Directions for Encyclopedias." *Publishers Weekly* 232 (Oct. 2, 1987): 40.

Herbert, Rosemary. "Checking It Out." *Publishers Weekly* (July 13, 1990): 18–26.

Irving, Richard D., and Bill Katz, eds. "Reference Services and Public Policy." *Reference Librarian* no. 20 (1987).

Katz, Bill, and Robin Kinder, eds. "The Publishing and Review of Reference Sources." *Reference Librarian* no. 15 (Fall 1986): entire issue.

Katz, Bill, and Ruth A. Fraley, eds. "Reference Services for Children and Young Adults." *Reference Librarian* nos. 7 and 8 (Spring/Summer 1983): entire issues.

Kemp, Barbara E. "Multiple Roles of Academic Reference Librarians: Problems of Education and Training." *Reference Librarian* no. 14 (Spring/Summer 1986): 141–149.

Kibirige, H. M. "Computer-Assisted Reference Services: What the Computer Will Not Do." *RQ* 27 (Spring 1988): 377–383.

Kroll, Rebecca. "The Place of Reference Collection Development in the Organizational Structure of the Library." *RQ* 25, no. 1 (Fall 1985): 96–100.

Leide, John E. "The Information Specialist and the Reference Librarian: Is the Complete Librarian Obsolete?" *Reference Librarian* no. 18 (Summer 1987): 87–94.

Library Journal. New York: R. R. Bowker, 1876–. Semimonthly. "Reference Books of [Year]" published annually in April issue.

Lukenbill, W. B. "Providing Community Information in the School Library Media Center." *Catholic Library World* (May/June 1986): 260.

McSweeney, L., and M. K. Cassell. "A Bare Bones Reference Collection." *Unabashed Librarian* no. 62 (1987): 27–28.

Mech, Terrence. "The Realities of College Reference Services: Case Study in Personnel Utilization." *Reference Librarian* no. 19 (1987): 285–308.

Miller, Richard R. "The Tradition of Reference Service in the Liberal Arts College Library." *RQ* 25, no. 4 (Summer 1986): 460–467.

Nichols, M. I. "Collection Development and the Core-Reference Collection." *Texas Library Journal* 63 (Winter 1987): 128–130.

Nichols, M. I. "Weeding the Reference Collection." *Texas Library Journal* 62 (Winter 1986): 204–206.

Orgren, Carl F., and James Rice. "The Current Trends and Controversies in the Literature of Reference Services and Their Implications for the Practice of Reference Work." *Reference Librarian* no. 14 (Spring/Summer 1986): 1–15.

Reference Services Review. Ann Arbor, Mich.: Pierian Press, 1973–. Quarterly.

Rettig, J. R. "Every Reference Librarian a Reviewer." *RQ* 26 (Summer 1987): 467–476.

RQ. Chicago: Reference and Adult Services Division of the American Library Association, 1960–. Quarterly.

Sabosik, P. E. "Reference Books in *Choice.*" *Choice* 23 (Nov. 1985): 404–405.

Schlachter, G. A. "Obsolescence, Weeding, and Bibliographic Love Canals." *RQ* 28 (Fall 1988): 7–8.

Schlachter, G. A. "Reference Books." *RQ* 26 (Spring 1987): 382–384.

Sexton, K. "Reference Work as a Teaching Tool." *Top of the News* (Fall 1983): 73–76. (The title of this journal changed to *Journal of Youth Services in Libraries* in 1987.)

Stevenson, Gordon, and Sally Stevenson. "Reference Services and Technical Services: Interactions in Library Practice." *Reference Librarian* no. 9 (Fall/Winter 1983): entire issue.

Tifft, Rosamond. "The Growth and Development of Information and Referral in Library Services: A Selective History and Review of Some Recent Developments." *Reference Librarian* no. 21 (1988): 229–259.

Watson, P. G. "Collection Development and Evaluation in Reference and Adult Services Librarianship." *RQ* 26 (Winter 1986): 143–145.

Wilson Library Bulletin. New York: H. W. Wilson, 1914–. Ten issues per year.

Appendix B

List of Publishers and Distributors

ABC-Clio
P.O. Box 1911
130 Cremona Drive
Santa Barbara, Calif. 93116–1911
(805) 968–1911
(800) 422–2546

America: History and Life
Arms Control, Disarmament, and Military Security Dictionary, The
Asian Political Dictionary, The
Biographies of American Women: An Annotated Bibliography
Dictionary of Classical Mythology: Symbols, Attributes, and Associations
Dictionary of Irish Mythology, A
Electoral Politics Dictionary, The
Focus on School: A Reference Handbook
Human Rights
Information Sources of Political Science, 4th edition
International Law Dictionary, The
International Relations Dictionary, The, 4th edition
Public Administration Dictionary, The, 2d edition
Public Policy Dictionary, The
State and Local Government Political Dictionary, The
U.S. Government: A Resource Book for Secondary Schools
World Economic Data

(See also Todd Publications)

Abingdon Press
201 Eighth Avenue South
Nashville, Tenn. 37202
(615) 749–6290

Interpreter's Bible, The
Interpreter's Dictionary of the Bible
Yearbook of American and Canadian Churches

Harry N. Abrams, Inc.
100 Fifth Avenue
New York, N.Y.
(212) 206–7715

Encyclopedia of Fashion, The

Academic International Press
P.O. Box 1111
Gulf Breeze, Fla. 32562

Encyclopedia of Physical Science and Technology
Encyclopedia of Telecommunications
Modern Encyclopedia of Russian and Soviet Literatures, The

Academy Chicago Publishers
213 West Institute Place
Chicago, Ill. 60610
(312) 644–1723

Guide to Non-sexist Children's Books, volume II: 1976–1985, A

Access Press
Distributed by Prentice-Hall Press

15 Columbus Circle
New York, N.Y. 10023
(212) 373–8000
U.S. Atlas

Addison-Wesley Publishing Company, Inc.
Route 128
Reading, Mass. 01867
(617) 944–3700
Associated Press Stylebook and Libel Manual, The, rev. edition
Encyclopedia of Physical Education, Fitness, and Sports (vol. 3)
Insider's Guide to Foreign Study, The
(See also Longman Publishing Group)

Africana Publishing Company
Subsidiary of Holmes & Meier Publishers, Inc.
IUB Building
30 Irving Place
New York, N.Y. 10003
(212) 254–4100
New Reader's Guide to African Literature, A, 2d edition
Reader's Guide to African Literature, A

Agee Publishers, Inc.
P.O. Box 526
Athens, Ga. 30603
(404) 548–5269
Boarding School Guide, The

AMACOM Books
(See American Management Association)

American Alliance for Health, Physical Education, Recreation, and Dance
1900 Association Drive
Reston, Va. 22091
(703) 476–3400
Encyclopedia of Physical Education, Fitness, and Sports (vol. 4)

American Association of Dental Schools
1625 Massachusetts Avenue, N.W.
Washington, D.C. 20036
(202) 667–9433
Admission Requirements of U.S. and Canadian Dental Schools

American Association of Engineering Societies
1111 Nineteenth Street, N.W.
Suite 608
Washington, D.C. 20036–3690
(202) 296–2237
Who's Who in Engineering, 7th edition

American Bankers Association
1120 Connecticut Avenue, N.W.
Washington, D.C. 20036
(301) 843–8800
Banking Terminology, 3d edition

American Collegiate Service
P.O. Box 442008
Houston, Tex. 77244
(713) 493–9863
Scholarships, Fellowships, and Grants for Programs Abroad: A Handbook of Awards to U.S. Nationals for Study or Research Abroad

American Geological Institute
4220 King Street
Alexandria, Va. 22302–1507
(703) 379–2480
(800) 336–4764
Glossary of Geology, 3d edition

American Guidance Service
Publishers' Building
Circle Pines, Minn. 55014–1796
(612) 786–4343
Bookfinder: A Guide to Children's Literature About the Needs and Problems of Youth Aged 2–15, The

American Hospital Association
840 North Lake Shore Drive
Chicago, Ill. 60611–2431
(312) 280–6000
American Hospital Association Guide to the Health Care Field

American Jewish Committee/Jewish Publication Society of America
765 East 56th Street
New York, N.Y. 10022–2746
(212) 751–4000
American Jewish Year Book

American Journal of Nursing Company
555 West 57th Street
New York, N.Y. 10019
(212) 582–8820
Facts About Nursing

American Law Book
Distributed by West Publishing Company
Box 64526, 50 West Kellogg Boulevard
Saint Paul, Minn. 55164
(612) 228–2500
(800) 328–9352
Corpus Juris Secundum

American Library Association
50 East Huron Street
Chicago, Ill. 60611
(312) 944–6780
ALA Filing Rules
ALA Glossary of Library and Information Science, The
ALA Handbook of Organization and Membership Directory
ALA World Encyclopedia of Library and Information Sciences, 2d edition
Business Serials of the U.S. Government, 2d edition
Dictionary of Literary Pseudonyms: A Selection of Modern Popular Writers in English
Exciting, Funny, Scary, Short, Different, and Sad Books Kids Like About Animals, Science, Sports, Families, Songs, and Other Things
Genealogical Research and Resources: A Guide for Library Use
Guide to Reference Books, 10th edition
Guide to the Literature of Art History
Museum of Science and Industry Basic List of Children's Science Books, 1988, The
Musicals: A Directory of Musical Properties Available for Production
Sources of Information in the Social Sciences: A Guide to the Literature, 3d edition

American Management Association
Distributed by AMACOM Books
135 West 50th Street
New York, N.Y. 10020
(212) 586–8100
Manager's Desk Reference, The

American Medical Association
(See Chicago Review Press)

American Psychiatric Association
1400 K Street, N.W.
Washington, D.C. 20005
(202) 682–6000
Diagnostic and Statistical Manual of Mental Disorders, 3d edition rev.

American Psychological Association, Inc.
c/o Publication and Communication Office
1200 Seventeenth Street, N.W.
Washington, D.C. 20036
(202) 955–7600
Psychological Abstracts
Publication Manual of the American Psychological Association, 3d edition
Thesaurus of Psychological Index Terms, 5th edition

Ancestry, Inc.
Box 476
Salt Lake City, Utah 84110
(801) 531–1790
(800) 531–1790
Ancestry's Red Book: American State, County, and Town Records
Concise Genealogical Dictionary
Library of Congress: A Guide to Genealogical and Historical Research, The
Source: A Guidebook of American Genealogy, The

Anchor Books
Division of Doubleday & Company, Inc.
666 Fifth Avenue
New York, N.Y. 10103
(212) 765–6500
(800) 223–6834, ext. 479
101 Stories of the Great Ballets
Dictionary of Geological Terms, 3d edition

Apollo Book
5 Schoolhouse Lane
Poughkeepsie, N.Y. 12603
(914) 462–0040
(800) 431–5003
(800) 942–8222 (N.Y.)
Dictionary of American Sculptors: 18th Century to the Present
Mantle Fielding's Dictionary of American Painters, Sculptors and Engravers, 2d edition
New York Historical Society's Dictionary of Artists in America 1564–1860

Appleton & Lange
Subsidiary of Simon & Schuster, Inc.
25 Van Zant Street
East Norwalk, Conn. 06855
(203) 838–4400
(800) 423–1359
Handbook of Poisoning: Prevention, Diagnosis and Treatment, 12th edition

Archon Books
Division of The Shoe String Press, Inc.
Box 4327
925 Sherman Avenue
Hamden, Conn. 06514
(203) 248–6307, 6308
Plots and Characters in Classic French Fiction

ARCsoft Publishers
Box 132

Woodsboro, Md. 21798
(301) 845–8856
Space Almanac

Ardis Publishers
2901 Heatherway
Ann Arbor, Mich. 48104
(313) 971–2367
Russian Romantic Fiction

Edward Arnold
Distributed by Routledge, Chapman & Hall
29 West 35th Street
New York, N.Y. 10001
(212) 244–3336
Student's Dictionary of Psychology, A

Association for Asian Studies, Inc.
University of Michigan
1 Lane Hall
Ann Arbor, Mich. 48109
(313) 665–4847
Bibliography of Asian Studies

Association for Computing Machinery
11 West 42nd Street, 3d floor
New York, N.Y. 10036
(212) 869–7440
ACM Guide to Computing Literature

Association of American Medical Colleges
1 Dupont Circle, N.W.
Washington, D.C. 20036
(202) 828–0400
Medical School Admission Requirements

Avon Books
105 Madison Avenue
New York, N.Y. 10016
(212) 481–5600
100 Best Treatment Centers for Alcoholism and Drug Abuse, The
American Almanac of Jobs and Salaries, The, 3d edition

Ayer Company Publishers, Inc.
50 Northwestern Drive, Number 10
P.O. Box 958
Salem, N.H. 03079–0958
(603) 898–1200
Italian Theatre

Bantam Books, Inc.
Division of Bantam Doubleday Dell
666 Fifth Avenue
New York, N.Y. 10103
(212) 765–6500
(800) 223–6834
Advice for the Patient: Drug Information in Lay Language, vol. 2, 9th edition
(See also Doubleday & Company, Inc.)

Barnes & Noble Books
Division of Rowman & Littlefield Publishers, Inc.
8705 Bollman Place
Savage, Md. 20763
(301) 306–0400
Dictionary of Philosophy
Poetry Handbook: A Dictionary of Terms, 4th edition

Barron's Educational Series, Inc.
250 Wireless Boulevard
Hauppauge, N.Y. 11788
(516) 434–3311
(800) 645–3476
Barron's Profiles of American Colleges: Descriptions of the Colleges, 17th edition
Dictionary of Advertising and Direct Mail Terms
Dictionary of Mathematics Terms

Basic Books, Inc. Publishers
Subsidiary of HarperCollins Publishers, Inc.
10 East 53d Street
New York, N.Y. 10022
(212) 207–7000
(800) 242–7737
American Handbook of Psychiatry, 2d edition

Baywood Publishing Company, Inc.
26 Austin Avenue
P.O. Box 337
Amityville, N.Y. 11701
(516) 691–1270
Abstracts in Anthropology

Beacham Publishing, Inc.
2100 South Street, N.W.
Washington, D.C. 20008
(202) 234–0877
Beacham's Guide to Key Lobbyists: An Analysis of Their Issues and Impact
Beacham's Guide to Literature for Young Adults
Research Guide to Biography and Criticism
(See also Research Publishing, Inc.)

Beacon Press
25 Beacon Street
Boston, Mass. 02108
(617) 742–2110

Nonsexist Word Finder: A Dictionary of Gender-Free Usage, The

Beaufort Books
226 West 26th Street
New York, N.Y. 10001
(212) 727–0190
Knock on Wood: An Encyclopedia of Talismans, Charms, Superstitions, and Symbols

Peter Bedrick Books, Inc.
2112 Broadway, Suite 318
New York, N.Y. 10023
(212) 496–0751
(800) 365–3453
Biographical Dictionary of Scientists, The

Frederic C. Beil Publishers, Inc.
414 Tattnall Street
Savannah, Ga. 31401
(912) 233–2446
Rookledge's International Type Finder: The Essential Handbook of Typeface Recognition and Selection

The Belknap Press of Harvard University Press
79 Garden Street
Cambridge, Mass. 02138
(617) 225–0430
Harvard Encyclopedia of American Ethnic Groups
Harvard Guide to American History, rev. edition
New Harvard Dictionary of Music, The
Notable American Women, 1607–1950
Notable American Women, The Modern Period

Betterway Publications, Inc.
Box 219
Crozet, Va. 22932
(804) 823–5661, 2047
(800) 522–2782
Crafts Supply Sourcebook, The

Bibliotheca Persica
Distributed by the State University of New York Press
State University Plaza
Albany, N.Y. 12246
(518) 472–5000
(800) 666–2211
Persian Literature

Billboard Books
Distributed by Watson-Guptill Publications
1515 Broadway
New York, N.Y. 10036
(212) 764–7300
(800) 451–1741
World Radio and TV Handbook

A & C Black Publishers, Ltd.
Imprint of Sheridan House, Inc.
145 Palisade Street
Dobbs Ferry, N.Y. 10522
(914) 693–2410
Black's Veterinary Dictionary, 16th edition

Basil Blackwell, Inc.
3 Cambridge Center
Cambridge, Mass. 02142
(617) 225–0430
(800) 445–6638
Blackwell Companion to Jewish Culture: From the Eighteenth Century to the Present, The
Blackwell Encyclopaedia of Political Thought, The
Concise Dictionary of Classical Mythology, A
Dictionary of Human Geography
Dictionary of Human Geography, The, 2d edition
Dictionary of Linguistics and Phonetics, A, 2d edition
Women's Studies: A Bibliography of Dissertations, 1970–1982

Blandford Press
Distributed by Sterling Publishing Company, Inc.
387 Park Avenue South
New York, N.Y. 10016–8810
(212) 532–7160
(800) 367–9692
National Anthems of the World, 7th edition

Blue Bird Publishing
1713 East Broadway, Suite 306
Tempe, Ariz. 85282
(602) 968–4088, 9003
Home Business Resource Guide

R. R. Bowker
121 Chanlon Road
New Providence, N.J. 07974
(908) 464–6800
(800) 521–8110
American Men and Women of Science 1989–90, 17th edition
Best Books for Children: Preschool Through the Middle Grades, 4th edition
Beyond Picture Books: A Guide to First Readers
Biographical Books, 1876–1949

Biographical Books, 1950–1980
Bookman's Glossary, 6th edition
Bowker Annual: Library and Book Trade Almanac
Business and Economics Books, 1876–1983
Code of Federal Regulations
El-Hi Textbooks and Serials in Print
Fantasy Literature for Children and Young Adults: An Annotated Bibliography, 3d edition
General Reference Books for Adults: Authoritative Evaluations of Encyclopedias, Atlases, and Dictionaries
Great Treasury of Western Thought: A Compendium of Important Statements on Man & His Institutions by the Great Thinkers in Western History
How-To: 1,400 Best Books on Doing Almost Everything
Literary and Library Prizes, 10th edition
More Notes from a Different Drummer: A Guide to Juvenile Fiction Portraying the Disabled
Reader's Adviser, 13th edition
School Librarian's Sourcebook, The
Science & Technology in Fact and Fiction: A Guide to Children's Books
Self-Help: 1,400 Best Books on Personal Growth
Software Encyclopedia 1989, The, 4th edition
Who's Who in American Art, 1989–1990, 18th edition
Who's Who in American Politics: 1989–1990, 12th edition

(See also K. G. Saur)

Brighton Press
P.O. Box 14501
Chicago, Ill. 60614
(312) 549–6808
Encyclopedia of Physical Education, Fitness, and Sports (vols. 1 and 2)

E. J. Brill, Inc.
P.O. Box 467
24 Hudson Street
Kinderhook, N.Y. 12106
(518) 758–1411
(800) 962–4406
Selective Guide to Chinese Literature, 1900–1949

Broadcasting Publications, Inc., Book Division
1705 DeSales Street, N.W.
Washington, D.C. 20036
(202) 659–2340
Broadcasting Yearbook, The

Brodart Company
500 Arch Street
Williamsport, Pa. 17705
(717) 326–2461
(800) 233–8467
Elementary School Library Collection: A Guide to Books and Other Media, 16th edition

Brooks/Cole Publishing Company
Division of Wadsworth, Inc.
511 Forest Lodge Road
Pacific Grove, Calif. 93950–5098
(408) 373–0728
(800) 354–9706
Dorsey Dictionary of American Government and Politics, The

Buros Institute of Mental Measurements
Distributed by the University of Nebraska Press
901 North 17th Street
Lincoln, Nebr. 68588
(402) 472–3581
Tenth Mental Measurements Yearbook, The

Business One-Irwin
1818 Ridge Road
Homewood, Ill. 60430
(708) 206–2700
(800) 634–3961
Dow Jones-Irwin Business and Investment Almanac, The
Handbook of Financial Market Indexes, Averages, and Indicators, The

(See also Dow Jones-Irwin)

Buteo Books
P.O. Box 481
Vermillion, S.D. 57069
(605) 624–4343
Dictionary of Birds, A

Butterworth-Heinemann
80 Montvale Avenue
Stoneham, Mass. 02180
(617) 438–8464
(800) 366–2665
Dictionary of Electronics, 2d edition
Dictionary of Mechanical Engineering, 3d edition
Information Sources in Engineering, 2d edition

Cambridge University Press
40 West 20th Street
New York, N.Y. 10011
(212) 924–3900
(800) 221–4512
'Abbasid Belles-Lettres, Cambridge History of Arabic Literature series
Arabic Literature to the End of the Umayyadd Period, Cambridge History of Arabic Literature series
Cambridge Ancient History Series, The, 1st, 2d, and 3d editions
Cambridge Atlas of Astronomy, The, 2d edition
Cambridge Encyclopedia of Africa, The
Cambridge Encyclopedia of China, The
Cambridge Encyclopedia of Earth Sciences, The
Cambridge Encyclopedia of India, Pakistan, Bangladesh, Sri Lanka, Nepal, Bhutan and the Maldives, The
Cambridge Encyclopedia of Language, The
Cambridge Encyclopedia of Latin America and the Caribbean, The
Cambridge Encyclopedia of Life Sciences, The
Cambridge Encyclopedia of the Middle East and North Africa, The
Cambridge Guide to Literature in English, The
Cambridge Guide to the Historic Places of Britain and Ireland, The
Cambridge Guide to the Material World
Cambridge Guide to World Theatre, The
Cambridge Historical Encyclopedia of Great Britain and Ireland
Cambridge History of Africa, The
Cambridge History of China, The
Cambridge History of Classical Literature
Cambridge History of Latin America, The
Cambridge Illustrated Dictionary of Natural History, The
Historical Atlas of Africa
Literary History of Persia, A
Literature in America: An Illustrated History
New Cambridge Bibliography of English Literature
New Cambridge Modern History, The
Poets of Modern Russia
Worldwide Government Directory, with International Organizations, 1990

Cambridge University Press
Distributed by UMI Demand
300 North Zeeb Road
Ann Arbor, Mich. 48106
(313) 761–4700
(800) 521–0600
Cambridge History of English Literature, The
(See also Melvett G. Chambers)

Careers
Imprint of Gorsuch Scarisbrick Publishers
8233 Via Paseo del Norte, Suite F-400
Scottsdale, Ariz. 85258
(602) 991–7881
Occu-Facts: Information on 565 Careers in Outline Form

Center for Latin American Studies, Arizona State University
Social Sciences Building, Room 213
Tempe, Ariz. 85287–2401
(602) 965–5127
Dictionary of Contemporary Brazilian Authors, A

Chadwyck-Healey, Inc.
1101 King Street, Suite 380
Alexandria, Va. 22314
(703) 683–4890
(800) 752–0515
Black Biography, 1790–1950: A Cumulative Index

Melvett G. Chambers
14502 East 47th Avenue
Denver, Colo. 80239
(303) 371–8729
Chambers Biographical Dictionary, rev. edition

Melvett G. Chambers
Distributed by Cambridge University Press
40 West 20th Street
New York, N.Y. 10011
(212) 924–3900
(800) 221–4512
Chambers Concise Dictionary of Scientists
Chambers World Gazetteer: An A–Z of Geographical Information, 5th edition

Chemical Publishing Company, Inc.
80 Eighth Avenue
New York, N.Y. 10011
(212) 255–1950
Chemical Formulary: Collection of Commercial Formulas for Making Thousands of Products in Many Fields, The

Chicago Review Press
Distributed by the American Medical Association

535 North Dearborn Street
Chicago, Ill. 60610
(312) 280–7168
(800) 621–8335
AMA Handbook of Poisonous and Injurious Plants

Children's Theatre Association of America
Theatre Arts Department
Virginia Tech
Blacksburg, Va. 24001
(703) 961–7624
Child Drama: A Selected and Annotated Bibliography, 1974–1979

Chilton Book Company
1 Chilton Way
Radnor, Pa. 19089
(215) 964–4000
Chilton's Auto Repair Manual 1983–90
Chilton's Import Car Repair Manual 1983–90
Chilton's Motorcycle and ATV Repair Manual 1945–85
Chilton's Truck and Van Repair Manual, 1979–86

Chinese University of Hong Kong
Distributed by the University of Washington Press
P.O. Box 50096
Seattle, Wash. 98145–5096
(206) 543–4050
(800) 441–4115
Twenty-five T'ang Poets: An Index to English Translations

CHOICE
125 South 9th Street, Suite 603
Philadelphia, Pa. 19107
(215) 592–7644
Building Women's Studies Collections: A Resource Guide

Christian Classics
Distributed by HarperCollins
10 East 53d Street
New York, N.Y. 10022
(212) 207–7000
(800) 242–7737
Butler's Lives of the Saints, 2d edition

Chronicle Publications
Distributed by Prentice-Hall Press
15 Columbus Circle
New York, N.Y. 10023
(212) 373–8000
Chronicle of America

CIBA-Geigy
Medical Education Division
14 Henderson Drive
West Caldwell, N.J. 07006
(800) 631–1181
Atlas of Human Anatomy

CineBooks, Inc.
990 Grove Street
Evanston, Ill. 60201
(312) 475–8400
(800) 541–5701
Motion Picture Guide, The

Clarendon Press
Distributed by Oxford University Press, Inc.
200 Madison Avenue
New York, N.Y. 10016
(212) 679–7300
(800) 451–7556
Bibliography of British History, 1789–1851
Concise Oxford Dictionary of French Literature, The
Oxford Classical Dictionary, The, 2d edition
Oxford Companion to Art, The
Oxford Companion to French Literature, The
Oxford Companion to Spanish Literature, The
Oxford History of English Literature, The
Oxford History of Hungarian Literature: From the Earliest Times to the Present, The

The College Board
45 Columbus Avenue
New York, N.Y. 10023–6992
(212) 713–8000
College Cost Book, The
College Handbook, 1990–1991, The, 27th edition
College to Career: The Guide to Job Opportunities

College Placement Council, Inc.
62 Highland Avenue
Bethlehem, Pa. 18017
(215) 868–1421
(800) 544–5272
CPC Annual, The

Columbia University Press
562 West 113th Street
New York, N.Y. 10025
(212) 316–7100
Bibliography of 17th–Century French Prose Fiction
Columbia Dictionary of Modern European Literature, 2d edition

European Historical Statistics, 1750–1970
Guide to Oriental Classics, 3d rev. edition
Short History of Opera, 2d edition
Twentieth-Century Russian Drama: From Gorky to the Present
Washington Representatives, 1989: Who Does What for Whom in the Nation's Capital, 13th edition

Congressional Quarterly Books
1414 Twenty-second Street, N.W.
Washington, D.C. 20037
(202) 887–8500
(800) 543–7793
America Votes 18: A Handbook of Contemporary American Election Statistics
American Leaders 1789–1987: A Biographical Summary
Congress and the Nation
Congressional Quarterly Almanac
Congressional Quarterly's Guide to the Presidency
Congressional Quarterly's Guide to the U.S. Constitution: History, Text, Index, and Glossary
Congressional Quarterly's Guide to the U.S. Supreme Court, 2d edition
Congressional Quarterly's Guide to U. S. Elections, 2d edition
Current American Government
Politics in America: 1990, the 101st Congress

Contemporary Books, Inc.
180 North Michigan Avenue
Chicago, Ill. 60601
(312) 782–9181
(800) 691–1918
Chase's Annual Events

The Continuum Publishing Corporation
370 Lexington Avenue
New York, N.Y. 10017
(212) 532–3650
Continuum Dictionary of Women's Biography, The, exp. edition
International Dictionary of Psychology, The

Copp Clark Pittman
Distributed by Gale Research, Inc.
835 Penobscot Building
Detroit, Mich. 48226–4094
(313) 961–2242
(800) 877–GALE
Canadian Almanac and Directory

Cornell University Press
Box 250, 124 Roberts Place
Ithaca, N.Y. 14851
(607) 257–7000
(800) 666–2211
Bibliography of Modern Icelandic Literature in Translation
Chronology of the Ancient World, 2d edition
Who Was Who in the Greek World, 776 B.C.–30 B.C.

Council of State Governments
Iron Works Pike
P.O. Box 11910
Lexington, Ky. 40578–1910
(606) 252–2291
Book of the States, The

CRC Press, Inc.
2000 Corporate Boulevard, N.W.
Boca Raton, Fla. 33431
(407) 994–0555
CRC Handbook of Chemistry and Physics
CRC Handbook of Mathematical Sciences, 6th edition

Crescent/Crown
Distributed by Random House, Inc.
201 East 50th Street
New York, N.Y. 10022
(212) 751–2600
(800) 726–0600
Atlas of the Ancient World

The Crossroad/Continuum Publishing Group
370 Lexington Avenue
New York, N.Y. 10017
(212) 532–3650
(800) 242–7737
British Women Writers: A Critical Reference Guide
Continuum Dictionary of Women's Biography, The, rev. edition

Thomas Y. Crowell Company
Distributed by HarperCollins
10 East 53d Street
New York, N.Y. 10022
(212) 207–7000
(800) 242–7737
Bulfinch's Mythology
International Thesaurus of Quotations

Crown Publishers, Inc.
Imprint of Random House, Inc.
201 East 50th Street
New York, N.Y. 10022

(212) 751–2600
(800) 726–0600
Consumer's Dictionary of Food Additives, A, 3d edition
Encyclopedia of Furniture, The, 3d rev. ed.
Kovel's Antiques and Collectibles Price List
International Encyclopedia of Astronomy, The
Theatre World
(See also Harmony Books)

CSA Publications of the State University of New York
Binghamton, N.Y. 13901
(607) 777–2119
Political Handbook of the World

Da Capo Press, Inc.
233 Spring Street
New York, N.Y. 10013
(212) 620–8000
(800) 221–9369
Encyclopaedia of the Musical Theatre
Encyclopedia of Jazz
Encyclopedia of Jazz in the Seventies
Encyclopedia of Jazz in the Sixties
Dictionary of Ballet Terms, A

F. A. Davis Company
1915 Arch Street
Philadelphia, Pa. 19103
(215) 568–2270
(800) 523–4049
Taber's Cyclopedic Medical Dictionary, 15th edition

Walter de Gruyter, Inc.
Distributed by Routledge, Chapman & Hall
29 West 35th Street
New York, N.Y. 10001
(212) 244–3336
American Universities and Colleges, 13th edition
New Dictionary of the Social Sciences, A, 2d edition

Dembner Books
Distributed by W. W. Norton & Company, Inc.
500 Fifth Avenue
New York, N.Y. 10110
(212) 354–5500
(800) 223–2584
(800) 233–4830 (orders)
Complete Book of U.S. Presidents, The, 2d edition

Dodd, Mead & Company
See Mead Publishing Corporation

Doubleday & Company, Inc.
Division of Bantam Doubleday Dell
666 Fifth Avenue
New York, N.Y. 10103
(212) 765–6500
(800) 223–6834
American Cancer Society Book of Cancer: Prevention, Detection, Diagnosis, Treatment, Rehabilitation, Cure
Amy Vanderbilt Complete Book of Etiquette: A Guide to Contemporary Living, The
Ocean Almanac, The
Walter Breen's Complete Encyclopedia of U.S. and Colonial Coins
(See also Anchor Books; Bantam Books, Inc.)

Dow Jones-Irwin
Distributed by Business One-Irwin
1818 Ridge Road
Homewood, Ill. 60430
(708) 206–2700
(800) 634–3961
Doing Business in New York City

Dun & Bradstreet Corporation
(See Dun's Marketing Services, Inc.)

Dun's Marketing Services, Inc.
Division of Dun & Bradstreet Corporation
3 Sylvan Way
Parsippany, N.J. 07054
(201) 605–6000
(800) 526–0651
Million Dollar Directory: America's Leading Public and Private Companies

The Dushkin Publishing Group, Inc.
Sluice Dock
Guilford, Conn. 06437
(203) 453–4351
Encyclopedia of Sociology
Global Studies: Western Europe

Editor and Publisher
11 West 19th Street
New York, N.Y. 10011
(212) 675–4380
Editor and Publisher International Yearbook
Editor and Publisher Market Guide

Educational Directories, Inc.
P.O. Box 199
Mount Prospect, Ill. 60056
(312) 459–0605
Patterson's American Education

William B. Eerdmans Publishing Company
255 Jefferson Avenue, S.E.
Grand Rapids, Mich. 49503
(616) 459–4591
(800) 253–7521
(800) 663–9326

Eerdmans Analytical Concordance to the Revised Standard Version of the Bible, The
International Standard Bible Encyclopedia, The, rev. edition

Elsevier
Imprint of Elsevier Science Publishing Company, Inc.
655 Avenue of the Americas
New York, N.Y. 10010
(212) 989–5800

Abbreviations Dictionary: Augmented International, 7th edition
Dictionary of Architectural and Building Technology

Enslow Publishers
Box 777
Bloy Street and Ramsey Avenue
Hillside, N.J. 07205
(201) 964–4116

Hazardous Substances: A Reference

Envoy Press, Inc.
Distributed by APT Books, Inc.
141 East 44th Street, Suite 511
New York, N.Y. 10017
(212) 697–0887

Latin American Writers: A Bibliography with Critical and Biographical Introductions

Eurail Guide Annual
27540 Pacific Coast Highway
Malibu, Calif. 90265
(213) 457–7286

Eurail Guide: How to Travel Europe and All the World by Train

Europa Publishers, Ltd.
Distributed by Gale Research, Inc.
835 Penobscot Building
Detroit, Mich. 48226–4094
(313) 961–2242
(800) 877–GALE

Africa South of the Sahara
Europa World Year Book, The
International Who's Who
Middle East and North Africa, The
South America, Central America, and the Caribbean, 2d edition

Everest House
Reprinted by Books on Demand
300 North Zeeb Road
Ann Arbor, Mich. 48106–1346
(313) 761–4700
(800) 521–0600

Dictionary of Terms and Techniques in Archaeology

Facts On File, Inc.
460 Park Avenue South
New York, N.Y. 10016
(212) 683–2244
(800) 322–8755

All About Tropical Fish, 4th edition
American Architects: A Survey of Award-Winning Contemporaries and Their Notable Works
Atlas of African History
Atlas of Ancient America
Atlas of Ancient Egypt
Atlas of Environmental Issues
Atlas of Medieval Europe
Atlas of the Bible
Atlas of the British Empire
Atlas of the Greek World
Atlas of the Islamic World since 1500
Atlas of the North American Indian
Atlas of the Roman World
Atlas of World Issues
Biblical Quotations
Birds: The Aerial Hunters
Birds: The Plant- and Seed-Eaters
Birds: The Waterbirds
Book of 1000 Plays: A Comprehensive Guide to the Most Frequently Performed Plays, The
Choral Singer's Companion, The
Companion to Chinese History
Complete Handbook of Garden Plants, The
Cultural Atlas of Africa
Cultural Atlas of China
Cultural Atlas of Japan
Day by Day
Dictionary of American Literary Characters
Dictionary of Cliches, The
Dictionary of Wars
Editorials on File
Encyclopaedia of Architecture
Encyclopedia of Alcoholism, The, 2d edition
Encyclopedia of American Journalism, The
Encyclopedia of Animal Behavior, The
Encyclopedia of Animal Biology, The
Encyclopedia of Animal Ecology
Encyclopedia of Animal Evolution, The

Encyclopedia of Aquatic Life, The
Encyclopedia of Birds, The
Encyclopedia of Censorship, The
Encyclopedia of Colonial and Revolutionary America, The
Encyclopedia of Drug Abuse, The, 2d edition
Encyclopedia of Evolution, The
Encyclopedia of Feminism
Encyclopedia of Historic Places, The
Encyclopedia of Insects, The
Encyclopedia of Jewish History
Encyclopedia of Mammals, The
Encyclopedia of Marriage, Divorce, and the Family, The
Encyclopedia of Native American Tribes
Encyclopedia of Reptiles and Amphibians, The
Encyclopedia of Second Careers, The
Encyclopedia of the Animal World (series)
Encyclopedia of the Renaissance
Encyclopedia of the Third World, 3d edition
Encyclopedia of Witches and Witchcraft
Encyclopedia of Wood: A Tree-by-Tree Guide to the World's Most Versatile Resource, The
Facts On File
Facts On File Dictionary of Archaeology, The
Facts On File Dictionary of Artificial Intelligence
Facts On File Dictionary of Astronomy, The, rev. edition
Facts On File Dictionary of Biology, The, rev. and exp. edition
Facts On File Dictionary of Botany, The
Facts On File Dictionary of Chemistry, The, rev. edition
Facts On File Dictionary of Design and Designers, The
Facts On File Dictionary of Geology and Geophysics, The
Facts On File Dictionary of Marine Science, The
Facts On File Dictionary of Public Administration, The
Facts On File Dictionary of Religions, The
Facts On File Dictionary of Science, The, 6th edition
Facts On File Dictionary of the Theatre, The
Facts On File Encyclopedia of World Mythology and Legend
Facts On File News Digest CD-ROM
Facts On File World Political Almanac, The
Facts On File—National Quotation Bureau Directory of Publicly Traded Bonds
Facts On File—National Quotation Bureau Directory of Publicly Traded Stocks
Fish
Handbooks to the Modern World: Africa
Historical Maps on File
History of Science and Technology: A Narrative Chronology, The
Human Body on File, The
Insects and Spiders
Larousse Gardening and Gardens
Life Sciences on File
Mammals: Primates, Insect-Eaters, and Baleen Whales
Mammals: The Hunters
Mammals: The Large Plant-Eaters
Mammals: The Small Plant-Eaters
Middle East, The
Musical Instruments of the World: An Illustrated Encyclopedia
New A–Z of Women's Health: A Concise Encyclopedia, The, rev. edition
New Book of American Rankings, The
New Book of World Rankings, The, 3d edition
Patient's Guide to Medical Tests, The, 3d edition
Pets and Farm Animals
Predators and Predation: The Struggle for Life in the Animal World
Quotable Woman, From Eve to the Present, The
Religions on File
Reptiles and Amphibians
Shakespeare A to Z: The Essential Reference to His Plays, His Poems, His Life and Times, and More
Simple Animals
Soviet Union and Eastern Europe, The
State Maps on File
Timetables of Sports History: Basketball
Trees of North America, The
Western Europe
Women's Atlas of the United States, The
World Encyclopedia of Police Forces and Penal Systems
World Encyclopedia of Political Systems & Parties, 2d edition
World of Games: Their Origins and History, How to Play Games, and How to Make Them, The
World Press Encyclopedia

Fairchild Books & Visuals
7 East 12th Street
New York, N.Y. 10003
(212) 887–1866
(800) 247–6622

Dictionary of Interior Design, The
Fairchild's Dictionary of Fashion, 2d edition
Fairchild's Dictionary of Textiles, 6th edition

Farrar, Straus & Giroux, Inc.
19 Union Square West
New York, N.Y. 10003
(212) 741–6900
(800) 631–8571
Literary Terms: A Dictionary, 3d edition

The Feminist Press at the City University of New York
311 East 94th Street
New York, N.Y. 10128
(212) 360–5790
Feminist Resources for Schools and Colleges: A Guide to Curricular Materials, 3d edition

J. G. Ferguson Publishing Company
200 West Monroe Street
Chicago, Ill. 60606
(312) 580–5480
Career Discovery Encyclopedia
Encyclopedia of Careers and Vocational Guidance, The, 7th edition

Fisher Books
5669 North Oracle Road, Suite 2103
Tucson, Ariz. 85704
(602) 292–9080
(800) 255–1514
Drugs, Vitamins, Minerals in Pregnancy

Focal Press
80 Montvale Avenue
Stoneham, Mass. 02180
(617) 438–8464
Focal Encyclopedia of Photography

Fodor's Travel Publications
Distributed by Random House, Inc.
201 East 50th Street
New York, N.Y. 10022
(212) 751–2600
(800) 726–0600
Fodor's Travel Guides (series)

Food and Agriculture Organization of the United Nations
Distributed by UNIPUB
4611-F Assembly Drive
Lanham, Md. 20706–4391
(301) 459–7666
(800) 274–4888
State of Food and Agriculture, The

The Foundation Press, Inc.
615 Merrick Avenue
Westbury, N.Y. 11590
(516) 832–6950
Fundamentals of Legal Research, 3d edition

The Free Press
Division of Macmillan Publishing Company, Inc.
866 Third Avenue
New York, N.Y. 10022
(212) 702–2000
(800) 257–5755
Encyclopedia of Bioethics
Encyclopedia of Crime and Justice
Encyclopedia of Educational Research, 5th edition
Encyclopedia of Philosophy, The
International Encyclopedia of the Social Sciences
Macmillan Encyclopedia of Architects

W. H. Freeman & Company Publishers
41 Madison Avenue
New York, N.Y. 10010
(212) 576–9400
Five Kingdoms: An Illustrated Guide to the Phyla of Life on Earth, 2d edition

Gale Research, Inc.
835 Penobscot Building
Detroit, Mich. 48226–4094
(313) 961–2242
(800) 877-GALE
Acronyms, Initialisms, & Abbreviations Dictionary, 15th edition
African Authors: A Companion to Black African Writing, Volume 1:1300–1973
American Architecture and Art: A Guide to Information Sources
American Writers for Children Before 1900 (Dictionary of Literary Biography, vol. 42)
American Writers for Children, 1900–1960 (Dictionary of Literary Biography, vol. 22)
American Writers for Children Since 1960: Poets, Illustrators, and Nonfiction Authors (Dictionary of Literary Biography, vol. 61)
Biographical Dictionaries and Related Works, 2d edition
Black African Literature in English: A Guide to Information Sources
Black Writers: A Selection of Sketches from Contemporary Authors
Bookman's Price Index: A Guide to the Values of Rare and Other Out-of-Print Books

Brands and Their Companies: Consumer Products and Their Manufacturers with Addresses and Phone Numbers, 8th edition
British Novelists 1600–1800
Characters in 20th-Century Literature
Cities of the World, 3d edition
Climates of the States, 4th edition
Contemporary Authors: A Bio-Bibliographical Guide to Current Writers in Fiction, General Nonfiction, Poetry, Journalism, Drama, Motion Pictures, Television, and Other Fields
Contemporary Authors, New Revision series
Contemporary German Fiction Writers [first series]
Contemporary German Fiction Writers [second series]
Contemporary Graphic Artists
Contemporary Literary Criticism: Excerpts from Criticism of the Works of Today's Novelists, Poets, Playwrights, and Other Creative Writers
Contemporary Musicians: Profiles of the People in Music
Dictionary of Literary Biography
Elizabethan Dramatists (Dictionary of Literary Biography, vol. 62)
Encyclopedia of American Religions, The, 3d edition
Encyclopedia of Business Information Sources, 6th edition
Encyclopedia of Occultism and Parapsychology: A Compendium of Information on the Occult Sciences, Magic, Demonology, Superstitions, Spiritism, Mysticism, Metaphysics, Psychical Science and Parapsychology, 2d edition
Executives on the Move
German Fiction Writers, 1885–1913
German Fiction Writers, 1914–1945
Hispanic Writers
Hobbyist Sourcebook
International Business Travel and Relocation Directory, 5th edition
Newsmakers: The People Behind Today's Headlines
Notable Black American Women
Passenger and Immigration Lists Index
Peoples of the World: Latin Americans
Picturesque Expressions: A Thematic Dictionary, 2d edition
Popular Music: An Annotated Guide to American Popular Song
Professional Careers Sourcebook: An Information Guide for Career Planning
Short Story Criticism: Excerpts from Criticism of the Works of Short Fiction Writers, vol. 1
Small Business Sourcebook, 3d edition
Something About the Author: Facts and Pictures About Authors and Illustrators of Books for Young People
Twentieth-Century American Dramatists
Video Source Book, 11th edition
Who's Who Among Hispanic Americans

(See also Copp Clark Pittman; Europa Publishers, Ltd.; Hurtig Publishers, Ltd.; Longman Publishing Group; St. James Press)

Garland Publishing, Inc.
136 Madison Avenue
New York, N.Y. 10016
(212) 686–7492
(800) 627–6273

Advertising Handbook
Afro-American Genealogy Sourcebook
Alcohol Use and Alcoholism: A Guide to the Literature
American Women Artists, Past and Present: A Selected Bibliographical Guide
Apartheid: A Selective Annotated Bibliography, 1979–1987
Biographical Dictionary of American Cult and Sect Leaders
Black Arts Annual
Black Authors and Illustrators of Children's Books: A Biographical Dictionary
Black Dance: An Annotated Bibliography
Blues: A Bibliographical Guide, The
Cuban Literature: A Research Guide
Encyclopedia of Human Evolution and Prehistory
Encyclopedic Handbook of Cults in America
Folk Music in America: A Reference Guide
Handbook of American Women's History
Handbook of Latin American Literature
Homosexuality: A Research Guide
Latinas of the Americas: A Source Book
New York Botanical Garden Illustrated Encyclopedia of Horticulture, The
Nobel Laureates in Economic Sciences: A Biographical Dictionary
Nobel Laureates in Literature: A Biographical Dictionary
Prevention Education: A Guide to Research
Rape and Sexual Assault: A Research Handbook
Research Guide to Argentine Literature
Sexuality Education: A Resource Book

Sociology of Aging: An Annotated Bibliography and Sourcebook
Women and Work, Paid and Unpaid: A Selected, Annotated Bibliography
Women of Color in the United States: A Guide to the Literature

Garrett Park Press
Box 190
Garrett Park, Md. 20896
(301) 946–2553
Where the Jobs Are: A Comprehensive Directory of 1200 Journals Listing Career Opportunities

Genealogical Publishing Company, Inc.
1001 North Calvert Street
Baltimore, Md. 21202
(301) 837–8271, 8272, 8273
(800) 727–6687
Burke's American Families with British Ancestry
Family Diseases: Are You at Risk?
International Vital Records Handbook
Managing a Genealogical Project

Geological Society of America/American Geological Society
P.O. Box 9140
3300 Penrose Place
Boulder, Colo. 80301
(303) 447–2020
(800) GSA–1988
Bibliography and Index of Geology

Glencoe/Macmillan
(See Visual Education Corporation)

Global Trade Company
5212 North Beaver, Suite A
Bethany, Okla. 73008
(405) 789–8943
1000 Cooking Substitutions

Gordian Press, Inc.
Box 304
85 Tompkins Street
Staten Island, N.Y. 10304
(718) 273–4700
History of French Dramatic Literature in the Seventeenth Century

Gower Publishing Company
Old Post Road
Brookfield, Vt. 05036
(802) 276–3162
Filmed Books and Plays: A List of Books and Plays from Which Films Have Been Made, 1928–1986
Harrod's Librarians' Glossary of Terms Used in Librarianship, Documentation, and the Book Crafts, and Reference Book, 6th edition
How to Use Chemical Abstracts, Current Abstracts of Chemistry and Index Chemicus

Greenwood Publishing Group, Inc.
Box 5007
88 Post Road West
Westport, Conn. 06881
(203) 266–3571
American Educators' Encyclopedia
American Popular Illustration: A Reference Guide
American Theatre Companies, 1931–1986
Biographical Dictionary of American Journalism
Biographical Dictionary of American Labor, rev. edition
Biographical Dictionary of American Sports: Baseball
Biographical Dictionary of Hispanic Literature in the United States: The Literature of Puerto Ricans, Cuban Americans, and Other Hispanic Writers
Biographical Dictionary of Latin American and Caribbean Political Leaders
Biographical Dictionary of Psychology, 2d edition
Dictionary of Albanian Literature
Dictionary of American Children's Fiction, 1859–1959: Books of Recognized Merit
Dictionary of American Children's Fiction, 1960–1984: Books of Recognized Merit
Dictionary of American Diplomatic History, 2d edition
Dictionary of American Nursing Biography
Dictionary of American Religious Biography
Dictionary of Brazilian Literature
Dictionary of British Children's Fiction: Books of Recognized Merit
Dictionary of French Literature
Dictionary of Gerontology
Dictionary of Italian Literature
Dictionary of Modern French Literature: From the Age of Reason Through Realism
Dictionary of Spanish Literature
Dictionary of the Black Theatre: Broadway, Off-Broadway, and Selected Harlem Theatre

East and Southeast Asian Material Culture in North America: Collections, Historical Sites, and Festivals
Eighteenth-Century Musical Chronicle: Events 1750–1799, An
Equal Rights Amendment: An Annotated Bibliography of the Issues, 1976–1985
Ethnic Genealogy: A Research Guide
Fifty Caribbean Writers: A Bio-Bibliographical Critical Sourcebook
Finding the Source in Sociology and Anthropology: A Thesaurus-Index to the Reference Collection
Guide to Folktales in the English Language: Based on the Aarne-Thompson Classification System
Guide to Research in Gerontology: Strategies and Resources
Handbook of United States Economic and Financial Indicators
Handbook on the Aged in the United States
Hispanic-American Material Culture
Historical Dictionary of North American Archaeology
Information Sources in Advertising History
Instrumental Virtuosi: A Bibliography of Biographical Materials
International Dictionary of Theatre Language, An
International Handbook on Aging: Contemporary Developments and Research
Literature for Young People on War and Peace: An Annotated Bibliography
Mythical and Fabulous Creatures
Notable Women in the American Theatre: A Biographical Dictionary
Nuclear Weapons World: Who, How, and Where, The
Peruvian Literature: A Bibliography of Secondary Sources
Political Leaders of the Contemporary Middle East and North Africa: A Biographical Dictionary
Public Interest Law Groups: Institutional Profiles
Puerto Rican Literature: A Bibliography of Secondary Sources
Radio: A Reference Guide
Reference Guide to Modern Fantasy for Children
Retirement: An Annotated Bibliography
Spanish Literature, 1500–1700: A Bibliography of Golden Age Studies in Spanish and English, 1925–1980
They Wrote for Children Too: An Annotated Bibliography of Children's Literature by Famous Writers for Adults
Toxic and Hazardous Materials: A Sourcebook and Guide to Information Sources
Twentieth-Century Musical Chronicle: Events 1900–1988, A
Twentieth-Century Shapers of American Popular Religion
United States in Africa: A Historical Dictionary, The
Women of Mathematics: A Bibliographic Sourcebook
Women of Northern, Western, and Central Africa: A Bibliography, 1976–1985
Women Writers of Spain: An Annotated Bio-Bibliographical Guide
Women Writers of Spanish America: An Annotated Bio-Bibliographical Guide
Women's Studies Encyclopedia, vol. 1: Views from the Sciences

Grolier, Inc.
Sherman Turnpike
Danbury, Conn. 06816
(203) 797–3500
American Presidents: The Office and the Men, The
(See also Scarecrow Press, Inc.)

Grove's Dictionaries of Music
Distributed by Macmillan Publishing Company, Inc.
866 Third Avenue
New York, N.Y. 10022
(212) 702–2000
(800) 257–5755
New Grove Dictionary of American Music, The
New Grove Dictionary of Jazz, The
New Grove Dictionary of Music and Musicians, The
New Grove Dictionary of Musical Instruments, The
(See also Stockton Press)

Hafner Press
Division of Macmillan Publishing Company, Inc.
866 Third Avenue
New York, N.Y. 10022
(212) 702–2000
(800) 257–5755
History of the Russian Theatre: Seventeenth Through Nineteenth Century

G. K. Hall & Company
70 Lincoln Street
Boston, Mass. 02111
(617) 423–3990
(800) 343–2806

American Women Sculptors: A History of Women Working in Three Dimensions
Bibliographic Guide to Anthropology and Archaeology, 1987
Bibliographic Guide to Dance
Dance Handbook, The
Dictionary of Anthropology
Dictionary of Women Artists: An International Dictionary of Women Artists Born Before 1900
Guide to American Poetry Explication, Colonial and Nineteenth-Century
Guide to American Poetry Explication, Modern and Contemporary
Guide to Japanese Prose, 2d edition
Newbery and Caldecott Medal and Honor Books: An Annotated Bibliography
Nobel Peace Prize and the Laureates: An Illustrated Biographical History, 1901–1987, The
World Atlas of Archaeology, The
World Atlas of Architecture, The

Hammond, Inc.
515 Valley Street
Maplewood, N.J. 07040
(201) 763–6000
(800) 526–4953

Times Atlas of World History, The, 5th edition, rev.

Harcourt Brace Jovanovich, Inc.
(See W. B. Saunders Company)

Harmony Books
Division of Crown Publishers, Inc.
201 East 50th Street
New York, N.Y. 10022
(212) 572–6120

Harmony Illustrated Encyclopedia of Rock, The, 6th edition
New Compleat Astrologer: The Practical Encyclopedia of Astrological Science, The, rev. edition

Harper & Row Publishers, Inc.
Distributed by HarperCollins Publishers
10 East 53d Street
New York, N.Y. 10022
(212) 207–7000
(800) 242–7737

American Sign Language: A Comprehensive Dictionary
Asimov's Chronology of Science and Discovery
Astrologer's Handbook, The
Bowes and Church's Food Values of Portions Commonly Used, 15th edition
Brewer's Dictionary of Phrase and Fable, 14th edition
Dictionary of Art Terms and Techniques, A
Encyclopedia of American Facts and Dates, The, 8th edition
Encyclopedia of Horror Movies
Essential Guide to Nonprescription Drugs, The
Essential Guide to Prescription Drugs, The
Funk & Wagnalls Standard Dictionary of Folklore, Mythology, and Legend
Harper Atlas of World History, The
Harper Dictionary of Foreign Terms, The, 3d edition
Harper Religious and Inspirational Quotation Companion, The
Harper's Bible Dictionary
Masterpieces of World Literature
Perennial Dictionary of World Religions, The
Radio Amateur's Handbook, 15th rev. edition
Rehab: A Comprehensive Guide to Recommended Drug-Alcohol Treatment Centers in the United States
Rock On: The Illustrated Encyclopedia of Rock n' Roll
Thesaurus of American Slang
Times Atlas of the Second World War, The
Woman's Encyclopedia of Myths and Secrets, The

HarperCollins Publishers
10 East 53d Street
New York, N.Y. 10022
(212) 207–7000
(800) 242–7737

Comparative Guide to American Colleges for Students, Parents and Counselors, 14th edition
Times Atlas and Encyclopedia of the Sea, The, 2d edition

(See also Basic Books, Inc. Publishers; Christian Classics; Thomas Y. Crowell Company; Harper & Row Publishers, Inc.; Zondervan Publishing House)

Hart Publishing
1900 Grant Street, Suite 400
P.O. Box 1917

Denver, Colo. 80201
(303) 837–1917
Encyclopedia of Design

Harvard University Press
79 Garden Street
Cambridge, Mass. 02138
(617) 495–2600
(800) 962–4983
American National Election Studies Data Sourcebook, 1952–1986
Bibliography of Studies and Translations of Modern Chinese Literature, 1918–1942
Brazil, Portugal and Other Portuguese-Speaking Lands: A List of Books Primarily in English
Contemporary Chinese Novels and Short Stories, 1949–1974: An Annotated Bibliography
Dictionary of Ethology, A
History of Italian Literature, A, rev. edition
Russian Literature Since the Revolution
(See also The Belknap Press of Harvard University Press)

Carol Hess Associates
Distributed by Political Resources, Inc.
P.O. Box 363
Rye, N.Y. 10580
(914) 939–0598
Political Resource Directory

Hilary House Publishers, Inc.
980 North Federal Highway, Suite 206
Boca Raton, Fla. 33432
(407) 393–5656
Direct Marketing Market Place

Hippocrene Books, Inc.
171 Madison Avenue
New York, N.Y. 10016
(212) 685–4371
Marvelous Journey: A Survey of Four Centuries of Brazilian Writing

The Hispanic Society of America
613 West 155th Street
New York, N.Y. 10032
(212) 926–2234
Spanish Drama of the Golden Age

Holmes & Meier Publishers, Inc.
30 Irving Place
New York, N.Y. 10003
(212) 254–4100
Africa Contemporary Record: Annual Survey and Documents
Black African Literature in English: 1977–1981 Supplement

Holt, Rinehart and Winston, Inc.
6277 Sea Harbor Drive
Orlando, Fla. 32887
(407) 345–2000
(800) 542–5479
American Political Dictionary, The, 8th edition
Dawn to the West: Japanese Literature of the Modern Era

Horn Book, Inc.
14 Beacon Street
Boston, Mass. 02108
(617) 227–1555
(800) 325–1170
Horn Book Guide to Children's and Young Adult Books, The

Houghton Mifflin Company
1 Beacon Street
Boston, Mass. 02108
(617) 725–5000
(800) 225–3362 (trade books)
(800) 257–9107 (textbooks)
(800) 255–1464 (college texts)
American Heritage Dictionary of Science, The
Atlas of the Living World, The
Encyclopedia of World History: Ancient, Medieval, and Modern, Chronologically Arranged, An, 5th edition
Information Please Almanac

House of Collectibles
Imprint of Ballantine/Del Rey/Fawcett/Ivy Books
201 East 50th Street
New York, N.Y. 10022
(212) 751–2600
(800) 638–6460
Official Overstreet Comic Book Price Guide, The, 19th edition

Human Kinetics Publishers, Inc.
(See Leisure Press)

Humanities Press International, Inc.
171 First Avenue
Atlantic Highlands, N.J. 07716–1289
(201) 872–1441
(800) 221–3845
Dictionary of Philosophy and Religion: Eastern and Western Thought

Hurtig Publishers, Ltd.
Distributed by Gale Research, Inc.
835 Penobscot Building
Detroit, Mich. 48226–4094
(313) 961–2242
(800) 877–GALE
Canadian Encyclopedia, The, 2d edition

Indiana University Press
10th and Morton Streets
Bloomington, Ind. 47405
(812) 855–4203
(800) 842–6796
Indiana Companion to Traditional Chinese Literature

Industrial Press, Inc.
200 Madison Avenue
New York, N.Y. 10016
(212) 889–6330
Machinery's Handbook: A Reference Book for the Mechanical Engineer, Draftsman, Toolmaker and Machinist, 23d edition

Institute of Electrical and Electronics Engineers
445 Hoes Lane
Piscataway, N.J. 08855–1331
(201) 981–0060
IEEE Standard Dictionary of Electrical and Electronics Terms, 4th edition

Institute of International Education
809 United Nations Plaza
New York, N.Y. 10017
(212) 984–5421
Academic Year Abroad
Teaching Abroad 1988–1991

International Youth Hostel Federation/American Youth Hostels
P.O. Box 37613
Washington, D.C. 20013–7613
(202) 783–6161
International Youth Hostel Handbook

Irvington Publishers, Inc.
522 East 82d Street, Suite 1
New York, N.Y. 10028
(212) 777–4100
Cyclopedia of Painters and Paintings
Outline History of Spanish American Literature, 4th edition

Jane's Information Group
1340 Braddock Place, Suite 300
Alexandria, Va. 22314–1651
(703) 683–3700
(800) 243–3852
Jane's Aerospace Dictionary, 3d edition
Jane's All the World's Aircraft, 1989–90, 80th edition
Jane's Fighting Ships
Jane's World Railways, 1989–90, 31st edition

The Johns Hopkins University Press
701 West 40th Street, Suite 275
Baltimore, Md. 21211
(301) 338–6900
Walker's Mammals of the World, 4th edition

Johnson Books
1880 South 57th Court
Boulder, Colo. 80301
(303) 443–1576
(800) 662–2665
Black African Literature in English Since 1952

Keats Publishing, Inc.
27 Pine Street
New Canaan, Conn. 06840
(203) 966–8721
Nutrition Desk Reference, The, rev. edition

Kennedy Institute of Ethics
Georgetown University
Washington, D.C. 20057
(202) 687–6689
(800) 633–3849
Bibliography of Bioethics

Kent State University Press
101 Franklin Hall
Kent, Ohio 44242
(216) 672–7913, 7914
(800) 666–2211
(800) 688–2877
Language of Journalism: A Glossary of Print-Communications Terms, The

Alfred A. Knopf, Inc.
Subsidiary of Random House, Inc.
201 East 50th Street
New York, N.Y. 10022
(212) 751–2600
(800) 638–6460
Audubon Society Encyclopedia of North American Birds
Audubon Society Field Guide to North American Birds: Eastern Region, The
Audubon Society Field Guide to North American Birds: Western Region, The
Ballet Goer's Guide

Familiar Flowers of North America: Eastern Region
Familiar Flowers of North America: Western Region
Familiar Trees of North America: Eastern Region
Familiar Trees of North America: Western Region

Kodansha International U.S.A., Ltd.
114 Fifth Avenue
New York, N.Y. 10011
(212) 727–6460
(800) 631–8571 (except N.J.)
History of Japanese Literature, A
Kodansha Encyclopedia of Japan
Reader's Guide to Japanese Literature, A

Kraus International Publications
Route 100
Millwood, N.Y. 10546
(914) 762–2200
(800) 223–8323
Bibliography of Creative African Writing
Bio-Bibliography of German-American Writers, 1670–1970, A
Writings on American History, 1962–1973: A Subject Bibliography of Books and Monographs
(See also UNIPUB)

Krause Publications
700 East State Street
Iola, Wis. 54990
(715) 445–2214
Contemporary Russian Literature, 1881–1925
Standard Catalog of World Coins, 17th edition
Standard Catalog of World Paper Money, 6th edition

Robert E. Krieger Publishing Company, Inc.
Box 9542
Melbourne, Fla. 32902
(407) 724–9542
Dictionary of Behavioral Science, 2d edition

Peter Lang Publishing, Inc.
62 West 45th Street, 4th floor
New York, N.Y. 10036–4202
(212) 302–6740
Bibliography of German Literature: An Historical and Critical Survey, The

Larousse
Distributed by BDD Promotional Book Company, Inc.
Division of Bantam Doubleday Dell
666 Fifth Avenue, 16th Floor
New York, N.Y. 10103
(212) 492–9487
(800) 223–6834
Larousse Dictionary of Painters
Larousse Encyclopedia of Archaeology, 2d edition
New Larousse Encyclopedia of Animal Life

The Lawyers Co-Operative Publishing Company
Aqueduct Building
Rochester, N.Y. 14694
(716) 546–5530
(800) 527–0430
American Jurisprudence Second

Lea & Febiger
200 Chester Field Parkway
Malvern, Pa. 19355–9725
(215) 251–2230
(800) 444–1785
Modern Nutrition in Health and Disease, 7th edition

Leisure Press
Division of Human Kinetics Publishers, Inc.
P.O. Box 5076
Champaign, Ill. 61825–5076
(217) 351–5076
(800) 342–5457
(800) 334–3665 (in Ill.)
Sports Rules Encyclopedia, 2d edition

Libraries Unlimited, Inc.
Box 3988
Englewood, Colo. 80155–3988
(303) 770–1220
(800) 237–6124
Critical Guide to Catholic Reference Books, 3d edition
Education: A Guide to Reference and Information Sources
Library and Information Science Annual
Microcomputer Software Sources: A Guide for Buyers, Librarians, Programmers, Business People, Educators
Philosophy, A Guide to the Reference Literature
Reference Works in British and American Literature
Social Sciences: A Cross-Disciplinary Guide to Selected Sources, The
Sociology: A Guide to Reference and Information Sources
Studies in Human Sexuality: A Selected Guide

Supernatural Fiction for Teens: 500 Good Paperbacks to Read for Wonderment, Fear, and Fun
Women's Studies: A Recommended Core Bibliography 1980–1985

J. B. Lippincott Company
East Washington Square
Philadelphia, Pa. 19105
(215) 238–4200
(800) 638–3030 (Mass.)
(800) 242–7737 (Pa.)
Lippincott Manual of Nursing Practice, The, 4th edition

Little, Brown & Company, Inc.
34 Beacon Street
Boston, Mass. 02108
(617) 227–0730
(800) 343–9204
Familiar Quotations: A Collection of Passages, Phrases, and Proverbs Traced to Their Sources in Ancient and Modern Literature, 15th edition
Originals: An A-Z of Fiction's Real-Life Characters, The
(See also Museum of Modern Art)

Live Oak Publications
1515 23d Street
P.O. Box 2193
Boulder, Colo. 80306
(303) 447–1087
(800) 365–3453
Work-at-Home Sourcebook, The, 3d edition

Llewellyn Publications
Box 64383
Saint Paul, Minn. 55164–0383
(612) 291–1970
(800) 843–6666
Heaven Knows What, 8th edition, rev.
New A to Z Horoscope Maker and Delineator, The, 13th edition

Longman Publishing Group
Subsidiary of Addison-Wesley Publishing Company
Longman Building
95 Church Street
White Plains, N.Y. 10601
(914) 993–5000
(800) 447–2226
Broadcast News Manual of Style, A
Longman Handbook of Modern British History, 1714–1986, The, 2d edition

Longman Publishing Group
Distributed by Gale Research, Inc.
835 Penobscot Building
Detroit, Mich. 48226–4094
(313) 961–2242
(800) 877–GALE
Agricultural & Veterinary Sciences International Who's Who, 3d edition
Annual Register: A Record of World Events, The

Macmillan Publishing Company, Inc.
866 Third Avenue
New York, N.Y. 10022
(212) 702–2000
(800) 257–5755
American Horticultural Society Encyclopedia of Garden Plants, The
Atlas of American Women
Atlas of Classical History
Atlas of Southeast Asia
Atlas of the Middle East
Baseball Encyclopedia: The Complete and Official Record of Major League Baseball, The, 8th edition
Battles and Battlescenes of World War Two
College Blue Book, The, 22d edition
Dictionary of Business and Economics, rev. and exp. edition
Dictionary of Contemporary Politics of South America, The
Dictionary of Medieval Civilization
Dictionary of Slang and Unconventional English: Colloquialisms and Catch-phrases, Solecisms and Catachreses, Nicknames and Vulgarisms, 8th edition
Educator's Desk Reference: A Sourcebook of Educational Information and Research, The
Elements of Editing: A Modern Guide for Editors and Journalists, The
Encyclopedia of Judaism, The
Encyclopedia of Religion, The
Encyclopedia of the American Constitution
Encyclopedia of the Holocaust
Guide to Schools of Nursing in Four-Year Colleges and Universities: Baccalaureate and Graduate Programs in the United States and Canada
Handbook to Literature, A, 5th edition
Historical Atlas of Political Parties in the United States Congress, 1789–1989, The
Hortus Third: A Concise Dictionary of Plants Cultivated in the United States and Canada
Macmillan Bible Atlas, The, rev. edition

Macmillan Guide to Correspondence Study, The, 3d edition
Macmillan Illustrated Animal Encyclopedia
United States Energy Atlas, 2d edition
We the People: An Atlas of America's Ethnic Diversity
Wyman's Gardening Encyclopedia, 2d edition
(See also The Free Press; Grove's Dictionaries of Music; Hafner Press; Schirmer Books; Charles Scribner's Sons)

Magna Carta Book Company
3716 Fieldstone Road
Randallstown, Md. 21133
(301) 466–8191
Genealogies in the Library of Congress: A Bibliography

Manchester University Press
Distributed by St. Martin's Press, Inc.
175 Fifth Avenue
New York, N.Y. 10010
(212) 674–5151
(800) 221–7945
Short History of Italian Literature, A

Mansel
Distributed by The H. W. Wilson Company
950 University Avenue
Bronx, N.Y. 10452
(212) 588–8400
(800) 367–6770
(800) 462–6060 (N.Y.)
Quantities and Units of Measurement: A Dictionary and Handbook
Translations of Bengali Works into English: A Bibliography

Marquis Who's Who
3002 Glenview Road
Wilmette, Ill. 60091
(708) 441–2387
(800) 621–9669
Who Was Who in America with World Notables
Who's Who in America
Who's Who of American Women, 16th edition

Marshall Cavendish Corporation
2415 Jerusalem Avenue
North Bellmore, N.Y. 11710
(516) 826–4200
(800) 821–9881
Great Writers of the English Language
Man, Myth and Magic: The Illustrated Encyclopedia of Mythology, Religion and the Unknown, 3d edition

Martindale-Hubbell
630 Central Avenue
New Providence, N.J. 07974
(201) 464–6800
Martindale-Hubbell Law Directory

Mayflower Associates
Distributed by Peter Smith Publisher, Inc.
6 Lexington Avenue
Magnolia, Mass. 01930
(508) 525–3562
Encyclopedia of Ancient Civilizations, The

McFarland & Company, Inc., Publishers
Box 611
Jefferson, N.C. 28640
(919) 246–4460
Black American Women in Literature: A Bibliography
College Majors: A Complete Guide from Accounting to Zoology
Magazine Writers Nonfiction Guidelines: Over 200 Periodicals Editors' Instructions Reproduced
Musical Terms, Symbols and Theory: An Illustrated Dictionary
Resume Reference Book, The
Science Fiction, Fantasy and Horror Reference: An Annotated Bibliography of Works About Literature and Film
Sports Quotations: Maxims, Quips, and Pronouncements for Writers and Fans
Symbolism: A Comprehensive Dictionary

McGraw-Hill, Inc.
1221 Avenue of the Americas
New York, N.Y. 10020
(212) 512–2000
American Electricians' Handbook, 11th edition
Artists' and Illustrators' Encyclopedia, 2d edition
Encyclopedia of Economics
Graphic Arts Encyclopedia, 2d edition
Grzimek's Encyclopedia of Mammals
Handbook of Mathematical Tables and Formulas, 5th edition
Handbook of Organic Chemistry
Jobs of the Future: The Five Hundred Best Jobs—Where They'll Be and How to Get Them
Lange's Handbook of Chemistry, 13th edition
Lectionary of Music

Marks' Standard Handbook for Mechanical Engineers, 9th edition
McGraw-Hill Concise Encyclopedia of Science & Technology, 2d edition
McGraw-Hill Dictionary of Earth Science
McGraw-Hill Dictionary of Modern Economics: A Handbook of Terms and Organizations, 3d edition
McGraw-Hill Dictionary of Physics
McGraw-Hill Dictionary of Physics and Mathematics
McGraw-Hill Dictionary of Scientific and Technical Terms, 4th edition
McGraw-Hill Encyclopedia of Astronomy
McGraw-Hill Encyclopedia of Electronics and Computers, 2d edition
McGraw-Hill Encyclopedia of Engineering
McGraw-Hill Encyclopedia of Ocean and Atmospheric Sciences
McGraw-Hill Encyclopedia of Physics
McGraw-Hill Encyclopedia of Science and Technology, 6th edition
McGraw-Hill Encyclopedia of the Geological Sciences, 2d edition
McGraw-Hill Encyclopedia of World Biography
McGraw-Hill Encyclopedia of World Drama: An International Reference Work in 5 Volumes, 2d edition
McGraw-Hill Handbook of Business Letters, The, 2d edition
McGraw-Hill Personal Computer Programming Encyclopedia
McGraw-Hill Yearbook of Science and Technology
Modern Electronic Circuits Reference Manual
New Catholic Encyclopedia
Perry's Chemical Engineers' Handbook, 6th edition
Standard Handbook for Civil Engineers, 3d edition
Standard Handbook for Electrical Engineers, 12th edition
Standard Handbook for Secretaries
Synopsis and Classification of Living Organisms
Television and Audio Handbook: For Technicians and Engineers

(See also Standard & Poor's; TAB Books)

David McKay Company, Inc.
Subsidiary of Random House, Inc.
201 East 50th Street, MD 4–6
New York, N.Y. 10022
(212) 751–2600
Civil War Dictionary, The

Mead Publishing Corporation
1515 South Commerce Street
Las Vegas, Nev. 89102–2703
(702) 387–8750
Encyclopaedia of the Musical Theatre

Medical Economics Books
680 Kinderkamack Road
Oradell, N.J. 07649
(201) 262–3030
(800) 223–0581
Physician's Desk Reference

Merck & Company, Inc.
Box 2000
Rahway, N.J. 07065
(201) 855–4558
Merck Index: An Encyclopedia of Chemicals, Drugs, and Biologicals, The, 11th edition
Merck Veterinary Manual: A Handbook of Diagnosis, Therapy, and Disease Prevention and Control for the Veterinarian, 6th edition

Merck Sharp & Dohme International
Professional Communications Department
West Point, Pa. 19486
(800) 323–7160
Merck Manual of Diagnosis and Therapy, 15th edition

Merriam-Webster, Inc.
47 Federal Street
Springfield, Mass. 01102
(413) 734–3134, 3148
(800) 828–1880
Webster's Medical Desk Dictionary
Webster's New Biographical Dictionary
Webster's New Geographical Dictionary
Webster's Secretarial Handbook, 2d edition

Merrimack Publishers
Distributed by State Mutual Book & Periodical Service, Ltd.
521 Fifth Avenue, 17th floor
New York, N.Y. 10175
(212) 682–5844
Popular Dictionary of Buddhism, A

Michelin Travel Publications
P.O. Box 19001
Greenville, S.C. 29602–9001
(803) 458–6470
(800) 423–0485
Michelin Hotel and Restaurant Guides (series); Michelin Tourist Guides (series); Michelin Maps (series)

Michigan Slavic Publications
The University of Michigan Press
Box 1104
839 Greene Street
Ann Arbor, Mich. 48106
(313) 764–4394
Czech Literature

The MIT Press
55 Hayward Street
Cambridge, Mass. 02142
(617) 253–5646
(800) 356–0343
Encyclopedia of Materials Science and Engineering
Encyclopedic Dictionary of Mathematics, 2d edition
Encyclopedic Dictionary of Psychology, The
Women in Science: Antiquity Through the Nineteenth Century—A Biographical Dictionary with Annotated Bibliography
(See also Pergamon Press, Inc.)

Modern Language Association of America (MLA)
10 Astor Place
New York, N.Y. 10003
(212) 475–9500
Guide to Reference Works for the Study of the Spanish Language and Literature and Spanish American Literature
Guidelines for Journal Editors and Contributors
Literary Research Guide, 3d edition
MLA Handbook for Writers of Research Papers, 3d edition
MLA International Bibliography of Books & Articles on the Modern Languages and Literatures
MLA Style Manual, The

Modern Library Prakasham
Distributed by South Asia Books
Box 502
Columbia, Mo. 65205
(314) 474–0166
Bibliography of Panjabi Drama

Moody's Investors Service
99 Church Street
New York, N.Y. 10007
(800) 342–5647
Moody's Manuals

Morgan & Morgan, Inc.
145 Palisade Street
Dobbs Ferry, N.Y. 10522
(914) 693–0023
Dictionary of Contemporary Photography

Mosby–Year Book, Inc.
11830 Westline Industrial Drive
Saint Louis, Mo. 63146
(314) 872–8370
(800) 352–4177
Mosby's Medical, Nursing, and Allied Health Dictionary, 3d edition

Motorbooks International, Publishers & Wholesalers, Inc.
Box 2
729 Prospect Avenue
Osceola, Wis. 54020
(715) 294–3345
(800) 458–0454
Classic Old Car Value Guide 1990, 24th edition

Mouton de Gruyter
200 Saw Mill River Road
Hawthorne, N.Y. 10532
(914) 747–0110
History of Bulgarian Literature, 1865–1944, A

John Muir Publications, Inc.
Distributed by W. W. Norton & Company, Inc.
500 Fifth Avenue
New York, N.Y. 10110
(212) 354–5500
(800) 223–2584
(800) 233–4830 (orders)
Traveler's Guide to Healing Centers and Retreats in North America

Museum of Modern Art
Distributed by Bulfinch Press
Division of Little, Brown & Company
34 Beacon Street
Boston, Mass. 02108
(617) 227–0730
History of Photography from 1839 to the Present, The, 5th edition

National Archives Trust Fund Board
National Archives Publications
7th and Pennsylvania Avenues
Washington, D.C. 20408
(202) 501–5235
Guide to Genealogical Research in the National Archives, rev. edition

National Association of Social Workers
7981 Eastern Avenue
Silver Spring, Md. 20910

(301) 565–0333
(800) 638–8799
Encyclopedia of Social Work, 18th edition

The National Council on the Aging/Sage Publications, Inc.
2111 West Hillcrest Drive
Newbury Park, Calif. 91320
(805) 499–0721
Current Literature on Aging

National Geographic Society
1145 Seventeenth Street, N.W.
Washington, D.C. 20036
(202) 857–7000
(800) 638–4077
Exploring Your World: The Adventure of Geography

National Journal
1730 M Street, N.W.
Washington, D.C. 20036
(202) 857–1400
(800) 424–2921
Almanac of American Politics 1990, The

National League for Nursing
350 Hudson Street
New York, N.Y. 10014
(212) 989–9393
(800) 847–8480
(800) 669–1656 (in N.Y.)
Scholarships and Loans for Nursing Education 1989–1990
State-Approved Schools of Nursing L.P.N./L.V.N.
State-Approved Schools of Nursing R.N.

National Register Publishing Company
3004 Glenview Road
Wilmette, Ill. 60091
(708) 256–6067
(800) 323–6772
Standard Directory of Advertisers
Standard Directory of Advertising Agencies

National Textbook Company
4255 West Touhy Avenue
Lincolnwood, Ill. 60646–1975
(708) 679–5500
(800) 323–4900
Dictionary of Advertising
(See also VGM Career Horizons)

National Urban League
500 East 62d Street
New York, N.Y. 10021
(212) 310–9000
State of Black America, The

Neal-Schuman Publishers, Inc.
23 Leonard Street
New York, N.Y. 10013
(212) 925–8650
Fiction for Youth: A Guide to Recommended Books, 2d edition
Medical Word Finder: A Reverse Medical Dictionary
Storyteller's Sourcebook: A Subject, Title and Motif Index to Folklore Collections for Children, The
This Day in Religion
(See also Third World Editors)

New American Library (NAL)
Division of Penguin U.S.A.
375 Hudson Street
New York, N.Y. 10014
(212) 366–2000
Complete Film Dictionary, The
Leonard Maltin's TV Movies and Video Guide

New England Historic Genealogical Society
101 Newbury Street
Boston, Mass. 02116
(617) 536–5740
American and British Genealogy and Heraldry: A Selected List of Books, 3d edition

New York University Press
70 Washington Square South
New York, N.Y. 10012
(212) 998–2575
Dictionary of the Environment, A, 3d edition

Nichols Publishing Company
11 Harts Lane, Suite I
East Brunswick, N.J. 08816
(201) 238–4880
Dictionary of Computing and New Information Technology, 3d edition
Dictionary of Energy, 2d edition

Nolo Press
950 Parker Street
Berkeley, Calif. 94710
(415) 549–1976
(800) 992–6656
(800) 445–6656 (in Calif.)
Family Law Dictionary: Marriage, Divorce, Children, and Living Together

Nordic Books
P.O. Box 1941
Philadelphia, Pa. 19105
(609) 795–1887
Bibliography of Danish Literature in English Translation, 1950–1980

Northern Cartographic, Inc.
3073 Williston Road
South Burlington, Vt. 05403
(802) 860–2886
Access America: An Atlas and Guide to the National Parks for Visitors with Disabilities

W. W. Norton & Company, Inc.
500 Fifth Avenue
New York, N.Y. 10110
(212) 354–5500
(800) 223–2584
(800) 233–4830 (orders)
Blue Guides (series)
Lives of the Painters, The
Yearbook of Astronomy
(See also John Muir Publications, Inc.)

NTC Business Books
(See National Textbook Company)

Octopus Books, Inc.
Distributed by Doubleday Canada, Ltd.
105 Bond Street
Toronto, Ontario M5B 1Y3
(416) 977–7891
Encyclopedia of Classic Cars, The

Official Airline Guides
P.O. Box 55664
Boulder, Colo. 80322
(800) 323–3537
OAG Planner Hotel and Motel Redbook

Ohio State University Press
1070 Carmack Road
Columbus, Ohio 43210
(614) 292–6930
Dictionary of Feminist Theory, The
Guide to Reference and Bibliography for Theatre Research, A, 2d edition

Oliver-Nelson Books
Nelson Place at Elm Hill Pike
Nashville, Tenn. 37214–1000
(615) 889–9000
(800) 251–4000
Dictionary of Biblical Literacy, The

Ortho Information Services
Building T
6001 Bollinger Canyon Road
San Ramon, Calif. 94583
(415) 842–5530
Ortho Problem Solver, 3d edition

The Oryx Press
4041 North Central at Indian School Road
Phoenix, Ariz. 85012–3397
(602) 265–2651
(800) 279–6799
(800) 279–4663 (orders)
AIDS Bibliography
AIDS Information Sourcebook, 2d edition
Contemporary American Women Sculptors
Core Collection in Nursing and the Allied Health Sciences: Books, Journals, Media
Directory of Pain Treatment Centers in the U.S. and Canada
Guide to Information Sources for Social Work and the Human Services
Handbooks and Tables in Science and Technology, 2d edition
Milestones in Science and Technology: The Ready Reference Guide to Discoveries, Inventions, and Facts
Setting Up a Company in the European Community: A Country by Country Guide
Statistical Handbook on Aging Americans
Video Classics: A Guide to Video Art and Documentary Tapes

Oxford University Press, Inc.
200 Madison Avenue
New York, N.Y. 10016
(212) 679–7300
(800) 451–7556
American Musical Theatre: A Chronicle
Atlas of Prehistoric Britain
Challinor's Dictionary of Geology, 6th edition
Concise Dictionary of Biology
Concise Oxford Companion to American Literature, The
Concise Oxford Companion to American Theatre, The
Concise Oxford Companion to the Theatre, The
Concise Oxford Dictionary of Ballet, 2d edition
Concise Oxford Dictionary of English Literature, The, 2d edition
Concise Oxford Dictionary of Opera, The, 2d edition
Concise Oxford History of Music, The
Dictionary of Genetics, A, 3d edition
Dictionary of Information Technology, 2d edition

Dictionary of Modern Legal Usage, A
Dictionary of National Biography
Dictionary of Superstitions, A
Dictionary of Surnames, A
Dictionary of the Physical Sciences: Terms, Formulas, Data
Encyclopedia of the Musical Film
Great Song Thesaurus, The
Heritage of Music (series)
New Oxford Companion to Music, The
New Oxford History of Music, The
Oxford Bible Atlas, 3d edition
Oxford Companion to American History, The
Oxford Companion to American Literature, The, 5th edition
Oxford Companion to American Theatre, The
Oxford Companion to Animal Behavior, The
Oxford Companion to Australian Literature, The
Oxford Companion to Canadian Literature, The
Oxford Companion to Children's Literature, The
Oxford Companion to Classical Literature, The, 2d edition
Oxford Companion to English Literature, The, 5th edition
Oxford Companion to Gardens, The
Oxford Companion to German Literature, The, 2d edition
Oxford Companion to Medicine, The
Oxford Companion to the Decorative Arts, The
Oxford Companion to the Mind, The
Oxford Companion to the Theatre, The, 4th edition
Oxford Companion to Twentieth-Century Art, The
Oxford Dictionary for Writers and Editors
Oxford Dictionary of English Christian Names, The, 3d edition
Oxford Dictionary of Music, The
Oxford Dictionary of Natural History, The
Oxford Dictionary of Quotations, 3d edition
Oxford Dictionary of Saints, The, 2d edition
Oxford Dictionary of the Christian Church, The, 2d edition
Oxford History of the Classical World, The
Psychiatric Dictionary, 6th edition
Social and Economic Atlas of India, A
World's Major Languages, The
(See also Clarendon Press)

Pantheon Books, Inc.
Division of Random House, Inc.
201 East 50th Street
New York, N.Y. 10022
(212) 751–2600
(800) 638–6460
Dictionary of Ornament

Penguin U.S.A.
375 Hudson Street
New York, N.Y. 10014
(212) 366–2000
Miller's International Antiques Price Guide
Penguin Guide to Compact Discs, Cassettes and LPs, The
Total Television: A Comprehensive Guide to Programming from 1948 to the Present, 2d edition
(See also New American Library)

The Pennsylvania State University Press
820 North University Drive, Suite C
University Park, Pa. 16802
(814) 865–1327
Minorities in America: The Annual Bibliography

Pergamon Press, Inc.
Maxwell House, Fairview Park
Elmsford, N.Y. 10523
(914) 592–7700
(800) 257–5755 (orders)
International Encyclopedia of Education, The

Pergamon Press, Inc.
Distributed by The MIT Press
55 Hayward Street
Cambridge, Mass. 02142
(617) 253–5646
(800) 356–0343
Concise Encyclopedia of Building and Construction Materials
Concise Encyclopedia of Composite Materials
Concise Encyclopedia of Mineral Resources
Concise Encyclopedia of Wood and Wood-Based Materials

Perigee Books
Distributed by The Putnam Berkley Group, Inc.
200 Madison Avenue
New York, N.Y. 10016
(212) 951–8400
(800) 631–8571
Dictionary of World Mythology, A

Peterson's Guides, Inc.
Box 2123
Princeton, N.J. 08543–2123

(609) 243–9111
(800) EDU–DATA
College Money Handbook
Peterson's Annual Guides to Graduate Study
Peterson's Guide to Four-Year Colleges
Peterson's Guide to Independent Secondary Schools

Pharos Books
200 Park Avenue
New York, N.Y. 10166
(212) 692–3700
(800) 221–4816
Coin World Comprehensive Catalog & Encyclopedia of United States Coins, The
World Almanac and Book of Facts, The

Pharos Books
Distributed by Ballantine
Division of Random House, Inc.
201 East 50th Street
New York, N.Y. 10022
(212) 751–2600
(800) 638–6460
Complete Book of Food: A Nutritional, Medical, & Culinary Guide, The

The Pierian Press
Box 1808
Ann Arbor, Mich. 48106
(313) 434–5531
(800) 678–2435
Library Research Guide to Psychology

Pocket Books
Division of Simon & Schuster
The Simon & Schuster Building
1230 Avenue of the Americas
New York, N.Y. 10020
(212) 698–7000
(800) 223–2348 (customer service)
(800) 223–2336 (orders)
Encyclopedia of Alternative Health Care, The

Porter Sargent Publishers, Inc.
11 Beacon Street
Boston, Mass. 02108
(617) 523–1670
Handbook of Private Schools: An Annual Descriptive Survey of Independent Education

Praeger Publishers
Reprinted by Hacker Art Books, Inc.
45 West 57th Street
New York, N.Y. 10019
(212) 688–7600
Pictorial Dictionary of Ancient Rome

Prentice-Hall Press
Division of Simon & Schuster
The Simon & Schuster Building
1230 Avenue of the Americas
New York, N.Y. 10020
(212) 698–7000
(800) 223–2348 (customer service)
(800) 223–2336 (orders)
Almanac of American Women in the 20th Century
Baedeker's Guides (series)
Costume Designer's Handbook: A Complete Guide for Amateur and Professional Costume Designers, The
Dictionary of Superstitions, A
Documents of American History, 10th edition
Encyclopedia of Telemarketing
Encyclopedic Dictionary of Accounting and Finance
Health Care U.S.A.
Kohler's Dictionary for Accountants, 6th edition
Mobil Travel Guides (series)
National Directory of Legal Services
National Park Guide
New Jerome Biblical Commentary, The
Places Rated Almanac: Your Guide to Finding the Best Places to Live in America, 2d edition
Portable Electronics Data Book
Prentice-Hall Dictionary of Nutrition and Health, The
Senior Citizen Handbook: A Self-Help and Resource Guide, The
Vogue/Butterick Step-by-Step Guide to Sewing Techniques, The
(See also Access Press; Chronicle Publications; Regents Publishing Company, Inc.; Stonesong Press; Webster's New World Dictionary)

Price Stern Sloan, Inc.
360 North La Cienega Boulevard
Los Angeles, Calif. 90048
(213) 657–6100
(800) 421–0892
(800) 227–8801 (in Calif.)
Complete Guide to Prescription & Nonprescription Drugs

Princeton Book Company Publishers
Box 57
Pennington, N.J. 08534–0057

(609) 737–8177
(800) 326–7149
Language of Ballet: A Dictionary, The

Princeton University Press
41 William Street
Princeton, N.J. 08540
(609) 258–4900
(800) 777–4726
History of Japanese Literature: Vol. 1, The Archaic and Ancient Ages, A
History of Japanese Literature: Vol. 2, The Early Middle Ages, A
Princeton Companion to Classical Japanese Literature
Princeton Encyclopedia of Classical Sites, The
Princeton Encyclopedia of Poetry and Poetics

PRO-ED
8700 Shoal Creek Boulevard
Austin, Tex. 78758
(512) 451–3246
Test Critiques
Tests: A Comprehensive Reference for Assessments in Psychology, Education, and Business, 2d edition

Prometheus Books
700 East Amherst Street
Buffalo, N.Y. 14215
(716) 837–2475
(800) 421–0351
Dictionary of Science and Creationism

Public Affairs Information Service, Inc.
521 West 43d Street
New York, N.Y. 10036–4396
(212) 736–6629
(800) 288–7247
Public Affairs Information Service Bulletin

The Putnam Berkley Group, Inc.
200 Madison Avenue
New York, N.Y. 10016
(212) 951–8400
(800) 631–8571
Almanac of American History, The
Book Collecting: A Comprehensive Guide
Columbia Encyclopedia of Nutrition, The
Definitive Kobbé's Opera Book, The
Great Composers
(See also Perigee Books)

Quadrangle
Distributed by the New York Times
229 West 43d Street
New York, N.Y. 10036
(212) 556–3664
(800) 631–2580
New York Times Manual of Style and Usage: A Desk Book of Guidelines for Writers and Editors, rev. edition

Quigley Publishing Company, Inc.
159 West 53d Street
New York, N.Y. 10019
(212) 247–3100
International Motion Picture Almanac
International Television and Video Almanac

Rand McNally & Company
8255 Central Park Avenue
Skokie, Ill. 60076
(312) 673–9100
(800) 323–4070
NBC News Rand McNally World News Atlas
Rand McNally Atlas of the Oceans, The
Rand McNally Atlas of World History, rev. and updated edition
Rand McNally Commercial Atlas and Marketing Guide
Rand McNally Interstate Road Atlas: United States, Canada, Mexico
Rand McNally's Children's World Atlas

Random House, Inc.
201 East 50th Street
New York, N.Y. 10022
(212) 751–2600
(800) 726–0600
American Medical Association Encyclopedia of Medicine, The
American Medical Association Family Medical Guide, rev. edition
History of Russian Literature from Its Beginnings to 1900
New York Times Theater Reviews 1870–1919
New York Times Theater Reviews 1920–1980
Official NBA Basketball Encyclopedia: The Complete History and Statistics of Professional Basketball, The
(See also Crescent/Crown; Crown Publishers, Inc.; Alfred A. Knopf, Inc.; David McKay Company, Inc.; Pantheon Books, Inc.; Pharos Books; Times Books; Villard Books; World Almanac)

Reed Publishing U.S.A., Inc. (Reed Information Services)
275 Washington Street
Newton, Mass. 02158
(617) 964–3030

International Year Book and Statesman's Who's Who, The

Reference Service Press
1100 Industrial Road, Suite 9
San Carlos, Calif. 94070
(415) 594–0743
Financial Aid Available Now for Research, Study, Travel, and Other Activities Abroad

Regents Publishing Company, Inc.
Distributed by Prentice-Hall Press
Division of Simon & Schuster
The Simon & Schuster Building
1230 Avenue of the Americas
New York, N.Y. 10020
(212) 698–7000
(800) 223–2348 (customer service)
(800) 223–2336 (orders)
Philosopher's Guide to Sources, Research Tools, Professional Life, and Related Fields, The

D. Reidel Publishing Company
Distributed by Kluwer Academic Publishers
101 Phillip Drive
Assinippi Park
Norwell, Mass. 02061
(617) 871–6600
History of Iranian Literature

Research Publishing, Inc.
Distributed by Beacham Publishing, Inc.
2100 South Street, N.W.
Washington, D.C. 20008
(202) 234–0877
Bibliographies in American History, 1942–1978: Guide to Materials for Research

Rodale Press, Inc.
33 East Minor Street
Emmaus, Pa. 18098
(215) 967–5171
(800) 441–7761
Encyclopedia of Organic Gardening, The
Gardener's Illustrated Encyclopedia of Trees and Shrubs, The

Roehrs Company
P.O. Box 125
136 Park Avenue
East Rutherford, N.J. 07073
(201) 939–0090
Exotica, Series 4 International: Pictorial Cyclopedia of Exotic Plants from Tropical and Near-tropic Regions

Rolling Stone Press
Distributed by Summit Books
Division of Simon & Schuster
The Simon & Schuster Building
1230 Avenue of the Americas
New York, N.Y. 10020
(212) 698–7000
(800) 223–2348 (customer service)
(800) 223–2336 (orders)
Rolling Stone Encyclopedia of Rock & Roll, The

Roth Publishing, Inc.
185 Great Neck Road
Great Neck, N.Y. 11021
(516) 466–3676
(800) 327–0295
Roth's American Poetry Annual: A Reference Guide to Poetry Published in the United States

Fred B. Rothman & Company
(See Weidenfeld & Nicholson)

Routledge & Kegan Paul
Imprint of Routledge, Chapman & Hall, Inc.
29 West 35th Street
New York, N.Y. 10001–2291
(212) 244–3336
Dictionary of Philosophy, A, 2d edition
Dictionary of Sports Quotations

Routledge, Chapman & Hall, Inc.
29 West 35th Street
New York, N.Y. 10001–2291
(212) 244–3336
Companion to the Physical Sciences, A
Concise Dictionary of Psychology, The, 2d edition
Dictionary of Gods and Goddesses, Devils and Demons
Dictionary of Modern Critical Terms, A, rev. edition
Dictionary of Organic Compounds, 5th edition
Dictionary of Scientific Units: Including Dimensionless Numbers and Scales, A, 5th edition
Industrial Medicine Desk Reference
(See also Edward Arnold; Routledge & Kegan Paul; Stein & Day; Theatre Arts Books)

Rowman & Littlefield Publishers, Inc.
8705 Bollman Place
Savage, Md. 20763
(301) 306–0400
Black's Agricultural Dictionary, 2d edition

Dictionary of American History, rev. and enl. edition
(See also Barnes & Noble Books)

Royal Boskoop Horticultural Society
Distributed by International Specialized Book Services
5602 N.E. Hassalo Street
Portland, Oreg. 97213–3640
(503) 287–3093
(800) 547–7734
Conifers

Running Press Book Publishers
125 South 22d Street
Philadelphia, Pa. 19103
(215) 567–5080
(800) 345–5359 (orders)
Computer Dictionary: A User-Friendly Guide to Language Terms and Jargon, The
Religious Writer's Market Place, 3d edition

Sage Publications, Inc.
2111 West Hillcrest Drive
Newbury Park, Calif. 91320
(805) 499–0721
Atlas of World Cultures: A Geographical Guide to Ethnographic Literature

St. James Press
Subsidiary of Gale Research, Inc.
233 East Ontario Street
Chicago, Ill. 60611
(312) 787–5800
(800) 345–0392
Annual Obituary, The
Contemporary Architects, 2d edition
Contemporary Artists, 3d edition
Contemporary Dramatists, 4th edition
International Dictionary of Films and Filmmakers, The
Political and Economic Encyclopedia of the Pacific
Thinkers of the Twentieth Century: A Biographical, Bibliographical, and Critical Dictionary, 2d edition
Twentieth-Century Science Fiction Writers, 2d edition

St. John's University Press
Grand Central and Utopia Parkways
Jamaica, N.Y. 11439
(718) 990–6735
Classical Greek and Roman Drama

St. Martin's Press, Inc.
175 Fifth Avenue
New York, N.Y. 10010
(212) 674–5151
(800) 221–7945
Complete Peerage of England, Scotland, Ireland, Great Britain and the United Kingdom: Extant, Extinct, or Dormant
Contemporary Novelists, 4th edition
Contemporary Photographers
Critical Dictionary of Educational Concepts, A
Dictionary of Contemporary American Artists, 5th edition
Dictionary of Philosophy, A, 2d edition
Encyclopedia of Pop, Rock and Soul, rev. edition
Golden Bough, The
Let's Go Guides
New Golden Bough, The, rev. edition
Rule Book: The Authoritative, Up-to-Date, Illustrated Guide to the Regulations, History, and Object of All Major Sports, The
Sports Encyclopedia: Pro Basketball, The, 2d edition
Sports Encyclopedia: Pro Football—The Modern Era 1960–1990, The, 8th edition
Sports Encyclopedia: Baseball 1990, The
Statesman's Year-Book World Gazetteer, The, 3d edition
Statesman's Year-Book: Statistical and Historical Annual of the States of the World, The
Twentieth-Century Children's Writers, 2d edition
Twentieth-Century Crime and Mystery Writers, 2d edition
Work, Study, Travel Abroad: The Whole World Handbook, 9th edition
(See also World Almanac)

Salem Press, Inc.
Box 1097
Englewood Cliffs, N.J. 07632
(201) 871–3700
(800) 221–1592
Critical Study of Long Fiction, Foreign Language series
Critical Survey of Drama, English Language series
Critical Survey of Long Fiction, English Language series
Critical Survey of Poetry, English Language series
Critical Survey of Short Fiction
Cyclopedia of World Authors
Great Events from History

Great Events from History, American series
Great Events from History, Ancient and Medieval series
Great Lives from History, American series
Magill's American Film Guide
Magill's Quotations in Context, second series
Magill's Survey of Cinema: English Language Films, [first series]
Magill's Survey of Cinema: English Language Films, [second series]
Magill's Survey of Cinema: Foreign Language Films
Magill's Survey of Science, Earth Science series
Magill's Survey of Science: Space Exploration series
Masterplots II, American Fiction series
Masterplots II, British and Commonwealth Fiction series
Masterplots II, Non-fiction series
Nobel Prize Winners: Chemistry, The
Nobel Prize Winners: Physics, The
Restoration Drama
Survey of Modern Fantasy Literature
Victorian Novel: An Annotated Bibliography, The
World Philosophy: Essay-Reviews of 225 Major Works

Howard W. Sams & Company
Box 775
Carmel, Ind. 46032
(317) 573–2500
(800) 257–5755
Computer Dictionary, 4th edition
Modern Dictionary of Electronics, 6th edition
Reference Data for Engineers: Radio, Electronics, Computer, and Communications, 7th edition

W. B. Saunders Company
Subsidiary of Harcourt Brace Jovanovich, Inc.
The Curtis Center
Independence Square West
Philadelphia, Pa. 19106
(215) 238–7800
(800) 545–2522 (orders)
Dorland's Illustrated Medical Dictionary, 27th edition
Encyclopedia and Dictionary of Medicine, Nursing, and Allied Health, 4th edition
Illustrated Dictionary of Dentistry, The

K. G. Saur
Division of R. R. Bowker
245 West 17th Street
New York, N.Y. 10011
(212) 337–7023
(800) 521–8110 (orders)
African Studies Companion: A Resource Guide and Directory
Annotated Bibliography of Exploration in Africa, An
Black African Literature in English: 1982–1986 Supplement
Information Sources in Physics, 2d edition
Information Sources in the Life Sciences, 3d edition
Who's Who in the Socialist Countries in Europe
Who's Who in the Soviet Union Today: Political and Military Leaders

Scarecrow Press, Inc.
Division of Grolier, Inc.
52 Liberty Street
Metuchen, N.J. 08840
(201) 548–8600
(800) 537–7107
20th Century Spanish-American Novel: A Bibliographical Guide, The
Advertising Slogans of America
American Women in Sport, 1887–1987: A 100-Year Chronology
Bookman's Guide to Americana, 9th edition
Chronology of the People's Republic of China 1970–1979
Cuban Exile Writers: A Bibliographic Handbook
Dickinson's American Historical Fiction
Dictionary of Mythology, Folklore, and Symbols
Drury's Guide to Best Plays, 4th edition
Educational Guide to the National Park System, An
Guide to Critical Reviews, A, 3d edition
Homosexuality Bibliography: Second Supplement, 1976–1982
Index to Fairy Tales, 1949–1972, Including Folklore, Legends and Myths in Collections
Index to Fairy Tales, 1973–1977, Including Folklore, Legends and Myths in Collections, 4th suppl.
Latin American Literary Authors: An Annotated Guide to Bibliographies
Make It—II: An Index to Projects and Materials, 1974–1987
Mexican Literature: A Bibliography of Secondary Sources
Radio Soundtracks: A Reference Guide, 2d edition

Research and Reference Guide to French Studies, 2d edition
Sourcebook for Hispanic Literature and Language: A Selected Annotated Guide to Spanish, Spanish-American and Chicano Bibliography, Literature, Linguistics, Journals, and Other Source Materials, A, 2d edition
Special Edition: A Guide to Network Television Documentary Series and Special News Reports, 1955–1979
T.A.P.P. Sources: A National Directory of Teenage Pregnancy Prevention Programs
Women in the World: Annotated History Resources for the Secondary Student

Schirmer Books
Division of Macmillan Publishing Company, Inc.
866 Third Avenue
New York, N.Y. 10022
(212) 702–2000
(800) 257–5755
Gänzl's Book of the Musical Theatre
Music Reference and Research Materials: An Annotated Bibliography, 4th edition

Scott, Foresman & Company
Division of HarperCollins Publishers
1900 East Lake Avenue
Glenview, Ill. 60025
(312) 729–3000
(800) 782–2665 (orders)
Robert's Rules of Order, rev. edition
Standard Postage Stamp Catalogue

Charles Scribner's Sons
Division of Macmillan Publishing Company, Inc.
866 Third Avenue
New York, N.Y. 10022
(212) 702–2000
(800) 257–5755
African American Writers
Album of American History
American Writers: A Collection of Literary Biographies
Ancient Writers: Greece and Rome
Biological Sciences in the Twentieth Century, The
British Writers
Civilization of the Ancient Mediterranean: Greece and Rome
Complete Guide to Furniture Styles, The, enl. edition
Concise Dictionary of American Biography, 3d edition
Concise Dictionary of American History
Dictionary of American Biography
Dictionary of American History, rev. edition
Dictionary of Comparative Religion, A
Dictionary of Costume, The
Dictionary of Scientific Biography
Dictionary of the Middle Ages
Encyclopedia of American Economic History: Studies of the Principal Movements and Ideas
Encyclopedia of American Foreign Policy
Encyclopedia of American Political History: Studies of the Principal Movements and Ideas
Encyclopedia of Asian History
Encyclopedia of the American Judicial System: Studies of the Principal Institutions and Processes of Law
Encyclopedia of the American Religious Experience
European Writers series
Halliwell's Film and Video Guide, 6th edition
Halliwell's Filmgoer's Companion, 9th edition
Latin American Writers
Modern American Women Writers
Presidents: A Reference History, The
Science Fiction Writers: Critical Studies of the Major Authors from the Early Nineteenth Century to the Present Day
Supplement to Music since 1900
William Shakespeare: His World, His Work, and His Influence

The Shoe String Press, Inc.
Box 4327
925 Sherman Avenue
Hamden, Conn. 06514
(203) 248–6307, 6308
American Drama Criticism: Interpretations 1890–1977, 2d edition
English Novel Explication: Criticisms to 1972
English Novel Explication Supplement III, Through 1984
Plots and Characters in Major Russian Fiction
(See also Archon Books)

Signet Books
Imprint of New American Library
1633 Broadway
New York, N.Y. 10019
(212) 366–2000
(800) 526–0275
Consumer Guide Automobile Book
Used Cars Rating Guide, 1990 edition

Simon & Schuster, Inc.
The Simon & Schuster Building
1230 Avenue of the Americas
New York, N.Y. 10020
(212) 698–7000
(800) 223–2348 (customer service)
(800) 223–2336 (orders)
Lovejoy's College Guide, 19th edition
Women in the World: An International Atlas
(See also Appleton & Lange; Pocket Books; Prentice-Hall Press; Rolling Stone Press; Summit Books; Touchstone Books)

Simon & Schuster Software/Brady Books
15 Columbus Circle
New York, N.Y. 10023
(212) 373–8093
(800) 223–2336
Computer Industry Almanac

Slavica Publishers, Inc.
Box 14388
Columbus, Ohio 43214–0388
(614) 268–4002
Comprehensive Bibliography of Yugoslav Literature in English, A, 1593–1980
First Supplement to A Comprehensive Bibliography of Yugoslav Literature in English, 1981–1985

Social Issues Resources Series, Inc.
P.O. Box 2348
Boca Raton, Fla. 33427–2348
(407) 994–0079
(800) 232–7477
Atmosphere Crisis: The Greenhouse Effect and Ozone Depletion, The

Society of Automotive Engineers, Inc.
400 Commonwealth Drive
Warrendale, Pa. 15096
(412) 776–4841
Dictionary of Automotive Engineering

Society of Spanish & Spanish-American Studies
University of Colorado
Department of Spanish & Portuguese
Campus Box 278
Boulder, Colo. 80309–0278
(303) 492–7308
Origins of Spanish Romanticism: A Selective Annotated Biography

Sociological Abstracts, Inc.
P.O. Box 22206
San Diego, Calif. 92122
(619) 695–8803
(800) 752–3945
Sociological Abstracts
Thesaurus of Sociological Indexing Terms, 2d edition

Sound View Press
170 Boston Post Road, Suite 150
Madison, Conn. 06443
(203) 245–2246
Who Was Who in American Art

Southeast Asia Programs/Cornell University
102 West Avenue
Ithaca, N.Y. 14850
(607) 255–4359
Introduction to Thai Literature

Southern Illinois University Press
P.O. Box 3697
Carbondale, Ill. 62902–3697
(618) 453–2281
Guide to Contemporary Italian Literature: From Futurism to Neorealism
Modern Italian Novel: Volume 3, From Pea to Moravia, The

The Spoon River Press
P.O. Box 3676
Peoria, Ill. 61614
(309) 672–2665
First Editions: A Guide to Identification, rev. edition

Springer Publishing Company, Inc.
536 Broadway
New York, N.Y. 10012
(212) 431–4370
Duncan's Dictionary for Nurses, 2d edition
Encyclopedia of Aging

Standard & Poor's
Subsidiary of McGraw-Hill, Inc.
25 Broadway
New York, N.Y. 10004
(212) 208–8581
Standard & Poor's Register of Corporations, Directors and Executives
Standard & Poor's Stock Market Encyclopedia, Including the S&P 500
Standard & Poor's Stock Reports

Standard Rate and Data Service
3004 Glenview Road
Wilmette, Ill. 60091
(800) 323–4588
Standard Rate and Data Service

Stanford University Press
Stanford, Calif. 94305
(415) 723–9434
Stanford Companion to Victorian Fiction, The

State University of New York Press
(See Bibliotheca Persica)

Stein & Day
Distributed by Routledge, Chapman & Hall, Inc.
29 West 35th Street
New York, N.Y. 10001–2291
(212) 244–3336
Dictionary of Catch Phrases: American and British from the Sixteenth Century to the Present Day, A, rev. edition

Sterling Publishing Company, Inc.
387 Park Avenue South, 5th floor
New York, N.Y. 10016–8810
(212) 532–7160
(800) 367–9692
Guinness Book of World Records
Illustrated Encyclopedia of Costume and Fashion: 1550–1920, The
(See also Blanford Press; Summerhill Press)

Stockton Press
Division of Grove's Dictionaries of Music, Inc.
15 East 26th Street
New York, N.Y. 10010
(212) 481–1334
(800) 221–2123
Directory of Economic Institutions
New Palgrave: A Dictionary of Economics

Stonesong Press
Distributed by Prentice-Hall Press
Division of Simon & Schuster
The Simon & Schuster Building
1230 Avenue of the Americas
New York, N.Y. 10020
(212) 698–7000
(800) 223–2348 (customer service)
(800) 223–2336 (orders)
New York Public Library Desk Reference, The

H. S. Stuttman, Inc.
333 Post Road West
Westport, Conn. 06889
(203) 226–7841
New Illustrated Science and Invention Encyclopedia: How It Works, The

Summerhill Press
Distributed by Sterling Publishing Company, Inc.
387 Park Avenue South, 5th floor
New York, N.Y. 10016–8810
(212) 532–7160
(800) 367–9692
Hockey Scouting Report

Summit Books
Division of Simon & Schuster, Inc.
The Simon & Schuster Building
1230 Avenue of the Americas
New York, N.Y. 10020
(212) 698–7000
(800) 223–2348
(800) 223–2336 (orders)
Art of the Piano: Its Performers, Literature, and Recordings, The
Month-by-Month Atlas of World War II, The

Swallow Press/Ohio University Press
Scott Quadrangle
Athens, Ohio 45701
(614) 593–1155
(800) 638–3030
American and British Poetry: A Guide to the Criticism 1925–1978

Swets North America
P.O. Box 517
Berwyn, Pa. 19312
(215) 644–4944
Dictionary and Encyclopedia of Paper and Paper-Making, 2d edition

Syracuse University Press
1600 Jamesville Avenue
Syracuse, N.Y. 13244–5160
(315) 443–5534
Critical Bibliography of French Literature, A

TAB Books
Division of McGraw-Hill, Inc.
113311 Monterey Avenue
Blue Ridge Summit, Pa. 17214
(717) 794–2191
(800) 233–1128
Encyclopedia of Electronics, 2d edition
Illustrated Dictionary of Electronics, 4th edition
Illustrated Dictionary of Microcomputers, The, 2d edition

Teachers College Press
Teachers College, Columbia University
1234 Amsterdam Avenue
New York, N.Y. 10027
(212) 678–3929
(800) 445–6638
Educational Software Selector, The, 3d edition

Ten Speed Press
Box 7123
Berkeley, Calif. 94707
(415) 845–8414
(800) 841–BOOK

What Color Is Your Parachute? A Practical Manual for Job-Hunters and Career Changers

Thames & Hudson, Inc.
500 Fifth Avenue
New York, N.Y. 10110
(212) 354–3763
(800) 233–4830

Illustrated Dictionary of Glass, An
Illustrated Dictionary of Jewelry
Middle Ages: A Concise Encyclopedia, The
Nineteenth-Century Painters and Painting: A Dictionary

Theatre Arts Books
Subsidiary of Routledge, Chapman & Hall, Inc.
29 West 35th Street
New York, N.Y. 10001–2291
(212) 244–3336

Theatre Language: A Dictionary of Terms in English of the Drama and Stage from Medieval to Modern Times

Third World Editors
Distributed by Neal-Schuman Publishers, Inc.
23 Leonard Street
New York, N.Y. 10013
(212) 925–8650

Third World Guide, The

Thomas Publishing Company
1 Penn Plaza
New York, N.Y. 10119
(212) 695–0500

Thomas Register of American Manufacturers

Three Continents Press
1901 Pennsylvania Avenue, N.W., Suite 407
Washington, D.C. 20006
(202) 223–2554

Asian/Pacific Literatures in English: Bibliographies

Times Books
Subsidiary of Random House, Inc.
201 East 50th Street
New York, N.Y. 10022
(212) 751–2600
(800) 726–0600

New York Times Career Planner: A Guide to Choosing the Perfect Job from the 101 Best Opportunities of Tomorrow

Todd Publications
Distributed by ABC-Clio
P.O. Box 1911
130 Cremona Drive
Santa Barbara, Calif. 93116–1911
(800) 968–1911
(800) 422–2546

Reference Encyclopedia of the American Indian, 5th edition

Touchstone Books
Subsidiary of Simon & Schuster, Inc.
The Simon & Schuster Building
1230 Avenue of the Americas
New York, N.Y. 10020
(212) 698–7000
(800) 223–2348 (customer service)
(800) 223–2336 (orders)

New Our Bodies, Ourselves; A Book by and for Women, The, rev. edition

Charles E. Tuttle Company, Inc.
28 South Main Street
Rutland, Vt. 05701–0410
(802) 773–8930, 8229
(800) 526–2778

Kabuki Handbook: A Guide to Understanding and Appreciation, The

Tyndale House Publishers, Inc.
Box 80
351 Executive Drive
Wheaton, Ill. 60189
(708) 668–8300
(800) 323–9400

New Bible Atlas

Ungar Publishing Company
370 Lexington Avenue
New York, N.Y. 10017
(212) 532–3650

African Literatures in the 20th Century: A Guide
American Women Writers: A Critical Reference Guide from Colonial Times to the Present
Critical Temper: A Survey of Modern Criticism on English and American Literature from the Beginnings to the Twentieth Century, The
Encyclopedia of World Literature in the 20th Century, rev. edition

Far Eastern Literature in the Twentieth Century: A Guide, rev. edition
Key Sources in Comparative and World Literature: An Annotated Guide to Reference Materials
Literature of Spain in English Translation: A Bibliography, The
Major Modern Dramatists
Modern American Literature, 4th edition
Modern Arabic Literature, A Library of Literary Criticism series
Modern British Literature
Modern German Literature, A Library of Literary Criticism series
Modern Latin American Literature
Modern Slavic Literatures: Bulgarian, Czechoslovak, Polish, Ukrainian, and Yugoslav Literatures, vol. 2
Modern Spanish and Portuguese Literature
Spanish American Writing Since 1941: A Critical Survey

UNIPUB
Distributed by Kraus International Publications
Route 100
Millwood, N.Y. 10546
(914) 762–2200
(800) 223–8323
Cuba, 1953 to 1978: A Bibliographical Guide to the Literature

United Nations
Sales Section, Publishing Service
Room DC2-0853
New York, N.Y. 10017
(212) 963–8302
(800) 553–3210
Demographic Yearbook

United States Government Printing Office (U.S.G.P.O.)
U.S.G.P.O. Stop SSMR
Washington, D.C. 20401
(202) 783–3238
Agricultural Statistics
Astronomical Almanac, The
Biographical Directory of the United States Congress, 1774–1989, 15th edition
Dictionary of Occupational Titles, 4th edition
Digest of Educational Statistics
Historical Statistics of the United States
Occupational Outlook Handbook
States and Small Business: A Directory of Programs and Activities, The
Statistical Abstract of the United States, 109th edition
United States Code
United States Government Manual, The
World Factbook, The
Yearbook of Agriculture

United States Pharmacopeial Convention, Inc.
12601 Twinbrook Parkway
Rockville, Md. 20852
(301) 881–0666
(806) 227–8772
Drug Information for the Consumer

University of Alabama Press
Box 870380
Tuscaloosa, Ala. 35487
(205) 348–5180
American Public Administration: Past, Present, Future

University of California Press
2120 Berkeley Way
Berkeley, Calif. 94720
(415) 642–4247
(800) 882–6657
Business Information Sources, rev. edition
Guide to Sources for Agricultural and Biological Research
History of Polish Literature, The, 2d edition

UCLA Latin American Center
405 Hilgard Avenue
Los Angeles, Calif. 90024
(213) 825–6634
Statistical Abstract of Latin America

University of Chicago Press
5801 Ellis Avenue
Chicago, Ill. 60637
(312) 702–7700, 7633
(800) 621–2736
Best in Children's Books: The University of Chicago Guide to Children's Literature, 1966–1972, The
Best in Children's Books: The University of Chicago Guide to Children's Literature, 1973–1978, The
Best in Children's Books: The University of Chicago Guide to Children's Literature, 1979–1984, The
Chicago Manual of Style, The, 13th edition, rev. and exp.
Critical Dictionary of Sociology, A
Manual for Writers of Term Papers, 5th edition
Requirements for Certification of Teachers, Counselors, Librarians, and Administrators

for Elementary and Secondary Schools
Twentieth-Century French Literature

University of Massachusetts Press
Box 429
Amherst, Mass. 01004
(413) 545–2217
Chinese Theatre in Modern Times: From 1840 to the Present Day, The

University of Miami Press
P.O. Box 4836
Hampden Station
Baltimore, Md. 21211
(301) 338–6952
New History of Spanish-American Fiction, A

University of Minnesota Press
2037 University Avenue, S. E.
Minneapolis, Minn. 55414
(612) 624–2516
History of Scandinavian Literature, 1870–1980, A
History of Swedish Literature, A
Searching for Your Ancestors: The How and Why of Genealogy, 5th edition

University of Nebraska Press
(See Buros Institute of Mental Measurements)

University of Texas Press
Box 7819
Austin, Tex. 78713–7819
(512) 471–7233
Bibliography of Latin American Theater Criticism, 1940–1974, A
Handbook of Latin American Studies
Mexican-American Literature: A Preliminary Bibliography of Literary Criticism
Selective Bibliography of Bibliographies of Hispanic American Literature, A, 2d edition

University of Toronto Press
340 Nagel Drive
Cheektowaga, N.Y. 14225
(716) 683–4547
Dictionary of Canadian Biography
Historical Atlas of Canada
Sexual Abuse of Children: A Resource Guide and Annotated Bibliography

University of Washington Press
Box 50096
Seattle, Wash. 98145–5096
(206) 543–4050, 8870
(800) 441–4115
Middle East Studies Handbook, A
(See also Chinese University of Hong Kong)

University of Wisconsin Press
114 North Murray Street
Madison, Wis. 53715–1199
(608) 262–4928
Latin America: A Guide to the Historical Literature

The University Press of Virginia
(see Winterthur Museum)

Van Nostrand Reinhold
115 Fifth Avenue
New York, N.Y. 10003
(212) 254–3232
Color Encyclopedia of Gemstones, 2d edition
Dangerous Properties of Industrial Materials, 7th edition
Encyclopedia of Climatology
Encyclopedia of Physics, The, 3d edition
Foods and Food Production Encyclopedia
Handbook of Aging and the Social Sciences, 2d edition
Handbook of Applied Mathematics: Selected Results and Methods
Hawley's Condensed Chemical Dictionary, 11th edition
Hazardous Chemicals Desk Reference
International Encyclopedia of Psychiatry, Psychology, Psychoanalysis, & Neurology
Mathematics Dictionary, 4th edition
Van Nostrand Reinhold Encyclopedia of Chemistry, 4th edition
Van Nostrand's Scientific Encyclopedia, 7th edition

Vanderbilt University Press
1211 Eighteenth Avenue South
Nashville, Tenn. 37212
(615) 322–3585
Comparative History of Slavic Literatures
History of Nineteenth Century Russian Literature

VGM Career Horizons
Division of National Textbook Company
4255 West Touhy Avenue
Lincolnwood, Ill. 60646–1975
(708) 679–5500
(800) 323–4900
VGM's Careers Encyclopedia, 2d edition

Viking Penguin
375 Hudson Street
New York, N.Y. 10014
(212) 366–2000
Complete Book of the Olympics, The
Guide to American Graduate Schools, 5th edition
Penguin Dictionary of Quotations
Penguin Encyclopedia of Popular Music, The

Villard Books
Division of Random House, Inc.
201 East 50th Street
New York, N.Y. 10022
(212) 751–2600
(800) 726–0600
Bill James Historical Baseball Abstract, The

Visual Education Corporation for Glencoe/Macmillan
15319 Chatsworth Street
Mission Hills, Calif. 91395–9509
(818) 898–1391
(800) 423–9534
Career Information Center, 4th edition

Wadsworth, Inc.
(See Brooks/Cole Publishing Company)

Walker & Company
720 Fifth Avenue
New York, N.Y. 10019
(212) 265–3632
(800) AT–WALKER
New York Philharmonic Guide to the Symphony, The

Warman Press
P.O. Box 1112
Willow Grove, Pa. 19090
(215) 657–1812
Warman's Americana and Collectibles, 3d edition
Warman's Antiques and Their Prices

Warren Publishing, Inc.
2115 Ward Court, N.W.
Washington, D.C. 20037
(202) 872–9200
Television and Cable Factbook

Watson-Guptill Publications/Billboard Books
1515 Broadway
New York, N.Y. 10036
(212) 764–7300
(800) 451–1741
Rock Movers and Shakers
(See also Billboard Books)

Webster's New World Dictionary
Distributed by Prentice-Hall Press
Division of Simon & Schuster
The Simon & Schuster Building
1230 Avenue of the Americas
New York, N.Y. 10020
(212) 698–7000
(800) 223–2348 (customer service)
(800) 223–2336 (orders)
Webster's New World Dictionary of Mathematics

Weidenfeld & Nicholson
Imprint of Fred B. Rothman & Company
10368 West Centennial Road
Littleton, Colo. 80127
(303) 979–5657
(800) 457–1986
New Everyman Dictionary of Music, The

West Publishing Company
Box 64526
50 West Kellogg Boulevard
St. Paul, Minn. 55164
(612) 228–2500
(800) 328–9352 (orders)
Black's Law Dictionary, 5th edition
Guide to American Law: Everyone's Legal Encyclopedia
United States Code Annotated
(See also American Law Book)

Western Publishing Company, Inc.
1220 Mound Avenue
Racine, Wis. 53404
(414) 633–2431
Guide Book of United States Coins, A

Westview Press, Inc.
5500 Central Avenue
Boulder, Colo. 80301
(303) 444–3541
Introduction to Library Research in Women's Studies
Middle East Contemporary Survey

Whitaker Publishing
19 Jersey Street
Denver, Colo. 80220
(303) 333–5233
Almanack, An

Whitston Publishing Company, Inc.
P.O. Box 958
Troy, N.Y. 12181
(518) 283–4363

Annotated Bibliography of the Novels of the Mexican Revolution of 1910–1917, An

Markus Wiener Publishing, Inc.
225 Lafayette Street, Suite 911
New York, N.Y. 10012
(212) 941–1324
(212) 347–6100 (customer service)
Japan's Economy: A Bibliography of Its Past and Present
Modern Hebrew Literature in English Translation

John Wiley & Sons, Inc.
605 Third Avenue
New York, N.Y. 10158
(212) 850–6000
Architectural Graphic Standards, 8th edition
Concise Encyclopedia of Psychology
Dictionary of Business and Management, 2d edition
Dictionary of Computers, Information Processing, and Telecommunications, 2d edition
Encyclopedia of Architecture Design, Engineering, & Construction
Encyclopedia of Artificial Intelligence
Encyclopedia of Psychology
Encyclopedia of Statistical Sciences
Family Mental Health Encyclopedia, The
Handbook of Engineering Fundamentals, 4th edition
Handbook of Plastic Materials and Technology
How to Find Chemical Information: A Guide for Practicing Chemists, Educators, and Students, 2d edition
International Dictionary of Medicine and Biology
Kirk-Othmer Concise Encyclopedia of Chemical Technology
World Facts and Figures, 3d edition
(See also Worldmark)

The H. W. Wilson Company
950 University Avenue
Bronx, N.Y. 10452
(212) 588–8400
(800) 367–6770
(800) 462–6060 (in N.Y.)
American Authors, 1600–1900: A Biographical Dictionary of American Literature, The Authors series, 8th edition
American Songwriters: One Hundred Forty-Six Biographies of America's Greatest Popular Composers & Lyricists
British Authors Before 1800: A Biographical Dictionary
British Authors of the Nineteenth Century
Children's Catalog, 15th edition
Current Biography Yearbook
Dictionary of Foreign Phrases and Abbreviations, 3d edition
Facts About the Presidents: From George Washington to George Bush, 5th edition
Facts About the States
Greek and Latin Authors 800 B.C.–A.D. 1000
Guide to the Ancient World: A Dictionary of Classical Place Names, A
Musicians since 1900: Performers in Concert and Opera
Reference Shelf
Sears List of Subject Headings, 13th edition
Sixth Book of Junior Authors and Illustrators
South American Handbook
World Artists, 1950–1980

Winterthur Museum
Distributed by The University Press of Virginia
Box 3608
University Station
Charlottesville, Va. 22903
(804) 924–3468, 3469
Decorative Arts and Household Furnishings in America, 1650–1920: An Annotated Bibliography

Woodley Publications
4620 DeRussey Parkway
Chevy Chase, Md. 20815
(301) 986–9106
Relocating Spouse's Guide to Employment: Options and Strategies in the U.S. and Abroad, The

World Almanac
Distributed by Ballantine
Division of Random House, Inc.
201 East 50th Street
New York, N.Y. 10022
(212) 751–2600
(800) 638–6460
Jobs Rated Almanac

World Almanac
Distributed by St. Martin's Press, Inc.
175 Fifth Avenue
New York, N.Y. 10010
(212) 674–5151
(800) 221–7945
World Almanac of U.S. Politics, The

World Book, Inc.
525 West Monroe, 20th Floor
Chicago, Ill. 60606
(312) 258-3700
(800) 621-8202
World Book Health and Medical Annual, The

Worldmark
Distributed by John Wiley & Sons, Inc.
605 Third Avenue
New York, N.Y. 10158
(212) 850-6000
Worldmark Encyclopedia of the Nations, 6th edition
Worldmark Encyclopedia of the States, 2d edition

The Writer, Inc.
120 Boylston Street
Boston, Mass. 02116
(617) 423-3157
Dictionary of Fictional Characters

Writer's Digest Books
1507 Dana Avenue
Cincinnati, Ohio 45207
(513) 531-2222
(800) 289-0963
Artist's Market: Where and How to Sell Your Graphic Art
Photographer's Market: Where and How to Sell Your Photographs
Poet's Market: Where & How to Publish Your Poetry
Writer's Market

Yale Far Eastern Publications
Yale University
340 Edwards Street
New Haven, Conn. 06520
(203) 432-3109
Chinese Fiction: A Bibliography of Books and Articles in Chinese and English
History of Chinese Literature: A Selected Bibliography, 2d edition

Yale University Press
302 Temple Street
New Haven, Conn. 06520
(203) 432-0960
Handbook of Russian Literature

Zondervan Publishing House
Subsidiary of HarperCollins Publishers, Inc.
1415 Lake Drive, S.E.
Grand Rapids, Mich. 49506
(616) 698-6900
(800) 727-1309
New International Dictionary of Biblical Archaeology, The

Out-of-Print Book Dealers

Ben Abraham Books for the New Age
97 Donna Mora Crescent
Thornhill, Ontario, Canada L5T 4K6
(416) 886-0534

Alec R. Allenson, Inc.
P.O. Box 133
Westville, Fla. 32464

Apollo Book
5 Schoolhouse Lane
Poughkeepsie, N.Y. 12603-4907
(914) 462-0040

Gordon Beckhorn Bookperson
23 Ashford Avenue
Dobbs Ferry, N.Y. 10522
(914) 478-5511

Blackwell North America
6024 S.W. Jean Road, Building G
Lake Oswego, Oreg. 97035
(503) 684-1140

Blackwell North America, Inc.
1001 Fries Mill Road
Blackwood, N.J. 08012
(609) 629-0700

The Book Mart
7 Billmore Plaza, Box 5094
Asheville, N.C. 28803-5094
(704) 724-2241

The Bookery
Dewitt Building
Ithaca, N.Y. 14850
(607) 273-5055

Christian Classics, Inc.
P.O. Box 30
Westminster, Md. 21157
(301) 848-3065

City Wide Book & Premium Company
Box 211, WMBG Station
Brooklyn, N.Y. 11211-0211
(718) 388-0037

Clergy Book Service
12855 West Silver Spring Drive
Butler, Wis. 53007
(414) 781–1234

Jean Cohen Books
P.O. Box 654
Bonita Springs, Fla. 33959
(813) 992–1262

Concord Books
P.O. Box 3380
Kailua Kona, Hawaii 96740
(808) 326–2514

Lew Dabe Books
R.D. 2, Box 388
Athens, Pa. 18810
(717) 247–7285

Friendly Frank's Distribution, Inc.
3990 Broadway
Gary, Ind. 46408
(219) 884–5052

Gull Book Shop
1547 San Pablo Avenue
Oakland, Calif. 94612
(415) 836–9141

Junius Book Distributors, Inc.
P.O. Box 85
Fairview, N.J. 07022
(201) 868–7725

John Justice Book Wholesalers
110 Exchange Place
Martinsburg, W.Va. 25401
(304) 263–3399

Eric Chaim Kline Bookseller
2221 Benedict Canyon Drive
Beverly Hills, Calif. 90210
(213) 395–4747

Larry Laster Old & Rare Books & Prints
2416 Maplewood Avenue
Winston-Salem, N.C. 27103
(919) 724–7544

Liberty Systems & Services, Inc. Bookstore
20251 Century Boulevard
Germantown, Md. 20874–1162
(301) 428–3400

Liberty Tree Network
134 Ninety-eighth Avenue
Oakland, Calif. 94603
(415) 568–6047

Christine Pegram Main Bookshop Out-of-Print Department
1962 Main Street
Sarasota, Fla. 34236
(813) 365–0586

Russica Book & Art Shop, Inc.
799 Broadway
New York, N.Y. 10003
(212) 473–7480

Sagebrush Press
P.O. Box 87
Morongo Valley, Calif. 92256
(619) 363–7398

Shuey Book Search
8886 Sharkey Avenue
Elk Grove, Calif. 95624
(916) 685–3044

Specialized Book Service, Inc.
1418 Barnum Avenue
Stratford, Conn. 06497–5403
(203) 377–6510

Square Deal Records Book Department
50 Prado Road
San Luis Obispo, Calif. 93401–1002
(805) 543–3636

Trophy Room Books
P.O. Box 3041
Agoura, Calif. 91301
(818) 889–2469

United Society of Shakers
R.R. 1, Box 640
Poland Spring, Maine 04274
(207) 926–4597

O. G. Waffle Book Company
897 Thirteenth Street
Marion, Iowa 52302
(319) 373–1832

Yankee Paperback & Text Company
38 Summer Street
Northfield, N.H. 03276
(603) 286–4840

Samuel Yudkin & Associates
2109 Popkin's Lane
Alexandria, Va. 22307
(703) 768–1858

Indexes

Index of Titles and Subjects

Entries in CAPITALS AND SMALL CAPITALS *are the titles of reviewed books;* **boldface** *page numbers show where reviews appear. Entries in* roman *type are topics discussed within the text. Entries in italic type are the titles of books mentioned in the text but not reviewed.*

Author Index

Index by Rating

The following is a list of all titles recommended in this book, organized by rating—core, supplementary, or new and noteworthy. **Boldface** *page numbers following the title show where reviews appear.*

Core Titles

Supplementary Titles

New and Noteworthy

Library of Congress Classification Index

The Library of Congress Classification heading indicates the topics of the books listed below the heading. In some cases, headings combine more than one LC grouping. The number in the heading states the first *number of any titles below; for the last number in the grouping refer to the number in the following heading. Titles are listed alphabetically under each heading. They are followed by the page number on which the review appears, in* **boldface,** *and by the title's full Library of Congress number, in parentheses.*

NA ARCHITECTURE

NB SCULPTURE

NC ILLUSTRATION

ND1 PAINTING

NK DECORATIVE ARTS

P LINGUISTICS (GENERAL)

PA CLASSICAL LITERATURE

PE ENGLISH LANGUAGE

PG RUSSIAN AND SLAVIC LITERATURE

PJ ORIENTAL LITERATURE (GENERAL)

PJ5021 SEMITIC LITERATURE

PK INDO-IRANIAN LITERATURE

PL49 FAR EASTERN LITERATURE

PL7 JAPANESE LITERATURE

PL2264 CHINESE LITERATURE

PL4200 THAI LITERATURE
Introduction to Thai Literature, **139** (PL4200.J6)

PL8010 AFRICAN LITERATURE
African Authors: A Companion to Black African Writing, Volume I: 1300–1973, **48** (PL8010.H38)
African Literatures in the 20th Century: A Guide, **50** (PL8010.A43)

PN LITERATURE (GENERAL)
Black Writers: A Selection of Sketches from Contemporary Authors, **83, 749** (PN490.B53)
Brewer's Dictionary of Phrase and Fable, **379, 740** (PN43.B65)
Characters in 20th-Century Literature, **749** (PN56.4.C4)
Columbia Dictionary of Modern European Literature, **734** (PN771.C575)
Contemporary Authors: A Bio-Bibliographical Guide to Current Writers in Fiction, General Non-fiction, Poetry, Journalism, Drama, Motion Pictures, Television, and Other Fields, **80, 157, 195, 735** (PN771.C66 X)
Contemporary Literary Criticism: Excerpts from Criticism of the Works of Today's Novelists, Poets, Playwrights and Other Creative Writers, **77, 195, 735** (PN771.C59)
Cyclopedia of World Authors, **742** (PN41.M26)
Dictionary of Modern Critical Terms, A, **742** (PN41.D4794)
Encyclopedia of World Literature in the 20th Century, **737** (PN771.E5)
European Writers, **743** (PN501.E9)
Guidelines for Journal Editors and Contributors, **446** (PN146.G8)
Handbook to Literature, A, **740** (PN41.H6)
Literary Terms: A Dictionary, **749** (PN44.5.B334)
Magazine Writers Nonfiction Guidelines: Over 200 Periodicals Editors' Instructions Reproduced, **447** (PN147.M33)
Masterpieces of World Literature, **749** (PN44.M3448)
Masterplots II, **78** (PN147.A28)
Masterplots II: Nonfiction series, **749** (PN44.M3448)
MLA Style Manual, The, **623** (PN147.A28)
New Reader's Guide to African Literature, A, **49** (PN849.A35)
Nobel Laureates in Literature: A Biographical Dictionary, **750** (PN452.P7)
Originals, The: An A–Z of Fiction's Real-Life Characters, **748** (PN56.4.A4)
Poetry Handbook: A Dictionary of Terms, **738** (PN44.5.D4)
Something About the Author: Facts and Pictures About Authors and Illustrators of Books for Young People, **254** (PN497.566)
Survey of Modern Fantasy Literature, **746** (PN56.F34.S97)
Writer's Market, **447, 622** (PN161.W956)

PN100 CHILDREN'S LITERATURE
Beacham's Guide to Literature for Young Adults, **259** (PN1009.A1)
Best Books for Children: Preschool Through the Middle Grades, **251** (PN1009.A1)
Best in Children's Books, The: The University of Chicago Guide to Children's Literature, 1966–1972, **251** (PN1009.A1)
Best in Children's Books, The: The University of Chicago Guide to Children's Literature, 1973–1978, **251** (PN1009.A1)
Best in Children's Books, The: The University of Chicago Guide to Children's Literature, 1979–1984, **251** (PN1009.A1)
Black Authors and Illustrators of Children's Books: A Biographical Dictionary, **256** (PN1009.A1)
Children's Catalog, **252** (PN1009.A1)
Exciting, Funny, Scary, Short, Different, and Sad Books Kids Like About Animals, Science, Sports, Families, Songs, and Other Things, **257** (PN1009.A1)
Fantasy Literature for Children and Young Adults: An Annotated Bibliography, **257** (PN1009.A1)
Fiction for Youth: A Guide to Recommended Books, **252** (PN1009.A1)
Guide to Non-sexist Children's Books, Volume II: 1976–1985, A, **258** (PN1009.A1)
Horn Book Guide to Children's and Young Adult Books, The, **259** (PN1009)
More Notes from a Different Drummer: A Guide to Juvenile Fiction Portraying the Disabled, **258** (PN1009.Z6)
Newbery and Caldecott Medal and Honor Books: An Annotated Bibliography, **253** (PN1009.A1)
Oxford Companion to Children's Literature, The, **253** (PN1008.5.C37)
Sixth Book of Junior Authors and Illustrators, **254** (PN1009.A1 F47)
Supernatural Fiction for Teens: 500 Good Paperbacks to Read for Wonderment, Fear, and Fun, **259** (PN1009.A1)
They Wrote for Children Too: An Annotated Bibliography of Children's Literature by Famous Writers for Adults, **260** (PN1009.A1)
Twentieth-Century Children's Writers, **255** (PN1009.A1 T9)

PN1021 POETRY
Critical Survey of Poetry, **83, 203** (PN1021.C7)
Poet's Market: Where & How to Publish Your Poetry, **621** (PN1059.M3 P59)
Princeton Encyclopedia of Poetry and Poetics, **746** (PN1021.E5)

PN1625 DRAMA
Critical Survey of Drama, **77, 201** (PN1625.C74)
Literary and Library Prizes, **620** (PN171.P75 L5)
Major Modern Dramatists, **745** (PN1861.M27 1983)
McGraw-Hill Encyclopedia of World Drama: An International Reference Work in 5 Volumes, **691, 738** (PN1625.M3)

PN1988 MOTION PICTURES, RADIO, TELEVISION
Complete Film Dictionary, The, **372** (PN1993.45.K66 1987)
Encyclopedia of Horror Movies, **376** (PN1995.9.H6 M5)
Filmed Books and Plays: A List of Books and Plays from Which Films Have Been Made, **373** (PN1997.85)
Halliwell's Film and Video Guide, **373** (PN1993.45.H27)
Halliwell's Filmgoers' Companion, **374** (PN1993.45.H3)
International Dictionary of Films and Filmmakers, **376** (PN1997.8.F555)
International Motion Picture Almanac, **377** (PN1993.3.I55)
Leonard Maltin's TV Movies and Video Guide, **377** (PN1988.M27)
Magill's American Film Guide, **377** (PN1997.8.M24)
Magill's Survey of Cinema: English Language Films, first series, **375** (PN1993.45.M3)
Magill's Survey of Cinema: English Language Films, second series, **375** (PN1993.45.M32)
Magill's Survey of Cinema: Foreign Language Films, **377** (PN1993.45.M24)
Motion Picture Guide, The, **377** (PN1995.N3460)
Radio Soundtracks: A Reference Guide, **211** (PN1991.9.P58)
Special Editions: A Guide to Network Television Documentary Series and Special News Reports, 1955–1979, **212** (PN1992.8.D6 E56)
Total Television: A Comprehensive Guide to Programming from 1948 to the Present, **209** (PN1992.3.U5 M3)
Video Classics: A Guide to Video Art and Documentary Tapes, **212** (PN1992.95.B6)
Video Source Book, **210** (PN1992.95.V53)

PN2035 THEATER (GENERAL)
Cambridge Guide to World Theatre, The, **696** (PN2035)
Concise Oxford Companion to the Theatre, The, **689** (PN2035.C63)
Facts On File Dictionary of the Theatre, The, **697** (PN2035)
International Dictionary of Theatre Language, An, **690** (PN2035.I5)
Oxford Companion to the Theatre, The, **693** (PN2035.H3)
Theatre Language: A Dictionary of Terms in English of the Drama and

Information Science, The, **492** (Z1006.A48)
ALA World Encyclopedia of Library and Information Sciences, **493** (Z1006.A18)
First Editions: A Guide to Identification, **178** (Z1033.F53 F57)
General Reference Books for Adults: Authoritative Evaluations of Encyclopedias, Atlases, and Dictionaries, **495** (Z1035.1.G45)
Guide to Reference Books, **495** (Z1035.1.S43)
Harrod's Librarians' Glossary of Terms Used in Librarianship, Documentation and the Book Crafts, and Reference Book, **496** (Z1006.H32)
Reader's Advisor, **744** (Z1035.B7)

Z1037 CHILDREN'S LITERATURE
Best Books for Children: Preschool Through the Middle Grades, **251** (Z1037.G48)
Best in Children's Books, The: The University of Chicago Guide to Children's Literature, 1966–1972, **251** (Z1037.A1 S9)
Best in Children's Books, The: The University of Chicago Guide to Children's Literature, 1973–1978, **251** (Z1037.A1 S92)
Best in Children's Books, The: The University of Chicago Guide to Children's Literature, 1979–1984, **251** (Z1037.A1 S93)
Black Authors and Illustrators of Children's Books: A Biographical Dictionary, **256** (Z1037.R63)
Bookfinder, The: A Guide to Children's Literature About the Needs and Problems of Youth Aged 2–15, **256** (Z1037.A1 D78)
Children's Catalog, **252** (Z1037.C5443)
Elementary School Library Collection: A Guide to Books and Other Media, **494** (Z1037.E4)
Exciting, Funny, Scary, Short, Different, and Sad Books Kids Like About Animals, Science, Sports, Families, Songs, and Other Things, **257** (Z1037.C29)
Fantasy Literature for Children and Young Adults: An Annotated Bibliography, **257** (Z1037.L97)
Fiction for Youth: A Guide to Recommended Books, **252** (Z1037.S485)
Guide to Non-sexist Children's Books, Volume II: 1976–1985, A, **258** (Z1037.A1 W64)
Literature for Young People on War and Peace: An Annotated Bibliography, **260** (Z1037.E38)
More Notes from a Different Drummer: A Guide to Juvenile Fiction Portraying the Disabled, **258** (Z1037.9.B36)
Newbery and Caldecott Medal and Honor Books: An Annotated Bibliography, **253** (Z1037.P45)
Supernatural Fiction for Teens: 500 Good Paperbacks to Read for Wonderment, Fear, and Fun, **259** (Z1037.K485)

Z1065 PSEUDONYMS
Dictionary of Literary Pseudonyms: A Selection of Modern Popular Writers in English, **742** (Z1065.A83)

Z1207 AMERICANA
Bookman's Guide to Americana, **177** (Z1207.H43)

Z1224 BIBLIOGRAPHIES—AMERICAN LITERATURE
American and British Poetry: A Guide to the Criticism, **81, 203** (Z1231.P7 A44)
American Drama Criticism: Interpretations 1890–1977, **81** (Z1231.D7 P3)
Bio-bibliography of German-American Writers, 1670–1970, A, **418** (Z1229.G3 W35)
Black American Women in Literature: A Bibliography, **83** (Z1229.N39657)
Contemporary Authors, **80, 195, 735** (Z1224.C62 X)
Dickinson's American Historical Fiction, **82** (Z1231.F4 D47)
Guide to American Poetry Explication, Colonial and Nineteenth-Century, **83** (Z1231.P7 R66)
Guide to American Poetry Explication, Modern and Contemporary, **83** (Z1231.P7 L46)

Z1236 BIBLIOGRAPHIES—UNITED STATES HISTORY
America: History and Life, **71** (Z1361.W39 S56)
Bibliographies in American History, 1942–1978: Guide to Materials for Research, **72** (Z1236.B39)
Harvard Guide to American History, **68** (Z1236.F77)
Writings on American History, 1962–1973: A Subject Bibliography of Books and Monographs, **71** (Z1236.W773)

Z1421 BIBLIOGRAPHIES—MEXICO
Annotated Bibliography of the Novels of the Mexican Revolution of 1910–1917, An, **474** (Z1424.F4 R88)
Mexican Literature: A Bibliography of Secondary Sources, **469** (Z1421.F63)

Z1511 BIBLIOGRAPHIES—CUBA
Cuba, 1953–1978: A Bibliographical Guide to the Literature, **461** (Z1511.C48)
Cuban Exile Writers: A Biobibliographic Handbook (Escritores de la diaspora Cubana: manual bibliografica), **475** (Z1520.M37)
Cuban Literature: A Research Guide, **471** (Z1521.F694)

Z1557 BIBLIOGRAPHIES—PUERTO RICO
Puerto Rican Literature: A Bibliography of Secondary Sources, **472** (Z1557.L56 F67)

Z1601 BIBLIOGRAPHIES—LATIN AMERICAN HISTORY
Handbook of Latin American Studies, **459** (Z1605.H23)
Latin America: A Guide to the Historical Literature, **461** (Z1601.G75)

Z1609 BIBLIOGRAPHIES—HISPANIC LITERATURE
Bibliography of Latin American Theater Criticism, 1940–1974, A, **472** (Z1609.D7 L9)
Latin American Literary Authors: An Annotated Guide to Bibliographies, **465** (Z1609.L7 Z82)
Peruvian Literature: A Bibliography of Secondary Sources, **470** (Z1861.F67)
Research Guide to Argentine Literature, **475** (Z1621.F22)
Selective Bibliography of Bibliographies of Hispanic American Literature, **473** (Z1609.L7 B77)
20th Century Spanish-American Novel, The: A Bibliographic Guide, **468** (Z1609.F4 F68)
Women Writers of Spanish America: An Annotated Bio-Bibliographical Guide, **474** (Z1609.L7 W63)

Z2011 BIBLIOGRAPHIES—LITERARY RESEARCH
Literary Research Guide, **744** (Z2011.H34)
New Cambridge Bibliography of English Literature, **197** (Z2011.N45)
Reference Works in British and American Literature, **204** (Z2011.B74)
Research Guide to Biography and Criticism, **745** (Z2011.R47)

Z2019 BIBLIOGRAPHIES—GREAT BRITAIN
Bibliography of British History, 1789–1851, **185** (Z2019.B76)
English Novel Explication: Criticisms to 1972, **203** (Z2014.F5 P26)
English Novel Explication Supplement III, Through 1984, **203** (Z2014.F5 P26)

Z217 BIBLIOGRAPHIES—FRENCH LITERATURE
Bibliography of 17th Century French Prose Fiction, **396** (Z2174.F4 B35)
Critical Bibliography of French Literature, A, **394** (Z2171.C74)
Research and Reference Guide to French Studies, **396** (Z2175.A208)

Z2231 BIBLIOGRAPHIES—GERMAN LITERATURE
Bibliography of German Literature, The: An Historical and Critical Survey, **418** (Z2231.A1 B37)

Z2551 BIBLIOGRAPHIES—ICELANDIC LITERATURE
Bibliography of Modern Icelandic Literature in Translation, **418** (Z2551.M57)

Dewey Decimal Classification Index

The Dewey Decimal Classification heading indicates the topic of the books listed below the heading. In some cases, headings combine more than one Dewey grouping. The number in the heading states the first *number of any titles below; for the last number in any grouping, refer to the Dewey number in the following heading. Titles are listed alphabetically under each heading. They are followed by the page number on which the review appears, in* **boldface,** *and by the title's full Dewey number, in parentheses.*

to Information Sources, **113** (016.709′73)
American Women Artists, Past and Present: A Selected Bibliographical Guide, **123** (016.704′042)
Decorative Arts and Household Furnishings in America, 1650–1920: An Annotated Bibliography, **299** (016.745097)
Guide to the Literature of Art History, **122** (016.709)
Make It–II: An Index to Projects and Materials, 1974–1987, **627** (016.7455)

016.78 BIBLIOGRAPHIES—MUSIC
Blues, The: A Bibliographical Guide, **601** (016.781643)
Folk Music in America: A Reference Guide, **600** (016.781773)
Instrumental Virtuosi: A Bibliography of Biographical Materials, **543** (016.780922)
Music Reference and Research Materials: An Annotated Bibliography, **541** (016.78)

016.79 BIBLIOGRAPHIES—PERFORMING ARTS
American Drama Criticism: Interpretations 1890–1977, **81** (016.792)
Black Dance: An Annotated Bibliography, **289** (016.7932)
Child Drama: A Selected and Annotated Bibliography, 1974–1979, **256** (016.792′0226′0973)
Guide to Reference and Bibliography for Theatre Research, A, **695** (016.792)
Leonard Maltin's TV Movies and Video Guide, **377** (016.79′43′7519)
Radio Soundtracks: A Reference Guide, **211** (016.79144′75′0973)

016.8 BIBLIOGRAPHIES—GENERAL LITERATURE
American Women Writers: A Critical Reference Guide from Colonial Times to the Present, **79** (016.8)
Bibliography of Creative African Writing, **50** (016.8088)
Drury's Guide to Best Plays, **689** (016.8)
Exciting, Funny, Scary, Short, Different, and Sad Books Kids Like About Animals, Science, Sports, Families, Songs, and Other Things, **257** (016.80806′8)
Filmed Books and Plays: A List of Books and Plays from Which Films Have Been Made, **373** (016.8088)

016.80883 BIBLIOGRAPHIES—YOUNG ADULT LITERATURE
Fantasy Literature for Children and Young Adults: An Annotated Bibliography, **257** (016.80883′876)
Fiction for Youth: A Guide to Recommended Books, **252** (016.80883)
Literature for Young People on War and Peace: An Annotated Bibliography, **260** (016.80883′0358)
Supernatural Fiction for Teens: **500** Good Paperbacks to Read for Wonderment, Fear, and Fun, **259** (016.80883′937)

016.809 BIBLIOGRAPHIES—WORLD LITERATURE
Guide to Critical Reviews, A, **690** (016.809′2)
Key Sources in Comparative and World Literature: An Annotated Guide to Reference Materials, **743** (016.809)
Science Fiction, Fantasy and Horror Reference: An Annotated Bibliography of Works About Literature and Film, **750** (016.8093′876)

016.810 BIBLIOGRAPHIES—AMERICAN LITERATURE
Best in Children's Books, The: The University of Chicago Guide to Children's Literature, 1979–1984, **251** (016.81′09′9282)
Black American Women in Literature: A Bibliography, **83** (016.810809)
Dickinson's American Historical Fiction, **82** (016.813)
Guide to American Poetry Explication, Colonial and Nineteenth-Century, **83** (016.811′009)
Guide to American Poetry Explication, Modern and Contemporary, **83** (016.811′509)

016.82 BIBLIOGRAPHIES—ENGLISH LITERATURE
Asian/Pacific Literatures in English: Bibliographies, **139** (016.820′8′095)
Black African Literature in English: A Guide to Information Sources, **49** (016.82)
Black African Literature in English: 1977–1981 Supplement, **49** (016.82)
Black African Literature in English: 1982–1986 Supplement, **49** (016.82)
Black African Literature in English Since 1952, **51** (016.82)
English Novel Explication: Criticisms to 1972, **203** (016.823009)
English Novel Explication Supplement III, Through 1984, **203** (016.823009)
Literary Research Guide, **744** (016.8209)
New Cambridge Bibliography of English Literature, **197** (016.82)
Reference Works in British and American Literature, **204** (016.82)
Research Guide to Biography and Criticism, **745** (016.8209)

016.83 BIBLIOGRAPHIES—GERMAN AND SCANDINAVIAN LITERATURE
Bibliography of Danish Literature in English Translation, 1950–1980, A, **417** (016.8398′1′9)
Bibliography of German Literature, The: An Historical and Critical Survey, **418** (016.83)
Bibliography of Modern Icelandic Literature in Translation, **418** (016.839′6980)
Bio-bibliography of German-American Writers, 1670–1970, A, **418** (016.83′08′0973)

016.86 BIBLIOGRAPHIES—HISPANIC LITERATURE
Annotated Bibliography of the Novels of the Mexican Revolution of 1910–1917, An, **474** (016.863′081)
Bibliography of Latin American Theater Criticism, 1940–1974, A, **472** (016.862)
Biographical Dictionary of Hispanic Literature in the United States: The Literature of Puerto Ricans, Cuban Americans, and Other Hispanic Writers, **83, 677** (016.86′09)
Cuban Literature: A Research Guide, **471** (016.86′09′97291)
Guide to Reference Works for the Study of the Spanish Language and Literature and Spanish American Literature, **673** (016.86)
Latin American Literary Authors: An Annotated Guide to Bibliographies, **465** (016.86′08′098)
Latin American Writers: A Bibliography with Critical and Biographical Introductions, **472** (016.86′09′98)
Literature of Spain in English Translation, The: A Bibliography, **674** (016.86′08)
Mexican Literature: A Bibliography of Secondary Sources, **469** (016.860′9′972)
Peruvian Literature: A Bibliography of Secondary Sources, **470** (016.860′9′985)
Puerto Rican Literature: A Bibliography of Secondary Sources, **472** (016.860′09′97295)
Research Guide to Argentine Literature, **475** (016.86′09′982)
Sourcebook for Hispanic Literature and Language, A: A Selected Annotated Guide to Spanish, Spanish-American, and Chicano Bibliography, Literature, Linguistics, Journals, and Other Source Materials, **467, 676** (016.86)
Spanish Drama of the Golden Age, **676** (016.862′4)
Spanish Literature, 1500–1700: A Bibliography of Golden Age Studies in Spanish and English, 1925–1980, **676** (016.86)
20th Century Spanish-American Novel, The: A Bibliographic Guide, **468** (016.863)
Women Writers of Spain: An Annotated Bio-Bibliographical Guide, **676** (016.86′09′9287)
Women Writers of Spanish America: An Annotated Bio-Bibliographical Guide, **474** (016.86′09′9287)

016.89 BIBLIOGRAPHIES—ORIENTAL LITERATURE
Bibliography of Studies and Translations of Modern Chinese Literature, 1918–1942, **135** (016.8951)
Chinese Fiction: A Bibliography of Books and Articles in Chinese and English, **140** (016.8951′3)
Comprehensive Bibliography of Yugoslav Literature in English, 1593–1980, A, **312** (016.8918′1)
Contemporary Chinese Novels and Short Stories, 1949–1974: An Annotated Bibliography, **140** (016.8951′3′09)

Atlas of Environmental Issues, **321** (363.7)
Atmosphere Crisis, The: The Greenhouse Effect and Ozone Depletion, **321** (363.739)
Directory of Pain Treatment Centers in the U.S. and Canada, **274** (362.1′960472)
Encyclopedia of Alcoholism, The, **301** (362.29′2′03)
Encyclopedia of Crime and Justice, **489** (364)
Encyclopedia of Drug Abuse, The, **301** (362.2′9)
Encyclopedia of Social Work, **669** (361.003)
Health Care U.S.A., **274** (362.1′02573)
100 Best Treatment Centers for Alcoholism and Drug Abuse, The, **303** (362.2)
Rape and Sexual Assault: A Research Handbook, **436** (364.1)
Rehab: A Comprehensive Guide to Recommended Drug-Alcohol Treatment Centers in the United States, **302** (362.2′9′02573)
T.A.P.P. Sources: A National Directory of Teenage Pregnancy Prevention Programs, **724** (363.9′6)
Traveler's Guide to Healing Centers and Retreats in North America, **275** (362.1′78)
World Encyclopedia of Police Forces and Penal Systems, **490** (363.2′03)

370 EDUCATION
Academic Year Abroad, **340** (370.1962)
American Educators' Encyclopedia, **330** (370.3)
American Universities and Colleges, **330** (378.73)
Barron's Profiles of American Colleges: Descriptions of the Colleges, **331** (378.73′219)
Boarding School Guide, The, **343** (373.222)
College Blue Book, The, **332** (378.73)
College Cost Book, The, **332** (378.3′0973)
College Handbook, The, **333** (371.214)
College Majors: A Complete Guide from Accounting to Zoology, **343** (378.1′99)
College Money Handbook, The, **341** (378.3097)
Comparative Guide to American Colleges for Students, Parents and Counselors, **334** (378.73)
Critical Dictionary of Educational Concepts, A, **341** (370.321)
Digest of Educational Statistics, **341** (370.212)
Educational Software Selector, The, **341** (370.2854)
Educator's Desk Reference, The: A Sourcebook of Educational Information and Research, **343** (370.7)
Encyclopedia of Educational Research, **334** (370.718073)
Focus on School: A Reference Handbook, **343** (370)
Guide to American Graduate Schools, **335** (378.1553′02573)
Handbook of Private Schools: An Annual Descriptive Survey of Independent Education, **335** (373.73)
Insider's Guide to Foreign Study, The, **342** (370.19′62)
International Encyclopedia of Education, The, **342** (370.3′21)
Lovejoy's College Guide, **336** (378.73)
Macmillan Guide to Correspondence Study, The, **337** (374.4′025′73)
Patterson's American Directory, **337** (370.25′73)
Peterson's Annual Guides to Graduate Study, **338** (378.73)
Peterson's Guide to Four-Year Colleges, **339** (378.73)
Peterson's Guide to Independent Secondary Schools, **339** (373.2′22′02573)
Requirements for Certification of Teachers, Counselors, Librarians, Administrators for Elementary and Secondary Schools, **340** (371.133)
Scholarships, Fellowships, and Grants for Programs Abroad: A Handbook of Awards to U.S. Nationals for Study or Research Abroad, **344** (378.34)
Teaching Abroad 1988–1991, **342** (370.19′63′024)
Tenth Mental Measurements Yearbook, The, **610** (371.26)

380 COMMERCE
Editor and Publisher Market Guide, **446** (380.122)
Standard Postage Stamp Catalogue, **627** (382.2)

384.5 BROADCASTING
Broadcasting Yearbook, The, **207** (384.554)
World Radio and TV Handbook, **211** (384.5)

385 RAILROAD TRANSPORTATION
Eurail Guide: How to Travel Europe and All the World by Train, **712** (385.22)
Jane's World Railways, 1989–90, **703** (385.254)

391 COSTUME AND PERSONAL APPEARANCE
Dictionary of Costume, The, **296** (391.003)
Encyclopedia of Fashion, The, **292** (391.003′21)
Fairchild's Dictionary of Fashion, **293** (391.003′21)
Illustrated Encyclopedia of Costume and Fashion, The: 1550–1920, **298** (391.009)

395 ETIQUETTE
Amy Vanderbilt Complete Book of Etiquette, The: A Guide to Contemporary Living, **431** (395)

398 FOLKLORE
Dictionary of Mythology, Folklore, and Symbols, **381** (398.03)
Funk & Wagnalls Standard Dictionary of Folklore, Mythology, and Legend, **382** (398.042′03)
Mythical and Fabulous Creatures, **385** (398)

403 LANGUAGE, LINGUISTICS
American Sign Language: A Comprehensive Dictionary, **450** (419)
Cambridge Encyclopedia of Language, The, **455** (403)
Dictionary of Linguistics and Phonetics, A, **451** (410.3′21)
World's Major Languages, The, **454** (409)

422 ETYMOLOGY OF STANDARD ENGLISH
Dictionary of Foreign Phrases and Abbreviations, **450** (422.4′03)
Harper Dictionary of Foreign Terms, The, **452** (422.4)

423 ENGLISH LANGUAGE—DICTIONARIES
Abbreviations Dictionary: Augmented International, **453** (423.1′19)
Dictionary of Catch Phrases, A: American and British from the Sixteenth Century to the Present Day, **453** (427.09)
Dictionary of Cliches, The, **454** (423.1)
Dictionary of Slang and Unconventional English, A: Colloquialisms and Catch-phrases, Solecisms and Catachreses, Nicknames and Vulgarisms, **452** (427.09)
Nonsexist Word Finder, The: A Dictionary of Gender-Free Usage, **454** (423)
Oxford Dictionary for Writers and Editors, **623** (423)
Picturesque Expressions: A Thematic Dictionary, **454** (428.3′19)
Thesaurus of American Slang, **455** (427.973)

500 PURE SCIENCES
American Heritage Dictionary of Science, The, **654** (503.21)
American Men and Women of Science 1989–90, **655** (509.2′2)
Asimov's Chronology of Science and Discovery, **664** (509)
Cambridge Guide to the Material World, **663** (500)
Cambridge Illustrated Dictionary of Natural History, The, **172** (508.03′21)
Companion to the Physical Sciences, A, **572** (500.2′03)
Dictionary of the Environment, A, **319** (508.03′21)
Dictionary of the Physical Sciences: Terms, Formulas, Data, **656** (503.21)
Encyclopedia of Physical Science and Technology, **656** (503.21)
Facts On File Dictionary of Science, The, **658** (503.21)
McGraw-Hill Concise Encyclopedia of Science & Technology, **664** (503.21)
McGraw-Hill Dictionary of Scientific and Technical Terms, **659** (503.21)
McGraw-Hill Encyclopedia of Science and Technology, **659** (503.21)